Aircraft Projects of the Commonwealth Aircraft Corporation

Joe Vella

Aircraft Projects of the Commonwealth Aircraft Corporation

© 2022 Joseph A. Vella
1st Edition
First published 2022 by Joseph Alfred Vella
Glen Iris, Victoria 3146, Australia
javella@tpg.com.au

ISBN 9780645185904 (paperback), 9780645185911 (hardback)

All rights reserved. No part of this publication may be reproduced, stored in a retrieval system or transmitted in any form or by any means, electronic, mechanical, photo-copying or otherwise, without the prior permission of the publisher.

Disclaimer:
The publisher will not be legally responsible in contract, tort or otherwise, for any statement made in this book. Material contained in this book is intended for historical reference and entertainment value only.

Additions or corrections are welcome, please send them to the publisher's email address above.

National Library of Australia Cataloguing-in-Publication entry:

Summary	The built & unbuilt aircraft projects, proposals & aviation related programs (1936-2000) of the Commonwealth Aircraft Corporation and its subsequent owners - A company history - Scale drawings, photographs, index & bibliographies.
Title	Aircraft Projects of the Commonwealth Aircraft Corporation / Joseph Alfred Vella.
Author	Vella, Joseph Alfred, 1944-, (author.)
Published	Glen Iris, VIC : Joe Vella, 2022.
Content Types	text
Carrier Types	volume
Physical Description	1 volume.
Language	English
Identifiers	ISBN 9780645185904 :, 9780645185911 :
Libraries Australia ID	69969400

Book and cover design by Joe Vella. Text set in 9 point Calibri.
Text and line drawings © Joseph A. Vella

About the author

Joe Vella graduated in Electrical Engineering design in High Voltage Distribution Systems Protection & Control, transitioning to military aircraft ground and air communications, aircraft wiring loom design and ground support equipment prototypes in the Department of Air/ RAAF HQ Support Command. He was Team Leader in Control Tower equipment projects, PCB design and East Coast radar coverage development in the Radar & Navigation Aids Engineering group of the Department of Civil Aviation, then Project Design Team Leader in an American owned energy distribution business. He established his own consultancy for suburban underground cabling infrastructure development projects.

His interest in aviation developed as a young child immersed in an aviation environment, living in walking distance to the Kalafrana Fleet Air Arm Maintenance Yard in south-eastern Malta where Royal Navy Fleet Air Arm aircraft carriers brought aircraft ashore for repair or replacement. All within the landing circuit of the adjacent airfield of RNAS *HMS Falcon* at Hal Far and the movements of new post-war era aircraft, the RAAF's 75 & 76 Squadron Vampires (86 Wing on temporary secondment to NATO) and the frequent majestic visitations of Shorts Sunderland Mk V flying boats of the Royal Air Force 201 and 230 Squadrons.

That early aviation exposure was later reinforced when living close to the commercial aircraft flight path of Essendon Airport (Melbourne), leading to the inevitable aviation photography, article writing, documenting aircraft markings artworks and contributing research to overseas publications. He has been a member of the Aviation Historical Society of Australia from 1969, sometime joint editor of Aviation Heritage and past Chairman and Public Relations Officer of the Moorabbin Air Museum.

Contents

Acknowledgements	iii
Preface	iv
Imperial to Metric Conversion Factors	v
Abbreviations	v
Introduction: A Brief Company History	vii
List of Aircraft Construction Projects and Proposals	xxxvi

Chapter 1. Pre-War and Wartime Endeavours	1
Chapter 2. First Generation Jet Fighters	9
Chapter 3. Basic Trainer Thinking	123
Chapter 4. Fast Jets and Sabre Prospects	143
Chapter 5. Winjeel Derivatives, Private Aircraft Venture and Naval Works	165
Chapter 6. Supersonic Trainer / Attack Aircraft	195
Chapter 7. Commuter Aircraft, Helicopters and Naval Exports	223
Chapter 8. System Upgrades, MB326H Concepts and Submarine Detection	244
Chapter 9. Light Transports and Light Military Aircraft	263
Chapter 10. Advanced and Basic Trainer Aircraft Concepts — A Last Fling	276
Chapter 11. Post Merger Projects	301
Chapter 12. Aero Engine Work	305

Appendices

1. CAC Company Data	318
2. The Government's Control of the Aircraft Industry	318
3. CAC Logos	319
4. Selected Design & Program Management Personnel	320
5. An Explanation of Constructor Number Revisions	321
6. Design Families	322
7. Organisation Charts	324
8. Factory Layout	325
9. Contract Number List (As issued by CAC)	326
10. Production Aircraft List (As issued by CAC)	327
11. Aircraft Constructor Numbers	328
12. CAC Project and Drawing Number Systems	334
13. Design Origin Background	334

Addenda	335
Photographic Addendum	336
Index	359

Acknowledgements

What was the reason and basis of this book?

The Aviation Historical Society of Australia (AHSA) editorial team, while searching for publication projects in 1983, took on the upcoming 50th anniversary of the Commonwealth Aircraft Corporation as a special edition of the society's Journal. At the time, CAC was clearing out old or superseded technical documents, some dating back to WW2.

In 1983 the new incoming CAC management requested an external (non CAC) independent technical assessment of the extent and merit of its extensive historical paper archive, which I performed. This long assessment over three years led me to unprecedented new material and generous levels of freedom of information from the individuals of the principal design group; mostly recently retired and still available for consultation.

This opportunity developed into a substantial compilation of historical engineering reference material well beyond the size of the planned special edition of the AHSA Journal. This led to the development of this book.

However patient, my family was right to be frustrated as the spare time between 1983 and 1987 was consumed by the amassed and emerging company material, multiple drafts, slow typing and the linking of it with an ever expanding volume of cross referencing with National Archive files.

Following its integration with HDH in 1985 and its considerable downsizing, CAC abandoned its notional financial support for the publication of this emerged history, as it was not a core activity for an engineering business. BHP, a share holder partner in CAC offered to publish ten copies of the research in 1986 to donate to ten significant Australian libraries. For various reasons my publisher and I rejected this invitation. CAC had a succession of new owners in the following 15 years through which its original project contract numbering system was maintained. For that reason this record was extended till the business as a unit ceased to exist. The subsequent demise of CAC saw its 'Historical Document Archive' move to different secure and insecure off-site locations, always inaccessible, until a brief period of access occurred sometime around 2015, then went into storage once again.

I am indebted to the assistance given by Wal Watkins A.R.M.I.T.(Aero); M.R.Ac.S; former CAC Project Support Engineer and leader of the Preliminary Design Study Group for the many evenings we spent in patient interview, recurring discussion, arranging interviews with retired staff, emergent new discovery of preliminary design information and the continual encouragement in his confidence in the project, when the end never seemed in sight.

To Ian Ring, Dip.Ae.E., B.Comm., C.Eng., F.R.Ae.S., A.E.A.I.A., CAC Chief Aeronautical Engineer from 1953 to June 1980 who was tasked by CAC management to proof read my multiple initial drafts. Ian was the invaluable private source of the politics, machinations and evaluation committees of the Australian aviation industry and a continual urging and driving inspiration.

In parallel was the interest shown and history guidance readily offered during many Saturday morning back garden conversations over coffee with Herbert Knight B.E.(Qld); F.R.Ae.S.; M.I.E.(Aust); F.I.Prod.E.; M.S.A.E.(US & Aust); former General Manager and member of the Board of CAC.

In addition the inputs and help provided by John Kentwell B.E.(Aero); M.R.Ae.S.; Ch.Eng; A.A.S.C.; Chief Design Engineer of CAC 1959 to 1977 and Manager Engineering and Chief Engineer CAC/HDHV 1977 to 1986. Also David Rees, Defence Marketing Manager and Public Affairs CAC; Jim Caterson, Chief Aircraft Engineer HDH (Vic.), Dennis Baker, Manager Historical Projects Group; Jack Kennedy, Dan McQuiggan, R.Bullen, J.Whitney, B.Cobham, Jeff Trusler and Charlie Sutton (CAC Librarians), Jerry McArdle, Leon McCoubrie, John King, Bill Skinner and Roger Ward(Quality Inspector). Roger was CAC's unofficial resident cartoonist. His generosity to allow the use of the superb artworks of his illustrated observations on company events is greatly appreciated.

Former CAC General Manager D.J. Dalziel, together with other ex-CAC personnel: Ern Jones, Reg Schulz, Lee Archer, Charles Reid, Neville Smith, Tony Mlinarich, Hugh Wright, Christine Adin-James, Frank Byrne,Tony Todaro (Engine Division) Michael Sullivan-Senior Manufacturing Planner (HDHV) for their individual history contributions, advice and assistance in response to my many enquiries. Trish McAvaney for her very early typing work.

With a continually evolving script, it was Roger McLeod's (AHSA) substantial voluntary typing effort from draft number three for the requested draft submission to the collapsed Putnam Aeronautical Publications that it became possible to produce a realistic manuscript as sections of research were completed, often revised and re-written. Anthony Carolan, General Manager (HDHV), for providing the typing services of his PA, Grace Watson, every two weeks in the third year of the project.

Richard Hourigan, the late Kevin Kerle, Mark Pilkington, Ron Cuskelly, Mal Davis, David Eyre, Alan Patching, David Anderson (AHSA members) and Dr Henry Millicer each made a significant contribution freely offering their research and photographs in areas of their specialty. Particular persons who responded to my newspaper requests for assistance and other forms of addressed inquiries include Alf Argent David Collier, Bob Dengate, Brigadier P.D.Lipscombe, Eric Sargeant, Allan Flett (graphic art proposals), Bob Parker, Alan Charnley (GAF-Administrative Chief Draftsman), Gus Moorees, Owen Jones, Ted Sedunary, Ken Silcock, G. Redding, D. Bury, D.J. Donaldson, Ian Johnson and L. Giles. Brendan Cowan, Campbell Rae, Reg Metcalf, Robert Anderson, Darren Tanner, Alan Ray, Ron Jenkins, Joseph Borg, Roger Meyer (Dept of Civil Aviation Vic/Tas Region & the Civil Aviation Historical Society); Jacques Chillon (Air Britain); Henri Suisse (Avidus Marcel Dassault Press Information); Headquarters Army Aviation Centre, Oakey Qld; Institution of Engineers (Aust); RAAF Historical Section; Defence Regional Library, Vic/Tas; Amalgamated Wireless of Australia.

Tony Cooney, Dept of Minerals & Energy, Vic. for his knowledge of the Fisherman's Bend site; Dr Barry Collett, Melbourne University History Department with his early advice and review of the initial text and possible research recognition; Brian Hill for his permission to use his CAC corporate charts; Mal Crozier and Robert Nash of the GAF Heritage Group; Richard Sanders for the frequent use of his vast aviation technical reference library; sadly to the late MacArthur Job originally approached to edit the manuscript; Judy Sullivan for her last minute special typing and the generous support of friend and colleage, the former CSIRO technical librarian Martha Hills, for her patient guidance and formatting of the entire large bibliography.

Derek Buckmaster (AHSA), having also travelled down the same self-publishing route, for his encouragement, mentoring support, formatting assistance, corrections and practical suggestions without whom this text would not have reached publication; Lil Mangoni of the National Archives Australia, Melbourne Branch (N.Melb) for her valued direction in the task of retracing the many NAA files that had acquired a different or revised identity in the intervening years between the time of the original research at the former Melbourne Brighton Archives and the elapsed time in storage, progressively updated before going to print.

Preface

This work presents the CAC company design activity in context with local political events, potential relationship with overseas design organisations and local operational needs and developments.

The principal sources of information were the company engineering reports, internal memoranda, correspondences, interviews, oral histories and the related National Archives of Australia correspondence files, reports, minutes of departmental and ministerial meetings.

In a number of instances the same event in a factory report has a date that is slightly different in a subsequent compilation created for Government records. Data will in some instances be at variance with previously published material. As a company with a large, continually changing workforce, it was not possible to know, locate, recall or to include the name of every individual taking part in a project.

The work is not intended to document the history of the defence units which operated the CAC-built aircraft, nor all the fasteners, rivets or bolts in a particular concept or project or a daily record of progress. It is intended to capture as many documents as possible from an enterprise that subject to economic forces was coming to an end. Because most factory original dye line drawings were too large, of poor quality and poor definition, it was not possible to reproduce them other than at a redrawn uniform scale, of either 1:72 or 1:144 for the original analogue publication. However in this digital based layout, the drawings may not be reproduced exactly to these scales. The two scale rules below are included for reference.

All of the designs described have been quantified in the original Imperial units in use at the time.

Monetary figures of pounds or dollars are left as found.

The text is presented in chronological date order representing the final compilation date of a numbered engineering report, project promotional material date or the start date for a concept which did not have an engineering report. Other methods of presentation which were considered but put aside were:

- Grouping into a family tree extension of a first design, ie showing all the derivatives of the one type together eg the Wirraway, Winjeel etc
- Grouping by aircraft role function, ie into trainer, fighter, transport etc categories.
- Grouping by the various different company report numbers.

Joe Vella
April 2022

*Company advertisement - **AIRCRAFT** journal May 1976*

*Company advertisement - **AIRCRAFT** journal April 1976*

Imperial to Metric Conversion Factors

Length/Distance/Area
1 inch (in) = 25.4 millimetre (mm)
1 foot (ft) = 30.5 centimetre (cm) or 0.305 metre (m)
1 statute mile (m) = 1.6 kilometre (km)
1 nautical mile (nm) = 1.15 statute mile (m)
1 nautical mile (nm) = 1.85 kilometre (km)
1 square inch (in²) = 6.45 square centimetre (cm²)

Speed
1 knot (kt) = 1 nautical mile per hour
1 knot (kt) = 1.85 kilometre per hour (kph) or (km/hr)
1 knot (kt) = 1.15 statute miles per hour (mph)
1 statute mile per hour (mph) = 1.6 kilometre per hour (kph) or (km/hr)
1 foot per second (ft/sec) = 0.305 metres per second (m/sec)

Volume/Weight/Pressure
1 Imperial gallon (gall) = 4.55 litre
1 pound (lb) = 0.45 kilogram (kg)
1 pound per square inch (psi) = 6.89 kilopascal (kpa)
1 ton = 1.02 tonne

Power
1 horsepower (hp) = 0.746 kilowatt (kw)

Abbreviations

AA	Anglo Australian
AAM	Air to Air Missile
AD	Aircraft Depot
AESL	Aero Engine Services Ltd
AFC	Air Force Cross
AFC	Australian Flying Corp
AFTS	Advanced Flying Training School
AHSA	Aviation Historical Society of Australia
AI	Airborne Interception (Radar)
Air Cdre	Air Commodore
AISG	Australian Industry Study Group
AM	Air Marshal
AoA	Angle of Attack
AOS	Air Observers School
APC	Aircraft Production Commission
APC	Aircraft Production Committee
APU	Auxiliary Power Unit
APU	Aircraft Performance Unit
ARDU	Aircraft Research & Development Unit (RAAF)
ARL	Aeronautical Research Laboratories, Fishermans Bend
AFST	Air Force Staff Target
AFSR	Air Force Staff Requirement
ASR	Air Staff Requirement
ASSY	Assembly
ASTA	Aerospace Technologies of Australia Pty Ltd (The former Government Aircraft Factories)
ATAR	Atelier Technique Aeronautique Reichenback
AURI	Angkatan Udara Republik Indonesia
AUW	All-up Weight
AVM	Air Vice Marshal
BAe	British Aerospace
BFTS	Basic Flying Training School
BHC	Bell Helicopter Company
BHP	Broken Hill Proprietary
BHAS	Broken Hill Associated Smelters Ltd.
BSEL	Bristol Siddeley Engines Ltd
BTH	British Thompson Houston
CAC	Commonwealth Aircraft Corporation
CAF	Citizen Air Force
CAS	Chief of Air Staff
CFS	Central Flying School
cg CG	Centre of gravity
c/l C/L	Centre line
CL	Coefficient of Lift
CMU	Central Maintenance Unit
CP cp	Constant pitch
CRD	Central Recovery Depot (or Repair Depot)
CRO	Cathode ray oscilloscope
CSIR	Commonwealth Scientific and Industrial Research
DCA	Department of Civil Aviation (Aust)
DCAS	Deputy Chief of Air Staff
DEPAIR	Department of Air
DHC	de Havilland Canada
DIFAR	Directional Low Frequency Analyse and Record
DoD	Department of Defence
DoS	Department of Supply
DRCS	Defence Research Centre, Salisbury (S. Aust)
DSTO	Defence Science and Technology Organisation
DTS	Directorate of Technical Services (RAAF)
EATS	Empire Air Training Scheme
ECM	Electronic Counter Measures
EE	English Electric
EEZ	Exclusive Economic Zone
EFTS	Elementary Flying Training School
ELINT	Electronic Intelligence
ext	external
ESAMS	Electronic Systems and Management Systems (Ltd)
ESM	Electronic Support Measures
FAA	Federal Aviation Administration (USA)
f/f	first flight
FFAR	Folding Fin Aerial Rocket
Flt Lt	Flight Lieutenant
ft	foot/feet
ft/min	feet per minute
g	gravity
GA	General Aviation
GAF	Government Aircraft Factories, Fishermans Bend
gall	gallons (Imperial)
GAMD	General Aeronautique Marcel Dassault (formerly Marcel Bloch)
GE	General Electric (USA)
GFA	Gliding Federation of Australia
GM	General Manager
GMH	General Motors Holden
GO	Gas Operated
GP	General Purpose
GRP	Glass re-inforced plastic
Grp Capt(GPCAPT)	Group Captain
HdH	Hawker de Havilland
HE	High Explosive

HF	High Frequency	OTU	Operational Training Unit
hp	Horsepower		
HSA	Hawker Siddeley Aviation	PAX	Passengers
HUD	Head-Up Display	PHI	Position Homing Indicator
		PNG	Papua and New Guinea
ICI	Imperial Chemical Industries	PR	Photographic Reconnaissance
IFF	Identification Friend or Foe	psi	pounds per square inch
IFR	Instrument Flight Rules		
Imp	Imperial (measure)	QEA	Qantas Empire Airways
in	inch (measure)		
int	internal	R & D	Research and Development
		RAAF	Royal Australian Air Force
kt	Knot (nautical mile per hour, measure of speed)	RAE	Royal Aircraft Establishment, Farnborough (UK)
		RAF	Royal Air Force
LASER	Light Amplification by Stimulated Emission of Radiation	RFC	Royal Flying Corps
		RFT	Request for Tender
lb	pound (avoirdupois)	RHS	Right hand side
lb/hp	Pound per horsepower	RNAS	Royal Naval Air Service
lb/sq in	Pound per square inch	RNZAF	Royal New Zealand Air Force
lb/sq ft	Pound per square foot	rpg	rounds per gun
lb s t	pound static thrust	rpm	revolutions per minute
LE	leading edge	RR	Rolls Royce
LF	Low Frequency	RSU	Repair & Salvage Unit
LHS	left hand side	Rtd	Retired
L/G	Landing gear		
LOX	liquid oxygen	SAP	Semi armour piercing
LOTEX	Life of Type Extension	SAR	Staff Air Requirement
		SAR	Search and Rescue
MAP	Military Assistance Program (USA)	SBAC	Society of British Aircraft Constructors
MAP	Ministry of Aircraft Production (UK)	SE Asia	South East Asia
max	maximum	SFC	Specific Fuel Consumption
MDAP	Mutual Defence Assistance Program (USA)	SFTS	Service Flying Training School
MHLS	Missile Handling & Launching System	SL	Sea level
min	minimum	SNECMA	Societe Nationale d'Etude et de Construction de Moteurs d'Aviation
min	minute		
Mk	Mark	spec	Specification
mm	millimetre	Sqdn Ldr(SQDNLDR)	Squadron Leader
MoD	Ministry of Defence (UK)	sq ft	square foot
MoS	Ministry of Supply (UK or Aust)	Sta	station
MR	Maritime Reconnaissance	STOL	Short Take-Off and Landing
MR	Military Rating		
MTBF	Mean Time Between Failure	TACAN	Tactical Air Navigation
MTF	Mobile Task Force	TBO	Time between overhauls
MTOW	Maximum Take-Off Weight	TE	Trailing edge
		TO	Take Off
NA	Not Applicable	TNI-AU	Tentara Nasional Indonesia-Angkatan Udara
NA	Not available	TRE	Telecommunication Research Establishment, (UK)
NAA	National Archives of Australia		
NAA	North American Aviation Inc.	UHF	Ultra High Frequency
NACA	National Advisory Council for Aeronautics	UK	United Kingdom
NAS	Naval Air Station	US	United States (of America)
NATO	North Atlantic Treaty Organisation	USAAC	United States Army Air Corps
NF	Night fighter	USN	United States Navy
NLA	National Library of Australia		
nm	nautical mile	VTOL	Vertical Take-Off and Landing
NRDO	Naval Research and Development Office	VWS	Variable Wing Sweep
ntu	Not Taken Up		
		WAGS	Wireless Air Gunners School
OCU	Operational Conversion Unit	WER	War Emergency Rating
OEM	Original Equipment Manufacturer	Wg Cdr(WGCDR)	Wing Commander
OR	Operational Requirement	WRE	Weapons Research Establishment

Introduction: A Brief Company History

The consequence of the disastrous economic depression of 1930-31 was to see Britain abandon her free trade policies and the nations of Europe raising high tariffs on farm and industrial products. The 1932 conference of Commonwealth ministers established the principle of preferential trade to promote a self-sufficient British Empire. Trade restrictions were having a serious effect on the RAAF, as it could only acquire English built aircraft most of which were not being delivered at the promised rate whilst the UK firms gave higher priority to their hugely expanded home defence demand and to lucrative commercial side orders; a topic raised by Archdale Parkhill, (Australia's Defence Minister 1934-37) at the 1937 Imperial Conference.

In his autobiography, 'These Are Facts,' Group Captain Richard Williams, the RAAF's first Chief of Air Staff had stated "*that from the time of the establishment of the Air Force, I had taken every opportunity to impress on ministers that the Service must have an aircraft industry behind it but none would take up the suggestion that the government establish such an industry. They were afraid of the cost. I know that the Munitions Supply board in the Defence department wanted to do so*". Adding that British manufacturers had approached the RAAF with the possibility of setting up an industry so long as they were assured of all RAAF orders – a monopoly Richard Williams would not recommend.

Similarly, Lawrence Wackett wrote that "*I learnt that advice from England on world re-armament had alarmed the Federal Government and assumed a new emergency*". Archdale Parkhill, had asked about the possibility of developing an Australian aircraft manufacturing industry and spoken to several industrial leaders. His motivation was the Chief of Air Staff's frustration and inability to obtain the selected British aircraft with which to expand the Air Force.

The CAS had also had discussions with Laurence Hartnett, the managing director of GM-H, a person with wartime flying experience in the RNAS. His involvement in the local production of cars was a determination to break away from a reliance on English imports to one of local self-sufficiency. He was sounded out as to whether the American General Motors (through its involvement in the Douglas Aircraft Corp) would possibly build aircraft in Australia. The answer was a definite no.

Essington Lewis, general manager of BHP, visiting Europe on business in 1934 returned in 1935 via Japan and the Far East and expressed concern at the rising industrialisation and heavy concentration on armaments in Japan. He had similar opinions about the situation in Europe, in London in mid 1934 with Sir Harry McGowan, Chairman and managing director of ICI (UK) and with W.S. Robinson, the well connected and influential joint managing director of Broken Hill Associated Smelters (BHAS) who was also visiting the UK. Together with Harold Darling, the managing director of BHP, W.S. Robinson and Laurence Hartnett, all understood the need for something to be done about the industrial military defence of Australia. As outlined by Professor J. McCarthy (UNSW) in his comprehensive and scholarly, *Australia & Imperial Defence 1918-39, A Study in Air & Sea Power Power;* the genesis of CAC is obscure. Individually Lewis, Robinson and Hartnett each lay claim to have started the industry. It was not until W.S. Robinson was in direct contact with PM Joe Lyons that any real progress could be made with this group of leading industrialists. The minister wrote to them.

A meeting on August 7, 1935 between Essington Lewis and Archdale Parkhill held at Defence Department Headquarters, Victoria Barracks, Melbourne, emphasised that efforts made over the previous 14 years to set up an aircraft industry had met with no success and that it was imperative that steps be taken without delay to alter the situation in view of the prevailing world conditions.

Harold Gordon Darling
L.J. Wackett/MS4858/NLA

The company representatives reminded the Defence Minister that they were producers of ferrous and non-ferrous metals and vehicle industry manufacturing. Whilst recognising the necessity of co-operating in the defence of the Commonwealth, it was not their policy. They did not desire to enter into what could be regarded as manufacturing munitions, an action which might be misunderstood by the public and their shareholders. They would co-operate if the Government invited them to meet an urgent national necessity and would be prepared to subscribe up to £1,000,000 ($98,456,600 in 2020 values based on the Reserve Bank inflation formula) to form a company to produce aircraft and aero engines. Discussions led to the formation of an industrial syndicate.

Over several meetings the tasks of the representatives of this initial industrial grouping, was to set out the legal requirements for a concept as proposed by the Minister as well as establishing the aims of a business which was much broader in scope than the sole purpose of building aircraft for defence. Other possibilities included the manufacture of aircraft for the civil aviation market; establishing flying schools, aerial photography, the carriage of mail, operation of landing grounds and in due course establishing an export business.

Essington Lewis.
L.J. Wackett/MS4858/NLA

This industrial group met for the first time in the 422 Lt Collins St, Melbourne head office of BHP on August 9, 1935. Also present were the Minister Archdale Parkhill; Malcolm L. Shepherd, secretary Defence Department; Essington Lewis and Frank M. Mitchell the secretary of BHP. The eventual shareholding companies were entering a venture not for large profits but for patriotic reasons expecting 4 or 5% return on capital, with optimism of future growth of civil aviation seen as a long term prospect by manufacturing British designs. The Minister assured the group of his personal support, since having come to office he had noted with concern the unsatisfactory situation regarding the supply of aircraft from Britain, with delivery promises based on half of the requirement being available the next year, and the balance on some future indeterminate date. Because of the worsening political situation in Europe and the possible eventuality of war, this supply of aircraft was not considered to be guaranteed. The group was asked to make their submissions for Cabinet consideration with a long term view to local self-sufficiency, reducing gradually the dependence on overseas suppliers, if possible even that of importing aircraft instruments.

The first of ten formal meetings of the consortium was held in the Melbourne offices of BHP on January 7, 1936. Those present, Sir Colin Fraser (BHAS), Sir Lennon Raws (ICI Aust), Harold G. Darling (BHP), Essington Lewis (BHP), Marshall L.Baillieu (BHAS), L. J. Hartnett (GMH), F.M. Mitchell and L. Bradford agreed to form a syndicate. Imperial Chemical Industries was added to the group at the second meeting of the Syndicate and a £36,000 three way-split working fund was created; the first task of which was to send out a world-wide technical evaluation mission. It was agreed to adopt the approach to create new aircraft designs in Australia to cater for local conditions

William S. Robinson, Joint Managing Director - Broken Hill Associated Smelters

Laurence Hartnett, Managing Director-General Motors-Holden

Sir Lennon Raws, Chairman & Managing Director - ICI Australia

making maximum use of local materials so that within five years of industry's initiation, first line defence aircraft could be in production. This was conveyed to the Minister in a formal letter of intent on January 25, 1936 also seeking co-operation and technical advice from the RAAF. (Other possible considerations had been the alignment with a British firm, importing its components or adopting and modifying overseas designs and manufacturing as much as possible in Australia.)

Hartnett's business and industrial experience was paramount in advising, writing and formulating the Syndicate's aims to Parkhill and others and it was hoped that GM-H with its production engineering know-how would manage the enterprise on behalf of the other Syndicate members whose predominant background and interest lay in mining. Requested, but unable and not wanting to take on the overseas mission himself, Hartnett sought advice from the CAS.

Richard Williams, promoted to Air Vice Marshal on January 1, 1935 immediately recommended Wg Cdr Lawrence J. Wackett (Rtd) to lead the mission in the selection of the 'lead-in' aircraft and engine for the embryonic industry. He was then running his own firm, the Tugan Aircraft Co. Ltd at Mascot Aerodrome but agreed on January 31, 1936 he would be ready to travel anywhere on one week's notice. Two other members of the mission were Sqdn Ldr H.C. Harrison (Tech Rtd) and Sqdn Ldr A.W. Murphy, the RAAF Chief Workshops Technical Officer, loaned specially for the purpose. They sailed from Melbourne for London aboard RMS Otranto on February 19, 1936. A letter of authority by AVM Williams on behalf of the Air Board, dated February 18,1936, sought assistance for the visiting mission from the UK Ministry. The Syndicate's intentions had been relayed by telegram to the Dominions Office in London on February 11, 1936.

Lawrence James Wackett was the obvious person with the practical local aircraft construction experience, a virtue which AVM Williams had sought so much to officially promote on an industrial scale. Born In Townsville, Qld in 1896, he was a technical graduate of the Royal Military College, Duntroon which was established to provide the future officer corps for the Military Service. Wackett was the only one of three graduates of the College to serve in the Australian Flying Corp (AFC) and the only one who continued his service into the RAAF.

He flew with No 1 and 3 Squadrons Australian Flying Corps, in Palestine, organised the repairs of crashed AFC aircraft and improved their operational effectiveness including the building of an elementary form of observer's gun turret and a synchronized machine gun. Leaving the AFC squadrons he spent a year on official

(Left): S. Barnwell. Bristol Aeroplane Co. Experimental Designer 1911-1914; Chief Designer 1915-1921, 1923-1936. Chief Engineer 1936-1938. Wackett's mentor in 1921-23. **Putnam Company.** *(Right): Lawrence Wackett at the Randwick Station in 1924.* **L.J.Wackett/MS4858/NLA**

technical training at the Orfordness Experimental Station in Suffolk an offshoot of the nearby Martlesham Heath Experimental Station (UK). All new British aircraft designs were tested at both stations as well as French and captured German aircraft. Aged 22, with the rank of Captain he was back in the frontline with No 3 AFC in France. At the request of General John Monash (AIF) he devised a method of aerial parachute delivery of 200,000 rounds of boxed ammunition by RE8 aircraft of the RAF and 3 AFC to troops in support of the 1918 battle of Hamel. The innovation earned him a £300 reward from the British Government. After graduating with a Bachelor of Science degree from Melbourne University in 1921, he spent two years in private postgraduate study in Melbourne in the practical aspects of aeroplane design guided by Frank S. Barnwell, better known then as the designer of the Bristol F2B Fighter of WW1 (and later the Blenheim) who was spending two unsatisfactory years in Australia. He had taken a short commission in the Air Force Technical branch, where he was just asked to design propellers. Resigning in disgust he returned home in 1923. Barnwell's tutoring led Wackett to the creation of the RAAF Experimental Section.

It was at about this time, as related in his November 1958 presentation 'Some Experiences of a Pioneer in the Aircraft Industry in Australia' to the Melbourne Branch of the RAeS, that Wackett had decided he was going to pioneer the aircraft industry in Australia and make his career not in the Air Force but in building aircraft for the Air Force. His first private design was the Warbler, an entry in the Light Plane Competition (won by Edgar Percival) for locally built aircraft sponsored by the NSW Aero Club in 1923. It incorporated his own Wizard engine, an unreliable two cylinder 20-30 hp invention, it being the only locally designed engine in the competition.

Persuading Defence Minister E.K. Bowden to acquire a dilapidated workshop in Randwick, NSW and the Controller of Civil Aviation to provide funding for the construction of an aeroplane, Wackett formed the RAAF Experimental Section at Randwick in 1924. The Widgeon I flying boat (G-AEKB) fitted with a 200 hp Siddeley Puma engine was completed in 1925, crashed on its attempted first take-off nearly drowning Lawrence. It flew on December 3, 1925; was then modified to an amphibian layout with an Aircraft Disposal Company (ADC) 300 hp Nimbus 6 cylinder in-line engine, dual controls and deeper floats. With a staff of 80 personnel, the station undertook engine and airframe repairs and the manufacture of wooden propellers for the RAAF. Wackett's second amphibian design, the Widgeon II with its larger 440 hp Armstrong Siddeley Jaguar engine flew on February 2, 1928. The RAAF accepted it on April 13,1928. Made from Australian beech and maple timbers, it was the first

Australian designed and constructed aircraft (engine excepted) to make a 9,000 mile round-Australia flight in 1928. The *Warrigal I* trainer (1929) with a 200 hp Armstrong Siddeley Lynx radial engine was most unpopular with RAAF pilots. It was underpowered and had dangerous spinning characteristics. The *Warrigal II* (1930) two seat, 400 hp Armstrong Siddeley Jaguar radial engined Army co-operation aircraft was flown as a possible replacement for the RAAF's DH9/DH9A. Because of its excessively heavy handling characteristics it was not developed further.

One of the recommendations of Air Marshal Sir John Salmond, Air Officer Commanding the Royal Air Force, sent out in 1927 by the Air Ministry to review the status of the RAAF and find ways of reducing costs, was to close down the Randwick Experimental Section saying that, *"if the object of the building of these machines is to prove that it is possible to build aircraft from materials in Australia, that objective has been attained."* Salmond's report upset the Government, stating the RAAF needed to expand its numbers. It was unfitted for war. The 1935 Australian economy was in still in the grip of austerity, hardship and frugality of the Depression. Hanging over it all to the mid-1920s, was the Australian Government's massive crippling cost of WW1 of some £377M, a large portion of which was borrowed from Britain in fighting its war. There was no moratorium on the paying of interest given to the Jim Scullin (1929-32)

CAC's first company building – the former Tugan Aircraft Co at Mascot Aerodrome some time after October 1936. An LJW6 Gannet stands outside, possibly one of either TG57, TG58 or TG59. **J.A..Vella Collection**

The deep yellow / gold of the logo is more discernable in the original coloured notepaper. **Tugan Aircraft Ltd NAA File: A5954, 873/1**

government which had been pursuing a low expenditure deflationary policy. Added to which up to 1938, had been the post war outlay of £156M for war pensions and veterans medical costs.

The Experimental Section had provided Wackett the experience of local aircraft design and construction but the Federal Auditor General found expenditures went well beyond planned figures. The closure of the Section led to Wackett, fifth in rank from the top of

the RAAF, to resign, leaving the Service in 1930 and moving with some equipment and staff to space at the languishing Cockatoo Dockyard, NSW, to work in a private capacity as manager of the aviation section of its workshops. Jack Payne, the yard's manager had pioneered naval and merchant shipbuilding with great success but all work had been stopped under pressure from British shipbuilders and been reduced to docking and repair activities. Wackett's October 1931 paper- 'Launching by Catapult' a mathematical study of various methods of launching aircraft from ships was published in 'The Aircraft Engineer'. Wackett's aim was to pioneer aircraft construction. He was the Aeronautical Superintendent in 1933 of C.G. Robinson's New England Airways which operated a fleet of tri-motored Avro X aircraft. The Air Force, losing its Experimental Station retained its confidence in Wackett and for three years diverted aircraft repair work to the Dockyard; Charles Kingsford Smith's crashed *Southern Cross* aircraft was also re-built there and the *LJW6 Codock*, a six-passenger touring aircraft with two Napier Javelin 160 hp engines was designed and first flown in March 1934 to Kingsford Smith's requirement. As the effects of Depression started to bite, the dockyard closed and Wackett, like thousands of others was out of a job. In the interim he dabbled in hydroplane racing boat designs fitted with aero engines including one boat for himself. Without support he continued airliner design on his own till he received backing to re-finance, re-open and utilize the hangar and workshops of the former General Aircraft Co Ltd. at Mascot Aerodrome.

Leo Turl and Frank Gannon, the principals of Tugan Aircraft Ltd backed Wackett as its Managing Director. The *LJW7 Tugan Gannet*, a revision of the Codock, flew in October 1935. Carrying a pilot and eight passengers and powered by two Gipsy VI, 200 hp engines, it was the first of eight to be built and received the first type Certificate of Airworthiness granted in Australia. The first five were built under Tugan Aircraft; the last three under CAC's name at Mascot. The second LJW7 built for the RAAF, received in November 1935 was the first monoplane acquired by that Service. Auxiliary fins were later fitted on the tailplane of all the examples (With the LJW6

Wooden aircraft work at Tugan Aircraft Ltd. **Tugan Aircraft Ltd. NAA File: A5954, 873/1**

Lawrence James Wackett first General Manager of the Company. Retired 1960. **HDHV**

A pristine Art Deco design first stage, Aircraft Factory 1 complex shortly after completion November 27,1936 viewed from the south east. **HDHV**

and LJW7 designations known to have been applied to the Codock and Gannet aircraft respectively, it is possible but not certain, that LJW1, 2, 3, 4 and 5 could have been applied to the earlier designs by Wackett but not acknowledged publicly). Little is known about Wackett's undated drawing of a twin RR Kestrel powered coastal defence monoplane to British Air Ministry Spec G24/35 issued in 1935. (This request led to the eventual Blackburn Botha and Bristol Beaufort medium bombers.) The recommendation by the CAS to the Department of Defence on March 6, 1935 that an aviation manufacturing industry be established in Australia, led J.R. Craig, chairman of Tugan Aircraft to write to Defence on July 8,1935:

> *"As we are the only firm in Australia at present actually engaged in aircraft production, we desire that our qualifications,intentions and proposals should be placed before you…"*

Repercussions from the Mother Country

The involvement of GM-H in the syndicate's plans was to set in motion a difficult and strenuous period of relations between the Joe Lyons Government of Australia and the British Government of Stanley Baldwin. The British reaction was mixed: yes, an Australian production capacity might be useful if it could be a source of supply to the Royal Air Force in wartime even though the Air Ministry refused to concede that Australian orders for British military aircraft had been repeatedly delayed; but American participation would preclude Australian access to British technical information (lagging as it was behind the American level of advancement of the day) and secrets to which M. L. Shepherd observed *"an obstacle invented by the UK Government for tactical reasons in an endeavour to get their own way"*. The original GM-H stake of 25% proposed by the Syndicate was reduced to 16% on June 18, 1935. Under Parkhill's suggestion the GM-H stake could not be more than 10% and all of the new company's upper management had to be British originated. It was not to be subject directly or otherwise to foreign influence (presumably American influence). The British Board of Trade was wary that the influence of GM-H, the only organisation in Australia with considerable experience in motor car body building engineering, would erode the prospects of the UK motor car trade in Australia. This was the background threat around which obstacles persisted. The sale of aircraft to the Dominion Governments was also regarded by the British industry as their close preserve and they showed great concern at the possibility that some of the aircraft required by the RAAF might in fact be made in Australia. A campaign of opposition was launched from within the British industry through Charles G.Grey, engineer, activist and editor of *Aeroplane* magazine and supported by the Australian representatives of British aviation firms of the Society of British Aircraft Constructors. An additional hindrance was Stanley Bruce, Australia High Commissioner to Britain (the former Australian PM 1923-29) who tended to identify himself with Britain. He was advised that such highly technical matters as aero engines could not be successfully built in Australia.

To calm the situation at home GM-H's 10% holding was offered to the British aero firm of Hawker Siddeley. Their local representative showed a slight interest in the proposal, qualified by the condition that they would only accept if aircraft of Hawker design were to be selected for local manufacture.

Sir Archdale Parkhill, Defence Minister 1934-37 supported the creation of local aircraft manufacture.

The Wackett led mission arrived in the UK where it was based at Austral Development Ltd at 95 Gresham St, London (the UK arm of C.L. Bailleau & L.R. Robinson's Collins House Group. It was to be a future semi-commercial base for CAC in the UK). The mission toured factories in the Netherlands, France and Germany, where Junkers Flugzeug & Motorenworke AG stood out with its production methods based on American industry ideas and concepts. Walter Werke in Prague, Czechoslovakia, were building airframes and (Bristol) radial engines under licence in the one plant, including forge and foundry facilities, which impressed Wackett greatly. The vast new facilities of the aviation companies of the United States of America where aircraft production was on a large scale and the use of stressed skin metal air-frames and other technical advances made it obvious this was the country with the latest ideas which to adopt. Information was available on aero engine and airframe workshop layouts, machine tools and manpower production data. Wackett was of the opinion that serious aircraft construction in Australia had to start within 3 years. On June 18, 1936 the Defence Minister (now Sir Archdale Parkhill) wrote to the secretary of BHP representing the Syndicate stating:

> "From the correspondences *and the discussions which have taken place, the Commonwealth Government understands that the Syndicate is prepared to assume full responsibility for the proposed activities and that the companies and interest comprising the Syndicate do not and will not expect the Government to assume any liability whatever in initiating and developing the enterprise."*

On the same day, the Prime Minister made a statement to the press to formally announce the Syndicate's intent to build both military and eventually civil aircraft and in due course to establish an export business. Names put forward for the new enterprise included :

The National Aircraft Company (L.J. Hartnett's suggestion);

Australasian Aircraft Development Co. Ltd;

Australian Aircraft Ltd;

Aircraft Manufacturers of Australia Ltd; and

Southern Aircraft Corporation Pty Ltd

The final choice of the Commonwealth Aircraft Corporation Pty Ltd was agreed to on September 10, 1936. Special permission by order-in-council had to be granted to allow the use of the word 'Commonwealth' in the name. It was an unfortunate selection as the Government did not have a financial stake in it and it was to

become the subject of long-running commercial confusion especially when the DAP/Government Aircraft Factory was built alongside CAC's a few years later to assist in the war effort.

The Dominions Office was informed on September 24, 1936 that a choice of engine and aeroplane had been made in favour of the North American NA-16 General Purpose Monoplane. To the opponents of the venture, in both Britain and Australia, the announcement came as a shock, for not only was GM-H part of the Australian Syndicate but also because the parent company, General Motors, had a 52% stake in North American Aviation. (The American bosses of GM took a dim view that L.J. Hartnett had dragged them into an aviation project in Australia's national interest, when they were trying to divest themselves of similar activities at home). The intervention of Prime Minister Joe Lyons was called upon once again to pacify British interests peeved that the Syndicate went their own way rather than through the Empire, selecting an aircraft best suited for Australia despite it being earlier promised of a UK aviation industry selection. The UK Air Ministry had been repeatedly assured by PM Lyons that only a standard type in use with the RAF would be produced. Joe Lyons then had to stand by the wishes of the Syndicate with the concurrence of the Air Board.

Paying the Price

It took two attempts for Minister Parkhill to convince the Cabinet and to receive its approval that the information, reasons and justifications given by AVM Richard Williams for the selection of the NA-16, a non-British Empire aircraft were entirely valid. When the British Air Ministry was asked by the Air Board as to which alternative aircraft would have been suitable for Australian manufacture, they could only offer the Westland Lysander, winner of Army co-operation Spec. A.39/34. First flown on June 15, 1936 it was rejected outright as being unavailable and totally unsuitable. Mentioned in dispatches following his visit to the Bristol Aeroplane company and re-acquaintance with his former tutor Frank Barnwell, was another entry in Spec. A.39/34, the Bristol Type 148, a one-off example with a layout configuration substantially similar to that of the NA-16. However it did not fly till October 15, 1937 and was well out of contention.

Sir Archdale Parkhill's own and the Cabinet's eventual approval to build this non-British entity by a private industry enterprise he had encouraged, lost him support within the Party, the deputy leadership of the United Australia Party in December 1935 and his Parliamentary seat in the upcoming Federal election of October 23, 1937. He had been a purposeful Defence and Cabinet Minister in his 1934-37 portfolios in the Joe Lyons Government.

Leading up to the Federal election the Minister addressed his Warringah (NSW) electorate conference held at the Mosman Town Hall on February 4, 1937. In part he stated *"that because of our sparse population, long distances and indifferent communications, the Air Force, by reason of its mobility, is of outstanding importance in our Defence preparations as Minister for Defence, I realised that it was my duty to go into this matter as soon as I assumed office (in 1934)"*. After explaining the background to the on-going delays, some of up to two years for the deliveries of aircraft orders placed in Britain he added *"some two years ago (1935), therefore, under my directions, a determined effort was made to have this industry organised on a sound basis, on modern lines, and utilising our own resources"*.

This was a detailed, combative speech, ranging over many aviation matters primarily related to the NA-16 aircraft, defending its selection, responding to many pro-Britain critics, the creation of CAC, the lagging technical state of the British aviation industry, defending Wackett's private non-government role and comparing the RAAF order of battle with other air force numbers around the world. In 'Aircraft Pioneer', Wackett gave high praise to Sir Archdale Parkhill for his courage in leading the way to establish an aviation industry and CAC. A suitably captioned portrait of Sir Archdale hung in Wackett's office for *"twenty-five years so that none might forget to whom credit was due"*.

The Company is Born

The Commonwealth Aircraft Corporation was registered under the Companies Act of Victoria and incorporated on October 17, 1936. The venture attracted a lot of interest from major businesses doubtless because the new enterprise would have a guaranteed market for its products especially after the stagnation of the Depression. There was also the prospect that eventual sales would come from civil aircraft production after tooling-up for military aircraft orders had been completed.

de Havilland proposed to CAC that it could build its engines in Australia but only so long as it was still able to import the identical engines from the United Kingdom in competition.

The original company had an authorised capital of £1,000,000 initially paid up to £600,000. BHP took 200,000 £1 shares and a similar number were shared between Broken Hill Associated Smelters Pty. Ltd. and the Electrolytic Zinc Co. of Australasia Ltd. ICIANZ had 90,000, General Motors Holden's 60,000 and the Orient Steam Navigation Co. Ltd. 50,000 shares. The directors were Harold Darling from BHP (Chairman); Essington Lewis (BHP), Sir Colin Fraser; M.L. Baillieu (BHAS), Sir Lennon Raws (ICI); L.J. Hartnett; Arnold Johnson and Arch G. Brown (Secretary) who was brought across from BHP. Its registered address was 422 Little Collins St, Melbourne. The Corporation's Board of Directors met for the first time on October 27, 1936.

The first acts of the Board were:

The adoption of the recommendations of the technical evaluation mission; the purchase of Tugan Aircraft and transfer of its staff as the technical nucleus of the new company and obtaining the Government's acceptance of the recommendation of the mission.

The Board agreed to purchase the assets and the manufacturing licence of the Tugan Aircraft Company for £20,000 effective as from November 7, 1936 and the Tugan Aircraft factory sign was replaced with that of Commonwealth Aircraft Corporation Pty Ltd. Three LJW7 Gannets were completed at Mascot with CAC documented as their build company. A14-3 was the first, going to the RAAF. One nearly complete Gannet and another just commenced were

On the left Archie Brown the long serving Company secretary to CAC with Herb Knight. **HDHV**

View of part of the early engine factory layout. **L. J. Wackett/MS4858/NLA**

stated as being moved to Fisherman's Bend but not completed. Both were eventually delivered to the RAAF in June 1940 as A14-6 and A14-7. Tugan Aircraft was wound up in April 1937 and closed its hangar doors in November at the end of Gannet production.

Constructive Moves

The process of establishing CAC as an operating concern was largely supervised by Wackett who was appointed its General Manager at a salary of £1,000 per annum (and later its managing director). Sqdn Ldr H.C. Harrison was offered the position of Supply Manager. Wackett had originally prepared a list of machinery, tooling and layout for a factory complex to produce both the P & W Wasp (USA) engine and de Havilland (UK) engines together with the NA-16 and the (Tugan) Gannet as a utility commercial aircraft. For the next two years there was an anticipated expenditure of £584,970 to build 40 military aircraft, 30 training aircraft, 50 radial engines, six commercial airframes (Gannet) and on expected licence from de Havilland (UK) - 40 Gipsy Major and 20 Gipsy Six in-line engines. Ultimately no de Havilland engines were built.

One of the major problems which had occupied the attention of the Syndicate for a considerable amount of time was the location of the proposed factory, a subject on which there had been much discussion on the formulation of the requirements for the site. The Syndicate solicited responses for a site of a preferred 25 acres in area from the Premiers of South Australia, Victoria and New South Wales, terms, or hopefully concessions and/or State Government assistance. It was necessary that the factory should be located on or near a landing field of about 70 acres in size and be in close proximity to a waterfront to launch seaplanes and flying boats, the types of aircraft in widespread service at the time for which a long future was predicted. Their pre-eminence was quickly eclipsed by the rapid development of the land based airliner after WW2. (The CAC factory and hangars fronted Lorimer St and piers in the Yarra River, but seaplanes were not a Yarra River activity).

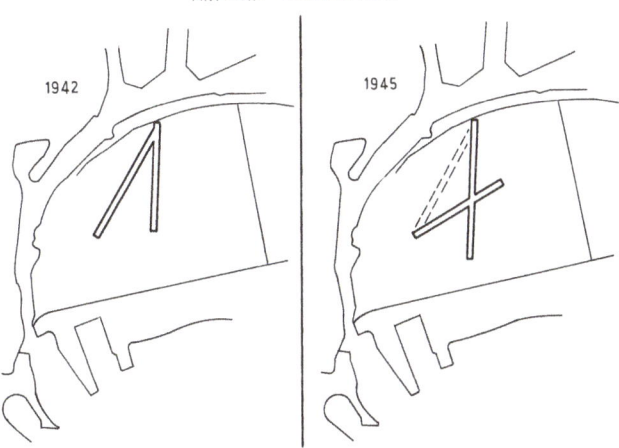

Manufacturing aero engines and spare parts. **HDHV**

Other considerations were close proximity to an industrial city and near the administrative offices of the Defence and Civil Aviation Departments. With both these located in Melbourne at that time the choice was clear. Whilst BHP was inclined to favour a site in New South Wales because of its large holdings in that state there was a good case for preferring Melbourne due to the greater availability of general engineering trades labour which could in time be trained to work on aircraft construction. The labour situation in Melbourne was also steadier and less extreme in its unionism.

Running through these discussions was the inclination to associate the future aircraft industry with the automobile industry and Laurence Hartnett with a strong advocacy of this association, had at an early stage in negotiations, tried to induce his GM Head Office to take an active interest in the matter. From the proffered sites of Perth, Alice Springs, Maryborough, Sydney, Newcastle and Port Adelaide, it was the Fisherman's Bend site at Port Melbourne in Victoria that was a clear favourite. Not only did it have a water frontage but it was also next door to the GM-H factory offering the possibility of an interchange of labour between the two complexes.

Additionally, there was ample unencumbered space. Nearby land had been used by Graham Carey from 1919 till 1921 for his Melbourne Air Service. In 1920 the Shaw-Ross Engineering & Aviation Company located between the Hobson's Bay waterfront and Williamstown Road established the Port Melbourne Aerodrome. It received Aerodrome Licence No 1 on May 30, 1921 for the Fisherman's Bend Aerodrome, the first such license in Australia. It became the Shaw Aviation Company on July 1, 1928, then relocated to the new Commonwealth Aerodrome at Essendon in 1929 but ceased operation in August 1931. Nearby on Coode Island on the Yarra River, the Larkin Aircraft Supply Co was founded on July 1, 1921. It obtained Aerodrome Licence No 22 and closed in May 1934.

The river frontage 31 acre site was purchased for £14,475 from the Commonwealth Government and contract settled on May 24, 1937, but the provision of the landing field on land owned by the Victorian State Government was the subject of drawn out negotiation. The site was a close 2.25 miles from the centre of the city of Melbourne. The State Premier Albert Dunstan refused in 1935 to allow the construction of an airport, agreed to reconsider the matter in May 1936 and settled on December 8, 1936 to reserve and lease 146 acres for use by CAC as its landing field and to level and grade the area at an estimated cost to the State of £20,000. Work on the factory's sandy site started in February 1937 and building of the £100,000 original factory complex commenced two months later.

Construction was an astonishingly smooth and fast achievement. Hartnett had transferred his GM-H construction engineer Eric Gibson and the contractors from the GM-H building down the road and the CAC factory went up in a matter of five months; an art deco era industrial design similar to that of the NAA Inglewood plant in California. Administration moved from Little Collins St, Melbourne to the new building at 304 Lorimer St, Port Melbourne enabling CAC to become an independent concern. Measuring 520 feet by 320 feet, it was ready for occupation in September. The engine, airframe factories and ancillary buildings amounted to an area of about 143,000 sq ft.

Runway layout 1944, looking north. **HDHV via Tony Todaro**

In retrospect the site by the river isolated the factory from the growth of labour source to the west and south-west of the city because of the lack of access. However the nearby GM-H factories became a major subcontractor to CAC during the war years.

Because of the preferential trade agreement within the British Empire and the refusal of the Customs Department to waive duty on American production machinery, the British Trade Commission in Australia had to be mollified by the preferential importation of machinery from Britain where there was an equivalent to the required American item in return for the purchase of primary products. Within the available finance there had to be the strictest economy in the amount of production capital to be purchased. The Engine Factory machine shop was organised on a functional rather than components basis, ie with separate turning, milling, grinding and drilling sections. Whilst this was inconvenient in production it did ensure the maximum possible use of each multi-purpose machine tool rather than the specialised machinery for specific tasks as was employed at the large North American Aviation complex.

Construction of the first test house commenced in April 1938. It comprised of two engine cells located on either side of a control room. Test test house fuel farm and storage sheds were erected on the vacant land beyond No 1 Engine Factory close to and almost in line with the first Butler hangar. It was used for the P & W R-1340 engine production tests; R-985 and R-1830 overhauls and R-2000 and Cicada development work.

Subsequently, when the scale of production was increased, the machine shop was re-arranged on a components basis, ie approximately six factory sections each equipped to suit the machining of similar types of components within each section. Originally, the Aircraft Factory was to obtain all machined components from the Engine Factory. This produced problems with regard to priorities and when the production rate increased, a separate machine shop was established in the Aircraft Factory.

Aircraft work started in April 1938 with 490 employees. The first Pratt & Whitney R-1340 radial engine was accepted by the RAAF on January 27, 1939. Thus aero engines were in mass production many years before any similar engine manufacturing activity had taken place in the local automobile industry.

Left: Thomas W.(Bill) Air, first Chief Engineer & Herb Knight. **RAAF**

The first Wirraway flew two months later on 27 March, six months before the start of the war, approximately two and a half years after the start of factory construction. The largest source of tradesmen was the Victoria Railways Workshops. The initial factory worker average age was 32 years. In the overall make-up of the workforce, about twenty individuals had any prior aircraft design and/or construction experience.

Frank T. Wheeler previously 12 years with the Douglas Aircraft Company(USA), was appointed manager of the Aircraft Factory from July 15, 1938; Thomas W. (Bill) Air, shipwright, naval architect, engineer associate of Wackett from Cockatoo Dockyard its first Chief Engineer, and Harry Becker Superintendent of the Aircraft Factory.

The Air Board was quick to see the value of the new venture. On May 10, 1938 AVM Williams sought CAC's thoughts on the Air Board's need for a Wirraway with a Twin Wasp engine; 80 to 90 twin engine general purpose reconnaissance aircraft and 24 to 30 two-seater fighters. The last two inherited Tugan Gannet aircraft were dismantled and placed in storage on November 17, 1939 to gain needed floor space. In 1938 CAC built replacements of the upwards folding trailing edge lower lower wing section of the RAAF's Supermarine Seagull V amphibian aircraft as well as replacement parts and new leading edge slats for the RAAF's 34 Avro Cadet biplane trainer aircraft.

Government Take-Over Bid

The Federal Government made its entry into aircraft production building the Bristol Beaufort Torpedo/Bomber aircraft. Co-ordination of wartime aircraft production effort was given to the Aircraft Production Commission (APC), a statutory body established on March 21, 1940, headed by Harold W. Clapp. This body, responsible to the Minister for Supply, replaced the earlier Aircraft Construction Branch. As the war situation for Britain worsened, the Beaufort program became a totally Australian effort without the major input of overseas material and components which had been originally intended.

When the John Curtin Labor Government came to office on October 7, 1941 the new Minister for Aircraft Production (Don

The early years. The many piers on the Yarra River. **HDHV via Tony Todaro.**

USAAC P-38 and C-47 aircraft outside CAC's camouflaged factory building. **Richard Hourigan**

Cameron) supported a move by the APC to compulsorily acquire the assets of CAC at or near the original establishment price, or to assume control of the company as a wartime emergency measure for the duration of the conflict. This move was seen as a way to exercise a more centralized control over manpower and resources in the industry due to the difficulties experienced by the Beaufort Division built next door, to find the manpower and sub-contractors to cope with the vast demands of constructing the bomber. Such was the pressure that covert inducements were made to CAC staff to transfer to the Government site. The proposition put to the CAC Board by the Minister on December 12, 1941 was rejected. On 15 December, using BHP's Lockheed 12A, VH-ABH, Harold Darling, Sir Colin Fraser and Wackett flew to Canberra to clarify the matter with Prime Minister John Curtin. Harold Darling also issued a statement strongly condemning the actions of Harold Clapp and his takeover proposals. He suggested the problems of the APC would be solved by the formation of a Production Advisory Committee comprised of Government, Service, industry and union participation but the Minister would not budge. The Prime Minister gave his assurance that there was no plan to nationalize the aircraft industry. The APC was abolished the next day and the Aircraft Advisory Committee created within the Department of Aircraft Production with Wackett as its Technical Adviser. Harold Clapp resigned.

Expansion

In the middle of 1939 CAC was told it was to build the Bristol Taurus sleeve valve engine for the Beaufort bomber, an engine of an entirely different engineering configuration to the P & W Twin Wasp which Wackett had previously suggested be selected to power the Australian built Beaufort. CAC had asked but was refused Beaufort production work. Aside from the initial 132 Wirraways on order, this engine would have been CAC's only other work. Following the 1940 UK export embargo of Taurus engines, the RAAF decided to re-engine the Beaufort bomber with the larger P & W R-1830 Twin Wasp radial. CAC's experience building the P & W R-1340 radial, placed it in the excellent position in November 1939 of setting up and running a special Government plant on a 20 acre site at Lidcombe, NSW, to produce this engine. Building construction commenced in June 1940. Start-up was initially slow as castings were being made in Melbourne until Lidcombe's foundry opened in 1941. The first of 870 engines was delivered in November 1941. James Kirby managed the plant till the end of the war. Back at Fisherman's Bend, large quantities of replacement cylinders for the Armstrong Siddeley Cheetah engines on the Air Force's Avro Ansons were manufactured and dispatched every week. The number of Gipsy engine crankcase castings produced by the end of 1940 had exceeded three hundred. With the Japanese entry into the Pacific War the extra demand could only be met with a 60 hour week of 12 hour shifts of 8.00am-8.00pm / 8.00pm-8.00am for 5 days a week. It changed to a 52 hour factory week of five days of 8 hour shifts and a 12 hour shift on Saturday but it was difficult to maintain worker interest and efficiency with this routine. Employee numbers were at 5,141.

Wackett ran into problems with a summons from the authorities on May 26, 1942 for not maintaining an effective wartime factory blackout. Once sufficient materials had been received the Aircraft Machine Shop became the largest fluorescent lighting installation in Australia enabling total blackout conditions to be established. The factory exterior was painted in two-tone camouflage colours, the electricity sub-stations were sand-bagged, air raid shelters erected, a Volunteer Defence Force of about 550 staff and employees was organised and armed to be available for all shifts. Slit trenches were dug beside the Yarra River. An enemy aircraft sighting tower was on location at the adjacent DAP factory site. The introduction of a 44 hour week increased work efficiency and the factory went to night shift in May 1942. Personnel numbers reached 5,900.

A significant decision was made when the company established its own foundries. The £100,000 aluminium casting foundry was established in March 1938 under licence from the Aluminium Company of America (ALCOA). This commenced operation in January 1939 and the first cylinder head for the single Row Wasp was poured in March 1939. In addition huge tonnages of bronze castings were poured. The casting of magnesium parts was enabled through a licence agreement from *Magnesium Elektron* of the United Kingdom. The raw metal was originally obtained from the UK; eventually a ten ton shipment was received from the United States in July 1941. Thereafter BHP was able to be the sole source supplier. Some 270,000 lb of the alloy had been cast to June 1943. CAC's aircraft designs and the engines in production needed a combined total of in excess of 1,200 castings in either aluminium or magnesium. To cope with the overall demand for casting work the Fisherman's Bend area was extended and a new foundry built in the Melbourne suburb of Highett, where foundation works commenced in June 1942 and the first magnesium pour took place eight months later. All the magnesium and aluminium castings for all aircraft and engine manufacture, repair and overhaul by the RAAF and all organisations and companies supporting the aircraft industrial war effort were supplied by CAC. When the company commenced work on Wirraway production it had the support of about 30 sub-contractor firms. The achievement of their results was impressive in that, starters, generators, tyres, rivets, spark plugs, batteries, bomb sights, compasses and instruments were all completely made in Australia. The range of alloy steels increased to match manufacturing demand. As its workload increased the firms engaged on sub-contract work climbed to number around 300 by the end of June 1943. Most of these firms were new to the industry, with some from Australian subsidiaries or licensees of overseas companies. Some of these firms owed their existence and subsequent good fortune because of the need to supply CAC's production lines. Eventually and realistically the majority of those firms found it unprofitable in the post war era to maintain manufacturing and servicing facilities for military products for which there was a very small and irregular local demand.

USAAC Support

The factory assembly and test of American aircraft which were arriving at the Melbourne wharves for use by the growing numbers of American service personnel in Australia was starting to reach significant proportions by April, 1942. A portable Butler hangar (informally known as the American hangar) relocated from the Philippines was erected with materials supplied by the United States Army at the NE corner of the airfield. This went a long way towards improving working conditions. A second example followed and was set up as the Flight Hangar and Experimental Section and much later the Structural Test Section eg the Spaceframes; Ikara Test Rig & Simulation and Wamira Basic Trainer Bird Strike Gun. A Bellman hangar was also in place by 1942. Once the USAAF vacated the first Butler hangar it was used to store CA-11 Woomera components, then dismantled in June 1945 and relocated to Garbutt Field, Townsville and replaced by a further two transportable Bellman hangars.

The 'Myer' pre-fabricated house built by CAC on display in the Melbourne Treasury Gardens-1947. *Reg Schulz*

Example of the "bread and butter" work with bus bodies in various stages of construction and the CA17/CA18 P51 Mustang production line to the left. *Reg Schulz*

Depiction of a homely interior inside the display house. *L.J.Wackett/MS4858/NLA*

stores buildings still to be built in the vicinity for the U.S. authorities, the DAP Advisory Committee rejected the proposal outright.

Examples of DC-2, DC-3, C-47, Hudson, Lodestar, B-25 Mitchell, B-26 Marauder, P-38 Lightning, P-39 Airacobra, P-43 Lancer, P-47 Thunderbolt, P-40 Kittyhawk, A-20 Boston, Beech UC-45, Vought Kingfisher, Curtiss CW-22 Demon, Stinson Vigilant and Cessna UC-78 Bobcat were assembled, repaired or modified for the USAAC. Airspeed Oxfords were put together for the RAAF. Long range tanks were fitted to Marauders and Bostons. Seven USAAC B-24 Liberators were delivered for fitment of nose turrets, and lower guns. Four were completed but as this required special design effort, CAC was happy to see this work transferred to the QANTAS workshops in Sydney. Two C-47's were completely refitted as personal aircraft for Vice Admiral Arthur Carpender (USN), Commander Southwest Pacific Force and General Douglas MacArthur. Another 14 DC-3's were modified to freighter C-47's with cargo doors. The number of USAAC aircraft which were assembled or modified is variously documented as between 280 and 300. A rudimentary control tower box stood on the southern corner of CAC and DAP.

All this work was in addition to building the Wirraway, Wackett Trainer and Boomerang, the design and development of the CA-4, CA-11, CA-15, establishing the production of the CA-11, and producing engine cowlings, cowl gills and exhaust collectors for the DAP Beaufort.

Sea borne supplies, equipment and American aircraft destined for CAC for assembly and test were off-loaded at Port of Melbourne then trucked or towed down Salmon St into the airfield to receive attention in the two American hangars to the east of the plant. Supplies for CAC were also discharged at the seven or eight piers which abutted the north-west river frontage of the factory.

As the tempo of aircraft arriving by ship transport increased Wackett was in contact with the Dept of Interior on March 26,1942 asking them build a 40 foot wide taxiway to facilitate movement of aircraft from Princes Pier on Hobson's bay to the rear of the company's factory and airfield (and to also include the DAP Beaufort Division workshops). He suggested it could run along Boulevard West to Williamstown Rd, or alternately using Howe Pde, a distance of about one mile for an estimated cost of £1,250. The Dept of Works responded that this was likely to create traffic congestion and put forward four alternative routes. With a number of proposed large

Proud employees in front of the 1,000th 37 passenger seater GMH Bedford bus to be completed-June 1950. *Reg Schulz*

DV-94. The only Deliverette van built. Note the CAC hub caps. It now resides with the Science Museum of Victoria. *J.A.Vella*

The aeronautical design group of CAC at June, 1942 was comprised of Thomas W (Bill) Air, Frederick (Fred) David, Ian Fleming, Edwin (Ted) Faggetter, Ralph Price, Allan Bolton, Doug Humphries and Ian Ring forming part of a combined total of 180 draftsmen and engineers from various disciplines.

At the peak of activity in January, 1944 there were 7,400 personnel at Fisherman's Bend of which 1,244 were female. A further 3,243 employees were located at Lidcombe. The third shift was discontinued in February. Aircraft and engine factories expansion had continued to such an extent that CAC owned in excess of 654,000 sq ft of covered buildings by June 1944 from the initial 163,770 sq ft in 1938. From 1943 Lidcombe produced Merlin Mk 31,61 and 85 /Packard spares for the DHA Mosquito, RAAF Spitfires and Mustangs and moved on to the fabrication of tooling for Fisherman's Bend.

The 1,000th aircraft was delivered on December 17, 1944 ending with a total of 1,187 aircraft for the RAAF by August 8, 1945. This achievement had been possible because of the initial philosophy which went into setting up the company as the nucleus of a key part of Australia's emergent defence industry. The new plant at Fisherman's Bend was possibly the only one in the world that could, under its own roof turn out both engines and airframes supported by the myriad activities such as foundry work, machine shops and sheet metal shops. Yet in reality it was a back-stop strategic support operation. As the availability of American combat aircraft numbers rose rapidly from their vast resources, CAC's wartime production numbers took on a continual downward slide. There was also production competition from both the Beaufort Division with the Beaufighter and de Havilland at Bankstown, NSW with the Mosquito bomber.

From June 1942 to May 7, 1945, throughout most of the war, the Aircraft Advisory Committee met on 77 occasions at '*Western House*' at 83 William St, Melbourne. CAC's permanent representative was Lawrence Wackett. In his rare absences he was replaced by Thomas W. (Bill) Air or Board member, H.G. Darling. Five company test pilots were employed during the war years; Hubert Boss-Walker, James Carter, Ken Frewin, Greg Board and James Schofield.

War's End and Frustration
Government expenditure incurred to the end of the war in the development of the overall aircraft industry totalled approximately £ 111,350,000. In addition, another £24.5M had been outlaid under United States Lend Lease and Canadian Mutual Aid conditions for aircraft engines, materials and parts.

The cessation of hostilities brought a sharp cut back and a slowdown in the CA-17/18 Mustang project. No new aircraft programs were in sight and 80 Mustangs had been delivered to the end of 1946. Added to the 755 Wirraways; 200 Wackett Trainers; the two CA-4 / CA-11; 250 CA-12,13,14,19 Boomerangs and the one CA-15, it brought production numbers to 1,290 aircraft.

A faint glimmer for the future was the secondment of CAC personnel under Government and MAP sponsorship for a period of jet engine and airframe study in the United Kingdom. Six engine division staff: Colin Bellward, Jim Melbourne, Richard Brooks, George Brown and George Foster led by Hugh Francis left Australia on November 20, 1945 for a course at Power Jets Ltd. Hugh Francis who for 15 years had been the Chief Engineer of the Technical Department of Armstrong Whitworth (UK), became the CAC Aircraft Factory Superintendent when Frank Wheeler ended his association with CAC in July, 1940. The team members were directly involved in the day-to-day design, research and work at Whittle's Power Jets, Rolls Royce Ltd, de Havilland and the Royal Aircraft Establishment.

Engine factory to the right of the initial low level admin building as seen in this early 1938 view. Lorimer Street & Yarra River at the top. Visible (top right) is one of the Port Phillip Bay excursions' famous paddle steamers. **L. J. Wackett/MS4858/NLA**

On 22 November, Ted Faggetter, Doug Humphries and Ian Ring left for their stint with Power Jets followed by placement at the RAE Farnborough, Lucas and Dunlop to further their experience on aircraft design, development and manufacture. Fred David (the team's deputy) and Ian Fleming followed in March 1946 after finishing some CA-15 trials. CAC paid a A£5,000 fee for their laboured tuition. In the immediate post-war period, Britain was in an age of austerity and rationing so the CAC team was most appreciative of the food parcels which the company sent them on repeated occasions.

Approval was given in June 1945 for the design and construction of jet engine Test House No 1 with two test cells at a cost of £31,000. Located east of the Wasp piston engine test house, adjacent to and west of No 2 and 3 Bellman hangars, it began testing the RR Nene 2-VH jet engine in 1948 for the DHA built Vampire.

The Highett foundry was closed in July 1946 and all the work was consolidated at the £28,450 Fisherman's Bend foundry that the War Cabinet had approved in 1945. Consideration was given within the company to thoughts of amalgamation as a consortium with de Havilland and the Government, with CAC placing a heavy emphasis on engine work, de Havilland on special types of aircraft and propellers and the balance for the Government. Wackett realistically had felt CAC did not have the essential aircraft R & D funding base to support a manufacturing industry on its own.

An unexpected development was the Government decision to accept Britain's request that Australia might undertake the development of a pilotless target aircraft for use at the guided weapons range then in the process of being established at Woomera, South Australia. For security reasons, it was decided that this task should be handled by the DAP's Beaufort Division (later GAF) where only quite limited original design capability existed, whereas CAC with its more experienced design and development history was left out. As DAP had built aircraft of British origin, the UK was not about to let its secrets escape to CAC with its industrial inclination towards America.

In order to bolster its design capacity the Ministry of Munitions sought and obtained in August 1947 the transfer of CAC's Fred David to ARL and Ian Fleming to the DoS (he later led the design of the Jindivik pilotless aircraft), a move with practical reality due to the lack of aircraft work at CAC. Because of it, Ted Faggetter also left to start Dunlop Aviation (Melbourne): Alan Bolton and Thomas Air moved to Technico who were producing aircraft instruments. Joe Solvey went to the Structures Division of ARL to eventually specialize

Participation in Fokker F27 Friendship local production had been considered in 1957. J. A. Vella

in structural analysis of aerial target aircraft shot down at the Woomera UAV trials.

Work on the production of the R-R Nene 2-VH jet engine for the RAAF's order of DH Vampire fighter was underway with the agreement of March 1947. CAC sent a study team to R-R in the UK. Quantities of new machinery and tooling was required to switch to gas turbine engine production. A total of 114 engines and spares were assembled and built between 1948 and 1954. Wackett's plans for the long term survival of his factories was to enter the field of commercial production of domestic goods, items which were in short supply and for which there was a ready demand. Personnel numbers were reduced and CAC turned out 65,000 aluminium kettles at the rate of 300 a day, 25,000 saucepans, 75,000 domestic pressure cookers, 1,000 metal roofs made up of different configurations of pressed steel tiles for the Victorian Housing Commission, 25,000 enamelled baths, wooden doors and 150 pre-fabricated *Myer* houses.

The *Myer Emporium* held a display of its three bedroom *Myer House* in the Treasury Gardens in March 1947 and 400 purchasers put down a deposit. For an exclusive supply of timber to CAC, the Toorongo Logging Co (£14,500) and Limberlost Lumber Mills (£12,500), trucks, saw mill, railway siding at Nayook (Victoria), near Noojee, were acquired in May 1947. The price of houses was set by the Prices Commission and having teamed with J. C. Taylor and Sons for the on-site work and building erection, the program ran into, objection from some councils, industrial strikes due to restrictive building regulations, building industry self-protection, hostility of the government to big business and refusal of plumbers, painters, bricklayers to co-operate on site. Output was delayed 12 months and after outlaying £75,000 CAC incurred heavy financial losses with only 50 built. The *Myer Department* homes were sold at a fixed price of £1,650 each (at a loss to CAC). An expansion of this concept was the design of a two storied pre-fabricated Type A concrete cottage. However the agreement with Myer was terminated on May 18, 1948. The production facilities were scrapped and its timber mill at Nayook was sold to home builder A.V. Jennings in June for £80,000. (Similarly by 1948, Vickers Aircraft Ltd (UK) had completed about 11,000 pre-fabricated houses for the post war UK Government.) CAC was making its baths for £14, they retailed for £17/3/6 but by the end of 1951 they

North American Aviation F-100 Super Sabre. Considered by Wackett as possible successor to CAC Sabre also to be fitted with a RR engine. J.A.Vella Collection

had become a loss venture, costing £18 each to produce. Examples of a modular kitchen and bathroom were constructed for the Victoria Housing Commission. In February 1946, CAC was contracted to GM-H to build passenger bus bodies. This was to be the long term bread and butter work that was to help provide the cushion between the highs and lows of future aircraft production work. The first of 2,177 of these (to October 1961) was delivered on October 15, 1946.

The two Lockheed 12A Electra aircraft of Broken Hill Associated Smelters' VH-ABH *Silver City* and BHP/Zinc Corp's VH-ASG *Silver Gull* of the Associated Airlines corporate fleet were based and maintained by CAC at Fisherman's Bend from 1946 till about 1957.

In July 1946, £10,000 was set aside for the development of a narrow aluminium body delivery van that could move down tight laneways. Its power was a (1938) 597cc BMW R66 motor bike engine and gear box, with the driver standing up or perched on a retractable saddle seat, while folding side doors provided easy access. The one *Deliverette* built in 1947 created business interest but production plans were shelved with the onset of the Korean war. Plans for a three wheeled postal delivery van for country mail distribution were also shelved. In 1948 GM-H decided to sell their shareholding in CAC. Their shares were acquired by Rolls Royce only after serious consideration as it had not previously invested in any overseas or aircraft manufacturing business, for which Wackett wrote in his autobiography *"Here was a famous British firm with a world-wide reputation being financially interested in an Australian firm, one which to build up had been my life's work. I gained much personal satisfaction. What would the critics say now? We had started exclusively with American help, but now we were linked with the very spirit of Britain, Rolls Royce".*

The CA-22/25 Winjeel project was given the go-ahead; the advanced CA-23 design was deeply researched, then ended. The CA-24 Hawker P1081 was to be built but eventually abandoned. To 1951, CAC had completed 278 DHA Vampire 100 gall drop tanks. The urgency of the Korean War brought about the serious work on the CA-26 / 27 Sabre. It was a time of new aerodynamics, new advanced engine types to take over from the initial Rolls-Royce centrifugal type Nene. Both the Canberra bomber and the CA-23, before its cancellation, were to be recipients of the RR Tay turbo-jet. However the RR Avon was built to power the CA-27 Sabre and also GAF's licence built Canberra bomber. Test House No 2 to test the Avon was designed and built by CAC to the east of the Nene Test House but with a wall in common. It was completed in December 1952 and also used to test RR Derwent, BS Viper and the Solar range of industrial engines.

Herbert Knight second General Manager of CAC, 1960-1969. J. A. Vella Collection

For the more powerful Avon Mk 109, CAC designed and built Test House No 3, located between the Wasp engine house and the engine factory. Overseen by Jim Melbourne (Engine Development & Test), this was upgraded from late 1957 and completed in 1962 to handle 30,000 lb thrust engines; was government owned and CAC paid to use it each time. Portion of the old piston engine test cells

Pre 1965 clear view of the expanded site with the three Bellman hangars and gun firing butts in the foreground. **HDHV**

structure was used during the upgrade. This enabled the provision of four fully silenced and acoustically treated inlet ducts. Hot engine gases were ejected via a massive detuner 6 feet in diameter at its entrance and 12 feet at the exit end. It was 104 feet long and weighed 55 tons. Jet engine Test Houses 1-3 were air and water cooled. Water was pumped and sprayed into the exhaust detuner from tank storage at the rear of the test houses.

Varied engine work had continued at Lidcombe on the RR Merlins for the GAF Lincoln bomber and the conversion of others for the CA-17/18 Mustang. Bristol Centaurus and Double Mamba, RR Griffon engines of the RAN Fleet Air Arm's Hawker Sea Fury, Fairey Gannet and Firefly aircraft were overhauled modified and returned to service on 3,792 occasions to 1960.

A Boost in Aircraft Work

The former Air Marshall George Jones was on the Board of CAC from 1952 to 1957 following his retirement from the RAAF. He believed in the Australian aircraft industry and strongly supported the local design of aircraft. The spurt of design activity to support the Winjeel, CA-23 all-weather fighter and the re-engineering of the F-86 Sabre meant a rebuilding of CAC's design team for the second time. Thomas Air returned as Chief Engineer of the Aircraft Division in November 1949 and stayed till October 1952. This work was accompanied by a five year engine and airframe overhaul program to refurbish 153 Wirraways for the RAAF and RAN.

With the CA-27 Sabre in production Wackett looked at the NAA F-100 Super Sabre as its successor but with a RR Avon RA-19R engine instead of its P & W J57. His next thoughts were to fit two of the Avons in a widened fuselage. Neither scheme went ahead.

Cars lining up for regular weekend racing on the quite Fisherman's Bend runways. Behind the Viv Payne's FL Holden is a model 250F Formula One Maserati; one of the 1957/58 World Championship cars. **Viv Payne**

In the first thirteen years of its use the Fisherman's Bend Airfield had been the take-off point for many types of one, two and four engine aircraft built and assembled by CAC and the adjacent DAP / GAF factory reaching up to the size of the GAF Lincoln bomber. Two 4,200 foot long paved runways were laid, together with a diagonal grass strip. By 1950 it had become clear that the replacement aircraft for the Lincoln and Mustang would be jet powered requiring longer, safer runways and creating an increased noise problem. As the English Electric Canberra bomber was to be the next manufacturing project at GAF, the DoS conducted a review in 1950 of airfields suitable for its flight testing. All used and disused airfields within a 50 mile radius of Melbourne were suggested including Pakenham East; Monomeith Park south of Koo-Wee-Rup (considered to be too marshy); an area south of Geelong; the Laverton RAAF Base and the rank outsider, Tocumwal, NSW, on the River Murray.

Whilst RAAF Laverton was considered to be the most attractive proposition, 4,300 acres of farmland was acquired at Lara to establish the Avalon Airfield. No jet engine aircraft used the Fisherman's Bend runways. The Winjeels and Ceres were flown from there and the 1965 decision to build the high span Lower Yarra Bridge across the river mouth sealed the fate of the wartime airfield necessitating its closure and eventual subdivision. Nevertheless, CAC conducted initial flight trials on all the CA-32 (Bell 206B-1) helicopters built at the factory. Air space and flight corridors were allocated for CAC's use.

To about 1962, the company ran a private ferry service across the Yarra River for its employees residing in the western suburbs and disembarked them at the Lorimer Street piers but with the upgrade of the Port of Melbourne to handle substantial container cargoes and the eventual opening of the Lower Yarra crossing bridge, the small Lorimer St piers were removed. The area of river immediately in front of the factory became a large, ship swinging basin.

Although the company had been established with the added aim of eventually becoming involved in civil aircraft, its formative years were in the war period. This meant a heavy concentration on military aviation products which led to the development of a style of industry which was different to what would have eventuated had it been an operation managed solely by market forces. There was generally only one customer...the Government, and ignoring the tiered structure within each level of Government; in simplistic terms, there were only three people needed to approve a decision to purchase - a politician, a member of the Armed Services and a Departmental member. CAC became subject to rigid governmental control over all its operations; over its cost accounting procedures and profits as though it were a section of the DoS. Profits of 5% did not take into account advertising or re-investment.

There was the trend for the levels of manufacturing technology to remain static until a new aircraft building program would be introduced in a hurry. Each program beginning with the Sabre and continuing with the Mirage, MB326H etc. presented a heavy financial burden to update manufacturing processes and maintain good productivity. The finance needed for the acquisition and operation of even more complex machinery and processes for a short run of more expensive military

ACM Sir Frederick Scherger. Chairman of the CAC Board, 1968-1974. **HDHV**

A89-903. The RAAF P-2V and SP-2H Neptune fleet received systems upgrades by CAC between 1957 and 1964. J. A. Vella

North American Aviation A-3 J/RA-5C Vigilante, US Navy nuclear strike bomber was offered to CAC to build to replace the EE/GAF Canberra. J.A. Vella Collection.

aircraft was beyond the resources of local companies comprising the small industry.

The Australian Government established the practice of purchasing the major machine tools which would then be available to the industry for use on Government work. It then encouraged the use of the equipment on commercial work for which use it sought to charge exorbitant and uncompetitive rental fees. There were constant arguments on cost detail as to whether items of a commercial nature had been fabricated on CAC owned machinery or Government purchased equipment for which there would then be a rental charge made based on the new price of the machinery concerned. There was a brief flirtation with civil aircraft roles. Preliminary design work was carried out on the Wallaby feeder liner and many possible Winjeel derivatives. In 1957, the Minutes of the Board made brief mention of the possibility of building the Fokker F27 Friendship airliner (or parts of it) but it could not safely allocate the floor space to do so as it waited to lead the build of the RAAF's next jet fighter. The directors were not keen to take the risk and lose. The F27's method of construction was not in CAC's engineering style and its market potential was judged to be low when the the similar Handley Page Herald and Aviation Traders Accountant designs had very short production runs. Many CA-27 Sabre enhancement proposals were put forward. Finally the CA-28 Ceres aerial agricultural spreading aircraft was started in 1956 as a private venture risk project. Only 20 examples were sold. All through the war years and immediately after there was a heavy reliance on cost plus defence work. Some of the shareholders representatives were in favour of cost plus, but the company management was not in favour. The bills were sent to the Government who audited, approved or reduced the figures and provided the funds a year or 18 months later. The quality was always good, the delivery not too bad, but the price was a real battle. It struggled with the start-up costs for a low production run.

There was no result to a plan of September 1959 to join with AWA for a co-production scheme of the Philco Sidewinder air-to-air missile. At the same time the position at Lidcombe had become critical. It had built undercarriage parts for the GAF Lincoln, DHA Vampire and CAC Winjeel and the work force fell from 1,000 in 1956 to about 300 in 1959. The decision was taken to end CAC's management of the factory. It was leased to de Havilland as of January 1, 1960. Recognition of the value of CAC was made by Sir Roy Fedden the famous Bristol Aero Engine chief designer during his private visit of Australia and New Zealand in 1959. In the July issue of '*Aircraft*' he voiced his concern at the agitation in the local Press about the future necessity of CAC: *"in my view Australia has an irreplaceable asset in the CAC set-up by Sir Lawrence who established a breed of men with pride and enthusiasm for the highest class of workmanship, second to none in the world...created through Aeronautics, and it has proved a high watermark for engineering quality throughout the country, which is a priceless asset."*

Between 1957 and 1964 the company carried out modifications on the twenty-four P2V-4 & 5 and SP-2H Neptune maritime patrol aircraft of the RAAF's No 10 and 11 Sqdns. This work undertaken at Avalon Airfield, took in revised and repaired engine mounts; new engine fire extinguisher systems (this followed the fatal airborne engine fire loss of A89-308 near Richmond, NSW on February 4, 1959) together with electrical and structural work to install the AF/ARN-801 '*Wombat*' Doppler navigational aid. This update was a precursor to similar major work CAC was to undertake some 10 years later on the successor P-3B/C Orion fleet.

In 1958, North American Aviation approached CAC for it to build 100 of its extremely advanced A3J Vigilante, the USN's carrier-borne strategic nuclear bomber (f/f 31/8/1958) with its unique rearward ejection bomb delivery system. In its later RA/5C reconnaissance/attack reconfiguration, it was selected by the 1963 AM Valston Hancock overseas mission; 36 aircraft for £88M were required but it was quickly dropped. It was not a tactical strike aircraft.

Wackett was raised to Knight Bachelor in the 1954 New Year's honours list. He retired from the management of CAC in December 1960 saying - *"its the end of an era..... I have had my day"*. He dominated CAC from 1936 to 1960 as its Chief Executive at a time when personalities rather than committees called the tune and in an era in which observers of the time, believed CAC to be the equal of the world's best (for its size) in the years 1948 to 1953. He did not work with the planned luxury of a deputy manager so relegated management functions during his absences, to the company's secretary. Described as the, *"won't be beaten personality, big, blunt and all Australian"* in his expressed contempt of meddlers and bureaucrats. He knew what was right and appropriate in an aircraft requirement sense and the observation was often made - was it he or the Air Marshals who ran the Air Force Requirements Branch? He was not a notable aircraft designer but he worked hard at it in his early days. He was more at ease in mechanical work, inventions and for his expertise in production engineering. In 1959 he received the Kernot Memorial Medal from Melbourne University for distinguished engineering achievement followed in 1967 by the Finlay National Award from the Institute of Production Engineers and in 1974 the Oswald Watt Medal for outstanding contribution to the development of aviation in Australia. His salary in August 1960 was £7,200. Whereas de Havilland (Australia), a subsidiary of the British parent firm also a prolific builder during WW2, was created to sell, assemble and to later make British designed aircraft. Its leaders and its aircraft escaped the public attention of Lawrence Wackett but the designs of its parent firm were world famous names. It became part of the Hawker Siddeley Group(UK) in 1959 and Hawker de Havilland Australia on January 11, 1963.

The Sixties

Herb Knight, Superintendent of the Engine Factories became CAC's second General Manager on January 1, 1961. A legacy of Wackett's long term management stint of almost a quarter of a century was that the degree of control and decision-making process which he had exercised had left many members of his senior management bereft of the major decision making process. The CA-29 Mirage sub-contract and accompanying ATAR 9C engine came on stream in September 1964 but without CAC as its highly anticipated project leader. CAC had a £10,000 work package(Project EX219) to design the rear fuselage, tail surfaces and General Electric engine installation in GAF's 1964 F.2 jet trainer design to ASR AIR 51 but it was cancelled on January 21, 1965 after the selection of the Italian MB326H.

Bill Abbott, CAC's third General Manager 1969 to 1976 came from the British Motor Corporation, Australia. **HDHV**

The CA-30 was the CAC-managed licence build for the RAAF of its new trainer, the Macchi MB326H and its Bristol Siddeley Viper engine. This contract provided a peak workload to 3,572 employees in 1967 as the production / assembly line pushed out three complete airframes and five engines each month.

In an opportunity to prepare itself for the chance to provide a light observation helicopter to the Armed Services, CAC assumed control of International Helicopters, the Australian agents for Hughes Helicopters on December 1, 1967. Its subsequent submission of the Hughes 369/500/OH-6A design lost out to Bell Helicopters.

The dependence on Air Force work caused massive variations in employment demand from the peak response to a national crisis of war, to the trough of frustration in political indecision in the post war years reaching in the surprise truncation of the CA-32 Bell 206 helicopter project. Being part of a techno-political industry meant a near to total dependence on political decisions not necessarily made on the basis of logic, good economics or even good reason. This fluctuation in hope and depression still left the company with a small nucleus of loyal, highly trained and skilled men who stayed on when outside industry or overseas opportunities might well have tempted them to seek areas of greater promise.

The Learning Curve effect

Because of the lack of continuity in aircraft production, CAC had to build up its work force three times up to 1970 with an obvious reduction in skills with each build-up campaign in the available class of labour. Because of the lack of job security, skilled men did not return. CAC was committed to minimum award wage rates with a nominal bonus. They could not always attract skilled labour with the consequence that semi-skilled men had to be trained for a particular task.

Under this less than ideal management of people, the only obvious virtue was production efficiency. In 1956, CAC and the industry in general held a 40% advantage over the United States in lower labour costs. The case for local production could definitely be stated to be in Australia's favour, ie a lower unit cost, provided the Government made an early decision to order in relation to the production status of the overseas design and the order was in the region of 100 aircraft. Engineering and tooling costs were still able to be absorbed.

However it was not these components which made the local product appear to be dearer, but the Learning Curve effect, brought about by the large numbers of aircraft ordered by, for example the U.S. Government. This effect of a reduction in man-hours needed for the production of a second item or unit, amounted to 80% of that of the first unit, and those for the fourth unit were 80% of the second unit with the hours progressively reduced to the stage where the 100th unit required only 22.7% of the hours required for the first unit. However, local orders seldom exceeded 100 aircraft first off.

This effect gave American products (or those of other countries) the high price advantage if Australia waited until 500 or more of the aircraft had been produced before purchasing our aircraft from them. The slender initial local orders, offset by the lesser labour cost could only be competitive if compared with the identical point on the learning curve of the original producer's production line. This was compounded by the need to train about 75% of recruited labour, causing time and cost lags and the reluctance of local component or raw material suppliers to set up for a short time to exacting standards on a stop-start basis...all problems associated with a lack of continuity of projects. Labour was frequently sought from the UK. Whilst secondary industries were protected by tariffs etc., aero engines produced in Australia for military purposes had no such protection and consequently suffered in direct comparison with overseas costs. Having built the Sabre here, CAC was able to modify and support it both locally and in the region for about 18 years, long after US production had ceased.

A Call For Recognition

Sir Frederick Scherger (Air Chief Marshall) former Chairman of the Chiefs of Staff, joined the board of CAC in March, 1967. On 2 October the Chairman of the Board, Sir Sydney Rowell told an assembled gathering at the handover ceremony of the first Macchi MB326H that he hoped the Government would not allow CAC to become a mere copyist, but one, which with original work and thought could capitalize on its wide range of engineering skills.

His words were almost echoed the following year by Ian Ring, the Chief Engineer who expressed the remarks in his Lawrence Hargrave Memorial lecture of September 19, 1968 that,

> *"CAC had shown initiative in design far in excess of what might have been expected for its size. It is regrettable that more use has not been made of the Australian industry's services. Much is made of the need for protection of the grossly expanded automobile and electronic and domestic appliance industries, but the aircraft industry has been made a political and Service football which nobody wants to hold. Major projects are based on Service requirements for new aircraft every eight years, but there is a pressing need for experimental and developmental work between these projects. Australia was able through the utilization of skills within its design force to achieve very low development costs unlike the United States where skill specialization puts up the cost of design overheads".*

Continuing with the bus production line, 442 COMAIR CAV 12,14,16,17,18,19,20 & 21 bodies were rolled out between 1960 and December 1970 supplied on Bedford and Leyland chassis. No longer a viable enterprise, this activity was terminated.

The deeply studied CA-31 private venture supersonic trainer was overlooked. The AA-107 collaborative project for close support swing-wing aircraft with the British Aircraft Corporation was also dropped for lack of international customer interest.

Sir Frederick Scherger commented again in 1971: *"that CAC....in general submitted design projects in line with advanced overseas technology, aligned to Australian requirements, have them discussed, advised and re-evaluated until time ran out too late or the Spec revised too late for local production."*

A Lack of Confidence

A significant pointer to the future after the demise of the AA-107 was given by David Fairbairn, the Minister for Air, Federal House of Representatives debate in July 1970 on a subject *of public importance,* when he said,

> *"the greatest drawback with local production is that you tend to get a set-up in which something designed in Australia almost inevitably turns out to be not as good as the best aircraft designed and flying overseas. Then, by pressure of events, the RAAF is forced to take something that is second best. We have to decide whether we want the RAAF to be just a public relations show for Australian industry or whether we want it to be the best equipped Air Force in the world".*

> *"There is a future for the industry in Australia. It lies in repairs, maintenance of modifications and in projects like Jindivik, Ikara, Turana and others. It also lies in making components. I believe it is essential that when we place orders for defence equipment overseas we have an agreement that many of the components that can be made in Australia should be made in Australia".*

During the ensuing debate, Defence Minister Malcolm Fraser said in part, *"Hawker de Havilland has, I think, shown more initiative than the other two sectors of the industry in achieving orders, even in the exceedingly difficult United States Aerospace market. If the rest of the industry can show the same initiative and enterprise, a healthier situation might develop".*

This latter situation had been partly brought about by the overload in the U.S. industry as a result of the demands by the Vietnam War and the need to find uncommitted production capacity. It was not CAC policy to enter the U.S. sub-contract market at that time preferring instead to improving RAAF and RAN support and letting others chase offset work and observing their experience.

Group Expansion

After ten years at the helm, Herb Knight stepped down on December 31, 1969 for his replacement, R. L. (Bill) Abbott with an advertised annual salary of $25,000 (*The Herald*) who came from the disbanded British Motor Corporation (Leyland). An active private pilot, Bill had been on the GM Holden car original design team, military truck work and also associated with rail and locomotive programs in Detroit, Michigan, USA. His brief was to take the company away from its near-to-complete dependence on cost-plus work. No long term commercial projects had been sought for a long time for fear that they might have stood in the way of effective tendering for Air Force contracts.

As *Aircraft* magazine put it in July 1969 when the vacancy of General Manager was advertised:

> *"he will be expected to increase profitable commercial manufacturing to maximize utilization of plant"* and *"an indication that the industry should be forced to this line having had no backing of Government and private capital for its own design talents - appropriately applied to both the needs of the RAAF and that wider field. If others can confidently accept such a challenge, why not Australia? Our wisdom and vision are little in evidence".*

Ian Ring, Chief Aeronautical Engineer to CAC 1953-1980. **HDHV.**

Personnel and management organisational changes were introduced. CAC had not previously had a specialized sales and marketing organisation. Until the advent of Bill Abbott, the Engineering Department practically ran the operations of the company, being involved in all the phases of design, production, marketing and costing. This was altered through a dispersion of personnel and responsibilities. The engine and airframe factories were combined into a single Production Engineering Group, one Machine Shop, one Tool Room and one Supply Purchasing System with Arthur Nash the Chief Production Engineer.

There were plans to change the company name. To the uninformed, the name *'Commonwealth'* gave the impression of a link with the Government. The profit margin was consistently falling over the years and at one stage no profit could be made over a set gross figure. Additional work was done at no profit. There were tight cost estimates prior to the start of a job and any subsequent variation had to be justified. Overhead costs were greatly increased by Government bureaucratic overseeing whilst engineering and manufacturing costs were remarkably good and competitive particularly in relation to HDH and GAF. CAC made less profit under cost plus than they would have made on fixed price contracts. In the first two years of commercial offset work it lost $790,000.

The basic problem always faced at CAC was one of amortizing the pre-production non-recurring costs, like organising and tooling over very small volume orders. Piece prices, ie direct labour, material and applicable overheads were fairly competitive with the United States (until about 1972), provided roughly equal volumes, were considered. To diversify its activities and redress the emphasis on military work, Rex Aviation, the Australasian distributor of Cessna aircraft was acquired and became part of the CAC group on July 1, 1971. Design studies were undertaken to try and incorporate Cessna components into CAC originated but Cessna based single and multi-engine aircraft.

Mergers, Rationalization and Specialisation Plans

There had been repeated plans to rationalize and rework the entire industry since the DAP established the Government factories in 1939. Ian Ring's extensive private papers set out his involvement in these continuous and repeated exercises. Their relationship with and effect upon CAC were paramount. In simplified form, the options which had been canvassed were:

- Take-over of GAF by CAC
- Take-over of CAC by GAF
- Merger of the two organizations with a single management board, incorporated as a private company
- Merger of the two organizations with the addition of an Australian electronics company
- Rationalisation by specialisation

No solution was ever found through the many committees that were set up. No proposal satisfied the financial and political interests of the parties involved nor those of their respective employee groups.

Proposals for restructuring of the industry seemed to come to prominence at times of low work-load and uncertain futures. The first instance of rationalization (as related previously) came in 1941 when the APC sought the enforced acquisition of CAC, but was squashed by the Prime Minister of the day, John Curtin. By 1958, the entire industry, having gone past the peak workloads of the Sabre, Winjeel, Canberra and Jindivik programs was expected to sink to non-viable levels. It was clearly the time to put the entire industry into a better organised status.

The only outstanding work was on the GAF Jindivik target aircraft and the Malkara anti-tank guided missile. Sir Lawrence Wackett was not convinced that there was no future for manned fighter aircraft as had been inferred earlier in a suggestion that GAF be restricted to being a guided weapons group requiring a small labour force and reduced floor space. CAC would take over all remaining aircraft work, overhaul and repair tasks from GAF in addition to embarking on the local manufacture of the Fokker F27 Friendship airliner, which idea CAC had financially considered in 1957 but put aside.

To determine the contraction of the industry the Government established the Fitzgerald Committee in March 1958. Led by Sir Alexander Fitzgerald, professor of accounting at Melbourne University it rejected any idea of mergers and recommended the closure of the Fisherman's Bend GAF factory and to transfer of all future aircraft, engine and guided missile contracts to CAC. The balance of the diminishing load would go to GAF at Avalon with the exception of the small design section which could have been absorbed by the Research and Development Group of the Department of Supply. The Fitzgerald Report also recommended that the DoS / Chrysler Motor Car Annexe in Adelaide be made available to CAC and that a progress review be held within two years. de Havilland Aircraft's chairman in Sydney, Lester Brain, urged CAC to continue in its bid to take control of GAF, which, set up as a wartime necessity (in the form of the DAP Beaufort Division), was enjoying continued favoured support by the DoS to the detriment of the private enterprise pair.

With its contents favourable to CAC, the report was never released or publicly discussed. As the time approached to decide on the Sabre fighter replacement, the Department told CAC that it wished to implement the project by spreading the work amongst the three factory groups, meaning the policy for rationalization had been ignored or revised.

Mr N. Hodgson, Manager of GAF headed a committee created in February 1960 to carry out the suggested review. It reported five months later that CAC's future appeared to be completely dependent on the new fighter decision, whereas GAF had good prospects for a substantial base workload. Further plans were to be left in abeyance pending the outcome of the Sabre replacement. The shock nomination of GAF as prime contractor for the Mirage fighter led to considerable argument and negotiation in order that CAC be allowed

A very busy Engine/Machine shop in the 1960s. **HDHV**

a share of the airframe work in addition to building its large new afterburning engine.

A DoS team established in the middle of 1961 to examine rationalization reported back in October with the conclusions:

- That a take-over of GAF by CAC was an unlikely possibility
- The formation of a joint CAC/Government company was not likely. To merge the two bodies into a commission would require a major investigation
- The most readily attainable degree of integration would be for the DoS to absorb most or all of the CAC establishment
- If a merger could not be achieved in the near future, then the principle of allocating projects to a selected prime contractor should be continued and reviewed within two years

This Departmental Committee had reversed the recommendations of the Fitzgerald Committee and gave its support to GAF, continuing to build up increasing excessive capacity to about 1976.

CAC then went through a stable period with the Mirage work and the design and manufacture of the Ikara and Branik missile handling systems for the RAN and Brazilian Navy. With the workload bottoming out in 1968 / 69 the Chairman of the Board, Sir Frederick Scherger addressed the Minister for Supply (Senator Ken Anderson) on June 26, 1968 urging rationalization with CAC as the predominating unit. This was followed up by a Departmental Working Party investigation which suggested that from a determined future date all work for the aircraft industry in Victoria should be the province of a new organisation based on the present CAC. Work then in progress with GAF at that date would be handed over to CAC. As there was not sufficient defence work for two organisations it was intimated that CAC ought to involve itself in commercial aircraft projects at its own expense.

The company re-submitted rationalization plans on May 27, 1969 asking for a merged CAC / GAF but with growth planned into it and seeking a government R & D expenditure of $400,000 per annum with the new grouping. Another Working Party led by K.D.Johnson was convened to work on this submission and it reported in September 1969 to an agreed merger with CAC as the surviving entity. The DoS under guidance from the Government sought to implement the necessary procedures, however the Department's Victorian Regional Director presented a paper with an excessively pessimistic outlook on workload and surprised the different participants by suggesting the formation of a joint company with government and private share holdings or a wholly owned government company. The CAC Board did not accept a minority shareholding but was willing to consider an equal shareholding.

Assisted by Working Parties and Sub-Working Parties each with joint CAC / GAF representation, each studying specialised aspects of amalgamation, the groups worked towards trimming resources but given this, the investigating committees saw the joint company as a viable and financially improved proposition. The estimated cost of operation was $33 million with the then current combined workload, employing 3,500 people, 400 less than the existing level. Financial assistance from the Government of $6.2M per annum would be required at the existing level of workload, compared with $9.2M being provided to the separate organizations. They estimated that assistance would not be required when employment reached 6,000.

In July 1971, a joint CAC/DoS study was set up to study the practical issues of amalgamation in detail followed in September 1971 by the Defence Industrial Committee under the chairmanship of industrialist Sir Charles McGrath (1969-77) to examine the position with particular reference to Defence requirements. It reported in August 1972. In September 1972 the Government gave conditional approval to Australian participation in multi-national collaborative arrangements and sanctioned the DoS to negotiate rationalization. CAC's workload in 1972 was comprised of 84% of Government work, 10% overseas offset contracts and 6% from local commercial need. At the same time, it was not able to attract the bright young qualified men as there was little confidence in an industry that was static.

In January 1973 the new Labor Government Defence Minister Lance Barnard, authorised further discussions to amalgamate the three major organisations under one management. The next Working Group which included CAC's General Manager Bill Abbott, was assisted by officers of the Development Finance Corporation. The Group based its deliberations on an industry workload of 4.5 million man-hours with a total 6.0 million man-hour capacity (reduced from the then 8.0 million hours). GAF's loss for 1971-72 was $443,000. CAC's profit was $218,000.

Federal Cabinet was not happy that two private sectors of the amalgamation should be guaranteed a profit from the combined body. The continued procrastination by the Government and the absence of any sort of stable policy was proving very irritating to the CAC Board. The Chairman expressed to the Minister of Defence in September 1973 that GAF be made a statutory Corporation, so as to create fair competition within the industry.

He added that the CAC Board had five alternatives before them:

- Go into a form of merger acceptable to CAC shareholders
- Sell out to the Government if an acceptable price could be negotiated
- Continue as is, assuming Reserve Capacity Funding remains
- Continue in existence, but only on specialised lines of manufacture (eg engines)
- Go out of business

The Minister responded to this appeal indicating a planned overall contraction to defence contracts then underway. CAC's employee numbers had sunk in 1970 to 1.3 million man-hours utilization per annum compared with 3.2 million man-hours in 1967.

It was decided that the move of HDH Lidcombe to Bankstown would proceed independently of Fisherman's Bend. At the same time CAC revealed its interest in moving to the largely then empty Essendon Airport and vacating the Fisherman's Bend site. This move was mooted as part of the RAAF P-3C Orion maritime patrol aircraft systems upgrade project that had been under investigation.

The new Government and the Minister clearly had no policy at all on rationalization of the industry.

Desperately, the CAC Chairman was again in touch with the Minister on October 12, 1973 stating that in view of the small projected workload and lack of overall planning there appeared to be three options available to CAC:

- For the Government to buy out all the CAC assets at Fisherman's Bend, and take over all CAC staff
- For the Government to buy out only those CAC assets necessary for planned defence support. CAC to dispose of the remainder of the property and staff as best it can
- For CAC to complete its non-aircraft work as quickly as possible, and reduce to a specialist organization in the field of engines and mechanical skills, located either at Essendon Airport or Fisherman's Bend (and still doing engine testing at Fisherman's Bend)

Answers were needed by February 1974 so as to enable a cessation of company operations by February 1976. (CAC's Rex Aviation and helicopter interests were not part of any negotiation agreement.)

In March 1974, the Department submitted to the Defence Industrial Committee its proposals for rationalization by:

- Consolidating the Lidcombe facilities into Bankstown
- Restructuring the facilities at Fisherman's Bend under one management with a potential capacity for 3.0 million man-hours a year

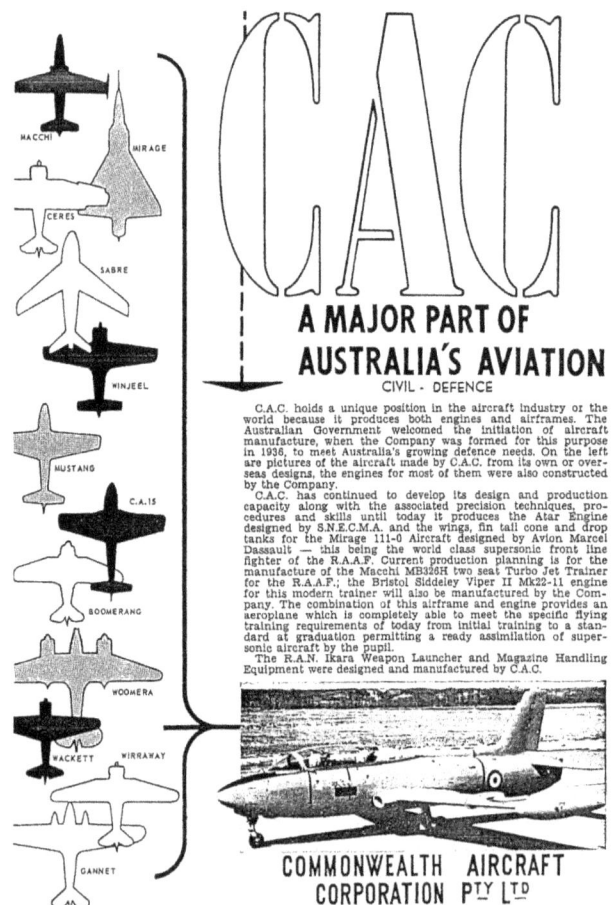

A frequent appearance of a CAC advert in AIRCRAFT magazine a consistent supporter of the Australian aviation scene.

It is not certain if what was intended was to be 'rationalization' or 'nationalization', as Clyde Cameron, Labor Minister for Science & Consumer Affairs, 1972-1975 in the Gough Whitlam government had a strong advocacy of nationalization of the industry with a majority Cabinet backing. His ideas imitated the take-over plans of CAC, by Don Cameron, (no relation) Labor Minister for Aircraft Production of 1941-45. In April 1974, CAC's newest move was to cut back the size of the plant by 50% and to concentrate primarily on engine and mechanical work, but to undertake aircraft and other work as could be obtained competitively. It also sought the transfer of certain relevant sections of GAF to CAC in return for CAC withdrawal. In May 1974 the Prime Minister Gough Whitlam decided the question of future assistance to the industry should be referred to the Industries Assistance Commission.

A paper based on the CAC proposal was considered by the Defence Industrial Committee in September 1974. The Committee:

- Endorsed that planning proceed for rationalisation of the facilities at Fisherman's Bend along the lines of the CAC proposal
- Endorsed the choice of CAC as the preferred contractor for manufacture and overhaul of all jet engines used by the Services, except those presently maintained by the Services themselves or the airlines
- Recommended that action take place as soon as possible

The answers to the entire aerospace industry were dependant on equipment needs for the Services, level of Service activity, partnership ratio between the private section and Government party and the return on investment for the private industry sector. By May 1974, the thoughts of merger had become politically and financially untenable to the Government. Initial costing had produced a figure of about $14M to buy out CAC, $4M to acquire Hawker de Havilland and a further $8M was needed to re-organise the Fisherman's Bend GAF and CAC dual complex.

The Minister agreed to the restructuring of the HdH and CAC facilities and stated that the Commonwealth would recognise the three organizations as having the following general capabilities:

CAC: The manufacture, repair and overhaul of jet engines, including associated sheet metal activities, together with capabilities for engine modification and spares production. The design and manufacture of systems and components involving like technology

John David Dalziel. CAC's fourth General Manager 1976- 1985. **HDHV**

HDH: Repair and overhaul of a wide range of piston, turboshaft, turboprop and small turbojet engines, helicopter transmissions and fixed and rotary wing airframes. Reduced manufacturing capacity for sheet metal and machine components, giving some capability for component manufacture including offset orders

GAF: Design, development and production of aircraft and guided missiles, together with capability for modification, spares production and airframe repair and overhaul

The Commission recommended that a 25% protective tariff on aircraft galleys CAC was producing should be available to the company when, and if they applied for it. This development created an outcry from CAC and initiated a period of intense hostility between the company and the Department of Industry and Commerce. It was a move which was to have a tremendous influence on the field of activities, arrangement policy and the success or failure of CAC.

The Government had completely wiped away the history of CAC successes in aircraft design, manufacture and overhaul, building helicopters, overhaul of helicopter transmissions and of small jet engines (BS Viper); production of sheet metal components and the analysis and control of fatigue in military airframes.

GAF would not be turned into a Statutory Corporation. A qualifying statement was released by CAC stating it was not company policy to vacate the province of aircraft design and manufacture, nor to abandon its aircraft sheet metal business; it would continue to seek such Defence work on a competitive basis. The following two years were of argument about the interpretation and implementation of the rationalization by specialization policy. The Department of Manufacturing Industries was perceived to be redistributing the existing capacity whilst that at CAC was not being fully used. GAF's machine shop and hydraulic component overhaul capabilities were expanded. It was given all new sheet metal work.

The Viper engine and Macchi trainer overhaul work for the west coast based fleet was allocated to HdH in Perth. The Department of Manufacturing Industry implemented the Government policy by trying to channel all new aircraft work to GAF and HdH. It advised American vendors for the New Tactical Fighter not to contact or discuss sub-contracts with CAC, except for those related to engine assembly and component manufacture. All indications were that the Department was bolstering GAF to the detriment of CAC, for although the Department applied its policy vigorously to CAC no consideration was given to an equal compensation of work transfer from GAF.

Union bans were in force by October 1976 on all work associated with the rationalization of the CAC / GAF facilities. The matter was chaotic. In the interim, workload increased significantly with decisions to extend the life of the Macchi and Mirage aircraft through their (LOTEX) programs and improved offset orders. CAC was able to win Defence contracts in spite of the limits placed upon it to be a big engine specialist.

The company often received the support of the RAAF, who stated a preference for working with CAC on the grounds of reliability and work excellence. The more important contracts were:

- Barra Sonobuoy - design and test
- Macchi life extension and modification program
- Mirage life extension and modification program
- P-3B Orion- Omega navigation system installation
- P-3C Orion - install new sonobuoy processing equipment
- Expansion of the work on aircraft fatigue life analysis and monitoring on Mirage, Macchi MB326, F-111, CT4 and C-130 Hercules aircraft
- Laser Airborne Depth Sounder system analysis
- Manufacture of Nomad components for GAF
- Manufacture of F/A-18 tactical fighter components
- Manufacture of *Snake Eye* bomb flip-out tail fin assemblies

As time went on it became more difficult to identify any specific aircraft Defence contract which had been lost by CAC as a result of the Government 'rationalisation by specialisation' policy.

Meanwhile CAC had established itself as a partner in the Australian Aircraft Consortium for the design and manufacture of the new Basic Trainer. Its work package allocation was however held within the unhappy messy constraints of the 1976 government policy (Refer to CA-36 Wamira).

Continuous investigation, justification and argument in the company's day to day dealings with the Department who took a very rigid and all-encompassing interpretation of the policy as expressed by the Minister resulted in many thousands of man-hours spent in wasteful effort to demonstrate CAC's ability to deal with aircraft contracts. The Parliamentary Joint Committee on Foreign Affairs and Defence of 1976 led by David J. Hamer was to examine the ability of the local aircraft manufacturing industry to support Defence in a time of conflict. The 1978 sub-committee chaired by Robert C. Katter was to investigate the organisation related to defence procurement, especially that of local versus overseas procurement. The prevailing view was that the country would rely on the design and production from overseas sources but would provide through-life local industry support. Both these committees had little influence on Government policies or Departmental interpretations of those policies. They did not affect CAC operations and their recommendations were largely used as background material as happened with the earlier McGrath report.

Don Eltringham, Deputy Defence Secretary advised CAC in May 1980 it would look at the distribution of work against anticipated Service demands in the 1980s. This interminable series of committees and ongoing machination created much wasted money and effort in argument and debate in an atmosphere of ingrained, unconcealed hostility and antagonism between Government Departments of frequently changing names and the company. Opportunities were squandered and precious time lost. Although personalities changed, the debate over rationalization continued, but probably decreased in importance as industry workload picked up with increased political support.

In the area of aircraft final assembly GAF had the advantage with their occupation of the Department owned Avalon Airfield at Lara, Victoria. Competition with GAF in terms of price remained impossible however because of Departmental control of costs, accounting practices and secrecy surrounding the subsidies paid to GAF. It was in CAC's strong opinion a question which could not be solved until the Government Department responsible for administering Government industrial policy, ceased to be manager of the over-manned Government owned aircraft factories. CAC's costs were a battle.

Had the recommendations of some of the reports been implemented, the structure of the industry may have ended up entirely different with the two private enterprise companies fiercely competitive and efficient. There had been little evidence of statesman-like political foresight that defence production capacity should be developed in up-to-date technology during periods of international peace, although the principle of Reserve Capacity Funding permitted the establishments to carry unused and obsolescent plant at little cost to current production. Had the various Liberal-Country Party Governments, the champions of free enterprise taken the steps as recommended by various investigating committees in the 1950's and 60's, then GAF would have been abolished.

In the 1976, Sir Lawrence Wackett Lecture by Sir Frederick Scherger recently retired as Chairman of CAC, he stated in part... *"our aircraft industry has rapidly gone the way ...of the car and truck manufacturing base... and will soon be incapable of carrying out those simple but vital tasks of maintaining and modifying the products of other nations which we have acquired."*

Commercial Work to Survive

During the tenure of General Manager Bill Abbot, the commercial work was based on whatever the company could bring in. It included the building of rotors, booms and barrels and the assembly of pumps for Squeeze Crete (Australia),aerodynamic sheet metal fittings for the Westgate Bridge lighting pylons, the dome of the Science Museum's Planetarium, FAA certified commercial aircraft galleys and food and liquor trolley modules for Trans Australia Airlines, Ansett and Qantas Airways (and some exports), Repco-Brabham and British Leyland Motors engine cylinder blocks, Frank Matich racing wheel castings, auto accessories, pistons and rings. Breech plugs for Ramset Fasteners, investment castings for underwater diving gear, vehicle bodies for 75 fire tenders (through Wormald Bros.) for the RAAF and Department of Civil Aviation, 8 mm film developing equipment for Kodak, Hyperbaric cancer treatment pressure vessel for Cancer Institute research, Phytotron environmental cabinets for the CSIRO, boom-gate control equipment, horsemeat mincers and rope making machines. It took over production of pressed metal parts and detail fittings for Jindivik from February 1963 then passed it to HdH. Between 1968 and 1973, Luigi Pellerini, (NSW) designer of the Transavia Airtruck had aspirational discussions with CAC on his various general aviation projects. In the early 1970s the company was promoting itself through its representative at the 'Australian Mission SNECMA' in Paris as *"the most versatile aircraft factory in the Southern Hemisphere"*.

Whilst not within the commercial category, the diversified engineering structure of CAC enabled it to be involved from the late 1960's on the design, production and installation of the launcher, automatic handling system and storage magazine for the Ikara anti-submarine missile/torpedo system for the RAN and the Branik, reduced cost, less automated system for the Brazilian Navy (refer to Ikara & Branik texts). The work for the Brazilian Navy was completed by August, 1977 boosting that year's profit to A$1.58M. Prospects of sales of the system to India and Argentina came to nothing because of apathy and ineptitude from within the Public Service.

This naval work ran in parallel with another very successful development project-the Barra sonobuoy in which CAC had complete responsibility for all the mechanical aspects of the project excepting the electronic system, power source and hydrophones. Barra had evolved as a joint DSTO and United Kingdom defence requirement.

There was a return to surface transport with the construction of 150 articulated bus bodies for use in the ACT to a design by the M.A.N. German mechanical engineering group. This brought the total of bus bodies built to 3,655. Roof beams were built for VicRail's series of stainless steel carriages. CAC entered into a technical agreement with M.A.N. for support in the design and possible manufacture of

Yakolev 40 demonstrator I-JAKA for co-production offer with CAC. Essendon Airport. July 3,1971. **J.A.Vella**

'Snake-Eye' low altitude release, retarding fin assembly on 500lb Mk 82 bomb. **J.A. Vella Collection**

electric rail cars for Queensland Railways and new trams for Melbourne. It did not win either bid. Investigations were undertaken into the Australian Urban Passenger Train concept.

In 1971 Russia's Aviaexport company sought discussions with CAC about the possible production and DCA certification of the 32 seater passenger Yakolev-40, three jet engine feeder liner in which TAA had shown interest. I-JAKA, the Italian registered demonstrator aircraft was present at Essendon Airport on July 3, 1971. DCA/TAA/CAC's drawn out hopeful interactions came to nothing in 1974.

Prosthesis replacement joints were manufactured; a patent was taken out in 1974 for *Calloy,* a steel with a wide industrial use particularly on high wear bearings and pivot components in the mining and maritime industries. Between 1975 and 1987, in excess of 1,340 aircraft sets of passenger evacuation slide containers were built for the McDonnell Douglas DC-10 / KC-10 wide body jets. Passenger doors were provided for the Lockheed Tristar airliner. The company also supplied most of the sheet metal pressings for the New Zealand built CT-4A Airtrainer and the Fletcher FU-24 agricultural aircraft; fuselage structural frames and wing components for the GAF Nomad N22 and N24. At GAF's request, CAC built the display mock-up of the Nomad N24. Plans were envisaged to establish a lost-wax type of foundry in Singapore and preliminary work was a carried out for a possible return into housing construction when patents and manufacturing rights were sought for the *Coombs Modular Steel House* for the Housing Commission of Victoria. The Ford and Mitsubishi motor car companies ordered brake bracket and calliper assemblies.

Two Sikorsky S61N helicopters were assembled for Ansett Airlines. The State Electricity Commission of Victoria provided ongoing work with needed repairs to turbine impellers and new maintenance manuals for its power stations. Manuals were also produced for the entire range of RAAF aircraft. A varied list of customers helped to maintain a flow of activity in the firm's foundries especially in aero engine component refurbishment. The Singapore Defence Force required 7,000 turbine blades for the RR Avon in its Hawker Hunter jet fighter fleet and Viper turbine blades for its BAC Strikemasters, valued at more than A$1M. There was the casting and

SAAB made a substantial effort in 1972 to have the JA37 Viggen & its Flygmotor RM8 engine co-produced by CAC to replace the Mirage IIIO.

L-R; Charles Reid; Walter Watkins and David Rees. **HDHV**

repair of 600 Allison T56 (C-130, P-3C aircraft) turboprop turbine blades; turbine blade refurbishment on RR Dart turboprop engines from Australia and Pacific user airlines. The fabrication of component parts for the GE CF6-80/CFM56 large turbofans; and casings and turbine blades for RR Spey turbofans. Pressed metal running wheels for the Australian Armoured Corp *Leopard* Battle Tank were produced in large quantity. Investment casting of parts for the French Matra 530 air-to-air missile, the McDonnell Douglas Harpoon anti-ship missile, the Nulka Active Ship Missile Decoy Rocket System and the Northrop Grumman High Performance Aerial Target System. Six fuel tank module pallets for fitment into the RAAF CH-47C Chinook helicopters were designed and built as well (for early offset) starting in February 1971, 80 fuselage fairings and panels. 4,032 flip-out tail, *Snake-Eye* low altitude release fin assemblies were built to fit the 500 lb Mk 82 GP bomb (Project EX368) started in December 1982, a mixture of work that was part offset and part Defence activities.

Other examples of early offset work included flap-drive gear boxes for the Boeing 747 airliner, pylons and stabilizers for the Sikorsky S61N helicopter and compressor blades for the Avco Lycoming T55 turbo shaft.

A Parliamentary defence sub-committee made public its hope that CAC's CA-X Universal Lightweight Trainer had a future prospect in defence acquisitions, whilst it also called for greater and more realistic funding for new plant than the annual figure of about $1M. The committee also called on the RAAF to reduce its depot level repair and modification work in favour of the industry. A parallel study for a Lightweight Jet Trainer (LWT) was targeted towards using less fuel and reducing operating costs.

SAAB-Svenska Aeroplan Aktieboget (Sweden), sent a high-level sales and management team to CAC in May 1975 to suggest a market for their *Safari* four seater touring aircraft and to embark on the design of a four engine utility transport. It was also to reinforce the previous agreement of March 1972 of the offer of offset work if their fourth generation JA37 Viggen combat aircraft was selected to replace the Mirage IIIO based on a production of 27,67 or 127 aircraft. The Viggen and the Mirage F1 had been short listed as the RAAF's contenders in late 1972. The SAAB 37AU co-production and joint development (primarily based on the JA37 variant) was of about 50% of the airframe or about 40% of direct labour including the transfer of design work to meet the RAAF request for air conditioning, an arrestor hook, an increase to 6,000 hours design life, greater all-up

RAF HS Nimrod MR1 XV241, from Kinloss visiting RAAF Richmond. October 15,1988. CAC built underwing pylons for the type. **J. A. Vella**

weight and higher speed variable geometry intakes. SAAB had teamed with Grumman Aerospace, USA to design and test the intakes. (According to *Aeroplane,* Vol 48/10, Grumman had built a full-scale mock-up). 70% of its Volvo Flygmotor RM8 engine was to be built by CAC. A revised test cell was needed to handle its greater physical size and thrust in relation to the then ATAR 9C. SAAB spent a lot of time, expense and resources on its approach to CAC with technical visitations in both directions but the RAAF were unsure of future reliable weapons support from Sweden. The aircraft was also built in distinct attack(AJ) and interceptor (JA) airframes. With the new Labor Government in office in December 1972, Defence took a big budget hit and the RAAF was warned by Defence Minister Lance Barnard it could not expect high price combat aircraft. It had not taken part in approved overseas co-production ventures. It was not until 1981 that the true multi-role, vastly superior F/A-18 Hornet was selected instead. For the year ending September 1976, the CAC Group consolidated profit was $934,000. After a lapse of some years Rex Aviation declared a dividend of 5 cents for each 50 cent share.

John David (Jock) Dalziel from BHP's Shipyard Division at Whyalla, South Australia took over as General Manager on September 1, 1976 following the retirement of Bill Abbott, by which time the emphasis on defence economic viability had been greatly altered. The workload had been 1.2M man-hours in 1972 and was expected to be about 1.7M in 1978 (about 20% of the capacity of the plant) too low for the company to operate on an economically viable basis. The hourly rate had climbed from £6.00 in 1968 to $19.50 in 1976, yet CAC had doubled its sales in the three years between 1969 and 1972. Nevertheless Jock Dalziel instigated a corporate development study for the company. This concluded that CAC should pursue technologies in the transport, medical and aerospace fields. Management consultants W.D. Scott recommended re-structuring of the company from a functional organisation to one broken into Operating and Corporate Divisions. The new line-up began operating on July 1,1978.

A bid was entered in January 1977 as sub-contractor firm to EMIE, Lorell Electronics and Grumman Aircraft Corporation for a A$3M work package to convert the RAN's two Hawker Siddeley HS748 navigation training aircraft to an Electronic Warfare System training layout; CAC lost out to HDH, who lost money on the project. The factory space at Fisherman's Bend in 1977 covered an area of 23 acres on 60 acres of land with a base load of gas turbine engine overhaul business covering the ATAR 09 , Viper 22-11, Avon Mk 26 and Mk 109 engine units. The Group with its subsidiaries had fallen to a combined 1,850 personnel.

In association with Rigfield Constructions Pty Ltd, of Huntingdale, Victoria, an agreement was struck in the latter half of 1976 to erect Spaceframes. CAC was responsible for the design, marketing and the building of the Spaceframes under licence from Mero Raurnstruktur GMBH (West Germany). Possibly the most visible examples of a number of these structures were the 400 foot high, 80 ton white enamelled tube frame spire surmounting the Victorian Arts Centre, the Illoura Plaza, St Kilda Rd Atrium and the Collins Place Plaza frame (Melbourne). These activities and the myriad commercial items big and small, simple or complex, listed in this summary had CAC labelled the *University of Fisherman's Bend* where a production engineer could be exposed to an impressive diversity of skills and engineering demands.

John Kentwell, Chief Design Engineer, Manager of Engineering & Chief Engineer 1980 to 1986. **HDHV**

More Subsidiaries

In the second half of 1978, Static General Engineering became the second subsidiary to be added to the Group. (International Helicopters with its Hughes outlet was absorbed into Rex Aviation when CAC became the manager of the Bell 206 helicopter program). Static General Engineering was an Adelaide, S.Aust based firm established by the Vershoor family in 1955 to build industrial handling equipment. Its annual turnover had been running in excess of $2M. The firm had produced a number of innovative, military and civil aircraft cargo handling ground-based equipment for the air forces of Sweden, Malaysia, Singapore, Egypt, USA as well as the RAAF.

In the same year Commercial Aviation Pty Ltd was formed. This was a Rex Aviation venture (50% share) with Evergreen Helicopters of Oregon, USA for the support of offshore oil drilling exploration work in the Timor Sea beginning in 1979. On contract with Australian Aquitaine Petroleum in 1981, two helicopters, a leased Bell 412 and an AS 330J Puma (VH-CRA) were employed. Extensions of this support to the Shell Oil rigs *Ocean Digger* and *Nymphea* operating in Bass Strait from Port Welshpool through 1982/83 brought into use two Bell 212s (VH-CRO, CRQ) and Sikorsky S61N (VH-CRU) helicopters.

Jock Dalziel brought about a second company re-organisation in 24 months which came into effect on July 1, 1980. The Industrial Operations Division had been making huge losses (mainly due to the M.A.N. bus project) whilst sales and profits within the Defence Operations Division under Ian Ring were growing very well. To capitalize on this growth more emphasis was placed on the Defence capabilities of CAC by the creation of a Gas Turbine Division managed by Gordon Doleman (from Rolls Royce, UK) and an Aircraft Division led by D.W.Burton after the retirement of Ian Ring. From this move and for the next five years the company showed a steady 12% growth in real terms with increasing export sales. The Industrial Operations Division was abandoned and all engineering activities' came under the umbrella of the Aircraft Division within the

Tony Carolan, General Manager of HDHV from April 1986. **HDHV**

new Operating Divisions. All other management activities came under the Corporate Divisions including the new Market Development under David Rees who was also the company's first Public Relations officer.

The Basic Trainer Aircraft got underway as a three-way shared split between GAF, CAC and HDH in the Australian Aircraft Consortium. It was a project for which CAC was the most appropriately equipped and experienced entity to take the design lead. Because of the 1975/76 Industry work rationalization plan it could not be seen by the Government to be the project leader, nor the builder of airframe assemblies. The consortium did not work as hoped. A relatively straightforward engineering exercise, became a tangled project mired by a multi-layered management process largely driven by an RAAF system lacking aircraft design experience.

A further incursion into the commercial field was building VOR Direction Finding equipment shelters for the Department of Civil Aviation. The Rex Aviation / CAC plan of establishing a Port of Melbourne Heliport on its land was approved in March 1981. It logged 296 movements in its first year of operation. CAC was one of a few companies still capable in 1982 of producing castings for R-1340, R-1830 and R-2000 radial engine cylinder heads. A successful initial sale of 450 units was made to Bachan Aerospace of Michigan, an agency acting on behalf of continental United States, Canada and European operators with the then prospects of a further order for 1,000 cylinder heads.

An Infusion of New Life?

The biggest change to the company's manufacturing capability was the long awaited injection of new machine tools and processes for the 1980s technology New Tactical Fighter which with 13 other local firms participated in the designated Australian Industry Participation (AIP) program. The Government's $50M and CAC's $8M went into upgrading and installing 190 new machine tools and process items to enable the construction of component parts as technology transfer from GE for the building/assembly of the F404-GE-100 turbofan engine for the F/A-18 Hornet fighter. Having originally bid to manufacture 52 engine components, 27 items were settled on, as the tooling costs for the larger bid were deemed to be disproportionate to the resultant technology transfer.

CAC also became a separate source competitive supplier of other F404 components and modules to the US Navy Supply Office. The airframe section of the work was comprised of 73 ship-sets of engine bay doors, six items for each aircraft as well as engine aft nozzle fairings. These items were sent for incorporation in the rear fuselage assembly of the F/A-18 at Northrop's Hawthorne (California) parent plant. Eight hundred and nineteen(819) ship-sets of engine bay doors and nozzle fairings and 202 wing weapon / fuel pylons were part of the F/A-18 work offset. This new technology was not without its price.

The GE F404 engine with its advanced six module replacement design was averaging 3,500 hours between major overhauls (from US Navy experience) and requiring only 600 man-hours to assemble in comparison to 600 hours between overhauls for the ATAR 9C of the Mirage IIIO and the 3,500 man-hours to assemble each engine. This reduced the RAAF's volume of the company's overhaul work with a consequent reduction of a large number of CAC personnel previously employed on refurbishment tasks. An $8.7M government, air-cooled engine test facility was opened in 1984 to accept engines up to 40,000 lb thrust, built on CAC land, leased and managed by CAC (the fourth engine test house). With an underground fuel storage capacity of 250,000 litres the test cell came into use in September, 1984 with each of the CAC assembled F404 engines (for the RAAF F/A-18 fleet only) requiring about ten hours of pre-acceptance test running. A $3M addition allowed it to test GE T700 helicopter turboshaft engines from 1988. It was demolished in 1995.

Both CAC's subsidiaries - Rex Aviation/Commercial Aviation and Static General Engineering were eventually taken out of the Group because of poor and fluctuating performance. Rex Aviation's yearly return for 1980 was the best since its takeover in 1971 but it was not

The pylons of the new Lower Yarra Crossing bridge to the rear approach to cross the Yarra River and put an end to the runways of the ARL, GAF and CAC complex after 1966. On a crisp Melbourne morning : (left) The new low level 'White House' admin building sits out front of the original admin offices; (right) three detuners of the engine test houses and two of the Bellman hangars. **HDHV**

Project EX385. Under construction the maintenance training rig (above) of the Automatic Flight Control System for the US Navy's Sikorsky MH53E Sea Dragon mine countermeasures helicopter (below). **Ron Jenkins**

able to offset cash flow problems for the Group. The return of a profit of $333,000 on Group assets of $8.5M in 1978 was a matter of concern as it had been in the previous year. In 1981 the Hughes Helicopter franchise was relinquished in favour of distribution rights for the more exciting Aerospatiale (France) helicopter products. For both Static and Rex, 1982 was a significantly bad year due to a business recession. Both subsidiaries recorded large losses. Static General Engineering losing $1.2M, was wound up at the end of the financial year. Rex lost $200,000 in selling only 30 aircraft. Approximately 50% of all Cessna deliveries by Rex Aviation (2,840 aircraft) took place in the ten years since CAC had assumed ownership. It was acquired by Australian Aviation Holdings Pty Ltd on August 9, 1984.

The long running and very large Service Life Monitoring Program (SLMP) for the F111C, Mirage, MB326H and CT-4A was joined by the British Aerospace (Aust) effort to develop and market the AFDAS (Aircraft Fatigue Data Analysis System) for which CAC provided the software design for the prediction of structure life. Leading edge flaps assemblies for the Boeing 747 was a significant manufacturing contract valued at $130M with first deliveries commencing in late 1987. A re-association was established with Sikorsky (Connecticut, USA) with the long term offset supply of 870 Blackhawk/Seahawk helicopter intermediate and tail rotor transmission gear box components. In 1987/88 in a further $6M offset deal, GE T700 turboshaft engine parts were manufactured. For $1.2M, 50 engines were assembled for the same helicopters with the RAAF and RAN.

In addition a start was made on November 12,1985 on a $6M contract also from Sikorsky to build two ground maintenance trainers (Project EX385) for the US Navy's MH53E Sea Dragon aerial towed sled, mine sweeping countermeasures helicopter (operational on June 6,1986). The walk-around 65 x 9ft module/platform had a multi-function capability incorporating the major MH53E mechanical and electrical systems, 3,000 psi hydraulic system, cargo winch system for the towed sled, two GE T64 turboshaft engines and transmission, rotors and folding tail boom...all non-flight rated components supplied from the USA. CAC's input was to build the frame and include three 3,000 psi hydraulic pumps. The second trainer module was for the Aircraft Automatic Flight Control System and the cockpit area. The project led by Jim Caterson, Bill Gornall and Peter Howell was delivered to the USN Station, Norfolk, Virginia on February 2, 1990.

A Need for New Capital

The obvious need to revise CAC's courtship with diversification activities was consolidated by the strategic business consultants Pappas, Evans, Carter and Koop's advice that the company was in a position to compete to advantage in some aspects of gas turbine and airframe systems work against overseas competitors. Concern was expressed for the need of substantial follow on work for the Gas Turbine Division following the expected 1987 phase-out of emphasis on the ATAR 9C engine. The problem was compounded by funding limitations for collaborative projects and the absence of synergy between aerospace work and the activities of the majority of the shareholder companies. The owners and shareholders in 1985 were:

BHP Nominees Pty Ltd	33.3%
North Broken Hill Limited	12.5%
Western Mining Corporation	12.5%
Electrolytic Zinc Company of Australasia Limited	8.3%
I.C.I. Australian Investments Pty Ltd	15.0%
Rolls Royce Limited	10.0%
Pacific and Orient Australia Holdings Pty Ltd	8.3%

From 1968 a long series of large engine development partnership proposals were put to the Board of CAC variously on the Rolls-Royce RB 211 series and GE CF6 variants with suggested 5% company project risk investments. Finally a concept with a lower company share was selected. This was to seek a 1.6% or $A11M stake in the development of the General Electric CF6-80 large turbofan engine during 1982/83 and become a revenue sharing partner with GE. The capital would be raised either by total borrowing or a combined selling of equity with reduced borrowing. General Electric was considered for the sale of equity. Rolls Royce objected to any such offer to a direct competitor as it had a 1984 revenue sharing agreement with GE on the CF6-80C2 and RB211-535E4 aero engines. Bank loans could not be arranged because of the high funding risk involved with the existing level of equity. It meant that funds to over 65% of the total assets of the company would have to be borrowed in order to finance the CF6-80 project. This was considered by the directors to be betting the future of CAC on just one project.

They formed a sub-committee to consider the financial re-structure of the company and the problems of a future reducing workload followed by an approach to the Federal Government through the Minister for Industry and Commerce, Senator John Button in February/March 1983 to obtain Government guaranteed backing to any possible loan. When this was refused they formed another sub-committee to recommend the sale of equity to likely interested parties and approached a number with a proposal. (The Senator may have encouraged HDH to acquire CAC at this juncture). Those interested were Australian National Industries, Commonwealth Steel, Westland Helicopters and Hawker de Havilland. Offers were received, refused, received again and then accepted from Hawker de Havilland. The end came before the directors' committee had made its final report.

In a press release of May 1985, Rollo Kingsford-Smith, Chairman of HDH and Neal Stevens, Chairman of CAC announced that agreement had been reached to merge the two companies as of June 30,1985, consistent with the Government Aerospace Industry Policy of Senator John Button of August 1984.

On July 1, 1985 after 48 years and 9 months of independent existence, the Commonwealth Aircraft Corporation became a wholly owned subsidiary of Hawker de Havilland Limited for a sum believed to be more than $25M financed from HDH internal resources. A year later CAC's name was changed to Hawker de Havilland (Victoria) Limited.

Figures published in the last available CAC Report (1983) placed the company as having:

Fixed Assets (including $3.4M freehold land valuation),total machinery, equipment, service plant, buildings and improvements of :
$16.62M

Current stock and work in progress, cash at the bank etc of:
$27.00M

Total Assets $44.83M

In the financial year 1983/84 profit was $929,000 on a sales revenue of $89M. Employees numbered 1,872.

After nine challenging years in charge, General Manager John David Dalziel, retired on July 31, 1985. This merger was part of the re-organisation (*Flight International*-Jan 4, 1986) that Senator John Button (Labor Government) had foreseen as so necessary in his industry review. David Rees, CAC's Corporate Manager for Market Development said of the merger:

"Emotionally, many of us felt a little disappointed, but equally, it was the right way to go".

Between 1980 (following the internal structural re-organisation) and 1985, CAC had demonstrated better sales performance growth than HDH but HDH's profit before tax and interest payment had been consistently higher than that of CAC. The efforts to re-align CAC back into predominantly aerospace work in the 1980's had reduced CAC's dependence on cost-plus work from 80% to 55% by 1985. Exports had grown from 1% of sales to 35% of sales. Aerospace components and services in the 5 years had grown from A$1M to A$31M with major sales going to the USA. But with the possibility of further cut back in Defence work, there was no assurance that the RAAF would continue to use Australia's aerospace industry in the same way as it had done in the past. It was necessary therefore, to adopt a more commercial, competitive tendering approach to obtaining work, which, since 1975 HDH, Bankstown had demonstrated it could do very well. Did HDH assist CAC in this transition ? Perhaps it was too late to restructure the business, the surplus assets and manpower to suit the needs of the company long-term in the kind of evolving specialist systems work, which it did in a small way.

Within a matter of months of the 1985 merger, the new grouping having become the majority operating shareholder of the AAC's Basic Trainer, re-submitted the design but lost out on its revised Wamira A10B bid. The Government cancelled the project in favour of the larger Swiss Pilatus PC-9A. Its ending was a bitter blow to Australian aviation. The loss of this indigenous work package together with the cut back in Mirage and ATAR engine spares production and overhaul, forced CAC's new acting Director & General Manager, Bruce Hattersley, from August 1, 1985 the highly charged task of reducing the workforce by about 20%. This was necessary to keep the facility functioning economically whilst preparations were underway to tool up for the PC-9/A trainer aircraft for which HDH was project leader.

Anthony Carolan, the thirty-eight year old former HDH engineer and manager was appointed GM of Fisherman's Bend in April 1986. Beyond the merger date an extensive workload in the four engine test houses continued with the GE F404 turbofan, the overhaul of

Electron Beam welding (above) & Numerically Controlled Machine centres-Engine maintenance (below). **Tony Todaro**

Caterpillar Solar, Saturn, Centaur and RR industrial gas turbines. It was handling 15% of the industrial gas turbine work in the Asia Pacific region; the GE T700 helicopter turboshaft ; testing of the Bell 206B-1 LOH and Blackhawk/Seahawk power trains; F/A-18 Airframe Mounted Accessory Drive; the Fuel Test Rig and Oil Rig Test rooms.

New offset credit work included ship-sets of the two- piece rear loading ramp for the RAAF's Alenia Aermacchi C27J Spartan battlefield airlifter (DHC Caribou replacement) ; underwing weapons pylons (four pylons set per aircraft) for the Royal Air Forces HS Nimrod maritime patrol aircraft in addition to airbrakes, wing flaps, horizontal tail fins and underwing pylons for the RAF, RAAF & Malaysian Air Force HS Hawk advanced trainer. The AH-64 Apache attack helicopter weapons pylons bid was abandoned. Composite and alloy components were built for the Airbus Industrie A320, A320, A330, A340 and A380 family, Bombardier, Boeing 737, B777, B787 as well as the initial fuselage design development and production of the McDonnell Douglas MDX Explorer helicopter. The B787 wing trailing edge movable surfaces were designed and built by HDH. In 1991, after some 20 years, civil aircraft offset work was brought to an end. With the eventual Boeing take over, all non-Boeing work was terminated.

Between 1989 and 1992, HDH(V) combined with Israel Defence Industries on a $15M contract to modify four of the RAAF's Boeing B707-338C transports into pod and drogue aerial re-fuelling tankers. Following its acquisition by Tenix Defence Systems, the company took on part of Project Echidna/AIR 5416, to install Radar Warning Receivers (RWR) and Electronic Support Measures (ESM) on the

RAAF's twelve C-130H Hercules tactical transports. Both projects were located at the new HDH(V) hangar erected at Tullamarine Airport. In the same time frame, Tenix Defence Systems, with Lockheed Martin and other contractors was involved in the Tactical Air Defence Radar System (TADRS) Mobile Radar Cabins, Project AIR 5375, for the RAAF. Four sets of stainless steel operations and storage cabins were built for this at Fisherman's Bend, outfitted at Tullamarine and delivered in 2001. The company was responsible for the integration and initial system testing for its eventual RAAF customers, Nos 3 and 114 Mobile Control & Reporting Units.

In a statement before his retirement, the last Chief Engineer of CAC, John Kentwell remarked that:

> "the business of Hawker de Havilland / CAC was to become more capital intensive combined with a high degree of staff training, re-training and a change in the nature of the staff. Fewer numbers were to be employed on recurring work but greater numbers would be committed to non-recurring and essential support activities. The nature and scope of the workload arising from local defence requirements, whilst demanding in the level of technology involved, was insufficient for economic viability. There was now a very limited prospect for complete aircraft design and virtually no prospect of complete engine design arising from local requirements. Work thus had to be in a continuity of more specialised aeronautical activity coupled with collaborative projects and offset work".

New Name – Hawker de Havilland Victoria Ltd

Bruce S. Price the Chairman of HDH notified the staff at CAC of the impending change in a written circular:

> CHANGE OF NAME OF COMMONWEALTH AIRCRAFT CORPORATION TO HAWKER DE HAVILLAND VICTORIA LIMITED
>
> 'It has been decided to change the name of Commonwealth Aircraft Corporation Ltd to Hawker de Havilland Victoria limited. The change in company name will be effective 1 July 1986. The company will remain a wholly owned subsidiary of Hawker de Havilland Ltd and a member of the Hawker Siddeley Group of Companies. . .
>
> A number of important advantages should result from the change. The merger of the two companies in July 1985 was aimed at integrating the two private sector companies to form Australia's largest aerospace organisation and to gain world-wide recognition. The adoption of a common company name should establish the merged Hawker de Havilland as the pre-eminent Australian aerospace in the eyes of our Australian military, domestic and overseas customers. At the same time it will remove a longstanding problem of recognition by those who confuse Commonwealth Aircraft Corporation with its neighbouring Government-owned competitor.
>
> There will be understandable nostalgia and all of us will be reluctant to see the CAC name disappear. Nevertheless we believe it is important for people in both CAC and HDH to relate to the merged organisation. The adoption of a common name should hasten that process. There are technical difficulties in a complete merger of the two businesses into a single company at this stage. As a result it is necessary to retain two separate companies, though both will be identified by the abbreviated name of 'Hawker de Havilland'. For administrative purposes the three primary activities will be designated Melbourne Operations, Sydney Operations and Perth Division.
>
> The General Manager of Commonwealth Aircraft Corporation limited will issue detailed administrative instructions to effect the change in the company name. This will entail formal advice to the appropriate regulatory authorities and advice to our customers, suppliers and other organisations with whom we associate. Considerable effort will be required to revise stationery, brochures, advertising material, signs and entries in publications. These changes will be effected as quickly as possible to minimise any likely confusion. B.S. Price ... Chairman ... 5 May 1986

CAC lasted on its own longer than some of its UK counterparts where rationalization of many well known companies had been a matter of slow fact since before WW2. There were about 15 aircraft manufacturers in 1954. The mergers of the British Aircraft Corporation and Hawker Siddeley Aviation groupings on April 29, 1977 brought about the nationalised British Aerospace (BAe) and one independent firm, Westland.

CAC, GAF and HDH had support through the maintenance of production capability payments, a scheme begun in the late 1940's following declining workloads with the aim to retain a level of skills and facilities in the industry which exceeded those required in peace time. This Reserve Capacity Funding was based on a formula (refer to page 335) which took into account Defence workload costs, the Defence Maximum Capacity for Mobilization and the commercial / offset workload. Funded yearly, CAC's share was $5.2M in 1985. Aside from its WW2 production and prototypes, the 1952 Winjeel was its last production indigenous military design. In 1960 it produced the short run Ceres aerial agriculture aircraft. It was the major contractor for the final assembly of the RAAF's American/Australian Sabre, Italian MB326H jet trainer and the American Bell 206B-1 helicopter.

The Government funded the large employer automobile industry, maintaining rocket ranges for outsiders, supporting the R & D for the discoveries of unseen stars, but in the practical business of backing local aircraft designs (GAF Nomad excepted), did not exhibit confidence in local engineering nor was it seriously fostered in between the cyclical need of the adaptation of foreign designs for the Armed Forces. In countries where technology and innovation was promoted not as a political expediency but as a planned policy of national development, the aerospace sector was a leader of new engineering. Locally, development was complacent, relying on mining with its low 2% employment base. What little R & D funding was available in Australia was directed almost exclusively to Government research bodies with little follow-through to industry for engineering development leaving the Australian aerospace component heavily dependent on the intermittent transfer of overseas technology. Due to the minuscule domestic defence market requirements, any hiccups or political interference generated a disproportionate set-back to any organisation which set out to be a specialist defence supplier. A vicious circle was created. Specialist suppliers or subcontractors became ultimately few in number and those manufacturers like CAC who stayed on, suffered indifference.

As the Wamira A10B project hung in the balance awaiting its final outcome, the September 1985 editorial of *Aircraft* stated... 'The basis for a viable for a viable, strategically important Australian industry is design and development. It should not forever build bits and pieces for others'.

Many ideas and concepts created by CAC were mostly glossed over. The CA-31 and AA-107 were significant hallmark designs. It was no longer possible to compare it with Sweden's aerospace industry or with SAAB, a company similar in size to CAC, established in 1937, into its sixth generation of jet fighter design and commuter airliners in its product line. Sweden's quasi-independence, different geopolitical and industrial outlook and a reliable client Air Force made it so technologically superior to Australia's aviation industry. There was no comparison with the passionate, successful constant output of the Canadian and Brazilian aerospace industries or the relatively newly emerged technological aviation products from Israel.

The volume of aerospace business in Australia had for many years been insufficient to sustain a dynamic industry. Without doubt, Hawker de Havilland as one third of the original major aircraft industry grouping was aware of this fact and kept away from local design initiatives. It sought and achieved a greater national and international presence with contracts independent of the needs of the Australian Armed Forces. The industry had as a whole been the subject of some 17 or 18 inquiries from 1958, reviews and unreleased reports, all to no productive outcomes. At the same time the RAAF moved towards maintenance and upgrades in contract partnership with new large private enterprises in a scattering of outsourcing that did away with the established local production facilities….the end of the aircraft building industry. By 1996 the RAAF was reduced by 22% of its personnel numbers to 17,300 members, losing some of its own work, an outcome that tacitly involved a lot of necessary future private commercial support.

The purpose of CAC was to build up a capability to manufacture military aircraft and engines in Australia thus decreasing its dependence on other countries in times of crisis. It remained mostly attached to Defence cost-plus work which was difficult to move away from; was reluctant to enter into serious independent civil aircraft work; worked within the constraints of its size; like most Australian companies wishing to put their ideas into production, had no access to risk/fail capital and as relayed to the author by Market Development Manager, David Rees…"it *lacked synergy amongst its establishment shareholders*". Fifty years later CAC had built a modest 1,750 aircraft and more than 2,500 aero-engines. The creation of CAC was a salutary, timely, turning point in Australian technological and industrial development.

On October 17, 1986 Hawker de Havilland Victoria celebrated the Commonwealth Aircraft Corporation's 50th Anniversary.

On July 1, 1987 the Government Aircraft Factories, the over-manned, unprofitable but probably more technologically advanced entity was corporatised as AeroSpace Technologies of Australia (ASTA) and acquired by Rockwell International on December 8, 1994 who had previously acquired North American Aviation. Boeing acquired Rockwell in 1996 and by default ASTA in 1997. In May 1988 CAC's highly successful foundry and metal casting hardware business was auctioned off. Earlier, Aircraft Factory No 3 along the Beaufort Place boundary had been hived off to the adjacent GAF/ASTA complex. Stripping leading hands, foremen, storemen and chasers (would chase shortages in parts, component drawings & work orders) of their roles and pay and replacing them by one third of their number by supervisors to change the CAC 'culture' failed. It led to a serious loss of expertise, productivity, safety, morale issues and possibly contracts. Attempts to lease out Aircraft Factory 2 failed.

The Hawker Siddeley Group's non-aviation and foreign interests (inc HDH) were acquired by BTR Nylex Ltd (UK) in 1992 for £1.5bn. The local HDHV was split into four business units: 1. Systems Engineering; 2. Aircraft Structures Manufacturing; 3. Engine Component Manufacturing and 4. Engine Overhaul & Repair. It discarded business units 3 & 4 probably in anticipation of asset stripping. The rest with a lot of vacant space was acquired by Tenix Defence Systems in May 1998. Tenix sold the business (less the site) for A$16.6M to Boeing in October 2000. It also disposed of the HDH civil aviation interests to BAe and the Hawker Pacific agency to Celcius Aerotech. With Tenix's approval HDH sold both the Bankstown and Fisherman's Bend aircraft manufacturing businesses to Boeing for a reputed US$40M. Interestingly HDH had approached Boeing in 1999 wishing to acquire its ASTA component but was refused. It traded combined with the former ASTA until 2007 as a division of Boeing, then as Boeing Aerostructures Australia in 2009.

There was a serious business case to relocate Systems Engineering to the Tullamarine Airport hangar and generous land deal offers by the Altona city council to relocate the Repair & Overhaul (Engine Shop) whilst still using the Test Houses at the Bend were not taken up. The Engine Division was the only Division making a profit when it was closed. Caterpillar Industrial wanted its commercial relationship with HDHV to continue, but to no avail.

BAE Systems acquired Tenix Defence Systems in January 18, 2008 and with it the former HDHV hangar at Tullamarine Airport. It relocated the staff of its Systems Engineering team led by Jim Caterson to offices in Melbourne city. Boeing chose to limit its Fisherman's Bend operation to the much upgraded former ASTA buildings and to dispose of the more commercially attractive former CAC site. HDHV left the site by the end of 2000 with new enterprises appearing by July 2001 completely transforming the site by October 2015 (via Google Earth). Between 2006 and 2009 the signature Butler hangar and two Bellman units were moved to Tyabb Airfield, Victoria; the other Bellman was taken to the cold and windy regional town of Cressy, Victoria for use as a shearing shed and farm machinery storage. The former CAC *'White House'* newer admin block located on 50 Wirraway Drive and some of the former aircraft street names are the only reminders of the CAC business at 304 Lorimer St, Port Melbourne.

Bibliography: A Brief Company History

Aircraft. Various.

Aircraft. Turbojet testing facilities at CAC (November 1957).

Aircraft Manufacture in Australia File No.2 Formation of CAC [NAA: A5954, 873/2]. Barcode:651873.

Aircraft Manufacture in Australia File No.1 (July 1935-November 1935). [NAA: A5954, 873/1]. Barcode: 209091.

Anderson, David. (1982) 'Foreign aircraft assembled by CAC during WW2' : *AHSA Journal* Vol.22 / 4.

Australia. Dept. of Aircraft Production (1937-68). Secretary DAP to Secretary Dept. of Air on aircraft production program-appendix 'A'(Sept 28, 1942).[NAA: MP 1472/1,15 part 1]. Barcode: 514588

Australia. Dept. of Aircraft Production (1937-68). [Memorandum of Dept. of Air conference re future aircraft production (October 7, 1942)]. [NAA: MP 1472/1, 15 part 1].Barcode: 514588.

Australia. Dept. of Aircraft Production (1937-68). Minutes of meeting. (May 25, 1944). [NAA: MP 1472/1, 15 part 1]. Barcode: 514588 .

Australia. Dept. of Aircraft Production (1939-45). Aircraft production & aircraft industry history in Australia. (August 31,1945) [NAA: MP 1472/1, item 15 part 4]. Barcode: 5798360

Australia. Dept. of Aircraft Production. (1942) Flight field Fishermans Bend. Proposal to connect with Princes Pier by taxiway to facilitate movement of aircraft. [NAA: MP287/1, 1577]. Barcode: 475675.

Australia. Dept. of Aircraft Production (1937-68) Director General of Munitions (July 20, 1942). Memorandum of meeting. [NAA: MP 1472/1, 15 part 1]. Barcode 514588.

Australia. Aircraft Advisory Committee (1942-46). Minutes of meetings-Aircraft Advisory Commission. Meetings 1-77. [NAA: B5028,1; B5028,2; B5028,3; B5028,4; B5028,5] Barcodes : 395652; 395653; 395650; 395651 & 395649 respectively.

Barnes, C.H. (1964) *Bristol Aircraft Since 1910*. Putnam, London.

Brown, A. G. (1943) Commonwealth Aircraft Corporation: A short history. [Unpublished] .

Caterson, J. (September. 17,1984) *The political influences upon the establishment of CAC, 1935-42* [Unpublished].

Commonwealth Aircraft Corporation. (undated) Files W1-W6; P2; 025a; 025b, T5.

Commonwealth Aircraft Corporation. *Annual reports, Air tales; Pursuit; From the Whitehouse* [In-house magazines].

Commonwealth Aircraft Corporation. (various) Commonwealth Aircraft Corporation. (1976) CAC & the future: a collection of papers from a seminar, August 21, 1976.

Commonwealth Aircraft Corporation. (1976) Notes on management meeting between SAAB- SCANIA and CAC, May 18, 1976.

Geoff Goodall's aviation history site (www.goodall.com.au)

Hartnett, Laurence, Sir, 1898-1986. (1964) *Big wheels, little wheels*. Lansdowne Press, Melbourne.

Kepert J.(1993) *Fishermans Bend - A Centre of Australian Aviation*. AR-008-377. ARL/DSTO, Melbourne.

Knight, Herb H. (1985) CAC Aero engine work: engine production history [Oral record & notes to the author].

Man & Aerial Machines. 1989-90 John Hopton, Prahran, Victoria.

Manufacture of Aircraft in Australia. History of formation of CAC [NAA: A5954, 873/5].Barcode: 651876.

Mason, Francis K. (1967) *The Westland Lysander*. Profile Publications No 159. Surrey, UK .

McCarthy,John (1976) *Australia & Imperial Defence 1918-39. A Study in Air & Sea Power*. University of Queensland Press.

McDonnell Douglas Explorer helicopter. *Jane's all the world's aircraft*. (1996/97). Jane's Information Group. Coulson,Surrey,UK.

Parkhill, Archdale Sir, 1879-1947. (1937) 'The manufacture of aircraft in Australia': address by Minister for Defence to the Warringah Electoral Conference, February 4, 1937.

Rayner, Harry (1984). *Scherger. A biography of ACM Sir Frederick Scherger*. Australian War Memorial, Canberra.

Rees, David. CAC Corporate Manager Market Development & Publicity [DRR/5.8.2 Correspondence].(1985-1987)

Ring I. H. (1985-1987) [Interviews].

Ring I. H. (1950) Report on the limitations of Fishermans Bend Airfield 1950. [Internal communication].

Ring I. H. (1958) The Fitzgerald Report [Internal communication]

Ring I H. (1961) The Mirage Contract Committee, 1960-61 [Internal communication].

Ring I. H. (1968) *Aircraft Project Design in Australia*. The Lawrence Hargrave Memorial Lecture to the Royal Aeronautical Society. (September 19,1968) [Melbourne].

Ring I. H. (1972) The McGrath report for the Defence (Industrial) Committee, 1972. [Internal communication].

Ring I. H. (1975) Industries Assistance Commission Inquiry, 1974-75 [Internal communication].

Ring I. H. (1978) Parliamentary Joint Committee on Foreign Affairs and Defence, 1976 and 1978. [Internal communication].

Ring I. H. (1982) The aircraft industry, leader in technology. [Internal communication].

Ring I. H. (1983) The rationalisation of the aircraft industry. [Internal communication].

Rotor & Wing. MD(McDonnell Douglas) reborn.(August 1999)

Royal Aeronautical Society (Aust). (1977) *Australian aeronautics, 1927-1977: a historical review*. The Society. Parkville , Victoria.

Stephens, Alan (2001).*The Royal Australian Air Force,1915-2000*. Oxford University Press, South Melbourne.

Todaro, Tony. CAC engine test cells. [Communications].

Vincent, David(1982). *Mosquito Monograph. A history of Mosquitoes in Australia & RAAF operations*. Koon Wah Printing Pty Ltd , Singapore.

Wackett, Lawrence James, Sir, 1896-1982. (1972) *Aircraft Pioneer: an autobiography*. Angus and Robertson, Sydney.

Wackett,Lawrence James, Sir. Some Experiences of a Pioneer in the Aircraft Industry in Australia. Journal of the Royal Aeronautical Society. May 1959.

Wackett, Lawrence James, Sir. *Launching by Catapult*. The Aircraft Engineer , UK .October 30 1931.

Williams, Richard, Sir,1890-1980.(1977) *These are facts: The autobiography of Air Marshall Sir Richard Williams, KBE,CB,DSO*. Australian War Memorial and Australian Publishing Service, Canberra.

Yule, Dr Peter(2001). *The forgotten giant of Australian aviation (ANA)*. Hyland House Publishing, Flemington, Victoria .

CAC Fiftieth Anniversary

HAWKER DE HAVILLAND VICTORIA LIMITED

The wrecking end

Engine factory at Lidcombe, NSW. **L.J.Wackett / MS4858 / NLA**

INVESTMENT CASTING, STEEL & NON-FERROUS FOUNDRY MACHINERY, PLANT & EQUIPMENT

(15) TO THE ORDER OF: HAWKER DE HAVILLAND VIC. LTD., who have closed their foundry operation and the COMMONWEALTH OF AUSTRALIA, who are disposing of surplus equipment.

Monday, May 30 at 11 a.m. 304 Lorimer Street, Port Melbourne

SHAW FOUNDRY AND MELT SHOP: 2 Inductotherm Electric Induction Melting Furnaces, 90 kg to 450 kg, Bank of 3 Inductotherm Electric Induction Melting Furnaces, 35 kg, 250 kg and 120 kg, Mould Firing Furnace, Monorail Blocks and Tackles, Scales etc., Shalco Continuous Sand Mixing Plant, Model Saturn 2, Warril Mould Rollover Plant, Fordath Pacemaker Screw Type Radial Sand Mixing and Slinging Plant, Sand Mill and Mixing Machine, Pascall Ball Mill.
PATTERN AND FETTLING SHOP: Archdale 36" Pedestal Drill, 2 - 24" Abrasive Cutoff Saws, 2 Bandsaws, Polishing Lathe, Pedestal Grinders, Arc Welding Plants, Gardiner Linisher, Macson 8" Centre Lathe, Pedestal Fans etc., Mega Master Linishing Machines.
LIGHT ALLOY FOUNDRY AND INSPECTION AREA: Bank of 2 Birlec Treatment Furnaces, Industrial Electric Tempering Furnace, Granowski Rotary Table Grit Blast Plant, Vacublast Manual Sand Blasting Plant, Portable Multi Arm Rotary Table, Desks, Benches, Cupboards, Stock Racks, Chairs etc.
INVESTMENT CASTING MELT AND POWER SECTION: 2 Inductotherm Metal Melting Furnaces, Mould Firing Furnace and associated equipment.
INVESTMENT REFRACTORY COATING AREA: Druville Type Rollover Furnace, 100 KW Inductotherm Stokes Vacuum Melting/Casting Furnace Model 900-437-524, Leeds & Bradfield Electrically Heated Autoclave, Sassi Refractory Grinder, Furnace Engineering Drying Oven, Wax Melting Tanks, Eke Overhead Raining Cabinet, Email Dust Collection Plant, Dip Coating Vats, Fume Extraction Cabinet, Mixing Tanks, Drum Stands, Stock Racks, Work Trollies, Benches etc.
WAX INJECTION MOULDING AREA: 2 Vertical Wax Injection Moulders, 1 Horizontal Wax Injection Moulder, 4 Vericast Injection Moulders, Epic Temcraft Horizontal Wax Injection Moulder, Austenal and Leyden Vertical Wax Injection Moulders, Wax Melting Vats, Torit Reverse Dust Collection Plant, Coolboy Cooling Towers.
GENERAL - SUPER FINISH FETTLING AREA: ES Inspection Unit, Servex 100 Ton Garage Press, Richardson Wet Scrubbing Plant, Miller Synchrowave 300 amp Tig Pulse Welder, Lakeside Water Cooling Tower, 50 Ton Vertical Hydraulic Press, Emery Grinder, Polishing Lathe, Meggamaster Twin Belt Linishing Machine, Webo Pedestal Drill, Arbour Press, Hercus Tool and Cutter Grinder.
PATTERN SHOP: 2 Macson 42" Bandsaws, Wadkin Vertical Router, Tanco 6" Buzz Planer, Macson ½" Pedestal Drill, McPherson 24" x 8" Panel Planing and Thicknessing Machine, Barker 18" Ripsaw Bench, Wood Turning Lathe, Grinders, Scales, Stock Racks, Benches etc.

On view Friday, 27th May 9 a.m. - 4 p.m. — Catalogues available.

The Age, Saturday 14 May 1988

Mason Gray Strange VIC. LTD.
91-101 Leveson Street
North Melbourne
Phone 329 9911 Fax 328 4292

Time for the Clowns to leave the business. **Roger Ward**

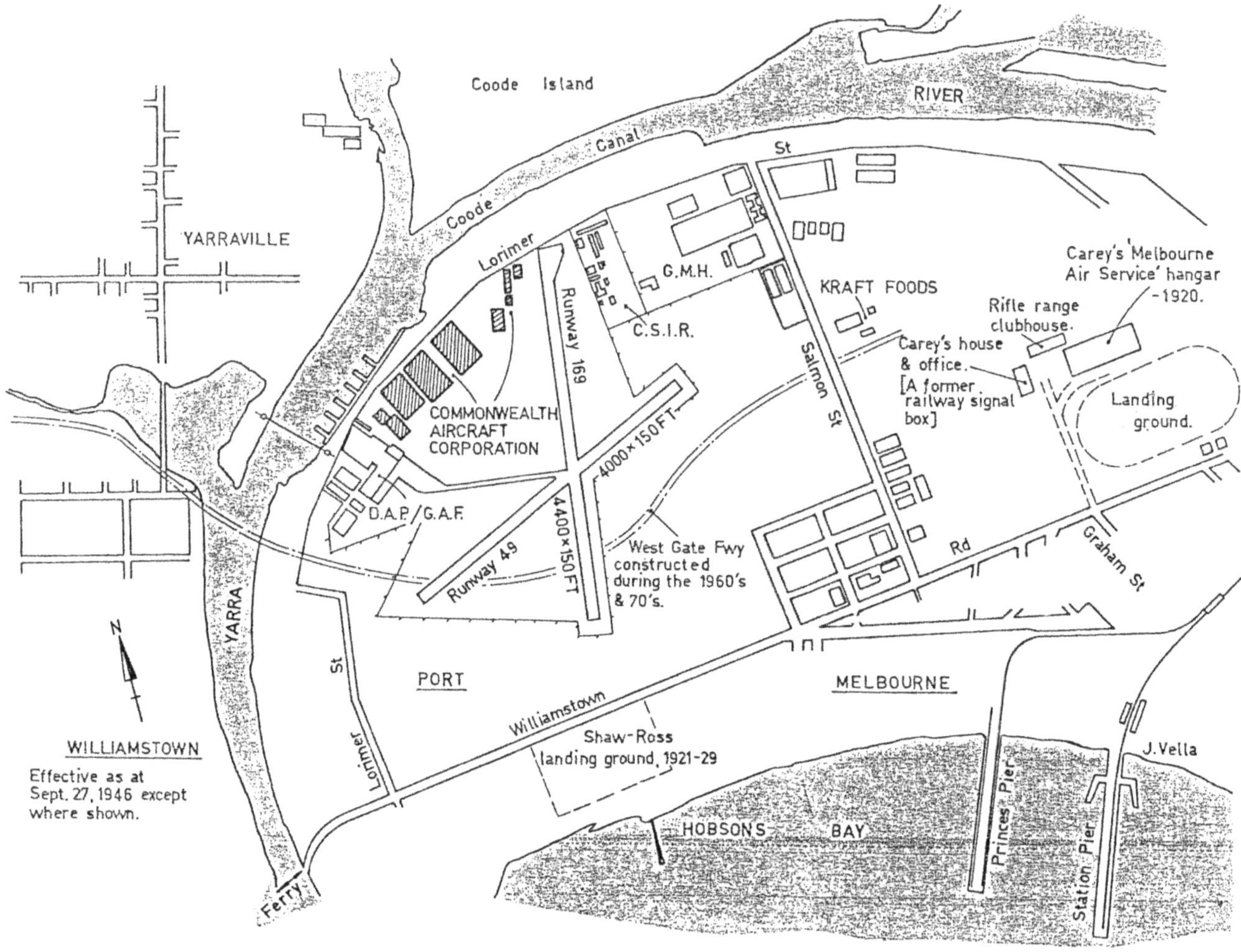

General area around CAC in 1946 except where noted. **J.A.Vella**

HDH-CAC company advertisement - AIRCRAFT journal April 1977. **J.A.Vella Collection**

List of Aircraft Construction Projects and Proposals

Chapter 1   BUILD-UP TO WAR
1. CA-1, 3, 5, 7, 8, 9, 10 & 16 Wirraway General Purpose / Trainer Aircraft	1936*
2. P143 Ab-Initio Trainer Aircraft	7 / 1938
3. CA-2 / CA-6 Wackett Trainer Aircraft	10 / 1938*
4. P144 / P148 Twin Engine Bomber Reconnaissance Aircraft	10 / 1938
5. P147 Single Engine Two Place Multi-Gun Fighter Aircraft	2 / 1939
6. P149 Twin Engine Fighter Aircraft	4 / 1939
7. P150 Twin Engine General Purpose Aircraft	5 / 1939
8. CA-4 Wackett Bomber / CA-11 Woomera Bomber	6 / 1940*
9. CA-12, 13, 14, 14A & 19 Boomerang Fighter Aircraft	12 / 1941*
10. P175 Anti-Tank Aircraft	7 / 1942
11. XP17 & P176 Wright Cyclone Boomerang Fighter Aircraft	5 / 1942
12. P178 / CA-15 Fighter Aircraft	10 / 1942*
13. P177 Four Engine Transport Aircraft	11 / 1942
14. CA-17, 18 & 21 North American P-51 Mustang Fighter	2 / 1944*

Chapter 2   FIRST GENERATION JET FIGHTERS
15. P189 / P193 CA-22 Winjeel Trainer Prototypes	11 /1947*
16. P182 / P184 / P186 Grumman Panther Derivatives	3 / 1948
17. P196 Twin Seat All-Weather Fighter Aircraft	10 / 1948
18. P223 / CA-23 All-Weather Fighter Aircraft	2 / 1950
19. CA-24 Hawker P1081 Day Fighter Aircraft	2/ 1950
20. CA-26 / CA-27 North American F86 Sabre Fighter Aircraft	4 / 1951*
21. XP46 Single Seat Day Fighter Aircraft	10 / 1951
22. Rocket Interceptor [1]	11 / 1951

Chapter 3   BASIC TRAINER THINKING
23. CA-25 Winjeel Trainer Aircraft	1 / 1952*
24. XP47 Rocket Interceptor [2]	4 / 1952
25. P247 / XP48 Winjeel, RR Dart Turboprop Aircraft	8 / 1952
26. P248 / XP49 Winjeel, RR Dart Turboprop Aircraft	8 / 1952
27. XP51 / XP52 Ram-Jet Helicopters	10 / 1952
28. XP53 Sabre RR RA-14 Avon Turbojet	10 / 1952
29. P256 / P267 Winjeel Twin Aspin II & Marbore II Jet Engines	2 / 1953
30. P260 / XP55, P266 / XP57, P269 / X259 Jet Trainers	3 / 1953
31. P265 / XP56 Wallaby Feeder Liner	8 / 1953
32. P271 / XP63 Jet Trainer, Derwent Turbojet	11 / 1953
33. P277 / XP61 Winjeel Ambulance	12 / 1953

Chapter 4   FAST JETS AND SABRE PROSPECTS
34. XP62 Four Engine Light Interceptor	12 / 1953
35. XP64 / XP65 / XP66 Warrior-Air Superiority Fighter Aircraft	5 /1954
36. XP67/ XP68 Fighter Aircraft	12 / 1954
37. P302 / XP69 Improved Avon Sabre	4 / 1955
38. P314 / XP70 Winjeel, Tricycle Undercarriage	11 / 1955
39. P312 / P313 Sabre, In-Flight Refuelling	11 / 1955
40. P321 / XP71 Sabre, Rocket Boost [1]	12 / 1955
41. P322 / XP72 Sabre, NASARR Installation	12 / 1955
42. P280 / P282 / P301 Sabre, Blue Jay Guided Missiles	12 / 1955*
43. Blue Jay Guided Missiles on DH Sea Venom Fighter	7 / 1956
44. XP73 Jet Trainer & XP74 Executive Transport Aircraft	8 / 1956

Chapter 5   WINJEEL DERIVATIVES, PRIVATE AIRCRAFT VENTURE AND NAVAL WORK
46. XP75 Winjeel, Utility Aeroplane [1]	8 /1956
47. XP75 Winjeel, Utility Aeroplane [2]	8 /1956
48. XP76 Winjeel, Agricultural Aircraft	9 /1956
49. XP77 CA-28 Ceres Agricultural Aircraft	9/1956*

50. P402 Sabre, Rocket Boost [2]	1 /1959
51. Sabre, Ramjet Thrust Augmentation	7/1959
52. CA-29 GAMD Mirage IIIO Fighter Sub-Contract	3/1960*
53. EX200 / EX220 - Ikara Missile Handling & Launch System	4/1960*
54. Conceptual STOL Feeder Liner	5/1960
55. P435 Sabre, Photo Reconnaissance	6/1960
56. Winjeel, Turboprop Agricultural Aircraft	2/1964

Chapter 6 SUPERSONIC TRAINER / ATTACK AIRCRAFT

57. CA-31 Supersonic Trainer / Close Support Aircraft	3/1964
58. An Aerial Top Dressing Aircraft	7/1965
59. CA-30 Aer Macchi MB326H Trainer Aircraft	9/1965*
60. The Hughes Helicopter Franchise	12/1967
61. AP1001-BAC / CAC AA-107 Close Support / Trainer Aircraft	1/1968

Chapter 7 COMMUTER AIRCRAFT, HELICOPTERS AND NAVAL EXPORTS

62. CA-28 Ceres Turboprop Conversion	6/1968
63. A Commercial Aircraft Replacement for Winjeel Trainer	10 /1968
64. Turbofan Boost on Short Haul Aircraft	11/1968
65. Britten-Norman Islander with Turboprop Engines	2 /1970
65. EX260 Branik Missile Handling & Launch System	1970*
67. GAC-100 Commuter Aircraft	4/1970
68. Winjeel, FAC101D Forward Air Control Aircraft	10/1970
69. GAF Nomad Technical Assessment	10/1970
70. CA-32 Bell 206B-1 LOH Kalkadoon	2/1971*

CHAPTER 8 SYSTEM UPGRADES, MB326H CONCEPTS AND SUBMARINE DETECTION

71. Macchi MB326H [Mod]	4/1971
72. EX300 Barra Sonobuoy	1971*
73. CAP 201-Macchi MB326H Replacement Trainer Aircraft	5/1971
74. Cessna Compacts, Aerobat A157, Twins & Glider Tug	7/1971
75. AP1002-CAC / HS 1182 [Hawk] Jet Trainer	8/1971
76. CA-30 Mk2, MB326H Trainer Aircraft	8/1972
77. Winjeel, Glider Towing	2/1973*
78. CA-33, P-3 Orion Systems Upgrade	1973*
79. Sarich Orbital Engine Aircraft Applications	1/1974
80. CA-36, Apprentice Training Project [PL-4A]	6/1974*

CHAPTER 9 LIGHT TRANSPORTS AND LIGHT MILITARY SUPPORT AIRCRAFT

81. Light Military Support Aircraft	6/1975
82. Light Military / Civil Transport	6/1975
83. Light Helicopter Crane/Jeep	6/1975
84. Light Surveillance Aircraft -Cessna 402 Mod	6/1975
85. A DHC-4 Caribou Transport Replacement Aircraft	9/1975
86. Light Utility Transport Aircraft	2/1976
87. C-130 'Tubby' Hercules Transport	10/1976

CHAPTER 10 ADVANCED AND BASIC TRAINER AIRCRAFT CONCEPTS- A LAST FLING

88. CA-X Universal Lightweight Trainer [ULWT]	1976
89. Lightweight Jet Trainer [LWT]	5 /1977
90. CAC / Short Bros. Ltd SD3-MR Seeker	3/1978
91. Winjeel Trainer- New Piston Engine	9/1978
92. Winjeel Trainer-Turboprop Engine	4/1979
93. AAC / CA-34 Wamira Basic Trainer	1979*
94. Winjeel-AFST 5044, Basic Trainer Proposal [1]	4/1980
95. Winjeel-AFST 5044, Basic Trainer Proposal [2]	1980
96. CA-35 LADS Installation	1980*
97. AP1035 Remotely Piloted Crop Spraying Helicopter	6/1980
98. AP1051 Project KAHU, RNZAF A-4 Skyhawk Modernisation	1983

CHAPTER 11   POST COMPANY MERGER PROJECTS

99.	CA-37 Pilatus PC-9/A Basic & Advanced Trainer Aircraft	1986*
100.	CA-38 Aerial Refuelling Tanker Conversions	1989*
101.	CA-39 McDonnell Douglas MDX/MD900 Explorer Helicopter	1989*
102.	CA-40 P3C Orion ESM Upgrade	1990*
103.	CA-41 General Dynamics F-111C AUP	1993*
104.	CA-42 Unknown	
105.	CA-43 Unknown	
106.	CA-44 Sikorsky S-70B-2 Seahawk & S-70-9 Blackhawk Helicopters	1988*

CHAPTER 12   AERO ENGINE WORK

107.	CAC Aero Engine Work	1936 - 1985*

* Built Projects

The Clowns reminisce the loss of a missed opportunity. **Roger Ward**

The inevitable reality. **Roger Ward**

CHAPTER 1: PRE-WAR AND WARTIME ENDEAVOURS

CA-1,3,5,7,8,9,10 & 16 WIRRAWAY GENERAL PURPOSE / TRAINER AIRCRAFT
1936

A formation of Wirraway aircraft from No. 2 Service Flying Training School, Wagga, NSW in 1941. **RAAF**

The formation of the Commonwealth Aircraft Corporation and the selection of the first aircraft for its manufacture, the North American Aviation NA-16, were two events interdependent on each other. The five-month mission which from February to July 1936 visited the UK, France, Holland, Czechoslovakia, Germany and the United States was led by Lawrence J. Wackett (Wg Cdr, Retd) RFC, AFC, BSc (then Managing Director of Tugan Aircraft Ltd, Sydney), who was joined by Sqn Ldr H.C. Harrison (Chief Draftsman at Boulton and Paul during WWI and retired RAAF Director of Technical Services) and Sqn Ldr A. W. Murphy (Chief Workshop Officer of the RAAF).

The government instructions to the mission were that it would be prepared to place orders for an aircraft of a developmental but useful type so that a well-organised and balanced expert manufacturing unit could be built up using materials indigenous to Australia wherever possible. Other considerations were:
1. An emphasis on the achievement at the earliest possible date of the complete manufacture of a range of types of aircraft.
2. Keeping to one method of manufacture (explained later as referring to the one form of engine i.e. radial or in-line).
3. Designs which, through appropriate tooling and jigging, would in an emergency be capable of production in considerably larger quantities by the use of semi-skilled labour.
4. The design to be adopted had to be engineered for quantity production rather than based on an accomplishment for performance.
5. Australia was not at that time well off in the availability of suitable timbers, non-ferrous alloys, aluminium or magnesium but was an excellent source for steel.

The Selection

Lawrence Wackett was under no illusion that the first step into military aircraft production had to be a prudent, measured one. His line of thinking is clear from his autobiography where he stated:

"While I was completely optimistic, having seen how production had been developed overseas, I felt it was unwise to attempt too much at the beginning. This had been a paramount consideration when choosing the aeroplane and engine for the initial venture. Some who could see value in the aeroplane only as an up-to-date military weapon, had little regard for the problems of aeroplane construction in a relatively non-industrial community such as Australia was at that time and conceded nothing in the nature of a compromise. I was fully aware that our initial aircraft was a second line weapon or merely an advanced trainer, but thought it was essential to confine our early efforts to this".

"By a fortuitous coincidence the selected aeroplane was fitted with an air-cooled engine that represented the modern technique of engine design and production, combined with methods that would involve us in relatively moderate outlay for plant in comparison with some contemporary engines of the liquid cooled type".

The airframe with its mixture of castings, stressed skin construction for the wings and tail surfaces, welded tube fuselage with fabric side panels, and variable pitch propeller blades would be both an advance of anything available from the United Kingdom as a general purpose aircraft but also develop a variety of fabricating skills.

The choice was also backed up by other attributes indicative of the new North American Aviation (NAA) company:
1. It possessed a very high appreciation, knowledge and effectiveness of organisation, not so markedly apparent in other factories visited.
2. Their design incorporated all-metal stressed skin construction, tubular steel fuselage frame.
3. Very strong emphasis had been placed on ease of production.
4. Very effective tooling, jigs and fixtures were employed.
5. The basic engineering and designs lent themselves to wider applications, thereby providing scope for future possible development.
6. The company was enthusiastic about assisting Australia to develop its industry and showed a strong support to the approach put forward.

The Syndicate's communication with Sir Archdale Parkhill, Minister for Defence, on July 30,1936 suggested an initial building program of at least 40 complete aircraft and 10 spare engines each year, of what was described as the NA-16 all-metal general purpose monoplane. Forty was considered to be the minimum number necessary in order to justify taking up the necessary manufacturing licences.

NAA was a new concern having come into existence in 1934. It was to get off the ground by virtue of the vast multitude of derivatives and large production numbers of its first design the NA-16, an all-metal, low wing monoplane with tandem open cockpits, a fixed undercarriage and powered by a 400 hp Wright R-975 radial engine. The original NA-16 made its first flight on April 1, 1935.

Improving on the selection

James H. 'Dutch' Kindelberger, President of NAA communicated with Wackett on July 23, 1936, offering a complete aircraft (NA-16-1A) with a two position propeller, 550 hp engine and fixed undercarriage for US$23,700 plus $720 for shipping freight costs. Drawings and information for a retractable undercarriage were offered at US$5,000.

The manufacturing rights to the North American design were not cheap. The licence fee sought and documented by CAC as at November 25, 1936 was US$25,000 for the specification and manufacturing data and a sliding scale of royalties based on the sale price of the airframe less engine and propeller. This was to be 5% on aircraft Nos 1 to 25; 4% on aircraft 26 to 50 and 3% on aircraft 51 to 100 and no payment thereafter. (Note that North American Contract Brief 51, as stated by J. McCarthy, (UNSW) Duntroon, gives the figures of US $100,000 in licence fees and royalties made up of US $30,000 for the specifications and manufacturing data, US $1,000 fee on each of the first 25 aircraft and US $600 each on the following 75 aircraft when royalty payments were to cease.)

CAC's tentative suggested prices to the Australian Government were £7,200 for each complete aircraft and £2,600 for each spare engine based on an aircraft, a development of the basic NA-16 design with a fixed undercarriage, two bladed variable pitch propeller and a Pratt & Whitney R-1340 radial engine. This was the NA-16-1A, serial 32-387, built to the charge number NA-32.

The new CAC received approval for their proposal in January 1937. On February 2, Sir Archdale Parkhill, in an address to his Warringah electoral conference at the Mosman Town Hall, NSW was defending the choice of aircraft, saying that the Government's hope and intention was that an English aircraft type be built and it was a surprise that the choice was American. However, the facts had to be faced, the UK's industry was in a rundown state; was concerned with its own defences and delays to Australian orders had ranged from 18 to 24 months.

The NA-16-A arrived at the Melbourne docks on August 9, 1937 and was first flown from RAAF Base Laverton, Victoria on September 3, 1937 by Sqdn Ldr Frederick Scherger. Given RAAF ident A20-1, the first of its line, the aircraft was taken on by the RAAF on February 2, 1938 and locally identified as the NA-16.

Wackett's second visit to North American was in March 1937 accompanied by Thomas W. (Bill) Air, E. J. Smith and Sam Bruce, ex-Tugan Aircraft Company workshop staff. On 10 March he signed the licence for the NA-16-A and the recent NA-16-2K (NA-33) demonstrator, serial 33-338. Wackett returned on September 6, 1937 and wrote to Parkhill on 29 September confirming the selection of the NA-33. This aircraft was more akin to the retractable-gear demonstrator NA-26 (which was not to fly until February 11, 1938) built for the NA-36 Basic Combat aircraft (BC-1), of NAA charge date March 16, 1937 fitted with armament and retractable undercarriage. Possibly because of this comparatively late availability of the BC-1, that North American Aviation offered to build the sole NA-33.

Both the NA-32 and NA-33 had the identical NAA charge number date of March 10, 1937. The latter was still a NA-16 but it was identified by its NA-33 charge number. (From 'NAA Training Aircraft' by Dustin Carter, AAHS /Summer 1979, it is obvious that many models were being developed simultaneously rather than in an orderly lineal manner. This renders the series confusing, with NAA charge numbers and types changing place out of sequence.) It was the entrepreneurial skills of NAA's president, that was to foster more than 17,000 examples of the trainer, with another 4,500 built under licence in four other countries. Aware that priority funding in the USAAC was earmarked for combat aircraft, not trainer aircraft, he convinced the US Army's Chief of Air Corps , Major General Henry 'Hap' Arnold that the aircraft he was building were not trainers but Basic Combat aircraft, thus bringing about the evolution of the BC-1.

The NA-33 was shipped out from the West Coast in September, flight tested by Sqdn Ldr F. Scherger on December 12, 1937, allotted ident A20-2, taken on charge on November 8, 1938 and eventually joined A20-1 as an instructional airframe at the RAAF Engineering School at Ascot Vale. RAAF test pilot Flt Lt Patrick Heffernan also carried out extensive testing of both the NA-16 and NA-33 at Laverton.

NA-16-1A, commonly known to the public as the NA-16, with fixed undercarriage and two-bladed propeller. **RAAF Museum**

Following a series of RAAF Hawker Demon accidents, the Government, without consulting the Air Board, sought a review by the Inspector General of the RAF, Air Marshall Sir Edward Ellington. The NA-16 and NA-33 were being test flown at RAAF Laverton during his visit from mid-June 1938. The antagonism from England toward the American aircraft continued. Edward Ellington, when invited, refused to watch the NA-33 being displayed for his benefit. He was critical of its selection saying the RAAF should have waited for a better British aircraft!

Local criticism also continued. The *Sydney Morning Herald* (Fairfax Press) was generally not in favour whereas Melbourne's *Herald & Weekly Times* press (Collins House Group) was in favour. Sydney based, patriotic newspaper-style magazine SMITH'S WEEKLY of January 16,1937 had its hostile say in a long piece about the scandal of building American aeroplanes in Australia for the RAAF:

To Sir Archdale Parkhill , Minister for Defence,

DEAR SIR ARCH - Certainly when you do change your mind you go the whole hog. It seems likely that poor "Smithy" was being snubbed and put in his place because he wanted to use American aircraft. Australia's greatest airman conceded that certain types were eminently suitable for use in the Commonwealth. Well now, sir, you have not only opened the door to American aircraft, but you and your cabinet colleagues have decided that Australia's first worthwhile aircraft factory is to build American -type war planes. Your' re sure a hustler when you do start!

The article went further - *"Candid Australian friends say the whole thing is a racket or graft-whichever one likes to call a deal in which politics, politicians and financiers are so mixed that one cannot tell the other from which"*.

And - *"In any case the decision to build American machines is a gross breach of faith with the British Air Ministry"*.

Followed by - *"We believe little manufacturing, in the sense of handicraft, is to be done at Fisherman's Bend. The Australian idea seems to be that the factory there will be merely an assembly depot..."*

Approval and Vindication

The Air Board comprising of AVM R. Williams (RAAF), AVM H.R Nicholl (RAF, on loan to Australia) and Grp Capt W.H. Anderson

(RAAF) agreed on January 14, 1938 to substitute the NA-33 for the earlier model with the recommendation that 40 aircraft of the type to be called the *Wirraway*, (an indigenous language word for *challenge*). The Minister for Defence approved this six days later subject to evidence supporting the *reasonableness of price quoted*. The estimate for the changes requested by the RAAF on the NA-33 were put at £548, raising the unit price to £7,550 and increasing it to £7,748 with modifications for a retractable undercarriage.

It was now possible to acquire an aircraft developed locally from the NA-33 for £8,098 (later increased by £46 to pay for additional equipment).

An order was eventually placed for :
40 complete aircraft at £8,144		£325,760
10 spare Wasp 'H' engines at £2,600		£26,000
Total		£351,760

In addition the establishment of an entirely new manufacturing complex in what has been described as the finest collection of engineering plant in Australia at the time, together with the recruitment and training of production personnel was a significant task. There was also the sorting and identifying the myriad collection of licensor samples of every individual part of both airframe and engine in every stage of the production process arriving from the United States about which L. J. Wackett states in his autobiography:

> "These varied from a sample complete aircraft and a spare complete engine to components in varying stages sufficient to build five complete aircraft when the detail parts were completed. We had forgings, castings and materials of all types sufficient for fifty aircraft and other raw materials from which finished parts would be produced at CAC as tooling became available".

March 27, 1939. Dignitaries outside the factory waiting for A20-3 to fly. **L. J. Wackett/MS4858/NLA**

A20-3. The first locally built/assembled CA-1 Wirraway I at Fisherman's Bend, 1939. **Richard Hourigan.**

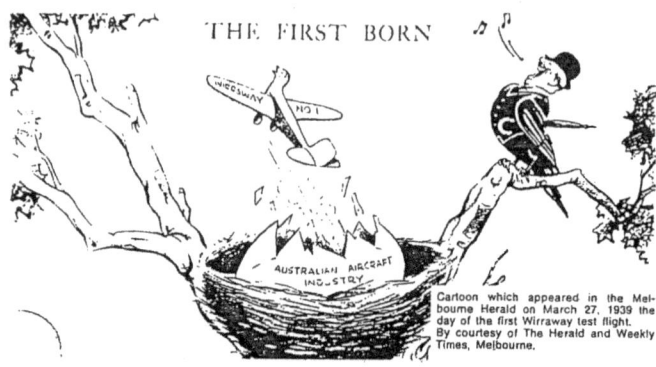

Cartoon depicting Archdale Parkhill which appeared in the Melbourne Herald on March 27, 1939 the day of the first flight of A20-3. **The Herald & Weekly Times, Melbourne**

A licence from the Aluminium Company of America set up the local production of aluminium castings and the establishment of a supply chain of sub-contractors. For many of these firms their very existence and future fortune came about because of the creation of CAC. They in turn, were to fill a very urgent need of engineering support during WW2.

Setting up the NA-16 production process cost £169,000. This was comprised of £8,500 for NA-16-2K airframe and engine, £16,000 for the licence, £15,000 for jigs and dies, £60,000 for parts and materials and £70,000 for plant and machine tools. The combined Wirraway and the P & W Wasp engine licence fees came to £20,400.

Ted Beck, from North American Aviation, was the original Wirraway Project Engineer, followed in 1939 by Reg Schulz, who had joined CAC in 1937 as a mechanical engineer/design draftsman. He was followed in turn by Maurice Lodge in 1940, when Reg Schulz assumed joint management of the CA-4 Wackett Bomber project.

The NA-32 had a direct drive R-1340 engine fitted with a two bladed propeller whilst that of the NA-33 was geared and drove a three bladed propeller with a combined weight considerably greater than that in the NA-32. As a result, gravity, torque, thrust and gyroscopic loads on the engine mounting and its attachment to the fuselage were greatly increased and it was felt prudent to revise the stress analysis of North American Aviation. This permitted an increase in maximum weight from 5,000 lb to 5,500 lb.

The NA-33 as delivered had a single exhaust and the location of the oil cooler was such that it interfered with access to the engine bay and also with the engine cooling system. The cooler was transferred to the bottom of the engine mounting in combination with the carburettor air intake. This meant splitting of the exhaust pipe and the modification of the engine cowling. The revised components were designed and fabricated at CAC.

Because of an anticipated increase in bomb carrying capacity the outer wing attachment and the undercarriage axles were strengthened in addition to modifying parts of the undercarriage to facilitate mass production by J. N. Kirby in Sydney. The internal structure of both outer wing panels was modified to fit two Universal Carriers internally for bombs up to 250 lb and the wing centre section was redesigned to fit six Light Series Carriers for bombs up to 40 lb. The centre section flaps were re-arranged to permit increased forward vision for the prone bomb-aiming position. Provision was made for a bomb sight below the floor of the second cockpit, and a camera and RAAF type landing flares in the aft fuselage. The NA-33 gun installation was re-designed to fit two forward firing pilot operated machine guns on either side of the front instrument panel with synchronising gear and 1,200 rounds of ammunition, as well as a hydraulic lift type flexible gun installation in the rear cockpit. A complete redesign of the electrical system with regard to bomb release (to operate from both cockpits), two radio sets and the camera installation was undertaken. The tailplane was strengthened to overcome likelihood of damage in service as experienced with the NA-32 (A20-1) design. All riveted joints were redesigned to replace the 17S type rivets with type A17S. The American SAE system of screw threads was changed to British Standard on the airframe but not on the engine. These extensive changes created a huge workload for the drawing offices.

The first R-1340 Wasp engine assembled by CAC (from imported components) was accepted by the RAAF on January 27, 1939. The second work shift was introduced on the previous day and the first Wirraway fuselage was mated to its centre section wing.

CAC spent an additional £1,000 improving the surface quality of the landing field which was not nearly enough to take away all the unevenness from the ground. The first flight of the first locally assembled Wirraway, A20-3, took place shortly before noon on Monday March 27, 1939 by CAC test pilot (Flt Lt) Hubert Boss-Walker taking off from the sandy, loose surfaced, potholed landing ground adjacent to the Fisherman's Bend factory.

Hubert Boss-Walker had been flying instructor at the Royal Victorian Aero Club (Essendon) from June 1937. In March 1939 Wackett passed aircraft handling notes and a copy produced by NAA for CAC of an engineering and construction file on the Wirraway and its engine for Boss-Walker to familiarize himself with the aircraft prior to its first flight. It was stolen from his locked car three nights later. Despite extensive inquires and police intervention the material was never found. Wackett was greatly upset describing Hubert as grossly careless and would have sacked him immediately had it been possible to find another person to take his place.

Richard Casey, Minister for Department of Supply and Development (wearing hat), and on his immediate left, Geoffrey Arthur Street, Minister for Defence examine a Wirraway and its dummy Lewis rear gun. **L.J. Wackett/MS4858/NLA**

As a temporary measure and with progressively increasing take-off weight, testing was transferred to RAAF Base Laverton. The RAAF billed CAC £21/11/10 for 183 gall of aviation fuel used during the testing of A20-3.

The flight was significant in that it marked a triumph for enterprise and technique and effectively answered both the critics and pessimists who argued that Australia was not capable of building such an aircraft.

Notable among the overseas critics was Britain's Charles Grey Grey, editor of the '*Aeroplane*'. His tirade did not let up, the most recent of the day was titled, 'American Profiteering in Australia'. The Australian aviation monthly '*Aircraft*' of May 1,1939 responded, arguing that England could not deliver the aircraft Australia had ordered and in any case, once converted to Australian currency, the A£6,250 cost of an English 'stick and string' aeroplane and added to it adequate instruments and a constant speed propeller the total price was not far removed from the A£8,098 estimated figure for the Wirraway, an aircraft which was an advance in its day for the purpose to which it was intended.

Commenting on the first flight, Wackett said,

> "we reached the production stage in less than 30 months. We had therefore accomplished something before war broke out in September. This was, in my opinion, the most important achievement of my life, for which I must claim credit for being the only person in Australia who trained himself for the task and got into a position to do anything at this critical time. There were others who realised the situation two years later, but this was too late".

Because the Air Board had not provided its military equipment, A20-3 had to be returned to CAC for fitment as CAC *"was concentrating on the manufacture of military installations of aircraft 2 to 5"*. The fact that British rather than US equipment was used meant that there was *"more work than was originally anticipated"* in the installation of military equipment.

It was to take about four years before an almost completely Australian airframe and engine could be produced.

Australia's declaration of war came on September 3, 1939 followed on 5 October by the approval of the War Cabinet of the formation of the Empire Air Training Scheme (EATS). Under this scheme which came into operation five days later, Australia was to furnish 10,000 pilots, navigators and air gunners for RAF service every year. The principal aircraft to be used in Australia for the Scheme were the DH82 Tiger Moth basic trainer before transitioning to the more advanced Wirraway aircraft.

Contractual Problems

On July 15, 1938 CAC was asked to quote prices and rates of delivery for another 60 aircraft and followed on June 8, 1939 by a request for a further 32 aircraft. No firm contract had been agreed

The Wirraway line. The temporary label on the rudder of the first airframe in the centre reads H2-506 indicating this aircraft was the second aircraft in production batch 'H' and became A20-506. **HDHV**

to for the first 40 aircraft so much so that the company secretary was forced to comment that *"the situation had changed so materially it would be advisable to hold a conference with your Department (Defence) for the purpose of arriving at a new basis for prices"*.

On August 1, 1939 the company was letting Defence know in general terms that it was seeking an increased unit price due to:
1. Increased wages.
2. Increased prices of materials.
3. Design changes.
4. Import duties on its plant and defence materials.

The increased prices of these items alone would leave CAC showing a loss on the first contract so it was not able to quote on the two new orders even though during July 1938 it believed the price of the batch of 60 would not be much in excess of £8,144 for each aircraft.

Richard G. Casey, Minister for the Department of Supply and Development, let it be known on August 31, 1939 that in requesting CAC to step up production he was not aware that extra capital expenditure would be needed and asked CAC to find this capital as the Government was not likely to be able to do so. To which Harold Darling eventually pointed out that the shareholding companies had gone into the aircraft industry for patriotic reasons and not large profits. To step up production to four aircraft and then six aircraft each week the Government provided the sum of £125,000. No corresponding working capital was, however, provided, and when it became evident that CAC had a payroll of 2,000 people and a wages bill of about £10,000 each week it was obvious that the company had been embarrassed by a shortage of working capital.

Draft copies of contracts were swapped back and forth between CAC's solicitors and the Deputy Crown Solicitor till the latter was forced to admit that due to the substantial additional work which CAC was being required to carry out, the question of price should be re-considered.

The degree of changes and requests for further alterations made Wackett comment, on August 24, 1939, in his factory work progress report to the Board of CAC, *"the Air Force is aiming at a degree of perfection which really cannot be achieved in this type of aircraft and will have to accept many compromises. They do not quite realise that we have gone a long way to adapt the NA-33 design to perform military duties but there is a limit to the possibilities. Their latest decision to extend the military duties to include flying over the sea in the 41st and subsequent aircraft is an attempt to extend the use of the aircraft for every form of military duty which an aircraft is called upon to perform"*.

Expenditure to December 31, 1939 was £583,940 with advances of £400,000 against £351,760 for agreed outlays. Up to 12 December

Partially completed Wirraway airframes. **L.J.Wackett/MS4858/NLA**

CA-1 Wirraways A20-4, 10 and 11 fresh off the production line flown by Hubert Boss-Walker; Sqdn Ldr P.Heffernan & Flg Off R. Hitchcock. **L. J. Wackett/MS4858/NLA**

when 26 Wirraways had been delivered, the cash overrun was real and serious.

S. V. Nixon, Chairman of the Accounting Panel of the Board of Business Administration was asked to give his comments on the expenditure problems of the Wirraway project. In his report of January 15, 1940 he indicated that consideration could be given for adjustment in payments for such things as jigs, special tools, gauges and the setting up of the drawing office as well as increases in wages payable to employees of the Australian Coach, Motor Car, Waggon Builders, Wheelwrights and Aircraft and Rolling Stock Wages Acts of 1935 although all of these items had been accepted by CAC as part of its overall estimate. S. V. Nixon also felt that the company may have overloaded the cost of training unskilled personnel to too high a figure, over too short a production period, ie the first 40 aircraft.

Orders for 92 extra aircraft and 20 spare engines had been put out without any price being agreed upon whilst the factory had now established that the average price of each Wirraway was nearer to £14,000. Finally, on August 5, 1940, Robert Gordon Menzies, the Minister for Munitions, signed on behalf of the Government a contract with supplementary agreements which paid CAC £8,144 per aircraft with an additional £3,366 for each of the 40 aircraft for contracted design, ground support equipment, tool kits for line, squadron and depot levels, technical training and supporting manuals. The War Cabinet was advised on September 27, 1941 that payments made to the company in respect of the first 40 Wirraways, all delivered by February 1940 and identified as the CA-1 Wirraway I, was to amount to £11,500 for each aircraft.

Subsequent approximate prices quoted by CAC were:
Aircraft 41 - 132	£12,250
Aircraft 133 - 232	£11,500
Aircraft 233 - 414	£10,500
Aircraft 415 - 481	£9,790

On June 3, 1941 CAC was seeking £115,341 incurred in establishing the manufacture of the Wirraway line. Included in this

Line up of Wirraway fuselage assemblies. **HDHV**

figure was a £11,092 component for continuing operations at the Tugan Aircraft works prior to embarking on Wirraway production. Having reached the expected £9,790 unit price, the company was proudly claiming on November 17, 1941 that the NAA Harvard trainer which was being supplied to the UK, was priced at £12,000, whereas CAC was able to deliver a Wirraway for under £10,000.

Production Momentum and British Demand

Sixty aircraft formed the CA-3 Wirraway II contract. The most noticeable external difference from the Mk I was the deletion of the corrugated surface on the Mk I empennage; some Mk Is were later modified to the standard surfacing. Aircraft A20-103 to 134 were the next 32 Wirraway II as contract CA-5. CA-7, CA-8 and CA-9 were further contracts for 100, 200 and 188 Mk II aircraft respectively. This brought total orders to be completed to June 1942 to 620 aircraft, peak production having been reached in December 1941 with the delivery that month of 42 aircraft.

CAC was not slow to offer the Wirraway for overseas sale. The the company's secretary, A. G. Brown, requested the Prime Minister, Joseph Lyons on March 23, 1937 to convey, when the opportunity arose, the attributes and merits of CAC and the NA-16 to the Prime Minister of New Zealand. The apparent response in press statements originating in New Zealand stated that New Zealand would first exercise the usual preference with Britain and only if Britain was not able to supply its needs would it look to other parts of the Empire.

The RAAF sought production of an additional 250 Wirraways as attrition replacements based on a need of 66 new aircraft each year. The Department of Aircraft Production however, had to implement a revised aircraft production program approved by Cabinet at the start of 1942 (post the attack on Pearl Harbour) which called for an end to the manufacture of trainers and concentrating resources on operational types, while at the same time undertaking an expansion program of the construction of hangars and workshops for repair and overhaul of airframes, engines and equipment to meet EATS and subsequently, RAAF and USAAC demand.

Ironically the British Purchasing Commission was to order the North American Aviation NA-49 (NA-16-1E) Harvard. The first of about 1,000 examples was to make its first flight on September 28, 1938.

This time the NA-16 found favour with Mr C. G. Grey. He announced *"that if the aircraft had the range to fly over Berlin, he was sure that all it would take to obtain a Nazi surrender would be to throw the propeller into low pitch and run it up to maximum revolutions; the noise would do the rest"*.

In June of 1940, the War Cabinet gave procurement approval for materials for 811 Wirraways although CAC was not authorised at that stage to proceed with production beyond 232 aircraft. Experience showed that Wirraway airframes could be produced more readily than the Wasp engines and that possible airframe production was considerably in excess of RAAF requirements for the type. So the UK government was offered all Wirraway production in excess of RAAF requirements provided the engine shortfall was made up from United States sources. The UK ordered 245 Wirraways to be delivered by the end of 1942 then increased that number by another 255 and was requesting a further 300 aircraft during 1943, giving a potential total Wirraway program of around 1,600 aircraft. On October 30, 1941, Wirraway numbers A20-565 to 1064 were expected to be allocated to the RAF order for 500 aircraft. Airframes were to be shipped out at the rate of ten aircraft each week. Of this weekly supply, six airframes would have had CAC built engines, the other four would have been without engines. Delivery of these airframes built to a CA-9 specification but with a possible variation in radios and the type of fixed forward armament, was expected to start in February or March 1942. CAC did not know where the aircraft were destined to be sent or operated. Details were at a higher Government decision level and remained so.

This export order was raised by Senator D. Cameron, the Minister for Aircraft Production in his meeting with the Board of CAC on December 12, 1941, during which the proposed take-over of CAC as a wartime emergency action was under discussion. He believed the British Government would probably set aside its order for Wirraways to help Australia concentrate its resources to the production of the Beaufort bomber. The Australian War Cabinet shifted its production priority to that of front-line combat aircraft soon after Japan entered the Pacific War on December 7, 1941, and the UK Government did abandon its orders for the Wirraway. The Royal Air Force had been allocated 245 serial numbers presumably for the first lot of aircraft they hoped to receive. The serial batches were: HP531-568; 584-627; 645-673; 687-736; 749-784 and 796-843. (It is not clear if Britain financed an alternate 245 Wirraway aircraft in lieu, as its contribution to the EATS.)

Following the departure of H. Boss-Walker on October 10, 1941, the work of production testing Wirraways and Wackett Trainers was left to James Carter. James had joined the company as assistant test pilot on September 26, 1941. This routine flight testing job was shared with service pilots.

Contract CA-10 and CA-20 earmarked for a production batch described as Wirraway dive-bombers did not eventuate but development problems with the CA-4 Wackett Bomber (dive bombing was to be one of its functions) brought about discussion on July 7,

The 500th Wirraway sometime in 1942. **HDHV**

CA-16 Wirraway

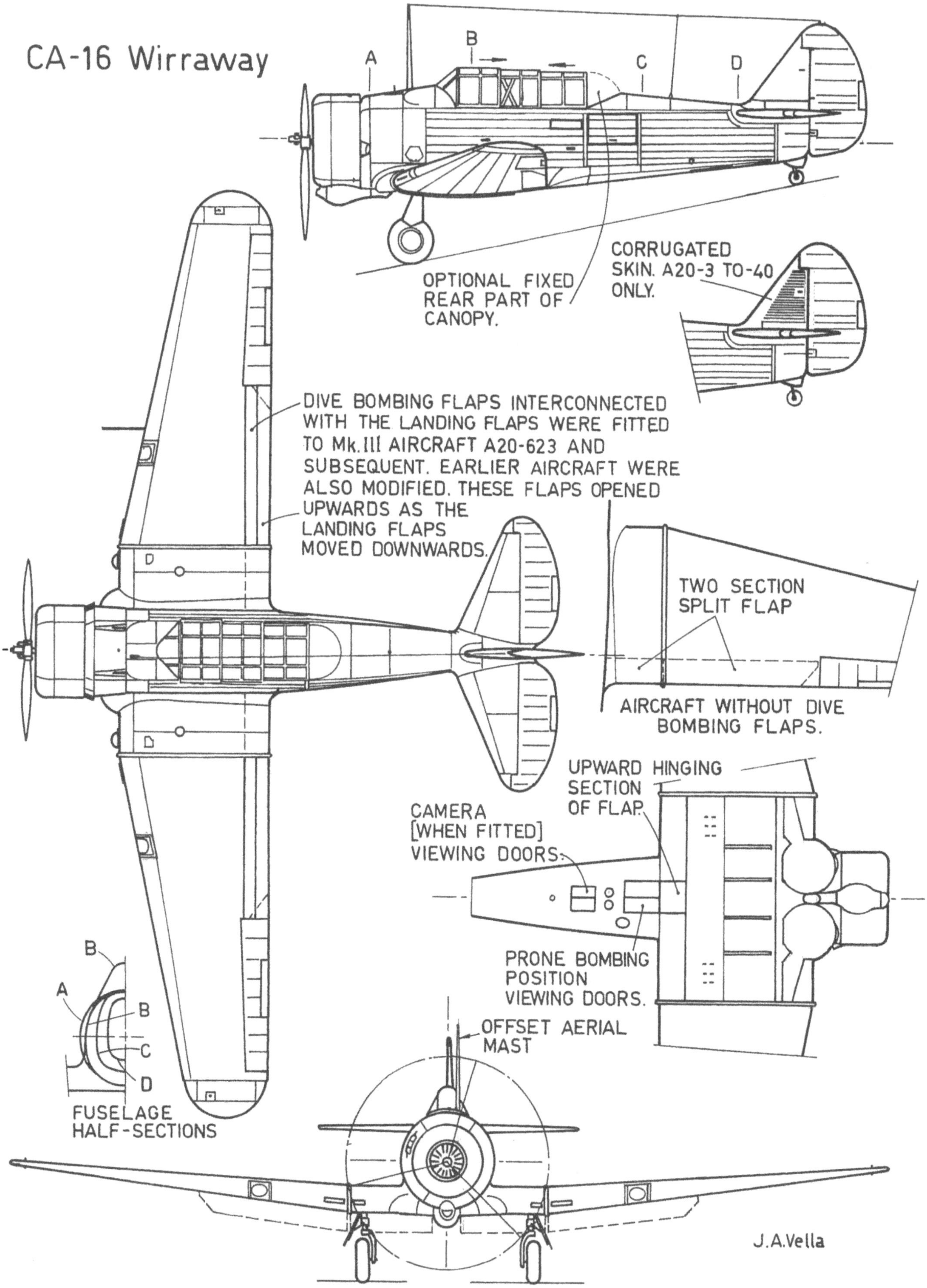

OPTIONAL FIXED REAR PART OF CANOPY.

CORRUGATED SKIN. A20-3 TO-40 ONLY.

DIVE BOMBING FLAPS INTERCONNECTED WITH THE LANDING FLAPS WERE FITTED TO Mk.III AIRCRAFT A20-623 AND SUBSEQUENT. EARLIER AIRCRAFT WERE ALSO MODIFIED. THESE FLAPS OPENED UPWARDS AS THE LANDING FLAPS MOVED DOWNWARDS.

TWO SECTION SPLIT FLAP

AIRCRAFT WITHOUT DIVE BOMBING FLAPS.

UPWARD HINGING SECTION OF FLAP.

CAMERA [WHEN FITTED] VIEWING DOORS.

PRONE BOMBING POSITION VIEWING DOORS.

OFFSET AERIAL MAST

FUSELAGE HALF-SECTIONS

J.A.Vella

A20-224. A CA-7 Wirraway II. **Frank Smith**

Wirraway CA-16, A20-707 fuselage on its floor handling trolley. **David Anderson. 548 722062008P**

1942 to fit dive brakes on some existing Wirraways. This it was hoped would fill the gap in defence needs until the CA-4 was steered through its design difficulties. The new work of modifying the wing centre section, fabrication and conversion to contract CA-10A was a source of difficulty to CAC as the factory was operating at a manning level several hundred below its intended requirement.

Approval was given for 500 modification kits to allow the aircraft to dive vertically without exceeding 245 mph. Clyde Engineering of Bankstown and Granville in NSW took over this Wirraway dive –bomber conversion work, fabricating the dive bombing flaps after 40 complete conversions had been carried out by CAC.

Ansett Airways were to take part in the conversion process, but when they were confronted by production difficulties the work was transferred to Richards Industries, who took on the job with enthusiasm. In contrast Clyde Engineering Industries, builder of locomotives and rolling stock were a lot slower in becoming adept with the engineering demands and the required quality of the finished aviation components.

Mating Wirraway CA-16, A20-707 fuselage frame to its wing assembly. **David Anderson. 548 722062009P**

The first CAC-modified machine was delivered at the beginning of October 1942. A combined total of 113 aircraft had been converted and returned to the RAAF by October 30, 1943.

These dive-bomber wings were of an internally strengthened centre section, the dive bombing flaps on the outer panels were interconnected with the landing flaps, operated by the same

Monthly Wirraway Deliveries 1939-1946								
Month	1939	1940	1941	1942	1943	1944	1945	1946
January		5	5	25			2	3
February		8	9	22			7	3
March		5	21	29		4	2	5
April		6	22	26		5	6	1
May		11	19	18		8	4	7
June		7	20	9		3	3	2
July	2	8	5			1	5	1
August	4	16	26			4	2	
September	6	15	36			6	5	
October	7	33	45			8	2	
November	6	34	37		5	9	5	
December	8	23	42		5	8	4	
Cumulative Total	33	204	491	620	630	686	733	755

Notes:
June 1942 - Production stopped at 620 aircraft
November 1943 - Production resumed
August 1945 - Pacific War ends, production at 717 aircraft
July 1946 - Production ended at 755 aircraft

hydraulic jack and opening upwards as the landing flaps moved downwards.

Operationally, the need for dive-bombing especially in the jungles of New Guinea and the islands started to assume a lower priority. It was hard enough to find the enemy in the jungles and mountainous terrain, let alone undertake a dive-bombing attack on him. The RAAF was also receiving the Vultee Vengeance specialized dive bombers in slowly increasing numbers and putting them into service as tactical strike aircraft.

The expected enemy incursions of the mainland had not occurred and this form of ground attack no longer held a priority production commitment. The dive flaps were locked shut and the mechanism disconnected; with the dive bombing role receiving limited training exposure at the various OTUs.

Army liason crew loading an RAF style delivery container under a No 4 Sqdn Wirraway at Gusap, New Guinea, 1944. **Richard Hourigan**.

A20-341, a CA-6 Wirraway II. **Frank Smith**

The company had also designed and produced, what Wackett described as an excellent wooden, two bladed propeller with the pitch change mechanism of a Hamilton Standard propeller and Curtiss bearings. CAC and de Havilland were to combine to produce 100 of these units if DEPAIR had the need.

Tooling for the hub was started in September 1941. The aim was to produce an alternate propeller which would take away the demand for metal units and leave the existing facilities to cope with the production needs of the Beaufort line. CSIR tested the propeller and found its performance comparable to that of the metal variant.

By May 1942 all the forgings necessary to meet the expected Wirraway production run were on hand and plans for this wooden propeller were put aside. However on May 25, 1942 the CAC Board was told that DEPAIR suggested the use of the CAC two bladed wooden propeller as de Havilland had been having initial production difficulties with the metal propeller. This was not taken up.

At about the same time as the dive bomber wings were put into production experiments were carried out in the CSIR wind tunnel on a system to operate the dive brake flaps and the main flaps by pneumatic means. The scheme devised by Ian Ring was to enclose a rubber bag within the flap cavity and inflating the bag through a ram air duct. To lower the flaps a cock would be turned to link with a suction point on the wing in lieu of the standard hydraulic flap system. Operation was very rapid and the concept offered a reduced structure weight and lesser maintenance. However the very best of rubberised silk was too thick a material and there were practical limitations to the folding of the bag volume in the retracted position.

Between December 1939 and April 1940, CAC built and supplied 29 collapsible instrument flying hoods. Aircraft A20-31 to 52 were amongst a group of mixed airframe numbers to be fitted with these hoods.

The Clowns take on aircraft movement. **Roger Ward**

Dust Problems

When Chief Engineer Thomas W. Air visited 2 SFTS, Wagga and 2 AD Richmond, NSW during February 1941, he was told of a shortage of Wirraway airframe and engine spares, technical information and drawings; lacking mainly due to the enormous rapid expansion of the RAAF servicing system. The situation at Richmond was not as bad as that at 2 SFTS.

The company's service engineer Ewart R. Chenery visited RAAF Pearce in WA on June 6, 1941 and commented on the good quality of the grassed aerodrome, the workshops and equipment. Their 17 Wirraways were well looked after by men who knew their job. At

A No 5 Sqdn Wirraway fitted with three storepedoes operating from Bougainville. **Richard Hourigan**

A20-570, CA-8 Wirraway II seen with underwing 0.303inch guns. Ammunition was stored in the wing, 1957. **Roger McLeod.**

RAAF Darwin on June 23, 1941 the scarcity of workshop tooling, working and finishing materials, a lack of engine spares from Stores Depots down south, improper and faulty work practices, engine parts covered in red dust and oil suggested the engines here be rescued and sent to a better equipped workshop, as loss of life may have occurred if present conditions were allowed to continue. RAAF Archerfield, Qld on July 3, 1941 was a better place with Wirraways clean and well looked after, the aerodrome in beautiful condition but the usual absence of wall charts, engine data service bulletins etc was very evident. Some of the aerodromes used in the Empire Air Training Scheme were little more than hastily prepared landing grounds from former wheat or grazing paddocks. Large volumes of raised dust were being ingested by the engines reducing the expected 400 hour life of a new engine. The adverse operating conditions and the intensive flying activity were lowering this life to around 100 hours creating a large demand on engine replacement and re-building.

A20-691, CA-9 Wirraway II on cross-country flight at RAAF Townsville, 1950s. **Richard Hourigan.**

The difficult summer conditions encountered by Chenery, in February 1942 at Deniliquin, NSW, were of dust clouds rising to hundreds of feet at a time. For six and seven days in each week one could not see across the aerodrome. 'Willy willys' of enormous size would sweep across it and sometimes through the hangar where the maintenance work was being carried out. Covers were placed on all equipment items in the hangars. At times the dust inside was so thick the lights had to be left on during daylight hours.

Conditions at Uranquinty,NSW were no better. Only 25 of the base complement of 120 Wirraways were operational. The rest were grounded due to engine dust problems and lack of engine spares. It was possible to locate the aerodrome at ground level by spotting the dust clouds from three miles away.

The factory work of producing replacement cylinder/ barrels was a huge undertaking which peaked around March 1942, co-inciding with a demand for a large quantity of engine spares and airframe parts, especially replacements for worn sliding canopy sections and tracks.

The incentive was such that if the life of each cylinder barrel in service could be extended by just 50 hours, then the production of cylinders would have been reduced by 5,000 units per annum. In practice the improved service life of the cylinders under dusty conditions went up from 100 hours to 500 hours.

Air to the carburettor was led to the engine through an unfiltered intake on the lower engine cowl. This was modified by placing an air cleaner element in a bulbous housing fitted below the other intake. A fast program for the production of filters and filter housings was started in May 1942 for retrospective fitting on aircraft already in service. An initial order for 500 modification kits at £35 each totalled £17,500. If the filters were used dry they would not trap the fine dust but if wet they became chocked in a relatively short time. When maintained frequently and properly the problem of wear was alleviated.

This engine wear created very heavy gas 'blow-by' with a consequent pressure rise in the crankcase which resulted in a reduction in the rate of return of oil from the rear section of the engine to the sump and retarded the rate of scavenging to the oil tank. In extreme cases the accumulation of oil in the rear section became so great that a quantity of it would be ejected from the engine breather onto the windscreen creating a serious operating danger for the pilot as it was likely to occur at take-off under conditions of high power and engine revolutions.

By drilling a one inch diameter opening high in the wall of the rear crankcase to balance the pressures in the crankcase and the rear section, the problem was overcome. These problems were in no way due to inherent shortcomings of the engine but were entirely due to the conditions under which they were operated, a significant departure from operating conditions in North America.

Production which had been completed to June 1942 at the 620th airframe resumed again in September 1943 on Wirraway IIIs of the CA-16 and final contract. This was an order for 150 aircraft fitted with dive brakes, part of the 250 additional aircraft sought by the RAAF as attrition replacements intended to take the total production figure to 870. The Wirraway III had the built-in armament deleted, the aft end of the cockpit framework enclosed by a streamlined perspex fairing and the dive brakes tied down to prevent their use.

This new workload helped to take up the slack in production until the anticipated start of the CA-17/18 Mustang in December 1943. With floor space allocated to the CA-17/18 line and the forthcoming CA-11 Woomera, erection commenced in the Wirraway Assembly Building. Aircraft output was dependent on the production rate at Richards Industries Ltd to whom the job of fabrication had been transferred so as to free up the capacity at Fisherman's Bend for the Mustang. Only 20 personnel were employed on this, primarily an assembly task. The initial output was a trickle at less than five aircraft each month and then, at the demand of the War Cabinet, was, by May 1945, deliberately slowed down to one aircraft each week.

The availability of ungeared Wasp engines, which had been imported for use in the Australian Cruiser Tank Mk 1 *Sentinel* construction program but were declared surplus when that project did not progress beyond an evaluation batch, made this extension in the Wirraway program possible. (See Chapter 12, Aero Engines; R-1340 engine).

CAC converted 350 of these engines to a geared drive between 1940 and 1945 (at a considerable saving to the Government) in addition to building 680 examples of the engine between 1939 and 1945 and carrying out overhauls on 545 similar engines.

The major sub-contractors for this and earlier phases included; GM-H at Woodville, South Australia, who produced 991 oil tanks and 908 pairs of fuel tanks; exhaust pipes from Myttons; cowlings from Richards Industries Ltd, South Australia, who also fabricated 415 wings, 258 Wirraway and Boomerang monocoques, 228 Wirraway and Boomerang centre sections and also delivering 6 pairs of wings, 5 Wirraway centre sections and 10 Wirraway monocoque fuselage sections each week; J.N.Kirby (Sydney) produced all Wirraway undercarriage units; de Havilland Aircraft fabricated 543 three bladed 3D40 metal propellers at their Alexandria, NSW, plant. They also built 57 examples of the metal 2D40 two-bladed variant when a shortage of forgings threatened the supply of the 3D model. They were not put into use. The Forest Products Division of CSIR built and tested a wooden bladed 3D40 propeller utilising Australian timbers.

CAC battling with manpower demands was not able to undertake the wartime overhaul of Wirraways although the subject had been repeatedly canvassed by the RAAF. The work was farmed out to Clyde Engineering at Bankstown and Granville in NSW. The 1,200 hours limit for a complete Wirraway overhaul was progressively advanced to around 1,900 hours. Clyde's concentrated on re-building crashed Wirraways, a task which employed 300 to 400 people.

By August 31, 1945, at the end of the hostilities in the Pacific, 97 CA-16s had been delivered bringing Wirraway production to 717. Work stopped in July 1946 after a further 38 aircraft had been built, ending at the 135th CA-16 rather than the intended 150, bringing the total of all variants to 757 aircraft (including the two imported sample aircraft).

*Fancy that! The Clowns accidentally discovered a forgotten restored Wirraway BF-F . **Roger Ward***

At the 620th airframe production break in June 1942, expenditure stood at:

	Total cost	Per Unit cost
Production cost	£5,433,437	£9,275
Profit margin	£189,593	£300
	£5,623,030	£9,575

Some Service Activities

12 Squadron was the first RAAF Wirraway operational unit. It was located at Darwin, NT, for patrol and convoy escort tasks soon after the outbreak of the War in Europe. In July 1940, 21 Sqn deployed to Singapore with 12 Wirraways (later replaced by Brewster Buffalo fighters) to aid in the defence of the Malayan Peninsula, subsequently operating from Seletar airfield on Singapore.

A detachment of six Wirraways from 12 Sqdn was operating in the advanced training role in Malaya at the time of the Japanese invasion and was raised to operational interdiction status, dive-bombing and strafing enemy landing barges and ground positions. Being the only aircraft with some sort of armament and reasonable, if limited performance, its early introduction in an operational role was to be expected.

*A20-715, 681, and others, starting up at RAAF Point Cook, 1956. **Roger McLeod***

With 209 Wirraways delivered by the time Japan entered the War these aircraft had equipped 4 Sqdn, Canberra (12); 5 Sqdn, Laverton (12); 12 Sqdn, Darwin (18); 21 Sqdn, Laverton; 22 Sqdn, Richmond NSW (17); 23 Sqdn, Archerfield, Qld. (12); 24 Sqdn, Townsville, Qld (12) and 25 Sqdn, Pearce, W. Aust (18).

24 Squadron deployed to Vunakanau, Rabaul, providing, the only 'fighter' defence when, from January 4, 1942, Rabaul came under Japanese attack. Two days later Flt Lt B.H. Anderson became the first RAAF pilot to engage in aerial combat in the South West Pacific when his Wirraway, A20-137 engaged a Kawanishi H6K4 'Mavis' flying boat. Between December and the end of January 1942 Japanese air attacks gradually destroyed most of the squadron's aircraft and it ceased to operate.

*An impressive line-up of 19 Wirraways at RAAF Point Cook with the kangaroo roundel & yellow fuselage training band, 12 Dec 1958, possibly in preparation for a massed fly-over Melbourne city prior to retirement, 19 aircraft to represent one for each year of service. **RAAF Museum.***

On March 5, 1942 following the return of the remnants of the squadron to Australia, Sqdn Ldr W. Brookes reported to HQ, North Eastern Area that their patrols were limited without an external fuel tank. In an attempt to remedy the situation, the unit had taken the step of removing the observer station seat, rear gun ammunition storage etc and fitted a standard 44 gall petrol drum, piping, air pump etc in a cradle secured to the bottom of the fuselage. This temporary fix increased range of the Wirraway by 50%.

Operationally, the aircraft's firepower was inadequate to harm Japanese flying boats, the only type of enemy aircraft that could be overtaken by a Wirraway in a pursuit.

When the Australian mainland came under air attack the aircraft of Darwin's 12 Squadron were ordered to remain on the ground. The only known successful downing of an enemy aircraft was by Wirraway A20-103, an aircraft from 4 Squadron, crewed by Flg Off J. S. Archer and Sgt J. Coulston who downed a Nakajima Ki-43 Oscar (initially thought to be and reported as a Mitsubishi A6M3 Zero) near Gona, PNG, on December 26, 1942. The Wirraway was circling above the bombed out hulk of a Japanese ship in the shallows near Gona when a Japanese fighter was sighted about 1,000 feet below. With the obvious element of surprise on their side, Archer dived on it letting off a fatal head-on burst with his front 0.303 inch machine guns; his speed then carried him on and past the Oscar.

The Wirraway was responsible for the success of the Australian section of the EATS in the role of advanced trainer with Nos 2, 5 and 6 Service Flying Training Schools in NSW at Wagga, Uranquinty and Deniliquin. The peak of flying activity at Deniliquin with 130 Wirraways on strength in June 1944 registered 7,000 flying hours for the month with an aircraft monthly average of between 45 and 50 hours. At Uranquinty, the aircraft monthly average for September was 58 hours.

A sustained operational commitment was Army co-operation work with 4 and 5 Squadrons. 4 Squadron in New Guinea and then Labuan Island worked the low level, ground strafing, target marking role. No 5 Squadron on Bougainville Island marked targets for RNZAF F4U Corsairs and was subsequently partnered in this role with the CAC Boomerang.

Capable of carrying a bomb load of up to 1,000 lb in overload condition, as well as reconnaissance flares and vital air dropped supply containers, the aircraft earned a reputation for outstanding work. There were also the early stints of mundane anti-submarine coastal patrol work.

Other units to use the aircraft in small numbers or short term attachments were: No 30, 54, 60, 78 and 82 Squadrons and 2, 3, 4 and 10 Communications Units.

Post War Service

The Wirraway was retained post war as an advanced trainer. For the role of armament training, it was proposed in late 1949 to fit an AN-N6 cine-camera gun, Gyro gunsight Mk IID and VHF radio. Two rocket launchers under each wing were to be secured using the existing bomb rack attachments. The concept was tested but did not see service.

Between July 1950 and July 1955, CAC overhauled and modified 153 Wirraways for the RAAF and RAN. The modifications, where not previously implemented, meant the removal of all internal armament items, fairing-in the rear gun emplacement by a clear Perspex canopy and in some instances mounting a 0.303 inch machine gun under each wing for gunnery practice. The latter installation was carried out at RAAF depot level.

The Fleet Air Arm operated seventeen Wirraways between 1948 and 1957 on shore based liaison work with 723, 724 and 816 Squadrons. These aircraft were: A20-28, 133, 139, 141, 145, 168, 176, 209, 211, 214, 225, 238, 250, 469, 490, 750 and 752 may have been provided under contract CA-20 in place of a previously cancelled

Specifications	Wirraway General Production CA-1,3,5,7,8,9,16			
Powerplant	One CAC/Pratt & Whitney 9 cyl Wasp R1340 S1H1G geared radial of 650 hp at take-off at 2,300 rpm and 600 hp at 7,000 ft			
Performance	Max speed at critical altitude (8,600 ft)	190.kt		
	Operating speed at SL at 2,100 rpm	150 kt		
	Operating speed at 9,000 ft	170 kt		
	Operating speed critical altitude (13,000 ft)	180 kt		
	Landing speed (flaps lowered)	56 kt		
	Max rate of climb	1950 ft/min		
	Endurance at 450 hp	3.07 hrs		
	Range at 450 hp at 13,000 ft	550 nm		
	Range at economical speed	735 nm		
	Service ceiling	23,000 ft		
	Fuel capacity	92 gall		
	Oil capacity	8.75 gall		
Weights	Normal gross	5,575 lb		
	Max gross	6,450 lb		
	Normal wing loading	21.8 lb/sq ft		
	Normal power loading	9.3 lb / hp		
	Empty	3,895 lb		
Dimensions	Wing span	43 ft	Wing area	256 sq ft
	Wing section(root)	NACA-2215	Wing section(tip)	NACA-2209
	Wing root chord	7 ft 6 ins	Wing tip chord	4 ft
	Length	27 ft 10 ins	Height	12 ft
Armament	Two fixed forward firing 0 303 in Vickers Mk V machine guns with 600 rpg			
	0.303 in Vickers G.O. Mk I machine gun in rear cockpit with 480 rounds			
	Max bomb load 1,000 lb			
Retrospective Designations	XP1 CA-1 Wirraway			
	XP5 CA-3 Wirraway			
	XP13 CA-9 Wirraway			
	XP14 CA-10 Wirraway			

A20-649 belonging to the Moorabbin Air Museum having its first engine run; an ambitious plan to return it to airworthy condition August 23, 1974 at RAAF Point Cook. J. A. Vella

CA-20 RAAF contract for 100 aircraft. All of the Navy's Wirraways were subsequently sold to Lund Aviation Inc. of New York in 1957. The Wirraway was kept on for liaison and advanced training work (1 BFTS & 1 AFTS) with the RAAF until 1959 when the last unit known to have operated the type was 23 Squadron at Mallala, South Australia. Its service replacement in the advanced training role was the de Havilland Vampire Trainer.

A number of airframes subsequently came on and off the civil aircraft register. Nine examples were listed in 2019.

General Purpose Aircraft Airframe Description

(The following is a summary from company aircraft notes)

The all metal wing was comprised of a constant chord centre section set at a 2° angle of incidence incorporating two fuel tanks of a combined 92 gallons capacity with a reserve 16 gallons in the port main tank as part of the total capacity.

Six light series stores carriers were built into the centre section of the wing aft of the rear spar. Each was to hold an 8.5 lb or 11.5 lb practice smoke bomb. Eight mechanically operated carriers or slips were mounted aft of the spar on the centre section fuel tank access panel. These were primarily intended for the carriage of pyrotechnics but could be used for small 20 lb HE bombs. A bomb release distribution circuit was also fitted for the electrically operated slips.

The outer wing panels, with detachable wing tips had a LE sweep of 12°51' and a dihedral of 5°. A pair of Universal Carriers was built into each outer wing panel to each lift 250 lb GP or SAP bombs. From aircraft A20-30 onwards the inner-most of these carriers were re-stressed to carry a 500 lb bomb.

Landing flaps were incorporated in the lower surface of the wing trailing edge extending between the inboard ends of the ailerons. The ailerons were fabric covered aluminium framed and incorporated booster tabs. A similar construction was used on the rudder and elevators and each was fitted with a trim tab, the entire empennage assembly being otherwise made of metal.

CAC added two forward firing 0.303 inch Vickers Mk V machine guns, one on either side of the front instrument panel aimed in a line outside the engine ring cowl with provision of 600 rounds of per gun, sighted by a standard ring and bead sight. Gun synchronising gear was added. Two easily detachable fabric covered aluminium alloy frame panels covered the fuselage sides. Aluminium alloy panels covered the upper surfaces, fore and aft of the cockpit enclosure. Three fuselage cowl pieces formed the engine nacelle enclosure ahead of the firewall. The engine cowl ring was a two piece assembly enclosing two exhaust outlets.

Specifications	NA-16-1A (Performance details as provided by NAA to CAC)	
Powerplant	One Pratt & Whitney 9cyl Wasp R1340 S3H1 radial of 550 hp driving a 2 bladed, 2 position, controllable pitch 9 ft diameter propeller	
Performance	Max speed at 5,000 ft	177 kts
	Cruising speed at 62.5% power at 16,000 ft	166 kts
	Landing speed (flaps lowered)	56 kts
	Max rate of climb	1,800 ft/min
	Service ceiling	26,000 ft
	Endurance at 5,000 ft at 62.5% power	3.4 hrs
	Range at 16,000 ft at 62.5% power	570 nm
	Range at econ speed	705 nm
	Fuel capacity	104 gall
Weights	Gross	4,500 lb
	Useful load	1,454 lb
	Wing loading	18.1 lb/sq ft
	Power loading	8.2 lb/hp

The forward and aft fuselage frame assembly sections were of welded chrome-molybdenum steel tubing with an aluminium alloy semi-monocoque construction to the bottom portion of the aft section. An overturn truss structure was incorporated in the forward fuselage frame, behind the front cockpit. Engine mount and wing centre section attachments were also part of the structure. Two forced-landing flare containers were located in the aft fuselage section as were the cut-outs for the camera, camera sight, bomb sight and flare discharge doors.

The part of the floor covering the course setting Mk VII or Mk IX bomb sight in the rear cockpit was arranged as a double-hinged door, which folded against the port side of the aircraft when the rotating seat for the second crew member was locked in the rearward facing position. Bomb sight doors (hinged along their length) in the fuselage bottom were interconnected with a section of the centre section landing flap which was arranged to swing upwards as the bombsight doors opened to permit a flat sighting angle from the prone position.

A 0.303 inch Vickers G.O. Mk 1, free gun mounted on a CAC designed, hydraulically elevated hoist moved on a circular track in the rear cockpit. Stowage for 480 rounds of ammunition was made up of eight 60 round capacity magazines clipped on the rear fuselage frame tubes below the gun scarf ring.

An F24 aerial camera on a Type 25 mounting could be installed in the rear fuselage on two rails between four vertical tubes when it was not intended to use the prone bombing position. It was reached via a large door on the port side. An Aldis camera aiming sight was fitted on a wedge plate mounting on the panel displaying the bomb-aimer's ASI and altimeter on the port side just forward of the camera.

The rear cockpit had a basic instrument flying panel together with generally, R1082/AT10TR (Australian built version of the T1083) HF main radio located between the front and rear cockpits. The VHF TR11B emergency receive and transmit set was aft of the rear cockpit, with its aerial mast in an offset position ahead of the front cockpit. The HF radio used a 235 foot long trailing aerial, drawn in and out of the starboard side of the rear cockpit opposite the bomb aimer's instrument panel by a Winch Type 5.

The main landing gear was hydraulically actuated and sideways retracting into the wing centre section ahead of the front spar. Each single leg of half-fork, fully cantilever design carried a 27 inch diameter tyre which remained exposed in its extended housing forward of the wing leading edge. The tailwheel assembly was a fully-castoring non-retractable unit with a 10.5 inch diameter tyre.

The tandem cockpits were under one enclosure incorporating individual manually sliding sections at each cockpit. The front seat occupant could be provided with a collapsible instrument flying hood.

Bibliography: Wirraway

Australia. Dept. of Aircraft Production. (various) [Correspondence.] [NAA: MP287/1,104]. Barcode: 469047.

Australia. Dept. of Aircraft Production (1937-68). Minutes of meeting. (May 25, 1944). [NAA: MP1472/1, 15 part 1].Barcode: 514588.

Australia. Dept. of Aircraft Production (1939-45). Aircraft production & aircraft industry in Australia (August 31, 1945). [NAA: MP1472/1, 15 part 4]. Barcode: 5798360.

Australia. Dept. of Aircraft Production. (1942) Director General of Munitions .Memorandum of meeting. (July 20, 1942) [NAA: MP1472/1, 15 part 1]. Barcode: 514588.

Australia. Dept. of Aircraft Production. (1940-44). Wirraway & Wackett Trainer aircraft : Reimbursement of development charges in connection with manufacture of.[NAA: MP287/1,1216]. Barcode: 441459.

Australia. Aircraft Advisory Committee (1942-46). Minutes of meetings-Aircraft Advisory Commission. Meetings 1-77. [NAA: B5028,1; B5028,2; B5028,3; B5028,4; B5028,5]. Barcode: 395652; 395653; 395650; 395651 & 395649 respectively.

Australia. Aircraft Production Commission (1940). Wirraway aircraft: Contract for the supply of by CAC.[NAA: MP287/1,104]. Barcode: 4609047.

Australian air log. (1965 -) Hurstville, N.S.W.: Australian Air Log.

Baillieu, Clive. (March 22, 1937) Development of CAC, choice of NA-16 and its characteristics [Letter from CAC to Col. Clive Baillieu, Austral Development Ltd].

Carter, Dustin. (1979) 'North American aviation training aircraft.' *American Aviation Historical Society Journal,* Vol. 24/2.

Commonwealth Aircraft Corporation. (Sept. 1941) Engineering report AA21. Detail specification for CA-9 general purpose aircraft.

Commonwealth Aircraft Corporation. (undated manual) Wirraway overhaul and repair manual.

Commonwealth Aircraft Corporation. (undated) CAC production file P2.

Commonwealth Aircraft Corporation. (undated) CAC Service Engineer file (Wirraway, Boomerang, Wackett Trainer).

Commonwealth Aircraft Corporation Board. (Dec 12,1941) Minutes of meeting with Senator D. Cameron, Minister for Aircraft Production.

Delivery of Wirraway Aircraft.[NAA:A705,9/15/75] Barcode:164040

Directorate of Technical Services(DTS)- NA16 [NAA:A705,9/15/5]. Barcode :164036.

DTS -Rockets provision for carriage on Wirraway aircraft .1949-52 [NAA: A705/1,9/15/980]. Barcode:164084.

en.Wikipedia.org / Sentinel Tank, 1942.

Hourigan, R. (1986) Production and technical data. [Unpublished notes].

Isaacs, K. (various issues) *'Aircraft of the RAAF.'* Canberra: *RAAF News.*

Knight, Herbert (General Manager CAC 1961-69) (Dec. 1986) [Interviews and correspondence].

McCarthy, John Malcolm, 1933- (1976) *Australia and Imperial defence 1918-39:A study in air and sea power.* University of Queensland Press, St. Lucia, Qld.

McVey, D. (Sept 28, 1942) Memorandum from Secretary Department of Aircraft Production to Secretary of Department of Air. [NAA: MP 1472/1, item 5 / box 4].

Manufacture of aircraft in Australia No. 2-1939 [NAA:A5954,883/2].Barcode:652190.

Mellor, D. P. (David Paver), 1903-1980. (1962) *The role of science and industry*. Australian War Memorial, Canberra.

Ohlrich, Walt; Ethell, Jeffrey L. (1983) *The incredible T-6 pilot maker.* Specialty Press. Osceola, Wiconsin, USA.

Parkhill, Archdale Sir, 1879-1947 (1937) 'The manufacture of aircraft in Australia' : Address by Minister for Defence, to the Warringah Electoral Conference, February 4,1937.

Parnell, Neville. (1974) 'Aircraft of the RAN.' *AHSA journal.* Vol. 15/1.

Parnell, Neville. (1974) 'The Fleet Air Arm.' *Air Pictorial*. UK. Vol. 36/2.

Parnell, Neville; Lynch, Clive, A. (1976) *Australian Air Force since 1911.* Reed Publications.

Rayner, Harry, (1914-),(1984) *Scherger : a biography of Air Chief Marshal Sir Frederick Scherger*. Australian War Memorial , Canberra.

Vella, J. A. (1983) 'Genesis of the Wirraway'. *Aviation Heritage*, Victoria. Vol. 23/1 & 2.

Vella, J. A. (2020) 'The Internment of CAC Test Pilot Hubert Boss-Walker'. *Aviation Heritage,* Victoria. Vol. 51/4.

Wackett, Lawrence James, Sir, 1896-1982. (1972). *Aircraft pioneer : an autobiography.* Angus and Robertson, Sydney.

Wirraway. 'NA-33 modification discussions'. (1991-93). *Man and Aerial Machines.* Issue Nos. 21 to 38.

A20-644. Post war at RAAF Laverton. **Lorrie Molent/ARL**

A20-757 in Trainer Yellow flying the last production Wirraway pennant. **David Anderson. 4782 722062007P**

P143 Ab-lnitio TRAINER AIRCRAFT
July 1938

This proposal appears to have been the first trainer aircraft investigation by CAC. It was submitted in response to the June 1938, RAAF Specification 3/38 for an Ab-Initio Trainer aircraft.

This specification, as set out made a constant requirement comparison with the layout and performance details of the English Miles Magister trainer aircraft. The Air Board ordered a Magister on October 1, 1937 to allow the RAAF to become acquainted with a monoplane layout for elementary training.

This aircraft A15-1 was received at 1 Aircraft Depot, RAAF Laverton on January 18, 1938 for trials and evaluation. It was passed to CAC in July 1938 for its own evaluation following which it submitted minimalist Proposal 143. The Magister served a period with 1 Flying Training School at Point Cook till April 1940 before ending up an instructional airframe at the 1 Engineering School, Melbourne Showgrounds, Ascot Vale.

Bibliography: P143 Ab-Initio Trainer Aircraft
RAAF (1938) Spec 3/38 for Ab-Initio Trainer.

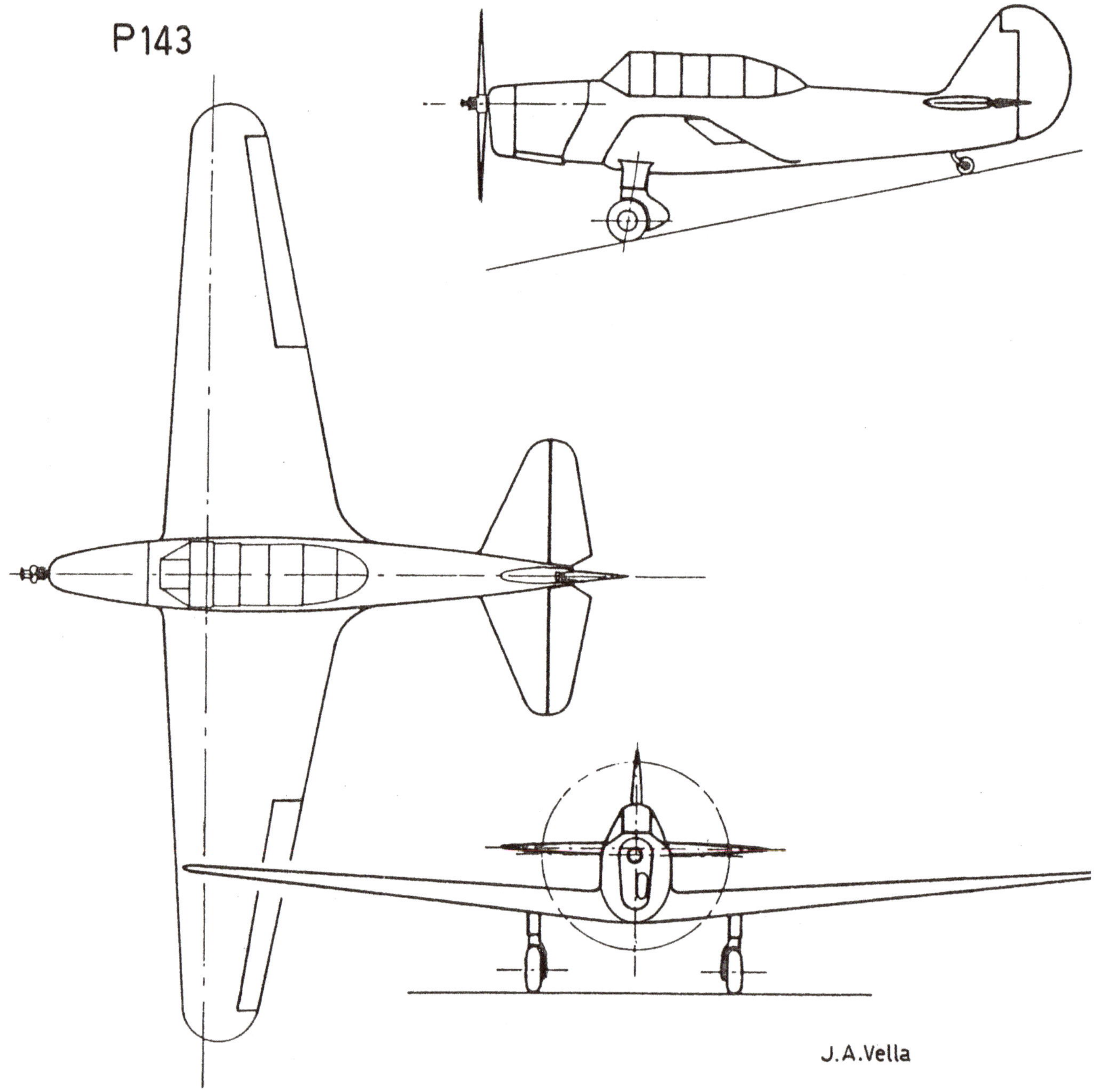

J.A.Vella

Specifications	P143 Ab-Initio Trainer Aircraft
Powerplant	One de Havilland Gipsy Major Series II in-line engine Two bladed de Havilland Series 1000 constant pitch propeller
Performance	Max speed not less than 112 kts (Specification requirement at normal load) Landing speed 43 kts (Specification requirement)
Weights	Max AUW 2,200 lb
Dimensions	Span 37 ft; Wing area 184 sq ft; Max chord 7 ft 6 in; Min chord 3 ft; Length 24 ft 4 in; Height 10 ft 3 in

CA-2 / CA-6 WACKETT TRAINER AIRCRAFT
October 1938

A formation of pilot-training all-yellow CA-6 Wackett Trainers. **Frank Smith.**

As early as July 30, 1936 in a letter to the Minister for Defence from the Syndicate establishing their intention to build the NA-16, mention was made of their desire to proceed with the production of a monoplane training aircraft simultaneous to the building of the NA-16.

The suggested asking price for the training monoplane was put at £1,500. When the company was informed on January 7, 1937 that it could proceed with the building of the Wirraway it was told that production of a training monoplane was to remain in abeyance. Design appears to have started in September 1937 and from a report in *'Aircraft'* magazine of May 1, 1939 there is evidence that a partial fuselage mock-up was in existence. CAC's early outline for the trainer is represented in Proposal 143 of July 7, 1938.

Ministerial approval for the construction of two trainer aircraft prototypes was given on October 10, 1938 with the Air Board issuing contract demand T.493 to the DoS on November 3, 1938 calling for the design of the two airframes generally in accordance with RAAF Specification 3/38. CAC's first estimate on costs was £5,000 for the first prototype but was to subsequently make a verbal agreement that it would construct two prototypes at an 'all-in' figure of £3,250 each, meaning everything connected with the design, material, equipment and completion of flight test would be done at CAC's expense with no support whatsoever from the RAAF. No completion date was offered or requested other than Wackett promising the completion of the first aircraft four months from the commencement date of construction; the second aircraft a month later. As an incentive to a short period of construction the Air Board withheld all payments until the aircraft were complete.

Ted Faggetter, Project Design Engineer (formerly of Westland Aircraft, UK); Ralph Price, Structures Engineer (also from Westland Aircraft) carried out the stressing on the Trainer in combination with L. J. Wackett and Thomas W. (Bill) Air. Gordon Fullerton, the company's first loftsman, graduated to be the CA-6 Project Engineer. Ern Jones replaced him as Project Design Draftsman.

Spinning tests of a model of the first designs were conducted at the RAE Farnborough, UK. The results suggested changes to the location of the tailplane. The aircraft was a low wing monoplane with a timber mainplane and empennage and a welded steel tube frame fuselage. Considerable experience had been accumulated on this form of construction at Tugan Aircraft in Sydney. It was a method which enabled construction to proceed with the minimum of delay with work on the metal tubing commencing in December 1938. However the promise of completion in four months from the start of work was optimistic.

Powered by a 140 hp (at 2,700 rpm) de Havilland Gipsy Major Series II in-line engine, it was overweight from the start. The first CA-2 (A3-1) took to the air for two circuits flown by Hubert Boss-Walker on September 11, 1939 (most likely, by inference from company factory progress reports, or according to other sources on September 19, 1939), five months later than originally promised. The take-off run was far longer than expected, the small engine had to be run at higher continuous revolutions with the conclusion, put forward by the RAAF, that the aircraft was about 50 hp short on what was thought to be the ideal for 'ab initio' training. On January 2, 1940 the Gipsy Major II was replaced by a 200 hp Gipsy Six engine and new propeller in a near identical cowling with additional venting.

Wackett Trainer CA-2, A3-1, with the Gipsy Major Series II in-line either at Point Cook or Laverton. **Frank Smith.**

The second prototype A3-2, also received a Gipsy Six. Both engines were from ex-Tugan Gannet A14-1. At an all-up weight of 2,402 lb including 100 lb of ballast in the rear cockpit, it had its first flight on November 11, 1939. However, the extra weight of this engine cancelled any improvement in the take-off run and raised the stalling speed higher than desired. The speed with the six cylinder engine was 140 knots (165 mph) and the climb rate of 1,000 feet per minute was a great improvement. Whilst the use of the Gipsy Six engine may have been acceptable it was no longer in production in the United Kingdom.

The gap between the desired and achieved performance pointed to a need for an engine of a size midway between 140 and 200 hp. Four fixed slots were built into the outboard wing leading edges of A3-2 in case more control was needed at the stall.

Alternative Engine

R. W. Cameron & Co. of New York, CAC's representatives in the United States were able to arrange the acquisition of the popular

CA-2 trainer fuselage mock-up. **David Anderson. 705091947N.PNG**

Ted Faggetter in his later years.- CA-2 Project Design Engineer. **The AGE**

Warner Super Scarab 7 cylinder radial engine. The output of this engine was about 35 hp less than the Gipsy VI figure. Twenty engines could be delivered each month within three months of an order being placed, stepping up three months later to 30 engines each month. On March 15, 1940 the Warner Aircraft Corp., Michigan invoiced CAC for two engines at US$2,706 each, including freight. Similarly, United Aircraft Corp, Connecticut arranged for the dispatch of two propellers for US$1,025 each to re-fit both CA-2 aircraft. The negotiations for the Super Scarab engine and accessories were carried out with Warner. As these engines were immediately available their use was accepted even though it was known the engine had a propensity to oil up on the lower cylinders.

The price set out on July 12, 1940 for the supply of 250 engines was:

Engines -	£176,800
Spares -	£38,340
Freight -	£17,840
	£232,980

The serial number grouping of the engines which were fitted to the airframes indicated they originated mostly as a large batch.

In order to establish a yardstick for the price to be charged for the expected production variant, Wackett sent a cable on January 24, 1940, to John Atwood, the President of North American Aviation requesting the price of 100 examples of their similar NA-35, all-metal tandem primary trainer fitted with the Ranger engine.

Atwood was reluctant to negotiate directly, preferring to work through the British Purchasing Commission. The intervention by the Minister for Air stopped any further inquiry as it would only have involved unnecessary work and unjustified expectations.

Trainer Employment Policy

As of March 20, 1940 both CA-2 Trainer prototypes were on RAAF strength and having completed their flight trials the RAAF was at a loss as to what to do with them. A3-1 was allotted to the Flying Instructors Course at Point Cook and A3-2 to the Communication Flight at Laverton. The Minister suggested that one be kept at Point Cook for flying practice by Senior Officers whose desk duties did not allow sufficient flying time or opportunity. On May 31, 1940 A3-1 was returned to CAC to be extensively modified to accept the shorter, lighter, Super Scarab radial engine and in this final form was test flown at Fisherman's Bend on June 28, 1940. A3-2 was likewise modified.

Meanwhile the Chief of Air Staff let it be known to the Minister for Air, on 12 April 1940 (he lost his life in an air crash on August 13, 1940) that he did not want the Trainer as it cost more than a DH82 Tiger Moth, of which the RAAF had adequate supplies. It also meant the introduction of another different aircraft type into the Air Force inventory.

In this the Minister concurred that: *"the greater installed power and double the price of the Tiger Moth, whilst in no way shortening the present EATS syllabus, one could not justify its substitution for the DH82. Were the RAAF to develop its own training syllabus there might have been room for the inclusion of an intermediate stage by the shortening of the course on the DH82".*

Director of Training (Wing Commander F. Scherger) had expressed his opinion that the trainer would, in spite of its initial cost, offer an improved standard of flying service; give a better appreciation of a heavy wing-loaded monoplane and a new graduate would only require half an hour dual on a Wirraway prior to first solo, whereas a DH82 trained pupil needed six to seven hours.

Wackett was also putting his argument to AVM Richard Williams. In a letter of May 23, 1940 he was extolling the virtues of the CA-2 concept and suggesting that since the aircraft was to cost so much less than a Wirraway it should be used as a step between the DH82 and the Wirraway (the cockpit control and instrumentation layout was meant to imitate that of the Wirraway) and leaving the latter to make up for the shortfall in deliveries from the UK of the Fairey Battle and the Avro Anson.

Production Approved

The decision to go to production was contained in the June 6, 1940 statement of the Minister for Air, that given the Government commitment to the Empire Air Training Scheme and the existing conditions in Britain, an examination of the training syllabus showed that as a temporary measure, approximately 3% of the operational exercises prescribed for the Advanced Training syllabus in the SFTS could be carried out in the Trainer.

The entry into service of the new trainer would release an equivalent number of Wirraway aircraft in lieu of Ansons and because of the composite nature of the construction of the airframe and the availability of materials from local sources, production was recommended without delay.

The previous day, under the terms of War Cabinet Agenda 118/1940 of June 5, 1940 approval was given to the ordering of 200

Wackett Trainer Order	
200 fully equipped Wackett Trainers at £3,000 each	600000
50 spare Scarab engines at £700 each	35000
Engine spares, instruments & tools	90000
Airframe spares & handling equipment	90000
Total	**815000**

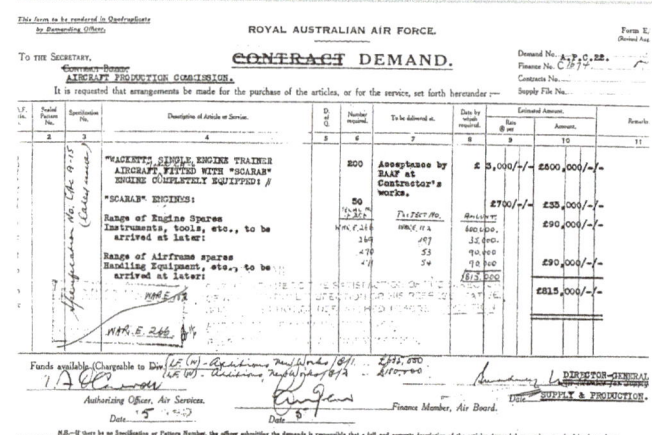

RAAF Demand paperwork No APC 22 for Aircraft Production Commission to provide 200 Trainers & 50 engines for £815,000

Fitting out Wackett Trainer production fuselages. **HDHV**

Trainer aircraft followed by a request placed on the APC on June 17, 1940. The production variant of the aircraft was identified as the CA-6 Wackett Trainer and both prototype CA-2 aircraft were re-numbered A3-1001 and 1002 in mid-1940 so as not to confuse them with the production aircraft numbering; the first application of the prototype series designation adopted by the RAAF. The name *Wackett Trainer* was given by the RAAF in recognition of the fact the design was largely the concept of Lawrence Wackett, the only significant member of staff who had prior practical experience of designing aircraft which had flown and gone into production.

The contractual letter to CAC on 11 July authorised the manufacture of the CA-6 to Specification A-15 (later revised to A-20) with deliveries required to commence on March 1, 1941 subject to the availability of engines and propellers. CAC proposed a cost plus 6% for aircraft 1 to 5 inclusive, of £6,000 each; a figure which the APC felt was too high and needed re-negotiation. The next batch, aircraft 6 to 50 and subsequent batches, each of 50 aircraft, were to be at fixed downward varying prices. The Aircraft Production Commission had expressed some concern in January when the development charges incurred with the preparation of the design of the two Wackett Trainer aircraft had advanced to £14,540, more than twice the original estimate.

These design and development expenses were, subject to the approval of the War Cabinet, to be included in the total cost of the order. A3-1001 resumed flight trials on July 26, 1940.

CA-6 final assembly with the adjacent Wirraway line on the right. **L.J.Wackett /MS4858 /NLA**

Once Laurence Hartnett became aware of the overseas engine order he offered the services of GM-H to the chairman of the APC for the possible building of the engine at his factories, suggesting first delivery four months after the receipt of drawings and material specifications. GM-H was by then well into the delivery of 500 Gipsy engines. The offer was turned down as the Scarab was not considered ideal for local manufacture and the possible role the CA-6 was to play in the EATS was limited.

Completed Trainer wing assemblies from GM-H awaiting assembly. **Ian Ring**

Only a matter of days after the go-ahead the APC suggested that the entire production be let out to sub-contract in order not to cause further slippage in Wirraway deliveries and it further proposed that the selection of sub-contractors be left to the Commission.

Wackett responded that if CAC was to deliver the aircraft as promised, the choice of subcontractor ought to be left to the company to decide, a process it had already initiated by making GM-H the major sub-contractor as builder of all the CA-6 wooden components, ie, the wings and horizontal and vertical tail surfaces. Spruce timber for the front and rear spars was imported from Canada. The CAC production line was to be functioning as soon as the planned building extensions were completed.

With CAC's magnesium foundry coming into production the opportunity was taken to modify the design of the trainer for mass production by replacing those components which on the prototype had been made of aluminium by ones cast in magnesium alloy, eg the undercarriage leg fork to help lower the aircraft empty weight.

Staff Decisions

A prolonged series of exchanges between CAC and de Havilland in Sydney and the APC as to who would assume responsibility for the production of the propellers was resolved in September. de Havilland was to carry out the machining of the blades and final assembly of five propellers a week at a cost of about £400 each, CAC to manufacture minor components and the Australian Drop Forging Co and BHP Whyalla to produce the hubs; other components to be imported. As this propeller problem dragged on, 12 pre-used 2B20s were imported to satisfy the original aircraft delivery schedule. Wackett's contingency plan was to propose ordering hubs for wooden propellers, but the Air Force vetoed the idea insisting on the variable pitch metal blades. The Forest Products Division of CSIR, using Australian timbers, had tested a wooden 2B20 propeller for the Trainer. Initial aircraft deliveries were still delayed until local propeller production caught up but even then the Air Force was still unresolved as to where it would allocate the 200 aircraft. de Havilland was to eventually deliver 220 metal propeller sets.

A3-2, second CA-6 production Trainer with the Warner Scarab radial engine. **Aust War Memorial via Frank Smith.**

Discussions resumed again on June 13, 1941 with the idea that the requirement was really for only 75 aircraft which could be a one for one substitution for DH82 Tiger Moth and Avro Cadets in the EFTS by the introduction of 5 hours of advanced flying towards the end of the course. Allowing another 39 aircraft for wastage over three years would leave the balance of the production as surplus, and then again it was suggested the type be deployed as 3 aircraft per half school.

The Air member for Organisation and Equipment requested a directive from the Australian CAS, Air Chief Marshal Sir Charles Burnett (RAF on loan) as to which way to go. He did not see the need for the aircraft being employed in EFTS units where, in the majority, they were up to strength in both aircraft and personnel numbers. However the SFTS units for whom the aircraft was originally proposed were in the opposite situation and could accommodate the new type.

Finally, on June 26,1941 the CAS settled the matter by declaring that the flying characteristics of the CA-6 were so dissimilar to that of the Wirraway that it could not be regarded as of great value as a substitute SFTS type. Its use would only be contemplated if flying time at the SFTS's had to be curtailed due to a shortage of available Wirraways. It would not substitute for the locally built DH82 of which there were ample numbers and cost about £1,000 less than the new aircraft. The CA-6 was to be used as a single engine aircraft at the Wireless Air Gunners Schools in lieu of the DH82 Tiger Moths previously earmarked for the role. It was to re-equip 3 EFTS at Essendon Aerodrome, 7 miles to the north of the factory as the initial service trials unit. The possibility of outfitting a second unit, the last of the unformed EFTS units with the CA-6 was still not entirely eliminated.

Foreign Sales Prospects

A less than serious attempt at selling the aircraft was initiated by John Storey of the Aircraft Production Commission (APC) when he informed Wackett that on 5 July he had discussed with the Secretary of State for India (in London) the possibility of acquiring Australian built aircraft, eg the Wackett Trainer. The APC forwarded a detailed specification copy to London offering either direct export or local production under licence.

On 5 November the Indian Government Department of Supply replied:

Subject: Monoplane Trainer Aircraft

> Sir,
> I am directed to acknowledge the receipt of your letter bearing no number or date, on the subject mentioned above.
>
> I am, Sir,
> Your obedient servant, (signed)
>
> Assistant Secretary to the Government of India.

In a similar vein, on September 11, 1941, John Storey passed CA-6 trainer data and offered production output to the Union of South Africa through its War Supplies liaison office in Melbourne.

The second prototype A3-1002 was retired in October 1941 as Instructional Airframe No 2 at the No 1 Engineering School, Melbourne Showgrounds, Ascot Vale, joining the evaluation Miles Magister.

Into Service

The first production trainer was flown on February 6, 1941. No 1 Aircraft Depot, Laverton, Victoria became the accepting facility for all CA-6. A3-2 and A3-3 were the first examples to reach 3 EFTS. The 50 hour syllabus of elementary flying was split into 25 hours of dual and 25 hours of solo flying. The CA-6 was the only aircraft type at the school, the previous DH60 / DH82 compliment having been dispersed to other locations. The built-in engine starter and wheel brakes were two features of the aircraft which helped cut down the manpower needed to ground handle the aircraft as compared to the previous biplanes and especially so in confined spaces.

Flying was at a very intense pace with the aircraft having to be available for morning and afternoon flying schedules. The daily maintenance and minor engineering rectifications were the responsibility of RAGNAH Pty Ltd (hangar spelt backwards), a subsidiary company of the Royal Victorian Aero Club formed for the purpose of maintaining the aircraft of 3 EFTS that had itself been formed from a nucleus of the RVAC (or the Australian National Airways Victorian Flying School).

The aircraft experienced its share of teething troubles with sudden forward collapses of either fixed undercarriage leg and splitting of the underwing ply covering which developed during aerobatics. This was rectified by changing the direction of the grain of some of the ply panels (7 October) from aircraft A3-114 onwards and on the upper surface of the wing starting from aircraft A3-140.

The Australian coachwood ply used for the outer skin covering being non-elastic in nature, turned the wing into a highly stressed assembly when it was applied to the wooden framework. There were reports of alarming sounds of loud cracks on some aircraft during flight as the stressed outer covering on

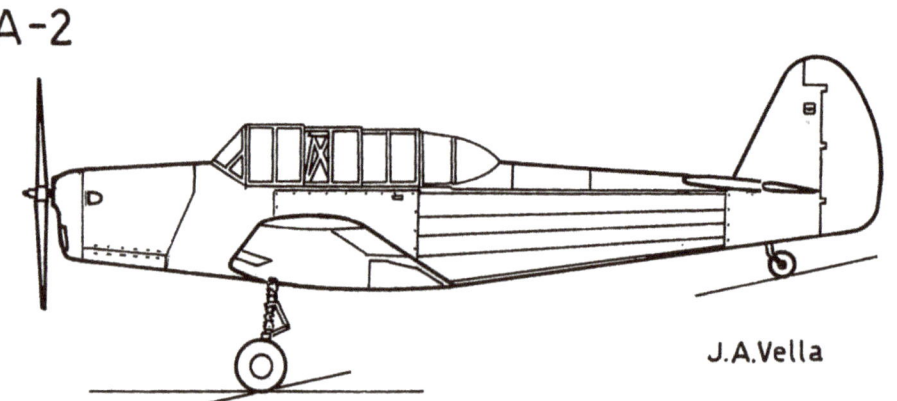

Wackett Trainer Deliveries 1941-1942		
Month	1941	1942
January		22
February		35
March	1	29
April		18
May	3	
June	9	
July	7	
August	13	
September	23	
October	14	
November	10	
December	16	
Cumulative Total	**96**	**200**

the wing's lower surface gave way. Prior to changing the direction of the ply panelling, Fred David and Ern Jones remedied the in-service aircraft at Essendon by introducing saw cuts in the lower surface ply covering along the chord of the wing between the main undercarriage legs.

Reinforcements were introduced between the wing spars and the fuselage attachment castings and alterations made to the main fuselage tube frames which were buckling under compression loads caused by heavy landings. (Failures documented February 21, 1942). There were instances of the hinge cut-out breaking away from the aileron spar causing local cracking in the ply covering (January 9, 1942). The fuel tank vents and overflow pipes projecting near the rear spar became blocked by the mud thrown up from the wheels of the aircraft. A winter of heavy rainfall had turned the surface of Essendon Aerodrome into mud so as the fuel was drawn out, the blocked vents caused the fuel tanks to collapse due to the resulting vacuum.

During the lay-up for overnight maintenance work, the vents were re-positioned to near the front spar (February 2,1942) and this overcame the problem. As at January 26,1942, 3 EFTS was operating thirty Trainers: A3-3, 9, 12, 15, 16, 21, 24, 25, 26, 28, 29, 31, 32, 35, 37-46, 50, 73, 75-78. One hundred and nine aircraft had been accepted to that date.

The official establishment of Wackett Trainers planned as at February 25, 1942 is shown in the table below.

Once the production hurdles had been overcome the delivery rate kept on increasing, reaching a peak of 35 aircraft in February 1942 and final completion in April 1942.

Unit	Initial Establishment	Initial Reserve
3 EFTS	18	9
11 EFTS	36	18
CFS	12	6
1 WAGS	22	10
2 WAGS	22	10
3 WAGS	22	10
Totals	**132**	**63**
Combined Total		195
On order		200
Available for Wastage		5

The service allocation varied from the planned theoretical distribution. 3 EFTS was officially disbanded on May 1, 1942. Some of its aircraft had already been transferred to Benalla in N.E. Victoria to form 11 EFTS. Aircraft had started arriving there in January 1942 and by June eighty-five Trainers had been received at the station.

However the number in service was lower than this through attrition and the subsequent diversion to No 1 and 3 WAGS of 20 of this number. From instructor pilots, trainee pilots' log books and RAAF records, 92 aircraft were with 11 EFTS between March and November 1942. These included A3-3, 4, 6, 9, 10, 12, 13, 15, 16, 19, 21, 24-26, 28, 29, 31, 32, 35-48, 50, 73-80, 81-99, 113-130, 143-153, 183, 190, & 198. Twenty of these were subsequently converted for radio training.

As of June 19, 1942 the seventy-nine aircraft which were to be converted by 1 Aircraft Depot to receive the T1083/R1082 transmitter and receiver wireless equipment installations were:

A3-61 to 72	12 aircraft
A3-101 to 112	12 aircraft
A3-131 to 142	12 aircraft
A3-154 to 165	12 aircraft
A3-167 to 177	11 aircraft
A3-181 to 200	20 aircraft
Total	**79 aircraft**

The RAAF modification kits assembled by 1 AD entailed some 61 man-hours of alteration work to the rear cockpit with the removal of the majority of flying instruments, throttle, flap lever and rudder pedals. The HF aerial mast fitted ahead of the cockpit was the same as that used on the Wirraway.

In addition to the 20 aircraft withdrawn from 11 EFTS and modified by CAC for wireless training, another 30 were converted bringing the total stated number for radio work to 129 aircraft. However, according to the A3 Series aircraft status cards only 118 aircraft were modified.

More Rectifications

More airframe rectification work was found necessary during 1942 including the introduction of a reinforced front fin attachment plate, a tailwheel centering device, strengthening of the carburettor air scoop mounting support and changes in the wing due to occasions of No 1 rib breaking or pulling away from the rear spar with the result that the outboard ribs also pulled away causing a gap of about one inch to appear between the trailing edge of the wing and the fuselage side fairing panel.

The one inconvenience that could never be eradicated was the need to work with US and UK tool standards on the aircraft, the airframe having naturally been designed to British Standards whilst the engines were imported American. Some of the Warner Super Scarabs developed internal cracking at the rear of the engine which was rectified by fitting a metal plate to which were welded a number of bosses. Those engines modified in this manner ended up being a fractional, 0.125 inches, greater in depth.

There was added alarm at the rate of cylinder wear on the engines. Whether the cumulative rectification changes could be partly to blame it is not clear, but the Department of Air was most concerned that the DAP expenditure on the CA-6 had, by April 16,1942 risen to £894,104, some £69,000 over budget.

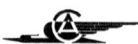

CA-6 Wackett Trainer

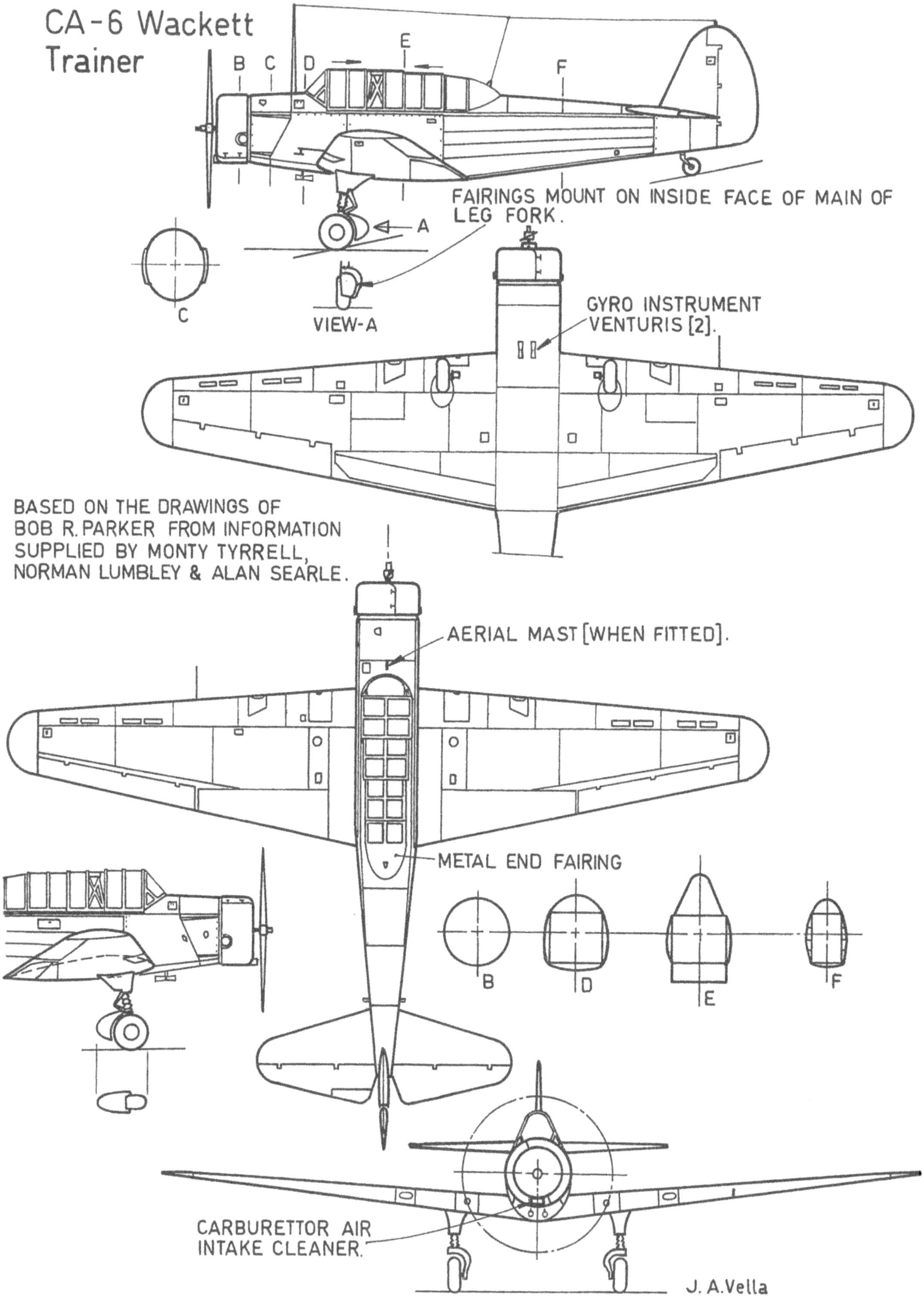
B
C
D
E
F
A
FAIRINGS MOUNT ON INSIDE FACE OF MAIN OF LEG FORK.
C
VIEW-A
GYRO INSTRUMENT VENTURIS [2].
BASED ON THE DRAWINGS OF BOB R. PARKER FROM INFORMATION SUPPLIED BY MONTY TYRRELL, NORMAN LUMBLEY & ALAN SEARLE.
AERIAL MAST [WHEN FITTED].
METAL END FAIRING
B
D
E
F
CARBURETTOR AIR INTAKE CLEANER.
J. A. Vella

Partly finished Wackett trainers looking to leave the factory.

HDHV

Work underway on one of the two CA-2 prototype airframes. Gypsy Major Series II engine cowling has been fitted. **L.J. Wackett/MS4858/NLA**

Above: Front cockpit panel. **Mark Pilkington**

Below: Rear cockpit panel. **Mark Pilkington**

Hubert Boss Walker in the first CA-6 production Trainer. Finished in Trainer Yellow, fitted with Warner Scarab radial engine sometime after May 31, 1940. **L.J.Wackett/MS4858/NLA**

The major sub-contracting work was carried out by GM-H. Agreement had been settled by June 14, 1940 by Lawrence J. Harnett GM-H's managing director whereby CAC was to supply all tools, jigs, fixtures, castings to be machined and eventually all the materials with the exception of paint and glue so as they could build the wooden components of the Wackett Trainer. GM-H had also offered to build the welded steel tube framework but after an initial enthusiastic response from Wackett this did not materialise. The GM-H factory complex at Fisherman's Bend built 249 wing and tail assemblies; at their Woodville plant in South Australia they fabricated 340 sets of oil and fuel tanks. The Trainer wings were constructed as a one-piece unit delivered for mating with the steel tube fuselage frames.

On November 4, 1942, GM-H billed CAC the sum of £63,565/13/8 for the labour component and although the shareholders of CAC received no dividend, it appears GM-H was allowed a profit margin of £1,503.

With the end of production on April 12, 1942, Department of Air final expenditure figures stood at:

	Total cost	Unit cost
Production cost	£619,613	£3,098
Profit margin	£26,540	£133
Total	£646,153	£3,231

Wackett Trainer spares were still in production as at the end of October 1942.

Service Use

The units which made prominent use of the CA-6 were 1 WAGS at Ballarat, Victoria; 2 WAGS at Parkes, NSW and 3 WAGS at Maryborough, Qld. The aircraft used for radio training were distinguishable by the tall radio mast located ahead of the front cockpit. 3 EFTS was initially at Essendon Aerodrome before being replaced by 11 EFTS at Benalla and those with the Central Flying School operated from either Point Cook, Victoria or Tamworth, NSW.

There were short term attachments to eight Elementary Flying Training Schools; two Operational Training Units; five Service Flying Training Schools and many short term placements at other smaller units but most of these appear to have been in the nature of temporary storage whilst awaiting an allotment to a private contractor for major overhaul or repair. These contractors spread around the eastern seaboard, were Ansett Airways; Butler Air Transport (Mascot); Victoria and Interstate Airways; Aircrafts Pty Ltd, Archerfield (Qld); National Aircraft Corporation; Clyde Engineering and the Newcastle Aero Club at Broadmeadow, NSW.

*A3-191 piloted by F/Sgt J.Birch with the radio trainee in the rear cockpit on a cross-country flight from No 1 WAGS, Ballarat, Victoria over rain flooded countryside, 1943. **Frank Smith***

*Wireless Trainer A3-139 with distinctive yellow undersurfaces and the tall radio mast ahead of the front cockpit. **Frank Smith***

At times these organisations were so stretched they were not able to cope with their very large service workload. In the case of the CA-6, those aircraft which had not received a complete overhaul fetched an eventual disposal price as low as £7/10/0. The majority of aircraft were retired to temporary storage at 8 OTU at Narromine and 8 EFTS at Narrandera, NSW.

Wireless Trainer

Australia's commitments under the Empire Air Training Scheme Agreement also brought pressure on the RAAF radio organisation for the establishment and manning of the wireless air gunners schools. In accordance with an agreement reached at a conference at Ottawa, Canada in November 1939, Australia undertook to recruit and train 7,056 wireless air gunners by March 1943, This undertaking meant establishing wireless air gunner schools and accepting 320 new recruits every four weeks.

The purpose of the schools was to administer courses in accordance with the RAF Standard Syllabus to such a level of proficiency in the manipulation and operation of the wireless telegraphy and associated installations, that the trainees would be able to maintain communications and make use of radio aids to navigate their aircraft.

The first wireless air gunner's school 1 WAGS, opened at Ballarat, on April 22, 1940. At the end of April 1941 its personnel strength numbered 1,352 . The school also had three Douglas DC-2 fitted out as radio classrooms. CA-6 examples there were A3-64, 71 and 191.

The majority of the DC-2 aircraft arrived via Australian National Airways off the Melbourne docks to 1 Aircraft Depot, Laverton for the installation of engines and wireless training equipment. Eight DC-2s served with the Signal Schools and the three WAGS on short term training attachments before being moved to their eventual transport roles. 2 WAGS at Parkes started training on February 6, 1941. On September 20, 1940 the school had four DH84 Dragon and twenty-five Wackett Trainers. 3 WAGS was formed at Maryborough on September 18, 1941.

When the program was fully established the 24 weeks of instruction at the air wireless schools was preceded by an eight week course at an initial training school, followed at the end by a four week course at a bombing and gunnery school. At the completion of this training, the wireless air gunner was posted to an operational training unit or was embarked for overseas posting.

Besides schooling in radio theory the ground training segment of this course included an intermediate phase for most students to be sent out to the country side in covered motor panel vans equipped with an AT5/AR8 radio installation and a suitable aerial to communicate from a moving vehicle to a base station. This practice went on for one course per month for 19 months in the instance of 1 WAGS. Toward the end of the stay at a WAGS establishment about 25 hours was set aside, spread over a four week period, for radio practice from an airborne Wackett Trainer.

The trainee sat in the rear cockpit, had his equipment checked out by the instructor prior to take-off and proceeded to follow a set of course exercises on the Morse key using the R1082/T1083 equipment, having, once achieved sufficient height reeled out the LF trailing wire antenna. If this was not done correctly or it was snagged, effective communication was difficult. It was however a more common occurrence for the radio set to ground-test perfectly well and then fail when airborne and again function properly when back on the ground. Of course the doubting instructors tended to put this down to the incompetence of the trainees.

Flying activity, carried out only during daylight hours, was continuous and intensive, hampered only by bad weather or serviceability, with the aim of allowing a trainee to gain the minimum proficiency of 20 words per minute. There was little interaction with the pilots in the front cockpit who merely acted the role of a taxi-driver. They were instructed to fly straight and level to allow the trainee to perform the radio exercises to best advantage.

The sending of morse-key messages could be affected by uneven flying to say nothing of other effects such as airsickness. During flight, the pilots communicated with the trainees by passing bits of paper indicating the current position. This the trainee coded and transmitted to base; for example, 'notpiks' would be sent when passing over the township of Skipton, south west of Ballarat. The instructor or radio operator back at the airfield would be in touch with two or three trainees simultaneously operating on the same frequency.

Air experience time was accumulated at random, flights ranging up to two hours duration, subject to aircraft availability and equipment reliability. Pilots and radio trainees were never a fixed crewing combination but subject to needs and availability. There were bored staff pilots for whom the entire wartime flying experience was to fly wireless trainees struggling with airsickness and the Morse code in the back of Wackett Trainers. For others, the sheer routine of the work would only be broken by an occasional stint of aerobatics well away from the airfield. A favourite variation was to fly low over Lake Learmonth (near Ballarat) and intentionally or otherwise to return back to base with a wet undercarriage.

The dummy undercarriage 'not down' warning signals originally built into the aircraft were deleted from the cockpit layout for the radio training aircraft pilot.

The radio equipment operated on four frequency ranges, A, B, C and D. Range was changed in the R1082 receiver by plugging in the appropriate coils. In the T1083 transmitter the plug-in element was not just a coil but a whole oscillator circuit, a bulky affair 5 inches square and 8 inches deep.

In July 1943, training was introduced at Ballarat for the new category of NAV-W(navigator-wireless). The main requirement for this category was for Vultee Vengeance and the Beaufighter crews. These aircraft carried a pilot and a member qualified both as a navigator and wireless operator. The NAV-W had the highest selection standards of all aircrew trainee streams and the top five or so graduates from each course on the Wackett Trainer went to this mustering. The Avro Anson was used for this task and the training was later moved to Mt Gambier, South Australia to become 1 Navigator Wireless School.

2 WAGS at Parkes, NSW, was disbanded at the end of 1943 and its Trainers dispersed to Ballarat and Maryborough, where at the latter, servicing of the airframes was provided by Aircrafts Pty Ltd, who were also maintaining the wooden framed Avro Ansons.

Ballarat's CA-6 complement had grown to 43 aircraft by January of 1944. Only 21 of these were serviceable. There were 16 at Maryborough and only one half of these could get into the air. This situation was an improvement over that which had existed in September 1943 when 91 CA-6s were grounded at three stations - 18 at Parkes, 62 at 7 Aircraft Depot, Tocumwal and 11 at Ballarat.

This had been brought about solely through a lack of serviceable engines caused by cracks in the pistons at the gudgeon pin boss. Locally made replacement pistons were coming forward in small quantities. These were a considerable improvement over the old style but were still showing evidence of cracks at the 120 hour inspection. Ansett Airways, Qantas and 7 AD were heavily committed re-building the Scarab engines whilst airworthy airframes languished, stored, waiting for re-conditioned engines. Every engine was re-built when it was discovered the main crankcase bearing was not receiving lubrication.

In contrast the wooden structure stood up to the task much better than anticipated. At the same time (September 1943) most airframes had clocked up 1,000 hours. When the 1,200 hour figure had been reached, the usual time for a complete overhaul, the work was generally deferred because of the excellent condition of the internal structure. Examples at Ballarat clocked up 1,680 hours before being grounded for a total overhaul.

By the end of March 1943, the original date for the termination of the EATS, 5,376 wireless air gunners had been trained and the wastage from all causes had been 11.3%. Although the EATS had been extended for a further two years; within one year, the need for aircrews to be sent to the European war theatre had been reduced. By August 1944, further new drafts for aircrews were cancelled under the EATS.

Pilot Trainer

11 EFTS at Benalla, Victoria was officially established on June 26, 1941. About one half of the complement of 3 EFTS, the initial trials unit, (refer to previous text) was transferred to 11 EFTS in 1942 and the former unit was disbanded.

Three patterns of pilot training evolved:

- The first was to introduce new recruits to the DH82 Tiger Moth and to graduate on the Tiger Moth. This was carried out done at about 12 Training Schools around Australia.

- The second was to introduce new recruits to the Tiger Moth and then to transition to the Wackett Trainer co-located at Benalla.

- The others went into their first flying experience straight onto Wackett Trainers and graduated on them.

Eventually the mixed DH82/CA-6 courses were abandoned in favour of specialization on either type.

Satellite airfields to Benalla were at Winton and Goorambat but the heavy wet weather of the early part of 1942 made flying very difficult from all three airfields. With compounding delays making a marked effect on the training schedule, some flying activity (in

A3-90 from No 11 EFTS in overall foilage green finish at Tocumwal awaiting its eventual post war fate. **Frank Smith**

DH82's) was shifted north to Deniliquin in NSW and its satellite field, Wandook. Wackett Trainers were then temporarily transferred back to Essendon in September to take advantage of better conditions there and returned to Benalla late in the following month. 11 EFTS had an association with the CA-6 which lasted about 15 months. The Wackett fleet was officially retired by April 1943.

The Air Board had decided with certainty by December 20, 1944 that no CA-6 would be retained for Elementary Training at the end of the war although the possibility of retaining 10 examples at the CFS was suggested in order to maintain four aircraft in flying condition. The availability of spares may have determined the future fate of the aircraft. An RAAF request for a large order of spares placed in November 4, 1943 was rejected by CAC on the basis that both the company and its subcontractors had put aside all production jigs and facilities and six months would be required to re-tool. A further proposition was to retain quantities of the aircraft for Citizen Air Force training provided a more satisfactory engine could be substituted.

The final action was the disposal document of October 1, 1945 through which the Commonwealth Disposals Commission offered to divest itself of 97 Trainers with engines from disposition centres at CMU Narrandera and 7 AD Tocumwal fetching prices ranging from £120 to £250. The 20 airframes without engines located at 2 CRD, Richmond; 3 CRD Amberley and 1 WAGS Ballarat ranged in price from £7/10/0 to £75. This accounted for 117 machines out of 202 CA-2 / CA-6 constructed. From 1 WAGS; CMU Tamworth and 2 CRD the Commission was disposing of 97 engines with a price variation ranging from £2/ 10/ 0 to £50. All items were sold ex-site in 'an as is, where is' condition advising prospective buyers to look first before they purchased. A3-1001 & 1002 were also disposed at Ballarat. The disposal action put an end to any post-war use of the CA-6 by the CFS or CAF.

A3-200. Last production Wackett Trainer over Port Phillip Bay flown by James Carter. April 22,1942.
John Harrison via Neil Follett Collection

B-307, the previous RAAF A3-30. Note the fairings/spats on the rear of the mainwheels, quickly discarded in Australian service because of muddy landing grounds. **Frank Smith.**

A line up of uncowled CA-6 in use by the Militaire Luchtvaart(ML) Air Force of the NEIA. **Frank Smith.**

Ninety-six airframes and the entire spares inventory were acquired by J. T. Brown (Kew, Victoria) of Kingsford Smith Aviation Services of Mascot and Bankstown airports, NSW. He requested DCA allocate a block of aircraft registrations for his new inventory. The majority were later revoked following their export. With other buyers in the mix, 43 CA-6 eventually came on the Australian civil aircraft register with 48 call sign allocations. (Table 1).

Evidence points to J. T. Brown also having had plans to export six Wackett Trainers to India but without success, as on December 17, 1945 he requested DCA allocate them Australian civil registrations instead. By the early 1960s the Department of Civil Aviation requirements of airworthiness for wooden sparred/plywood/glued type of aircraft construction had made it difficult to keep the CA-6 on the civil aircraft register.

Four examples of the KS-1,KS-2 & KS-3 Cropmaster, an aerial agriculture derivative of the CA-6 were produced from 1957 by the Kingsford Smith Aviation Service, NSW with a hopper installed in the previous rear cockpit position with a cutout of the centre section of the wing and still retaining the Scarab engine. All were retired by May 1961. Yeoman Aviation, an associate company to KSAS was formed in 1958 to also specialize in aerial agriculture aircraft. It produced the YA-1 Cropmaster using the basic steel tube fuselage frame, undercarriage and the original tailplane fin and rudder of the CA-6 with new metal wings, metal and fibreglass body panels and modern six cylinder engines. Further development introduced a new metal swept fin and rudder retaining the fuselage tube steel frame and undercarriage. Twenty examples were built with six exported to New Zealand.

In Foreign Service

CA-6 Wackett Trainers next saw service with the Netherlands East Indies Army Air Force, Militaire Luchtvaart (ML-KNIL).

Table 1
POST WAR CIVILIAN WACKETT TRAINERS

	Constructor Number	RAAF Identification	Civil Registration		Constructor Number	RAAF Identification	Civil Registration
1	243	A3-9	VH-AFG	22	348	A3-114	VH-AFF
2	244	A3-10	VH-AKG	23	353	A3-119	VH-AFB
3	247	A3-13	VH-AIS	24	362	A3–128	VH-AFC
4	238	A3-14	VH-EAY	25	263	A3-129	VH-AMA
			VH-AIO				VH-DGR
5	254	A3-20	VH-AQB	26	264	A3-130	VH-AIM
6	256	A3-22	VH-ALV	27	366	A3-132	VH-BQL
7	257	A3-23	VH-AIV	28	372	A3-138	VH-AGE
8	265	A3-31	VH-AIY	29	373	A3-139	VH-BEC
9	269	A3-35	VH-AFL	30	374	A3-140	VH-AKK
10	274	A3-40	VH-AJB	31	379	A3-145	VH-AFD
11	276	A3-42	VH-AIG	32	380	A3-146	VH-BCP
12	283	A3-49	VH-AJH	33	381	A3-147	VH-BAW
13	304	A3-70	VH-APD	34	382	A3-148	VH-AHU
14	309	A3-75	VH-AOO	35	385	A3-151	VH-AKT
15	310	A3-76	VH-AJU				VH-WFM
16	317	A3-83	VH-EAZ	36	393	A3-159	VH-AFI
			VH-AIQ	37	401	A3-167	VH-AGP
17	319	A3-85	VH-BLV	38	402	A3-168	VH-ALD
18	321	A3-87	VH-BLV	39	406	A3-172	VH-AKF
			VH-BLV	40	408	A3-174	VH-APC
19	341	A3-107	VH-BLV	41	432	A3-198	VH-AHX
			VH-BLV	42	433	A3-199	VH-ARH
20	342	A3-108	VH-BLV	43	101	A3-1001	VH–AHV
21	247	A3-113	VH-BLV				

The full details of this occurrence are not clear because of the political history of the time and the loss and destruction of Dutch documentation. Whilst the Indonesian population was seeking post war independence, the Dutch colonial power was reluctant to give in to this demand. The labour on Australia's wharves was known to be sympathetic to the Indonesian cause and in strong opposition of the Dutch stand. Disruptive action on Australian wharves to Dutch shipping or ships operating on behalf of the Dutch Government made things difficult for the departure of Dutch Air Force units resident in Australia and their supporting infrastructure. It is not clear by what channels, 56 CA-6 aircraft managed to leave Australia having been acquired by the ML-KNIL from J. T. Brown.

These aircraft left Sydney in April 1947 with the NEI Army acting as shipping agents arriving at the port of Tanjung Priok, north Djakarta on the passenger/cargo vessel M.V. Tjibesar to be re-assembled at Tjililtan (Djakarta, West Java ML) aerodrome. Thirty aircraft were put into service, of which 15 were stationed at Kalidjate and five at Andir, both airfields also in West Java. Ten were held in reserve. The fate of the others is not known.

Table 2
RAAF Identities & ML-KNIL Markings Or Roles

A3-3	B-301	A3-45	B-311	A3-100	B-322	A3-149	B-328
A3-5	W/T SP	A3-47	B-312	A3-111	W/T SP	A3-152	B-329
A3-7	B-302	A3-51	W/T SP	A3-112	W/T SP	A3-154	W/T SP
A3-8	W/T SP	A3-53	W/T SP	A3-116	B-323	A3-157	W/T SP
A3-11	B-303	A3-54	B-313	A3-117	W/T SP	A3-162	W/T SP
A3-18	B-304	A3-55	B-314	A3-118	W/T SP	A3-163	B-330
A3-19	B-305	A3-60	B-315	A3-121	W/T SP	A3-165	W/T SP
A3-27	B-306	A3-68	W/T SP	A3-122	W/T SP	A3-169	W/T SP
A3-30	B-307	A3-73	B-316	A3-123	B-324	A3-173	W/T SP
A3-34	B-308	A3-86	B-317	A3-124	B-325	A3-178	W/T SP
A3-37	B-309	A3-89	B-318	A3-125	B-326	A3-180	W/T SP
A3-41	B-310	A3-93	B-319	A3-127	B-327	A3-182	W/T SP
A3-43	W/T SP	A3-97	B-320	A3-135	W/T SP	A3-184	W/T SP
A3-44	W/T SP	A3-99	B-321	A3-136	W/T SP	A3-196	W/T SP

It was planned to use the aircraft as an intermediate step between the Piper Cub and the N.A. Harvard but were operated more as a 'club' type aircraft to keep fighter pilots proficient when operational flying was not possible at the ML-KNIL Central Flying School (see Table 2).

Due to the local hot conditions the Trainers were flown with the engine ring cowl removed. Initially their engines and to a lesser extent the airframe were a nightmare and a source of despair for the maintenance crews. Whilst the aircraft was considered pleasant to fly, it was underpowered for the climate of the region and its poor maintenance reputation hard to eradicate. (All the airframes had come from CDC disposals and each varied as to the degree of airworthiness quality).

The aircraft carried markings B3-0l, B3-02 etc, but these were subsequently changed to B-301, B302 etc. Twenty-seven CA-6 are known to have become part of the Indonesian Air Force with the establishment of that service on July 1, 1950. The later Indonesian designed and built Nurtanio NU-200 Sikurmbang had some construction features similar to those of CA-6.

Aircraft Description

The construction of the airframe was conventional for the period of the late thirties, being a composite mix of wood, steel, fabric, aluminium and magnesium alloy. An important feature of the design for its training role was that in the event of damage to the wings, the fuselage was designed to be lifted clear with the minimum of disassembly, leaving the control system together with the fuel tanks intact. The fuselage could then be placed on a new wing ready for flight.

The all wooden wing was a one piece unit with a continuous front box spar of laminated spruce booms and plywood ribs, webs and detachable wing tips. The rear spar stopped at the aileron cut-out and an auxiliary spar carried the wooden framed and ply covered ailerons. The electrically operated wooden flaps extended from the inboard ends of the ailerons to the side of the fuselage.

Four fixed narrow 'letter-box' slots were incorporated into each outer wing leading edge (not on the first prototype CA-2, A3-1). Ply covered the entire wing, with the exception of aluminium inspection doors and alloy covers to the tops of the two 17 gallon capacity fuel tanks. These covers were integral with the wing surface and formed part of the walkways. Fuel contents reading gauges were let into their upper surfaces. The fuel was fed from the two independent tanks by an engine mounted fuel pump; five gallons from the contents of the starboard tank comprised the reserve.

The engine mounted oil tank had a service capacity of 3.5 gallons. The fixed landing gear, part supplied by J.N. Kirby & Co had oleo shock absorbers, brake drums and 19 x 17 inch smooth contour tyres operating at 30 psi. Both the front and rear spars supported the main undercarriage attachment alloy fittings. The tailwheel was a non-retracting non-steerable fully swivelling unit with a 10.5 inch diameter tyre of 40 psi pressure. Wheel spats or fairings which enclosed a mud scraping plate to the rear face of the mainwheel tyre were sometimes fitted, although in service they defeated the intent of their application as they readily packed up when the mud was of a heavy sticky consistency (as found in the north Essendon area).

Fuselage frame assembly comprised of welded chrome steel tubing with an overturn structure incorporated in the frame behind the front cockpit. The fixed skin cover was an aluminium alloy framework covered in fabric, and secured to the fuselage frame with clamps. This covering, on the starboard side of the fuselage extended from midway along the front cockpit aft to the leading edge of the tailplane. On the port side of the fuselage the covering extended aft from the rear of the second cockpit.

A factory fresh just rolled out CA-6, A3-158. Destined for eventual factory conversion for the wireless training role. **HDHV**

The engine was enclosed by a removable ring cowl and backed up by four access panels ahead of the cockpit. Two removable alloy panels on the port side and one on the starboard side ahead of the fixed fabric covering gave reach to instrumentation and control runs. Upper fuselage surfaces fore and aft of the cockpits were aluminium alloy.

Tandem cockpits were under one enclosure incorporating individual manually operated sliding sections at each cockpit for entrance and exit of the crew and terminating in an alloy fairing at the rear of the second cockpit. An instrument flying hood was provided in the front cockpit and when not in use the folded hood was stored aft of the front seat.

The tail assembly, with the exception of two removable aluminium inspection panels at the lower rear, was made entirely of wood with the fin offset 2° to port. A trim tab was provided on the port elevator. Throttle, mixture and propeller control levers, trim tab, flap and engine start controls were included in both cockpits. The front cockpit was intentionally similar to the Wirraway in both layout and instrumentation, the CA-6 had 10 instruments. There were 13 in the Wirraway. The instructor in the CA-6 rear cockpit was there largely to monitor the pupil, not to fly solo. He had 5 instruments; there were 6 in the Wirraway. Warning lights were provided for landing gear, flap, bomb, camera gun firing and battery condition.

As part of the preparation for transition to the Wirraway, a dummy set of undercarriage retraction controls were fitted. A red light would appear and a warning horn would sound if the dummy undercarriage lever was not operated when the engine had been throttled right back.

For some aspects of the training function, the aircraft could be fitted with a camera gun in each wing and four racks for light practice bombs under each outer wing.

Flight Testing

It was not until the last aircraft had been delivered in April 1942 that the Aerodynamics Section of the CSIR was able to release its report on the handling trials of the CA-6 (A3-14). This delay was caused by the large amount of performance testing needed on the DAP Beaufort. The report on the CA-6 was critical of its poor brakes, nose heaviness and an undercarriage that gave a very hard ride which made taxying over uneven ground at speeds greater than 10 mph distinctly unpleasant, causing the whole machine to vibrate and clatter most disconcertingly. The forward view in flight was considered to be good from the front seat but very poor for the rear seat occupant.

Specifications CA-6 Wackett Trainer

Powerplant	One Warner Super Scarab 165D, seven cylinder air-cooled radial engine of 175 hp at 2,250 rpm at SL or 165 hp at 2,100 rpm at SL driving a Hamilton Standard (DHA) constant speed Series 2B2D two bladed propeller of 7 ft 6 in diameter			
Performance	Max speed at 175 hp at 2250 rpm at SL	40 kt		
	Cruising speed at 165 hp at 1950 rpm at SL	95 kt		
	Cruising speed at 165 hp at 1950 rpm at 10,000 ft	91 kt		
	Cruising speed at 165 hp at 1950 rpm at 4,000 ft	70 kt		
	Approach speed with 60° flap (max)	69 kt		
	Endurance at 78 kt	4.5 hrs		
	Max absolute range at economical speed	370 nm		
	Range with reserves	300 nm		
	Fuel load 34 gall (includes 5 gall reserve)			
	Average fuel consumption rate 8.5 gall/hr			
Weights	Empty	1,906 lb		
	Normal gross	2,590 lb		
	Normal wing loading	14.1 lb/sq ft		
	TO power loading	15.7 lb/hp		
Dimensions	Wing span	37 ft	Chord at root	7 ft 6 in
	Area	184 sq ft	Dihedral	5°
	Aspect Ratio	7.45	Airfoil section NACA 'M' Series	
	Wing LE sweep	3° 49'	Wing TE sweep forward	11° 20'
	Incidence at root	4.5°	Incidence at tip	1.5°
	Total flap area	14.6 sq ft	Flap travel	0°- 60°
	Height (tail down)	6 ft 9 ins	Height (tail up)	9 ft 10 ins
	Area of fin and rudder	15.98 sq ft	Tailplane area (total)	36.3 sq ft
	Length	26 ft		
Armament	8 x 10 ½ lb practice bombs on two Light Series Carriers, one under each wing			
Retrospective Designations	XP2 CA-2 Wackett Trainer Prototype – Gipsy 4 engine			
	XP3 CA-2A Wackett Trainer Prototype – Gipsy 6 engine			
	XP4 CA-2B Wackett Trainer Prototype – Warner Super Scarab engine			
	XP12 CA-6 Wackett Trainer Production			

Instrumentation and arrangement of cockpit controls was considered to be less than admirable. Reading of the fuel contents gauges on the upper surface of the wing was often difficult due to a combination of placement and reflections from the glass on the faces of the gauges. The aircraft was statically and dynamically stable and the effects of slipstream and flaps on flying trim were small. Directionally and laterally the aircraft was stable and considered to have suitable characteristics for blind flying training. Ailerons were very light and effective.

The aircraft was thought to be unstable in a flat turn and if a wing was allowed to drop it would spin out of the turn. Type trials were complicated by difficulty experienced in obtaining satisfactory engine operation, probably due to an inherent-defect in the mixture distribution of the Super Scarab engine. This last problem appears to have plagued the aircraft throughout its service life, tending to give the CA-6 a bad reputation on account of its engine.

An unusual item of comment concerned a length of brass chain about 18 inches long which was hung from the rear end of the fuselage to give electrical discharge contact with the ground because the tailwheel of the aircraft was of a non-conducting type. Once airborne this chain flapped around and thrashed against the metal inspection panels near the tail in an irritating and alarming manner.

In general, the aircraft had satisfactory handling characteristics although service pilots tended to find its take-off performance with full fuel load and the compliment of two-crew, hair-raising. Its stalling characteristics were less pleasant than in a Tiger Moth, but it was easy to make it enter into and exit from a spin. Cross-wind take-offs and landings were to be avoided and the aircraft had to be 'flown' into a landing. It was not a spectacular performer on a go-round circuit with constant speed propeller and flaps lowered. Compared to a Tiger Moth, the design had the extra operational features of built-in engine starting, brakes, flaps, propeller pitch control, undercarriage retraction (simulated) and fuel tank switching, operating items which caused handling problems for some first time fliers at 3 EFTS. Whilst the CA-6 was designed as a primary training aircraft the degree of additional flight control functions found in the aircraft, as compared to those in a Tiger Moth, allowed it to be identified as an Intermediate Trainer - a halfway step between the DH82 and the Wirraway.

David Donaldson, a graduate of 11 EFTS, kept a diary of events of his time at the school. His recollections on graduating to the CA-6 were: *"the cockpit drill is considerably more complicated than the old Tiger but they are much more comfortable and steady on the controls'"*.

It was an aircraft whose significance is generally overlooked or overshadowed by the larger more widely used Wirraway. The CA-6 was the first all Australian designed aircraft (with the exception of its engine) to reach significant mass production numbers. It was operated by the armed forces of two countries, post war aero clubs and private fliers during a span of thirty years and was the basis of further small scale aerial agriculture aircraft derivatives, the Kingsford Smith KS-3 and CA-6 structural parts in the new Yeoman YA-1 Cropmaster series.

Bibliography: CA-2 & CA-6

Air Board. Air Member for Organisation & Equipment (1939-45). Wackett Trainers - Employment Policy. [NAA: A705, 9/26/25]. Barcode:164237.

Australia. Aircraft Advisory Committee (1942-46). Minutes of meetings of Aircraft Advisory Commission. Meetings 1-77.[NAA: B5028,1; B5028,2; B5028,3; B5028,4; B5028,5]. Barcodes: 395652; 395653; 395650; 395651 & 395649 respectively.

Australia. Dept. of Air. (1940). Wackett Trainer order and general policy. [NAA: A705, 9/26/5].Barcode: 164234.

Australia. Dept. of Aircraft Production (1940-44).Wirraway & Wackett Trainer aircraft: Re-imbursement of development charges in connection with manufacture of.[MP287/1,1216]. Barcode: 441459.

Australia. Aircraft Production Commission (1940). Warner Scarab engines for Wackett Trainers- purchase of 250. [NAA: 287/1,322]. Barcode: 469284.

Australia. Aircraft Production Commission. (1940). Wackett Trainer aircraft. War Cabinet approval of the ordering of 200 Warner Scarab engines [NAA: MP287/1,411].Barcode: 469584.

Australia. Aircraft Production Commission. (1940). Warner Scarab engines-complete parts list. [NAA: MP287/1,466]. Barcode: 469653.

Australia. Dept. of Aircraft Production. (1941).Wackett trainer structural glue tests by CSIR. [NAA: MP287/1,798]. Barcode: 471202.

Australia. Dept. of Aircraft Production. (1941).Wackett Trainer aircraft. Detail specification of aircraft supplied by CAC. [NAA: MP287/1,915]. Barcode: 471446.

Australia. Dept. of Aircraft Production. Trainer memorandum meeting (January 11,1941). [NAA reference lost]

Australia. Dept. of Aircraft Production.(1941). Wackett Trainer aircraft. (1941). Suggested Supply of aircraft to South Africa.[NAA: 287/1,1155]. Barcode: 471691.

Australia. Dept. of Aircraft Production (1941).Wackett Trainer aircraft. Possibility of Supply to India. [NAA: MP287/1,1188].Barcode: 471803.

Australia. Aircraft Status cards (1941-42) Wackett Trainer Scarab A3-1 to A3-99.[NAA: A10297 Block 4]. Barcode: 3045769.

Australia. Aircraft Status cards (1942-44) Wackett Trainer Scarab A3-100 to A3-200.[NAA: A10297 Block 5]. Barcode: 3045770.

Australia. Aircraft Status cards (1939-46) Wackett Trainer Scarab A3-1001 & A3-1002. [NAA: A10297 Block 25]. Barcode: 3045792.

Berry D. (1987) [Communication re: WAGS trainees/pilots/instructors]

Boer, P. and Casius, G. W. (1975) 'NEIAF (Part III)', Air Combat, UK Vol.3/4.

Brown, J. T. (1990) 'Acquisition of CA-6 Trainers', Man & Aerial Machines, AHSA No.13.

Commonwealth Aircraft Corporation. (1938) Engineering report A-4: November 15, 1938. Detail specification for model CA-2 to RAAF specification 3/38.

Commonwealth Aircraft Corporation. (1940) Engineering report A-15. (January 4, 1940) Detail Specification for Wackett Trainer model CA-6.

Commonwealth Aircraft Corporation. (undated) CA-2. Flight test reports.

Commonwealth Aircraft Corporation. Update service Wackett Trainer overhaul and repair manual.

Commonwealth Aircraft Corporation. (undated) CAC production files P2; M5.

Commonwealth Aircraft Corporation. (undated) CAC Service Engineer file S5.

Commonwealth Aircraft Corporation. (undated) Second and subsequent contracts for Wackett Trainer and Wirraway.

Commonwealth Aircraft Corporation. (undated) Wackett Trainer Information sheets 3.1 to 3.8.

Commonwealth Disposals Commission (Australia). 'Wackett Trainer, disposal document October 1,1945.' *ASHA Newsletter Vol. 2/3 (1986)*.

Council for Scientific and Industrial Research. Aerodynamics Section. (undated). Report F.4. Summary of type trials A3-14.

Donaldson,D.J.(1987)[Communication re: WAGS trainees/pilots/instructors].

Geoff Goodall's aviation history site (www.goodall.com.au)

Hall, E. R. GRP CAPT, C.O. RAAF Radio School (1987) [Communication re: WAGS trainees / pilots / instructors].

Hooftman, Hugo. (1967) Van Glenn Martins en Mustangs. Alle vliegtuigen die hebben gevlogen bij het K.N.I.L., de Indische Militaire Luchtvaart. Zwolle: La Rivìere & Voorhoeve. [Translations for NEI CA-6 aircraft operations by A. D. (Gus) Moorrees, Melb,1986.]

Johnson, Ian (1987) [Communication re: WAGS trainees/pilots/instructors].

Jones, Owen. (1985) Lecture to the Aviation Historical Society of Australia, Victoria Branch.

Mellor, D. P. (David Paver), 1903-1980. (1962) *The role of science and industry*. Australian War Memorial, Canberra .

Pilkington, Mark Giles L. (1986) [Wackett Trainer technical and reference material].

Redding,G.(1987)[Communication re: WAGS trainees/pilots/instructors].

Royal Australian Air Force. Directorate of Technical Services. (1940-41). CAC Trainer Aircraft suitability for intermediate & advanced training-Service flying & handling trials [NAA: A705, 9/26/6]. Barcode :164235.

Royal Australian Air Force. Wackett Trainers to NEI. (*Adf.messageboard.com.au*).

Royal Australian Air Force. Directorate of Technical Services. (1941-44). Use of Wackett Trainer Aircraft at Wireless Air Gunners Schools. [NAA: A705, 9/26/24]. Barcode:164236.

Royal Australian Air Force. Directorate of Technical Services. (1941-44). Wackett Trainer aircraft mainplanes.[NAA: A705, 9/26/45]. Barcode: 164246.

Royal Australian Air Force. Directorate of Technical Services. (1941-43). Wackett Trainer aircraft fin & tailplane.[NAA: A705, 9/26/51]. Barcode: 164248.

Royal Australian Air Force. Directorate of Signals.(1942-44) Wackett Trainer aircraft - Promulgation of wireless aircraft borders. [NAA: A705, 9/26/107].Barcode : 164264.

Sedunary,E.(1987)[Communication re: WAGS trainees/pilots/instructors].

Sergeant,E.(1987)[Communication re: WAGS trainees/pilots/instructors].

Sillcock,K.(1987)[Communication re: WAGS trainees/pilots/instructors].

P144 / P148 TWIN ENGINE BOMBER–RECONNAISSANCE AIRCRAFT
October 1938

Released on October 23, 1938 this company specification covered a twin engine, three aircrew aircraft intended to perform day bomber, night bomber, reconnaissance and dive bombing roles.

The layout of P144 was of a low set wing on top of which was located a narrow fuselage with a long glass house cabin. This cabin had a similar but longer arrangement of sliding canopy sections as used on the Wirraway. Like the Wirraway the retracted main wheels were housed in fairings in the leading of the wing ahead of the front spar. The fuselage ended in a twin finned tail arrangement.

For the observation / bombing role a glazed gondola formed part of the lower mid-fuselage structure below and to the rear of the wing. Two P & W Wasp engines powered the aircraft. The wing trailing edge was an unbroken straight line with any form of sweep. Armament was to be a single Vickers machine gun with 400 rounds of ammunition and two flexible mount Lewis guns with 700 rpg. The disposition of these guns was to have been in the rear of the upper crew compartment and in the gondola. Fuel provision was for 220 gallons.

P148

The P144 specification was quickly followed on February 2, 1939 by that for P148. The dive bombing role had been discarded, the wing span increased by 6 inches and the engines changed to the P & W Twin Wasp, effectively almost doubling the built-in engine power. The wings now had taper on the trailing edge and the armament provision revised. There were to be two forward firing Vickers Mk V machine guns with 500 rpg and two Vickers 'K' machine guns on flexible mounts in the extended cabin. Four underwing bomb carriers were to each carry a 250 lb bomb. Consideration was to be given for the installation of a 37 mm cannon.

Bibliography: P144 / P148 Twin Engine Bomber

Commonwealth Aircraft Corporation. Engineering Report AA10 (A5). Twin Engine Bomber- Reconnaissance Aircraft (October 1938).

Commonwealth Aircraft Corporation.(undated). Engineering Report AA8 (A9). Provisional Specification for Twin-Engine Bomber-Reconnaissance Aircraft (Twin Row Wasp Engines).

P147 SINGLE ENGINE TWO-PLACE MULTI-GUN FIGHTER AIRCRAFT
February 1939

On June 23, 1938 the Secretary of the Air Board requested from CAC the performance figures resulting if a Wirraway was to be fitted with a Twin Wasp radial engine. Wackett sent back a favourable reply on 5 July with an outline specification prepared by Herbert Knight for a two seater fighter having two fixed 0.303 inch machine guns, a flexible gun operated by the observer and an estimated all-up weight of some 6,250 lb.

This information was upgraded and re-issued seven months later on February 1,1939 for an aircraft now equipped with four Vickers Mk V machine guns in the outer wings, a flexible gun in the rear

Specifications	P144 Twin Engine Bomber-Reconnaissance Aircraft	
Powerplant	Two Pratt and Whitney R-1340 Wasp radial engines of 700 hp each at TO	
Performance	Max speed at 11,000 ft	236 kts
	Cruise speed at 15,000 ft	214 kts
	Max range at 15,000 ft	1,080 nm
	Range day bomber/recon (9,886 lb)	880 nm
	Range night bomber/recon(9,968 lb)	880 nm
	Range day bomber (10,131 lb)	780 nm
	Range night bomber (10,213 lb	700 nm
	Range dive bomber (9,022 lb)	780 nm
Weights	Normal loaded	9,500 lb
	Max loaded	11,000 lb
Dimensions	Wing span	54 ft
	Wing area	350 sq ft
	Length	32 ft 2 ins
	Height	11 ft
Armament	One Vickers m/g with 400 rounds & two Lewis m/gs with 700 rpg	
Retrospective Designation	XP6	

Specifications	P148 Twin Engine-Bomber Reconnaissance Aircraft	
Powerplant	Two Pratt & Whitney R-1830 S3C4-G Twin Wasp radial engines of 1,200 hp each.	
Performance	Max speed at 5,000 ft	273 kts
	Cruise speed at 15,000 ft	253 kts
	Range at econ cruise speed	1,080 nm
Weights	Normal	10,500 lb
	Max loaded	12,500 lb
Dimensions	Wing span	54 ft 6 ins
	Wing area	363 sq ft
	Length	34 ft 2 ins
	Height	11 ft
Armament	Two Vickers Mk V m/gs with 500 rpg. Two Vickers 'K' flexible mount vm/gs. 37 mm cannon possible option. 1,000 lb bomb load	
Retrospective Designation	XP7	

Specifications	P147 Single Engine Two Place Multi-Gun Fighter Aircraft	
Powerplant	One Pratt and Whitney R-1830 S1C3-G Twin Wasp geared radial of 1,200 hp at TO at 2,700 rpm; 1,050 hp at 7,500 ft & a cruise rating of 700 hp at 15,000 ft at 2,325 rpm	
Performance	Max speed at 5,000 ft	250 kts
	Cruise speed at 15,000 ft	226 kts
	Max rate of climb	3,700 ft /min
	Endurance at cruise speed	2 hrs
	Range at economical speed	650 nm
Weights	Empty	4,752 lb
	Normal gross (inc 92 gall of fuel)	6,325 lb
Dimensions	Wing span	43 ft
	Length	28 ft 6 ins
Armament	Four 0.303 in wing mounted Vickers Mk V m/gs with 500 rpg. One 0.303 in Vickers 'K' flexible mounted m/g in the rear cockpit with 600 rounds.	
Retrospective Designation	XP8	

cockpit but with a taper on the trailing edge of the Wirraway outer wings, together with a necessary increase in operating weight.

Bibliography: P147 Single Engine Two Place Multi Gun Fighter

Commonwealth Aircraft Corporation. (undated). Engineering Report A4A. Preliminary Specification for Wirraway Two-Place Fighter.

Commonwealth Aircraft Corporation. (1939) Engineering Report A8, (February 1,1939) Provisional Specification for Single-Engine, Two Place, Multi-Gun Fighter Aircraft.

Commonwealth Aircraft Corporation (June 23, 1938). Correspondence from the Air Board to L. J. Wackett.

Wackett, L. J. (July 5, 1938). Correspondence to the Air Board.

P149 TWIN ENGINE FIGHTER AIRCRAFT AIRCRAFT April / May 1939

P149 and P150 shared a near common configuration layout and a basically identical gun installation.

P149 was issued on April 12, 1939 and it was a brief for a twin engine, two place interceptor and convoy escort fighter. There was a choice of two radial engine type; the Pratt & Whitney R-1830 S3C3-G Twin Wasp or the Bristol Taurus III.

The outline of P149 depicted a narrow fuselage terminating in a twin finned tail assembly as in the P148 Proposal, a shorter glass house two crew compartment and retaining the similar main undercarriage wheel stowage arrangement. Four fixed forward firing Vickers Mk V machine guns with 500 rpg were located in the outer wing panels. The Vickers 'K' machine gun on a flexible mount with its 480 rounds of ammunition in the rear of the crew glass house was intended to offer some minimal rearward defence. The ventral gondola was deleted and crew reduced to two.

Specifications	P149 Twin Engine Fighter Aircraft	
Powerplant	Two Pratt & Whitney R-1830 S3C3-G Twin Wasp radial engines of 1,100 hp each at TO or: Two Bristol Taurus III radial engines of 950 hp at TO	
Performance	Max speed at 9,000 ft	301 kts
	Cruise speed at 700 hp per engine at 16,000ft	281 kts
	Range at econ cruise speed	1,200 nm
Weights	Interceptor: Empty	7,366 lb
	AUW	9,470 lb
	Convoy Escort: Empty	7,366 lb
	AUW	10,913 lb
Dimensions	Wing span	50 ft
	Wing area	314 sq ft
	Length	32 ft 9 ins
	Height	10 ft
Armament	Four Vickers Mk V m/gs with 500 rpg. One Vickers 'K' flexible mount m/g with 480 rounds	
Retrospective Designation	XP9	

For interception, the internal fuel was to be kept to 110 gallons whilst the long range convoy escort was to have up to 290 gallons. It is not known which engine installation is depicted in P149.

Bibliography : P149 Twin Engine Fighter

Commonwealth Aircraft Corporation. (1939). Engineering Report AA11 (A10). (April/May 1939). Preliminary Specification for Twin-Engine Fighter Aircraft.

P144

J.A.Vella

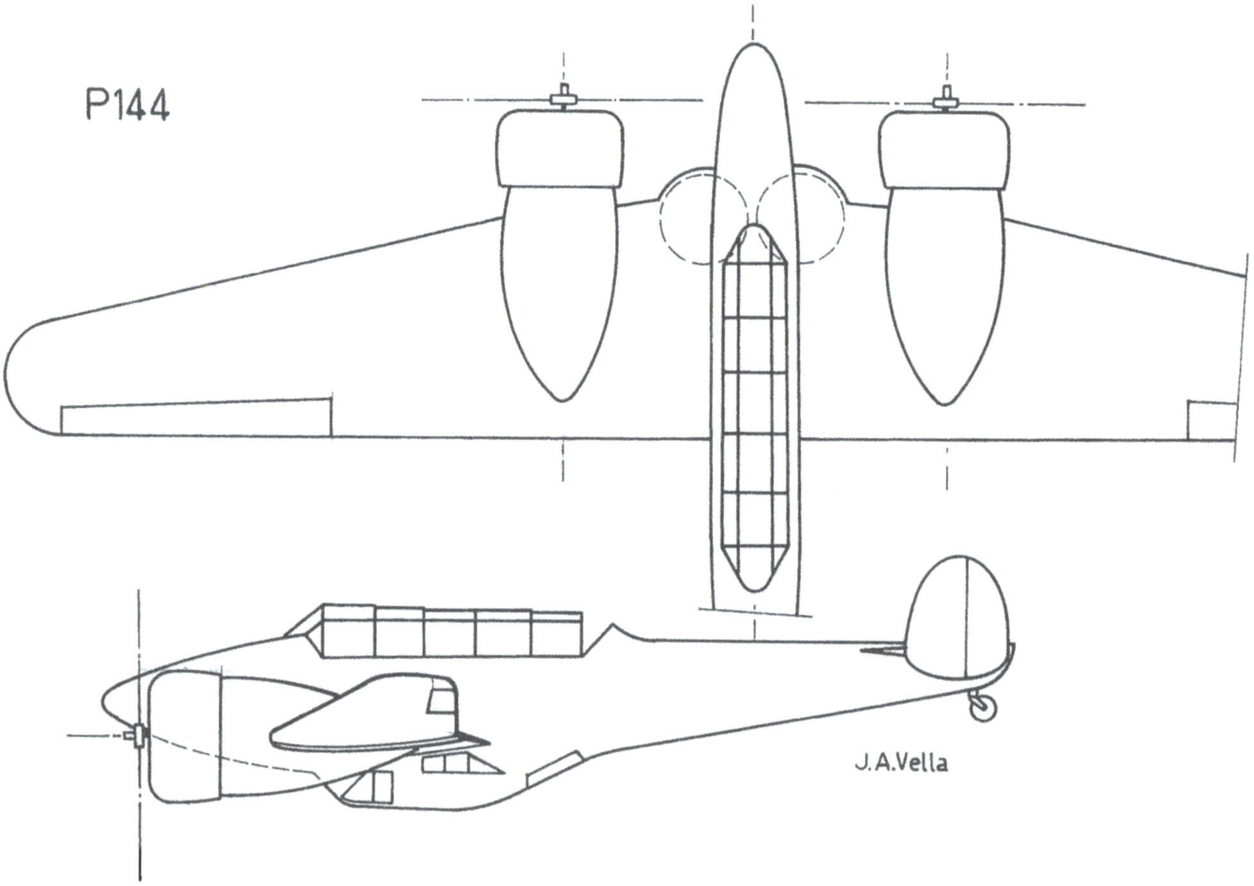

P148

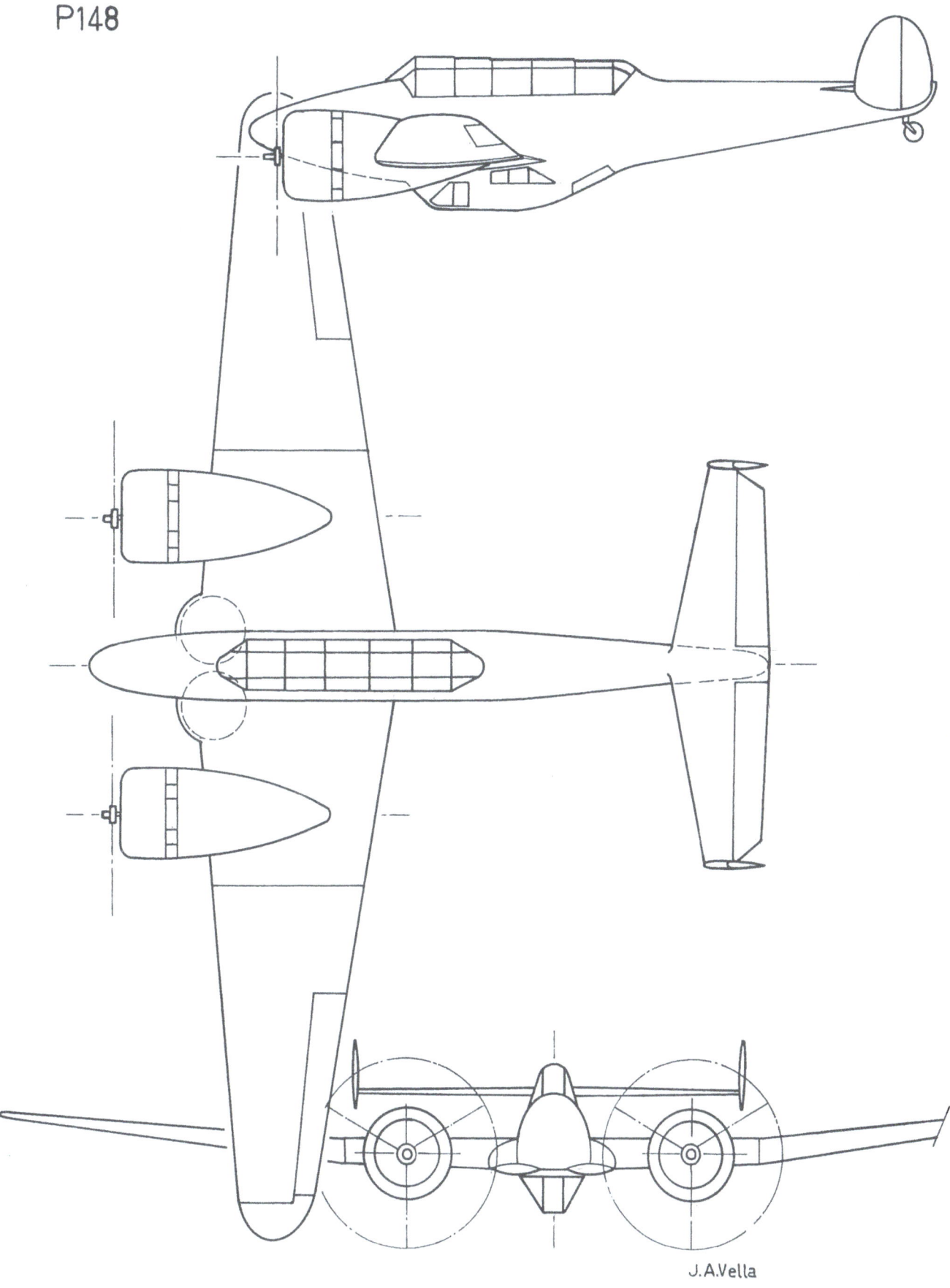

J.A.Vella

P150 TWIN ENGINE GENERAL PURPOSE AIRCRAFT
May 1939

Proposal P150 was an extension of design P149 to perform other likely roles. This specification was an updated variation for that of P144 / P148.

The roles of day or night fighter, day or night reconnaissance, day or night bomber and dive bomber were still suggested but the engine power (of the P150 interceptor proposal) was dropped back to use two of the 650 hp CAC R-1340 Wasp radial engines. With the ventral gondola removed and replaced by a bomb sight and prone bombing position immediately aft of the rear cockpit, crew complement was now reduced to two as compared with that of the P144 / P148. A 20

P147

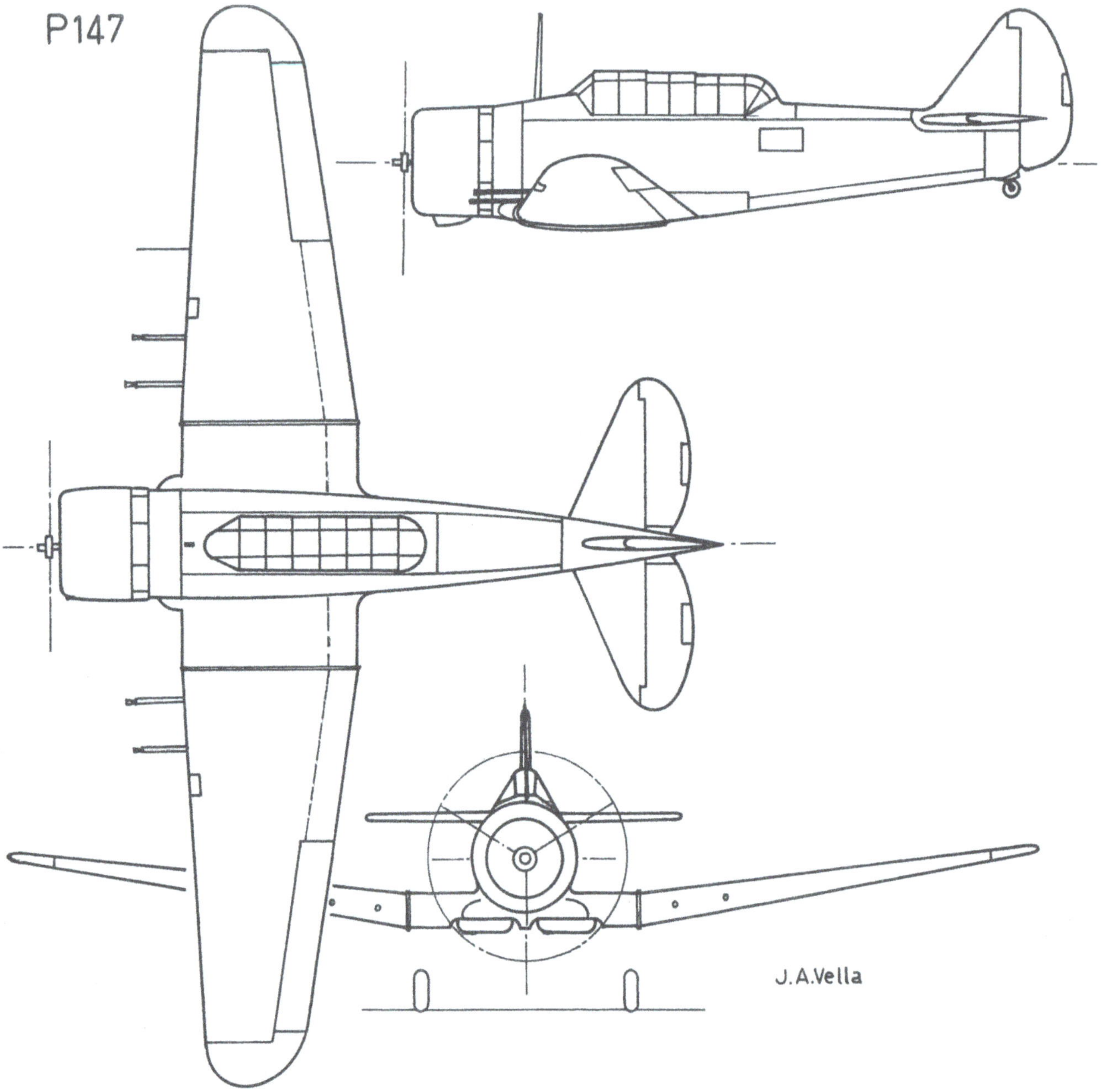

Specifications	P150 Twin Engine General Purpose Aircraft
Powerplant	One CAC/Pratt and Whitney R-1340 S1H1-G Wasp radial engine of 650 hp at TO at 2,350 rpm
Performance	Max speed at 7,000 ft 243 kts Cruise speed at 14,000 ft 232 kts Range at econ cruise speed 1,200 nm
Weights	Empty 6,438 lb AUW day/night fighter(130 gall fuel) 8,500 lb AUW day/night recon (220 gall fuel) 9,263 lb AUW day/night bomber (220 gall fuel) 10,230 lb AUW dive bomber (220 gall fuel) 9,570 lb
Dimensions	Wing span 50 ft Wing area 314 sq ft Length 32 ft 6 ins Height 9 ft 6 ins
Armament	20 mm forward firing cannon 1,500 lb bomb load
Retrospective Designation	XP10

mm cannon was to be located in the extreme fuselage nose. The other gun armament was identical to that of P149. Universal Carriers under the fuselage and wing centre section were to take a maximum 1,500 lb bomb load.

The weight variation in the different roles was due to the differing quantity of fuel carried assuming there was an identical amount of ammunition but ignoring the bomb load capacity, F.24 reconnaissance camera and bombing flares.

Bibliography : P150 Twin Engine General Purpose Aircraft

Commonwealth Aircraft Corporation. (1939) Engineering Report AA9 (A11). (May 1939).   Preliminary Specification for Twin-Engine General Purpose Aircraft.

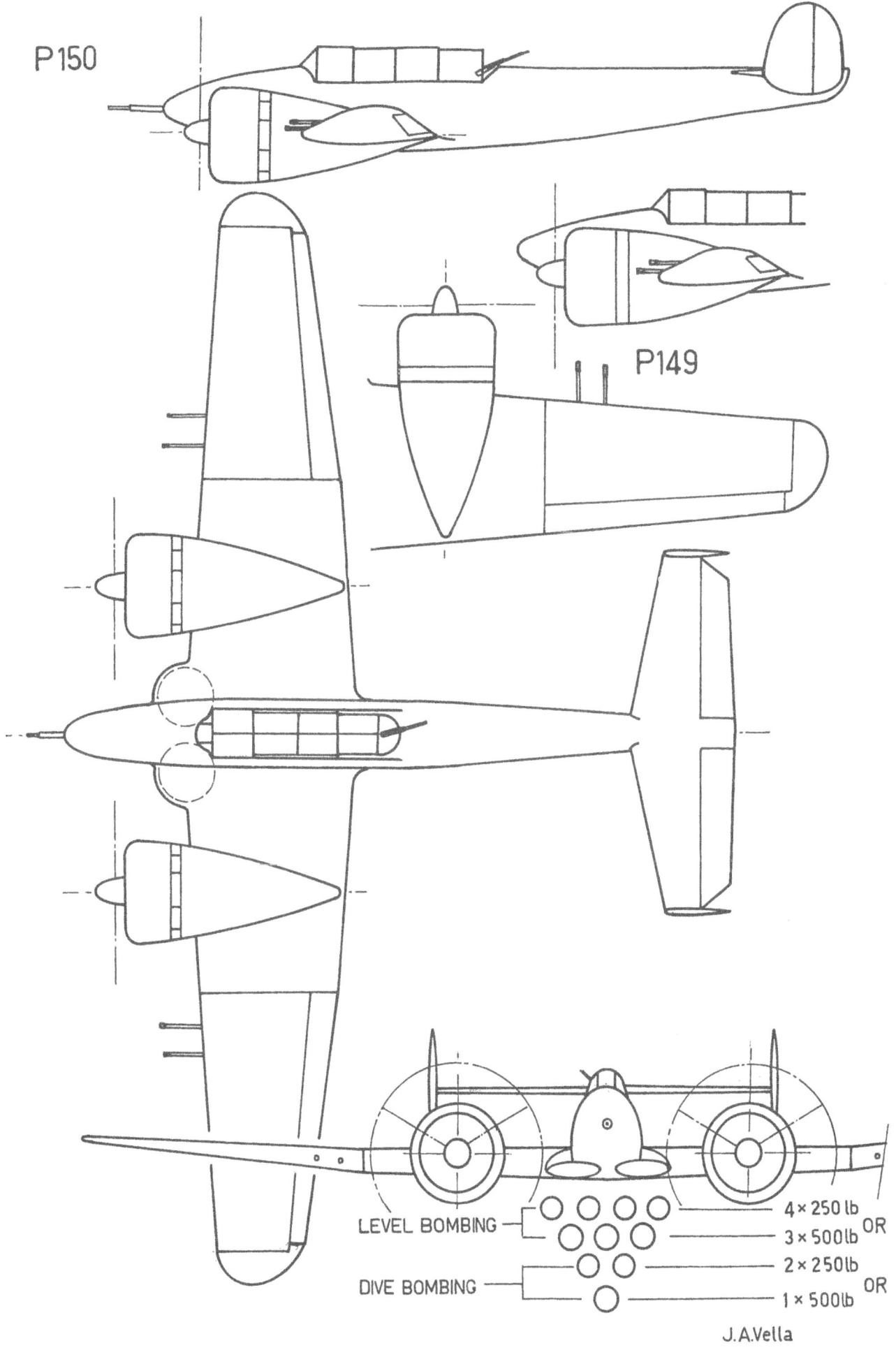

CA-4 WACKETT BOMBER & CA-11 WOOMERA BOMBER
June 1940

In June of 1940 the Australian War Cabinet voted CAC a sum of £50,000 for the construction of an aircraft to meet RAAF Development Specification No 241 (dated April 23, 1940) which called for *a twin engine dive-bomber, torpedo carrying, general bombing and reconnaissance prototype aircraft.*

The Cabinet had acted on the recommendation of the Air Board who had been impressed by the claims made by the company with their private initiative bomber preliminary design work. The Air Board ordered a prototype on May 31, 1940 followed closely by War Cabinet's approval on June 5, 1940 for the CA-4 Wackett Bomber. The company had encouragement from both the Government and the RAAF in view of the many problems faced in Britain and Australia with starting the local production of the Bristol Beaufort.

The RAAF Technical Services Directorate was given the task of developing the RAAF technical specification. Soon after this, the project came under the control of the Aircraft Production Commission and its development was suddenly beset by management and control problems in communications between the RAAF, APC and CAC. The APC aware of all the initial planning and early design on the CA-4, tended to bypass the RAAF and CAC and placed the responsibility of design approval, stress calculations and fatigue testing of the CA-4 with the CSIR; activities which had not been included in its limited charter for basic research in its barely established facilities.

The APC ignored the standing of CAC with the RAAF as an Approved Firm for aircraft design whose design authority with an

A partial view of the CA-4 mock-up built out of the cheapest materials. **Reg Schulz**

The forward fuselage assembly resting on a wooden representation of the wing. **Reg Schulz**

RAAF / CAC based Resident Technical Officer had already been well established with the Wirraway and Wackett Trainer contracts, well before the CSIR Division of Aeronautics had been created. This led to a strained relationship between the RAAF and the APC. Arbitrarily, the latter went so far as to divert part of the £50,000 funding for the CA-4 to ARL to achieve its self-assigned fatigue testing role.

Following the visit to Australia by H.E. Wimperis, Director of Scientific Research at the UK Air Ministry, the Joseph Lyons Federal Government adopted its recommendations in December 1937 to establish the Aeronautical Research Laboratory (ARL) beside the CAC factory. It was to include a large wind tunnel, engine test bed, physics Laboratory and an instrument section along similar lines in its equipment and test procedures to the RAE at Farnborough (UK).

Construction work did not begin until August 1939 and the large capacity 9ft x 4ft wind tunnel had its first run on December 15, 1941 two days before the Japanese attacks on Malaya and Pearl Harbour. On completion, the Research Laboratory became headquarters of the Division of Aeronautics, of which ex-RAE Laurie Coombes was appointed Chief.

On August 5, 1940 the Board of CAC had noted that responsibility for the success of the design lay with the role of CSIR affirming the view of APC. Wackett did not like the inclusion of a government controlled civilian organisation in his dealings. His relations with Laurie Coombes whilst not always cordial improved slowly and the new wind tunnel was to feature in the search for answers with the troubled aerodynamics of the CAC bomber.

The enormity of the task in the project could only be put in perspective by taking into consideration the fact that CAC had only been in existence for 44 months. The fledgling design staff was led by Thomas W. (Bill) Air (Chief Engineer); Friedrich (Fred) David (Chief Designer); Edward F. Faggetter (Design Project Engineer); Ralph Price (Stressing), Lionel Stern, Project Engineer Hydraulics; Doug Humphries; Joe Solvey (Structures) and Reg Schulz (CA-4 Bomber Project Engineer).

It was possible to work within what, in today's terms, seems such a small funding allocation of £50,000 for such a large undertaking only because the leading personnel directly associated with the construction of the aircraft pursued their task with an extraordinary dedication and measure of self-sacrifice. Working exceptionally long hours for no overtime penalty pay, going short on sleep, they strived for the success of the project during a period of national crisis. At a time when the pressures on the embryonic CAC team were suddenly so urgent, the CA-4 was an example of outstanding inter-departmental co-operation within the organisation of the company. The company also needed future new work.

The background ideas for the layout of this type of aeroplane had been with Wackett for some time. It was left to his designers to translate those ideas and his latest innovation and most unique feature of the CA-4, the remotely controlled power operated gun turrets, into practical reality.

The Chief Designer, responsible for the overall configuration, was Friederich Wilhelm Dawid who had qualified as an engineer in Austria in 1922, worked at the establishments of Ernest Heinkel and Fiesler in Germany. Ernest Heinkel with business contacts in Japan from 1925, supplied a series of reconnaissance aircraft to Aichi suitable for catapult launching. To escape the Nazi concentration camps he was able to place Friederich Dawid as a consultant aerodynamicist with Aichi Tokei Denki K.K. (Aichi Electric Clock & Electric Co Ltd) on behalf of the Imperial Japanese Navy where in strict secrecy he worked on the design of the wing of the Aichi D3A1 'Val' navy

Friedrich(Fred) David. **Neil Follett Collection**

dive-bomber. When Japan joined the war with Nazi Germany his position was not safe. He came to CAC in April 1939, having been recommended to Wackett by the resident Australian Consul in Japan. He quickly changed his name by deed poll to Frederick (Fred) William David.

A 1:48 scale model of the bomber was tested in the small wind tunnel of the Engineering School of Melbourne University toward the end of 1939. The faculty had received £1,500 from RAAF funds in December 1921 to enable a small wind tunnel of 6 sq ft cross section area to be built and assist in the development of the science of aeronautics.

The wood and cardboard full scale mock-up of the CA-4 built to examine the cockpit and internal layouts was inspected by RAAF staff at the start of February 1940. With the granting of the Development Specification rapid steps were taken to establish full scale mock-up and engineering test rigs for the fuel system, engine installation and controls, equipment runs, the remote gunnery mechanism and an experimental section of the integral wing fuel tank.

Professor Thomas Laby (Physics Department of Melbourne University) contributed to the design of the mirror sighting devices for the remote turret armament.

CA-4 Project Organisation

Following the submission of the preliminary design proposal in October / November 1940, and its acceptance by the RAAF in the middle of December, special project organisational methods were implemented. (Refer to Fig 1.) Because of the size of the project and the conscious decision to complete the aircraft in nine months, two project engineers were appointed. Ted Faggetter was to manage liaison between the design and drawing offices and Reg Schulz was the Project Engineer to liaise between the Design Project Engineer, the Chief Draftsman, Drawing Office section leaders and the manufacturing and development activities. Both Project Engineers reported to Thomas (Tommy) Air, CAC's Chief Engineer.

The first priority was to establish a company experimental department. Harry Becker, Principal Superintendent and Wackett's workshop leading hand since the days of the RAAF Experimental Station at Randwick in 1924, had the task to equip the new department with machinery, layout tables, benches and a project planning office. The shortage of draftsmen did not allow the preparation of all complete structure drawings so that it became necessary to just release basic layouts and small centre-line drawings with reference stations, grid lines, group numbers, material size, specification, special treatment etc.

The stress related design decisions, such as rivet pitch, would then be added in the experimental shop as the data became available. In contrast, all machined components were fully detailed. An engineering order system was also created to cope with the more than 3,000 serial numbered engineering sketches. These sketches were to be formally drawn when the pressure of work on the prototype had eased. CAC was simultaneously designing, developing and constructing the prototype aircraft. The wing centre section was a complex 26 foot wide structure fitted with castings and machined components to mount the undercarriage, flaps, turrets, bomb pick-up points, fuel tanks, engines, control runs and armour plating.

This assembly was built up on a large steel rig made up of two 30 foot long, 12 inch high structural I-beams. Aluminium alloy spar boom extrusions were obtained from Alcoa. Due to wing taper a twisting device was built to rework the extrusions to correspond to angular change at each rib station. Castings required for the undercarriage mounts, wing to fuselage attachments, control surface supports, forgings for the undercarriage leg were some of the many new items needed for the task from an industry which, four years previously had not existed as an organised industrial entity. The rear fuselage and wings were joined to the centre section assembly at the end of June and it was a sense of satisfaction to confirm prior to roll out in September 1941 that the CA-4 came out within predicted weight estimates. The aircraft was finished in dark earth brown, dark green and sky blue camouflage, carrying the RAAF experimental aircraft serial A23-1001.

CA-4 Aircraft Description

The construction of the CA-4 was divided into basically four sections: wings, fuselage, tail unit and control surfaces. The low cantilever wing was comprised of a centre section with dihedral outer units. The space between the two spar stressed skin structure of the centre section was almost an entire integral fuel tank, the first integral fuel tanks constructed in Australia.

The main tanks, on either side of the longitudinal centre of the aircraft, were each of 105 gallon capacity; the No 2 or mid-section tanks were each of 99 gallon capacity, whilst the outer, or No 3 reserve tanks of 62 gallons each were located behind the engines. These were also referred to as the engine nacelle tanks. This gave a total internal fuel capacity of 532 gallons. The outer wing panels, with a plan form similar to those on the Wirraway but with increased chord, were of a single spar structure with spaced ribs and stressed skin covering. The internal fuel capacity could be boosted by two 293 gallon drop tanks carried under the wing centre section on the outer two of four pick-up points. With this total 1,118 gallons of fuel the CA-4 had a much extended radius of operation.

The technique of constructing the integral tanks was to seal all stringers and other junctions with Butyl rubber moulded seals contained within separate riveted aluminium alloy pressings. All mating faces of the structure were dismantled after drilling, cleaned and sealed with Fullers Compound – a rubber base sealant which was applied with a CAC developed gun. The entire assembly was then placed into a rotating jig and a rubber base slushing compound applied to coat the whole interior of the fuel tanks. Sealing of the integral fuel tanks was not only a mechanically difficult task but one that was hampered by slow curing due to a cold and wet winter. A persistent series of fuel leaks were to be encountered during the trials of the CA-4 and this method of proofing the fuel tanks was subsequently to be abandoned on the succeeding CA-11 Woomera in favour of the new development of rubber fuel cells.

The Trimotor Layout

The Pratt & Whitney R-1830 S3C3-G Twin Wasp engines, each of 1,100hp were mounted on the centre line of the wing thickness although more of the side area of the each nacelle was above the wing than below it. Shortly after the original design had been finalized, the supply of P & W R-1830 engines from the United States (pending the start of local production under licence) was threatened.

As CAC was then producing the S1H1G Wasp for the Wirraway, Wackett decided in August 1940 that three of these 650 hp engines would be installed. Consequently both engine stations were moved outwards on the wing centre section by an amount sufficient to clear the propellers from interfering when running three engines. The central engine was to be mounted on the front end of the tubular fuselage replacing the streamlined monocoque nose intended for the twin engine configuration.

This precautionary measure accounted for the rather wide centres between outboard engines on both the CA-4 and CA-11. All engine attachments were interchangeable for use of either the Wasp or Twin Wasp. CAC's production of the Twin Wasp eventually came on line and the three engine layout did not eventuate but there was no going back. However its legacy was to manifest itself during the flight test phase. (The engine cowlings and exhaust designed for the CA-4 were used on the competing DAP Beaufort.)

The chrome-molybdenum steel tube framework of the fuselage was built in two sections joined by a semi-monocoque bottom cowl over the rear lower fuselage. The upper fuselage decking behind the cockpit enclosure was metal covered. The side panels consisted of fabric covered ply on wooden frames. The tail unit was a cantilever two spar stressed skin unit. The trailing edge of the wing was not faired into the fuselage.

The leading edge portions of the ailerons, elevators and rudder were metal covered whilst that aft of the control surface spars comprised of aluminium ribs with a fabric covering. (This method of assembly for the fuselage, wings and control surfaces was retained for the later CA-11). The lower flaps were used for take-off and landing and in conjunction with upper surface flaps, for dive bombing and torpedo dropping. Flap positions were Shut; Take Off-17°; Landing-45°; Diving (flaps down 64° and dive brakes up 45°).

The gun turrets were domed and prominent, and the oil cooler exhaust above the centre of the engine stopped just to the rear of the cowl gills.

The pilot's vision from the multi framed glasshouse cabin was good except when taxying, when the high pointing nose obstructed forward vision. For recce work an F24 vertical camera was set 32 inches aft of the nose tip beneath the front guns and behind two outward opening, hydraulically operated doors 6.5 inches wide and 16.5 inches long. The location did not provide for in-flight access as the operation was controlled by the bomb-aimer and sighted via an Aldis sight 18 feet 5 inches to the rear of the nose tip. Film / camera access was through the nose port side.

Test pilot Hubert Boss-Walker inspects cockpit progress. A young Reg Schulz on the right is engaged on paper work. **Reg Schulz.**

Both at the mock-up conference and following the subsequent CSIR trials it was suggested that the camera be relocated in the rear of the fuselage in a retractable mount above the ventral rear defence gun doors and that nose cannon armament be a future possibility as their availability became more certain.

In the retracted position the dual wheels of the main undercarriage protruded about nine inches below the lower surface of the engine nacelle to minimize structural damage in the event of a wheels-up landing. The wheels on the CA-4 were ex-Tugan Gannet aircraft items.

As the main undercarriage was lowered it pushed open the spring loaded doors. The larger doors into which the narrow undercarriage doors were incorporated opened only for bomb release. The tail wheel was not retractable. An extensive 3,000 psi Dowty live line hydraulics system was provided. In comparison with the 1,000 psi systems fitted to the Wirraway and Boomerang, the CA-4 installation was intended to offer a substantial weight saving.

Part of the starboard upper & lower surface airbrakes in the open position. **Reg Schulz**

Crew Functions

The allocation of functions for the three members of the aircrew was unusual. There was to be a first pilot/forward gunner; a co-pilot / wireless operator / rear turrets gunner (a mustering which had not yet been established in the RAAF) and the navigator/ bomb-aimer / ventral defence gunner. Handholds, footholds and sliding canopy sections provided entry into the cabin. The pilot, seated behind a bullet proof windscreen operated the four nose mounted Browning Mk II 0. 303 machine guns aiming through an open ring and bead sight. Each gun was provided with 800 rounds of ammunition. To allow the pilot to gain sight of any other aircraft approaching from below and out of sight under the wings, a clear vision panel was fitted into the lower fuselage under his seat.

The CA-4 on its undercarriage for the first time. The rear fuselage is still to be fitted. **Reg Schulz** .

The co-pilot was provided with a permanently installed rudder bar, a storable control stick, throttle and propeller controls, trim tab

CA-4, A23-1001 prototype. Outside for the first time. Low dihedral wing angle. **David Anderson. 707072010P**

Engine running tests on the prototype. Note the exposed domed starboard turret & short oil cooler duct. **Reg Schulz.**

The CA-4 before its first flight with the starboard remote turret sitting prominent, un-faired at the rear of the engine nacelle. **Reg Schulz.**

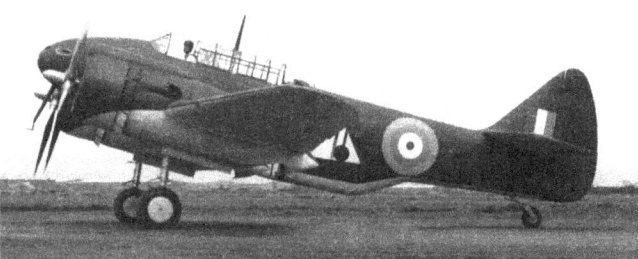

CA-4, A23-1001 taxying on September 19, 1941 for its first flight, Fisherman's Bend. **David Anderson. 157 29012028P**

A happy throng of CAC employees greet the prototype CA-4, A23-1001 at the end of its first flight. It has the domed turrets & short engine oil cooler ducts. **Reg Schulz.**

A smiling Hubert Boss-Walker and a happy employee crowd after the CA-4 first flight. **Reg Schulz.**

A23-1001 on the CAC landing ground at the end of its first flight with the CAC factory staff running across to meet it. The old Newport power station is in the background. Wirraway A20–366 in the foreground. **Reg Schulz.**

Note the extended oil cooler duct on top of the engine, the revised turret top, the clear vision panels to the sides and top of the navigator's space with the right side gun aiming periscope enclosure jutting out from the rear of the glasshouse. **Reg Schulz.**

wheels, a range of flying instruments and undercarriage controls. His forward vision was virtually non-existent because of armour plate and a turn-over truss structure. He was to help fly the aircraft on long range missions should the automatic pilot fail. His radio gear was positioned at the rear of the second cockpit, made to swing out and be operated in a rear facing position then stowed to one side when no longer required. There was also a folding table, a transmitting key and an aerial cable winch on the starboard side above the left foot well.

The last duty of the second crew member was to man the rear hemisphere defence of the aircraft using the remote operated turrets. It was Wackett's concern for the safety of a rear tail gunner which made him decide that his safety would be enhanced if he was located in the central body of the aeroplane. In addition his effectiveness would be greatly increased if he was to operate two turrets protecting a greater volume of sky whilst minimizing crew numbers.

Wackett's idea was of a major defence based on a gun turret (or barbette) at the rear of each engine nacelle. Each turret was to have two Vickers Mk V 0.303 inch machine guns and 1,070 rounds of ammunition (four guns were initially proposed). Each turret was 9 feet 7 inches from the centre of the aircraft, inclined 10° downward and mounted on a central pivot on the rear face of the centre section rear spar. The turret cylinder was comprised of a four spoked wheel resting on ten rubber tyred rollers running in a track above the skin. The starboard gun of each turret was to be used for synchronization of turret and harmonization of sights whilst the port gun adjustable in elevation had the starboard gun slaved to it. The ammunition boxes and chutes were mounted to the cradle and moved with it. To use the guns the co-pilot rotated his seat to face aft and positioned himself in two foot wells in the fuselage floor in order to manipulate a fold-away turret control column. This column operated the turret hydraulic control valve which with fore/aft movement elevated and depressed the guns and with side to side movement swept the turrets in azimuth. The turrets operated in azimuth by means of jacks, rods and chains around a sprocket at the turret pivot. The port, control or reference turret, was raised via a hydraulic jack. An arm connected directly by a chain to the turret so that it was always parallel to it in elevation was mounted on the starboard turret. There was no manual back-up in the event of a hydraulic failure.

A Wackett-designed sight head was mounted on a Wirraway rear gun track coupled by a system of chains to the port turret so that it moved in harmony with the guns in both horizontal and vertical planes but was maintained parallel with the longitudinal axis of the aircraft by means of a pantograph. This sight head which was made up of two sights was located 30.5 inches aft and 42.3 inches above the turrets when the fuselage datum was horizontal. The upper of the two sights was used in direct vision, whilst the other 7.5 inches lower and 3.5 inches to the right was to be used to look into the blind area beneath the tail via two periscopes comprised of a mirror on either side of the fuselage. (During WW1, Wackett had made an attempt at devising a system of aerial attack from below another aircraft when he was stationed at Orfordness with its scientific staff, learning of various types of guns, sighting devices, gun mountings etc.)

This periscope assembly on the CA-4 was mounted across the rear of the cabin glasshouse. The sight head contained a system of levers, pinions and cams to form a no-allowance sight ie one in which direct aim is taken at the target aircraft. The sight however had been designed to give a correct no-allowance sighting for firing for just two conditions of flight either of which may have been set up for by selection of a lever on top of the sight head.

These conditions were for:
- Parallel Course: In which the CA-4 is flying at 260 kts (300 mph) at 15,000 ft whilst the target aircraft is flying a parallel course at the same speed at a distance of 1,200 ft either above, below or on either beam.
- Attack Course: In which the CA-4 is flying at 260 kts (300mph) at 15,000 ft and the target aircraft is making a front gun attack from either quarter at a speed of 320 kts (375mph). Further, it was assumed that at a distance of 1,200 ft the CA-4 opens fire and that at all ranges less than 1,500 ft, the target aircraft is pursuing a path on which it can fire at the CA-4

The electrical interrupter gear allowed the guns to fire so long as the system was functioning. Any defect, fault or damage to the system would prevent the guns from firing. (This method of operation did not find favour during the CA-4 armament trials due to the possibility of the tail assembly taking own hits).

Ian Grant was the engineer responsible for the design and practical development of the sight head. He was installed with his drawing board adjacent to Wackett's desk so that he could work in close proximity with the inventor of this extremely complex idea.

The third member of the crew, the navigator/bomb aimer/ventral defence gunner was provided with a Mk IXA bomb sight in the forward section of the under fuselage compartment. To reach this position he had to fold up his seat, turn around and lie on the floor placing one leg on either side of the ventral defence gun. Other items for his use included fusing switches and a bomb distribution board.

The Vickers G.O. Mk 1 0.303 inch machine gun for ventral defence was situated at the rear end of the nav compartment. It was fired through a 15 inch by 28 inch opening which was covered by a pair of hydraulically operated outward opening doors (the mock-up conference had asked that these doors be made to slide upward internally conforming to the curved lines of the fuselage). The mounting was a gun pivot carried at the bottom of a tubular steel swing which was hinged at each side of the fuselage 34 inches above the floor. The assembly was held rigid by a quick release anchorage in the floor just ahead of the opening.

To engage a target it meant disconnecting the front legs of the nav table, the quick release at the other end and sliding it up into the roof held by catches; fold the seat up against the fuselage port side and provided the gun was in its un-stowed location under the nav

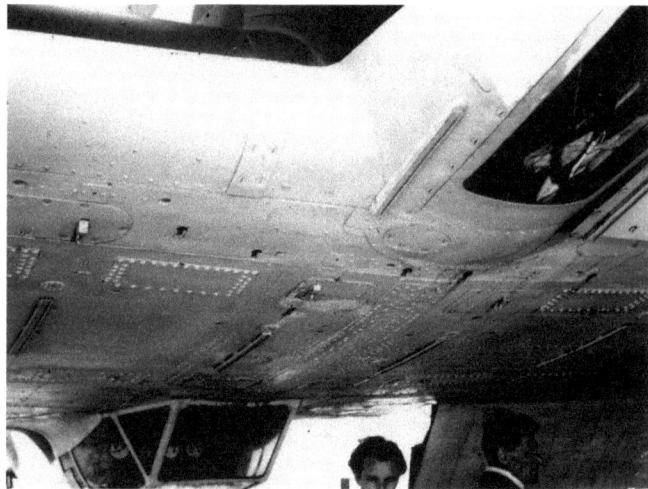

CA-4, A23-1001. The original flat screen of the rear ventral bomb-aimer's compartment & the pilot's undersurface viewing panel. November 12,1941 **David Anderson. A211 32715012011P**

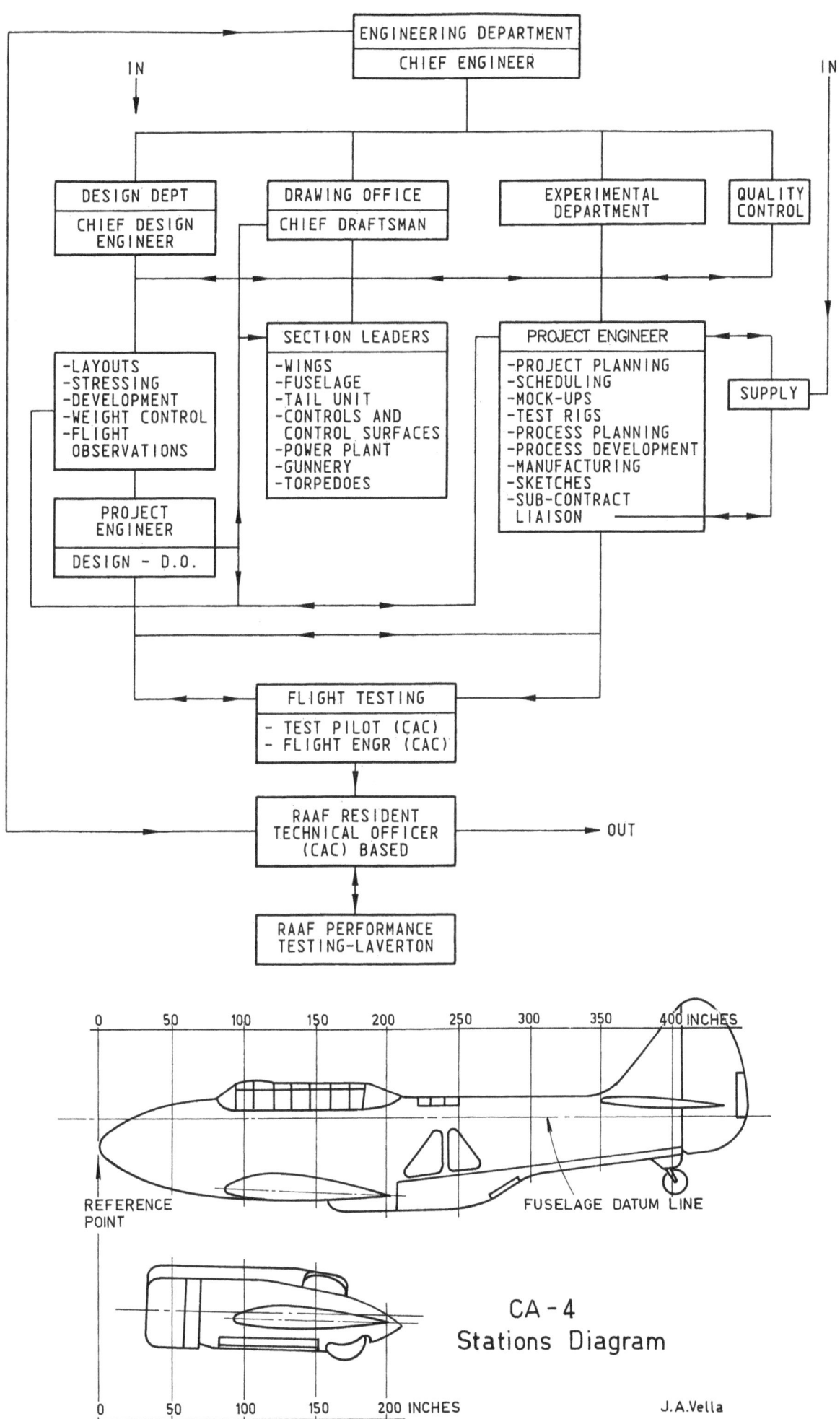

table, to then open the gun doors. The whole motion was timed to take 12 seconds. There was storage space for six 100 round ammunition magazines. To assist with navigation sight taking, large triangular clear vision panels were located on either side of the fuselage as well as a clear panel in the upper fuselage. Lacking a conventional bomb bay the CA-4 was designed to carry its bomb load under its centre section as well as four 250 lb bombs suspended one on either side of each main undercarriage leg in an enclosed lower engine nacelle. The outer wing panels fitted with light bomb carriers were limited to lifting a total of 8 x 40 lb bombs. The maximum bomb load was 3,320 lbs. Based on the CA-4 empty weight of 12, 385 lbs, a series of suggested mission / weapon loadings was:

Torpedo dropping (AUW 20,122 lb): Two Mk 12 or Mk 13 Model 1 torpedoes, each of 1,719 lb and 355 gall of fuel
Dive bombing (AUW 18,125 lb): Two 500 lb bombs and 420 gall of fuel
Long Range Bombing (AUW 20,124 lb): Four 250 lb bombs in the engine nacelles; two 500 lb bombs and 532 gall of fuel

Flight Testing

Company test pilot (Flt Lt) Hubert Boss-Walker carried out the first taxying trials on September 14, 1941 and again four days later. The wheel brakes were found to be inadequate in holding the aircraft at full throttle or in providing differential braking. The epic day for CAC for the first flight of A23-1001 was September 19, 1941 with all employees given time off to watch the event. Some 17 months had elapsed since plans were formulated and about ten months since the start of fabrication work.

Ian Fleming flew as test observer on nearly all occasions although Fred David flew twice to observe for himself a worrying and uncomfortable airframe vibration of a frequency of about five cycles per second. Wool tufting gave no indication of disturbed airflow over the tail surfaces in any flight condition but as the shuddering continued in the engines-out condition the problem was believed to originate from some aerodynamic disturbance. Most test flights had mechanical problems.

Two guns & ammunition chutes in place in each turret. The original intent was to fit four guns in each turret. *Reg Schulz.*

The vacant space above each wing behind each engine intended for the gun turret. The original engine oil coolers shown were subsequently modified. *Reg Schulz.*

Navigator's viewing panels seen to the rear of the cabin glasshouse. *Richard Hourigan.*

Mock-up of a torpedo carrying installation with a steadying arm braced at the navigator window frame. *David Anderson. 72412012P*

As the flight department grappled with the aerodynamic problems, Wackett felt progress was too slow as he wished to sell his bomber idea to the RAAF quickly. He needed new shop floor work. He blamed Hubert Boss-Walker for not having *his heart and soul* in the CA-4 and told him he was to be replaced on the project. Boss-Walker's pay was £650/year and £1 per flying hour plus £2/hour for CA-4 flight tests. The aircraft's mechanical problems frustrated Boss-Walker. He resigned immediately on October 10, 1941, rejoined the RAAF and moved to flight testing at 1AD, RAAF Base Laverton on November 18, 1941 from where he was to be eventually interned for eight months till December 1942. His place was taken by Ken Frewin, formerly with Holyman Airways Ltd and test pilot for Australian National Airways of their locally assembled Douglas DC-2s. His first flight on the CA-4 on October 11, 1941, was the CA-4's twelfth.

The gun turrets were removed to assist with isolating the source of the aerodynamic disturbance. Observations and handling anomalies included extreme turbulence and buffeting at around 103 kts (120mph) on the leading edge of the tailplane when the flaps were raised and lessening as the flaps were lowered; at the stall of 55 kts with engines on and flaps down, the aircraft would get very tail heavy and then drop on its nose with a rocking movement in the elevator. The airflow forward of the wing root trailing edge and around the rear engine nacelles was disturbed and this was attributed to a breakdown in the boundary layer when the aircraft approached the stall speed. This was caused by the 'wash' which occurred between the high set engine nacelles, the high fuselage sides and the low set wing. The immediate solution was to delay or eliminate the separation of the airflow by installing fairings at the previously un-faired fuselage / wing trailing edge and engine nacelle / wing junctions. Fairings had been proposed at the design stage but had been rejected for fear that they would impede on the navigator's side and downward vision. Random aerodynamic vibration was now thought to be linked with the tops of the un-faired ball-domed turrets, as dummy torpedoes which had been flight tested on two occasions produced no handling difficulties.

The aircraft was grounded for 21 days to carry out some engine maintenance and angling the main undercarriage legs forward an

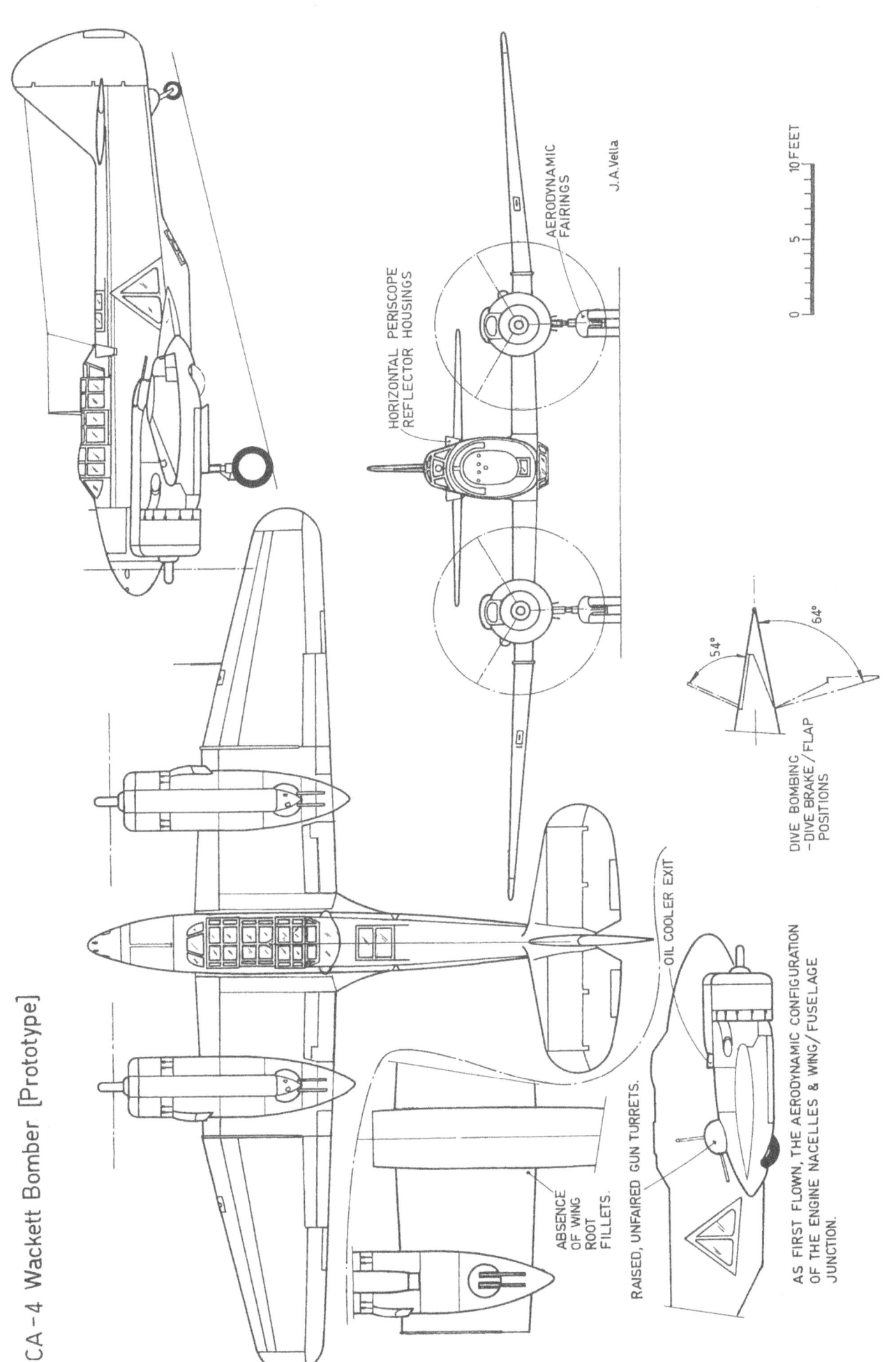

CA-4 front panel. Criticised by Special Duties Flight pilots at RAAF Laverton for 'its lack of systematic grouping of instruments' after having been earlier accepted by the RAAF. **Reg Schulz**

extra four inches to reduce the tendency of the aircraft to want to stand on its nose following the application of heavy braking. The aerodynamic fairings were put on the wing and the tops of the turrets were faired in by extending the oil cooler duct rearwards. Flight testing now revealed an improved fore and aft control but the turrets were still a source of turbulence. Flight 23, on November 13, 1941 was planned as a short demonstration flight for the benefit of the Australian Prime Minister, senior defence personnel and the visiting Air Chief Marshal Sir Robert Brooke-Popham, Air Officer Commander- in- Chief Far East (Singapore). It provided some surprises.

Following lift-off at 1105 hrs at the end of a 1,290 foot run, the aircraft was displayed then dived three times at 206 kts (242 mph) in front of the viewing audience but as it prepared to land at 1120 hrs the port undercarriage would not lock, in-spite of its appearance to be fully lowered. Attempts to lock down the leg through violent pitching movements were to no avail; the emergency hand pump produced no result. An attempt was made to release the four dummy 250 lb weight bombs in the engine nacelles also failed. (Subsequent investigation revealed the circuit had not been wired in.)

The flight observer Ian Fleming dropped a notebook over the airfield outlining the crew's situation and their proposed plan of action. The aircraft was then flown down to impact the lowered port leg with the runway. This kicked back the leg through three quarters of its travel and it stuck there confirming the lack of down-lock. The aircraft landed on the retracted right undercarriage. Both wheels cushioned the impact with minimum damage after the aircraft slid some 540 feet to a stop.

This episode was quickly discovered to have been a case of sabotage. The sequence valve on the strut down lock had been deliberately hammered; sand placed in the top of the strut and brass machine turnings put in the hydraulic reservoir. This event, together with a number of his other personal activities and without sufficient proof was to bring Hubert Boss-Walker under suspicion from the authorities.

Replacement engines were promised by DAP and sent overnight as rail freight from Lidcombe, NSW to Melbourne's Spencer Street railway station. Wackett raised a storm when he discovered the wrong engines had been sent causing a delay of four days. The aircraft flew again on December 8, 1941 fitted with an aerodynamic fairing between the twin wheels of the main undercarriage. Dural hydraulic pipe lines were replaced by steel lines to prevent further leaks. These new fairings increased the aerodynamic pressure on the undercarriage and the hydraulic pressure was insufficient to lock it down at the usual speed of 130 kts.

The following day the aircraft took off at a weight of 18,250 lb corresponding to full load for maximum range, full crew complement, all guns and ammunition, representing an aircraft taking off from Darwin for a non-stop flight to Singapore. The take-off run was 1,460 ft. At maximum design diving speed of 208 kts (240 mph), the CA-4 showed admirable handling qualities with a dive commencing at 10,000 ft followed by pull-out at 3,000 ft with a further 1,000 ft needed to flatten out. Deceleration from diving speed to torpedo dropping speed was also very rapid. From this flight on the aircraft was to be plagued by hydraulic system problems interfering with the planned flight routine. The CSIR were introduced to the CA-4 for a short series of performance and handling trials on three days commencing on December 16, 1941. It amassed 3.5 hours over three flights, two of which had to be cut short because of engine problems and more failures in the extremely complex hydraulic system. The aircraft was flown by CAC's Ken Frewin, flight observer Ian Fleming together with T. Laurence, the observer from CSIR.

Metal propellers of 11ft 6ins diameter were fitted prior to the start of these trials. It was found to have extremely poor brakes. The elevator control was deemed inadequate to lower the tail down for a three point landing. Fuel was seeping from the upper surface of the port wing at the intersection of the walkway and front spar. Brief handling trials were then conducted on 19 December by Flt Lt James Harper, Officer-In-Charge of the Special Duties Flight at Laverton. The RAAF became involved so as to form a judgement if the multi-role design should continue. He noted lateral instability, a lack of a true stall even with the stick held right back and successive stalling and un-stalling of the tailplane. Because of a very heavy aileron circuit he

A23-1001, November 13,1941 the wheels-up landing following u/c failure at Fisherman's Bend airfield. Periscope housing on either fuselage side casts a dark shadow above the navigator's viewing panel. **Reg Schulz.**

CA-4. CAC staff inspecting the splintered wooden props. November 13,1941 after test Flight 23. **David Anderson. A211 25715012004P**

recommended the use of spectacle type of control in lieu of the control stick.

The cockpit layout was criticised for its lack of systematic grouping of instruments in spite of its earlier acceptance by the Air Force mock-up conference. Even with the cowl gills fully-open engine cooling was not adequate for standard summer temperatures. On Flight no 43, the first for 1942 on 3 January, new fairings were fitted between the wheels of the main undercarriage. These were an improvement eliminating wheel buffet and allowed the undercarriage to be down and locked at 120 kts in six seconds. Hydraulic problems persisted and these were seen as a possible big hurdle in the future deployment of the aircraft. A horizontal tail of increased area was flown on February 5, 1942. This gave better feel and balance and it was now possible to sort out other handling shortfalls which called for an increase in outer wing dihedral and an enlarged fin. Further refinement eight days later saw a reduction of tail incidence from 5° to 2° 30' bringing an immediate steadier ride and elimination of the fore/aft hunting.

It was also decided to revert to the original smaller tail and elevators with the reduced incidence setting and to install P-40 Kittyhawk style large wing root/fuselage fairings. On April 20, 1942 the prototype CA-4 was delivered to 1 AD, Laverton, were it sat in storage for long periods. In November it suffered a taxying accident with the port undercarriage leg and was returned for repairs to CAC on 22 December.

Armament Trials -The Turret and Sight Systems

Armament trials were conducted over a three day period while the aircraft was attached to the Special Duties and Performance Flight at Laverton. To check the correctness of the no-allowance cam sight head it was necessary to set up the conditions for which the sight operation had been designed. In the first instance the CA-4 was not able to fly at the optimum 260 kts at 15,000 ft, whilst for the attack case it was not possible to make a towed target sleeve perform the desired evolutions. Of 4,350 rounds fired at a sleeve towed by a Fairey Battle at 100 kts at 2,000 ft only 13 hits were obtained – a completely unsatisfactory result.

Independent trial of the turret control system by Flt Lt W.Davenport-Brown DFC (RAF), an air gunner with extensive operational experience with various gun turrets resulted in no hits from 1,460 rounds fired during simulated fighter runs against a sleeve target. The Vickers guns in the turrets jammed frequently when tilted to steep firing angles and were replaced by Browning Mk II 0.303 inch guns. In flight, the turrets would not follow the control stick in simultaneous elevation and traverse. They would not traverse at a constant angle but would depress immediately the stick was pushed across for traversing and would then elevate again to the original position as soon as the traverse movement ceased. This aspect made accurate and quick sighting extremely difficult.

The upper sight was good to use but the lower sight and the view through the periscope of an evading target was greatly hampered by a loss of transmitted light and whilst the gunner scanned the sky for a target the guns wondered randomly off the target until they reached their traversing limits needing to be brought back to point at a selected target. This brought about a consequent loss of opportunity because of the time taken to slew the guns to the selected target.

Expansion of the hydraulic lines and an acknowledged lack of system rigidity contributed to the slow control response. As the attacking fighter manoeuvred and the CA-4 evaded, the gunner found it impossible to keep track of the target through his sights, climbing in and out of the deep foot wells, swinging the sight head on its circular track with one hand and operating an oversensitive turret control stick and the gun firing button with the other hand. A fighter 3,000 ft astern weaving moderately against an earth background was easily lost sight of, creating a frantic searching between left and right periscope reflectors and /or viewing through the upper direct sight.

The maximum rates of turret rotation were:
Traverse   (through 150 ° in both directions) was 33 °/sec
Depression (through 94°) was 27 °/ sec
Elevation   (through 94°) was 14°/ sec

These were judged to be too slow and the generalizations / limitations set by Wackett as to the expected fall of the bullets were easily swept aside if either or both the CA-4 and the attacking aircraft did not fly to the design criteria to which the sight head had been set. The defensive fire of the guns was limited to 75° forward from the tail; where 90° was needed.

Davenport-Brown rejected the no-allowance sight head completely. He suggested a simpler version with an increased field of view and replacing the turret control stick by a fixed twist grip alternative. To combat the effects of fatigue and provide for greater aiming accuracy a rotating seat was suggested. Another point of concern was the integrity of the interrupter gear, which though robust would, If not properly maintained or if it failed in flight, result in the tail of the aircraft or the navigator being shot up. Re-arming of the turret guns was very slow and very difficult. Links and spent cases lying on the wing surface under the turret could only be scooped out by hand via a small access hole which added to the precariousness of the operation by the 26 °of down slope on the upper wing.

Other Armament and Ordinance

The field of fire of the ventral gun was good but firing it from a kneeling position of maximum depression angle under manoeuvring high g-forces was almost impossible. The forward guns were satisfactory in the air but were a maintenance, access and re-arming nightmare, requiring the manhandling of heavy items in tight confined working spaces some eight feet above the ground. The ammunition and gun cowlings needed the releasing and tightening of over 100 fasteners. Re-arming into ammunition bins in situ was not possible.

The bomb carrier installation was similar to that on the Wirraway with release slips built into the wing and nose/tail steadies and fusing rails screwed on externally. Bombing up in the engine nacelles ie stations 5, 6, 7 and 8 was awkward because of the small confines and the presence of oil seepage. The CA-4 was assessed to be a fair, low and high level day bomber and dive bomber. It exhibited sloppy rudder control with a series of swings as the rudder was used

	DAP Beaufort VIII	CAC CA-4 Wackett Bomber
Engines	2 x 1,200 hp P & W R-1830 S3C4-G radials	2 x 1,100 hp CAC R-1830 S3C3-G radials
Crew	Four	Three
Max speed	230 kts (268 mph)	236 kts (275 mph)
Wing Span	57 ft 10 ins	59 ft 2.5 ins
Length	44 ft 3 ins	37 ft 3 ins
Height	14 ft 3 ins	13 ft 6 ins
Weight loaded	22,500 lb	20,124 lb
Guns	Four	Nine
Torpedoes	One	Two
Bombs	1,500 lb	2,000 lb

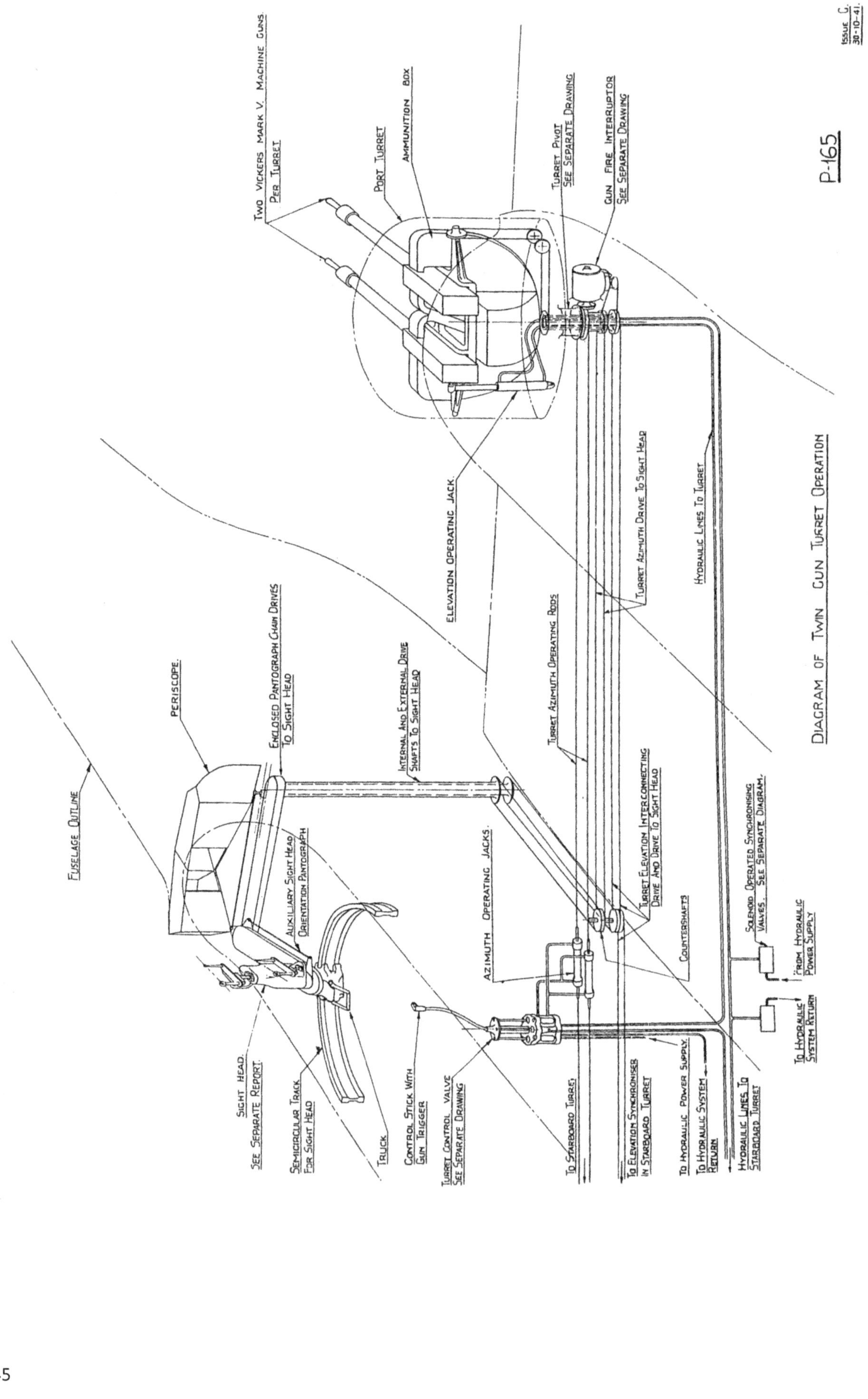

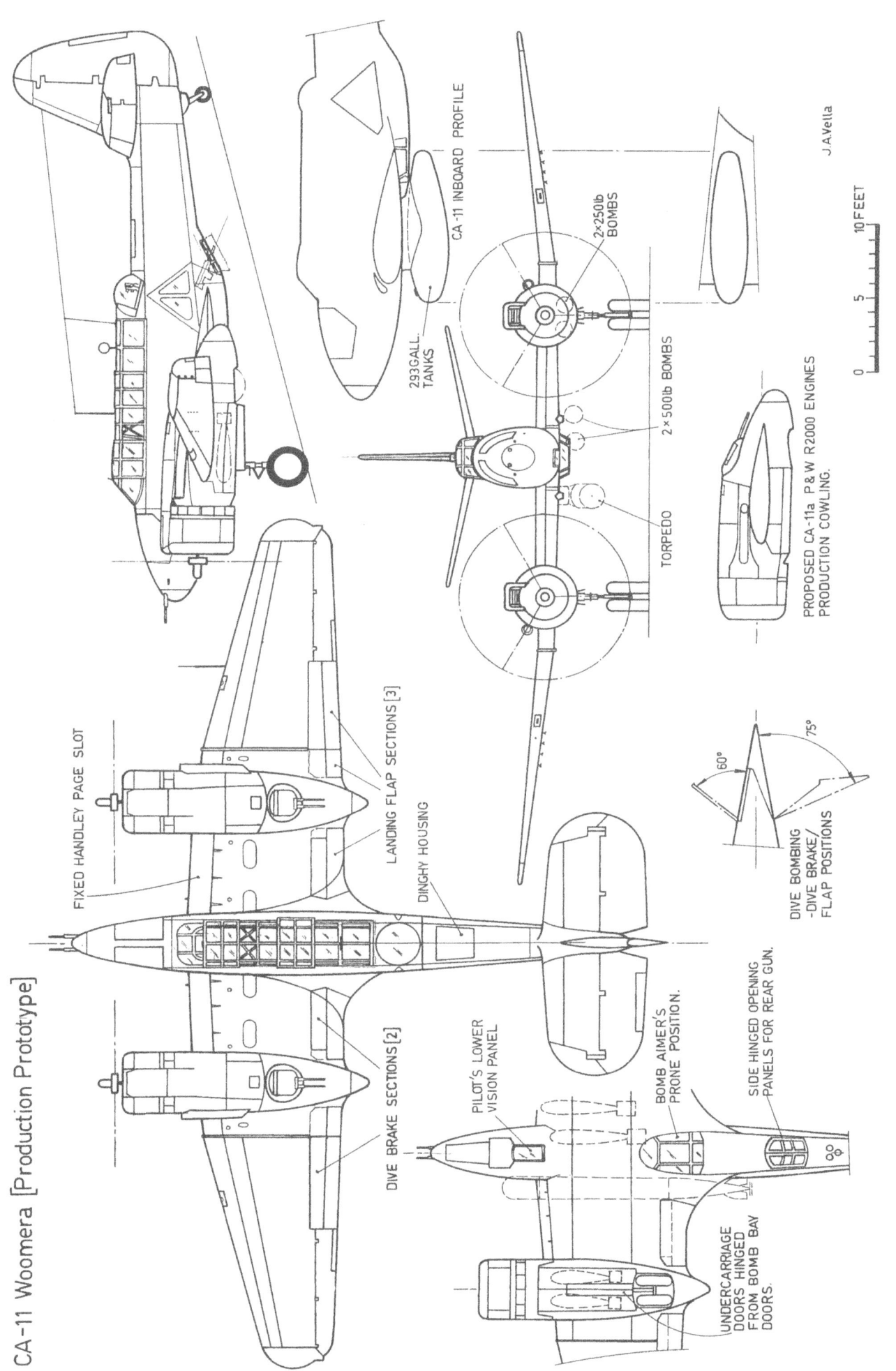

Repaired after its bell-landing accident. New Curtiss Electric metal props, gun ports sealed, pilot's lower clear vision panel under the nose & the bomb-aimer's viewing panel is now curved. The CAC logo is in the centre of the landing gear covers **Reg Schulz**

A23-1001, repaired after the belly-landing accident. . **Reg Schulz**

CA-4 over the Werribee racecourse, west of CAC. Clear view of the dummy torpedoes without any steadying arms.
David Anderson. 31717012072P

Test pilot Ken Frewin. December 1941. Left side periscope assembly at rear of cabin glasshouse **David Anderson CAC Neg 14-724012033P**

to counter two engines spaced 19 feet apart. In aspects of re-arming, bombing up and defence armament maintenance the CA-4 was considered unsatisfactory. Wackett submitted four patent applications (nos 414,486,459,968) of two parts of his gun-sighting mechanism to the USA on September 28,1942 . There was no take-up.

CSIR Wind Tunnel Investigations

The Division of Aeronautics of the CSIR carried out a series of wind tunnel investigations into the handling problems of the CA-4 in the first half of 1942. Using one-sixth and one-tenth scale wooden models it was possible to see the very bad wing / fuselage junction which together with the engine nacelles was causing a premature airflow separation at low angles of attack followed by a sudden loss of lift and a wide turbulent wake in the region of the tailplane. No fillets of a reasonable size would completely remove the stall. The most effective manner of improving the flow conditions was to raise the wing to the mid fuselage position but as this was not likely to happen the next most effective solution was to install a fixed leading edge slot between the fuselage and the engine nacelles.

Ken Frewin was dismissed on 14 July and following his subsequent resignation on August 18, 1942 corresponded directly with the Minister of Aircraft Production on July 23, 1942. He commented on his heavy test workload; the disintegration in flight of the untested wooden propeller on the CA-12; the manner of the CA-4 test flights, highlighting his differences with CAC management about his requests for, but non-response for alterations he had wanted carried out on the CA-4 before his test flights. Ken also wrote to Charles Lumby at the US Lend Lease Mission in Sydney on September 16, 1942 critical of the experimental nature of the CA-4 and the need for there to be a lot to be done to bring it up to production standard.

Aircraft Lost

Tragedy struck the CA-4 program on January 15, 1943 part way through its armament trials. The aircraft had lifted off from Fisherman's Bend flown by the recently promoted Sqdn Ldr James Harper. The flight had a dual purpose. It was to familiarize CAC's new test pilot, James Carter prior to his taking charge of CA-4 testing. This was his first flight in the CA-4.

The second reason was to evaluate the aerodynamic performance of a fixed wing leading edge slot (as suggested by the CSIR) which had been fitted on 1 January. Lionel Dudgeon, the section leader draftsman responsible for the design of the slot went along as observer. Ted Faggetter and Reg Schulz were last minute withdrawals from the flight.

The aircraft had completed the test and was returning home when fuel was seen seeping out of the port engine area. With reluctance because of the high weight of the aircraft, the electric feathering switch on the Curtiss propeller was activated. The immediate internal explosion from the petrol fumes in the cockpit blew Harper clear of the aircraft to a lucky escape. Flying at 1,000 ft altitude, Carter's parachute hadn't had time to fully open and Dudgeon down in the bomb aiming part of the fuselage did not escape. Both were killed, the only occasion CAC was to ever lose its flight test personnel in an accident. Fuel leakage and its build up in the tail section had been reported previously. Reg Schulz told the author he had (as was to be expected) developed serious concern

The degree of build complexity is apparent in this view of open panels and hydraulic piping in the CA-11. **HDHV**

A23-1 on display resting on jacks displaying good detail of a long range tank to port & a torpedo to starboard underside. **HDHV**

Open access panels on the forward armament bay as final assembly on the CA-11 continues. **Reg Schulz**

The rear gun aimer's position has been revised & the glass house canopy has been extended. Pressure rake struts are mounted ahead of the horizontal tail to test for disturbed air flow. **Reg Schulz.**

The CA-11 resting on its undercarriage for the first time. Note the larger oil cooler intakes and the nose cannon **Reg Schulz.**

A23-1 close-up of the much revised and improved engine cowlings for the CAC P & W R1830-S1C3-G engines. Aircraft CA-11A, A23-2 was fitted with the CAC R2000 engines. **David Anderson.**

Two 293 gallon long range tanks on the CA-11 main under-fuselage pick-up stations. **Reg Schulz.**

Dihedral has been applied to the horizontal tail. The aircraft is in all-over foliage green camouflage finish with the yellow prototype 'P' symbol. RAAF Laverton. **David Anderson**

CA-11 Woomera Front Cockpit Layout and Instrumentation

1. Flaps control lever
2. Throttle controls
3. Pitch controls
4. Elevator trim tab control
5. Hydraulic hand pump
6. Undercarriage selector lever
7. Tail wheel lock
8. Rudder trim tab control
9. Aileron trim tab control
10. Compass
11. Control grip
12. HF wireless control box
13. Airspeed indicator
14. Artificial horizon
15. Rate of climb indicator
16. Altimeter
17. Directional gyro
18. Turn and bank indicator
19. Automatic pilot control panel
20. Magneto switches
21. Feathering buttons
22. Gills control lever port
23. Gills control lever starboard
24. Suction gauges
25. Cylinder temperature gauges
26. Outside air temperature gauge
27. Magnesyn compass
28. Hydraulic pressure gauge
29. Port/starboard inner and outer fuel contents gauges
30. Oil shutter control
31. Bomb selector switches
32. Mixture controls
33. Manifold pressure gauges
34. Engine tachometers
35. Oil and fuel pressure, and oil temperature gauges combined
36. Dashboard light
37. Starter buttons
38. Undercarriage, bomb doors, camera door position lights
39. Aircraft voltmeter
40. Fuel cock controls
41. Selector switches
42. Generator main switch
43. Fuel cock control panel
44. Bomb distributor panel
45. Engine fire extinguisher
46. Cockpit lighting rheostat
47. Formation lights
48. Pilot's seat

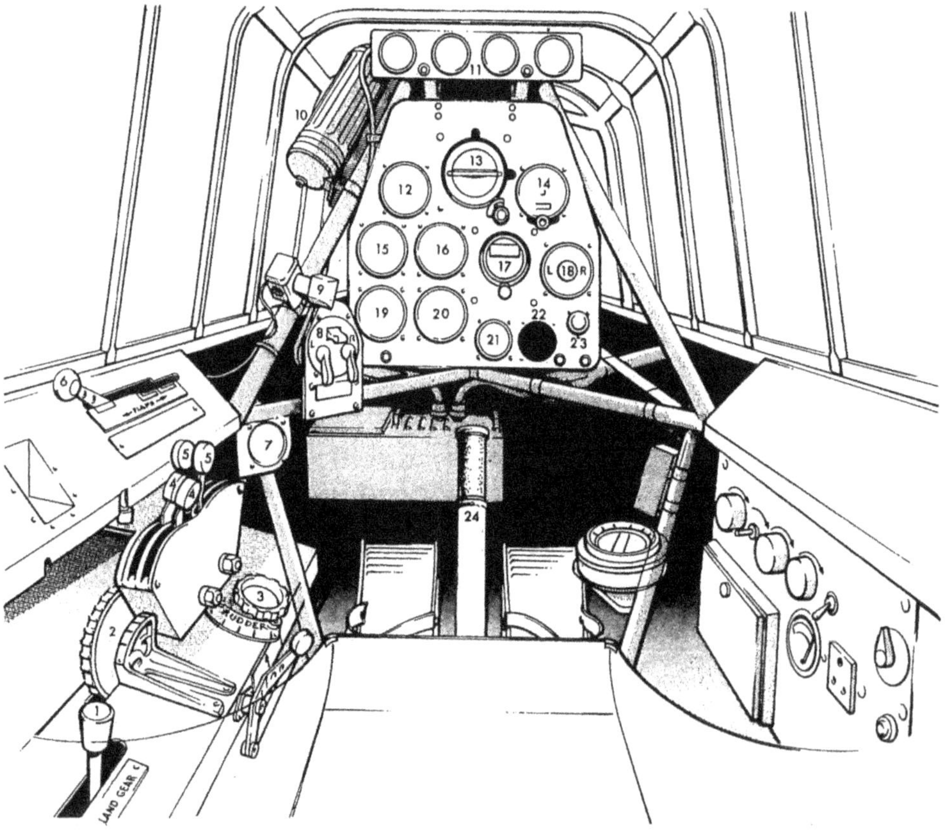

CA-11 Woomera Rear Cockpit Layout and Instrumentation

1. Undercarriage selector lever
2. Elevator trim tab control
3. Rudder trim tab control
4. Pitch controls
5. Throttle controls
6. Flaps control lever
7. Hydraulic pressure gauge
8. Magneto switches
9. Dashboard light
10. Fire extinguisher
11. Fuel contents gauges
12. Airspeed indicator
13. Artificial horizon
14. Altimeter
15. Port manifold pressure gauge
16. Starboard manifold pressure gauge
17. Directional gyro
18. Turn and bank indicator
19. RPM indicator port
20. RPM indicator starboard
21. Suction gauge
22. Position of aircraft clock
23. Undercarriage warning light
24. Control column

Reproduced from AIR ENTHUSIAST QUARTERLY No. 1

Specifications	CA-4 Wackett Bomber			
Powerplant	Two Pratt & Whitney R1830 S3C3-G Twin Wasp 14 cyl radial engines with a single stage (8:1) supercharger driving 3 bladed Curtiss Electric constant speed, fully feathering 11 ft 6 inch diameter propellers.(Clockwise rotation as viewed from the pilot's position). Rated at 1,100 hp at 2,700 rpm at TO. 950 hp at 2,700 rpm to 14,000 ft in continuous climb. Cruising at 700 hp at 2,200 rpm to 13,200 ft. (Port engine no. 1443. Starboard engine no. 1340– Ref. CSIR Report F.1)			
Performance	Max speed (clean)	230 kts		
	Max speed with two torpedoes at 9,000 ft	228 kts		
	Initial climb rate (clean)	1,900 ft/min		
	Initial climb rate with external stores	1,600 ft/min		
	Service ceiling	22,000 ft		
	Max range, one torpedo & 293 gall external tank	1,720 nm		
	Internal fuel capacity	532 gall		
	Oil capacity	32 gall		
Weights	Empty	12,385 lb		
	Loaded	20,124 lb		
Dimensions	Wing span	59 ft 1 in	Wing root chord	9 ft 6 ins
	Mean chord	7.44 ft	Tip chord	4 ft 1 in
	Aspect ratio	7.95	Wing area	440 sq ft
	Airfoil section NACA 2218.6 (Root)		Airfoil section NACA 2209 (Tip)	
	Centre section dihedral	1° 1.5'	Outer panel dihedral	5°
	Sweep back centre section at 25% chord	1° 28'	Sweep back outer panels at 25% chord	9° 37'
	Length	39 ft 6.75 ins	Height (tail down)	13 ft 9 ins
	Height (tail up)	18 ft 3 ins	Upper outer flap span	71.5 ins
	Upper mid flap span	29.5 ins	Upper inner flap span	61.5 ins
	Lower outer flap span	71.5 ins	Lower mid flap span	29.5 ins
	Lower inner flap span	61.5 ins	Diving flap area	19.65 sq ft
	Lower flap area	48.8 sq ft	Track	19 ft 3 ins
	Main wheels dia	31 ins		
Armament	Four fixed, nose mounted, 0.303 in Vickers Mk V m/gs with 800 rpg. One Vickers 'K' Mk 1 G.O. m/g in rear of ventral step with 600 rounds Two 0.303 in Browning Mk II m/gs in each of two remotely controlled barbettes with 1,070 rounds in each turret Four 250 lb bombs in engine nacelle bays Eight 20 lb or 40 lb bombs under the outer wing panels Four 500 lb bombs (or two 1,000 lb or one 2,000 lb bomb) or two Mk 12 or Mk 13 Model 1 torpedoes under centre section Combinations of these loads to a maximum of 3,420 lb including carriers, cradles etc.			
Retrospective Designation	XP11			

The only CA-11 to be fully completed and fly. A markedly different looking aircraft to the earlier CA-4 prototype. **Reg Schulz.**

Specifications	CA-11 / CA-11A Woomera Bomber			
Powerplant	CA-11: Two CAC Pratt & Whitney R1830 S3C3-G Twin Wasp 14 cyl radial engines with a single stage (9.15:1) supercharger driving 3 bladed De Havilland Hydromatic 23E50 fully feathering 11 ft 6 inch diameter propellers.(Clockwise rotation as viewed from the pilot's position). Rated at 1,200 hp at 2,700 rpm at TO. 1,050 hp at 2,250 rpm to 7,500 ft in continuous climb. Cruising at 700 hp at 2,250 rpm to 13,500 ft. (Port engine no. 84. Starboard engine no. 420 – Ref. RAAF Report) CA-11A: Two CAC R2000 Twin Wasp 14 cyl radial engines rated at 1,350 hp for TO			
Performance	Max speed (clean)		240 kts	
	Max speed with two torpedoes at 9,000 ft		234 kts	
	Cruising speed at 8,000 ft		195 kts	
	Initial climb rate (clean)		2,090 ft/min	
	Initial climb rate with external stores		1,750 ft/min	
	Service ceiling 23,500 ft			
	Max range, one torpedo & 293 gall external tank		1,900 nm	
	Internal fuel capacity		596 gall	
	Oil capacity		44 gall	
Weights	Empty		12,756 lb	
	Loaded		2,885 lb	
Dimensions	Wing span	59 ft 2.5 ins	Wing root chord	9 ft 6 ins
	Mean chord	7.41 ft	Wing tip chord	4 ft 1 in
	Aspect ratio	8.0	Wing area	440 sq ft
	Airfoil section NACA 2218.6 (Root)		Airfoil section NACA 2209 (Tip)	
	Centre section dihedral	1° 1.5′	Outer panel dihedral	5°
	Sweep back centre section at 25% chord	1° 28′	Sweep back outer panels at 25% chord	9° 37′
	Height (tail up)	17 ft	Height (tail down)	13 ft 6 ins
	Upper outer flap span	69 ins	Upper mid flap not fitted	
	Upper inner flap span	49 ins	Lower outer flap span	69 ins
	Lower mid flap span	24 ins	Lower inner flap span	56 ins
	Track	19 ft 2 ins	Main wheel dia	31 ins
	Tail wheel dia	18 ins	Length	37 ft 3 ins
Armament	Two fixed, nose mounted, 20 mm Hispano cannon with 120 rpg Two fixed nose mounted 0.303 in Browning m/gs with 600 rpg Two 0.303 in Browning Mk II m/gs in each of two remotely controlled barbettes with 1,070 rounds in each turret (but could possibly have been replaced by 0.50 in calibre) Four 250 lb bombs in engine nacelle bays Eight 20 lb or 40 lb bombs under the outer wing panels Four 500 lb bombs (or two 1,000 lb or one 2,000 lb bomb) or two Mk 12 or Mk 13 Model 1 torpedoes under centre section Combinations of these loads to a maximum of 3,420 lb including carriers, cradles etc.			
Retrospective Designation	XP15			

Gregory Board. CA-11 test pilot; Wirraway & Boomerang production test pilot. **HDHV**

CA-11 rear cockpit front instrument panel. **Reg Schulz**.

waiting for news past the bomber's four o'clock scheduled return time.

The aircraft crashed in a flat attitude three miles south-west of Kilmore, Victoria. On January 18, 1943, 26 RSU (Repair & Salvage Unit) recovered the virtually intact wreck and delivered it to 1 AD the following day followed by approval to convert it to components on 26 February.

The CA-11 Woomera

In the interim and as an outcome of the tests with the CA-4, plans had been formulated for the production variant, the CA-11 *Woomera* (an indigenous aboriginal language for 'throwing stick').

An order for 200,000 lb of aluminium was placed with Alcoa in January 1942. RAAF Specification 2/42 for a long range fighter/ torpedo/ dive bombing aircraft issued on March 8, 1942 requested 105 production examples, A23-1 to 105, construction of which was expected to start in January, building up to 20 aircraft each month.

Five days earlier on March 3, 1942 the DAP Demand No 715 on CAC valued the forthcoming CA-11 production as:

105 complete aircraft at £32,500 ea.	£3,412,500
Spares	£52,500
210 engines & propellers	£1,835,000
Total	£5,300,000

The production order was not an easy task to take on with an estimated 800,000 hours or 80 weeks required for production tooling. This was impossible to achieve within the given time. The factory had a production capacity of 300,000 hours each month which could be realised as either 40-50 fighters requiring 6,000 - 7,000 hours each or 12-15 bombers requiring 20,000 -25,000 hours each but not both types simultaneously. Parallel fighter and bomber production would have needed an outlay of £80,000 on new buildings and the employment of 2,200 additional personnel.

The output of 15 aircraft each month fell short of the RAAF requirement of 20 aircraft so the gap was to be made up by a scheme of external sub-contracting of almost the entire bomber. CAC would manufacture a first batch to verify engineering and production methods and would also provide the space for final assembly. Whilst the company's pre-occupation was with the initial start-up of the Boomerang fighter production, the whole of the machine tools were transferred from the aircraft factory to a new machine shop building so as to allow fuselage assembly to take place. The difficulty in locating the extra toolmakers that were needed was a matter of great concern as was the Chief of Air Staff's (Air Commodore George Jones) expressed worry in November 1942 at the slow progress with the CA-4 trails added to the criticisms raised by the CSIR.

Wind tunnel testing at ARL commenced in February 1943 but a letter from the DAP of 10 February advised of the Air Board's decision to limit production to an initial 20 aircraft pending verification of the CA-11's ability to meet its operational role. However it was not till August 2, 1944 that the RAAF officially released Manufacturing Specification 2/42 (Issue 2) concerning the 20 aircraft.

Priority in the drawing offices was given to CA-11 over the parallel CA-15 fighter design so as to be able to release drawings to the sub-contractors, whereas on the shop floor there was still Government indecision as to whether CAC was to build the CA-11 or the Douglas C-47 under licence. This situation was not clarified until Douglas Aircraft (USA) made it known in February 1943 that Australia could not expect to receive any material, engineering, tooling or manpower assistance whatsoever with this large undertaking unless the US Government insisted that the Douglas Company had to do so; Douglas was very hard pressed.

The war equipment situation in the Pacific had started to change. Torpedo and dive bombers were superseded by heavily armed attack bombers such as the B-25 Mitchell and A-20 Boston. There was also the promise of B-24 Liberator heavy bombers for the RAAF and the RAAF's perceived need was for a dive bombing / attack aircraft rather than a torpedo carrier. In spite of numerous difficulties created by sub-contractors failing to succeed with development work the pressure was still maintained until the tooling task was finally completed in January 1944. Some of the larger outside contractors which as of February 17, 1943 had become designated suppliers of major CA-11 components were:

Australian Metal Productions- bomb and undercarriage doors, gun turrets
Brookes Robinson - cockpit enclosures, bomb aimer's windscreen and ventral enclosure
Shell Australia - gun turrets
Southern Panel - ventral gun doors
Myttons Pty Ltd - flaps
James Kirby - main undercarriage
Australian Chemical Industries - wheel hubs
Dunlop - tyres, self- sealing tanks
General Motors- Holden (Woodville, S.Aust) - external fuel tanks (50 units delivered), oil tanks (60 units delivered) and monocque nose
Ruskins Motor Bodies - wingtips
Richards Industries Ltd (Mile End, S. Aust) - ailerons, complete empennage

Sufficient components had been received at the beginning of November 1943 to commence assembly of ten aircraft. A23-1 had its wing centre section fitted and was sitting on its undercarriage by January 4, 1944. Nine fuselages were in evidence by the end of February and whatever manpower could be spared was directed towards bringing the first Woomera to flying status.

This aircraft was powered by a pair of Pratt & Whitney R-1830-S1C3-G engines whereas the definitive production model was to have CAC built R-2000 radials. By July 1944 two of the five test R-2000 engines had been installed in the CA-11A, A23-2, the second Woomera on the line. The front of its engine nacelles had been altered to accept the geared cooling fan of the R-2000. Additionally it was hoped to fit the so called CAC 40°, three bladed wooden propellers on the aircraft. The choice of engine for the CA-11 was the subject of long speculation. Production of the Bristol Beaufort bomber by the DAP factories was as of June 1942 expected to cease with the 450th example. It would then have been succeeded by a higher powered Wright Cyclone R-2600B variant or by an entirely new aircraft such as the CA-11. 252 examples of the Twin Wasp engine including spares were needed for the CA-11 but the planned S1C3-G local production could not meet the demand for both the CAC bomber and the production blocks of the DAP Beaufort.

To help alleviate this difficulty 600 Wright Cyclone (1,600hp) engines were sought from the USA in February 1942. The Joint Aircraft Committee in the United States agreed to supply 145 examples but then refused (on March 1942) to make any further allocations beyond ten Wright R-2600B-8 or -13 engines for use in CA-4 development until such time as trials had taken place. As time moved on this prospect lapsed.

There were structural differences between the CA-11 refined for production and the CA-4 which had served its purpose as a trials and development machine. The opportunity was taken to include a

number of quick release or hinged access panels to reduce the large number of fasteners; to incorporate fixed slots on the wing leading edge; to increase the outer wing dihedral and completely redesign and enlarge the tail assembly. The rear fuselage upper decking was cut and a dinghy stowage compartment created in the area where there had previously been a navigator's clear vision sighting panel. The glass house canopy enclosing the three crew members was almost doubled in length. Plans to incorporate a locally developed two pounder gun as front armament were abandoned in favour of two Hispano 20mm cannon.

The remote gun turrets were retained, but R. W. Cameron & Co Inc, CAC's representatives in the USA and Austimpro in Washington were experiencing difficulties trying to acquire the General Electric fully automated, remotely operated turrets developed for the B-29 Superfortress bomber to replace the CA-4's troublesome hydraulic turret control. Electrically driven, with two 0.5 inch m/gs and targeting calculated by analogue computers, the system had impressed Wackett during his overseas aircraft evaluation mission of 1943. Two sets of the GE remote control units would not be available till December 1944.

Following the improvement suggestions made about the CA-4, the rear gunner was now seated under a moulded Perspex sighting turret. The pilot's instrument panel was re-organised according to function; a spectacle type control wheel was introduced; an automatic pilot was installed and a reflector gun sight was fitted on a swivel arm that could be swung across out of the way when not required.

Wing fuel capacity was increased slightly to 596 gallons. On July 1, 1944 Reg Schulz was appointed Production Superintendent of the Aircraft Division and Les Scascighini became the bomber's project engineer. The aircraft was ready to fly on May 3, 1944 but the self-sealing fuel tanks were leaking badly due to faulty workmanship and needed rectification. Wackett warned that their contractor provider would not be trusted with similar work on the follow-on CA-17 Mustang.

At 1150 hours on July 7, 1944 CAC test pilot, Greg Board, flying solo, lifted A23-1 at an all up weight of 16,150 lb into a grey morning sky. The flight lasted 35 minutes. The CA-11 showed improved rudder and elevator control and better ground handling, but there was a new slow, uneven aerodynamic vibration which persisted up to about 220 kts. To obtain a second opinion on the source and extent of the vibrations, Sqdn Ldr Derek R. Cuming from 1 Aircraft Performance Unit with previous CA-4 handling experience took the aircraft up on 20 July . Greg Board flying a Boomerang accompanied the Woomera for close-in aerial observations. This was fruitful as he saw the tips of the tailplane moving vertically through about six inches and the entire rear fuselage vibrating in a torsional mode. Tufting attached to the engine nacelles / gun turrets showed a violent pattern of airflow similar to that of the CA-4, only worse.

From the eight to the thirteenth flight, observations were taken with a cine-camera and a pressure rake strut mounted ahead of the horizontal tail. This revealed the presence of disturbed air under the tail which subsequent alterations to the contours of the rear of the nacelles had not eliminated. It wasn't until the 17th flight on 27 October that a marked improvement was observed when 12° of dihedral was applied to the horizontal tail. Wind tunnel tests had missed this. The problem of fuel leakage returned (which was not expected with rubber self-sealing tanks) necessitating the temporary isolation of the outer nacelle fuel tanks. Empty external 293 gallon capacity long range tanks were air tested and found to reduce airspeed by 10-15kts. The Air Board approved the name *Woomera* on August 9, 1944.

The Inevitable End

The project was terminated on September 27, 1944 (as had the CA-15 fighter). In an operational sense dive bombing was no longer an urgent requirement so late in the war. The DAP Beaufort, although criticized by the American S.W. Pacific Command for some aspects of its performance was to remain the mainstay torpedo bomber for the RAAF. The need was for offensive defence aircraft, where both the operationally tested de Havilland Mosquito and the DAP Beaufighter built locally, fitted the requirement. It had been claimed in July 1943 that the CA-11 was to be capable of twice the range of the DAP Beaufort when used as a torpedo carrier. With the demise of the CA-11 the Australian War Cabinet hoped for the release of about 400 personnel to the more urgent task of producing the CA-17/18 Mustang.

Twenty Woomera fuselages were complete but only ten centre sections had been finished to September, the rest of the major components including all completed outer wing sections, were put into storage pending disposal action. CAC completed two more flights on 1 & 2 November prior to grounding the aircraft for rectifications by which time Greg Board had built up 17.4 hours of air time on 18 flights. On November 21, 1944 the aircraft was handed over to 1 APU at RAAF Laverton where further flying was to be carried out to complete type trials and form a brief performance assessment. Flying went from April to August 1945 at a slow pace, hampered by bad weather and poor serviceability mainly attributable (again) to the hydraulic system. Reports of the day indicate that the CA-11 possessed more predictable and improved ground and air handling qualities than displayed by the CA-4.

With the conclusion of the trials the aircraft was transferred to 1 Central Recovery Depot at Werribee, Victoria on December 20, 1945 where it was to remain until the decision was made in January 16, 1946 to convert it to components and scrapped in 1950.
A23-2, the CA-11A was on its undercarriage as were the first 5 airframes. The remaining airframes on the line were dismantled during the week following cancellation, stored in a the ex-USAAC Butler until the end of the war, when they were sold for scrap. The destruction of assembly jigs was rapid. The remains of the aircraft and what would appear to be the commencement of others were located at the rear of the premises of Ready Mix-Concrete Pty Ltd at Nunawading, Victoria some years later and in a nearby scrap yard in 1952. The incomplete fuselages did not carry construction number plates but the figures 5, 6, 8, 9, 10, 12, 15, 16, 17, 18 and 20 were painted on the frames. Thirteen airframes were traced; the frame work and the metal skin under the fuselage was complete in each case.

With the demise of the CA-11 went the endeavours, innovations and hopes of what was seen to be a design of greater potential than its contemporaries of 1940. An insufficiency of design staff numbers and skilled production workers were the two main factors which contributed to the slow development schedule. It was not that the problems of the CA-4 or CA-11 were insurmountable but their presence made it impossible to bring the aircraft into service for the war. As it was, the CA-4/CA-11 called for as much in the way of imported material and human resources (with the exception of the big design element) as did the DAP Beaufort torpedo/reconnaissance bomber that was being produced next door to CAC. On those facets the two aircraft became competing airframes.

The aircraft had its problems with its unfortunate original proposed three engine layout developed as a twin engine machine with its then attendant aerodynamic problems; the failure of the first attempted local use of integral fuel tanks and the extremely complex and useless mechanical remote gun turret aiming system. The RAAF allowed this project to continue without too much involvement or oversight possibly as it had AM Sir Charles Burnett on loan from the RAF as its CAS from February 11, 1940 till May 1942. It was an appointment which brought with it a lot of acrimony. Unwanted by his own service, Burnett gave his greatest attention to the implementation of the EATS as quickly as possible with a reputation of riding roughshod over the Air Board.

Through the agency of a wartime inventions review board it was possible to make known those inventions which could support the cause of the allied nations, Wackett's invention of his periscope/reflector sight system was rejected outright by the UK.

On August 6, 1945 the company's secretary advised the DAP the costs of establishment of the truncated CA-11 production line, materials, tooling etc. was put at £2,123,776/2/8 and were seeking their recompense share of £120,558 /2 /8.

The bomber project was of such a magnitude, organisation and potential that it warranted the praise of Professor D. Mellor in his study 'The Role of Science and Industry-Australia in the War-The Government and the People, 1942-45'. In summing up if the war had resulted in any change with relation to the design and development of armaments, Prof Mellor concluded that:

> "with a few notable exceptions, such as the Owen gun, the short 25 pounder artillery and the Wackett Bomber, little had been achieved in the way of new designs during the war of 1939-45".

(PS: A large volume of CAC, RAAF & CSIR flight test, engineering and aerodynamics reports was available in 1986 from which to compile the many problems and solutions encountered with this aircraft design. It was only possible within the scope and size of this history to document the essential markers).

Bibliography CA-4 Wackett Bomber & CA 11 Woomera Bomber

Australia. Dept. of Aircraft Production (1942). Local Manufacture of a new aero engine. [Letter from L.J.Wackett to Secretary Dept. of Aircraft Production] (November 9,1942).

Australia. Dept. of Aircraft Production (1942). CA-11 Bomber aircraft. Contractual Arrangements with CAC. [NAA:MP287/1,1465].Barcode: 475383.

Commonwealth Aircraft Corporation (Undated). CA-4 Test Flights No.1-56. Pilot & Observer's reports.

Commonwealth Aircraft Corporation (Undated). CA-11 Test Flights No.1-19. Reports.

Commonwealth Aircraft Corporation (1944). CA-11 Special Flight Test Reports 1, 2 & 4.

Commonwealth Aircraft Corporation (1943). Major Assemblies Under Sub-Contract for CA-11. Engineering order 5080. (February 17,1943)

Commonwealth Aircraft Corporation.(various) [In-House Memoranda related to aero engines].

Commonwealth Aircraft Corporation (various). [Collection of meeting extracts relating to aero engines. CAC file TRA6].

Council for Scientific & Industrial Research. (1942). Report A.8 - Wind tunnel investigation on the design of the fuselage of the Medium Bomber CA-4 (March 1942).

Council for Scientific & Industrial Research (1943). Report A.9 - The Stalling characteristics of a low wing Twin-Engine Bomber (Feb 1943).

Council for Scientific & Industrial Research, Division of Aeronautics (December 1,1941).

Part 1 - Preliminary type trail model CA-4

Part 2 - General description, cockpit layout, loading & photographic trials

Part 3 - RAAF armament trials (March 1943)

Crotty, D. (undated) *Aeronautical Research in Australia 1939-45.*

Isaacs, Keith (1974). 'Wackett's Wonder'. *Air Enthusiast Quarterly.* No.1.

Mellor, D.P. (David Paver), 1903-1980(1962). *The role of science and Industry.* Australian War Memorial, Canberra.

Royal Australian Air Force. Directorate of Technical Services (1945--1947). No.1 APU   Performance Report Type Trials of CA-11. [NAA: 1472 /1,21]. Barcode: 514432.

Royal Australian Air Force. (1941). Development Specification No. 2/41 (April 23, 1941).

Royal Australian Air Force. (1944). Manufacturing Specification 2/42, Issue 2. The Manufacture of aircraft type CA-11 bomber (August 2, 1944).

Schulz, Reginald (1986). 'The CA-4 / CA-11 bomber project'. Lecture to the AHSA, Victoria Branch (Sept 1986).

Schulz, Reginald (1987). [Interview].

'The CAC Woomera'. *Aviation Historical Society of Australia.* Vol. 15/3. (July-August 1974).

CA-12, 13, 14, 14A & 19 BOOMERANG FIGHTER AIRCRAFT
December 1941

The only fighter aircraft to be both designed and produced in Australia is the CA-12/CA-13/CA-19 *Boomerang* series. The combination of the suddenness of the Japanese assault and their subsequent fast advance; the obvious lack of any significant air defence in Australia and the realisation that both traditional supply sources, Great Britain and United States of America, were fully committed to supplying their own defence needs, prompted the decision to attempt the design and construction of a fighter aircraft in Australia.

The RAAF wanted an aircraft of good performance, manoeuvrability, a stable gun platform combined with ease and simplicity of maintenance. But overall it had to be available quickly. This emphasis on speed of availability led to the misplaced label of *panic fighter* being attached to the design.

There had been the previous company Proposal P147 to turn a modified Wirraway airframe with a larger engine and five 0.303 machine guns into a fighter configuration. The ideas behind what became was to become the Boomerang were in part initiated by the Chief Design Engineer, Fred David.

Internal studies commenced within days of the Japanese attack on the United States Fleet at Pearl Harbour committed the design staff to using what was available in the country as the basis for further development. It was natural that the attention would turn to the Wirraway airframes that CAC was building and the P & W R-1830 S1C3-G Twin Wasp 1,200 hp, 14 cylinder radial engine the company was also producing at its new factory at Lidcombe, NSW, for installation on the DAP Beaufort bomber.

Preliminary sketches and figures submitted to CAC management by the design team on December 14, 1941 showed that many Wirraway parts could be used directly in the new aircraft. The major change exceptions were:

- The use of a P & W R-1830 Twin Wasp radial engine, the installation work for which had been similarly applied on the CA-4 bomber
- The creation of a completely new outer wing of reduced span and area, stressed to 10g for best performance and agility and incorporating a built-in armament of two 20 mm Hispano cannon and four 0.303 inch Browning machine guns rather than one with eight 0.303 machine guns
- A strengthened wing centre section within the original Wirraway aerodynamic outline to exploit the existing Wirraway jigs
- A shortened welded steel tube frame fuselage covered mainly in plywood to obviate a metal monocoque structural development and testing commitment. This new section would also house a new 70 gall self-sealing fuel tank in the place where the Wirraway rear seat would have been located to supplement the original two 45 gall tanks in the aircraft centre section
- The self-sealing of the wing section fuel tanks and the provision for a flush fitting, jettisonable ventral fuel tank
- The addition of cockpit armour plate and armour glass in the windshield, and
- A general strengthening of the structure to absorb the increase in power, speed and weight

Management gave the go-ahead for the start of detail design on December 21, 1941. In relative terms but through no fault of CAC, as the Government had done little to seriously prepare by way of fighter defence, this was a very late start for a new fighter design. Official correspondence between the Government and CAC referred to the design as the *'Wirraway Interceptor'*. Chief Design Engineer Fred David headed the project team. Thomas W. (Bill) Air, the company's Chief Engineer was the person in charge. Arthur Williams was the initial Project Engineer and Maurice Lodge, Project Liaison officer. Alan Bolton, Project Design Engineer was responsible for the structural integrity, engine mount, new tail and outer wing assembly and general detail; Doug Humphries for the revision and strengthening of the centre section and the undercarriage; Joe Solvey, wing aerodynamics and Chief Draftsman Ern Jones for evolving the concept into engineering build documentation.

Others in the team were Ian Ring, Ian Fleming, Lionel Stern, Herb Knight, Ralph Price and Ted Faggeter all supported by Factory Superintendent Hugh Francis. Fred David, classified as a resident enemy alien was expected to report himself every week to the police station at either Port Melbourne or St Kilda.

A pair of Hispano cannon had been brought back from the Western Desert by a member of the RAAF. CAC examined them and provided drawings and tooling by which Lionel Stern arranged for mass production by Harland Engineering at Footscray, Victoria.

Construction progress on the prototype A46-1. **Richard Hourigan**

With wind tunnel tests as a guide, the Chief of the CSIR Division of Aeronautics was of the opinion that the adaptation proposed by CAC was an excellent method of building, in a reasonable time, a substantial number of high performance aircraft.

Fred David emphasised to the author in 1986:

"that the design and construction work of the first prototype was done very quickly, it was also done very carefully. We could not afford, at that time, to have a fatal accident with the CA-12 otherwise it would have destroyed all self-confidence in what we were doing. Therefore, the emphasis was placed on ensuring that it should be structurally able to withstand what it should. If an accident had occurred everyone would have held it against us but since we were fortunate not to have one, nobody took any notice. At that time we were in the region of relatively low speeds, the wing loading was well known and could be calculated and there were no fatigue complexities".

He also confirmed no assistance came nor was it requested in any form from North American Aviation. Suggestions that the design of the Boomerang was descended from the NA-50 single seat fighter are without foundation. Derived from the BC-1 Basic Combat aircraft, seven examples of the NA-50 were sold to Peru in 1938 and another six intended for Siam (Thailand) were embargoed and went to the US Army as the P-64 training aircraft.

With great tenacity, hectic pace and seven day working weeks in the design and drawing offices, engineering drawings were released to the factory in mid-February. The production contract was awarded on February 18, 1942. Arthur Williams was to later recall *"we worked so hard you only knew it was Sunday because you did not have to wear a tie"*.

On 29 May, in an elapsed time of 117 days the first CA-12 (A46-1) made its initial 20 minute flight piloted by Ken Frewin. On 2 June the DAP approved the name *Boomerang* at the suggestion of the Air Board.

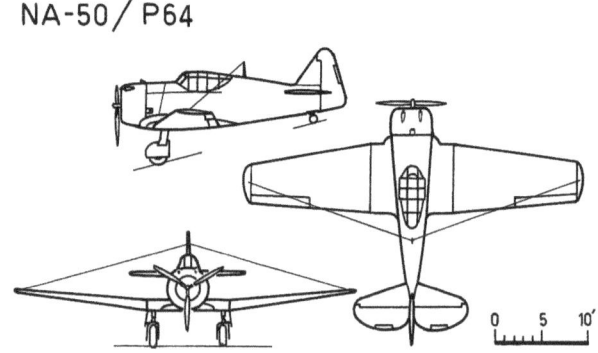

NA-50 / P64

Boomerang / Wirraway Comparison:		
	Wirraway	Boomerang
Engine rated power	550 hp	1,200 hp
Weight maximum	6,450 lb	8,032 lb
Wing area	265 sq ft	225 sq ft
Wing span	43 ft	36 ft
Fuel capacity	92 gall	160 gall (internal)

Complete CA-12 A46-1 under inspection prior to first flight. Visible on the rudder is the batch number A1. **HDHV**

On test flight No 8 the canopy flew off, hit Ken on the head and face as he approached from over the nearby Newport power station. At 1450 hours on June 25, 1942, Ken Frewin took A46-1 on flight No 32 to test an 11 feet 6 in diameter, CAC designed, wooden bladed propeller made by W. J. Manufacturing Ltd of Sydney fitted with a Curtiss electric hub instead of the Hamilton Standard unit. At 20,000 ft the aircraft lurched violently; experienced severe vibrations; lost radio contact and the starboard side tailplane was hanging loose and fluttering badly. Unable to return to Laverton, an emergency landing was made at the Werribee satellite airfield.

The trailing edge of one prop blade had completely disappeared, the glue bonding of which was found to be negligible; the other blades also showed cracking; three engine mounts were broken; the horizontal tailplane spar was fractured held on by the front attachment; the broken pitot held on by its electrical wires. The aircraft was returned by road, repaired and flying again in two weeks.

In June 1942 the CAC Board gave Ken Frewin a £100 bonus for his part in the hurried and pressured pace of test flying the CA-12. The near catastrophic in-flight emergency on A46-1 and his heavy test workload had stressed Ken. He had medical advice for a month's sick leave and a three month spell from test flying. The company thanked him for his services and dismissed him with one month's notice on July 14, 1942. (Ken also had a previous drinking problem from his earlier time flying with Holyman Airways). He resigned on August 8, 1942 having joined CAC on October 9, 1941, one day before Hubert Boss-Walker also resigned from the company following a disagreement with Lawrence Wackett due to a perceived lack of commitment to the testing of the CA-4 bomber.

Testing moved at a rapid rate. By July 11, 1942 when it was delivered to RAAF Laverton, A46-1 had accumulated 15 hours and 40 minutes of air time in 42 flights. Flt Lt James Harper from the Special Duties & Performance Unit took on the flight testing as temporary replacement. A46-1 had been the progressive mock-up airframe as its construction advanced, the prototype, service evaluation and first production airframe. It subsequently served its way through No 1 Aircraft Depot, 2 OTU at Mildura and the Central Flying School.

In July the CA-12 was demonstrated for Lt General G.H.Brett, USAAC (Deputy US/British/Dutch/Australian Command). He was impressed. Lawrence Wackett was happy as the CA-12 had shown a top speed of 310 mph, 10 mph better than predicted.

The start of Boomerang production co-incided with the end of the CA-6 Wackett Trainer work in April and the temporary halt in Wirraway production in June of 1942.

The Department of Aircraft Production felt it was imperative to hold together the Wirraway workforce that had practically completed the detail parts manufacture for the planned order of 620 Wirraways. Only general assembly now remained. Without a follow-on project, 2,000 to 2,500 personnel would have to be laid off for some three months at the rate of 200 per week. On February 2, 1942 the War Cabinet decided, as recorded in Agenda No 46/1942, to build 105 'Wirraway Interceptors' to insure against possible delays in the delivery of other overseas fighter aircraft whilst reviewing the performance and desirability of the new design. (At the same time the delivery prospects of the P-40 Kittyhawk were also to be considered. The RAAF accepted the first hastily delivered batch of Curtiss P-40E Kittyhawk in March 1942, the start of a massive delivery total of 838 P-40E/K/M/N variants to 1945. Spitfires also started arriving in August 1942.)

The engine Wackett wanted in the 'Wirraway Interceptor' was the P&W R-1830 S3C4-G variant of Twin Wasp which would have had to come from imported stocks earmarked for some of the DAP Beaufort bomber production.

Five engines were readily diverted following the War Cabinet's approval of January 26,1942 which allowed for:

105 complete aircraft @ £12,000 each	£1,260,000
20 spare engines @ £5,500 each	£110,000
Airframe & engine spares	£280,000
Total	£1,650,000

Wackett's desire to employ the S3C4-G engine was backed by the Chief of CSIR when he pointed out on March 26, 1942 that this engine produced 100 hp greater output and a 500 ft/min better climb rate than the S1C3-G.

Whereas the Air Board had suggested a variant with the alternate Wright Cyclone R-2600B which in its various forms offered 1,600-1,700 hp at take-off, far in excess of that required for the CA-12. These higher ratings were more suitable for a twin engine bomber and there was little to be gained on a CA-12 above 15,000ft when fitted with a Wright Cyclone let alone the introduction and support difficulties for a different engine.

The estimated performance figures given on April 7, 1942 for the three engines types were:

CA-12 Engine Selection Considerations			
Unit	P & W S1C3-G Twin Wasp	P & W S3C4-G Twin Wasp	Wright Cyclone R2600 (Supercharged)
Speed at 13,000 ft	258 kts (300 mph)	265 kt (309 mph)	300 kts (345 mph)
Rate of Climb	2,500 ft /min	3,000 ft /min	4,000 ft /min

To achieve the best performance with the Wright Cyclone engine the design would have had to undergo extensive refinement. Speedy delivery was sought from the USA on February 2, 1942 of an additional 150 S3C4-G engines.

CA-12 Boomerang

The early CA-12 contract examples off the production line were used by the RAAF to establish whether any major problems existed which would have to be rectified before the production sequence had gone too far but no modifications were requested.

By Christmas Day of 1942 the RAAF had accepted 23 Boomerangs. The initial batch of 105 CA-12 (A46-1 to A46-105) was complete in June 1943. The first two aircraft featured an external lower oil cooler intake. Subsequent production aircraft had the intake incorporated in the engine cowl inner surface and A46-1 and -2 were likewise brought up to this standard. Initial monthly deliveries were expected to be 20 aircraft each month but the realised monthly average for the first six months was only 4.5 aircraft. Engine deliveries did not match the pace of airframe delivery; only 47 units had arrived by the beginning of February 1943.

Several problems and undesirable characteristics did show up when the aircraft was established in service and brought to the attention of CAC service Engineer Maurice Lodge during his April and July 1943 visits to 2 OTU, Mildura and 84 Sqdn on Horn Island. Cracking of the spinner back plate; guns that froze at altitude; a gun-sight that was difficult to use, so moved forward 3 inches. A recurring problem of fading brakes led to the re-design of the brake drum and the subsequent change of liner material. Failure of the ventral fuel tank retaining pins were problems that arose and were solved. Propeller spinners had been introduced to improve engine cooling during a sustained climb. Inexperienced pilots had difficulties with the aircraft's short wheel base in cross-wind conditions, resulting in many repeated ground loops and blown tyres; best rectified by a change in handling technique. Throughout Maurice's extensive unit visits he was confronted by the recurring complaints of the lack of sufficient spares, the appropriate tools and paucity of maintenance charts. Due to the rapid expansion of aircraft numbers, RAAF personnel were learning their trades on the job in sometimes trying and difficult operating conditions.

A tendency for the aircraft to go into unexpected full rudder lock during the climb or in sharp turns at speeds below 180 mph was also encountered. Methods of managing rudder and trim were released by the Special Duties & Performance Unit in May 1943 with the expectation of a retrofit of a new revised fin which would provide an airframe solution. There was also a separate significant aerodynamic buffet which showed up as a very high frequency vibration in the controls circuit.

The performance of the Boomerang was close to anticipated. Speed was modest, but in areas of rate of climb and manoeuvrability it was better than its contemporaries in the P-40E Kittyhawk and the P-39 Airacobra in comparative aircraft handling trails which gave assurance to the Air Board. Mock combat and dog-fights were flown with the weights of the trial aircraft adjusted to be as close to each other as was practical. Evaluation pilots were RAAF Sqdn Ldr A. Rawlinson & Flt Lt W. J. Arthur and USAAC, Capt A. W. Lunde. The flight trails were overseen by CSIR Division of Aeronautics research officer Thomas Lawrence and reported on July 30, 1942. When tested against Brewster Buffalo (A51-6) the CA-12 had a speed advantage, but was outmanoeuvred in diving and zooming and at no time was it able to gain the initiative in combat. The comparison was largely inconclusive but after the tests the Air Board felt the CA-12 was good enough and was prepared to accept as many as 200 aircraft, anxious to stress the necessity to proceed.

CA-12 Airframe Description

The wing group was of a fixed centre section with two fuel tanks of a total 90 gall capacity, detachable outer wing panels and wing tips. Construction of the wing was metal throughout. The exception was the metal framed, fabric covered Frise type ailerons. The two 20mm Hispano cannon with 60 rpg and four 0.303 in Browning machine guns with 1,000 rpg were accessed and re-armed from above the wing. There was no internal structural similarity between a Wirraway outer wing and the shorter span outer wing on the CA-12. The fighter wing was of a smooth finish; that on the Wirraway was

CA-12 test pilot Ken Frewin talks with USAAC Lt.General George Brett after a July flight demo--nstration. **HDHV**

covered in raised rivet heads. The tail group was strengthened, surfaces were of metal construction with fabric covered elevator and rudder. The latter and the port elevator were fitted with a trim tab, whilst a servo trim tab was fitted on the starboard elevator. The fuselage was a welded steel tube framework with the bottom aft portion covered by a stressed aluminium alloy skin, whilst the side and top fairings were of plywood with wooden formers and stringers. The fairing ahead of the cockpit was of aluminium. The aft-sliding, readily jettisonable canopy could be locked in flight in any one of three intermediate positions. The windscreen was shielded by 1.5 inch bullet proof glass. Armour plate to the rear of the pilot, was 11 mm thick above the top longeron and 6 mm in front of the fuselage fuel tank and down below the pilot to the level of the wing. (Metric and Imperial units are as described in the Maintenance Manual). There was a 70 gallon fuel tank behind the cockpit and a 70 gallon impregnated wood external fuel tank could be carried on a centre-line bomb shackle. Oil capacity was 14 gallons.

A HF radio transceiver was located in the mid-rear fuselage. The main undercarriage was a fully cantilever single leg fork type with 27 inch diameter tyres, each assembly attached to the front spar and retracting inwards into the centre section leading edge. The 11 inch diameter tailwheel was able to swivel through 360°, was steerable through the rudder control, but was not retractable.

The CA-12 carried navigational lights on the wing tips and the side of the fin; a white identification light on the rear upper fuselage; three identification lights on (CA-13 & 19; one on the CA-12). A formation light was on either side of the fuselage in line with the front of the windscreen. Each wing incorporated a landing light and

Rate of Climb (ft/min) versus Altitude (ft)	CA-12 (A46-1)	P-40E (A29-129)	P-39 (BW 127)
Sea level	2,500 ft	1,850 ft	2,000 ft
15,000 ft	2,080 ft	1,400 ft	1,550 ft
20,000 ft	1,550 ft	1,000 ft	1,100 ft
30,000 ft	500 ft	150 ft	200 ft
Weight	7,358 lb	8,417 lb	7,777 lb
Speed (kts) versus Altitude (ft)	CA-12 (A46-1)	P-40E (A29-129)	P-39 (BW 127)
Sea level	223 kts	240 kts	270 kts
15,000 ft	253 kts	275 kts	310 kts
20,000 ft	258 kts	266 kts	280 kts
30,000 ft	310 kts	236 kts	266 kts

A46-1 receiving the admiration of CAC's employees on roll-out from the camouflaged factory on May 29,1942. **Richard Hourigan**.

a mechanically operated Type 045 camera gun was located in the outer port wing.

CA-13 Boomerang II

On October 5, 1942 the War Cabinet gave its approval for 95 aircraft (A46-106 to A46-200) to be built. The aircraft of this contract CA-13, incorporated modifications found necessary by service use. These included:

- The replacement of the metal wing tips with laminated timber items
- Fitting of a Beaufort type flame damper exhaust tube instead of the original simple exhaust (Introduced from c/n 949, A46-126)
- The substitution of metal covered ailerons instead of the fabric covered originals
- The provision of an external rear vision mirror
- The removal of the hydraulic cocking mechanism on the cannon and the substitution of a mechanical pre-flight cocking system in its place
- Change from plain to ribbed tyres
- The relocation of the reflector gun sight for easier use and pilot safety and
- Ducting hot exhaust air to the gun bays to eliminate gun freezing at altitude

This second order that brought production numbers to 200 had been expected to be completed by June 30, 1943. However, a shortage of labour and uncertainty of engines supply made this impossible until on June 7, 1943 the Boomerang was allocated the higher priority to all imported S3C4-G engines in preference to that of the Beaufort bomber production with which the allocation had been previously shared.

The RAAF introduced changes to airframes on the production line such as the inclusion of a new rudder pedal assembly; the raising of the hydraulic shelf necessitating a change in a fuselage fairing and various other minor alterations. This manner of operation annoyed Wackett immensely as it disrupted and delayed the production line. He was at a loss to understand why the RAAF would not accept the overseas method of introducing such changes by the use of Air Force maintenance depots. The latter were hard pressed with their own workload and demands of rapid maintenance expansion. Production slowed toward the end of the year with preparations under way for the local manufacture of the P-51 Mustang. The first CA-13 was delivered in August 1943, the last in May 1944 quoted at £6,500 for an airframe, £5,250 per engine and £900 for each propeller.

CA-14

An improved version of the CA-12 was seen as a first priority on August 8, 1942 employing either the existing type engine with an exhaust driven turbo supercharger or a R-2600 Wright Cyclone, whichever could be implemented first with Wackett promising in War Cabinet Agenda No 397/1942 an example of either aircraft would be completed by December 31, 1942.

In an effort to improve the Boomerang's performance at altitude, work started in late 1942 on an experimental airframe in which turbo supercharger gear was to be fitted. This followed War Cabinet's backing of it as a high priority project on September 26, 1942 with funding for £15,000. As the Twin Row Wasp was a medium supercharged engine giving its greatest output with the high speed geared supercharger at about 15,000 feet, it limited the performance of the aircraft.

To overcome this, a General Electric B-2 turbo supercharger (the only kind available) was installed in the rear fuselage and fed by an intercooler air scoop on the left side of the fuselage in line with the rear of the cockpit. The Harrison intercooler (from a Boeing B-17 Fortress), the only type to hand, was not the ideal match. For the R-1830 the correct unit would have raised the critical altitude by between 4,000 to 5,000 feet. Its exhaust duct flap was located immediately behind the cockpit roof. The Curtiss Electric three bladed propeller was accepted, there being no other choice. The unusual layout of the intakes and ducting, the design responsibility of Ian Ring, was to rapidly demonstrate the turbogear, its complex system, provide heat transfer safely through the airframe and prove its performance before embarking on a more refined aerodynamic fix. Test pilot James Carter lacked experience of supercharger gear operation so Wackett would not allow him the initial testing . He had been unable to secure flying time and local experience for him on the RAAF's small fleet of Republic P-43 Lancers that were fitted with turbo superchargers.

On January 13, 1943, the CA-14 (serial A46-1001) was test flown by Flt Lt John J.Holden, RAAF Resident Technical Officer at CAC. FLt Lt Holden was the RTO from February 1942 till early 1945. In addition to his normal duties he performed a lot of test and acceptance flying when a company test pilot was not available. Flt Lt Jim Carter died on January 15, 1943 in the crash of the CA-4.

Ten flights were amassed over the next fourteen days. A badly mounted shroud on the turbo nozzle box was replaced and the two lower cowl gills on the port side were removed to improve the airflow

Boomerang Deliveries 1941-1945				
Month	1942	1943	1944	1945
January		3	4	13
February		13	5	1
March		21	6	
April		18	12	
May		16	5	
June		10	5	
July		4	6	
August	1	22	3	
September	3	14	2	
October	5	7	4	
November	4	9	5	
December	11	8	7	
Cumulative Total	24	169	235	249

CA-12, 13, 14 & 19 Boomerang

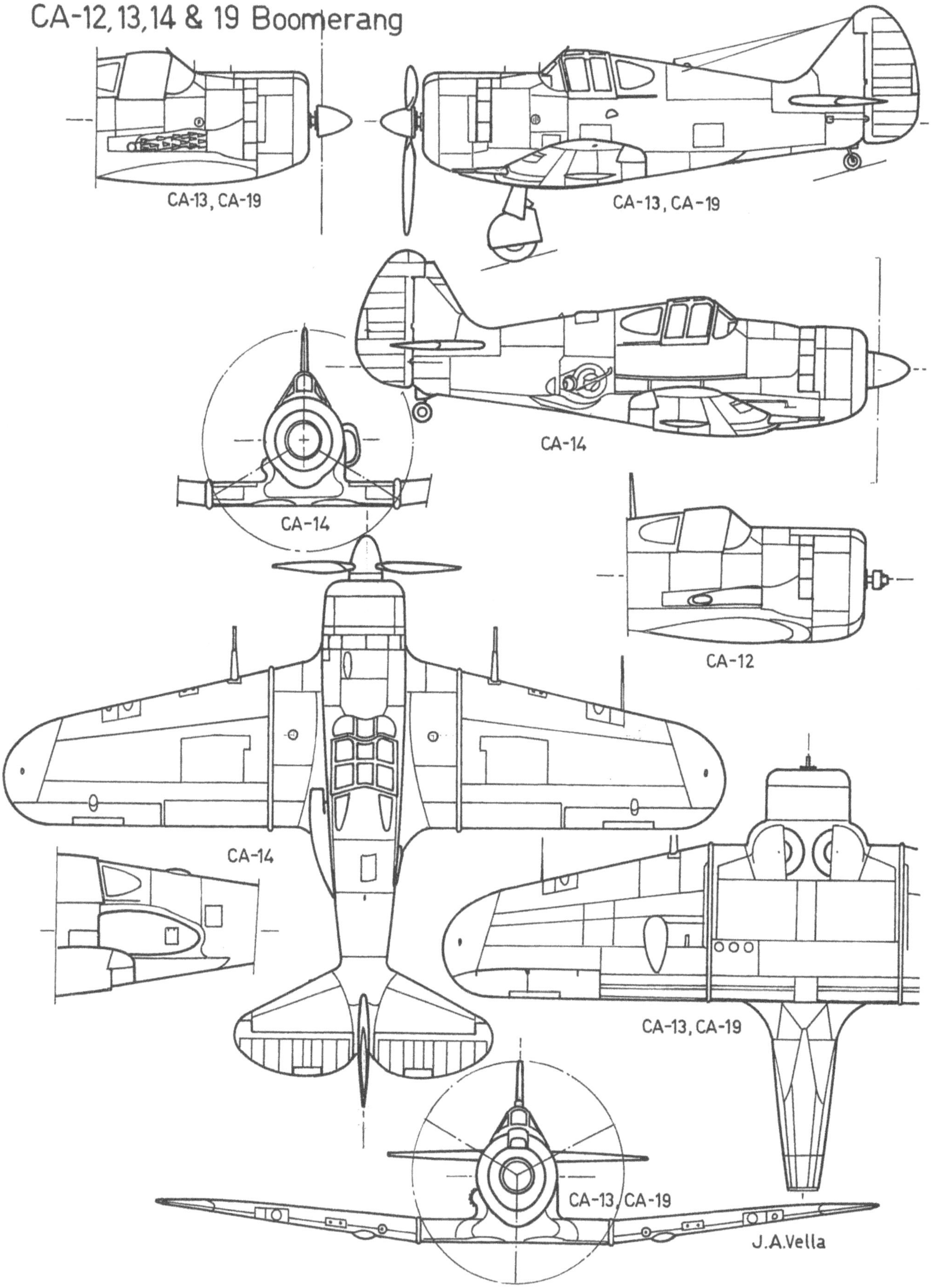

CA-14a Boomerang

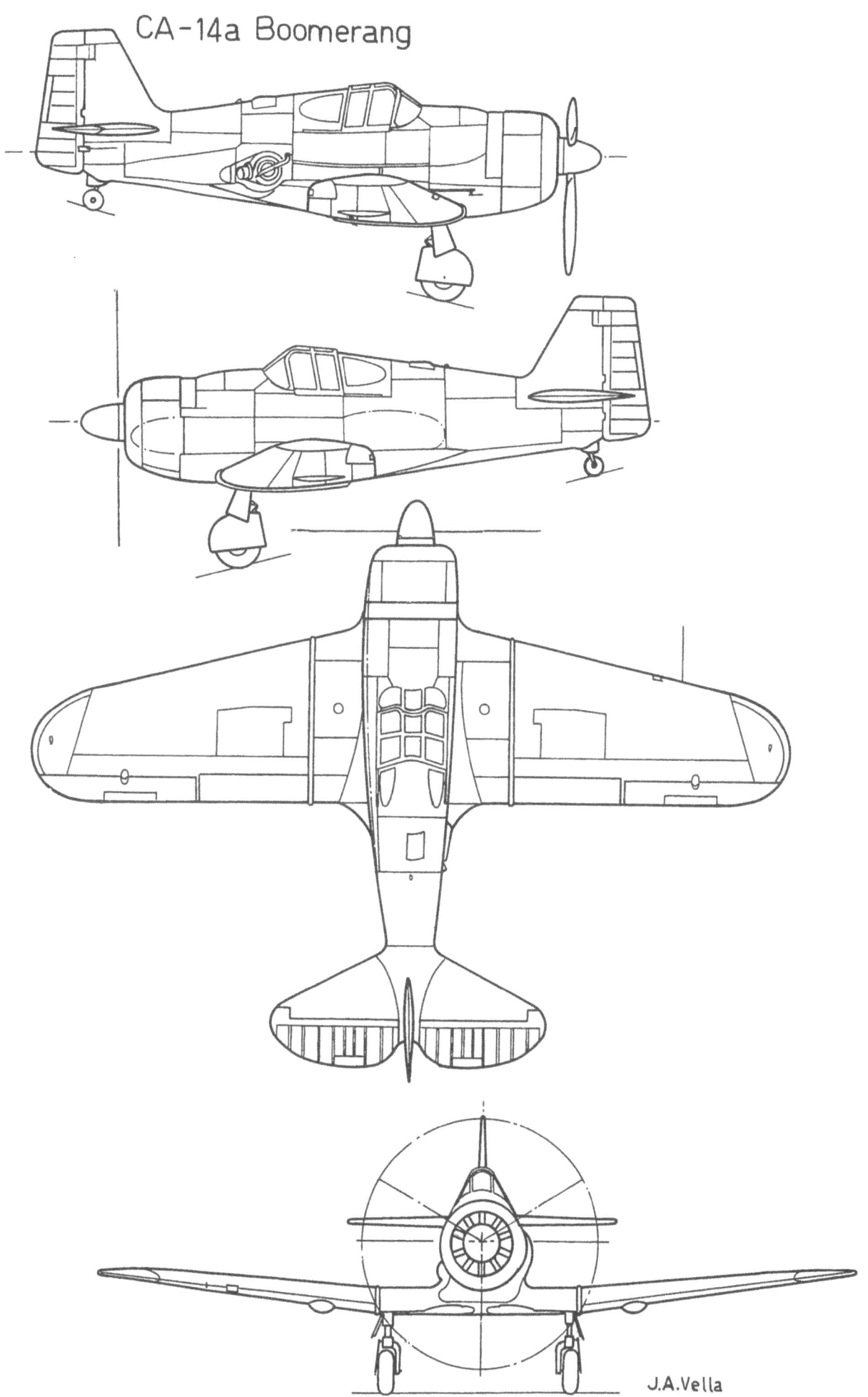

Specifications

	CA-12	CA-14	CA-14A
	Single seat interceptor & fighter bomber Powerplant: P & W R1830-S3C4-G Twin Wasp, 14 cyl. Twin row air cooled radial of 1,200 hp at 2,700 rpm driving a Hamilton Standard 3 bladed propeller of 11 ft dia	Experimental P & W R1830-S1C3-G Twin Wasp with G.E. Type B-2 Turbosupercharger driving a Curtis Electric 3 bladed propeller of 11 ft dia	Experimental P & W R1830-S1C3-G Twin Wasp with fan cooling & G.E.Type B-9 Turbosupercharger driving a de Havilland 3 bladed propeller
Weights:	Empty -5,373 lb Max. AUW- 8,249 lb	5,723 lb 8,249 lb 7,744 lb(combat). Data is based on the combat weight	5,823 lb N/A 7,844 lb (combat). Estimated data is based on the combat weight
Speed:	238 kts (275 mph) at SL 257 kts (295 mph) at 7,600 ft 262 kts (305 mph) at 15,000 ft	233 kts (269 mph) at SL 270 kts (311 mph) at 15,000 ft 302 kts (347 mph) at 28,200 ft	248 kts (285 mph) at 27,000 ft 322 kts (372 mph) at 27,000 ft
Service Ceiling:	31,000 ft	36,000 ft	37,000 ft
Climb Rate:	2,450 ft /min at SL 1,760 ft/min at 15,000 ft 380 ft/min at 28,200 ft	2,150 ft /min at SL 1,640 ft/min at 15,000 ft 1,180 ft/min at 28,200 ft	2,100 ft /min at SL 2,770 ft /min at 30,000 ft
	Time to 20,000 ft -9.2 mins	Time to 28,600 ft - 17.2 mins	Time to 30,000 ft- 15.2 mins
Range:	810 nm at 165 kts at 15,000 ft	N/A	N/A
Endurance:	4.9 hrs	N/A	N/A
Wing Span:	36 ft 0 ins	36 ft 0 ins	36 ft 0 ins
Length:	26 ft 5.5 ins	27 ft 5.5 ins	27 ft 3 ins
Height:	11 ft 7 ins (Tail up)	N/A	N/A
Wing Root Chord:	90 ins	N/A	N/A
Chord Incidence:	2°	Ditto	Ditto
Wing Dihedral:	7° on outer wing	Ditto	Ditto
LE Sweep:	12° 45'	Ditto	Ditto
Wing Twist (outer wing panel):	1.5°	Ditto	Ditto
Aspect Ratio:	5.76	Ditto	Ditto
Wing Root Section:	NACA 2215	Ditto	Ditto
Wing Tip Section:	NACA 2206.11	Ditto	Ditto
Horizontal Tail Area:	45 sq ft	Ditto	Ditto
Horizontal Tail Span:	13 ft	Ditto	Ditto
Vertical Surface total area:	20.3 sq ft	Ditto	Ditto
Vertical Surface offset:	1° 8' to port	Ditto	Ditto
Armament:	2 x 20 mm Hispano cannon with 60 rpg & 4 x 0.303 Browning m/gs with 1,000 rpg	Ditto	Not fitted
Retrospective Designation:	XP16	XP18	N/A

A line-up of factory fresh Boomerang aircraft. **HDHV**

L.J.Wackett (in black hat),CAC Board members & USAAC representatives discuss the CA-12. **HDHV**

to the inter-cooler. The CA-14 was handed to the RAAF on April 17, 1943.

Its climbing performance was degraded by having to make use of the conventional style of cowl gills to induce sufficient cooling to the engine. Some aerodynamic cleaning up of the engine cowl and wing contours was attempted and whilst the use of turbo supercharging improved the speed of the aircraft by 20%, the manner of the installation created trim, directional instability and tailplane buffet problems. The results of these tests (Refer to Specification table) of the CA-14 fitted with all military equipment, guns (and finished in camouflage paint) were sent by telegram on April 15, 1943 to Wackett in the United States where he was part of a mission embarked on the selection of new aircraft types for the RAAF. He was asked to investigate a source of four bladed 11 foot diameter propellers in the event of the CA-14 entering series production.

CA-14A

To clean up the aerodynamics of the CA-14 and increase its performance airframe changes were outlined:

- To use the CAC R-2000 radial engine with its axial flow cooling fan
- Replacement of the intercooler air scoop by an intake located within a modified engine cowl
- Fitting a General Electric Type B-9 turbosupercharger
- Fit sliding cowl gills to realise a 6% reduction in drag in level flight and about 18% reduction during the climb phase
- Installing a Curtiss metal, four bladed 11 ft diameter propeller and
- Enlarged more angular, vertical tail surfaces

These changes were expected to raise the aircraft empty weight by about 100 lb. The support of Lt General G. Kenney, commander of Allied Air Forces South West Pacific Area and that of General Douglas MacArthur was sought to obtain the turbosuperchargers. Their approval was given with reluctance as it was judged that any future Australian requirements would be at the expense of United States production as it had considered Australia was incapable of building superchargers, a contention strongly refuted by CAC.

Lend-Lease then gave its approval to procure 125 GE Type B-9 exhaust driven turbosuperchargers at a total cost of £145,000 but on February 2, 1944 it informed it was unable to supply them. A Type B-9 turbosupercharger gear was installed at the end of March. The B-9 and the earlier type B-2 are believed to have both originated from unserviceable USAAC B-24 Liberator bomber aircraft operating in Australia. Air to the turbosupercharger was conveyed through a faired duct on the left side of the fuselage which when viewed from above gave the aircraft a slightly asymmetric bulged appearance.

A beautiful view of a new factory interior with the CA-12 final assembly line. **HDHV**

Following the departure of Ken Frewin most of the specialised Boomerang test flying was conducted by Greg Board who took up his appointment as the new test pilot on March 1, 1943 having previously been an instructor at 2 OTU at Mildura, northern Victoria and flown Buffaloes in combat in Malaya. He took over the testing of the CA-14A. Not all the other modifications went according to plan. A larger spinner and the enlarged new square fin and rudder was fitted and flying in the week of Monday May 24, 1943 performing very well, followed a week later by the fitting of a ten bladed axial flow fan in front of the R-1830 engine. This operated at three times the speed of the propeller. Fixed fairings were fitted in place of the conventional (or as proposed, sliding) cowl gills and a three bladed de Havilland propeller substituted for the much preferred four-bladed unit. The intended CAC R-2000 engine could not be fitted; its testing was still

A46-128 BF-N in 5 Sqdn formation, Mareeba, N.Qld, March 3, 1944. **John Harrison via Neil Follett Collection**

CA-12 pilot instrument panel. **HDHV**

A46-105/MH-E of 83 Sqdn receiving its 40 hourly inspection at Menangle, NSW, between Feb & Sept 1945. **Richard Hourigan**.

CA-12 cockpit right side. **HDHV**

CA-13 A46-157, CAC engine cooling fan trials aircraft. Wirraway A20-652 to the left outside the Butler hangar. **HDHV**

A factory fresh CA-13 A46-163 Batch 'K' on pre-delivery test. **HDHV**

CA-13 A46-121/QE-N, Batch 'H', 'Olga', of 4 Sqdn. Sepinggang Airfield, Borneo. July 25, 1945. **Stuart Kirkham via Derek Buckmaster**

CA-13 A46-199/ QE-Y, Batch 'M,' 'Home James' of 4 Sqdn **Derek Buckmaster**

Completed aircraft receiving pre-flight adjustments outside the factory. **LJWackett/MS4858/NLA**.

The B-2 supercharger on the starboard side. **HDHV**

The large square duct reaches up to the intercooler at the rear of the cockpit, the design work of Ian Ring. **HDHV**

CA14A, A46-1001 with the enclosed intercooler duct from the engine cowl down its fuselage side and the modified fin & rudder as tested on A46-27. **Richard Hourigan**

A casual Lawrence Wackett & a defensive looking Boomerang test pilot Greg Board in an informal chat. **LJWackett/MS4858/NLA**

The engine cooling fan and square fin stand out in this view at Fisherman's Bend. **Reg Schulz.**

A46-1001/CA-14 with the small fin forward extension. **Richard Hourigan**.

A46-1001 with intercooler air scoop on mid port fuselage side & extended spinner. **Reg Schulz.**

A No 5 Sqdn Boomerang leads out a strike flight of New Zealand Air Force F4U Corsairs from Torokina airstrip on Bougainville. **RAAF via Barry Pattison.**

in progress. Although first mention of the CAC R-2000 occurred on October 7, 1942, its development had been underway for some time. The engine division had bored out five R-1830 engines to 2000 cu in capacity for this installation and that in the eventual CA-11A, but it struck lubrication problems on test.

The War Cabinet allocated £15,000 for development of the CA-14A with the P & W Twin Wasp engine and £25,000 for the fall-back alternate with the R-2600B Wright Cyclone.

Recommendation was made on July 5, 1943 that production should eventually change over to the CA-14A model. However with the availability of imported high altitude fighters the CA-14A was swept aside. Had the decision been made to put the CA-14 into production it would have also been necessary to incorporate cockpit pressurization to reach and sustain altitudes in the region of 40--45,000 ft. As it was, the aircraft was able to achieve altitudes of 40,000 ft with limited onboard oxygen supplies and perform a lot of useful flying for the Meteorological Bureau to eventually be scrapped at Laverton in 1948 or 1950.

CA-19 Boomerang

In July 1943 CAC endeavoured through the DAP to build another 120 Boomerangs, the last fifty to be fitted with the fan assisted CAC built R-2000 engine without supercharging. The War Cabinet gave approval for only 50 aircraft authorising £939,000 including spares on 16 September. This construction was sanctioned even though the CAS had advised that no further Boomerangs were required.

The value of this limited order was that it would keep the factory floor staff together while CAC tooled up for the Mustang. The War Cabinet insisted that all Boomerang production was to cease on January 31, 1945. When plans to put the CA-14A into production did not materialize the contract CA-19 (A46-201 to A46-249) for 49 aircraft reverted back to the CA-13 configuration with minor alterations. The last 39 aircraft in this order, A46-211 to 249, were fitted with an F24 vertical camera in the rear fuselage. The CAC design office hoped that an interim surplus of engineering effort might be directed towards incorporating the square fin and rudder to the CA-19 batch and Boomerangs already in service. The first CA-19 was delivered on May 25, 1944; the last on February 1, 1945. In an effort to make production match the available manpower, the jigs for the Boomerang centre section were transferred to Richards Industries in South Australia midway through the CA-13 contract. Likewise GM-H's Woodville plant in South Australia built 396 pairs of fuel tanks, whilst at their Fisherman's Bend factory they fabricated fuselage, wing spar and flap assemblies and some complete wings. de Havilland supplied 302 examples of the Model 3E50 propeller.

Some Experimentation

CAC's endeavours to be independent in the supply of propellers led them to develop a three bladed, variable pitch (40°) wooden propeller (metal blades were a possible option) along the lines of the earlier two bladed model built for possible Wirraway application. Development was complete by August 27, 1942 and plans were to use it on both the R-1830 and R-2000 engine.

Flight proving of the propeller on Boomerang A46-27 that had been taken aside for the trials, got off to a bad start. The CAC factory progress report of March 11, 1943 noted: when the pilot set out on the first test for the wooden propeller a mishap resulted in damage to the wooden blades and damage (flying debris) to two other nearby parked Boomerang aircraft. The replacement blades which were to undergo trials in the engine test house were in turn rendered non-airworthy by flying debris when a cooling fan for the R-2000 engine under trial in the test house disintegrated. With new blades the propeller was finally air tested on June 8, 1943 and although it was considered to be satisfactory it was the subject of continuous modification. This development did not result into a demand or production order. de Havilland had also successfully flight tested a four bladed lightweight (Hydromatic) propeller on Boomerang A46-27 and planned in March 1944 to seek approval to build another 25 propellers for trial purposes. The CA-14A enlarged tail configuration was also tested on A46-27, as was new brake lining material and cockpit carbon monoxide contamination tests. On completion of the trials with the Special Duties and Performance Unit the aircraft was issued to 2 OTU.

A46-157 also had a temporary share of test flying. In November 1943 the aircraft's cowl and gills were altered to accommodate the geared cooling fan which had previously been fitted on the CA-14A. The propeller shaft was extended and the cowl lengthened forward three inches. It also tested two hydraulically actuated sliding cowl gills in place of the standard gills that created a lot of drag on the CA-14. It also tested a four bladed Curtiss Electric propeller. Following successful initial trials A46-157 was handed to the RAAF Aircraft Performance Unit in June 1944, then released to 83 Sqdn in July 1945. The May 1943 recommendation by the APU for a new revised fin and rudder was possibly tested on A46-47. Greg Board left CAC on February 2, 1945 after Boomerang production had come to an end.

Some Service Use Details

Although intended from the outset to be a fighter, no Boomerang aerial victory was ever achieved. It lacked sufficient all-out speed and enemy incursions over the mainland became fewer and far between. From 2 OTU at Mildura, Vic and 8 OTU at Parkes, NSW, newly converted pilots went to form 83 Squadron at Gove, NT for North-Western area defence; 84 Squadron at Horn Island for protection of the North-Eastern area and eventually moving to Papua New Guinea and 85 Squadron at Guilford and RAAF Pearce for the defence of Western Australia. Nos 4, 5 and 84 were the only units to confront the Japanese advance. 8 CU, a hybrid communications unit used some examples of the Boomerang on Goodenough Island.

The Boomerang's best performance was at sea level where it could outrun the Spitfire Mk VIII. Its performance died away after 11,000 ft altitude as the engine became overheated. It could be coaxed higher and slowly once the cowl gills were opened, the throttle eased off, and the engine allowed to cool down a little, then resuming the climb and so on, but it was outclassed at the altitudes at which air superiority dog-fighting took place.

It became a second line fighter with a front line role in the ground support war of Army co-operation duties. The aircraft of No 4 and 5 Squadrons, together with Wirraways, established their niche in the ground war in Papua New Guinea, Borneo and the Solomon Islands. The Boomerangs of 4 Tactical Reconnaissance Sqdn were especially heavily tasked on Army co-operation work in the Huon Peninsula campaign in the north-east of Papua Guinea in support of the Australian 7th and 9th Division with each pilot amassing high flying hours.

With its good manoeuvrability, rate of climb and general sturdiness, the aircraft was exceptional and ideal for operations in valleys, mountainous and jungle terrain. It was recognised and affectionately known by ground troops, flew low level photographic reconnaissance sorties; strafed gun emplacements and pockets of sniper fire and with their cannon marked enemy gun or troop emplacements for artillery strike or low level bombing by P-40 Kittyhawks, most of the flying for this sort of work having to he carried out at tree top level. Beleaguered troops or ground patrols were assisted by aerial drops of specially packed food, medicine and urgent supplies. The need for photography work raised by the 9th Aust Division in Papua New Guinea, led to Tsili-Tsili based 4 Sqdn to develop a camera installation in the Boomerang's (A46-156) under-fuselage belly tank. In addition to control boxes and motors, two standard F24 cameras were installed, one at the front for forward oblique and vertical images the other in the rear portion of the tank for vertical and side oblique photography. The advantage of this installation was that it removed the need for major structural alterations. However when the aircraft was flown in dirty weather, mud thrown up by the wheels blotted out the lenses of the cameras. (Refer to above; late CA-19 examples had a camera built in).

Across all units which operated the Boomerang, the in-service dispatch figure had reached 85% by 1944.

The cost of the entire production of 250 aircraft amounted to £6,277,000 at an approximate unit cost of £21,250 excluding spares.

Final Word

The Boomerang was a successful design born out of necessity and alarm at a time of national wartime crises with an enemy seemingly closing in on the northern regions and no true fighter aircraft available. The distinctly unusual situation was that Australia's one and only indigenous fighter design to enter production was the inspiration of a man whose original aeronautical background experience stemmed from Australia's two wartime antagonists, Germany and Japan.

With the end of the war, the Commonwealth Disposals Commission set out the detailed guidelines for the disposal of equipment and aircraft. Together with DCA, it was stated no ex-combat aircraft were to be allowed to come into civil operation. All types had to be written off. This included the destruction of the Boomerang project technical data.

Bibliography: CA-12 to CA-19 Boomerang Fighter

Aero Supercharging. Multiple source extracts-(1937-1980) via Sanders, Richard.

Australia. Aircraft Advisory Committee (1942-46). Minutes of meetings of Aircraft Advisory Commission, Meetings 1-77. [NAA: B5028, 1; B5028,2 B5028,3; B5028,4; B5028,54]. Barcodes: 395652; 395653; 395650; 395651 & 395649 respectively.

Australia. Dept. of Aircraft Production (1942). Aircraft Production in Australia. [NAA: MP407/1, 6] Barcode: 368351.

Australia. (September 26, 1942) Boomerang interceptor, War Cabinet agenda No 397/1942.

Australia. (August 24, 1943) Proposed Extension Order for Manufacture of Boomerang aircraft. War Cabinet Agenda No 365/1943.

'Australian Operated Aircraft' (1974-1979) - *Aviation Historical Society of Australia*.

Commonwealth Aircraft Corporation. Engineering Report AA27. CA-12 Detail Specification.

Commonwealth Aircraft Corporation. Engineering Report AA28. CA-14 Preliminary Performance Report.

Commonwealth Aircraft Corporation. (Undated) CAC Production file P2.

Commonwealth Aircraft Corporation. (Undated) Pilot report files T5 & 026a.

Commonwealth Aircraft Corporation. (April 24, 1942). Future Program Policy Memoranda.

Commonwealth Aircraft Corporation.(1941-1944).CAC Interceptor Project (CA-12) Boomerang Aircraft. Part 2[NAA: A1196, 1/502/21 Pt 2.] Barcode: 199203.

Cumming, D.R. 'Rudder locking on CA-12' (May 2, 1945). Aircraft Performance Unit. RAAF HQ file No.9/18/4.

David, Friedrich, (1986). [Interview].

Francis, H. (March 29, 1943). CA-14 progress of flight testing.

Grantham, Gregory (1930-); Bushell, Edward. J. (1931-). (2004) *Shaft of the Spear: Evolution of the RAAF technical services to the end of WW2*. Acme, Canberra.

Hourigan, R. (Richard) (1961, -62, -63 & -64.) [Correspondence from Dept. of Supply on CAC Boomerang aircraft constructor numbers].

Mellor, D.P. (David Paver), 1903-1980(1962). *The role of science and industry*. Australian War Memorial, Canberra.

Royal Australian Air Force. No.4 Tactical Reconnaissance Sqdn -Huon Peninsula Campaign. (January 24, 1945). Report of effort.

Wings. (June 1986).Vol. 16/5: Sentry Books.

P175 ANTI-TANK AIRCRAFT
July 1942

It is not known what requirement was responsible for the creation on July 16, 1942 of a layout for an anti-tank and ground attack aircraft. Two variants were put forward differing one from the other in the choice of engines.

The first one proposed the use of two Pratt & Whitney R-1340 Wasp radial engines. These were mounted below a mid-set wing which was of a similar planform to that of the CA-4 bomber. The pilot sat under a framed canopy in the forward nose, with the gunner member of crew positioned further aft under a mid-upper fuselage clear vision cupola. From this location he was to direct rearward-gun fire with a 0.5 inch machine gun mounted in a remote ball turret in the extreme tail. There was provision for 1,500 rounds ammunition.

The floor of the cockpit was placed above the centre line mounted single barrel 40mm Bofors anti-tank gun, with its firing mechanism and store of 80 rounds of ammunition. There was

Specifications	P175 Anti-Tank Aircraft	
Powerplant	Version 1: Two Pratt & Whitney R-1340 S1H1-G Wasp radial engines of 600 hp each	
	Version 2: Two Pratt & Whitney R1-830 Twin Wasp Twin radial engines of 1,200 hp each	
Performance	N/A	
Weights	Version 1:	
	Empty	7,591 lb
	Gross	13,262 lb
	Version 2:	
	Empty	9,050 lb
	Gross	13,262 lb
Dimensions	Wing span	50 ft 8 ins
	Length	36 ft 3 ins
	Height	10 ft
Armament	Forward firing 40mm Bofors anti-tank gun with 80 rounds. 0.5 in m/g in remote operated tail turret with 1,500 rounds	
Retrospective Designation	NA	

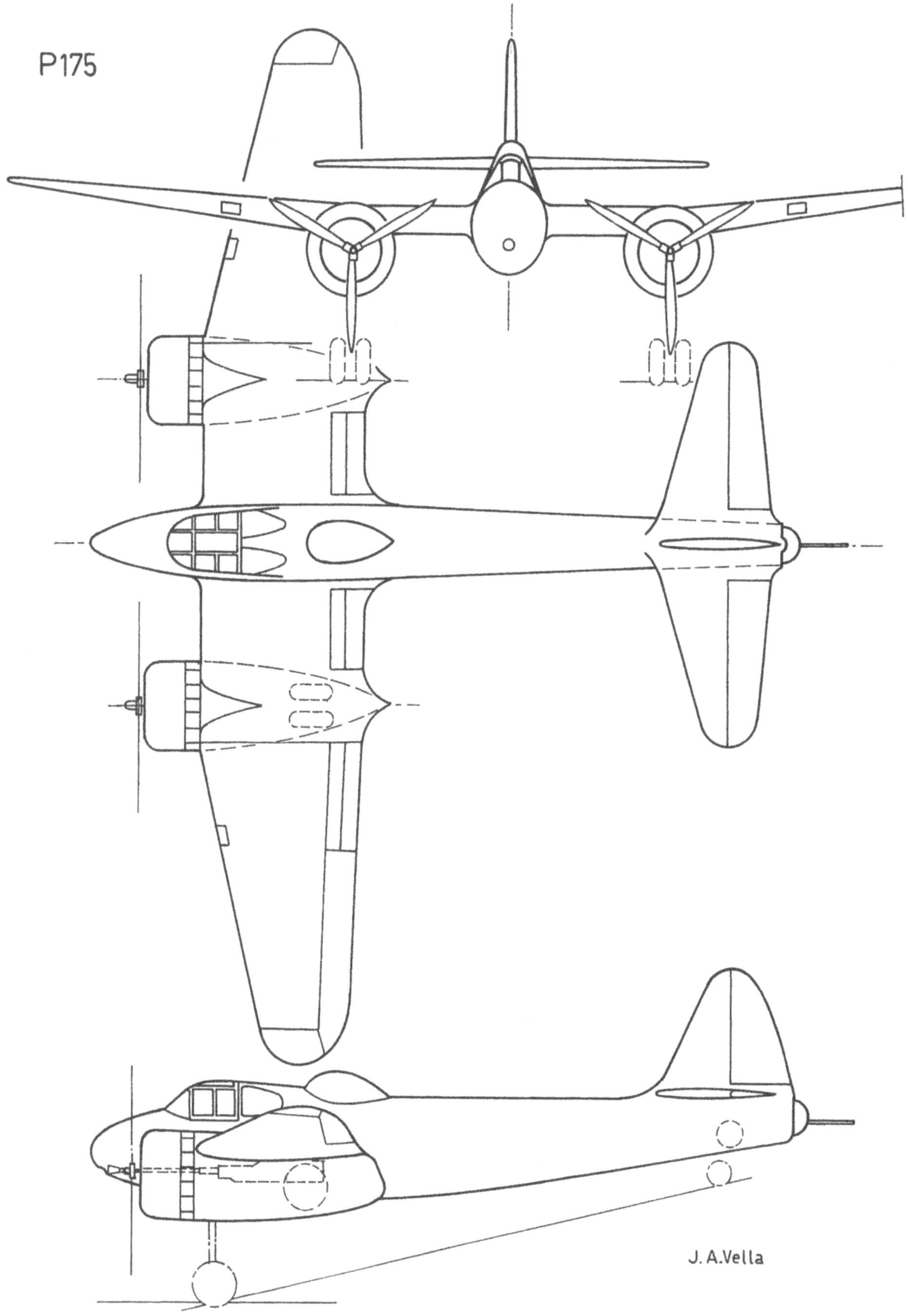

P175

J.A.Vella

XP17
28-5-42

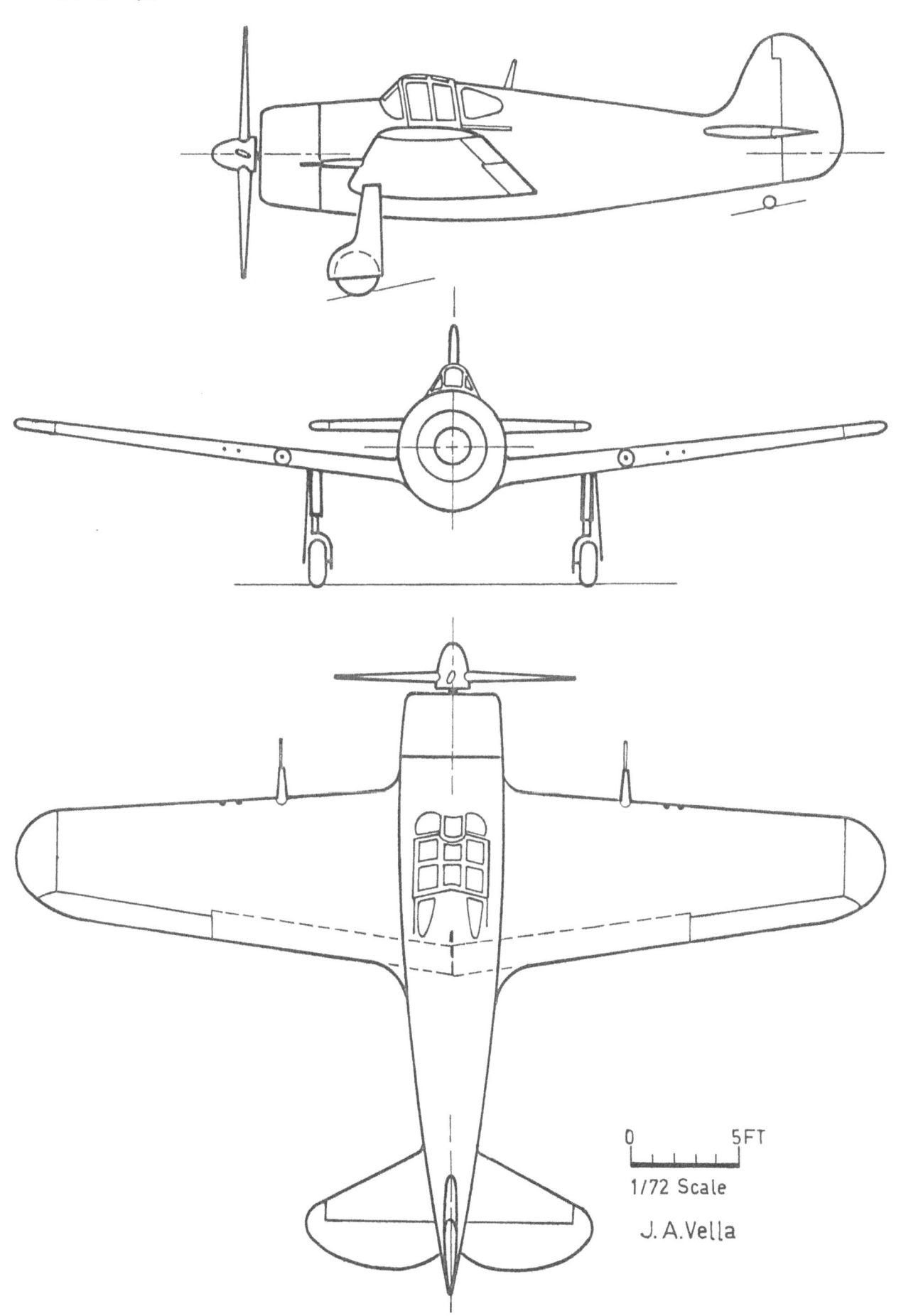

1/72 Scale

J. A. Vella

P176
8-8-42

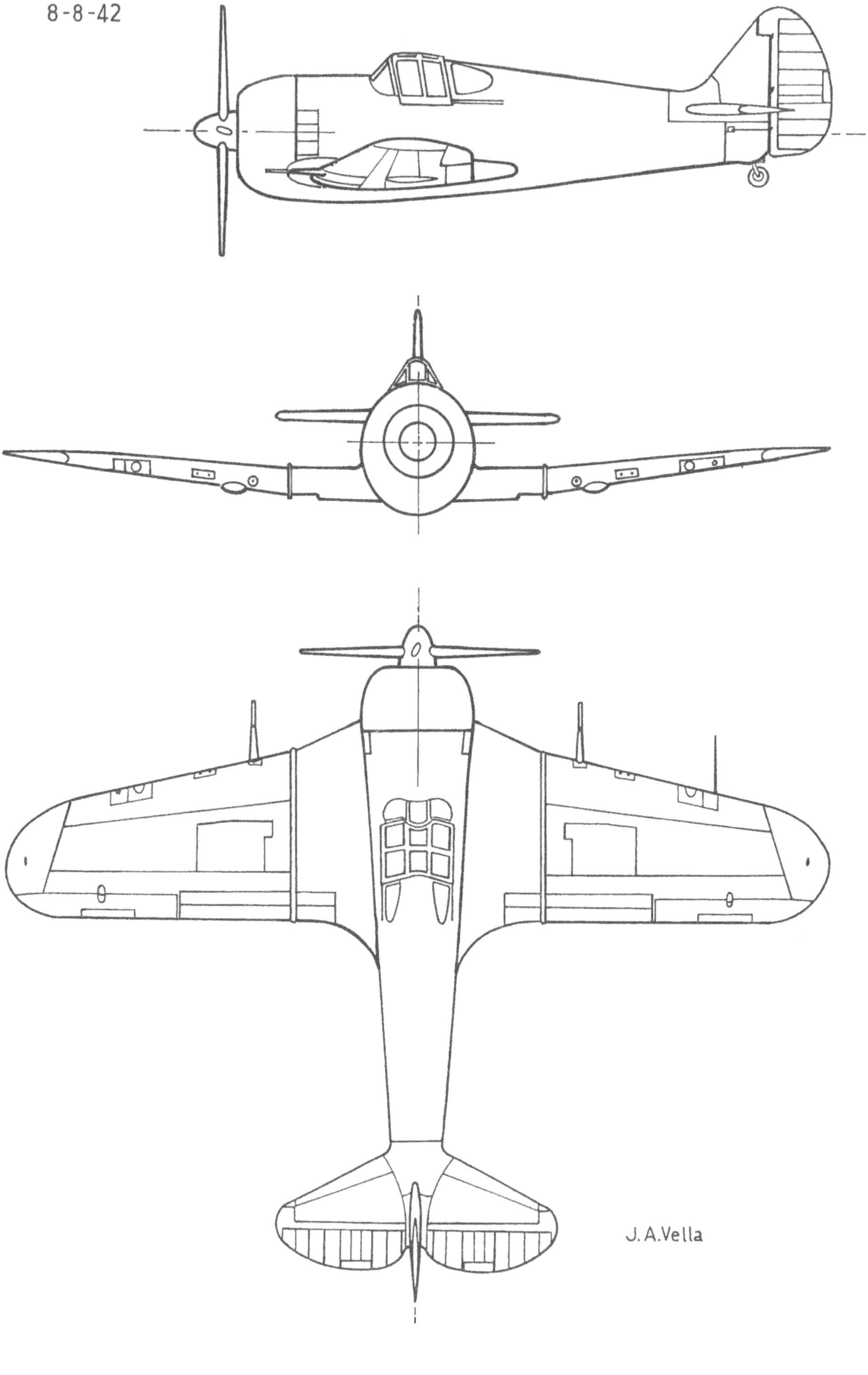

J.A.Vella

provision for 200 gallons of fuel. The rearward retracting main undercarriage was to have twin wheel assemblies. The tail wheel was also to be retractable.

In the second version the engine of choice was two of the P & W R-1830 S3C-4G Twin Wasp radials each of 1,200 hp doubling the installed take-off power. The offensive armament load was the same but the fuel capacity was increased to 300 gallons.

Bibliography: P175 Anti-Tank Aircraft
Commonwealth Aircraft Corporation. (1942) Engineering Report AA15. (July 1942). Anti-tank aircraft project.

XP17 & P176 WRIGHT CYCLONE BOOMERANG FIGHTER
May 1942-Aug 1942

By April 24, 1942 follow-on work, general factory output and new aircraft tooling capacity over and beyond the order for 105 examples of the CA-12 had become a matter for detailed consideration. The tooling manpower requirement indicated that CAC did not possess the capacity to cope with the CA-4 / CA-11 bomber adequately to 1943, however it did have sufficient capacity to handle tooling for fighters but not two distinct projects simultaneously. Propositions were put to undertake a limited tooling upgrade on the CA-12 along the lines :

1. The installation of a Wright Cyclone engine in a CA-12 with minimum sheet metal change would require eight weeks and 75,000 man-hours of new tooling work

2. A re-designed, improved new fighter for 1943 service requiring 20 weeks and 20,000 man-hours of new tooling

3. The installation of supercharger gear to either of the above or the CA-12 during 1943

Item (3) received the go-ahead as the prototype CA-14 / CA-14A and Item (1) had some traction as it generated at least two aircraft outlines by the company and pressure from Australia on the USA from mid-1942 to source 145 Wright Cyclone radial engines. An improved conversion of the CA-12 was a government first priority as at August 8, 1942 with either an exhaust driven turbo supercharger model or a Wright Cyclone powered variant, whichever could be implemented first. The latter had the support of the CAS, AVM George Jones.

From September 1942, the USA had, with great difficulty, allocated the Australian Government 25 Wright Cyclones each month for use on a new Boomerang Interceptor. This was well below the expected factory capacity of 40 to 50 fighter aircraft each month after the completion of the CA-12 contract. If this offer had been taken up it would have been much easier to justify requesting the supply of superchargers as preliminary indications were that the 1,700 hp class Wright Cyclone without supercharging would have been inferior especially at altitude when compared with the existing P & W 1,200hp Twin Wasp fitted with a geared supercharger.

To take on a CA-12 enhancement as described here, the factory was to embark on 10,000 hours of production tooling each week and 20 weeks of preparation time. This would have co-incided with the time required to resolve the engine mounting alterations, aerodynamic refinement and the expected arrival of the first of the Wright Cyclones in September 1942. Supercharger gear was anticipated to arrive sometime in 1943. This did not happen as Lend-Lease informed on February 17, 1944 of its inability to supply. In the event of the local manufacture of a new and larger engine, the Wright Cyclone was considered to be a complex difficult undertaking in comparison with the larger P & W R-2800 Double Wasp. The latter followed the lines of the smaller P & W R-1340 with its simple spur gears. Building the R-2800 locally would have seen a saving of about four months of tooling preparation time because of existing, basically similar facilities for the R-1340 engine. For the first time on October 7, 1942, Wackett, at a meeting with the Department of Air in the context of engine production, mentioned the existence of the CAC R-2000, a local upgrading of the R-1830 expected to deliver 1,350 hp for take-off.

XP17
A brief undocumented outline existed dated May 28, 1942. It was given the XP17 retrospective designation after the war. It depicted a smooth cowled fuselage with a radial engine driving a four bladed CAC wooden propeller with a mid-fuselage located cantilever wing devoid of a centre section together with a retractable tailwheel and the outline of the CA-12 cockpit canopy. The general spec date was April 1942.

P176
By contrast the later August 8, 1942, P176 outline revealed distinctive but enlarged Boomerang outlines. This was the work of Doug Humphries and carried the mixed label of Type CA-12 Model CA-15.

An engineering progress report of 9 August stated that the aircraft was to incorporate the latest aerodynamic principles including a laminar flow airfoil, efficient engine ducting design and a retractable tail wheel (but depicted as non-retractable on the company document). Wackett had suggested the CA-12 could be cleaned up to improve its performance by using a wooden bladed propeller; fit the CAC R-2000 engine or quicker still to install the Wright Cyclone R-2600B-13 engine.

Daniel McVey, secretary to the Aircraft Advisory Committee wrote to the secretary of the Department of Air on September 28, 1942 recommending this upgraded Boomerang, suggesting the construction of a prototype as well as installing a similar engine in the DAP Beaufort bomber, thereby achieving an upgrade of performance in two warplanes with an identical engine.

Specifications	XP17 Wright Cyclone Boomerang Fighter	
Powerplant	Wright Cyclone R-2600-B radial engine of 1,700 hp	
Performance	Max speed at 30,000 ft	344 kts
	Cruise speed at 30,000 ft	330 kts
	Range at 2/3 power at 15,000 ft	600 nm
	Range at 2/3 power at 30,000 ft with external fuel	860 nm
	Range at 450 hp at 15,000 ft	1,300 nm
	Range at econ power at 30,000 ft with external fuel	1,500 nm
Weights	NA	
Dimensions	Wing span	40 ft
	Length	28 ft 9 ins
	Height	NA
Armament	Wing mounted two 20 mm cannon with 200 rpg & four m/gs with 1,000 rpg	

Chief of Air Staff AVM G. Jones, stressed the urgent need for a long range fighter with a single radial engine (the liquid-cooled twin engine de Havilland Mosquito not fully meeting the requirement) and backed the Boomerang upgrade idea; whilst AVM W. D. Bostock, Air Officer Commanding RAAF Command with operational control over all RAAF squadrons in the SW Pacific Area, suggested otherwise and supported the Mosquito. There were ongoing, well documented differences and a prolonged degree of antagonism between these two senior officers throughout the war.

On September 19, 1942 the War Cabinet allocated £25,000 to CAC in support of the investigation it had already started to deal with of the consequences of installing the Wright Cyclone engine. If approved Wackett had promised he would have a prototype completed by December 31, 1942 ie in four months, and in production in six months. The company attempt to economise and make use of some 75% of production components of the CA-12 was fraught with a stream of development outcomes. The increased all-up weight of this engine installation and its four bladed CAC wooden propeller would have been too heavy for the existing undercarriage assembly and brakes. This called the need for a new centre section, new engine cowl, gills exhaust, new fuselage with revised cockpit, a heavier duty undercarriage, larger wheels, the extended wing leading edge space into which to retract them and a revised geometry for their retraction mechanism. It would use the CA-12 outer wings and empennage. Span and length were necessarily increased. In practical terms it was essential to have an entirely new wing structure.

The Advisory War Council had approved further development with the Wright R-2600-B (1,700 hp) engine in November 1942 but once CAC had advised the impracticality of persisting with this design, it gave consideration to allow a local development of an interceptor fighter with the P & W R-2800-43 (1,850 hp) engine. This brought to an end the XP17 / P176 proposals for CA-12 airframe based enhancements with a Wright Cyclone engine and led to the concentration of new design effort on the P178 / CA-15 concepts.

Specifications	P176	
Powerplant	Wright Cyclone R-2600-B radial engine of 1,700 hp	
Performance	340 mph at 30,000 ft	
	Climb rate at 35,000 ft	4,100 ft/min
Weights	Empty	6,200 lb
	Combat	7,900 lb
Dimensions	Wing span	38 ft 4 ins
	Length	29 ft 4 ins

Bibliography : P176
Australia. Dept of Aircraft Production (1942-42). Aircraft production policy, Air Board & War Cabinet Agenda No 46/1942 & No 469 / 1942. [NAA: MP407/1, 5]. Barcode: 368331.

Commonwealth Aircraft Corporation. CAC Interceptor project (CA-12) Boomerang Aircraft Part 2. [NAA: A1196, 1/502/21 Pt 2]Barcode: 199203.

Humphries. D. (August 8,1942).Wright Cyclone R2600B-13 Type CA-12 Model CA-15. [NAA: A1196,1/502/21 Pt 2]. Barcode: 199203.

P178 / CA-15 FIGHTER AIRCRAFT
October 1942

When the RAAF issued Specification 2/43 in 1942 it sought an interest in a fighter with an airframe and engine combination capable of producing a worthwhile leap in all-round performance over that of the CA-12 Boomerang. Various avenues of upgrading the performance of the Boomerang were pursued; the most significant being the built experimental CA-14 /14A turbo-supercharged variant. This approach was however considered to be the limit of experimentation to extract maximum performance from a small airframe. In spite of the success of the CA-14A, the recommendation in July 1943 for its series production was not implemented, the Air Force having already accepted the North American Aviation P-51 Mustang as its next significant fighter aircraft for local production.

CAC pursued Specification 2/43. Their submission made it a late starter in wartime fighter aircraft design. This was no fault of CAC. It was its response to the urgent operational need as perceived in 1942.

P178
The P178 outline of October 30, 1942 as had been suggested by L. J. Wackett was of a compact, short fuselage faintly reminiscent of the Focke Wulf Fw190 in plan and profile, with a low set below mid-fuselage located wing with a semi-elliptical shaped trailing edge (similar to the P-47), two cannon and four machine guns. Intended for the high altitude role, power was to be provided by a P & W R-2800-21 single speed, single stage, engine with an exhaust driven turbo-supercharger (as used on the USAAC Republic P-47 Thunderbolt).

Dimensions: Span- 40 ft 0 ins   Length-30 ft 7 ins

It had been Wackett's long held contention that if a new large radial engine was to be built at CAC it would be the Pratt & Whitney R-2800 Double Wasp as there was considerable engineering similarity between it and the R-1340. At the same time CAC's engine facility at Lidcombe was already heavily committed overhauling R-2800 engines for the USAAC in their SW Pacific area of operations.

Ted Faggetter and Fred David were the authors of a preliminary in-house CA-15 specification approved on January 25, 1943 which now described the aircraft as a low and medium altitude fighter, high speed dive bomber and ground strafing aircraft. Powered by a Pratt & Whitney R-2800-43 single stage, two speed supercharger radial engine, it was to be armed with four 20 mm cannon and four 0.5 inch machine guns.

Dimensions: Span   40 ft 0 ins
              Wing area   263 sq ft
              Length   34 ft 4 ins
              Height (tail down), to tip of propeller   12 ft 4 ins

On an unknown date, this internal report A87 was declared obsolete in favour of Specification Report A94, with the R-2800-21 engine. Design work continued on the layout with the -21 engine with wind tunnel tests scheduled for the second half of February 1943. The DAP advised CAC on February 17, 1943, that the War Cabinet had given its approval to the development of the CA-15.

Development was funded to £50,000 for equipment and materials including the work on a mock-up, a start on which had been made in February. This was inspected on 21 May. The design team was comprised of Fred David, Chief Designer; Ian Ring & Doug Humphries, Design Engineers; Harry Becker, Experimental Section Superintendent and Ian Fleming of Flight Test.

CAC's drawings (15-03002, 003, 00110) of May and June 1943, showed the aircraft had taken on the proportions and appearance of the P-47 Thunderbolt, with a turbo-supercharger stowed internally in the mid fuselage below and slightly to the rear of the pilot seat. Complex ducting from the large (380 sq in) air intake below the engine with its oil coolers, was routed (through 60 sq in) ducts along the bottom and both sides of the fuselage level with the cockpit floor to the intercooler and supercharger.

Exhaust gases were piped back separately to the turbine and expelled through a waste gate in the bottom of the fuselage. Ducted air was fed to the centrifugal impeller and returned via the intercooler, (which had its own waste gate behind the turbine) to the engine under pressure. Waste air from the oil coolers was vented through a duct to the lower port side of the fuselage in front of the wing.

The wing planform was now shown to have an angular trailing edge comprised of two forward sweep angles. The wing leading edge had root extensions for undercarriage stowage. Of necessity the previous CA-12 construction of welded steel tube frame, fabric, ply and aluminium construction had given way to that of semi-monocoque stressed alloy skin. Armament was two 20 mm cannon and two 0.5 inch machine guns. The CAC drawing of June 4, 1943 showed it fitted with an eight gun armament (cannon protruding) and powered by the R-2800-22W (not the -21) with water injection without any change of outline.

Dimensions: Span-39 ft 0 ins   Length-34 ft 0 ins.

Specifications	CA-15 with P & W R-2800-10W	
Powerplant	One P & W R-2800-10W Double Wasp 18 cyl radial engine with 2 speed, 2 stage mechanical supercharger of 2,000 hp & 2,300 hp with water injection driving a CAC 12 ft 9 ins diameter 4 bladed Jablo propeller	
Performance at aircraft weight of 9,360 lb	Max speed at SL	306 kts
	Max speed at 20,000 ft	345 kts
	Max speed at 27,000 ft	357 kts
	Max speed at 30,000 ft	349 kts
	Rate of climb at SL	4,700 ft/ min
	Rate of climb at 30,000 ft	1,800 ft/min
	Time to 10,000 ft	2.3 min
	Time to 20,000 ft	4.8 mins
Weights	Combat	9,360 lb
Dimensions	Wing span	36 ft 0 ins
	Length	34 ft 9 ins
	Propeller tip height	14 ft 2 ins
Armament	Eight 0.5 inch m/gs	

The First Change

Wackett was the Technical Adviser to the DAP, a member on the overseas mission that set out in January 1943 to select a long range escort fighter, a heavy bomber and a high altitude interceptor fighter. Wackett's interest lay mainly in the selection of the high altitude fighter. The team visited widely, taking in development trends in new aircraft design, armament and engines in the United Kingdom and USA.

The North American Aviation P-51 Mustang was selected to fill the high altitude fighter role. Although no specification had been issued for a low and medium altitude fighter it was considered that such an aircraft should have a radial engine in preference to an in-line design which would be more vulnerable to damage from ground fire in low altitude combat. The mission did consider the Hawker Tempest II, Curtiss P-69 and the CA-15 for the low altitude role. Nevertheless, it was concluded that a decision on the type should be deferred as the need for a high altitude fighter was more urgent. With most fighter aircraft in the SW Pacific area already operating in the low / medium altitude role, there was a sufficiency in numbers.

CA-15 mock-up. Early configuration possibly the R-2800-21. **HDHV**

At the Board meeting of June 16, 1943 the company was confirmed as the builder of the P-51 interceptor under contract CA-17.

On Wackett's return to Australia to his position on the Aircraft Advisory Committee he suggested on 5 July that the revised Specification 2/43 Issue 1 now calling for a Medium Altitude Fighter (leaving the high level cover to the P-51) was inconsistent with the design which had been underway for some six months. Wackett had firmed the opinion based on his overseas tour that a two stage supercharger installation in a radial engine aircraft with liquid cooled intercoolers would have the advantage over air cooled intercoolers through a great reduction of bulky duct work. Geared fan forced cooling would also reduce drag by doing away with exterior flap type gills allowing the use of sliding shutters to control the dumping of cooling air.

The CA-15 design would have to be altered to take an engine without turbo-supercharging. The revised Specification required optimum performance at or about 20,000 ft and the essential characteristics at this altitude were to be:
- A high rate of climb coupled with a high rate of acceleration
- Good fighting manoeuvrability particularly in the rolling plane
- High speed

By 16 August, DEPAIR had agreed to the engine change and was willing to build two airframe prototypes (subject to War Cabinet approval) to test out different armament combinations. Although

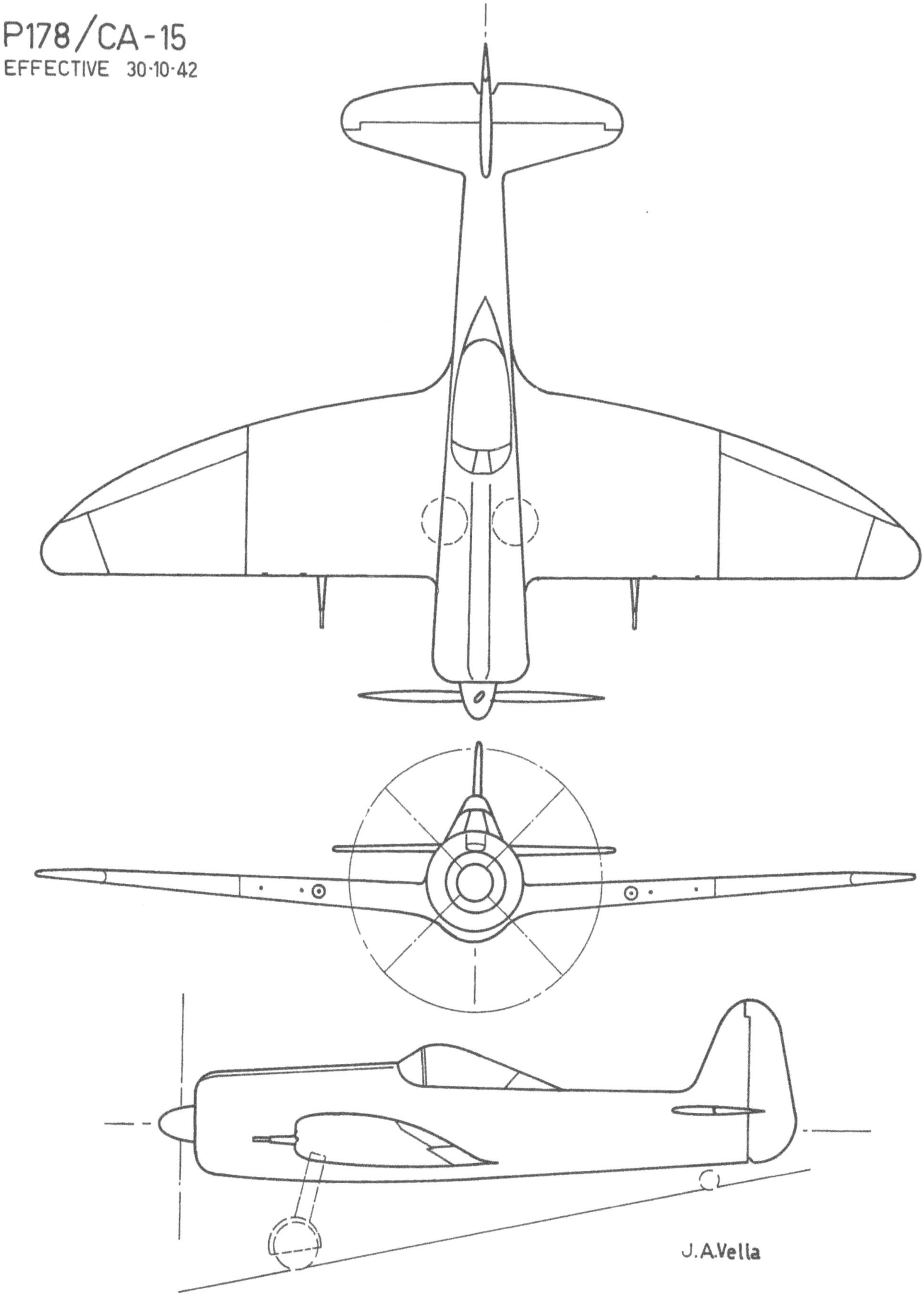

P178/CA-15
EFFECTIVE 30·10·42

J.A.Vella

much of the previous detail design work could be utilized, the revised specification dictated fundamental changes amounting to a new design and some twelve months of extra work. By mid-October, with a firmed outline, the design concept was passed to the drawing office. It was considered it would eventuate to be the best performance low-altitude fighter in existence. Two mock-ups of the CA-15 were in the Experimental Section (Department), where the aircraft was being built, one with an exhaust driven turbo-supercharger, the other one without.

The wing platform was changed to have an unbroken trailing edge and a three foot reduction in span due in part for the demand of good roll and turning performance. The fuselage was extended nine inches with the intention to now install the R-2800-10W Double Wasp, 18 cylinder radial engine. This unit with a two speed, two stage mechanical supercharger with fan cooling, nine liquid cooled aftercoolers combined with an underslung air-cooled radiator in a bulky front end was deemed capable of delivering 2,000 hp and up to 2,300 hp with water injection. The R-2800-10 and -25 engine variants had also been considered.

CAC's 12 ft 9 in. diameter, 40° propeller fitted with Jablo blades was to be used. (Jablo ie laminated, densified compressed wood – after Bruno Jablonsky, 1938 .)

Defensive armament was to be eight 0.5 inch machine guns enclosed completely inside the wing with no muzzles protruding on the leading edges so as to maintain the laminar flow over the high speed wing section. Fred David carried out the engine installation design during August and September 1943.

Following General George Kenney's (Commander-Allied Air Forces South West Pacific Area) recommendation on the range requirements for fighter aircraft, the fuel capacity of the CA-15 was increased to provide a cruising endurance of five hours and a combat time of 45 minutes.

While this CA-15 activity was underway, the aircraft factory's high priority was to keep the preparation of the initial CA-11 Woomera bomber production uppermost.

In August 1943 the design of the CA-15 was reduced in priority to the status of an exercise In engineering design technique. Building of frame jigs had begun by the last week of November; engineering drawings issued and parts manufacture commenced in January 1944. It had been Wackett's suggestion of September 27, 1943 that two prototypes still be built to test the performance of two forms of the proposed armament combinations. Meanwhile the CSIR Division of Aeronautics investigated the efficiency of the intercooler duct location following the change from the 'original' engine, as well as the full scale retraction testing of the CA-15 undercarriage with its door panels.

The design of this configuration was attributed to Ted Faggeter and Stan R. Brookes.

Up until this stage, some £31,512 had been spent in developing the design mock-up with emphasis on the high altitude role. The requirement was now to be for low-to-medium altitude.

Engine Changes Continue

By the beginning of 1944 the airframe was ready to receive its engine installation and two R-2800-10W engines were sought through Lend-Lease and the United States Naval authorities. On June 1, 1944 CAC learned the -10W engine production was to be discontinued and Pratt & Whitney recommended its equivalent replacement, the -22W. (CAC documents show these change dates in reverse order.)

On data then available, this engine was expected to show an unfavourable drop in output even at medium altitudes and its application was discarded. The design progressed to using the R-2800-57W Double Row Wasp with its single speed, single stage supercharger, water injection and external boost.

The supercharger was mounted beneath the engine and the cooling system consisting of two aluminium air-to-air intercoolers also in the engine bay offering:
- A compact arrangement to maintain pitching inertia
- Short lengths of ducts ensuring a quick response to throttle movement
- Complete flame damping (as requested in the Specification) due to a submerged arrangement

All this forward located equipment added to the frontal bulk of the airframe. The unit had a brochure military rating (MR) of 2,200 hp up to 25,000 ft and a war emergency rating (WER) of 2,800 hp to 25,000 ft, driving a four bladed propeller as in the previous -10W installation but of 12 feet diameter. On WER power the very high climb rate of 5,800 ft /min was expected.

The effect of thrust recovery from a turbo-supercharger jet exhaust installation was not known except through calculation. Exact data was not expected until an engine was available. However, from information available on June 3, 1944, calculating an average performance for the engine with and without thrust recovery, the expected figures were :

CA-15 with R-2800-57W			
Altitude (Ft)	Climb Rate (ft/min) W.E.R.	Climb Rate (ft/min) M.R.	Max Speed (kts) W.E.R. without Jet Exhaust
Sea Level	5700	4400	345 kts (398 mph)
5000	5600	4300	360 kts (415 mph)
10000	5400	4100	373 kts (430 mph)
22000	5000	3700	404 kts (465 mph)

W.E.R. War Emergency Rating

M.R. Military Rating

Specifications	CA-15 P & W R-2800-57W	
Powerplant	One P & W R-2800-57W Double Wasp 18 cyl radial engine with single stage, single speed turbo supercharger, with water injection & external boost of 2,200 hp to 25,000 ft & a WER of 2,800 hp to 25,000 ft driving a CAC 12 ft 9 ins dia 4 bladed Jablo propeller	
Performance	Refer to tables above	
Weights	Combat	9,686 lb
	Wing loading	8 lb /ft
Dimensions	Wing span	36 ft
	Length	34 ft 9 ins
	Height	11 ft 7 ins
Armament	Six 0.5 inch m/gs	

Both the -10W and -57W engines had a cooling fan with reduction gear and propeller shaft extension. The differences in weight between the two power groups was 4,343 lb for the -10W and the lighter 4,257 lb for the -57W. Combat weight of the CA-15 with the

CA-15
R2800-21
4-6-43

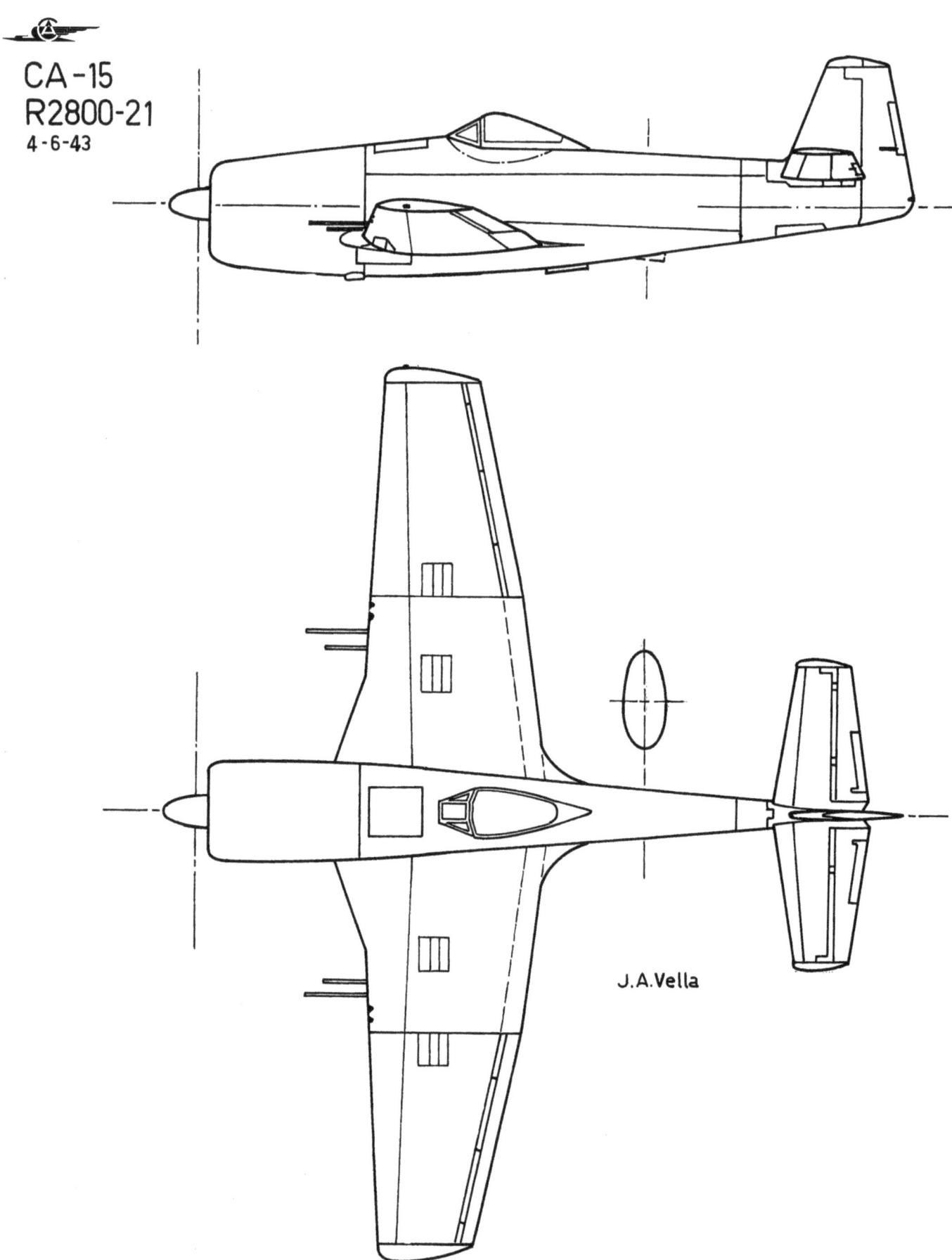

J.A.Vella

R-2800-57W was 9,686 lb including 90 gallons of fuel, 20 gallons of oil and six 0.5 inch machine guns.

Although chronologically the -57W engine was to replace the -10W variant; CAC documents show these dates (as depicted here) in reverse order. Multiple engine selections were investigated in close and urgent succession and the respective internal engineering documentation did not always keep pace.

The powerful Pratt & Whitney R-2800 had been in use in vast numbers of United States aircraft. To list a few is to indicate the reliability and service strength of this engine. The -10W was in the F6F-5 Hellcat; -10 in the Curtiss XP-60E; -34W in the F7F Tigercat and F8F Bearcat; the -21 and -59 in the P-47B,C & D; -8W in the F4U-1 Corsair; and the -57C in the XP-47J, P47M & N Thunderbolt.

The Air Board and the DAP had now agreed in principle that three prototypes of the CA-15 be built. This was strange in view of the lowered status of the project.

In July, CAC was informed that the -57W was not yet in production and would not be available.

As of August 15, 1944 a record of work on the first prototype showed progress towards completion as follows:

Detail tooling	75%
Assembly jigs	85%
Fabrication of wing	20%
Fuselage	60 %
Fixed tail surfaces	40%
Control surfaces	25%
Surface controls	50%
Landing gear	60%

CAC's representative in the United States, R. W. Cameron & Co, Inc. advised that acquisition of R-2800 engines was difficult and a hold-up was expected. A short time later the conclusion must have been reached that no alternative suitable production variant of the R-2800 engine would be available. CAC had fabricated an engine mount for the R-2800 based on one example of this engine at Fisherman's Bend that had been sent from Lidcombe on April 15, 1943, on loan from the USAAC for use in mock-up trials. (Two intercoolers were also loaned). The secondary reason for the loan was to evaluate the R-2800 and its suitability for local manufacture within CAC's existing facilities. These items were sent back in February 1945.

Centaurus and Griffon

The immediate reaction to this setback was to propose an alternate radial engine. This time as conveyed in Report A100 of August 15, 1944 by Doug Humphries, the choice was the 2,300 hp Bristol Centaurus CE-12SM 18 cylinder, two row, sleeve valve, single stage, two-speed mechanical supercharger radial as flown in the experimental Hawker Sea Fury prototypes.

Apart from engine controls no structural alterations were required aft of the firewall. The engine was to be moved back approximately ten inches causing a rearward shift of centre of gravity. The cowling was shortened by ten inches and due to another increase in the diameter of the frontal area the vision over the nose would have been reduced from 8° to 7.65°. This engine in Proposal P181 gave a much reduced performance.

By September 29, 1944 an investigation was underway to consider fitting the liquid cooled Rolls Royce Griffon 125, two-stage, 3 speed, supercharged, 12 cylinder engine.

Setback But Work Continues

The change to the Griffon was followed almost simultaneously by the decision of the Prime Minister, that, *having regard to the manpower requirements* and with the War Cabinet and the Advisory War Council's approval, both the CA-15 and sister project the CA-11, bomber, be abandoned. This directive of September 27, 1944, was vigorously attacked by the management of CAC. It was a decision that would virtually put an end to the wartime design and development work of CAC, the only aircraft establishment that was involved in major design.

Whilst 300 to 400 people would be released from the CA-11 project, the CA-15 was moving along with 60 personnel, 15 or 16 of which were University of Sydney graduates. Their involvement in the design was part of the aeronautical development work attempted by the University, where a Chair of Aeronautics had been established.

Even Sidney Camm, the English designer of the Hurricane, Typhoon and Tempest fighters was quoted by L.P. Coombes, Chief of Aeronautics, CSIR as saying that *"Australia could not get far in aircraft production if it did not encourage original design and development".*

That near prophetic statement was made on October 23, 1944.

The situation was pulled back from the brink by re-instating the CA-15 as a development project (acknowledging the fact that jet aircraft were likely to offer the improvement of performance that was sought) still subject to the development ceiling of £150,000. This figure had been based on the use of radial engines. With the changes to fit the Griffon, costs escalated. £136,235 had been spent of an estimated final £207,000. To sort this out the project overhead charges were changed from that of an aircraft in full production to that of a one-off item on April 9, 1945.

Work continued on the engine installation. Alteration of the structure aft of the firewall was limited to radiator modification in the form of two frames below the lower longerons. With the thrust line raised 5.5 inches, a larger diameter propeller could be considered. The installation of the engine was simpler and access was also easier.

Loaded for combat with 90 gallons of fuel the comparison was:

	R-2800-57W	Griffon 125
Weight	9,686 lb	9,033 lb
Wing Loading	38 lb / sq ft	36 lb/ sq ft

This latest engine change meant another disruption and another load on a meagre number of available design staff. The engine was to be located so as to have the same forward vision as on the R-2800 installation. With its reduced oil consumption, the Griffon 125 needing only 15 gallons of oil and no necessity for tankage space for water injection, it was possible to find new space for a fuselage located self-sealing fuel tank with a capacity of up to 40 gallons. (Although this extra fuel space was accounted for in general weight estimations, flight test reports quote only a total internal fuel capacity of 220 gallons, ie only the wing tanks which leaves the conclusion that if fitted, and there is doubt about this, the tank was not used.)

The maximum fuel requirement for long range escort or ferry was now reckoned at 450 gallons; comprised of 220 gallons in the wings, 30 usable gallons from the fuselage cell and two 100 gallon external tanks on wing station 119. Alternatively two 40 gallon external tanks were optioned for wing station 82.

Comparison with the P-51H with a 2,200 hp Packard Merlin and using data then available to the RAAF gave confidence of good prospects for the CA-15. The P-51H first flew on February 3, 1945 and had a normal loaded weight of approximately 9,500 lb. The CA-15 was expected to be superior to the P-51H over a complete altitude range for the same propeller efficiencies and superior in maximum speed between 10,000 and 28,000 feet.

Pending the availability of the promised contra-prop RR Griffon 125 as stipulated in the altered requirement RAAF Spec. 2/43 (Issue 3) the decision was taken to accept on a no-cost loan basis the interim the use of two Griffon 61 engines, with two-stage, two speed mechanical superchargers with four bladed propellors from the Ministry of Aircraft Production . The Griffon 61 was the engine in use in the RAF's Supermarine Spitfire Mk 21 and planned for the Supermarine Spiteful, the first of which (NN660) had its maiden flight on June 30, 1944. For the CA-15, the ancillaries were different and of

Static load testing the CA-15 wing. **HDHV via David Anderson.**

Model of the R2800-57W variant. **Kevin Kerle.**

Model views possibly of the model R2800-21. **HDHV via Derek Buckmaster.**

CA - 15

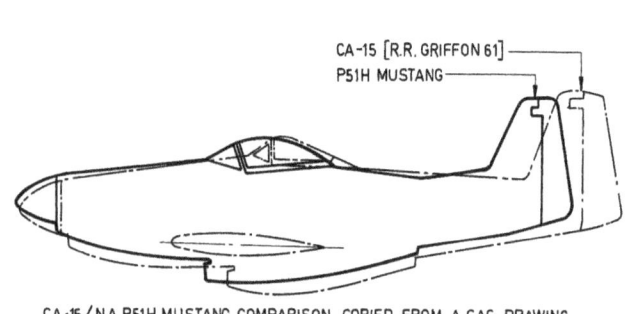

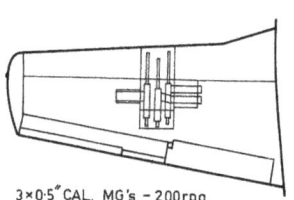

3 × 0·5" CAL. MG's – 200 rpg

1 × 20mm CANNON – 140 rpg
1 × 0·5" CAL. MG – 260 rpg

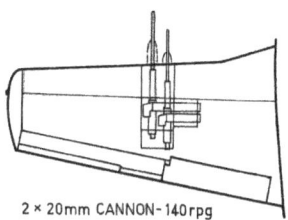

2 × 20mm CANNON – 140 rpg

Armament Installation Alternatives

J. A. Vella

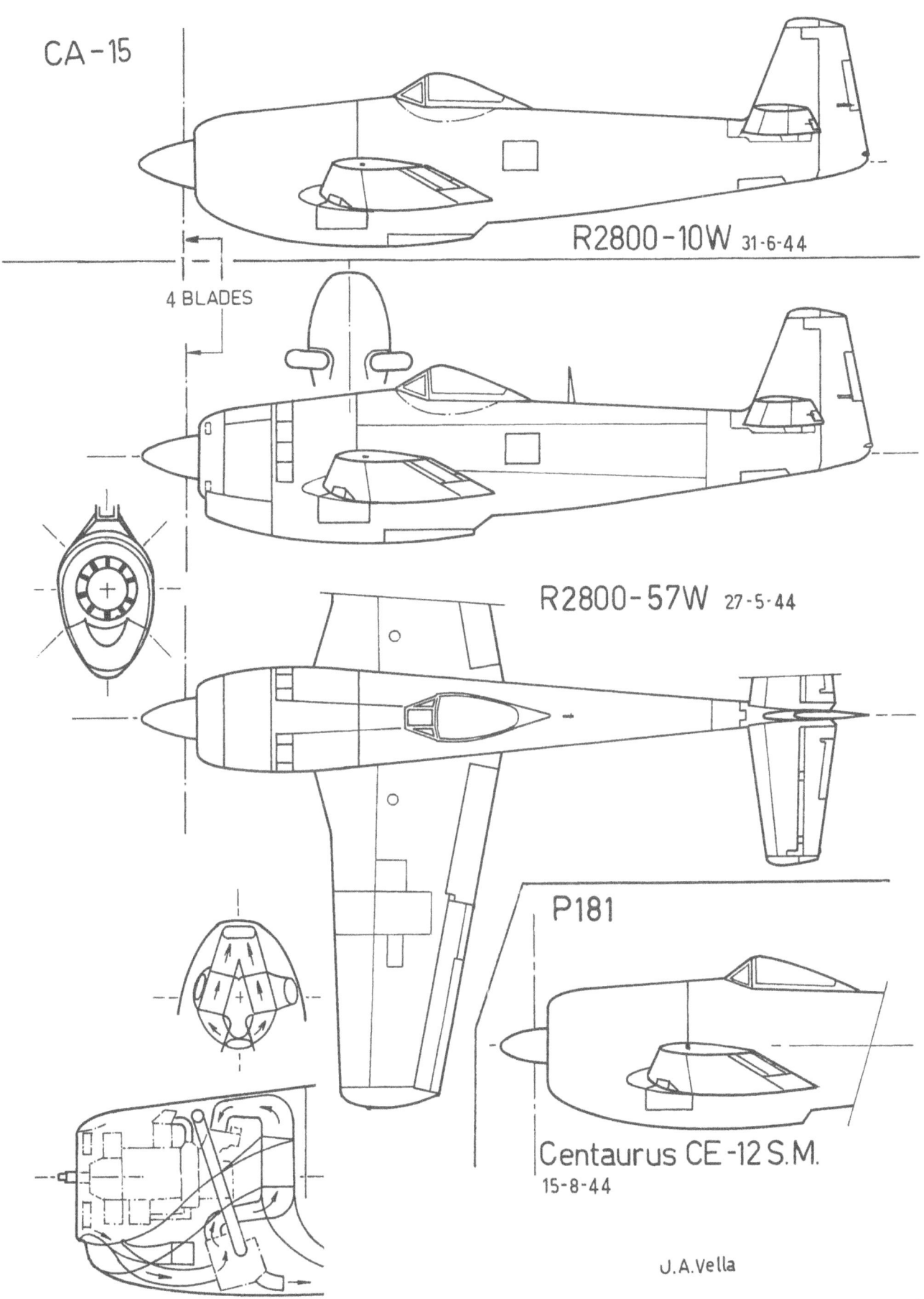

CA-15

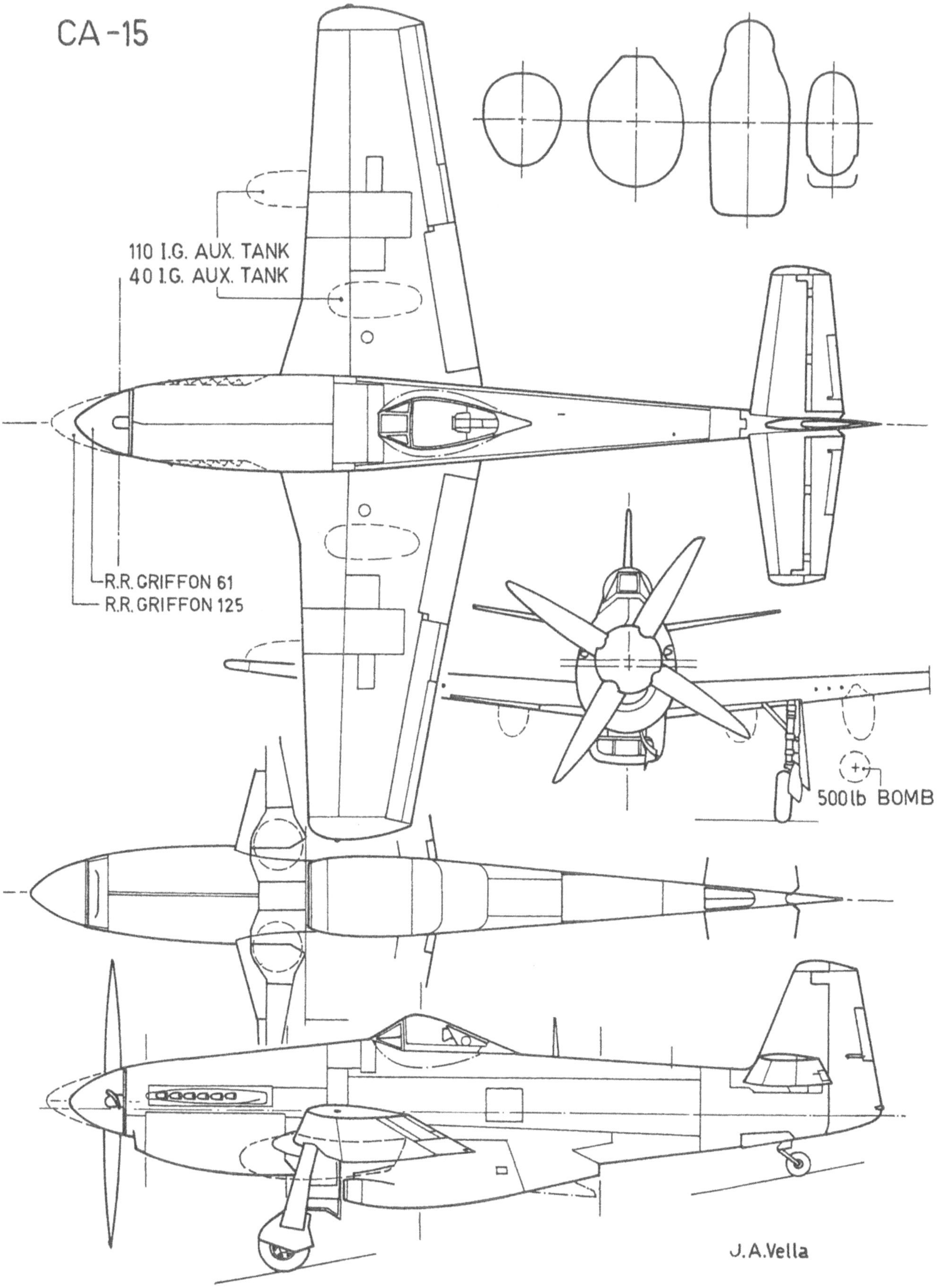

- 110 I.G. AUX. TANK
- 40 I.G. AUX. TANK
- R.R. GRIFFON 61
- R.R. GRIFFON 125
- 500 lb BOMB

J.A.Vella

Port cockpit console. **HDHV via Derek Buckmaster.**

Pilot instrument panel. **HDHV via Derek Buckmaster.**

Starboard cockpit console. **HDHV via Derek Buckmaster.**

The bold impressive lines of a well thought out & designed fighter aircraft. **HDHV**

Above & below: Line maintenance by staff of the CAC Experimental Department. **HDHV**

Jim Schofield taxying A62-1001 at Fisherman's Bend. **HDHV**

The aircraft at an unflattering angle after its forced landing at RAAF Point Cook, December 10, 1946 flown from Fish Bend by Flt Lt Lee Archer. **Richard Hourigan**

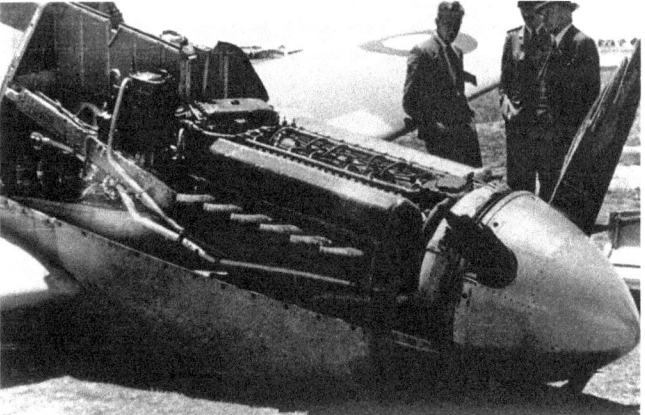
CAC's test pilot Jim Schofield leaning on the wing of the seriously damaged aircraft with its splintered Jablo propeller. **HDHV via David Anderson.**

Specifications	CA-15 - RR Griffon 61			
Powerplant	One Rolls Royce Griffon 61, 12 cyl liquid cooled vee engine of 1,540 hp at TO; 2,305 hp at 7,000 ft and 1,820 hp at 21,000 ft driving a 12 ft 6 inches diameter 4 bladed Dowty Rotol Jablo propeller			
Performance	Max speed at SL	319 kts		
	Max speed at 26,400 ft	389 kts		
	Max speed at 32,700 ft	374 kts		
	Time to climb to 20,000 ft	5.5 mins		
	Max rate of climb rate (without armament)	4,900 ft/min		
	Max rate of climb (with armament)	4,000 ft /min		
	Service ceiling	39,000 ft		
	Range with 220 gall internal fuel	1,000 nm		
	Range with external fuel	2,200 nm		
Weights	Empty equipped	7,540 lb		
	Normal loaded	10,764 lb		
	Max overload	12,340 lb		
Dimensions	Wing span	59 ft 1 in	Wing area	253 sq ft
	Root chord	10 ft 3 ins	Tip chord	4 ft 9 ins
	Aspect ratio	5.12	Wing LE sweep	3° 11'
	Wing dihedral	5°	Airfoil section NACA Laminar Flow Drag-66 Series	
	Length	36 ft 2.5 ins	Height (tail down) to tip of propeller 14 ft	2.75 ins
	Height (tail down) to top of fin	9ft	Tailplane span	13 ft 10 ins
	Horizontal tail area	45.7 sq ft	Aspect ratio	4.19
	Tailplane LE sweep	8° 8'	Tailplane dihedral	10°
	Wheel base	23 ft 7 ins	Track	14 ft 0.5 ins
Armament	Six wing mounted 0.5 in Browning m/gs with 250 rpg. Provision for 10 rocket projectiles, two 500 lb bombs or two 1,000 lb bombs			
Retrospective Designation	XP20 CA-15 Pratt & Whitney R-2800 engine XP21 P181 CA-15 Bristol Centaurus engine XP22 CA-15 RR Griffon 61 engine			

necessity, arranged differently. With an identical fuel load the Spitfire Mk 21 was 87 lb lighter than the CA-15.

Empty weights for a three aircraft comparison were:
  CA-15   7,151 lb
  P-51H   6,481 lb
  Spitfire Mk 21 6,853 lb

No Griffon 125 Engine – More Alternatives

The trauma of engine choice and installation still persisted. The Griffon 125 would not be available for about eight months but Rolls Royce was building a small number of Griffon 121 engines (believed to be two or three examples) for application in the Australian CA-15 and an experimental Spiteful. One engine with its two, three blade, 11 foot diameter, contra-rotating propellers of the same kind as fitted on the Seafire Mk 46, was promised, albeit not very convincingly, for delivery in January 1946.

RR reneged; the Griffon 125 was not going to be built. Little is known of this variant. (The author's correspondence with Rolls Royce UK in 1983 suggested all its documentation was lost).

Meanwhile to assist with the engine installation work, CAC was sent drawings of the engine mounting for the Spiteful. The CAC engineering team that had gone to England in August 1945 to investigate the theories and application of the new era of jet propulsion was busy sending back to the company data on the efficiency and performance of various four bladed, five bladed and contra-rotating propellers for possible application on the CA-15. The two Griffon 61 engines had arrived by sea at CAC on June 28, 1945 and on September 20, engine number 17072/A487149 was lifted into the revised engine bay compartment and the start of the big effort of fitting its cooling system. It had now also become apparent that the Griffon 121 had a drastically different rear end mounting arrangement from that built for the Griffon 61. This was deemed necessary in order to eliminate persistent vibrations in the Griffon 61 at around 2,400 rpm. Direct acquisition of the Griffon 121, its propeller and set of spares, now threatened to exceed the £150,000 expenditure limit placed on the CA-15 design. A spare 12 ft 6 inch diameter four bladed propeller with Jablo constructed blades and spinner were received and an order was placed for two Rotol, 11 ft diameter, five bladed, wooden propellers (as used on the Spitfire Mk 21) to be sent out for eventual installation as an alternative to the four bladed propeller. Rotol could not comply with this request as it found it was not possible to fit the correct profile spinner capable of accommodating five blades on the CA-15. Eventually, with some modifications, a spinner as was fitted on the Westland Welkin, was found to be acceptable.

During his visit to Rolls Royce, Hugh Francis was to learn that the Griffon 121 was never going to be put into production. Its development was only kept active in order to test the three speed supercharger. Another possible engine variant was then mooted. By fitting conversion gearing to the Griffon 61, this engine became the Griffon 85 with contra-rotating propellers improving the perceived take-off, climb and handling characteristics of the CA-15. The propellers had to be made of metal as it was now considered no longer prudent to operate wooden bladed propellers in tropical climates. Also, the onset of flutter in wooden blades greater than 11 feet in diameter added to this changed operational demand. (The RR Griffon 85 with six-blade Rotol contra-props had been flight tested in the UK on the third Hawker Sea Fury F2/43 prototype [LA610] on November 27, 1944.)

On October 23, 1945 CAC sought to extricate itself from installing the Griffon 121/125 series engines and on 12 November the DAP conveyed the willingness of the Department of Air to meet this request, adding also the cancellation of both the five bladed propellers and the conversion gearing offered for possible use on the Griffon 61.

The future prospects of the CA-15 performance were awaited eagerly both in Australia and in the UK. The British Air Ministry showing more than a superficial interest had considered the possibility that once local trials had been satisfactorily accomplished, the aircraft would be shipped to England for further flight test and development. But with only one example flying this was not viable.

During his visit to Australia and CAC, the Managing Director of Rolls Royce Ltd., Ernest W. Hives, remarked that, in his opinion, the installation of the Griffon engine in the CA-15 was the best example of work of its kind.

Aircraft Description

From most angles the aircraft had the looks of a portly P-51H Mustang, but much larger and sat on an undercarriage of 14 foot track giving exceptional stability on uneven ground. The fuselage was built around four longerons. The engine drove a four bladed Rotol constant speed propeller. Two fabricated beams joined the front and rear engine supports to the lower firewall joints with tie members from the rear supports to the upper firewall joints. The firewall width was greater than needed for the slim engine fitted, but nevertheless the aircraft still looked slim due to the increase in length from the liquid cooled engine.

The pilot was seated over the wing trailing edge at the top of the deep fuselage. The area below where the sliding track of the bulged teardrop canopy met the top of the fuselage was faired by almost vertical panels into the apex of the fuselage. Entry was from behind the port wing. The windscreen was of 1.5 inch thick laminated bullet proof panel. The specification called for armour protection against 20 mm cannon rounds from 300 feet astern at angles of 20 degrees to the aircraft centre line. The realised protection for the body provided cover to only 12.5 degrees, with two plates 0.25 inch thick placed 6 inches apart. Head and shoulder protection limited by the need to provide adequate rear vision was achieved by using a 0.75 inch thick plate.

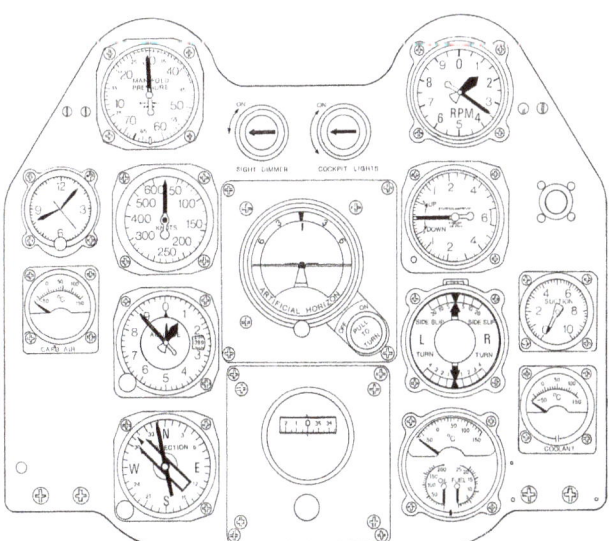

The wing was a two piece NACA 66 series laminar flow aerofoil section. Metal skinned ailerons covered 48% of the span with the remaining space occupied by hydraulically operated flaps. The wing, like the fuselage and tail assembly, was of all metal flush riveted stressed skin.

Fuel was in two tanks each of 110 gallons capacity, self-sealing by a lining of sandwiched layering of synthetic rubber (inner lining) nylon fibre and natural rubber to a thickness of 0.345 inches.

A similar self-sealing tank of a nominal 30 gallons capacity was to be located in the fuselage behind the pilot. The 100 gallon jettisonable underwing tanks were of wooden construction.

The undercarriage was of a cantilever oleo strut with an articulated side brace, retracting inboard into the wing structure. Goodyear 27 inch diameter Smooth Contour tyres inflated to 60 psi were on the main landing gear. The forward retracting Dowty tail wheel unit was a fully castoring, self-centering, lockable, levered suspension type.

Armament Choice

The choice of armament seemed to have given some difficulty as the initial request for eight 0.5 inch machine guns was not proceeded with beyond the specification. It requested the first aircraft to fly would have six 0.5 inch calibre Browning machine guns with 250 rpg and alternative fittings for four 20 mm Mk V cannon with 120 rpg. In the event of a second aircraft flying, the first was to have six 0.5 inch machine guns whilst the second aircraft was to have a mixed armament of two 20 mm cannon with 120 rpg and two 0.5 calibre machine guns with 250 rpg with alternative mountings for the installation of four 20 mm Mk V cannon-all very complex.

The complete mid-fuselage cooling duct was aerodynamically similar to that of the P-51 and use was made of North American data from the P-51B No 1 aircraft to predict performance. Both the intercooler and engine radiator were standard Morris type design and similar to units in the de Havilland Mosquito and Supermarine Spitfire. This was an integrated radiator that managed both the intercooler and oil systems. The exit to the ventral radiator duct incorporated a shutter which could be varied in area from 157 sq in to 388 sq in. The opening was controlled from the temperature of the engine coolant entering the radiator. An electrically operated actuator, thermostatically controlled, would adjust the exit shutter to the required opening. The intercooling system incorporated the heat exchanger for oil cooling. The engine coolant flowed from the intercooler to the oil heat exchanger; to the radiator and back to the intercooler. Engine oil was pumped from its tank to the engine and returned via the oil heat exchanger back to its tank.

Trials, Tribulations and Late Success

With the Pacific War ended, work on the prototype, A62-1001, proceeded with decreased urgency combined with reduced labour availability. Nevertheless taxying trials commenced in February 1946. Poor braking performance necessitated a change from the original 10 inch diameter wheel and disc brake assembly to a temporary fitment of P-51 Mustang, seven inch diameter units, pending a satisfactory resolution with the larger brakes. The aircraft made its fifteen minute first flight at around 6.00pm on March 4, 1946 in the hands of CAC test pilot, James Schofield.

James Schofield's post flight words were quoted in a Melbourne newspaper:

> "She is a very nice aircraft and I was well satisfied with her. She will do everything that is expected of her and I think she will show a better performance than any other single engine aircraft I have flown"

The aircraft was flown with its propeller reduced to 12 feet 1 inch diameter. (A damaged blade and subsequent repair meant cropping by five inches). The CAC Board gave James a £100 bonus. Changes

introduced as a result of the first dozen flights included the alteration of the angle of incidence on the tailplane (as had been predicted at a late stage in wind tunnel testing) and moving the line of the aileron hinges to give better control balance. A ground towing incident caused one propeller blade to tangle with a trestle as a consequence of which the spare full 12 feet 6 inch diameter propeller was installed. The aircraft took part in the Victory Day flypast over Melbourne on June 10, 1946 and manufacturer's trials continued until 27 June. It was handed over to Sqdn Ldr D. Cuming at 1 Aircraft Performance Unit on 2 July for calibration and performance trials. It had logged 18.35 hours in 23 flights with CAC confirming a max speed of 448 mph at 26,400 feet; 4,900 ft/min rate of climb; service ceiling of 39,000 feet and a range of 2,540 miles, all substantially better than the P-51D.

It was flown by RAAF test pilots Wg Cdrs James Harper and G. Marshall; Sqdn Ldrs Derek Cuming, G. Brunner, C. Stark, G. Shiells, and Flt Lt J.Lee Archer at 1 APU, Point Cook. Minor shortcomings which were repeatedly highlighted, were the lack of a clear vision panel; aileron, rudder and elevator control heaviness; the inability to open the hood in flight; the need to keep the hood closed whist engine running to stop exhaust fumes entering the cockpit. Forty three hours of air time were accumulated before the loss of hydraulic fluid was to cause a wheels-up, flaps-up landing at RAAF Point Cook on December 10, 1946 when being flown by Lee Archer. The estimate to rectify the damage and restore the CA-15 to an airworthy condition was put at £3,000. After months of vacillation as to whether it would be repaired even though there was still a need to validate the design parameters as urged and requested by 1 APU, CAC and CSIR, the Department of Air relented and on April 29, 1947 authorised rectification work. The airframe was moved by road to CAC on June 2,1947.

The tooling required for the repair had already been sold by the DAP Disposals Branch in January 1947 but was still stored in the Butler hangar. It was purchased back and work commenced in CAC's Experimental Section. Progress was slow taking 8,600 manhours. The spare Griffon Mk 61 was installed and another £1,000 was allocated to complete the task.

The aircraft was returned 17 months later on May 19, 1948 to 1 AD at RAAF Base Laverton and handed over to ARDU on the following day. John Miles, DAP/GAF's chief test pilot flew the aircraft on four occasions in early May, prior to its return to the RAAF. It was in his opinion and experience, the finest piston engine fighter he had ever flown.

Testing continued on till early 1950. On 7 February, the program was stopped due to difficulty in obtaining spares (especially for the hydraulics system) and in May the aircraft was returned to 1 AD to be reduced to components. The Griffon engines and propellers were to have been returned to the UK.

Official reports credit the aircraft as being very pleasant to fly, possessing good in-flight vision, and handling that was marred only by excessive change of rudder trim with variation of power and/or speed. The CA-15 was the last new piston engine single seat fighter prototype to fly anywhere in the world. There was the belief that had the aircraft flown with the R-2800-57W engine, the maximum level speed would have exceeded the 389 kts (448 mph) level flight figure reached by the Griffon engine prototype. It was claimed to have been the fastest piston engine fighter of WW2.

In the CA-15, CAC was able to demonstrate its ability to produce a design of comparable weight and certainly better performance than its overseas contemporaries. The RAAF stayed with the CA-17/CA-18 built P-51D Mustang, then went on to fly Vampires, Meteors, etc –

it was the new beginning, the jet age. There have been stories that the CA-15 airframe still exists, secreted away. It was last sighted In May 1950 dismantled, engineless and crated in the 1 AD hangar.

The CA-15 total project cost (including its repair) was put at £142,935, well inside the War Cabinet expenditure limit of £150,000.

Bibliography: CA-15

Australia. Aircraft Advisory Committee (1942-46). Minutes of Meetings of Aircraft Advisory Commission. Meetings 1-77.[NAA: B5028,1; B5028,2; B5028,3; B5028,4; B5028,5]. Barcodes: 395652; 395653; 395650; 395651; 395649 respectively.

Australia. War Cabinet. (1942). Aircraft Production Policy (December 7,1942), War Cabinet Minute no.2503, Agenda no. 469/1942.

Australia. War Cabinet. (1943). Manufacture of CA-15 Prototype Fighter Aircraft (January 14, 1943). War Cabinet agenda no. 36/1943.

Commonwealth Aircraft Corporation. (Undated). Engineering reports AA29 to AA41, A94, A100, A101, A106 and A111.

Commonwealth Aircraft Corporation. (Undated). CAC Production file F2.

Commonwealth Aircraft Corporation. (Undated). CAC General CA-15 file-A18C.

Council for Scientific & Industrial Research (1943-43).Forward copies of reports prepared by the Division of Aeronautics.[NAA: MP287/1, 3477]. Barcode: 484516.

David, Fred. Commonwealth Aircraft Corporation. Engineering Report A102 (October 16,1944) Analysis CA-15 Griffon.

Grantham, Gregory (1930-); Bushell, Edward J.(1931-).(2004) Shaft of the Spear: *Evolution of the RAAF Technical Services to the End of WW2*. Acme, Canberra.

Humphries. D. (August 8,1942).Wright Cyclone R2600B-13 Type CA-12 Model CA-15. [NAA: 196,1/502/21 Pt 2]. Barcode : 199203.

Miles, John (1979). *Testing Time*. Neptune Press,Belmont, Victoria.

Royal Australian Air Force. Directorate of Technical Services (1945-47). No 1 APU Performance Report Type Trial of CA-15.[NAA: MP1472/1,21]. Barcode: 514432.

P177 FOUR ENGINE TRANSPORT AIRCRAFT
November 1942

The background to this proposal was a memorandum of October 30, 1942 from the Air Board stating the urgent need for transport aircraft capable of rapid local manufacture, making use of local resources but without delaying any existing or future aircraft manufacturing activity. P & W R-1340 Wasp radial engines had to be used, 473 imported, ungeared examples of which (intended originally for the cancelled 'Sentinel' local design armoured vehicle project) were immediately available together with another 100 engines which were subsequently received and held in USAAC storage in Sydney.

Four submissions were presented at a DAP discussion meeting on November 24, 1942:

- de Havilland to build the Canadian Norduyn 'Norseman' utility aircraft under licence. Approx. payload 3,000 lb. (Mk IV was built with the R-1340 engine)
- A DCA design based on the DC2 fuselage, DAP Beaufort centre section, wings, undercarriage and P & W R-1830 Twin Wasp engines (this was the quickest solution but was

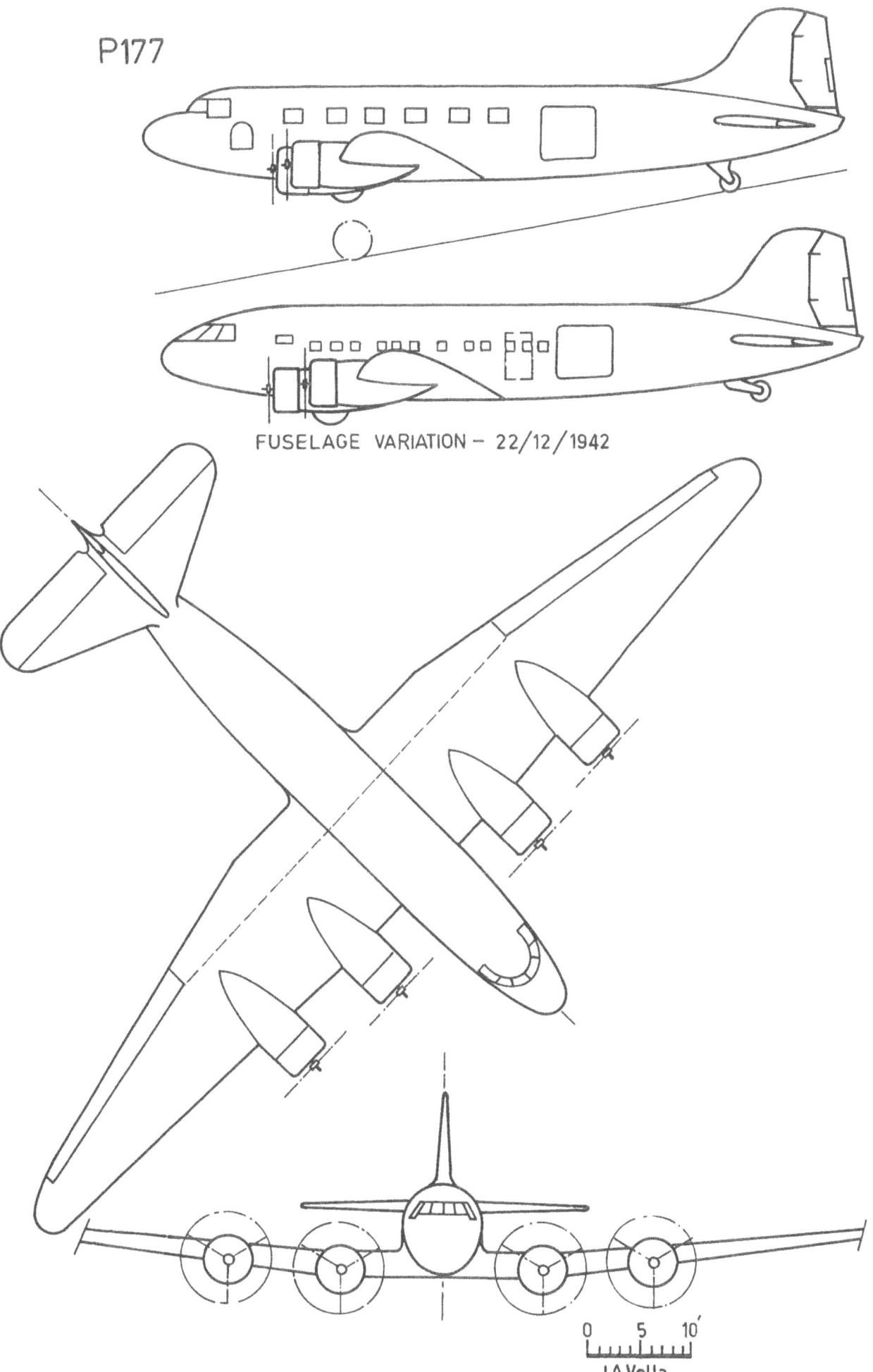

P177

FUSELAGE VARIATION – 22/12/1942

inappropriate because of the non-availability of dural material and Twin Wasp engines).
- The DCA3, which was an aircraft aerodynamically similar to the DC3 but constructed in timber
- The DCA5, also constructed in timber and powered by two R-1340 Wasp engines but which Wackett pointed out was 1,000 lb heavier than the metal variant and considerably underpowered

By contrast, CAC in the P177 proposal put forward on November 9, 1942 followed the outline of the requirement with a four engine design of basic simplicity and maximum use of available materials. The fuselage was based on the aerodynamics of the DC3 but built up of welded chrome molybdenum steel with an outer fabric covering. This method of construction was far quicker than the wooden monocoque technique suggested for the DCA3 and was preferred by the RAAF despite of its uneconomic use of internal space. The one piece wing and the tail assembly were to be of timber construction covered in stressed plywood. (There were later statements hinting to adopt a metal copy of the DC3 tail unit). All control surfaces were to be of aluminium alloy sheet metal construction with fabric covering. Four of the Wirraway engine installations were to be used and the wing was to house 550 gallons of fuel.

Maximum use would be made of Wirraway tools, fittings etc but the company lacked the capacity to build the aircraft. CAC was able to design the fuselage but sought the assistance of the Department of Civil Aviation (DCA) to help with the wing. The DCA had been engaged on design work with the proposed installation of Wright R-2600 Cyclone engines on the DAP Beaufort bomber. The GM-H factory at Fisherman's Bend with its wood working experience (as the major sub-contractor building all the wooden components of the CA-6 Wackett Trainer), was considered to be the prime candidate for building the wing. The first aircraft was planned for 18 months delivery but the site for final assembly had not been selected. Production was expected to be at the rate of two aircraft per week to a total of 80 aircraft for a unit price of £40,000. A revised outline blended the cockpit area and its glazing into the fuselage (Curtiss C-46 style); smaller but extra passenger cabin windows were incorporated and the mountings for engines no 2 and 3 were extended forward, all of these variations were dated December 22, 1942.

Daniel McVey, Secretary to the DAP and Arthur Corbett the Director General of Civil Aviation were not in favour of the design, judging it to be below the prevailing standards for transport aircraft. DCA would assist in whatever way was necessary but would not sponsor the proposal nor allow for its post war civil use. A fully fledged design was better than the expedient solution conveyed in the P177 concept. (The insistence of making use of surplus P & W Wasp engines would have come to nothing as CAC fitted reduction gearing to 350 of the engines which allowed it to extend the production of its Wirraway trainer.)

The P177 ended suddenly on January 25, 1943 with the joint recommendation by the Air Board and the Vice President of Douglas Aircraft Corp that CAC should embark on an alternative program, that of building 100 C-47 transports powered by P & W Twin Wasp radial engines. However because of lingering doubts about the availability of the Twin Wasp, Wackett made the strange proposal the C-47 be powered by four of the smaller Wasp engines. The plan to build the C-47 airframe in Australia was also scrapped when it was made very clear to Wackett in February 1943 during his visit to the Douglas plant that there was a serious doubt as to Australia's ability to produce the C-47 and CAC was not to expect any help from Douglas whatsoever in regard to materials, engineering or tooling for such a venture. Assistance would only be given under a strong directive from the United States Government as Douglas was already fully committed to the war effort.

In April 1943 General Douglas MacArthur vetoed the wartime building of transport aircraft in Australia in favour of continued fighter aircraft production. The growth in capacity of larger transport aircraft was such that it was now considered feasible to fly them in from the United States freeing up valuable shipping space.

Specifications	P177 Four Engine Transport Aircraft	
Powerplant	Four Pratt & Whitney R-1340 S1H1-G Wasp radial engines each of 650 hp at TO	
Performance	Max speed at 5,600 ft	182 kts
	Initial climb rate at 25,000 lb	1,500 ft/min
	Max range at econ cruise speed of 121 kts at 7,000 ft	1,510 nm
Weights	Total structure	7,455 lb
	Empty	15,096 lb
	Freighter	26,708 lb
	Paratroops	26,708 lb
	Ambulance	25,258 lb
Dimensions	Wing span	95 ft
	Wing area	987 sq ft
	Length	64 ft 6 ins
	Height	16 ft 11 ins
	Tailplane span	26 ft 8 ins
Retrospective Designation	XP19	

The P177 Roles:
- Freight Transport: The cargo floor load capacity was to be 7,000 lb with a floor distribution of 100 lb / sq ft. Loading was through a rear side door assisted by floor rails and a winch attached to the forward bulkhead. There was to be the facility to carry two 13 ft diameter propellers lashed externally.
- Troop Transport: A maximum of 26 fully equipped troops could be carried
- Paratroop Transport: Fifteen fully equipped paratroops and one jump controller were to be carried. Exiting the aircraft was through a 54 in by 30 in starboard side hatch. Eight universal carriers were required for the carriage and dropping of supply containers
- Ambulance Transport: A maximum combined capacity of 21 stretchers and three sitting patient cases
- Glider Towing: The P177 was to be capable of towing two transport gliders

Bibliography: P177 Four Engine Transport Aircraft

Australia. Aircraft Advisory Committee.(1941-46).Minutes of meetings of Aircraft Advisory Commission. Meetings 1-77. [NAA: B5028,1; B5028,2; B5028,3; B5028,4; B5028,5] Barcodes: 395652; 395653; 395650; 395651 & 395649 respectively.

Australia. Aircraft Advisory Committee.(1942-43). Minutes of meetings of Aircraft Advisory Commission-Meetings 19-34.[NAA: B5028, 2].Barcode: 395653.

Australia. Aircraft Advisory Committee.(1944-46).Minutes of meetings of Aircraft Advisory Commission-Meetings 65-77.[NAA: B5028,5]. Barcode: 395649.

Commonwealth Aircraft Corporation. (1942) Engineering file AA15 (A881) (November 1942). Preliminary Specification for Four Engine Transport Aircraft.

Commonwealth Aircraft Corporation. (undated) CAC Production file P2. Commonwealth Aircraft Corporation. (undated) CAC files – W1a to W6g.

CA-17,18 & 21 NORTH AMERICAN P-51 MUSTANG FIGHTER AIRCRAFT
Feb 1944

On December 7, 1942 the Australian War Cabinet gave approval for a technical mission to visit Great Britain and the United States of America to evaluate and if possible make recommendations for the selection of a high altitude interceptor fighter, a long range escort fighter and a heavy bomber. Led by Daniel McVey, Secretary of the Department of Aircraft Production with L. J. Wackett (CAC) deputy leader, and technical adviser to the DAP. Also part of the mission were AVM A. T. Cole; Grp Cpt W. S. Armstrong; Wg Cmdr J. P. Ryland and D. Callinan (Assistant Supervisor of Area Operations, Beaufort Division). The team left Australia on January 28, 1943 to begin the American part of its tour at Los Angeles on February 2, 1943; arrived in Scotland on 16 March before returning to Australia on 17 June via the United States.

The main contenders for the interceptor fighter choice were the Republic P-47 Thunderbolt, North American P-51 Mustang and the Supermarine Spitfire Mk VIII.

The P-47 Thunderbolt was judged to be the least desirable because of its lower operating ceiling and slower rate of climb although it possessed great range on externally carried fuel. The P-51 Mustang possessed good speed, range and altitude performance combined with a middle of the road armament package. Wackett felt it was a waste of valuable time to cross the Atlantic to evaluate the Spitfire Mk VIII knowing that the ease of manufacture of the P-51 made it a foregone conclusion. Nonetheless, the Spitfire had the higher rate of climb to 20,000 feet, a heavier armament than either the P-47 or P-51 but had the lowest speed and range on external fuel tanks. The Spitfire was 30 mph slower than the P-51, was a complex build and well into its development and service life whereas the P-51 was the aircraft with new aerodynamics. Nevertheless, the RAAF did receive 410 Spitfire Mk VIII in three different variants in direct transfer from the UK beginning late in 1943 to mid-1945.

Together with Spitfire Mk Vs they were used mainly for Northern Area local defence and in the South-Western Pacific, island hopping campaign to regain lost territory, even then their endurance was not of a very practical level. The RR Merlin 70 engine was fitted in the HF Mk VIII variant of delivered Spitfire. This aspect has some significance in this account on the CA-17/CA-18 as related in the latter part of the text.

Daniel McVey recommended the selection of the P-51 as the *'middle of the road'* design choice possessing a good range and ease of manufacture. The delegation on the strong technical confirmation advice given by Wackett, agreed. Whilst admitting that it did not completely fulfil the Air Board specification (but no aeroplane that was then in production could), Daniel McVey, still on the UK part of the evaluation mission informed Essington Lewis that Australia should build the Mustang with the Packard Merlin 61 engine. This action would also extend the productive liaison already established with North American Aviation and capitalize on the relative proximity of the west coast of America to Australia.

As this was perceived to be the fighter which was to bear the brunt of the remaining years of the war for Australia, the original

L-R. L.J.Wackett; James Kindelberger(President North American Aviation) & Daniel McVey. **L.J.Wackett/MS4858/NLA**

'Prototype' pattern aircraft A68-1001. **HDHV**

contract called for 690 Mustangs, a significant order, to be built locally with 790 Packard Merlin engines coming from American production, deliveries of complete aircraft to commence in 1944. Arrangements were entered into for the supply of tooling, production data and the completion of initial component parts. The War Cabinet gave its approval on June 14, 1943 for CAC to build the P-51 under licence under contract CA-17. In spite of the detail arrangements it was unclear (as is apparent from internal documentation at CAC) as of September 1943 if the model to be built under licence was to be the P-51B, P-51D or P-51F variant. The extensive documentation and technical report made out by Wackett following his visit to North American Aviation described the P-51B and the planned differences for the upcoming P-51D, the prototype of which did not make its first flight till November 17, 1943. This uncertainty must have accounted for the delayed signing of a contract with North American Aviation but final arrangements were reached sometime in November. Production rights ran to approximately US$2M and US$1,000 per built aircraft together with 5% of the value of built spares.

At CAC, advance preparations were underway. By February 1944 the whole of the company's toolmaking facilities were concentrated on the production of jigs and assembly tooling. The Department of Aircraft Production meeting of May 25, 1944 let it be known that the manufacture of the 690 Mustang aircraft and spares was to be accorded the highest priority. There was to be no delay in the transference of personnel previously employed on CA-12 to CA-19 Boomerang production contracts. This directive was further reinforced by statements issued in September by the War Cabinet.

A Commencement

Plant re-arrangement involved a considerable amount of internal structural work to install a new moving assembly line with tracks and overhead gantry runways as had been evaluated at North American Aviation. Production was to be divided into two stages.

Stage 1, the CA-17 contract provided for the assembly of 80 aircraft from 100 sets of imported semi-finished components of the P-51D from the earliest production block, the P-51D-5-NA. These component sets were in the North American Aviation constructor numbers group 110-34386 to 110-34485 (these numbers did not line up with the subsequent CAC c/ns, being merely representative of sets of aircraft parts).

Three hundred and forty six crates of component parts had arrived at CAC by February 1944. By June 1944, one thousand personnel or about 25% of the factory establishment was committed to P-51 preparation work and CAC had received pattern aircraft, P-51D-5-NA ex USAAC 44-13293, renumbered locally as 'prototype' Mustang A68-1001. It was finished in dark green, dark sea grey and sky scheme, the only Australian P-51 to be camouflaged; the rest were left in bare metal.

The CA-17/18 project design engineer was Ern Jones. Maurice Lodge was its first project engineer, subsequently followed by Murray Bishop. There was dismay at the extent of modification work needed on the parts that had been shipped out and doubt that the aircraft assemblies would readily come together. North American Aviation P-51D engineering drawings showed changes which were not in the parts received. These parts had to be modified or new ones substituted and missing details manufactured as the build-up of tooling allowed.

In August, General Douglas MacArthur informed the Prime Minister that in view of the delays in local P-51 production of about 12 months (beyond the control of CAC and DAP) the Lend Lease arrangement was to be restricted to 350 complete aircraft assemblies and spares. General George Kenney was no longer prepared to support the local project in view of the ready availability of aircraft deliveries from the United States.

On January 1, 1945, Wackett listed his production problems of shipping delays; delays in deliveries of specialist tooling, equipment and machine tools; faulty supplied parts; mixed P-51B and P-51D model parts. 1,200 engineering changes had taken place since the start of local work. Delays crept in as CAC endeavoured to produce and update some 3,000 drawings and revise tooling. It was a time of intense frustration. Some parts were specially flown in from the United States to assist in the assembly of the first ten aircraft.

Labour Problems

Due to the actions of the Manpower Directorate, personnel who had earlier been released as the result of the cancellation of the CA-11 Woomera project were not directed in sufficient numbers to the P-51 line as had been expected. The situation worsened so that by March 1944 personnel numbers were 224 down on quota because the Directorate had been compelled to divert workers to the production of fertilisers and the preservation of fruit, both activities rating a higher priority at that stage of the war rather than the production of aircraft. It was also strongly noted as absolutely necessary that the 400 men engaged in the completion of the 250 Boomerang aircraft order be available to carry out the P-51 project.

The matter was referred to the War Cabinet for resolution. The first twenty sets of components were used for the initial tooling up prior to quantity manufacture. A68-1 Mustang Mk 20, powered by the Packard Merlin V1650-3 was identical to the P-51D-5-NA in all respects with the exception for slight cockpit equipment changes. CA-17, A68-1 flew on April 29, 1945 piloted by CAC's new test pilot James Schofield. It was handed to the RAAF on 4 June. James Schofield had completed his initial flight training with the RAAF; flew with the RAF 451 & 127 Sqdns between September 1941 and November 1944, taken part in the Hawker Typhoon trials in the Middle East and returned to complete No 4 Test Pilots Course at Laverton on January 29,1945 prior to joining CAC as its civilian test pilot shortly after. Test pilot Greg Board had left CAC on February 2, 1945.

A congratulatory telegram was sent to DAP Secretary Daniel McVey, following the successful flight of the first P-51. *"Our most sincere congratulations on your wonderful achievement in setting up the first Mustang production line in Australia and best wishes for continued success-North American Aviation Inc. USA-James Kindelberger, President"* May 2,1945.

Eighteen CA-17s had been delivered by the end of the Pacific war.

As the critical labour situation eased and showed improvement, tooling commenced in anticipation of Stage 2 of the production phase, the CA-18 contract. In the meantime the order had been further cut back to 250 aircraft in October 1945, and then further adjusted to two hundred aircraft. The CA-18 batch comprised of 120 aircraft, A68-81 to 200. In contrast to the CA-17 Mustang, the CA-18 was to be locally manufactured, but both groups were to use imported engines. That this contract should have been allowed to proceed with the war well and truly ended and with a very large number of American built Mustangs on hand, can only have been justified on the grounds of keeping CAC's workforce together till the next peacetime project came along.

Drawn Out Deliveries

Consequently, with war's end CA-17 / CA-18 deliveries became a slow trickle. Production of the CA-17 was completed in April 1946. The 80th and last CA-17, (A68-80) was handed over to the RAAF on July 30, 1946. Fifty seven CA-18 were delivered in 1947-48; 31 in 1949 and the final 32 CA-18 in 1950-51. CAC delivery dates were not always the RAAF acceptance dates, due to a mix of late aircraft and engine technical glitches, lack of available RAAF pilots and record entry keeping delays by RAAF administrative staff.

After the delivery of A68-80, production of the CA-18 was stretched out to four aircraft each month till June 1949 and slowed down further after that. Jim Schofield carried out the production flight testing of the first 90 aircraft assisted later by John Miles who accumulated 385 flights on 98 Mustangs. James Schofield departed CAC in 1947 to join the then Department of Civil Aviation as an Inspector of Aircraft Accidents.

One possible development that did not progress was the April 13, 1948, inquiry by Wackett of the DAP wishing to know if the RAAF was going to order 50 examples of the TP-51 two-seater trainer variant. Anxious to keep the factory floor staff together,it would provide CAC with another year's work and utilize common materials and tooling. Within nine days the CAS had vetoed the idea. There had been some minor RAAF consideration for an advanced trainer. This included the new Avro Athena T1 / T1A / T2 side by side advanced trainer, a mere 22 examples of which were built for the RAF. Both the Athena and the Boulton-Paul Balliol were the outcome of RAF Spec T7/45. Wackett had plans to re-configure the internal layout of the TP-51 and believed it would have been a fast, ideal, advanced trainer far better than the RR Merlin 35 powered T2 variant of the Athena. The TP-51 concept was considered again by Ern Jones in 1951 when visiting North American Aviation Inc in preparation for the CAC

A68-1 undergoing hydraulic function testing. **HDHV.**

CA-17 Mustang Mk 20 A68-1 first flight from Fisherman's Bend. **Reg Schulz.**

Mustang production line. A68-200 on the mechanised overhead gantry above A68-57. **David Anderson. 5925 720062099P**

CAC test pilot James Schofield ready to make the first test flight. **HDHV via David Anderson.**

The CA-17/CA-18 Mustang production line. **Reg Schulz.**

James Schofield taxying A68-1 the first CA-17. **Richard Hourigan.**

CA-18 Mk22 Photo Reconnaissance aircraft A68-187 c/n 1512 at Bankstown, NSW September 22, 1964. **Richard Hourigan.**

CAC Assembled & Built P-51

Contract & Mark	RAAF Identity	Engine Model	CAC c/n	Quantity
CA-17 Mk 20	A68-1 to 80	Packard Merlin V1650-3	1326-1405	80
CA-18 Mk 22 Photo Recon A/C ex-Mk 21	A68-81 to 94	Packard Merlin V1650-7	1406-1419	14
CA-18 Mk 21	A68-95 to 120	Packard Merlin V1650-7	1420-1445	26
CA-18 Mk 23	A68-121 to 186	Rolls Royce Merlin 66 or 70	1446-1511	66
CA-18 Mk 22 Photo Recon A/C ex Mk 21	A68-187 to 200	Packard Merlin V1650-7	1512-1525	14
Total				200

CA-17 & CA-18 Mustang Deliveries 1945-1951

Month	1945	1946	1947	1948	1949	1950	1951
January		3		1	1		1
February		11		2	1	3	1
March		8		3	5	4	1
April		3		3	2	2	1
May	1	3		1	2	2	2
June	3	4		3	7	2	1
July	7	3	7	1	2	3	3
August	7		5	4		1	1
September	5		3	4	3	1	
October	5		3	2	3	1	
November	8		7	4	2	2	
December	9		2	2	3		
Cumulative Total	45	80	107	137	168	189	200

Specifications CA-17, 18 & 21 Mustang

Powerplant One Packard Merlin V1650-3, 12 cyl liquid cooled vee engine of 1,400 hp at TO or V1650-7 of 1,490 hp at TO driving a 4 bladed Hamilton Standard (Hydromatic) 24D50 propeller of 11 ft 2 inches diameter or:

One Rolls Royce Merlin 66, 12 cyl liquid cooled vee engine of 1,315 hp at TO or Merlin 70 of 1,250 hp at TO driving a De Havilland propeller of 11 ft diameter

Performance
Speed at SL to 14,000 ft	390 kts
Speed 20,000 ft to 26,000 ft	304 kts
Speed 32,000 ft to 40,000 ft	226 kts
Max rate of climb speed SL to 15,000 ft	150 kts
Max rate of climb speed 20,000 ft to 25,000 ft	145 kts
Max rate of climb speed 30,000 ft to 40,000 ft	130 kts
Appoach speed (flaps lowered)	100 kts
Speed for max range	185 kts
Internal fuel	220 gall
External fuel jettisonable combat tanks 2 x 62 gall	

Weights
Basic	7,635 lb	Combat (clean)	10,500 lb
Normal loaded	9,500 lb	Max landing	8,500 lb

Dimensions
Wing span	37 ft	Wing area	235 sq ft
Root chord	8 ft 2 ins	Tip chord	4 ft 2 ins
Aspect ratio	5.12	Wing Incidence	1°
Wing LE sweep	3° 35'	Wing dihedral	5°
Height (tail down) to tip of prop	13 ft 4 ins		
Height (a/c horizontal) to fin top	12 ft 2 ins	Tailplane max chord	2 ft 6 ins
Length	32 ft 3 ins	Tailplane span	13 ft 2 ins

Armament Six wing mounted 0.5 in Browning m/gs. 400 rpg for inboard guns. 270 rpg for centre & outer guns
Provision for 3 zero rail launchers under each wing for 5 inch HVAR

Retrospective Designation XP23 / CA-17 Mk 20

A68-67 on test over Port Philip Bay with the runways visible on the upper right. **HDHV.**

Sabre project. By that time the trainer was too late to be of any practical value to the RAAF.

The second development which was started, but curtailed, was the incorporation of Dowty power controls in A68-170 at the request of the RAAF. This was an exercise in preparation for the CA-26 Sabre power operated control surfaces. It remained untested. CAC also built 328 P-51 drop tanks. The CA-21 contract for additional Mustangs was cancelled on September 18,1944.

CA-18 Contract Aircraft

There were three variants within the group of 120 locally manufactured Mustangs : Mk 21, Mk 22 and Mk 23. Aircraft A68-81 to 120 (40 aircraft) were built as Mk 21 with the Packard Merlin V1650-7 engine. The first fourteen were then retro-modified to accept aerial cameras and re-designated Mk 22 (A68-81 to 94). A68-121 to 200 (80 aircraft) were to be built as Mk 22 and for the sake of uniformity with the earlier fourteen photo reconnaissance aircraft A68-187 to 200 were also fitted with the Packard Merlin V1650-7. Only the sixty-six CA-18 Mk 23 Mustangs had the Rolls Royce built Merlin engines that were sourced from RAAF WW2 Spitfire spare engines suitably modified by CAC at their Lidcombe plant. They were fitted with de Havilland propellers, distinguishing them from the Hamilton Standard Hydromatic units on the Packard Merlin engine machines. The engines also differed in their accessories. This change of engine had become necessary because the United States Government terminated the supply of Packard Merlin engines when the war came to an end. Australia received 130 of the Merlin V1650-3 engines for the CA-17 and was intended to receive 293 examples of the V1650-7 model for the CA-18.

The switch to Rolls Royce Merlin 66/70 engines was confirmed at a meeting held at RAAF Headquarters on April 6, 1946 which had been preceded by a visit to CAC on 18 March by Ernest Walter Hives, the managing director of Rolls Royce. Hives was of the opinion that CAC should curtail its RR Merlin engine building program and resort to the 1,000 or so uncommitted Rolls Royce Merlin engines available to it in Australia and the United Kingdom through the Lend-Lease scheme. (CAC had started on the Merlin 102 engine for the GAF Avro Lincoln bomber aircraft and the later cancelled local production of the Avro Tudor transport aircraft. Large quantities of Spitfire Mk VIII were received by the RAAF and delivered straight into storage. The HF Mk VIII variant was fitted with the Merlin 70 engine.)

The meeting of 6 April resolved that for the CA-18, from the 121st Mustang, Merlin 66 and 70 Rolls Royce engines were to be used after the conversion of spare engines into complete power assemblies. The prototype or pattern aircraft, A68-1001, became a development trials machine and was re-fitted with a Rolls Royce Merlin 70 to assess the suitability of the engine for the Mk 23 variant. Two hundred and twenty four engines were received by CAC for conversion. Fifty six were cannibalised for spares, one was returned to the RAAF and 167 earmarked for installation and attrition. (All the engines used in both the CA-17 and CA-18 contracts were overseas built.)

CA-18 Mk 2

The camera installation in the Mk 22 enabled the aircraft to perform survey and tactical reconnaissance missions. The F24 cameras for vertical and oblique photography could be mounted in the rear fuselage, above and behind the radiator scoop intake. The oblique viewing eight inch camera was positioned to point from behind a window on the port side of the fuselage. It was possible to mount this camera to achieve 9, 15 or 30 degree angle view settings from the horizontal.

To assist the pilot sighting lines were painted on the port wing and the cockpit canopy for the three viewing angles. Alternate 5, 8 or 14 inch lenses could be fitted to the vertical F24 camera. An optically flat viewing window protected by an electrically actuated sliding door was positioned in a removable fairing immediately aft of the coolant shutter. For rearward facing oblique photography a rear facing prism would attach to the eight inch vertical lens. Mounted in a different fairing, this lens was protected by a door which slid open through a linking to the tail wheel undercarriage strut. The lens was exposed as the undercarriage retracted.

Propeller Development

The prospect of the initial large order for 690 Mustangs to be manufactured locally brought forth from CSIR plans for the development of a light weight, variable density wooden propeller for use on the P-51. CSIR had been involved with this line of development of forest products and the propeller that was proposed for the P-51 was 120 lb lighter than the metal equivalent. Yet because of its lightness the RAAF considered it to be deficient in coping with the weight of a P-51 when it was configured as a long range fighter.

The Mustang had a known problem of an aft placed centre of gravity condition if the rear/centre fuselage fuel tank was filled to its maximum of 90 US gallon capacity as this was likely to occur for the long range mission. The use of a lighter propeller would therefore have not helped but most certainly aggravated the problem. The concept was dropped on this account. Nevertheless the RAAF did introduce handling procedures and fuel quantity limits to maintain satisfactory handling conditions with the aircraft. de Havilland's Alexandria plant in NSW built the 24D50 propellers for the P-51s fitted with the Packard Merlin engine.

The P51 Mustang in RAAF Service

The RAAF ran out of war by the time the Australian production of the P-51 had got into its stride and while it is not directly related to the CAC production of the P-51 it is appropriate to include a mention of the additional quantities of direct delivery P-51s which went to the RAAF so as to distinguish them from the CA-17/ CA-18 aircraft.

RAAF serials A68-1 to 200 were allocated to CAC assembled/manufactured P-51s whilst serials in the range A68-500 to 583 (USAAF c/n's 44-12474 to 44-12473) were given to eighty-four P-51K-10/15s.

Serials A68-600 to 813 (USAAF c/n's 44-12861 to 45-11483) were given to 214 examples of the P-51D-20/25/30 model. These 298 aircraft were shipped from North American production lines and delivered between April and September 1945 to RAAF No 1, 2, 3 and 6 Air Depots for assembly, flight test and in a lot of instances straight into storage. These Mustangs were to be the basis of the reformation of 84 and 86 Squadrons (part of 78 Fighter Wing) in the middle of 1945. However with the ending of the war these squadrons were very quickly disbanded without seeing any action. Instead 81 Fighter Wing, comprising of 76, 77 and 82 Squadrons was established with these P-51 to comprise part of the Allied Occupation Force in Japan that was to remain in being until October 1948. This force, after the earlier withdrawal of the UK component, was then reduced to just 77 Squadron. It unexpectedly found itself committed to the Korean conflict from its beginning with the first action on July 2, 1950. Some 56 Mustangs were rotated through 77 Squadron's nine months of operations with the P-51 in Korea. A68-121,123, 125,128 and 131 were five of possibly six CAC built Mustangs that arrived in Korea or Japan in March 1951. After flying close to 4,000 sorties with the P-51 and losing eighteen of its aircraft, the unit was recalled to Iwakuni, Japan in April 1951 to reform on Gloster Meteor F.8 jets.

The CA-17/CA-18 Mustang on Home Territory

The use of American built Mustangs came to an end with the withdrawal of 77 Squadron for its re-equipment with jet aircraft. Meanwhile back home the Permanent Air Force reformed 78 Fighter Wing comprising of 75 Squadron (from August 1946); 76 Squadron (from January 1949) and 78 Squadron (from 1946) on CAC Mustangs. In addition, 4 Tactical Reconnaissance Squadron operated Mustang Mk 20 and Mk 22. It was subsequently renamed 3 Tactical Reconnaissance Squadron. A reduced size Permanent Air Force did not have a need for the Mustang due to the on-going re-equipment program with the de Havilland Vampire jet fighter-bomber . It was then possible to reform the disbanded Citizen Air Force units associated with five 'City' squadrons. 21 City of Melbourne (Fighter) Squadron; 23 City of Brisbane (Fighter) Squadron were re-formed on April 19, 1948. 22 City of Sydney (Fighter) Squadron re-formed on April 19,1948 and the final unit 24 City of Adelaide (Fighter) Squadron came together on April 30, 1951. All the CAF units operated the CAC P-51s exclusively.

The many other post-war units or detachments to which CAC P-51s were deployed included, Base Squadron Flights, Central Flying School, Communication Units, the Aircraft Performance Unit/ Aircraft Research Development, RAAF Base Laverton and the Target Towing Flight based at RAAF Richmond whose five or six aircraft were fitted with a target sleeve towing frame to provide high speed air-to-air and ground-to-air gunnery practice to requesting units.

Six aircraft, A68-1, 7, 30, 35, 72 & 87 were placed at Emu Field at Maralinga, South Australia as static ground test blast specimens during Britain's nuclear bomb tests conducted in 1953. All the aircraft were recovered intact many years later and exported to the USA. Ironically, in 1967 when A68-1 was retrieved and being flown out to Parafield Airport, it was escorted part of the way by the DCA Region Aero Commander 560E piloted by the original test pilot of A68-1, Jim Schofield, Superintendent of Operations (from 1958) of the South Australia / Northern Territory Civil Aviation Region.

By late 1958 nearly all the CA-17 and CA-18 Mustangs had been withdrawn from service. A number were sold overseas for civilian flying, some took part in international air races and seven examples were on the Australian Civil Aircraft register as of 2015.

Outside of the United States, it was only Australia and more particularly CAC that had undertaken production of the P-51.

Bibliography: CA-17, 18 & 21 P-51 Mustang Fighter Aircraft

Anderson, Peter N. (1975) *Mustangs of the RAAF and RNZAF.* ,Sydney Reed, Sydney.

The scene at Tocumwal, NSW. Fifteen CAC built P-51 awaiting disposal. **Richard Hourigan .**

Australia. Aircraft Advisory Committee. (1942-46). Minutes of meetings of Aircraft Advisory Commission. Meetings 1-77.[NAA: B5028,1; B5028,2; B5028,3; B5028,4; B5028,5]. Barcodes: 395652; 395653; 395650; 395651 & 395649 respectively.

Australia. Dept. of Aircraft Production.(1944-45). Aircraft production policy. Production of CA-17 in Australia.[NAA: MP287/1, 3046A]. Barcode: 364109.

Australia Dept of Aircraft Production.(1944-45). Aircraft production & aircraft industry in Australia.(August 31, 1945).[NAA: MP1472/1,15 part 4]. Barcode:579360.

Baker, Dennis (1989) 'CAC Mustang delivery dates.' *AHSA newsletter*, Vol. 5/3.

Commonwealth Aircraft Corporation. (Undated) CAC production files P2 and M5.

Commonwealth Aircraft Corporation. (Undated) 'Mustang overhaul manual- Mk 20 & 21'.

Commonwealth Aircraft Corporation. [Production reports to DAP 1946-53.]

Fleming, Ian (CAC). 'A Survey of Recent UK Aircraft Projects' (unnumbered) (June 1947).

Jones, Ern J. (1985) [Correspondence].

Lukasik, Mariusz. (2015) *North American P-51 Mustang B/C/D/K Models: Topdrawings 28.*[Unknown place] : Kagero Oficyna Wydawnicza; Ian Allen (possible distributor) Birmingham, UK.

Miles, John. (1979). *Testing Time*. Neptune Press, Belmont, Victoria.

RAAF. Dept of Air. Pilot's handling notes.

RAAF. Headquarters. (1946) Meeting of engine requirements (April 5, 1946).

Schofield, James E. (1939-48). Service record. [NAA:A9300].Barcode: 5255670.

CHAPTER 2. FIRST GENERATION JETS

P189/P193/CA-22 WINJEEL TRAINER PROTOTYPES
November 1947

In February 1948 the RAAF issued Technical Requirement AC77 for a modern elementary trainer aircraft. With the Tiger Moths, Wackett Trainers and Wirraways declared obsolescent, the new specification was drawn up with the object of replacing them with a single aircraft, capable of handling the flying duties of the earlier

P189

P193/CA-22 Winjeel Prototype

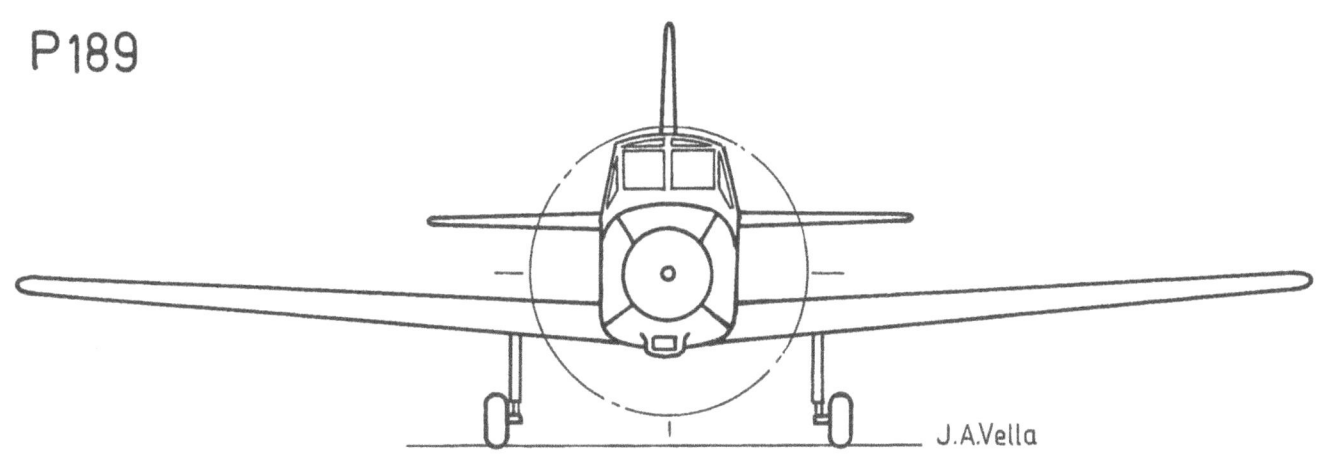

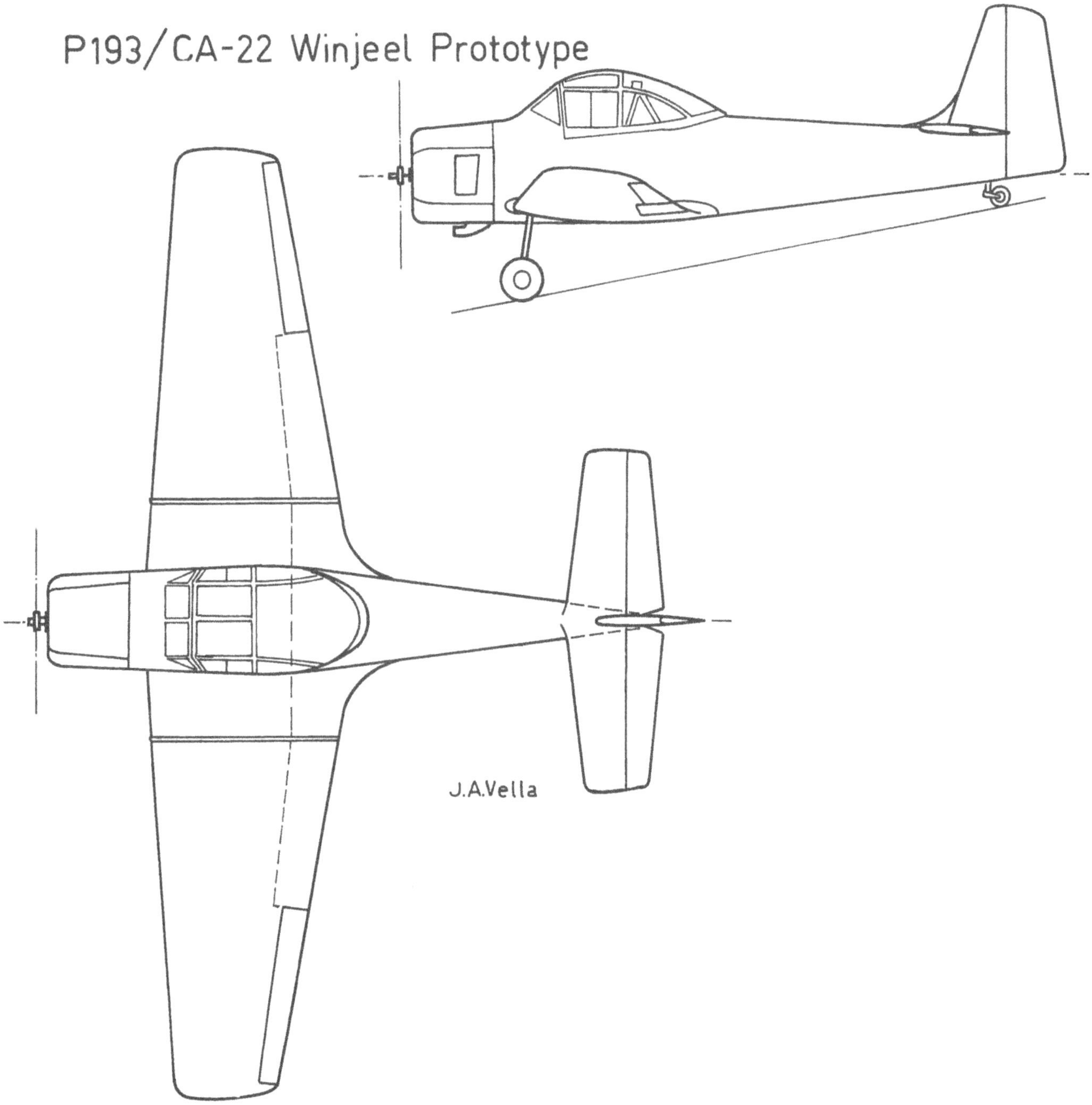

types and equipped to cover the latest training requirements. The RAAF had informed the management of CAC on October 15, 1947 that it wanted the company to build the new training aeroplane, subsequent to which a new design section was established with an allocation of £2,000 to carry out preliminary investigation work.

The new trainer was to be capable of accommodating three persons (although there was space provision for four), to be of simple and robust construction with good flying characteristics. The third seat was to allow a second pupil to watch and study the activity in the two front seats. Economy of operation and ease of maintenance and repair were to be paramount considerations.

Agreement was reached between CAC and the RAAF in May 1949 to the building of two prototypes to contract CA-22. Thomas (Bill) Air was Chief Engineer. Design direction was led by Chief Design Engineer Doug Humphries with Ian Ring the Project Senior Design Engineer / Chief Stressman and E.M. Bishop, Project Chief Draftsman. As Doug Humphries became progressively more involved in the CA-23 All-Weather Fighter Proposal, Ian Ring took over the design responsibilities on the trainer.

Layouts of September 16, 1948 depicted an aircraft in Proposal 189 of the familiar CA-22 outline but with the wing lacking the horizontal centre section as was eventually to appear on P193. Earlier in April 1948, outline P190 suggested a sideways retracting undercarriage. Wind tunnel and structure tests at ARL tests were completed by June 1950. Construction of the first prototype A85-618, commenced in July 1949, was completed 20 months later on January 26, 1951 and made a 12 minute duration first flight on February 3, 1951 flown by GAF and CAC (1947-53) chief test pilot, John Miles. He continued the testing process till November 1951 and amassed 156 flights on the type, assisted by Bill Herbert, GAF's deputy test pilot.

The aircraft underwent a long series of trials of finding the optimum fillet shapes to the wing/fuselage and fin/fuselage locations. Likewise, the rearward set fin and rudder was constantly modified by increasing the rudder chord; increasing the height of the fin and rudder and finally testing a small dorsal fin extension of 11.5 inches up the leading edge of the fin, then another 36 inches forward of the fin and 13 inches up the leading edge (P231). These were done as part of the spin / stall test routine for which a spin recovery parachute housing was located on the upper rear fuselage. The aircraft was reluctant to enter a spin, an excellent feature in a private aircraft, but not so in a basic military trainer. By February 22, 1952, the first prototype had accumulated 171 flight hours during 244 flights. Wg Cmdr Geoff Marshall, Sqdn Ldr Ken Robertson, Flt Lt James Rowland and Flt Lt Bill Scott participated in the long CAC/RAAF test regime at the Aircraft Research and Development Unit.

Sir James Rowland, the eventual RAAF CAS in 1975, commented in his biography 'Pathfinder,"Kriegie" & Gumboot Governor' on the RAAF's *"crazier proposition of carrying a second pupil in a third seat so as to save time when the pupils changed over, which had bugged the Winjeel design. Can you imagine sitting for an hour behind an instructor and pupil while they did spins and aerobatics, then for another hour while you did them ? Or how much use the first pupil would be after sitting in the back until you had finished ?"* He also attributed the few faults of the CA-22 *"largely due to the confused RAAF requirements at the time of design"*

(Initially, all wartime testing and trials were conducted by the Special Duties and Performance Flight of 1 Aircraft Depot. As the volume of research and development increased, 1 Aircraft Performance Unit [APU], an independent organisation to test all RAAF aircraft, equipment and modifications was formed in December 1943 led by Sqdn Ldr J.Harper. In September 1947 the APU was renamed

Specifications	P189 / P193 /CA-22 Winjeel Trainer Prototypes	
Powerplant	One Pratt & Whitney R985-AN2 Wasp Junior, 9 cyl radial engine of 445 hp at TO	
Performance	Max speed	145 kts
	Cruise speed	130 kts
	Climb rate at SL	1,500ft /min
Weights	Normal AUW	3,997 lb
Dimensions	Wing span	38 ft 9 ins
	Wing area	250 sq ft
	Aspect ratio	6.0
	Wing join chord	7 ft 7 ins
	Fuselage/wing chord	8 ft 9 ins
	Wing LE sweep	4° 5'
	Height	8 ft 3 ins
	Length	29 ft 4.5 ins
	Fin & rudder area	23 sq ft
	Tailplane area	46.5 sq ft
	Wheelbase	18 ft 10 ins
	Track	10 ft
Retrospective Designations	XP28 / P189 Basic Trainer XP29 / P193 CA-22 Winjeel Trainer Prototype XP38-Winjeel, Forward Fin, Cicada Engine	

the Aircraft Research and Development Unit [ARDU]. It remained at RAAF Laverton until 1977).

Company development trials were carried out on canopy separation which for its time was a very large single piece unit. A85-618 was tied down in a simulated low power glide angle directly behind a RAAF Lincoln bomber on the Fisherman's Bend aerodrome. The airflow from its four engines (approx 80 kts) simulated the canopy jettison conditions. Seven successful separations were carried out with the canopy sailing backwards through the air to be captured on a large net slung between the jibs of two mobile cranes.

The second prototype, A85-364 flew on August 29, 1951 similarly fitted with the P & W R-985 Wasp Junior radial engine and with its fin and rudder also located at the extreme end of the fuselage. The reluctance of the aircraft to enter a spin was partly due to a deep keel below the horizontal tailplane and a rudder of insufficient area to overcome the excess side area. In addition, there was a lack of experience in testing to be able to find the correct technique for the placement of the control column in just the right position to neutralize wing twist to be able to initiate the spin. The shape of the

L-R. Ian Ring, Harry Becker, John Miles (seated), Douglas Humphries.
AIRCRAFT Herald & Weekly Times

The test canopy is sailing towards the safety net. **Richard Hourigan**

The CA-22 first prototype A85-618 in its original form with a spin recovery parachute housing on mid upper fuselage.
L. J. Wackett/MS4848/NLA

The early vertical tail location and a dorsal fin is evident on the first CA-22 prototype A85-618 over-flying Port Melbourne. **HDHV**

The CA-22 second prototype A85-364 displaying engine accessibility, the tail fin in its final location & the spin recovery parachute housing in the extreme tail. **Richard Hourigan.**

canopy was altered slightly at the rear. Both aircraft were tufted for airflow examination. The fin and rudder were moved forward 38 inches on the basis of data supplied by ARL. Former ARL structures experimental officer Alan Patching, recalls that in the immediate post-war era when CAC and the Government Aircraft Factories talked to each other, GAF's Chief Aerodynamicist Henry Millicer, solved the Winjeel aircraft spinning problem by re-arranging the empennage assembly. The chord of the fin had been increased and the fin and rudder assembly moved forward on the fuselage to a point where the leading edge of the fin was ahead of the tailplane. The engine was moved forward 7 inches and given a downward thrust line. It had taken till late 1952 to solve the aerodynamic problem. (Henry Millicer had previously worked on the Hunting Percival T.1 aircraft in the UK and solved an identical problem on their Provost, their new RAF post war basic trainer aircraft, re-positioning the location of its horizontal tail).

However, spin was induced once the correct technique had been established and this was even before the fin was moved forward. Spin entry was natural and similar for both installations with an almost identical number of turns for either fin location before a normal recovery. A benefit of this change was a re-balanced improvement in the appearance of the aircraft.

Towards October of 1952 aircraft A85-618 was taken for a tour of operational evaluation and opinion gathering at different RAAF stations. Most time was spent at Uranquinty, NSW. It returned to CAC in September 1953 to be fitted with one of the two CAC designed Cicada prototype radial engines. This was to be an engine flight test research phase. However the Cicada was never flight tested due to a recurring series of mishaps during its ground testing phase.

Aircraft A85-364 was predominantly used by ARDU on engine airflow cooling tests; followed at their conclusion by tropical trials in Northern Australia.

The new aircraft was given the name W*injeel* (an indigenous language word for Young Eagle).

Bibliography: P189 / P193 / CA-22 Winjeel Trainer Prototypes

Commonwealth Aircraft Corporation. (1951). Design Summary 22-29. CA-22. June 21, 1951.

Commonwealth Aircraft Corporation. (Udated). CA-22 Flight trials, design & serviceability changes introduced during test flights.

Commonwealth Aircraft Corporation. Production Reports to DAP 1949-53.

Miles, John. *Testing Time* (1979).Neptune Press. Belmont, Victoria.

Patching, Alan. [Discussion] (2016).

Rowland, James (1922-99) & Yule, Dr Peter (1954-). *Pathfinder, 'Kriegie' & Gumboot Governor(2018). The Adventurous Life of Sir James Rowland. RAAF AM CAS.* Air Force History & Heritage Branch, Canberra.

P182 / P184 / P185 / P186 FIGHTER AIRCRAFT GRUMMAN F9F PANTHER DERIVATIVES
March 1948

Based on an endorsement by the Defence Committee and recommended by the Minister of Defence with approval from the Department of Air and the Department of Supply and Development, CAC was sponsored with the design and development of a jet fighter aircraft and the building of two such prototypes.

The basic requirements were for airborne radar gear for location and identification; pilot, radar equipment operator and a jet engine preferably with the intent to use the RR Nene engine then in production in Australia. (The F9F Panther engine was the J48 Tay, a development of the RR Nene.)

Initial studies, configurations and available information on proposed overseas designs led Thomas W. (Bill) Air in March 1948 to favour the prospect based on the Grumman XF9F-2 Panther of the United States Navy to replace the RAAF's Vampire and CA-17/18 Mustang. The lack of Government foreign dollar reserves were a problem. This did not deter Wackett as he offered to produce an Australian equivalent of the machine provided one example could be acquired. The quoted price less installed military equipment was £40,000. Though official Government representations were made, the US Defence Department, due to security restrictions forbade any transfer of data or hardware. CAC's ideas which had surfaced for the development of the Panther airframe had been formulated on the expectation of American assistance.

The first Proposal P182 relocated the six 0.5 inch guns from the nose of the aircraft to the wing or their replacement by rockets, freeing up the forward fuselage space to locate a 30 inch diameter radar scanner and the observer station ahead of and below the pilot in the body of the nose. The fuselage would have had to be lengthened by four feet.

In Proposal P184, with the forward fuselage kept at its original length and the mid-fuselage extended, the observer was located behind the pilot.

Fighter Proposal No 3, P185 of September 7, 1948 had both crew members seated side by side and built-in armament changed to two 30 mm cannon with 200 rounds of ammunition. Fuel capacity in the fuselage tanks was 350 gallons with the provision of another 120 gallons of fuel or water for water injection.

Proposal P186 appeared on September 10, 1948. Like P185 it employed a large diameter radar dish which made it possible to use the large frontal area to seat the two crew members side by side, a formula that had been tried with success on the Douglas F3D Skyknight. The British AI Mk 9D radar which was an advance on the unit fitted in the de Havilland Mosquito NF Mk 30 of 1945 was planned for both the P185 and P186. Martin Baker ejection seats were also to be fitted. P186 introduced a wing of greater area combined with moderate sweepback and a narrowed taller fin emulating the manner in which the Panther evolved into the F9F-6 Cougar by September 1951. The fuselage was increased in length by some two feet, the cannon armament was retained but the fuel capacity was raised slightly to 380 gallons. The original US Grumman F9F Panther had engine suction relief doors on the dorsal fuselage. Suction relief to the Nene turbojet on P186 was to be via a ventral

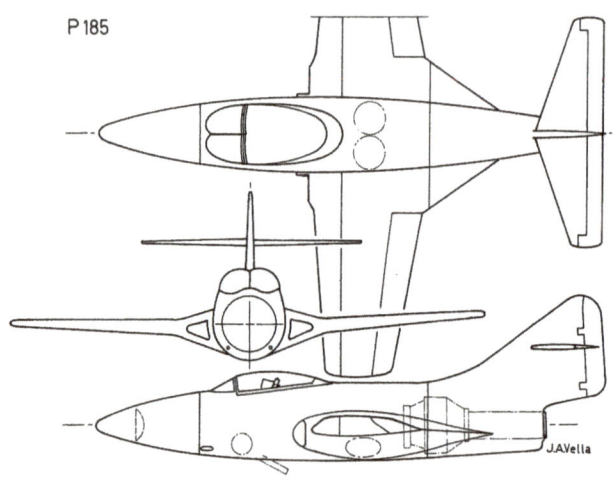

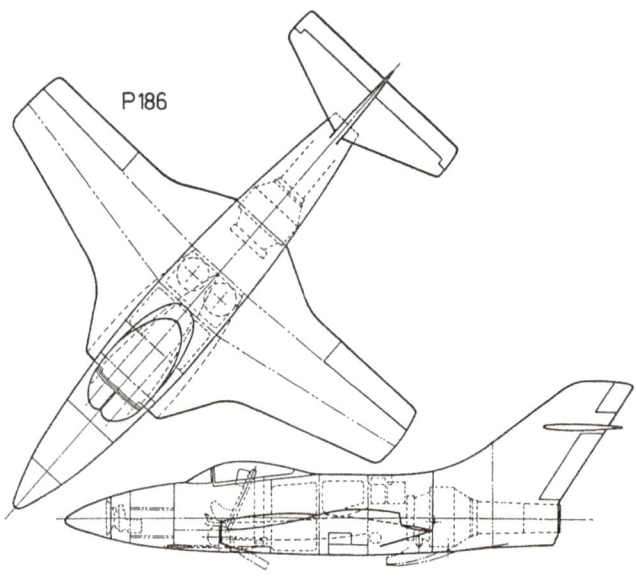

retractable intake behind the trailing edge of the wing. None of the proposals showed the wing tip fuel tanks of the US original.

Retrospective Designations :
XP24 / P182 Grumman Panther No 1
XP25 / P184 Grumman Panther No 2
XP26 / P185 Grumman Panther No 3
XP27 / P186 Grumman Panther No 4

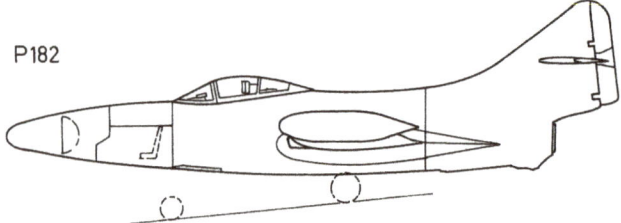

Grumman Panther F9F-5P, 126277, at Planes of Fame Museum, Chino, California. **J. A. Vella Collection**

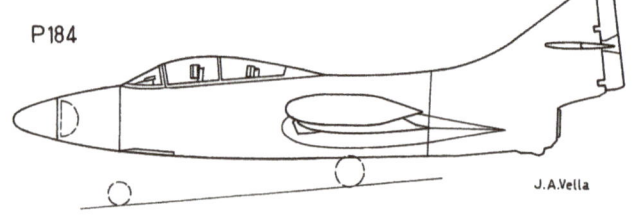

Bibliography : Grumman F9F Panther Derivatives
Commonwealth Aircraft Corporation. (undated). Engineering Report AA45 (A118). Fighter Aircraft Proposal, Grumman F9F Panther Modification.

P196 TWIN SEAT ALL-WEATHER FIGHTER AIRCRAFT
October 1948

The P185 / P186 Grumman Panther layouts rapidly gave way in 1948 to P196 as CAC design ideas moved towards an independent, larger and better aircraft for this role.

The most striking element of P196 was the thin, shoulder mounted 40° sweptback wing, the reversion to tandem crew seating, the side by side arrangements of the developed Nene engines and the high-set sweptback horizontal tail. The all-weather radar was the AI Mk 9C with a 28 inch diameter scanner. A 10 inch gun laying radar scanner was to be located in the inboard wing leading edge.

The one-piece unit wing was attached to the fuselage at four points and the rear of the fuselage could be detached at the main engine mounting points when major maintenance was required. A rocket augmentation engine could be fitted in the extreme tail cone. The nosewheel rotated through 90 degrees as it retracted backwards so as to use the available fuselage width to lie flat and not intrude into the cockpit space. Likewise the main units rotated forward through angled pivots to lie flat within the lower fuselage box.

Four 30 mm cannon and their total 1,200 rounds of ammunition were located in the mid-lower fuselage with their barrels exiting below the engine intake ducts.

A relatively large 720 gallons of fuel capacity was intended to be distributed between wing and fuselage thin wall cells. The detailed weight summary had arrived at an all-up normal loaded weight of 23,325 lb. All the general specification figures came out better than the official request.

Bibliography: P196 Twin Seat All Weather Fighter Aircraft
Commonwealth Aircraft Corporation, Engineering Report AA51 (A124). Twin Seat All- Weather Fighter Proposal. October 1948.

P223 / CA-23 ALL-WEATHER FIGHTER AIRCRAFT
February 1950

The year 1949 saw the beginning of the most ambitious and advanced aircraft design project ever undertaken in Australia. This was to be the CA-23 all-weather jet fighter, the culmination of a diverse series of investigations into the concept of the all-weather fighter that had its beginnings in Proposals 185,186 and 196.

In May 1949 the Defence Research and Development Committee awarded CAC the design and construction of two prototypes at a cost of £450,000. Approval followed from the Minister for Defence in July 1949 and contract CA-23 was agreed on September 16, 1949.

P202 and Radar Relay Concept
By the time Air Force Specification AC79 had been issued in August 1949, CAC had had access to a large number of current aerodynamic reports emerging from Britain and the USA. Work on the all-weather fighter design recommenced at the close of the year and by February 11, 1950 design proposal P202 had emerged. The aircraft was essentially of low aspect ratio, moderate 55°sweepback on a thin shoulder mounted wing with 3° of anhedral angle and a horizontal tail set on top of a highly swept 66° vertical fin. As such the layout represented in a more conservative fashion, the shape of aircraft predicted by the RAE in its Fighter Report, Aero 2300. Wind tunnel testing carried out during July 1950 at ARL revealed instability at moderate to high angles of incidence combined with wing tip stalling.

The increased downwash at the wing root caused the tail to destabilise the wing-body combination. Examination of this downwash pattern made it evident that lowering the tailplane to the wing chord plane was essential. This involved lengthening of the fuselage to provide sufficient structural support. P202 was to be powered by two Rolls Royce Avon turbojets each of 7,000 lb thrust with provision for reheat, although at the request of the RAAF the use of Rolls Royce Tay engines was also investigated.

The specification called for the British Mk 9C search radar with the possible provision for a Mk 16 and a 36 inch diameter dish located in a large conical radome inset in the centre of the dual engine intake duct. One wing was to have a 10 inch diameter gun laying radar housing located in the leading edge. Performance estimations had in the meantime indicated a diminishing likelihood of the aircraft being able to meet the important aspect of 530 kts cruise speed at 45,000ft. This was mainly attributed to the high drag of the fuselage intake when combined with the inset radar housing. Design took a different turn with the advent of development work led by Dr. Edward G. Bowen of the Radio Physics division of the CSIR of a new method of airborne interception of enemy aircraft. This was to be enabled by transmitting radar data gathered by a ground radar station and displaying it on a plan position indicator in the rear or observer cockpit of the aircraft. This concept, although experimental, led after consultation with the RAAF to the deletion of bulky search radar in the nose intake; its place taken by a 15 inch diameter gun laying radar dish. It is believed that ARDU had achieved successful interception tests.

A New Design
This alteration at the intake affected the whole outline of the fuselage and had repercussions on the wing, tail and undercarriage that was tantamount to a new design. The arrangement did not settle down until early in 1951 and was the subject of new model testing.

In August 1950, the RAAF issued the revised and final form of the specification. On the following month CAS Air Marshall George Jones remarked that the fighter should be good, as it incorporated the latest overseas ideas, but if it was scrapped, local design experience would be set back some 10 years.

RAAF Requirement (OR AIR 7) and Specification AC79A were basically similar to the British F4/48 Day - Night Fighter Landplane requirement; although some of the performance criteria for the Australian aircraft were more severe, especially on range.

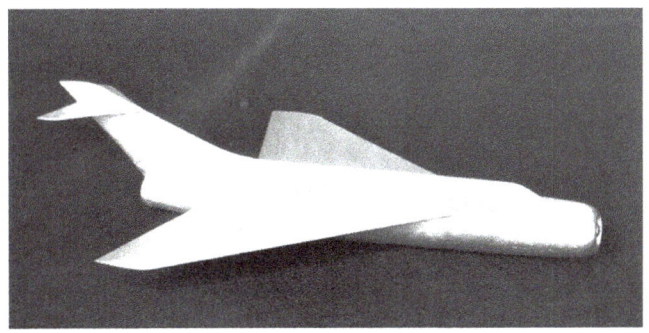

Model approximating Proposal P202. **HDHV**

P196
All Weather
Fighter

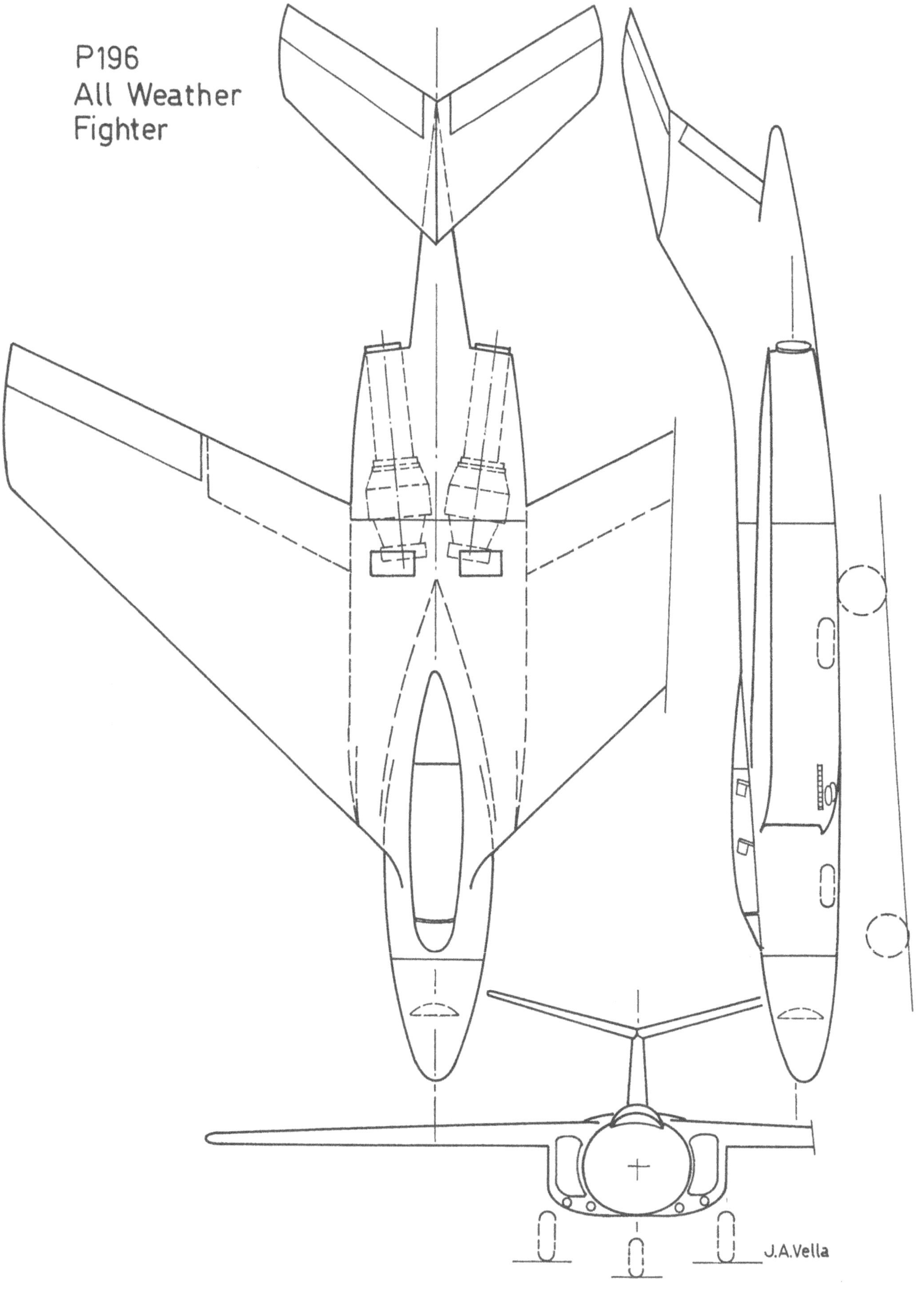

J.A.Vella

97

Specifications	P196 Twin Seat All-Weather Fighter	
Powerplant	Two Rolls Royce Nene turbojets (Variant unknown. Thrust was in 5,000 lb category)	
Performance	Max speed at SL	574 kts
	Max speed at 25,000 ft	559 kts
	Max speed at 45,000 ft	533 kts
	Rate of climb at SL	10,600 ft/min
	Rate of climb at 25,000 ft	6,000 ft/min
	Rate of climb at 45,000 ft	1,500 ft/min
	Time to 45,000 ft	10.6 mins
	Operational ceiling	47,000 ft
	Max range at 40,000 ft with 720 gall internal fuel	1,000nm
	Endurance at 40,000 ft with 70 gall internal fuel	3hrs
	Max range at 40,000 ft with 360 gall external fuel	1,500 nm
	Endurance at 40,000 ft with 360 gall external fuel	3.95 hrs
	TO distance	2,580 ft
	Approach speed	113 kts
Weights	Normal AUW	23,325 lb
	Max AUW inc 2 x 1,000 lb bombs	25,370 lb
	Combat (normal AUW less 200 gall fuel)	21,685 lb
	Wing loading (combat weight)	39.5 lb/sq ft
Dimensions	Wing span	44 ft	Wing area	50 sq ft
	Root chord	10 ft 3 ins	Tip chord	4 ft 9 ins
	Aspect ratio	3.5	Wing LE sweep at 25 % chord	40°
	T/C ratio	8 %	Tailplane span	22 ft
	Tailplane LE sweep at 25 % chord	42°	T/C ratio	7%
	Length	54 ft	Height	12 ft
	Wheel base	12 ft	Track	9 ft 6 ins
Armament	Four 30 mm cannon with 300 rpg	
	Provision for 10 rocket projectiles, two 500 lb bombs or two 1,000 lb bombs	
Retrospective Designation	XP30	

AC79A requested a jet propelled, long range all-weather, subsonic attack fighter capable of operating in all parts of the world. The primary roles were given as:
- Interception at long range of enemy air striking forces under all weather conditions
- Protection of allied air striking forces at long range and
- Attack of enemy surface targets at long range.

Tactical reconnaissance and dual training varaints were also envisaged.

The new specification requested a speed of 539 kts at 45,000 feet. This sort of performance was what was to be expected from this type of aircraft using un-reheated engines of the Avon or Armstrong Siddeley Sapphire type. However, to achieve this performance, drag had to be kept to a minimum, in spite of the large fuselage cross-section containing the side by side engines. Of necessity the swept back, low thickness/chord ratio wing with a high taper low aspect ratio of 2.0 was chosen that resulted almost in a delta planform with a quarter chord sweepback of 47° 45'.

To improve wing torsional stiffness and to prevent a change in stability due to tip stall, the ailerons cum flaps were moved well inboard. The thickness chord ratio of the wing varied from 7.3% at the tip to 3.7% at the root. For a number of reasons, chief among which were the minimization of bending shear stresses and the ability to absorb the transverse loads in fuel pressurisation, a multi-spar extruded stringer form of construction was adopted for the wings. Skin gauge was to vary from 0.048 to 0.25 inches, with the heavy gauge material across the centre section to be machine tapered.

A similar form of structure was adopted for the horizontal tail halves and the fin. Proposal P222 differed from the final configuration P223 of July 11, 1951 in having a span of 38 feet. In Proposal P223, the wing span was reduced to 33 feet. In October 1950, it was decided to put aside any further detail design work for 12 months in order to concentrate on the more immediate Winjeel production work. CAC management discussions in December 1950 anticipated possible new work on an F-86 Sabre project and re-scheduled P223 detail design to sometime around June, 1951. The company's design and engineering staff was stretched to cope with three simultaneous projects. The allocated expenditure limit of £450,000 still applied.

Aircraft Description

Data analysis was assisted through the use of a 1/8.54 scale model tested by the Aeronautical Research Laboratories at Fisherman's Bend in their 9 feet by 7 feet low speed tunnel. High-speed wind tunnel tests (1/16 scale model) and spinning trials (1/40 scale models) were conducted at the Royal Aircraft Establishment at Farnborough,UK. The availability and application of specialized aircraft equipment and hardware items was investigated by Ian Ring (Chief Aeronautical Engineer 1953-1980) on his engineering equipment sourcing and evaluation tour during 1951.

His UK visits took in Rolls Royce for engine data; Hobsons for flight controls; air conditioning at Normalair; Dowty for the undercarriage; Graviners for fire extinguishers; Smiths for instruments; windscreens from Triplex and Rotol. He continued to the United States on November 30, 1951 for discussions with amongst others, Goodyear for undercarriage and hydraulics; Bendix and AiResearch for electrical gear, returning to Melbourne on December 24, 1951. Herb Knight was also at Rolls Royce in the UK.

The 55 foot long fuselage of the P223 was a complex structure with ducts for the two engines, a wing cut-out, four gun package and undercarriage mounts and stowage. The front and rear fuselage load

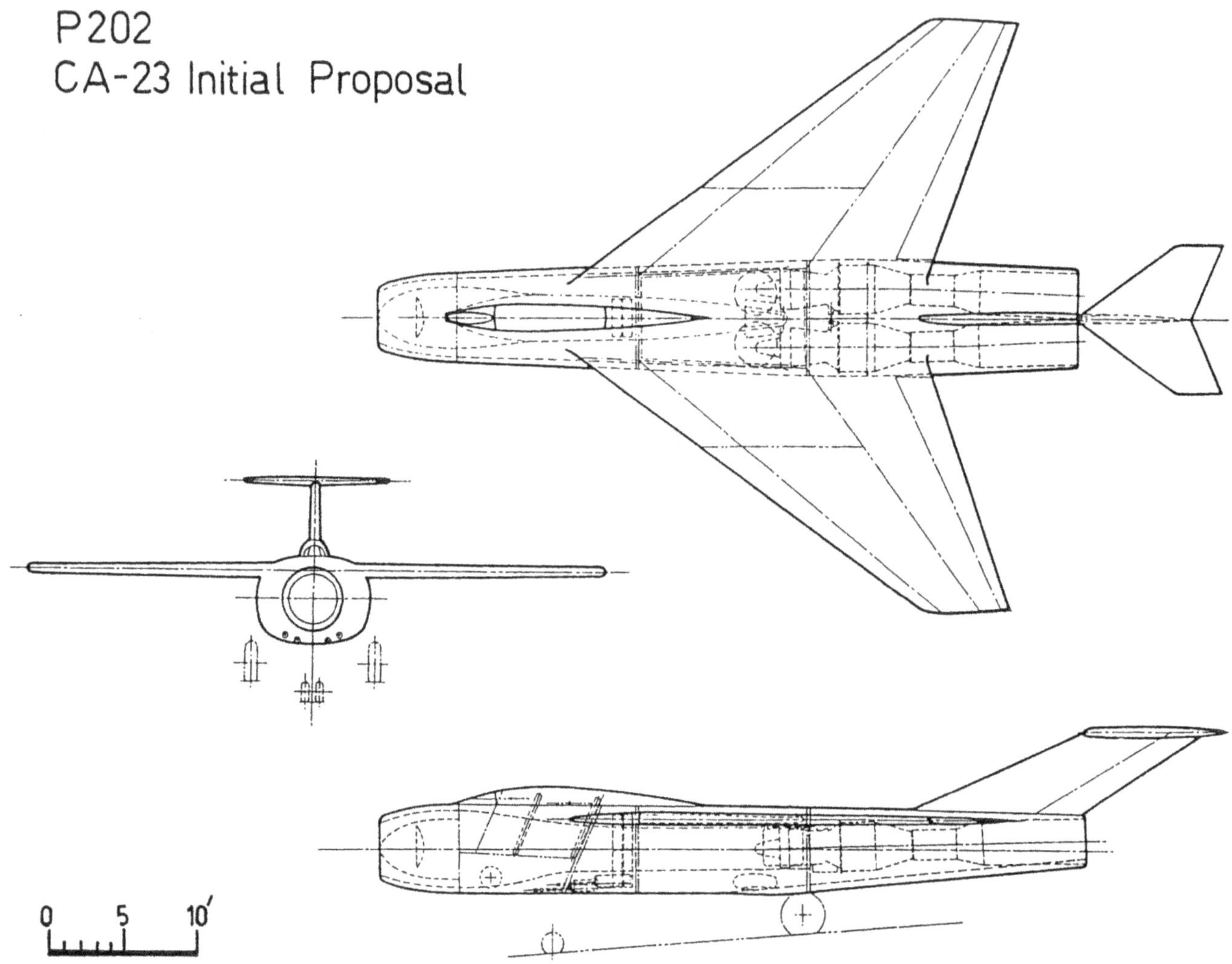

P202
CA-23 Initial Proposal
0 5 10′

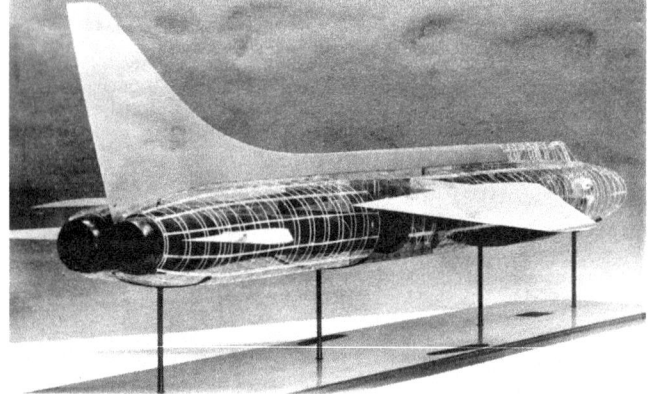

A view of the fuselage frames. ***Walter Watkins***

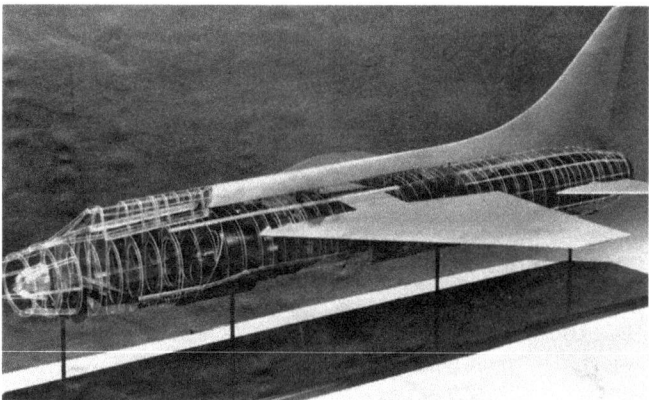

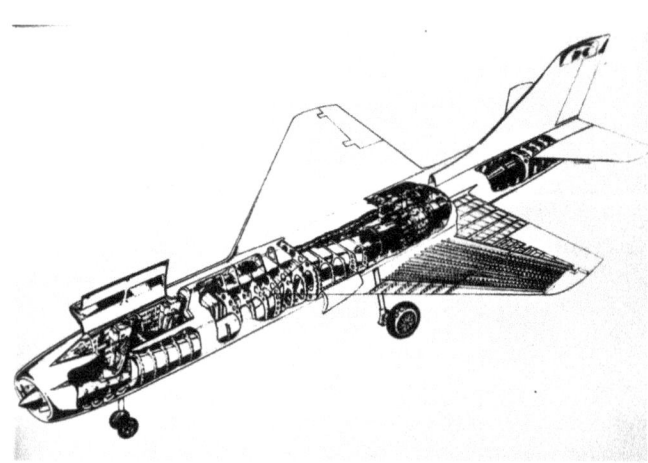

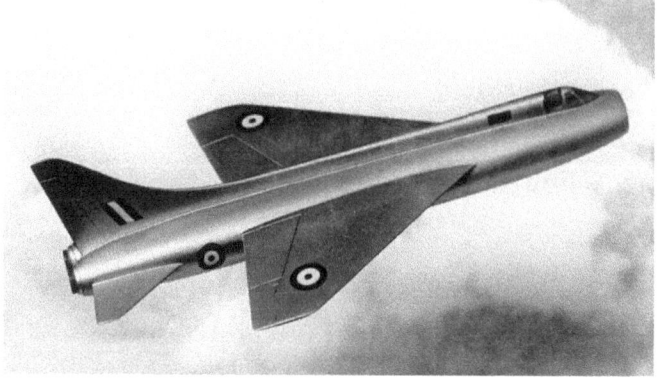

In its final configuration the CA-23 was a large airframe. ***HDHV***

P223 / CA-23

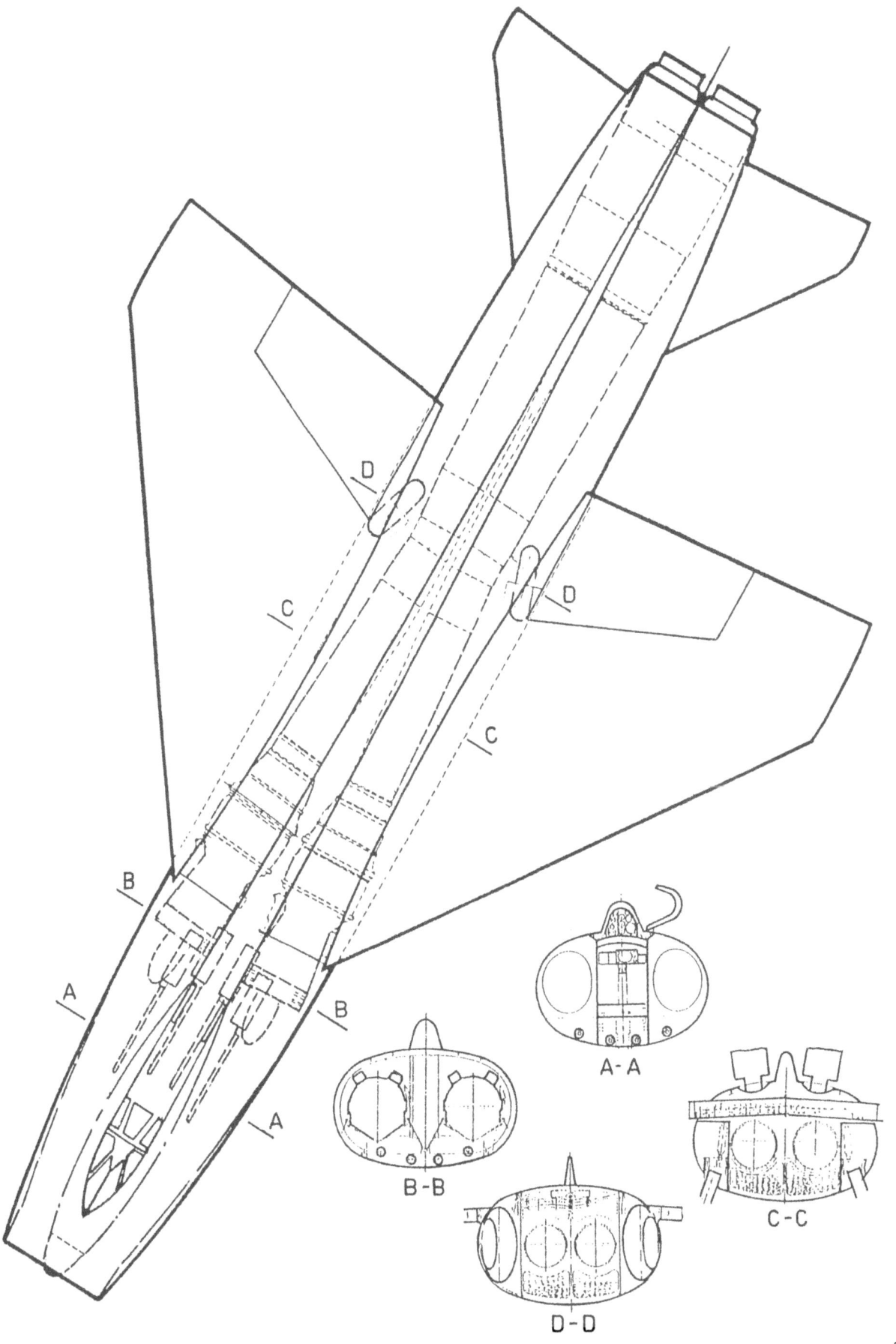

P223 / CA-23

Specifications P223 / CA-23 All-Weather Fighter Aircraft

Powerplant	One Rolls Royce Avon RA.7 turbojet of 7,500 lb thrust. SFC 0.92 lb/hr/lb		
	One Rolls Royce Avon RA.7R turbojet of 7,500 lb (dry) and 9,500 lb (reheat) static thrust at SL		
Performance at combat weight		With Avon RA.7	With Avon RA.7R
	Max speed at SL	620 kts	645kts
	Max speed at 45,000 ft	35 kts	NA
	Rate of climb at SL	9,300 ft/min	34,000 ft/min
	Rate of climb at 25,000 ft	9,000 ft/min	16,000 ft/min
	Rate of climb at 45,000 ft	710 ft/min	3,800 ft /min
	Time to 25,000 ft	2.8 min	2.05 min
	Time to 45,000 ft	8.1 min	4.3 min
	Combat ceiling	45,000 ft	50,000 ft
	Absolute ceiling	46,500 ft	51,000 ft
	TO dist over 50 ft	3,000 ft	2,430 ft
	Landing dist over 50 ft	3,060 ft	3,060 ft
	Approach speed	135 kts	135 kts
	Stalling speed	92 kts	92 kts
	Lift-off speed	154 kts	NA
	Approach angle	3°	3°
	Endurance with 1,600 gal	3 hrs	2.25 hrs
Weights	Empty	17,000 lb	NA
	Max TO	29,210 lb	NA
	Overload AUW (inc 2 x 1,000 lb bombs)	31,255 lb	NA
	Combat (less 40% fuel)	25,466 lb	NA
	Normal landing (less 75% fuel)	22,190 lb	NA
	Fuel capacity	60 gall	160 gall
	Wing loading at TO weight	56.2 lb/sq ft	NA

Dimensions	Wing span	33 ft	Wing area	520 sq ft
	Wing dihedral	3°	Root chord	8 ft 2 ins
	Tip chord	5 ft 6 ins	Aspect ratio	2.08
	Taper ratio	0.206	Wing LE sweep	54° 30′
	Sweepback at 25% chord	47° 45′	TE sweep	7° 54′
	T/C ratio at root	3.7 %	T/C ratio at tip	7.4 %
	Tailplane span	17 ft 8 ins	Tailplane area	54 sq ft
	Tail aspect ratio	2.242	Tip chord	2 ft 3 ins
	Tailplane LE sweep	54° 30′	Sweepback at 25 % chord	47° 45′
	Tailplane TE sweep	6.1°	Fin area	57.8 sq ft
	Fin LE sweep	48° 30′	Height	18 ft
	Fuselage length	32 ft 3 ins	Overall length	5 ft 9 ins
	Wheelbase	17 ft 3 ins	Track	9 ft 6 ins

Armament	Four 30 mm Aden cannon with 200 rpg. Provision for 2 x 1,000 lb bombs & air -to-ground rockets
Retrospective Designations	XP31 / P202 Twin Tay engines
	XP32 / P223 CA-23 Twin RR Avon RA.3 engines
	XP33 / P223 CA-23 Twin RR Avon RA.7 engines
	XP34 / P223 CA-23 Twin RR Avon RA.7R engines
	XP35-NTU

was to be borne by stringers and skin but in the centre section, the longerons were to be used to cross the large cut-outs for the wing, undercarriage and gun package. A large number of access panels/openings were provided. The pilot sat behind a vee-shaped four panel windscreen with the navigator/radar/systems operator in the rear cockpit. Both were provided with ejection seats and were enclosed by a one piece, starboard hinged metal framed canopy. The pilot position had three clear panels; the second crew member was provided with a window on either side.

Conventional light alloy sheet and extrusions were to be used throughout. Two petal type airbrakes (of 5% wing area in size) were positioned on the upper fuselage either side of the dorsal spine above the undercarriage mounts. Various forms of undercarriage arrangements were considered, but with the need to allow for maximum fuel space, single wheel main units were chosen. Location of the main landing gear pivots within the fuselage was made possible because of the ample width of the fuselage. This mounting allowed reasonable stability during ground roll. The main units as well as the twin steerable nosewheel were of the levered suspension type, the nosewheel retracting forwards, the main units to the rear. Tyre pressure for the main undercarriage was 130 lb/sq in and 100 lb/sq in for the nose gear. Nosewheel steering was through an angle of 60˚.

Fuel storage was divided into wing integral tanks containing a total of 700 gallons. Upper and lower fuselage flexible bag tanks housed the balance of 460 gallons. For twin engine safety, the fuel system was split left and right down the fuselage centre with 580 gallons supplying each Avon and provision for automatic fuel cross-over in the event of an engine failure or the failure of one fuel system. To minimise the shift in centre of gravity, the fuel cells were grouped as closely together as practicable. Transfer of fuel from the wing tanks to the fuselage collector tanks was through pressurization because the wing was too thin to permit the installation of the then available

A wind tunnel model. Proposal number not known. **ANAM**

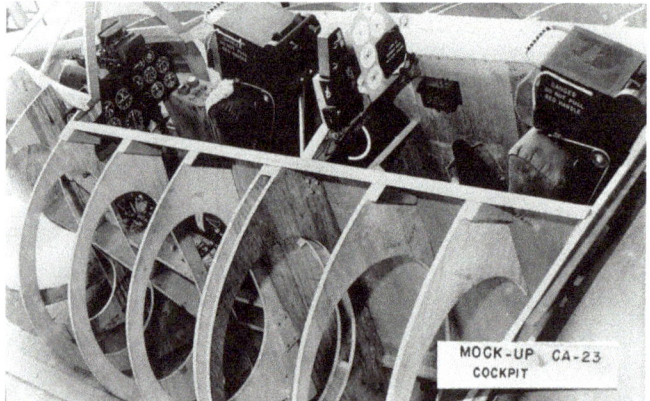

Visible are the inlet trunking frames, the pilot's Vee windscreen, front and rear ejection seats and instrumentation mock-ups. **Walter Watkins**

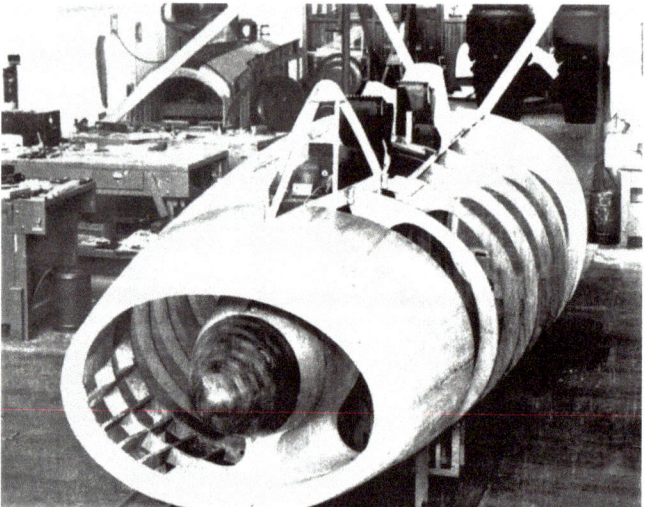

Full scale wooden mock-up of the revised intake. Wooden mock-ups of two Avon engines stand in the background. **Walter Watkins**

air turbine pumps. Ground pressure re-fuelling was specified to be at the rate of 300 gallons/min through two fuselage couplings. Air to the engines was ducted to each engine face via a single pitot entry, past the conical centre body housing for the 20 inch diameter gun laying radar dish and the tandem cockpits. The ducting was designed for the Avon RA-7 with built-in allowance for the greater air mass-flow required if a reheat variant was installed when it became available.

The engine compartments were split into three fire protection zones with each zone having its own its own flush air inlets and exits to ensure an adequate flow of cooling air under all conditions. The fuselage was split at the front engine frame mount to enable removal of the engines. The rear section was slid rearward with the engine tailpipes and the engines moved back on rails onto a supporting trolley.

A 3,000 psi hydraulic system powered the flaperons, all-moving tail, speed brakes, undercarriage, etc with an air driven pump as an emergency back-up. The substantial weight of the 30 mm ammunition was such that the only practical way to re-arm the aircraft was to lower the ammunition boxes as an assembly, through the lower fuselage.

Because of the non-availability of 30 mm calibre cannon at the time of the design, the specification allowed the initial use of 20 mm calibre units and anticipated the future provision for a form of multi-barrel recoilless gun. Provision for the carriage of bombs (2 x 1,000lb); air-to-ground unguided rockets (10 x 60 lb warhead) and two packs of unguided FFAR was allowed for in the design. However, only the cannon armament was mentioned in the final specification.

With the start of the CA-26/27 Sabre project, it was expected that the experience gained in installing the replacement Avon engine in that airframe would be transferred across to the CA-23. The entire design staff had been diverted to the urgent Sabre /Avon conversion work and no further items of equipment or materials were ordered beyond October 1951 pending a policy decision. By the following month, the design study which had been led by Doug Humphries in association with Charles Reid on the aerodynamics was considered complete. With nearly all the technical staff needed elsewhere, work was put aside but with its expected resumption in 1953. On-off assistance was provided by Ian Ring during the initial design phase when time could be spared from the design and test trials of the CA-22 Winjeel prototypes. The preparation of working drawings had commenced and it was the design group's opinion that the airframe of the CA-23 could be built for a total cost considerably less per pound weight than other current, similar designs. Judged in relation to contemporary designs in other countries, the CA-23 was a very advanced concept. No other design nearing the flight test stage approached the performance which was planned for the CA-23.

UK Evaluation

The first Aircraft Development Mission from the UK visited Australia in November / December 1951, and discussed, amongst other things, the projected CA-23 fighter. It was then agreed that the British Ministry of Supply would examine the CA-23 design data material and prepare an appreciation. This was provided on March 6, 1952.

This evaluation was carried out both for the design on its own merits and in comparison with the British aircraft being designed for the RAF Specification F4/48 ie the de Havilland DH110 and the Gloster GA-5 Javelin. It was somewhat critical. Of the criticisms which were raised, with the exception of the anticipated weight of the wing structure, CAC found it to be open to a number of ways of interpretation and there was a lack of understanding by the MoS of the CAC design team's approach to the aerodynamics of the fighter.

The MoS report concluded the wing planform, with its low aspect ratio and high span loading was more appropriate to a supersonic design. It considered the wing planform gave high maximum speeds, but was a penalty in most other respects. Manoeuvrability as indicated by the large turn radii even with reheat would limit the aircraft to combat heights of not more than 40,000 feet. Criticism was levelled at the practicality of a low set tailplane, the long intake duct and tail pipes. The undercarriage track was narrow; the combined aileron/flap low speed control was judged undesirable for an all-weather operations aircraft.

It suggested the CA-23 would be heavier than stated assuming the probable use of similar identical equipment to that planned for their Gloster aircraft design. However, it conceded that the weight of the wing was difficult to quantify since no design of that kind had ever been previously undertaken in the UK. Nevertheless it felt that CAC had gone into the weight analysis in quite some detail.

There was the additional and probably valid conclusion that the all-weather CA-23 would only be a success if the video presentation of radar data came up to expectations. If this failed a major redesign of the fuselage would have been necessary to accommodate the bulky AI equipment. If major structural alteration could not be contemplated, then the aircraft, because of its perceived lack of high altitude agility, would be best suited for medium and low altitude roles.

The concept of relaying radar information in the form of video presentation was a significant departure from the accepted method of collecting radar data. The system was theoretically investigated by the Telecommunication Research Establishment (TRE), Malvern, UK. On operational grounds, they were not impressed. Nevertheless, they were eager to see the system developed further and would seek out more details as time went on. The radar relay video system weighed approximately 250 lb less than the 750 lb weight of the Westinghouse AN/APQ-43 AI radar intended for the Gloster Javelin. There was a feeling that the MoS report had been a less than accurate attempt to discredit the CA-23 on the new ground broken by the design in some areas of the airframe layout, such as the intake duct radar conical centre body housing, the long engine ducts, the highly swept wing and the low set tailplane, all of which had received their share of criticism from the MoS. Wackett was not impressed. CAC read it as a lack of understanding by the MoS of its approach to the aerodynamics of the fighter.

Yet, in the same time frame the English Electric (EE) aero company was proceeding towards the P-1B, the pre-production prototype of the subsequent production EE Lightning UK point defence interceptor. This aircraft had shared similarities with the CA-23 of a radar conical housing in the engine nose intake, long engine ducts, the highly swept wing and the low set tailplane to escape wing downwash at high AoA. The major internal difference was the one crew station in the EE Lightning and the unique vertical stagger of its twin jet engine arrangement. That aircraft with powerful reheat engines eventually became Britain's first locally designed, post war, Mach 2 interceptor; an aircraft of very limited range but with a spectacular intercept performance. In spite of a number of errors in the MoS report, it was quite clear to CAC that the CA-23 would have exceeded the performance level of both the DH 110 (and its eventual production derivative, the DH Sea Vixen) and the Gloster Javelin as then planned.

(PS: Avro Canada had succeeded with the more conservative twin engine all-weather fighter CF-100 Canuck of 1950 (692 built) but failed with the 1959 magnificently ambitious CF-105 Arrow).

The End

Work proceeded slowly toward the prototype start stage. Because of the large ratio of chord to depth characteristics of the wing, development of the envelope construction technique was tested on a full scale part wing specimen. Full scale mock-up work commenced in 1950 and included areas of the wings, cockpits, cannon package, undercarriage, intake duct, the engines and a full size fuel system.

As a means of assisting with the stressing a 1/8th scale perspex model of the fuselage was prepared in the Loft department. Great advances were made in the methods of stress analysis of a highly swept wing and very extensive physical tests were carried out by strain-gauging and photo-elastic techniques on full scale airframe pieces and models.

All of this activity took place in parallel with the two programs; the CA-22/25 Winjeel Basic Trainer development and the CA-26/27 Sabre fighter, with its own design challenges. Wackett had admitted in 1952: *"that the CA-23 was a very big aircraft which may be beyond our capacity to produce with the facilities available and with other urgent work going on at the time…"*

Air Marshall George Jones, CAS since 1942, retired and was replaced from January 1952 by the controversial two year term appointment of Air Marshall Sir Donald Hardman of the Royal Air Force. Like George Jones, he also supported the local aircraft industry. When AVM Frederick Scherger was acting in the role in the absence of AM G. Jones who was ill, he discovered that Sir John Slessor, the RAF Chief of Air Staff, had advised members of the Australian Government against the CA-23 proposal for the RAAF. The RAAF had not been approached directly nor was it subsequently informed of this action. AVM Scherger made known to the British Defence Liaison Staff in Australia his strong displeasure of this unethical intrusion into his domain.

The RAAF Operations Branch had thoughts of abandoning the CA-23 on June 6, 1952 in that it would take not less than three and a half years to produce a prototype; it did not meet the all-weather requirement since it could not be fitted with a suitable AI;(the RAAF had allowed this) and some overseas projects could be in production well ahead of the CA-23. Officially all work on the project had been put on hold in April 1952 and an investigation had commenced on a smaller jet design, the XP46 Single Seat Day Fighter. Cancellation was confirmed on May 19, 1953 together with the suspension of £15,000 of development funding allocation for the financial year 1952 / 53.

Whilst funding had been provided for design study, research and development, there was no funding for prototype hardware. The RAAF had put up obstacles to any build funding and the requirement was allowed to lapse. The concept, its overall complexity and the likely small quantity that would have been ordered was beyond the peace time budget of a small Air Force the size of the RAAF. At no time did Ian Ring or CAC have any knowledge of the EE P1 design. The Short SB5 developmental aerodynamic test bed for the EE P1 did not make its first public appearance till September 1953. Even though the UK & Australian projects had totally different operational intentions, Ian Ring was surprised by the UK's comments on the design. With his significant contribution into the practical engineering build of the CA-23 he resolutely believed it could have been been managed by the company (in contrast to Wackett's doubts) but the economics of it at the time were dubious to its client, the RAAF. Five years, £163,195 and some 150,000 man-hours of work had gone into the project.

The prospect for the aeroplane was such, that Stewart Scott-Hall, the then Director-General of Technical Development(Air) at the Ministry of Supply, UK, who led a delegation to Australia early in 1952 to examine the local aircraft manufacturing facilities and establishments was moved to make a very flattering commentary on CAC 's capabilities.

In his summary of the Australian tour in the English journal, 'The Aeroplane,' he said : '*Mr Wackett and his project team are full of new ideas and evidently watch European and American aerodynamics with an intensity which is surprising when one bears in mind the distances which separate them from these activities. They are swift to apply the results of their study and their latest project is a most ambitious*

design for a night fighter, which in concept, is as advanced as anything yet seen in any other part of the world'.

Bibliography: P223 / CA-23 All - Weather Fighter Aircraft

Commonwealth Aircraft Corporation. (1951). Engineering Report AA58. Fighter Report Vols. 1,2 & 3, November 1951.

Commonwealth Aircraft Corporation.(1951). CA-23 Fighter Report A131. Vols. 1,2 & 3, November 1951.

Commonwealth Aircraft Corporation. Production reports to DAP 1949-53.

Commonwealth Aircraft Corporation. (1952). Engineering Report AA55-A. A Review by Ministry of Supply (UK). An Appreciation of All-Weather Fighter. July 1952.

Fighter type aircraft. Future development policy. [NAA: A1196, 1/501/586 Part 1]. Barcode:636278.

Ministry of Supply (UK). (1952). An appreciation of the CA-23 All-Weather Fighter. March 1952.

Production of two prototypes of a long range all-weather attack fighter-aircraft CA-23.[NAA: A5799,129/1953]. Barcode:525005

Rayner, Harry (1984). *Scherger. A biography of ACM Sir Frederick Scherger*. Australian War Memorial, Canberra.

Ring I. H.(Ian) (1985-1987) [Interviews]

Royal Aircraft Establishment, Great Britain. (1954) Report AERO 2498. Tests to High Subsonic Speeds. January 1954.

Royal Australian Air Force Tech. Specification. (1949). AC79, Two-Seater, Long Range, All-Weather, Attack Fighter. February 2, 1949.

Scott-Hall, S. (April 18,1952).'Aircraft Development in Australia'. *The Aeroplane*

CA-24 HAWKER P1081 DAY FIGHTER AIRCRAFT
February 1950

Hawker Siddeley Group's Australian representative for the South Pacific, ACM Sir Keith Park was invited to present an update of the Group's post war jet engine aircraft developments in an address at a restricted post-war aircraft production conference hosted by CAS AVM George Jones on January 30, 1948. This was probably part of Plan 'D', the RAAF's post-war organisation and requirements study set up in 1947 by George Jones. An operational version of their research P1052 aircraft was the preferred type, two examples of which (VX 272 and VX 279) had flown on November 19, 1948 and April 13, 1949 respectively. By October 1948 CAC was told the RAAF would take up the type and an immediate start would be necessary. The outcome of this and other meetings saw AM George Jones (now promoted to AM) and two senior RAAF technical staff undertake an evaluation visit in the UK in April-June 1949 to investigate its jet powered combat aircraft program. These took in the Supermarine Type 541; new variants of the Vampire / Venom; Meteor and the Hawker P1052, a swept wing version of the eventual Hawker Seahawk. It was the P1081, the next development, that was considered to have the best all-round performance. To assist AM Jones and needing to discover the status of the airframe development program and manufacturing processes of this unfamiliar English design, CAC sent Ern Jones-Assistant Factory Manager (nephew of AM George Jones) and E. J. (Jack) Smith-Chief Tooling Superintendent to evaluate the P1081, departing by Qantas Constellation on April 4, 1949 and arriving in England on 12 April. (Each return Melb-Syd-UK airfare cost £596/1/0). The pair returned from the UK on May 29, 1949 without much optimism but happy to leave behind the bleak English post-war living conditions. (The Canberra bomber was also selected in this mission and GAF's test pilot, John Miles flew the P1052 in the middle of 1950 as part of a Government funded tour of UK aircraft companies and the RAE.)

Sir Keith Park met with Prime Minister Ben Chifley on October 14, 1949 to discuss the Hawker Siddeley Group's offer to build their companies' aircraft in Australia. The Air Board recommended the P1081 and sought 72 aircraft at an estimated total cost of £5,140,750 including 96 Nene engines in submission no. 1347D to Federal Cabinet on November 19, 1949. The RAAF allocated it the Aircraft Series 2 identifier, A86. Following a change of Government from Labor to Liberal in December 1949, Hawker Siddeley renewed its offer in January 1950. The new Minister for Air, Thomas W. White was one of a number of individuals intent to put Australia back into the British sphere of defence equipment acquisition as Australia lacked US foreign exchange Reserves.

CAC aware of the government's intention to acquire a manufacturing licence from the Hawker Aircraft Company was not involved in the selection process of the P1081, the new day fighter it was to build under contract CA-24 but it was seriously short of work. Wackett was left out of the aircraft selection loop or perhaps George Jones was exercising his authority as Air Marshall. The Department of Air had been voted the sum of £5,120,000 for the P1081 for the years 1959-1956 from which CAC requested an allocation of £422,000 from the Department of Supply for the provision of jet engine test facilities.

Federal Cabinet (Agenda No 13) gave its approval on February 2, 1950 to build the 72 aircraft in Australia. Production planning was for 24 aircraft to be delivered each year with first delivery commencing in July 1951 and ending by June 30, 1954.

Unexpected Problems

By January 1950, following several months of flight testing, Hawker proposed to fit a Rolls Royce Tay engine in place of the RR Nene turbojet with which the P1052 was being tested. The RR Tay was a centrifugal flow gas turbine development of the Nene with an expected thrust of 6,250 lb, some 20% greater than that of the Nene and was the outcome of a performance investigation to meet an inquiry by the Australian Government. (The RR Tay was being developed at the request of P & W who subsequently took on its development and US military application as the J48. It was not used or built in the UK.)

Because of delays in its development program, Hawker were obliged to retain the Nene turbojet. The prototype, VX279, was rebuilt; its bifurcated tailpipe was replaced by a straight-through jet pipe and a new swept tail was fitted. Consideration was given to the RAAF's request for the installation of reheat or afterburner in a dedicated Australian prototype airframe. At an estimated £4-5M and development time in excess of two years, Rolls Royce refused the request as it would have diverted reheat development effort from their new axial flow series of Avon engines. The modified VX279, now designated the P1081, made its first flight on June 19, 1950.

The RAAF Specification document AC85 dated July 12, 1950 laid down the technical requirements for a land based day interceptor fighter for operation in temperate, tropical and sub-arctic conditions. The design was to be a development of the Hawker Type 1052 (E38/46) swept wing experimental aircraft: *"It should be the Hawker Type 1081 as described in the Hawker Aircraft brochure dated January 1950, except where varied to meet the requirements of Specification AC85"*. Specification AC86 which was released three months later requested minor equipment and acquisition changes.

CA-24 Hawker P1081

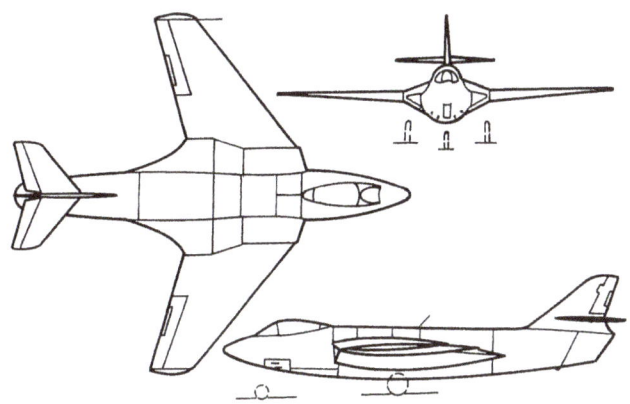

Specifications	CA-24 Hawker P1081 Day Fighter	
Powerplant	One Rolls Royce Nene R.N.2 turbojet of 5,000 lb s.t.(SL)	
Performance	Max speed at SL	604 kts
	Max speed at 36,000 ft	Mach 0.9
	Time to 35,000 ft	9.2 min
	Service ceiling	45,600 ft
	Fuel capacity	400 gall
Weights	Empty	11,200 lb
	Loaded	14,480 lb
Dimensions	Wing span	31 ft 6 in
	Wing area	258 sq ft
	Wing LE sweep at 25%	35°
	Length	37 ft 4 ins
	Height	13 ft 3 ins
	Track	8 ft 8 ins
Armament	NA	
Retrospective Designation	XP36	

From the outset Wackett was not happy or impressed with the P1040, P1052 or their latest derivative for the RAAF, the P1081 which he suggested did not fit the RAAF Specification.

Ern Jones went back to Hawkers in April 1950 to negotiate the best price production contract for a fitted-out fuselage front end, stub wings and outer wings shipped out to CAC as a means to verify the expected production drawings. There was no prototype. The rear fuselage and centre section were not representative of the Australian aircraft. Until the aircraft production plans had advanced the RR office in Collins St, Melbourne cautioned Wackett on May 24, 1950 against CAC being too hasty to make a start with production of the new Nene IV which was now destined for the P1081. Herb Knight with other engine factory personnel also visited RR to study the 5,000 lb thrust Nene IV which had only some 20-25% commonality with the Nene 2-VH being built by CAC for the Vampire FB30 etc series. Some 150 design changes had been introduced.

Without any P1081 orders placed on behalf of the Royal Air Force, this was expected to mean that impending development work would lead to delays in reaching full production efficiency and considerably greater expenditure than would be encountered in engineering a fully developed aircraft. On August 2, 1950 sensing what was probably an over optimistic delivery start date for the P1081, the Government authorised a stop-gap increase in the local de Havilland Vampire fighter-bomber production orders from 50 to 80 aircraft.

At Hawker Siddeley Aircraft Again

On June 6, 1950, Wackett, frustrated by reports he was receiving reported to the DAP, *"the Hawker quote for a complete sample aircraft is outrageous. We agree to carry out the task with the samples mentioned and it seems, that although the quotes are still outrageous we could achieve the objective for this approved expenditure ie the front fuselage and stub wings for A£100,000, fully fitted out (to assist production of the aircraft in Australia) for delivery on January 31,1951 and September 30,1951 respectively".*

CAC staff were sent to join and relieve Ern Jones at Hawkers in June 1950 comprising of Chief Draftsman Edward Bishop; Project Engineer Maurice Lodge and R. Holland, Engineering Administration followed in September by Production Engineer Reg Schulz; Tooling Engineer J.Morey and Project Design Engineer Arthur Williams. Living conditions in the immediate post-war years in Britain were so austere and unsatisfactory, that in order to supplement the group's living conditions the company sent them food parcels.

What the CAC team discovered about the P1081 was disappointing. £30,000 had been paid for a licence on an aircraft which was experimental in nature and the Hawker organisation was in no position to suggest when it would be in a fit state for production. Down payment of £150,000 and £5,000 for each of 5 years was expected. The Avon engine to be built at CAC for the Canberra bomber was seen as a possible future substitute for the Nene.

Back home, thinking all was well with the P1081, AVM R. L. Atcherley, interim CAS of the Pakistan Air Force sent a telegram on August 17, 1950 to Victor Letcher, Director of Aircraft Production asking the estimated cost and possible delivery of the P1081 from CAC's upcoming production line. Wanting to re-equip with jet fighters, his inquiry followed an earlier visit and meeting in Australia with both AM George Jones and V. Letcher. The prospect of any aircraft following to Pakistan was too early to contemplate!

On September 11, 1950 the DAP had the contents of an observation received from Wackett, *"as no speeding up of the project will be achieved whilst Hawkers insist on more than 12 months to produce a sample to prove the correctness of the drawings, we request that the meetings at Hawkers be discontinued as they appear to waste our officers time. We do not need multiple copies of these meetings minutes".*

Frustrated, he told the CAC Board on 20 September *"We now know the facts of the Hawker licence. The Government has bought an idea only, for which no production drawings exist. It happens that about 10% of the production drawings of another aircraft are applicable, and we will get these right away, but 90% are still to be made and the Hawker intention is only to give second priority to it. It is only an idea, based on a similar aircraft flown only two months ago with no military features built in".*

By October 6, 1950 CAC had received 822 engineering drawings. This grew to 3802 of an estimated 4,600 and Wackett expressed disquiet on the delay. He was irritated at the inability of the Hawker Aircraft Company to supply technical data in accordance with the agreed schedule nor the sample aircraft centre section which was not expected to arrive till September 1951. Parcels of drawings arrived in dribs and drabs. This meant that all tooling drawings could not be regarded as proven and local tooling for this major component could not get underway till 1952, a hopelessly delayed proposition. To add further frustration, Hawker Aircraft informed CAC that it could not deliver the front fuselage before March 1951 and had put back further the delivery of the centre fuselage section with stub wings to

November 30, 1951. Both sections fitted out with service equipment were to cost a combined £100,000.

Backing Out

Hawkers indicated that for work to proceed at a faster pace, CAC should send some design drafting staff to England. As this was not part of the contract agreement, CAC would not comply. As a measure of the exasperation being felt by Wackett, he, in company with Victor Letcher, felt obliged to make a personal assessment of the situation by visiting the Hawker Company at Kingston. Flying with QEA, Wackett departed on October 13, 1950 equipped with a daily UK £5 allowance plus board and fares with the expenses of the trip allocated 50% to Hawkers and (strangely) 50% to RR Avon engine development.

They arrived in the UK on 17 October. It soon became evident to both gentlemen that an error of judgement of a serious nature had been perpetrated by both Hawkers and the Australian Government as to the very early stage of development of the P1081 and that it was unlikely that there would be an Australian built P1081 flying before July 1952. Sidney Camm, Hawker's principal designer and Hawker's management understood the anomalous situation in which the Australian Government was now placed. The deposit funding was returned and work on the Australian project was stopped on November 14, 1950 with the Federal Cabinet confirming its cancellation on December 13, 1950. No aircraft hardware had reached CAC.

The Hawker company admitted that work on the P1081 was hindering its concentration on Specification F.3 / 48 for which it had orders to build three prototypes (P1067) for the RAF. This was to be the eventual very successful Hawker Hunter fighter. Not wishing to completely lose out, it offered the Hunter to the Australian Government as an alternative to the P1081 with a possible attainment of production in Australia by mid-1953.

The F.3 / 48 prototype was some months away from completion (first flight July 20,1951), and whilst with its Rolls Royce Avon engine it was the best fighter that Britain could offer it was not in Wackett's view the aircraft the RAAF should be acquiring. He also examined the production prototype of the Supermarine Swift Type 541, the swept wing development of the straight wing Attacker. It had fundamental shortcomings; did not impress him and he admitted the planned Hunter with its Avon engine was a far better prospect. His primary intent however was to compare and inspect the North American F-86 Sabre. On November 16, 1950 after a month in the UK, he left England on the liner *Queen Elizabeth*, bound for New York and Los Angeles.

A week before all work at CAC had ceased, a report received on November 7, 1950, stated that the Hawker Company had been

Hawker P1081, serialled VX279. **Clive Lynch**

VX279 at Heathrow, UK June 23, 1950. **David Molesworth**

busy building the front fuselage for their first Hawker Sea Hawk (P1040) fighter to Spec N.7 /46, developed for the Royal Navy Fleet Air Arm order of November 1949 (528 examples eventually built). This was ahead of the similar fuselage unit of the P1081 for CAC. The Australian High Commission in London stated in part of a long response to the Prime Minister's Office on January 30, 1951, that both the Hawker P1081 and the Supermarine Type 541 aircraft were built for research purposes and were not intended for production.

In January 1951, P1081, VX279 was passed to the RAE for further handling trials. On the 3rd of April, during a routine test flight the aircraft crashed at Norlington, Sussex, killing (Sqdn Ldr) Trevor Wade, Hawker's chief test pilot. The RAE report suggested the aircraft was in a near-vertical M 0.98 dive; the ML Aviation Ltd ejection seat had operated normally, but at 2,000 feet with the seat tumbling at 2.3 revolutions/sec it was too late for the parachute to open. Interestingly, the wing flaps were found to be in the fully-down position. Hawkers had, at one stage, anticipated using the flaps as air-brakes , a concept that had earlier been deemed a bad decision.

There was speculation as to the Hawker Siddeley Group's intentions. Were they using delaying tactics with the research P1081 airframe in a ploy to win an Australia order for their new definite Hawker Hunter? Rolls Royce had no long term plans for the Nene engine. The future lay with the Avon axial flow engine series. Some 3,066 engineering man-hours had been spent at CAC on the P1081. This included converting Hawkers use of decimals to fractions on their drawings. All documentation and drawings for initial tooling and airframe work disappeared quickly and quietly without a trace. Did it all go back to Hawker Aircraft or was it taken to the Government's Defence storage facility at Oaklands, NSW ? Most likely it was ordered be destroyed.

Zephyr was supposedly the name given to Australia's P1081 by the UK Government....a security ploy so as inquisitive poking into

VX279 in the air before its loss and that of Hawker chief test pilot Trevor Wade on April 3, 1951 . **Clive Lynch**

the crates labelled Zephyr would lead people to believe it was parts for the English made Ford motor car of the same name.

Bibliography: CA-24 Hawker P1081 Day Fighter
Aircraft:(August 1950, January 1951, February 1951.)

Australia. Dept. of Supply (1949-50). Overseas travel: General New Aircraft Projects. E.J.Jones.[NAA:MP287/1,5713].Barcode: 426608.

Australia. Dept. of Supply (1950-51).Hawker Aircraft Co. Fighter Project-Miscellaneous Correspondence, Data etc.[NAA: MP287/1, 5756/1].Barcode: 364158.

Australia. Dept. of Supply (1950). Hawker Aircraft P/L Project-Importation of Sample Components.[MP287/1, 5756/3].Barcode: 364144.

Australia. Dept. of Supply (1950). Hawker Aircraft Project-RR Nene Engine Type Required For.[NAA:MP287/1,5756/4].Barcode: 364154

Australia. Dept. of Supply (1950).Hawker Aircraft P/L- Interceptor Fighter- Reports from E.J.Jones.[NAA:MP287/1,5650/11]. Barcode: 426605.

Australia. Dept. of Supply (1950). Air Headquarters, Pakistan-Inquiry for the Supply of Hawker aircraft. [NAA: MP287/1, 5820]. Barcode: 363853.

Australia. Dept. of Aircraft Production (1937-68).Miscellaneous reports, minutes of meetings, historical notes dealing with aircraft production.[MP1472/1,15 part 1]. Barcode: 514588.

Carter, Graham (2006). *ML Aviation- A Secret World*. Keyham Books, Chippenham, UK.

Commonwealth Aircraft Corporation. (Undated) CAC file. Officers abroad - 025a/025b.

Commonwealth Aircraft Corporation. Plant Progress Reports(various)

Green, William; Cross, Roy. (1955). *The Jet Aircraft of the* World. MacDonald, London.

Jane's All the World's Aircraft (1949/50, 1954/55). Jane's Information Group : Coulson, Surrey, UK.

Mason, Francis K. (1971). *Hawker Aircraft Since 1920*. 2nd edition. Putnam, London.

Miles, John.(1979). *Testing Time*. Neptune Press, Belmont, Victoria.

Royal Australian Air Force. (1950) Tech. Specification AC85 (July 12, 1950). Land Based Interceptor Fighter.

Royal Australian Air Force. (1950) Tech. Specification AC85 (Oct. 1, 1950). Land Based Interceptor Fighter.

'Trevor Wade, Death of a Brilliant Test Pilot'. April 13,1951. *Flight*. .

Wackett, L. J. CAC. (1950-1952). Abroad File No 3/File W.5.

CA-26 / CA-27 NORTH AMERICAN F-86 SABRE FIGHTER AIRCRAFT
April 1951

A major change of direction, in the RAAF's fighter aircraft production program took place on February 21, 1951 the day on which the Australian Government decided that the Service's new fighter was to be the North American F-86 Sabre. This decision was the culmination of a series of separate events namely, the lack of satisfactory progress with the earlier decision to licence-build the Hawker P1081; the start of the Korean conflict midway through 1950; the RAAF's 77 Squadron's involvement in Korea flying P-51s and their replacement by the lack-lustre and subsequently out-classed Gloster Meteor F Mk 8 fighter jets, 36 examples of which announced in December 1950 by the new Menzies Liberal Government would be transferred from the inventory of the RAF.

A lot of the groundwork for the adoption of the Sabre was due in no small way to initiatives set in motion by Wackett. The aircraft had made a good showing in aerial fighting with the USAF in Korea against the Mig-15. An event of some significance was the decision by General Motors- Holden to relinquish its shareholding in CAC and for those shares to be offered and accepted by aero engine manufacturer Rolls Royce following a visit to CAC by Ernest W. Hives (later Lord Hives), chairman of Rolls Royce. RR bought in after very serious consideration. It had not previously as a prime aero engine builder, invested in any overseas or UK aircraft construction firm from the risk of alienating its competitors.

Having completed his official visit to Hawker Siddeley Aircraft to evaluate the troubled P1081 project for himself (Refer to CA-24 Hawker P1081), Wackett extended his tour to the USA to examine the production of the NAA F-86 Sabre. This was a private initiative, without any request from the Australian Government, but the decision was not without previous consideration. When General George Kenney, the wartime commander of Allied Air Forces in the S.W. Pacific, visited the CAC establishment in 1950, Wackett had expressed his desire to see the F-86 follow the P-51 in RAAF service rather than the shaky proposition surrounding the P1081. Wackett's letter to General Kenney of October 17, 1950 asked his permission to visit the Pentagon and North American Aviation's plant at Los Angeles. All was arranged by US Air Force Staff. It was the third time he was visiting NAA with the prospect of CAC once more building one of their designs. He crossed the Atlantic on the liner *Queen Elizabeth* to New York, visited CAC's US agents Messers R. W. Cameron in New York and arrived at the Los Angeles plant on November 24, 1950. Six days later on 30 November, business completed, he flew home aboard a B.C.P.A. flight.

The only reservation that the defence staff at Washington had about the sale of the F-86, was the demand and consequent non-availability of its General Electric J47 jet engine from US sources. Ernest Hives had already made approaches to NAA about the possibility of installing a RR Avon engine in the Sabre hoping to repeat the great success of the RR Merlin which had been used in the P-51 Mustang. On January 15, 1951 the anglophile Liberal Country Party Prime Minister, Robert Menzies, asked for advice, comments and suggestions through the Australian High Commissioner in London from the UK Ministry of Supply and the Air Ministry in respect of British aircraft likely to meet the RAAF Spec. for a jet fighter. It also had to be suitable for Australian production capacity in peace and war with the potential of it being a source of supply to the rest of the Commonwealth. The detailed response of January 30, 1951 was that UK capacity was committed to the new Hawker Hunter till August 1953, so tooling up for the Hunter in Australia as was previously hinted, would start some 18 months later than setting up for Sabre production.

The UK report derided the F-86 as being light and deficient in its armament; was likely to be slower and more difficult to build than the Hunter and would not recommend Australia build it as it would be obsolete by the time it was produced. As its production in the USA far outstripped the supply of its GE J47 engine, it was suggested finished airframe parts be sourced from North American Aviation or Canadair but its engine be built in Australia. However should Australia go down the path of the Sabre it should re-engine it with the RR Nene that CAC was building for the Vampire as Australian RR Avon production was fully committed to the GAF/ EE Canberra bomber program. The RAAF refuted the obsolescence claim and suggested it was the Sabre that would be easier to build. There was no way an audacious F-86E Sabre/Nene II-VH combination would be acceptable

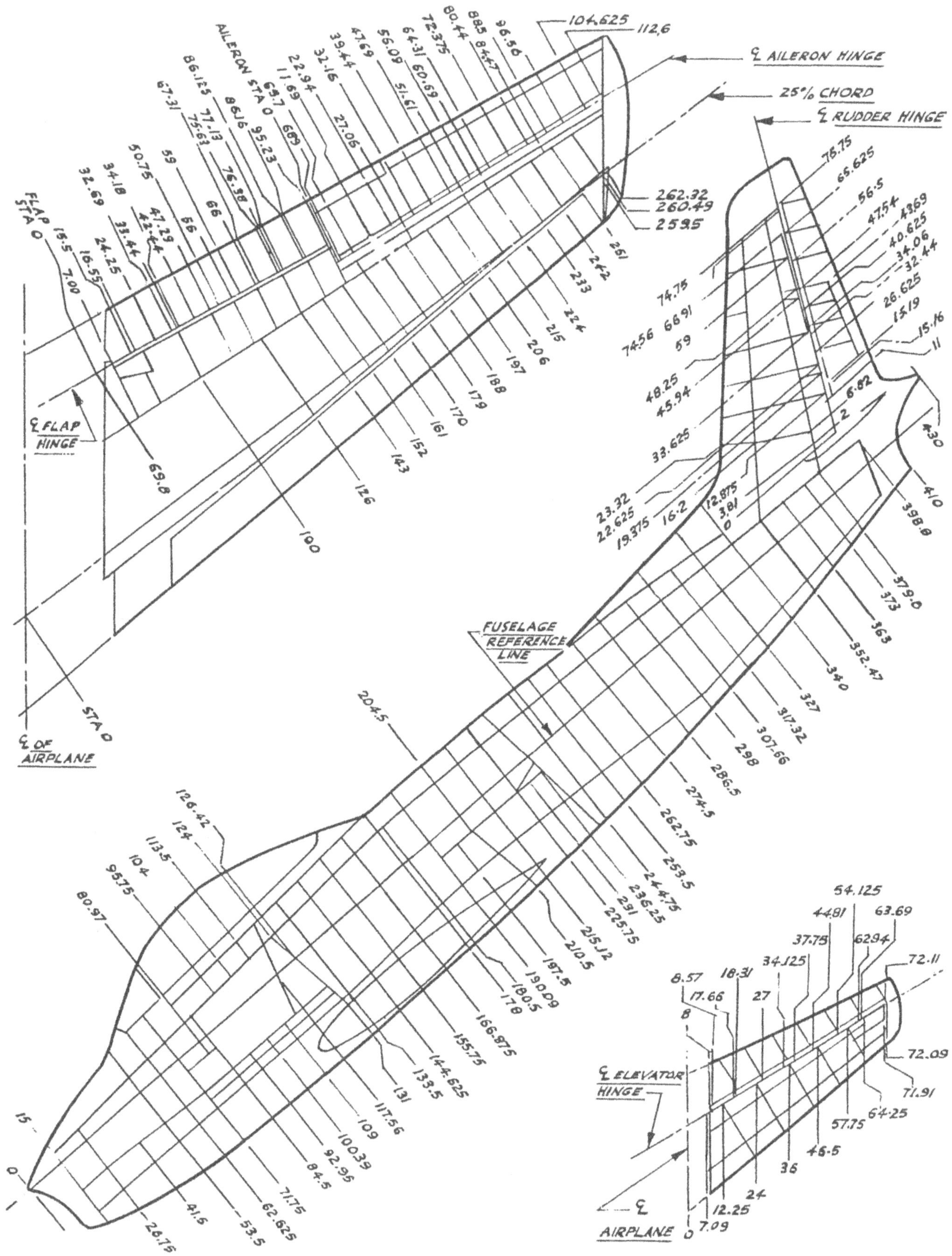

AIRCRAFT STATIONS

as it would be inferior to any other current combat type and North American Aviation Inc. would not under any circumstance approve or assist with the design installation of this dated engine.

Ironically, in a bid to span the gap in its own air defences, the UK had placed an interim order for 420 Canadair built Sabres until the Hawker Hunter entered service.

It was at this crucial juncture that the possibility of fitting an alternatively sourced engine in the form of a RR Avon first began to assume reality. With the concurrence of Ernest Hives who promised full engineering support and was prepared to supply an initial 12-20 Avon engines for the RAAF's initial requirement of 72 aircraft, the CAS AM George Jones through the Minister for Air, Thomas W. White endorsed the acquisition of the F-86E / Avon engine combination on February 2, 1951. This was viewed in many quarters as a prickly process in view of Australia's patriotic leaning towards equipment purchases from British manufacturers, but taken together with the selection of the British Avon engine it helped to mollify those critics.

The calculations for the Sabre evaluation based on comparisons between the original GE J47 and the RR Avon replacement engine were carried out by Charles Reid. Working on his own from late on Friday night, through the weekend he completed his report in time for the RAAF Melbourne engineering conference at 10 o'clock on the Monday morning. Victor Letcher reported on March 1, 1951 that North American Aviation was proceeding with its own design evaluation study for the installation of the Avon in the Sabre.

Licence Agreement

The mission to seal the licence deal left Sydney on April 19, 1951 on the Pan-Am Stratocruiser service. (The date of May 13, 1951 given in Wackett's book *'Aircraft Pioneer'* is incorrect. The company's travel arrangements file, passport and travel diary of Ian Ring who sat in the same row with Wackett, all show the date of 19 April.) The team was led by AVM Frederick Scherger and included L. J. Wackett, V. J. Letcher, Air Cdre E. Hay and Ian Ring. It was Ian's task to examine the project in more detail from his position of Project Manager and Design Engineer. The group was met at the North American Los Angeles, Inglewood Plant by representatives from Rolls Royce. The manufacturing licence was negotiated by Wackett and V. J. Letcher on behalf of the Department of Supply. Ian Ring and Wackett were back in Melbourne on 19 May, whilst Ern Jones departed for NAA on 20 June to examine the aircraft production process. A large supporting team numbering some 24 CAC technical and engineering personnel was sent to the USA in the follow-up study and familiarization process.

CA-27 Sabre Planned Cumulative Delivery Schedule
First & Second Orders 1954-1956

	1954	1955	1956
June	1		
September	5		
December	12		
March		18	
June		27	
September		36	
December		45	
March			54
June			66
September			78
December			90

The licence agreement of May 23, 1951 cost US$500,000 spread into three instalments; US$250,000 on signing; US$200,000 in the following nine months provided that substantially all the manufacturing data had been supplied; US$50,000 upon complete delivery of all manufacturing data and US$S6,500 for each airframe produced, plus 5% on the Australian cost of spare parts. All these outlays were borne by the Department of Supply. The manufacturing data included all the engineering detail of the F-86E Sabre, drawings, stress and weight analysis, flight test development reports, material and process specifications, tooling requirements and design as was production information such as the layout of production lines, flow charts, planning time estimates, assembly and inspection procedures.

Above all it allowed the company to acquire detail parts in the formed state and a considerable quantity of assembled tooling and specialized machine tools. This all helped to meet the RAAF request for an early in-service date. In spite of all this assistance from the parent design organisation, the CAC Sabre was not merely an assembly task. Considerable structural changes were set in train. CAC, with support from Rolls Royce, was to install the Avon turbojet in place of the original General Electric, 5,910lb thrust, J47 engine. It was envisaged that the early Sabres would utilize the RA-3, 6,500lb thrust Avon, but RR promised to supply 12 to 20 Avons of the model in current production when they were required. By the time the engines were required the current model in production in England was the Avon RA-7 of 7,500lb thrust without reheat or de-icing. Twenty examples were supplied as the RA-7 Avon Mk 20.

USAF combat reports from the fighting over Korea suggested that the F-86 would be the perfect aircraft if it possessed an engine of an extra one ton of thrust and heavier calibre ammunition than the 0.5 inch machine guns. While the change of engine in the Australian Sabre was due to the non-availability of the US engine and not these combat reports, the idea to upgrade the armament of the CAC Sabre was a direct response to the combat reports. By July 1952, the RAAF had firmed up on its recommendation that the original fixed gun armament of six 0.5 inch machine guns was to be replaced by two 30 mm Aden cannon. This revision was to add to the existing engineering tasks, significant as they were. The extensive changes to the engine and armament installations meant that only about 40% of the original fuselage design unaltered. The scale of engineering change required 150 toolmakers during 1952 to establish production for the following year.

Engineering Changes

The alternative engine brought with it many problems. What appeared to be the most serious of these, the provision of extra air mass to the engine (the Avon consumed 25% more air than its GE counterpart) was overcome fairly simply. By splitting the intake horizontally, inserting in the split a wedge of structure and so dropping the lower line of the fuselage by 3.5 inches at the front, the required extra air intake area was obtained. The intake duct area was now 435 sq ins. The increase in duct cross-sectional area faded out as it went back to the engine face. This 'split' was achieved by letting extension pieces into the sides of the fuselage frames in the vicinity of the nose. These were then covered by extensions to the skin panels on the outer surface. Inside the duct, the formed duct skins in their untrimmed state, as supplied by NAA, were of sufficient extra area to just cover the 3.5 inch increase in height.

While of greater thrust than the GE J47, the Avon engine occupied approximately the same space as its overall dimensions were similar. It weighed 460 lbs less than the GE J47. To preserve the original centre of gravity, leave the basic lines and flight characteristics of the Sabre undisturbed the lighter engine had to re-positioned further aft. The new location of the main engine trunnions made it convenient to move the transport joint by which

the whole rear end of the fuselage is removed, further aft, from Station 236.25 to Station 262.75 allowing the engine to be fully supported in the front fuselage structure.

The Avon had its own requirement of fuselage cooling and venting, as well as the considerations of access and installation. The fuselage fuel cells had to re-arranged and accessories and equipment relocated. The access doors for the J47 were not suitable for the new installation. Fuselage side panels were completely redesigned to incorporate access for the relocated services on and around the Avon engine. The increase in thrust meant a larger diameter tailpipe was required. To help solve these problems a series of fuselage mock-ups were built. One was to determine the repositioning of the electrical and hydraulic systems made necessary by the new engine and armament installations. It was also used as an assembly jig for the first-off hydraulic and fuel lines and electrical cables, to allow these to be tailored to fit before being placed on the prototype aircraft.

The second airframe fuselage complete in the main structural components, was used in a static test rig to check, the primary structure, the design of the skin cut-outs, altered frames and other local alterations. Other fuselage test sections were constructed to verify the aerodynamic changes created by the change of engines. Two of these sections, one for the revised intake contours, the other of the intermediate fuselage from the engine face to the propelling nozzle, were shipped to RR (UK) for investigations to provide a sufficient flow of cooling air along the fuselage interior to protect the structure from excessive temperatures both on the ground and in the air. These were carried out with an Avon fitted in the intermediate fuselage. The cooling air intakes were revised and two extra ventilation doors were placed in the top of the fuselage above the jet pipe. These were wired to open when the undercarriage was extended to prevent local overheating due to lack of circulation after the engine was shut down. The electrical starter was replaced by an iso-propyl-nitrate liquid fuel type to enable engine starting independent of electrical support.

Slow Deliveries

North American Aviation had quoted US$S8,057,200 for 100 sets of fabricated details and assemblies which were purchased with the Minister's approval on June. 6, 1951. The arrival of hundreds of cases in three shiploads of these parts in Port Melbourne in December 1951 should have been a boon to the program but as the result of the engineering changes much of this shipment was now unusable. Substitution of the Avon engine alone caused 100 sets of 2,340 items to be made redundant. Further, the sorting, identifying and storing of the excess parts was very time consuming and unproductive. The Government sought to return to North American Aviation and even to Canadair (which was building Sabres) those parts which had inadvertently been sent to Australia, but there was no call for the excess parts.

On November 5, 1951, J. L. Atwood, the president of NAA allowed a significant reduction of US$758,538 from the parts bill. The surplus items were written off as scrap and for the rest of production, only parts that were to remain unchanged were sent out.

For the prototype aircraft the wings, tail assembly, undercarriage, fuel tanks and the front fuselage top deck etc. were supplied as complete assemblies, but the rest of the fuselage was supplied as detail parts which had to be modified and assembled by CAC. Twenty-nine (F-86E listed) complete sub-assemblies for this one airframe cost US$42,164.

Production start-up was further assisted with 15 jigs and tool masters which cost US$121,500 and milling, stretch-wrap forming and roll forming machines which cost a further US$126,000. Of all the parts needed for production, 75% were imported from the USA as separate items requiring local assembly. A small minority of the 60% of the fuselage parts which had to be modified were actually worked on, the rest were put aside for locally fabricated alternatives. Parts for the production as a whole were persistently slow in arriving, creating an on-going concern, for the production engineering team. This problem manifested itself early creating a three month delay in the first flight of the local prototype. A long awaited shipment of 900 cases of parts and tools finally arrived in October 1952. All records detailing received model assemblies, parts, tooling and material were referred to as being F-86E; however as the aircraft was updated with the revised wing leading edge it took on the F-86F designation. (An undated company retrospective technical history summary states 100 sets of F-86F major structural items were ordered.) The dust had hardly settled on all the problems of installing the RA- 7 Avon engine than Wackett was propositioning the DAP (October 23, 1952) with the idea of installing the RA-14 Avon in the follow-on contract after the first 70 aircraft order. (Refer to XP53 Proposal).

Schedules

The RA-7 Mk 20 Avon delivery schedules set out on December 16, 1952 was to see the first two engines arriving by February 1953 and the other 18 coming in intervals by December 1953. The first engine was dispatched by sea from the UK on December 18, 1952.

To March 1953, some 10,000 hours had been expended in unforeseen tooling rectification work. 438 men were on the project on that month. There was acrimony on the creeping delay, however, Wackett often repeatedly defended his position by laying the blame on funding shortfalls within the Government departments concerned because they had not allocated the Priority One status that was needed to implement the RAAF schedule. With the first flight a matter of weeks away the prototype was still short of six component parts from the American suppliers.

Prototype Flies

The prototype given the CAC model number CA-26, the RAAF serial number, A94-101 and identified as a Sabre Mk 30, was ready for the AID inspectors on July 7,1953. The engine was run for five minutes on 20 July followed by the first taxi run on 29 July and by others on 31 July and 4 August . These runs were made from the flight hangar to the east-west runway at Fisherman's Bend. The aircraft was then partially dismantled and taken by road to the Avalon Department of Supply airfield at Lara, 35 miles south west of Melbourne.

The short runways at the factory were unsafe for test flying an aircraft with the performance of the Sabre. On the eve of the first flight quick action by Wackett averted disaster. One side of the undercarriage caught fire through overheated brakes from a prolonged series of taxi runs. A bystander was seen preparing to douse the flames with a bucket of water but Wackett intercepted him and heaved a bucket of sand on the flames. Overnight, new tyres and brakes were fitted on both main undercarriage units and Flt Lt W. (Bill) H. Scott took A94-101 on its 30 minute maiden flight on the following day, August 3, 1953. Bill Scott was released from his RAAF commission on January 22,1954 to become the Chief Test Pilot for the Department of Defence Production (Aircraft) taking over as Chief Test Pilot of GAF from John Miles. He was to perform the bulk of the CAC Sabre and the GAF Canberra bomber production flight tests. The UK-Commonwealth Relations Minister, Duncan Sandys, MP congratulated CAC on September 12, 1953 on their successful first flight. At the end of its acceptance trials, A94-101 was delivered to the RAAF Aircraft Research and Development Unit (ARDU) at Laverton, Victoria.

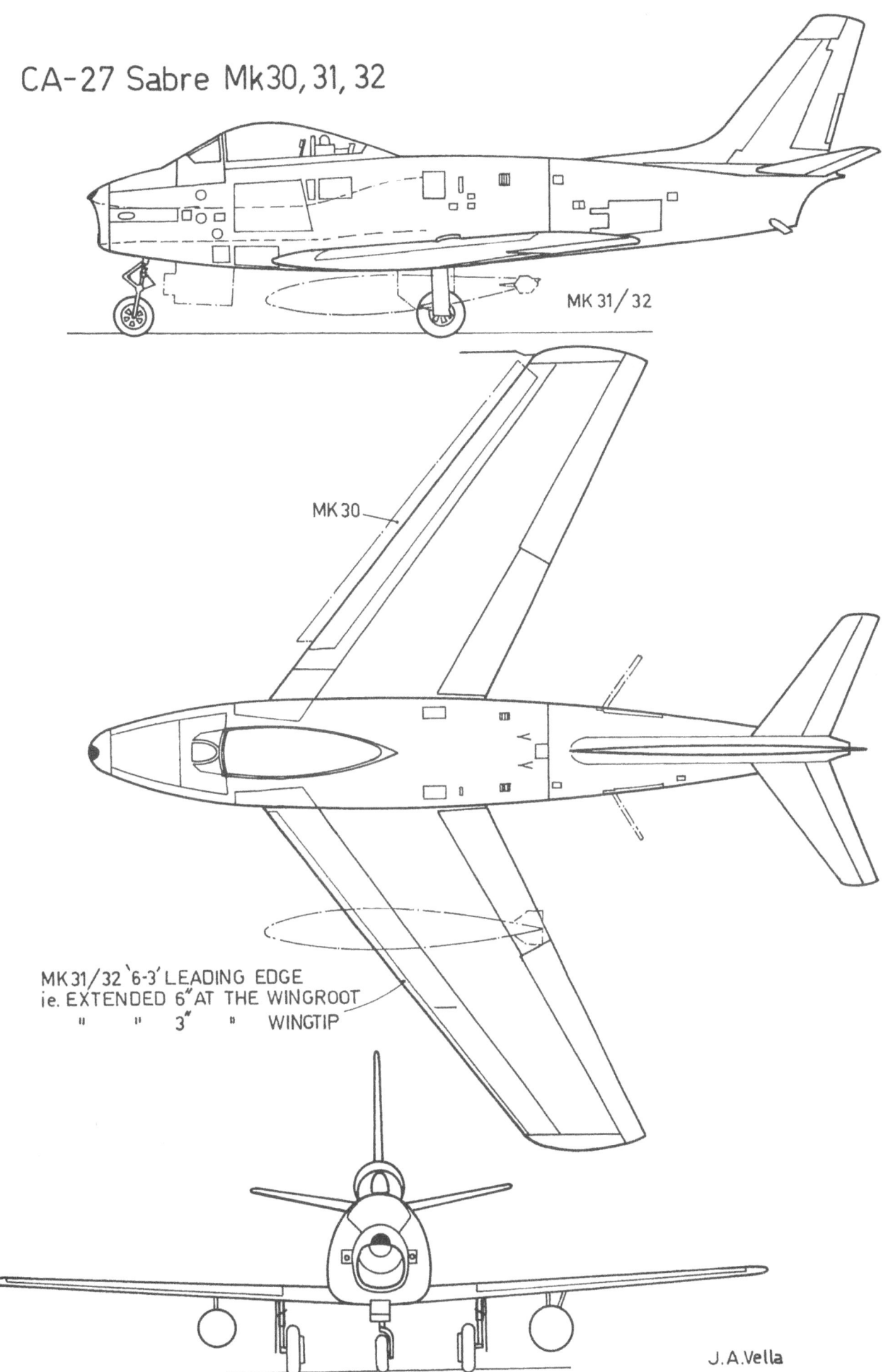

Electrical, hydraulic and fuel line systems etc installation test wooden mock-up. **HDHV**

A cold and gloomy winter's day. The sole prototype CA-26, A94-101 on the day of its first flight from Avalon on August 3, 1953. **RAAF/HDHV**

Another mock-up build underway. **HDHV**

CA-26 Sabre Mk 30 prototype A94-101. **RAAF/HDHV**

A94-902 the second production CA27-2 at the front of the assembly line. **HDHV**

Test Pilot Flt Lt W.(Bill) Scott. **LJW Collection/NLA**

CA-27 Sabre wing assembly area. **HDHV**

Armourers loading air-to-ground rockets on 3 Sqdn Sabres at RAAF Williamtown, March 1958. **J.A.Vella Collection**

A94-946 in the red trim of the ARDU overflying the MCG displaying its new Raytheon Sidewinder missile installation. **RAAF**

The black and white markings of A94-968 C A-27 Mk32 of 75 Sqdn with its complement of air-to-ground rockets at the ARDU, RAAF

FM1364 of 11 Sqdn Royal Malaysian Air Force, the previous A94-364. **J. A. Vella Collection**

A brief reference by John Kentwell from Los Angeles on December 15, 1953 provided a summary of the performance figures and engineering data for the prototype two-seater TF-86F Sabre variant that had recently been flown.

Armament problems

The satisfactory installation and operation of the Aden 30mm cannons was the cause of a further frustration and unexpected delay. For the trial installation CAC received one of the two English prototypes of the cannon. But the first two production examples delivered differed in outline from the prototype sample creating more delays and necessary changes. The firing of flight rated cannons caused the engine compressor to stall because of the sudden ingestion of muzzle gases. A threefold solution was put in motion. The early troublesome gun blast panel was gradually refined in various evolving stages to a baffle muzzle design able to direct gases

An RAF Hawker Hunter FGA 9 of 8/43 Sqdn. **J.A.Vella Collection**

away from the intake; Rolls Royce altered the design of the engine compressor so as to improve its level of tolerance and a fuel cut-off valve (dipper) was included to momentarily interrupt the fuel flow to the engine at a predetermined moment in the gun firing sequence. Aircraft A94-101, 903, 910 and 928 were used in the firing trials which commenced in March 1955 and ran to more than 200 test flights in the next 12 months spread between RAAF Base Laverton in the south and tropical Darwin in the north. From October 1955 the RAAF introduced the compressor 're-matching' alterations to modify those airframes and engines on the production line It frustrated Wackett as it was slowing up the planned delivery schedule. These alterations cost £556,000.

The operational suitability was verified to temperatures down to -90˚C at 54,000 ft in the tropics over Singapore. (It was a matter of some satisfaction to the CAC team that the equivalent clearance trials for the UK Hawker Hunter with its four 30 mm Aden cannon had at that time been only cleared to an altitude of 24,000 feet.) In the early test firings structural stress failure occurred in the rear section of the gun bays. A mock-up of the front fuselage to a station aft of the gun bays was built for ground testing and structural reinforcement was added to withstand the heavier recoil of the cannons. Whilst all of the company's engineering effort was being directed to solving the engine and structural problems and getting the production to flow on time, the Canberra bureaucracy and departmental machinery was frustrating possible sales of the Sabre to interested parties.

Overseas Sales Denied

The Indian Government had sought to place an order of 60 to 100 Sabres with North American Aviation Inc. in 1954 but had been turned away due to NAA's pre-occupation with the new F-100 Super Sabre. NAA suggested that the Indian Government might consider the CA-27 Sabre. The Foreign Affairs Department vetoed the approach due to the state of unease and risk of potential conflict between India and Pakistan. India eventually acquired the Hawker Hunter and GAMD Mystere fighters. In the mid-1960s the Pakistan Air Force considered the CAC Avon Sabre as a potential addition to its North American Sabres but pressure was reputedly applied by the Indian Government to disallow the sale. Pakistan ultimately settled for Canadair built Sabres.

An approach by the Government of South Africa was also turned down. The South African AF acquired Canadair CL-13 Sabres instead.

Production Orders

The initial order granted on February 22, 1951 (Contract CA-27) was for 70 aircraft (many contemporary references quoted a first order for 72 aircraft). The first 22 aircraft A94-901 to 922 Mk 30 were fitted with the imported RA.7 Avon Mk 20 engine and wing leading edge slats. A94-901 the first production aircraft flew on July 13, 1954 and was delivered to the RAAF on August 19, 1954. The Hawker Hunter F.1, suggested British alternative with its own development problems, entered RAF service in July 1954, just eclipsing the CA-27.

The green and white markings of A94-963 CA-27 Mk32 of 77 Sqdn RAAF Butterworth, 1968. **J.A.Vella Collection**

The blue and white markings of A94-915 CA-27 Mk30 of 5 OCU RAAF Laverton, April 18, 1971 towards the end of its service career. **J.A.Vella**

The 'AIRCRAFT' monthly magazine was a regular advertising space for CAC's products. **Herald & Weekly Times**

With red around the intake duct, the white Southern Cross superimposed on the striking bright red tail of A94-958 CA-27 Mk 32 of 3 Sqdn, RAAF Butterworth, Malaysia displays its inert Sidewinder AAR missile. **RAAF**

The company Clown happily off to a round of golf in the new Sabre golf buggy. **Roger Ward**

Above & Below: 79 Sqdn formed from 77 Sqdn was located at Ubon, Thailand from May 1962 to July 1968 to patrol the Thai-Laos border from a base largely improved by the RAAF. A94-980 Mk 32 is flying with live round Sidewinder AAM. **Barry Pattison (above) & RAAF**

A94-942; 960 & 969 over-flying their birthplace CAC at lower left. **RAAF/HDHV**

The 'AIRCRAFT' monthly magazine carried this advertisement in praise

AVIATION BP SERVICE

SUPPLIERS OF FUEL FOR THE ARDUOUS PROTOTYPE
TESTING AND FLIGHT-TESTING OF THE
AVON-SABRE JET FIGHTERS

congratulates

on the celebration of 21 years of service
to aviation in Australia

BP AVIATION SERVICE is operated in Australia by
The Commonwealth Oil Refineries Ltd, an associate of The British Petroleum Company Ltd

CA-27 cockpit front panel. **Reg Schulz**

Sabre Production

Model	Mark	RAAF Identity	Quantity	CAC c/n	Remarks
CA-26	Mk 30	A94-101	1		Prototype
CA-27	Mk 30	A94-901 to 922	22	1 to 22	All converted to Mk 31 standard by RAAF. RR Avon Mk 20
CA-27	Mk 31	A94-923 to 942	20	23 to 42	CAC Avon Mk 20
CA-27	Mk 32	A94-943 to 970	28	43 to 79	CAC Avon Mk 26
CA-27	Mk 32	A94-971 to 990	20	71 to 90	Second order
CA-27	Mk 32	A94-351 to 371	21	91 to 111	Third order

Specifications CA-27 Sabre Mk 30 / 31 / 32

Powerplant One Rolls Royce Avon RA.7 Mk 26 turbojet of 7,500 lb thrust (SL)

Performance
- Max speed at SL — 608 kts
- Max speed at 10,000 ft — 584 kts
- Max speed at 38,000 ft — 527 kts
- Average cruise — 470 kts
- Rate of climb at SL — 12,000 ft/min
- Service ceiling — 5,000 ft
- Range (2 x 100 gall drop tanks & 2 Sidewinder missiles) — 250 nm
- Range with 167 gall drop tanks — 340 nm
- Ferry range — 990 nm
- Fuel capacity (internal) Mk 30 — 352 gall
- Fuel capacity (internal) Mk 31 — 422 gall
- Fuel capacity (internal) Mk 32 — 412 gall

Weights
- Empty — 12,120 lb
- Loaded — 15,990 lb
- Max loaded — 18,560 lb

Dimensions
Wing span	37 ft 1.25 ins	Wing area	302 sq ft
Wing dihedral	3°	Root chord	10 ft 10 ins
Tip chord	5 ft 6 ins	Aspect ratio	4.53
Wing sweepback at 25% chord	35°	Airfoil section at root	NACA 0012-64
Airfoil section at tip	NACA 0011-64		
Tailplane span	12 ft 10 ins	Tailplane incidence	6° up to 10° down
Tailplane root chord	3 ft 10 ins	Tailplane tip chord	1 ft 9 ins
Tailplane dihedral	10°	Tailplane sweepback at 25% chord	35°
Fin height	7 ft 6 ins	Chord at root	6 ft 5 ins
Fin chord at tip	2 ft 4 ins	Height (overall)	14 ft 5 ins
Height (Lower fuse. tbo canopy top)	6 ft 7 ins	Length (overall)	37 ft 6 ins
Length (without empennage)	5 ft 10 ins	Track	8 ft 4 ins

Armament Two 30 mm Aden cannon with 170 rpg. Provision for 20 (max Mk 32) air-to-ground 3 inch or 5 inch rockets; two Sidewinder air-to-air missiles or bombs to 1,200 lb

Retrospective Designation
- XP40 — CA-26 Sabre Prototype
- XP41 — CA-27 Sabre Mk 30
- XP42/43 — CA-27 Sabre Mk 31
- XP44/45 — CA-27 Sabre Mk 32

The second batch, A94-923 to 942, twenty Mk 31s were fitted with the CAC built Avon Mk 20 engine and the '6-3' fixed wing leading edge in place of the leading edge slats for enhanced manoeuvrability at high altitude and high Mach numbers. This was at the expense of low speed docility and a higher stalling speed. Deliveries commenced in July 1955. The '6-3' designation referred to the American design alteration of adding a six inch increase in the wing root chord and three inches at the wing tip. The leading edges provided space for an extra 35 gallons in each wing raising total internal volume to 422 Imp gallons. New wing tips were necessary. A94-901 to 937 were brought up to this standard by the RAAF during major maintenance.

Up to this point each wing was provided with only one stores station. Twenty-eight Mk 32 aircraft, A94-943 to 970 ended the second batch. These aircraft received the RA-7 Avon Mk 26 engine with improved compressor handling characteristics to alleviate the cannon firing problems. In addition to the wet leading edges each wing structure was altered to carry two underwing stores. This reduced the capacity of the leading edge tanks to 60 gallons.

The CAC work load looked grimly thin beyond the initial order; then in May 1954 it received a request for another 20 Mk 32 airframes, A94-971 to 990. The funds allocated for these 20 aircraft were £1.5M for the airframes (£75,000 each) and £1M for 24 engines (£41,669 each) with the last of this batch A94-990 handed to the RAAF on June 17, 1959.

The production delivery program for the first 90 aircraft had been expected to be completed by December 1956 but it slipped by 24 months. The slippage could not be blamed to a lack of labour, rather it was that early technical problems had produced a cumulative delay. Also the large quantity of tooling and individual component errors; the time that was needed to unpack, identify, evaluate and store the thousands of delivered parts created massive delays.

Delays in selecting a successor to the Sabre and rejecting the F-104 Starfighter saw Federal Cabinet give approval on July 26, 1957 to a third and final order for 21 CA-27 Mk 32 aircraft, A94-351 to 371. A94-371, completed its acceptance trials at Avalon on December 19, 1961. Deliveries had fallen away to one aircraft each month as employee numbers dropped sharply. In contrast to a later ministerial statement the cost for each aircraft of this order was given as £526,044.

Manufacture of the aircraft was carried out at CAC's Fisherman's Bend factories. Final final assembly and flight testing was undertaken at Avalon to where all the airframe assemblies and engines were taken by road transport.

Into Service

On November 1, 1954 a Sabre Trials Flight was formed as part of 2(F) Operational Training Unit to introduce the aircraft into the RAAF. 75 Squadron was the first unit to equip at RAAF Base Williamtown, NSW on April 4, 1955 followed by 3 Squadron on March 1, 1956; 77 Squadron in 1959 and 76 Squadron in 1960.

In October 1958, 3 Squadron transferred to RAAF Base, Butterworth in Malaya, followed by 77 Squadron in February 1959. These two squadrons formed 78 Fighter Wing and shortly after their arrival in Butterworth both units commenced ground support operations with rocket and bomb attacks on Communist terrorists in the Malayan jungle. This campaign came to an end on July 31, 1960. On May 29, 1962 eight Sabres from 77 Squadron at Butterworth were relocated to Bangkok in response to a request from Thailand for help in maintaining the integrity of its borders with nearby troubled Laos. This detachment subsequently moved to its tactical location at Ubon and was renumbered 79 (F) Squadron.

On July 31, 1968 the unit was withdrawn back to Butterworth and re-absorbed into 77 Squadron. 2(F) OTU was renamed 2 OCU in 1958 and was eventually replaced by 5 OCU in 1970.

Armament Upgrade

To prolong the useful life of the Sabre and provide a measure of improved aerial defence as an interim step before a replacement air superiority fighter was selected, the RAAF decided in 1959 to equip the aircraft with two Raytheon AIM-9B Sidewinder, heat seeking, air-to-air guided missiles.

One Sidewinder was carried under each wing on pylons manufactured by CAC. A94-946 was the installation test aircraft modified by CAC at ARDU, Laverton. It was then flight tested at the Woomera Weapons Research Establishment where a Sidewinder successfully downed a GAF Jindivik target aircraft. The aircraft publicly displayed the Sidewinder installation in a low level demonstration flight over Melbourne on July 30, 1959. ARDU's other Sabre, A94-949, was similarly modified by unit personnel at RAAF Laverton.

A team of RAAF and CAC armament specialists was sent to Malaya late in 1959 to carry out the necessary modifications on the aircraft of 78 Fighter Wing. The first batch of Sidewinders was flown by two RAAF C-130A Hercules transports direct from the USA to Malaya in late February 1960. Sabres already in service were retrofitted by the RAAF, whilst CAC incorporated the modification in all airframes under construction. An earlier 1956 CAC study proposed an armament of four Sidewinders on separate pylons.

Two Sabres, A94-915 and A94-922, were modified to carry out air trials of the Firestreak missile at the WRE in Woomera, South Australia. CAC was responsible for the design of the aircraft installation and the incorporation of test and recording equipment. (Refer to P280 / P280 / P301 Sabre, Blue-Jay Installation.)

Foreign Aid

Retired CAC Sabres were donated by the Australian Government as a form of military aid to neighbouring SE Asian countries. The first recipient in September 1969 was the Royal Malaysian Air Force with refurbished, operational and instructional airframes: A94-353, 354, 356, 357, 359, 362, 363, 364, 365, 367, 369 & 371. Two years later another six examples followed : A94-946, 948, 978, 979, 983 & 987. CAC provided continual technical support from 1968.

Diplomatic relations with Australia returned to normal following the end of the *Konfrontasi* period of hostilities between the British Commonwealth and Indonesia in its failed attempt to prevent the creation of the Federation of Malaysia so 16 refurbished Sabres and instructional airframes were also passed to the Indonesian Air Force (AURI) at the Iswahyudi Air Base in East Java on April 9, 1973. In 1972 RAAF HQ Support Command S1/S4 Engineering unit in Melbourne produced a VHF communications upgrade mod (in which the author took part) for this batch of aircraft prior to their handover.

Airframe numbers were then increased to 20 aircraft: A94-361, 366, 368, 370, 945, 949, 952, 955, 957, 963, 968, 969, 970, 971, 972, 975, 980, 988 & 990. Sabre A94-352 crashed on take-off from Den Pasar in Bali on its delivery flight and was immediately replaced. The AURI fleet amassed between 1,500 and 2,000 hours of flying each year from 1973. CAC was contracted to repair and overhaul their engines and maintained an Indonesian liaison office until March 1981. All of the gift CA-27 Sabres were of the Mk 32 variant. The program of diversion of these CAC Sabres to Malaysia and Indonesia was negotiated and supported by the endeavours of Lee Archer in his company role of Manager for South-East Asia 1967-82.

Final Note

Twenty nine Sabres were lost through various causes from the 112 built. Twelve pilots lost their lives. The Minister for Air, Peter Hawson in a ministerial statement to the House of Representatives on October 20, 1964 quoted the original cost of the CAC Sabre as £263,518 without offering the full meaning of the figure (but it was probably not inclusive of production set-up, tooling, training aids and documentation). It took four years for the aircraft to reach service with the RAAF a delay that was not entirely due to the major engineering design changes which were undertaken.

Contributing factors were an insufficiency of Government funds to support the project; Department of Defence hindrance in the decision making process causing frequent and recurring delays and a difference of opinion between the technical and operational branches of the RAAF on the necessity of the engineering changes.

The CAC Sabre airframe originally to be based on the F-86E but subsequently identified as the F-86F, had undergone some 364 changes from the initial decision to adopt the design to RAAF requirements and through subsequent operational service updates.

Both the Sabre build project and the parallel Canberra bomber licence manufacture work were major undertakings and required significant industrial inputs, yet there was an apparent lack of associated technical benefit from these projects. Once they were completed the industry looked merely to save itself from total

oblivion whilst it marked time till the next Government funded project came along.

The CA-27 received the accolades of the aviation fraternity for what was considered to be the best variant of the F-86 Sabre in the world with a 30% increase in rate of climb, service ceiling, radius of action and 50 kts faster than US variants.

In terms of operational effectiveness the variant held its own for two years. A grateful Federal Government awarded Lawrence J. Wackett a knighthood for CAC's engineering effort. For the RAAF, the CA-27 was too late for the Korean War. For CAC it was an exercise in engineering management that was within reach of the size of the company such as it was in the years 1951 to 1954.

Sadly and in retrospect, outsiders were to comment that such a major design change would not be contemplated again in the future. Far easier to develop and build mining equipment and let other countries do the hard engineering thinking that creates alternative technological advancement.

Bibliography: CA-26/CA-27 NA F-86 Sabre Fighter Aircraft

Aircraft. Producing the Sabre, (April 1952, July 1953, October 1953).

Australia. Dept. of Supply.(1951). Aircraft Production Part 1A- Question of whether the Sabre should be manufactured in Australia if indeed there should be an aircraft industry.[NAA: 1472/13, 41].Barcode: 429232.

Australia. Dept. of Supply.(1951-54). Sabre Project-orders placed in the USA. [NAA: MP287/1, 6027/12].Barcode: 353455.

Australia. Government Aircraft Factories, Fishermans Bend, Victoria.(1955). Sabre project: orders placed in the USA. (1955-56). [MP319/1, 6027/12C].Barcode: 343832.

Australia. Government Aircraft Factories, Fishermen's Bend, Victoria.(1950).Canberra project: Engines-general, Sabre-Canberra-Avon 1952 programs chart (1950-52).[MP1070/1, CF380/10 Part 1].Barcode: 411699.

Australia. Government Aircraft Factories, Fishermans Bend, Victoria.(1954). Canberra project: Engines-general, Sabre-Canberra-Avon 1955 programs chart (1954-57).[MP1070/1, CF380/10 Part 4].Barcode: 41167.

Australia. Government Aircraft Factories, Fishermen's Bend, Victoria.(1951).Record of Avon Engine Discussions (1951).V.Letcher; M. Woodfull; L.Wackett; H. Knight; Wg. Cmdrs Mason; Birch, August 23,1951. [NAA: MP1070 / CF380 / 10 Pt.1]. Barcode: 411699.

Carter, A.H. 'The CAC Sabre.' AHSA presentations, April 26,1962; May 24,1962.

Commonwealth Aircraft Corporation, (Undated). Engineering Report AA64 (A133), Engineering Summary Avon Engine Installation in Sabre.

Commonwealth Aircraft Corporation. [Production reports to DAP 1949-53].

Commonwealth Aircraft Corporation. (Undated). CAC File - Officers abroad-025a.

Hourigan, Richard, 'The CAC Sabre', *AHSA Journal*, March/April 1966.

Kentwell, John. Correspondence to CAC from USA. (1953). The Two-Seater F- 86F Sabre, December 15,1953.

North American Aviation Inc. (undated). Data furnished under S.O. 5455-F86E licence agreement.

Wackett, L. J. CAC. Abroad File No 3.(1950-1952). File W5.

Wagner, Ray. *The North American Sabre* (1963). Macdonald, London.

XP46 SINGLE SEAT DAY FIGHTER AIRCRAFT
October 1951

This proposal of October 1951 was for a high performance day fighter with an economy of dimensions and structure weight and of a similar performance to the early models of the North American F-86 Sabre. The objective was to design the smallest possible airframe around the Rolls-Royce Avon RA-7R reheat turbojet. This resulted in an aircraft with minimum military equipment and an all-up weight of 10,735 lb, slightly heavier than the combat weight of a P-51 Mustang.

A 7% thick wing with 45°sweepback on the leading edge and a span of 19 feet 3ins was selected to minimize Mach compressibility effects. The low wing aspect ratio of 1.6 provided sufficient volume for the 350 gallons of fuel, as well as the placement of the main undercarriage units at the extreme wing tips where they lay flat after rotating through 90° during their rearward retraction. This undercarriage mount location simplified the structure of the wing and allowed the use of a shorter undercarriage since no allowance was required for aileron clearance during the ground roll. The main and rear wing spars attached to the engine fuselage mounts. Fitting 140 gallon fuel tanks on each wing tip was an option. Engine air was through an annular pitot nose intake duct in which a conical centre body for a ten inch diameter gun laying radar was located. The cockpit canopy faired into a dorsal tunnel, stretching the length of the fuselage to the base of the swept leading edge of the fin. This housed items of military equipment.

For economy of development, the design was to use Sabre hardware such as the ejection seat, aileron and elevator power boost controls, hydraulic pumps and air-conditioning. With minor modifications, the main undercarriage was based on P-51 Mustang main units. Primary armament consisted of two 30 mm cannon with 150 rounds per gun, this package located immediately behind the pilot with a fixed two degrees downward inclination of the barrels deemed sufficient to cope with both sea level and high altitude targets.

An engine change would be managed by removing the rear fuselage (no detail). The structural weight of 27.8% of the all-up weight was representative of current practice and could be achieved by engineering simplicity and careful attention to detail.

The XP46, the work of Doug Humphries, was planned as a low cost Sabre follow-on design to insure against the possibility of the loss of the large CA-23 project. The proposal was not followed through.

Secondary Role

Another role put forward was to convert the XP46 into a pilotless atomic bomber with a warhead located in the cockpit space. Having removed the canopy, the fuselage would be faired over to gain extra speed and the vehicle would discard its undercarriage on takeoff or lift off from a jettisonable trolley. Using reheat in continuous cruise at 45,000 feet, a range in excess of 220 nm was expected.
(This was a highly speculative secondary role that had no political, practical or economic support in that era.)

Bibliography: XP46 Single Seat Day Fighter Aircraft

Commonwealth Aircraft Corporation. (1951) Engineering Report AA57 (A129) (Oct 1951). Single Seat Day Fighter.

XP'46 – Single Seat Day Fighter

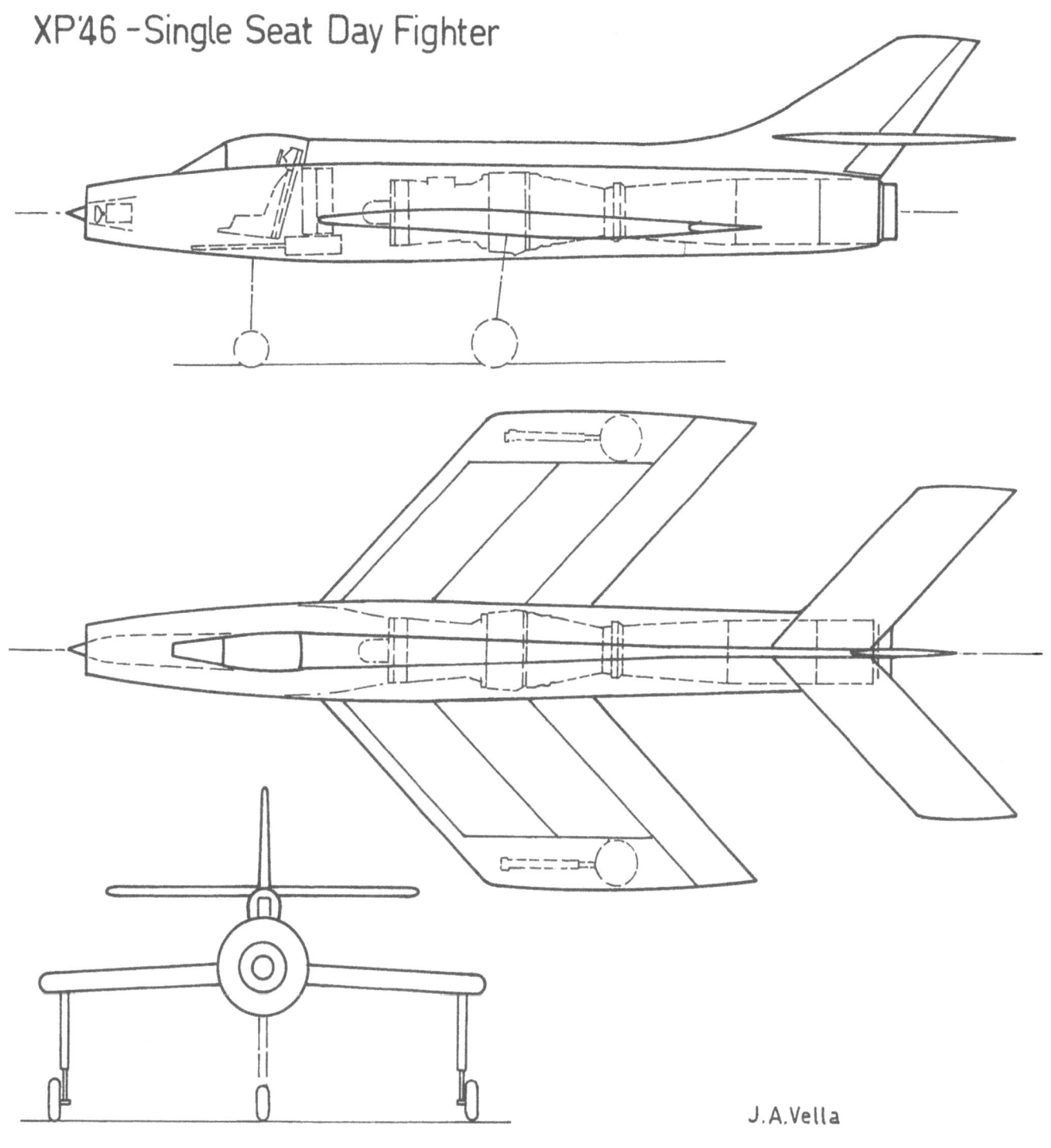

J.A.Vella

XP 46 Radius of Action on Internal Fuel			
Unit	Minutes	Nautical Miles	Fuel Consumed (Gall)
Take-off		0	15
Climb to 43,000 ft	4.5	0	42
Cruise out	60	515	220
Combat with reheat	5	0	86
Cruise return	60	515	190
Total	**135.5**	**1030**	**553**

Specifications	XP46 Single Seat Day Fighter Aircraft	
Powerplant	One Rolls Royce Avon RA-7R turbojet of 7,500 lb (dry) & 9,500 lb(reheat) static thrust at SL	
Performance	Max speed at SL	660 kts
	Max speed at 45,000 ft	750 kts
	Rate of climb at SL	40,500 ft/min
	Rate of climb at 45,000 ft	5,000 ft/min
	Time to 45,000 ft	2.85 min
	Turn radius at 520 kts at 45,000 ft	3.3 nm
	TO dist	750 ft
	Landing dist	1,995 ft
	Fuel capacity 350 gall internal & 280 gall external	
Weights	Empty	6,760 lb
	Service load	3,975 lb
	AUW	10,735 lb
Dimensions	Wing span	19 ft 6 ins
	Wing area	230 sq ft
	Wing LE sweep	45°
	Fin area	32.5 sq ft
	Fin LE sweep	6°
	Tailplane area	60 sq ft
	Tailplane LE sweep	45°
	Length	41 ft 6 ins
	Height	13 ft
	Wheelbase	10 ft 6 ins
	Track	17 ft 9 ins
Armament	Two 30 mm Aden cannon with 150 rpg	

ROCKET INTERCEPTOR [1]
November 1951

An enemy bomber approaching at 600 mph at an altitude of 55,000 feet was the threat scenario perceived by most Western defence analysts of the early 1950s as their biggest challenge. This threat was spoken of seriously in Australia because of concentrated industry groupings on the eastern seaboard. Limited in the choice of design and power in available jet engines, CAC brought out a study in November 1951 (the first of two) to use rocket power for a point defence interceptor with a very limited flight profile, somewhat reminiscent of the German Messerschmitt Me 163 of WW 2. This was the work of Doug Humphries and Charles Reid.

A high rate of climb could be achieved by the use of rocket power with interception on a collision course either from above or below. Australia was not unique in the possible use of rocket powered aircraft. France had been active in the area and the United States had both the flight experience and hardware in the shape of the Bell X-1 with engines of proven reliability and safety. The technology for the CAC design originated mainly from the USA and was to use 5,000 lb of the bi-propellant combination of diluted ethyl alcohol and liquid oxygen. The propellant was to be stored in two cylindrical fuselage tanks separated from each other by the wing front spar carry through structure. To the rear of the oxygen tank was the propellant pumping system and the mounting of two 7,000 lb thrust rocket motors arranged in a vertical pairing. Radio, radar processing and ancillary services were to be located behind the cockpit bulkhead. The main undercarriage was positioned near the extremities of the wing and rotated through 90° to lie flat in the wing. Allowance was made for

Rocket Interceptor [1]

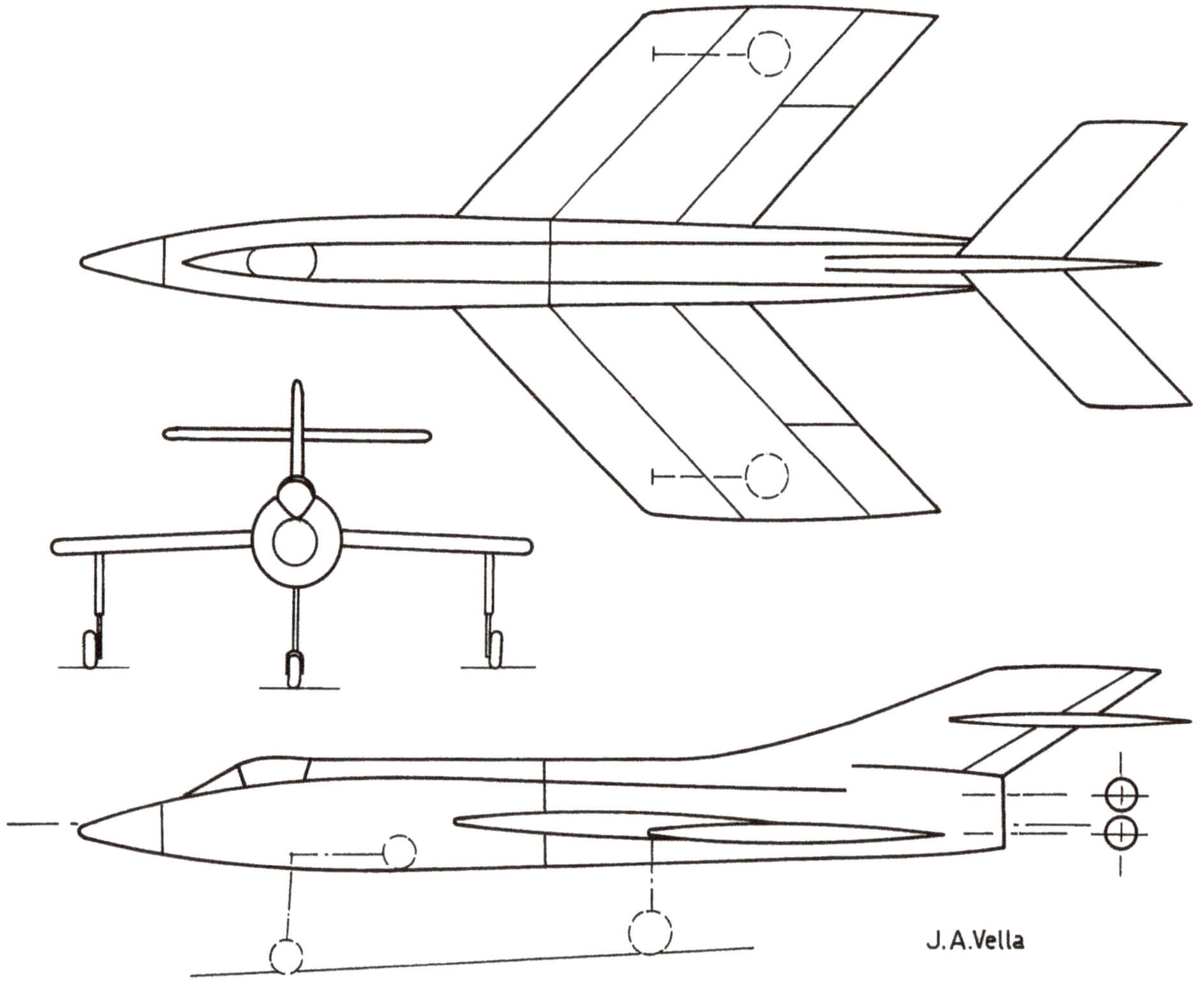

J.A.Vella

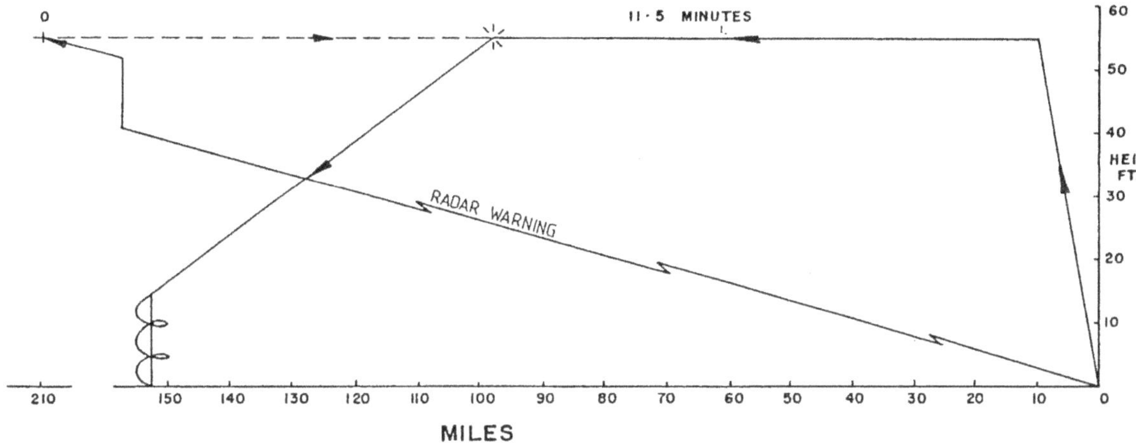

FIG. 1

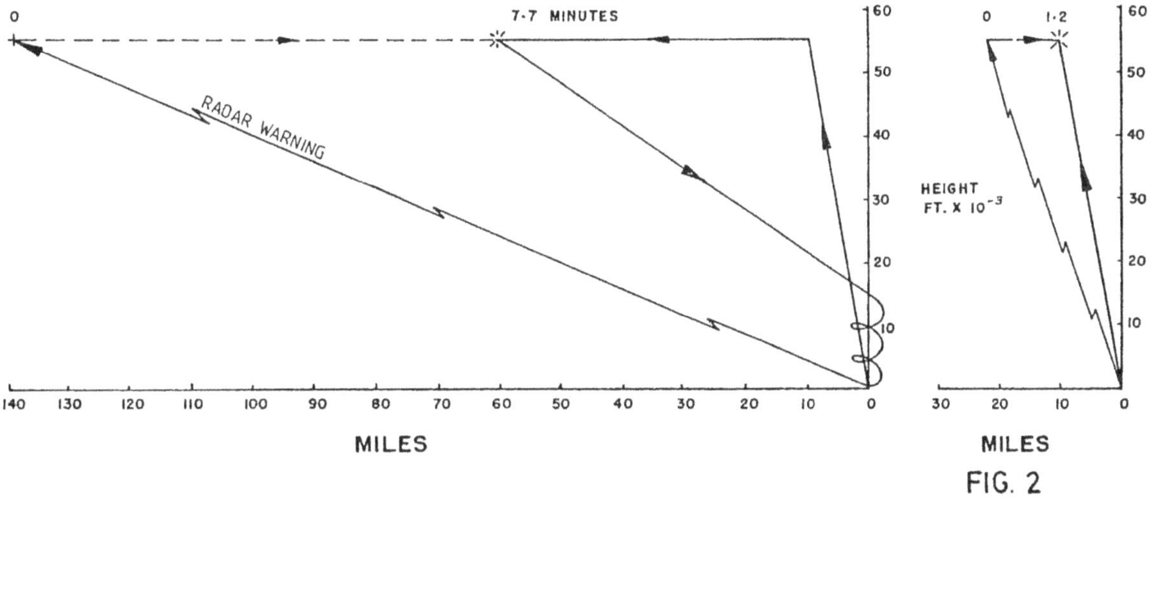

FIG. 2

Specifications	Rocket Interceptor (1)	
Powerplant	Two, four chamber Reaction Motors Inc bi-fuel rocket engines of 7,000 lb thrust each	
Performance	Max speed	562 kts
	Max speed at 45,000 ft	750 kts
	Rate of climb at SL	40,500 ft/min
	Rate of climb at 45,000 ft	5,000 ft/min
	Time to 10,000 ft	32.5 secs
	Time to 50,000 ft	68 secs
	Time to 70,000 ft	80 secs
	Max ceiling	185,000 ft
	TO dist	330 ft
	Landing dist	6,00 ft
Weights	Empty	2,545 lb
	Service load	5,605 lb
	AUW	8,159 lb
Dimensions	Wing span	18 ft
	Wing area	200 sq ft
	Aspect ratio	1.64
	Thickness	6 %
	Length	41 ft 3 ins
	Wheelbase	13 ft 6 ins
	Track	15 ft 3 ins
Armament	Air-to- air proximity fused rockets	

300 lb of armament weight in the form of air-to-air proximity fused rockets housed at the wing tips. The design aim was towards simplicity and small size to achieve a fast take-off and climb with high speed acceleration for combat.

A low aspect ratio of 1.64 was selected for improved stability and control and to minimize shift of the aerodynamic centre in the transonic range. At a gliding angle of 1:8 to achieve a lower sink rate and landing speed when both fuel and armament was expended, the wing loading was kept to 14.5 1b/sq ft. Two graphs (Fig 1 and 2, see previous page) highlight the estimated parameters for a long range and a short range intercept. In the first instance with a radar warning of the intruder at a range of 210 miles with about 21 minutes to spare, a head-on approach intercept was possible 11.5 minutes after first detection. Following combat and fuel exhaustion, a glide to a landing at an alternative airfield would have been necessary. For the short range intercept of an intruder 20 miles from its target at an altitude of 55,000 feet, interception 1.2 minutes after first warning was possible ten miles from launch base. Little more was done to this proposal aside from a detailed structural analysis. It was rapidly overtaken by a more refined and practical design five months later.

Bibliography: Rocket Interceptor [1]
Commonwealth Aircraft Corporation. (1951) Engineering Report AA59 (A132). (November 1951). Rocket Interceptor.

CHAPTER 3. BASIC TRAINER THINKING

CA-25 WINJEEL BASIC TRAINER AIRCRAFT
January 1952

Engineering preparation for an anticipated production run of 160 Winjeel trainer aircraft had commenced in February 1951. But contract CA-25 of January 1952 requested only 62 production aircraft powered by either the CAC R795 Cicada seven cylinder radial or the P & W R985 Wasp Junior nine cylinder radial engine.

Limited R & D funding for developing the Cicada engine did not stretch enough to solve a number of major mechanical failures during test running. Importation of used P & W Wasp Junior engines from Babb Co. Inc. of California came under consideration on July 18, 1951 as a result of a visit by Ern Jones, CAC's Administrative Chief Draftsman on F-86 Sabre business in the USA. He had been instructed by Wackett to seek out aero engine stocks in the region of the Los Angeles plant during his visit to North American Aviation.

Babb Co. Inc. held stocks of several hundred used P & W Wasp Junior R985-AN2/AN3 engines, engine mounts and propellers from retired Vultee BT-13 Valiant Trainers. Sixty-two engines for the production run and 38 spares were ordered on February 15, 1952 but this was cut back to 40 engine sets in anticipation that the Cicada engine would be available starting on airframe No 31. The RAAF extended limited development time and finance for the Cicada in May 1953. The first 30 Winjeels were to have the Wasp Junior. Charles Babb was the American used aircraft engines equivalent of Kevin Dennis' used motor cars business. (Kevin Dennis was an enterprising and colourful, used car dealership in Melbourne of the 1950s and '60s.)

The aerodynamic modifications generated during the flight trials of the two CA-22 prototypes were retained for the production aircraft, the RAAF Technical Specification AC91 which merely requested that any change to the design as a result of flight and evaluation trials of the prototypes should be considered, and where agreed to, incorporated in the production aircraft whilst still adhering to the original requirements of Technical Requirement AC77.

Obvious external changes were the increase in areas of the horizontal tail, fin and rudder. The engine cowl profile, gills and carburettor intake outline were revised and the sweep back on the leading edge of the wing was increased so as to correct a centre of gravity problem.

In all, some 96 modifications were required for production configuration. Despite the order to proceed in January 1952, tooling up was postponed for six months because of the greater priority attached to the companion Sabre project. Nevertheless material orders were released and tooling production and minor parts fabrication was underway by Christmas. 1,600 engineering drawings were released for production.

Airframe Description
The aircraft was of all metal construction featuring side by side adjustable seating for instructor and pupil with a third seat (non-adjustable) for an additional pupil. The wing was in three sections, the centre section containing two fuel tanks with a total capacity of 69 gallons and the two outer sections attached immediately outboard of the landing gear. Spars and ribs were formed in aluminium alloy sheet. Split flaps were fitted to the centre section and slotted flaps extended over 50% of the span of the outer panels.

Semi-monocoque construction was used for the fuselage with a tubular steel turnover truss built in for crew protection in the event of a crash. The canopy unit slid rearwards on three rollers. For instrument flying instruction with the pupil wearing blue tinted goggles, the windscreen and-canopy was provided with clip-on removable amber panels. The top of the canopy was initially fitted with a permanent amber-tinted perspex screen, later replaced by an overhead retractable sunshade. The engine cowls were arranged in four sections, able to open in 'petal' fashion for easy access to the engine and accessories. A two bladed, constant speed, Hamilton Standard propeller was used. The fixed landing gear cantilever shock strut with a streamlined fairing was attached to the centre section front spar.

*The Winjeel production line gaining momentum. **Richard Hourigan.***

*A85-434 in post RAAF retirement Warbirds category in vintage markings at RAAF Point Cook. **J.A.Vella***

*CAC production employees lined up with Ern Jones Admin Chief Draftsman, Lawrence Wackett and Ian Ring standing to right of the cowl/prop, 1957. **Reg Schulz***

Production Starts

Government money was tight and a financial clamp which had affected various defence projects allowed Winjeel production to languish between September 1953 and April 1954 which meant aircraft deliveries slipped back by 10 months until restrictions were lifted in July 1954.

de Havilland at Bankstown, NSW was the major subcontractor, responsible for building the wings, centre section, flaps and ailerons. Fuselage components such as the firewall, bulkheads, cockpit floor and windscreen were built by Chrysler Australia in South Australia. The empennage and fuselage rear cone were provided by Victorian & Interstate Airways of Essendon, whilst CAC built the undercarriage at their Lidcombe, NSW plant. Dunlop Rubber (Aust) supplied the fuel cells, main and tail wheels, tyres and disc brakes; Pilkingtons the windscreen and canopy toughened and laminated glass. At least 24 subcontractors were involved in the project. The first components from de Havilland were received late in 1953; those from Chrysler arrived in May 1954. CAC built the fuselage and assembled each aircraft.

*Winjeel A85-450 in post RAAF retirement Warbirds category flown by restorer Richard Hourigan in RH seat . Sept 20,1986. **K.Limon***

After repeated mishaps, the Cicada engine project came to an end on February 7, 1955. The full order of refurbished Wasp Junior engines was fulfilled by Babb Co. Inc. of California and Lund Aviation Inc. of New Jersey. The Bristol Aeroplane Co. (Aust) in Sydney tested the engines, their accessories and propellers when they reached Australia. Although the United States airworthiness authorities had given these engines a clean bill of health, some showed signs of internal corrosion when inspected after their arrival. The blame for this was attached to CAC but the company was insistent that the cause was due to insufficient or bad inhibiting procedures for their transportation to Australia. This meant extra incurred costs to strip down and re-build the engines.

In Service

The first production Winjeel, A85-401, was completed on February 8, 1955; made its first flight on 23 February, delivered to the RAAF in August 1955 and officially handed over to AM Sir John McCauley by Sir Lawrence Wackett on September 16, 1955. Twelve Winjeels were completed before the end of the year. The last aircraft, A85-462 made its first flight on November 21, 1957 and was accepted by the RAAF early in 1958. The program had stretched for 8.5 years from 1949. John Miles was both the GAF and CAC test pilot. He made the initial test flights assisted by Bill Herbert, GAF's deputy test pilot. The completed aircraft were tested at CAC's Fisherman's Bend factory and flown out from the airfield adjoining the premises.

*The last Winjeel built. A85-462 of No.1(B)FTS at RAAF Point Cook,November 8, 1970 . **J. A. Vella***

CA-25 Winjeel

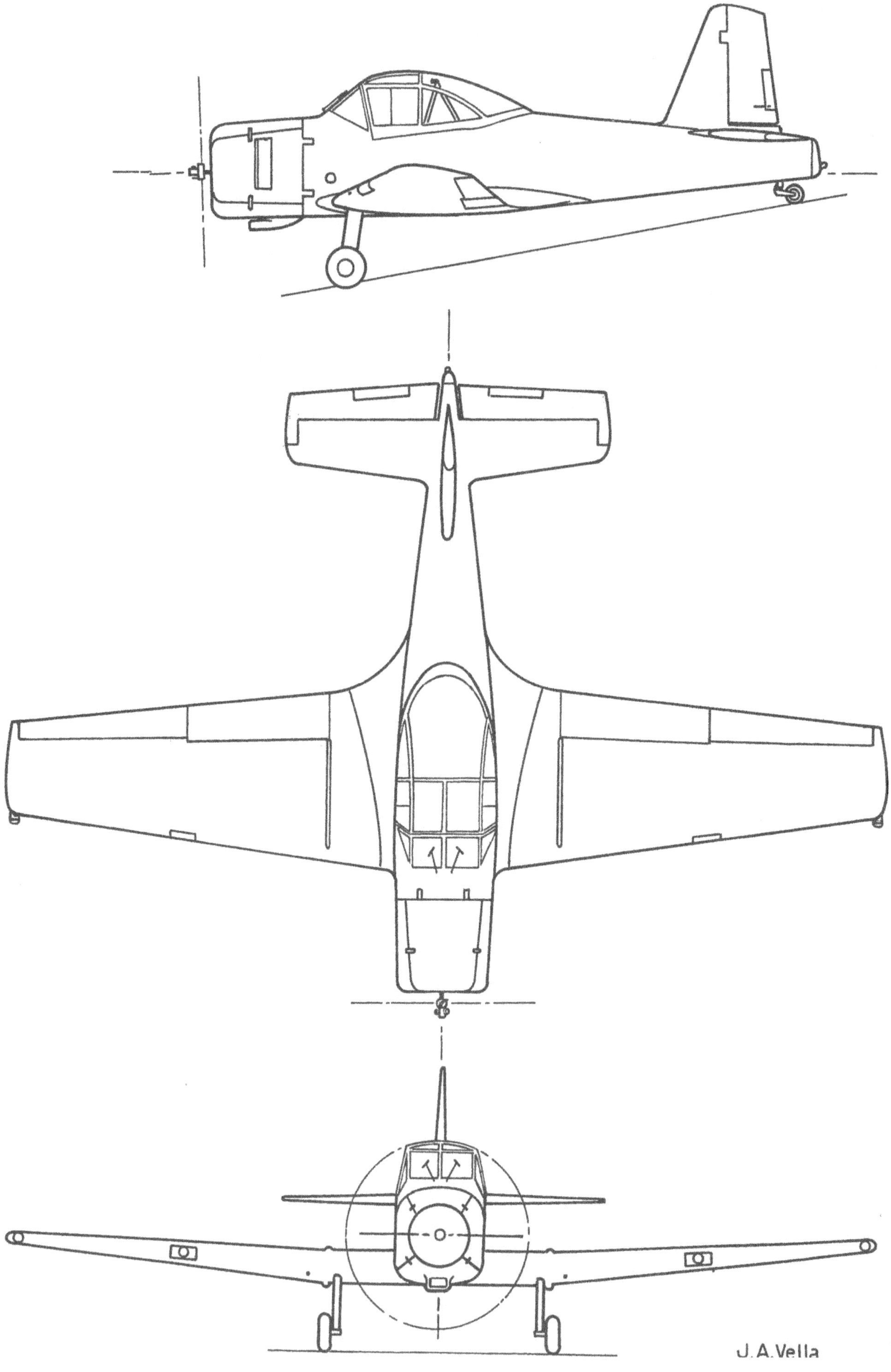

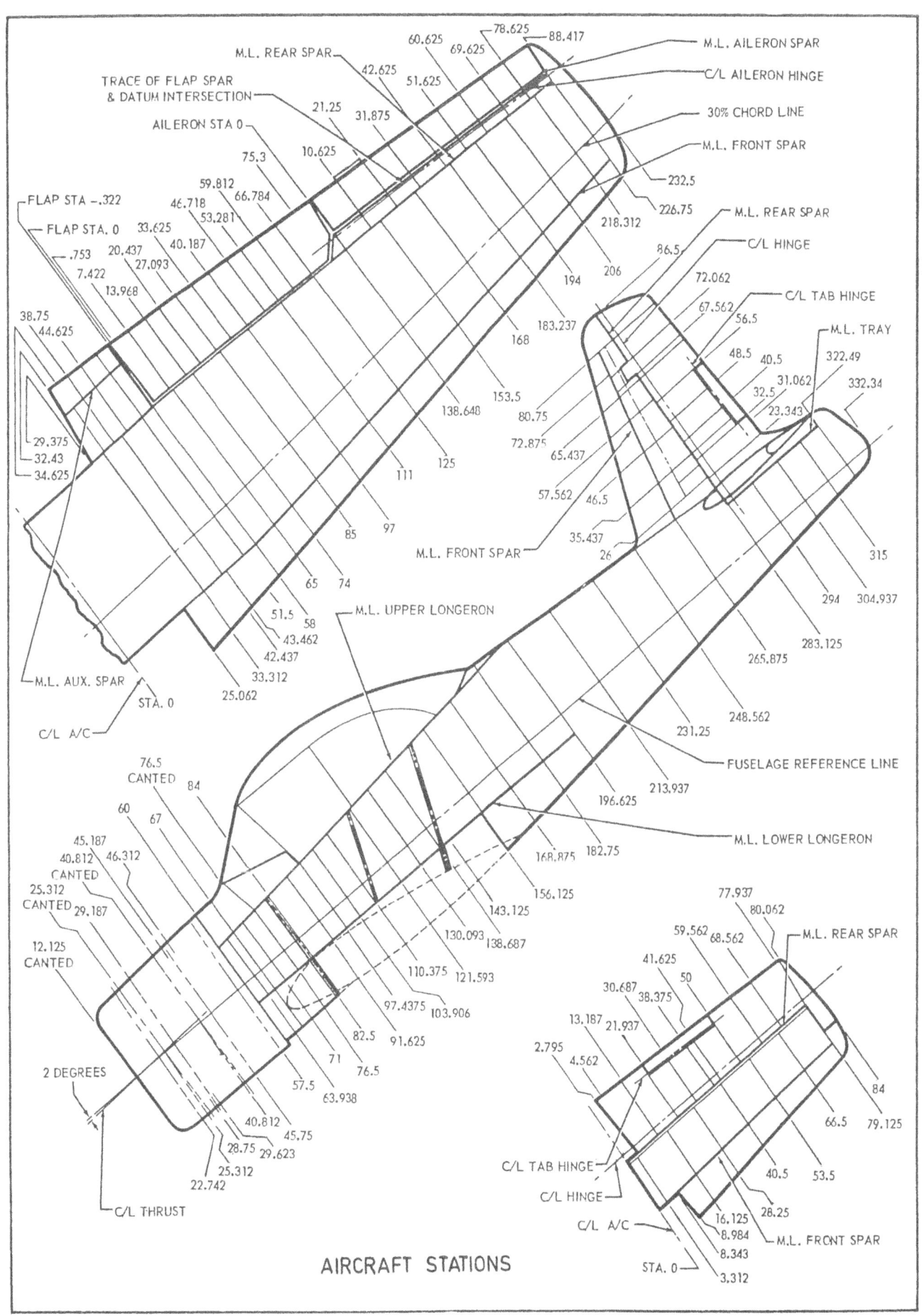

Specifications	CA-25 Winjeel Basic Trainer Aircraft	
Powerplant	One Pratt & Whitney R-985-AN2 Wasp Junior, 9 cyl radial engine of 445 hp at TO driving a Hamilton Standard 2 bladed constant speed propeller of 8 ft 3 inches diameter	
Performance	Speed at SL	106 kts
	Speed at 10,000 ft	107 kts
	Never exceed speed	220 kts
	Average cruise speed	115 kts
	Stall speed (flaps lowered)	50 kts
	Rate of climb at SL	1,000 ft/min
	Time to 10,000 ft	25 min
	Range at SL	598 nm
	Range at 10,000 ft	567 nm
	Endurance at 5,000 ft	5.5 hrs
Weights	Empty	3,400 lb
	Max AUW	4,300 lb
	Wing loading	174 lb/ sq ft
Dimensions	Wing span	38 ft 9 ins
	Wing area	250 sq ft
	Airfoil section	NACA 23014.7
	Aspect ratio	6.03
	Wing LE sweep	7° 5'
	Fin & rudder area	30.85 sq ft
	Tailplane area	49.78 sq ft
	Tailplane span	14 ft
	Length	29 ft 4.5 ins
	Height	8 ft 3 ins
	Wheelbase	18 ft 10 ins
	Track	10 ft
Retrospective Designations	XP37 CA25 Winjeel rear located Fin XP39 CA25 Winjeel, P & W Engine	

The first aircraft went to 1 Basic Flying Training School (BFTS) at Uranquinty, NSW, where trainees would fly 50 hours in the Winjeel, then convert to the Wirraway for a further 55 hours. When enough Winjeel numbers were on strength the type assumed the full basic training spectrum before pilot trainees converted to the two-seat Vampire. The average time to solo on the first Winjeel course was 8 hours 40 minutes.

Winjeels were also operated by the Central Flying School (CFS) at RAAF Base East Sale, for instructor training and by the RAAF College, Point Cook (X Flight). 1 BFTS transferred from Uranquinty to RAAF Base Point Cook in September 1958.

The aircraft was used in the base communication role; for pilot continuation training at RAAF bases such as Townsville and Pearce and in search and range clearance at the Woomera Rocket Range. The plan of all-through jet training that was implemented when the Macchi MB326H was introduced, was abandoned after a few initial courses, and a 15 hour flight assessment on the Winjeel was introduced into the syllabus for RAAF and RAN pilot trainees. The Army trainees continued to train to the pre-Macchi syllabus, completing 120 hours on the Winjeel before going to Oakey, Qld, to finish off their conversions. Winjeels were modified for Forward Air Control training with 2 OTU RAAF Williamtown from March 1969, then with 4 Flight in 1970, included as 'D' Flight in 77 Sqdn in 1987 and as the newly reformed 76 Sqdn in January 1989. Four Winjeels were used on a fatigue rotation basis from some 14 airframes. This activity extended to 1994 well past the time when all other Winjeels had been withdrawn from basic training nineteen years earlier in 1975. This took the service life of the type to 39 years.

The Winjeel was retained in the primary training role till January 1975 when its replacement the AESL CT-4A Airtrainer started entering service. Fourteen Winjeels were lost in accidents or extensively damaged and withdrawn from service. A massed formation flyover by 23 Winjeels over Geelong and Laverton on March 25,1976 marked the CA-25's official training role farewell. After disposal and in some instances of restoration, at least 30 examples had appeared on the Australian Civil Aircraft register.

The successful, basic Winjeel layout was to lead the company to many proposed design iterations as is related later in the text.

Bibliography: CA-25 Winjeel Basic Trainer

Australian Operated Aircraft, (1974-1979). *Aviation Historical Society of Australia.*

Commonwealth Aircraft Corporation. Cicada & imported engines for Winjeel (Undated & unidentified files).

Commonwealth Aircraft Corporation. Winjeel reference material notes.

Hourigan, Richard. (1986). CA-25 Winjeel Production Brief Histories. *AHSA Newsletter.* Vol. 2/1 & 2/2, 1986.

XP47 ROCKET INTERCEPTOR [2]
April 1952

Since the conceptual ideas for a rocket interceptor were formulated five months earlier, it was found possible to reduce the dimensions of the airframe without compromising performance in the intercept role by using one rocket motor powered by diluted ethyl-alcohol and liquid oxygen with a combined propellant volume of 375 gallons. Because this scheme had a lower thrust to weight ratio there would have been an increase in the time to altitude parameter although this was offset by a gain in cruise duration time. The maximum operational range was now 90 miles; 10 miles more than in the previous proposal.

The design team of Doug Humphries and Charles Reid felt there was sufficient amount of American wind tunnel data available on which it was possible with a considerable degree of confidence and reliability to achieve their anticipated aerodynamic and operational characteristics. The stability characteristics of the XP47 had been tested at CAC using catapult launched glider models. (In January 1952 the Royal Air Force Specification F124T sought a rocket powered interceptor as a last ditch line of UK defence. The rocket engine and turbojet powered evaluation Saunders-Roe SR53 flew in May 1957.)

Airframe Description

The XP47 had a sleek, three foot diameter monocoque form fuselage with a T-tail set on a rakish fin. Cabin pressurisation was to be maintained by sealing the rear hinged canopy prior to take-off and the use of a pressure suit. A metal framed canopy windscreen was made of 0.375 inch thick toughened glass intersecting in an invisible joint at the centreline, behind which was a small instrument panel and the pilot's North American Aviation type ejection seat. Mainwheel tyre pressure was a low 90 psi and either 4 inch diameter twin or single 12.5 inch diameter, 70 psi nose wheels were considered.

The Reaction Motors Inc. XLR-11-RM-5, four chamber, rocket motor was the same unit as was used on the Bell X-1, X-1A, X-1B and X-1D research aircraft in the United States. Thrust management was only possible by switching on each individual chamber as required to reach the eventual maximum 6,000 lb of thrust. A rubber bag type

XP47-Rocket Interceptor [2]

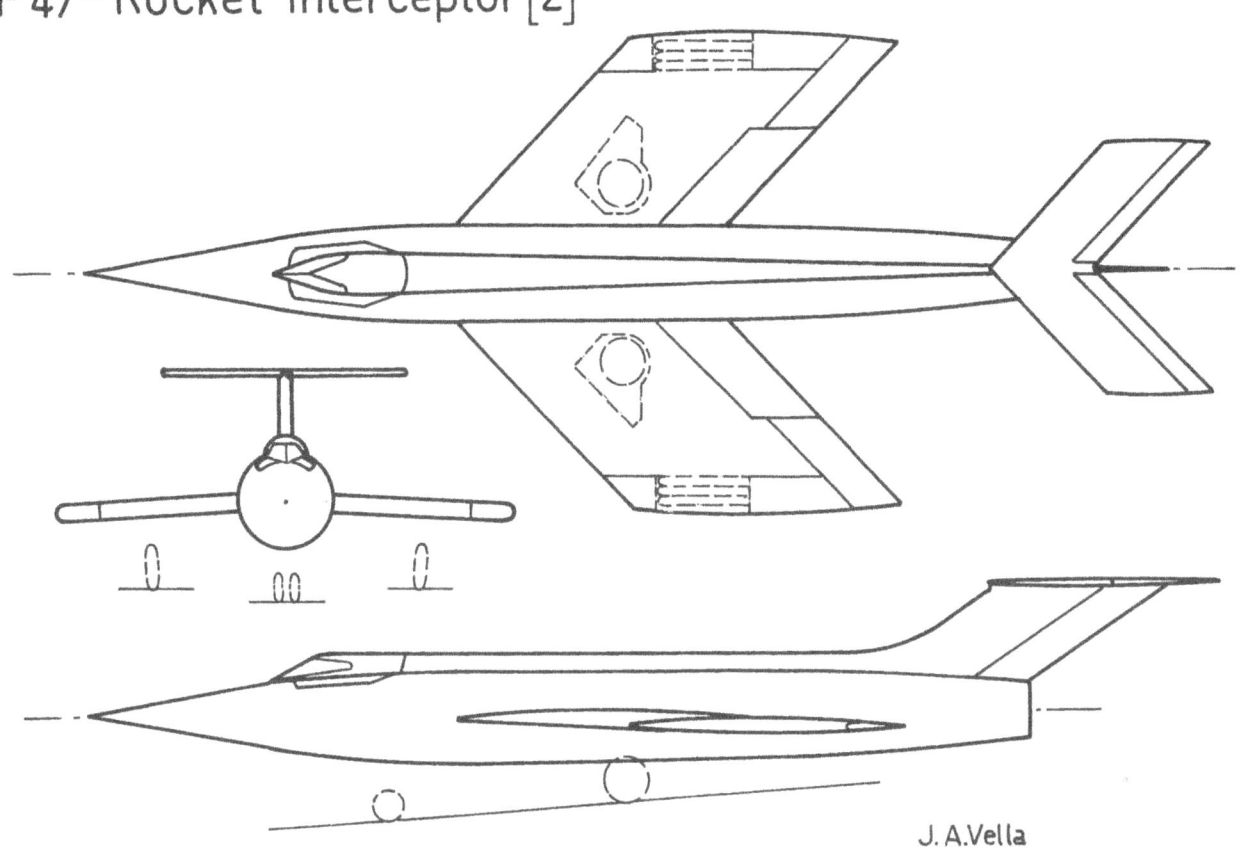

J. A. Vella

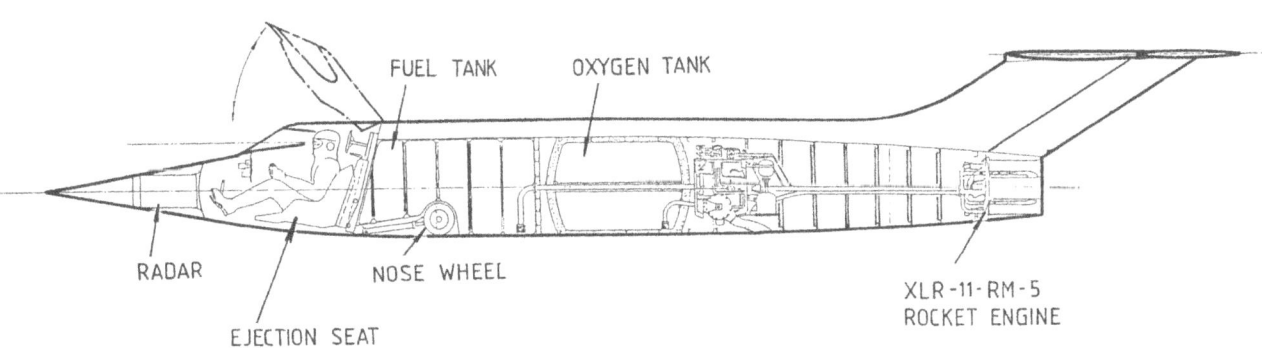

CA-25 WINJEEL AND XP47 SIZE COMPARISON

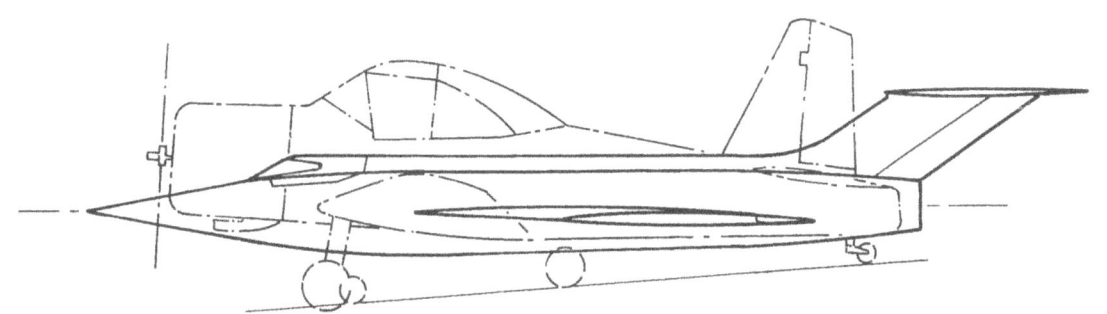

Impression of the XP47 vehicle based on the catapult test launching models. **Walter Watkins**

A rudimentary full scale mock-up of the front end of the XP47. Difficult to discern is Wal Watkins sitting behind the windscreen wearing an oxygen mask.. **Walter Watkins**

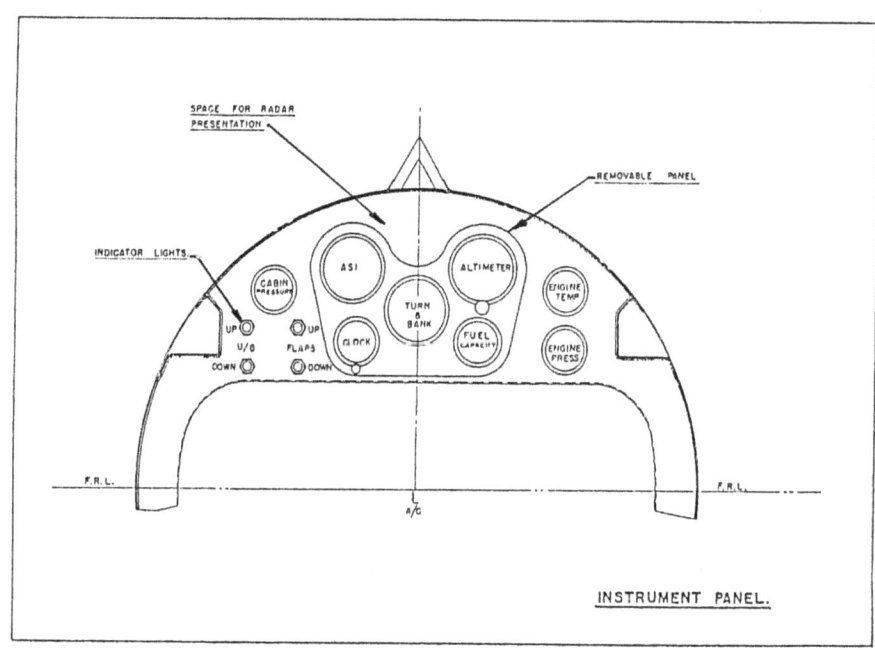

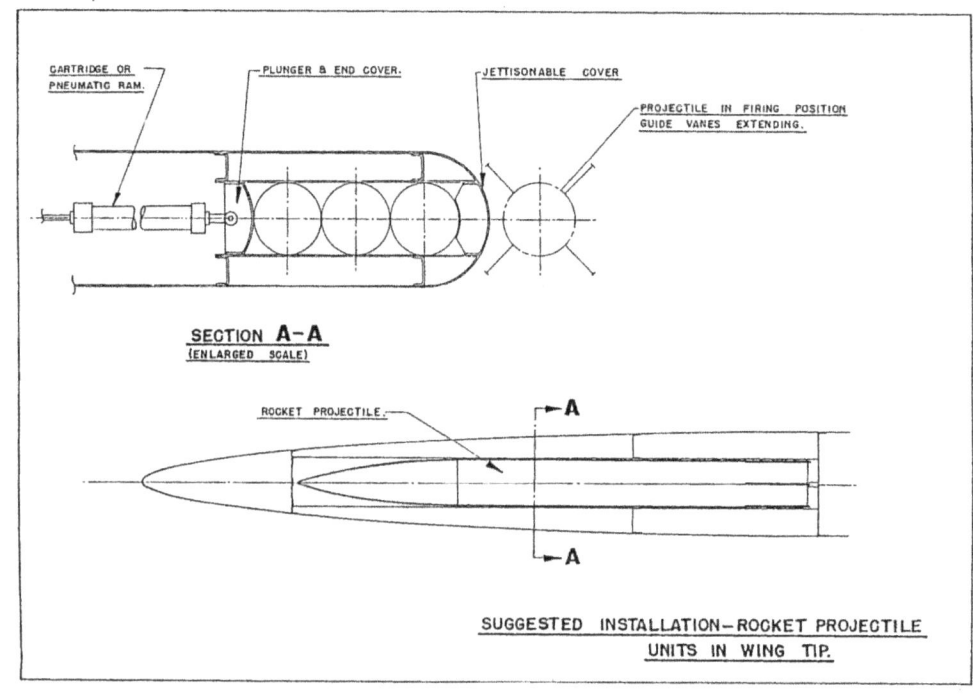

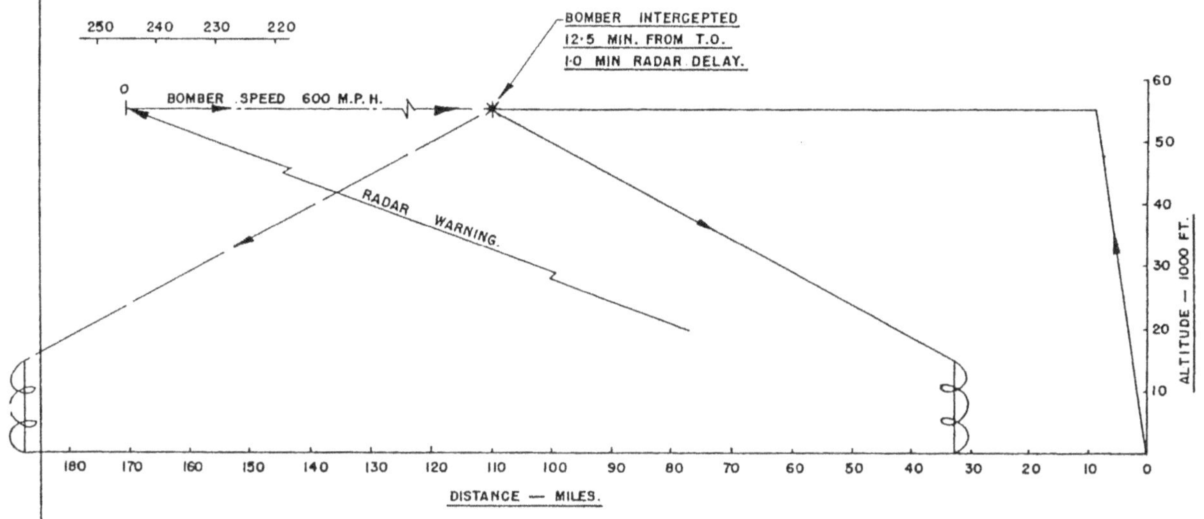

INTERCEPTION DIAGRAM.

SECTION A-1.32-2
SHEET No. 40

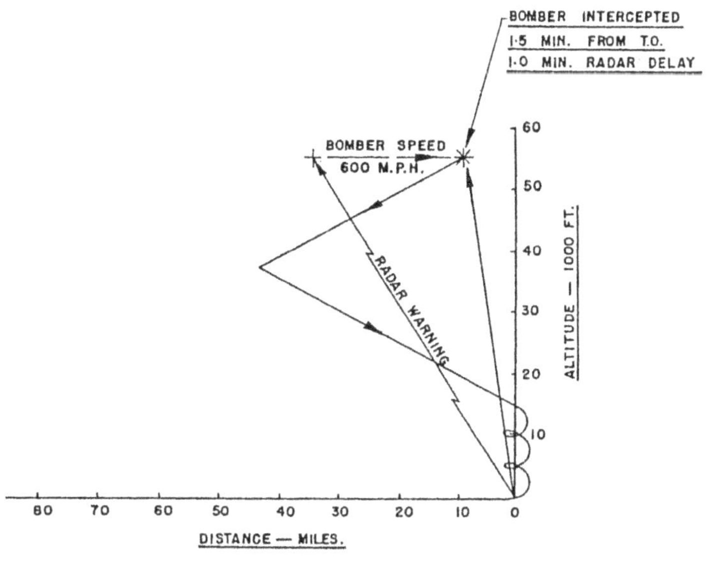

INTERCEPTION DIAGRAM.

SECTION A-1.32-2
SHEET No. 38

tank behind the cockpit held the ethyl alcohol fuel, followed immediately by the liquid oxygen tank which was to have a 0.036 inch thick aluminium wall encased by 2.0 inches of fibreglass insulation. It was expected that there would only be a liquid oxygen evaporation loss of about 1 lb per minute when the surrounding air temperature was 80°F. A small radar package in the extreme nose was to assist in the close intercept final phase.

The low aspect ratio, mid-set, swept wing of 7% thickness ratio and large chord permitted the complete stowage of the wheels leaving valuable space in the fuselage for the carriage of propellant.

To provide a smooth exterior surface under load, skin and close stringer construction using light alloy from both 24ST and 75ST spec was to be used with skin thickness ranging from 0.016 to 0.081 inches. All control surfaces were to be plain mass balanced and manually operated. Trimming of the all-moving tail was via an irreversible screw jack.

Six three inch Oerlikon or 2.75 inch Mighty Mouse unguided FFAR were the only armament. Armed with proximity fuses, three rockets on each wing tip were to be ejected sideways at one hundredth second intervals by a 400 lb thrust air-operated ram. The total structure weight of 840 lb was 37% of the empty weight with a load factor of 10 at a combat weight of 2,200 lb.

Flight Performance

The wing stiffness criteria dictated a limiting speed of 520 kts EAS. In giving emphasis to a low aspect ratio in the interests of stability and control at high speed, some sacrifice had to be made in the low speed characteristics. Glide and approach wing loading was to be 13.5 lb/sq ft with the gliding angle reduced from the 1: 8 of the previous Rocket Interceptor proposal to 1:4.5 by the higher induced drag.

The approach speed with flaps down was estimated to be 100 kts with a touchdown at 10° incidence of 75 kts. This corresponded to a lift co-efficient of 0.8. At take-off, both flaps and tailplane trim would have been used and the aircraft was to unstick at 110 kts following a run of 600 feet. Level flight would then be maintained until the airspeed approached 430 kts when the pull up to a vertical climb would be made. This technique would remove weight off the surfaces, thereby removing the induced drag and an increasing acceleration would result from increasing rocket thrust and diminishing weight as fuel was expended. Acceleration was to be limited to 1.6 g. After levelling out, the tailplane would again be used until the speed fell below Mach 1.0 at the beginning of the cruise phase. Climb to 55,000 feet to intercept an approaching 520 kts target was in the short time of 86 seconds. Closure speed was to be held to around 520 kts (M0.9), limited to the ability to make visual judgements and to maintain a moderate turning radius.

Interception Profiles

Two profiles, one of extreme late interception, the other of maximum warning time, exemplify the intended role for the aircraft. For the case of minimum warning time of 60 seconds, interception would take place 10 miles from base which would allow a return to the launch base with the aircraft having 15,000 feet in hand over the landing point.

In the situation of maximum warning time with interception taking place at around 100 miles, the landing would have had to be made at an alternate site. It was considered feasible and economical to return the aircraft back to its operating base by aerial towing, the speed necessary for adequate control was around 105 kts. The advantage of the rocket motor was that at the combat altitudes that were being envisaged it would have been possible to achieve

Specifications	XP47 Rocket Interceptor [2]	
Powerplant	One Reaction Motors Inc bi-fuel XLR-11-RM-5 rocket engine of 6,000 lb thrust	
Performance	Max speed in vert climb at 60,000 ft	730 kts
	TO speed	110 kts
	Time to 30,000 ft	62 secs
	Time to 50,000 ft	82 secs
	Time to 60 000 ft	90 secs
	Landing dist	750 ft
	Landing speed	75 kts
Weights	Empty	1,496 lb
	Service load	4,141 lb
	AUW	5,637 lb
Dimensions	Wing span	15 ft
	Wing area	135 sq ft
	Wing LE sweep	45°
	Aspect ratio	1.67
	Airfoil section	NACA 64A007
	Tailplane span	8 ft
	Tailplane chord	3.5 ft
	Tailplane aspect ratio	2.28
	Tailplane sweepback	45°
	Fin area	18 sq ft
	Fin chord	6 ft
	Length	31 ft
	Wheelbase	8 ft
	Track	8 ft 6 ins

accelerations at combat weight of 2.5g and hold turn radii at around 3g. Whereas at the same altitude the acceleration of a typical jet fighter of the period, powered by an Avon RA-7 engine with reheat would have produced an acceleration figure of only 0.125g. The performance expected at 55,000 ft would have been the equivalent of a turbojet powered aircraft at a considerably lower altitude.

The flying surface planforms of the XP46, XP47 and Rocket Interceptor [1] were nearly all identical to each other, displaying Doug Humphries and Charles Reid's design family trend line.

Bibliography: XP47 Rocket Interceptor [2]

Commonwealth Aircraft Corporation. (1952), Engineering Report AA60 (A132), (April 1952). Rocket Interceptor.

P248/XP49

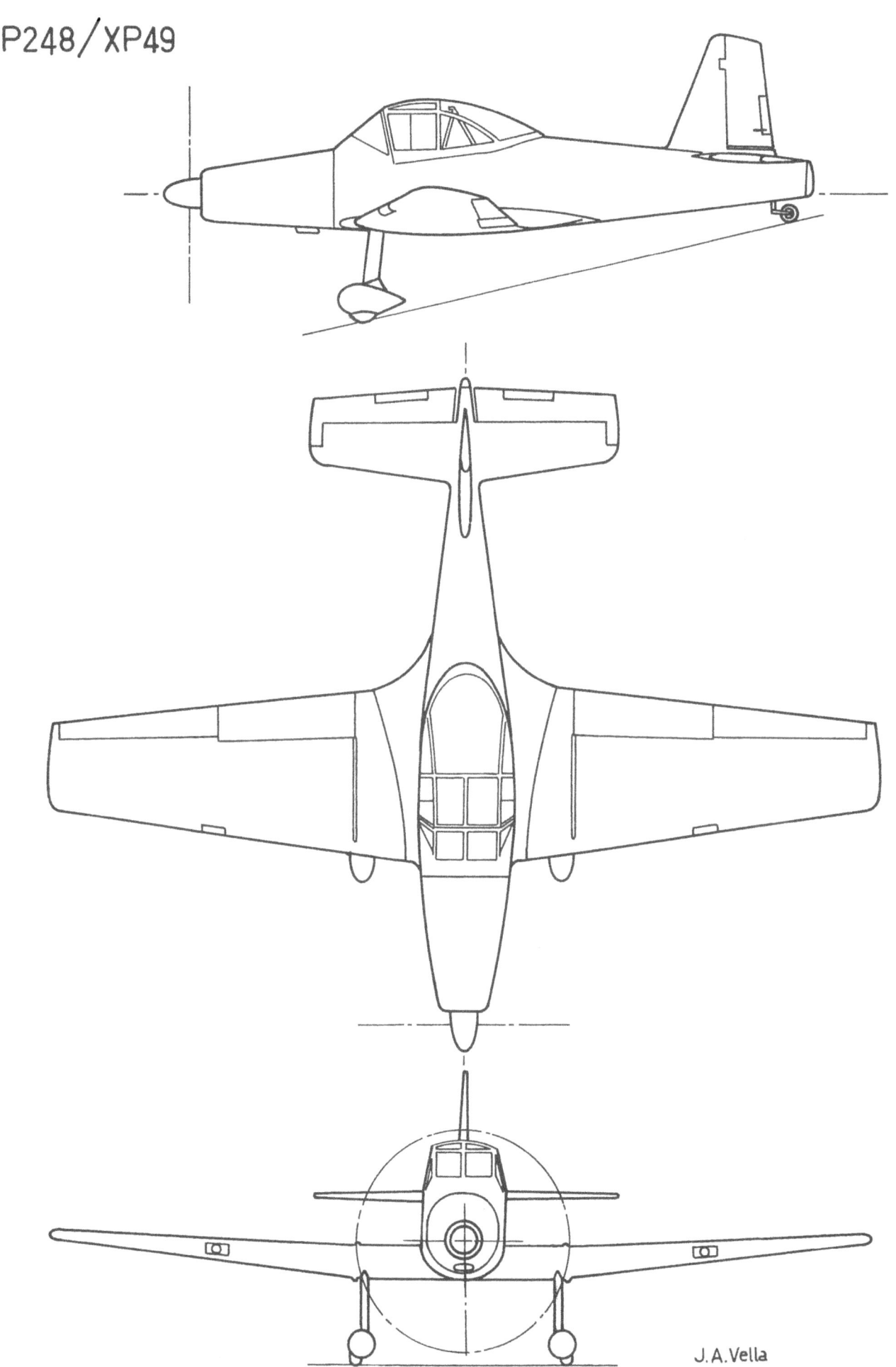

P247 / XP48 & P248 / XP49 WINJEEL RR DART TURBOPROP TRAINER AIRCRAFT
August 1952

With the completion of design of the Winjeel Basic Trainer and production planning well underway, attention turned to the concept of all-through gas turbine flying training in the expectation that this would become a long term operational requirement. CAC's first attempts at this were to propose the installation of a de-rated Rolls Royce Dart turboprop engine.

However, at 10,000 feet, where most of the training sequence was to take place, the fuel consumption of the Dart would have been far too high. The Dart's best altitude for least fuel consumption was 30,000 feet. It was an operational compromise at best.

Two configurations were envisaged, the P247 with a retractable undercarriage and P248 with a fixed spatted undercarriage The dates of the proposals were August 11 and 12, 1952 respectively. Work was halted at the end of September.

XP51 / XP52 RAM-JET HELICOPTERS
October 1952

These two unofficial schemes were ideas of C.J. Reid to establish a familiarity in the then new concept of tip driven ram-jet helicopters. They were no more than an exercise in aerodynamic computation to have some established local data in case there was an opening for an official requirement.

These type of ramjets had been tested in Europe. However due to their high level of uncomfortable noise such concepts were quickly out of favour throughout the world.

Bibliography: XP51 / XP52 Ram Jet Helicopters
Commonwealth Aircraft Corporation.(October 10,1952).[In-house memoranda notes].

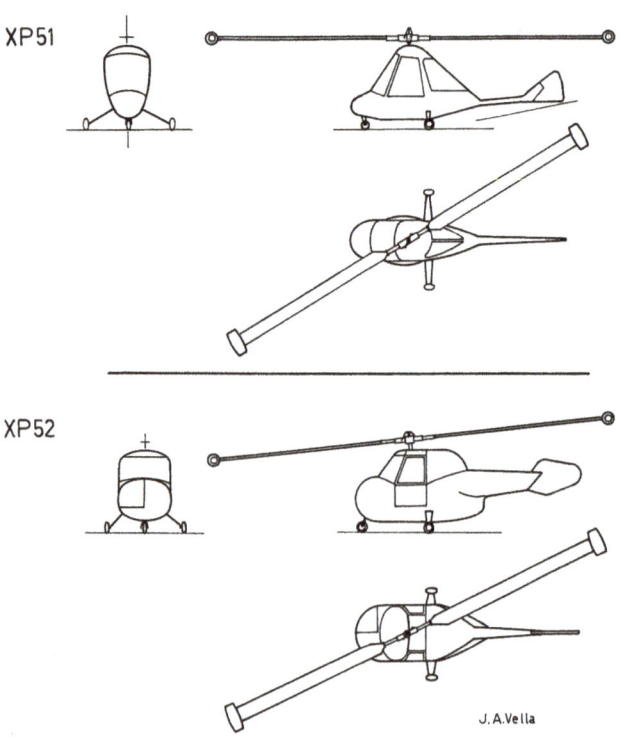

J.A.Vella

Specifications	XP52 Ram-Jet Helicopter No 1 Aerial Observation Post	
Powerplant	Rotor tip ram jets	
Performance	NA	
Weights	AUW	1,200 lb
Dimensions	Rotor diameter	28 ft
Specifications	XP52 Ram-Jet Helicopter No 2 Ambulance	
Powerplant	Rotor tip ram jets	
Performance	NA	
Weights	AUW	1,200 lb
Dimensions	Rotor diameter	28 ft

XP53 SABRE, RR RA-14 AVON TURBOJET
October 1952

This preliminary study of October 22, 1952 was undertaken by Ian Ring ten months before the first flight of the prototype CA-26 Sabre, to show the possible operational gain of fitting the Rolls Royce Avon RA.14 turbojet in the Sabre airframe in place of the chosen RA.7 Mk 20.

Compared with the 7,500 lb sea level thrust of the RA.7, the RA.14 200 Series delivered 9,500 lb thrust, a 25% increase. It incorporated an isopropyl-nitrate starter whereas the RA. 7 Mk 20 was fitted for electric starting but later converted to the liquid fuel starter (CAC Modification No 73). Full local production of this entirely different engine (which was also given some consideration for installation in the GAF Canberra bomber in a RAAF engineering conference held on October 24, 1952) could have been underway by July 1956.

The installation of the RA.14 in the Sabre was to incur further structural redesign making use of some 60% of the new tooling created for the RA.7 Avon Sabre fuselage. It would have been necessary to enlarge the intake duct area once more by 25%, from 435 ins² to 550 ins² by dropping the lower lip line a further 3.5 inches as in the previous re-design. The heavier RA.14 meant it had to be moved forward ten inches in relation to the RA.7 installation. All fuselage frames past Station 327 would have had to be enlarged to accommodate a tailpipe of increased diameter.

By extending the rear fuselage fuel cell higher up the sides of the fuselage it raised its capacity to 229 gallons. That in the wings totalled 206 gallons. At this juncture it was considered opportune to increase the number of cannon to four and provide sufficient ammunition for

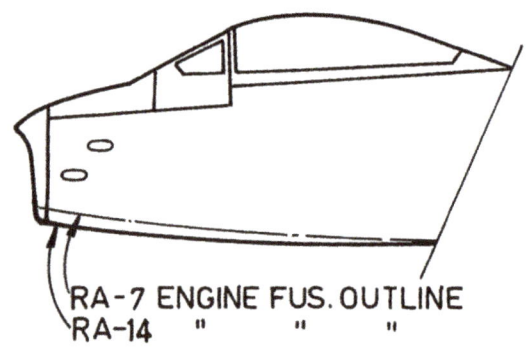

four seconds firing time. The engine installation would have incurred a 445 lb increase in weight; the gun installation 400 lb and another 205 lb for structural work. The design work for the new fuselage was planned to be complete by the second half of 1953 with the hope this uprated variant would be requested for the second Sabre production order.

Bibliography: XP53 Sabre, RR RA-14 Avon Turbojet

Commonwealth Aircraft Corporation. Production Report to DAP. 1949-1953.

Ring, I.H. (October 22, 1952). Engineering Report AA61 (A135). Preliminary Design Study RA.14 Avon Engine. Commonwealth Aircraft Corporation.

JET TRAINER
P260 / XP55   March 1953

Proposal 260 / Experimental Project 55 was one of a series of studies for a jet trainer to meet RAAF Specification AC 94. It featured a pressurized side by side cockpit arrangement, sweptback wings and twin Turbomeca Aspin II turbofans each of 759 lb thrust. This scheme was current in March 1953.

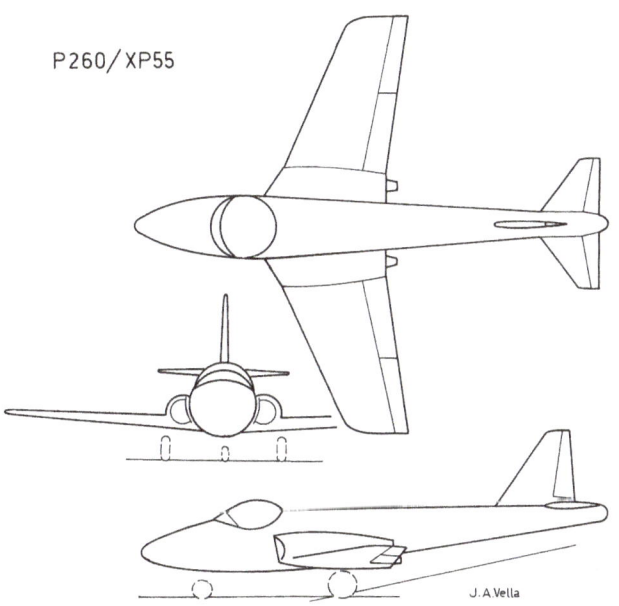

JET TRAINER
P266 / XP57 March 1953

A trainer variation based around an unidentified Armstrong Siddeley Engines Viper turbojet was dated June 1953. It was a more compact design than the P260.

JET TRAINER
P269 / XP59 July 1953

The July 1953 variation still used the A.S. Viper turbojet but with a low set tailplane. The common theme through the three studies P260 / P266 / P269 was a spherical shaped canopy. Intentionally, its inspiration was the similar shaped canopy found on the GAF assembled Canberra bomber. The shape was selected as it had minimum weight, minimum surface area and low cost.

Specification and dimensional data for the above three proposals. was lost by CAC.

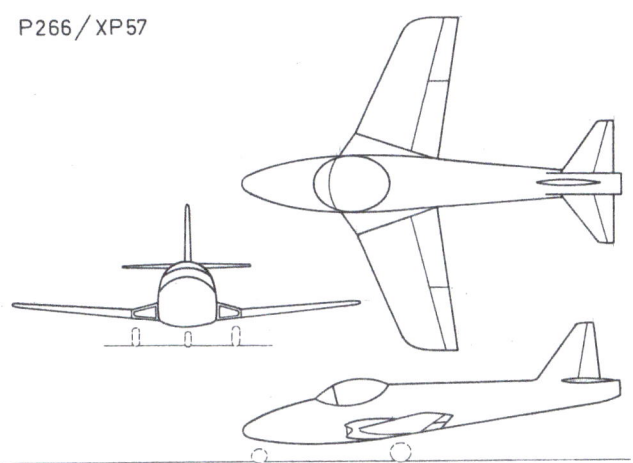

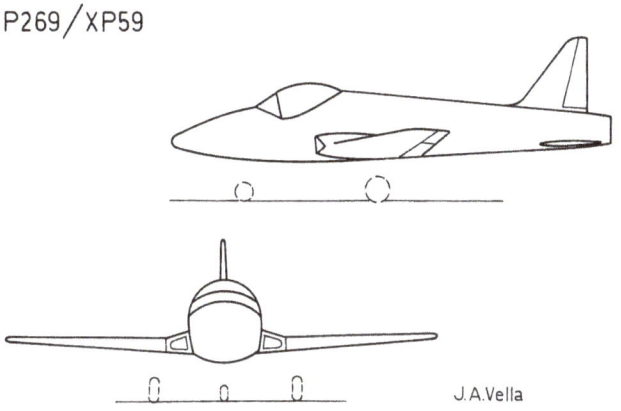

P256 / XP54 WINJEEL-TWIN ASPIN II TURBOFAN
P267 / XP58 WINJEEL-TWIN MARBORE II TURBOJET
February-June 1953

The avenue of gas turbine training utilizing the Winjeel airframe was taken up again in the earliest schematic outline drawings of January 1953 making use of two small jet engines.

They were not identified by any project numbers portraying the installation of Turbomeca Aspin II turbofan engines of 800 lb thrust in podded nacelles on the centre section/wing outer panel join line. One scheme depicted long slim cowls, the other shorter, more rounded pods. With a faired-in nose section to house various items of equipment and a tricycle undercarriage, the Winjeel had taken on the appearance of a boxy, squat, uncomplimentary derivative of the German Me 262 jet fighter of ten years earlier.

In the P256 / XP54 concept of February/March 1953, two of the same small (60 in long, 27 in diameter) Turbomeca Aspin II turbofans were located side by side in the nose of the Winjeel in place of the radial engine. Covered-over exhaust pipes terminated under the centre fuselage in line with the trailing edge of the wing. The mainwheel assemblies retracted forward into fairings built into the leading edge of the wing.

Winjeel-Turbomeca Aspin II
Initial Proposals
JANUARY 1953

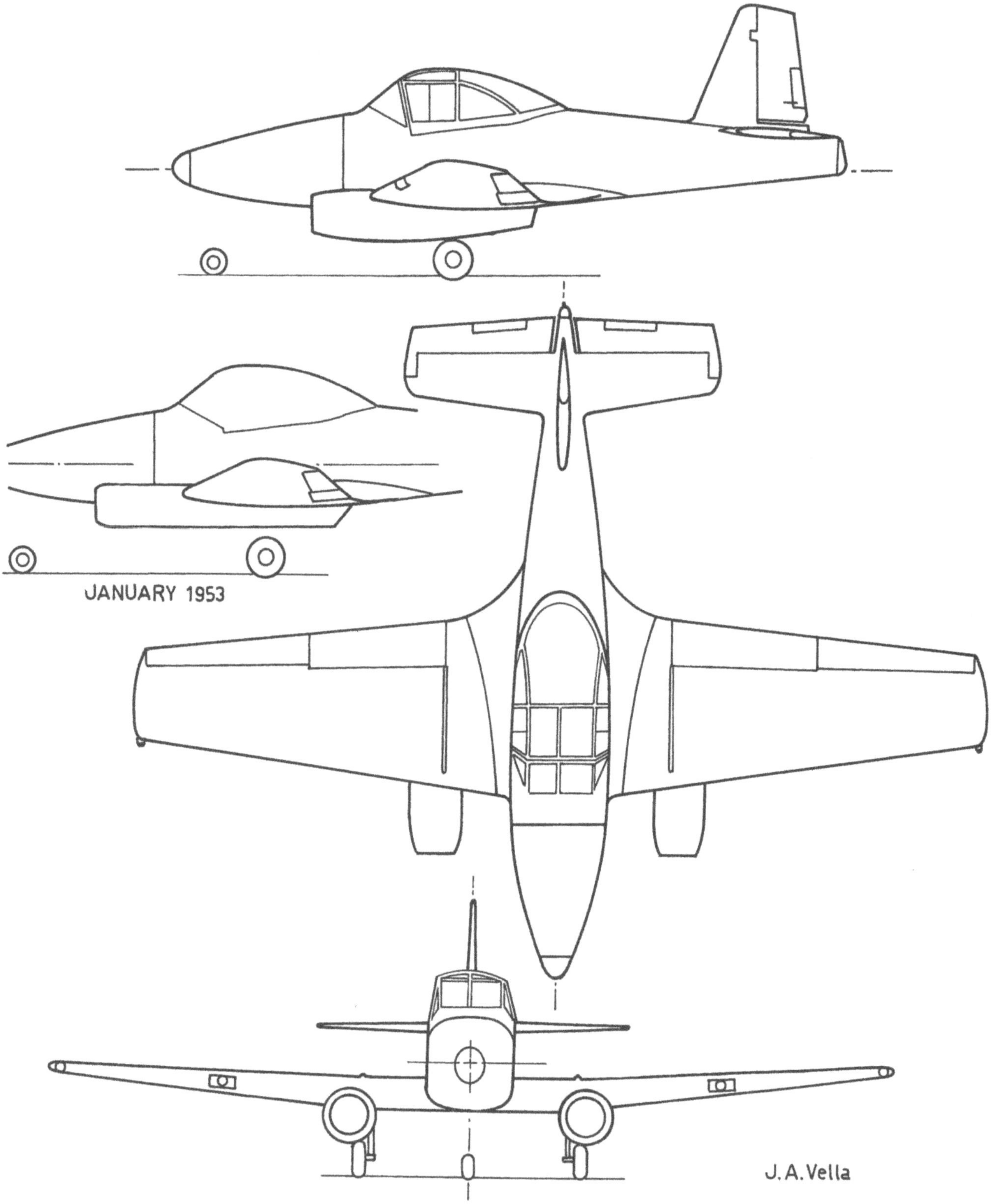

JANUARY 1953

J.A.Vella

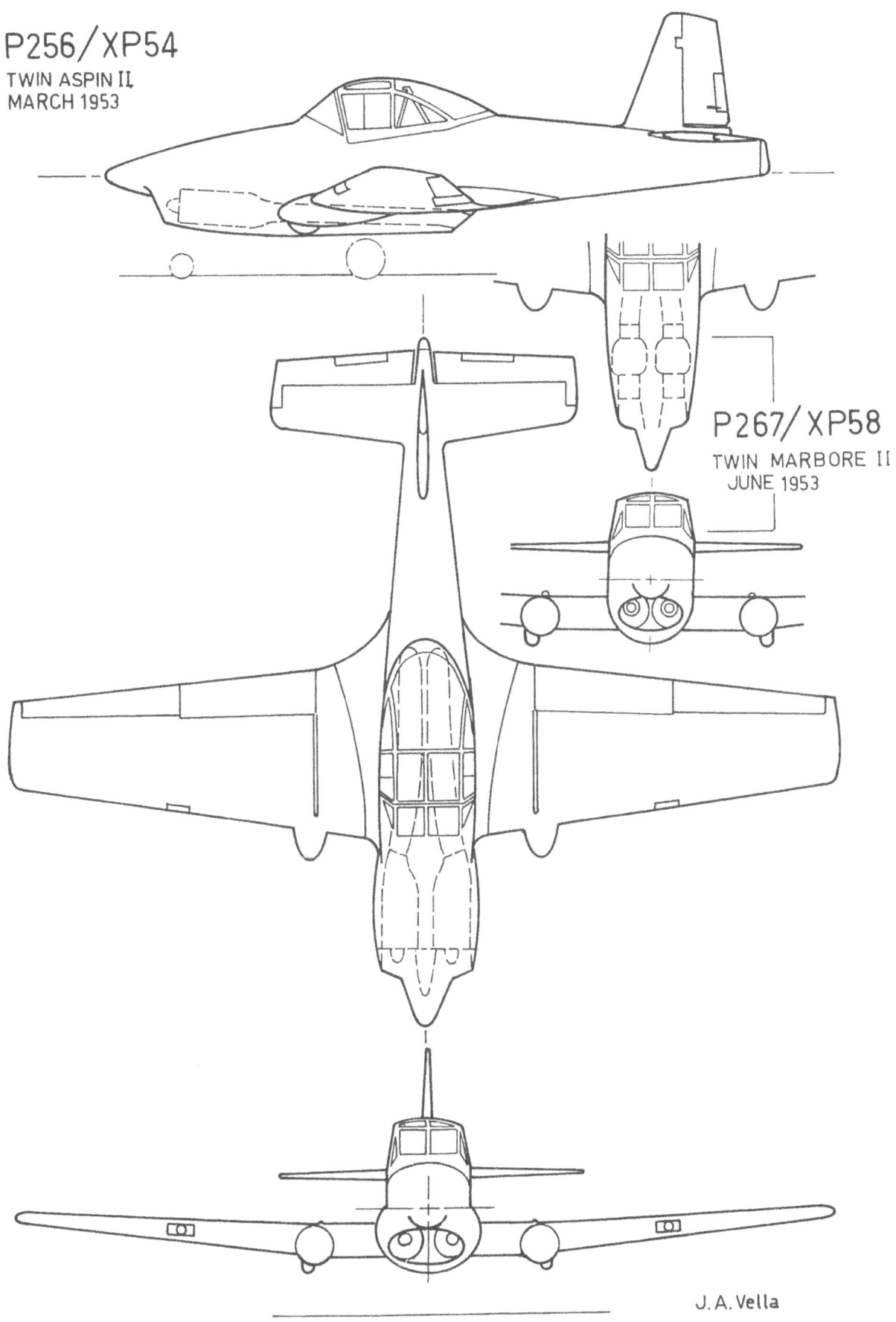

Specifications	P256 / XP54 -Winjeel Twin Aspin II Turbofan	
Powerplant	Two Turbomeca Aspin II turbofans each of 790 lb thrust at SL	
Performance	Max speed at 35,000 ft	329 kts
	Cruise speed at 35,000 ft	286 kts
	Rate of climb at SL	4,100 ft/min
	Stall speed at SL	45 kts
	Endurance(at 164 kts) with 72 gall of fuel	2.1 hrs
Weights	Max AUW(approx)	7,500 lb
Dimensions	Wing span	38 ft 9ins
	Length	30 ft 10 ins
	Height	11 ft 6 ins
	Wheelbase	8 ft 6 ins
	Track	10 ft 1 in

A nose wheel (replacing the original tailwheel) retracted to the rear. The XP54 suggested a performance similar to that of the Cessna T-37 turbojet trainer. In P267/XP58, the alternate twin engine arrangement was the 880 lb thrust Turbomeca Twin Marbore II, (Continental J69) turbojet, as used in the Cessna T-37 Trainer. This proposal was dated June 1953.

Both concepts were an innovative way to use the Winjeel airframe.

Bibliography: P256 / XP54 Winjeel Twin Aspin II Turbofan
Commonwealth Aircraft Corporation. (February 4, 1953). Engineering Report AA63 (A138). Trainer Aspin installation.

P265 / XP56 WALLABY FEEDER LINER
August 1953

In August of 1953 CAC released a promotional brochure and data for a small feeder airliner. From its beginning the company had of necessity concentrated on military projects and this proposal was its first official venture into the commercial aircraft scene with Wackett its principal instigator. It was his dual hope to launch the new design and to utilise it as the vehicle for the possible continued production of the CAC developed Cicada radial engine.

Given the name *Wallaby*, the design under the leadership of Doug Humphries was offered in three variants, namely:
- a twelve to seventeen passenger airliner,
- an executive transport and
- a freighter

The aircraft was intended for lower and middle level airlines as replacement for uneconomic feeder service DC-3s. With a reasonable sized order it was expected to have a price tag of around £A39,000.

Aircraft Description
The Wallaby combined utility and comfort in a very large degree and the nearest competition would have come, from the DH 104 Dove / DH 114 Heron family. Its unpressurised fuselage was short with large internal proportions of a basically square configuration, ample rounded upper and lower corners and finished off with an adaptation of the elegant nose contours of the DH 106 Comet airliner. Wal Watkins, Preliminary Design, had spent 1946-51 with the de Havilland, Hatfield, UK, on the design development of the Comet airliner.

The pilots were accommodated behind a multi-panelled flat windscreen arrangement in a cockpit which was reached via the passenger cabin. An avionics compartment was located beneath the floor of the cockpit. The passenger cabin was 23 feet long, 6 feet 3 inches wide and 6 feet high and featured a forward located toilet/washroom and a front luggage compartment of 28 cubic feet capacity, positioned across the aisle from the toilet. On the starboard side to the rear of the cabin and opposite the main entry door was a second and larger baggage compartment of 60 cubic feet capacity. Both compartments had external access. The cabin was provided with five generously sized rectangular windows down each side of the fuselage.

The main cabin entry door on the port side was 60 inches high and 48 inches wide, hinged downward and incorporated integral steps. It was to be capable of being held in a horizontal position to act as a freight loading platform. In the 15 seat passenger layout, five seat rows at 36 inch pitch would line up with each of the five windows in a 1-2 configuration, the twin seats along the starboard fuselage side. The elimination of the rear baggage compartment would allow the addition of an extra two seats.

An unusual feature was the incorporation of a third engine for take-off assistance, the centrifugal flow Turbomeca Palas turbojet of 350 lb thrust was to be installed in a plenum chamber in the lower rear fuselage cone. Air to the engine was provided via twin spring loaded doors which opened when the compressor started running. This third engine enabled an increase in passenger loading whilst at the same time allowing the aircraft to meet ICAO requirements for the engine-out case. It would also provide better take-off and climb performance from hot and high altitude airfields. Rubber bag type fuel tanks in the wings outboard from the engines held 90 gall each divided into 40 and 50 gall compartments. The Palas boost turbojet was also fed from these tanks.

Small Steps Philosophy
The Wallaby design followed the established CAC philosophy of taking small risk design steps whenever possible with each concept so as to minimize the overall risk and development cost and, therefore, the ultimate price tag. This approach was most obvious in the design of the wings, engine installation and undercarriage. CAC was proposing the use of its own radial engine, the Cicada, in an installation very similar to that of the Winjeel and using the same easy access four fold-back cowling panels.

The parallel chord wing centre section to well outboard of the engines, and incorporating dihedral, was an extension of that of the Winjeel Trainer design. The tapered outer wing panels were basically Winjeel components and the main undercarriage members were CA-18 Mustang units with revised tyre pressures. The nose wheel was to be from the CA-27 Sabre fighter.

The company had envisaged it would break even with as short a run of 30 aircraft being sold at £60,000 each, such was the belief in its approach to making use of previous production components. Regrettably, to the disappointment of the company, development of the troubled CAC Cicada engine ceased on February 7, 1955 when Government funding for its intended application in the CA-22 Winjeel prototype came to an end. (Refer to CAC Engine Work).

Market Response
Although local airlines showed some interest, their pre-eminent concern was whether CAC was intent on setting up a permanent or long term servicing and spares support facility to back up the aircraft.. This attractive scheme did not advance beyond the preliminary proposal/brochure phase.

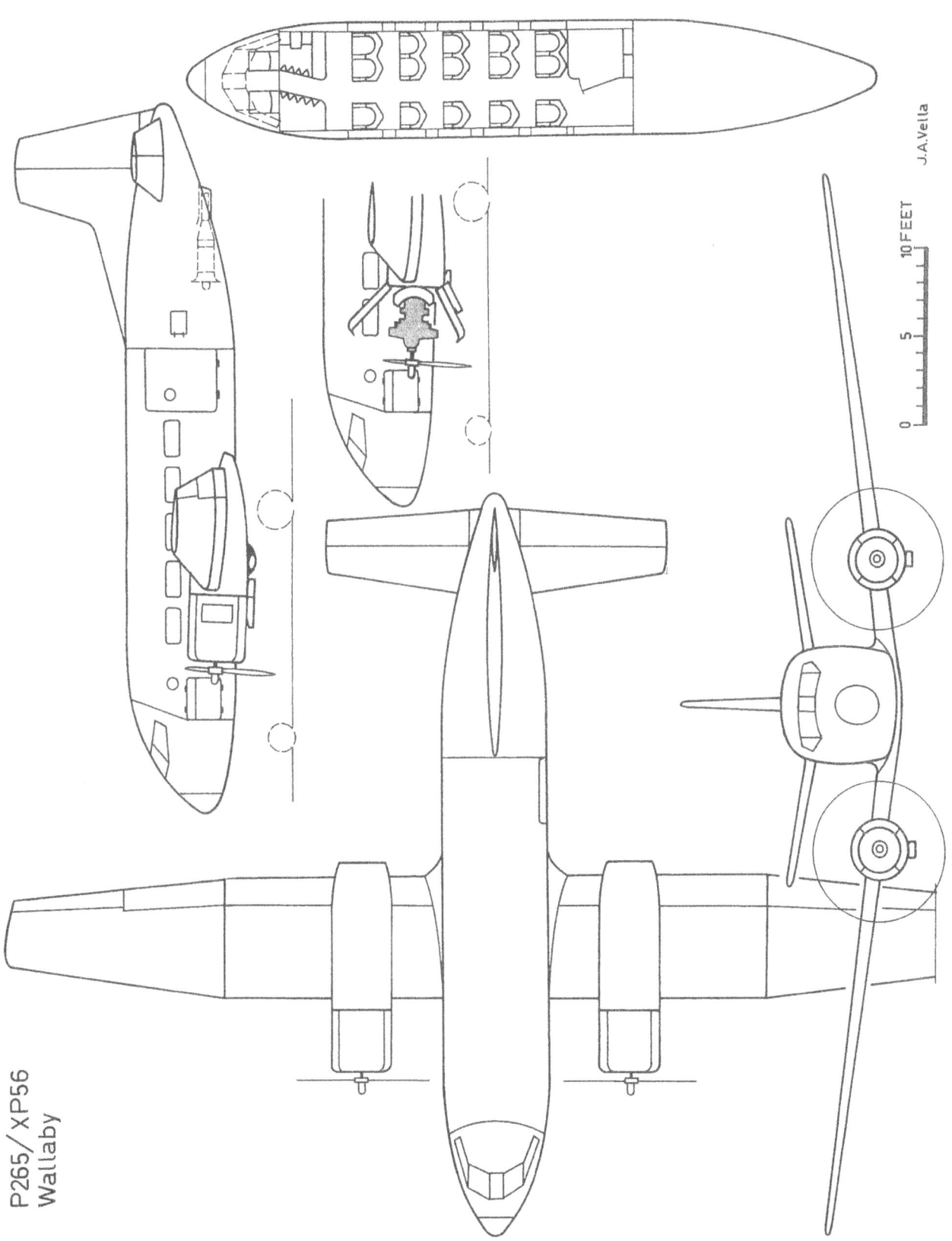

P265/XP56 Wallaby

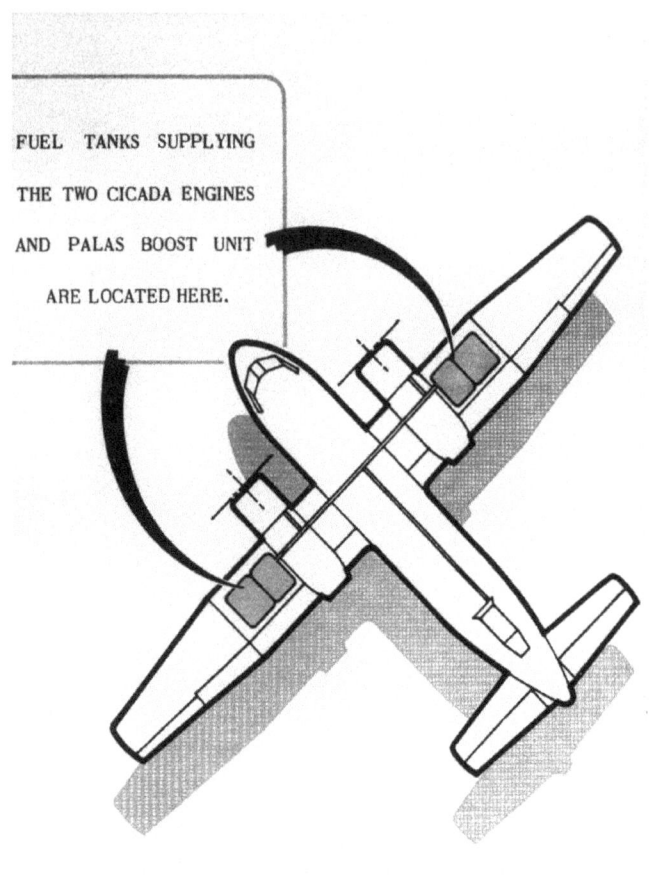

FUEL TANKS SUPPLYING THE TWO CICADA ENGINES AND PALAS BOOST UNIT ARE LOCATED HERE.

The interior layout of the Feederliner as portrayed in the CAC sales /promotion booklet. **HDHV**

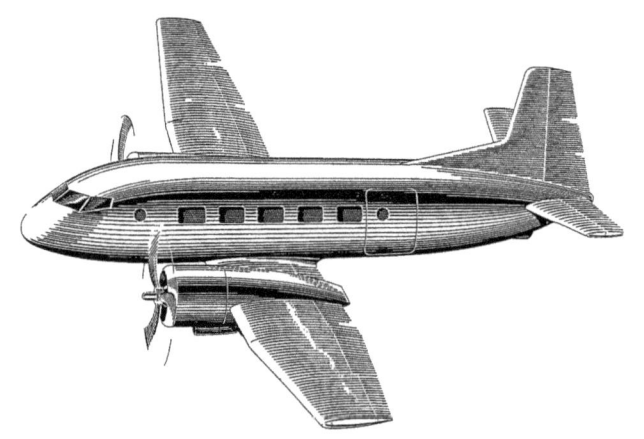

Specifications	P265 / XP56 Wallaby Feeder Liner			
Powerplant	Two CAC R795 Cicada 7 cyl supercharged radial engines of 450 hp each driving 3 bladed De Havilland fully feathering and reversing propellers. Max continuous cruise rating of 320 hp at 8,500 ft at a fuel consumption rate of 20 gall/hr			
	Also one Turbomeca Palas centrifugal flow turbojet booster engine of 350 lb (140 ehp) SL thrust with a Specific fuel consumption of 1.22 lb/hr/lb thrust			
Performance	Max speed at SL		164 kts	
	Design limit speed		180 kts	
	Economical cruise speed at 8,500 ft		138 kts	
	Rate of climb at SL		1,200 ft /min	
	Rate of climb, one engine out at SL		300 ft /min	
	Service ceiling		15,000 ft	
	Still air range at 62 % power at 8,500 ft with 12 pax		625 nm / 4.5 hrs	
	Still air range at 62 % power at 8,500 ft with 15 pax		350 nm / 2.5 hrs	
	Still air range at 62 % power at 8,500 ft with 17 pax		270 nm / 2.0 hrs	
	TO dist at SL (all engines)		1,170 ft	
	TO dist (SL) over 50 ft (all engines)		1,800 ft	
	Landing dist at SL		600 ft	
	Landing dist at SL over 50 ft		1,350 ft	
Weights	Empty		7,620 lb	
	Max payload		3,000 lb	
	Max TO		11,600 lb	
	Wing loading (at max TOW)		26.7 lb/sq ft	
	Total fuel (180 gall)		1,290 lb	
	R795 Cicada engine dry weight		780 lb	
	Turbomeca Palas engine dry weight		190 lb	
Dimensions	Wing span	64 ft	Wing area	435 sq ft
	Wing section NACA 23 Series		Tailplane area	100 sq ft
	Vertical fin area	50 sq ft	Length	44 ft 6 ins
	Height	18 ft 6 ins	Wheelbase	13 ft 6 ins
	Track	17 ft		

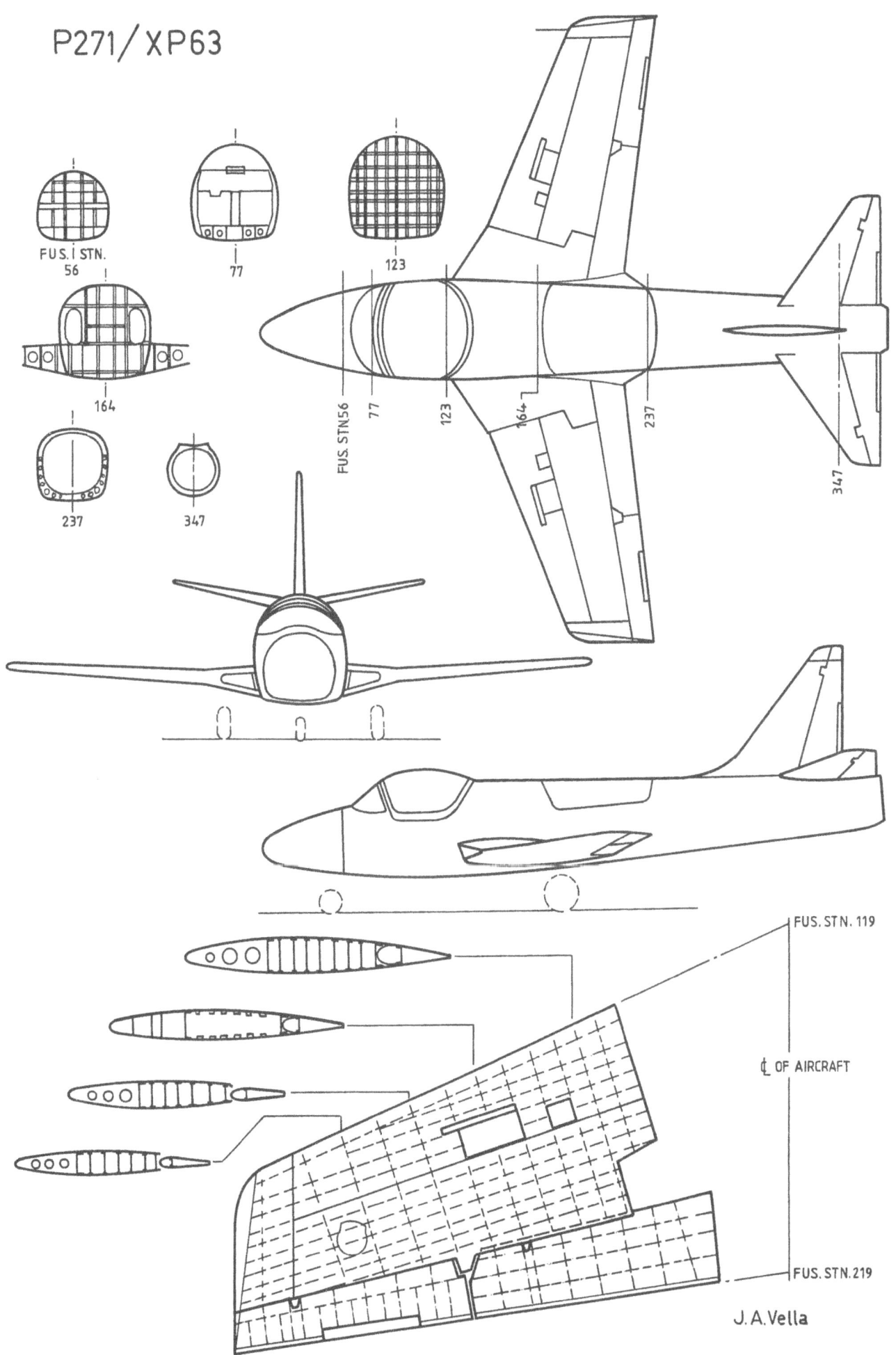

FUSELAGE

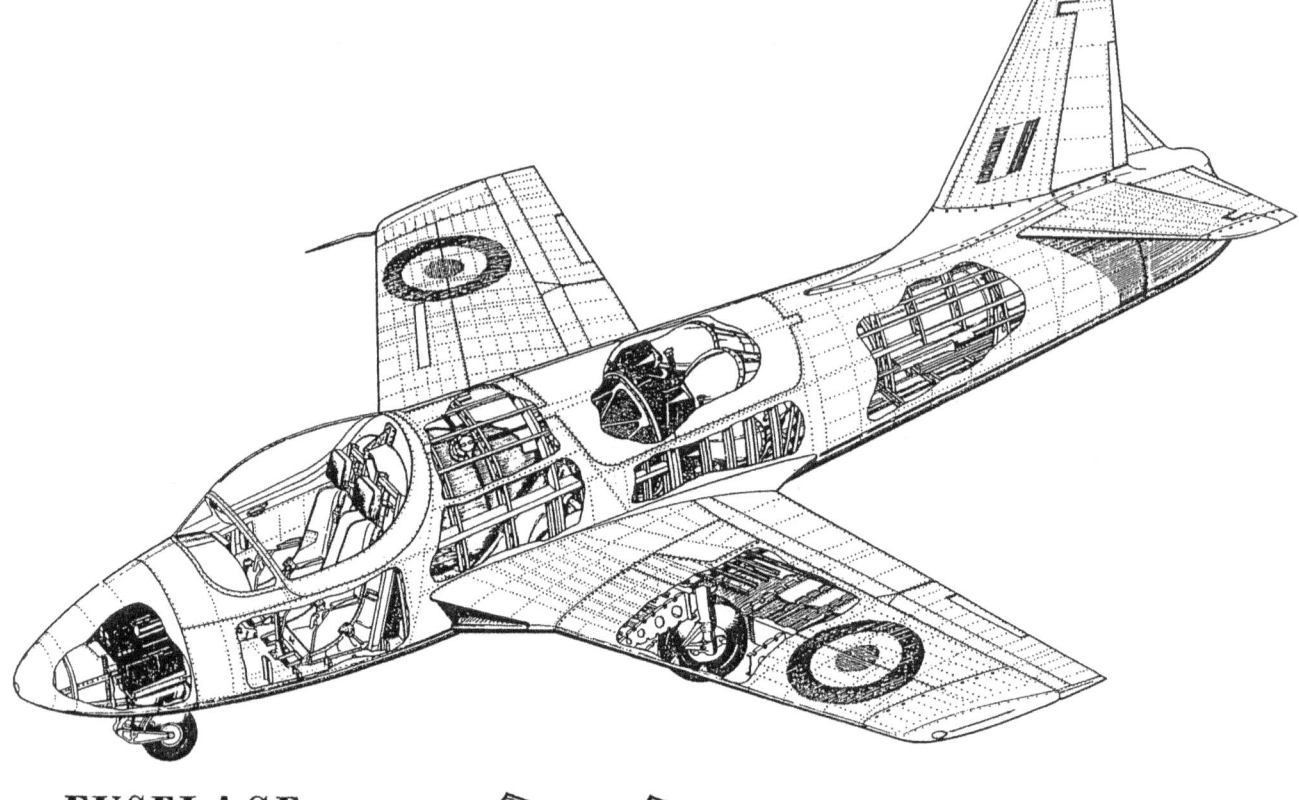

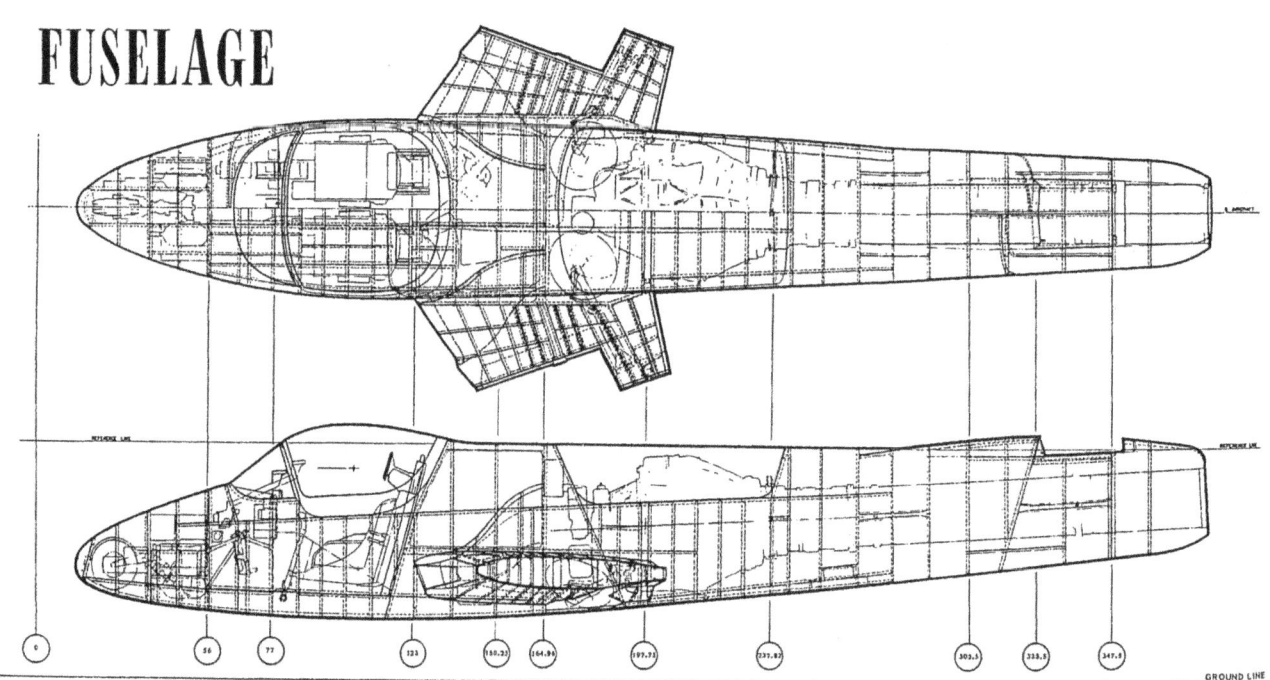

P271/XP63 with frame & stringer locations drawn on the model.

A smarter more sleek configuration than the early model Hunting Percival Jet Provost of 1953. **Walter Watkins**

Bibliography: P265 / XP56 Wallaby Feeder Liner
Commonwealth Aircraft Corporation. (August 1953). Engineering Report AA98. Wallaby Airliner.

P271 / XP63 JET TRAINER, RR DERWENT TURBOJET
November 1953

The XP63 was the final, definitive proposal and detailed jet trainer design study for RAAF Specification AC94. CAC Report AA97, released in November 1953, defined the general scope of this study. Like the earlier lead-up proposals, this study was under the design leadership of Doug Humphries and Charles Reid. The major change in this scheme was the selection of the Rolls Royce Derwent 8 RD7 turbojet, an engine of proven reliability and lower operating cost as it would not be pushed to its maximum limit in the training role. A considerable degree of interchangeability and accessibility was designed into the airframe to achieve ease of maintenance and simplify demands on the tooling requirements during manufacture. A smaller stockholding of spare parts would also be realised.

The XP63 was the CAC entry in the Department of Supply funded design study. GAF and de Havilland (Sydney) were likewise funded £6,000 each to submit their ideas on the project for competitive evaluation. Employing up to 12 draftsmen and four engineers over the design period, CAC was able to provide a fully detailed layout design on all aspects of the airframe and systems in just six months. The design went further than a mere paper study. It was an in-depth financial and technical assessment.

Aircraft Description
The fuselage was semi-monocoque, incorporating two large doors in the mid-upper surface to allow for rapid installation and removal of the engine. The forward fuselage incorporated a pressure cockpit with a ceiling limit of up to 50,000 ft, side by side seating, ejector seats, air conditioning and a rear hinged bubble canopy which lifted back to an angle of 50 degrees. An emergency canopy jettison release handle was located on top of the instrument panel. The windscreen was one piece of curved safety glass with provision for defrosting. The forward sliding section of the nose cone provided access to the radio, radio compass, batteries and oxygen bottles, all located above the nose wheel bay.

A large part of the fuel was carried in a fuselage cell behind the cockpit. A forward firewall separated the engine from the rear of the fuel tank. The fuselage also incorporated short stub wings from the extreme ends of which were pivoted the main landing gear legs. These retracted inwards to lie under the engine air intake ducting which was fed via simple intakes adjacent to the fuselage side. This stub wing arrangement made for an easier assembly, handling and transportation task.

The landing gear was fully enclosed, the wings were fully cantilevered, flush riveted and designed as a distributed loading system utilizing a multiple stringer/skin system of a main spar and large top and bottom booms, the whole attached to the fuselage via a continuous plate attachment joint achieving low stress concentration. An unusual feature of the wings was the symmetrical airfoil selected to minimize Mach effects at high speed. This made the outer wings including the ailerons and flaps interchangeable. Three fuel cells were located in each wing and narrow airbrakes which extended into the airflow were positioned on both upper and lower wing surfaces. Immediately behind these was an ammunition compartment to supply two 0.5 inch guns (when fitted) one under each wing in an external, quickly removable streamlined pod; all expended links and cases being retained in the pod. The horizontal tail was to be constructed in a similar manner with identical port and starboard halves positioned with 10 degrees of dihedral. The fin had a 30 degree sweep-back angle. A comprehensive instrument layout was provided to allow for night or blind flying training.

The overall program slipped back and it appears the requirement changed and the specification lapsed. However, late in 1953, Air Marshal Sir Donald Hardman had been succeeded by Air Marshal Sir John McCauley, as Chief of Air Staff. Whilst Sir Donald Hardman (on secondment from the RAF) and previously Sir George Jones, had both been strong supporters of the Australian aircraft industry, Air Marshal McCauley was not as enthusiastic.

The Robert Menzies Liberal Country Party Government had, on July 13, 1950 earmarked the de Havilland DH115 Vampire Trainer for possible acquisition by the RAAF as part of the post war general build-up. In November 1955 the Minister for Air, Athol G. Townley announced an order for 100 T33/T35 Vampire Trainers, and subsequently increased it to 110 aircraft.

Bibliography: P271 / XP63 Jet Trainer RR Derwent Turbojet
Commonwealth Aircraft Corporation. (November 1953). Engineering Report AA97. The Jet Trainer.

P277 / XP61 WINJEEL AMBULANCE
December 1953

This was a modification to the Winjeel Basic Trainer proposed by Ian Ring in December 1953, for the carriage of a stretcher patient. There was to be no major alteration to the structure with the exception of the provision of an entry cut-out and door on the starboard fuselage side.

Specifications	P271 / XP63 Jet Trainer RR Derwent Turbojet	
Powerplant	Rolls Royce Derwent 8 RD7 turbojet of 3,600 lb thrust	
Performance	Max speed at SL	465 kts
	Max speed at 35,000 ft	480 kts
	Rate of climb at SL	8,000 ft/min
	Rate of climb (45,000 ft)	1,500 ft/min
	Time to 45,000 ft	14.2 min
	Service ceiling	50,000 ft
	TO dist at SL	1,050 ft
	TO dist at SL over 50 ft	1,350 ft
	Landing dist at SL	1,050 ft
	Landing dist at SL over 50 ft	1,650 ft
	Landing speed	56 kts
	Range with max fuel	700 nm
Dimensions	Wing span	28 ft 6 ins
	Aspect ratio	4.5
	Wing LE sweep	20°
	Wing area	178 sq ft
	Wing dihedral	3°
	Mean chord	6 ft 3 ins
	Wing section	NACA 0012 Mod
	Flap area	25 sq ft
	Tailplane span	12 ft
	Tailplane area	45 sq ft
	Vertical tail area	22.5 sq ft
	Length	31ft 6ins
	Height	12 ft
	Wheelbase	10 ft 6 ins
	Track	7 ft

P277/XP61

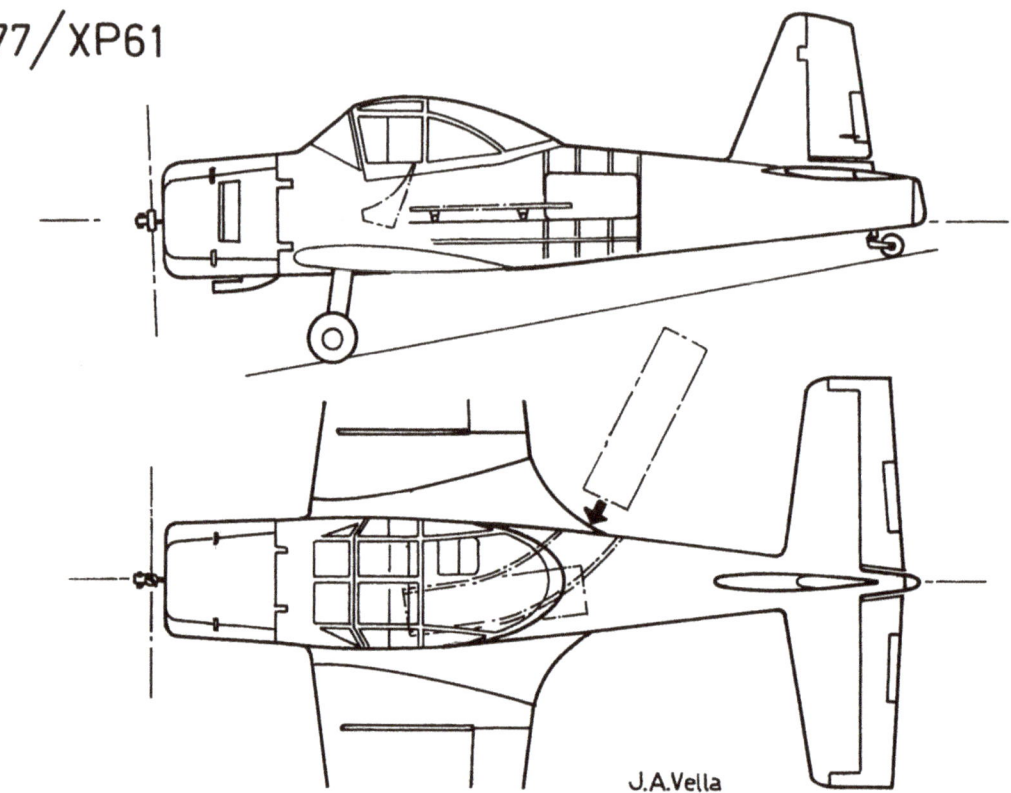

For ease of entry and exit a curved set of tracks were located on the cabin floor to just behind the pilot's station to place the stretcher parallel to the fuselage side. The turnover truss would have been deleted and other equipment relocated.

Specifications	P277 / XP61 Winjeel Ambulance	
Powerplant	One Pratt & Whitney R985-AN2 Wasp Junior 9 cyl radial engine of 445 hp	
Performance	Cruise speed at 5,000 ft	137 kts
	TO dist to 50 ft	1,170 ft
	Stall speed flaps lowered	47 kts
	Stall speed flaps raised	55 kts
	Endurance	3.5 hrs
Weights	Max TO	4,460 lb
Dimensions	As per CA-25 Winjeel Basic Trainer	

Bibliography: P277 / XP61 Winjeel Ambulance
Ring, I.H. (1986). [Interview]

CHAPTER 4. FAST JETS AND SABRE PROSPECTS

XP62 FOUR ENGINE LIGHT INTERCEPTOR
December 1953

This four engine aircraft was intended to have a similar role to that of the XP47 Rocket Interceptor – point or area defence but with a greater degree of operational flexibility. This light interceptor study was not as fully developed as were the CAC Rocket Interceptor ideas.

The availability of the very light weight expendable Rolls Royce RB93 Soar axial flow turbojet for missile, target aircraft and VTOL jet-lift application created the opportunity to consider this engine for short- life interceptor aircraft application.

The RB93, flight tested in the UK in 1954, an engine of small dimensions – 62 inches in length and 15 inches in diameter – was to deliver 1,810 lb thrust for an installed weight of 267 lb, representing a power/weight ratio of 6.77:1. Four engines were required to provide sufficient thrust at take-off and for the high speed (in excess of Mach 1.0) interception dash to target at altitude.

With a take-off weight of approximately 7,500 lb and a maximum take-off thrust of 7,240 lb the T/W ratio was near 1.0. This was required to provide a short take-off and rapid rate of climb. The T/W ratio with one engine operating and climb fuel expended was to be better than 0.25, providing for high cruise, for radar target check and later, controlled and selective return to base.

Rolls Royce had not at that time clearly defined the maximum thrust life of the RB93 engine but had indicated it to be between two to three hours. The aircraft was expected to require an engine change after four or five intercept missions. An intercept mission was expected to be of 20 to 25 minutes duration and the operating time of each engine was to be monitored to ensure safe operations. The specific fuel consumption figure of 1.26 for the engine was high, but by operating four engines in any combination of one to four it would have been possible to plan a mission of maximum effectiveness, with a greater versatility than would have been possible with rocket power alone.

The suggested engine management profile during intercept operations was:

Take-off and climb to altitude	4 engines
Cruise for radar directions	1 engine
High speed cruise to target area (near Mach 1 0)	2 engines
Dash to target and weapons release (Mach 1.2+)	4 engines
Return to base	1 engine

XP62 FOUR ENGINE LIGHT INTERCEPTOR

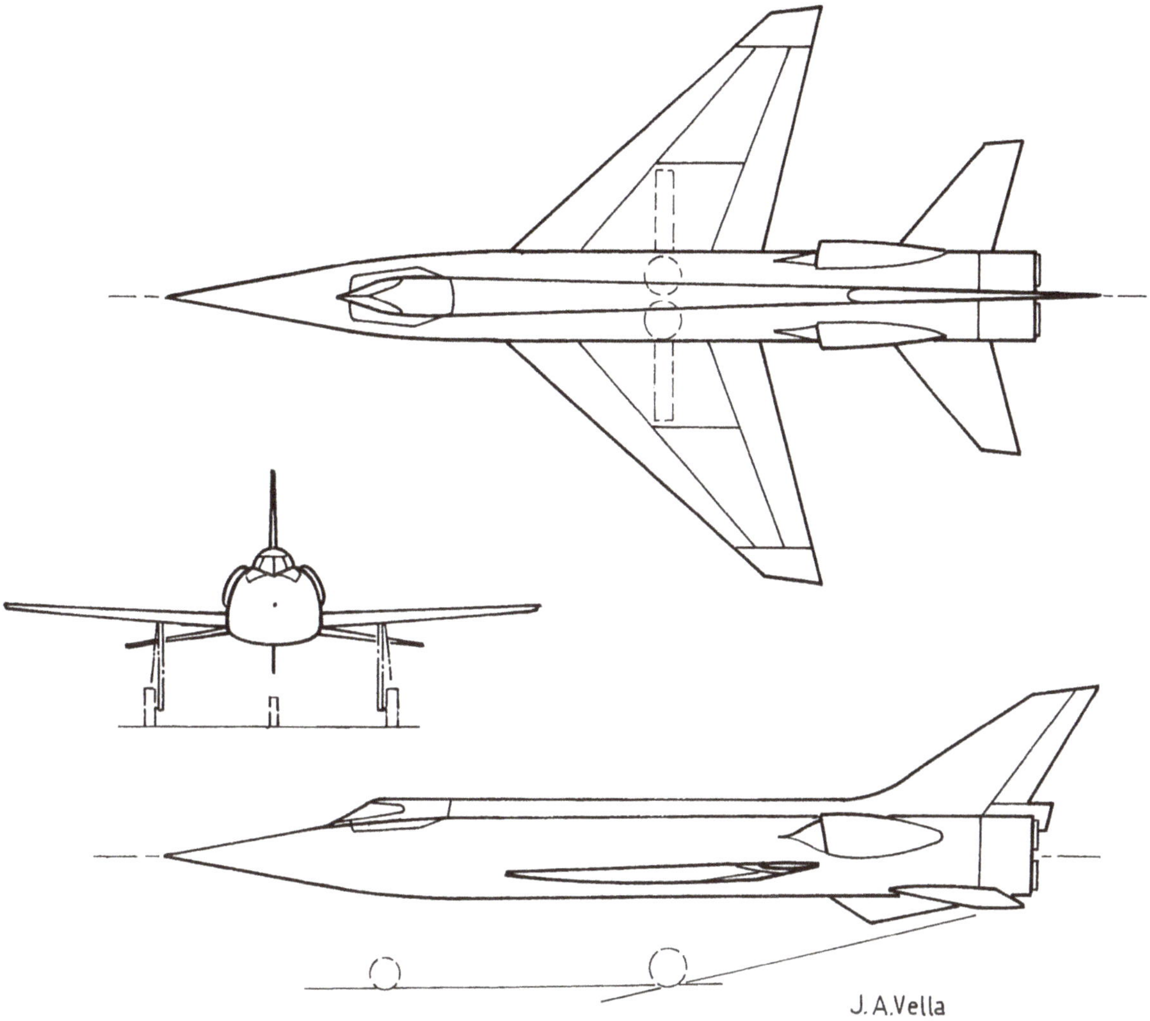

J. A. Vella

Aerodynamics and Structure

The aerodynamic configuration was influenced by the work on the CA-23 and based on a reduced size North American Aviation F-100 Super Sabre configuration (from which some engineering data had been made available to CAC). The aspect ratio and span on the XP62 were higher than the figures for the rocket interceptor ideas providing better subsonic L/D ratios.

The structure was to be entirely conventional with a fuselage of basically similar front end configuration to that of the XP47. However, the cross section from a point at the leading edge of the wing to the main spar of the horizontal tail was similar to that of the F-100 Super Sabre, i.e. a half-round top with flat sides and bottom. It was 40 inches wide, comprised basically of a fuel tank bay, an automatic sealing pressurized cockpit as on the XP47 and provision in the mid lower fuselage ahead of the main undercarriage bay for an enclosed rocket armament magazine. The one piece 20 foot span wing had a cut out for the main landing gear and was to be attached to the fuselage structure through four vertical bolts. Flaperon and taileron control surfaces were to be used as had been planned for the CA-23. The engines were grouped as a readily removed cluster of four, arranged in pairs on either side of the fin carry-through support structure. A single air intake on each side of the fin fed the two engines on that side. (Consideration was given to using a common intake plenum chamber but the study did not define that detail).

The Threat

The period of the early 1950s was one in which the fear of a nuclear bomber attack was a matter of paramount concern with defence authorities. Consequently, innovative interceptor solutions were given careful consideration. This particular proposal was a preliminary study to illustrate the feasibility for CAC to design a low cost specialized interceptor aircraft capable of intercepting and destroying a 500-600 mph, high flying bomber, some 150-200 miles from its anticipated target.

A North American Aviation F-100D Super Sabre. Its fuselage structure was to be the notional design basis for the XP62.
Gerhard Joos via J. A. Vella

These interceptors were to be stationed some 50 miles around a target city centre and were to be one-firing-pass vehicles. (Not dissimilar to the Luftwaffe Me 163 of WW2). With three interceptors each homing in on the same bomber target the probability of success was considered to be good.

Bibliography: XP62 Four Engine Light Interceptor

Green, William; Cross, Roy. (1955) *Jet Aircraft of the World*. Macdonald, London.

Watkins, W. (December 1953). Advice to the author on lost company computations of a C.J.Reid design study. Commonwealth Aircraft Corporation.

Specifications	XP62 Four Engine Light Interceptor	
Powerplant	Four Rolls Royce RB93 Soar Lightweight turbojet each of 1,810 lb thrust at SL	
Performance	Mach 1+ at altitude	
Weights	Max AUW(approx)	7,500 lb
Dimensions	Wing span	20 ft
	Length	34 ft
	LE sweep	43°
	Height	10 ft
	Wing area	130 sq ft
	Tailplane span	11 ft
	Wheelbase	10 ft
	Track	9 ft

FIGHTER REQUIREMENTS CRITERIA 1953-1960

PART 1: Formal Requirements

The 1950s were the halcyon days of CAC 'going it alone' with combat aircraft proposals. The XP46 Day Fighter, two Rocket Interceptor concepts, the Warrior and XP67/XP68 Tactical Fighters did not progress sufficiently and the state-of-the-art CA-23 was cancelled at the pre-prototype build stage. The reason for the existence of two of these proposals and the cancellation of another can best be explained by putting them into the context of three Air Force documents of July 1953, namely, 'The Fighter Aircraft Required for the RAAF as a Replacement for the RAAF Sabre'; 'A Summary on the Role and Employment of the RAAF', and the 'Air Staff Requirement for the Air Superiority or Offensive Fighter to Replace the Sabre in 1958'.

The 1953 Royal Australian Air Force was approved to be a seventeen squadron peacetime organisation of which five Citizen Air Force interceptor squadrons were included in the Home Defence structure. Other fighter elements were to be part of the Mobile Task Force (MTF) to be employed in tactical roles in the Middle East and SE Asia.

The CA-27 Sabres then coming into service were to form the MTF until the beginning of 1958 when a maximum of £A23M was earmarked for the start of a replacement cycle for the aircraft by its relegation to Home Defence squadrons and Fighter OTUs.

Six fighter aircraft design philosophies were examined to arrive at the one type affordable and able to meet the peace time needs of Australia. The arguments for and against the range of options were:

- The <u>All-Weather Fighter</u>, whilst it might ultimately have met all the requirements of the RAAF and may even have become essential for offensive fighter operations beyond friendly radar coverage was considered unlikely as a Sabre replacement as its day operation suitability was unproven; was handicapped for mobile operations due to the extra labour requirement to service its electronics; was far more costly than a day fighter of equivalent performance and would be beyond the purchase capacity of a RAAF peace time budget. Further, the provision of such costly specialist aircraft was thought to be the responsibility of the larger powers in theatres of joint defence operations.

- The <u>Day Interceptor</u> was considered to be a short ranged vehicle specializing in defence and unable to carry the war to the enemy.

- Similarly the <u>Rocket Interceptor</u> was a specialized defence fighter best left to the RAF and USAF to investigate to meet their more urgent defence requirement. Australia lacked sufficient research and production capacity for such a design and the RAAF was to keep a watching brief on overseas development but would stay out of any involvement-hence the lack of interest in the CAC Rocket Interceptor proposals.

- The <u>Simplified Day Fighter</u> was typified in the UK through the Folland Gnat but it lacked official government support. The US had abandoned the concept, and airframe size considerations were such as to minimize fuel capacity and armament and limit the aircraft to a defensive role, therefore there was to be no XP46 or XP62.

- The <u>Long Range Fighter</u> like the CA-23 was an offshoot from the All-Weather concept and would meet the needs of the RAAF with the exception of the limited all-weather requirement for the defence of Australia. In the 1953 concept however, such aircraft were beyond the capacity of Australia to produce or purchase on a peace-time budget — hence the cancellation of the CA 23. Only second-hand or dated examples of this type of aircraft were affordable.

- The <u>Air Superiority</u> or <u>Offensive Fighter</u> was thought to be the most suitable of the types considered for all conflicts in the Middle East, SE Asia, global or home defence.

The ASR for the aircraft to replace the CA-27/F-86 requested a speed of not less than M1.5 and preferably M2.0; a capability of operation at 60,000 ft; a time to climb to 40,000 ft at normal AUW of not more than 4 minutes and the ability to operate from hastily prepared surfaces at low tyre pressure loadings in distances of less than 6,000 feet.

The radius of action when carrying basic armament and overload tanks was not to be less than 500 nm and preferably ought to be 750 nm, with allowance for a reduction when carrying external stores or weapons. Because of limitations on the peacetime budget of the RAAF the overall size and complexity of the aircraft was to be kept to a minimum and the aircraft was to cost no more than £250,000 each, preferably much less.

CAC proposals XP64 / XP65 / XP66 Warrior and XP67 / XP68 Fighter were unsolicited submissions to the ASR and on paper went a long way towards fulfilling that requirement.

However by virtue of the miniaturisation of electronics (which was anticipated in 1953) the RAAF was able to acquire in 1960 the Mirage IIIO, an all-weather, multi-mission aircraft but at a unit price about twice the figure suggested in 1953.
(Refer to CA-29 Mirage sub-contract).

PART 2: Informal Developments

A number of the CAC proposals, for example the XP51 / XP52 Ram Jet Helicopter, some of the Sabre update and improvement ideas, the investigation into the use of rocket power, the tracked undercarriage on the XP67, would come about because of informal comment through the RAAF Technical Branch of an overseas development in a particular area. It would then be prudent that the initiative or topic be followed up so as some preliminary awareness and design would be underway should the idea become a formal local request. The 1950s were also a time of rapid advance on all aeronautical fronts by the design offices of the West's aircraft production centres. However, it was not easy to acquire much detailed data due to national security restrictions, so that if basic local research was lacking so also would be any large initiatives from industry.

XP64/65/66 WARRIOR-AIR SUPERIORITY FIGHTER AIRCRAFT
May 1954

A comprehensive study of fighter aircraft development was undertaken by the Operations Directorate of the RAAF in 1953. This review reached a number of conclusions as to the type of aircraft to be employed by the Mobile Task Force from January 1957 as set out in their Fighter Requirements Criteria 1953-1960. Following the analysis of these conclusions, CAC's Preliminary Design Group put forward ideas for a supersonic aircraft which would supplement and eventually replace the CA-27 Sabre that was just entering service.

The first proposal was circulated as a brochure dated May 1954 outlining the detail of an aircraft intended to fulfil a number of operational roles ranging from high rate interception and high speed, high altitude reconnaissance to tactical nuclear strike and long range (up to 600 nm radius) interdiction where some sonic dash performance was needed. With this spectrum of operational roles and built-in performance capability, the aircraft could have been the Australian equivalent of the North American Aviation F-100 Super Sabre which was a new design for the air superiority role and a supersonic successor to the F-86.

The intention of CAC's Preliminary Design Group was to produce a new airframe envelope utilizing a combination of existing CA-27 Sabre systems and equipment to minimize development costs and risks. It was hoped this commonality of systems would enable the new design to be introduced into the existing RAAF Sabre maintenance and support infrastructure.

Named *Warrior*, the unique aspect of the design was the plan to fabricate the entire structure out of stainless steel. Aluminium alloys were then considered less than ideal to be taken into serious consideration because of their rapid deterioration in strength with increase in surface temperature at speeds in the M1.5 to M2.0 range. CAC felt confident in promoting the use of the metal in aircraft structures and skins through its extensive jet engine manufacturing experience. Nevertheless a lot of development work would have been required beyond the brochure stage to establish the practical limits of working with the metal on a production basis. It was at least expected to be easier and less costly to work with than titanium.

Aircraft Description

The distinguishing structural feature of the aircraft was the thin unswept parallel chord wing with large tip mounted fuel tanks. To achieve supersonic flight, the fuselage was to have an extreme fineness ratio with all flying surfaces kept to a minimum thickness. The fuselage of the XP56 had a constant cross-section over a considerable portion of its length with the aim of keeping the amount of skin forming to a minimum. The very thin skin was to be stiffened by closely spaced stringers. To minimize the fuselage cross section area the bulk of which was to be occupied by the Avon 200 series RA-24R turbojet of 11,250 lb reheat thrust, all internal fuel was to be carried in streamlined wing tip tanks, each of 305 gallons capacity. (This was just prior to the discovery and application of the NACA area rule principles.)

The extreme nose contained a small AN/APG-30 ranging radar and the retracted, CA-27 Sabre nosewheel component. The pressurized cockpit, most of the instrumentation and ejection seat (now automatic) were of Sabre origin. The streamlined canopy comprised of a Vee-shaped thick glazed windscreen and a jettisonable, rear hinged, metal decked canopy, with a semi-elliptical window panel on each side.

Air conditioning, radio communication equipment, various ancillary items, twin guns and 340 rounds of ammunition were located aft of the cockpit and forward of the engine. The barrels of the two 30mm Aden cannon exited on the sides of the fuselage below the cockpit in a shallow depression angle. Access to the guns was through the sides of the fuselage but re-arming was via the upper fuselage. Air to the engine face was supplied from an oblique shock ramp type entry underneath and in line with the rear of the cockpit. A one piece petal style airbrake hinged downward from the lower fuselage immediately aft of the intake lip.

The entire lower fuselage was flat, identical to the construction used on the F-100 Super Sabre. The wing was to have a low aspect ratio of 2.75 and a thickness/chord ratio of 3.5%. Because of this thinness the required rigidity could only be achieved by the use of a relatively (0.125 inch) thick skin. As the wings were unswept and lacking dihedral, a one-sheet, one-piece style of construction could be adopted for its low set location. Construction complexity and cost would consequently be reduced. In the previous XP64 variant (documents lost), the identical wing was set high up on the fuselage side.

No ailerons were fitted with both trailing and leading edges of the wing being entirely occupied by segmented high lift flaps were operated by hydraulic jacks located in two fairings under each wing. An underwing stores station was to be co-located on each of these external fairings.

The four compartments in each wing-tip fuel tank were designed to minimise fuel loss as a result of combat damage. Fuel was fed from these wing-tip tanks through a central collector tank. Propyl-nitrate engine starting was incorporated in the RA-24R Avon engine.

The main landing gear legs, modified CA-27 items, retracted forwards into vacant space inside the wing tip tanks. A brake retarding parachute was to be deployed during the landing run. *The Douglas X-3 Stilletto stainless steel experimental test aircraft test results were received by CAC.*

XP65 Warrior

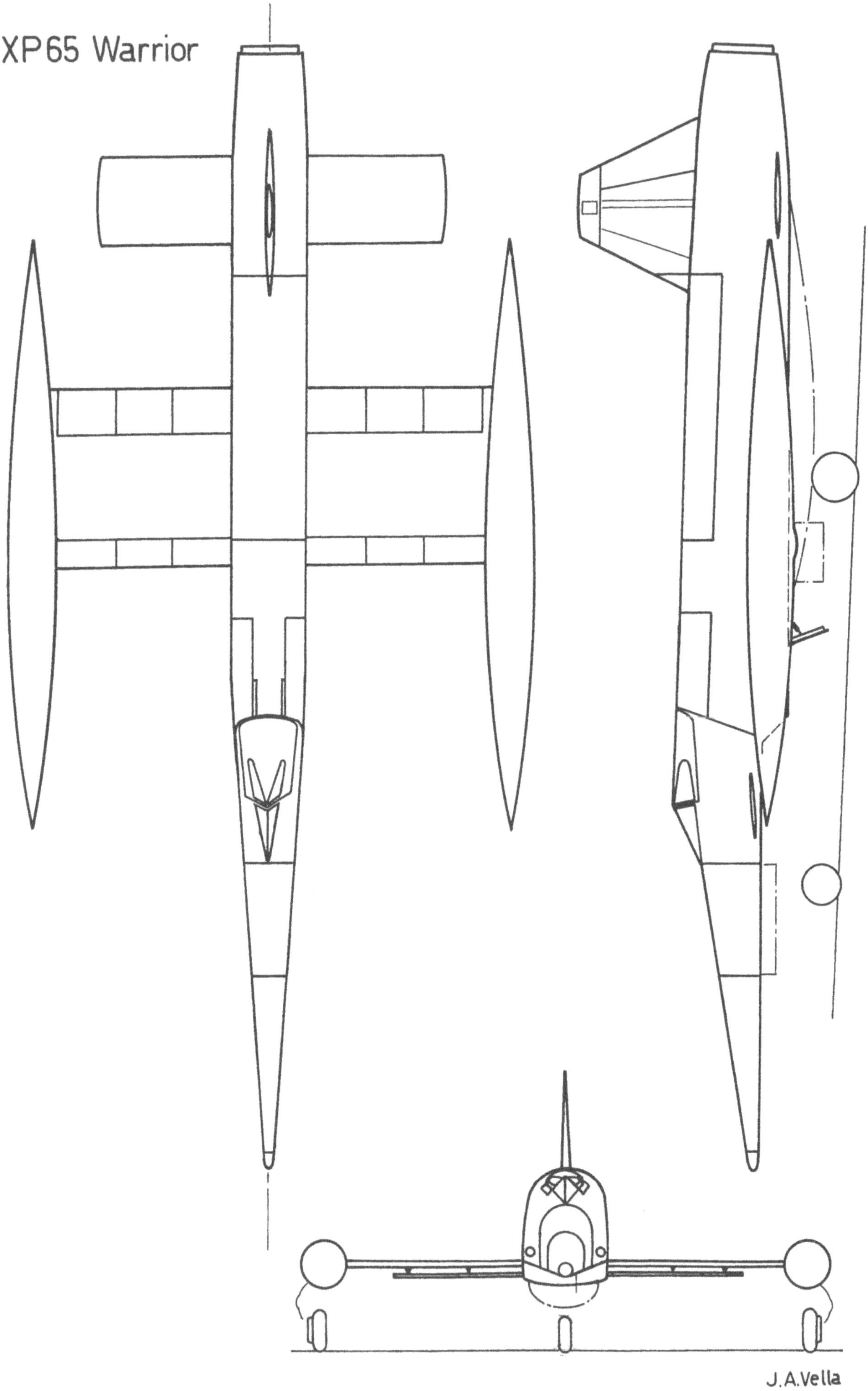

J.A.Vella

XP65 Warrior

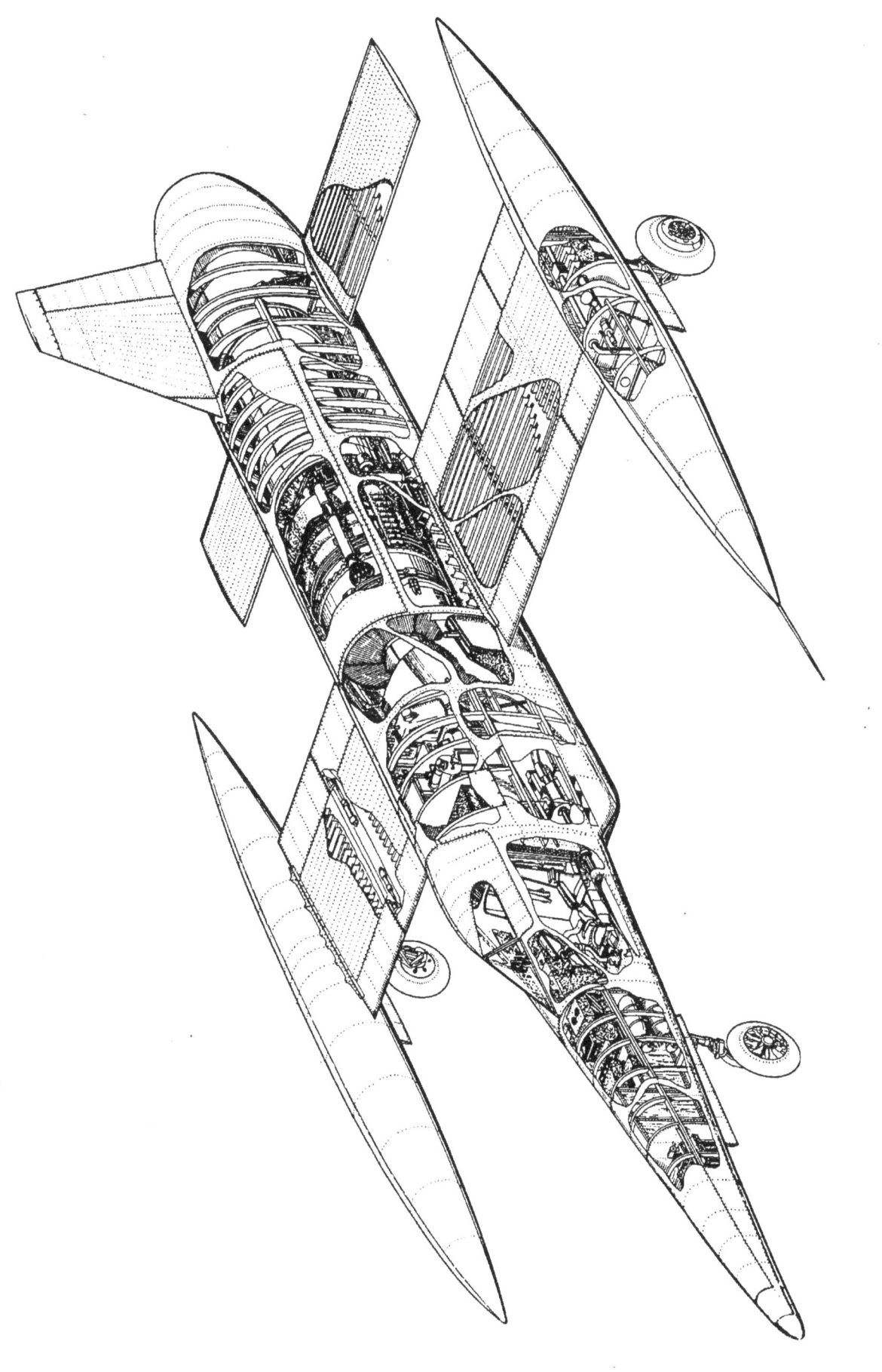

XP65 Warrior

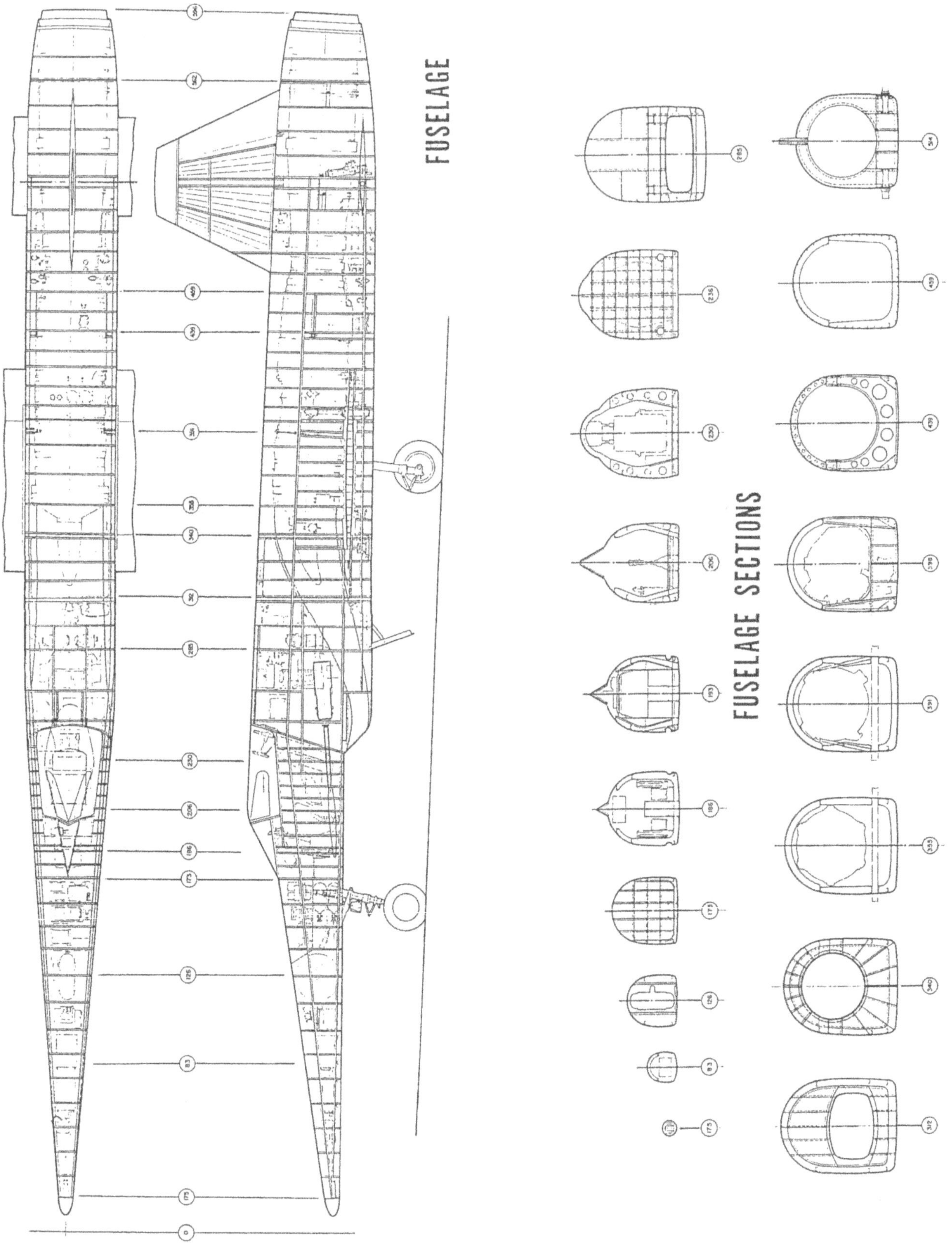

XP65 Warrior

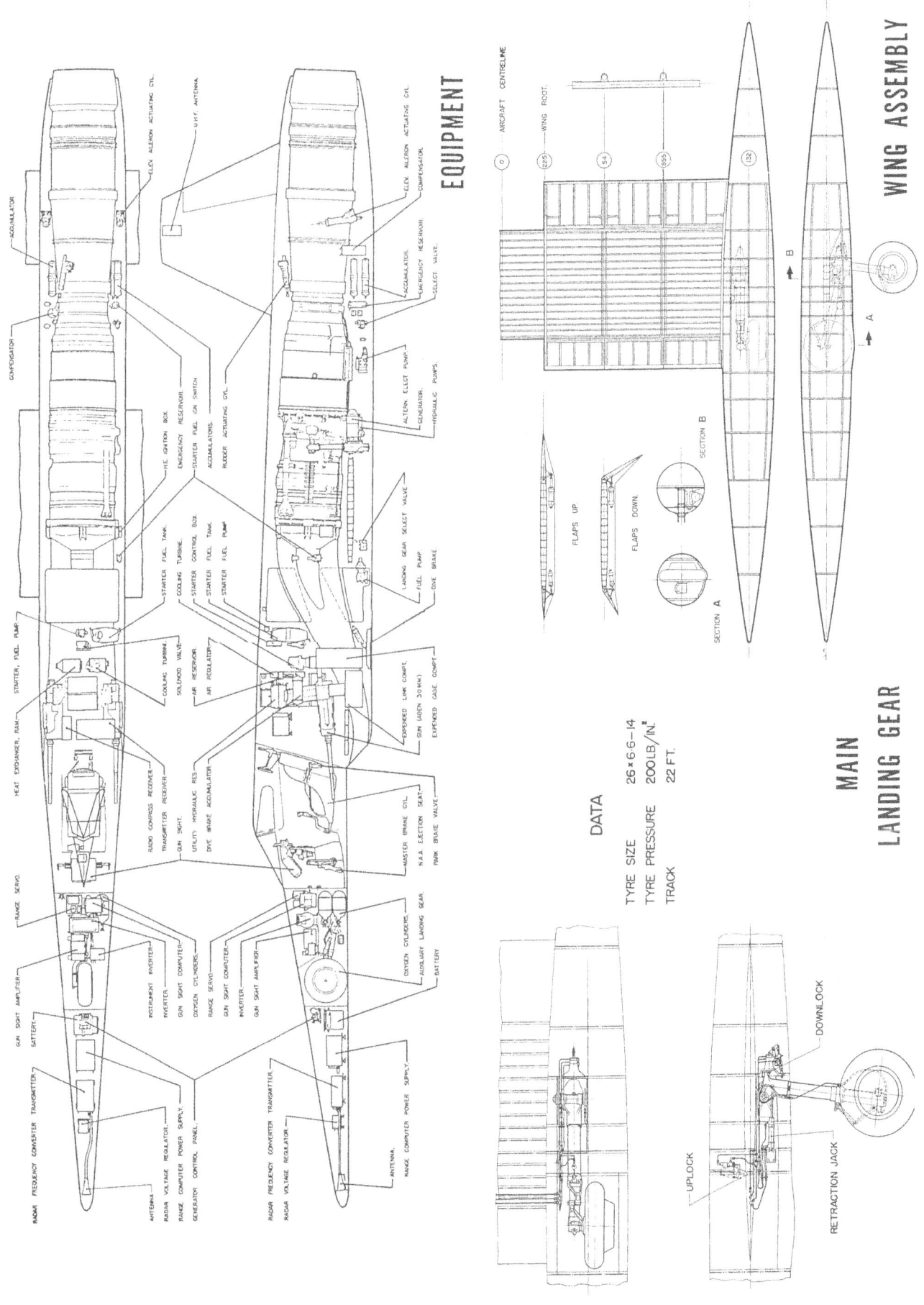

XP65 Warrior

A company 1/24th scale model of the XP65 concept showing the aggressive look of its fast combat jet concept. **J.A. Vella Collection**

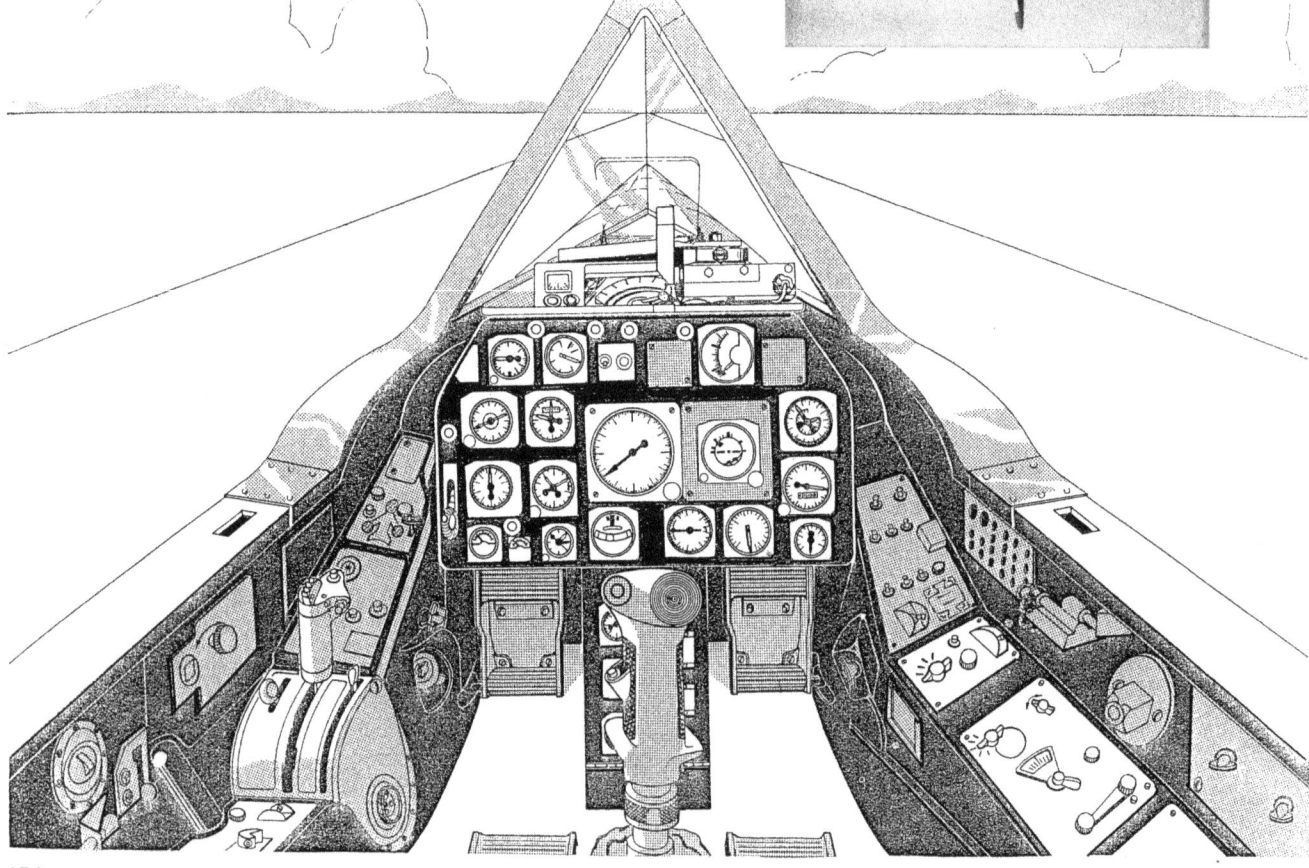

XP66

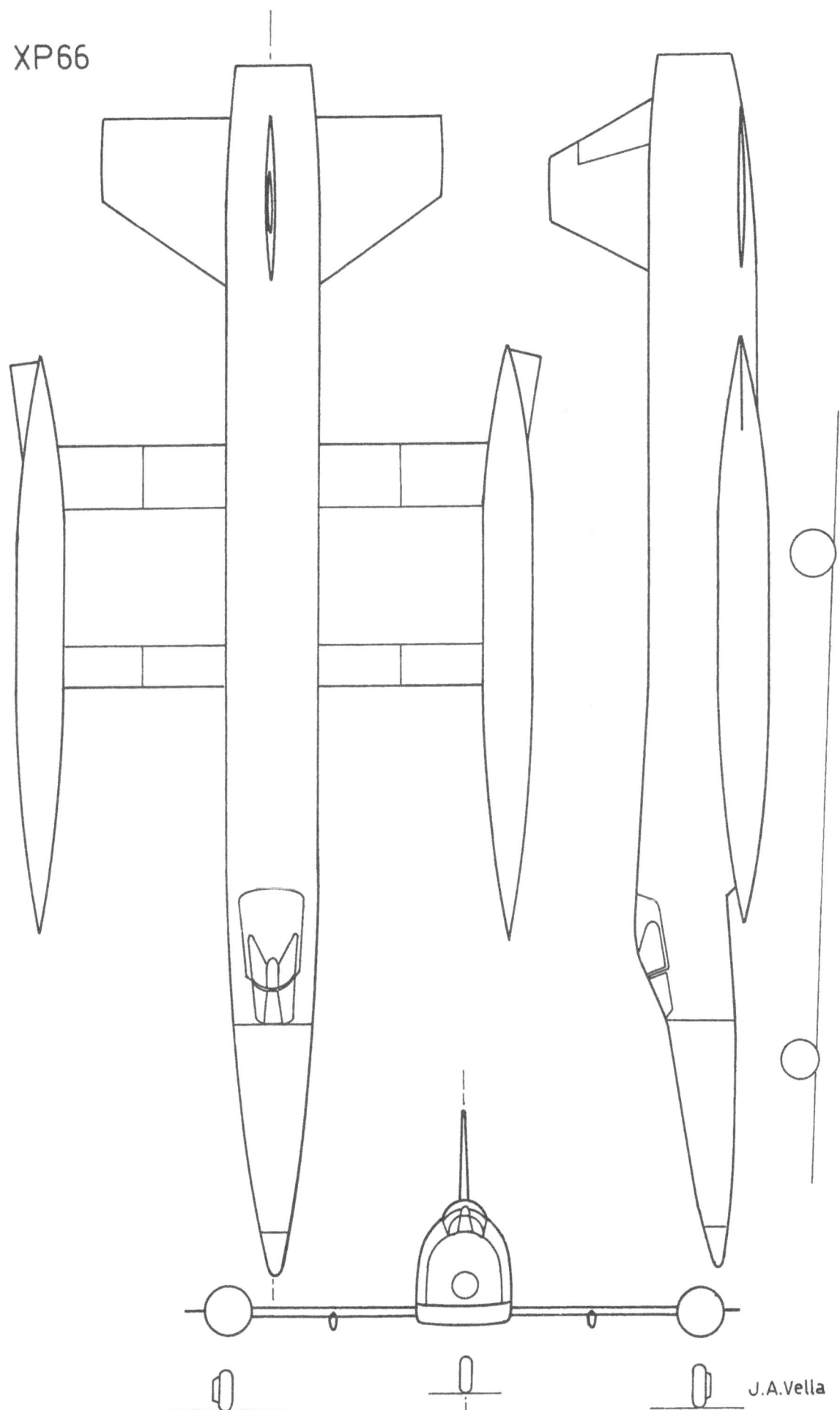

Specifications	XP65 Fighter			
Powerplant	One Rolls Royce Avon RA-24R turbojet of 10,000 lb thrust dry and 11,250 lb thrust with reheat Specific fuel consumption 0.88 lb/hr/lb			
Performance	TO dist (at 18,820 lb)	1,800 ft		
	Climb speed	520 kts		
	Approach speed	140 kts		
	Landing dist (at 12,870 lb)	1,800 ft		
	1. <u>Air Superiority Mission</u>: TO initial rate of climb 34,000 ft/min. Cruise at Mach 0.85, drop fuselage tank & accelerate to Mach 1.5 to Mach 2.0 at 45,000 ft. Combat radius 400 nm with 2 cannon & 860 gall fuel			
	2. <u>Fighter Bomber Mission</u>: TO initial rate of climb 27,700 ft/min. Cruise at Mach 0.85; SL attack with 2 cannon & two 1,200 lb bombs & 860 gall. Combat radius 250 nm.			
	3. <u>Ground Attack Mission</u>: Eight 3 in rockets, 2 napalm bombs, 860 gall fuel. Combat radius 250 nm			
	4. <u>Long Range Mission</u>: TO initial climb rate 28,000 ft/min with 2 cannon & 980 gall fuel. Five minutes at 45,000 ft at sonic speed. Combat radius 600 nm.			
	5. <u>Ferry Mission</u>: With 980 gall fuel, range 1,400 nm			
Weights	Empty	11,060 lb		
	Combat	14,710 lb		
	Disposable load	5,550 lb		
	AUW with 610 gall fuel	6,610 lb		
	AUW with 860 gall fuel	18,820 lb		
	Landing	12,870 lb		
Dimensions	Wing span	23 ft 3 ins	Aspect ratio	2.75
	Mean chord	8 ft	Wing area	176 sq ft
	T/C ratio 3.5% Modified Bi-convex			
	Tailplane span	14 ft 6 ins	Tailplane Aspect ratio	2.26
	Tailplane area	54 sqft	Chord	3ft 9 ins
	Vertical fin area	25 sqft	Length	47 ft
	Max fuselage width	3 ft 9 ins	Max fuselage depth	5 ft 2 ins
	Height	12 ft 9 ins	Turning circle	32 ft
	Main wheel pressure	200 psi	Nose wheel tyre pressure	80 psi
	Wheelbase	17 ft 6 ins	Track	22 ft
Armament	Two 30 mm Aden cannon. Eight 3 inch Mk 3 rockets in 4 vertical pairs. External stores limit to 2,400 lb ie 2 x 1,200 lb or 2 x 60 gall fuel tanks on inboard wing stations.			

The horizontal tail of a similar parallel chord layout to the wing was to provide both pitch and roll control through differential action. The power to drive the flaps, undercarriage, airbrake and control surfaces was derived from a 3,000 psi hydraulic system identical to that on the CA-27 Sabre.

Because the lower mid-fuselage was free from major intrusions, such as the main undercarriage units, it was possible to fit a flush, jettisonable, low drag, auxiliary fuel tank of 250 gallons capacity. Further fuel could be carried in two underwing 60 gallon tanks. Delivery of nuclear weapons was promoted but this was well outside the Government national and foreign defence policy of that era.

XP66

The XP66 was a growth derivative and although it retained the basic shape of the XP65, it introduced a slightly more curvaceous nose/windscreen/canopy combination and a horizontal tail with leading edge sweep set directly in line with the wing. Its technical spec data was not locateble. The XP66 was dated August 18, 1954.

Bibliography: XP64/65/66 Warrior Air Superiority Fighter
Reid, C.J., (May 1954). Engineering Report AA96. Air Superiority Fighter. Commonwealth Aircraft Corporation.

XP67 / XP68 FIGHTER AIRCRAFT
December 1954

The AA95 engineering brochure simply called it the *Fighter*. The XP68 was put forward to the same Air Staff Requirement as for the previous XP65 *'Warrior'* Air Superiority Fighter, but it was to have a cleaner wing design. It was a concept intended to challenge the performance of the Lockheed F-104A Starfighter, the aircraft which caught some initial lukewarm attention within the RAAF as a possible replacement for the CA-27 Sabre.

Aircraft Description - XP67

The XP67 was the initial, October 1954, lead-in idea from the CAC Preliminary Design Group. Little information has survived. Intended engine selection is not recorded. It was a long, strangely proportioned vehicle with a 25 ft span, an overall length of 51 ft 6 ins and an internal fuel capacity for 680 gallons. An upward hinging canopy that almost blended into the upper fuselage decking gave restricted rearward pilot vision. The most unusual element was the tracked wheel arrangement on the main undercarriage legs which permitted the aircraft a low footprint loading of 50 psi, a complicated concept tested overseas with limited success.

The RAAF requested that its next air superiority and offensive fighter be capable of operating from hastily prepared surfaces at low tyre pressures in distances of less than 6,000 feet. The rubberised,

XP67

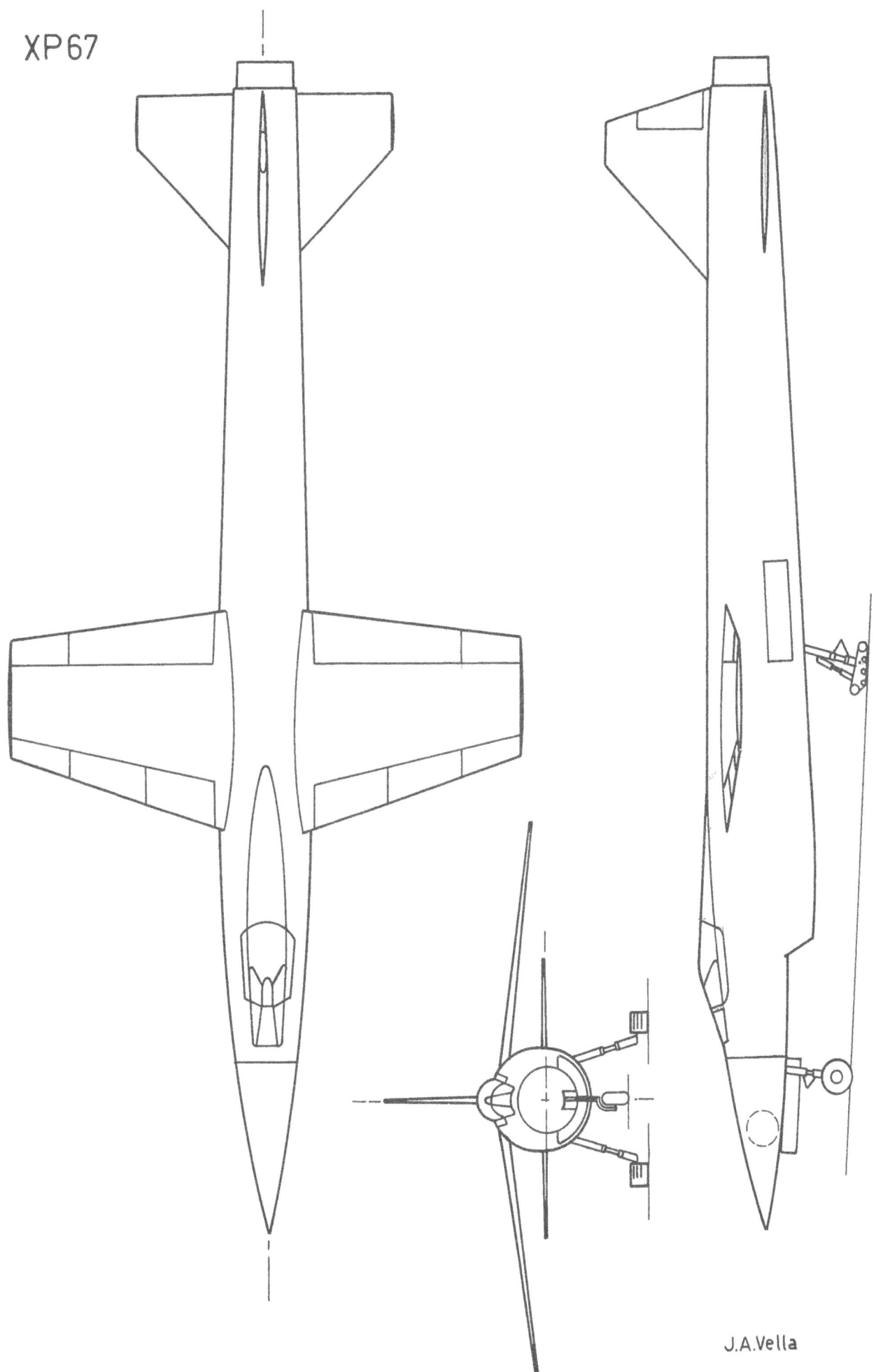

J.A.Vella

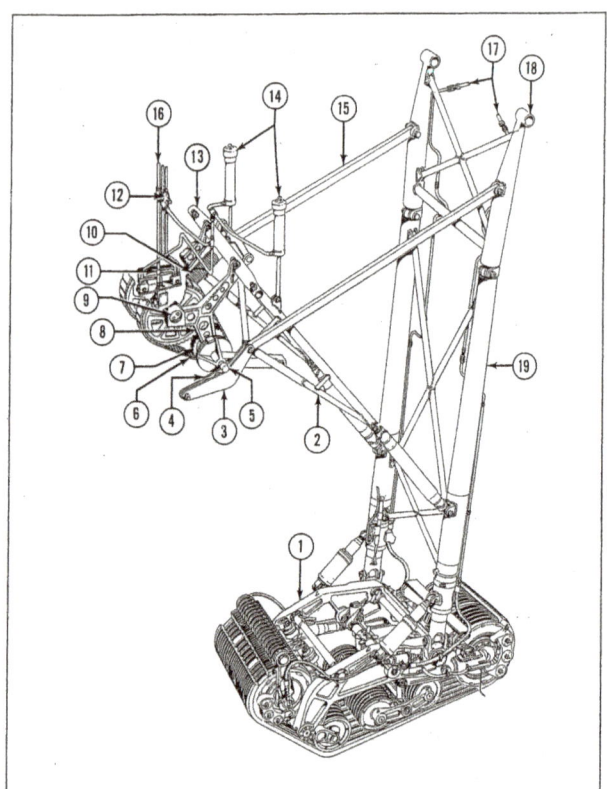

Figure 86A. Main Landing Gear (Track type airplanes)

1. Track unit
2. Drag strut
3. Locking link
4. Retracting arm
5. Torque shaft
6. Chain
7. Small sprocket
8. Retracting mechanism support
9. Adjustment pivot
10. Actuator
11. Three-way valves
12. Pressure relief valve
13. Cross tube
14. Emergency extension shock absorbers
15. Connecting link
16. Retraction booster hydraulic lines
17. Hydraulic brake lines
18. Upper truss
19. Shock struts

Above: Detail of main undercarriage for soft field operation tested on the Fairchild C-82A Packet transport aircraft. This style of main undercarriage was suggested for the CAC XP67 fighter. **Fairchild Aircraft Corp C-82, 1955 Maintenance Manual via Richard Sanders**

steel wire caterpillar belt undercarriage was seen as doing away with increasing large diameter low pressure tyres, requiring less stowage space and capable of handling a variety of soft surfaces. Military application started with George H.Dowty, the English undercarriage specialist firm. It tested tracks prepared in 1938 for the Westland Lysander. After WW2, Douglas A-20 Boston (4466) with main undercarriage tracked units was extensively tested and flown to take-off speeds from mud and soft sand surfaces. In the USA Goodyear and Firestone installed nose and massive main gear tracked units on Boeing B-50 (BK-118) and a Convair XB-36. Fairchild C-82A Packet (45-57746) was tested during 1948 and 18 aircraft were to be retrofitted with the caterpillar units. Twelve were completed but USAF trials revealed the complicated track mechanism to be most unreliable in the field.

Aircraft Description - XP68

The XP68 was the follow-on, detailed and documented concept put forward in December 1954. The operational functions of the design for an aircraft powered by a Rolls Royce Avon RA-19R afterburning turbojet were for the vehicle:

- To attain combat altitudes and sustained supersonic flight at levels in excess of 60,000 ft.
- To be a primary missile carrying interceptor with a secondary low level offensive capability
- To retain the take-off and landing characteristics of the existing CA-27 Sabre

The resultant configuration did not lack for an aggressive appearance. The core of the engine sat under a square-ended one piece wing of equal leading and trailing edge sweep angles with a small anhedral angle and a 23 ft span – a planform very similar to that of the F-104A. The 4.5 foot diameter fuselage with its long reheat tailpipe extended 48 feet in length. The vertical and horizontal tail surfaces had the same 3.75% thickness modified biconvex aerofoil section of the wing. As with the previous XP64/65/66/67 ventures, the structure and skin was to be of stainless steel stiffened by closely spaced stringers.

An attack and search radar of ten miles range was located ahead of a one piece, upward hinging, slightly raised canopy. Its integral sharply raked vee windscreen almost blended into the upper fuselage decking. Engine air was fed via a simple ramp intake created by flattening the round under surface of the cockpit enclosure, creating a shock wave which slowed down the speed of the air entering the engine duct. Two petal-type ventral airbrakes were positioned a short distance behind the lower leading edge of the intake duct.

The planned Rolls Royce 10,700 lb dry thrust Avon RA-19R afterburning turbojet appears to have been an offer (to CAC) of a special design derived from the RA-7R or the RA-14 (Mk 201), type tested in April 1953 at a dry thrust rating of 9,500 lb. (The RA-19R engine is not recorded in RR engine technical documents or mentioned elsewhere.)

Fuel was stored in three fuselage tanks; one immediately behind the cockpit above the engine inlet face, the other two above the engine and tailpipe. The main undercarriage units positioned at mid-fuselage in line with the trailing edge flap hinge line, retracted rearward to rest at an inclined angle above the tailpipe. Below and to the rear of the undercarriage storage space were two semi-externally mounted Aden 30mm cannon inclined at a shallow depression angle to aid in the low level attack role. Access to the cannon was from below the fuselage and through upper fuselage doors in the voluminous rear fuselage to re-arm with 150 rounds of ammunition for each gun.

Access to the wing surface powered controls and the mounting of the one-piece wing was through an upper centre fuselage panel whilst a large ventral door opened to the engine auxiliaries, batteries, hydraulic pumps, heat exchangers and the removal of the engine. The engine reheat pipe was reached through a removable rear fuselage section. A brake chute was to be used following touch down.

The low set horizontal tail was an all-moving one piece unit driven by a single jack. In the air intercept mission, one missile was to be mounted on each wingtip and another could be carried in a semi-recessed manner under the centre fuselage.

Like the XP65 Warrior before it, the XP68 was to be capable of carrying a nuclear weapon. This weapon, a 1,000 lb conventional bomb load or a retractable unguided rocket battery was to be carried in the semi-flush bay in lieu of the gun package. The nuclear weapon capability was ahead of its time, as the UK had still not yet produced the tactical small 2,000 lb weapon for the Canberra bomber. It was a promotion selling brochure. However Australia had already become the testing ground for the many series of British atomic weapons tests. The RAAF Air Staff were certainly anxious to obtain a nuclear capable aircraft should this option have become available. The 1954/55 Aircraft Mission to the UK and USA led by AVM A.M. Murdoch had settled for either the the UK's nuclear capable Avro Vulcan or the Handley Page Victor should the Australian technical, political and economic conditions allowed it.

In the traditional step-by-step CAC philosophy of incremental design, the cockpit layout was nearly identical with that of the CA-27 and equipped with Sabre systems. Almost all the mechanical components of the electric, hydraulic and power systems together

XP68

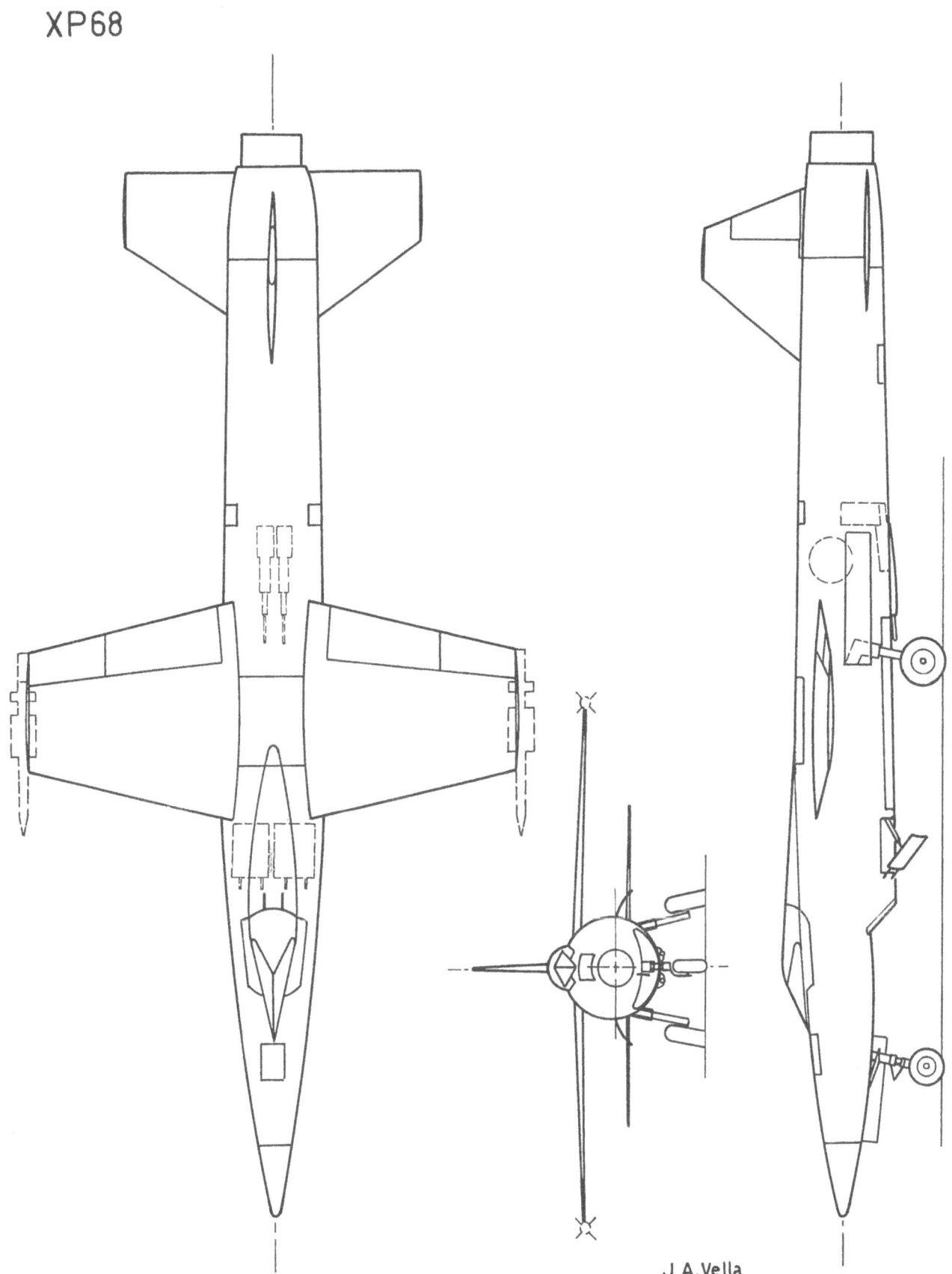

J.A.Vella

XP68

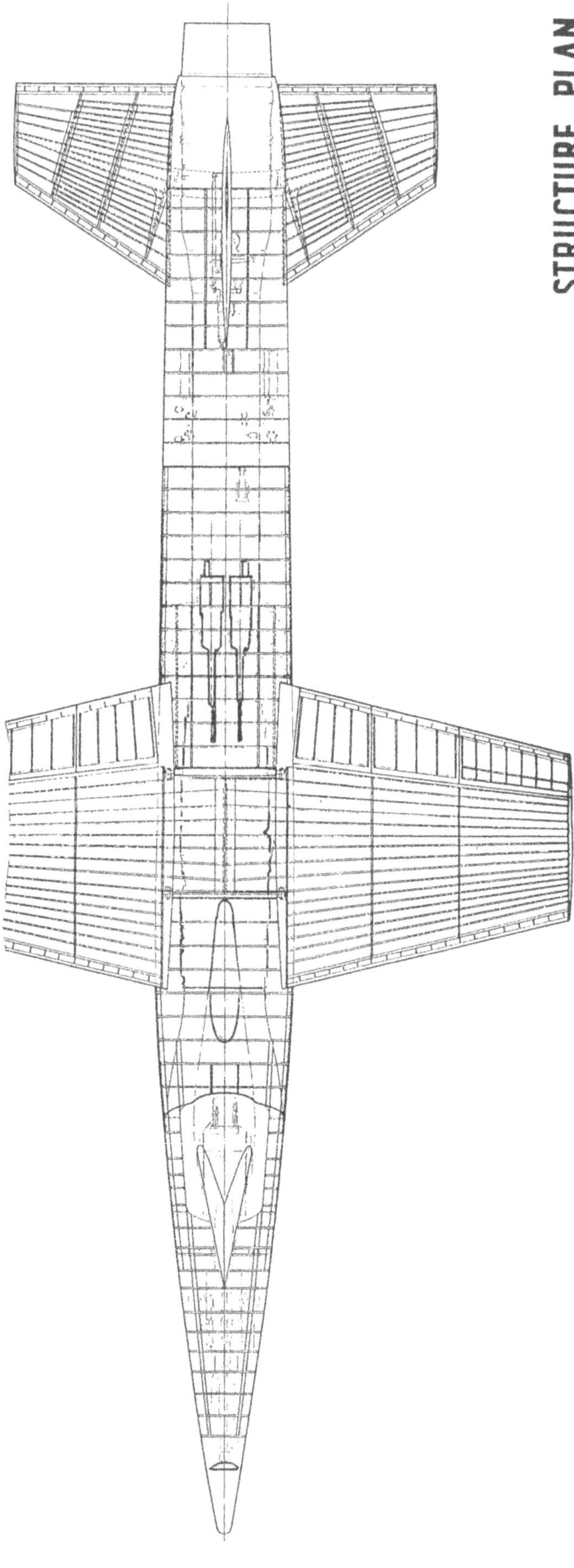

STRUCTURE PLAN

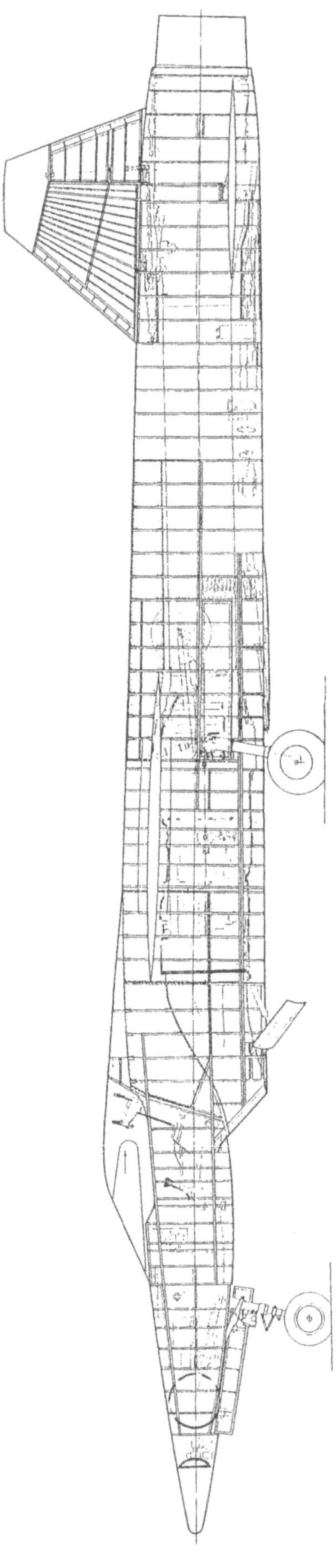

STRUCTURE ELEVATION

XP68

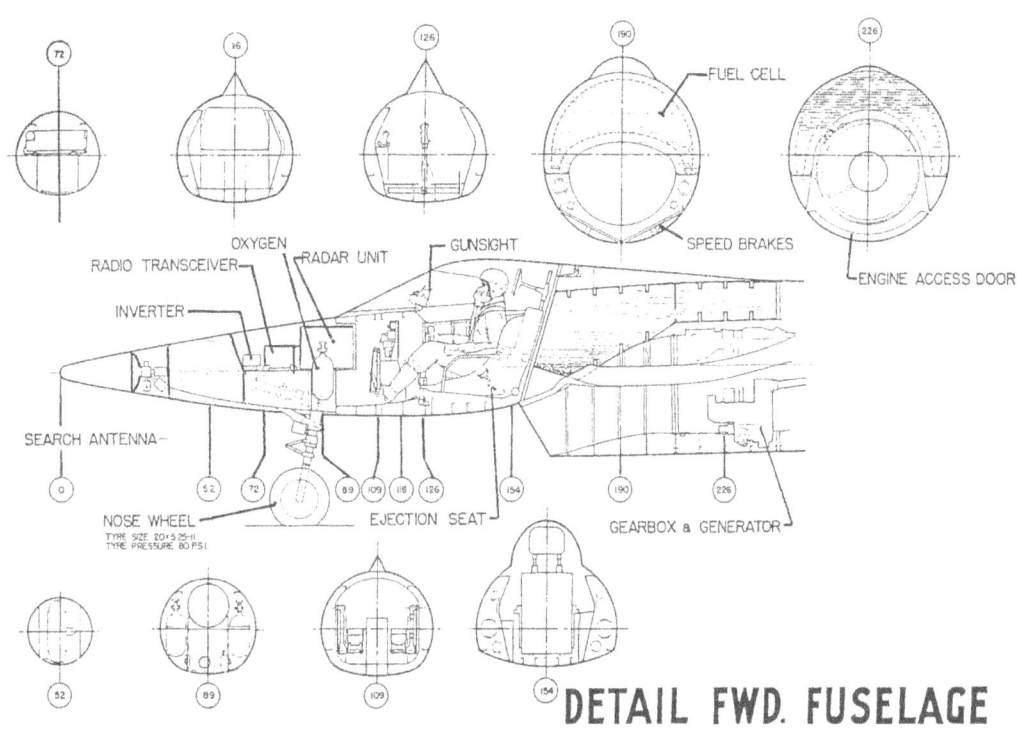

DETAIL FWD. FUSELAGE

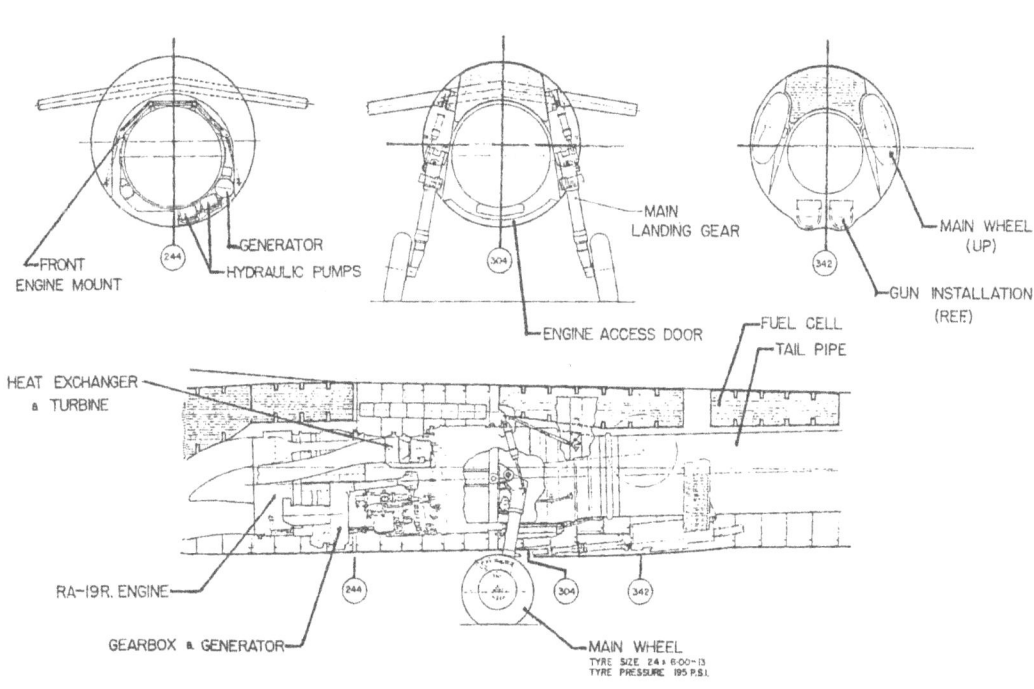

DETAIL MID. FUSELAGE

XP68

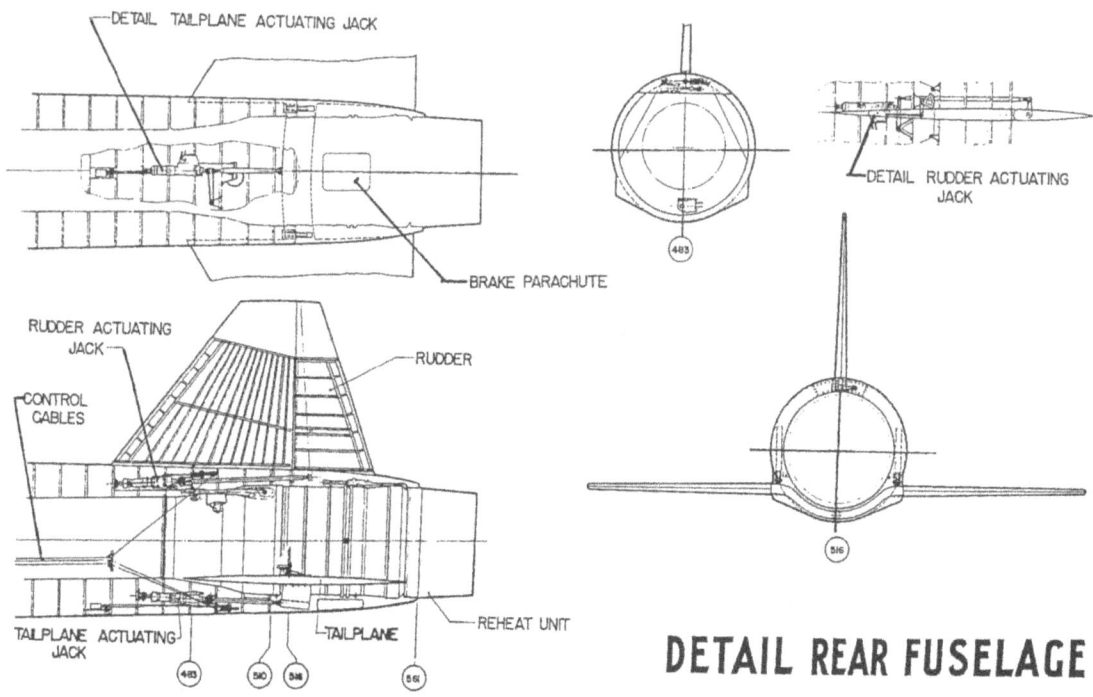

DETAIL REAR FUSELAGE

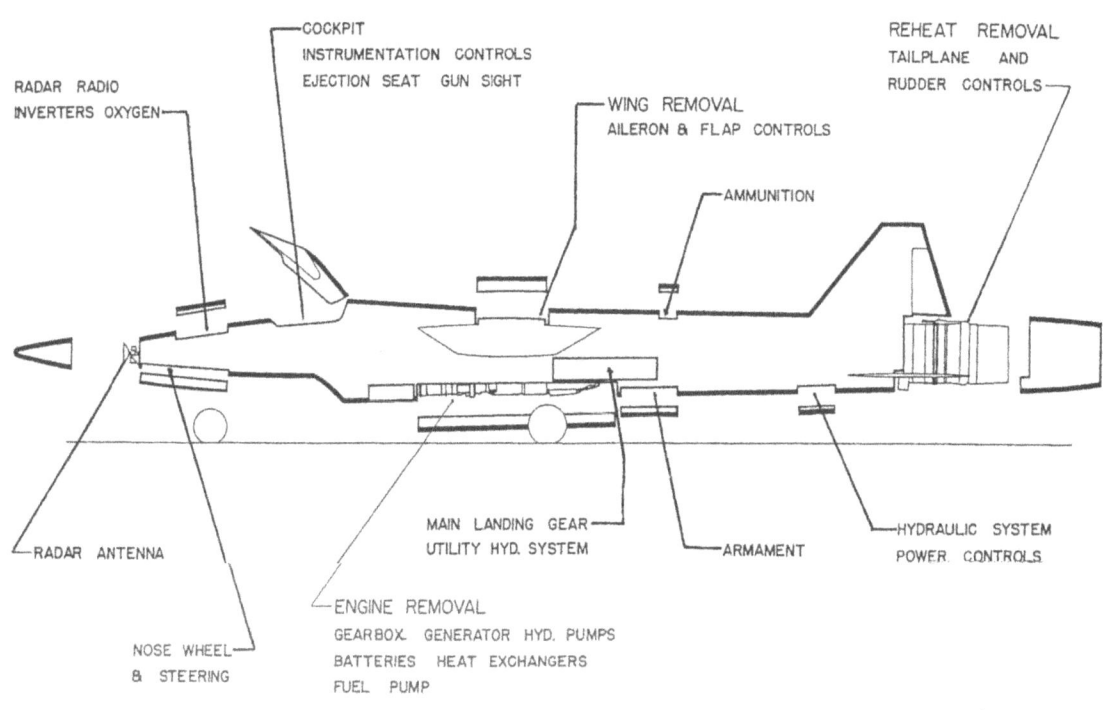

SERVICEABILITY

Specifications	XP68 Fighter Aircraft			
Powerplant	One Rolls Royce Avon RA-19R turbojet of 10,700 lb thrust dry and 12,500 lb thrust with reheat Specific fuel consumption 0.88 lb/hr/lb			
Performance	Max speed (dry) at 45,000 ft	Mach 1.5		
	Max speed (reheat) at SL	Mach 1.2		
	Max speed at 35,000 ft	Mach 2.0		
	Max speed at 60,000 ft	Mach 2.0		
	Rate of climb SL at M 0.9	50,00 ft/min		
	Rate of climb at 35,000 ft at M 0.9	13,000 ft/min		
	Rate of climb at 35,000 ft at M 1.5	28,000 ft/min		
	Rate of climb at 35,000 ft at M2.0	3,000 ft/min		
	Rate of climb at 60,000 ft at M 2.0	5,000 ft/min		
	Time to 35,000 ft	2.0 mins		
	Time to 60,000 ft	5.2 mins		
	TO dist	1,400 ft		
	TO dist over 50 ft	2,000 ft		
	Landing dist at 11,350 lb	1,500 ft		
	Landing dist over 50 ft	3,000 ft		
	Design diving speed at SL	Mach 1.3		
	Load factor proof	6.66		
	Load factor ultimate	10		
	Combat radius	300 nm		
Weights	Empty	10,350 lb		
	Engine dry weight	3,300 lb		
	Disposable load	5,150 lb		
	Normal TO	13,000 lb		
	Max TO (with 550 gall fuel)	15,500 lb		
Dimensions	Wing span	23 ft	Aspect ratio	2.88
	Root chord	9 ft 10 ins	Tip chord	5 ft 4 ins
	Wing area	117 sq ft	Wing T/C ratio 3.75% Modified Bi-convex	
	Wing LE sweep	7°	Wing TE sweep	-7°
	Tailplane span	14 ft	Tailplane aspect ratio	2.26
	Tailplane area	50 sq ft	LE sweep at 25% chord	27°
	Tailplane root chord	6ft 6 ins	Tip chord	3 ft 4 ins
	Height vertical fin	4 ft 6 ins	Tailplane T/C ratio 3.75% Modified Bi-convex	
	LE sweep at 25% chord	26°	Vertical fin area	21.8 sq ft
	Tip chord	2 ft 4 ins	Root chord	7 ft 6 ins
	Length	48 ft 4 ins	Vertical fin T/C ratio 4% Modified Bi-convex	
	Height	11 ft	Max fuselage dia	4 ft 8 ins
	Nose wheel tyre pressure	80 psi	Main wheel pressure	195 psi
Armament	Two 30 mm Aden cannon with 150 rpg; two air-to-air missiles. Alternate internal rocket battery pack, conventional bombs or a nuclear weapon to a load of 1,000 lb			

with those of the air-conditioning were basically CA-27 derived. The main landing gear with modified pivot and axle was CA-27, as was the nose wheel installation. The attack and search radar was the new element as was the proposed use of stainless steel, the material which had been tested and flown on the research aircraft, the Douglas X-3 Stilletto. CAC had received the research test results of this aircraft.

The XP68 was not fully designed but the accompanying drawings show the detail location of stringers and spars etc determined from preliminary stress analysis data.

The XP64 / 65 / 66 / 67 / 68 series with its exciting Mach 1.5 to Mach 2.0 expectations did not proceed. The RAAF did not have the faith (or the finances) to believe that the local designs could match or exceed the performance of the Lockheed F-104A Starfighter.

Bibliography: XP67 / XP68 Fighter Aircraft

Reid, C.J. (December 1954). Engineering Report AA95. Fighter. Commonwealth Aircraft Corporation.

Dowty, George, H. (September 30, 1943). Track Landing Gear. *Flight & Aircraft Engineer*.

Fairchild Aircraft Corporation. (January 15, 1955). *C-82A Packet Transport, Erection & Maintenance Instructions .T.O.1C-82A-2 (Revised)*. Fairchild Aircraft Corporation. Maryland, USA.

'Favonius', (July 7, 1949). American Notebook, Some Caterpillars Fly. *Flight & Aircraft Engineer*. London

Maclaren, O.F. (June 1949). Caterpillar Tracks. *Aeronautics*. Mitchell, Kent, A. (Spring 1993). Endless track Landing Gear. *American Aviation Historical Society Journal*.

P302 / XP69 IMPROVED AVON SABRE
April 1955

1955 could be classified the banner year for the CAC Sabre so numerous were the reports and studies that the design group originated in order to extend the performance of the airframe without incurring major structural change. All of these studies were of a short term nature but some were more intense than others.

The first of these dated April 19, 1955 was to upgrade the equipment fit of the aircraft, at the same time reducing its empty weight. By the installation of different radio navigational bearing equipment, a new VHF transceiver, revised braking units, high velocity Aden cannon, alternative ranging radar and power supply, and utilizing a thinner fuel cell lining material, the weight of the empty airframe could be reduced by 480 lbs whilst providing a useful 50 gallon increase in fuel capacity.

Increasing the wing area by the addition of 12 inches to each wing tip would have raised the service ceiling by 1,000 feet (the latter modification was a feature of the established North American F-86H and L variants and data was available to CAC from NAA). Two extra weapon pylon stations were suggested and a Solar jet pipe was to be introduced.

Bibliography: P302 / XP69 Improved Avon Sabre
Commonwealth Aircraft Corporation. (April 19, 1955). Engineering Report AA70. Improved Avon Sabre. Preliminary Design Study.

P314 / XP70 WINJEEL-TRICYCLE UNDERCARRIAGE
November 1955

To bring about an early familiarity with handling a tricycle undercarriage type aircraft during flying training, CAC designed a modification to fit a nose-wheel on its CA-25 Winjeel Basic Trainer.

Report AA74 of November 22, 1955 suggested the benefits of such a modification included improved forward vision on the ground, reduced take-off run, less tendency for the aircraft to bounce on landing, more efficient use of the main wheel brakes and easier handling in cross wind landings.

The obvious changes were a rearward retracting, dual wheeled, castoring nose leg assembly (60° on either side of centre); relocation of the main undercarriage legs three feet further aft to permit forward retraction; the storing of the retracted mainwheels ahead of the front spar in streamlined fairings and the addition of a tail bumper.

In the retracted position the nosewheel storage space would have meant the relocation of the battery, the carburettor air control box, the oil cooler location and its intake.

A 3,000 psi hydraulic system driven by an engine pump was selected. The overall penalty was a 100 lb increase in weight offset by a seven knot increase in maximum level speed. A large amount of

Specifications	P314 / XP70 Winjeel, Tricycle Undercarriage	
Powerplant	One Pratt & Whitney R985-AN2 Wasp Junior 9 cyl radial engine of 445 hp.	
Performance	Max speed at 4,460 lb	158 kts
Weights	Max TO	4,460 lb
Dimensions	Wing span	38 ft 9 ins
	Length	29 ft 6 ins
	Height	9 ft
	Wheelbase	6ft 6.5 ins
	Track	9 ft 8 ins
	Main wheel tyre dia 7.25-7.75 ins	46 psi
	Nose wheel tyre dia 5.7-6 ins	50 psi

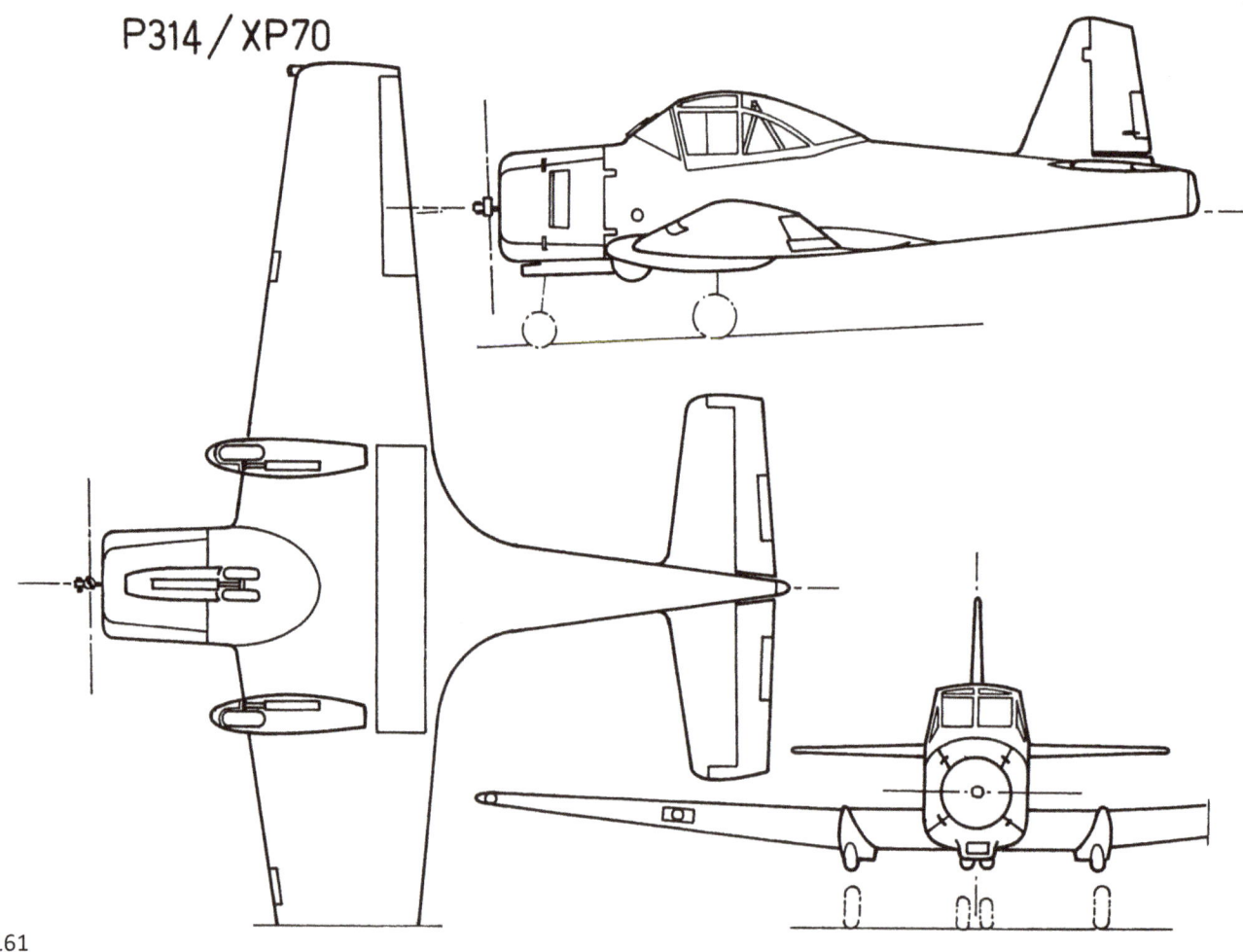

Two artist's impressions of P314 in flight and on the ground. **HDHV**

detail design had been completed but the RAAF lacked the funds to take up the proposal.

Bibliography: P314 / XP70 Winjeel, Tricycle Undercarriage
Humphries, D. (November 2, 1955). Engineering Report AA74. Winjeel Tricycle Undercarriage. Commonwealth Aircraft Corporation.

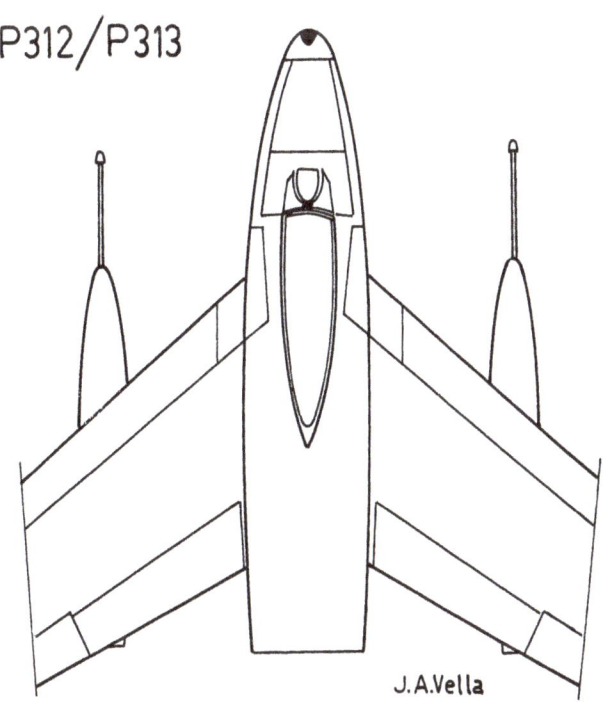

P312 / P315 SABRE, IN-FLIGHT REFUELLING
November 1955

Proposal P302 Improved Avon Sabre was followed by two interesting appraisals by H. Mann, Group Leader-Power Plants and Ian Ring, Chief Engineer, whose suggestion of November 9, 1955 was to install an in-flight refuelling capability to the Sabre Mk 31 and Mk 32. Deployments of the Sabre to the SEATO areas of responsibility were to become repeated and complicated undertakings.

This capability was to be achieved by installing a refuelling probe and the required valves to the nose of each of the two 166 gallon underwing tanks (each 99.5 inches from the aircraft centreline) as well as extra valves, switches and vents to the wing LE tanks. Each probe would have only supplied the underwing tank and the wing leading edge tanks on its particular side. With a tanker delivery rate of 280 gall/min it would have filled one side of the aircraft in 90 seconds. At this stage in its flight the optimum profile would have put the aircraft 600 nm away from base at a height of 25,000 feet. The extreme range of the aircraft with underwing tanks jettisoned when emptied would have been 2,400 nm. No mention was made of the aircraft handling considerations when receiving fuel load one wing at a time.

Significant design work was carried out on this proposal but the RAAF's shortage of funds would not allow it to follow through with this low risk operationally viable idea. (The US Navy's NAA FJ-3 Fury had been fitted with a probe directly under the port wing.)

Bibliography: Sabre, In-Flight Refuelling
Ring, I.H.(November 9, 1951). Engineering Report AA72. In-Flight Refuelling of Sabre Mk 31. Commonwealth Aircraft Corporation.

Ring, I.H. (November 9, 1951). Engineering Report AA73. In-Flight Refuelling of Sabre Mk 32. Commonwealth Aircraft Corporation.

P321 / XP71 SABRE, ROCKET BOOST [1]
December 1955

The essence of Proposal P321 by John Kentwell, Senior Design Engineer (Structures) was to improve the Sabre fighter's interception performance by the addition of a single chamber Napier Scorpion (Luton, UK) rocket booster engine (this engine had its first test run in May 1956). The upper portion of the rocket pack was to fit into a shallow recess in the lower fuselage surface behind the mid fuselage break. The rocket engine of 2,250 lb thrust ran on 64 gallons of High Test Peroxide and kerosene, the latter to be tapped from the engine fuel supply line.

The weight of the unit would have caused a rearward shift in the centre of gravity which would have been partially alleviated by leaving the rear fuselage 77 gallon fuel cell empty but this was not sufficient in itself. The other alteration would have been to extend each wing tip by 12 inches to restore the aerodynamic balance. The engineering data to modify the wing tips was available to CAC from North American Aviation Inc. The distribution of the cross-sectional area of the pack was to be arranged so as to conform to the new NACA 'area rule' principle keeping the aircraft drag increase to a minimum. Aircraft so equipped would have been returned to their original configuration relatively easily by removing the rocket pack and sealing over the recess with a new cover panel.

It was expected the aircraft would operate with the de Havilland Firestreak missiles which would have required an equipment pod ahead of the rocket pack. The performance of the modified aircraft

P321/XP71

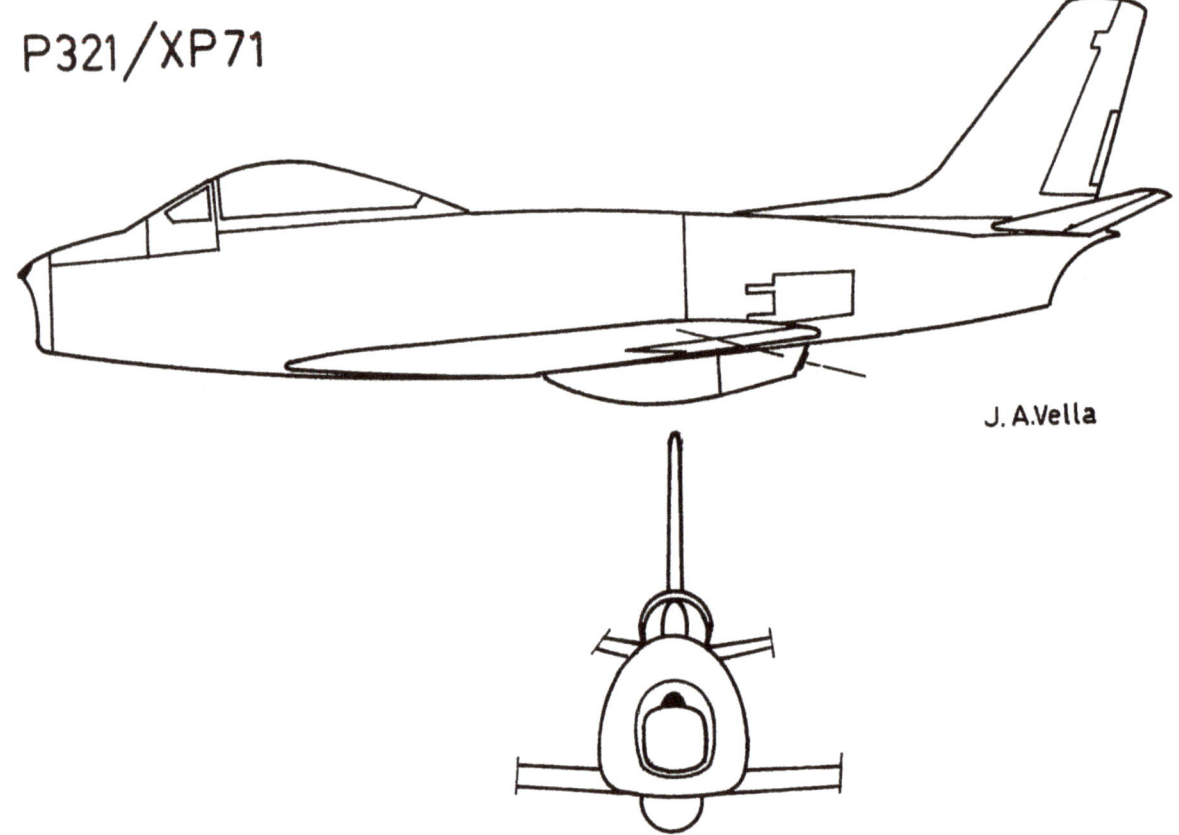
J.A.Vella

Unit	Without Rocket	With Rocket
Weight	14,900 lb	14,900 lb
Total thrust at 35,000 ft	2,420 lb	4,670 lb
Climb rate at 35,000 ft	3,850 ft/ min	11,000 ft/min
Time to 35,000 ft	9.25 min	1.6 min
Time to 50,000 ft	14.1 min	6.4 min
Turning radius at 35,000 ft	1.45 miles	1.74 miles
Turning radius at 50,000 ft	4.10 miles	6.35 miles

was expected to be constrained by the maximum useable lift co-efficient of 0.6 at 50,000 feet, the limiting Mach Number at that altitude and by the rocket's burn duration time of 96 seconds. The engineering report gave estimates for the enhanced performance. These show an increased combat turning radius for an increased total thrust. The aircraft weights were identical due to the planned reduction in internal fuel load. Some of the expected salient performance figures are shown in the table above.

Bibliography: P321 / XP71 Sabre, Rocket Boost [1]
Kentwell, J. (December 7, 1955).Engineering Report AA76. Rocket Boost for Avon Sabre. Commonwealth Aircraft Corporation.

P322 / XP72 SABRE, NASARR INSTALLATION
December 1955

The report of December 13,1955 for the replacement of the AN/APG-30 gun ranging radar on the CA-27 was the work of D.Humphries, Chief Engineer and J.Kentwell (Design Engineer). Its alternative, the North American Search and Ranging Radar (NASARR) had a fighter sized target detection range of approximately 8 nm and incorporated blind firing capabilities together with immediate transition to optical mode under suitable weather conditions.

This all offered a greater improvement in the detection / destruction of aerial targets in conjunction with the possible use of guided missiles as would have been necessary to take full advantage of the work underway to integrate the test installation of the Blue Jay (Firestreak) guided missiles (Proposal P280). All changes to the fuselage structure would have taken place above the upper longeron, together with a re-arrangement of the gunsight components, battery and inverter and the addition of a radar indicator screen in the cockpit. A fractional lengthening and raising of the upper intake nose contours were the minor fuselage alterations.

By combining the practical results from the de Havilland Firestreak configured test aircraft and the study reports of Proposal 321 for rocket boost, when fitted with the NASARR, it was estimated that Avon Sabres in this configuration could intercept a bomber cruising at 50,000 feet at Mach 0.85. This was only possible if the Sabre, in order to overcome its small speed margin and lack of

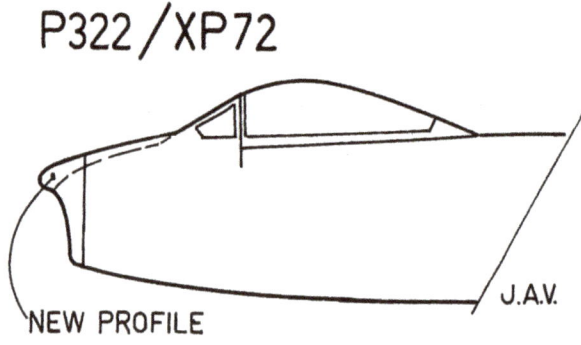
P322/XP72
NEW PROFILE / J.A.V.

manoeuvrability at bomber altitude, was able to position itself at lower altitude in front of the bomber, then turn beneath it and climb under rocket augmentation in true pursuit course to bomber altitude.

Bibliography: P322 / XP72 Sabre, NASARR Installation

Humphries, D. (December 13, 1955). Engineering Report AA77. Interception Analysis, Avon Sabre. Commonwealth Aircraft Corporation.

Commonwealth Aircraft Corporation. (December 13, 1955). Engineering Report AA78. NASARR Installation - Avon Sabre.

P280 / P282 / P301 SABRE, BLUE JAY MISSILE INSTALLATION
December 1955

One of the two Blue Jay missile test Sabres.
L. J. Wackett/MS4858/NLA.

A94-915 with Blue-Jay missile test rounds under both wings.
J. A. Vella Collection

The Sabre fuselage centreline pod fitted with control and test recording equipment. **Frank Smith**

The specialized modifications undertaken by CAC on two CA-27 Sabre aircraft to carry the Blue Jay (development code name for the de Havilland Firestreak), a first generation, infra-red, heavy, guided AAM missile were so complex, that turning the installation into a service reality was no easy undertaking.

Two airframes, A94-915 and 922 had their armament and oxygen systems removed so as to fit missile control equipment, test instrumentation and telemetry equipment for flight trials at the Woomera test range. A centreline pod was required to carry a decoder and sequencer, receiver, transmitter, recording equipment, two cameras and gyroscopes. This necessitated a small ventral fin under the rear fuselage to compensate for the forward side area of the pod and the two missiles, carried one on each underwing pylon, offset 99.5 inches from the aircraft centreline. Each missile was suspended 16.5 16.5 inches from its centre to the wing under surface.

Cooling air to the heat seeking sensors in the missile heads was supplied from high pressure air bottles located in the fuselage whilst hot air for missile control surface de-icing was routed from the engine. A94-922 flew in February 1956 in its modified form, followed in June by A94-915. Development testing continued into 1957 providing the RAAF with some operational missile operation experience. To maximize the efficiency of the installation a new ranging radar with a range of about five miles was suggested (the Sabre AN/APG radar was inadequate for the task) adding further equipment location and structural alterations.

The arrangement of equipment for operational service use would have been tackled in a different manner. The heavier, more powerful and long range capability of the Firestreak, lost out in 1959 to the relatively simple adaptation of the Raytheon Sidewinder AIM-9B heat seeking AAM to the Sabre.

Bibliography: P280 / P282 / P301 Sabre, Blue Jay Missile Installation

Commonwealth Aircraft Corporation. (December 1955). Engineering Report AA75. Sabre Blue Jay Carry-On Trials.

Commonwealth Aircraft Corporation. (December 14,1955). Engineering Report AA79. Sabre Blue Jay Installation, Avon Sabre.

BLUE JAY MISSILES ON DH SEA VENOM FIGHTER
July 1956

CAC was requested by the RAN Fleet Air Arm in 1956 to also evaluate the possible installation of the Blue Jay guided missile on its newest fighter acquisition, the de Havilland F (AW) 23 Sea Venom fighter. The only underwing station from which the missile could be supported was between the undercarriage fairing door and the wing fold break joint. The missile control equipment required space at the expense of two of the four 20mm cannon. Severe difficulties were anticipated in providing the complex routeing of hot and cold air and electrical services to the missiles through the region of the wing fuel cells.

The de Havilland Ghost engine was also totally inadequate as a source for increased hydraulic, pneumatic and electrical services. The concept was dismissed as being unworkable. However de Havilland, Christchurch, UK, successfully modified five Sea Venoms F (AW) 21 for each to carry two Firestreak missiles. They were part of the Royal Navy's Fleet Air Arm 700 and 893 Squadrons in late 1958 and successfully fired live Firestreak rounds at Fairey Firefly U9 drones flown out of RNAS Hal Far, Malta.

RAN's Fleet Air Arm DH. Sea Venom FAW 23 WZ930/804 on HMAS Melbourne, Port Melbourne. **J. A. Vella**

Bibliography: Blue Jay Missiles on DH Sea Venom Fighter

'De Havilland Sea Venom'.(1990). *Air International* Vol. 39/2.

Lindsay, Roger (1973). *De Havilland Venom*. Edward Appleby. Stockton-on-Tees, UK.

Ring, I. H. (July 18, 1956).Engineering Report AA104. Fitment of Blue Jay Missiles to De Havilland Sea Venom F (AW) 53. Commonwealth Aircraft Corporation.

XP73 JET TRAINER & XP74 EXECUTIVE TRANSPORT AIRCRAFT
August 1956

XP73 was an extension of the work carried out on the XP63 Turbojet Trainer. Led by Doug Humphries and finalized by August 22, 1956, it was a much refined and updated concept. The unsolicited design was centred on the Rolls Royce RB108 Lightweight turbojet engine, an engine designed primarily for VTOL application.

The XP73 was one half of a dual design approach, two airframe configurations, one a side by side military trainer, the other a four seater executive transport. This executive transport would have been CAC's second attempt at the civil aircraft market after the P265 Wallaby.

Common to both the XP73/XP74, was the use of boundary layer control ie blowing air tapped from the engine compressor over the wing trailing edge flaps to achieve higher lift co-efficients for a lower stalling speed from a smaller wing. The high set horizontal tail location was to avoid or lessen the aerodynamic influence of the wide fuselage. The main landing gear, control locks and control system were components from the design for the Winjeel Tricycle proposal P314.

In its XP74 four seater, pressurized, executive transport configuration with luggage and operating from a grass strip, a range of 1,050 nautical miles was expected. For this sort of operation, the aircraft was to have an on-board engine starting capability, low pressure 45 psi tyres and the ability to operate from grass fields of 2,400 feet balanced field length.

The design changes for the executive transport would come about by deleting the two ejection seats and on-board 140 gallon capacity fuel cells. Four passenger seats would be installed in this space and baggage storage provided above the nose wheel bay. Fuel would then be accommodated in two 96 gallon capacity wing tip tanks. The two cabin layouts represented two distinct aircraft types, not an interchangeable configuration from one layout to the other. The most striking feature of the design was the very large rearwards sliding canopy. This was provided to satisfy an Air Force request for sufficient cockpit cooling and ventilation whilst taxying during high ambient temperatures.

Bibliography: XP73 Jet Trainer & XP74 Executive Transport Aircraft

Commonwealth Aircraft Corporation. (August 22,1956). Engineering Report AA82. Primary Jet Trainer / Four Seat Light Transport.

CHAPTER 5. WINJEEL DERIVATIVES, PRIVATE VENTURE AIRCRAFT AND NAVAL WORK

XP75 WINJEEL, UTILITY AEROPLANE [1]
August 1956

"A bushman's aeroplane; the aeroplane for the man on the land, the aeroplane for rugged terrain."

This is how a new variant of the Winjeel Basic Trainer was being promoted in August 1956. Following the Wallaby commuter aircraft and the XP73 Executive Transport, this concept was the company's third attempt at a possible civil oriented market entry.

Unofficially dubbed the *'Camel'* it was to carry the pilot and five passengers or alternately up to 1,000 lbs of freight. The original layout of the Winjeel trainer was not lacking in space with a built-in provision for three seats and a small amount of luggage, virtually the space needed for a complement of four.

To increase this capacity it was proposed to remove some 54 inches of structure from behind the front seats and insert 72 inches of new structure, thereby increasing the overall length by 18 inches. This new insertion would have incorporated a large, side hinging, loading door on the rear port side, a new cabin roof, new floor, additional windows and a hinged section in the framed canopy for pilot entry. Two baggage areas were envisaged; one forward of the front passenger position, the other to the rear starboard side of the cabin.

The retractable sun blind covering used in the Trainer would still be retained. All five additional seats were to be easily removable so as to offer alternative freight load combinations such as two 44 gallon fuel drums or two passengers and a stretcher on the starboard side. Other necessary changes would have taken account of the need to re-establish the original cg position by moving the

Specifications	XP75 Winjeel Utility Aeroplane [1]	
Powerplant	One Pratt & Whitney R985-AN2 Wasp Junior 9 cyl radial engine of 445 hp.	
Performance	Cruise speed at 8,500 ft	137 kts
	Service ceiling	15,200 ft
	TO dist at SL	870 ft
	Endurance with 69 gall of fuel at 130 kts cruise at 5,000 ft	3.5 hrs
Weights	Max TO	5,215 lb
Dimensions	Wing span	38 ft 9 ins
	Length	29 ft 6 ins
	Height	9 ft

XP73/XP74

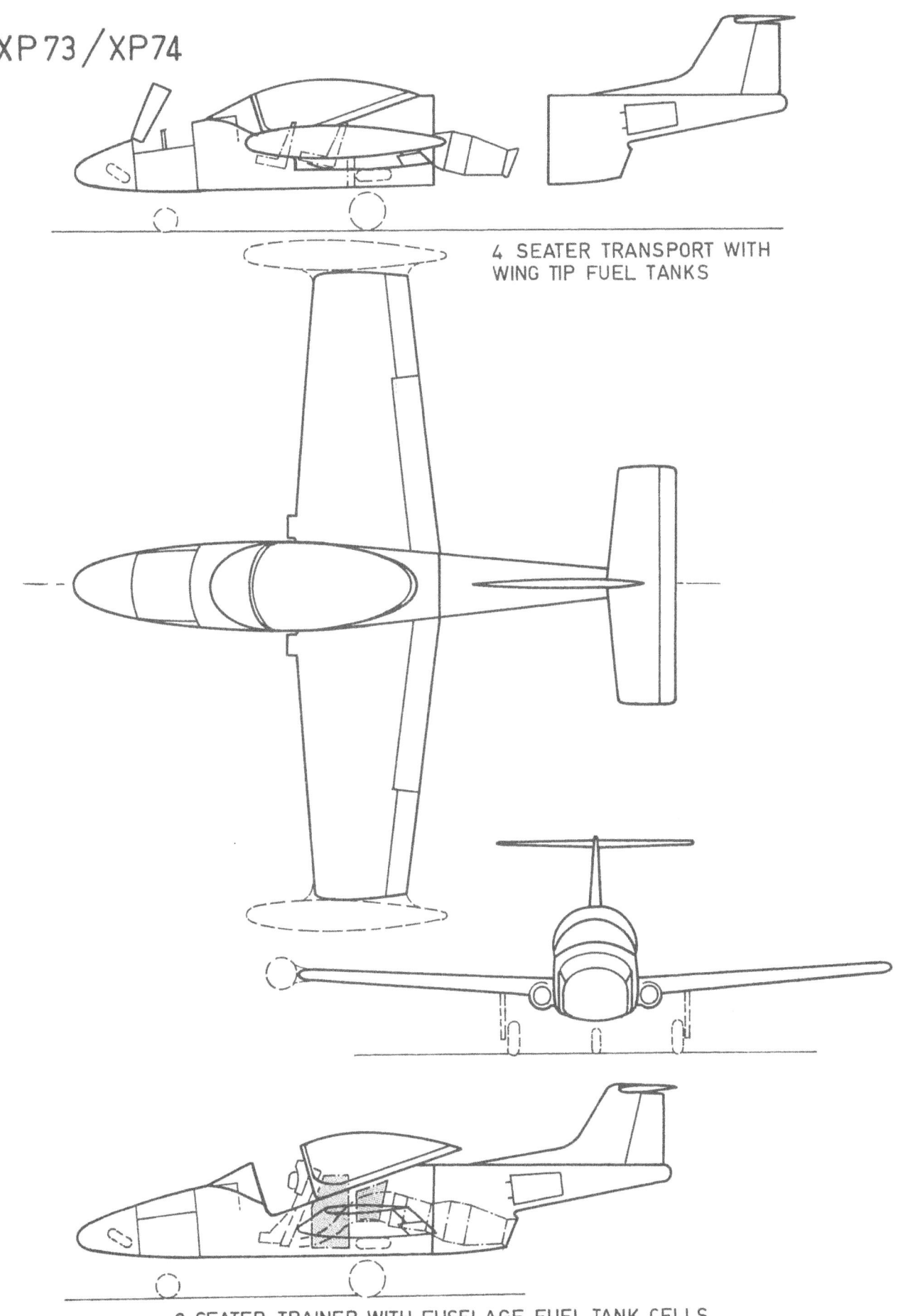

4 SEATER TRANSPORT WITH WING TIP FUEL TANKS

2 SEATER TRAINER WITH FUSELAGE FUEL TANK CELLS

J.A.Vella

Specifications	XP73 - Jet Trainer / XP74 - Executive Transport Aircraft			
Powerplant	One Rolls Royce RB108 lightweight axial turbojet of 2,340 lb thrust			
Performance		Trainer XP73		Transport XP74
	Max speed at 30,000 ft	430 kts		420 kts
	Rate of climb at SL	5,300 ft / min		4,200 ft /min
	Time to 30,000 ft	9 min		12 min
	Endurance at SL	1.25 hrs		NA
	Endurance at 30,000 ft	1.5 hrs		NA
	TO distance	360 ft		525 ft
	Range	NA		1,050 nm
Weights	TO	4,315 lb		5,510 lb
Dimensions	Wing span	28 ft 6 ins *		
	Aspect ratio	5.10	Wing area	160 sq ft
	Height	9 ft 6 ins	Length	29 ft
	Wheelbase	8 ft	Track	7 ft
	Uncertain in this includes wing tip tanks *			

wing six inches to the rear. Even though the maximum take-off weight of the aircraft was to be increased by 850 lb, there was no planned increase in engine power.

Bibliography: XP75 Winjeel Utility Aeroplane [1]
Commonwealth Aircraft Corporation. (August 1956). Engineering Report AA84. Winjeel Conversion.

XP75 WINJEEL, UTILITY AEROPLANE [2]
August 1956

By retaining the wing in the rearward shifted position as in the XP75 / Utility Aeroplane [1] proposal, another avenue for further development was considered. The role for this Winjeel Basic Trainer derivative was for rough field operation (particularly in PNG) and as a light military transport vehicle. This relatively unknown design extension would have meant a drastic alteration to the rear end of the Basic Trainer. With the possible exception of the horizontal and vertical tail surfaces all of the fuselage structure from a line about 36 inches to the rear of the windscreen frame would have been new work.

The layout comprised of a basic, box frame enclosed cabin with windows along each side and terminating in a large rear passenger/cargo entry and exit behind the wing trailing edge. This exit could be closed off by an optional, sideways hinged aerodynamically faired door. A small bench seat was to be located inside the door fairing for use by a medical attendant or small children. Six individual seats including that of the pilot, supplemented this small bench seat. A modified Winjeel tailwheel on an extended oleo leg was positioned at each corner of the exit opening forming a pair of elevated tailwheels. The pilot had an entry option on the port side via a centre line hinged canopy panel. The cabin roof was to continue in line with the new canopy frame terminating in a rectangular box boom on top of which was placed the horizontal tail unit. High lift wing devices were planned to be part of the design.

In a para-trooping role, the passenger seats would have been left out or bench seats substituted and the fairing door left off.

This scheme was a short five day study.

Bibliography: XP75 Winjeel Utility Aeroplane [2]
Watkins, W. (August 1956). Commonwealth Aircraft Corporation. Design Notes.

XP76 WINJEEL, AGRICULTURAL AIRCRAFT
September 1956

The first attempt at an agricultural variant of the Winjeel, dated September 1956, retained the basic outline of the Winjeel Basic Trainer but had a single seat cockpit located high over the wing trailing edge. A hopper of a one ton capacity was positioned ahead of the cockpit and over the main wheels. Its location would have requred making a 15 inch square cut-out on the centre line and leading edge of the tanks for the agricultural material dump gate. This would have meant a redesign of the Winjeel fuel tank cells.

XP76 was CAC's first flirtation at the agricultural aircraft market and incorporated the ideas being then advocated in the United States of America on the AG-1 design, the first attempt at seating the aircrew behind the hopper for the enhancement of crash protection and crew survival. XP76 was a study of about one week's duration and was rejected by the design group because of the high initial cost for a new Winjeel airframe. At about £160,000, this was approximately 5.9 times the purchase price of the DHC-2 Beaver agricultural application aircraft.

Bibliography: XP76 Winjeel, Agricultural Aircraft
Watkins, W.(September1956). Commonwealth Aircraft Corporation. Design Notes.

Specifications	XP76 Winjeel Agricultural Aircraft	
Powerplant	One Pratt & Whitney R985-AN2 Wasp Junior 9 cyl radial engine of 445 hp.	
Performance	Power to weight ratio	13.5 lb/hp
	Landing wing loading	14.3 lb/sq ft
	TO wing loading	24.2 lb/ sq ft
Weights	Empty	3,140 lb
	Hopper load	2,245 lb
	Max TO	6,090 lb
Dimensions	As per CA-25 Winjeel Basic Trainer	

XP77 / CA-28 CERES AGRICULTURAL AIRCRAFT
September 1956-1963

XP76 was considered in September 1956 but rejected due to the extreme cost of using new Winjeel Basic Trainer airframes as the basis for an aerial agriculture aircraft for spreading liquids and solids (superphosphate). CAC's engineering design group turned its attention to the Wirraway General Purpose airframe of WW2. Not

XP 75 / Winjeel-Utility Aeroplane (1)

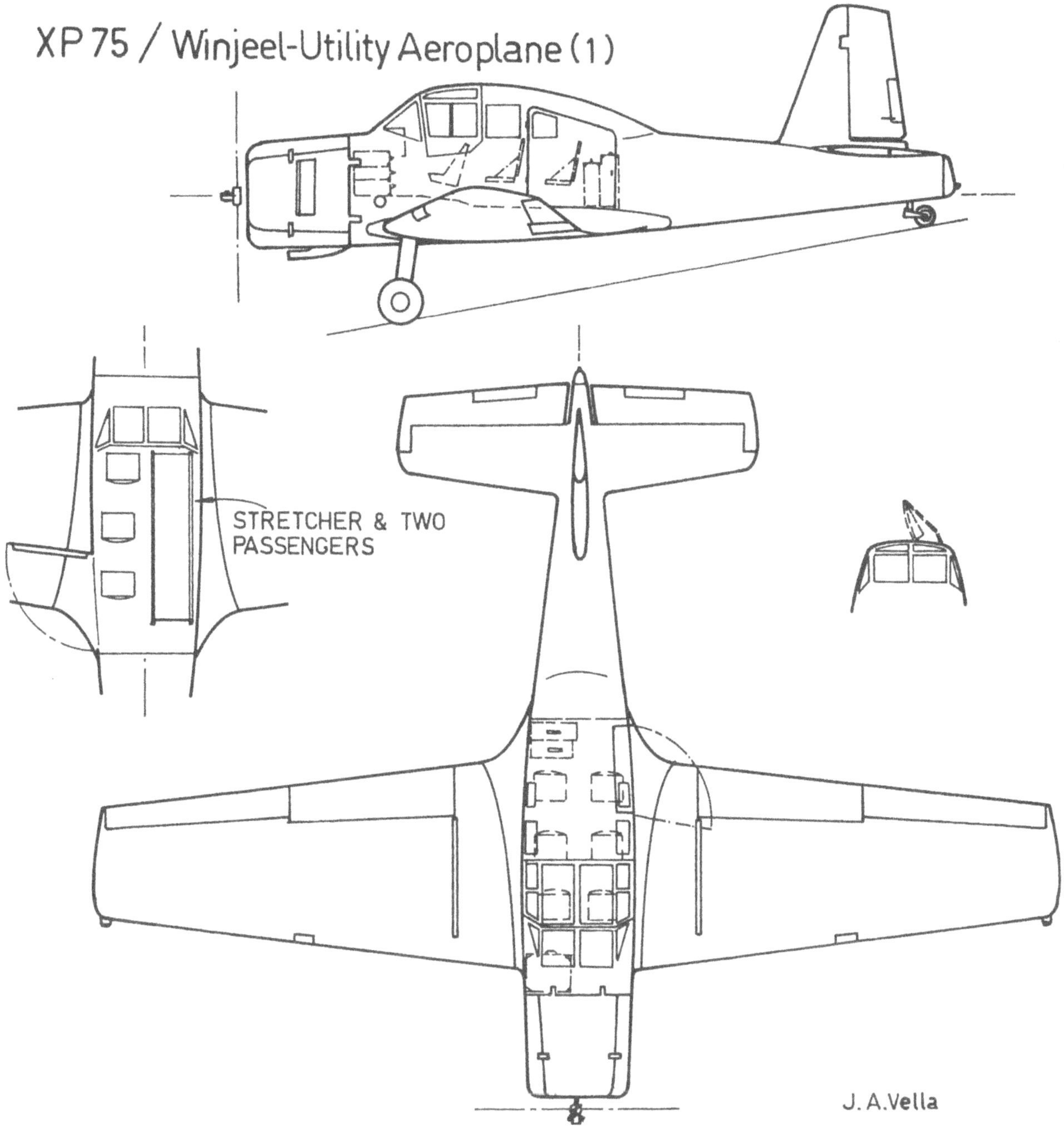

STRETCHER & TWO PASSENGERS

J. A. Vella

Winjeel-Utility Aeroplane [2]

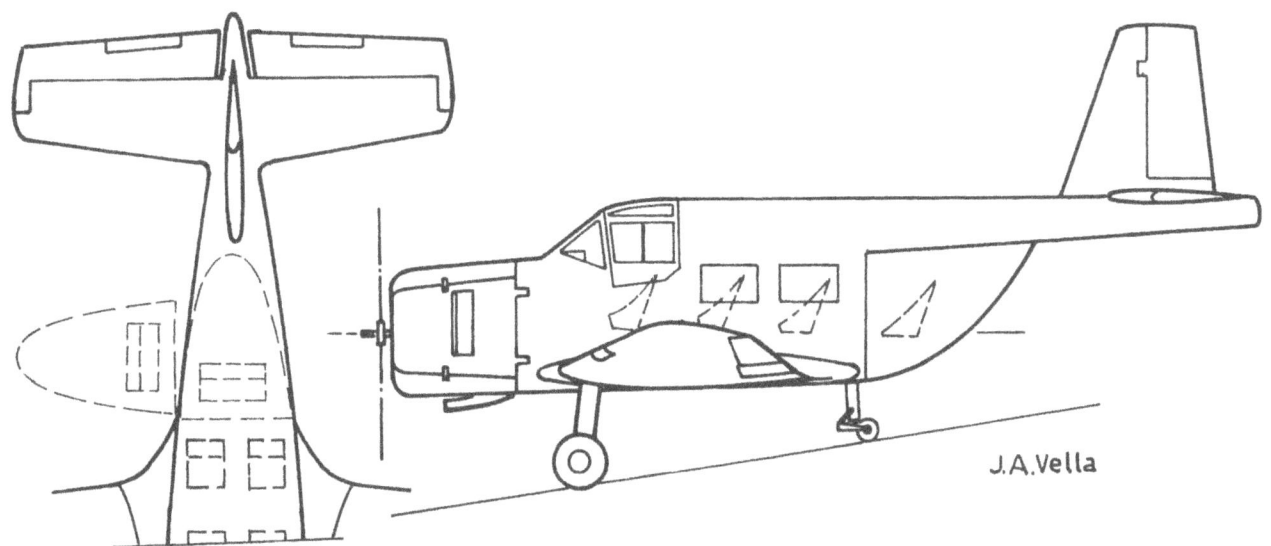

J. A. Vella

XP76

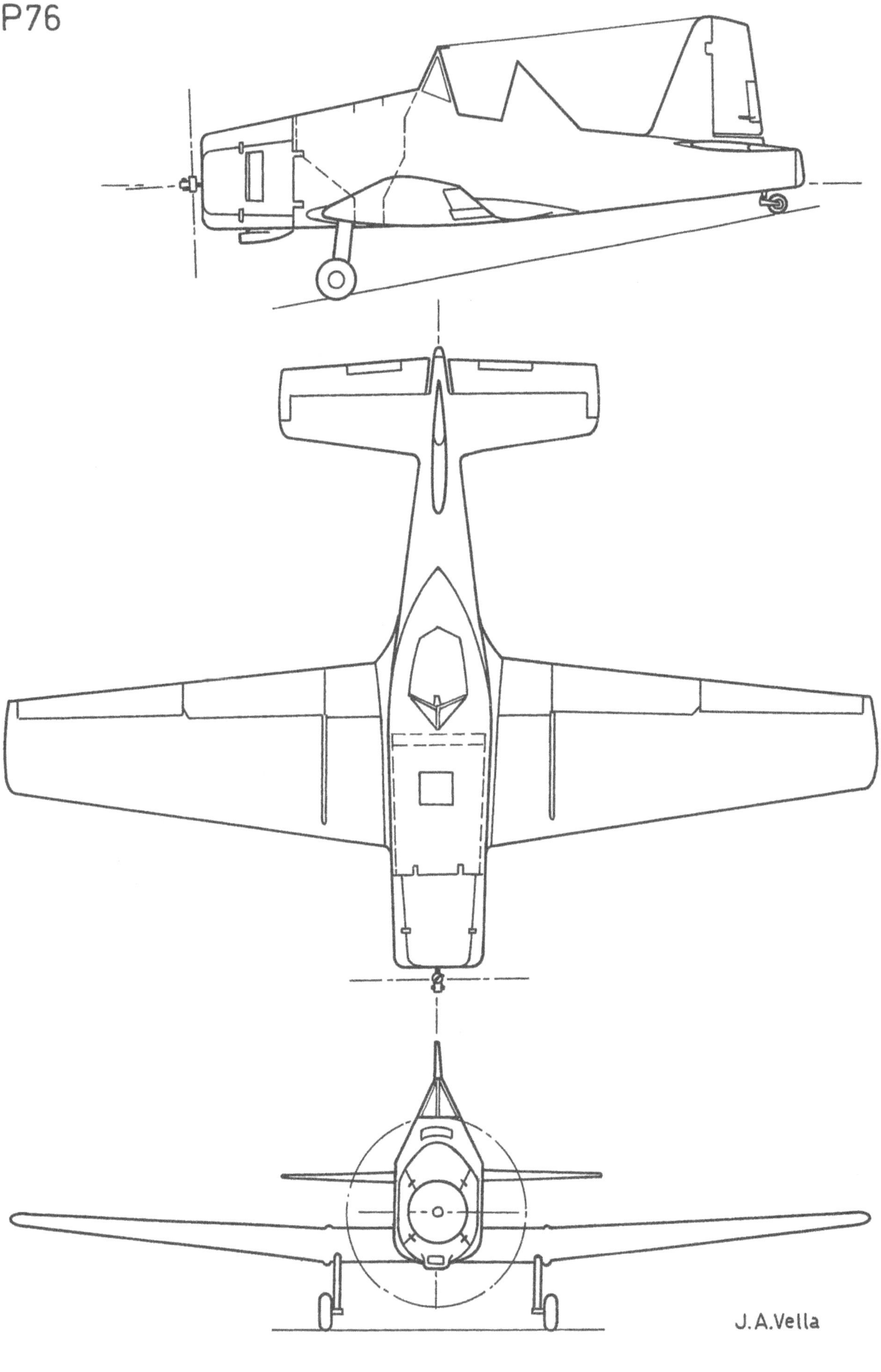

only was this seen to be a possible way to enter into the commercial sphere but shop floor work was needed as a stop gap measure between the end of CA-27 Sabre production and the start of its hoped- for fighter aircraft successor project.

The North American Aviation Harvard had been used in Brazil and Argentina with underwing tanks for crop spraying operations. Closer to home, Super Spread Pty Ltd at Moorabbin Airport had been operating two Wirraways (VH-SSF & SSG) between 1954 and 1956 spraying weeds and locusts. Several different herbicide carrying tank configurations were tried. A 60 gall tank was installed in the rear cockpit or a 60 gall tank could be carried on the centreline and under each wing. An air driven pump and different spray boom configurations had been tested. The configuration was not very successful needing careful handling of take-off weight and air speed.

Rather than adopt any similar strap-on arrangement with the Wirraway, the design team of Ian Ring, Chief engineer; Doug Humphries; Chief Design Engineer (later replaced on the project by John Kentwell); Charles Reid, Chief Aerodynamicist; R.Byron; Geoff Barrett and Wal Watkins aimed specifically at a dedicated new airframe based on the Wirraway structure in combination with structural robustness, simple systems, economic viability and the best possible performance and handling characteristics. Industry consultations with the large local aerial spread firms of Super Spread Aviation and Airfarm Associates suggested to CAC the need for a large aircraft for improved productivity.

ICIANZ, one of the shareholder owners of CAC and the producer of superphosphate fertilizer, ran a market survey for Australia and New Zealand. According to Geoffrey Richardson,* CAC's newly appointed sales engineer for the project (previously CAC's Flight Hangar Inspector), this survey optimistically suggested demand for 80-100 new aircraft capable of delivering a one ton load. Geoff's personal opinion was the aircraft was going to only achieve one sale in its first year. Up to this time CAC had never had an aircraft sales promotion element as the Federal Government was its prime customer and all promotion was handled by the engineering design group.

For the industry, which had a big reliance on the smaller Tiger Moths, Cessna and Piper type of aerial delivery aircraft, CAC's new aircraft venture was a big step up in work capability and an unknown quantity as far as the new airframe's maintenance overhead was concerned. Sir Lawrence Wackett, aware of this doubt wanted this future maintenance work brought back to either CAC's Fisherman's Bend or Lidcombe, NSW factories and not be carried out by the operators in the field.

In February 1957, CAC's board gave a not very enthusiastic approval to spend £5,000 for the production design of two prototypes without the basis of any firm orders but raised this to £8,000 whilst the market survey was still underway. Company secretary A.G. Brown was against the proposal. Ken Begg, the ICI member on the CAC Board suggested the aircraft be called Ceres, the Roman goddess of agriculture.

Wirraways A20-680 and A20-697 were purchased for £750 each from the Commonwealth Disposals Commission in March 1957 as the basis for prototypes of the new design. If flight tests were successful, the production rate was to be one aircraft every six weeks and thereafter one every two weeks. So as to allay any fears about supply and spares, CAC let it be known it did not have its own store or supply of Wirraway airframes but the Government had enough surplus airframes in storage to provide the basis for 120 Ceres. The Board authorised the spending of £41,000 on the construction of the two prototypes a jump from the earlier £28,500 estimate. (Another CAC document gives £58,000 as having been spent on the first prototype and £25,000 for the second CA-28 Ceres).

CAC made an initial purchase of 35 airframes with engines and 16 airframes without engines. More followed bringing the total to 61 airframes, paying £750 for each airframe. It also acquired 47 engine sets. P-51D Mustang wheels and disc brakes for the main undercarriage were purchased from the USA. The aim of the CA-28 project was for a basically new design making use of many perfect condition ex-Wirraway parts in order to arrive at a competitive new aeroplane selling price. The wing had to be enlarged to lift the heavy aerial drop load, operate out of small fields and fly safely at lower speeds. A completely new centre-section was extended by 48 inches to create space for the hopper and dump gate and moving the two existing 43 gall fuel tanks outboard within the section. Wing area was increased by adding large chord slotted flaps with 25 degrees range of travel on a modified trailing edge on the outer wing panels. These flaps were divided into three segments that spanned the entire trailing edge between the ailerons. The centre section of flap had a cut-out on its trailing edge to allow space for the dump gate mechanism push rod. The ailerons were extended to increase banking power; fixed leading edge slats were added to improve low speed handling and increase lift. The revised wing with a four foot greater span and an area of 312 sq ft was 22% larger than the Wirraway's.

The fuselage was considerably altered with a modified centre fuselage frame whilst retaining the engine mount. The raised superstructure cockpit with its excellent view and substantial turn-over truss to offer protection to the pilot was now set back on the wing trailing edge and on the prototype was fitted with the Wirraway style curved windscreen and framed canopy. Entry was via fuselage built-in step and hand grips. Controls and instrumentation were standard for a piston engine aircraft with the exception of the direct reading fuel gauges fitted on the upper surface of each wing above each fuel tank.

The rear fuselage was extended 29 inches behind the cockpit constructed in the same manner as that of the Wirraway with welded steel tube framework and a mixture of fabric covering and aluminium alloy panels. Later in its service life, some operators replaced the fabric panels by sheet metal alternatives. The large seam welded, externally reinforced stainless steel hopper of 41 cu ft capacity was located aft of the engine directly over the aircraft cg and ahead of the cockpit.

The forward hinging hopper lid in front of the windscreen was mechanically operated via push rods. Material delivery was via a controllable, mechanically operated discharge dust gate and a larger emergency dump gate that was to empty the hopper contents in less

*In 1937 Geoff Richardson designed and built the Golden Eagle, the first modern glider in Australia, now preserved at the Australian Gliders Museum, Bacchus Marsh, Victoria.

Super Spread's Wirraway VH-SSF at Moorabbin Airport. **Neil Follett Collection**

XP77/CA-28 Ceres

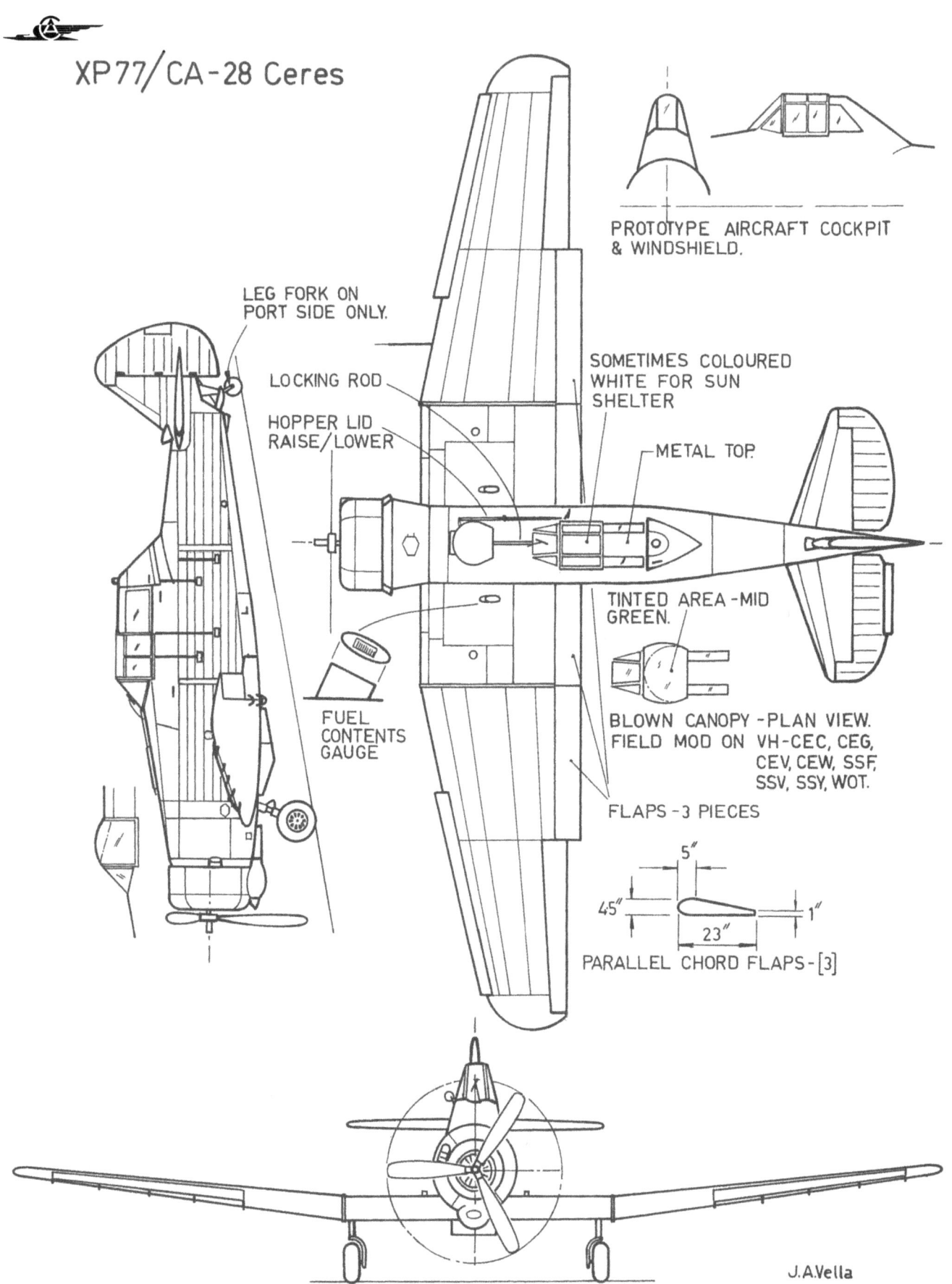

than five seconds. The hopper was supported inside of, but not part of the aircraft structure. It held 2,000 lb, subsequently increased to 2,240 lb or 232 gallons of liquid materials discharging the latter at variable rates via an air driven pump and 39 equally spaced spraying nozzles on three interconnected booms on the trailing edge of the flaps. This was to produce a maximum width swath of 90 feet when the aircraft was flown at 92 kts at an altitude of 5 to 10 feet.

The changeover from solid to liquid load was readily achieved by the replacement of the dust gate and dump door on the hopper with the combination air driven 4 bladed centrifugal pump, filter and sump unit. Initially the pump was to be driven via a flexible shaft from the engine through the left cowl and down under the wing. To simplify maintenance, all Wirraway hydraulics and electrical systems (where possible) were removed so that the flaps were now extended by a chain driven screw jack.

The wider track, non-retractable, fixed undercarriage units were Wirraway items whilst the tailwheel was a fully castoring lockable unit, generally left exposed. The fin and rudder were standard Wirraway assembly but the elevators were increased in area. A later mod increased the area of the horizontal tailplane.

The P & W R1340 Wasp 600 hp radial engine was retained but modified by removing the original reduction gearing (which drove the propeller at 0.66 engine speed) so as to extract some 30% or 500 lb extra static thrust driving its 10 feet diameter standard propeller. In its direct drive form the engine was identified as the S3H1-GMD Wasp. At the time the Ceres was the largest most powerful new aerial agriculture aircraft planned.

VH-CEA the first prototype rolled out in July 1957 for the workforce to admire, underwent a lengthy period of pre-flight ground testing prior to arriving by road at Avalon Airfield on January 17, 1958. CAC's Flight test engineer Louis Irving was to oversee the company's flight testing regime. Use of the government's Avalon airfield meant CAC had to pay an apportioned amount for its use and for the presence of personnel manning the airfield. DCA had prohibited any initial test flying over the built-up Fisherman's Bend area.

W. (Bill) H.Scott, Chief test pilot for Department of Defence Production (Aircraft) flew the aircraft for a weather curtailed first flight of 20 minutes duration in the late afternoon of February 18, 1958. The aircraft's propeller blades tip noise generated by the installation of the ungeared engine was most uncomfortable. Bill Scott's heavy workload with the CA-27 Sabre and GAF Canberra bomber flight testing limited him to 13 evaluation flights in the first six weeks, a figure CAC considered unsatisfactory.

The test tempo picked up and 31 flights were amassed in the following six weeks after Roy Goon, former Sqdn Ldr (83 Sqdn, Boomerang) RAAF, RVAC and McKenzie Flying School, Moorabbin flying instructor was appointed temporary test pilot on April 3, 1958. Sir Lawrence Wackett had initially asked Austin Miller, ex-RAAF pilot, whose firm Super Spread P/L had operated the Wirraway crop spraying aircraft, to be the Ceres test pilot but Austin declined because of his own heavy workload. By this time the aircraft was back at Fisherman's Bend.

For weight reduction and easier maintenance the engine cowling was left off taking away the integral air cleaner. Filtered air was then found to be inadequate so it was re-instated by positioning two new rectangular air cleaners in front of and either side of the oil cooler. Oil cooling was also a problem without the presence of air being forced past the cylinder heads by the engine cowling.

The rate of climb had decreased. Repeated cooling and climb performance testing was carried out on the company Wirraway CA9-763 (A20-570) and this verified the need to revert to flying the Ceres with Wirraway cowlings installed. The small air filters were removed after the engine cowling was re-instated.

Initial attempts were made on 11 April to tackle the prop tip noise problem by first cropping 6 inches, then 10 inches from the 10 feet diameter to bring it back to 9 feet 2 inches, all to no avail.

The aircraft was displayed by Roy Goon to a large aviation and aerial agriculture press gathering at Fisherman's Bend airfield that included superphosphate drop demonstrations. Organised by Geoffrey Richardson for a wintry July 1, 1958, Geoff's effort impressed CAC's board. Company secretary A.G.Brown awarded him an immediate pay rise of £1 (his weekly salary had been £7. A.G.Brown's annual salary was £4,968). It was also announced in April 1958 that CAC had considered an initial production batch of 40 aircraft with a selling price of £13,500 each. This was raised on June 24, 1958 to £14,000 each for the first 10 aircraft. For those beyond 1960, it was to be £15,000 in an authorised production of 18 aircraft. The spray gear kit of air driven pump, spray booms and accessories were extras. By comparison the DHC-2 Beaver in the same role, with a 450 hp engine (against the 600 hp Ceres) and a 300 lb smaller payload, was being offered at £27,000.

Certification flight testing ran from March to June 1958. The aircraft was certificated on August 13, 1958 at 6,640 lb, later raised to 7,150 lb as the direct drive, ungeared Ceres 'Type A'. It was used for the large volume of tests of dry material delivery measurements taken across a marked test area laid out on the Fisherman's Bend airfield followed by the aerial pumped spray tests with differing nozzle and boom arrangements all flown by Roy Goon at specified heights of between 5 to 15 feet.

VH-CEA reverted to the geared drive R1340 with the 10 ft diameter Hamilton Standard propeller and engine cowls reinstalled on September 5, 1958. The geared engine was designated the P & W S3H1G-CER Wasp.

Meanwhile, VH-CEB, the ungeared second prototype took to the air on June 6, 1958 and was delivered to Airfarm Associates of Tamworth, NSW for extensive field trials following more superphosphate drops at an aerial agricultural symposium at Hawkesbury, NSW on July 9, 1958. It amassed 600 hours in very quick time and impressed with its size, ruggedness and delivery but it lacked initial ground run acceleration and the propeller noise was highly objectionable. A suggested increase in the dump load to one ton was seen to offer better economics, so it was decided to test broader paddle bladed propeller blades to handle this load.

VH-CEB was certificated as Ceres 'Type B' with geared drive and standard propeller on December 19, 1958 (having had the reduction gear fitted in July) at an all-up weight of 7,350 lb some 700 lb above the original estimate. The engine cooling improved a little when the cowling was re-installed but not sufficiently so. It remained a problem on hot days and was solved by mounting an additional oil cooler in line behind the original item. 300 hours of flight test were completed during 1958. The slip-stream driven pump and spray booms created longitudinal instability as did the hopper depth projecting below the fuselage. The latter was cut back from 18 inches to 12 inches. Extending the wing/fuselage fillets (made out of fibre glass) to the rear beyond the flaps worked well to cure both sources of instability. An extended leading edge and increased mass balance was added to an enlarged horizontal tailplane and P-51 Mustang disc brakes were fitted as a better proposition. An electrical system was now re-introduced as a useful option following the Tamworth field trials.

A flat armour glass windscreen with a squared top replaced the original curved windscreen and curved upper frame. Superphosphate

General Comparison	
CA-28 Ceres	**DHC-2 Beaver**
Low wing - excellent visibility under all conditions	High wing – limited visibility in turning flight
Flap protection plates fitted to prevent stone damage. Ground clearance, flaps down - 7 inches	
Hopper in front of pilot, in conjunction with a low wing, guarantees pilot protection in crash situation	Hopper behind pilot, with high wing leaves pilot with less injury protection in a crash situation

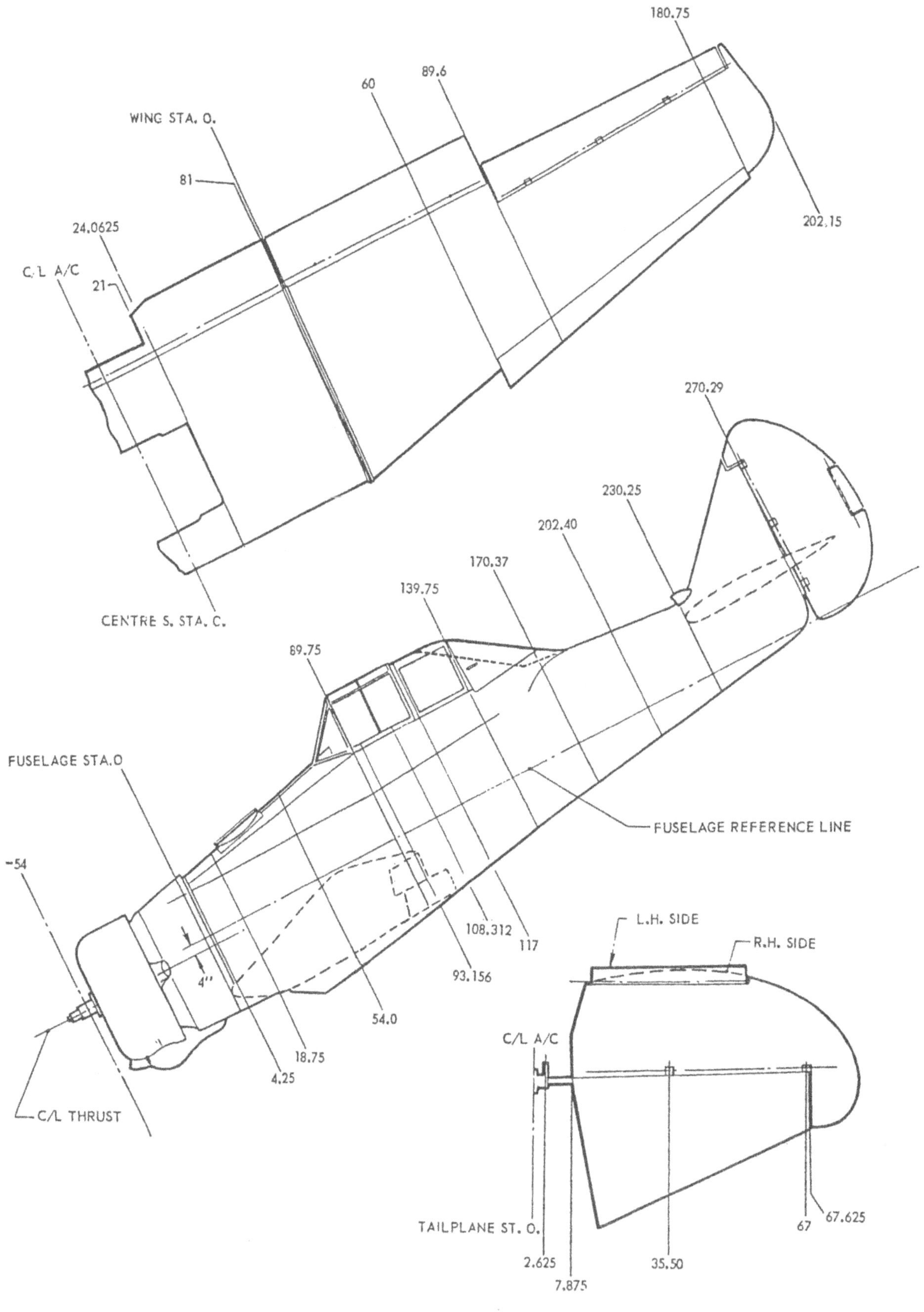

COMMONWEALTH AIRCRAFT CORPORATION PTY., LTD.
CERES MAINTENANCE MANUAL

dust from the loader/hopper could then be cleared away more easily with windscreen washers and wiper blades. The canopy was broadened at its apex to provide more headroom and the low hung flaps which cleared the ground by just seven inches were re-inforced with a stainless steel strip to prevent damage caused by stones thrown up by the main wheels and the strong blast of the propeller.

The estimated production cost for the following 18 aircraft was put at £295,000. Production was broken down into batches of three aircraft each. Batch No 2 (aircraft 4 to 6) was estimated to require 22,500 hours to fabricate, whilst Batch No 6 (aircraft 16 to 18) was expected to tally 16,000 hours.

Roy Goon carried out the conversion and familiarisation flights with the pilots of purchasers of the Ceres on the company's standard Wirraway with its strange flight test registration CA9-763 and call sign VH-AAZ. The former A20-570, it was acquired in July 1958 and issued a limited experimental permit to fly in the Fisherman's Bend area by DCA. As a military aircraft it could not, in that era, be placed on the civil aircraft register. Many flights were given, not all resulting in a subsequent sale. Some were flyers who saw it as an opportunity to revisit a military Wirraway experience of earlier times. On other occasions CA9-763 was the project camera ship and Roy's accompanying aircraft when a new Ceres was in the air in the hands of a new purchaser or their pilot.

VH-CEA was sold to Proctor's Rural Services of Alexandra in N.E. Victoria after it had been brought up to 'Type B' status; VH-CEB went to Airfarm Associates. VH-CEC, the first production machine flew on April 28, 1959 was also delivered to Airfarm Associates but returned to the factory to become the test bed for high solidity (paddle bladed) wider chord propellers. Three different sets of propellers blades were tested all cut down to 10 feet in diameter. Those sourced from the PBY Catalina blades were tried from 19 August; GAF Lincoln bomber blades from 26 August and from the P-51 Mustang on August 31, 1959. All exhibited unsatisfactory control characteristics; nevertheless 24 sets of Lincoln bomber blades were acquired. They produced a 500 lb increase in static thrust, a 15% reduction in the ground run but reduced the rate of climb. Finally a switch was made to using the modified 10 feet diameter, high solidity Hamilton Standard DA5080A propeller.

Five 'Type B' Ceres were built before the 'Type C' was introduced and certificated to an AUW of 7,410 lb. The hopper load for dusting was 2,243 lb; for spraying 2,720 lb.

An early criticism by operators of the initial batch of aircraft was the lack of passenger accommodation for the loader/driver or aircraft engineer on ferry flights. With DCA's approval, CAC built a removable seat for the inside of the aircraft hopper where farm tools etc were sometimes carried. Creature comfort was low, although the air inside the hopper was usually still, a fair amount of dust would be present making it necessary to wear a breathing mask and googles when using the space. The anti-surging baffles for liquids load were removed and the dump door was left unlatched to provide an exit in the event of a turnover on the ground. In flight, the airflow held the door closed but in the sometimes wintry climate of the South Island of New Zealand, sitting in the hopper was described as a form of physical torture.

Flight testing had tapered off by the time aircraft CA28-6 had flown and whilst Roy Goon returned to his flying instructor work at the McKenzie Flying School at Moorabbin, he was available to flight test each Ceres as it was completed. Passenger comfort level went up a notch when an extended cabin was flight tested on April 28, 1960 on CA28-6 (VH-CEG), the first 'Type C' to fly. The pilot's turn-over truss was modified to include a passenger seat with its occupant facing to the rear within the space formed from clear acrylic panels extending to the rear from the pilot's cabin and terminating in a starboard hinged, metal entry/exit door fairing. As the seat in the hopper was still permitted, the Ceres was DCA approved to carry two passengers. The development of the rear seat position was a two stage affair. The initial fairing was short and created aerodynamic instability at high weights and power settings but following a rearward extension tested on CA28-7 (VH-CEH), stability was regained. Aircraft CA28-6 to 21 inclusive were 'Type C'.

Heating to the cockpit and rear passenger was supplied by air drawn from the rear of the oil cooler. Another modification was to introduce ram air pressurisation of the rear fuselage (with an exit at the base of the fin) to prevent the entry of airborne superphosphate dust. Early examples of the Ceres had been building up so much dust in the rear fuselage that the aircraft cg was becoming uncontrollable. Attempts at sealing the airframe were not successful. The air intake originally located on an upper fuselage inspection panel was moved to the base of the fin when the rear cabin was extended for the second time.

Airfarm Associates of Tamworth was the largest operator of the Ceres. Pilots had commented on the narrow confines of the tapered cockpit canopy and the firm installed their own full blown sliding canopy to the pilot's position to provide the increased headroom and better visibility when wearing a crash helmet. These improved tinted canopies were retained when aircraft ownership changed hands. Airfarm Associates also subsequently replaced the fabric panels on the fuselage sides with sheet metal panels .

The Ceres was safe and very stable in the air; it had light and responsive controls and excellent low speed handling characteristics. The stall in particular, was vice-less. The large fixed leading edge slats on the outer wing panels eliminated the wing drop, one of the essential characteristics on the Wirraway in its pilot training role. Stall speeds ranged from 58 kts at max AUW to 50 kts with hopper empty. In the application role the aircraft was flown at 80 kts with 15 degrees flap set at take-off and left there. Full 25 degree flap was selected for landing. All the design evaluation and flight testing was carried out without the benefit of any wind tunnel model testing. However, it was considered heavy on the controls, heavy on fuel consumption, tiring to fly, a rough ride when taxying and required a long runway denying its safe operation into short fields. Early operating data suggested that hopper maximum load was only feasible when the on-board fuel was about half. This provided an hour's intense operation with an ample reserve.

The Forests Commission of Victoria was seen as a possible customer with a fire-fighting version of the Ceres put forward on January 11, 1962. CAC offered a conversion kit by dispensing with the emergency liquid loads dump doors, sealing the existing dust pump and spreader doors for fluids and installing an adjustable opening to control the dumping rate of retardant chemicals. This was proposed as a quick, one hour, change-over exercise to load 'Firebreak' fire retardant. There was no take-up of the idea.

Hire purchase arrangements were available between the company and potential buyers based on a plan of 47 monthly payments varying between £270 and £283 before the fluctuating commercial interest rate was applied or an outright purchase was made. Some indicative company agreements were as shown in the accompanying table.

The CAC Board cancelled further work on May 21, 1963 and Ceres aircraft production came to an end in July as the work tempo on the CA-29 Mirage IIIO fighter aircraft airframe and its engine contract took hold. Forty Wirraway airframes were used to produce the Ceres

Ceres revised and new wing centre-section. The leading edge points toward the floor. **HDHV**

Prototype VH-CEA under assembly and test. **HDHV**

The tall roll-over structure. **HDHV**

Lawrence Wackett (right) at the hand-over of Ceres VH-CEA to Wynne Proctor (centre) of Proctor's Rural Services, April 16, 1959. **HDHV**

The aerial spray pump and spray gear out to the ends of the lower wing surfaces of VH-CEC. June 3, 1959. **HDHV**

Above: Roy Goon walks way after handing over VH-CEA on April 16, 1959. **HDHV**

Left: VH-CEG in the distinctive deep red and yellow colours and bubble canopy mod of Airfarm Associates at Tamworth, NSW, September 24, 1972. **J.A.Vella**

CAC c/n	Type	Registration	First Flight	Further Registrations
CA-28-1	A	VH-CEA	18/02/1958	Crashed 22/03/1961. Rebuilt as CA-28-18
CA-28-2	B	VH-CEB	06/06/1958	
CA-28-3	B	VH-CEC	28/04/1959	
CA-28-4	B	VH-CED	21/08/1959	ZK-BPU
CA-28-5	B	VH-CEF (NTU)	04/11/1959	VH-SSZ, CDO
CA-28-6	C	VH-CEG	28/04/1960	
CA-28-7	C	VH-CEH	20/07/1960	ZK-BXW
CA-28-8	C	VH-CEI	01/09/1960	ZK-BXY
CA-28-9	C	VH-CEL	20/09/1960	ZK-BZO
CA-28-10	C	VH-CEK	20/10/1960	VH-SSY
CA-28-11	C	VH-CEM	07/02/1961	ZK-BSQ
CA-28-12	C	VH-CEN	06/02/1961	ZK-BVS
CA-28-13	C	VH-CEO	15/02/1961	VH-SSF
CA-28-14	C	VH-CEP	16/03/1961	VH-DAT
CA-28-15	C	VH-CEQ	07/12/1961	VH-WAX
CA-28-16	C	VH-CER	14/12/1961	
CA-28-17	C	VH-CET	20/02/1962	VH-WHY
CA-28-18	B	VH-CEX	25/08/1961	VH-CEA rebuilt, VH_SSV
CA-28-19	C	VH-CEU(NTU)	30/03/1962	VH-WOT
CA-28-20	C	VH-CEV	18/03/1963	
CA-28-21	C	VH-CEW	25/07/1963	

Front to rear VH-CEQ,CER,CET respectively the 15th,16th and 17th airframes. **HDHV**

VH-CEH makes a low level pass over the Fisherman's Bend runways on August 2,1960. **HDHV**

Single seater VH-CED CA28-4. **HDHV**

VH-CEC of Airfarm Associates at a RAAF Point Cook air display, March 7, 1960. **Roger McLeod.**

Select CA-28 Ceres Workloads

CAC c/n	Country	Super Dropped (Tons)	Aerial Work (Hours)	Aver Load/Hr (Ton/hr)
CA-28-4	NZ	(1962-65) / 17,972	1496	12
CA-28-7	NZ	(1962-65) / 29,166	2416	12
CA-28-12	NZ	(1962-65) / 18,461	1542	11.9
CA-28-10	Aust	(1962-65) / 13,799	1659	8.3
CA-28-11	NZ	(1962-65) / 20,150	1611	12.5
CA-28-19	Aust	(1964-65) / 10,936	1270	8.5
CA-28-5	Aust	(1965) / 7,000	800	8.75
CA-28-14	Aust	(1962-65) / 15,636	2033	7.7
Total		**136120**	**12836**	**10.2**

CA-28 Ceres / DHC-2 Beaver Operating Comparison

		With High Solidity 3D40 Prop	DHC-2 Beaver
Performance			
	Powerplant	600 hp	450 hp
	TO distance	1,050 ft	855 ft
	Rate of climb (SL) 0° flap	830 ft / min	879 ft / min
	Landing run (2 hr fuel reserve)	540 ft	465 ft
	Cruise at 5,000 ft (60% power)	114 kts	106 kts
	Fuel consumption (Cruising)	22 gall / hr	18 gall / hr
	Fuel consumption (Air spreading)	20 gall / hr	22 gall / hr
	Range at 5,000 ft	310 nm	385 nm
Weights	Empty	4,670 lb	3,050 lb
	AUW agricultural operations	7,410 lb	5,490 lb
Other	Purchase price	£15,000	£27,000

Specifications — XP77 / CA-28 Ceres Agricultural Aircraft

Powerplant One (CAC) Pratt & Whitney R1340-SH1G-CER Wasp 9 cyl radial engine of 600 hp at 2,250 rpm at TO (SL) driving either a 3 bladed high solidity 3D40, 10 ft diameter propeller or a Hamilton Standard 3D40 10 ft diameter propeller. Power loading 11 lb/hp

		With High Solidity 3D40 Prop	With Hamilton Standard 3D40 Prop
Performance			
	TO dist (SL) no wind 15° flap at 7,410 lb	1,050 ft	1,221 ft
	TO dist (SL) no wind 25° flap at 7,410 lb	525 ft	525 ft
	Rate of climb (SL) 0° sweep flap at 7,410 lb	660 ft / min	712 ft / min
	Rate of climb (SL) 0° sweep flap at 5,000 lb	1,520 ft / min	1,575 ft / min
	Ferry range with two passengers	450 nm	450 nm
Weights	Empty	4,670 lb	4,400 lb
	AUW agricultural operations	7,410 lb	7,410 lb
	Hopper load (with 4 hr of fuel)	2,000 lb	2,075 lb
	Max hopper cap of dry materials	2,243 lb	2,500 lb
	Max hopper cap of liquid materials	232 gall	232 gall
	Wing loading at 7,410 lb	22.22 lb / sq ft	22.22 lb / sq ft

Dimensions				
	Wing span	46 ft 11 ins	Max chord	8 ft 3 ins
	Wing tip chord	3 ft 8 ins	Wing area	312 sq ft
	Wing LE sweep	12° 51'	Wing outer panel dihedral	7° 4'
	Ground angle	12° 54'	Tailplane span	13 ft 3.75 ins
	Tailplane area	50 sq ft	Height to top of cabin	9 ft
	Height to top of fin	7 ft 1 in	Height to top of fin fuselage level	12 ft 5 ins
	Length	30 ft 8.5 ins	Wheelbase	21 ft 11 ins
	Track	12 ft 6.75 ins		
	Main wheel tyre dia 27 ins	28-35 psi	Tail wheel tyre dia 10.5 ins	35-50 psi

Basic Layouts

SPRAY EQUIPMENT

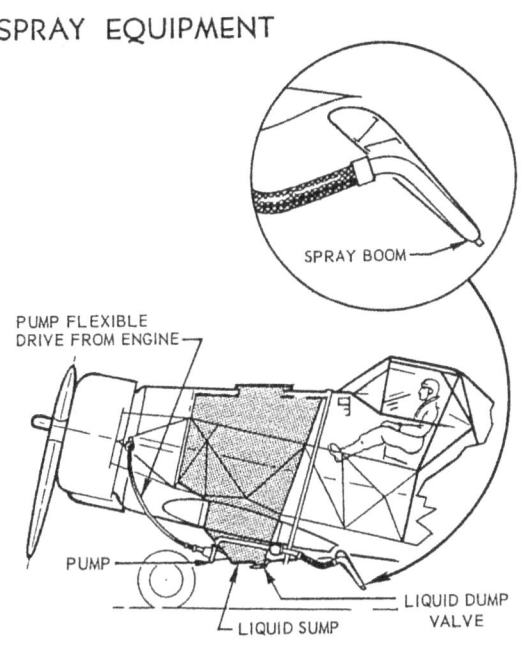

DUSTING LAYOUT

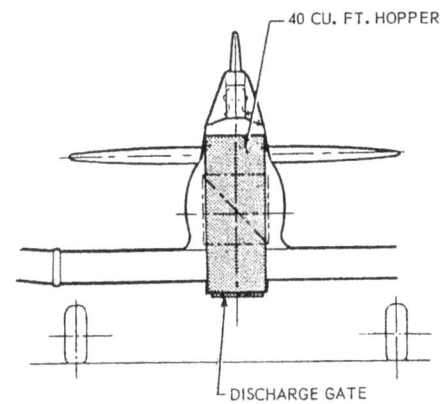

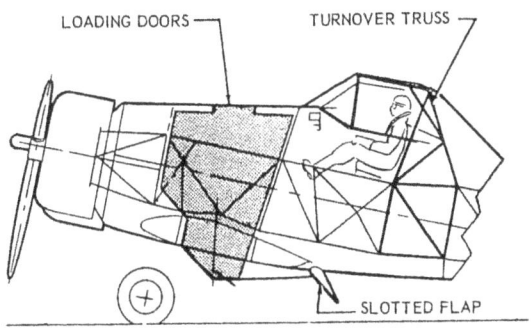

VH-CEG, CA-28-6, the last of the Type B model to fly was the test aircraft for the two seater cabin. **HDHV**

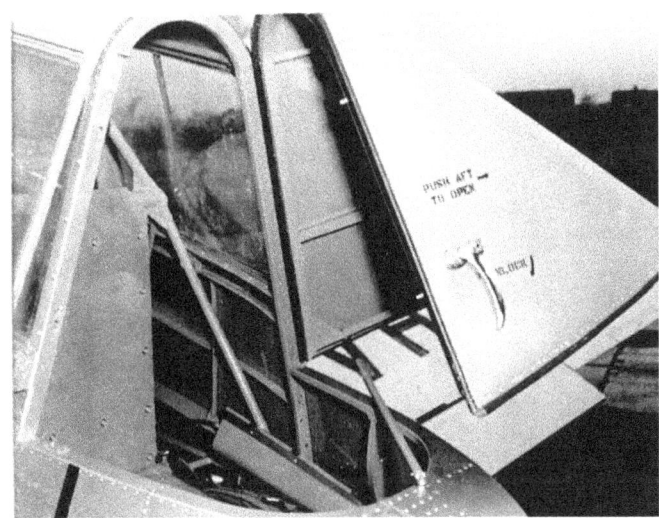

The rear seat installation and the rear fairing locked up in the open position. **HDHV**

CA-28-4, ZK-BPU in the red trim of Aerial Farming sometime in 1960. **HDHV**

CA-28 Ceres Purchase Agreements

Date	Registration	Hire Purchase (£)	Outright Purchase (£)
12-Sep-1960	VH-CEG	N/A	13800
22-Dec-1960	VH-SSY	16249	13800
15-Nov-1961	VH-CEP	16249	11702
18-Dec-1961	VH-CER	16249	11702
03-Jan-1962	VH-CEQ	16249	11702
10-Dec-1962	VH-WOT	16249	11702
05-Mar-1963	VH-WHY	16249	11702
12-Apr-1963	VH-SSF	15964	11450
05-Aug-1963	VH-CEW	16586	12000
10-Mar-1964	VH-SSF	N/A	10263

line. By October 1963, disposal action started of unused airframes, engines and the pilot conversion Wirraway. According to Geoff Richardson the program ended with a loss of some £400,000.

The prototype CA28-1(VH-CEA) which crashed on March 22, 1961, was e-built as CA28-18 and registered as VH-CEX. Seven Ceres were exported to New Zealand through the persistent efforts of Geoff Richardson. Thirteen others were operated locally.

The Australian operators and changing ownership of the Ceres were: Airfarm Associates (operated 8 Ceres); Super Spread Aviation Pty Ltd (4 Ceres); Coondair Pty Ltd (1 Ceres); Doggett Aviation (3 Ceres); Airland/Airland Improvements (6 Ceres); Marshall's Spreading Service (2 Ceres); Proctor's Rural Services (2 Ceres) and New England Aerial Topdressing and Superair Australia (1 Ceres).

The New Zealand operators were: James Aviation; Aerial Farming Ltd; Wanganui Aero Work Ltd; Cookson Airspread Ltd and Manawatu Aerial Topdressing Co Ltd.

Whilst the Ceres lifted a sizable load as a single engine aircraft, it was to be eclipsed locally by three Noorduyn Norseman aircraft VH-GSE; GSF & GSG, former WW2 RAAF aircraft powered by the identical Wasp engine as used on the Ceres and converted with a hopper positioned behind the pilot for the Pay and Williamson Pty Ltd company of Narromine, NSW. These aircraft operated between 1963 and 1967 were dropping superphosphate (only) loads of between 2,800 and 3,580 lbs at a lower operating cost than the Ceres.

CA28-21 (VH-CEW), the last private venture aircraft off the line was delivered to Airfarm Associates; the eighth Ceres registered with this operator. Had a trickle rate of production been maintained it may have been possible for the aircraft to find new operators as the economic climate improved and an alternative engine was possibly selected but CAC was locked in government cost-plus work. On November 6, 1962 the Minister for Civil Aviation had announced that the DH82 Tiger Moth must be removed from agricultural work.

The fickle nature of the local weather being prone to upset major portions of the rural economy was no exception for the year of 1959. Having experienced two consecutive bad seasons, a credit squeeze and a drop in aerial agricultural demand, the anticipated rapid run for orders for the Ceres evaporated. Twenty Ceres were built, although 21 construction numbers had been allotted.

Not exactly a 'private owners' dream aircraft using fuel at the rate of 22 gall/hour, the Ceres was labelled by one aviation publication as the possible *country cousin* of the Wirraway.

Bibliography: XP77/ CA-28 Ceres Agricultural Aircraft

Aircraft. (October 1957, May 1958, July 1958, August 1958, December 1959, January 1961, April 1962).

Australia. Department of Defence (1958). Agreement, Ceres Agricultural Aircraft. CAC. [MP1005/1, LO8050]. Barcode: 685060.

Australian Operated Aircraft. (1974-1979). *Aviation Historical Society of Australia.*

Buckmaster, Derek, 1964-(2017). *CAC Ceres-Australia's Heavyweight Crop Duster*. Derek Buckmaster. Glen Iris, Victoria.

Commonwealth Aircraft Corporation (September 18, 1959). Engineering Report AA102. Lincoln Bomber Blades for Ceres propeller.

Commonwealth Aircraft Corporation. (October 1959). Engineering Report AA103. Modication to 3D40 Propeller for Ceres.

Commonwealth Aircraft Corporation. (September 11, 1962). Engineering Report AA118. Proposed Modification of Ceres for Fire Fighting Duties.

Commonwealth Aircraft Corporation. (July 1958. Ceres Brochure.

Commonwealth Aircraft Corporation. (June 1961, Dec 1961). Ceres Operating Notes.

Commonwealth Aircraft Corporation. (1960-61). Flight Test Results. Reports AF6, 9, 10, 11.

Commonwealth Aircraft Corporation. (1958-60).Type Test Inspection Sheets: CA28-1, 2, 3, 5, 6.

Geoff Goodall aviation history site (www.goodall.com.au)

Richardson, Geoffrey. CAC. (January 1992).[Presentation to AHSA, Melbourne Branch].

P402 SABRE, ROCKET BOOST [2]
January 1959

A second more detailed and officially requested investigation into the use of rocket boost on the Avon Sabre came about on January 23, 1959. This was at the request of the RAAF Director General of Engineering for a performance analysis of the aircraft fitted with a Napier Single Scorpion rocket engine. The variation from the 1955 proposal was the use of two underwing tanks similar to the then existing 100 gallon fuel tanks to carry 200 gallons of High Test Peroxide, nitrogen pressure bottles and propellant transfer equipment.

An internal re-arrangement of equipment, ballast and a necessary reduction of fuel was mandatory to overcome the

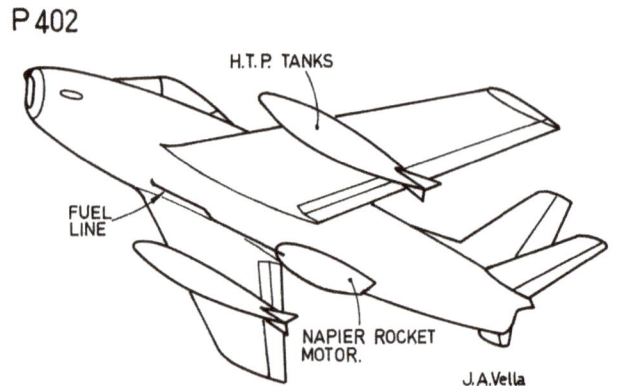

rearward displacement of the aircraft centre of gravity. Intercept armament was to be two Sidewinder heat seeking missiles.

Bibliography: P402 Sabre, Rocket Boost [2]
Kentwell, John. (January 23, 1959). Engineering Report AA99. Scorpion Sabre Performance. Commonwealth Aircraft Corporation.

SABRE, RAMJET THRUST AUGMENTATION
July 1959

Undoubtedly the most exotic and outlandish dream of the Sabre enhancement ideas was that from Charles Reid with his study into the application of ramjet propulsion to the aircraft. Two avenues of approach existed; that of fitting an external (available) 15 inch diameter ramjet under the fuselage and the alternative of converting the existing power plant into an integral turbojet with reheat and ramjet.

The first approach was not of any practical value and the operational characteristic of ramjets was the need for a high Mach number at the intake face for initial operation, something the Sabre could not achieve. The second approach was to realize the need of the required increase in thrust of somewhere near 300% by the integration of a conventional turbojet with reheat inside a ramjet casing of approximately five feet in diameter and 35 feet in length.

The intake and nozzle areas would have had to be increased to cope with a 140% increase in mass flow. At 35,000 feet the Avon engine in the standard Sabre would have been delivering 2,800 lb thrust. In an integral ramjet unit this figure would have been 14,000 lb thrust but the engine specific fuel consumption would have leaped from 1.16 to 3.20. The dimensions of the combined power plant would have been approximately the maximum external dimensions of the Sabre fuselage (Station 190 ie the rear of the closed canopy) and have been very large at the jet nozzle. This idea was not feasible because the rear fuselage was not capable of containing the required size of power unit within its contours.

Bibliography: Sabre, Ramjet Thrust Augmentation
Reid. C.J. (July 28, 1959). Engineering Report AA100. Ramjet Thrust Augmentation Study. Commonwealth Aircraft Corporation.

CA-29 GAMD MIRAGE IIIO FIGHTER SUB-CONTRACT
March 1960

On September 28, 1954 a seven member overseas mission led by AVM Alister Murdoch and including Doug Humphries left Australia to seek a replacement for the CA-27 Sabre. In a field which offered little choice in interceptor aircraft, Air Marshal Sir John McCauley, the RAAF Chief of Air Staff, favoured the unreliable Lockheed F-104A Starfighter, a daylight, point defence intercepter with the USAF Air Defence Command. In June 1957 AVM Frederick Scherger and Alister Murdoch travelled again. It was now the F-104C entering service with Tactical Air Command. The replacement decision was postponed again as missions went abroad and came back without any resolution.

The Northrop Corporation had lobbied strongly for the RAAF to take an interest in their new design, the N156F. Northrop's Vice President and General Manager visited CAC on March 2, 1959 with the view of establishing the N156F for offshore procurement from an Australian production line. Alternative production from a Japanese industry line was also given consideration.

Vital to the outcome of the discussions was the economics of producing 300 of the fighters in Australia as compared with the cost of a similar number in the United States. Because of the implications of committing this new aircraft to the facilities of CAC and of the consequences to interruptions to production which would result if the RAAF did not to select the N156F as its Sabre replacement, the Defence Department suggested that no decision be made until the aircraft had at least embarked on its test flying program.

In May 1959, the Lockheed and Northrop companies sent independent technical teams to Australia to stimulate RAAF interest in their respective aircraft. To analyse the information and technical data which these teams provided, the Department of Supply called on the expertise of CAC and established a working party, which over a two month period, produced a report entitled 'Preliminary Study of Production Costs of Northrop N156F and Lockheed F-104 Fighter Aircraft'. This was presented to the Secretary, Department of Supply, at the end of July 1959. It is not clear if this applied to the F-104C or the emerging F-104G Starfighter (The N156F made its first flight on July 30, 1959 but was shelved until May 1962. The US Department of Defence then selected it as the F-5 Freedom Fighter for supply to favoured nations under the MAP. Initial production deliveries commenced in October 1962.)

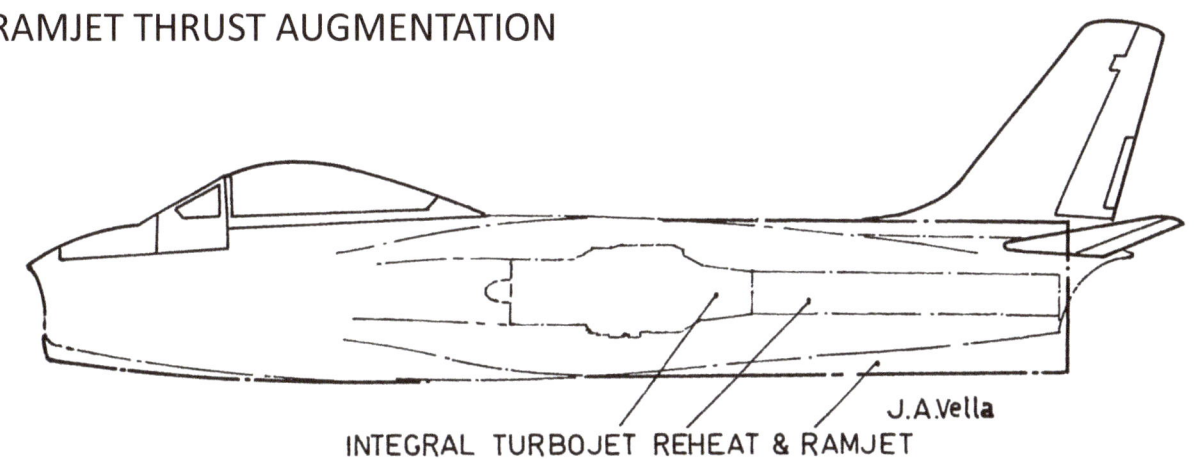

RAMJET THRUST AUGMENTATION
INTEGRAL TURBOJET REHEAT & RAMJET
J.A.Vella

Towards the end of 1959 a small RAAF team visited Sweden, then Belgium where the F-104G was to be built, and flight tested a Mirage IIIA in France. Production investigations were made for SAAB J-35 Draken and General Aeronautique Marcel Dassault Mirage III but not to the same extent as had been taken with either Northrop or Lockheed. The report from this European visit led to the six person Fighter Evaluation Team headed by Air Marshal Sir Frederick Scherger; Grp Cpt D. Cuming, Wg Cdr A. Hodges (test pilots) and Herb Knight, Engine Factory Superintendent co-opted by the Department of Defence to tour Europe and the USA from 22 May to August 1960 to look at the EE Lightning, Mirage IIIA/C, Republic F-105 Thunderchief, Northrop N156 and Lockheed F-104G.

Once the Mirage III came into contention it immediately attracted RAAF interest as the N156 aircraft was losing local favour.

March 1960 estimates for acquiring 30 aircraft, spares, tooling and licence fees for the F-104G and the Mirage came out greatly in favour of the Mirage. As it became obvious that the 1960 evaluation mission was to be the one to come at a definite choice of fighter aircraft, GAMD requested the Department of Supply send a senior Australian engineer to work with them in Paris to present their proposals for the sale of 100 Mirage aircraft, with manufacture substantially in Australia. Government reliance on CAC expertise was again demonstrated when the company was asked to release their Chief Engineer, Ian Ring, for this task. Ian left Melbourne on May 2, 1960 to spend two months with GAMD assisting them to complete their technical, manufacturing and financial submission to the Fighter Evaluation Team which visited France in June 1960.

So much investigative work had been carried out at CAC on behalf of the Department of Supply in preparation for the licence manufacture of the next fighter, that the company had become known as the '*Fighter Factory*'.

Aircraft	Imported ($ Million)	Australian Built ($ Million)
Lockheed F-104 Starfighter	$US68.17 $A30.40	$US80.17 $A35.80
GAMD Mirage	$US56.17 $A25.10	$US60.70 $A27.20

Avon Engines in Mirage and F-104 Aircraft

The battle for re-equipping the NATO air forces was decided in favour of the new tactical strike variant F-104G Starfighter, a model very different to the earlier inflexible F-104A. The attention then turned to Australia. Wackett showed a slight interest in involving Rolls Royce in the F-104 Starfighter and an installation arrangement for an Avon RA-19 with afterburner was drawn in 1954 and again in 1956 by Wal Watkins with an Avon RA-14 but the matter was not pursued. (Rolls Royce documents itemize the RA-27 Avon 64 and RA-24 Avon 63 as having been offered for powering the F-104 but there is no data to confirm this as a link with CAC.)

The RAAF sought an aircraft capable of flying from Darwin to Singapore without refuelling, a distance of 2,000 miles. The F-104 could not do this; neither could the Dassault Mirage III. Rolls Royce's UK senior management also felt that the installation of an Avon engine would offer the required range due to a stated 15% better fuel consumption than the SNECMA ATAR 9B. There was also the possibility it could establish a pattern for the prospect of Avon-Mirage sales to other Commonwealth countries should Australia set the lead. Rolls Royce was hoping for a repeat performance of change of fighter engine in their favour as had occurred with the CAC Sabre.

It is not known if the preliminary CAC investigation of installing an Avon engine into the F-104 had an influence or was the catalyst for Rolls Royce to enter into a 50:50 private development venture with GAMD in December 1959 to utilize and test a Mirage III airframe fitted with a Rolls Royce RA.24-28 Avon 67 (RB146) similar to the Avon 301 units used in the SAAB J-35 Draken and English Electric Lightning F.3. GAMD had also felt the need to offer an engine more powerful than the ATAR 9B. The RB146 was expected to provide both an increase in thrust and a lesser dry specific fuel consumption figure of 0.86, as compared with about 0.98 for the lower rated ATAR 9B. They were also convinced the RAAF with its long connections operating UK and USA aircraft would not acquire a French aircraft without a major British component. Combining the Avon turbojet with the British Ferranti Airpass radar was considered to offer a more acceptable package than the standard French Air Force Mirage IIIC with its Cyrano radar.

Herb Knight first visited Rolls Royce to evaluate the alternative RB146 engine. On May 31, 1960 he was at St. Cloud, outside Paris to inspect the mock-up installation of the RB146 in a Mirage. From CAC's jet engine manufacturing experience the Rolls Royce engine was considered to be a more complex and difficult manufacturing task than would be experienced on the SNECMA ATAR 9B or 9C.

The Scherger mission came out strongly in favour of the GAMD Mirage III over the rival, Lockheed F-104G Starfighter. The latter was very different to the F-104A variant with its unusual downward firing ejection seat seen during the 1954 and 1957 overseas missions. It was now an all-weather, expensive multi-role aircraft, possibly biased towards tactical strike. The Mirage was cheaper, simpler, with as good or better performance in the air, possessing superior landing and take-off capabilities. At maximum all-up weight it operated with much lower tyre pressures of 80 psi as against 135 psi for the F-104G. The F-104G required a 4,800 foot take-off run, whereas the 3,100 feet used by the Mirage fitted the Australian role in SEATO with lesser shortcomings.

Federal Cabinet endorsed the selection of the Mirage III on November 22, 1960. The next decision was the choice of engine.

Rolls Royce Engine Evaluation

The Mirage IIIO Rolls Royce Avon testbed airframe, (finished with RAAF insignia and named the 'City of Hobart', the home town of Athol Townley - the Minister for Defence) had its first engine run on February 8, 1961. The Australian markings were not official or connected in any way with the Australian Government. The III'O' designation was allocated by GAMD for 'Ostralia'. The 'A' was already in use and 'AU' was reserved for Austria, although Austria was never to operate the Mirage.

(The origins of the Avon testbed airframe have varied. Suggestions were it was a modified Mirage IIIA, one of ten built or one of five or six Mirage IIIC which were not accepted by the French Air Force but for which funds were provided in lieu to create the Mirage IIIS c/n 96; IIIR c/n 97; IIIB c/n 98; IIIE c/n 99 and possibly the Mirage IIIO c/n 100 (A3-I) prototype.) In 1987 the GAMD press office informed the author the Avon-Mirage was built from Mirage III early mass production parts and after completion of the test phase with the Avon engine became the Mirage IIIO-3 airframe. GAMD issues constructor numbers by owners; not by production line positions).

First flight took place on February 13, 1961 and four flights on the same day took the performance to Mach 2.05 and 50,000 ft. The external appearance of this aircraft was a hybrid, with a Mirage IIIC fin, a new IIIE longer forward fuselage and restyled undercarriage mounting to permit the carriage of a 1,300 litre centreline fuel tank.

The Avon engine installation completed in 28 days had presented no difficulties or structural alterations.

A nine member Australian technical equipment evaluation team led by Air Marshal I. D. McLachlan and Grp Cpt Ron T. Susans (who was also to test fly the aircraft) arrived in France on February 2, 1961. The Avon-Mirage was flown by senior aeronautical engineer and test pilot, Wg Cdr James Rowland on three occasions, one in a clean configuration Mach 2 run, the other two with underwing tanks and bombs. Because the engine as installed in the E.E. Lightning was 29.5 inches in diameter it left an annular gap of about 5 to 6 inches between the tailpipe and the Mirage rear fuselage, contributing drag. It was 640 lb heavier than the ATAR. Acceleration time from M0.9 to M2.0 at 36,000 feet was reduced in the clean configuration from 3 minutes 40 seconds to 3 minutes. Mach 1.32 was attained in 12,500 lb dry heat at 36,000 feet. It was rated at 15,650 lb with reheat and testing registered Mach 2.1 at 36,000 feet. A low altitude range of 430 nm and a high altitude range of between 860 and 1,000 nm was recorded. Testing and performance monitoring continued for many weeks.

Both James Rowland and GAMD's test pilot, Jean-Marie Saget thought so highly of the straight out performance of the Avon-Mirage that they planned an attempt at the world altitude record assisted with the boost of the aircraft's SEPR rocket motor, to go to 115-120,000 feet. The attempt did not take place.

GAMD's enthusiasm of two years earlier in 1959 for the involvement with Rolls Royce was no longer present. It had become politically obvious that GAMD was not now in a position to support anything other than a totally national product in view of President Charles (General) de Gaulle's strong emphasis on France's national pried and prestige. The French Air Force was also GAMD's best and first customer.

Shock to CAC and Rolls Royce Loses

On December 15, 1960 the Minister for Defence made the public statement announcing the selection of the Mirage as the new combat fighter. The CAC Board however had received earlier advice of this decision, when the Chairman, Sir Sydney Rowell and board member Ian McLennan, were invited to meet the Prime Minister Robert G. Menzies and Alan S. Hulme the Minister for Supply, in Canberra on 13 December. (L. J. Wackett was to retire on 30 December)

The Ministers dropped a bombshell. They wanted to rationalize the industry by directing all new aircraft work to GAF. CAC would build the engine for the Mirage and concentrate on follow-up airframe work on the Winjeel and Sabre.

CAC's directors objected strongly and angrily to this unsuspected turn of events which it was believed was sponsored by GAF in a blatant example of 'empire building'. The Board of CAC took this development very seriously believing that the lack of airframe work would signal the end of the company.

The Government responded to CAC's concern by agreeing to form a joint CAC and DoS committee to examine the possible breakdown of work. It was the contention of DoS that there was only enough aircraft work for one organisation. With GAF's concentration on the designs of the Jindivik guided target aircraft and the Malkara guided anti-tank missile, together with the claimed belief that the Mirage would be the last manned fighter for the RAAF, so GAF, as the manufacturer experienced in missile work had the greater potential to expand to cater for any future unmanned aircraft requirements. However most of this future workload was based on conjectural projects. CAC representatives forced and

The Northrop N156F evolved into the F-5 Freedom Fighter. **Gerhard Joos via J. A. Vella**

claimed the attractive GAF hourly cost rate was so because it was falsified; lacking such consideration such as taxes, rent, superannuation, depreciation etc.

CAC stuck firm to its insistence on full responsibility for the Mirage project whereas GAF conceded to off-load the manufacture of the fin and wings to CAC. The impasse was broken on April 18, 1962 by the Chairman of the Board agreeing to the company building the engine, wings, tail fin, elevons, tail cone, drop tanks and fuel system components.

The Avon 67 / RB146 did not offer significant improvement over the Mirage IIIE whereas overall performance at altitudes above 40,000 ft, for interception was inferior but was able to achieve higher speeds below 45,000 ft without afterburner. Whilst these trials went off very well, the French now armed with Avon performance figures counter-offered their aircraft with the marginally greater thrust Mirage IIIE / ATAR 9C or the experimental 9K variant.

The proposition put forward by Rolls Royce was to develop a 36 inch diameter afterburner with a convergent-divergent nozzle which would reduce the base drag, raise the level of static thrust to 16,600 lb and improve the performance above Mach 1.3. Neither Rolls Royce nor the British or Australian Governments were willing to enter into a development program which did not have the mutual support of two or three of the parties concerned. Australia's share of the development was estimated to be about £A500,000 but the risk was not warranted. Australia did not want to upset an established engine/airframe combination having in mind the previous experience with the Avon Sabre. SNECMA had meanwhile accelerated their work on the ATAR 9D intended for the Mirage III and hoped to offer the engine in the Australian Mirage as the ATAR 9K (it has been quoted as 'K' for 'Kangoarou'). The 9K planned for the Mirage IV strategic nuclear bomber could not be considered as it had not reached an acceptable level of development.

After a strong presentation in Canberra by the SNECMA team, Australia negotiated a reciprocal primary industry trade agreement with France and SNECMA reduced the price on the simpler ATAR 9C with the result that a ministerial statement of May 17, 1962,

The initial F-104A Starfighter interceptor of 1956 evolved into the heavier multi-role F-104G. **Gerhard Joos via J. A. Vella**

confirmed the elimination of the more expensive and complex Avon engine.

The designation IIIO was retained for the 'true' RAAF production configuration, minus the RB146. The unit cost for the ATAR / Mirage combination was some £A400,000. This was a lot less than the estimated £A500,000 for the Mirage / RB146 Avon combination.

Some of the other technical decisions settled were;
- to favour the Cyrano II attack radar in preference to the British offered alternative-the Ferranti Airpass II
- to choose the airframe of the Mirage IIIE rather than that of the IIIC as the basis of the Australian IIIO production variant
- to institute about 150 equipment changes including the selection of Sperry Twin Gyro platform, PHI, TACAN, Doppler radar and radar altimeter

Mirage A3-1 had its first flight in France on March 14, 1963. It preceded the April 5, 1963 first flight of the Mirage IIIE on which it was based. The initial contract order of March 31, 1961 was for a mere 30 aircraft which would be manufactured to a substantial extent in Australia.

CAC Airframe Work

A3-1 was the first of two French assembled prototypes of the Mirage IIIO. This aircraft, together with A3-2, set out to verify the modifications requested by the RAAF. A3-1 was air-freighted to Avalon, Victoria on November 27, 1963. Airframes 3 and 4 were shipped from France as fully equipped major assemblies of wings, fuselage, engines, etc. Airframes 5, 6, 7, and 8 were sent out as major assemblies ex-jigs. Aircraft 9 and 10 came out in half-shell condition. Airframe 11 and onwards were assembled from primary components and airframe 16 was the first example with some primary components made in Australia.

Mirage A3-3 made its first flight from Avalon, which was the GAF final assembly area for the Mirage, on November 16, 1963 and was officially handed to the RAAF on January 29, 1964, by the Minister for Air, David Fairbairn. For CAC, as well as for GAF, the French technical language and the Metric units of measurement were a new element never before encountered in aircraft licence production in Australia. In addition, the training of a new large workforce in the complex fabrication and assembly of what was essentially another stop-start defence project, all contributed to present major areas of difficulty.

CAC's policy was to fabricate all assembly jigs and to carry out all airframe jig assembly in Australia. Based on the initial small order or 30 aircraft, the majority of detailed fabricated parts were produced overseas with the exception of those items requiring frequent replacement, which were produced locally. Had the information to eventually increase the order to 116 aircraft been known earlier, the number of items to be completely manufactured in Australia would have been considerably increased.

The order was raised to 60 single seaters in October 1962 and increased again to 100 aircraft by February 20, 1963 followed by 16 dual-seater trainer aircraft. The local content of the entire airframe was 75% of the required total man hours, whilst only 10% of the primary parts were made in Australia.

The polyurethane sealing of the integral wing tanks on a production basis was a new technique. It required a controlled temperature and humidity space. Applying fresh sealant, closing the wing, pressure testing, filling with sealant, mechanically rotating the wing to slosh the sealant, draining it and days of curing. The major taper milled skin panels for the wings and fin and the wing spars machined from solid billet were fully imported as separate items. The Department of Supply considered the machinery necessary to produce this machining process as too expensive to import and set up. In simple terms, an advance in technology transfer as part of the manufacturing process was quickly by-passed and the aircraft manufacturing sector started its rapid decline in areas which mattered. The sheet metal items such as the elevons and rudder were fabricated locally and 25 additional sets were built; 16 sets were for the Mirage IIIOD dual seater aircraft and 9 were as a spares holding. Wing flaps were built as offset and sent to Nord Aviation in France.

Additional work included the fabrication of 174 x 500 litre, 243 x 1,300 litre and 132 x 1,700 litre drop tanks/long range tanks in addition to the rocket bay space fuel tanks, fuel tank and bomb rack pylons and airbrakes (less their hydraulic components).

Engine Builder

The nine stage axial flow compressor/two stage turbine SNECMA ATAR 09C3/03Z turbojet (ATAR: Atelier Technique Aeronautique Reichenback) for which CAC was the prime contractor was built with a chain of local supply companies to an initial 80% local content value but ended up nearer to 90%.

The ATAR engine series stretched back to the 1945 French nationalised SNECMA engine consortium whose technical director from 1950 was Dr Herman Oestrich formerly of BMW (Germany, WW2) aero engines.

The first three engines were received complete with accessories. The next 15 arrived in an almost complete state and from the 19th unit local manufacturing content was progressively increased until by the 32nd engine, almost all the chosen components were being manufactured in Australia. The original Metric dimensioned production drawings were all converted to Imperial measurement. Component manufacturing maintained full interchange with the identical French produced engine parts. Engine testing was carried out in the engine test house at CAC. The quantity of engines comprising of bought in complete units, assemblies and local manufacture totalled 192 units. The 09C3 was the initial model of the ATAR. Progressive SNECMA modifications took the engines through 09C4 and 09C5 configuration. Some were modified to 09C8 standard but 09C6 and C7 changes were not applied locally. Modifications were a combination of locally raised and/or major adaptions of SNECMA origin. All primary components for the engine assembly program were delivered by the end of 1968.

The first 50 aircraft Mirage IIIO (F) were fitted with the Cyrano 2A radar optimised for air-to air operations. Mirages IIIO (A) A3-51 to A3-100 had the Cyrano 2B radar that incorporated the ground

Mirage IIIO general final assembly by the Government Aircraft Factory at the Avalon Airfield, Victoria site.
ADF Serials Image Gallery, Bob Nash

mapping function which together with Doppler radar was intended for the ground support, Army and Navy co-operation roles.

In practical terms the local build content of airframe parts came to about 30% overall for the total airframe construction program (excluding the engine). An early estimate of the cost disadvantage for the local manufacture of the first 30 aircraft was put at 21%. No further estimates were available for the additional 86 airframes which were assembled because of the uncertainty as to what comprised local content and to what degree. However, the program was completed over 13 years within the approved funds of A$270M for 116 Mirage at an average cost per aircraft of A$2.43M which included the aircraft, spare engines, build equipment, initial maintenance and long term spares. In 1969 it was decided to convert all the IIIO (F) to IIIO (A) standard, reduce logistics and develop the advertised multi-role capability. This conversion was carried out at Avalon during major servicing.

Performance enhancement and updates were introduced during the production phase and service life of the Mirage. To increase the internal fuel capacity by some 55 gallons, wet wing leading edges were introduced from aircraft No 48 with slow retrospective modification to the earlier aircraft. Some 1,000 modifications were issued, the majority being adopted. Mirages were returned to the GAF and CAC factories for servicing and modifications on 348 occasions.

That is not to say the program went smoothly. Up to March 18, 1965, only 13 Mirages had been delivered. A3-1, the prototype, had crashed near Avalon in December 1964 during its flight trials. There was an unforeseen lag in initial deliveries caused by a lack of local skilled labour due to the severe run-down of the industry during the 1950s. Management skills had become rusty and the program was brought back to schedule by the recruitment of about 600 tradesmen from the UK. This problem at GAF did not affect CAC to the same degree, the latter being able to fabricate the extra wing sets for the Mirage IIIOD dual seaters but complete fuselages had to be fully imported from France so as to get around the severe production manpower problems at GAF. This delay meant that CAC Sabres had to be overhauled, at a high cost to the RAAF, for a further period of service beyond their planned retirement date.

New Developments

In August 1967 shortly after the June 1967 Six Day War between Israel and its Arab neighbour countries unconfirmed reports were circulating within RAAF Support Command (these did not originate from CAC) that the Australian Government had been approached by Israel for the possible immediate acquisition of spares and/or Mirage aircraft from the RAAF's fleet. These were needed to make good the losses in the Israeli Air Force Mirage IIIC fleet, but hindered from doing so by an arms embargo imposed by the French Government. However, this possible extra work for the local industry in support of the IAF was unlikely to have materialised due not only to the nature of the Australian assembly program that included the importation of much specified French sourced avionics and flight control systems but also of the politics and embargo restrictions that could then also have been extended to Australia. The Air Board considered the approach in September, possibly as a way to lower its own outlay on local support costs. The Department of External Affairs would have rapidly vetoed the proposition.

Later, in a reversal of roles, the firm of Israel Aircraft Industries sought to have the Kfir-C2, a highly modified Mirage 5 airframe with fixed canards, strakes, extended wing leading edges and a General Electric J79 turbojet, built under licence in Australia. IAI was anxious to export the expertise garnered in modifying and re-engining the Mirage. Mounting fixed canards on the delta winged Mirage

*CAC's Atar 9C engine and examples of external tanks on display in the No 1 Aircraft Depot hangar at RAAF Laverton. **J.A.Vella***

dramatically reduced the approach speed whilst enhancing such aspects of performance as the sustained turn rate, the low speed manoeuvrability and increasing the angle of attack capability.

CAC was also left considering newspaper reports that the Prime Minister of New Zealand, Keith Holyoake would be deciding if it would acquire 16-25 Mirage from Australia. Long term credit arrangements had been drawn up involving GAMD with the Department of Supply; a deal considered to be more attractive than the abondoned alternate USA offer of the F4 Phantom II.

The subject of using the SNECMA ATAR 9K was raised again in March 1978 where CAC, to an official request, analysed the possible changes or effects if the 9K50 turbojet was fitted as an alternative engine. The take-off distance, climb time and fuel consumed in the climb would have all been reduced, whilst the sustained level turn normal acceleration at altitude would have been increased by about 25% at the expense of an increased fuel flow. The only way to make use of the available excess power was to increase the fuel capacity of the Mirage IIIO even further beyond both existing internal and external fuel tank capacities at the expense of supersonic performance.

The Mirage fleet was put through a LOTEX program commencing in 1979 for the refurbishment by CAC of 96 wing halves for a flying life gain of 1,500 hours. Wings halves were examined, stripped down, the sealant removed, refastened and resealed. More right side wings were found stressed than left wings due to the flying pattern. All were completed in 1984. At the same time the RAAF sought 12 sets of new wings but was delayed due to a lack of parts from France. This $A8M contract eventually got underway in June 1983 with the delivery of a set of wings each month but was suspended when RAAF funding fell short and it would accept only six sets of wings. The other six remained in a partially complete state at CAC awaiting a decision on outstanding payments or eventual fate. Work restarted in late 1987 to build the wings for air freighting and resale to GAMD. The LOTEX program was possible because the original local manufacture had brought with it all the necessary jigs and tooling to support the aircraft throughout its service life.

*Mirage IIIO(F) A3-22, 76 Sqdn, RAAF Williamtown. October 14, 1969. **J.A.Vella***

Mirage IIIO (F) A3-29, 75 Sqdn, RAAF Williamtown. October 14,1969. **J.A.Vella**

Mirage IIIOD, A3-106, 2(F)OCU. RAAF Williamtown, April 7,1973. **J.A. Vella**

Mirage IIIO (F) A3-44, 76 Sqdn, RAAF Williamtown. October 14,1969. **J.A.Vella**

Mirage IIIOD, A3-106, in the earlier 2(F)OCU markings. RAAF Williamtown, October 14,1969. **J.A.Vella**

Mirage A3-27,-65, 2(F)OCU, RAAF Butterworth. **Air Commodore John Jacobs via J.A.Vella**

Mirage IIIO(A) A3-75, 77 Sqdn fitted with the longer photo reconnaissance camera nose. RAAF Fairbairn. April 3, 1971. **J.A. Vella**

Mirage A3-49, 2(F)OCU, RAAF Williamtown. April 7,1973. **J.A.Vella**

Mirage IIIO (A) A3-56, -58,-53,-85 formation of 75 Sqdn. **RAAF**

Left: CAC Mirage ATAR turbojet production advertisement in AIRCRAFT magazine October 1962. **Herald & Weekly Times**

A vertical fin frame structure build progress underway. **David Anderson. 704072053P.**

Below: The vertical fin on the Mirage IIIO was the second significant airframe component the company was to construct in the Mirage fighter sub-contract.

The Clowns helping the company dispose of unused Mirage product. **Roger Ward**

CA-29 Mirage IIIO wings under construction.
David Anderson. 704072054P

Mirage IIIO wings coming together. CAC's largest airframe components as the major sub-contractor to GAF. **HDHV**

The graceful looking Mirage was much liked by the RAAF. Its selection brought to the Service the opportunity to move from transonic speed to Mach 2; the introduction to an engine with afterburner and associated very high fuel consumption; introduction of TACAN and computer navigation; familiarity with combined air intercept and ground attack radar together with two different forms of missile homing characteristics. However the reliability and effectiveness of its primary air intercept armament, the Matra R530 and the Sidewinder AIM-9B missiles was very low. Very late in its service life the Matra Magic R550 missile was introduced.

The multi-mode Cyrano 2B radar with the combined ground mapping and air intercept radar capability notionally gave the aircraft a multi-role capability but with very real practical limitations of the almost manual technology of the day. Initially two squadrons operated in the specialized air intercept role, the other two in ground support. In merging the roles together it became very difficult for pilots to become proficient in the new full spectrum of the dual role in their mandated six months training cycle which also included tactical, visual and some photographic reconnaissance. Coupled with reductions in fighter pilot flying hours from 22.5 hours (although most were getting 30 hours) to 17 hours per pilot each month and the sudden disbanding of 76 Squadron on August 22, 1973 all created significant operational difficulties. These Defence cutbacks were brought on by the new Federal Labor Government looking for cut-back in defence spending in support of new urgently needed public social change initiatives. With the 'multi-role' capability, less was seen as the new norm. With the fighter force reduced to three squadrons, the high level skill emphasis in air combat tactics, intercepts and visual strike capability meant low-level all-weather operations became virtually beyond the fighter force to achieve and were hardly practiced. Efficiency decreased as pressure increased to maintain exercises and deployments.

The Mirage served with Nos 3, 75, 76, 77 and (much later) 79 Fighter Squadrons, 2(F) OCU and ARDU.

Bibliography: CA-29 Mirage IIIO Fighter Sub-Contract
Aircraft. (Various 1961,1963,1964,1966).

Cobban, B.(1986). Manager, HdH Manufacturing & Services. [Correspondence].

Chillon, Jacques. (1986). Mirage IIIO type origins.[Correspondence].

Commonwealth Aircraft Corporation. (March 1978). Engineering Report AA379. Basic Air Combat Performance Relativity between the RAAF Mirage IIIO powered by either the SNECMA Atar 9C or Atar 9K50.

Fleming, I. B. (1971). [Presentation to the Royal Aeronautical Society, Australian Division, Melbourne Branch].

Harker, Ronald, W. (1976) *Rolls Royce from the Wings, Military Aviation 1925-1971*. Oxford Illustrated Press, UK .

Jones, Ern R. (1986). CAC Production Manager. [Correspondence].

Park, R. (1986). HdH Design Engineering- Engines. [Correspondence].

Ring, I. H. The Mirage Contract Committee 1960-1961. [Internal communication].

Ring, I. H. (1986).[Interviews].

Rowland, James. Air Marshall, CAS (1922-1999). Mirage questions. (Undated).[Correspondence].

Suissue, Henri. Directeur Presse Information AMD & Breguet Aviation, Paris. (1987) [Correspondence].

Susans, M. R. (1990). *The RAAF Mirage Story*. Royal Australian Air Force Museum, Point Cook.

The Myth of the Mirage Spares Embargo (August 2017). Air Power Development Centre Bulletin, Canberra.

EX200 / EX220-IKARA MISSILE HANDLING AND LAUNCH SYSTEM
1960

From the middle of 1961, the protection of shipping convoys and naval task forces of the Royal Australian Navy against attack by enemy (Soviet) submarines was to be the role of the British derived Whitby Class, Australian built Type 12S, River Class Destroyer Escorts (DE), six of which were to join the Service.

These ships were fitted with hull mounted acoustic detection systems. Pre-set depth charges were ejected on a ballistic trajectory from their relatively short ranged, triple-barrelled 'Limbo' Mortar Mk 10 system towards the detected near position of the submarine. As this lacked the range to exploit the longer distance detection capability of the DE, it was decided in 1959 during the construction of the third ship, to seek a new weapon which could use the new family of lightweight torpedoes which were becoming available. Two existing systems were examined and rejected.

The US Navy's ASROC (Anti-Submarine Rocket), a solid fuel rocket motor arranged in tandem with a homing torpedo made a ballistic unguided flight to a pre-determined point to allow the release of the torpedo. Because of its long period of unguided flight, its age and the need for longer range, it was out of favour.

Manned helicopters delivering homing torpedoes were rejected due to low reaction time, the time taken to reach a fast moving, highly manoeuvrable underwater target, a lack of all-weather capability and the need for extensive structural alterations to the aft end of the ships to provide a helicopter launch and recovery pad.

Australia's decision was to develop an actively guided missile platform with in-flight target information updates, processing this information and directing the missile so that the American lightweight Mk 44 acoustic homing torpedo could be dropped into the water at a point as close to the target as possible. The project was a combination of the Departments of the Navy and Supply, with major assistance from industry. The DoS assumed responsibility for the research, development, design and manufacture of the airborne vehicle (missile less torpedo), the associated data processing, tracking, command guidance systems and the evaluation of system performance. These responsibilities were shared between the Aeronautical Research Laboratories, the Weapons Research Establishment and the Government Aircraft Factories, the latter for the Ikara delivery vehicle, Project M4. (*Ikara* is a central Australia indigenous language word for a throwing stick; a length of wood shaped to hold a spear so as to effectively extend the thrower's arm, thus extending the range and effectiveness of the spear.)

Ikara
The Ikara missile/delivery vehicle (DWB 1101) was a minimum size and weight vehicle fitted with readily detachable wings and fins. It was 25% the weight of ASROC and its magazine handling and launcher complex was 66% the weight of ASROC system. The adoption of twist and steer aerodynamic controls led to a minimum number of control surfaces. With the Mk 44 homing torpedo weighing 432 lb, 12.75 in diameter, 8.2 feet long, slung underneath the main body of the vehicle, there was a minimisation of aerodynamic instability following the dropping away of the ventral stabilizing fin, torpedo release, jettison of its rear covering and its

lowering by parachute at a maximum range of 10 nm and a maximum height profile of 1,100 feet. The AUW was 1,131 lb.

As part of the overall aim to reduce departure from the nominal flight path, both the boost Mattina and the Murawa sustainer, twin stage, solid fuel rocket engine developed by Bristol Aerojet Ltd (UK), formed an integral part of the vehicle structure, without the need for any jettison complications and side force effect. Production of about 1,400 units began in 1963 at the Maribrynong Explosives Factory in Melbourne. The vehicle had been designed for future growth potential to permit the carriage of alternative or heavier payloads at some later stage. The lead contractor for the RAN's guidance and fire control was EMI (Australia) Ltd. This initial analogue control computer system was eventually superseded by a digital update. The system used computations and real time command guidance sent to the electronics package located in the dorsal fin via a shipborne broad beam tracking antenna for launch and missile flight path correction updates which may have become necessary due to target manoeuvring. In this manner the optimum point for torpedo separation could be selected, based on the latest shipborne sensor information.

CAC's Primary Role

CAC was first approached by the Naval Research and Development Office (NRDO) on April 8, 1960 with indications that it was advocating the services of CAC as the prime contractor for the Ikara Magazine Handling and Launch (DW7831) System (MH & LS).

In August, the Department of Defence allotted funds for the concept, followed on 29 August with the handover to CAC of the Navy's preliminary design studies and specifications. The contract awarded on 20 September asked CAC to fully design, develop and manufacture a prototype system against this requirement specification suitable for installation on the Type 12S River Class Destroyer Escort ships. The company's basic design was approved nine months later on June 15, 1961 with its completion promised for February 28, 1963. This was a major undertaking for CAC, having had no previous experience in designing such large and heavy (by aeronautical standards) mechanical systems.

A number of key experienced mechanical and hydraulic system design personnel were recruited, of whom Tadeusz (Tad) A. Kowalewski and Geoff Aarons, Senior Mechanical Engineer led the design team together with Chief Engineer John Kentwell for this and subsequent Ikara system installations.

The principal features of the EX200 Missile Handling and Launching System (MHLS) for the Destroyer Escorts were:

- System almost entirely automated, hydraulically powered, electrically controlled, having the capacity for a high rate of continuous delivery of a relatively large number of missiles

*IKARA torpedo carrying guided missile. **IWM***

- Missile bodies (with its torpedo already attached by a shore weapons establishment) suspended on carriages in two rows at right angles to the ship's keel in a sealed magazine room. They could be automatically cycled to bring any particular missile to the extraction station
- An extraction trolley brought the missile bodies into a two stage missile assembly room where the flying surfaces were attached to them manually
- They were then automatically loaded onto the tilted all-weather capable, external launcher. After shutting the outside blast proof doors, the launcher was trained into its azimuth and elevation firing position
- The entire system was located on the aft starboard quarter deck well cut-out, on the Destroyer Escorts (where it replaced the previous Limbo Mortar installation)

The design established a number of precedents for naval systems and installation techniques in Australia. For example:

- The provision of a pump room where high pressure (3000 psi) lightweight hydraulic systems based on aircraft principles were employed. These proved to be very effective, relatively silent and virtually leak proof.
- The entire ship space for the system was simulated in a rig at CAC where all interfaces between the ship and the new CAC system were accurately located and then faithfully reproduced by the ship builder in each vessel.
- Each system was built in the rig at CAC and put through an extensive acceptance test program in the rig before being dismantled into large sub-assemblies for re-erection in a ship in minimum time.
- Much of the supporting structural bracketry was manufactured as high tensile steel castings, using CAC's Shaw Process casting technique. This work in cast high tensile steel was a big metallurgical challenge which was successfully achieved, including as it did, difficult welding processes. The implementation of aeronautical design techniques resulted in considerable weight saving in the magazine and the handling and launch system, enabling it to meet tight weight limitations as well as underwater explosion shock impact requirements.

The design, manufacture and subsequent development of the prototype system progressed rapidly and compared more than favourably with similar system development in the UK and USA. This was greatly helped by an efficient decision-making process within the NRDO office. Virtually all decisions, whether they were financial, technical or operational, were decided upon in a matter of hours by the Navy Office which had been located in Melbourne with that precise intention. The benefits of such a straightforward management system were lost or never learned by the Defence Department bureaucracy as each subsequent major project undertaken by CAC suffered an increasing weight of bureaucratic interference, lack of insight, understanding and remoteness.

The prototype system completed its acceptance tests at CAC in late 1963 and was installed by a CAC team in HMAS Stuart at Cockatoo Docks and Engineering, NSW early in 1964. Following successful sea trials, appproval was given for the production of six additional single launcher units, five for installation on HMAS Parramatta, Yarra, Derwent, Swan and Torrens and one system located at the CAC premises as a shore based training rig.

Further RAN expansion

At the peak of the design and development activity the project employed some 30 engineers, 100-120 design draftsmen and technical officers. With the impending delivery of three new Charles

F. Adams class (DDG) guided missile destroyers from the United States, the RAN began investigating on August 4, 1961 the fitting of the Ikara installation in these ships in place of their original ASROC ASW system. The first launcher was delivered on February 1, 1963 followed by first shipboard missile firing on 27 February.

While the same fundamental elements of the (DE) EX200 system were to be used, modifications to the new design (DDG) EX220 were necessary to cater for:

- the available location on the DDG on the upper deck approximately amidships, and
- the results of Service experience which showed that, provided the first two missiles could be launched quickly, a high continuous rate of fire was not necessary

Consideration of the available space led to the development of a duplex system, ie twin magazines, assembly rooms and launchers, one on either ship side, each covering approximately half the possible target area, whilst a revision of the firing rate, led to each magazine having approximately half the capacity of that on the DEs and each assembly room having only one missile assembly station. In other respects this DDG Ikara system was the same as on the DEs with the same degree of automation and method of control.

Three systems were built for HMAS Perth, Hobart and Brisbane using an identical approach to factory assembly, testing and installation as with the DEs. Two complete spare launcher assemblies were manufactured and held by the Navy as first and second reserve spares for both DE and DDG usage. The magazine capacity of the RAN ships was not revealed nor was the firing rate.

Testing Procedures

The whole of the Engineering Test Section of CAC's Engineering Department was involved in testing the Ikara MHLS. In the early stages of the prototype system development, vibration and heel (ship lean) test rigs were used. Testing was carried out on the performance validation of the hydraulic system and its individual components.

Dummy Ikara missile on port side mid-ship location on RAN's three DDG class destroyers. Missile assembly room to the right. An identical launcher was located directly opposite on the starboard side. Port Melbourne. March 14,1988. **J.A.Vella**

The location of the Ikara system was in the aft part of each ship in the River Class Destroyer Escorts in the proximity of the propeller drive shafts where the hull was subjected to the turbulent wash from the propeller. This required a means of verifying the integrity of the design against this possible source of vibrational influence.

CAC developed a low cost mechanical vibration table that amassed more than 300 hours of testing of the missile carriage, trolley and rail tracks with only minor changes being necessary on the Ikara components and no structural or equipment resonance was found to be present. During long sweeping turns the ship heeled over and the sideways load became significant for the transverse motion of the missile carriage in the magazine. This load was replicated through the heel testing rig, it being one of the requirements for the acceptance tests in the factory of all the individual RAN systems. It was also used to check the integrity of the hydraulics when holding an unlocked row of carriages in the event of either a hydraulic or electrical failure during transfer motion.

The Launch Process

The missile/torpedo weapon was loaded into the launcher from the assembly room trolley, rear end first, with the launcher cradle in a tilted position. After loading and return of the empty trolley, the launcher cradle was elevated and locked into a firing position after the blast doors were closed. Launcher elevation was at 45 deg with electrically powered fixed azimuth stops at 45 deg intervals.

The launcher, with its own independent hydraulic system was elevated or depressed by two jacks. In turn, the rotation and elevation of the launcher was controlled to avoid collision of the launched missile with parts of the ships superstructure on the DDG destroyers and to avoid wind-up of connecting cables. At the moment of firing (after an override lock ensured there was sufficient build-up of thrust to enable a successful launch) the first movement of the missile was along the supporting rails and as the pins of the ascending vehicle left the rails, these rails hinged away to ensure that they did not come into contact with the tail of the Ikara in free space due to the relative motion between the free missile and the ship.

The buffer stop of the launcher's azimuth rotation and the damping motion of the rails as they hinged out of the way were part of the CAC equipment testing process. Fore and aft travel of the carriages and trolley was by hydraulic motor and continuous chain drive. In the event of chain breakage, liquid spring buffers prevented damage which could result as part of the ship's pitching motion. All hydraulic valve functioning was validated through electrical testing of each installation; in addition the system was required to operate smoothly, as quietly as could be expected to minimize noise transmission underwater and without shocks that would have damaged the missile whilst performing to an overall expected time cycle both in the check-out rig and as installed on board ship.

HEY GUESS WHAT, SOMEONE JUST BLEW UP THE NEW CANTEEN! Rog

The Clowns are out of control. Having been barred from the in-house Navy training rig classes, carry out their own tests. **Roger Ward**

Looking aft. Launcher with a dummy round on stern of HMAS Torrens(DE). Port Melbourne, November 6, 1988. **J.A.Vella**

Rear view of an empty Ikara launcher on HMAS Brisbane (DDG). The large door in the superstructure to the left led to the missile magazine and assembly room. **J.A.Vella**

The front end of an empty launcher showing the launch rails and the cutout in the launcher housing for the missile's snap-on wings. Starboard side on HMAS Brisbane,(DDG) Port Melbourne November 29, 1970. **J.A.Vella**

The only 'complaint' from the RAN was that the MHLS 'did not leak' oil. This held back the standard navy practice of wiping metal surfaces in mechanical systems with an oily rag. This letdown was a minor grumble in return for safer floor compartment spaces. An outstanding feature of the MHLS was that no major changes were needed between the prototype and the production systems.

United Kingdom Adaptation

An agreement between the UK and Australian governments allowed for an exchange of technical data on the Ikara between the two parties. Bristol/BAC were the UK Ikara agents. Around 1962 the RN adapted its own variant of the Australian design for installation in the planned CVA-01/02 aircraft carriers (cancelled) and the Type 82 destroyers. Only HMS Bristol (D23) was fitted when the Type 82 class was also cancelled. Left with systems and a committment to buy the missiles, the RN then fitted Ikara as an expensive mid-life modernisation update, from June 1970 to October 1978, to eight Leander Type 121 class frigates, F10, F15, F18, F38, F39, F104, F109 and F114, the first of which was not completed until several years after the RAN had some of its own systems in service. Their missile storage and handling arrangements were changed to allow the loading/unloading of the torpedoes etc to be done on board ship. The UK systems had a 23 or 24 round capacity.

The UK's Ikara vehicle, GAF Project M5, had different (NATO) computer systems and command frequencies and were also intended to deliver, if required, the 600 lb WE177A Nuclear Depth Bomb. The Royal Navy used its own Vickers built ML & HS which was based on CAC's concept but changed to be pointed precisely to within minutes of azimuth launch arc, whereas the simpler RAN system relied on post launch, mid-course trajectory signal corrections. Built in boiler-plate, heavy type, construction it had to also withstand North Atlantic icing conditions. It weighed a lot more than CAC's design and reverted back to Royal Navy traditional heavy, low pressure, noisy hydraulic systems whose operation former submariners reputed could be heard from 10 miles away(unverified) under water. Comparisons between the RAN and Royal Navy systems by officers of both navies and by CAC, showed the system in the Australian ships in a very favourable light; particularly for the integrity, quietness, light weight and reliability of their hydraulic systems.

ARL and GAF Project M6, were studies for Extended Range Ikara (1974-75), that was to make optimum use of the heavier Mk 46 or Stingray torpedoes but it did not advance further, so by 1990 Ikara's role diminished. To June 30, 1974, 1004 missiles had been ordered by the UK, Australian and Brazilian Navies. (Refer to BRANIK text)

In part of the rundown of the UK Navy in 1981 to pay for their nuclear submarines deterrant, their Leander class frigate F104 HMS Dido was sold to new Zealand and became HMNZS Southland in 1983. Its UK fitted Ikara system was incompatible with the RAN's.

Proven in service, Ikara was unmatched for range, accuracy and reliability by any other ASW system in service or under development in the West. The RAN withdrew Ikara by 1991. It had not been updated and it became increasingly expensive to maintain.

The RAN/GAF/DSTO's follow-on, Turana Target drone based on the Ikara was test launched from HMAS Swan's ML & HS in January 1974 but was cancelled in September 1979 after 24 examples built.

The shore-based training aid (which mostly followed the internal layout of the DE ships) was located and operated by CAC inside the Butler hangar in the corner of the property leased from the State Government. HDHV continued this support on behalf of the Navy. until the Navy, not wanting to incur the costs of relocating the training aid, had it dismantled and broken up.

Bibliography: EX200 / EX220 Ikara Missile Handling & Launch System

Australia. Department of Defence. Directorate of Public Relations. [Correspondence] (1988).

Australia. Department of Supply. (Undated). *Ikara, Australian Long Range ASW System.*

Byrne. F. (1988). CAC Test Engineer.[Correspondence].

Collections. Transport & Engineering. Museums Victoria.

HARS Aviation Museum.

Kentwell, John. (1988). CAC Chief Design Engineer. [Correspondence].

Turana. Fleet Air Arm Association of Australia.

CONCEPTUAL STOL FEEDER LINER
May 1960

On May 4, 1960 the CAC Design Office Study Group held an informal meeting with DCA officials to discuss operational and design problems connected with STOL (Short Take-Off and Landing) passenger aircraft.

Staff present at the meeting were: J. Kentwell (Chairman); B. Carr; A.Fisher; H.Gorjanicyn; L.Irving; C.Reid; D.Simmons; W.Watkins and D. Whitaker, with guest Peter Langford, DCA Director of Airworthiness.

Peter Langford attended to gather general thinking on the subject matter with regards to operational control and to provide the official view concerning STOL operations for which CAC were considering proposals. The summary of the discussion did not formulate any far-reaching conclusions except to clear the way for some sort of general initiative being created. During a private visit in 1959 to both CAC and DCA, Sir Roy Fedden the former chief engineer of the Bristol Aero Engine Company had mentioned the general industry need for a 10-14 seater feeder liner. His thinking was based on working partnerships within the British Commonwealth to create and sustain a mutual viable aviation industry.

The broad consensus was that the Fokker F27 Friendship aircraft being operated by both TAA and Ansett airlines on feeder type operations was not, in spite of its extra speed, comfort, etc, attracting any more passengers than the old DC-3s.

TAA and Ansett had indicated an interest in a 10 seater aircraft with each airline needing about five examples. The need for a 14 seater aircraft was also likely but STOL capability was not essential. Private companies were also seeking a 10 seater aircraft for executive travel. DCA did not see any restrictions to the operations of STOL aircraft in a close urban environment envisaged the need for such an aircraft and offered the suggestion that to be effective, such aircraft had to be competitive with equivalent rail fares and the cost to passengers should approach road taxi fares.

DCA would have permitted a 'bus service' nature of fare collection by a single pilot operation. However, the single pilot operation in IFR conditions would probably not have been allowed if the aircraft was to operate into congested approach control zones.

CAC's thinking centred around the use of cross-coupled Allison Engine turboprop installations (as had been tested experimentally in

S.T.O.L. Concept Study - 8 Seat Commuter Aircraft
[Pressurized Cabin]

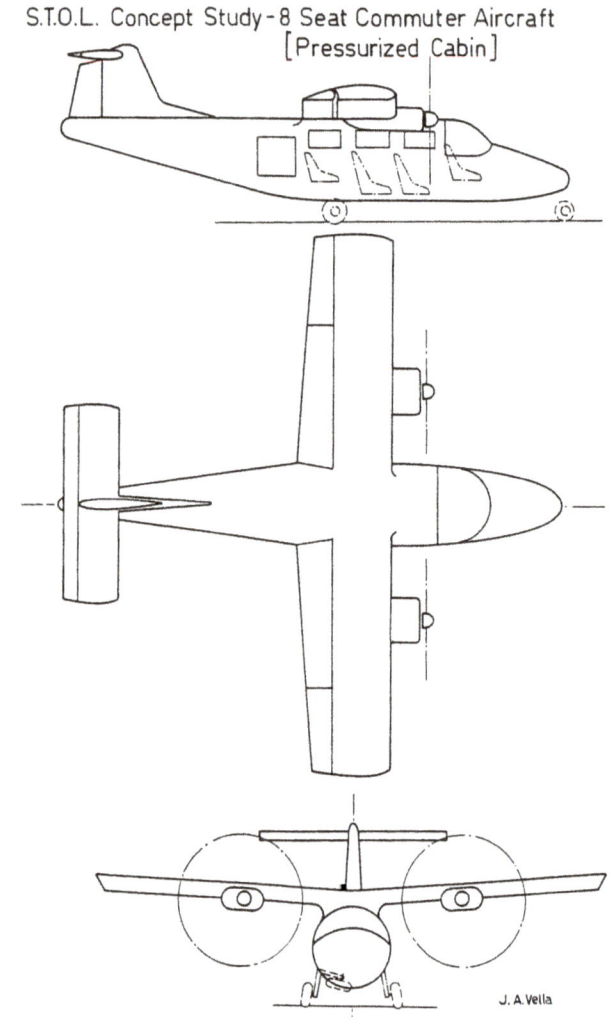

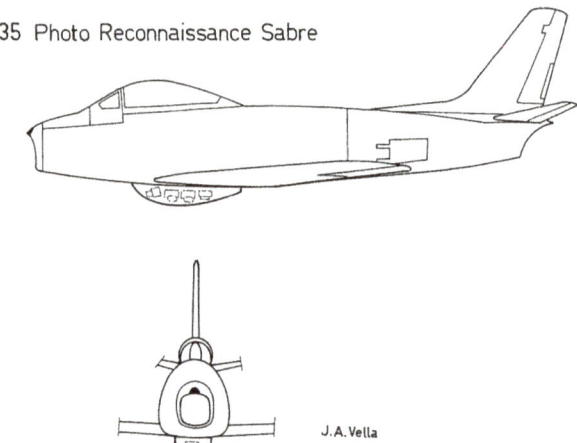

P435 Photo Reconnaissance Sabre

the USA) in which shaft failure on one engine would have been compensated by the second engine cross-drive shaft.

The need for operator backing by the manufacturer was seen as a paramount requirement for any company attempting a civil aircraft venture. To break the Cessna / Piper / Beechcraft nexus the potential operator had to have confidence with any possible new aircraft manufacturer for on-going service support.

Bibliography: Conceptual STOL Feeder Liner
Commonwealth Aircraft Corporation. (May 4, 1960).[Minutes of meeting held with Department of Civil Aviation].

P435 SABRE, PHOTO RECONNAISSANCE
June 1960

Three oblique mounted, forward facing and left and right side pointing model F95 four inch lens camera units were proposed for fitment in an under-fuselage flush fitting reconnaissance pod on the Sabre. This layout, to satisfy an official requirement for a photo reconnaissance platform was refined and expanded on June 30, 1960 (Drg 27-L7301) to also incorporate the vertical stereo KB-8A, 76 mm lens camera, its computer and a tape recorder package.

The location for the front of the pod was fuselage Station 85. The rear reference was Station 176. The pod was identical to the item used during the Sabre Blue Jay missile (DH Firestreak) trials.

The plan to use the Sabre as an aerial reconnaissance platform was not taken any further but the requirement was not abandoned. When the Mirage IIIO came into service some aircraft were reconfigured with tactical reconnaissance cameras in lieu of their nose radar equipment whereas the Wild RC10 vertical, high altitude cameras fitted to some RAAF Canberra bombers were used for cartographic survey work and not for tactical reconnaissance.

Bibliography: P435 Sabre, Photo Reconnaissance
Commonwealth Aircraft Corporation.(June 1960). Sabre Drg.27-L301, Layout Photo Recon. Equipment Container.

Winjeel, Turboprop Agricultural Aircraft
February 1964

On the second occasion that an agricultural derivative of the Winjeel Basic Trainer was contemplated, the original Pratt & Whitney Wasp Junior radial engine was to be replaced by a Pratt & Whitney (Canada) PT6 turboprop engine.

The basic configuration of the aircraft was of a hopper located over the main undercarriage, its upper rear surface faired into the fuselage decking. The pilot sat in front of the hopper and above the body of the engine. A second crew seat for the loader / flagman was located behind the hopper. This position was enclosed under a rearward sliding acrylic canopy.

Because of the much lighter weight of the PT6 engine in comparison with the Wasp Junior, its installation had to be much further forward, the tip of the spinner finishing up about 10 feet ahead of the existing engine firewall. The hopper load of 3,360 lb was significantly greater than that of the standard Ceres whilst the take-off weight would have been less.

Specifications	Winjeel, Turboprop Agricultural Aircraft	
Powerplant	One Pratt & Whitney (Canada) PT6A turboprop engine	
Performance	Cruise speed	160 kts
	Range at cruise speed	280 nm
	Landing speed	48 kts
	TO dist at 7,200 lb	1,050 ft
Weights	Empty	2,800 lb
	Hopper load	3,360 lb
	TO	7,200 lb
Dimensions	Swing span	38 ft 7 ins
	Wing area	250 sq ft
	Length	32 ft

Bibliography: Winjeel, Turboprop Agricultural Aircraft
Reid, C.J. (February 15, 1964) . Engineering Report AA178. Turboprop Agricultural Aircraft. Commonwealth Aircraft Corporation.

Winjeel-Turboprop Agricultural Aircraft

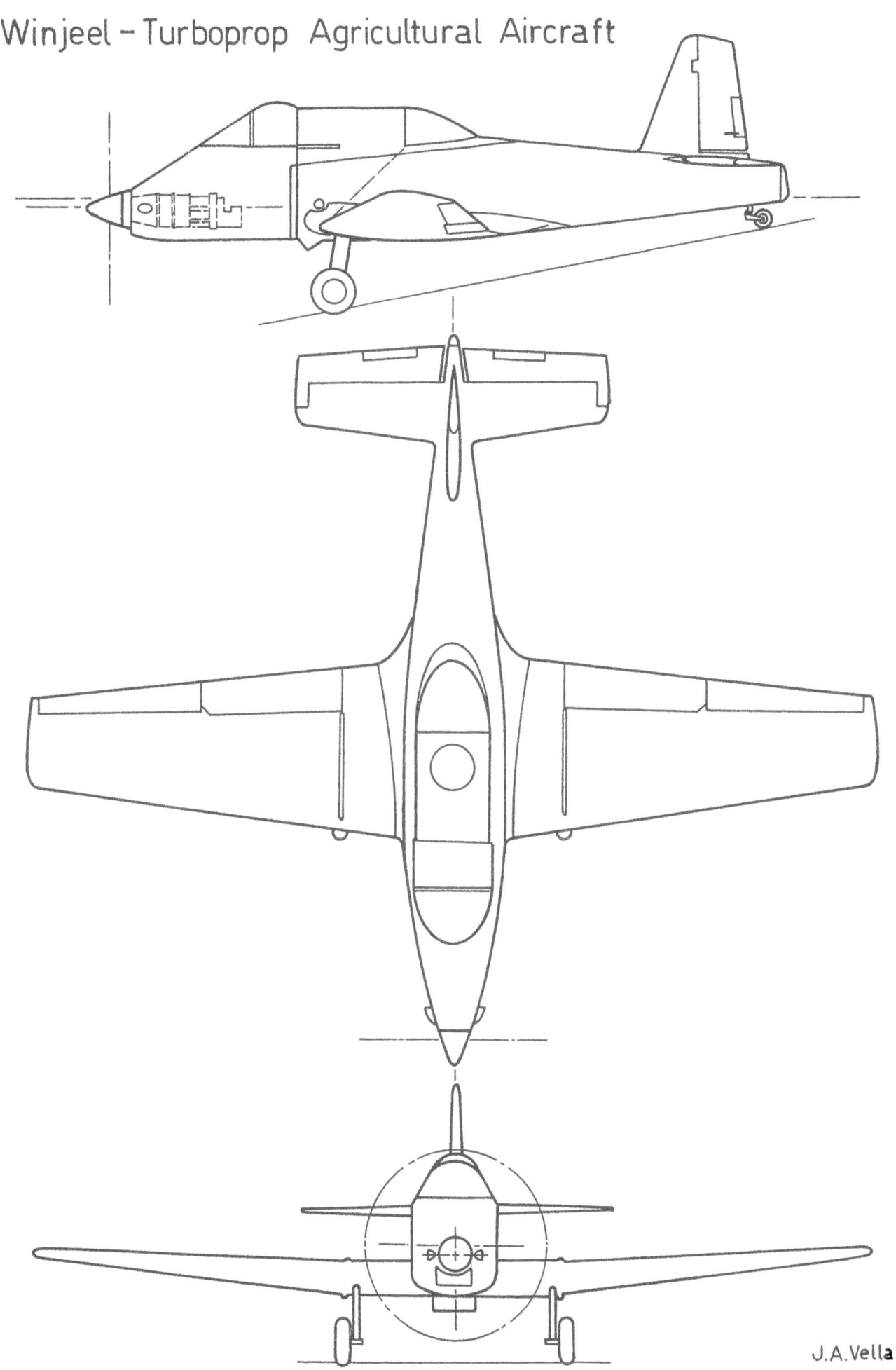

J.A. Vella

CHAPTER 6. SUPERSONIC TRAINER / /ATTACK AIRCRAFT

CA-31 SUPERSONIC TRAINER / CLOSE SUPPORT AIRCRAFT
March 1964 - December 1969

The CA-31 was the most important, detailed and largest aircraft design study for the company between 1964 and 1968. It marked the peak of progressive trainer study, design and building experience from the first ab initio trainer of 1938. The company's MB326H construction/assembly program was expected to provide work to 1970 but a new project needed to be available to phase into production during 1968/69.

The CA-31 proposal for a transonic trainer was one attempt to seek interest within the RAAF for an aircraft that would help in the advanced training role as a transition phase between the MB326H basic trainer, the Mirage IIIO fighter and the F-111C attack aircraft. As the Mirage IIIO began entering service, the CA-27 Sabre was relegated to the role of advanced trainer/close support aircraft. It was the replacement of this aircraft, operating in this short term role that CAC considered was a business opportunity worth studying. From the large quantity of company information gathered it is possible to see the project presentation as having been split into three phases, all linked together by an almost identical approach but separated in time due to a perceived change in operational requirement and some advances in aerodynamic and handling ideas.

Within these phases existed parallel designs for a dual-seat advanced trainer and a single seat combat aircraft and within the first phase, a proposal for a fighter interceptor to operate from small aircraft carriers.

First Phase - General Description and Overall Design Philosophy

Managed by John Kentwell and initiated under the leadership of Charles Reid, Senior Design Engineer-Aerodynamics and Propulsion, the earliest CAC ideas (AA 126 Jet Trainer) of March 1964 were centred on the primary role of that of a supersonic trainer.The rest of the team were Wal Watkins; Bill Gornall; Harry Gorjanicen; David Martin; Brian Keevers and Cec Billington. David Rees' task was to assess the flight dynamics of the CA-31 coming from a similar UK projects role on the HS P1127, Harrier and P1154.

The appearance of the design for the phases considered did not alter significantly. There were changes in the choice of engine, layout of internal equipment, size and weight. The earliest layout was for a delta wing with a curved blending of the root into slender intakes for one General Electric J85-13 turbojet, a curved sweep to the leading edge of the fin and a sharp uniformly tapered nose section (Fig 1).

This progressed by subtle refinement to a basic concept of a double delta wing design of a degree of complexity no greater than was essential to meeting the company specification, this being to provide the simplest and lowest cost aircraft. The choice of the double delta wing configuration was based on the CAC Mirage wing building/assembly program experience and its tested aerodynamics. Additionally, sufficiently proven practical aspects existed and research data was available. This combined with the realistic handling characteristics it would impart to the pilot stream destined for the delta winged Mirage IIIO; the first of which had been accepted by the RAAF in late 1964 as well as the yet to arrive F-111C with its variable geometry wing.

However in its simplest form the delta wing presented different handling characteristics when being flown at comparatively slow speeds, in that it sets the aircraft into high angles of attack due to a forward shift of the centre of lift. To alleviate this, to increase landing lift coefficient with positive control throughout the speed range the double delta design was chosen. Its main attributes, as against a conventional swept wing, was that the fixed leading edge strakes or leading delta would create a leading edge vortex which improved the lift capability, stability and handling qualities whilst compensating for the rearward shift of the aerodynamic centre at transonic and supersonic speeds. This vortex would remain intact to angles of attack up to 36 degrees and as it swept outboard along the top surface would produce higher suctions and therefore higher lift, the increase being as much as 20%. In addition:

- The effective inherent landing flare-out properties of the wing in ground effect would enable the aircraft to be driven onto the runway, without manual flare check by the pilot
- The lack of a longitudinal tail reduced the number and complexity of movable surfaces
- The high taper and large root chord of the delta enabled the greatest possible area of surface to be included in the effective wing area thus reducing the size of the actual wing panels required to achieve a given total wing area
- The large chord, short span nature of the wing allowed the use of the low thickness/chord ratio required for supersonic flight whilst still providing sufficient depth for the inclusion

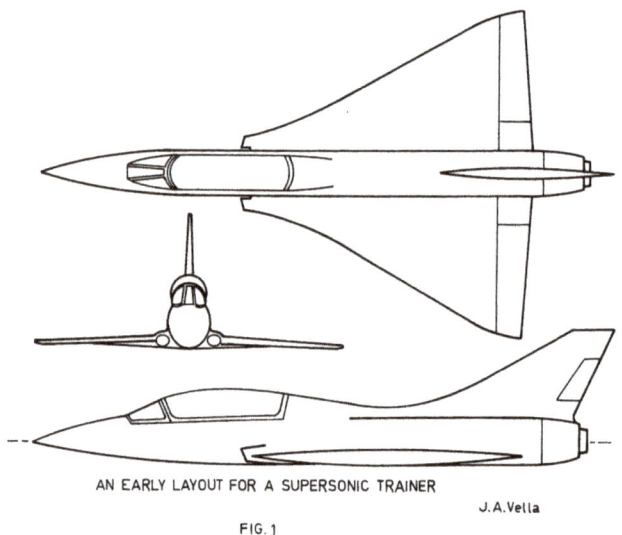

AN EARLY LAYOUT FOR A SUPERSONIC TRAINER
J.A.Vella
FIG. 1

of the main undercarriage
- Area ruling was applied to meet wave drag cancellation requirements
- Reheat was only to be used at take-off and to achieve supersonic speeds

First Phase - High Performance Trainer

Tandem cockpits were to be fitted with zero-zero ejection seats covered by a one piece side hinged canopy. This layout was not unlike that of the Northrop T-38 Talon or F-5B in that the rear seat occupant was not seated at a much higher level than the front seat pilot. The GE J85-J1A engine was in widespread use and of proven reliability. Engine replacement was through a built-in track/roller system which allowed it to slide out horizontally after the removal of the rear fuselage fairing. Simple pitot intake ducts under the wing leading edges were proportioned to obtain high pressure recovery. Internal fuel capacity was planned for 250 gallons with the option of an additional 200 gallons in external tanks (Figs. 2 & 3).

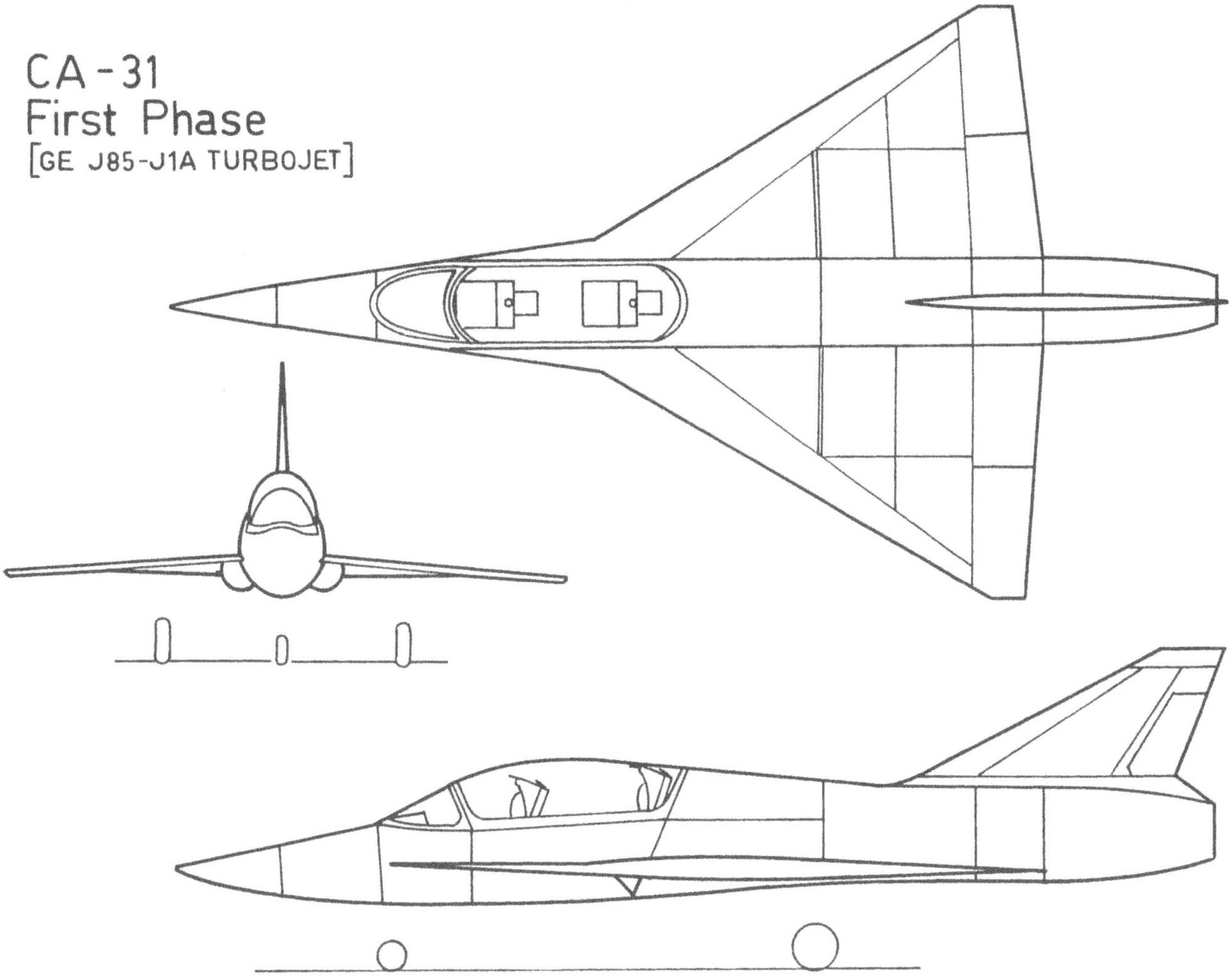

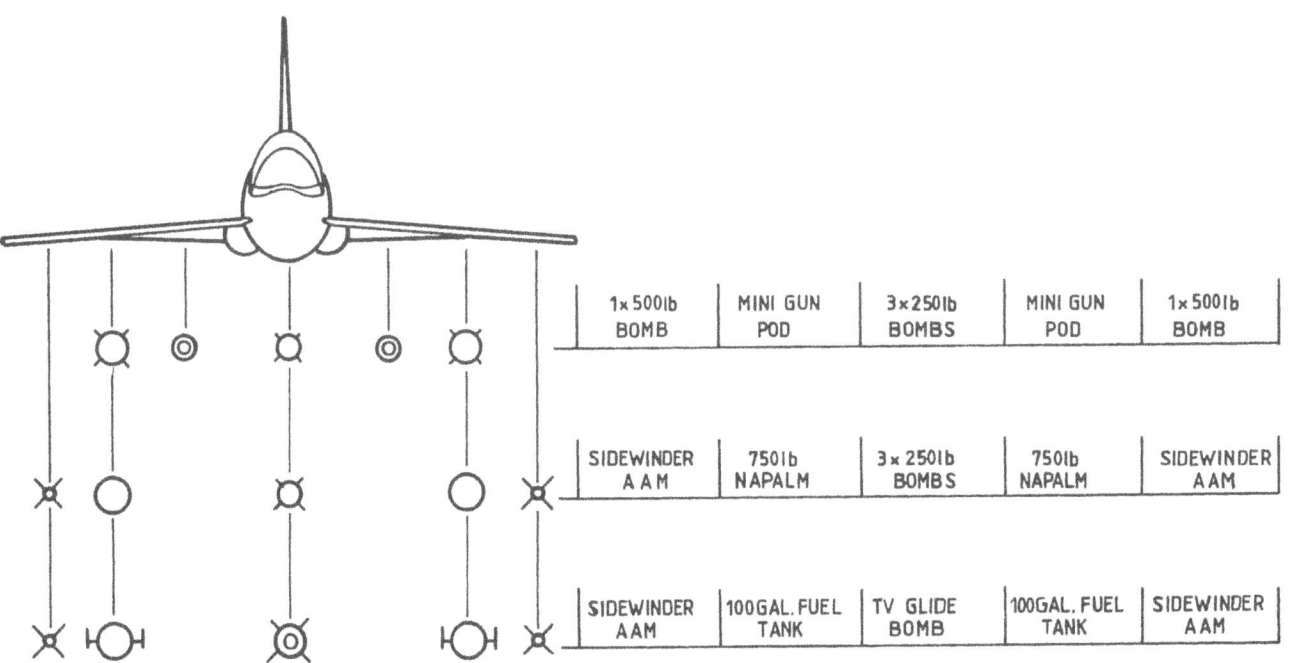

A typical high speed training mission would have been of 62 minutes duration, with 6 minutes of supersonic work, 10 minutes of high subsonic routines all at 36,000 feet, 10 minutes of general air work at 25,000 feet, two touch and go landings and the remainder of the time spent in climbing to and descending from altitude.

First Phase - Single Seat Combat Aircraft

To minimize costs the twin canopy arrangement was to be retained but the second seat would be replaced by mission related avionics and a 100 gallon auxiliary fuel tank. There was no provision for internal armament. For self-defence and intercept missions a Sidewinder air-to-air missile could be carried on wing stations 1 and 7, two of the seven underwing and fuselage hard points. A ferry range of 2,090 nm at 40,000 feet was expected using three 100 gallon external tanks. With a range of underslung weapon combinations (Fig. 3) it was posssible to offer many mission profiles. (Figs. 4 & 5)

First Phase - Naval Interceptor

This variant was put forward to capitalise on the small dimensions of the airframe and its probable suitability of operation from a small deck of Majestic class light aircraft carriers eg - HMAS Melbourne and INS Vikrant etc. Single and dual seat variants were proposed with the rear seat occupant performing the navigation/intercept role. Infra-red tracking / seeking, radar ranging, TACAN and UHF radio were located in the nose, whilst a HUD display and sight were also planned. If the second seat was deleted its place would be taken by a fuel tank of 120 gallon capacity. Catapult launch bridle attachment was made to two retractable hooks on the wing main spar. An arrester hook (not on the land variants) was to be added and immediately forward of this a fuselage fitting for the hold-back restraining cable and launch weak link (Figs. 6, 7 & 8).

An intercept profile of maximum capability was given as: Launch at a weight of 10,180 lb with 2 x 100 gallon external tanks, 2 x Sidewinder air-to-air missiles and an additional 120 gallons (either in the rear cockpit or as an additional external tank) with a wind over the deck of 18.5 kts, then proceed to a patrol position 50 nm from the carrier at 40,000 feet altitude, intercept a target at 200 nm from the carrier with an attack phase at Mach 1.1, to land back on deck at a weight of 5,400 lb; the entire flight lasting 2.6 hours. This would have been reduced to 1.5 hours if the speed was increased to Mach 1.5 (Fig. 9).

First Phase - Overall Production Planning

CAC's estimation of the development costs for the design, testing, mock-up, production tooling, fatigue testing and prototype was $5.9 million at 1966 prices. Envisaging a production run of five years duration after two years of design and prototype test flying, the unit average cost per aircraft was estimated to be $413,800, based on a run of 100 aircraft. Total costs for the entire program, excluding spares, was in the vicinity of $42 million at 1966 values.

Further Development

Whilst Air Staff Target AIR/64 for a high performance trainer existed, its near short term implementation was, in official circles, felt to be 'pie in the sky' and beyond 1975.

By April 1967, as part of CAC's continuing design refinement process, the preferred engine had become the Rolls Royce/Turbomeca RB172 / T260 Adour turbofan, with alternatives in the BS Viper 600; the BS/SNECMA M45 or the GE J85-J1A. Due to the greater power and increased weight over the J85 there was a corresponding enlargement of the airframe, span was 21 feet, length 37 feet 8 ins and height 10 feet 9 ins. Normal TO weight figure was now 8,500 lb and the maximum TO weight 12,500 lb.

The armament layout was revised to include a nose mounted 20 mm cannon with 100 rounds of ammunition, the gun barrel exiting on the upper surface of the nose cone and the number of strong points was reduced to three, one under each wing and one under the fuselage centre.

Other changes included the widening and deepening of the intake trunking to allow for a turbofan's increased air mass flow and the smoothing out of the leading edge strakes into a more blended curve whilst at the same time extending them further forward along the side of the fuselage. Re-contouring of the rear fuselage was necessary to fit the larger diameter engine (Fig. 10).

Airframe Description (RB172 Engine)

A basically circular cross section was used for the front fuselage and cockpit area to minimise pressurization loading, a maximum pressure differential of 3.00 psi. The fuel tank bay had an inner and outer skin to cater for fuel pressure loads and to provide a smooth iinner surface for contact with the bag type fuel cells. The fully machined main spar centre section unit was supported between two frames to make up the main spar frame assembly. The wing's three main elements were: a centre section spar assembly built integrally with the fuselage and two easily detachable outer wing assemblies each with two control surfaces and a fixed cambered leading edge. The rest of the wing was made up of a sharply swept front spar and a rear spar with an intermediate structure of an 'egg-crate' distribution of spanwise members and chordwise ribs (Fig. 11). It was was connected to the fuselage at the three spars only, with all bending loads being carried through the main spar. Torque reactions were carried via the pin joints at the front and rear spars. The fin structure and materials were similar to that of the wing except that a swept main spar was used.

All undercarriage members were of the levered suspension type, the single nose wheel retracting forwards into the nose bay and the main undercarriage legs, mounted on the main spar on inclined

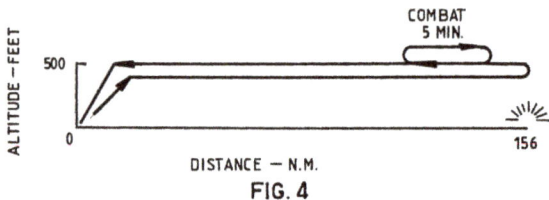

FIG. 4

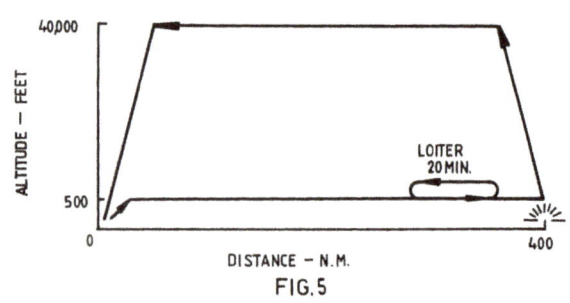

FIG.5

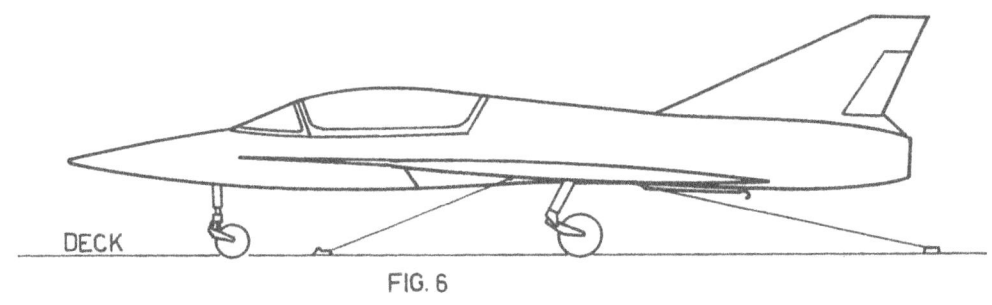

FIG. 6

Naval Intercepter Equipment
2 Seat

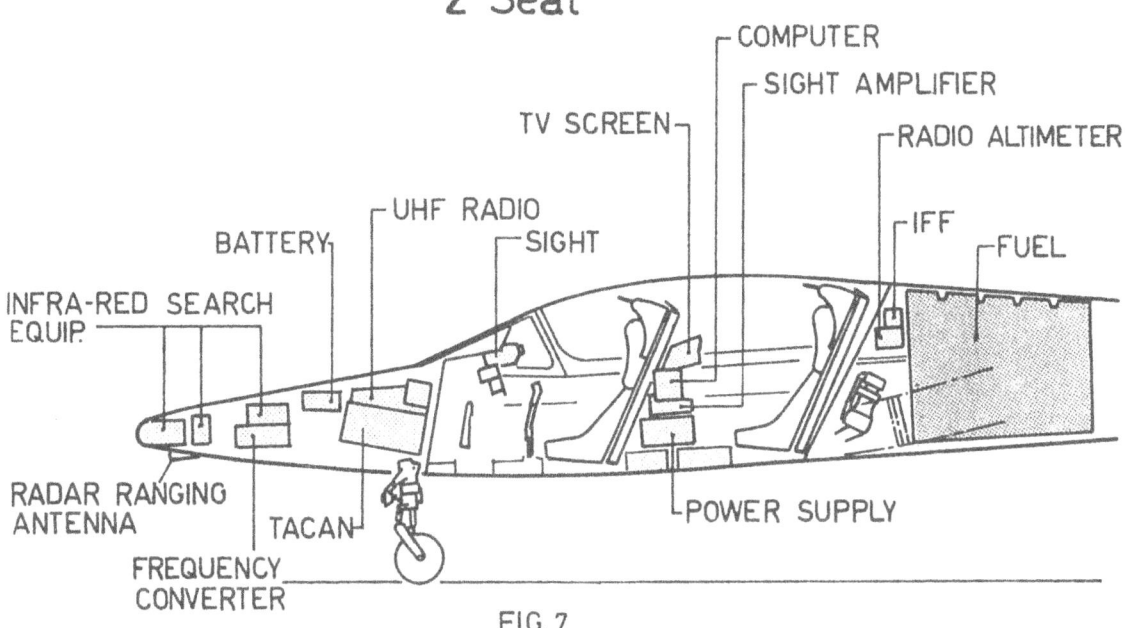

FIG. 7

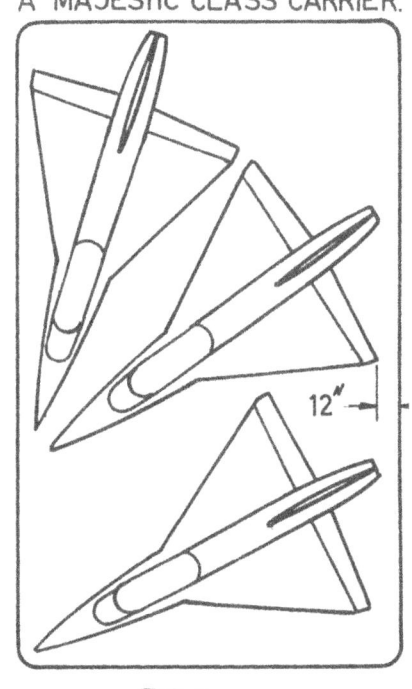

AIRCRAFT ON THE LIFT OF A 'MAJESTIC' CLASS CARRIER.

FIG. 8

Intercept Diagram

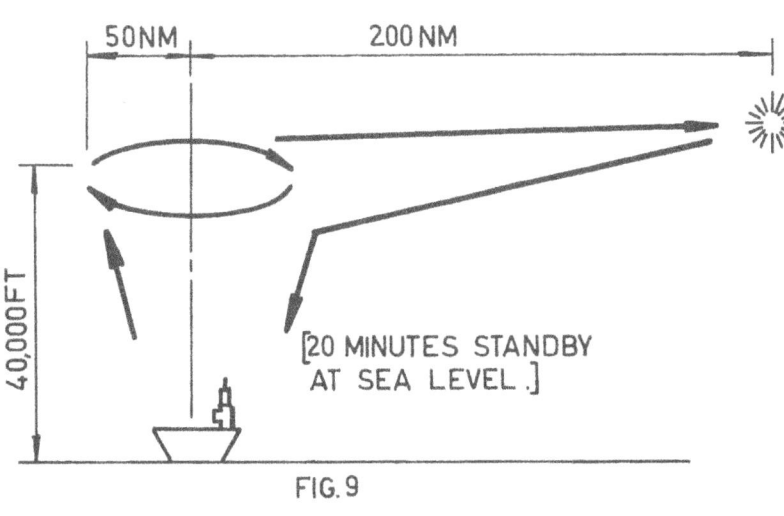

[20 MINUTES STANDBY AT SEA LEVEL.]

FIG. 9

spindles, retracted inwards into the wing space. Main wheel tyre pressures were in the region of 130 psi. For simplicity, the wings were devoid of internal fuel tanks. Removal of the rear fuselage fairing allowed installation or removal of the engine vertically through large, ventral access doors. Normal sheet metal skins and conventional aluminium alloys were to be used throughout, the intention being to build the airframe within the manufacturing capability of CAC without using heavy forgings or milled skins larger than the capacity of existing facilities.

Official Acknowledgement

In the Federal Parliament on May 2, 1967 the Minister for Air, Peter Howson, acknowledged the existence of the CAC design study and that it was a private venture ahead of any official requirement. The RAAF's intention was to continue using the CA-27 Sabre in the advanced training role until about 1974 / 75, even though it lacked a second seat. The requirement for a replacement training vehicle, if any, would have resulted in a very small aircraft order as the RAAF's sole Operational Conversion Unit / Ground Attack Squadron, 2 (F) OCU, was operating with a complement of 28 Sabres.

The Minister for Defence, Allen Fairhall, was still uncertain as to what line of future requirements lay ahead for the RAAF when he spoke in the House of Representatives on August 30, 1967:

> "The Commonwealth stands in no doubt about the capacity of the Commonwealth Aircraft Corporation to do a first class job in the aircraft industry. In respect of the aircraft to which the honourable member refers, however, this was a private venture entered into by the Commonwealth Aircraft Corporation on its own initiative and ahead of any Air Staff requirement for that particular type of aircraft. At this moment the Air Force is not able to say what type of aircraft it will need or when it will be needed. There is, therefore, no basis on which to negotiate with the Commonwealth Aircraft Corporation. All this is well known to the company."

However on 6 September , the Minister for Air was able to state that a revised Air Staff Requirement had been issued for an aircraft of an enhanced strike capability with an approximate requirement date of 1974, thus giving the industry about seven years lead time. He added, *"that other things being equal-that is, having regard to relative cost, delivery date and so on, we shall certainly aim to give preference to the Australian aircraft industry. No indication has been given to any aircraft industry overseas other than what I have conveyed to the House this afternoon."*

In another part of his statement he denied UK reports which said, *"the RAAF was about to place a $75 million order for the BAC Jaguar supersonic trainer / strike aircraft."*

The seven years of lead time was in direct contrast to the hurried demand which led to the acquisition of the Italian MB326H trainer. Other inferences drawn from the statement, *"that other things being equal etc"* were that the development costs of the supersonic multi-purpose aircraft would be so high that no Australian company could afford to go it alone and local involvement could only go ahead if generous Government development funding was provided. This, at a time when the RAAF budget was facing controversial acquisition cost overruns with the F-111C bomber, meant that development funds were not expected to be readily forthcoming. CAC, with its CA-31, had been given 7 years to produce a result for the RAAF but unless it could find a foreign partner to support the development of the CA-31 the future of the aircraft looked forlorn.

Following the release in August 1967 of Issue 2 of the RAAF Air Staff Requirement AIR/64 which changed the primary role of the aircraft from Operational Trainer to Close Air Support, CAC embarked on further studies to match this requirement.

Second Phase - General Description and Design Philosophy

Meeting the revised needs of AIR / 64 meant increasing the size of the airframe and by February 1968 the company had set out its revised ideas. The internal layout was changed, but the double delta formula was retained.

To meet or exceed the specification with the range of available engines the design would have had to incorporate two engines. This, on the basis of extra costs, size and complexity, was ruled out, but it was nevertheless offered as an option. To use a single engine of what was available in the chosen range was to fall lower than the needed requirement but it was the most economical and practical approach. The engines considered in order of preference were:

- A single Rolls Royce / Turbomeca RB172 / T260 Adour, rated at 5,250 lb dry and 8,200 lb in full afterburner
- Two Bristol Siddeley BS358 high by-pass ratio turbofans of 8,200 lb maximum installed reheat thrust, and
- Two General Electric J85-15 turbojets of a combined maximum reheat thrust of 8,600 lb (Fig 17).

Compared on an identical mission profile throughout and with identical wing and thrust loadings, the differences in fuel consumption between the three engines showed up as reduced or increased weapon load capacity. The economical RB172 Adour was in service building up flight time, whereas the BS358 was a new design with no known airframe application at that stage but it enabled the CA-31 to lift an extra 450 lb of weapon load over the RB172. The turbojet J85 was well proven in service but its high fuel consumption made the aircraft weapon load 590 lb less than that of the RB172. So the RB172 became the preferred baseline engine.

Second Phase - Single Seat Close Air Support

With a canopy and cockpit arrangement revised for a one seat occupant the neat good looks of the aircraft seemed to be further enhanced. Front end equipment revisions included a nose mounted 30 mm cannon (or 2 x 20 mm alternative) and a new twin nose wheel undercarriage. Internal fuel capacity was raised to 350 gallons boosted further by a 140 gallon cell behind the front cockpit. This area would also house the major portion of electronic equipment, aft of which were the air conditioning, oxygen and battery systems. The cockpit was equipped with a Martin-Baker zero-zero ejection seat, an electronic sight with a CRO output projected for a HUD and a sight computer together with a ranging radar in the extreme nose.

Electronic countermeasures equipment was to be carried in an underwing pod. The engine air intake contours were revised again, the deepened section was extended further back under the wing and the rear fuselage/engine fairing separation break was revised. A runway arrestor hook and a nine foot diameter ribbon brake chute were added. In conjunction with the operational role change the maximum take-off weight of the aircraft had climbed to 14,750 lb.

Likewise the overall dimensions had been increased from the similarly engined Operational Trainer in Phase 1. In relative size to aircraft in service with the RAAF, the CA-31 was larger than the CA-30 / MB326H but smaller than the CA-27 Sabre. It was low to the ground to permit chest height maintenance access (Figs. 12 & 13). Two support mission profiles flown at maximum take-off weight are shown in Figs. 15 & 16.

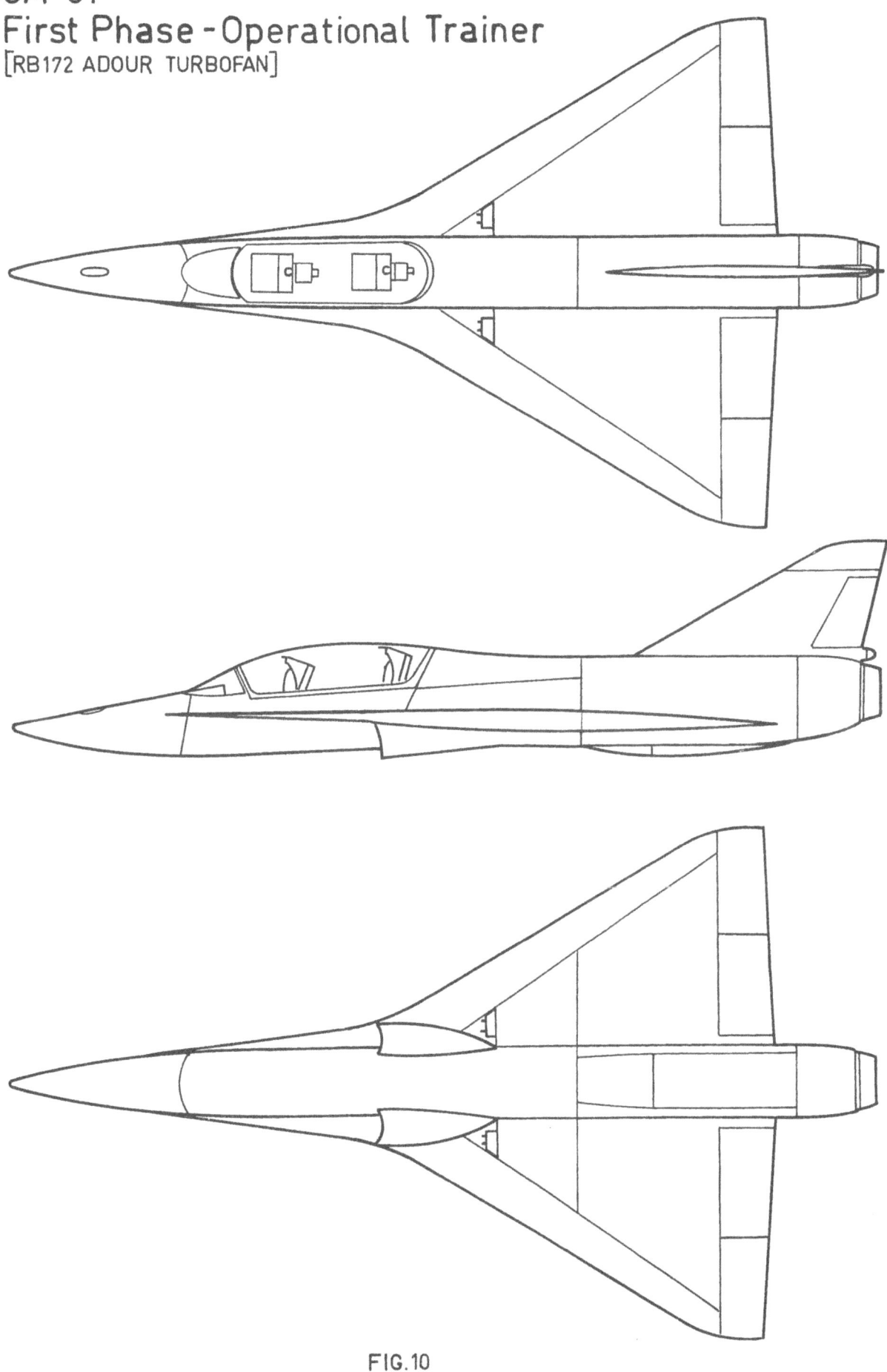

FIG.10

Second Phase - Twin Seat Conversion Trainer

A single piece side-hinged canopy fitted over tandem zero-zero ejection seats. Armament was reduced to one 20 mm cannon. The space previously meant for the 140 gallon auxiliary fuel tank and the electronics bay was given over to the instructor's position who's forward vision was raised slightly but was nowhere as pronounced as seen on later-aircraft like the HS Hawk, the MB339 or the CASA 101 Aviojet.

Both the single and dual seat aircraft were to be identical internally aft of the rear cockpit bulkhead and both were to be capable of the fitment of five external store stations, on the fuselage centre and two under each wing. Up to 360 gallons of external fuel could be carried on stations 2, 3 and 4. In both variants the cockpits were roomier than that of the Mirage IIIO. (Fig. 14).

Second Phase - Third Option, Twin J85 Engines

As related earlier to meet or exceed the Close Air Support specification would have entailed the use of two engines such as the J85 in a twin installation although this was not considered to be a satisfactory solution (Fig. 17).

Specifications	CA-31 Supersonic Trainer / Close Air Support Aircraft Second Phase-Third Option: Twin GE J85 Engines	
Powerplant	Two General Electric J85-15 turbojets of 4,300 lb thrust each. SFC 1.03 lb/hr/lb	
Performance	NA	
Weights	Empty	7,000 lb
	TO	15,500 lb
	Fuel capacity	615 gall
Dimensions	Wing span	23 ft
	Wing area	290 sq ft
	Height	12 ft
	Length	41 ft 8 ins

Second Phase - Overall Production Planning

The program to build was set a notional starting date of July 1, 1968, with two prototypes making their first flight in April and October of 1971. A production rate of three aircraft per month was planned with the first aircraft delivered by July 1973 if design was frozen by January 1971. Allowing for a run of fifty aircraft this would have cost $37.5 million at 1963 values or $63.6 million for one hundred aircraft. This was for construction of either the single seat and/or dual seat derivative. The production costs did not take into account the $9.6 million estimate for the development phase that would have included all design, test, structural test equipment, production tooling for both versions and the manufacture of two prototypes with minimal tooling. Production of one hundred aircraft would have been accomplished by October 1976.

Third Phase - Canard for More Lift

In order to extract more lift from slender delta winged aircraft, designers have resorted to fixed fuselage strakes as on the Concorde and retractable canards as fitted on the Tupelov Tu-144 and GAMD Mirage V Milan (Kite).The latter was built in a bid to improve the sales potential of the Mirage III to the Swiss Air Force in view of their severe physical operating environment in the Swiss Alps. CAC saw this overseas development as a possible application to the CA-31 scheme and in October 1969 issued a report prepared by David Rees proposing the aerodynamics for a canard.

Mounting a retractable canard on the CA-31 meant the low speed performance of the aircraft would have received a considerable increase in lift coefficient. The whole concept revolved around the allowable centre of gravity margins of the aircraft which was in turn controlled by elevon trim travel limits and the angle of incidence of the canard. The canard was to have leading edge slats so as to produce as high a stalling angle as possible; have an span of 8 feet and an area of 10 square feet; set at 20° dihedral, 9 inches below the fuselage datum and at an angle of incidence of 4° (Fig. 18).

For no change in the centre of gravity margin, the gain in lift would have been 17.2%. For a landing approach angle of 15° aircraft incidence, the lift increase would have been 9%, which would have allowed a reduction of 20 knots in the approach speed. Sealing flaps in the front fuselage would cover the retracted wings. Extension would be at speeds below 200 knots.

Computer Studies

Considerable work was done on the preparation of computer programs for the stress analysis of the CA-31 structure, as CAC policy was laid down that manpower costs would be a critical factor in the overall success of the project. A number of general purpose programs were established, but the greatest effort went into the analysis of the stress distribution in the delta wing. The outstanding work done by Louis Irving, Brian Keevers and Univeristy of NSW on this subject was one of the significant features of this project. As a result of this early work the design team had computerised the analysis that would disclose stresses and deflections at any point in the structure of the wing for any of the applied loading cases. It also introduced early CAD-CAM work to CAC.

Epilogue

What happened to the project? Obviously no CA-31s reached the hardware stage. After the project design had shifted into its second phase, with the emphasis on Close Air Support, the RAAF decided the aircraft was too small and allowed the design to fade out. Although the CA-31 double delta wing planform was ideal for an Advanced Supersonic Training aircraft, it is not the best plan form for Close Air Support where a conventional wing does better. The small size of the CA-31 restricted its ability to carry a sufficient quantity of externally mounted weapons.

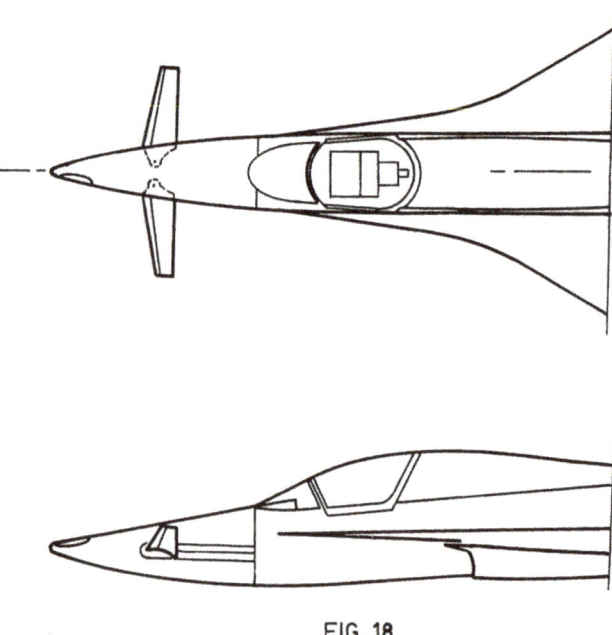

FIG. 18

J.A.Vella

Meanwhile most of the CA-31 design team travelled to the UK to co-operate in the study of the AA-107, the possible successor to the CA-31 and to hopefully open up a larger world market with that design. The RAAF filled its advanced trainer need by increasing the initial order for the Mirage IIIOD dual seat variant from ten to sixteen aircraft. These aircraft, combined with the use of effective simulators, served as the Operational Conversion Unit for the Mirage and F-111C fleets. The Macchi MB326H aircraft served in the light ground attack role when it was fitted with the 7.62mm underwing mini-gun pods.

The only tangible evidence of the existence of the CA-31 project was a full scale wooden mock-up on which some 1,600 workshop hours and 160 engineering hours had been expended. In the middle of 1974 this was donated to the Australian Aircraft Restoration Group at Moorabbin.

Specifications	CA-31 Supersonic Trainer / Tactical Stike First Phase- General Specification (July 1966)			
Powerplant	One General Electric J85-J1A turbojet of 4,100 lb thrust with reheat			
Performance	Max speed at 36,000 ft		Mach 1.50m	
	Cruise speed at 36,000 ft		Mach 1.07	
	Rate of climb at SL		29,500 ft / min	
	Rate of climb at 36,000 ft		13,600 ft / min	
	Time to 36,000 ft		2.0 mins	
	Max ceiling		57,000 ft	
	T.O. dist (normal weight & ISA day)		1,400 ft	
	T.O. dist (max weight & ISA day)		3,000 ft	
	Approach speed with 30% fuel		110 kts	
	Touchdown speed		90 kts	
	Range (2 crew & internal fuel)		930 nm	
	Ferry range(1 crew, 250 gall internal fuel, 100 gall aux fuel & 3 x 100 gall external tanks		2,090 nm	
Weights	Normal TO		7,000 lb	
	Max loaded TO		10,500 lb	
Dimensions	Wing span	20 ft	Wing area	200 sq ft
	Wing dihedral	3°	Root chord	10 ft 10 ins
	Tip chord	5 ft 6 ins	Aspect ratio	2.00
	Wing LE sweep	60°	Wing TE sweep	-4°
	Wing dihedral	-1°		
	Tailplane LE sweep	60°	Tailplane TE sweep	20°
	Tailplane dihedral	10°	Tailplane sweepback at 25 % chord	35°
	Tailplane area	27 sq ft		
	Max fuselage depth	4 ft 7 ins	Max fuselage width	2 ft 9ins
	Length	36 ft 6 ins	Height	10 ft 6 ins
	Track	9 ft	Base	15 ft 3 ins

Specifications	CA-31 Supersonic Trainer/ Close Air Support Aircraft Second Phase - Close Air Support - General Specification (Feb 1968)			
Powerplant	One Rolls Royce /Turbomeca RB 172/T260 Adour turbofan of 5,250 lb thrust dry and 8,200 lb thrust with reheat Specific fuel consumption 0.81 lb/hr/lb			
Performance			Close Air Support Aircraft	Trainer Aircraft
	Max speed at 36,000 ft		Mach 1.5	Mach 1.5
	Cruise speed at 36,000 ft		Mach 0.9	Mach 0.9
	Max speed at SL		Mach 0.9	Mach 0.9
	Rate of climb at SL at (9,250 lb)		29,000 ft/min	29,000 ft/min
	TO distance (ISA + 25°C)		3,080 ft	30 ft
	TO distance over 50ft (ISA+25°C)		5,100 ft	1,560 ft
	Landing distance (ISA+25°C)		2,000 ft (with 1/2 fuel)	2,200 ft (with 2/3 fuel)
	Approach speed		140 kts	148 kts
	Touchdown speed		117 kts	124 kts
	Max ceiling		63,000 ft	63,000 ft
	Fuel capacity		460 gall	340 gall
Weights	Empty		6,780 lb	6,910 lb
	Fuel		3,680 lb	2,730 lb
	TO		14,750 lb	10,200 lb
	Thrust/weight ratio		0.56	0.80
	Wing loading		54.5 lb/sq ft	37.8 lb/sq ft
Dimensions: Applicable to both aircraft	Wing span	22 ft 6 ins	Wing area	270 sq ft
	Aspect ratio	1.9	Length	39 ft 6 ins
	Height	11 ft 6 ins		

First Phase – Operational Trainer Structural Features

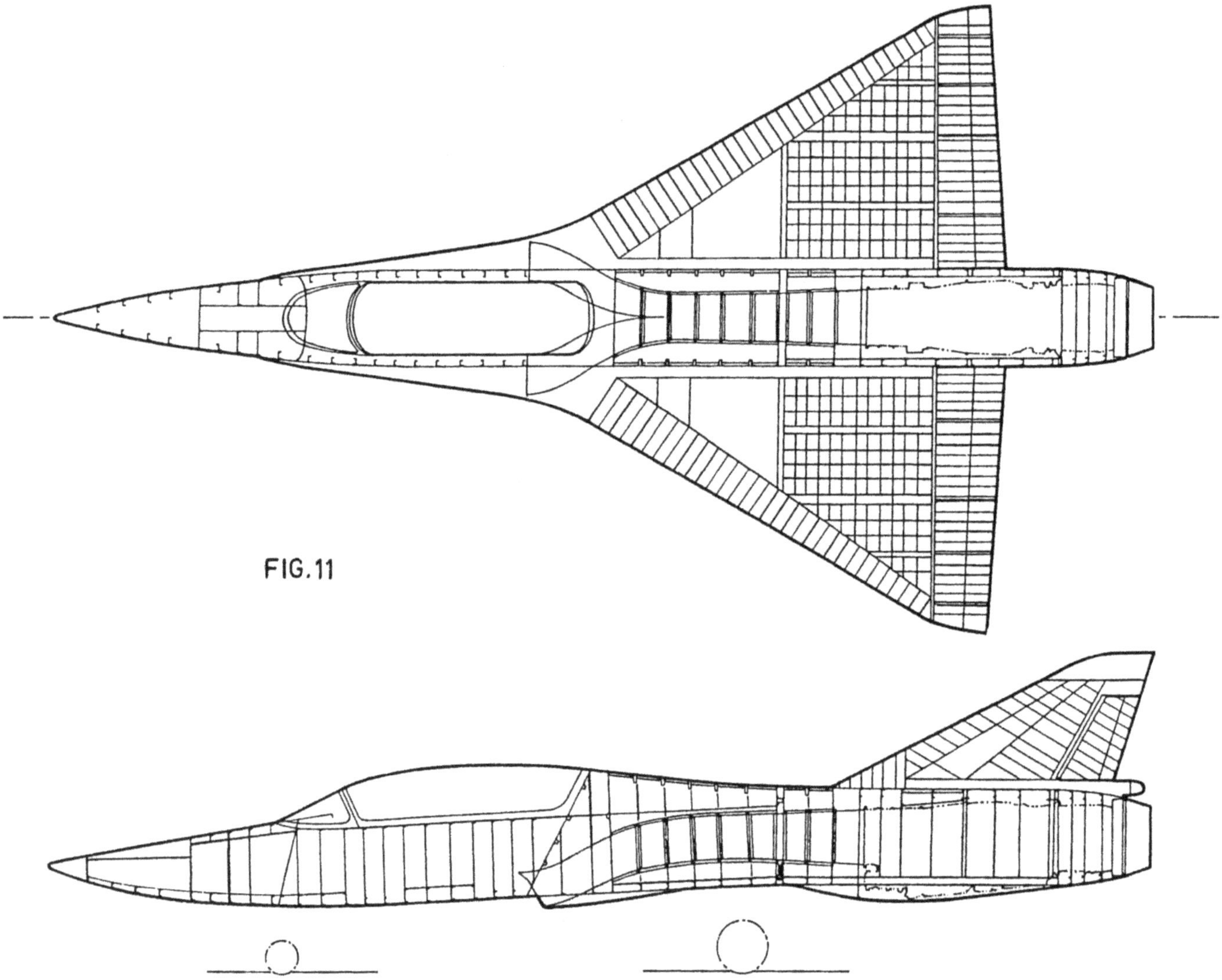

FIG. 11

Walter Watkins examining progress on the construction of the full scale wooden mock-up of the First Phase CA-31 with J85 engine, August 1966, with Les Stapleton foreman of the wood working shop.

Ian Ring and the neat lines of the small size initial configuration CA-31.
Walter Watkins

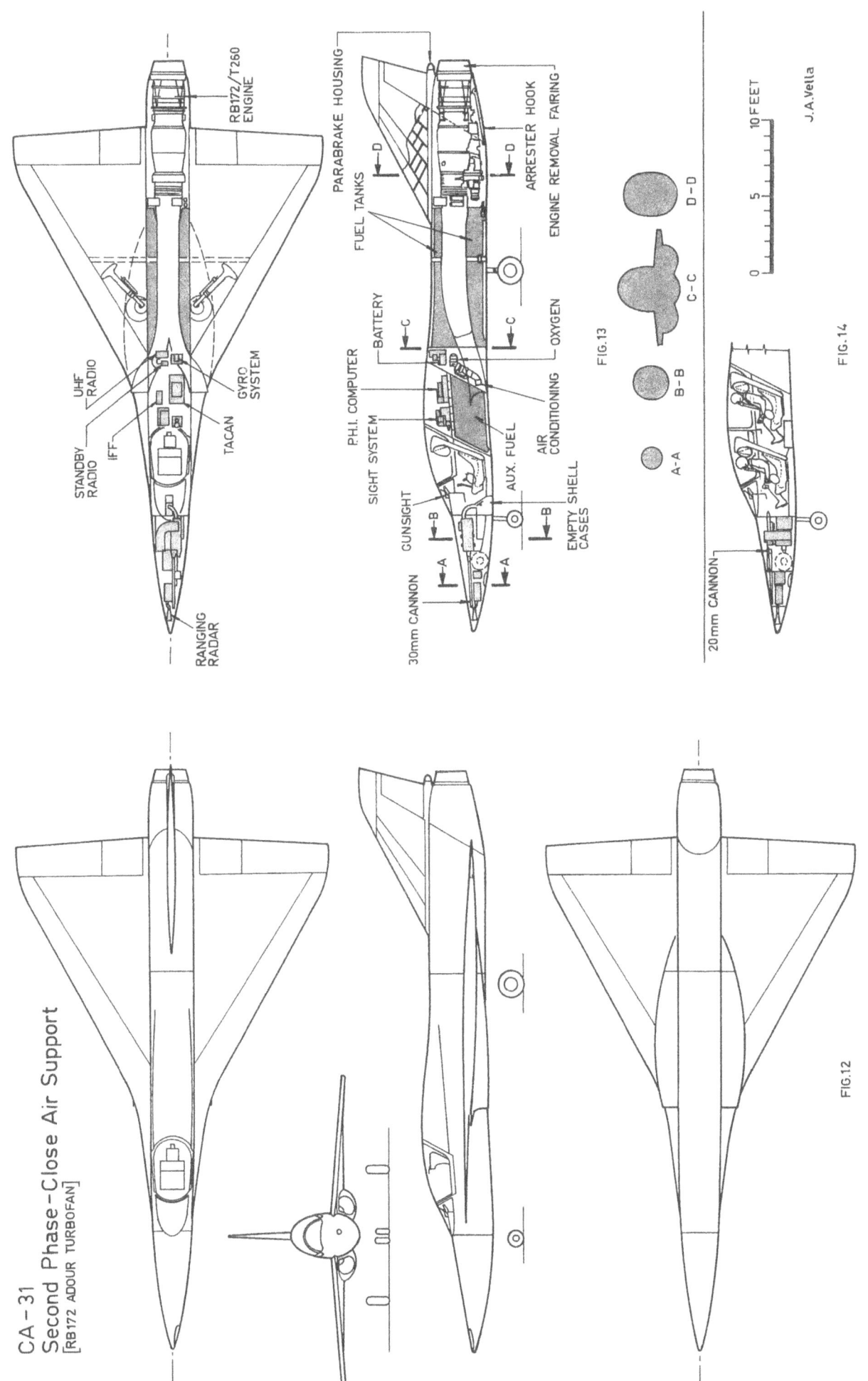

Lo-Lo Mission
T.O.W. 14,750 lb
MIL. LOAD 4960 lb
FUEL 360 GAL
I.S.A. +25°C

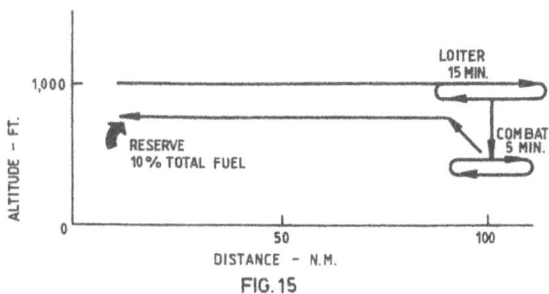

FIG. 15

Hi-Lo-Hi Mission
T.O.W. 14,750 lb
MIL. LOAD 4090 lb
FUEL 470 GAL.
I.S.A. +25°C

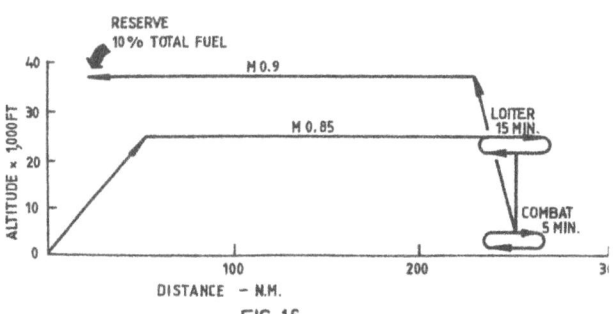

FIG. 16

CA-31 Second Phase Third Option
[2 × GE J85-15 TURBOJETS]

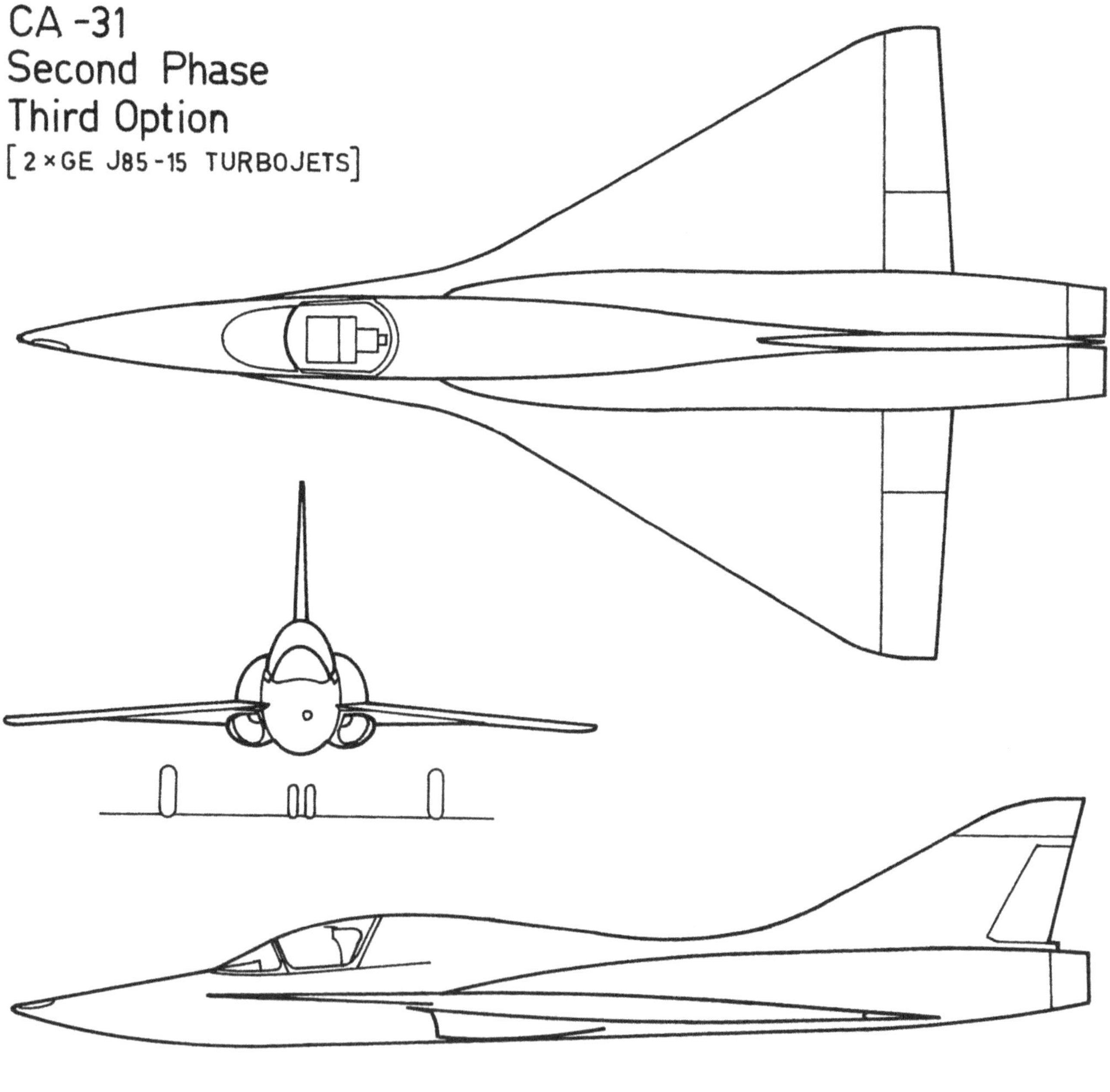

FIG. 17

J. A. Vella

If the project achieved nothing else it did focus an international interest in CAC, as well as establishing its own computer based, structural stress analysis program.

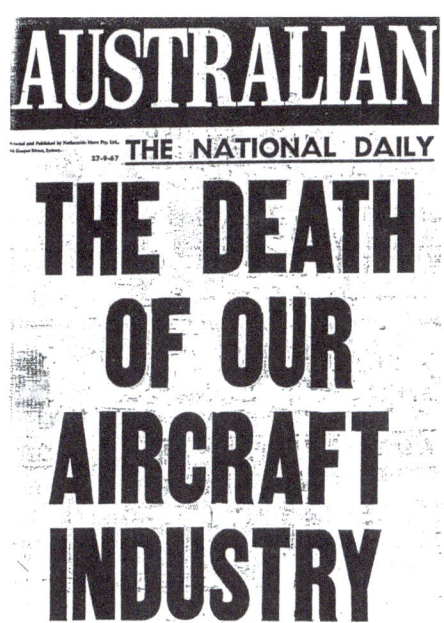

The newsagent's news stand headline of Wednesday September 27,1967 following the end of the CA-31. **J. A. Vella Collection**

Bibliography: CA-31 Supersonic Trainer/Close Support
Aircraft : (Various)

Australia. Parliament. House of Representatives (May 2, 1967). Reply to question re CAC aircraft] by the Hon. Peter Howson. Hansard.

Australia. Parliament. House of Representatives (August 30, 1967). [Ministerial Statement re CAC aircraft] by the Hon. Allen Fairhall. Hansard.

Australia. Parliament. House of Representatives (September 6, 1967). [Reply to question re future RAAF trainer aircraft] by the Hon. Peter Howson. Hansard.

Commonwealth Aircraft Corporation. (March 1964). Engineering Report AA126. Jet Trainer.

Commonwealth Aircraft Corporation. (July 1964). Engineering Report AA127. Supersonic Trainer.

Commonwealth Aircraft Corporation. (July 1966). Engineering Report AA150. CA-31 Supersonic Trainer / Attack Proposal.

Commonwealth Aircraft Corporation. (April 1967). Engineering Report AA155. CA-31 Operational Trainer.

Commonwealth Aircraft Corporation. (April 1967). Engineering Report AA156. CA-31 Operational Trainer Program & Cost Analysis.

Commonwealth Aircraft Corporation. (February 1968). Engineering Report AA176. CA-31 Close Support / Operational Trainer Aircraft.

Rees, D. R. (October 1, 1969). Engineering Report AA205. CA-31 Investigation Into the Use of a Canard. Commonwealth Aircraft Corporation.

Ring, I. H. (1968) 'Aircraft Project Design in Australia'. The Lawrence Hargrave Memorial Lecture to the Royal Aeronautical S o c i e t y , Australian Division. [Melbourne]. (September 19, 1968).

AN AERIAL TOP DRESSING AIRCRAFT
July 1965

During July 1965 CAC management sanctioned the beginning of what could have been the company's second strongest private venture bid into the agricultural aircraft market.

Market Survey

As a follow on to the CA-28 Ceres, Charles Reid and Walter Watkins carried out an extensive market survey on the Australian requirements for top dressing aircraft (superphosphate spreading only). This was based on the proportion of air dropped superphosphate, compared with the total Australian production. No allowance was made for spraying, seeding or other forms of aerial agriculture or for exports. The superphosphate component was considered large enough on its own if the current trends were to continue.

The summary of the basic criteria was:

- Australian superphosphate production would increase by an annual average of 200,000 tons based on the history of the previous seven years and extrapolated for future production. Figures were established for a fifteen year time span but only the data for three widely separated years is shown (Table 1)
- The percentage of air-dropped superphosphate compared with total production would increase at an approximate annual average of 2% and was expected to continue doing so for at least 10 years to about 1975, and
- The work capacity of a 1 ton hopper capacity spreader aircraft was assumed to be an annual average of 5,000 tons.

The analysis indicated that for the 6 years between 1967 and 1972 inclusive there would be an equivalent of 220/1 ton capacity spreader aircraft added to the aerial agricultural industry (Table 2). This number of aircraft, however, could only be regarded as 'equivalent tonnage required' and the actual distribution between various sizes, ie 0.25 ton, 0.50 ton and 1.0 ton capacity aircraft had to be established.

Any number of combinations of the three sizes of hopper equipped aircraft could be proposed. On the assumption that local industry was capable of supplying 50% of the total requirement, ie 110 / 1.0 ton aircraft, then such a combination would result in:

- 110 / 1.0 ton capacity aircraft or
- 220 / 0.5 ton capacity aircraft or
- 70 / 1.0 ton, plus 80 / 0.50 ton capacity aircraft

The third combination although conservative, was considered to be the most favourable mix, as aerial spreading operators tended to favour the larger aircraft for dusters.

Provided the local selling price for a CAC design was competitive with the DHC-2 Beaver, then a minimum planned output of 12 units per year could have been considered as a low risk commercial venture. The conclusion was that the local industry would place orders for at least 70 / 1.0 ton, plus 80 / 0.5 ton capacity spread aircraft over the period 1967 to 1972.

Aircraft Description

With the design work of Charles Reid on aerodynamics, the configuration arrived at was for an all metal (primarily 24ST Alclad) cantilever low wing monoplane based on the aerodynamic layout of

the Piper Cherokee. The planned engine was the 400 hp Avco Lycoming IO-720-A1A.

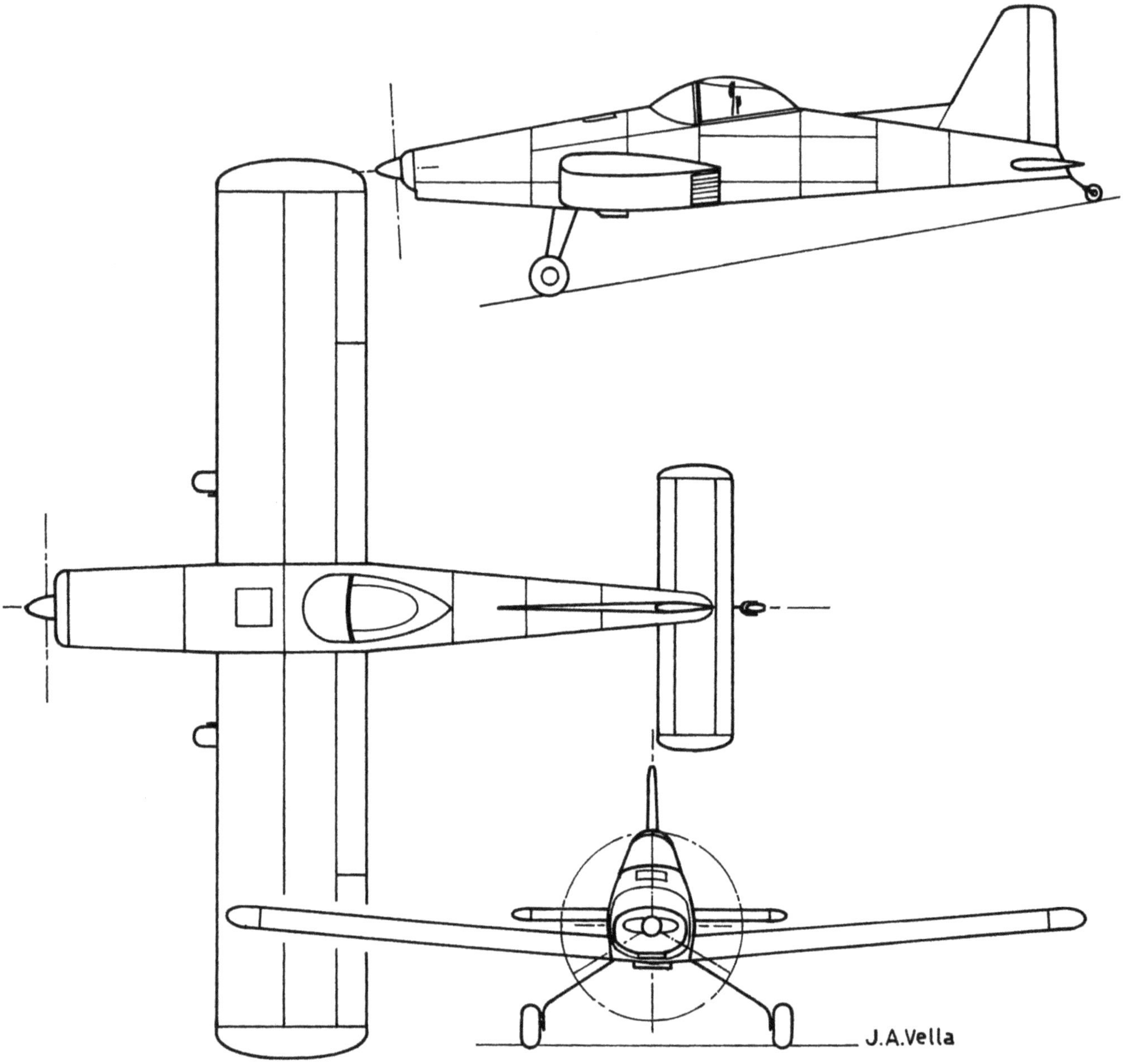

Single slotted flaps of 20% of the wing chord covered 60% of the wing trailing edge. The readily removable hopper of 2,000 1b capacity, to be made out of fibreglass, was located over the wing on the aircraft's centre of gravity and in front of the crew compartment. This compartment, straddling the trailing edge of the wing provided accommodation for the pilot and one other passenger seated behind the pilot facing aft. The canopy was a one piece clear vision rearward sliding unit with an overhead tinted segment. Fuel capacity was 60 gallons held in two wing root tanks.

Specifications	An Aerial Top Dressing Aircraft	
Powerplant	One Avco Lycoming IO-720-A1A, eight cylinder 400 hp piston engine driving a CS propeller of 6 ft 5 in diameter	
Performance	Max speed at SL	150 kts
	Cruise at 75% power at 7,000 ft	140 kts
	Initial rate of climb	1,250 ft/min
	TO dist at SL	970 ft
	TO dist over 50 ft at 4,500 lb	1,060 ft
	Range at 55% power	520 nm
Weights	Empty	2,200 lb
	Hopper load	2,000 lb
Dimensions	Wing span	36 ft
	Wing constant chord	6 ft 5 ins
	Wing area	230 sq ft
	Aspect ratio	5.65
	Tailplane span	11 ft 6ins
	Tailplane constant chord	3ft
	Wing section	NACA 652A415
	Height	8 ft 6 ins
	Length	29 ft 6 ins

Table 1

Year	Total Production Tons (Million)	Air Dropped	
		Total Air Dropped Tons (Million)	As % of Total Production
1958	2.0	0.06	0.03
1964	3.2	0.48	0.15
1972	4.8	1.49	0.31

Table 2
Crop Duster Annual Requirement
Aircraft of 1 Ton Hopper Capacity & 5,000 Ton Annual Work Capacity

Year	Air dropped Ton (Million)	Active Aircraft Required	Increase to Existing Fleet	Additions Due to Depreciation	Total New Aircraft
1965	0.58	226	20	4	24
1966	0.68	136	20	5	25
1967	0.8	160	24	6	30 new aircraft
1968	0.92	184	24	8	32 new aircraft
1969	1.05	210	26	9	35 new aircraft
1970	1.19	238	28	10	38 new aircraft
1971	1.34	268	30	12	42 new aircraft
1972	1.49	298	30	13	43 new aircraft

A significant amount of preliminary design work was carried out on all areas of the structure, engine mount, undercarriage, wing spar boom and general structural sizing for structural sufficiency and fatigue life together with work undertaken on the estimation of the size and cost of the development and production programs and the anticipated basic and operating costs.

Development cost was estimated at £322,000 and to require 12,000 hours of engineering time, 23,000 hours of drawing office time and 3,000 hours for the creation of manuals.

Another Abrupt Ending

Work on this scheme ceased in December 1965 when CAC management decided to divert all available design manpower to the military CA-31 project. Had this aerial agriculture aircraft been developed it would have been the equal to anything produced anywhere in the world at that time. The aircraft also had the potential for utility or military application roles.

Bibliography: An Aerial Top Dressing Aircraft
Reid, C. J.; Watkins, W. (July 1965). Unpublished Design Memoranda & Work Notes. Commonwealth Aircraft Corporation.

CA-30 AERMACCHI MB326H TRAINER AIRCRAFT
September 1965

On November 10, 1964 the Australian Government gave the go ahead for the RAAF to start the process of acquiring a new jet trainer aircraft to replace the Vampire T35 in use for many years by the RAAF flying training schools. When the ASR was released late in 1964 the time scale set for service introduction was so short that it would have excluded any local design. The Government and the RAAF were to come in for a considerable amount of criticism for the approach taken by the Service. One example of this was the statement made by Graeme A. Bird, Professor of Aeronautical Engineering, University of Sydney, in his address to the Canberra Branch of the Royal Aeronautical Society in 1966 where he said :

> "...it was by far the most serious planning and policy failure (ie the Government's).The Government Aircraft Factories had made several design studies and were well advanced with a final design (GAF F.2 turbofan all-through jet trainer) when the decision was made to build the Macchi trainer under licence... the RAAF perhaps through incompetence, but more likely by deliberation, failed to formulate a firm requirement well in advance, so that any design put forward within Australia could be ruled out by a newly revised requirement... the fault lies with the Government for allowing them to get away with it".

The RAAF planned for all-through jet training from 1968 and evaluated the concept with a Hunting Percival Jet Provost T2 (A99-001) leased from the UK and tested on Pilot Course 35 at 1 BFTS Pt Cook from April 20, 1959 to December 7,1959. It did not work well.

Six potentially suitable contenders for a Winjeel (piston) and Vampire (turbojet) advanced trainer replacement were examined by a joint Department of Air/Department of Supply team in March 1965. This overseas mission which left Australia on 27 February led by Air Commodore Brian Eaton, Director General of Operational Requirements, included a representative from the RNZAF.

Under consideration were the BAC Jet Provost, Canadair CL-41 Tutor, Fuji T1F-3, Aermacchi MB326, Potez 94 and SAAB 105. There was a narrow selection margin over the whole range of contenders, but the final choice was a decision between the CL-41 Tutor and the MB326H. Canadair and aero engine builder General Electric made a very determined local build and component buy-back proposal but the Aeronautica Macchi MB326 was regarded as the more suitable and cheaper aircraft. This selection was announced on August 27, 1965 by Defence Minister Senator Shane Paltridge.

The Selection
The MB326 was already in quantity production for the Italian Air Force and had been ordered by the South African, Ghanian and Tunisian Air Forces. The Australian Government considered that it would cost about the same or slightly more to build the aircraft in Australia rather than import an assembled product. Ten years later, in 1975, an Industry Assistance Council report gave 29% as the local cost disadvantage by the DoS to the building of the initial 75 MB326Hs as compared to direct importation. In the case of the ultimate 97 aircraft total production run the estimated cost penalty fell from 29% to 13%.

The acquisition price of an airframe from Aermacchi less engine and government furnished equipment, was about A$198,000 at 1965 prices. Such was the low workload level in the Australian aviation industry at the time the jet trainer was contemplated, that the Minister for Supply, Senator Norman Henty, was later to comment that it had reached the point where the capacity needed to support the RAAF would have been jeopardized had new work orders not been placed. (The Australian Aircraft Industry total work load figures for 1965/66 were at a significant high 7.81M man hours [8,930 personnel] and had fallen away to 4.01M man-hours in 1973/74 after CA-30 production had come to an end.)

CAC was formally informed on September 22, 1965 it was to be the prime contractor to build the (CA-30) MB326H trainer and its Bristol Siddeley Engines Ltd Viper 22-11 turbojet engine. Hawker de Havilland Australia was its major subcontractor with a 30% share of the production work in an initial building/assembly program of 75 airframes and 120 engines with an expectation that another 33 aircraft would be ordered. An anticipated RNZAF order of 20 aircraft concurrent with the order placed by the RAAF did not materialize.

The agreement to acquire the MB326H was for an aircraft in accordance with the RAAF's Technical Requirement Spec AC143, a complicated series of licence fees, together with the arrangements of the 'lead-in' aircraft and components to enable a graded familiarity to be built up with the new airframe. The right to its local manufacture and the transfer of technical support was ratified by the Australian Government and Aeronautica Macchi Societa per Azione of Milan (Aermacchi SpA) on November 1, 1965. For this the Government paid an opening fee of US$141,000 to build the airframe followed by US$64,000 on receipt of all technical data and continuing fees of US$15,000 on the 4th to the 8th anniversary of the signing of the agreement. In addition there was to be US$11,900 paid for each of the first 75 aircraft built plus US$6,000 for every aircraft beyond that quantity. 5% of the Aermacchi ex-works selling price was requested for all manufactured spare parts.

The Commonwealth was allowed the non-exclusive right to sell the trainer to countries bounded by the latitudes 10° south and 25° north and longitudes 90° east and 150° west encompassing Burma, Thailand, Malaysia, Singapore, Indonesia and the Philippines.

Colin Bellward, Engine Factory Superintendant went to Bristol Siddeley,UK to prepare for the Viper material. Bill Downes (HdH) and Aircraft factory Manager Ern Jones went to AerMacchi at Varese to set up the acquistion process. Due to the required in-service date of October 1967, a number of fully complete and near complete airframes were imported. This took the form of six fully assembled aircraft in fly-away condition ex-works AerMacchi; three sets of fully installed airframe assemblies, tested with fairings fitted and a further three aircraft sets of assemblies not fitted with fairings. All were shipped from Genoa, the first shipment left for Melbourne on June 26, 1967; the last departed at the end of September. Fifteen airframe packages comprised of uninstalled major assemblies and sub-assemblies with all the material and equipment to enable completion of the aircraft, were also shipped out.

The first two of the assembled aircraft, A7-001 and 002 had made their initial flights in Italy. A7-001 flew at Varese, 55km north of Milan, on February 11, 1967. It was tested locally on 18 September by ARDU test pilot Sqdn Ldr Maxwell Loves and handed over to the RAAF, at Avalon Airfield on October 2, 1967. The first two courses, 59 weeks long, re-introduced all-through jet training. Found too expensive they were discontinued and training reverted in 1969 to using the Winjeel basic trainer at RAAF Point Cook.

By the time the 31st CA-30 airframe had been assembled, the level of local production content was around 85%. The balance was made up of bought-in items because of a lack of suitable production facilities or equipment suppliers and/or the need to reduce the level of and therefore the cost of the local tooling program.The initial order for 75 aircraft was expected to be complete by December 1969, a target that was missed.

The first 34 engines were imported as complete items in order to give the RAAF a sufficient initial spares holding. Eight of these engines went direct to Aermacchi, the rest coming to CAC. The local production content of Australian produced/assembled engines reached a level of 95% by the 81st engine of the 147 ordered of

A7-003. One of the six received, fully assembled MB326H on test flight from Avalon Airfield, Lara,Victoria. **David Anderson. 724081623P**

which 113 were produced by CAC. For Australian service some 114 airframe and 90 Viper engine modifications were introduced, the majority of the latter as a result of Bristol Siddeley initiatives.

The aircraft was designed for ease of maintenance access, the fuselage being divided into four sections for production purposes. The forward sections accommodated the nose landing gear and electronic equipment, followed by the pressurised tandem seat cabin with its Martin-Baker ejection seats and starboard hinging single piece canopy. Fuel cells were to the rear, followed by the Viper engine installation and the rear fuselage unit.

Of the basic airframe, the manufacture of the wings, tailplane, wing tip 30 gall fuel tanks for training and 70 gall tanks for ferrying, horizontal control surfaces in addition to various engine components and undercarriage hydraulic items was undertaken by HdH at Bankstown. Dunlop's Aviation Division supplied the wheels, brakes, tyres, fuel cells and hydraulic components. GAF was the source for the clear one piece canopy. A mix of imported small jigs and tooling and manufactured large jigs was employed. As time went on the 70 gall tanks became a standard fit.

The airframe / engine build was carried out at Fisherman's Bend with the assembly of the complete aircraft for system function testing. Once this was complete the wings and horizontal tail units were removed and each aircraft was trucked to Avalon Airfield, Lara for re-assembly and pre-flight prior to handover to the receiving Service. Company Flight Test Engineer Lou Irving took part in each aircraft's flight test from the rear seat. With his death, Jim Caterson took over the role.

The Royal Australian Navy Fleet Air Arm was the second customer for the aircraft with the receipt of N14-075 on July 25,1970, the first of 10 examples for the FAA's land based VC-724 training squadron at HMAS Albatross, Nowra, NSW. It replaced their Vampire T22 & T34 serving as a lead-in trainer for the A-4G Skyhawk fighter/bomber. These 10 aircraft in addition to a further 12 for the Air Force brought total production to 97 aircraft. The serial range for the RAAF aircraft was A7-001 to -072; -079 to -083; -088 to -097. That for the RAN was N14-073 to -078 and -84 to -087. Production ended with the delivery of A7-097 on September 27, 1972. The RAN aircraft were transferred to the RAAF (and reverted to the A7 serial prefix) when the Robert Hawke Labor Government stopped FAA fixed wing operations.

On the earlier date of November 8, 1967, the Air Attache at the Italian Embassy to Australia visited Wellington, New Zealand, to discuss with the Royal New Zealand Air Force their outstanding requirement for a new jet trainer and the possible adoption of the CAC built MB326H as had been expected.

Above: Aircraft A7-014 and A7-015 at the head of this production line view at the CAC plant. **HDHV**

A7-002 of the CFS 'Telstars', the first RAAF MB326H display team at Avalon. March 23, 1968. **J.A. Vella**

A7-013 undergoing undercarriage retraction test in pre-delivery hangar at Avalon. March 23, 1968. **J.A. Vella**

A7-026 in the White & Orange 'Fanta Can' drink colours at RAAF Richmond. April 4, 1971. **J.A. Vella**

A7-067 of 2 Operational Conversion Unit. **J.A. Vella**

The Defence Minister, Malcolm Fraser, addressed Parliament on June 5, 1970 on the topic, *'Australian Aircraft Industry — Discussion of Matter of Public Importance'*,.... a very long speech, in part of which he stated:

> " I hope very much that New Zealand will believe that it is in its interests to buy Macchi aircraft from Australia rather than from Italy or the United Kingdom"

In his reply to the House of Representatives, Paul Keating, Deputy Leader of the Opposition slammed the very late formal tender request and therefore the inevitable decision to adopt another overseas design and added further:

> "to add insult to injury, the Government bungled the possible Singapore outlet for the Macchi and thus denied the local aircraft industry a much needed workload. The Government is now desperately trying to sell the plane to New Zealand".

The *Australian Financial Review* had stated that because of a lack of Government finance for the export of military equipment, the DoS had been unable to conduct negotiations on a government to government basis. CAC reverted to raise export finance at 7.5 % interest for 7 years through commercial channels with Bill Abbott (GM) flying to NZ to impress a sale. Whereas the UK offer through their Export Credit Guarantee Department was at 5.5% for 10 years. CAC made a second attractive formal presentation in July 1970 to supply 24 MB326H to the RNZAF. Deliveries were to start in the latter part of 1972 with the completion by the middle of 1974. No order came. The NZ Government was concerned for the future export market of its primary produce products after the UK joined the European Union so it leaned to the UK in its negotiations. In 1972 it started receiving 16 BAC 167 Strikemaster Mk 88 basic trainer/light attack aircraft at a lower unit price than the MB326H. They were replaced in 1991 by the later model Aermacchi MB339.

In RAAF service a number of shortcomings quickly arose. The nosewheel tyre threw up jets of surface water into each intake when operated in wet conditions. AerMacchi and Dunlop developed a chine tyre and CAC improved it with a metal and fibre glass sprayguard attachment. It was not Italian Air Force practice to fly in the wet. The extremely hot confined cockpits in local summer temperatures of 43°C were discomforting. Ventilated flying suits were tested but cooling air ducted from the engine at low altitude would leave the aircraft with insufficient flying power. Vision from the rear cockpit, always poor, was judged horribly dangerous during take-off and landing, especially at night.

The RAAF's original Unit Aircraft Establishment was for 66 aircraft. The planned distribution was: the new 2 FTS from January 1, 1969 (RAAF Pearce, W.Aust) - 45 aircraft; CFS (RAAF East Sale, Victoria) - 11 aircraft; 2 (F) OCU (RAAF Williamtown, NSW) - 8 aircraft and ARDU (RAAF Laverton, Victoria and later at RAAF Edinburgh, S. Aust) - 2 aircraft.The remaining aircraft were to be held in reserve.

Seven aircraft had been lost in accidents to January 1973 with the lead airframe amassing 2,000 flying hours by December 1972 showing signs of surface cracking in the wings and wing root fittngs. Metallurgical problems were first discovered in November 1968. The RAAF was concerned the trainer would not reach its safe operational life of 5,000 hours. From mid 1969, together with CAC and ARL/DSTO, it went on alert after discovering that under the RAAF's operating spectrum, fatigue problems were to be expected, at the very least in the lower main spar boom in the wing centre section, wing attachment and internal wing bracket mounting holes.

New Life

One of the possible contenders for a Jet Trainer replacement was an updated version of the MB326H. To enable an objective assessment of the aircraft to be made against other competition, a feasibility study was requested by the Department of Defence on August 1976.

In this study, CAC categorised the changes into groupings of:
- Essential change
- Desirable change - Low cost
- Desirable change - High cost

Many areas of equipment were considered to be in need of essential change or rectification. These ranged from fatigue life components, improved air conditioning and desirable changes ranging from a wheel anti-skid system to an increase in rear seat visibility, a liquid oxygen system, improved panel lighting and the possible fitment of a General Electric J85-4A turbojet which could offer up to a 25% gain in aircraft performance for a weight increase of 80 lb. Its smaller size compared with the Viper 22-11 wou1d have provided new space for enhanced equipment installation. These options was rejected by the RAAF.

Some of the structural upgrading recommended in this funded study to rectify airframe fatigue problems was carried out in the extensive $26M LOTEX (Life of Type Extension) program of March 1977 for which CAC was the design authority; a minimum cost refurbishment program to extend the aircraft safe life to 1988. It established an MB326H overhaul facility detachment at RAAF Laverton, using the former ARDU and 21 Sqdn hangar. It went from September 1978 to 1985. The turn around time of about 14 weeks for each aircraft was to repair the east coast fleet operated by the Central Flying School; 2(F)OCU; ARDU at RAAF Laverton (and later from RAAF Edinburgh) and the RAN's VC-724 from Nowra NAS.

The aircraft arrived at RAAF Laverton; the wings removed and returned to HdH at Bankstown,NSW and the fuselage transported by road to the Fisherman's Bend factory for insertion into the fuselage mating jig. The work at CAC consisted of upgrading the upper longerons in the forward nose area around the cockpit, a new centre section, centre frame, new canopy latches, torque tube in the tail, the fuselage fin frame and pick-up attachments together with a rebuilt fin with a new spar.

HdH's work on the wings included a new spar and new wing/ fuselage and wing/tip tank attachments. A7-019 was the first aircraft modified and was handed back in the middle of 1981. Forty-two trainers based around the eastern seaboard were modified by CAC who in turn also produced the 40 kits for the HdH Perth Airport site in Western Australia who managed the LOTEX program for the west coast based fleet. An ergonomics update schedule was introduced towards the end of the LOTEX program. This meant a change of cockpit lighting from red to white, de-sealing and re-sealing of the canopy and the deletion or re-arrangement of some of the cockpit instrumentation. There was a close to 50 / 50 split in the workload share between the east and west coasts.

The original planned life of type for the MB326H was to end in December 1980. Although the fatigue spectra of some aircraft flown by the CFS, (F) OCU and the Navy was above expectation, the RAAF was confident that the CA-30 would reach and go beyond the planned life to about 1984 through a policy of inspection and repair of critical fatigue areas - a policy that was actively pursued.

In the latter part of 1985, CAC / HdHV was awarded a $1.5m two year contract to carry out a Durability and Damage Tolerance Assessment (DADTA) analysis on the airframe to make it possible for

CA-30 MB326H, A7-024 in the main body jig during the Macchi LOTEX program. Macchi tip tanks can be seen on the line to the rear of the jig.. Located in Aircraft Factory 1, Fisherman's Bend. **Robert Anderson. 20200921**

MB326H in the CAC hangar at RAAF Laverton, Victoria receiving line and general maintenance. **Robert Anderson**

The comprehensive MB326H maintenance tool board managed through the use of allocated coloured tags. CAC hangar RAAF Laverton. **Robert Anderson**

Servicing Manager Rod Evans & CAC team at the CAC hangar, RAAF Laverton, responsible for bringing MB326H out of storage back to flying condition, 1970s & 1980s. **Robert Anderson**

The end of general MB326H & CT4A servicing by CAC (outside the repainted CAC hangar), RAAF Laverton. **Robert Anderson**

(L-R). CAC apprentice graduates - Peter Ibbotson, Ross Quick & David Anderson producing MB326H jet pipe insulating blankets made from heat insulating material sandwiched between two rolled, dimpled, stainless steel sheets. **David Anderson**

A7-068. Central Flying School, RAAF East Sale, Victoria. September 26, 1974. **J.A. Vella**

LOTEX rectification work at CAC's overhaul facility at RAAF Base, Laverton & (immediately above) at HDH, Perth. **Tony Todaro**

A7-080. 76 Sqdn. Avalon Airfield, February 2001. The last public appearance of the type. **David Anderson. JH03091503P**

The revised nosewheel chine tyre and water spray guard developed by AerMacchi, Dunlop and CAC.
David Anderson. 712122007D; 712122008D

CA-30 Macchi MB326H Deliveries

Year	Yearly	Cumulative
1967	5	5
1968	29	34
1969	32	66
1970	13	79
1971	10	89
1972	8	97

the type to (hopefully) continue flying to the end of its economic service life of around the year 2000. From 1989 the Pilatus PC-9/A replaced the MB326H in the advanced training role and left it in the lead-in-fighter work with attachemnts to Nos 25,76 and 79 Squadrons.

Following the in-flght wing failure and fatal loss of A7-076 in November 1990 the fleet was grounded. Examination of the wreckage discovered a mis-drilled hole during LOTEX which led to a crack-propagating wing failure. Numerous mis-drilled holes were then found in close to 30 airframes. Finding a repair fix for the remaining small fleet was futile so the RAAF ordered 27 new wing sets from AerMacchi. The original locally built jigs and program tooling had been destroyed sometime prior on Government instruction. Meanwhile Macchi operations were severely 'G' limited, held to nine aircraft in 1992 in the vital lead-in-fighter role and leaving it with 12 airworthy examples in 1993. HdHV fitted these wings at RAAF Laverton to meet the Service requirement for 30 servicable aircraft. The last Macchi flights were in February 2001. Finally in 1997, after decades of deliberation, the BAE Systems (HS) Hawk 127 was selected as the new lead-in-fighter trainer with a fleet of 33 aircraft entering service in November 2000.

The MB326H had been used by 2 FTS, 2 (F) OCU, 5 OTU, 25, 76 & 77 & 79 Sqdns; ARDU; the CFS with its Telstars & Roulettes display teams and VC-724. One VC-724 aircraft had the electronic systems of the DoS / Navy Ikara ASW guided weapon fitted in the rear cockpit to check and verify early remote guidance and system calibration.

For weapons training, 2(F) OCU aircraft were fitted with two pylons for Mk12/A7 Light series practice bomb carriers and the GAU-2B/A 7.62mm mini-gun pods. Twenty six aircraft were lost in accidents. The early ones related to a series of engine fires caused by high-pressure fuel leaks and some to icing induced engine flameouts.

Specifications	CA-30 AerMacchi MB326H	
Powerplant	One CAC (Bristol Siddeley) Viper 22-11 turbojet of 2,500 lb thrust	
Performance	Max speed at 19,700 ft	440 kts
	Rate of climb at SL	4,420 ft/min
	Stalling speed	84 kts
	Service ceiling	40,000 ft
	Range	600 nm
Weights	Empty	5,027 lb
	Max TO	8,560 lb
Dimensions	Wing span	32 ft 11 ins
	Span over wing tip tanks	34 ft 9 ins
	Wing area	204 sq ft
	Length	34 ft 5 ins
	Height	11 ft 4 ins

Bibliography : CA-30 AerMacchi MB326H Trainer Aircraft

Aircraft : (March 1966, September 1966, October 1967).

Anderson D. (1982). Macchis in Australian Service. *AHSA Journal* .Vol 21/3.

Australia. Parliament. House of Representatives. Australian Aircraft Industry. Discussion of Public Importance.(June 5,1970). [By the Hon. M. Fraser]. Hansard.

Australia. Parliament. House of Representatives. Australian Aircraft Industry. Discussion of Public Importance. (June 5, 1970). [By the Hon. P. Keating]. Hansard.

Australian Financial Review. (August 5, 1970).

Commonwealth Aircraft Corporation. (January 27, 1977). Engineering Report AA361. Update of the Macchi MB326H Feasibility Study.

Commonwealth Aircraft Corporation. *Pursuit*. [In-house magazine].

Eyre, David. (1983). *Illustrated Encyclopedia of Aircraft in Australia & New Zealand*. Sunshine Books, Sydney.

Macchi MB326H Agreement between Australia and Aeronautica Macchi Spa. (November 1, 1965).

RAAF News. (Various).

THE HUGHES FRANCHISE — A CONFLICT OF HELICOPTER INTERESTS
December 1967

International Helicopters Pty Ltd of Moorabbin was the Australian agency for Hughes Helicopters, co-owned, managed and established in 1961 by J.A. Lee Archer.

There was a general expectation in the late 1960s that the Federal Government was to request proposals from the industry for the supply of a light turbine helicopter for use by the Army Aviation Corp and the Fleet Air Arm. The introduction of the gas turbine powered helicopter into the Hughes range required an increased financial commitment from the agency and this co-incided with a desire of the partner in the business to move away from the agency.

CAC was interested in possible future involvement in a military helicopter program. General Manager, Herb Knight and the Board of Directors considered the acquisition of the Hughes agency to be an opportue move. However, the Hughes parent company in America was reluctant to transfer a distribution agency to what was considered by them to be the non-commercial structure of CAC. The stipulation to the take-over which came into effect on December 1, 1967, was conditional on the co-transfer of Lee Archer to continue as part of the helicopter group. He was appointed Commercial Manager of the Helicopter Division.

In January of 1968 the Department of the Navy issued Staff Requirement, NSR 4/67, for a Light Helicopter for use in non-operational roles from ship or shore base locations followed by the Department of Air on December 10, 1968, with a similar request in Air Staff Requirement No.55 (Issue 2) to meet the need for an Army helicopter intended for the carriage of freight, personnel, observation and evacuation of casualties.

CAC made their submission to the Requirement on behalf of their agency with the Hughes 369 / 500 / OH-6A Cayuse, powered by an Allison 250 turboshaft of 317 shp. In comparison with the two other contenders, the Hughes 500 design possessed a simple structure of excellent integrity formed from a truss with a deep beam and torque box, a simplified four blade 'Flexrotor' of reduced maintenance and lower weight. Overall it presented as a lower unit cost. A smarter airframe package which together with the benefits of technology transfer were plusses for the adoption of the design.

CAC and Hughes lost out in their submission to the rival Bell 206. The Army revised the selection criteria during the evaluation process and laid emphasis on the helicopters with the larger rated engines, ie the Westland Sud-Aviation SA341 Gazelle, powered by the 523 shp Turbomeca Astozou turboshaft and the Bell 206B with the 420 shp Allison 250-020 engine. (Refer to CA-32/Bell 206B-1) In spite of this loss, CAC ended up with the build management contract for the Bell 206, on behalf of the Department of Manufacturing Industry.

This arrangement created a situation which was untenable to the Hughes parent company. CAC was the Australian distributor for its helicopters whilst at the same time preparations were underway for the construction of a product from a rival firm. For ethical reasons CAC had to distance itself from its Moorabbin Airport operation. In 1972 the Hughes franchise was transferred to CAC's autonomous subsidiary, Rex Aviation, at Bankstown Airport, NSW and the International Helicopters hangar was sold to Jayrow Helicopters.

As a business venture the Hughes franchise had been a successful and profitable undertaking for CAC.

Bibliography: The Hughes Franchise - A Conflict of Helicopter Interests
Archer, J.A.L. (June 1986). [Interviews].

Commonwealth Aircraft Corporation. (December 1967). Engineering Report AA192. Hughes LOH for Australian Army.

Commonwealth Aircraft Corporation . (December 1967). Engineering Report AA1202. Hughes LOH for Royal Australian Navy.

AP1001-BAC/CAC AA-107 CLOSE SUPPORT/ /TRAINER AIRCRAFT
January 1968

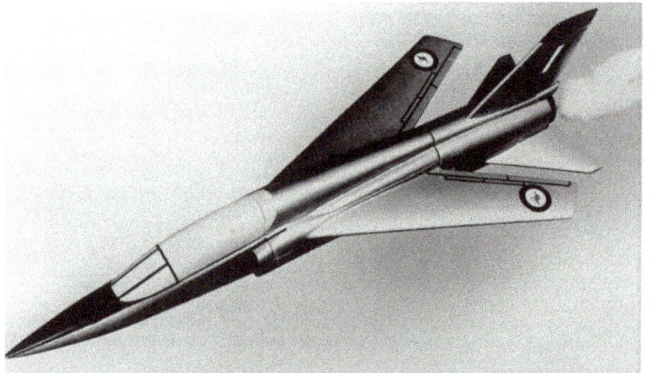

Two weeks following the Ministerial statement of September 1967 announcing the issuing of a revised Air Staff Requirement for a Close Support/Trainer aircraft (refer to CA-31), Australia was paid a visit by the British Minister for Defence (Equipment), Roy Mason from the UK Government of Labor Prime Minister Harold Wilson. The significance of his visit was the declaration that Australia and the United Kingdom may co-operate on a joint development of defence equipment for mutual and world-wide use, the detail of which was not made public. (but was most likely to be the eventual placement of Australian design personnel at BAC on new jet trainer designs and for the eventual invitation for co-production from HSA on the new HS1182 Hawk advanced trainer).

Meanwhile CAC had continued to work on the revised CA-31 and in the late half of 1967 the company was visited by Ray Creasey, Director of Advanced Systems and Technology of the British Aircraft Corporation (BAC), Warton, UK. Ray Creasey's visit was at the instigation of the Australian Government and the development work on the CA-31 impressed him. Part of BAC's design division was in a state of flux due to the collapse of the MRCA Anglo/French variable geometry combat aircraft collaborative program.

In view of the outstanding RAAF Air Staff Requirement AIR/64 Issue 2 (August 28, 1967) for an aircraft able to meet the dual roles of Close Air Support and Advanced Operational Training, CAC was invited to join in a collaborative program with BAC. This co-incided with the Royal Air Force's own draft Air Staff Target 362 of 1964 requesting a 1974 entry into service of a supersonic replacement for the Jet Provost / Hunter T.7 / Gnat T1 and the expected RAF AST 397 for a new Trainer / Close Air Support aircraft.

BAC was anxious to put into practice the extensive background it had built up in variable geometry wing design and it was its belief that the RAAF's Air Staff Requirement could only be met by the use of such a design. Working with CAC's small preliminary design team, BAC would capitalize on the extensive CA-31 design experience and at the same time hope for the possibility of spreading any future development risk with Australia or CAC.

This was Australia's first attempt at a joint venture with the UK in the design, possible development and production of an advanced military aircraft. Sponsorship was to be under the Department of Supply with a preliminary CAC team led by John Kentwell, Chief Design Engineer. It was the Australian Department of Supply's view, as expressed through Ian B. Fleming, Controller, Guided Weapons and Electronics:

> "that for the Australian aircraft industry to remain effective it must from time to time undertake major design and development projects. Never-the-less a limitation is imposed by technical competence and economics in relation to the type and quantity of aircraft required."

With the total number of aircraft required by the RAAF to this specification likely to be no more than 100, and could have been as few as 25 aircraft, the Department considered that 'going it alone' would stretch the available technical resources and would be unlikely to gain the necessary financial approval from the Government. So the Australian Government entered into a jointly funded venture with the UK Government for the equal sharing between the two countries of costs, development effort and production workload. The ultimate objective was to develop the cheapest and smallest aircraft that would meet the requirements of ASR AIR/64 and at the same time have the characteristics necessary to appeal to the widest possible export market.

The Anglo - Australian project got off the ground in January 1968 when John Kentwell, Chief Design Engineer; Charles Reid, Senior Design Engineer Flight Technology and William Gornall, Chief Structures Engineer left for BAC's Preston Division at Warton, Lancashire. The Division was managed by Frederick W. Page, head of the English Electric Lightning Mach 2 fighter design team. As the work on the CA-31 design tapered off at Fisherman's Bend, four other members of that team: Cecil Billington, Group Leader Structures; David Rees, Senior Aerodynamicist; Wal Watkins, Design Engineer, Configuration Development and Brian Keevers, Design Engineer, Structures, arrived in the UK on June 19, 1968.

The combined team was led by Ray Creasey of BAC. Other non-CAC personnel in the project were Tom Shelton, Chief Structural Designer (GAF) who was to assess the production viability for the Australian defence manufacturing facilities; to assist in the market survey for the final proposal and to act as liaison between the CAC team and the Department of Supply. Tom Trimble, Experimental Officer from the Aeronautical Research Laboratories was in collaboration with the Royal Aircraft Establishment at Farnborough as an independent assessor to evaluate the new design against the Air Staff Requirement.

With an in-service date of mid 1974 required by the RAAF and with that Service's first preference for a twin engine layout (although a single engine layout would have been given consideration) only engines which were in production or in an advanced stage of development would be taken into consideration. Once again, the preferred engine was the RB172 in a single engine installation or the twin J85 engine in a twin-engine configuration. The new General Electric GE-1 / J1A1 of 5,000 lb dry thrust and 7,500 lb with reheat was also a potential contender.

In this preliminary evaluation phase no existing aircraft type was considered suitable. The Northrop F-5A/B fell well short in a number of important respects while the in-house BAC / SEPECAT Jaguar over-matched the RAAF requirement, was far too expensive and was expected to have the very high UK operating cost of £1,400 per flying hour (1968 values).

The Anglo/Australian programme was split into three phases with approval being required from both governments before proceeding to a next phase.

- Phase 1 with an estimated Australian Government commitment of $100,000, was a six month design study in which developed layouts and possible variable geometry techniques would be investigated as well as making certain that the design agreed upon would be both smaller and cheaper to acquire and operate than the highly sophisticated SEPECAT Jaguar
- Phase 2 was to lead to the mock-up build stage, manufacture of a structural test airframe and the construction of two prototypes
- Phase 3 was to be the funding for production

The combined team using only the Australian ASR 64 as a yardstick worked through variations of design from AA-101 through to AA-107.

The AA-107 (Anglo/Australian 107) was the seventh variant of a line that evolved. A layout of the AA-106 with twin J85 turbojets is shown in Fig. 1.

The basic differences in these AA variants were in changes to wing area. Constant throughout was the use of a fixed fin, a slab tailplane, a high-set variable sweep wing, high lift leading edge and full span single slotted trailing edge flaps. Spoilers on the upper surface of each wing were to provide low speed roll control. When swept back, the trailing edge of the wing moved into a sealable slot in the side of the fuselage. The inboard wing swing pivots were to be made from FV520 stainless steel. The wing sweep range was 27° maximum forward and 69° maximum rearwards. Additional items were a runway arrestor hook and air brakes positioned under the lower front fuselage. The engine was a single Rolls Royce RB172 / T260 Adour afterburning turbofan fed via lateral pitot inlet ducts.

A dorsal spine of considerable depth was to house the heat exchangers and hydraulic reservoirs and faired into the vertical fin under which was located the landing brake parachute container. Fuselage side area was kept to a minimum by inclining the two seats 29° to the rear and still having the rear seat raised 9.5 inches in relation to the front seat.

The area-ruled mid-fuselage housed three fuel tanks (the wings were not plumbed) and two 20mm cannon with a minimum provision of 120 round of ammunition for each gun. A single 30mm cannon gun pack was an alternative. A recessed flat lower section of the fuselage allowed the use of a specially contoured weapons pallet capable of carrying a military payload of 5,000 lb dispersed across 7 stores stations. This would have included conventional munitions, overload fuel tanks or rocket, flare and reconnaissance pods. Under fuselage stores ground clearance was 40 inches. Customer choice and depth of expenditures would dictate the degree of sophistication of strap-on or pallet-mounted specialized equipment. The main undercarriage was to be capable of absorbing a vertical descent rate of 12 ft/sec for the trainer variant and 8.5 ft/sec for the close support variant.

The Doppler radar and processor, the liquid oxygen tank and convertor were positioned in the extreme nose. The cockpit layout features were based on that of the CA-31 and what could be transferred across from the new BAC Jaguar advanced trainer design. Tandem ejector seats were housed under a starboard hinging one piece canopy of a similar configuration to that on the Macchi MB326H.

Maximum speed was to be around Mach 1.5 at altitude with a design life of 4,000 hours in the trainer role.

Simplicity, light weight and ease of maintenance were the paramount design aims for the AA-107, the same design criteria as had been applied in the CA-31. Whilst it may have seemed to be an over-complication to design a VG wing into a small airframe intended to perform a training role, BAC was also trying to meet the Royal Air Force's outstanding Air Staff Target 362 of 1964 which called for a successor to the Jet Provost etc but with a performance better than that of the Northrop T-38 Talon.

At the same time the French Air Force was looking for a training aircraft to replace its Lockheed T-33 and the relegated fighter/advanced trainer Dassault Mystere IV, but this was secondary to their requirement for large numbers of cheap tactical aircraft to supplement the planned, complex V/ STOL Mirage IIIV.

Hopes were also held for sales in Spain, Canada, Malaysia, Singapore, New Zealand and various South American countries. In October 1968, D. Rees; C.Billington and W.Watkins returned to CAC for mock-up development, drawing office establishment and in-depth design. In great haste to complete the work for review before the end of November 1968, a full scale wooden mock-up was completed. J.Kentwell and W.Gornall returned in November. Brian Keevers remained at BAC for another year till the end of 1969. Charles Reid stayed on till the end of 1971 to assist with the initial phase of BAC's own P.59 / P.62 trainer projects.

Other events had now intervened to cast a new slant on the project. The BAC / SEPECAT Jaguar design (first flight of the French prototype was on September 8, 1968; the British prototype flew on October 12, 1969) was turning out to be so expensive an aircraft, that the initial intention of its use as an advanced trainer was dropped and its new role was to be a dedicated close support, highly advanced strike aircraft to be employed by nine squadrons in the RAF and fifteen squadrons in the French Air Force. This action immediately removed any prospect of the adoption of the AA-107 by the RAF as a close air support aircraft.

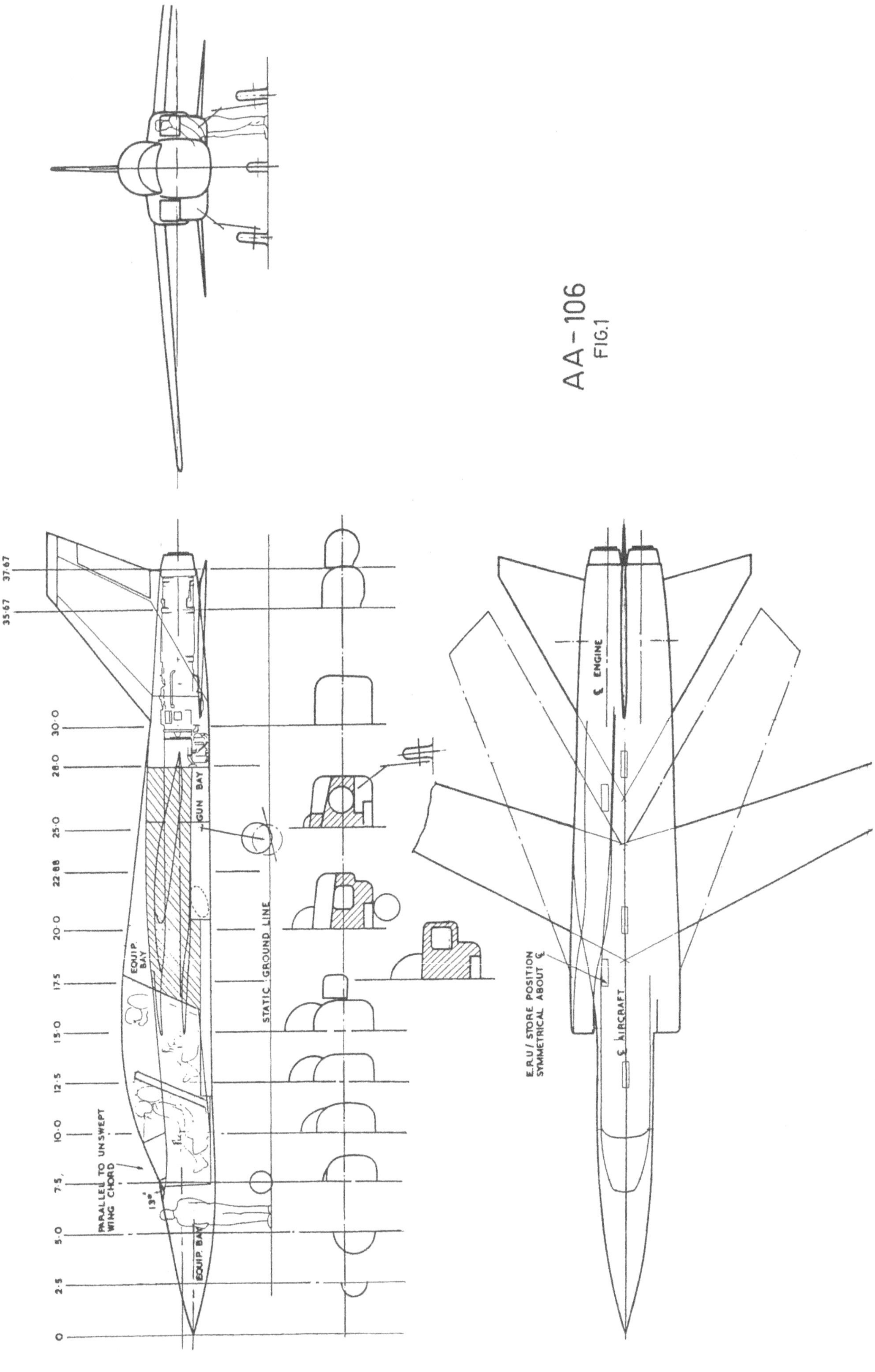

AA-106
FIG.1

AP1001 - BAC/CAC AA-107

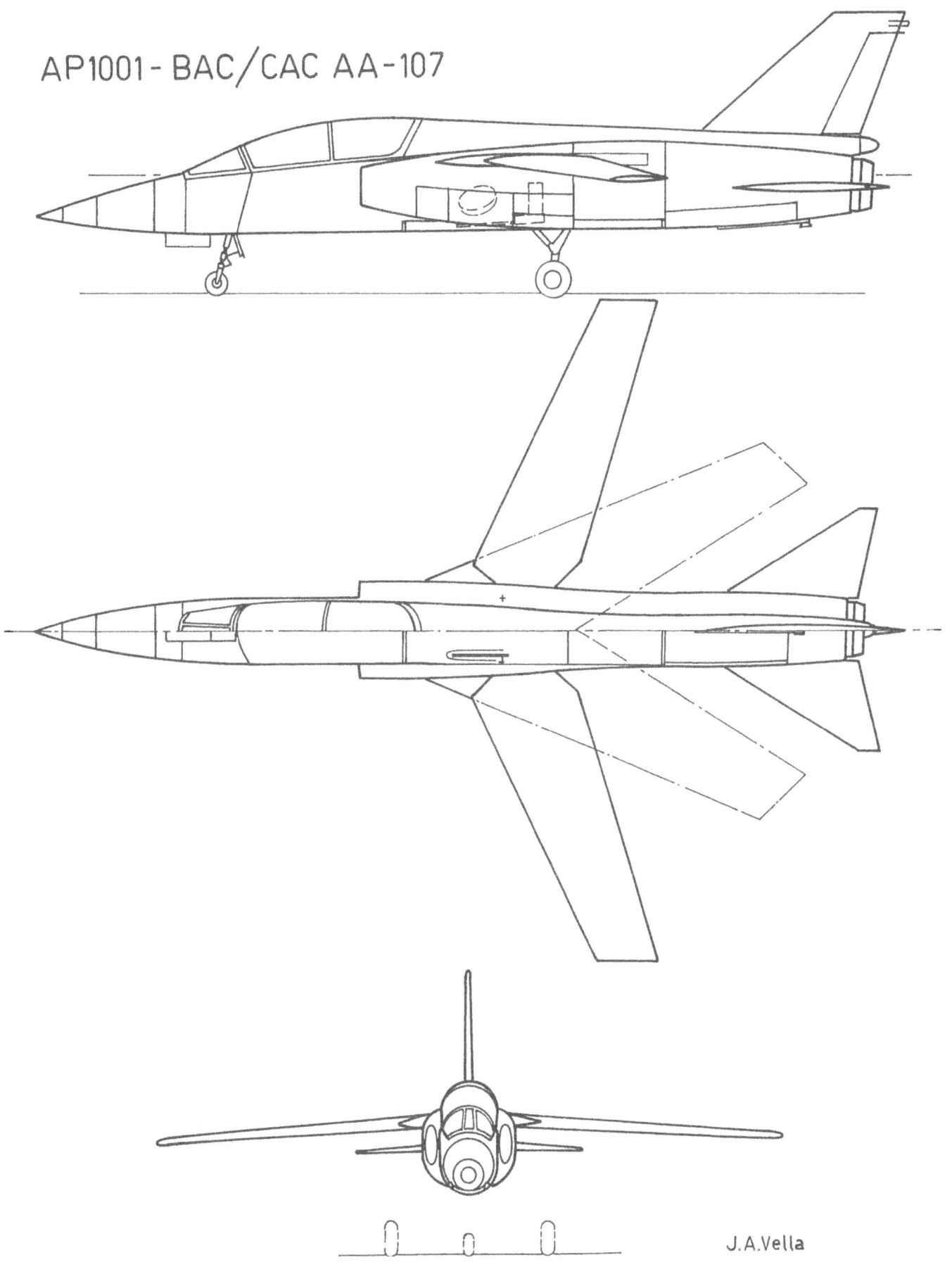

In January 1969 Senator Ken Anderson, the Australian Minister for Supply visited Warton to discuss the future of the AA project. BAC's preferred Variable Wing Sweep (VWS) trainer ideas were not going to be adopted by the RAF leaving them only for the possible miniscule RAAF light attack aircraft requirement.

By the middle of 1969 design work on the AA-107 had tapered off after a period of very intensive effort. In August 1969 BAC entered into a collaborative agreement with Aermacchi of Italy to possibly combine in the building of both a basic jet trainer, the P.59 powered by the Viper 632 turbojet and the P.62 Adour turbofan powered advanced trainer. With the possibility of there being other partners, especially on the advanced trainer, CAC was left with the vague possiblity of other partnership options.

With the BAC / SEPECAT Jaguar removed from its previously intended training role, the RAF needed an advanced high subsonic trainer to replace the Folland Gnat T1 etc. The UK / Italian partnership was also aimed at producing a new design to supersede the RAF's Jet Provost and the Aeronautica Militare Italiana's MB326 basic jet trainers. Whilst the P.59 was a separate new design, the P.62 used the fuselage and tail configuration of the Anglo / Australian AA-107 but did away with the swing wing in favour of the alternative more conventional fixed wing (Fig. 2).

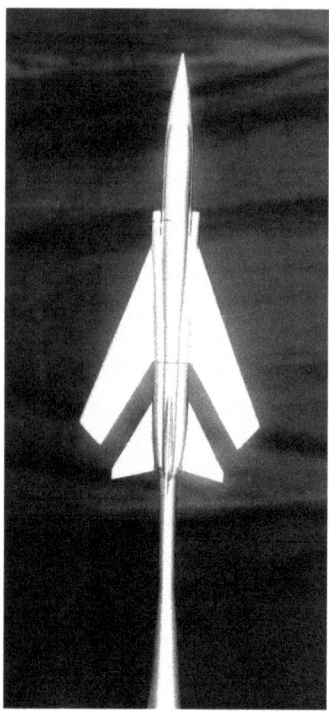

This approach of two widely disparate designs in the one package differed from the Hawker Siddeley plan offer of one airframe. Their HS1182 fixed wing Hawk, considered to be cheaper than any other type, was selected in October 1971 as the eventual winner of the Royal Air Force ASR 397 issued in January 1970.

In the meantime the combined design team waited on the Phase 2 deliberations of the Australian Government. Program cost figures were now claimed to be near to A$100M with a need of an order of at least 100 aircraft for a go-ahead. The desirable acquisition price was of less than A$1M per aircraft (1969 values). The RAAF's requirement was still for around 30 advanced trainers but there was not an urgent need for close support, as the Mirage IIIO was capable of providing this role even if the Army was not as convinced of its suitability.

In a ministerial statement to the Senate on May 22, 1970, Minister for Supply, Senator Ken Anderson advised the end of Australian Government's interest in the joint study by saying, in part:

> "it is the practice of my Department to seek, where possible, projects which might result in the local design, development or production of defence equipment. I emphasise that the purpose of the exercise was not to design a specific aircraft but rather to study the feasibility of a particular design concept and the market it would attract. In the event we have not been able to obtain sufficient assurances of overseas sales. Furthermore, there has been a re-thinking of the RAAF requirement for Close Air Support and Advanced Training and as a result continued work on the project could not be justified".

The RAAF had apparently withdrawn the ASR.

June 5, 1970 was a significant aviation topic day in the Federal Parliament. The cancellation of the study was sized upon by Paul Keating, Deputy Leader of the Labor Opposition as he spelled out a long critique of the *"criminal neglect of Australia's defence industries..."* by the years in government of the Liberal / National Parties coalition. The House of Representatives topic was 'The Australian Aircraft Industry - A Matter of Public Importance.' . David Fairbairn (the previous Minister for Defence) gave a generalised reply followed in turn by a long, wide ranging detailed historical defensive response of the industry by the Minister for Defence, Malcolm Fraser, highlighting the various industry programs then underway and planned.

He challenged by saying:

> "The Deputy leader of the Opposition did not say whether or not we should have gone ahead with the AA-107 the advanced supersonic trainer and ground support aircraft. I think his omission to say that the Opposition

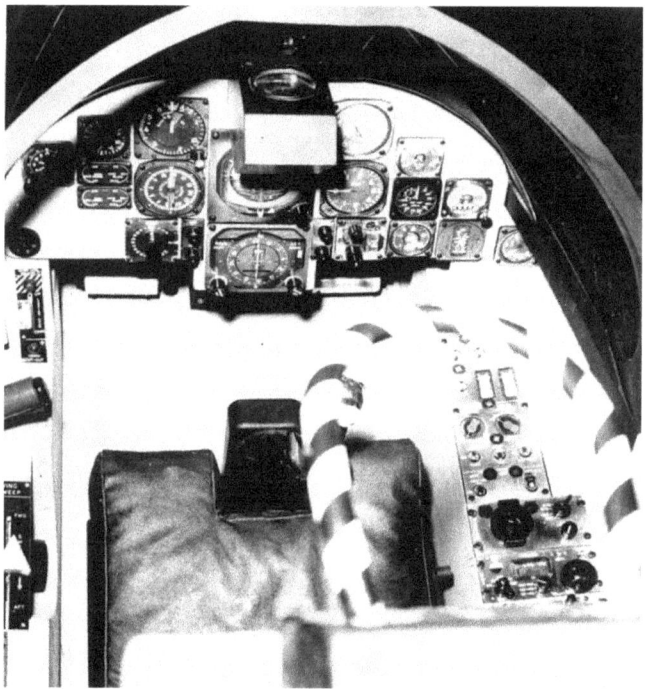

The front cockpit mock-up of the AA-107. **Walter Watkins**

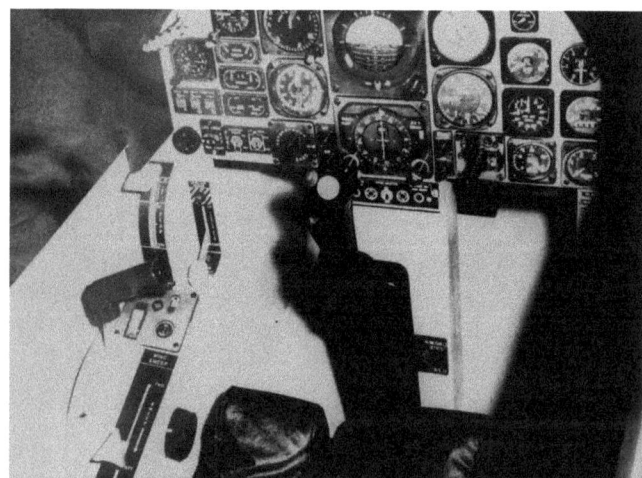

The rear cockpit mock-up of the AA-107. **Walter Watkins**

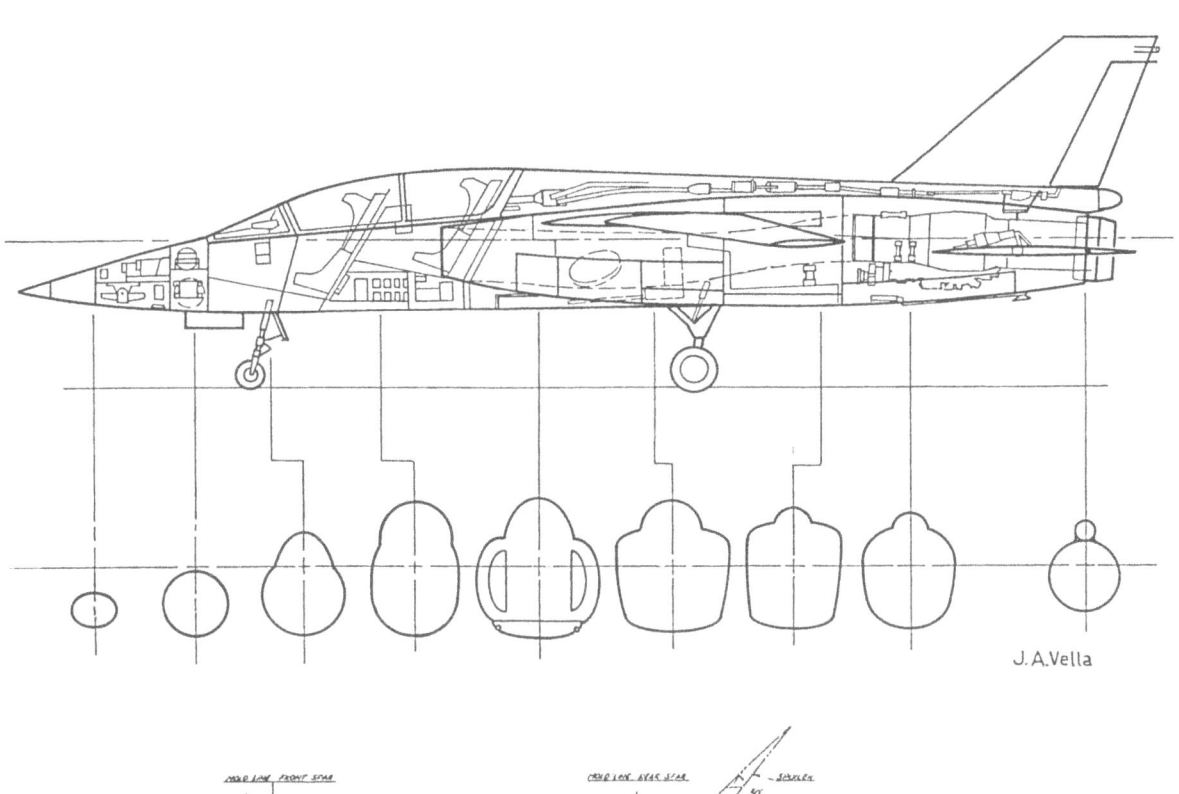
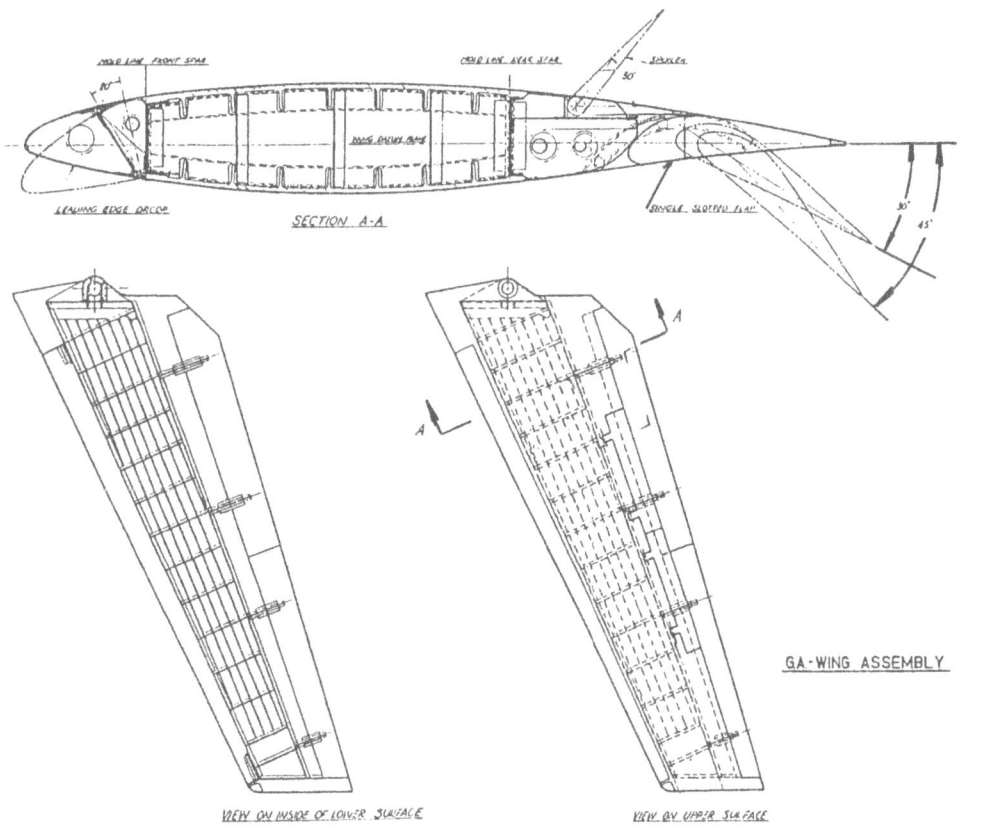

GA-WING ASSEMBLY

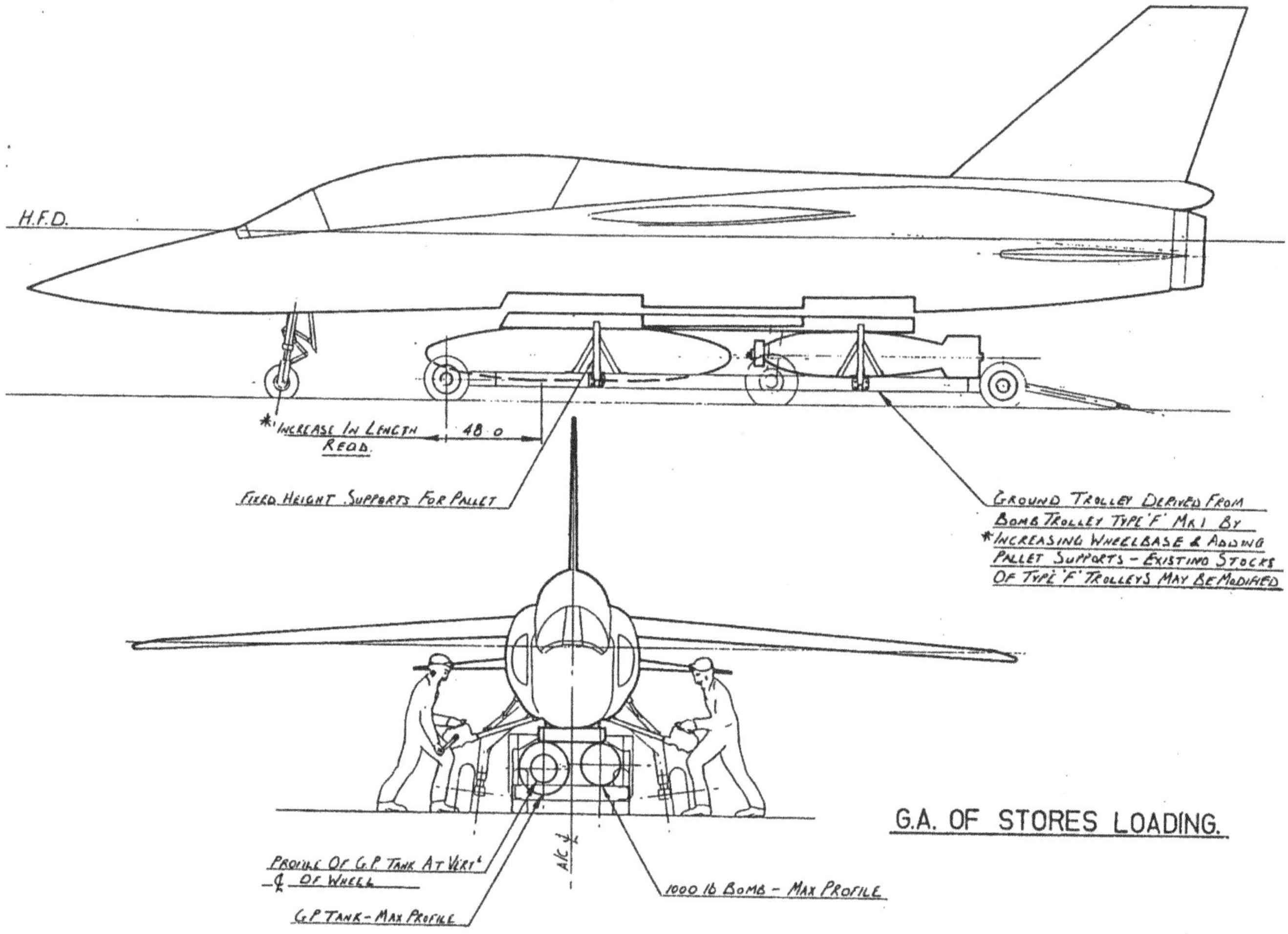

G.A. OF STORES LOADING.

Specifications	AP1001-BAC / CAC AA-107 Close Support / Trainer			
Powerplant	One Rolls Royce/Turbomeca RB172/T260 Adour turbofan of 5,250 lb thrust dry & 8,200 lb thrust with reheat Specific fuel consumption 0.81 lb/hr/lb			
Performance	Based on a TO weight of 12,000 lb ie trainer configuration of 2 crew, no external stores:			
	Max speed at SL with 69 ° sweep		Mach 1.05	
	Max speed at altitude with 69 ° sweep		Mach 1.48	
	Max ceiling with 27 ° sweep		51,000 ft	
	Max rate of climb with 69 ° sweep		25,000 ft/min	
	TO distance with 27 ° sweep , max reheat		1,620 ft	
	Duration, Trainer sortie at 12,000 lb		3 hrs	
	Range, Close Support, Hi-Lo-Hi strike at 16,000 lb		250 nm radius	
	Range, Close Support, Lo-Lo strike at 16, 100 lb		185 nm radius	
	Max ferry range		1,500 nm	
Weights	Trainer Aircraft empty	8,344 lb	Trainer aircraft TO	12,000 lb
	Close Support Aircraft empty	8,357 lb	Close Support Aircraft TO	16,100 lb
Dimensions	Wing span (unswept)	30 ft	Wing span (swept)	17.2 ft
	Wing area (unswept)	130 sq ft	Wing area (swept)	148 sq ft
	LE sweep	20 ° min; 69 °max	Wing root chord (unswept)	5.42 ft
	Wing tip chord	2.9 ft	Wing anhedral	4 °
	Aerofoil section	NPL/BAC Sect 12%		
	Taileron span	10.8 ft	Taileron anhedral	4 °
	Length	40 ft	Height	12.8 ft
	Wheelbase	16 ft	Track	7.4 ft
	Main wheel tyre dia	21 ins	Nose wheel tyre dia	13.5 ins

A composite wide angle view of the full scale AA-107 mock-up built at CAC. The small confines of the space and the camera wide-angle view distorts the much finer lines of the fuselage. Walter Watkins examines the wing pivot glove area.
Walter Watkins

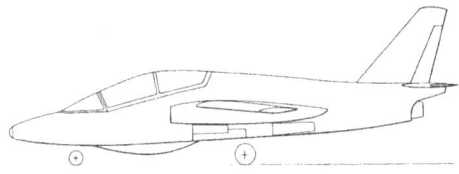

P.59

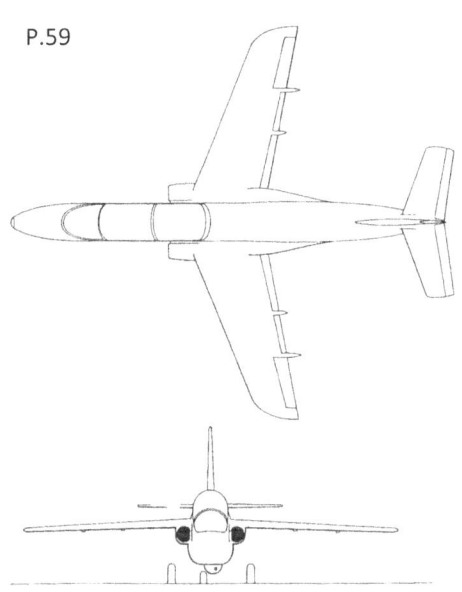

P.62

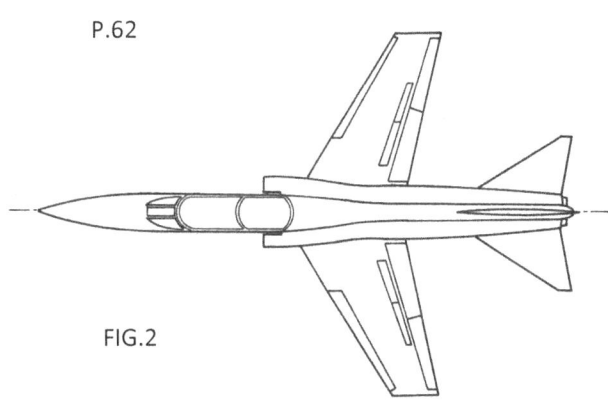

FIG.2

Above: The BAC P.59 trainer. CAC design staff worked for a short time on both the P.59 & P.62 trainer projects after the termination of the AA-107. **HAWK British Aerospace - Roy Braybrook**

Above: The BAC P.62, simpler fixed wing alternative trainer variant of the AA-107 proposed for the RAF after cancellation of the AA-107. **HAWK British Aerospace - Roy Broybrook**

Looking forlorn the AA-107 mock-up resides in a dismantled state at the Ballarat Aviation Museum, Victoria. **Roger McLeod**

supported the design and construction of this aircraft in Australia is the most significant weakness in the Opposition's attack because this attack has been hinged on the Government's refusal to proceed with a project which was in fact not viable."

and he continued :

"But if there is any person in the industry who believes that because he designs an aircraft there is an obligation on the Government to buy that aircraft and an obligation on the Royal Australian Air Force to fly that aircraft, that would in some circumstances be committing the Air Force to buying inferior aircraft and committing it to inferiority in air operations. I know that the Deputy Leader of the Opposition and his Party would not want that any more than the Government would want it."

(In the same speech he also applied an identical production warning proviso to GAF's Project 'N', the Nomad, then underway). The AA-107 project could not have succeeded, but criticism had continued. On 1 June in an address to the Australian Industries Development Association in Melbourne, Malcolm Fraser warned that too great a preoccupation with Australian-made labels could result in *"mediocrity"* in some areas of defence equipment and in its approach to such matters in the future, the nation would have to be more willing to discard *"sluggish and unattractive"* projects.

In an apparent change of heart on the training spectrum, the RAAF had arrived at the same conclusions as had the Royal Air Force in that supersonic capability was not necessary for flying training. The USAF syllabus included only one supersonic training sortie in their Northrop T-38 Talon as a result of the high cost of fuel. This decreased sortie time length was of limited training value.

As for the close support role, the Australian involvement in combat in South Vietnam had indicated a swing towards using dedicated armed helicopters. Eleven Bell AH-1G HueyCobras were ordered in December 1970. They were subsequently cancelled.

Fifteen months of design and negotiation work had been funded by the Australian tax-payer but the Federal Government could not afford the development cost of around A$50M even though this was one half of the combined Anglo - Australian figure. However American sources had suggested that likely development costs were more akin to reach A$250M. This figure was circulated around the Supply and Defence Departments and it caused a great deal of further apprehension.

Almost seven hundred general and detail engineering drawings were produced. All were subsequently destroyed. Photographs of the wooden mock-up which was erected in CAC's experimental shop do not do justice to its outline shape. A large airframe, it took up all the available floor space and photography was possible only with a distorting wide angle lens generating an uncomplimentary image. The dismantled mock-up resides with the Ballarat Aviation Museum in Victoria.

Throughout the time of the dual design effort a good rapport was established between both the BAC and CAC teams and the CAC members hoped a future occasion for co-operation would re-occur again.

Bibliography: AP1001 BAC/CAC AA107 Close Support Trainer
Aircraft. (June 1970)

Air International (Various). Key Publishing. Lincs, UK.

Australia. Parliament. Senate, Joint Design Study AA-107. (May 22, 1970). [Ministerial speech by Senator Ken Anderson].Hansard.

Australia. Parliament. House of Representatives. Australian Aircraft Industry. Discussion of Matter of Public Importance.(June 5,1970).[by the Hon M. Fraser]. Hansard.

Australia. Parliament. House of Representatives. Australian Aircraft Industry. Discussion of Matter of Public Importance.(June 5,1970) [by the Hon D.Fairbairn].Hansard.

Australia. Parliament. House of Representatives. Australian Aircraft Industry. Discussion of Matter of Public Importance.(June 5,1970).[by the Hon P. Keating].Hansard.

Braybrook, Roy. (1984). *British Aerospace Hawk*. Osprey Publishing. Oxford.

Commonwealth Aircraft Corporation. (May 1969). Engineering Report AA193A. Provisional Spec.for Anglo/Australian Trainer/Close Support Aircraft.

The Australian Financial Review. (June 2, 1970).

CHAPTER 7. COMMUTER AIRCRAFT, HELICOPTERS AND NAVAL EXPORTS

CA-28 CERES TURBO PROP CONVERSION
June 1968

An exercise to fit an alternate engine in the Ceres was completed by Charles Reid in August 1965. This meant replacing the R-1340 Wasp radial engine with a P & W PT6A, 500 shp turboprop.

There would have been a reduction of engine weight but the specific fuel consumption would increase by 32%. However the use of aviation kerosene would lower the operating cost by 30%. It would also have been necessary to reduce the PT6 compressor scream by placing the rear intake inside the engine cowling and to protect the air inlet by installing a perforated steel screen. The noise reduction exercise would have brought the noise level down to 93 decibels at a distance of 75 feet.

Specifications	Turboprop Conversion to CA-28 Ceres - A Comparison	
Powerplant	One Pratt & Whitney (Canada) PT6A-20 turboprop engine rated at 500 shp	
Performance	NA	
Weights	PT6A-20	R1340 Wasp
Empty	3,740 lb	4,647 lb
TO	7,000 lb	7,410 lb
Payload	2,230 lb	2,230 lb
Fuel	640 lb	284 lb
Engine installation	660 lb	1,625 lb
Dimensions	Length 35 ft (spinner tip to rudder)	

Bibliography: CA-28 Ceres Turboprop Conversion

Reid, C.J. (June 6, 1968). Engineering Report AA179. Preliminary Design Study, Turboprop Conversion to CA-28 Ceres. Commonwealth Aircraft Corporation.

A COMMERCIAL AIRCRAFT REPLACEMENT FOR THE WINJEEL TRAINER
October 1968

The Royal Australian Air Force's need for an ab initio training aircraft to replace the CA-25 Winjeel Basic trainer was expressed in Air Staff Requirement AIR/67 of March 1968 raised from Project AIR/4, was put aside, then updated as AFSR Air/67 in January 1971. Sixty-five examples were requested.

The main requirements of AFSR Air/67 were:

- Maximum AUW-2,500 lb (2,000 lb in 1968 release of AIR/67)
- Maximum manoeuvrability +6.0g, -3.0g
- Maximum cruise speed - 115 kts
- Maximum level flight speed - 125 kts
- Maximum diving speed - 220 kts
- Stalling speed - 45 kts
- Rate of climb - 1,000 ft / min
- Service ceiling - 12,000 feet
- Endurance with 10% fuel reserve - 5 hrs
- Side by side seating
- Tricycle undercarriage
- Stowage space for 100 lb of luggage
- IFR or night flying capability
- Fully aerobatic

The Commonwealth Aircraft Corporation's response of October 28, 1968, followed a detailed examination of about thirty existing and proposed training and general aviation aircraft that could meet the criteria.

Its final choice for consideration was narrowed down to five aircraft, namely the Cessna 172 (T-41A or B); Fuji FA200 (modified); AESL Airtourer (modified); Victa Aircruiser (modified) and the Beagle Pup, modified and morphed by 1971 as the Scottish Aviation Bulldog.

- Cessna 172 (T41A or B Mescalero). This was in service with the USAF, Ecuador and Peru. It had special crew seat backs and shoulder harnesses which were requested by the ASR but it was considered below par in terms of climb rate, stall speed and acceptable weight.
- Fuji FA200. Considered to have many attributes meeting the requirement and may have been a contender if trade imbalance considerations between Japan and Australia (then 50% in Australia's favour) were a major criteria.
- AESL Airtourer. A fully aerobatic and structurally sound design fitted with 100 or 115 hp engines. If it was to be fitted with a 150 hp engine it would have met the ASR very well. However in the opinion of RAAF test pilot reports including that of Air Cdr D.R. (Jell) Cumming, the Airtourer was too small and underpowered to be a military trainer.
- Victa Aircruiser. Built as a four seater it was owned by Victa Pty Ltd, Sydney who possessed the one prototype and $250,000 worth of tooling drawings and jigs. The offered unit selling price on the civil market was to be $18,000. Both CAC's Jim Caterson and Harry Gorjanicyn had worked on its design and the previous Airtourer.
- Beagle Pup. Beagle Aircraft Ltd were in the process of building a military variant of the civilian Beagle Pup with a clipped wing, a sliding canopy and a 210 hp engine, but the investment for the necessary design changes was slow in forthcoming.

Aircruiser Favoured

The proposal was to take the opportunity to purchase the existing tools and jigs of the Aircruiser from Victa Pty Ltd, modify the airframe so as to have only two seats and add dual controls. In addition to special seat backs and shoulder harnesses, a sliding canopy would be fitted.

The benefits of this choice were that the Aircruiser was an Australian design, built and certified under FAR23 rules backed with a considerable amount of available design and wind tunnel data to verify its handling characteristics. If further interest was shown, CAC could have gone on to produce a variant for the civil market and possibly, fitting a gas turbine engine in the 220 shp range which could have opened up new possibilities.

At a meeting in May 1966 between AVM Brian Eaton, head of the Air Force Technical Branch, Gary Richardson, Victa's Aircraft Division chairman and Henry Millicer its Chief Designer, there was the spoken belief that the Victa Aircruiser prototype had potential as a possible replacement for the RAAF's Winjeel Basic Trainer.

A lot of investigative work was undertaken by CAC from late in 1966 into a plan floated by Sir Lawrence Wackett with Dr Henry Millicer to form an aircraft fabrication syndicate. Sir Lawrence (retired from CAC in 1960) suggested Henry Millicer should re-work the Aircruiser into a military aircraft and rename it the *Airtrainer*.

The Aircruiser first flown in July 1966 did not have a commercial future with the Victa Aviation Division as it was exiting the aviation business in January 1967. This was a surprise but it had foreseen the rejection by the Tariff Board of any protection to be paid to Australian light aircraft manufacturers against intensified price competition from multiple US imports.

The syndicate's plan was to form a company at Moorabbin Airport to assemble both the Aircruiser and the still to emerge

Ceres Turboprop Conversion

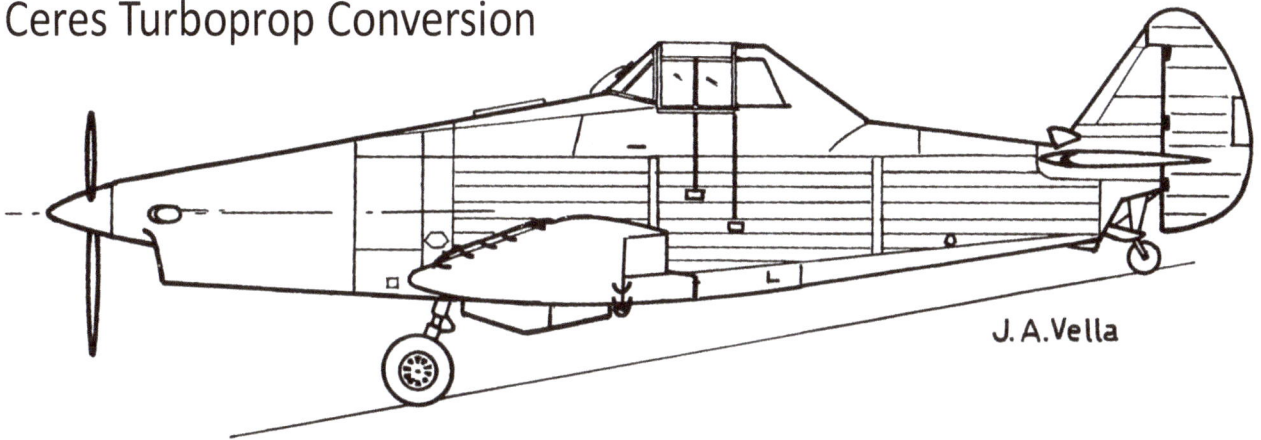

J. A. Vella

Airtrainer from parts manufactured at CAC and elsewhere. The syndicate was comprised only of the two principals, their two lawyers and a representative of the Federal Government. It met twice for discussions in legal Chambers in Melbourne and detailed cost estimates were prepared for a serious CAC engineering evaluation of the concept.

Victa was seeking the very high price of $750,000 for the design rights and manufacturing jigs of the Aircruiser and no matter how hard the idea was studied there was no solution to justify the enormous initial capital outlay for the design rights and the formation of a new company. It had become clear that to develop the military variant for which there was no specific order, without producing the civilian aircraft at the same time, against a small market demand, was not a viable proposition. CAC turned its back on the prospect.

The prototype Aircruiser T4 gained its type certificate in March 1967 and languished whilst Henry Millicer, with input from a number of specialist aviation individuals worked on the Airtrainer idea until his resignation from Victa later in the year.

Airtrainer Emerges

The design rights to the Airtourer and Aircruiser had been sold to Aero Engine Services Ltd, Hamilton, New Zealand in May 1971 nearly a year earlier, when AIR/67 was re-issued, seemingly written around the performance and weight capabilities of the shelved Airtrainer design.

AESL pulled out all stops at the realisation of a new military / civil market opportunity. Led by Pat Monk it revised Dr Henry's design with extensive structural changes including a jettisonable canopy, revised seating and about 100 engineeering and other detail modifications to make it a better platform for aerobatics and to meet the RAAF specification. It was still built to FAR23 civil airworthiness regulations.

The Airtrainer made its first flight on February 23, 1972 followed two months later by a comprehensive RAAF flight test evaluation. The Liberal Country Party Defence Minister David Fairbairn followed up quickly on July 24, 1972 with an order of 37 CT-4A aircraft (A19-027 to 063) for an outlay of A$3.25M in preference to the Scottish Aviation Bulldog, the development of the Beagle Pup. The Air Board confirmed the acquistion in March 1973. The incoming new Labor Federal Government then tried without success to reduce the order to 28 airframes. Production deliveries were to commence in 1973 but were held up for some requested aircraft rectification and further testing. The first CT-4A from the initial batch was received on January 15, 1975. Early serviceability problems including exhaust and fuel fumes leaking into the cockpit and fuel starvation problems delayed and interrupted the training courses so much that training intakes were reduced from four to three per year with just 37 aircraft.

Luckily, another batch of 14 aircraft (A19-064 to 077) was acquired in 1981 with the last example delivered on June 26, 1982. This later batch had been ordered by a shelter company on behalf of a Swiss flying club which was acting as cover for the Rhodesian Air Force trying to evade sanctions placed on it by the United Nations. When this was discovered the NZ Government embargoed the sale and placed the aircraft in storage until they were modified with two underwing hardpoints and an increase of 250lb in MTOW for the RAAF. All the Airtrainers were flown across the Tasman Sea to Australia fitted with long range tanks for the journey.

Part of the offset agreement with New Zealand was for CAC to provide CT-4A components to AESL to an initial value of about $250,000. AESL and Air Parts (NZ) Ltd had merged to become NZ Aero

A19-050 in the original Yellow & Deep Bronze Green service finish. RAAF Point Cook. December 6, 1976 **J.A. Vella**

Aircraft crewed, canopies raised, still some Winjeels in the background in preparation for a midday take-off April 7,1976. **J.A. Vella**

A19-073 in the second 'Plastic Parrot' paint scheme. RAAF Point Cook. December 1982. **J.A. Vella**

A19-074 in the White & Light Orange second colour scheme taxies past A19-072. RAAF Point Cook May 1,1988. **J.A. Vella**

Space Industries (NZAI).

Raw material was shipped from New Zealand to be reworked as finished or semi-finished pressings, castings, fuselage frames, spars, longerons and sheet metal work etc. The first work package was received in February 1973 for 40 sets of 260 items totalling some 10,000 formed parts and 2,000 castings. The offset work included items for the 24 CT-4 Airtrainers destined for the Royal Thai Air Force and for all other orders for the aircraft.

Slightly underpowered it performed well in RAAF service but had some residual limitations requiring flight restrictions. The side-by-side seating arrangement was much liked by instructors. It was extremly difficult to get into a full spin and inverted spins were banned. It was designed as a civil aircraft, with civil aircraft handling charateristics. It served with 1 FTS at RAAF Point Cook from 1975 till December 1992 as well as the Central Flying School at RAAF East Sale and provided the basic flying training for 64 RAAF and 55 Army pilot's courses as well as students from Malaysia and PNG.The Airtrainers were retired, stored and the majority sold at auction to private buyers at Bankstown Airport on May 23, 1993.

The Australian Defence Force Basic Flying Training School (BFTS) with a new fleet of civil registered AESL CT-4B aircraft took over the flight screening role in January 1993 in a BAE/Ansett Flying College industry training venture established at Tamworth Airport, NSW.

Sir James Rowland, RAAF Chief of Air Staff from 1975 and former ARDU test pilot was of the opinion the Winjeel should have been replaced by a proper military trainer with a 500-600 shp turboprop and a little bite in its handling:

"Unfortunately, the moment I mentioned that terrifying word 'design' with its connotation of risk, they all turned pale and changed the subject."

Bibliography: A Commercial Aircraft Replacement for the Winjeel Trainer

Aircraft: (July 1965, June 1966, September 1966, January 1967, January 1972, March 1972, April 1972).

Institution of Engineers Australia. (March 1987). Aerospace Industry Working Party [Report].

Millicer, Henry Dr. (August 9, 1987).[Correspondence].

Parnell, Neville; Boughton, Trevor (1988). *Flypast, a Record of Australian Aviation*. AGPS, Canberra.

Rees, D.R. (October 28, 1968). Engineering Report AA185. Light Aircraft to Meet ASR Air/67. Commonwealth Aircraft Corporation.

TURBOFAN BOOST ENGINE ON SHORT HAUL TWIN TURBOPROP AIRCRAFT
November 1968

One method of improving the take-off, range and payload characteristics of a feeder-liner type aircraft is to fit a boost engine that can be switched on for take-off and switched off during cruise. This kind of auxiliary power was first considered by CAC as a built-in item on the 1953 design of its P265 Wallaby Feeder Liner.

Considerations to using a booster jet engine on short haul aircraft have appeared from time to time. CAC made a brief assessment on the implications of fitting a third engine to the French (Aerospatiale) Nord 262 twin turboprop feeder airliner (f/f December 24, 1962), of which a total of 110 were eventually built. The reason for the CAC investigation is not clear, nor remembered although CAC staff had a presence and an office in France during the Mirage IIIO build years. Nord was a sub-contractor to GAMD building Mirage III wings and CAC was in an offset arrangement

Third production Nord 262 F-BLHQ on lease as a demonstrator aircraft by Japan Domestic Airlines. Mascot Airport, NSW. March 2,1966.
Roger McDonald Collection

fabricating components for Nord. This may have brought on this connection to an aircraft that was selling very slowly. The November 1968 study was to suggest installing an unidentified Pratt & Whitney turbofan boost engine of 2,200 lb thrust in this 29 pax aircraft, built for the DC-3 (21-32 pax) replacement market and powered by two (not very popular) Turbomeca Bastan 1,065 ehp turboprops.

Investigation Summary

The general conclusion was that improvements in payload and range obtainable with an auxiliary jet engine could be quite substantial if the installation of the unit is considered as part of the initial design of the aircraft. Its cost may well be justified in terms of the payload and range gains obtained. However, if the unit was fitted retrospectively, the modifications necessary to strengthen the structure and undercarriage and to also provide the extra fuel capacity to improve the range could result in far too costly an exercise on an existing aircraft. The cost penalties involved would not compensate for the improved performance obtained.

This would be particularly significant in passenger operating conditions where the load factor is low and increased passenger accommodation is not really a necessity. In cargo operations however, the increased payload capacity would more than likely be an advantage in obtaining more trade.

Bibliography:Turbofan Boost Engine on Short Haul Twin Turboprop Aircraft

Rees, D.R. (November 24,1968).Tech. Memo 011/4/DRR. Effect of Installing a Turbofan Boost Engine on the Performance of Short Haul Twin Turboprop Aircraft. Commonwealth Aircraft Corporation.

BRITTEN-NORMAN ISLANDER WITH TURBOPROP ENGINES
February 1970

The Britten Norman Islander ten seater aircraft designed and built (initially) at Bembridge on the Isle of Wight, UK first flew on June 12, 1965.

It was a small twin engine feeder liner aircraft of 6,000 lb max AUW (1970 figures). In its initial form it was powered by two 260 hp Avco Lycoming 0-540 series engines. So far as was then known, development of the aircraft was restricted to the future installation of supercharged engines to improve its performance in hot and high operating conditions.

The aircraft was considered to be one type that could benefit from the fitment of turboprop engines in place of its existing piston engines. Since ten standard examples had been sold in Australia to

the end of 1969, CAC felt it was appropriate to determine if improvements in performance would follow the installation of the alternate engines and if that gain could justify a larger market for this feeder transport in the less than 12,000 lb AUW category.

Turboprop Engines

Since 1960 many light executive and feeder transport aircraft had been fitted with turbine engines. The trend had been slow, attributed mainly to the higher acquisition cost of the turbine engine and the lack of appropriately small-sized turboprop engines in the 300 to 500 shp class. Three of the turbine engines which had made the grade in this small field were:

- PT6A Series engine
- Garrett AiResearch TPE-331 Series engine, and
- Allison 250

Both the PT6A and Garrett AiResearch engines were too powerful for the Islander and their installation would involve considerable structural redesign to the rest of the aircraft. The Allison 250 engine however, provided an effective 22% increase in rated power, as compared with 15% for the proposed supercharged Lycoming O-540 engine. It was decided to consider the installation of the Allison 250 and determine its operating and installation modification costs.

The Model 250-1315 engine had an effective maximum power rating of 317 shp and development was in hand to increase that to 370 shp. The engine dry weight was 139 lb, 40.8 inches in length, 19 inches wide and 22.5 inches high, with a power to weight ratio four times greater than that of the Lycoming O-540.

Operating costs

It was assumed that if the average utilisation would be 800 hours per annum and the stage length was 200 statute miles, then the direct operating cost would be 30 cent / ton-mile for the piston engine and 27 cent / ton-mile for the re-engined aircraft with the Allison 250 engines.

Conclusions

The Investigation came to the conclusions:

1. By re-engining the Britten-Norman Islander aircraft with two Allison 250-B15 turbo-prop engines it would have been possible to improve on the short haul payload/ range characteristic by as much as a 20% increase in payload for ranges up to 400 miles. Cruise speed would be increased by 20% and take-off distances by 20% if the maximum AUW of the aircraft was retained at 5,995 lb.
2. The unit cost of conducting the modification on 100 aircraft would have been A$60,730 which would require a retail selling price increase of 70% on the existing figure of A$90,000 for the unmodified aircraft. By comparison the expected price of the GAF Project 'N' (Nomad) was to be about 250% greater. The estimated total development cost of the B-N Allison engine modification was $105,440; made up of $50,000 for the alteration cost of the first prototype, $55,040 for the engines and $400 for ancillary equipment.
3. Operating costs for stages of 200 miles and an 800 hours per annum utilization would be reduced by 9% by using the engine modified aircraft.
4. If the fuel capacity of the Islander was increased to 160 gall its potential range would have been improved to 500 nm from the 325 nm with the standard fuel capacity of 114 gall, which was sufficient for 690 nm when flown in the piston engine form.
5. Modifying the complete aircraft structure and providing a retractable undercarriage so as to increase the maximum AUW and cruise speed was not considered worthwhile, since it would involve considerable extra modification cost.

The investigation did not eventuate into hardware. It was nevertheless an indication of development in the right direction as shown by events which did take place at Britten-Norman five years later.

Overseas Turbine Islanders

On October 29, 1975 Britten-Norman announced the development of the Turbo Islander powered by two Lycoming LTP 101 turbo-prop engines flat rated at 400 shp. This aircraft made its first flight on April 6, 1977 but did not enter production.

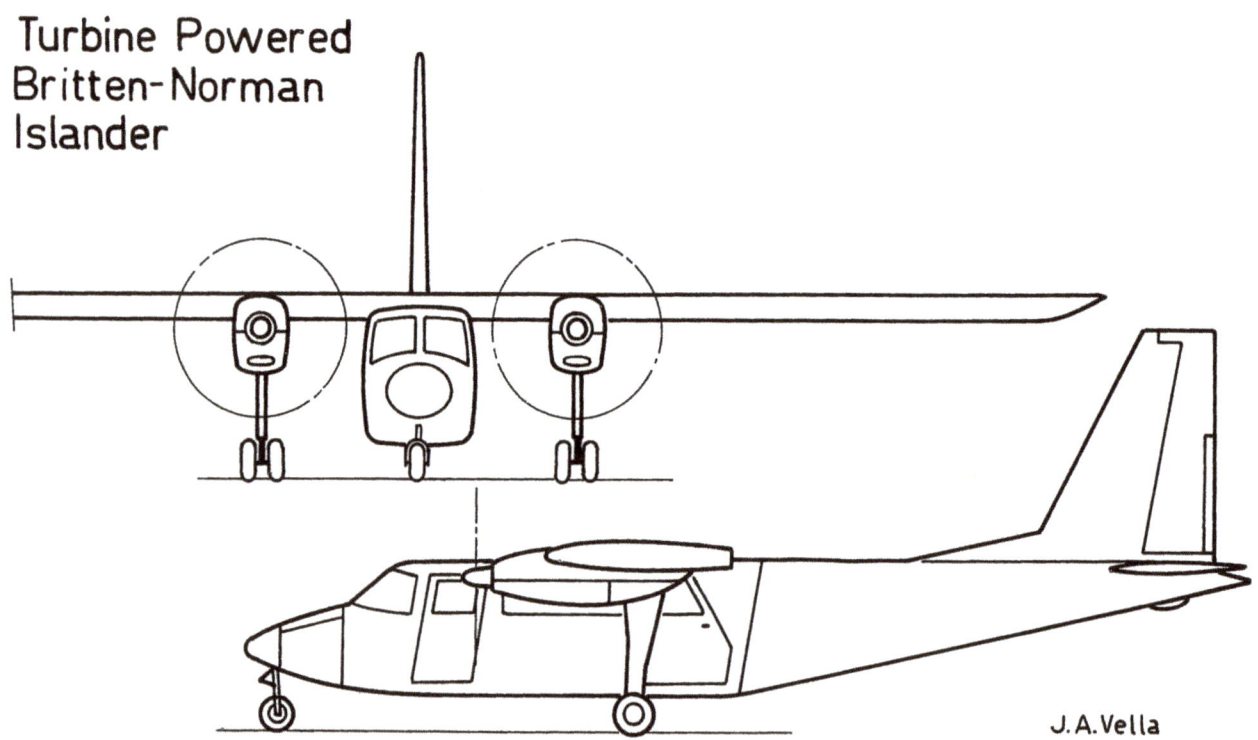

Turbine Powered Britten-Norman Islander

J. A. Vella

BN Islander VH-IGT.(Piston engine) Rottnest Airlines, September 1,1985. **Roger Mc Donald Collection.**

On August 2, 1980 the BN-2T Turbine Islander powered by two Allison 250-B17C turbo-props flat rated at 320 shp made its first flight. This version went into production. The problem of extra internal fuel was met by providing optional auxiliary tanks in extended wing tips, increasing the span by four feet and raising the internal wing fuel capacity from 114 gall to 163 galls. This figure is very similar to the capacity envisaged by CAC (item 4 above).

Bibliography: Britten-Norman Islander with Turboprop Engines

Jane's All the World's Aircraft. (1978/79, 1980/81, 1985/86). Sampson Low, London..

Rees, D.R. (February 25, 1970). Tech. Memo 011/5/DRR. Proposal to Re-engine Britten Norman Islander with Turboprop Engines. Commonwealth Aircraft Corporation.

EX260-BRANIK MISSILE HANDLING AND LAUNCH SYSTEM
1970

In 1970, CAC became aware of Brazilian Navy interest in Ikara and its possible use on their Vosper Thornycroft Ltd.(UK) designed and built frigates. Competitive design proposals were submitted to Vospers and the Brazilian Navy by CAC and from Vickers Barrow (UK) who had taken over the installation of Ikara for the Royal Navy. CAC's fixed price contract submission came out the winner and the EX260 BRANIK 102 (Brazilian Navy Ikara) project began with two systems installed in the UK during the ship building process.

Arthur Williams, the veteran former Tugan staff member was was project manager for this rigidly price-controlled and managed program. Experience from both the RAN and RN had made it obvious that Ikara was a potent and reliable weapon and that neither the carriage of large numbers of missiles nor continuous rapid launching was necessary, so some modifications were appropriate, particularly by simplifying the handling process in the weapon magazine, to minimize system costs. These Vosper Thornycroft frigates with a displacement of 3,800 tons placed them midway in size between the RAN's River Class and the DDG destroyers. In comparison with the original RAN River Class installation, the BRANIK had a reduced 10 round capacity magazine. The missiles were mounted in a single transverse row in individual stands shock-mounted to the deck. They were picked up, transported to the central extraction station by a simple, manually controlled, hydraulically powered overhead hoist and transferred to a single station assembly room by a deck-mounted trolley and automatically loaded to the launcher. This was in a similar fashion to each half of the Australian DDG system. Again, similar manufacturing, testing and installation techniques to the previous systems were retained however unit testing was simpler because of the manually operated transfer of missiles to the extraction station.

Four ship systems were ordered, although five were built when the first ship-set was lost at sea. Their transportation containers fell overboard when a heavy gale off the North Island of New Zealand shifted the deck cargo (the containers were subsequently found by the New Zealand Navy). Final system delivery was in 1977. The four Brazilian Navy frigates to be fitted with the single BRANIK launcher and its missile magazine were the F40-Niteroi, F41-Defensora, F44-Independencia and F45-Uniao. The lead ship Niteroi went through its successful Ikara trials in state 5 and 6 seas. Managed on-site by Arthur Williams from April 1977, Roger Lee and then Ken Gee from January 1978, were present at the Arsenal de Marinha, Rio de Janeiro to provide technical support to the Brazilian teams installing two ships systems. Tad Kowalewski followed in 1979 to observe and advise during the final testing phase.

The various Ikara handling and launching system projects were of considerable importance to CAC. They were largely instrumental in the company being able to retain a competent design team during the 1960s and early '70s, when aeronautical design activity was very low. It provided a significant manufacturing workload over a span of some 15 years with the fixed price BRANIK contract being an especially profitable venture.

The projects were recognised as of world class technical standard.

Bibliography: EX260 Branik Missile Handling & Launch System

Jane's Fighting Ships. (1987/88). Sampson Low, London.

Kentwell, J. (1988). CAC Chief Design Engineer. [Correspondence].

Ikara missile leaving CAC stern launcher on Brazilian Navy frigate F-45 Uniao.

THE GENERAL AIRCRAFT CORPORATION
GAC-100 COMMUTER AIRCRAFT
April 1970

A certain amount of optimism and possibly an equal amount of uncertainty surrounded the press release on behalf of the Australian Government's Minister of Supply, Senator Ken Anderson and Dr Lynn Bollinger, President of General Aircraft Corporation of El Segundo California, that had provisionally committed part of the Australian aircraft industry to a risk-sharing building program of a small airliner.

That date in California was February 7, 1969. The commitment was for the Government Aircraft Factories to build the complete wing of the General Aircraft Corporation GAC-100 and the engine nacelles for its PT6 turboprop engines. One hundred wing and engine nacelle ship sets were to be built at an initial rate of four sets per month beginning towards the end of 1969 and continuing through to 1972. The value of the production contract with GAF was put at approximately US$15 million but a start was conditional on the receipt of fifty definite aircraft orders.

This project was directed by the GAC Transport Division (a sister division of Helio Aircraft Company, both subsidiaries of General Aircraft Corporation) although production and final assembly were to be contracted out on a risk-sharing basis to other companies.

GAC, with the assistance of engineering and design staff of the Convair Division of General Dynamics Corporation schemed a 32 to 36 passenger STOL turboprop transport aircraft (the extra 4 seats being available if the galley, toilet and coat modules were deleted) aimed primarily at the third-level, commuter and local airline market. Passenger accommodation was four abreast with a centre aisle and a flight deck for two crew members. Four Pratt & Whitney (Canada) 800 shp PT6-30 turboprop engines provided the motive power. Special features were the advanced high lift wing devices for STOL performance from unimproved strips.

Dr Lynn Bollinger previously the founder (in 1948) and President of the Helio Aircraft Corporation and the principal designer of that company's 'Courier' STOL light plane joined with Kornel J. Fehr the chief design engineer for the GAC-100.

This risk sharing arrangement was the first offered to Australia for an American designed commercial aircraft. Pacific Airmotive Corporation of Burbank, California was to be the major subcontractor and builder of the fuselage, the tail assembly and a quick change engine installation kit. GAC formed an Australian subsidiary, GAC (Aust) Pty Ltd in April 1969. Its manager, Keith Goddard (a local business start-up entrepreneur) developed the ambitious plan for Australian production on an expanded scale.

Australia As Risk Partner

Some of the reasons put forward for seeking out Australia for involvement in the project were; its 'highly developed and relatively unrecognized' capacity for modern aircraft manufacturing at highly competitive overall costs, quick delivery of components by QANTAS Airways to California (where final assembly was to take place) and the perceived significant market for this type of aircraft in Australia and in Australia's sphere of influence in the South Pacific. Further explanations were given 15 months later on June 18,1970 through a paper presented to the Melbourne Branch of the Royal Aeronautical Society on the subject, *'The Opportunity for Australians to Attain World Leadership in an Important Sector of the Transport Aircraft Manufacturing Industry'*. Through this venue it was possible to expand on a number of doubtful areas and concerns.

The Government was to be asked to fund a A$100,000 feasibility study for which GAC suggested several eminent names in the United States transport business, including Donald Douglas Snr in order to give a level of credibility to such a small little known company. Financial estimates placed the maximum capital requirement at A$30M when the aircraft was in full production, but before any cash flow had been received from delivered aircraft.

GAC (Aust) was to purchase the design rights from the American company for A$3M and raise private capital to A$10M. The rest was to come from merchant banks. The Department of Trade was interested in the project as it would represent an equivalent of A$60M a year in funds saved by the otherwise importation of aircraft in the category.

A letter of intent for the sale of five aircraft from an undisclosed operator had lapsed and no effort was being made to sell the aircraft until production arrangements had been settled. Marketing was not considered to be a great problem as personnel from Boeing, Convair and Douglas who were well known and respected could have been recruited from these sources.

The rate of production was initially to be two aircraft per month to a maximum of eight each month within 18 months. There were about 22,000 man-hours of construction work on two test airframes, one for static and one for dynamic testing, three prototypes and 6,000 man-hours in final assembly and flight test of the prototypes which would be flying by end of 1971. But searching examinations which the industry had conducted showed that the amount of original design work to be offered or carried out in Australia was minimal and limited.

During the prevailing period, the economic recession affecting the United States and Europe had not yet affected Australia but that situation was expected to alter by 1972 and if the project was delayed by that length of time it would most likely be abandoned. A country with a possible domestic market and an experienced aircraft industry was considered a necessary criteria for the construction of the aircraft. Europe in general was not seen as having an internal domestic market. Germany's labour rate was too high. Sweden had the industry base and was planning to build the SAAB 1071 (it developed as the SAAB Fairchild 340 commuter aircraft).The Japanese industry had already received government funding for a commercial aircraft project and no further proposals could be considered whilst Beechcraft Corporation (USA) was not able to gear up for such a project.

By American standards, the Australian industry labour rate was favourable when compared with the large American companies, with specialized design entities, very high tooling support prices and whose productivity was consequently higher. The market potential for this type of aircraft was seen as 3,000 aircraft, with penetration of 800 by the GAC-100. By June 1969, wind tunnel tests in the USA were showing indications of better than design expectations.

CAC's Market Survey

When it appeared likely that the Commonwealth Aircraft Corporation could be a subcontractor to the Government Aircraft Factories on the wing building program, the company undertook its own forecast market study and made comparison with the market forecast data supplied by GAC, which included figures supplied by the Boeing Airplane Company. The minimum baseline profit load factor for the aircraft was 14 passengers on a stage length as low as 100 miles.

From CAC's figures it was assessed that for the United States local market operating at the then average 15-20 passengers per flight there could have been a need for about 150 GAC-100s. The aircraft seemed primarily aimed at replacing the DC-3 and Fokker F-27 Friendship and possibly the DHC-6 Twin Otter in some special circumstances.

TAA was looking at it as a Fokker F-27 replacement (100-160 mile stages) and also for some of the Twin Otter routes (60 mile stages). Ansett-ANA were sceptical about the design ideas, operating costs, reliability, sales support and the quoted all-weather equipped price of A$1.2M, which they considered to be too low. Their attitude was that no order could be forthcoming until there was:

- confirmation of the A$1.2M fully equipped price,
- that it would be competitive in operating costs relative to depreciated F-27s,
- availability of spares and service, and
- availability of the aircraft by 1973-74.

As of December 1969, an estimated 42 GAC-100 may have been sold in Australia for the RPT market (Table 1).

Table 1
Passenger Aircraft in RPT Service

Type	Trans Australia Airlines	Ansett-ANA	Others	Total
Fokker F-27	15	22	7	44
DHC-6 Twin Otter	8	2	0	10
Douglas DC-3	10	8	30	48
Total	33	32	37	102
Estimated Potential Sales of GAC-100 in Australia	18	22	2	42

Both domestic airlines thought the STOL characteristics of the GAC-100 were not essential when the aircraft came to operate out of the airstrips then in use by the F-27. Because the aircraft take-off weight was far in excess of the 12,500 lb permitted by the Department of Civil Aviation for commuter type operations, there was a limitation on possible other operators coming on the scene. Yet with Jetair Australia Ltd founded in May 1969 having been granted a commuter airline licence to operate DC-3s, there was considerable speculation as to what would replace the DC-3 on their routes. The other interesting speculation was that potential local operators which had until then faced restrictions by import and exchange controls to protect the Two Airline Policy, would have had access to a suitable type with possible repercussions to the accepted Policy. The local production of the GAC-100 was an aircraft suitable for these secondary air services.

In May 1970, one month after their market survey, CAC undertook a weight analysis of the design. In the report by Wal Watkins it was suggested that the figure given by GAC for maximum take-off weight of 26,500 lb was a low estimate for an aircraft intended to lift a maximum payload of 7,380 lb. Total equipment weight was felt to be low and at that stage of the design there was the belief that the maximum take-off weight should have been approximately 28,000 lb. The CAC survey was most comprehensive in its comparison with other aircraft in the same category. This was done to gauge the reliability of the initial General Aircraft Corporation data. At the same time, San Diego Aircraft Engineering Inc. California conducted a credibility check of the design and concluded that the 26,500 lb maximum take-off weight could be held to a 10% increase (very close to the CAC estimate).

CAC pointed out that the recession affecting the United States air transport industry could lead to mergers or increases in subsidies but that this problem, whilst generally affecting the major carriers was not going to have a profound effect on third level commuters who were in any case small in relative numbers. Alternatively, the overall reduction in economic confidence expected to last till 1974 was likely to retard interest in the GAC-100. The possible delay of its production by at least a year could put it in a favourable position without any planned competition when the recession lifted.

The RAAF was also known to be considering proposals for a maritime patrol version of the GAC-100. A small force of around 24 aircraft would be dispersed around the coastline to operate from the many unprepared airstrips to perform the in-shore-patrol task. Operational figures for the role were the ability to take-off fully loaded within a distance of 2,500 feet, a maximum cruise speed of 290 kts to the patrol area and the capability of loitering on only two of its four engines for a period of some four hours on 70 kts at a 430 nm radius from base. Ideas of a rear loading ramp GAC-100M variant had arisen for which 50 were seen as possible sales to the RAAF and Army. CAC's production set-up cost estimate for it came out at A$1.15M.

The aircraft had now received a 3 foot fuselage stretch from the original 64 ft 4 ins. This allowed it to be a true 36 seater with galley, toilet and coat compartments. The passenger seats were to be on tracks so as to enable rapid conversion for freight. Passenger entry and exit was via a rear port side door with integral stairs. Cabin pressurisation was to a maximum differential of 6.5 lb/sq in and total fuel capacity in four integral wing tanks was 660 US gallons. Rated horsepower had been increased by the choice of the 850 shp PT6A-40 turboprop engines (Fig. 1)

Manufacturing Re-arrangement

In May 1970 the prime contractor, Pacific Airmotive Corporation withdrew from the project having been unable to find the capacity to handle the work rate of eight aircraft each month. Grumman Aircraft, Bethpage, New York announced on June 8, 1970 it was prepared to take over production rights to build the GAC-100 on the US east coast. CAC was now invited to join in the risk sharing program to build the fuselage, engine installation and possibly components or major portions of the PT6A turboprop engines but told Grumman it would only be a sub-contractor if offered. New Zealand National Airways Corporation at Christchurch was to build the tail assembly. Aero Engines Services Ltd of Hamilton, NZ and Amalgamated Wireless Australia (AWA) were to particpate. A decision to build the aircraft locally had to be made by June 12, 1970.

CAC's general manager, Bill Abbott, envisaged customer commercial doubts in the venture. They had to be confident of guaranteed back-up whilst in service, especially if there was the likelihood of a takeover of General Aircraft Corporation (Aust).

CAC's Turbofan Engine Derivative

Sensing an obvious market coolness about the design, CAC put up an alternative up-market variant (released on July 3, 1970) powered by two rear fuselage mounted Roll Royce MH45-04 turbofans of 8,112 lb thrust each, together with a cleaned up 64 ft span wing of moderate leading edge sweep (17°) and trailing edge (8°) sweep angles (Fig 2). The aircraft was about 1,000 lb lighter but was calculated to have 50% greater seat mile costs based on the same load factor as the basic model and probably equal if differential load factors were used based on the jet appeal of the turbofan. Block times and speed were better for stage lengths of 100 nm and longer.

Government Backs Away

The fate of all the negotiations, discussions, etc was sealed on June 9, 1970 when it was disclosed in Parliament by the Minister for Defence, Malcom Fraser, and the Minister for Supply, Senator Ken Anderson, that there was *"no demonstrable market for the aircraft that would give the Government confidence the project should proceed"*. There was also a considerable amount of money which the Government and industry had to find together with other reasons for the cessation of the project and not supporting a feasibility study.

CAC/GAC-100

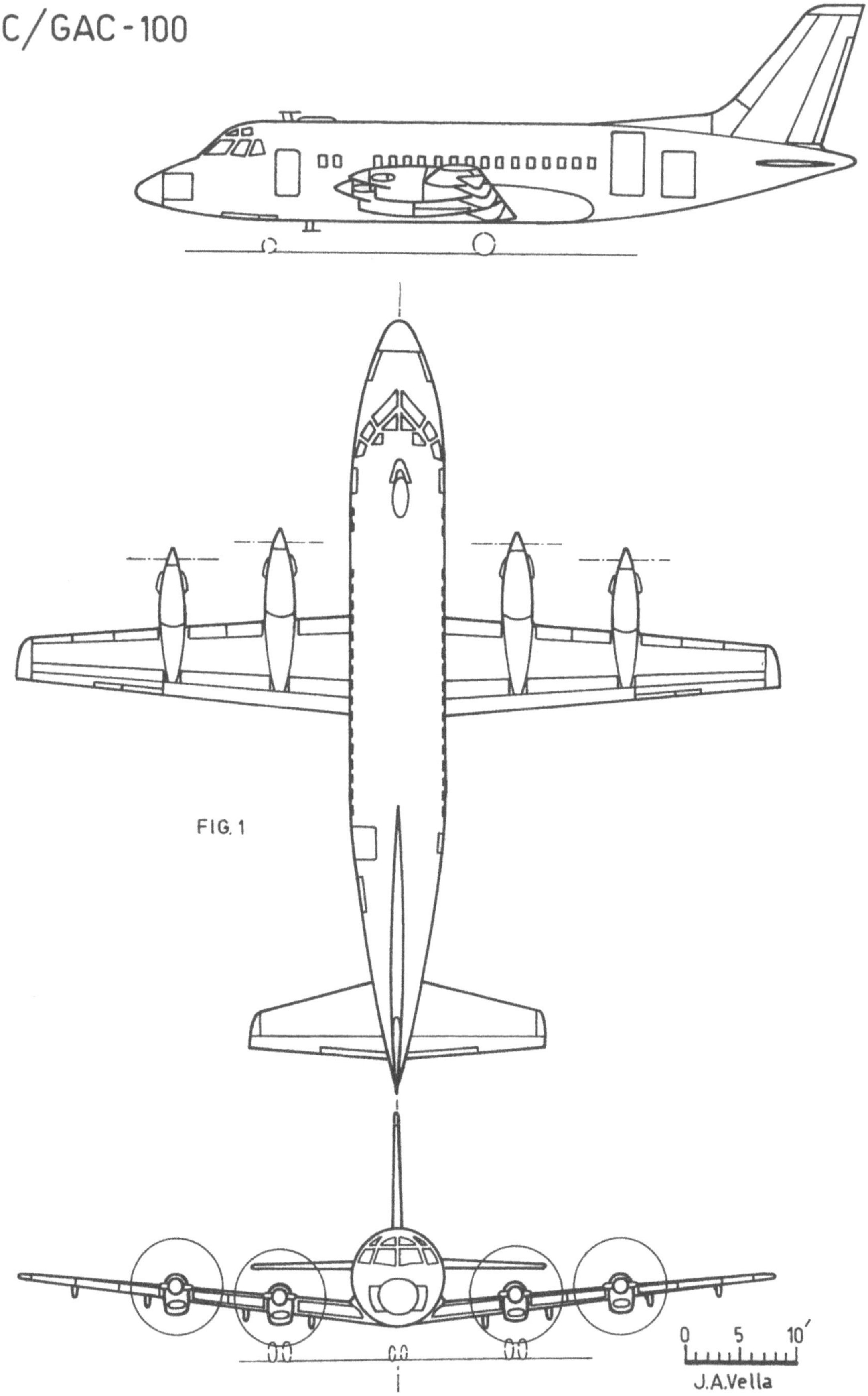

FIG. 1

J.A.Vella

The GAC-100 was coming in at a time when the GAF STOL Project 'N' (Nomad) had also been funded to prototype production. There was a doubt in the ability of the Australian industry to produce the GAC-100 on a commercial basis and maintain reasonable delivery rates. It doubted the validity of some performance claims made by GAC. There was a fear that possible operators would be prejudiced because GAC was a small unknown company and that Australian based production might add to this scepticism. Repercussions on the American market were feared if it was promoted and sold in the United States and it then became the negative target for the lobby of the run-down American aircraft industry, even though it was felt that 50% of the aircraft by value of equipment could have been of American origin. The Government considered the risk element of GAC(Aust) being taken over was quite high. GAC(Aust) quickly closed down on June 30, 1970.

CAC/GAC-100 [Turbofan]

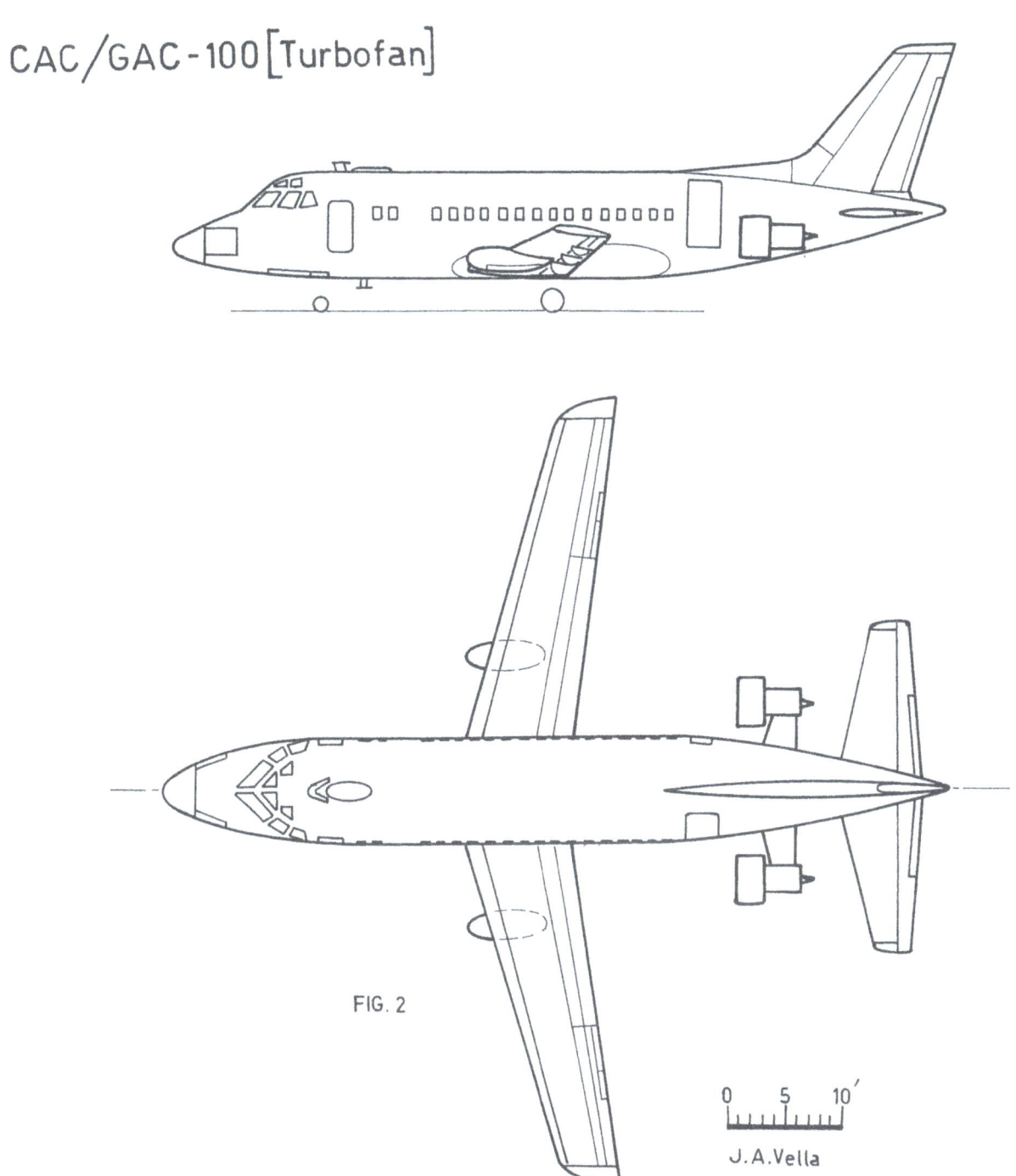

FIG. 2

J.A.Vella

Whilst the project hung in abeyance, a rival design broke into the market. The Canadian Government provided the major R&D funding for the four engined DHC-7 (later to be known as the 'Dash 7') in 1970. In their different design approaches, both the GAC-100 and the DHC-7 were intended for the STOL role. (105 examples of the DHC-7 had been sold by October 3, 1986 the date on which the highly successful, well established, de Havilland Canada company had delivered its 7,000th aircraft.)

At this stage in the project the aircraft size was increased slightly. The length was now 70 feet, internal fuel capacity went up to 1,150 US gallons and the aircraft was being offered as a 36 to 40 passenger seater. CAC had no design involvement in the GAC-100. The future likelihood of any design input might have arisen with the take-up of the military variants. Had the plan to build the GAC-100 fuselage come to fruition, it would have been shop floor work that would have taken over from the tapering off in the MB326H jet trainer builld project.

Postscript

The end of the Australian manufacturing plans did not mean the demise of the GAC-100. Indeed design refinement continued and in late 1973 a twin engine variant, the GAC-100-2 was to be built, whilst the original design was to move ahead in July 1974. However in the following year all production resources of the company were channelled towards the construction of the Helio Super Courier and Model H-550A (AU-24) Super Stallion.

In August of 1979, Commuter Aircraft Corporation announced plans to manufacture a commuter aircraft and for deliveries to start in 1983. At an estimated unit price of US$2.6M, the funding required to start production was US$S30M. This aircraft was described as

Specifications	GAC-100 Commuter Aircraft (1969-70)	
Powerplant	Four Pratt & Whitney (Canada) PT6A-40 turboprop engines each rated at 850 shp driving 3 bladed reversal pitch propellers of 9 ft diameter	
Performance	Max cruise speed at 15,000 ft	286 kts
	Approach speed at SL	74 kts
	TO field length at max TO weight	2,300 ft
	Range with max fuel	700 nm
Weights	Empty operating	13,605 lb
	Max payload	6 240 lb
	Max TO	23,500 lb
	Fuel load	660 US gall
Dimensions	Wing span	70 ft
	Aspect ratio	10.6
	Incidence	3°
	Dihedral at 40 % chord	7°
	LE sweep at 25 % chord	1° 30'
	Wing area	460 sq ft
	Cabin length	31 ft
	Max cabin height	6 ft 3 ins
	Fuselage length	67 ft 4 ins
	Height	22 ft
	Wheelbase	18 ft 6 ins
	Track	22 ft
	Main wheel tyre pressure	45 psi

'based on an old Douglas Aircraft design for a DC-3 replacement which was never produced '. But it was none other than the GAC-100 with a widened fuselage. The previous 104 inch external diameter was now 111 inches. Accommodation had crept up to 40 to 44 passengers (at reduced pitch) with extra exits added.

Chairman of the company was the same Dr Lynn Bollinger. A new 250,000 sq ft facility for the final assembly of the GAC-100 was to be built at Youngstown, Ohio. The US Department of Commerce would have guaranteed 90% of the US$30M of private capital conditional on the company being able to attract 25 firm orders.

Commuter Aircraft Corporation was still promoting the GAC-100 at the 1981 Paris Air Show. It was now a lengthened 60 seater, selling for US$5M. The PT6A-45A turboprops were rated at 1,173 shp each and maximum take-off weight had climbed to 34,000 lb. The Youngstown final assembly building was well underway by December 1981 and there were further design revisions of a more extensive nature that included a new wing, a new fuselage and further increases in installed power with the 1,409 shp PT6A-45R turboprops that altered the external appearance of the airframe. The load capacity was kept at 60 passengers. By mid-1983 work on the aspiring airliner had been suspended.

This was the 'Irrepressible Phoenix' paper project that spanned more than 14 years. With changing economics its original passenger capacity had doubled as nearly had the intended motive power. It was one of those proud projects from an unknown entity motivated by a determined individual that fell by the wayside because of inadequate financial resources and uncertainty in the market. For CAC this turned out to be yet another project evaluation study.

Bibliography: The General Aircraft Corp GAC-100 Commuter Aircraft

Aircraft. (June 1970).

Air International. (September 1981, September 1982, July 1983). Key Publishing, Lincs, UK.

Australia. Department of Supply. (February 1969). Press Release. Government Withdraws backing for GAC-100.

Aviation Week & Space Technology. (February 1969).

Flying Review International. (September 1969, December 1969, May 1970). Key Publishing, Lincs, UK.

Interavia Air Letter (1968, 1969, 1979). *Jane's All the World's Aircraft.* (1963 to 1983). Sampson Low, London.

Rees, D. R. (June 3,1970). Tech Memo 021/8/DRR -Proposal for a Turbofan Version of the GAC 100 Aircraft. Commonwealth Aircraft Corporation.

The Age. (June 6, 1970).

The Australian Financial Review. (June 8, 1970).

Watkins, W. (April 1970). Review of Aircraft Market Forecast. Commonwealth Aircraft Corporation.

Watkins, W. (May1970). Preliminary Weight Analysis. Commonwealth Aircraft Corporation.

WINJEEL FAC 101D FORWARD AIR CONTROL AIRCRAFT
October 1970

On October 16, 1970 D.Rees and D.Viner put forward a report to meet Air Staff Requirement AIR 65 issued in May 1969 for a forward air control (FAC) aircraft to be used by the RAAF in locating and identifying ground targets and directing offensive air operations onto targets. Because of the likely small number of aircraft required, it was expedient to propose using components from the Winjeel Basic Trainer aircraft to achieve a significant cost saving.

For Proposal FAC 101D parts of the Winjeel airframe that were to be incorporated included an unmodified empennage and the two Winjeel outer wing sections including the ailerons to form a three piece wing. The cantilever wing was located above the new two person tandem crew cabin beneath a new 9 ft 4in span centre section. Narrow section steel members formed the framework of

Specifications	Winjeel FAC 101D Forward Air Control Aircraft	
Powerplant	One Avco Lycoming IO-540-K piston engine of 300 hp driving a 7 ft diameter CS propeller	
Performance	Max speed at 100% rating	142 kts
	Speed at 75% at 4,000 ft	135 kts
	Speed at 20,000 ft at TO weight of 3,490 lb	120 kts
	Time to 14,000 ft	15 min
	Rate of climb at 14,000 ft	500 ft/min
	Service ceiling	20,000 ft
	TO dist (ISA) at SL to 50 ft	1,000 ft
Weights	Empty	2,552 lb
	TO	3,490 lb
Dimensions	Wing span	38 ft 6 ins
	Wing dihedral	0°
	Mean chord	5.86 ft
	Wing LE sweep	5°
	Wing dihedral	0°
	Tailplane span	14 ft
	Tailplane LE sweep	7°
	Tailplane dihedral	0°
	Height	9 ft
	Length	32 ft

FAC 101D

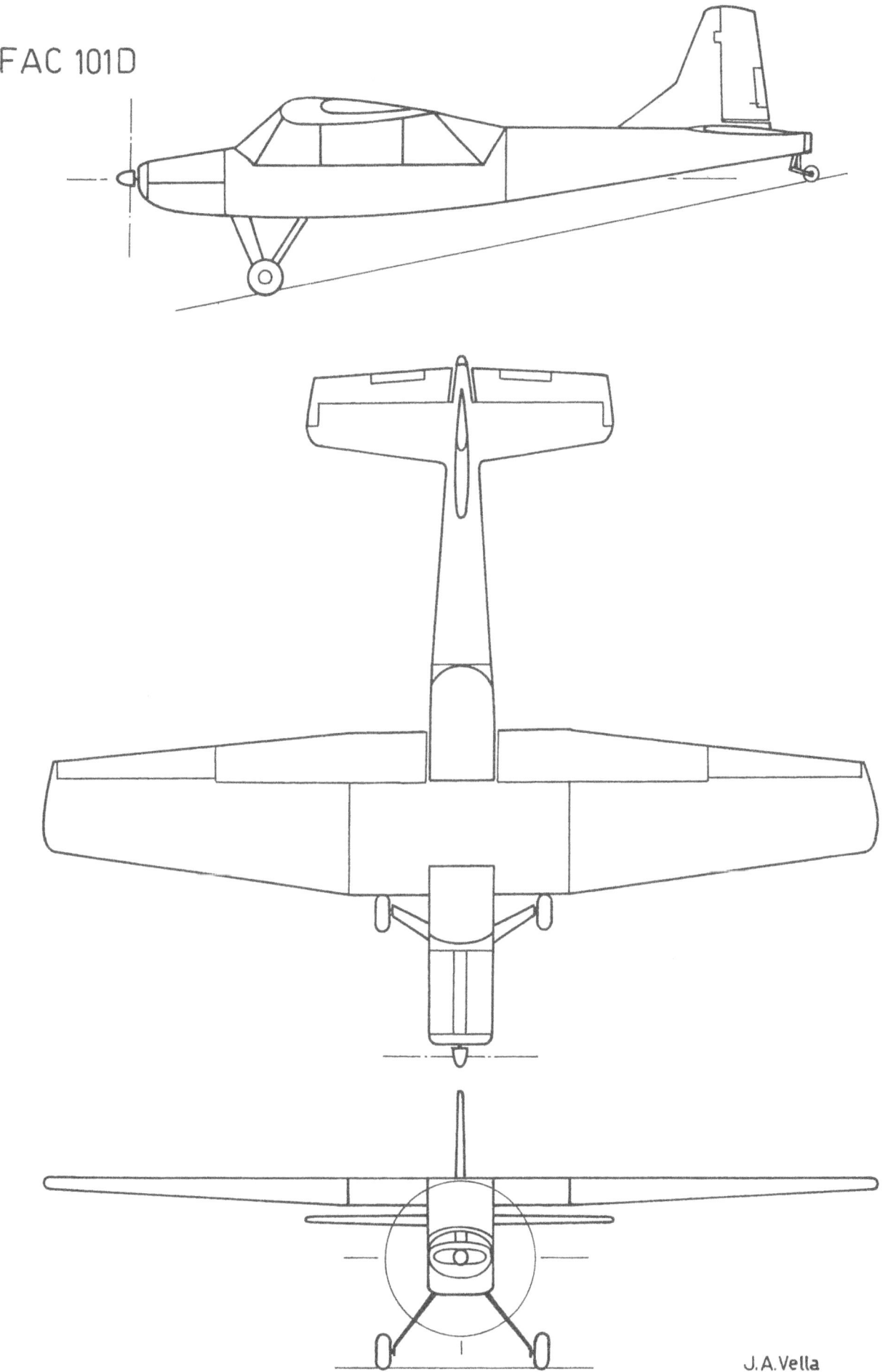

J.A.Vella

the cabin selected to give minimum obstruction observation. Fuel was contained in two integral wing tanks each of 35 gall capacity to supply a 300hp Lycoming piston engine. It was thought at the time of issue of the ASR, that the parameters requested were closely based on those of the USAF twin engine Cessna 0-2A observation aircraft used widely in the Vietnam war.

CAC's initial study concluded it could not produce a design with all the requested performance figures. This was because in trying to maintain a low budget based on a notional requirement for 25 aircraft, certain major economies had to be achieved eg: the use of a piston engine. A longer design study and the possible use of the Allison 250, a 317 shp turboprop engine, would have raised the performance and the unit cost.

The initial costing for a production run of 25 aircraft gave a unit price of $83,850 per aircraft, based on existing tooling and existing Winjeel parts but not allowing for profit. This represented a saving of $28,000 per aircraft over a design using new tooling and no Winjeel components.

Bibliography: Winjeel FAC101D Forward Air Control Aircraft
Rees. D. R. (October 16, 1970). Tech. Memo DRI 011/13/DRR. Commonwealth Aircraft Corporation.

GAF NOMAD TECHNICAL ASSESSMENT
October 1970

Prior to the Government Aircraft Factory's Project 'N' Nomad being released to production, the Federal Government funded CAC to provide an independent analysis into the concept and the design.

The Independent Technical Assessment Committee comprised of four company engineers: J. Kentwell (Chief Design Engineer); C. J. Reid, Senior Design Engineer(Flight Technology); W.(Bill) J. Gornall, Senior Design Engineer(Structures) and Wal Watkins, Design Engineer (Weights with D. Martin, Development Engineer (Current Projects) of Qantas Airways included in the group.
[The assessment start date is not known]

This report released on October 30, 1970 looked into the planned structure weights, performance estimates, general engineering features and operating costs, the latter in comparison with the DHC-6 Twin Otter and BN Islander.

The Nomad was still in the active design stage and working with this knowledge the engineering review committee recommended that for competitive economical operations the design take-off weight be raised from the initial 7,000 lbs to 7,700 lbs. This would permit the carriage of thirteen passengers with baggage for a range of 210 nm under VFR conditions. The original capacity was for ten passengers. Under the circumstances of increased payload, the direct operating costs per seat mile would have been comparable with the 20 seat DHC-6 Twin Otter(turboprop engines) and the nine-seat Britten-Norman BN-2 Islander(piston engines).

The engineering of the aircraft structure and systems was considered to be sound but with the recommendation and reservation that the aircraft roll control system as well as those of pitch and yaw were in need of a considerable development time and effort. Further detail design consideration was advised be given to the effect of the undercarriage loads and stub wing deflections on the bracing strut and structure of the wing.

Strong attention was also suggested be applied to the size of the tailplane carry-through torsion box in relation to the torsional stiffness requirements of the all-moving tailplane. There was also concern about the large area of cockpit transparency and the effect this would have on the pilot's comfort from the combination of engine/propeller noise and solar heating.

A separate second investigation highlighted the concern of the basic cost of the Nomad. As a substantial proportion of the potential civil market for commuter operations appeared to arise from small operators with a small capital investment, first cost was a prime consideration. Unit cost of the aircraft had already begun to be of concern before the first flight of the prototype on July 23, 1971. The major contributing factors to the expected high basic price omitting the aspect of amortisation appeared to come from the use of turboprop engines, the retractable landing gear and the complicated STOL devices.

This assessment sought to reduce the basic price by the substitution of piston engines, a fixed landing gear, conventional aileron roll control and a simplified STOL mechanism. The biggest departure from the original concept was to suggest the adaption of the lightweight Teledyne Continental Tiara turbocharged piston engines. Of 450 bhp, the T8-450 eight cylinder units were a new range of engines, unique because of a 2:1 gear reduction system on which there had been a large investment. Substituting the T8-450

VH-SUP, cream & orange painted GAF Nomad N22 prototype outside the assembly hangar, Avalon Airfield, Lara., Victoria. March 26, 1972. **J. A. Vella**

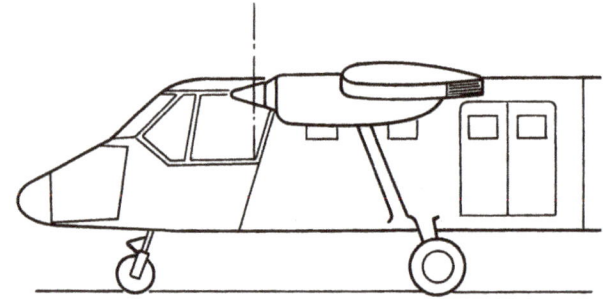

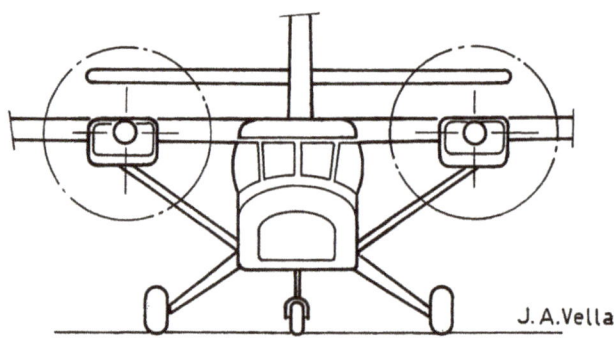

Project 'N' configuration as suggested in the review by CAC with piston engines and fixed undercarriage.

VH-SUP, at Avalon Airfield, October 25,1975. **J. A. Vella**

engines in place of the 400 shp Allison B-17 turboprops would have saved $50,000 for each aircraft installation, but at the expense of an increase in installation weight from 885 lb to 1,440 lb. However the weight of fuel which was then required was considerably reduced. (Production of the Tiara engine series ceased in 1980. It was commercially unsuccessful due to a disappointingly high fuel consumption and not a significantly improved performance over existing piston engines).

In the undercarriage group, reversion to fixed main and nose-wheel units (as on the DHC Twin Otter and BN Islander) by the elimination of the outrigger pods, retraction mechanism and re-arrangement of the wing strut location would have realised a saving of some $11,000 per airframe. Changes to simplify the STOL control mechanism was expected to nett a further $6,000 reduction.

The combination of these alterations would have resulted in a reduction of the quoted basic price of the Nomad from a brochure figure of $230,000 to that of $163,000, with no change in payload but at the expense of an increase of 210 lb in maximum take-off weight and a minor degradation in performance. This 29% overall reduction in price was considered to be attainable. There would also have been a consequent 14% reduction in direct operating costs. GAF, however, was not interested in other than the use of turboprop engines, the original flight control configuration and the original undercarriage layout.

Bibliography : GAF Nomad Technical Assessment

Commonwealth Aircraft Corporation. (October 30, 1970). Engineering Report AA236. GAF Project N24, Independent Technical Assessment.

Reid. C.J. (January 27,1971). GAF Project N24. Report on the Feasibility of Reducing the Presently Indicated Basic Price. Commonwealth Aircraft Corporation.

CA-32 BELL 206B-1 LIGHT OBSERVATION HELICOPTER (KALKADOON)
February 1971-1977

The Department of the Navy issued Staff Requirement NSR 4/67 in January 1968 for a Light Helicopter for use in non-operational roles from ship or shore locations. On December 10, 1968 the Department of Air released ASR No.55 Issue 2 to meet the need for an Army Light Helicopter intended for the carriage of freight, observation and evacuation of casualties. (Refer to 'The Hughes Franchise - A Conflict of Helicopter Interests', December 1967).

These requirements sought a total of 84 helicopters to replace the Army's 65 old Bell 47G-2 Sioux and the two Westland Scout helicopters of the Fleet Air Arm. Such a small order did not warrant setting up a local production line to cover all aspects of construction. Nevertheless this was seen to be the first opportunity at closing a gap in local defence support capability; that of the fabrication of rotor blades and rotor transmission gear systems.

A surprising plan was revealed on March 16, 1970 by Malcolm Fraser, the Defence Minister for the Liberal Government saying that *"final selection was to be made on the basis of the best prospects for local manufacture, including commercial sales"*. To this end, Request for Proposals for the local manufacture of 200 helicopters was issued. Seventy-five airframes were for the Army, nine for the Navy and the balance of 116, for commercial use. By the time the final selection had been reached, the Armed Services had rationalised their separate training helicopter requirements and reduced to 75 their number of helicopters and therefore the production total to 191 helicopters.

The finalists were the Bell 206B / OH-58 and the newer Sud Aviation / Westland SA341 Gazelle. Selection of the latter was doubtful because of uncertainty of overseas European support for the type in the event of its use in a conflict. (Pilatus Aircraft Works of Switzerland had already withheld support for the Army's Turbo Porter aircraft due to Australia's involvement in the Vietnam conflict). The Hughes 500 and Bolkow 105 were dropped early.

On February 18, 1971 the announcement was made to acquire 75 Bell 206B Light Observation Helicopters at a contract price of A$37M. The 'off the shelf' price for unmodified aircraft from the US production lines was A$25M. The A$37M figure was bluntly described as a subsidy to the Bell Helicopter Company (BHC) of Fort Worth, Texas as it included the offset for the 'learning curve effect', the transfer of new fabrication techniques as well as A$6.3M to allow the production line costs to be gradually reduced in order to sell the commercial Bell 206 at a price competitive with the American built equivalent aircraft.

Market information at the time indicated a sales potential in the Australasian region in excess of 100 aircraft up to 1980. Bell Helicopters was to be responsible for the marketing and sales of the Australian built civil variant. A commercial contract (with no US military involvement) was established between the Australian Government through the Department of Productivity and the Bell Helicopter Company, the design authority throughout the program. CAC was participating only as the major sub-contractor. The RAAF acted as the engineering authority on behalf of the Australian Army and the Fleet Air Arm.

Up to the time of the go-ahead decision, the status of the BHC light helicopter line-up was comprised of:

- 1969 - OH58A Kiowa (Model 206A-1) with an Allison 250-C18 engine
- 1971- JetRanger II (Model 206B) with an Allison 250-C20B engine

The Australian model of the helicopter was a hybrid incorporating the better aspects of the American OH-58A Kiowa and the civil JetRanger II Model 206B. High inertia longer main rotor blades with swept tips from the OH-58 gave a quieter and improved performance. The 400 shp Allison 250-C20B turboshaft from the Model 206B would permit better 'hot and high' performance and an increase in all-up weight. These differences were to make the Australian variant the best performing Model 206 in the world in 1972. There would be differences in the avionics, radio, interior appointment, landing skids and the colour of the transparencies between the civil variant and the aircraft destined for the Armed Forces which were to be used for training, command and control, artillery observation, reconnaissance,

casualty evacuation, limited photography and Army field-cable laying. It was also to be readily adaptable for utility tasks at the combat company level without the use of special kits or attachments.

To achieve an early service introduction, BHC agreed to supply the first 12 aircraft, modified OH-58s built to RAAF Spec. Eng. AC163 of an interim Bell 206B-1 standard until subsequent modification to the final Spec. Eng. AC159 outline. In addition, two of the Spec. Eng. AC159 aircraft (Bell c/ns 44513, RAAF serial A17-013 and 44514, A17-014) together with one commercial aircraft (c/n 44701, N14820) were built by BHC as production prototypes. These differed from contemporary Bell 206 / OH-58s to the extent that BHC promoted the Model 206B-1 as the OH-58 Kiowa II. BHC was responsible for the FAA certification and accomplished this complicated civil / military mix using a specially modified (but unidentified) American registered commercial Bell 206 to a basic 206B-1 layout to which the Spec. AC159 aircraft were related. Type certificate H2SW was then endorsed to cover the new variant and the production of the 12 Spec. AC163 helicopters was authorised. The matter was complicated by particular items in the aircraft such as armour plate and avionics which were regarded by the FAA as non-certifiable so this led to the raising of a 'mythical' configuration - a detailed description to which a Spec. AC159 aircraft covered by a separate set of drawings was a combination of the 'mythical' layout and a series of exemptions pertaining to extra items fitted to the military helicopters.

Aircraft A17-013 was used to guarantee the integrity and operating characteristics of the electrical and avionics systems and A17-014 for conformity inspections of those certifiable installations which were different to the civilian airframe, c/n 44701. BHC needed to maintain current FAA certification of the 206B-1 for the possible importation of Australian built civil helicopters into the United States so it instituted a procedure to process all production changes through both the FAA and the Australian DCA. The majority of test flying necessary to obtain the type certificate was carried out in the United States by BHC and some Australian personnel including Army pilot, Paul Lipscombe on the commercial airframe 44701 during 1972 / 73. This culminated in the award of FAA type approval in February 1973 followed by Australian certification on May 10, 1973, a first for an Australian built helicopter.

Army Acceptance

The dates of manufacture of the BHC produced aircraft, Kiowa II A17-001 to A17-014 were as shown in the table below:

Bell 206B-1 Identification	BHC Manufacture Dates
A17-001; A17-002; A17-003; A17-004	11 Nov 1971
A17-005; A17-006; A17-007; A17-008	6,7,8 & 9 Dec 1971
A17-009; A17-010; A17-011; A17-012	5,5,5 & 7 Jan 1972
A17-013	17 July 1972
A17-014	14 Sept 1972

Aircraft A17-001 to -012 were air freighted in assembled form to the Bell Australia (BA) facility at Brisbane Airport. They were delivered in three consecutive numeric lots each of four aircraft commencing with A17-001 in American Airlines B707-323C, N8417. This aircraft made three trips into Brisbane on November 15, 1971, December 13, 1971 and January 16, 1972 and the three groups of helicopters were each taken on by the Army in the same month of their arrival. They were all pre-flighted by BA and test flown by BA's pilot Ray Hudson together with Pat Long, John Stanwycks and Army pilots Bob Rich and Jim Campbell.

The BA 206B-1 was formally accepted by the Army on November 22, 1971. Meanwhile the 161 Independent Reconnaissance Squadron of the Australian Army in Phuc Tuy province in South Vietnam was able to acquire early operational experience on the type from July 1971 to the end of withdrawal of Australian forces in December 1971 on eight (70-15238 to 70-15243) Kiowa on loan from the US Army.

CAC Contract and Assembly Lead-in

Early in 1970 Bell Australia approached CAC for possible civil Bell 206 production and sales. The agreement concluded in June 1971 was for program manager and primary contractor CAC, to build/ /assemble 179 helicopters ie 63 in military configuration and 116 for the civilian market. CAC was responsible for the production planning, training, tooling, testing and engineering support. The new workload was welcomed by the company's general manager as a 'wonderful morale booster' and 'a new era of high precision modern technology' for the industry. Ian Ring was the initial CA-32 Bell 206B-1 project manager and he continued this role from his newly created administrative post of General Manager, Defence Division until Neville Smith assumed the position in 1972. Les Scascighini was the chief project engineer.

Arthur Williams, Aircraft Factory Superintendant, Ian Ring and Colin Bellward (Engines) visited Bell Forth Worth to examine B206 production methods. There was to be an orderly production build-up to three aircraft each month by the end of the program's second year. This was based on the capacity of a single main assembly jig worked on a single shift basis; the size of the aircraft precluded the presence of more than four men working on it at any one time. Any delays on the assembly line prior to this jig affected the total program thereafter because time could not be made up through the rate determining main jig. A shortage of skilled tradesmen and supervisors together with a general dislike for shift work, made it impossible to introduce a second shift. To achieve the delivery target the program followed the usual pattern of receiving aircraft from the originating company in increasing degree of sub-assembly breakdown. Simultaneously the fabrication of parts commenced locally. The levels at which overseas items were progressively reduced to complement increasing local content were:

Level	Fabrication Content
0	2 complete military aircraft 1 complete civil aircraft (These aircraft were use at BHC for type development and approval exercises before delivery)
1	5 military aircraft 1 civil aircraft (These aircraft were supplied in increasing degree of sub-assembly as lead-in to Level 2)
2	14 aircraft in which airframe details, main & tail rotor blades, minor machined parts & assemblies, control tubes, electrical harness & hydraulic lines were locally manufactured
3	20 aircraft in which main & tail rotor hubs & the swashplate were locally manufactured
4	136 aircraft in which main transmission, free wheeling unit, input drive shaft, tail rotor gear box were locally manufactured

All change points through to Level 3 were achieved. Level 4 was cancelled in its entirety in June 1974 and Level 3 was amended to include one additional aircraft. Avionics, windscreens, windows, tail rotor shaft and turboshaft engines were to remain imported items throughout the project. The only raw materials from Australian sources were items of paint, sealant and lubricant. However in the matter of paint, difficulty was encountered where the quantities fell short of normal commercial batch volumes, a typical example of the Australian situation in regard to small batches of aircraft quality materials.

After the initial submission of bids to BHC for five separate packages of work, CAC was directed to incorporate sub-contractors.

Sub-contractors

On the basis of this project the Government Aircraft Factories (GAF) undertook an expansion of its existing bonded panel fabrication departments to enable the construction of the complex main and tail rotor metal adhesive bonded blades and bonded honeycomb structural panels such as the cabin roof and floor, fuel tank bay, seat structure, nose fairings, rear fuselage fairings, baggage compartment floors and vertical fin.

From the start of the work, the development of panel and blade production was in trouble and was never able to match the assembly schedule requirements, so much so, that production ceased completely in November 1975 when it became evident that processing at GAF was out of control and quality control broke down. Two hundred main rotor blades were set for delivery but only seven examples were judged as flight acceptable. The balance of the rotor blade and bonded panel order was eventually filled from BHC sourced components.

Hawker de Havilland was contracted to supply five packages:
1. Minor machined details
2. Minor machined assemblies
3. Main rotor hub, tail rotor hub and swashplate assembly
4. Swaged control tubes
5. Tail boom

However after production difficulties were encountered, HdH subsequently sub-contracted package No 1 to GAF and packages 2, 4, 5 and part of 3 to CAC. Other companies were contracted for minor plastic parts, tube bending and chemical milling and it was in this area that the difficulties in controlling disinterested or commercially oriented minor sub-contractors was of a strong concern.

CAC's fabrication work included the items mentioned above together with the cabin doors, horizontal tail and the intended spiral bevel gears for the engine transmission and tail rotor drive shaft.

Tooling and Production Activity

A quantity of basic master tool shapes and templates was provided by BHC. All assembly and fabrication tooling was built at CAC and HdH. At CAC alone, some 4,570 tools were made for assembly and fabrication of the structure and another 770 for transmission component manufacture and assembly. When the contract was let, the BA 206B-1 was only a specification aircraft based on the OH-58, so there followed a period of design and prototype manufacture at BHC Texas reflected in 3,700 engineering changes.

Collectively, well over A$1.5M was spent on tooling with a similar amount expended on capital equipment of which half was to provide facilities for the government-supplied Speco & Gleeson gear cutting machinery and other high quality items in the engine transmission. CAC was eventually responsible for about 80% of the local manufacture/assembly input. Production tooling fabrication work commenced at the company in April 1972 and was complete by December. Airframe production was expected to be well advanced on the learning curve by the 57th airframe.

From the outset, parts and material shortages from BHC and American suppliers were a matter of concern to CAC, its sub-contractors and the customer as a result of pressures created by the war in Vietnam on the economy of the United States. BHC with a strongly developed commercial sense was insistent on the isolation of CAC from the ultimate customer throughout the contract. They were very sensitive of commercial liability and therefore erred heavily on the conservative side in any marginal decision with regard to errors of workmanship; ie repair by replacement was used in preference to rework. This attitude caused difficulty in the contract due to limited parts and material availability which could not tolerate even minimum scrappage. BHC did not maintain shelf stocks of all parts but built to order with a long lead time. Parts which were peculiar to the BA 206B-1 were not available from BHC. A further limitation was the inability to bring parts from BHC to solely gain a cost advantage whilst maintaining the mandated Australian content level.

In November 1973, Federal Parliamentary budget estimates were being prepared to consider various levels of reduction in the military side of the program whilst still leaving the civil component intact. On June 11, 1974 the request for 75 aircraft for the Army was cut back to 56 machines. All civil program work and Level 4 activity ceased on the same day. The civil component was cancelled entirely. The new Gough Whitlam Federal Labor Government (1972-75), looking for defence budget cutbacks to support its new considerable social welfare changes in society, withdrew the subsidy for the production of the civil helicopters as costs had become progressively unbalanced by a high level of local monetary inflation. The local economy had been driven into recession following big wage rises and a 400% fuel price increase. BHC withdrew from the civil production commitment; there was no commercial viability in it any longer.

Aside from the twelve Spec. Eng. AC163 helicopters and A17-013 (the US built prototype) which was handed over on April 10, 1973, fourteen other aircraft had been delivered to the Army and three civil airframes had been completed. c/n 44702 was registered VH-AJC in November 1973 but c/ns 44703 and 44704 were not registered and 44705, 44706 and 44704 were part completed. All the finished and part completed commercial airframes were to be converted to military configuration. VH-AJC was also duly returned from Textron Pacific Ltd (Qld) on May 9, 1975 for conversion. N14820, c/n 44701, the civil prototype arrived from the USA and on subsequent conversion became A17-055. Transition to an all military program was achieved in September 1974. Work on the retro-modification of the first eleven (A17-009 had been lost in an accident) helicopters to the equipment standard of A17-013 commenced in June 1975. This entailed radio and wiring loom changes to bring the aircraft to IFR standard, removal of the XM-27E-1 mini gun armament system and installing the taller skid undercarriage which was intended to protect the under surface of the helicopter from damage in the event of alighting on debris or unseen tree stumps in tall grass.

These aircraft also had the removable port side door post fitted. This particular feature of the Australian helicopter permitted the rear port side cabin door to swing on its rear hinges and to carry the centre post with it when there was a need to load two stretchers, stacked one above the other on the left side of the cabin. The door would then be closed re-instating the centre post which was a structural load carrying member. The helicopter was not allowed to fly with the door post removed. In ordinary circumstances this door which was double hinged, would swing from its front hinges. All aircraft still retained the capability of having pintle-mounted hand-operated machine guns.

A re-negotiated contract schedule set December 1975 as the completion of the entire program. However this was not achieved because GAF's problems with metal bonding were almost insoluble as was the resultant long lead time incurred on BHC supplied panels

CA-32 Bell 206B-1

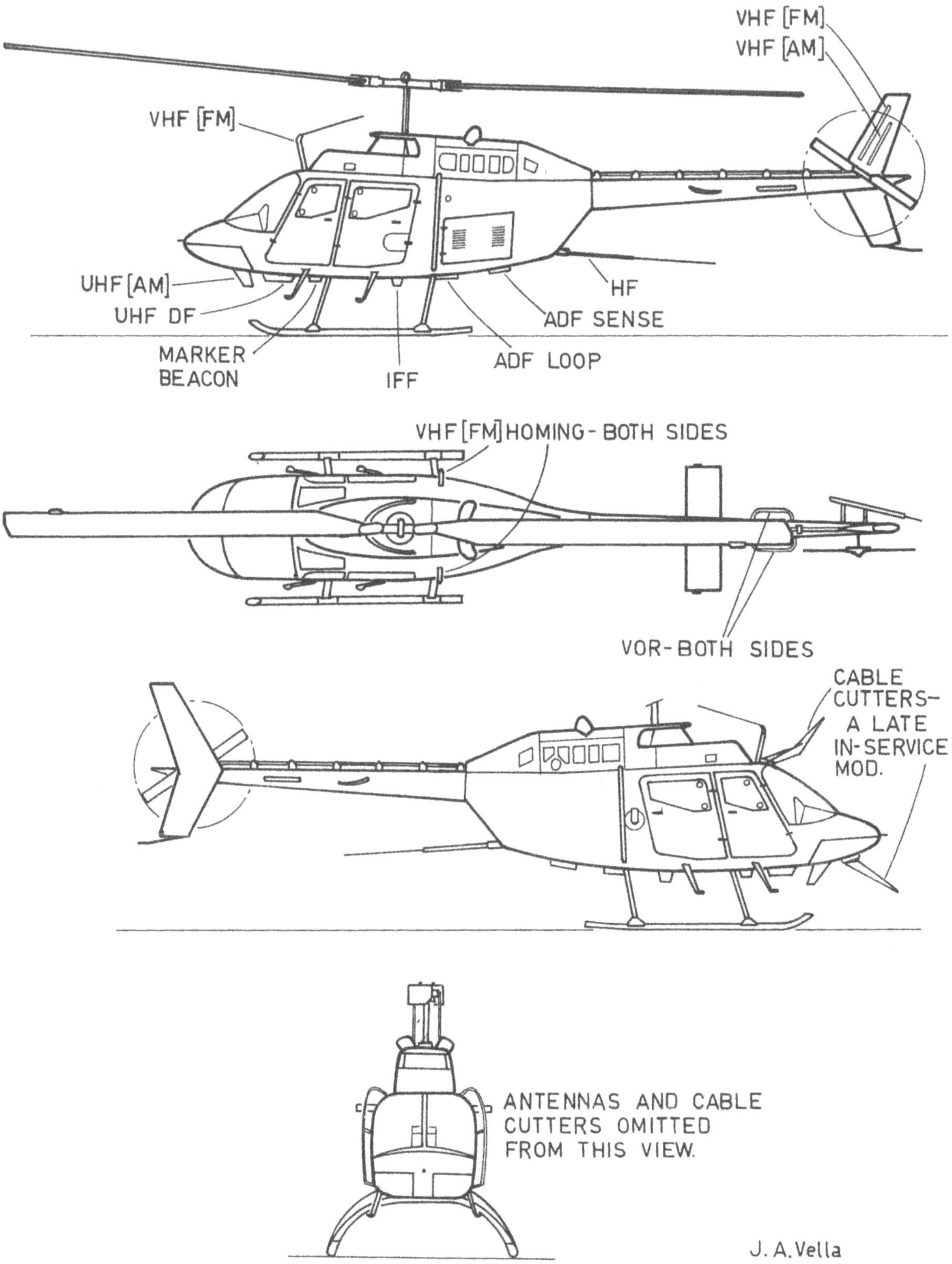

and other Bell sourced items of equipment. Piecemeal assembly and fabrication work continued as events allowed. The cut-back in the program came in just as production of the Australian produced transmissions was starting to get underway. Only a few test examples had been tried out on the Government supplied gear cutting plant. All transmission gears had then of necessity to be imported, defeating one of the primary reasons for local production. (The machinery was eventually put to use in the production of the Mirage IIIO/SNECMA ATAR engine auxiliary gear drives and Sikorsky S-70 Black Hawk/Seahawk helicopter transmission gears offset work.

When shortage items such as honeycomb panels and rotor blades arrived from BHC their use was interrupted by a six week long industrial dispute at CAC. The entire program including the conversion of four civilian aircraft was finally completed on March 8, 1977 with the delivery of aircraft c/n 44549, A17-049. The problems in the fabrication of the airframe and the difficulties created by the Government cut-back caused havoc with the delivery schedule. Taking into account the converted aircraft and those retro-modified; 8 aircraft were delivered in 1973; 11 in 1974; 18 in 1975; 20 in 1976 and 2 in 1977.

At the presentation of the Type Certificate for the Bell Helicopter 206B/1 in the office of the then Director General of Civil Aviation.

L to R: Herb Waldrup, Project Engineer, Bell Helicopter, Aust; Earl Zelt, Project Manager, Light Helicopters, Bell Forth Worth, Texas; Joe Moharich, Manager, Bell Helicopter, Aust.; Ian Ring, Bell 206B Program Controller, CAC; Sir Donald Anderson (D.G.). **Val Foreman Photography via HDHV**

A17-045 receiving a pre-flight inspection by Bob Trease, CAC's helicopter test pilot prior to the Army acceptance check flight from the CAC heliport. **HDHV**

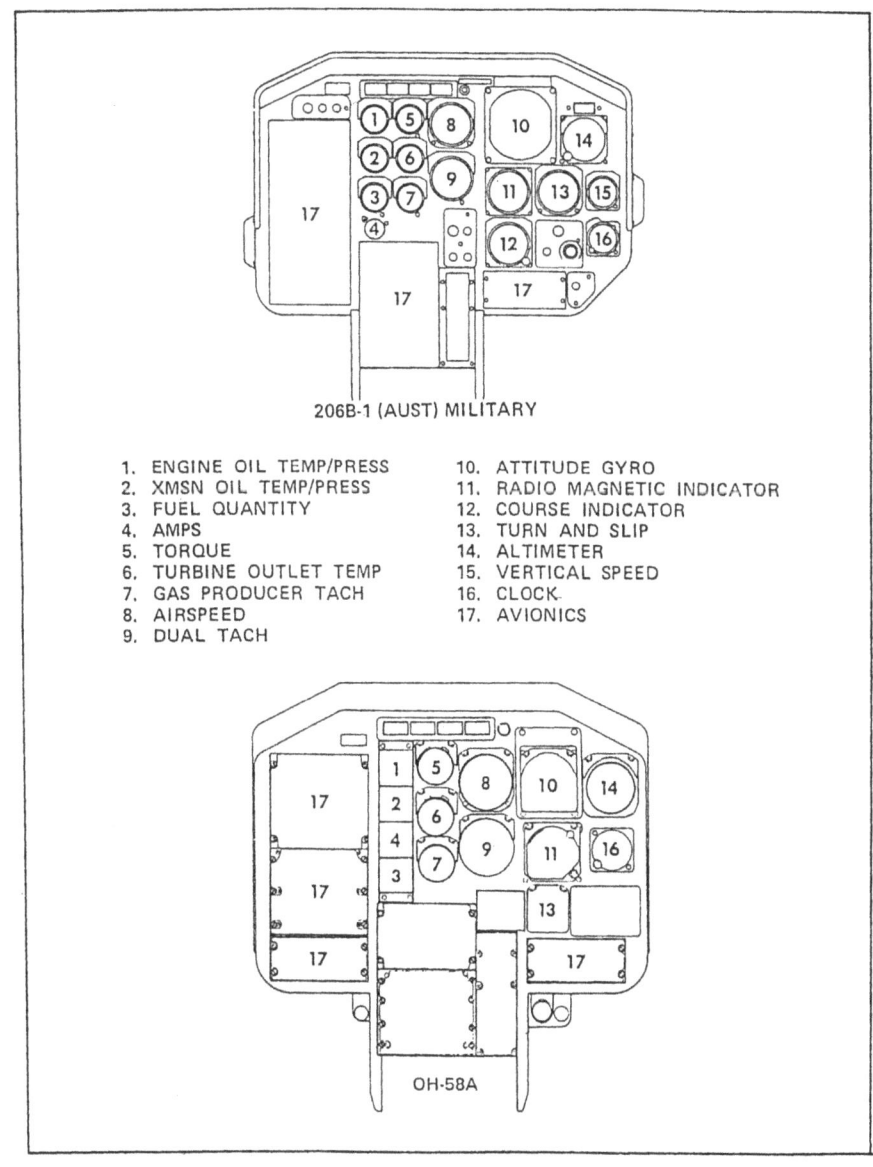

Differences in the cockpit instrument panel between the Australian built 206B-1 military helicopter and the USA OH-58A variant

In total, 58 aircraft were test flown at CAC between April 1973 and March 1977. Approximately 200 hours of air time and 60 hours ground running time were amassed in that period. Test flying facilities were based on the 1,400 feet by 400 feet open area to the south of the property. A non-magnetic helipad for engine ground running and compass swinging was located in front of the main CAC assembly hangar. Test flying of the early Australian assembled aircraft was carried out by BA pilots until Bob Trease was appointed Company Helicopter Test Pilot. He joined on September 11, 1972 and with Jim Caterson spent familiarisation time at Forth Worth from December 1972. Jim, the aircraft Flight Test Engineer till the end of 1975, took part in the flying as assistant to Bob Trease. Bob left CAC in December 1974 but would return to test when available. Towards the end of the retro-modification phase test flying was once again put in the hands of Bell Australia pilots. The Port Melbourne heliport was later established in the south-east corner of the CAC land.

Aircraft A17-004 and 021 were attached to ARDU and carried out the initial performance trails at RAAF Base Laverton and in Papua New Guinea in 1975. Over a period, eight aircraft ie N17-005, 006, 013, 025, 031, 034, 049 and 056 served in the Fleet Air Arm with HC-723 squadron on short term ship detachments till September 2000, then were handed over to the Army. The Army Aviation Corp 161,162 and the 1st Aviation Regiment Recce Squadrons, 171 Operations Support Squadron, School of Army Aviation and 11 Supply Battalion operated the Bell 206B-1. At the end of its operational life some remaining airframes ended up with various museums whilst 22 others were disposed of through an on-line auction in March 2019.

Kiowa, the indigenous American Indian tribal name used for the military OH-58 was considered inappropriate for Australia and was not officially sanctioned. On October 7, 1972 the Army chose the Australian name for the aircraft – *Kalkadoon*. The dedication ceremony took place with A17-007, at Kalkadoon Park in Mount Isa, Queensland in the electorate of the then Army Minister, Robert C. Katter. The name was not popular. It was not adopted for the Australian Bell 206B-1 Light Observation Helicopter (LOH). Kalkadoon was the name of an indigenous mountain warrior tribe located north of Cloncurry, Qld. In a fierce frontier war battle with white settler pastoralists in 1884, the tribe was nearly wiped out.

Airframe Description

The Bell 206B-1 was a five place helicopter powered by a single Allison Division of General Motors Corp 250-C20B turboshaft 400 shp engine. The pilot's station was to starboard; co-pilot/passenger to port. The area aft could be used as a passenger/cargo compartment, including an auxiliary 20 gallon fuel cell, all to a maximum load of 950 lbs. The two-bladed main rotor was of an all-metal, D-shaped aluminium spar, honeycomb core with a bonded aluminium alloy outer skin construction. The fuel system comprised of a single bladder, self-sealing, crashworthy cell of 60 gallons capacity and a 16 gallon reserve located below and aft of the passenger seat.

The basic structure was a mix of aluminium beams, aluminium skinned monocoque tail boom and multiple aluminium honeycomb sandwich panels. All the Bell 206s were fitted with cabin attachment points for medical stretcher kits. Optional fitting included an electric hoist with a 300 lb lifting capacity; a support frame for a slung hook load of 1,500 lb and multi-cell inflatable floats. When fitted, a passive defence kit comprising of armour plate fixed to the sides, bottom and back areas of the crew seats and the engine compressor section was intended to give small arms fire protection. All aircraft had the ability to carry pintle mounted, hand operated machine guns.

The Army Aviation helicopters were fitted with the taller skid undercarriage to provide safety clearance when landing in tall grass whereas those operated by the Navy were fitted with a rotor brake and the standard low skid to facilitate on-board ship hangar storage.

Summary

Shortly after the curtailment of the project, the then Defence Minister Lance Barnard stated in Parliament:

> *"The estimate of cost should the original project run to completion is $45.6M including an amount to assist the commercial production of 116 civil helicopters, support costs for the 75 military helicopters and expected escalation; while not final, the expected order of project costs for 56 helicopters is about $32M"*

This was a saving of $13.6M, later reduced by the IAC.

The program ran to 56 airframes including conversions and retro-modifications but CAC was involved in the assembly / component manufacture of 41 airframes. The military order was 19 aircraft or 25% less than originally requested, cutting back the initial $12M contract value to CAC as well as removing 640,000 man hours from the original 1,400,000 man hours needed to complete the task. The program failed in its original objective to embark on the satisfactory production of bonded panels, rotor blades and transmission gear systems.

The Industries Assistance Commission (IAC) undertook a retrospective examination of the cost disadvantage incurred by entering into local production. Based on Department of Manufacturing Industry (DMI) figures that disadvantage was put at 37% or 137% as a base unit cost when compared to a direct purchase through the DoD/US Army. However, for the program to be completely viable with the US main JetRanger production a premium of 57% would have had to be paid on each military helicopter so that BA could offer the local civil JetRangers at the standard commercial price of about A$140,000 each. Considering the well aired Government hopes for the rationalization of the aviation manufacturing industry, the cut-back in the helicopter program was also seen by some observers as the opportunity for Ken Enderby, the

Specifications	CA-32 Bell 206B-1 LOH Kalkadoon	
Powerplant	One GM Allison (GM) 250-C20B turboshaft of 400 shp derated to 350 shp. Transmission limited to 317 shp for TO & 270 shp for continuous operation	
Performance	Max speed SL to 3,000 ft	120 kts
	Max rearward speed	30 kts
	Max sideways flight	35 kts
	Rate of climb	26 ft/sec
	Ceiling	10,000 ft
	Range	300 nm
	Endurance	3.9 hrs
Weights	Empty	1,540 lb
	Useful load	1,250 lb
	Gross	3,212 lb
	Max with external load	3,600 lb
Dimensions	Main rotor dia	35 ft 4 ins (Military) 33 ft 4 ins (Civil)
	Rotor chord	1 ft 1 in
	Tail rotor dia	5 ft 2 ins
	Tail rotor chord	5.27 ins
	Height to top of rotor mast	10 ft 7 ins
	Height to top of vertical fin	9 ft 2 ins
	Fuselage width	4 ft 4 ins
	Length (extreme overall)	41 ft

Three CAC/Bell 206B-1 outside the factory await flight test. The new Lower Yarra Crossing bridge can be seen cutting through the end of the airfield runways. **HDHV**

Army A17-018 with the Army's tall skid undercarriage, door removed & a more representative external antenna array. **Kevin Kearle**

N17-013/892 of RAN Fleet Air Arm HC-723 Squadron at Nowra NAS. The FAA helicopters had the standard low skid for ship hangar storage, blue & white paint colour scheme & large HF antenna under rear fuselage. **J.A. Vella**

A17-004 arrived in the first airfreight delivery from the Bell parent company to Bell Australia's Helicopter base at Brisbane's Eagle Farm Airport on November 20, 1971. **Ron Cuskelly**

The CA-32 helicopter assembly area. Airframe CA-32-16 leads the line. January 19, 1972. **HDHV**

Minister of Manufacturing Industry, to push CAC to the brink of a merger with GAF. This did not eventuate. The Bell 206B-1 was to be the last new-build aircraft assembly project for CAC.

Besides the complicated dual type prototype construction and dual certification process, there was the immediate hiatus caused to the management of CAC in trying to finalize the truncated program with its attendant pressures on BHC to supply the unexpected import components. There was also the economic loss to the country in terms of outgoing capital to import the more than 80 civilian Bell 206 JetRanger helicopters that came to be registered locally to June 1981.

The program was also victim to the usual government short-term expediency, stop-start defence planning and a lack of industrial economic foresight. According to the IAC report, in making its cutback, the Government made a saving of 9.6% or about $9M at 1971 prices.

(In August 1982, Defence placed a separate total importation order for 18 Aerospatiale AS350B Ecureuil [Squirrel], an aircraft the equivalent of the Bell 206 for Defence basic helicopter training and general utility use, including limited naval deployment.)

Bibliography: CA-32 Bell 206B-1 LOH Kalkadoon

Aircraft : (February 1968, November 1968, April 1970, July 1970, January 1971, March 1971, December 1971, February 1972, July 1972, January 1973, July 1974, May 1976).

Archer, L. J. (1986).[Interview].

Anderson, David. (October 15,1980). Letter to Mal Davis. Civil airframe conversions to military configuration.

Argent, A. Australian Army Aviation pilot. [Correspondence].

Army Aviation in Australia. (October 1972). *AHSA Journal* Vol. 13 4/5.

Australia. Industries Assistance Commission. *Industries Assistance Commission Report*. (Date unknown). AGPS, Canberra.

Australia. Embassy, (United States). (September 18, 1972). 'Light Observation Helicopter Certification & Qualification'. 2501/7/Tech (September 13, 1972). Embassy correspondence to RAAF Engineering, Department of Air.

Australian Operated Aircraft. (1974-1979) Aviation Historical Society of Australia.

Australia. Air Board. (August 1987). Bell 206B-1 Flight Manual. Defence Instruction (Air Force) AAP 7210.010-1. Canberra : Department of Air.

Bell 206B-1 Flight Test Schedule. Defence Instruction (Air Force) AAP 7210.010-6-15. Canberra : Department of Air.

Caterson, J. (1986). Project Flight Test Engineer. [Interview].

Commonwealth Aircraft Corporation. (April 16, 1980).[Company project notes].

Currie, Richard (NZAHS); Davis, Mal (AHSA). (1987). Bell A17-001 to A17-014, Aircraft Builder's dates.

Cuskelly, Ron (1987). Air freighting of helicopters to Brisbane, Australia. [Correspondence].

'Kalkadoons-The Land of the Blacks' Last Stand '(December 3, 1987) .*The Age*

Lipscombe, P. (1986). Brigadier, Australian Army Aviation test pilot [Correspondence].

Metcalf, R. Bell Helicopters Pacific, Chief test Pilot. [Correspondence].

Ring I.H. (1986). CAC Bell 206B-1 Program Controller. [Interviews].

Royal Australian Air Force Eng. Spec. AC159. (June 7,1970). LOH Model 206B-1 (Incorporating BHC Report 206-947-085).(Revised April 21,1971).

Royal Australian Air Force Eng. Spec. AC163. (March 23, 1971). LOH Model 206B-1 Phase 1 (Incorporating BHC Report 206-947-084). (Revised April 21,1971).

Royal Australian Air Force, CAC Resident Engineer; Bell Helicopter Company. (September 13, 1972). Aspects of Federal Aviation (USA) Certification Bell 206B-1.

Smith, N.A. (April 16, 1980). CAC Bell 206B-1 Project Manager. Project History correspondence to Argent, A., Department of Science & the Environment, Antarctic Division. [Australia].

CHAPTER 8. SYSTEM UPGRADES, MB326H CONCEPTS AND SUBMARINE DETECTION

Macchi MB326H (Modification)
April 1971

The first of the company's Macchi MB326H jet trainer performance enhancement plans was an unofficial, general, idealistic schematic outline produced by the Chief Aerodynamicist, Charles Reid in April 1971. This was 15 months before the start of the first of the official schemes described later under the generic series CA-30 Mk 2. It was a more aerodynamic advance than those later schemes. The fuselage front end modification entailed the raising of the rear rear instructor pilot position to create 10 °of forward downward vision over the head of the front seat occupant. This would have meant new structural work on the cockpit sides and the design of a more refined nose cone to also increase the downward vision for the student pilot. The radiused under cockpit surface was reminiscent of that employed on the earlier CA-31 design. The fuselage aft of the rear cockpit bulkhead would be unchanged with the exception of the use of the more powerful Bristol Siddeley Viper 500 or 600 engine and the addition of under fuselage strake/s.

For fatigue considerations, in view of the problems that had arisen in the CA-30, the wing centre section main spar would be changed to be a steel component. The outer wings would no longer be fitted with tip tanks but would be modified to have a leading edge curved wing tip to reduce drag. No substitute was offered to the loss of the wing tip fuel tanks although that is not to say it was not considered. The intake duct-to-wing leading-edge junction was also to incorporate a minor root extension. The physical changes in this outline were probably the most far-reaching and most ideal. No technical or performance data has survived to support these changes.

Bibliography: Macchi MB326H (Modification)
Reid, C. J. (April 1971). Commonwealth Aircraft Corporation. [In-House Project Design Notes].

EX300-BARRA SONOBUOY
1971

Early in 1971 a diverse number of companies were invited by the then Department of Supply to a 'live-in' session at the Weapons Research Establishment (WRE) at which the preliminary scientific work that had been carried out on a passive submarine detecting device, a sonobuoy, was presented. The companies were encouraged to form consortium groupings and to present competitive proposals for the engineering development and pre-production manufacture of the unit. CAC, intending to assume responsibility for the mechanical and hydrodynamic aspects of the device teamed up with Philips Industries who were to undertake the electrical / electronic aspects of the design.

After reviewing the various proposals the WRE selected the preferred concepts from a number of submissions and re-arranged the final grouping for the sonobuoy development contract so that project management was entrusted to ESAMS Ltd. Aust (Electronic Systems and Management Services), a project and systems engineering management company, part of the GEC- Marconi Group (UK).

Almost 90% of the mechanical and aero / hydrodynamic facets of the buoy were entrusted to CAC. Amalgamated Wireless of Australasia (AWA) was responsible for the power supplies and electronic system in which CAC had a 10% share. The hydrophone array suspension cable was to be the work of Cable Makers Australia. With Plessey Electronics (Aust), CAC had a 10% stake in the development of the unit's hydrophones.

The SSQ-801 Barra Sonobuoy was part of a joint Australian / British government development in submarine underwater detection. The new higher performance sonobuoy was needed to capitalize on improved noise processing techniques and hardware as typified in the Marconi (UK) developed AN/AQS-901 airborne signal processing and display system. This was to be installed in the RAF's all-jet Hawker Siddeley Nimrod MR.2 maritime patrol aircraft and

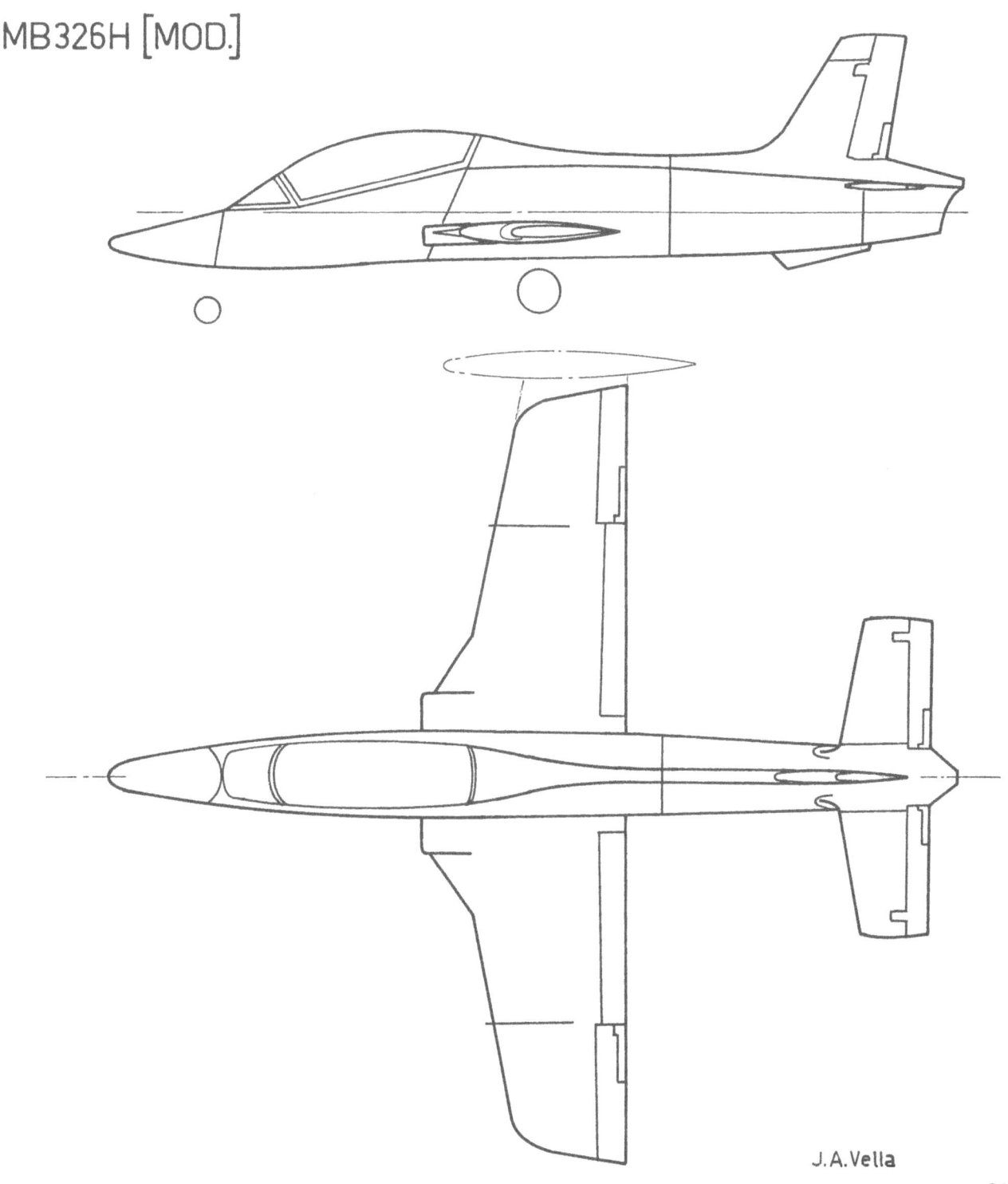

MB326H [MOD.]

J.A.Vella

also to be fitted in the RAAF's forthcoming fleet of the turboprop Lockheed P-3C Orion maritime patrol aircraft.

The name *Barra* originated from an Australian indigenous language. There is however, uncertainty, depending on which tribal nation language is consulted. It refers to 'water' in one instance or 'to listen' in another application or usage. Whatever the origin, the Barra sonobuoy did both, ie it operated in water and it listened. It was not the only sonobuoy type intended to be carried by the P-3C but it was one of a number of active and passive buoy devices which were released as required to detect, classify and locate a quarry.

Barra was a passive, broad-band operation, significant range, direct-bearing type of buoy. Its design permitted the use of just one or two of the buoys in an operational environment where a field pattern was previously required. The smaller the number of sonobuoys dropped in the sea around a suspected submarine, the lesser the chance of the submarine becoming aware through the noise of the buoy hitting the water that it is being tracked or hunted. The ability of the one buoy providing detection, classification and unambiguous bearing information was an advance of the then, conventional target localization method with either a mix of sonobuoy types or tactics which were often time consuming and sometimes inaccurate. Deploying two Barra sonobuoys in an operational setting would result in rapid, accurate, passive target localization even in a noisy ocean environment.

This was achieved by appropriate processing of information gathered through beam forming the outputs of 25 sensitive hydrophones arranged in a passive, horizontal, planar array of five telescopic arms so as to provide high gain and bearing accuracy.

The work was unique in that CAC was entrusted with a development concept to create the physical parameters of the sonobuoy, unlike their earlier Ikara naval project where the concept had originated from the Departments of the Navy and Defence.

Work on EX300 commenced at CAC in 1972 under the leadership of Ek Lemberg who had been responsible for the original CAC concept proposals submitted to the WRE.

Some of the key CAC people on the project Design and Development were Peter Howell, Chief design Engineer; Royce Dellar & Leigh Pfitzner, Design Engineers; Peter Foden, Chief Test Engineer; Leon McCoubrie, Senior Test Engineer; Keith Lunney & Dennis Baker, Mechanical Test Engineers; Ian Mole, Electrical Test Engineer; Sid Marshall, Electronic & Electrical Engineer; Les Hutchinson, Workshop Manager & Machinist; Alfred Chittock and Alf Cassar, Machinists.

The mechanical / electronic systems of the new sonobuoy were highly complex and ingeniously assembled to a very tight and dense package measuring 914 mm in length, 124 mm in diameter and weighing 12.7 kg. Dropped in the sea from low altitude under a cruciform parachute to provide a stabilized entry into the water, this standard aircraft Type 'A' store separated into two parts. The casing became the surface buoy and data transmitting platform with a pre-selected operating life and a large submerged, suspended, hydrophone sub-assembly giving target positional information by digital multiplexing of the hydrophone data with data from an internal magnetic compass. Azimuth coverage of both broadband and spectral information was transmitted to the aircraft acoustic processor on one of 50 VHF channels. The unfolded assembly was stabilised in the water by a drogue anchor. Operating life and depth were pre-selected on the buoy prior to ejection from the launch aircraft.

Development involved a considerable amount of testing of the concept and the gradual evolution of a tightly packaged mechanical assembly that would be self-sufficient and once it impacted the water, it would unfold and erect itself into its operational configuration. The bulk of the testing was carried out in the water, but aerodynamic and parachute performance development trials were carried out at Woomera, South Australia.

From about June 1974 the controlled underwater testing took place in a temporary de-mountable 150,000 gallon capacity hydrodynamics test tank, 30 feet in diameter and 35 feet deep.

As first envisaged it was to be located in the Butler hangar at CAC but due to its large size it was erected within a new purpose-built, tall enclosed structure on the south side of No 3 Bellman hangar. The Defence Department outlaid $110,000 for its construction. There was a site establishment for four divers to work on and evaluate the sonobuoy's underwater unfolding process. Engineers Leigh Pfitzner and Ian Mole took part in the underwater work.

Testing was cold work with periods of prolonged immersion. For personal comfort, CAC spent $1,600 on plumbing for new male and female toilets and warm showers for use by the divers after their cold underwater test sessions.

With the built-in facility to perform underwater photography, this tank served to accomplish some 75% to 80% of the buoy testing phase. The balance was carried out at sea and at Kilsby's Hole, a Defence Research Centre, Salisbury,(DRCS) natural undisturbed fresh water cavern near Mt. Gambier in South Australia. WRE had installed an underwater viewing and filming chamber to observe various sonobuoy water entry speeds.

Progress was slow for about eighteen months, due in part to the physical separation of the team groupings at various parts of the project. In 1974 E. Lemberg left CAC to take up employment in the United States and largely at the instigation of ESAMS, the design teams were consolidated at the AWA company site in Sydney, NSW. J.D.Burgess managed the project from mid-1974.

Charles Reid, Senior Design Engineer, Flight Technology (former Chief Aerodynamicist) led and managed the CAC design activity and with a number of other key CAC design personnel also transferred to the AWA plant, while the development test team remained at CAC with the test facility but still under Charles Reid's technical direction. Most of the new ideas and thinking for the ingenious mechanical configuration package of the sonobuoy originated from Melbourne as a result of the test and development trials.

At the peak of development activity, CAC had some forty engineering and technical personnel involved in the work, about one third of them located in Sydney. Activity there finally ceased at about 1980. Flight and development trials took place between 1976-1979 in St Vincent Gulf off Kangaroo Island, South Australia filming sonobuoy flight trajectory, whilst tracking and buoy performance trials to test aircraft drop behaviour using the RAN's UH-1B Iroquois helicopters and FAA Grumman S-2E/G Tracker aircraft were centred in Jervis Bay, NSW. Naval recovery craft were in use to retrieve and examine the dropped specimens. An RAAF P-3B Orion operating out of RAAF Base Richmond was also used. CAC Flight Test Engineer, Dennis Baker was responsible for gathering the test drop data.

For six weeks between June and August 1978, a CAC test engineer was attached to Hawker Siddeley Aviation in the UK for Barra aircraft qualification trials flown on the RAF's Hawker Siddeley Nimrod aircraft based at Woodford, Manchester to verify North Sea cold water operations.

Barra drop parachute testing rig at CAC. **Dept of Defence /HDVV**

The lower portion of the sonobuoy showing the deployed telescopic five arm microphone array assembly. Aerospace Trade Display, RAAF Richmond 1988. **J.A. Vella**

Unidentified RAF; UK & Australian civilian test evaluation team at Woodford, Manchester UK with a BAe Nimrod MR Mk1.

In 1976/77, AWA was appointed prime contractor for the production of the SSQ-801 sonobuoy and although CAC considered making itself available for the task, the company's management decided that it was not appropriately set up to take on this type of quantity production. CAC was then in the position where, in its own right, it had design and development responsibility for the structure and mechanical systems of the unit as well as sub-contractor responsibilities to AWA for production of a limited range of mechanical components through to about 1987. Test tank work went on as part of a continuing development process. Production of the sonobuoy then became the province of Sonobuoys Australia, a partnership of AWA and Plessey Pacific responsible for the electronic work. 66,000 units had been produced by 2007 when deliveries ended. The average unit cost to the RAAF (in 1995) for 13,000 sonobuoys was $3,800.

The YS-503 and AQA-801 airborne processors were part of the Barra detection system fitted to the Sikorsky S-70B Seahawk helicopters taken on by the RAN in 1988.

Barra had eight years of excellent service and outstanding reliability in both the air forces of Australia and the UK (and possibly others), offering an economy of use through its greater efficiency. Quoting from the Pacific Defence Report Journal,1988:

> *"the buoy continues in production having proved to be an international success with many thousands sold".*

For CAC, the complex development task shielded in security and secrecy went on largely unknown, very successful and totally removed from public recognition and awareness.

Bibliography: EX300 Barra Sonobuoy

Forecast International. Anti-Submarine Warfare (October 2011).

Australia's Barra Sonobuoy. (Undated). Sonobuoys Australia (AWA-Plessey) document, 102SA 3M8.88.

Commonwealth Aircraft Corporation. Miscellaneous aerial test program correspondence.

Jane's Avionics. (1986/87). Jane's Information Group. Coulsdon, Surrey UK.

Kentwell, J. (1988). CAC Chief Design Engineer.[Correspondence].

Pacific Defence Reporter. (December 1987, January 1988).

CAP 201 – MACCHI MB326H REPLACEMENT TRAINER AIRCRAFT
May 1971

CAP 201 – Commonwealth Aircraft Proposal 201 – was a brief study into the need of a Macchi MB326H replacement making use of components from the MB326H but introducing new elements to achieve the desired performance without incursions into a totally new design. This was done so as to utilize some of the existing MB326H tooling and to be able to amortize the new tooling and development costs over what would be expected to be a small production run.

This May 14, 1971 investigation by D. Rees and D. Viner was in a similar time scale, but independent of the MB326H (MOD) design concept of C. J. Reid and well ahead of the large studies initiated in 1972 on the CA-30 Mk 2 updates. Approximating in size the MB326H with a span of 33.9 feet and a length of 40 feet, the fuselage of the CAP 201 differed markedly from that of the MB326H in having a finely tapered, stepped cockpit with the rear seat occupant elevated 9 inches above that of the front seat datum. Both cockpits were to be fitted with Martin-Baker Mk 4 ejection seats. The rear fuselage was also of a new design to move the horizontal tail to the bottom of the fuselage in order to keep both wing and tail mean chords in the same horizontal plane. The vertical and horizontal fixed and control surfaces were to be Macchi units.

Pitot air intakes located on either side of the fuselage were to deliver air to the 4,000 dry thrust RR / BS Viper 600 engine. 148 gallons of fuel was divided into two fuselage tanks. The wings were to be partly based on Macchi units, low set on the fuselage but swept back 20° and finished off with rounded tips to improve the drag

CAP 201

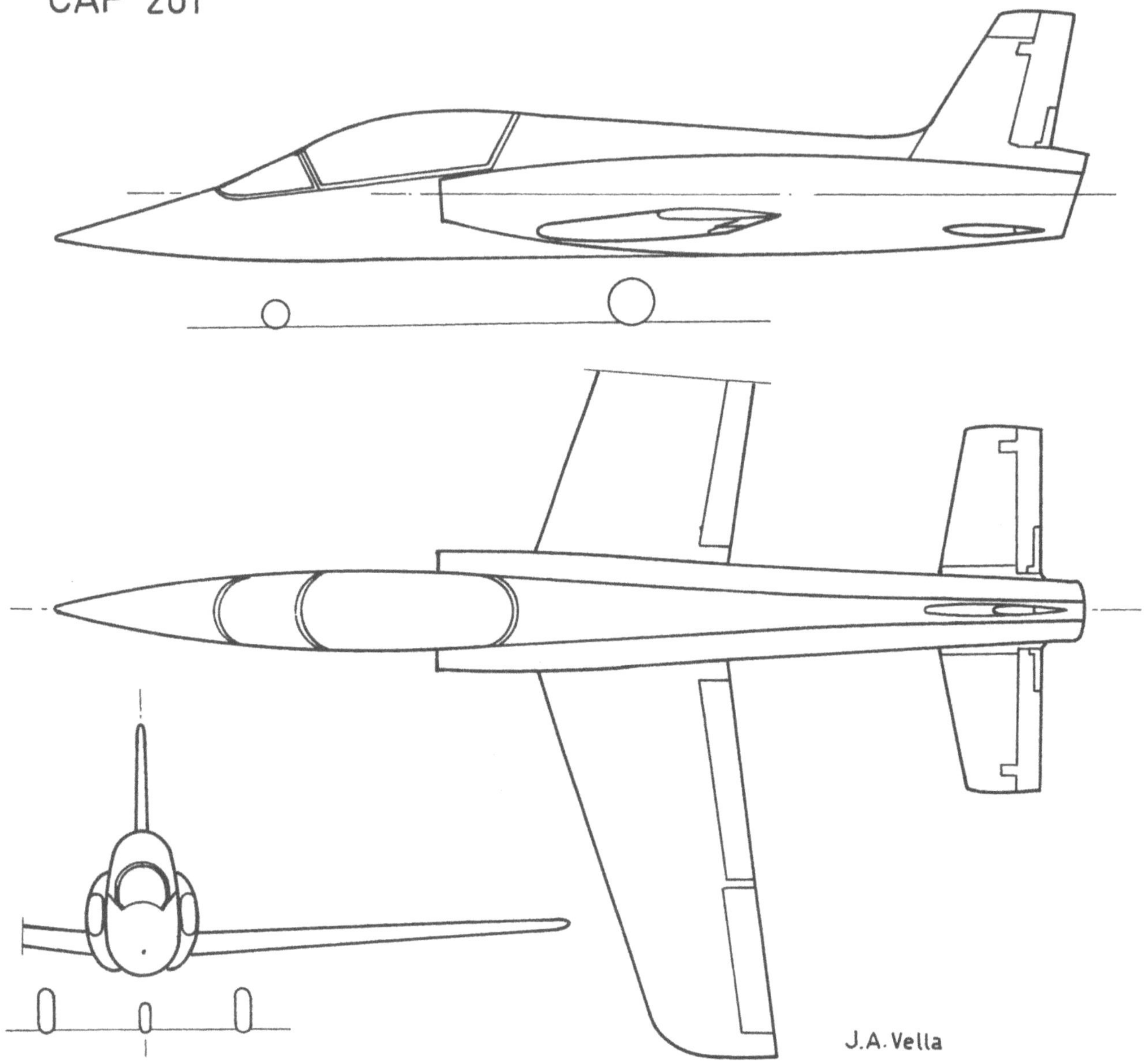

Specifications	CAP 201 MB326H Replacement Comparison			
Powerplant	One Rolls Royce (B.S.) Viper 600 turbojet of 4,000 lb thrust			
Performance			CAP 201	CA-30 MB326H
	Max speed TAS at SL		495 kts	400 kts
	Max speed TAS at 10,000 ft		490 kts	418 kts
	Max speed TAS at 30,000 ft		470 kts	414 kts
	Rate of climb at SL		7,000 ft/ min	3,700 ft/ min
	Rate of climb at 10,000 ft		5,600 ft/min	3,000 ft/min
	Rate of climb at 20,000 ft		4,200 ft/min	2,000 ft/min
	Time to 10,000 ft		1.9 mins	3.5 mins
	Time to 20,000 ft		4.0 mins	8.0 mins
	TO distance over 50 ft		1,700 ft	1,900 ft
Weights	Empty		5,970 lb	5,350 lb
	TO		8,806 lb	7,136 lb
Dimensions, CAP 201	Wing span	33.9 ft	Mean chord	6.4 ft
	Wing area	218 sq ft	Wing LE sweep	20°
	Dihedral	2.9°	Aspect ratio	5.26 sq ft
	Tailplane span	14.6 ft	Tailplane mean chord	3.74 ft
	Tailplane area	54.50 sq ft	Tailplane LE sweep	11.6°
	Dihedral	0°	Aspect ratio	3.9
	Fin height	7.7 ft	Fin mean chord	4.2 ft
	Fin & rudder area	36 sq ft	Fin LE sweep	32°
	Tail plane aspect ratio	2.9	Length	40 ft

characteristics. The main wheels retracted into the wings, each of which was to be fitted with two (optional plumbed) stores pylons.

Utilizing existing tooling for the wings and tail components, the estimated cost of producing 100 aircraft at a basic labour cost of $2.2 (1971) per hour with a 100% overhead, was of the order of A$40M, excluding spares.

This mix of some existing tooling, MB326H components and new build items, represented a saving of approximately $27,400 per aircraft on development and $11,800 per aircraft on tooling amounting to $39,200 or 9% of the 'new-design' cost per aircraft, the estimated unit cost being $387,000.

The estimated overall financial figures (production and launching costs) are shown in the tables below:

Production Cost (Total average cost of 100th Aircraft)	
New tooling	$426,488
Existing tooling	$387,290

Launching Costs	
New tooling	$7,123,682
Existing tooling	$4,385,048

The CAP 201 would have out-performed the MB326H by a substantial margin. The latter was a lighter, lower powered aircraft with less leading edge wing sweep.

Bibliography: CAP 201-Macchi MB326H Replacement Trainer Aircraft
Rees, D.R.; Viner, D. (May 14, 1971). Tech. Memo DRI 011/14/DRR. Commonwealth Aircraft Corporation.

CESSNA COMPACTS, AEROBAT, TWINS & GLIDER TUG
July 1971

Rex Aviation Holdings Ltd-Cessna aircraft distributors went into receivership on January 15, 1971 following a loss of about $318,000 during the previous 18 months. This was a reflection of the strain being experienced in General Aviation operations due to the very low growth, an overstocking of some aircraft types (in Rex Aviation's case of second hand aircraft) and the very expensive and sophisticated twin types which sold at irregular intervals and stretched the financial resources of most GA distributors.

CAC's take-over offer to Rex Aviation's Australian distributorship, 57% owned by Rex Aviation, New Zealand, was based on 20 cents for each 50 cent share in the Sydney firm. The bid totalled about $368,000. General Manager, R.W. (Bill) Abbott hoped that the eventual take-over which was to come into effect on July 1, 1971 would lead to future local production of Cessna components or aircraft such that economic manufacture could be undertaken on a cost basis at least equal to the landed cost in Australia of imported Cessna types.

Bill Abbott was made Chairman of Rex; David Irons, General Manager and Walter Watkins, CAC Project Support Engineer, held two shares. Walter's role was to promote the production change ideas that could result in a reduced aircraft selling price.
In the 1971 calendar year CAC / Rex had sold 268 new Cessna aircraft and 23 second hand examples. David Irons continued as General Manager of the separate division but with financial underpinning by CAC and hopes for a continued 60% share of the local market. At a Cessna-Rex dealer conference held in the Royal Victorian Aero Club on 30/31 May, 1972, Bill Abbott expressed the idea that Australian Cessna dealers should be thinking about Cessna models for specific Australian needs by the slow development process of importation and the building of a locally developed model, a process he had set in motion in September 1971. This was to find ways and means for Rex Aviation to sell more Cessna aircraft, more profitably.

At least two earlier expressions of interest in local Cessna work involvement failed to reach fruition. The first was reported in 'Aircraft' magazine of April 1961 about a proposal by Cessna Aircraft Co. to establish a factory in South Australia for the construction of a four seat aircraft ie the C172 or C175, for the Asian , Australasian, and South African region. Cessna anticipated building 50 aircraft in the first year and 150 each subsequent year. With the existing alignment of Beech Aircraft with the French Morane Saulnier and de Havilland (Aust), the suggestion was that CAC should perhaps align itself with Cessna. The possible production link could have been helpful following the eventual run-down on the GAMD/GAF Mirage sub-contract.

The second opportunity presented itself shortly before the Rex take-over. Rossair Ltd of Parafield, South Australia, had shown an interest in building Cessna 150 modifications (through Doyn Conversions), manufactured by AVCOM Industries of Kansas, USA. As Rossair lacked the engineering back-up to design conversions to meet DCA's approval, CAC seemed set to move in, but it didn't.

However the retail prices for the Cessna line-up in Australia in 1971 was causing concern as they slowly got out of reach of more and more people including the rural community and the small business sector where used aircraft were selling very well and where the price was felt to be right. In relation to the American market, the average Australian income was much lower and the price of the imported aircraft re-assembled by Rex Aviation, after having been dismantled and crated in Wichita, Kansas was becoming unattractive. There was market room for a much down-graded C172 in terms of options and CAC considered the economics of local assembly of a select Cessna range, including high usage spares in competition with imported spares and complete aircraft through Rex Aviation.

However Cessna Co. was loath to allow an Australian program when local demand was so low and Cessna's Wichita plant was suffering severe under-utilisation. CAC was a fully approved civil aircraft manufacturing complex eg, building of the CA-28 Ceres and commercial aircraft galleys. DCA also had reciprocity certification arrangements with the UK and USA authorities.

All of the Cessna based proposals were referred to Dr. R. Gray of the Corporate Planning Group appointed to CAC from BHP to assist and offer advice on diversification and new commercial products for possible future development at or by the company.

CAC / Cessna 'Compact' & 'A157'
To find the lower priced aircraft, the Cessna 'Compact' proposal of Charles Reid emerged on December 1, 1971 as a more competitive Trainer / Commuter aircraft with a basic list price of $15,000. This was principally the 150 Aerobat enlarged into a three seater. The 1971 Australian GA basic list prices were C150-A$12,700; C172-A$17,500 and Piper PA28-140C-A$13,000.

The C150 was considered to be small in relation to the Cherokee P28-140C and could be usefully enlarged provided that Cessna would supply the majority of assembly components at factory prices. It was to be a minimal change modification replacing the 100 hp engine by

Cessna Compact
CESSNA C150 AEROBAT AIRFRAME

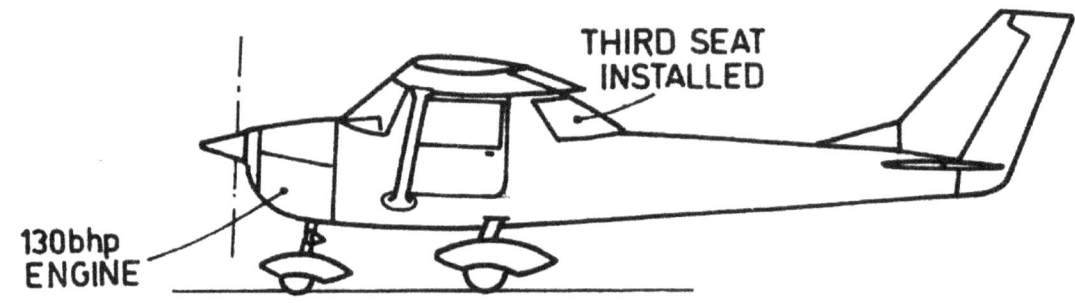

| | Cessna C150 | CAC/Cessna 'Compact' | | CAC/Cessna Aerobat 'A157' |
		Trainer	Commuter	
Date	1970	December 1971	December 1971	February 1972
Power-hp	100	130	130	130-150
Seats	2	2	2	3-4
Weight empty (lb)	1030	1080	1080	1100
Useful load (lb)	530	510	680	900
TO weight (lb)	1560	1590	1760	2000
Span (ft)	33	33	33	30
Wing area (sq ft)	155	155	155	135
Rate of climb (ft/min)	670	810	700	NA
Fuel (US gall)	26	26	26	NA
Max speed at SL (kts)	105	115	115	130

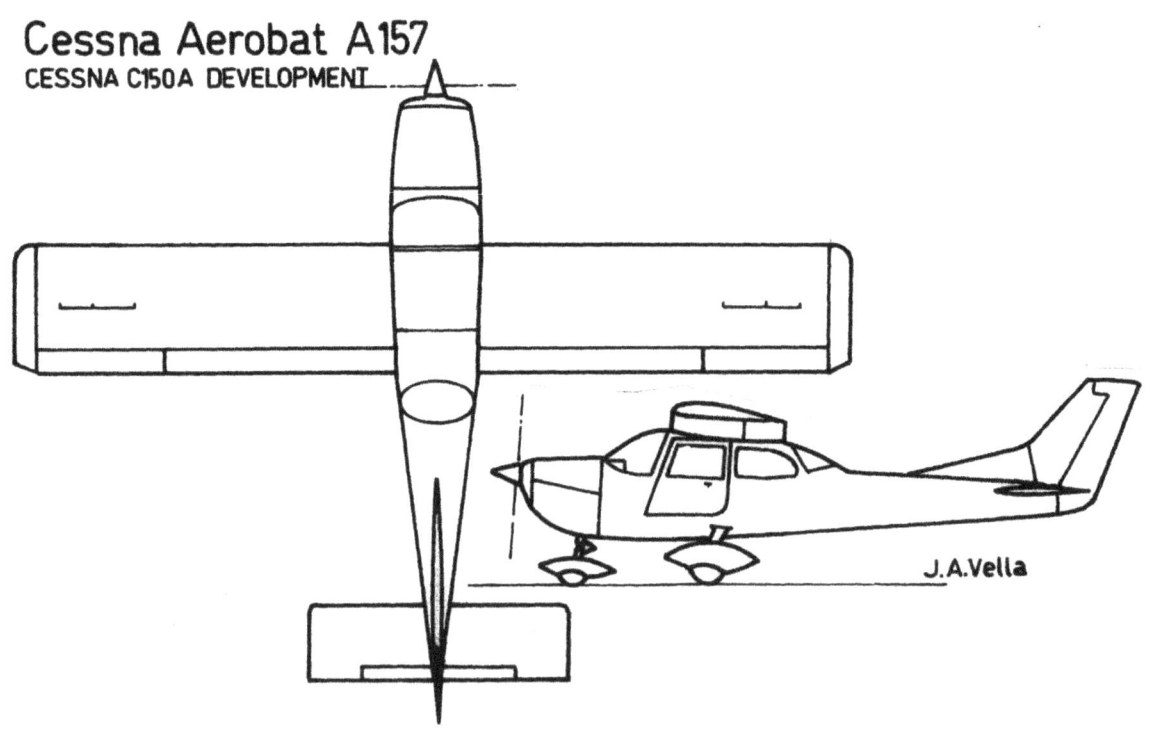

Cessna C172 Light Twins Derivatives

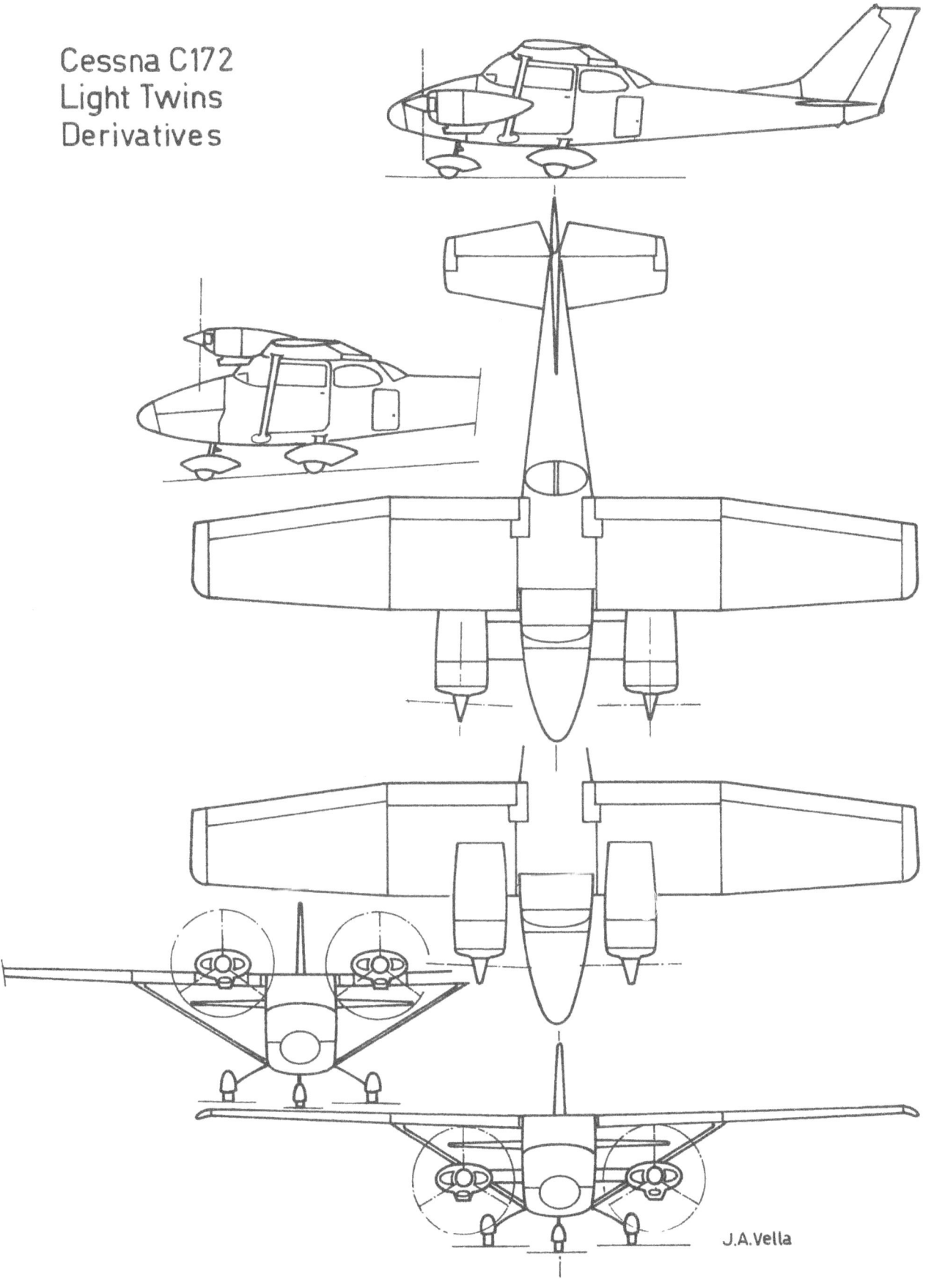

J.A.Vella

Glider Tug

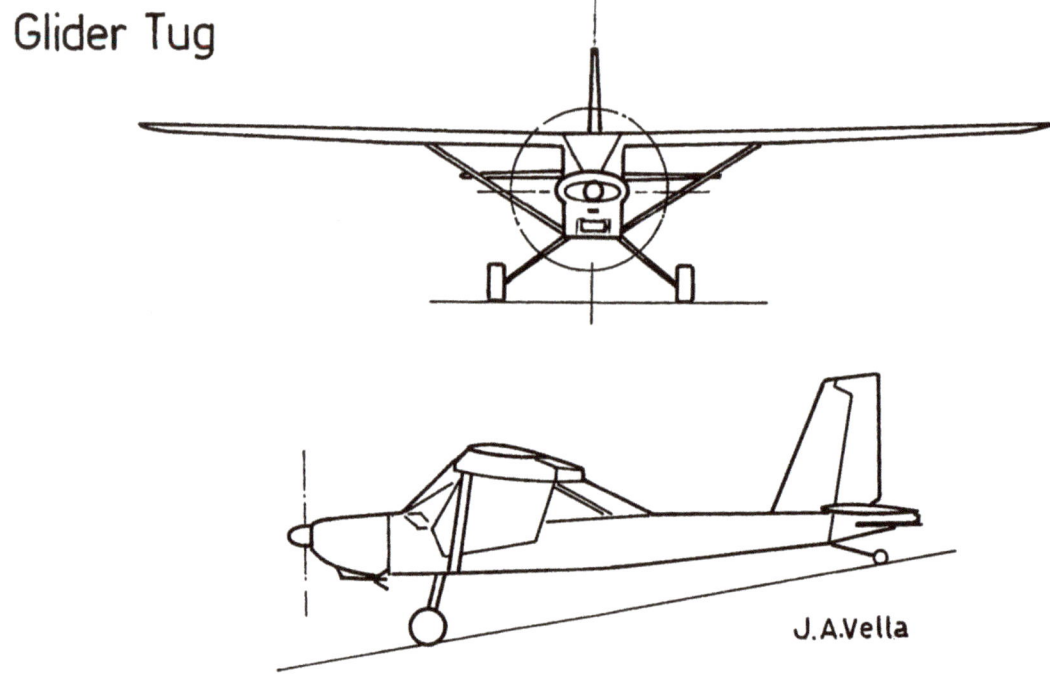

J.A.Vella

a 130 hp Franklin 4A-235B or a Rolls Royce Continental 0-240A such as had already been fully certificated by Reims Aviation in France on a C150. A third adult seat or space for two children would have been included by minor re-contouring of the acrylic rear cabin window and slight strengthening of the undercarriage to improve the C150 commuter capacity by 130 lbs.

This it was felt would open the market to the family oriented flier, especially in Australia. Rolls Royce, shareholders in CAC were consulted extensively on the engine change throughout the month of January 1972. The following month on February 2, 1972 another follow-on 4 seat C150 development proposal was put forward by W. Watkins. This required a new parallel chord cantilevered wing of less area and an all-moving tail. It was designated 'A157'.

Up to the time of these proposals, of the 15,000 Cessna C150 built, 260 had been sold in Australia and 380 Cessna C172 had appeared on the local register from the 18,000 manufactured.

Cessna C172 Light Twins & Glider Tug

In 1975, Bill Abbott requested ideas for a simple twin engine aircraft using Cessna components to offer the local market a cheaper 'Cessna' light twin. The basis of one scheme was to use the original Cessna C172, install two Rolls Royce 0-200, 100 hp engines above the wing inboard of the struts and fairing over the original nose engine installation. It looked messy, top heavy and unflattering. (A similar exercise had been carried out by the Swiss Pilatus firm in 1968 in creating the one example PC-8D Porter, by deleting the centre engine from the Turbo Porter and mounting two Lycoming IO-540 engines on the high wing).

An alternative idea was to support the two engines on the ends of a beam carried through the nose of the aircraft ahead of the engine firewall. This gave the aircraft the appearance of the Dornier Do 28.

More practical perhaps and a design for which there was an immediate demand, was a glider tug. There had been expressed by the Gliding Federation of Australia a need for fifty (50), low cost, rugged all metal aircraft not requiring overnight shelter (to preserve any fabric panels), developed for use as a Glider Tug and selling for no more than $16,000. Preference was for a 180 hp engine installation to enable the ferry towing of two gliders to competition areas, but a 150 hp engine would have been considered adequate. The disadvantages of the types of aircraft then in use for the role were high maintenance costs and inadequate spares availability. Again due to the low volume of sales the only way to design to a price was to incorporate components from existing production aircraft. The essential need was for good visibility and this was apparent by the developing trend to adapt aerial agriculture aircraft as glider tugs as they were generally of a narrow fuselage, single seat configuration.

CAC responded in June 1975 by suggesting the use of the Cessna C150 Aerobat wing, struts, tailplane and fuel tanks and the Cessna 172 fin, rudder, engine mount, fuel system, control features and undercarriage. The fuselage, to a CAC design, consisted of a simple, sheet metal, square corner, box configuration approximately 12 feet by 4 feet and 2 feet wide, with a cabane superstructure of chrome molybdenum steel tube construction. Tandem seating was intended, but a single seat was preferred. This proposal created interest amongst some gliding clubs who were prepared to put down 25% deposit, 12-15 months in advance, provided the sale price would not exceed $16,000 (1977).

Certification flying would have been carried out by GFA officials and this aspect was not expected to create any difficulties. But Rex Aviation was not in favour of the general idea suggesting instead the use of pre-owned Cessna 180 and C182 aircraft. However Alan Patching, the Gliding Federation's Technical Officer advised these older aircraft had a corrosion problem that resulted in high maintenance and operating costs.

Specifications	CAC Glider Tug	
Powerplant	One Avco Lycoming O-360 180 hp engine	
Weights	Empty	900 lb
	TO	1,400 lb
	Wing loading	9.5 lb / sq ft
	Power loading	9.3 lb / hp
Dimensions	Wing span	30 ft
	Wing area	147 sq ft

The other plan was the Cessna 402A Mod from CAC's Light Surveillance Aircraft program (Refer to Light Surveillance Aircraft text).

The Cessna distributorship remained viable and healthy. During September 1976 Rex Aviation made the 2,000th sale since its inception at Bankstown, NSW in 1954. Eventually, the serious down turn in general aviation activity made the agency a liability to CAC and disposal action was finalised by June 30, 1984.

Bibliography: Cessna Compacts

Aircraft. (1971, 1972, 1973, 1976).

Commonwealth Aircraft Corporation. (Undated). [In-House Memoranda notes].

Reid, C.J. (December 1971). Cessna Compacts (C150). Commonwealth Aircraft Corporation.

Watkins, W. (May-June 1975). Glider Tug - Low Cost/Low Risk Approach. Commonwealth Aircraft Corporation.

Watkins, W. (February-May 1976). Commonwealth Aircraft Corporation. Glider Tug, Cessna Components.

Watkins, W. (May 1977). Glider Tug. Commonwealth Aircraft Corporation.

AP1002-CAC / HAWKER SIDDELEY AVIATION HS1182 JET TRAINER
August 1971

The British Aircraft Corporation, Warton, UK, failed to elicit any local interest with their AA-107, P.59 and P.62 trainer projects.(Refer to AP1001-BAC/CAC AA-107 text). It was then the turn of the opposing British aerospace combine, the Hawker Siddeley Aviation Group (HSA) to solicit Australian interest.

The Royal Air Force had issued the draft ASR No 397 for a Folland Gnat Trainer replacement in January 1970 followed in September 1970 by the Request for Proposals to industry. Hawker Siddeley, having worked on many possible design variations since 1965, was favoured by the Service with their Hawker Siddeley 1182 project. The Group was also interested in involving the Australian aerospace industry in what they considered to be a project with vast potential.

During the early part of 1971, CAC was approached by the Australian Department of Supply (DoS) through Ian Fleming to seek its interest for a possible collaborative proposal with HSA (UK) in designing and manufacturing a variant of that aircraft for the RAAF. On August 3, 1971 CAC agreed to participate as the Australian prime contractor and junior partner to HSA with GAF and HdH nominated as sub-contractors to CAC.

August 1971 was four years into the offered seven year time frame commencing in September 1967 when the Minister for Air had challenged the local aircraft industry to come forward with possible plans for the RAAF's eventual advanced strike / trainer replacement of the MB326H.

John Kentwell (Engineering Manager); D. Rees (Program Manager); C.Reid (Design Engineeer Flight Technology) and W.Gornall (Design Engineer Structures) had the task of making a preliminary assessment of the HS 1182AJ (AJ stood for Adour powered, July 1971).

It had been agreed that the base configuration criteria for the aircraft would be a Rolls Royce Adour turbofan engine, an AUW of 10,500 lb and a wing area of 194 sq ft. Australia was expected to receive a 30% share in the design, development, tooling and production work including design of the complete wing structure, tailplane, rudder, nose and tail cone, wing pylons, main undercarriage installation and doors as part of the breakdown of a 250 aircraft order for the RAF and a notional (optimistically high) order of 75 aircraft for the RAAF. Complete fatigue, static testing, air-conditioning and third prototype aircraft tropical trials would have also been Australian development tasks. (The latter two trials were eventually carried out in Malta).

A crucial aspect to the viability of the project was the critical local shortage of design and production engineers and design drafting staff, about 105 of whom were required. Less than half of these could have been recruited in Australia but only if existing projects like the GAF Nomad were terminated. Even then, the local aviation industry was in such a low active state it would still have been necessary to obtain an appreciable percentage of the required expertise from overseas. Eleven members of CAC's design group were earmarked to be located at HSA Kingston, UK on the initial design phase for a period of four months from November 1971.

In October 1971 the UK Ministry of Defence selected the HS1182 Hawk and approved a fixed price development contract the equivalent of A$42M. Australia's share of this was to be A$12.6M and a rapid decision on a commitment of the development of the wing was required by the Royal Air Force so as to keep their program on track. However the Australian Department of Supply(DoS) attempted to play off the HSA Kingston project against the P.59 of BAC Warton looking for better unknown offers from either group.

The RAAF issued their ASR 120/78 in December 1971. The Australian DoS stepped back from any further involvement in March 1972 claiming inherent design shortcomings (with respect to the RAAF requirement) such as inadequate internal fuel and oxygen supplies. There were also obvious untested production and logistical handling problems. A 1972 RAAF overseas evaluation team eliminated the aircraft and other possible advanced trainer contenders and deferred the replacement decision by opting to fund the cheaper LOTEX program option for the CA-30 / MB326H jet trainer.

HSA proceeded alone in the venture and the HS1182 Hawk made its first flight on August 21, 1974. It went on to be a most successful design, winning considerable export orders for Great Britain. For CAC it was a lost economic opportunity. Would it have come off ?

Ironically the RAAF then selected the BAE Systems (HS) Hawk in June 1997 as its new lead-in fighter trainer aircraft with the first of 33 examples (plus one static test airframe) entering service in November 2000 operated by Squadrons 76 and 79. This selection

HS Hawk XV156. Third prototype on warm weather trials at Luqa, Malta, July 2,1975. **J. Spiteri via J. A. Vella**

resulted in the usual mandatory local industry offsets. HDHV became the sole supplier to the UK production line of the horizontal stabilizers, wing flaps, airbrake panel and underwing stores pylons for the RAF/RAAF/Malaysian Air force HS Hawk trainer orders.

Bibliography: AP1002 CAC/Hawker Siddeley Aviation HS1182 Jet Trainer

Rees, D.R. [DRR/5.8.2 In-House Memoranda notes dates unknown] & (Aug 1986) correspondence with the author. Commonwealth Aircraft Corporation.

Braybrook, Roy.(1984). *British Aerospace Hawk.* Osprey Publishing, Oxford.

Sullivan, Michael. (1991-2000).HDHV Senior Production Planner. [Discussions].

CA-30 Mk 2 MB326H JET TRAINER
August 1972

The matter of replacing the CA-30 / Macchi MB326H in RAAF service was the subject of a lot of official vacillation. CAC undertook a major investigation to remain in touch with the anticipated requirement through a possible existing airframe re-building program that was structured to have a small impact on the RAAF expenditure budget and allow time for the future development of a new advanced local industry trainer design. The RAAF issued Air staff Requirement ASR 120/78 late in 1971 in which it set out the performance and capability requirements anticipated for a 1978-80 aircraft replacement of the MB326H. It was to be subsonic and to provide both basic and operational combat training. The HS 1182 Hawk (UK) or Dassault / Dornier Alpha Jet (France/Germany) were seen as filling the role but following an evaluation mission to Europe in early 1972 these aircraft were deemed unacceptable.

In August 1972 CAC presented a preliminary study in which six different modification schemes were considered. These were intended to satisfy a large proportion of the ASR requests via a low cost, low development risk venture.

Configuration Studies

A variety of CA-30 modifications and configurations were examined, each differed from the other due to the relative technical complexity or the type of engine that was selected. The design aims in each case were basically:
- To improve the fatigue life of the aircraft
- To improve the performance of the aircraft
- To provide a better view for the rear seat occupant

Three of the six configurations investigated employed the Rolls Royce / Bristol Siddeley Viper 500 engine; the other three were to use the new Viper 632 engine:

Viper 500 series engine: CA-30 Mk 2A / 2C / 2E variants
Viper 632-43 engine: CA-30 Mk 2B / 2D / 2F variants

The airframes of configuration pairs 2A and 2B were similar, as were 2C / 2D and 2E / 2F. Each configuration featured a wing of reduced span and differed only in the shape of the front fuselage alteration and the engine installation.

AP1003 / CA-30 Mk 2A & Mk 2B

The front fuselage changes for these configurations centred on raising the position of the rear seat by 11 inches and providing a new canopy of modified profile. The major obstacles were in trying to limit the amount of structural change around the sloping bulkhead to minimize costs and to limit the amount of side area increase so as to maintain adequate directional stability with the existing fin. The differences between the engine installations were minor.

CA-30 Mk 2C & Mk 2D

The front fuselage outline for the MK 2C and Mk 2D was a complete revision resembling the front fuselage of the later MB339 production variant (as acquired by the RNZAF). By providing a

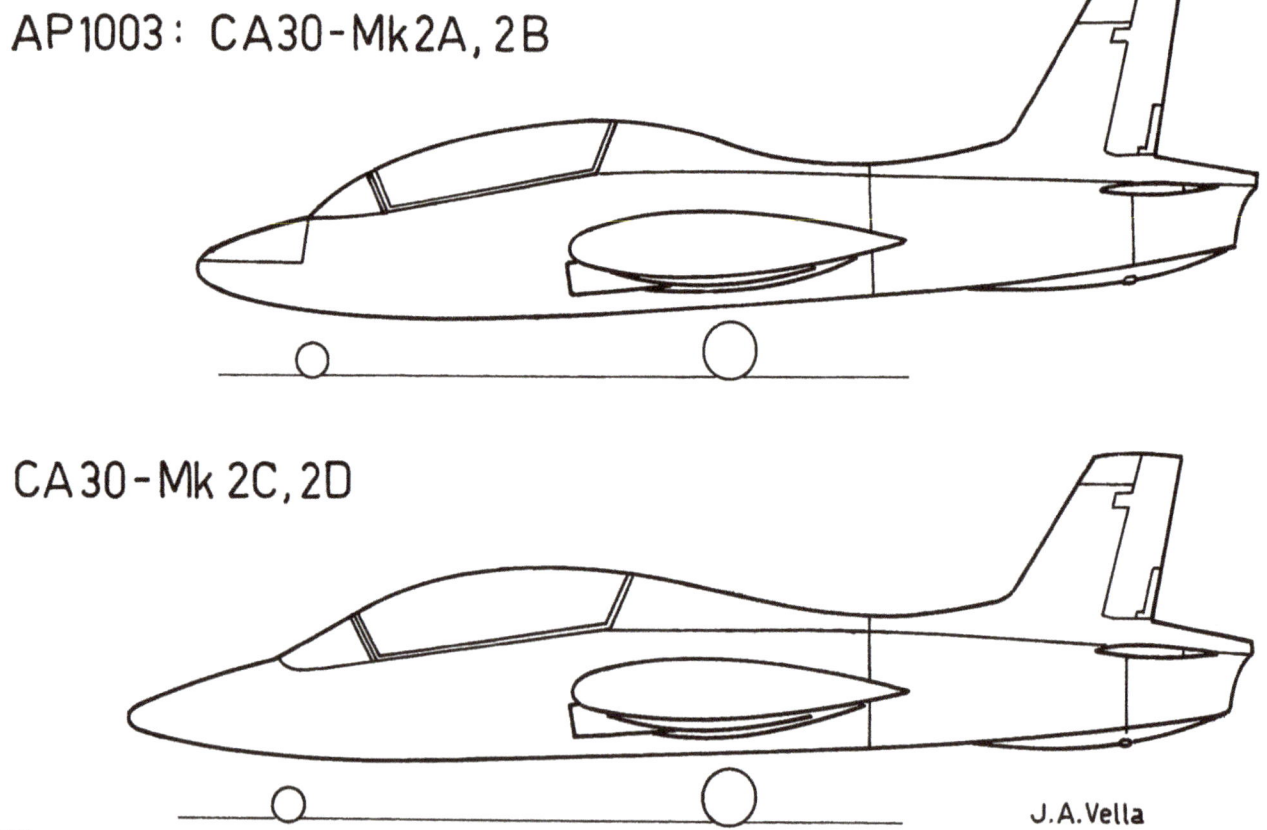

J.A.Vella

AP1005: CA30-Mk2F

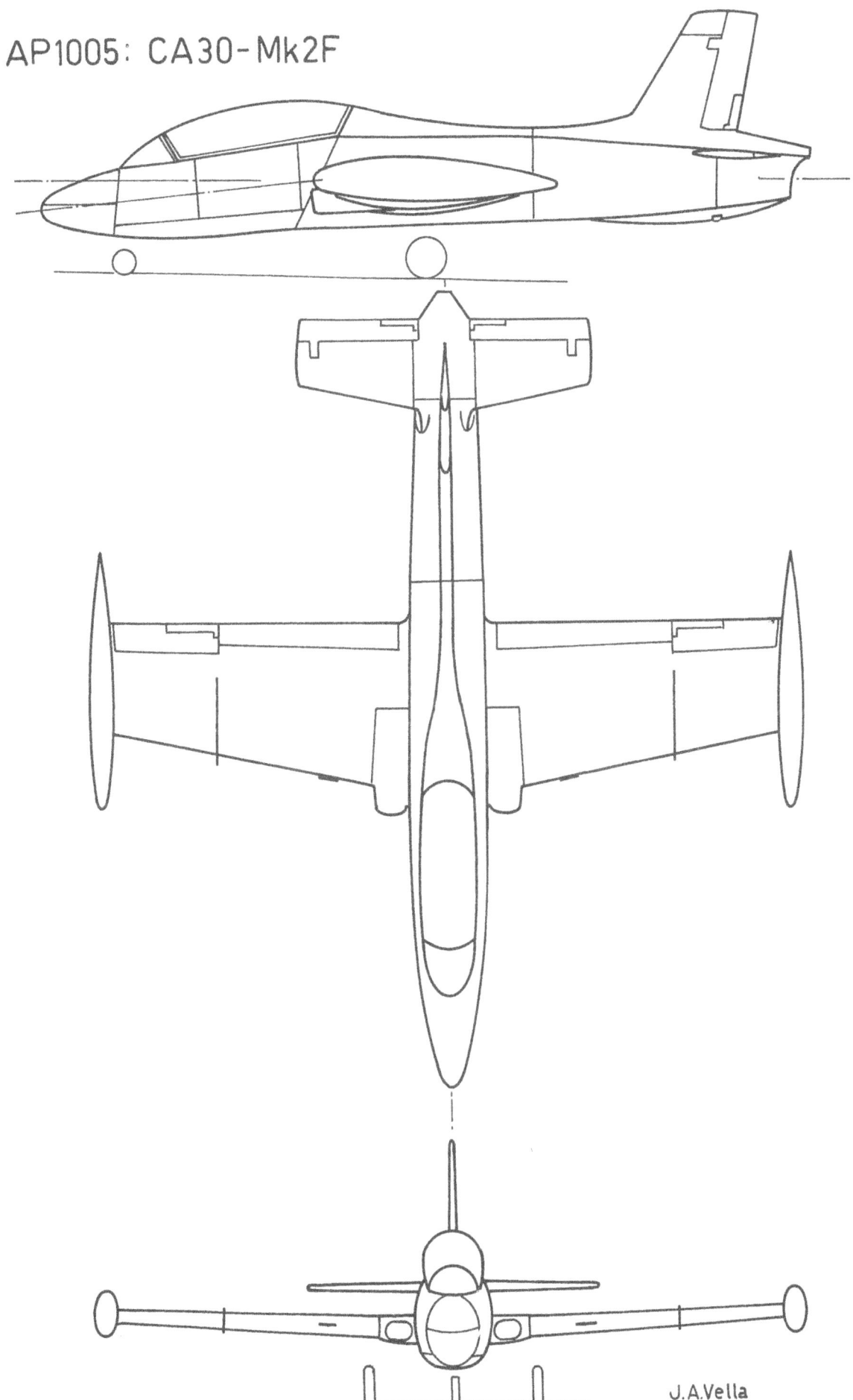

completely new cockpit arrangement the front and rear seats could be positioned to provide the best possible forward vision options. The differences between the engine installations were minor.

AP1004 / AP 1005 CA-30 Mk 2E and Mk 2F

For these configurations, the fuselage nose and cockpit area were tilted downwards by 6° relative to the fuselage datum line and only minor changes were made to the structure around the sloping bulkhead. The Mk 2E mod was considered to be the cheapest way of providing a better seat view and the Mk 2F to be the most cost effective.

The CA-30 Mk 2E alteration was comprised of:
- The replacement of the original Viper 22-11 engine with a Viper 500 or 600 series item requiring a mid and rear fuselage structure similar to that on the MB326G and K (overseas variants) at the same time improving the fatigue life of wing / fuselage attachment frames.
- The modification of the cockpit so as to give the rear seat occupant a ten inch increase in vertical vision over the head of the front seat occupant. This was to be done by raising the rear seat by three inches and depressing the nose section of the fuselage by an angle of six degrees. There would have been a new canopy and an extensive re-arrangement of equipment in the rear cockpit and a lesser amount of change in the front cockpit.
- Eighteen inches removed from each wing tip and the tip tank structure refitted. This would have allowed the aircraft to operate at much higher weights with improved ride qualities and an increase in fatigue life.
- The incorporation of fatigue life extension alterations.
- An improved air-conditioning package.
- Improving the roll power control system and installing a rudder yaw damper.

The foregoing analysis study indicated the CA30 Mk 2E offered the lowest cost solution whilst the CA-30 Mk 2F was the more cost effective and resulted in a further study to investigate the cost and technical aspects.

The aim of the extended study into the Mk 2F configuration was:
- To conduct a development program using two prototypes built to the Mk 2F standard; and
- To modify a notional 60 RAAF CA-30 aircraft to the Mk 2F standard. This number was chosen as it was the approximate number of aircraft that had not already been fatigue modified.

The Viper 632-43 engine of 4,000 lb thrust (60 % more than the Viper 22-11) was the same as installed in the single seat MB326K (overseas variant) and for the 60 units involved it was considered to be more economic to import the engines as its commonality with the Viper 22-11 on the existing RAAF fleet was only 5%.

New (MB326G) centre sections with enlarged air intake ducts and strengthened spars were to be acquired from Aermacchi. The other major alterations that were outlined were the 6° droop on the front fuselage; a canopy of increased length and revised cross section at the rear; a micro detonating cord for emergency shattering of the canopy; a transparent safety blast panel between the cockpit stations; a 16.2 inch reduction in the span of each half wing to improve the roll rate whilst reducing the wing root bending moments and gust response. The air conditioning system would have been upgraded.

The combination of these changes would have raised the AUW from 8,560 lb to 8,950 lb. Other changes mooted but held back to keep the modification costs to a minimum, would have been to swap to an on-board LOX system; provide a yaw damper; fit the larger 103 gallon tip tanks to meet the ASR requirement; an updated gun sight; nose undercarriage steering and control and new flight instruments.

A three phase development program was planned consisting of:
- Project definition from October 1972 to April 1973.
- Full scale design and development from March 1973 to August 1975 costed at $1.73M to include two prototype test aircraft, the first of which was to fly on June 4, 1974.
- Production modification to 60 aircraft from April 1975 to December 1978 at a rate of two aircraft per month to a total outlay of $17.5M.

The average cost for the modification of each aircraft when development cost was amortized and engine cost included would have been $324,000 with a total project cost of $19.4M.

This was considered to be 32% of the cost of a new aircraft of the HS Hawk/Dornier Alpha Jet category. A new aircraft would have a life of 10-15 years; the CA-30 Mk 2F was to extend the useful life of the CA-30 by 10-12 years.

The Macchi modified to Mk 2F standard would have resulted in reduced conversion training for pilots because of aircraft familiarity; better maintenance because of crew familiarity with the aircraft; less need for new special tools and lower pre-production tooling and plant investment.

The result of the changes would have given the CA-30 Mk 2F an aerodynamic performance comparable with the Macchi MB339 but it was not comparable with the HS Hawk / Alpha Jet in terms of thrust and wing loading.

By the end of February 1973, the Department of Defence, on advice from both the Department of Air and Department of Navy turned down the work of CAC on technical, operational and economic

Mk	Modification	Engine Viper	Cost (1972) $AM
1	Continued production of the CA-30 with Viper 22-11 engine	22-11	33.3
2A	Mod. to cockpit by raising rear pilot & modifying canopy shape. Installation of new engine & clipped wing	500	26.9
2B	Same as 2A but with 600 series engine	632	29.6
2C	Completely redesigned cockpit & nose similar to MB326N, new engine & clipped wings	500	34.9
2D	Same as 2C but with 600 series engine	632	37.6
2E	Mod. to cockpit by rotating nose & cockpit through 6° nose down & repositioning pilot seats. Installation of new engine & clipped wings	500	17.1
2F	Same as 2E but with a 600 series engine	632	19.4
New A/C	Completely new aircraft such as MB339, HS1182, Alpha Jet etc		

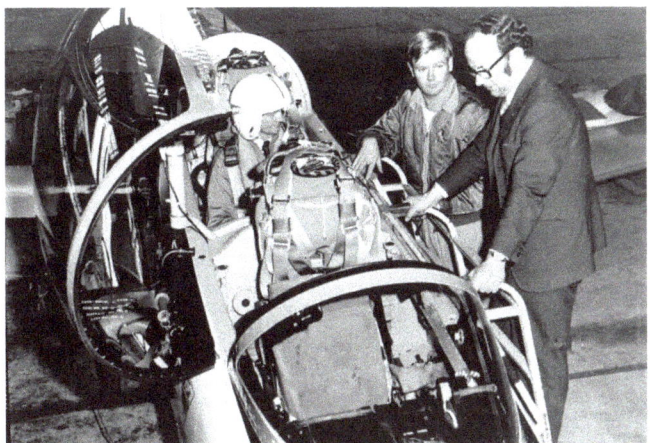

Charles Reid, CAC Senior Aerodynamicist in the rear seat of an RAAF MB326H & Walter Watkins (far right) discussing the cockpit up-date studies in the project study CAC pursued with a lot of vigour.
Walter Watkins

grounds. It had tentatively decided not to proceed with a $147,700 project definition phase for which funding had been sought by the Department of Supply on December 22, 1972.

The main problem arose from the manner the RAAF evaluated the company submission. The Service perceived the studies as an absolute answer to its requirement for a new trainer, whereas CAC contended that it was a concept which only came close to achieving that target. Thus the RAAF evaluated the proposal from the high ground and sought to include every aspect as one of equal importance or weight in the Air Staff Requirement by highlighting that 53 out of 97 aspects of the ASR 120 / 78 were not met, nor were the requested 1980 type handling qualities. CAC was mystified.

Both the RAAF and the RAN disagreed with CAC's fatigue assessment of the airframe and the need to undertake major structural replacement (the RAN operated the aircraft as a shore-based aircraft). The Viper 623 was considered an untried, little developed engine and most unlikely to be available for a June 4, 1974 first flight as proposed. (It did achieve production status on Aermacchi developments of the trainer).

In addition the RAAF with 80 MB326H on strength but with a Unit Aircraft Establishment of 66 aircraft required in the mid-1980s, felt that attrition rates might preclude the availability of that number of modified aircraft still being available during the required period. There could, at worst, be no aircraft still in reserve.

CAC's detailed study into the Mk 2F concept occupied nine members of the aircraft engineering staff. It was intended to be a forerunner and the basis from which to seek further discussions with the customer if it wished. It was a project well within the capabilities of the company and would have employed about 150 personnel.

Other CA-30 modification ideas included extending the wing leading edge, deleting the wing tip tanks, incorporating the Mk 2E fuselage proposals and installing the fuel economical Turbomeca Larzac turbofan. Implementing these would have extended the limiting Mach No, increased maximum speed, range and altitude and improved the handling qualities.

Reluctant to let the Mk 2F work just disappear, another submission was put forward on October 23, 1973. This time it put together an Industry Work Package concept where two CA-30 aircraft would be modified as Trainer Evaluation Aircraft by incorporating into them the Mk 2F outline package changes. This would build up the industry skills in those areas and verify the effectiveness of the RAAF requirement. The project was to cost $1,920,000.

Nothing came of this approach till May 1975 when the topic was resurrected as a potential Australian total industry project where the design and development experience could then be applied to Australia's future Macchi trainer replacement. This would have provided the RAAF operational experience with particular new features such a turbofan engine, improved flying controls and glass /electronic cockpit instrumentation for evaluation purposes. It would also have given the Australian industry a continuing experience with design and development.

The extended effort spent by the management of CAC to make a viable entity of the CA-30 update / replacement was formally ended on November 4, 1977 by the RAAF Chief of Air Force Materiel.

Whilst appreciating the significant amount of time and planning that was undertaken, the Government would only embark on structural and equipment refurbishment to extend the operational life of the CA-30. It would not offer any long term planning advice which would assist the local industry in making future re-equipment submissions.

Specifications	CA-30 Mk 2F MB326H Trainer	
Powerplant	One Rolls Royce (B.S.) Viper 632-43 turbojet of 4,000 lb thrust	
Performance	Max speed at SL	470 kts
	Max speed at 30,000 ft	450 kts
	Vne	480 kts
	Cruise speed at 35,000 ft	M0.62/360 kts
	Rate of climb at SL	6,200 ft /min
	Rate of climb at 30,000 ft	2,750 ft/min
	Time to 30,000 ft	7 min
	Service ceiling (clean)	51,000 ft
	TO dist (ISA) at SL over 50 ft	1,700 ft
	Landing dist (ISA) at SL	2,000 ft
	Ferry range	1,180 nm
Weights	Max TO	8,950 lb
Dimensions	Span (over tip tanks)	30 ft 2ins
	Wing area	195 sq ft
	Length	35 ft

Bibliography: CA-30 Mk2 MB326H Jet Trainer

CA-30 Modification Proposal for Australian Aircraft Industry. (May 1975). [In-House Memoranda notes].

Commonwealth Aircraft Corporation. (August 1972). Engineering Report AA266. Jet Trainer Project CA-30 Modifications, Preliminary Study.

Commonwealth Aircraft Corporation. (October 1972). Engineering Report AA269. Feasibility Study for a Jet Trainer.

Commonwealth Aircraft Corporation. (April / May 1973). Engineering Report AA297. CAC Comments on RAAF Assessment of CA-30 Mk 2 Feasibility Study.

Rees, D.R. (December 1972). Engineering Report AA284. Cost Estimate for Project Definition of CA-30 Mk 2. Commonwealth Aircraft Corporation.

Rees, D.R. (February 1973). Engineering Report AA290. Study on Effect of Increased Local Manufacture on CA-30 Mk 2 Program Cost. Commonwealth Aircraft Corporation.

Watkins,W.(November 1973). Engineering Report AA307. RAAF Trainer Evaluation Aircraft Commonwealth Aircraft Corporation.

Watkins, W. (May 1977). Engineering Report AA357. CA-30 Larzac Modification. Commonwealth Aircraft Corporation.

WINJEEL FOR GLIDER TOWING
February 1973

A number of Winjeel derivative role applications were put forward by CAC to 1973. None were implemented and only one advanced further than a paper study. Ironically that one was not initiated by CAC but by the Gliding Federation of Australia (GFA).

The Federation was to host the 1974, World Gliding Championships to be held at Waikerie in the NE corner of South Australia. The Federal Government was providing funding assistance to help in conducting the event and in the lead up to the Championships the GFA sought Government support to a plan to use RAAF Winjeel Trainer aircraft to tow the gliders. The request was based on the desire to provide a uniform towing aircraft for all competitors and to provide one of sufficient power to uplift gliders which were anticipated to have the highest wing loadings ever flown by competition gliders anywhere in the world up to that time.

On February 8, 1973 CAC was requested by the RAAF to carry out a feasibility study on the modifications to enable Winjeels to be used for the glider towing proposal to satisfactorily achieve a manual tow release and to employ an emergency system of cutting the tow rope. The study was to include production planning, costs and time required to provide modification kits for 15 aircraft.

The Aircraft Research and Development Unit at RAAF Base Laverton was tasked to test the Winjeel, required the following flight test parameters be met when towing a Blanik glider:

- A total of six launches over a period of one hour
- Calibrated airspeed to be 70 kts
- Climb rate to be 500 to 600 ft / min
- Release height to be carried out at the highest possible ambient temperature

The preliminary flight tests were conducted at RAAF Base Laverton on October 17, 18 and 19, 1973 using Winjeel A85-442. This aircraft was fitted with a glider towing attachment designed and built by CAC. The equipment was fitted by ARDU personnel under the direction of RAAF Support Command.

Two gliders available for the test, an all-metal two place high wing conventional Blanik and a fibre glass single seat Salto assessed the effect of aero-tow modifications on the aircraft's handling characteristics (the effect was negligible), the functioning of the emergency release mechanism aboard the Winjeel, the handling characteristics of the Winjeel with a representative glider in tow, the handling characteristics of the glider whilst under tow by the Winjeel and the effect of glider tow on Winjeel engine performance.

The flight trials which were limited to a maximum encountered temperature of ISA+8°C, precluded a valid assessment of the Winjeel aircraft in the role of a glider tug when operations to be carried out at Waikerie, South Australia in the summer of January 1974 where temperatures were expected to be at higher ambient levels (NB: ISA at Sea Level is 15°C).

The Winjeel was flown at 65 kts in the climb, close to the aircraft stall speed of 55 kts. Because of this low air speed and the inability of the canopy to jettison below the minimum required airspeed of 80 kts, a recommendation was made that the canopy side panels be removed for tugging operations to allow pilot egress should the aircraft have overturned following a forced landing. An internal rear view mirror was suggested because the towing pilot's rear vision was restricted by the bulk of the aircraft's overturn safety structure.

The test results indicated that the aircraft was capable of glider tug operations without exceeding engine handbook operating limits when ambient temperatures were close to those for an ISA standard day. This made it essential that further flight trials be carried out under more representative conditions, ie at high ambient temperatures and testing a second aircraft to represent the other extreme of the structure age spread of the Winjeel fleet to be used for tugging. So Winjeel A85-451, with greater engine and airframe hours than A85-442 was also fitted with aero-towing gear.

The gliders towed were Salto, Libelle and Vasama, single place moderate performance types. In these a higher climb speed of 75 kts was used as it increased the stall margin, improved aircraft handling and was preferred by the glider pilots. At 65 kts an increase in ambient temperature by 8°C significantly reduced the height at which the limiting cylinder head temperature (CHT) was reached. At higher ambient temperatures (about ISA+ 15 C) when climbing at 65 kts the CHT limit of 260°C was reached at heights between 700 ft and 1,300 ft above ground level. Increasing the airspeed to 75 kts had a beneficial effect on CHT. The CHT limit however was still reached before 2,000 ft above ground level. Extended climbs were also carried out.

The available testing conditions records were:

Date	Aircraft	Duration	Temp	Location
30 Oct 1973	442	0:30	ISA+8° C	Laverton
5 Nov 1973	451	1:10	ISA+6° C	Bacchus Marsh
7 Nov 1973	451	2:00	ISA+15° C	Bacchus Marsh
15 Nov 1973	451	1:30	ISA+16 °C	Waikerie
N/A	451	N/A	N/A	Benalla

Under the best conditions filtered air could not be used on the ground since the carburettor air temperature limit was rapidly reached. As filtered air would have had to be used in dusty conditions likely to be experienced at Waikerie during the summer this was almost certainly expected to be an aircraft limiting factor. Whilst the oil temperature upper limit was not reached, a temperature of ISA+20°C would have limited the operation of the aircraft. It was concluded that any further increase in ambient temperature above ISA+15°C would have adversely affected the operations of the aircraft. At ISA+15°C, the required climb rate of 500 - 600 ft / min could not be achieved consistently due to the presence of vertical air currents.

CAC was eager for the exercise to go through for the publicity which could have resulted and if the GFA was able to find a sufficient number of volunteer Winjeel pilots to fly the aircraft during the Championships.

A85-442 airborne trailing the Salto glider. **RAAF/ARDU**

Preparing the single seat Salto glider for its Winjeel aircraft tow. **RAAF/ARDU**

The Blanik glider starts to lift off on the tow. Scene at RAAF Base Laverton. **RAAF/ARDU**

Notwithstanding the reservations highlighted by the ARDU report, there was the added complexity which was created when the RAAF contingent of around 70 personnel was needed to fly and service 12 flying and 3 reserve aircraft, together with a standby crash rescue launch on the nearby Murray River. There was already great pressure to house and feed all the competitors, supporting crews and officials. The GFA could not cope with the added RAAF personnel numbers. On that basis alone, the scheme was dropped and aerial agriculture type towing aircraft used in place of the RAAF Winjeels.

Bibliography: Winjeel for Glider Towing

Australia. Aircraft Research and Development Unit. (February 1974) Technical Investigation No 439 Pt 1 & 2.

Patching, Alan.(1973). Technical Officer, Gliding Federation of Australia. [Interview].

Royal Australian Air Force, Resident Engineer (CAC). (Undated). [RAAF correspondence with CAC management].

CA-33 P-3 ORION SYSTEMS UPGRADE 1973

To satisfy the RAAF ASR 120 / 72 for a long range Maritime Patrol aircraft to replace the ageing Lockheed SP-2H Neptune aircraft of 10 Squadron operating out of RAAF Base Townsville, Lockheed Aircraft Corp of Burbank, California had proposed a joint airframe integration proposal to the RAAF and Australian Government. It would deliver to the RAAF ten basic P-3C Update II Orion aircraft with flight instrumentation, navigation and communication equipment installed. The Air Force would then transfer them to Lockheed Australia who, with the assistance of an Australian prime contractor, would install and integrate all the specific RAAF required Weapons System equipment in the aircraft for final return to the RAAF during 1977.

Planning included an Integrated Test Facility and Avionics Laboratory Facility. Aircraft detailed new design, development, manufacture, installation, management and test would be carried out at a temporary CAC facility set up at Essendon Airport in Melbourne. The main airline activities of the airport had vacated some five years earlier to the new Tullamarine Airport. The accommodation sought at Essendon included nearly all of the Main Terminal Building No 68; hangar buildings Nos 12, 81, 85, 86, 88, 91, and 102. The indicative estimate of the CAC co-production package of 1.8M manhours of work was estimated at A$14.8M.

However the work on this first P-3C batch did not develop in this manner. The system integration project was revised to only include the upgrading of part of the aircraft submarine detection system to incorporate the alternate Marconi (UK) developed AN/AQS-901 acoustic signal processing and display system linked with the Australian developed Barra sonobuoy in place of the standard American AN/AQA-7 DIFAR sonobuoy system.

Major Avionics Change

The AN/AQS-901 system was also to be installed by the UK industry in the Hawker Siddeley Nimrod MR2 maritime patrol aircraft of the Royal Air Force as part of the upgrade from the MR 1 to MR 2 standard. AN/AQS-901 was the only processing system in service able to handle data from all advanced types of sonobuoy in the NATO inventory, that were intended to identify the movement of quieter submarines in deeper waters. It was also the only system that could process the signals of the new Barra passive directional sonobuoy.

It exploited digital processing techniques and displayed the data in the aircraft platform on heavy cathode ray screens and chart recorders. Three passive (via buoy) location processing techniques were employed and when these were not sufficient, or during the attack phase, active sonobuoy processing was used which employed different methods of analysis. The AN/AQS-901 was built by Elliot Bros (later GEC-Avionics).

The RAAF also sought the establishment of the P-3C Compilation, Mission Support, Integration and Training (CMI) facility that took in the aspects of P-3C ground training, testing and maintenance support at RAAF Base Edinburgh.

From about 1975 onwards, CAC formed a team led by Project Engineer Des Lynch to plan the $6.2M contract integration work of the twin AN/AQS-901 installation for the P-3C Update II Orion patrol aircraft on order and expected to arrive from May 1978. This was to run nearly in parallel with the company's part in the Barra sonobuoy development program.

A Substantial Work Package

The work on systems of the ten P-3C Update II Orion, A9-751 to A9-760 was a much bigger undertaking than was readily apparent. A9-751 arrived at RAAF EDN on May 26,1978. Fundamentally the job was to install approximately 2,200 lbs of electrical equipment comprising the AN/AQS-901 system that was based on a pair of Marconi 920 air traffic control computers. However, the space, electrical and heat load implications of this meant that a large proportion of the internal layout of the aircraft had to be modified to accommodate the new equipment and to provide for its impact on all the other operating stations within the aircraft. This led to major changes to the electrical system and most particularly the environmental control system (ECS). Not only were additional electrical and heat loads imposed on other systems by the AN/AQS-901 equipment but the changes to crew stations meant the relocation of these electrical supplies, in addition to which the RAAF called for a general upgrading of the ECS to meet Australian operating conditions.

The detail design tasks that were undertaken included:

- The design of the racks for mounting of the AN/AQS-901, incorporating special cooling provisions.
- Sonic systems operation stations for two operators and an instructor/operator position (this was originally laid out for two operators but two years into the project, the RAAF decided to install a third seat with monitoring and control equipment for an instructor member of crew).
- Modifications to two other operator stations.
- Modifications to the pilots' instrument panels.
- Modification of two external antennas.
- Electrical system changes and load calculations.
- Re-design of the Environmental Control System. This included the fitment of a larger engine driven compressor, water spray unit and an extensively revised control system, as well as the physical relocation of the air supplies to the various operating systems.
The ECS as supplied by Lockheed functioned but did not meet the Australian climate requirements as set out in MIL STD 210. In addition the water spray/heat exchanger combination had its own shortcomings. CAC in conjunction with ARL and ARDU as advisers, created a revised system and produced a prototype installation that was tested in Darwin on P-3C, A9-751.
The new design worked very well and the data was forwarded to Lockheed who built production kits for the RAAF in addition to units for the United States Navy and Canadian Aurora P3C patrol fleets. CAC installed the kits in the RAAF P-3Cs and carried out its own acceptance tests.
- Structural modifications and confirmatory stressing to cater for all changes.
- Weight, balance and performance calculations to cover all changes made.
- The production of drawings covering all of the above.

Testing included :
- Desk analysis, ground and flight vibration tests.
- Detail testing of cooling system in the racks.
- Flight testing of ECS-development and acceptance trials carried out variously (for cooling) in Darwin, in Central Australia and (for heating) south of Macquarie Island (54° 30′ S; 158° 57′ E) in the SW Pacific Ocean approaching Antarctica maintaining an altitude of around 50,000 feet for a night cold-soak flight.

Hardware and fabrication included:
- The fabrication and assembly of all racks, looms, ducts and structural reinforcements.
- The installation in the first 10 airframes was followed later by the work on the next 10 aircraft. (From 1985, 11 Sqdn had ceased to be an operator of the P-3B Orion model. The 10 aircraft of this variant which it had operated since 1968 were traded-in with the acquisition of 10 of the P-3C Update III/2 model, bringing up the P-3C fleet to a total of 20 aircraft).

Work Underway

Work on the first ten P-3C Update II aircraft (10 Squadron) commenced in November 1979 with final assembly/system integration undertaken at RAAF Base Edinburgh, S. Australia, which for the consolidation of maintenance and management of assets was to become the nucleus base for both P-3C maritime patrol squadrons from December 1984. Preparatory work had been underway at CAC since April 1977, although in March 1973 the company was investigating the new possibility of acquiring a long term lease on Hangar 103 at Essendon Airport, to allow it to do this work in Melbourne. Ultimately Essendon was not used because of difficulties managing RAAF airframe maintenance away from the P-3 Orion home base. CAC's team of ten to twelve personnel experienced in aircraft modification delivered the first modified aircraft A9-755 in January 1980 and completed the lot by March 1982.

With a gap between the installation work on the first ten P-3C aircraft and the delivery of the second batch, CAC's modification crew had been disbanded. It was necessary to re-group a team for the work on the second batch of P-3C Update III/2 Orion, A9-656 to A9-665 which began arriving at Edinburgh from December 1984. Work commenced in March 1985 on the first arrival, aircraft A9-656. CAC also trained ex-RAAF technicians in the work. In both instances, the P-3Cs were received with sensor crew stations laid out to American requirements ie DIFAR etc, but these were removed and reworked as stated previously. However, the second group of aircraft were delivered without the American sonobuoy data processing electronics but with the improved, CAC derived, ECS modification kit already in place. Whilst the aircraft's ECS was primarily intended to cool the aircraft and its on-board equipment, it was also to be capable of heating the aircraft when operational need dictated it.

The company was awarded the work on the second P-3C batch because of its excellent performance on the previous P-3C conversion project. The alterations to A9-656 were completed in July 1985 and all ten aircraft had been modified by November 1986, a contract valued in excess of $6M to CAC.

Senior Flight Test Engineer Dayle Betts and Assistant Flight Test Engineer Dennis Baker spent four years in South Australia between 1979 and 1983 overseeing the ground and air testing of the prototype P-3C installation via data logging equipment and subsequently the qualification and acceptance testing of all 20 Orion. As each aircraft installation was completed it underwent a week of ground test prior to an acceptance flight of about one hour duration.

Some 13 CAC personnel were constantly on site at Edinburgh during the entire length of the project. Design work was overseen by Jim Caterson and Dennis Baker. New documents or altered drawings were sent back and forth to base at Fisherman's Bend via a dispatch bag on the Greyhound interstate overnight bus until the availability of facsimile machines finally improved the exchange of information.

The introduction of Data Conditioning Unit III equipment on the second tranch of P-3C resulted in further modifications to the wing wiring looms on the AN/AQS-901 processor (the DCU was an item of equipment built by Marconi that translated sonobuoy transmitted data into an acceptable computer language format). The first ten P-3C Orion which had the DCU Unit II level equipment installation were retrospectively upgraded.

AWA was responsible for the design and manufacture of the ground based Compilation, Mission Support and Integration Facility (CMI) for which CAC built the AN/AQS-901 rack and console with the wiring, cooling etc to fit into the CMI and the update for DCU III. Computer Sciences of Australia provided the software.

Thorn-EMI Electronics were subcontractors to CAC for the general installation and the development of some of the electronics, eg: the provision of the Aircraft Interface Unit (ACIFU) which was designed to enable the British designed AN/AQS-901 to communicate with the United States originated Central Processing Unit. A Ground Integration Rig (GIR) representative of the proposed P-3C installation was also designed and constructed at Fisherman's Bend.

The P-3C enhancement project was the largest such undertaking embarked on by the RAAF to that time. It was concluded to the great satisfaction of the customer and gained substantial merit for CAC.

OMEGA Global Navigation Task

Much earlier than the AN/AQS-901 work, CAC was responsible for the installation of Omega navigation equipment in the ten P-3B model aircraft. Omega was a UK designed, US Navy developed, extremely long range all-weather navigation system. Eight global transmitting stations sent time shared, phase differentiated sequence signals in the 10khz-14 kHz range for use by aircraft, submarines and surface ships providing a positional accuracy of 1-2 nm. It operated between 1991 and 1997 and preceded the satellite derived Global Positioning System. The Australian Omega transmitting station/tower was located at Woodside, eastern Victoria.

CACs function (EX366) included the installation work, cockpit alterations and the low level flight testing of the equipment across specially laid out markers in Spencer Gulf, South Australia. In conjunction with the RAAF, Dennis Baker developed the Flight Test profile that from Edinburgh, took the P-3B to the top end of the Yorke Peninsula, to the west coast of Spencer Gulf, down to the Kangaroo Island lighthouse at Cape Willoughby, to Victor Harbour and return to RAAF Base Edinburgh.

The RAAF P-3 Orion Fleet

P-3B A9-291 to 295; 297 to 300; 605. 11 Squadron operated the P-2E Neptune from RAAF Base Townsville. From May 9, 1968 it received the P3B Orion and relocated to RAAF Base Edinburgh. The P-3B was not an economic proposition to update. Lockheed took them back to rework them for new operators. Six were transferred to 601 Squadron of the Portugese Air Force refurbished as P-3P; one went to 5 Squadron of the RNZAF; another was damaged by fire at RAAF Edinburgh; two went to the US Customs.

P-3C Update II A9-751 to A9-760. 10 Squadron operated the SP-2H Neptune from RAAF Base Townsville. From May 1978 it took on the P-3C operating from RAAF Base Edinburgh. Aircraft A9-754 ditched at Cocos Island as a result of a heavily loaded, mid-air high 'G' manoeuvre, part wing break-up on April 26, 1991.

P-3C Update III /2 A9-656 to A9-665. This second batch of Orion replaced the P-3B variant from December 1984. To distinguish them in their different Update status from the previous batch and to avoid confusion during maintenance and parts ordering, 492 Maintenance

Orion P-3C, A9-754, 10 Sqdn. RAAF Edinburgh, April 7, 1979. **J.A. Vella**

Orion P-3B, A9-291. 11 Sqdn, RAAF Edinburgh April 7, 1979. **J.A. Vella**

Orion P-3C, A9-753. 10 Sqdn, RAAF Point Cook, August 21, 1983. **J.A. Vella**

Marconi AN/AQS-901 operator stations in RAAF P-3C Orion. **RAAF**

CA-33. Hand-over of Orion A9-758, first completed AN/AQS-901 system P-3C upgrade, RAAF Edinburgh. CAC technician team L-R .Mick ?; Ron Jenkins; John Underhill; Peter Flounders; Kerrie Spinks; Alan Timmins; Bob Willoughby; Ron Ferris; Jim Adams; Howard Reynolds; Arthur Moody; Col Stones; John Toma & Peter Spinks. **Ron Jenkins**

RAAF P-3 Orion Fleet	
1. Lockheed Model Number	RAAF Identification
P-3B - 95 - LO	A9 - 291 to 296
P-3B - 100 - LO	A9 - 297 to 300
P-3B - 105 -LO	A9 - 605
2. Lockheed Model Number	RAAF Identification
P-3C - 180 - LO	A9 - 751 to 754
P-3C - 185 - LO	A9 - 755 to 760
3. Lockheed Model Number	RAAF Identification
P-3C - 220 - LO	A9 - 656 to 659
P-3C - 225 - LO	A9 - 660 to 665

Squadron re-designated them P-3W. This designation did not last and the entire fleet was re-titled the AP-3C in 2002.

TA-P3B A9-434;438;439. Were late 1996 acquisition refurbished ex-US Navy aircraft acquired for crew training and transport so as to preserve and extend the life of the active squadron airframes. Although the RAAF P-3C fleet carried the different markings of two squadrons, the aircraft were pooled and with the inclusive 292 Training Squadron, operated as part of 92 Wing.

Next Update

Project Air 5276 signed on January 24, 1995 set out to extend to 2015 the Orion's life span and fatigue life through the installation of a lighter,(by 3,500lb)more reliable range of equipment. In a multi-phased project all the RAAF P-3C underwent the extensive electronics upgrade led by L-3 Communications Integrated Systems (Raytheon), ASTA and AWA Defence Industries. The AN/AQS-901 was replaced by the lightweight, less energy consuming colour displays and environmentally cooler, Computer Devices of Canada's (CDC) UYS-503 acoustic processing system which was also capable of processing all type sonobuoys including, Barra. The ELTA ALR-2001 ESM was also added as Air 5140 with HDHV involvement. Most of this work was done by ASTA at Avalon Airfield. Two aircraft, AP-3C(EW), A9-657 & 660 were converted for dedicated Elint gathering and electronic land warfare surveillance.

HDHV by then owned by BTR Nylex (UK) was being reduced for further on-selling and had lost workforce expertise.

Bibliography: CA-33/P-3 ORION Systems Upgrade

Australian Aviation. P3 & AP-3C Orion. (July 1993, April 1995).

Baker, Dennis. (1988-2018). Flight Test engineer/Manager, HDH/Vic Historical Projects. [Correspondence].

Chartres, John. (1986*)*. *BAE Nimrod*. Ian Allan, London.

Commonwealth Aircraft Corporation. (August 5, 1977). Statement of Work Task No.3/76.

Commonwealth Aircraft Corporation. (Undated). Configuration Management Plan for Project AIR 72- P3C [Issue 2].

Commonwealth Aircraft Corporation. (October 1985, February 1986) *Air Tales*. [In-House magazine].

Jane's Avionics. (1986/87). Jane's Information Group. Coulsdon, Surrey, UK.

Omega Navigation System (1969). United States Navy Training Film (U-Tube).

RAAF A9 Orion (www.adf-serials.com.au)

Rees, D.R. (January 1973). Engineering Report AA285. Proposal for Participation in the Lockheed P-3C Orion Co-Production Program. Commonwealth Aircraft Corporation.

SARICH ORBITAL ENGINE FOR AIRCRAFT APPLICATION
January 1974

Part of the company's continued diversification process into commercial ventures was to investigate the possible aviation applications of the Ralph Sarich Orbital petrol engine, the development of which had been taken over by the Broken Hill Pty Ltd Company. This was at the instigation of Dr R. G. Ward, BHP's General Manager of Planning and Research Management. The Orbital engine invented in 1972 worked on the principle of orbital (rotary) rather than reciprocating motion of its internal parts.

Ken Hunter, John Ellem (Engines), Wal Watkins (Project Support Engineer) and Louis Irving (Chief Engineer), initiated a preliminary study in mid January 1974. After five weeks investigation based on limited technical data provided by Ralph Sarich, it produced an extensive report of the engine design changes needed for its application in aircraft roles as well as assessing CAC's engineering capacity to cope with possible changes to its revolutionary engine design. It concluded the design of the engine warranted undertaking a detailed Feasibility Study.

In comparison with aero engines of similar output a Sarich aero engine would have been smaller, lighter and possessed a better power / weight ratio, have fewer parts and therefore offer better reliability and improved maintenance. Additionally, the engine did not present any special airframe installation problems and was

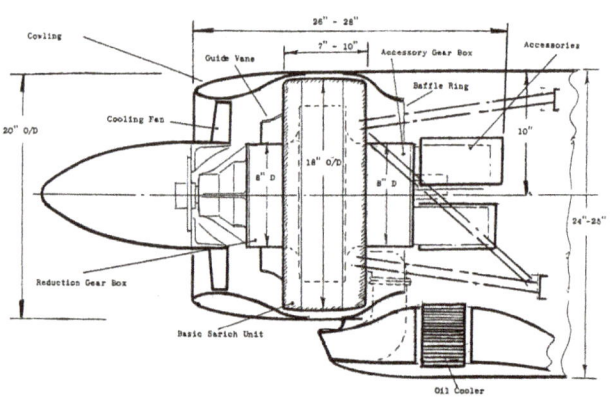

TYPICAL IDEALISED INSTALLATION
SARICH AERO -ENGINE

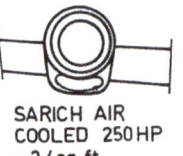

SARICH AIR
COOLED 250 HP
- 2·4 sq. ft.

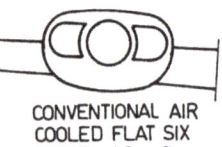

CONVENTIONAL AIR
COOLED FLAT SIX
260 HP - 4·3 sq. ft.

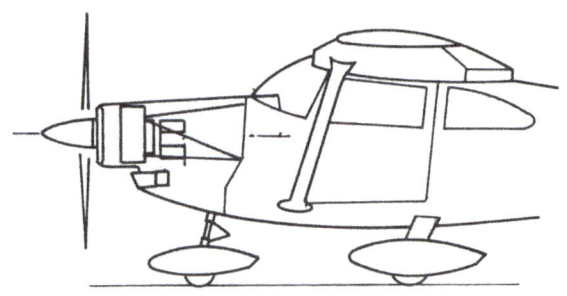

considered to offer the biggest performance gain when applied as a wing installation. The major change required would have been the conversion of the design from water to air cooling and although not an easy undertaking, it was within the capabilities of the CAC's Engine Department.

The Basic Engine

The engine was described as a single row, seven chamber, poppet valve, water cooled unit. With a customer preference overwhelmingly in favour of using air cooling, the advantages for the conversion of the engine from water cooling were the self-contained nature of the unit, lighter weight than a liquid cooled unit of equal output, simpler installation, increased reliability and less vulnerability in military operations. Conversely liquid cooling offered a reduced frontal area, more even cooling of the combustion area and better fuel consumption at higher compression ratios. Without adequate data of torque and SFC characteristics it was not possible to know if a direct or geared drive system was needed. Both were given consideration. Both were very compact packages with the geared drive assembly possibly needing a cooling fan.

Air cooled Sarich engines would have achieved significant frontal area drag improvements and were not expected to exceed 55% of that of the equivalent piston engines. This drag reduction would have permitted an increase in cruising speed of 8 kts when fitted in a light twin (Cessna 340). Similarly, in weight comparison, a direct drive, water cooled Sarich aero engine would have matched the installed weight for the existing aircraft piston engines of 100 hp and upwards. The air cooled variant would have shown an improvement, whilst a geared air cooled drive unit would have significantly improved on the newly developing Teledyne Tiara range of engines.

A comparison of centre-line tractor engine installations:

Cessna 172	Installed Weight
Original engine Lycoming O-320 (150 HP)	400 lb
Sarich Aero Engine (150 HP)	335 lb

The report concentrated on the comparison of developed Sarich aero engine horsepower outputs against existing aero engine equivalents. The suggestion was made to concentrate on the lower power units (150 hp and less) due to expected competition from the Teledyne Tiara. (The Tiara series was eventually discontinued.)

The indication was that there was a vast potential market for the home aircraft constructor, with for example the Bede Aircraft with their BD-5 and Bensen Aircraft with their Gyrocopter, searching for 5,000 - 8,000 engines in the 40 hp to 100 hp range. Other possible uses were in inboard/outboard marine, snowmobile and industrial applications.

With little by way of direct competition except from a 65 hp Hirth and VW conversions, there was a definite niche for the aero Sarich with a similar but perhaps lesser market potential in the 100 hp to 150 hp range. However the 180 to 300 hp power range was difficult to penetrate until there was a proven history of operational experience with the lower powered variants. (Project Support Engineer, Wal Watkins, was also the Federal Secretary of the Ultra-Light Aircraft Association of Australia).

Sarich Orbital Engine Specification			
Diameter	18 ins	RPM	5,000
Length	9.75 ins	HP	150 to 200
Displacement	200 cu in	HP/lb	1.1 to 1.4
Weight	140 lb	HP/cu in	0.75 to 1.0

Market Costs

To be competitive, the price of the Sarich aero engine had to be near to that of the existing piston engines as tabulated below.

Original Equipment Manufacture Price(1973)

Aircraft Engine	HP	OEM Price (A$)
O-200A	100	3000
O-300D	145	1900
IO-360C	210	2600
IO-470D	260	3000

Sarich Unit	HP	Target OEM Price (A$)
Direct drive 214 cu in	105	1450
Direct drive 305 cu in	150	2000
Geared drive 214 cu in	175	2250
Geared drive 305 cu in	250	3000

Management assistance and technical advice was sought from Rolls Royce Light Aircraft Engine Division, (UK) on the subjects of distribution, marketing, prices, air cooling problems etc. Rolls Royce experience was also sought on the organisational and commercial aspects of the design and production of light engines, cost control and the times for possible development and production cycles.

Bibliography: Sarich Orbital Engine for Aircraft Application
Commonwealth Aircraft Corporation. (January 1973). Engineering Report AA314. Sarich Engine Development for use in aircraft.

CA-36 APPRENTICE TRAINING PROJECT
(Pazmany PL-4A)
June 1974

This project had its beginnings on June 3, 1974 when Wal Watkins, CAC Project Support Engineer and also the Federal Secretary of the Ultra-Light Aircraft Association of Australia (ULTA) informed CAC that the Association's advice had been sought concerning a proposal by CAC apprentices to scratch build an ULTA sports aircraft which could be considered as an Apprentices Training School Project.

The investigation into various makes and types of sport aircraft and their constructional techniques combined with their likely educational merit, led to Wal Watkins suggest adoption of the Pazmany PL-4A, a design by Ladislao Pazmany, resident of San Diego, California,USA. The Board of CAC gave their consent on March 1976 for construction of the PL-4A as part of the first year apprentice training program. Progress was slow. A Revmaster R2100D (VW)

VH-XAP, the smart looking Pazmany PL-4A, first of type on Australian civil aircraft register. It carries the CAC logo and contract no. CA-36 on the fin & the text 'Commonwealth Aircraft Corporation Apprentice Training Project' on the fuselage side. **J.A. Vella**

engine was chosen. This selection entailed an approved but detailed modification to the mounting of the engine, its controls and fuel lines. These changes coupled with doubts on the mechanical integrity of some components of the particular bought-in engine, combined to add unexpected delays and to draw out the aircraft completion date.

Built along conventional management lines, with the apprentices carrying out all the functions of estimating, scheduling, planning and inspection, the project was given the CA-36 designation. Construction picked up momentum in 1982 but was limited by the number of apprentices who could work on the small plane at any one time.

The PL-4A was the first of its type on the Australian civil aircraft register. VH-XAP made its first flight on May 16, 1983 and was subsequently offered for private sale for $10,000. After a time in private ownership it was donated to the Australian National Aviation Museum (formerly the Moorabbin Air Museum) in 2016. It was kept in airworthy condition and makes special air show appearances attracting a lot of attention due to its smart, nifty rarity.

Bibliography: CA-36 Apprentice Training Project
Commonwealth Aircraft Corporation. Pazmany PL-4A Training Project General Files (2).

CHAPTER 9. LIGHT TRANSPORTS AND LIGHT MILITARY SUPPORT AIRCRAFT

THE LIGHT MILITARY SUPPORT AIRCRAFT
June 1975

Lee Archer, former RAAF/ARDU, CA-15 test pilot, former co-owner of International Helicopters and CAC's South East Asia Manager, was the driver of a perceived need for a counter insurgency type aircraft in the South East Asia region. The first official moves within the company to sanction this idea started in June 1975 when the suggestions for a brief technical outline were considered. Lee Archer's sketches of possible configurations had already been discussed with Wal Watkins, CAC's Project Support Engineer in January 1974. The experience in the air war over South Vietnam was that most of the dedicated ground support combat aircraft were far too complex, heavy, expensive and hardly ever required to operate above 10,000 feet. It was Lee Archer's view that future conflicts in the region would be of a similar guerrilla infiltration by land and sea. This made the role of combat helicopters new and paramount and also introduced the new Cessna O-2 and North American Aviation OV-10 Bronco fixed wing aircraft in the light support / observation roles.

A tactical choice for similar future circumstances suggested two options. The first, a small number of sophisticated and therefore expensive aircraft with their ground support infrastructure or secondly, the use of a larger number of simple, less expensive aircraft of an easily handled and maintained nature. In the low level roles, a versatile low cost, multi-purpose aircraft appeared to be a more effective proposition. CAC, greatly in need of stable non-Government supported work load, knew that its industry experience would adequately qualify it to design, develop and manufacture an aircraft that came within the second less sophisticated option.

Archer's vision was that such an aircraft should have maximum versatility by designing it as a 'prime mover concept' (as employed in the heavy trucking industry) with extensive use of 'off-the-shelf' components for minimum cost and maximum reliability in continuation of CAC's traditional project design philosophy. In June 1975, Wal Watkins was asked to expand Lee Archer's proposals for a light multi-role military support aircraft. His report AA332 dated July 24, 1975 provided preliminary information to engender interest and discussion.

Sir Laurence Hartnett CBE who had been involved as a consulting industrialist to the Singaporean Government for the establishment of several enterprises was made aware of the project by Lee Archer and the resulting discussions suggested the project could be of interest to ASEAN nations. It was considered that such an aircraft could be a collaborative design and development training program for Singapore industry. This would advance Singapore's objective to establish a self-supporting aircraft industry. Their cost of labour was low and development of the project in Singapore would provide a competitive product on world markets.

Co-inciding with these discussions was the announcement on August 7, 1975 by the Defence Minister, Bill Morrison that the Government was to impose a 200 mile Exclusive Economic Zone (EEZ) around the 12,000 mile coastline of Australia. This would require the setting up of surface and air patrol infrastructure of the coastal area along similar lines to that of the US Coast Guard. This announcement provided further company impetus for the Light Military Support (LMS) aircraft concept.

On September 11, 1975 Lee Archer and Wal Watkins gave a presentation of the LMS aircraft in Canberra to Don Eltringham, Deputy Secretary, Department of Defence. He suggested that CAC approach the three Defence services as there was a requirement for both a Forward Air Control Aircraft and a Coastal Surveillance Aircraft and whilst it was considered that the GAF Nomad would not be suitable for FAC work, it would be a competitor to the company's proposed LMS aircraft in the coastal patrol role. The DoD would not allocate funding for the LMS aircraft unless the Defence forces requested a need for the aircraft. A$45M had been spent from the Defence budget vote to develop the Nomad and some of these aircraft were given away in overseas aid programs. Such an occurrence was not likely to be repeated. In the same way, aid funds for Singapore and Malaysia were fairly well committed in other directions and were not likely to be diverted for setting up the LMS project.

Thoughts were also expressed that CAC, under the Industries Assistance Commission recommendations, was not expected to be in the airframe development business in the future but would be specialising only in engines, spare parts and support for other programs if the mooted industry rationalization plans were implemented. Lee Archer believed that the greater part of the expected market was to be found in SE Asia, not in Australia, even if a coastal patrol variant was to be accepted. As such, CAC as a private company was quite justified in seeking external commercial business. It wanted this project to be developed along a 'skunk works philosophy' with a small competent team using a maximum amount of 'off-the-shelf' components preferably of Cessna origin eg: engine installation, controls, undercarriage and putting it all together down to a price and not to an ideal specification.

The initial target selling price was to be no more than A$200,000. The company management wished to investigate a collaborative proposal with Singapore and to proffer their technical expertise and advisory services as project designers and consultants for a training project in all areas of design, development and production, including the Type Certification processes.

CAC's Engineering Manager, Louis Irving and Lee Archer briefed the Department of Foreign Affairs in Canberra on September 23, 1975. They received a cautious response with regard to the anticipated production of the LMS aircraft and its export to the SE Asian region. In this respect, with the stated built-in versatility of the design and its military counter insurgency capability, the Australian Government would not grant a blanket arms export approval. There was however, little that could be done to stop the company manufacturing the aircraft overseas, there being no restraint in discussing the options with Singapore, Malaysia, Thailand or Indonesia.

It was therefore decided to continue with the project and firmed up on plans to have discussions with the Singapore Government with the assistance of Sir Laurence Hartnett. CAC would act as designers and consultants in collaboration with Singapore to develop and produce the LMS under licence for themselves and the SE Asian countries. The prototype was to be manufactured at CAC and fully certificated in Australia. It appeared that from the strength of the arguments being put forward, that CAC was very determined to make an impact with this project, as it considered this would assist to:

- Re-establish CAC as an aircraft design organisation
- Enter the export market and
- Help obtain further Australian Defence contracts

Whilst contributing to Regional Defence by:

- Assisting with the establishment of aircraft industries in SE Asia and
- The design and development of a Light military Surveillance aircraft

It was estimated it would cost $5.9M Singapore dollars (A$2.0M) in October 1975 values to launch the program on a pre-production commitment.

Aircraft Description

The general objective of the design was to provide a low cost versatile aircraft to satisfy low key surveillance and 'police patrol' actions, with provision for quick conversion to other utility applications. The concept was not to display an overly offensive profile. Wal Watkins was responsible for the configuration design, market survey and cost / labour / programming predictions.

The aircraft was a light, twin piston engine aeroplane with a simple high wing, T- tail unit, a pod fuselage with a stiff tail boom, an all- weather capability and tandem aircrew seating.

All load carrying structures were of to be single curvature panels in conventional aluminium alloy sheet with all complex shaped fairings formed in GRP. The parallel chord wing incorporated the new NACA GAW-2 Series 17% aerofoil section with a 12 inch deep main spar providing ample fuel tank capacity. Maximum span flaps were possible by utilising spoiler ailerons on the wing upper surface together with short span feeler ailerons to provide pilot control force feel. Built-in fittings for simple wing-tip extensions were incorporated. The 36 in wide 'pod and boom' fuselage was to be built from heavy gauge sheet skins with a minimum of supporting frames, finished off in a boom on top which was located a T-tail of conventional construction and a forward retracting nose wheel in the GRP nose fairing.

The two 300 hp Teledyne Continental engines together with their cowlings were 'off-the-shelf' Cessna 402 installations as were the single wheel main undercarriage units that retracted rearward into the engine nacelles. Turbo supercharged piston engines were selected in lieu of turboprops to reduce the procurement cost and maintain maximum power output on hot days.

To this basic 'prime mover', various fuselage modules or pods designed for specific operations were to be quickly attached in-the-field as required. The basic 'prime-mover' module was self- sufficient and capable of operating with its crew of two. For direct military / customs surveillance duties, a small calibre gun turret module would be mounted under the rear fuselage pod and if necessary this could be supplanted with underwing mounted rocket armament. Alternatively, vertical and sideway looking survey camera modules could be installed in place of the gun module.

Missions and Roles

The utilitarian capabilities envisaged of the aircraft are listed in the Defence and civil applications table. Some applications would require variations of the fuselage pod module and specialised equipment fit.

Disposable loads would include: Military stores and weapons; food and medical supplies; fire-fighting equipment; power generating packs and delivering livestock fodder supplies.

With the Ferranti Seaspray airborne search radar installed for coastal patrol and flown with a crew of three, it was estimated that a coastal / sea area of 50,000 sq miles could be surveyed during a 7.5 hour mission, cruising at 150kts.

A comparative estimate between the GAF Nomad N22B and the CAC LMS indicated:

Unit	GAF Nomad N22B	LMS
Weight (TO)	8,500 lb	6,300 lb
Cruise speed	145 kts	180 kts
Range with 1,300 lb equipment weight	700 nm	700 nm
Cruise speed	145 kts	180 kts
Range with 800 lb equipment weight	900 nm	1,250 nm

Costs and Program Estimates

Commercial viability of the LMS would only have been a reality with a minimum run of 100 units within a production period of five years and it was on this basis that costs and program estimates were calculated, a run for which no sophisticated tooling was required.

Detail design and development was to be achieved by Singaporean personnel joining with the CAC design team as understudies for training in all aspects of the project. Production was estimated to commence about 30 months after the start of initial detail design.

A Singapore based production line would bring about a unit cost of S$420,000 (A$137,000), compared with CAC's unit production cost of S$500,000 (A$162,000). The 'design-to-a-cost' Target Basic Sale price was set at S$625,000 (A$203,000). These costs did not include possible military role operating equipment of about A$161,000 (all costs in October 1975 values).

Negotiations and Outcome

Bill Abbott, CAC's then General Manager and Lee Archer made a first visit to Singapore with the proposal in December 1975 to initiate official discussions with introductions provided by Sir Laurence Hartnett.

The moment of truth came on January 23, 1976. The Singapore Minister for Science and Technology, through the Chairman of the Economic Development Board (Dr L. C. Meng), informed Sir Laurence

Hartnett that for the project to be successful, there had to be an extensive marketing support and servicing network, an activity for which Singapore was totally lacking. He also pointed out that the type of aircraft design being offered was considered to have a sale potential mainly with military aid programs and such aid would not be supported by the Government of Singapore. The LMS concept was considered to be technically feasible and acceptable as would have been a more complex and advanced design. Provided that design, manufacture and certification training were included and that CAC participated with negotiated terms and a risk sharing capital involvement, then co-operation was possible.

By April 1976 some six months after the estimates prepared for the December 1975 presentation by CAC in Singapore, the exchange rates had changed dramatically to increase the Singaporean costs by some 50%. The new April 1976 estimates projected a production unit cost of S$640,000 (A$233,000) a little less competitive relative to an acceptable 1976 sale price of S$660,000 (A$230,000) for this type of military aircraft.

Defence Applications	Civil Applications
Visual Reconnaissance	Ambulance
Armed Reconnaissance	Utility Transport
Close Support	Survey & Mapping
Forward Air Control	Bush Fire Surveillance
Forward Command Mission	Pest Control
Border Surveillance	Aerial Search
Coastal Surveillance	Air Sea Rescue
Radar/Photo Surveillance	Disaster Evacuation
Supply Support Drop	Pollution Patrol
Paratroop Drop	Police Patrol
Helicopter Escort	Direct TV Reporting
Aircrew Navigation Training	Pilot Training

Jock Dalziel CAC's new General Manager, visited Singapore during April / May 1977 for a series of business discussions but the LMS had dropped out of consideration toward the end of Bill Abbott's tenure. Cancellation of the LMS was made known in a press release of September 26, 1976.

This unique proposal did not progress beyond desk-top display models which showed an aircraft of neat functional lines. A good deal of preliminary design data had been established to develop the specification, with feasible, continuing development proposals in the form of a small twin engine, eight passenger utility civil / military commuter aircraft and a larger four engine 20 passenger light utility transport aircraft (Refer to later descriptions).

This was CAC's last large, significant and serious initiative to get back into aircraft design and development operations with its own exclusive creative proposals-within its scale of capability and financial resources.

LMS Aircraft Postscript Comments

On March 30, 1977, the Grumman Aerospace Corporation of Bethpage, New York, through their office of Offset Development, provided a cursory written critique of the LMS engineering proposal. This informal summary was the result of an approach a few weeks earlier by Ron Westrup, CAC's Marketing Manager during a visit to Grumman.

Specifications	Light Military Support Aircraft (LMS)	
Powerplant	Two Teledyne Continental TSIO-520 E/600 turbo charged piston engines of 300 hp each at 2,700 rpm driving 3 bladed CS propellers of 6 ft 4.5ins diameter	
Performance	Max speed at SL	210 kts
	Max speed at 10,000 ft	230 kts
	Rate of climb	1,700 ft/min
	Cruise speed at SL	160 kts
	Range (2 crew, 1,200 lb mission equip't) at 150 kts	1,200 nm
	Endurance (47% power at 10,000 ft)	7.6 hrs
	Ferry range	2,500 nm
Weights	Empty	3,600 lb
	Mission load	1,540 lb
	Useful load (Aircrew & equip't)	2,700 lb
	Max TO	6,300 lb
	Fuel load	1,160 lb
	Wing loading	35 lb/sq ft
	Power loading	10.5 lb/hp
Dimensions	Wing span	30 ft
	Wing chord	6 ft
	T/C ratio	17%
	Wing area	180 sq ft
	Tailplane span	12.1 ft
	Tailplane chord	4.1 ft
	Tailplane area	50 sq ft
	Length	35 ft

There was not much material available for Grumman Aerospace to work with other than CAC's technical brochures, artist impressions and general arrangements. A serious critique would have required more detailed description of the aircraft and a more involved effort on Grumman's part. Informal comments by Grumman technical specialists in the areas of aerodynamics, propulsion, structures and controls were not overly critical. They noted the choice of a T-tail design, whilst improving spin / stall behaviour, might have been too heavy for a light aircraft and the use of a conventional tail from an existing design might have been considered worthwhile. It was also felt there may have been weight / cost penalties due to the need to cater for basic torsional stiffness for the fuselage boom design; further aggravated perhaps by the presence of a T-tail.

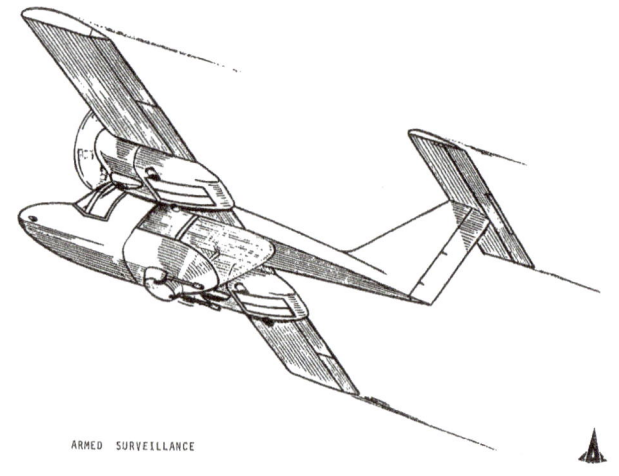

The LMS in the armed surveillance role .HDHV

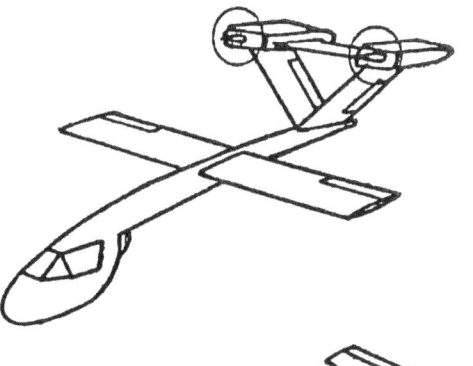

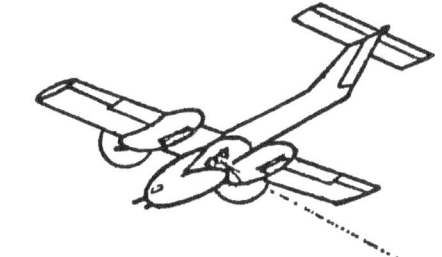

Various layout configurations as seen on the designer's sketch pad.

The original pencil outlines were too faint to reproduce and have been overdrawn to make them more legible. **Walter Watkins**

In the armed support/coastal patrol role with twin cannon turret. **Walter Watkins**

The LMS with the minimum add-on pod in place. **Walter Watkins**

Walter Watkins

The plain airframe prime mover configuration. **Walter Watkins**

For the carriage of passengers, a wide body lock-on module was envisaged. **Walter Watkins**

The prime mover fitted with a cargo/supply drop platform. **Walter Watkins.**

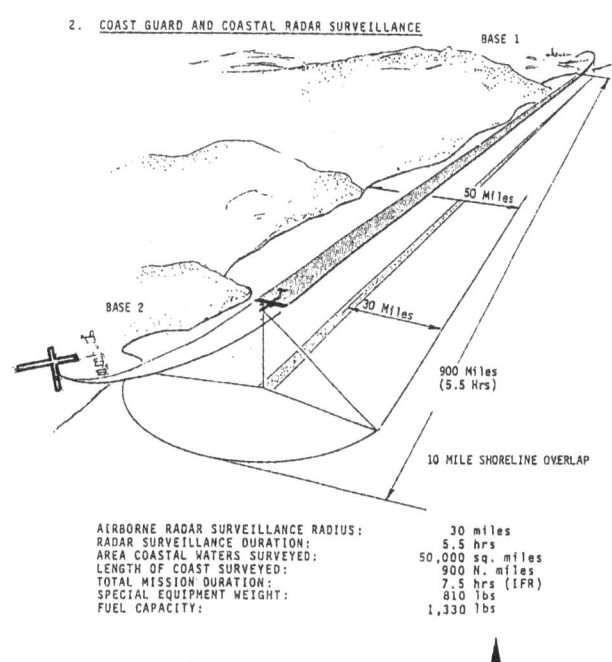

Typical Naval Radar Surveillance Missions diagram.

Light Military Support

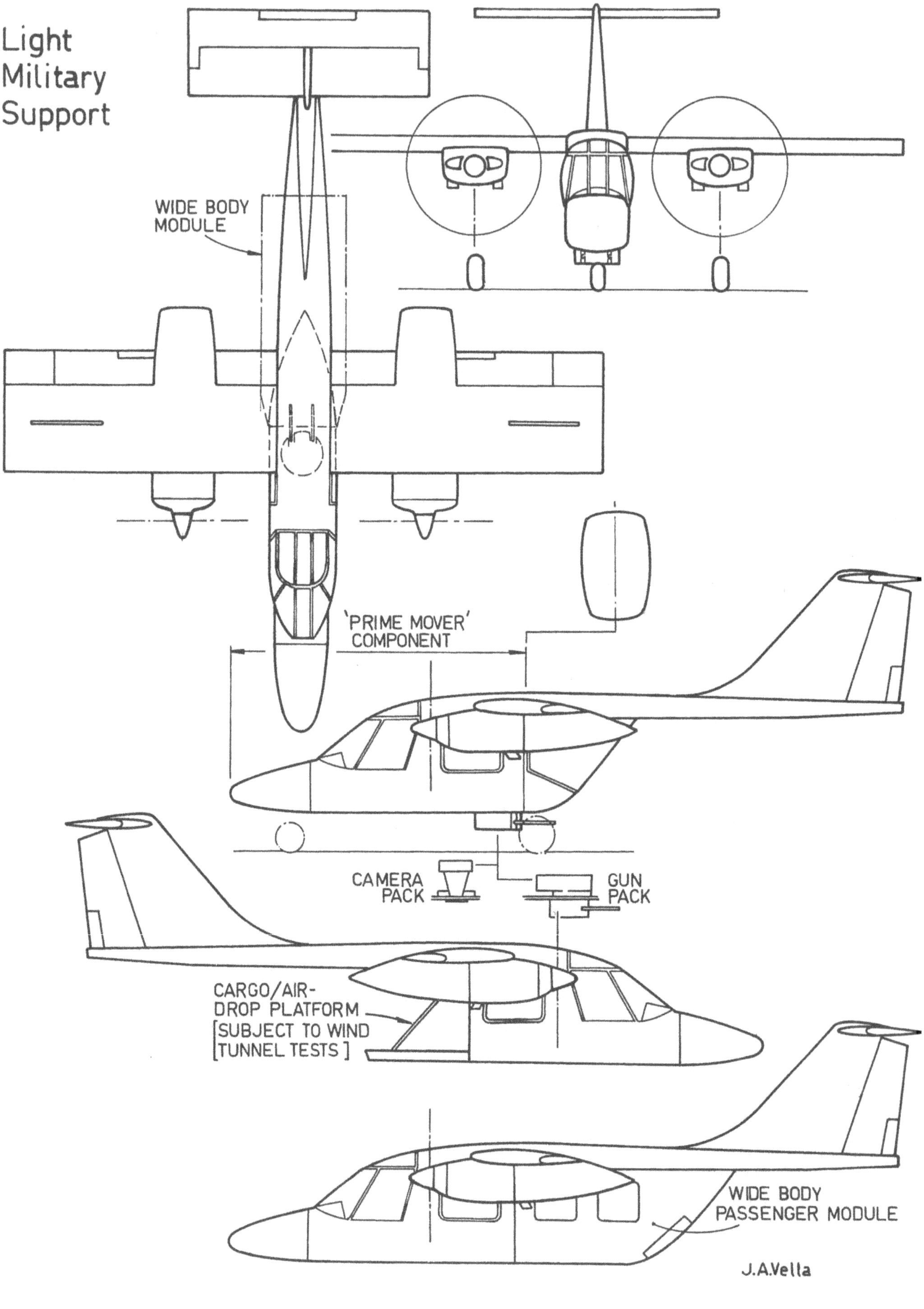

Labels on drawing:
- WIDE BODY MODULE
- 'PRIME MOVER' COMPONENT
- CAMERA PACK
- GUN PACK
- CARGO/AIR-DROP PLATFORM [SUBJECT TO WIND TUNNEL TESTS]
- WIDE BODY PASSENGER MODULE

J.A.Vella

Other points raised on cg consideration, the possible use of turboprops, the positioning of the nose wheel and the use of long main undercarriage units were not of great concern.(the undercarriage in use on the Aero Commander was not all that different from that planned for the LMS).

Walter Watkins later related to the author that the helpful comments by Grumman were interesting but not valid, having regard to the proposed sizing of the components concerned.

Bibliography: The Light Military Support Aircraft

Dalziel, J. (1987). CAC General Manager. [Correspondence].

Watkins, W. (July 24,1975) . Engineering Report AA332. A Proposal for a Light Multi-Purpose Support Aircraft. C o m m o n w e a l t h Aircraft Corporation.

Watkins, W. (November 1975). Engineering Report AA336. An Aircraft for a Singapore Aircraft Industry. Commonwealth Aircraft Corporation.

LIGHT MILITARY / CIVIL TRANSPORT (LMS DERIVATIVE)
June 1975

The possibility of creating a civil / military transport aircraft derivative of the LMS concept was a short exploration study for the maximum possible utilization of LMS based airframe components.

The plan was to use the LMS wing, undercarriage, engine installation and tail assembly but to change to a new, wider conventional fuselage to seat eight to ten passengers. For utility work a rear loading ramp was included. The potential of the aircraft lay in commuter / light transport work and coastal surveillance.

Specifications	Light Military /Civil Transport	
Powerplant	Two Teledyne Continental TSIO-520 E/600 turbo charged piston engines of 300 hp each	
Performance	With 1,000 payload in IFR conditions:	
	Cruise speed	190 kt
	Range	1,200 nm
Weights	Max TO	6,300 lb
Dimensions	Wing span	33 ft
	Wing area	200 sq ft
	Cabin length	12 ft
	Cabin width	5 ft

Bibliography:LMS Military/Civil Transport

Commonwealth Aircraft Corporation. (Undated). [Project study notes].

LIGHT HELICOPTER CRANE / JEEP (LMS AIRCRAFT ADDENDA)
June 1975

Early in 1975 the CAC Inter-Union IAC (Industries Assistance Commission) Enquiry Committee requested the company's Design Engineering Department assess the feasibility of small helicopter development. With CAC's agency representation for Hughes Helicopters and a production commitment with the Bell 206, the suggestion was worthy of study.

During the LMS aircraft definition period, the subject of a three-

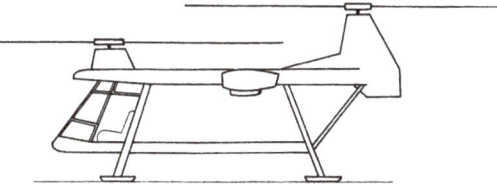

Crane/Jeep Helicopter [Type A]

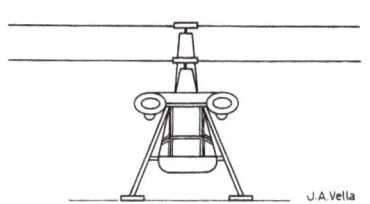

J.A.Vella

Specifications	Light Helicopter Crane/Jeep Proposal A	
Powerplant	Two Teledyne Continental piston engines of 210 hp each	
Performance	Max speed	78 kt
	Endurance	3.5 hrs
Weights	Lift capacity 1,000 lb on a 12 ft x 4 ft loading platform or a 2,200 lb sling load	
Dimensions	Rotor diameter	2 x 25.4 ft
	Rotors	2 x 3 blades
	Height of front rotor	9.5 ft
	Height of rear rotor	12 ft

Specifications	Light Helicopter Crane/Jeep Proposal B	
Powerplant	Two GM Allison 250 (C20) turboshaft engines of 400 shp each	
Performance	NA	
Weights	Lift capacity 3,700 lb on a 15 ft x 4 ft loading platform	
	Empty	1,800 lb
	Useful load	4,500 lh
	TO	6,300 lb
Dimensions	Rotor diameter	2 x 26.3 ft
	Rotors	2 x 4 blades

nation (Australia, USA and Singapore) small helicopter co-operative program in the utility crane category was discussed. With only 126 helicopters of all categories operating in Australia in 1975, the local market was not commercially viable. From a survey of world-wide helicopter operations, the prominent gap existed in the small tandem rotor / crane jeep category with a one ton payload capacity selling for around A$130,000. There was also no twin engine helicopter with a payload capacity 30% greater than the Hughes 500C and selling for no more than A$230,000.

Lee Archer suggested that a tandem rotor helicopter loading platform configuration for study should make use of the rotor systems of the Hughes 300 and 500 series. Two configurations were casually schemed during September 1975; the principal differences lay in engine selection. In both proposals the loading platform would carry fully equipped troops or be fitted out as a gun platform.

(In October 1976 a nearly identical idea to the CAC's Crane / Jeep was documented and circulated by the American Jovair Corporation of California with their J-12 'Air Mule').

Light Military/Civil Transport

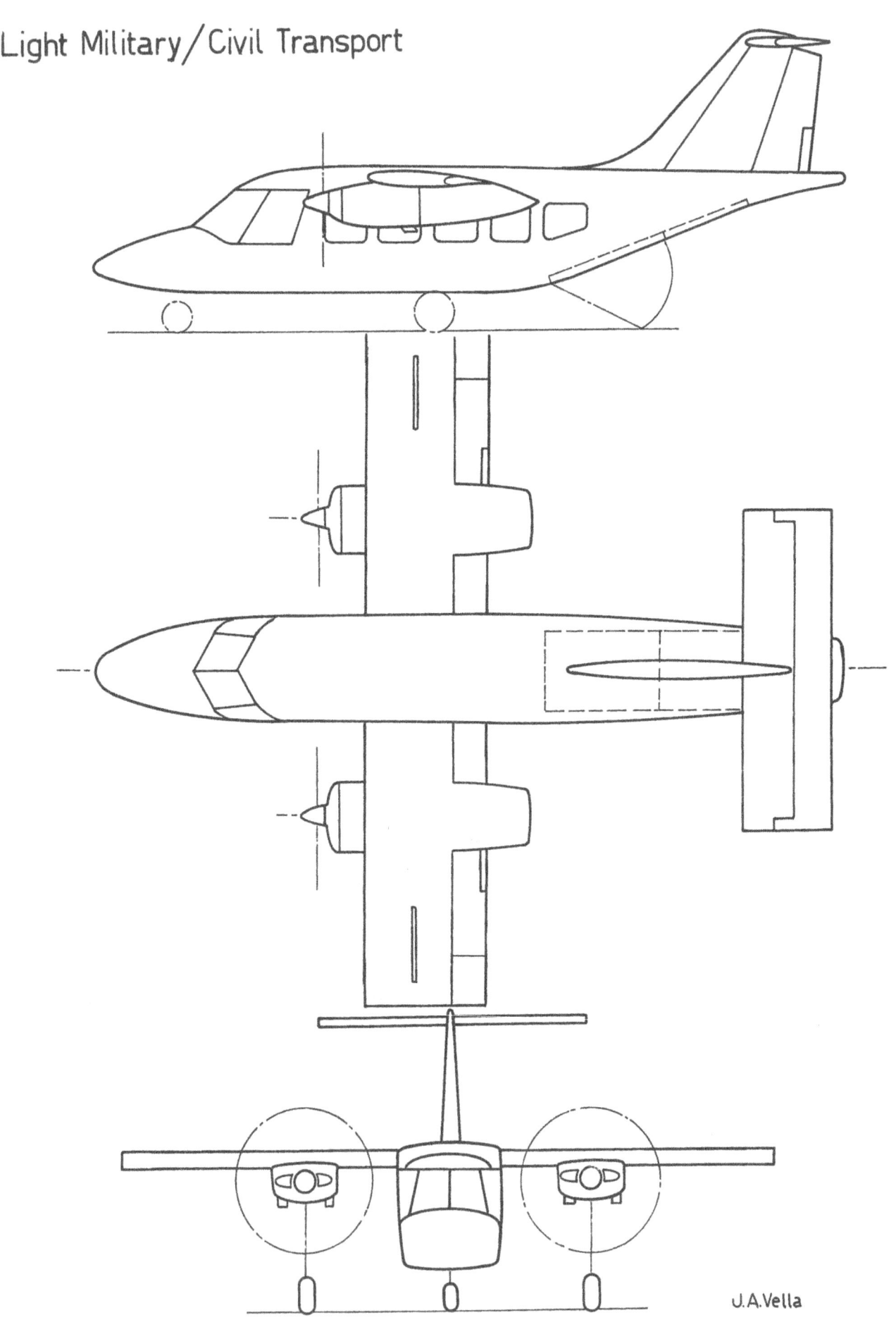

J.A.Vella

Bibliography: Light Helicopter Crane/Jeep

Commonwealth Aircraft Corporation. (Undated). [In-House Memoranda Notes].

Commonwealth Aircraft Corporation. (Undated). Design Notes.

Watkins, W. (April 1975). Potential Feasibility Projects on Helicopters. Commonwealth Aircraft Corporation.

LIGHT SURVEILLANCE AIRCRAFT (CESSNA 402A MOD)
June 1975

During August 1975 and before a commitment was made to concentrate on the new LMS Aircraft study, Project Support Engineer, Wal Watkins undertook a casual evaluation for an alternative low cost Cessna 402A conversion into a Light Surveillance/Patrol Aircraft.

The Cessna 402A was a well-established light twin with accommodation for 10 passengers. Its payload /cruising speed/range productivity was superior to the Nomad N22 and as a consequence for any operations not requiring STOL capability, a structurally modified Cessna 402A could prove versatile.

The conversion envisaged a new rear fuselage structure widened into a 'beaver tail' configuration and tilted upwards to form a continuous new profile in line with the cabin upper surface. The lower surface would incorporate a 36 inch wide, inward opening door to enable the easy loading of stretchers and long bulky cargoes. This opening would also permit para-drops and other aerial deliveries as well as provide an observation aperture for any specialized cameras, infra-red detector equipment etc.

Many of the existing structural frames would have been utilized with minor re-working. It was intended that this conversion would be carried out on used aircraft with low hours on their airframe. As proposed this variant would have enhanced the utility of the aircraft where a fleet was required for a wide range of special operations.

Rex Aviation, the Australian agents for Cessna advised that it was unlikely that Cessna Aircraft Co. would give its co-operation and technical data for such a conversion but this was not tested at the time.

No further time was spent on the idea due to the greater emphasis on the development plan of the more versatile LMS aircraft.

Bibliography: Light Surveillance Aircraft (Cessna 402A Mod)

Commonwealth Aircraft Corporation. (Undated). [Project study notes].

DHC-4 CARIBOU TRANSPORT REPLACEMENT
September 1975

The DHP-72 was a 1974, de Havilland Canada STOL follow-on project to replace their company DHC-5, turboshaft powered Buffalo tactical transport. Australian industry participation was sought in the development of this advanced STOL design proposal.

This complex aircraft was to be powered by two modified, split-flow, Roll Royce Spey turbofans with Bristol Pegasus type jet exhausts (as used on the HS Harrier VTOL tactical fighter) and bypass blown air ducted across the upper wing surfaces. The aircraft was to have a work capacity of 4,900 ton miles/hour, about eight times the capability of the DHC-4 Caribou transport then in service with two squadrons in the RAAF.

Whilst the RAAF was yet to issue its requirement for a Caribou replacement, such a request was expected to surface between 1979 and 1983. Working on the assumption that such an aircraft would not be expected to lift a single mission load greater than 50% of the in-service DHC-4 capacity, the CAC Aircraft Design Study Group concluded the DHP-72 aircraft had a capability and complexity far in excess of likely Australian defence needs and set out to propose a smaller but still capable alternative in the form of a modification

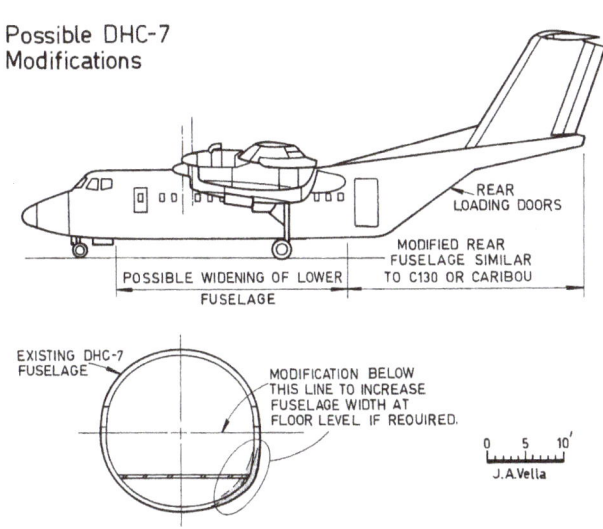

RAAF DHC-4 Caribou, A4-159 at Ballarat Airfield, VIC. Sept 25,1971.
J.A.Vella

Unit	DHC-4	DHC-7	DHP-72	C-130	CH-47A
Military payload (Tons approx)	4	5.5	10.6	20	3
Cruise speed (kts)	158	240	460	320	130
Work capacity (Ton miles/Hr)	630	1500	4900	6400	390

based on the 54 passenger, DHC-7 STOL airliner aircraft that had made its first flight on March 27, 1975.

The DHC-7 was powered by four 1,120 shp turboshaft engines. The study suggested a rear loading ramp, the possible widening of the cabin at floor level and a 3 ft increase in wing span. Alternatively, a completely new wide body fuselage would have worked well for military roles. This early assessment suggested pursuing Defence Department interest with the view of structuring a feasibility study to determine the validity and market potential of the modified DHC-7 as a replacement of the STOL DHC-4 Caribou. Such a study was expected to provide useful experience and guidelines for future collaboration with Canada, particularly for the DHP-72 if that was to be pursued. The idea went no further. The DHP-72 was also dropped.

Bibliography: A DHC-4 Caribou Transport Replacement Aircraft

Aircraft. Another Opportunity Is Knocking. December 1974

De Havilland Canada DHC-7. *Air International*: Vol 19 (September 1980) Key Publishing, Lincs. UK.

Watkins, W. (September 5, 1975). Engineering Report AA333. A Proposal for a Caribou Replacement Aircraft. Commonwealth Aircraft Corporation.

LIGHT UTILITY TRANSPORT AIRCRAFT

February 1976

The Light Military Support (LMS) aircraft was a concept that was capable of further development or could be taken to new directions.

This applied to the Light Utility Transport Aircraft (LUTA), a configuration with minimal manufacturing complication, provided the concept was economical to operate and competitive with similar aircraft. The added advantage in this scheme was that it might have provided the Singapore Government with a possible construction follow-on project to the previous LMS (had it been embarked upon) of a larger and more productive airframe type.

Department of Transport (the former DCA) figures for direct operating costs of commuter aircraft were used by the CAC Aircraft Design Study Group in a long term 'long shot' investigation of the sort of light transport / commuter aircraft that would be required at around 1980 to 1985 with a 16-18 seat payload and a cost in the vicinity of $30,000 per seat. At the same time a 5% to 10% improvement in seat / mile costs over existing types was sought ie 'Design to an Operating Cost Comparison' philosophy (Table 1).

The trend towards increasing fuel costs, labour costs and higher loan repayment rates indicated the need for an aircraft of:
- low initial capital cost
- low operating cost
- rugged construction with simple maintenance and
- moderate economical cruising speed

A generalised operating cost study of existing and projected aircraft designs pointed to the application of piston engines to achieve the desired parameters. Existing aircraft in commuter operations were considered to offer a low capacity eg BN Islander or GAF Nomad or were too expensive to acquire with their turboshaft engines eg the DHC-6 Twin Otter, GAF Nomad or Shorts Skyvan.

From the survey of 'Design to Operating Cost Comparison' (Table 1) it became apparent that the original design parameters put the cost / seat mile in an unfavourable situation. However, by reducing the capital investment figure from $696,000 to $641,000 and accordingly dropping the basic aircraft cost from $554,000 to $505,000 (Table 2) the cost / seat mile figure of 8.0 cents could only

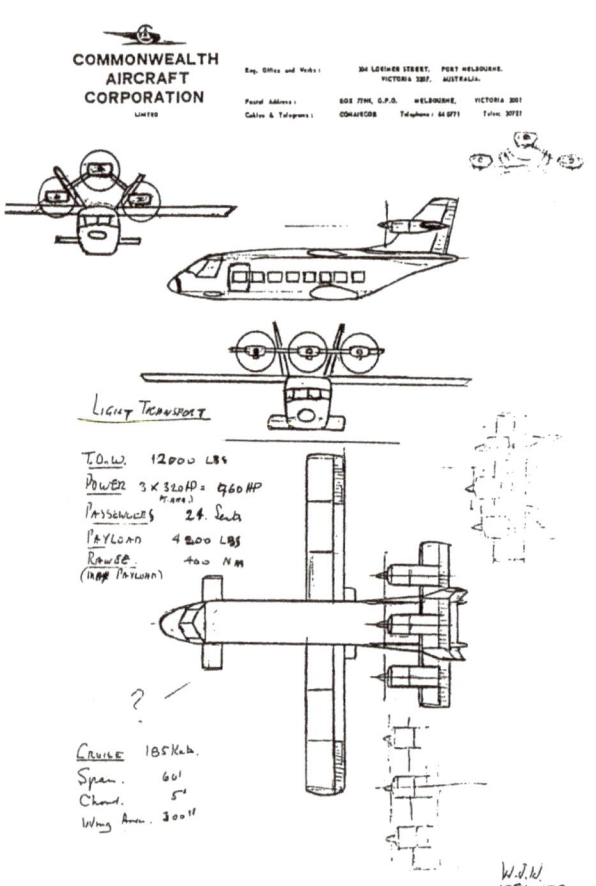

Early suggestion outlines from the designer's sketch pad.
Walter Watkins/CAC

Table 1: Design to Operating Cost Comparison

	Capital Investment ($)	Passenger Seats	Max. Cruise (Kts)	Cost/Seat Mile (Cents)	Total Cost/Hr ($A)
LUTA Project (Original)	696000	20	200	8.4	329
LUTA Project (Revised)	641500	20	200	8	312
B-N Islander	232000	9	139	9.5	116
B-N Trislander	402700	17	156	8.9	212
Cessna 402B	239000	9	187	8	134
DHC-6 Twin Otter	798000	20	177	9	333
GAF Nomad N24	535000	15	173	8.2	194
Saunders ST-27	737000	22	200	8.3	355
Saunders ST-28	944000	22	200	9.6	412
Short Skyvan	1042000	22	173	11.9	445
Short SD3-30	1481200	30	195	8.8	505

be equalled by the Cessna 402B. This, however, could only carry nine passengers, less than half of that intended for the LUTA.

Cost analysis Report AA338 carried out in December 1975 analysed at least four differing payload / weight combinations of the LUTA. The cost data for only two of the layouts is shown, the original and the preferred model (Table 2).

By increasing the passenger number to 21, an unrivalled competitive cost / seat mile figure of 7.6 cents could be expected. Total capital cost / passenger seat mile came out at $32,050, close to the desired objective of $30,000. All operating costs were based on a load factor of 100% for all examples tested in order to establish a common base comparison. With actual operations it was unlikely that the average load factor for any competitive aircraft would exceed 60%.

Aircraft Description

Overall, the design was to be as simple and easy to manufacture as was possible. The wing of the LUTA was to be a larger span version of the LMS wing retaining the same section, planform, spoiler ailerons and feeler ailerons offering a maximum span of wing trailing edge flaps. Power was to be provided by four 300 hp Continental TSIO-520 piston engines. The 'off-the shelf' levered suspension landing gear retracted into outrigger fairings on the sides of a simple box section, straight sided fuselage. Twin outward canted fins positioned on the extremities of the rear fuselage sides were intended to give improved yaw control over the broad rear fuselage.

The cabin, unobstructed by wing or undercarriage structures was to be 20.5 feet long, 66 inches wide and 72 inches high. Passenger seating was a 2-1 arrangement with provision for a toilet, coat storage and baggage space at the rear of the cabin above the integrally hinged

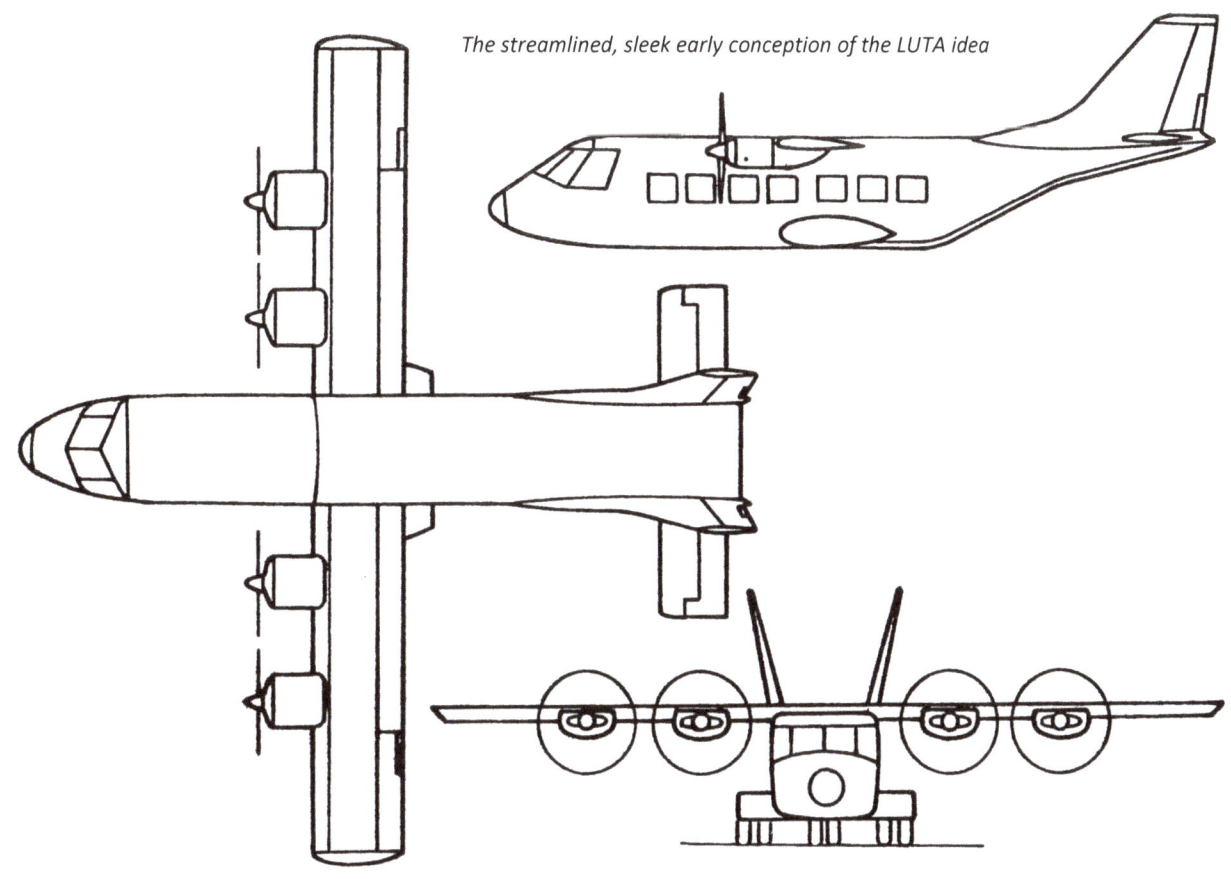

The streamlined, sleek early conception of the LUTA idea

Table 2: Cost Summary	LUTA Project (Original $)	LUTA Project (Revised $)
Number of passengers	20	20
Airframe cost	500000	450000
Total basic aircraft cost	554000	505000
Spares cost	86000	81500
Avionics	55000	54500
Total capital cost	696000	641000
Total cost/hour	329	312
Cost/seat hour	16.5	15.6
Capital cost/seat	34800	32050
Airframe cost/seat	25000	22500
Cost/seat mile (20 pax)	8.4 cents	8.0 cents
Cost/seat mile (21 pax)	8.0 cents	7.6 cents

Specifications	Light Utility Transport Aircraft (LUTA)	
Powerplant	Four Teledyne Continental TSIO-520 E/600 piston engines of 300 hp at 2,700 rpm, driving 3 bladed CS propellers of 6 ft 4.5 ins diameter	
Performance	Max speed at SL	200 kts
	Cruise speed on 75% power at 10,000 ft	210 kts
	Rate of climb at SL	1,600 ft/min
	IFR range with standard reserves	350 nm
Weights	Basic empty	7,100 lb
	TO	12,500 lb
	Total useful load	5,400 lb
	Payload capacity	4,200 lb
	Internal fuel capacity	2,400 lb
	Wing loading	40.5 lb/sq ft
	Power loading	10.4 lb/hp
Dimensions	Wing span	51.5 ft
	Wing area	310 sq ft
	Length	47 ft
	Height	16 ft

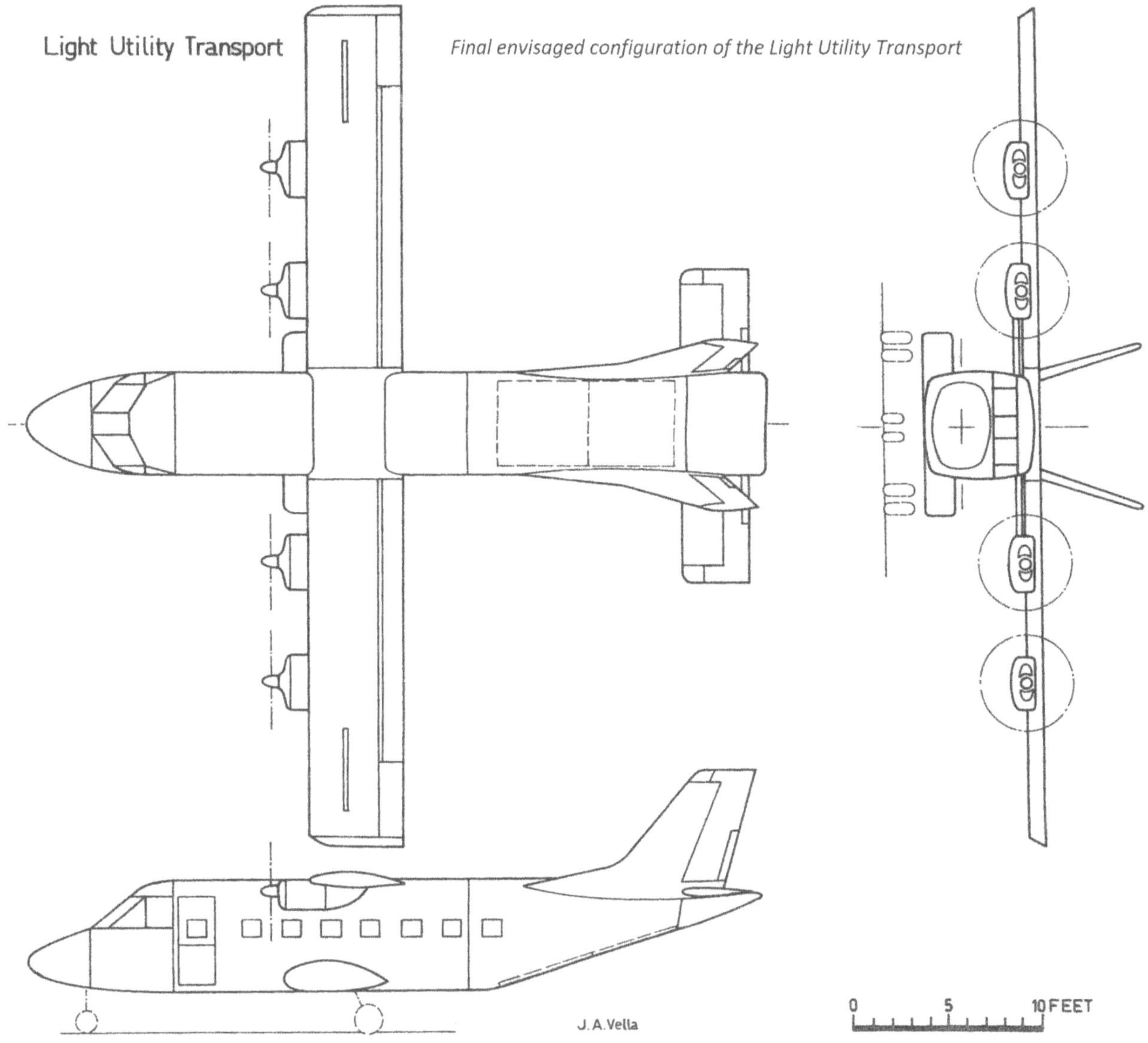

Final envisaged configuration of the Light Utility Transport

J.A.Vella

rear loading ramp. This ramp was to allow maximum versatility for the utility / freight or military applications. The forward port side door with integral steps led to the cockpit and passenger cabin.

At the conclusion of the study on April 9, 1976 the launch cost for prototype construction and development over an elapsed 30 to 36 month period was estimated at $4M to $5M assuming that the LMS had been certificated. 100 to 150 ULTAs could have been delivered over five years.

Bibliography: Light Utility Transport

Watkins, W. (February 1976). Engineering Report AA338. Operating Costs, Light Transport Aircraft. Commonwealth Aircraft Corporation.

Watkins, W. (April 9, 1976). Engineering Report AA341. Light Transport Aircraft, Preliminary Study. Commonwealth Aircraft Corporation.

C-130 'TUBBY' HERCULES TRANSPORT
October 1976

The Tactical Transport Aircraft (TTA) Industry Feasibility Study organised by the Federal Government in 1976 left CAC with no identifiable specialist involvement. GAF and HDH had each received a $25,000 funding package to specifically collate performance data and provide a market assessment. CAC was allocated a similar funding but for a subsidiary support role by Walter Watkins to GAF.

This study was intended to provide background data and information of existing aircraft variants or proposals that would by 1984, satisfy the RAAF Air Staff Target AST 120/84 to replace their versatile DHC-4 Caribou STOL transport aircraft.

The lack of specialist involvement for CAC caused concern for the company as it would set a precedent to their disadvantage when other future feasibility studies were to be offered. It would deny them vital leadership experience, upgrading of its expertise and possibly reduce their commercial status for future negotiations and participation with this and similar collaborative programs.

Partly to minimize this situation and to capitalize on the impending withdrawal from service (in 1978) of the RAAF fleet of its twelve C-130A Hercules transports, CAC's Aircraft Design Study Group put out its own proposal in October 1976 to use these, soon to be redundant aircraft as a possible TTA contender. Adopting Lockheed's style of 'stretch/shrink' design development process would bring these C-130A airframes closer to the AST 120/84 requirements. This was during the time when the company was intensely involved in worldwide investigations for commercial diversification opportunities to broaden its operational and financial base. This diversification initiative was made known to Lockheed Aircraft Corp and their interest, approval and possible collaborative support was essential if the '*Tubby*' C-130A proposal was to proceed beyond the preliminary paper stage. The expected advantages in converting the forthcoming C-130A airframes was in providing a lower cost development of a proven aircraft and a commonality of aircraft spares and ground handling and cargo restraint equipment with the RAAF's other C-130E Hercules fleet. No mention was made of the structural integrity or the available operating life left on the airframes.

In October 1975, twelve months prior to CAC's conceptual ideas, Lockheed Georgia Corp publicized its forthcoming new design, a twin engine derivative of the C-130 and proposed this to the Government's TTA study. CAC, fully aware of the L-400 configuration took a different economical approach. It planned making use of the C-130A's outer wings, fuel system, engine installation and reducing the centre section span to the width of the fuselage deleting two of the engines resulting in an overall span of 100 feet. The fuselage would be reduced by 7 feet ahead of the wing and by 4.5 feet aft, eliminating the paratrooper exit doors. These structural alterations together with equipment changes would have resulted in a take-off weight of 74,000 lbs, almost half the 155,000 lbs for the C-130E Hercules, a bigger payload than the AST 120/84 requirements but at a lower cost than for the new and smaller DHC-5 Buffalo turboshaft powered tactical transport seen as the family successor to the radial engined DHC-4 Caribou. The RAAF found the DHC-5 lacking.

As early as April 2, 1968, seeking to fill this specialised role, Canadian Air Force CV-7A/DHC-5 Buffalo, registered CF-LAQ, was flown from Essendon Airport and impressively demonstrated from a prepared rough muddy field, adjacent to the Bacchus Marsh airfield landing strip, displaying (empty) its very steep STOL handling characteristics in wet and gusty conditions. (The author experienced the unsettling transit flight which nevertheless was far more stable than previous flights on the much slower Caribou in better weather conditions).

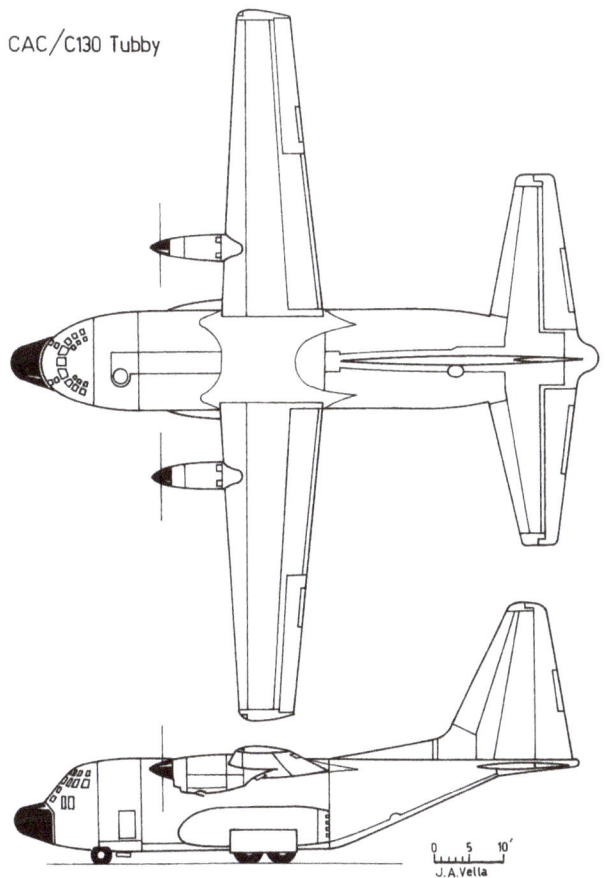

CAC/C130 Tubby

Lockheed Hercules C-130A. A97-205 & A97-206 of 36 Sqdn RAAF Richmond. April 04, 1976. **J. A. Vella**

CAC's C-130A *Tubby* proposal was officially conveyed to Lockheed in December 1976. Their response of February 1977 did not agree with CAC's entire expectations. Lockheed advised they had considered the kind of C-130 version presented by CAC with their own conceptual studies leading up to their L-400, including a shortened fuselage variant. They preferred the retention of the paratrooper exit side doors and suggested adverse stability and control problems might arise as a result of the shortened fuselage.

It was also Lockheed's opinion that fuel weights being about equal for the short or long fuselage C-130 for a given payload and range, the weight penalty of 2,500 lbs for the longer L-400 fuselage was not significant when compared with the greater loading versatility for the L-400 design and the expectation of greater commercial applications. Table 1 provides a three-way Lockheed Hercules comparison.

The CAC investigation was not an in-depth study but an initiative to seek interest and future work. It needed Lockheed's support for its success. As this was not forthcoming the idea was abandoned.

Table 1: C-130 Hercules Variants Comparison			
	Lockheed C-130E	CAC/C130A 'Tubby'	Lockheed L-400
Wing span (ft)	132	100	109.5
Wing area (sq ft)	1745	1360	1470
Length (ft)	120	86.5	97.8
Cargo cabin length (ft)	41.3	30	41.3
Engine TO power (hp)	18000	9000	9300
Weight engines (lb)	16654	8190	8400
Weight equipment (lb)	13608	8000	N/A
Weight empty (lb)	69180	47480	53800
Weight max TO	155000	74000	84000

Lockheed L-400 Background

Proposed to fly in the northern Spring of 1982 the L-400 was to retain the standard fuselage of the four engine Hercules; the front wheel from each of the two wheel tandem bogies was to be deleted together with a 22.5 foot reduction in span, creating a new centre section but retaining the outer wing sections from the standard C-130 and adding new parallel chord 4.5 foot long wing tip extensions and upgrading with two Allison 501-D22F turboshaft 4,910 eshp engines and 14 foot diameter propellers. Development had been underway for about nine months before positive sales prospects declined and the program was closed down.

Bibliography: C-130 'Tubby' Hercules

Air International. (October 1975, April 1977, March 1980, November 1980). Key Publishing, Lincs, UK.

Commonwealth Aircraft Corporation. (Undated). In-House Memoranda & Discussion Notes.

Flight International. (February 1969): ILLIFE Transport Publications, UK.

CHAPTER 10.   ADVANCED AND BASIC TRAINER AIRCRAFT CONCEPTS – A LAST FLING

CA-X UNIVERSAL LIGHTWEIGHT TRAINER 1976 - 1977

The aviation industry expected there would be a call to replace the CA-30 Macchi MB326H trainer in the same time frame as the RAAF was acquiring its New Tactical Fighter to replace the Mirage IIIO. It was known the New Tactical Fighter would be an aircraft of significantly advanced technology and operational capability as compared to the Mirage, so it was considered that a Macchi trainer replacement should or would reflect a similar forward advance in training capability.

These studies, begun in 1976, and proposed by Jim Caterson, Senior Engineer Flight Technology (successor to Charles Reid) in August 1977 indicated that the use of new aerodynamics, technology, a turbofan engine and lightweight structures could be combined to achieve this greater trainer performance capability.

Dubbed the Universal Lightweight Trainer (ULWT), this concept was thought to have more relevance as to what kind of aircraft could meet the future needs of the RAAF rather than the crop of available trainers which were considered at the time of their inception to be logical developments of the aircraft they were intended to replace.

The RAAF pilot training syllabus (as at 1977) lacked a dedicated advanced trainer beyond the MB326H stage. This was a measure of economic necessity based on a likely very small number of aircraft needed for the advanced training role. The basic training spectrum was 60 hours flown in the CT4A Airtrainer and 150 hours on the turbojet powered CA-30 / MB326H. With the technology that could be incorporated into the new trainer it seemed feasible that the 'Universal Trainer' would reduce the role of the CT4A or its equivalent to a 'screening' aeroplane to help in the early filtering of unsuitable pilot candidates. But the inherent built-in versatility of the ULWT would enable it as a single type with different developments of a chosen engine or a different engine, to be quite capable of performing the roles of:

- Primary training
- Basic training
- Advanced training
- Continuation training

The cost of any aeroplane but especially that of military aircraft with a high density structure is in direct proportion to its total weight. Two basic ways of improving the military aircraft cost/weight factor was to lower structure and fuel weights. Selecting a turbofan engine would result in a lesser fuel demand and a lower fuel weight which gave scope for a reduction in structure weight eg for a similar or better performance to the MB326H with its BS Viper 22-11 engine and a take-off weight of 8,530 lb. The ULWT was expected to have a take-off weight of only 4,500 lb.

The use of a turbofan engine leads to a lesser fuel load and the dynamic performance of the airframe is enhanced through an improved thrust-to-weight ratio eg an increase climb rate capability could be utilized to repeat training manoeuvres more often during a single mission. As it was not envisaged the RAAF would seek a supersonic training capability the early dynamics of this design were MB326H related and geometrically similar to it ie the same approximate wing and tail assembly and leading edge sweepback.

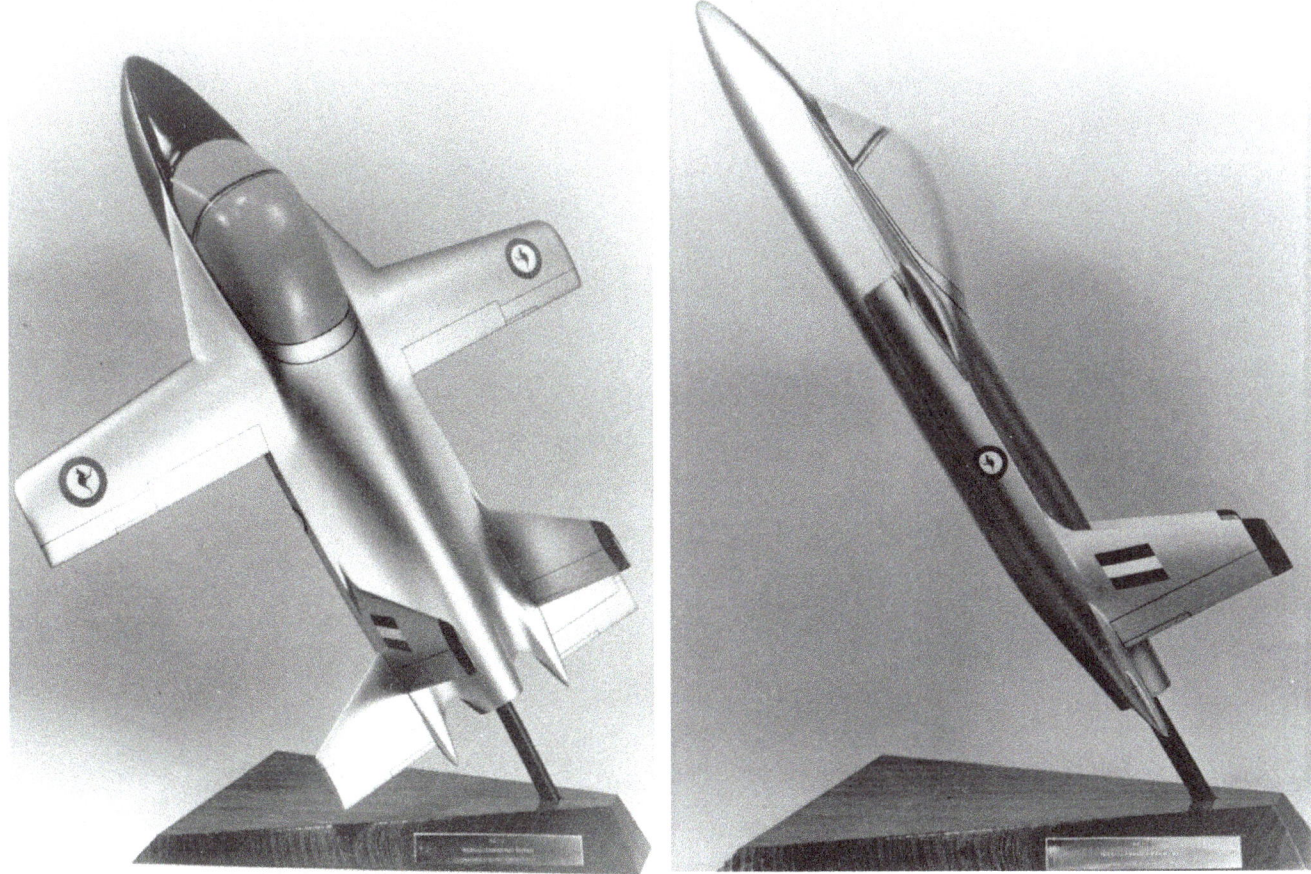

*The CA-X Universal Lightweight Trainer ULWT with its capacious engine space & the similarity to the Macchi MB326H aerodynamic flying surfaces. Credit both photographs **Walter Watkins**.*

This also applied to the company stablemate of the ULWT, the Light Weight Trainer (LWT).

Aircraft Description

The preferred engine was a P & W (Canada) JT15D-5 turbofan, supported not by an enclosed load structure but located between the main rear fuselage load-carrying beams behind simple lateral air intake ducts (with lips of large radii to prevent duct airflow separation) which passed beneath the wing structure. The load carrying beams thus formed a twin boom layout of box spars attached to the main wing spar forming the structural load element of the ULWT. The large space available between the lateral boom spars made it possible to fit bigger or different engines without structural change. The 'twin boom' spars were enclosed by 'D' shaped exterior skin panels blended into the non-structural skin above and below the engine. Space within the booms housed the main undercarriage units, the doors of which deployed independently of the undercarriage sequence to act as airbrakes.

Wing leading edge strakes extended the fuselage/wing blended concept further, providing a lift vortex which helped to delay the wing stall at high incidence. A supercritical wing section was selected combined with a geometry based on approximately the same as that of the MB326H. Likewise the tail surface shapes were MB326H related but with twin fins positioned on the extreme ends of the structure booms to overcome directional instability which was

Specifications	CA-X Universal Lightweight Trainer (ULWT) Comparison		
Powerplant	1. CA-X ULWT: Pratt & Whitney (Canada) JT15D-5 turbofan of 2,600 lb thrust 2. CA-30 MB326H: Bristol Siddeley Viper 22-11 turbojet of 2,500 lb thrust		
Performance		ULWT	CA-30 MB326H
	Max speed at SL (Mach No/kts)	M 0.57/376	M 0.57/376
	Max speed at 30,000 ft (Mach No/kts)	M 0.75/442	M 0.70/412
	Time to 30,000 ft	6.5 mins	18.5 mins
	Speed for max climb angle	9 kts	145 kts
	Max climb rate	6,532 ft/min	2,940 ft/min
	Max climb rate angle /ratio (deg / ft/min)	23.4°/3,660	9.2°/2,382
	Stalling speed	90 kts	95 kts
	Service ceiling (60% fuel remaining)	47,800 ft	37,000 ft
	Fuel to reach 30,000 ft	250 lb	700 lb
Weights	Max TO	4,500 lb	8,711 lb
Dimensions	ULWT not available CA-30 MB326H as per type		

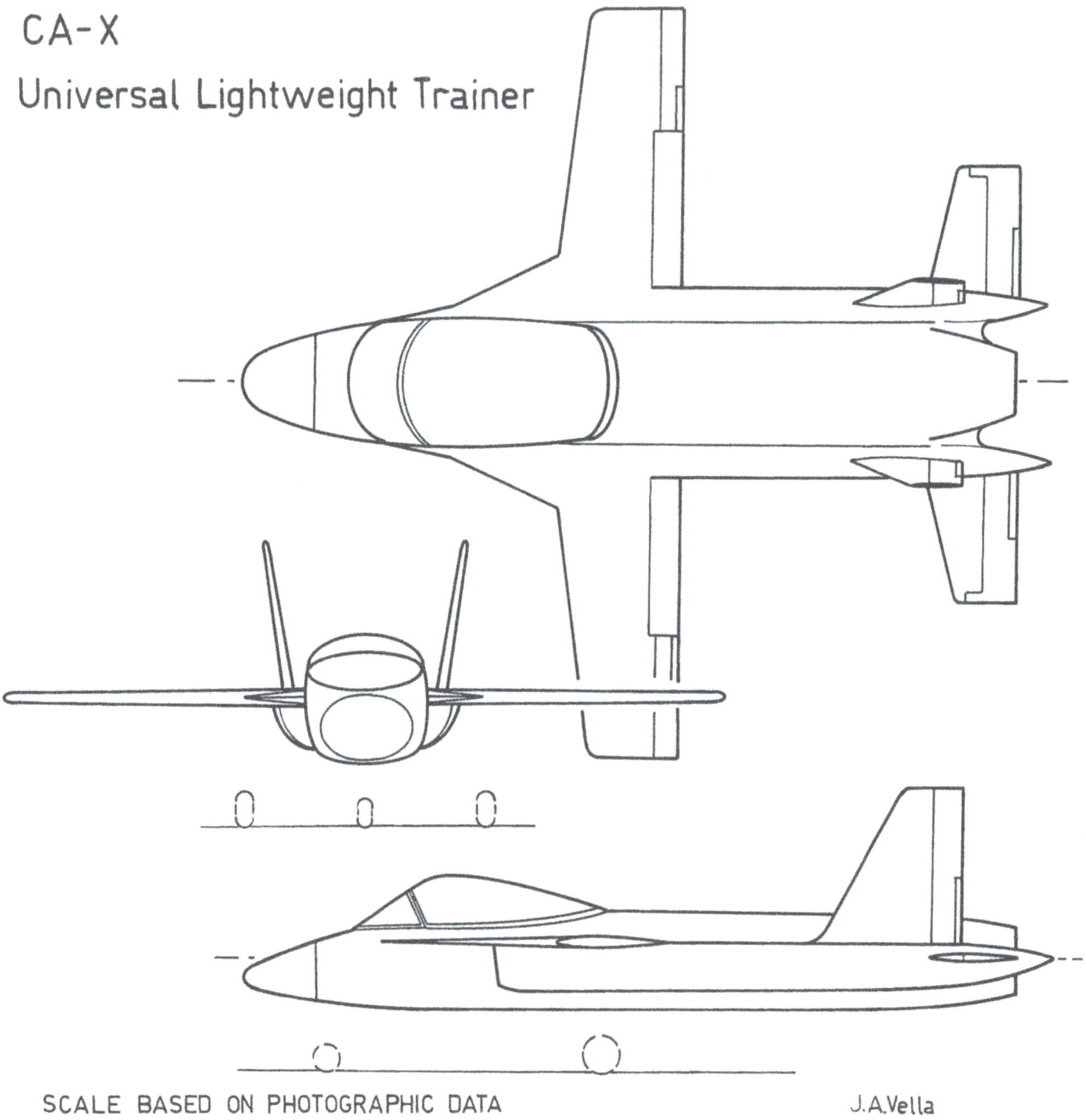

CA-X
Universal Lightweight Trainer

SCALE BASED ON PHOTOGRAPHIC DATA J.A.Vella

sometimes encountered at high angles of attack on aircraft with a wing-body blended design and a single fin. Fuel was housed in the mid-fuselage and wing centre section. Side by side cockpit seating was the most practical means of training in a multi-type training fleet with its improved cockpit communications, identical cockpit forward vision for both occupants especially during continuation training, a minimum of duplication of instruments, displays, avionics controllers etc and improved sortie efficiency.

The significant feature of the ULWT was its potential low fuel consumption and high performance relative to the CA-30 as shown in the Specification CA-X ULWT Comparison table.

The ULWT created a lot of interest within the RAAF Technical Branch and the Parliamentary Defence Committee but it was not taken further due in part to the large financial outlay/overrun on the acquisition of the F/A-18 Hornet fighter and supporting infrastructure. A scale model of the ULWT was displayed at the 1979 Paris Air Show.

(Because of commercial restrictions on releasable dimensional data, the accompanying drawing is scaled from photographs of the display model based on the given cabin exterior width of 50 inches.)

Bibliography: CA-X Universal Lightweight Trainer

Caterson, J. (1986). [Interview].

Ring, I.H. (1981) 'Opportunity of the Century - CAC's Advanced Trainer Projects'. *Aircraft* (March 1981).

Light Weight Jet Trainer

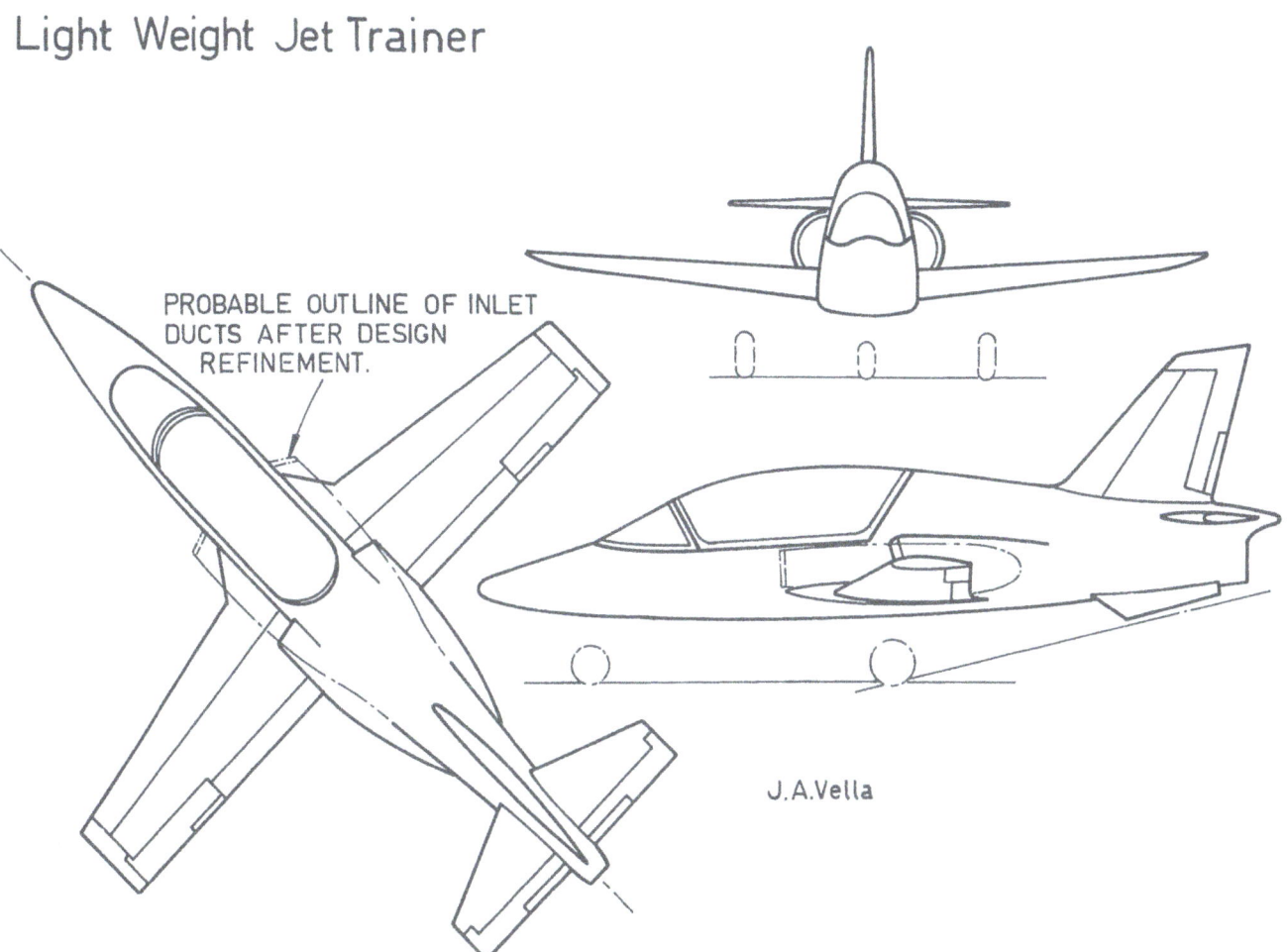

J.A.Vella

LIGHT WEIGHT JET TRAINER
May 1977

On April 4, 1977, the Cessna Aircraft Company gave a presentation at CAC of their plans to re-engine their established and long serving T-37B Tweet jet trainer to compete for the USAF's Next Generation Trainer requirement. This upgraded aircraft, the TFT-37 was to be powered by two of the new proposed 1,250 lb thrust Garrett AiResearch TFE-311 turbofan engines.

Bill Patterson, a Vice-President of Garrett AiResearch also took up the proposal with enthusiasm. He visited and suggested that CAC could contribute by developing the design of the fan for this new engine, a task which Bill Patterson considered to be well within CAC's capability. This proposal needed the USAF to be the launch customer for the re-engineing of the T-37B. In the engine development and initial production program of US$25M, CAC's participating share was put at approximately A$4M. Instead, the USAF selected the new design Fairchild Republic T-46. It flew, was cancelled in 1986 and then replaced by the Beechcraft T-6A Texan II based on the much modified Pilatus PC-9 as the new USAF trainer aircraft.

Whilst these outcomes in the United States were still sometime in the future, an alternative proposal for the use of the new engine was put forward by Lee Archer (CAC Manager, SE Asia Region) who foresaw an opportunity for an ailing CAC which was without a self-generated aircraft project to develop a new fuel efficient jet trainer around the TFE-311 turbofan engine. When the earlier CAC proposal for the joint development of the Light Military Support (LMS) was turned down by the Singapore Minister for Science and Technology, it was indicated there was still interest in collaborative ventures especially if they were for the development of a more sophisticated aircraft. The impetus for formulating the light jet trainer idea was to regain Singapore's interest and to capitalize on the forecast downturn of the availability of fuel in the 1980's, coupled with its predicated higher cost in five years' time.

This avenue presented a potentially low development and procurement cost and a vast reduction in fuel consumption using a turbofan engine. The market for the lower priced jet trainer was, subject to future analysis, optimistically put at 600 units and considered to be especially attractive as the existing major aircraft manufacturers were then committed to the development and production programs over the next 10 years for larger and more costly training/support aircraft such as the HS Hawk; Dornier Alpha Jet, Breguet/Dassault/BAC Jaguar, CASA 101 etc.

The Light Weight Trainer (LWT) project became the work of Project Support Engineer Wal Watkins, a long-time proponent for the less sophisticated, less costly aircraft packages within the capability of CAC. It was aimed at the basic and continuation end of the training spectrum with a thrust/weight ratio, wing loading and span loading chosen to provide similar performance and handling characteristics to the CA-30/MB326H but at an AUW of 3,600 lb, approximately half that of the MB326H. Maximum wing span was set at 24 feet with a wing area of 100 sq ft. Development to construct five prototype airframes was expected to be about A$20M with a unit production cost of $555,000 at 1977 prices in a production run of 200 aircraft. It was estimated there would a saving of some 55 million gallons in fuel for a fleet of 100 aircraft with a 5,000 hour operating life cycle spanning 12 to 15 years as compared with a similar fleet of MB326H. The LWT ran in parallel to but separate from the ULWT the other CAC concept for a fuel efficient trainer.

With the RAAF moving at a glacial pace to select an MB326H replacement to accompany the move into their new fourth generation fighter combat aircraft, the LWT figures were seen as a

Life Cycle Cost Comparison for 100 Aircraft
(Based on a Fuel Cost of 45 cents/gall)

	A$ Million (1977 Values)		
	CA-30 (Update)	MB326H (New)	LWT
Procurement cost ($M)	60	130	80
Fuel costs -5,000 hours ($M)	33.8	33.8	9
Total life cycle costs ($M)	93.8	163.8	89
Fuel used in 5,000 hours (M gall)	75	75	20
Fuel quantity saved (M gall)			55
Fuel costs ($M)	4.8	74.8	

smart approach in the direction of operating economics. (The RAAF selected the BAE Systems (HS) Hawk in 1997.)

Potential Savings: If the fuel price rose to 76 cents /gall due to the adoption of the World Parity ratio (as happened in 1985), the savings were expected to be:

LWT versus CA-30 Update $21.9M
LWT versus CA-30 New $91.9M

However the Singapore Government was not going to be rushed into a joint development. The Australian Department of Defence was uncommitted and did not encourage interest. The company came to the conclusion that by the time the fledgling Singapore aviation industry had been taught how to approach the design and manufacture of the aircraft, if that was their intention (as had been suggested and proposed with the earlier LMS project) then, well-established other manufacturers, recognising the demand could have taken up the concept and beaten CAC to that market. CAC was not going it alone.

The LWT was earlier in concept from its likely direct equivalent, the SIAI Marchetti S211, first flown in 1981 and described as the world's first true very light (4,070 lb) weight jet, which (ironically) was subsequently selected, co-developed and operated by the Republic of Singapore Air Force. From 1984 the RSAF acquired 32 examples of which 24 were assembled locally. Only about 60 examples were built in contrast to the optimistic 600 aircraft suggested for this class.

The main feature of the whole CAC proposal was its delightful simplicity, not just in the design sense but in the logical opportunity that it presented to an ailing aviation company to recover its standing in a world market by participating for the first time in jet engine design and development with an established engine manufacturer. The market potential was considered (though not established) to be the best of any peacetime aircraft project proposed by CAC.

Specifications	Light Weight Jet Trainer (LWT)	
Powerplant	One Garrett TFE-331 turbofan rated at 1,250 lb thrust at SL	
Performance	Not available	
Weights	TO	3,600 to 4,200 lb
Dimensions	(Dimensions are initial approximations)	
	Span	24 ft
	Wing area	100 sq ft
	Length	28 ft

Bibliography: Light Weight Jet Trainer

Commonwealth Aircraft Corporation (April 1977).[Minutes of CAC Board Meeting].

Dalziel, J. (1987). CAC General Manager. [Correspondence].

Ring I.H. (1981) 'Opportunity of the Century - CAC's Advanced Trainer Projects'. *Aircraft.* (March 1981).

Watkins, W. (May 1977). Engineering Report AA359. Preliminary Proposal for Light-Weight Jet Trainer. Commonwealth Aircraft Corporation.

CAC / SHORT BROS LTD SD3-MR SEEKER
March 1978

In December 1977 the Government Aircraft Factory announced its intention to release the Nomad Searchmaster 'L' coastal surveillance model fitted with a 360° search radar.

This development would contribute to further employment and extension of Nomad production work. It was also publicly stated (Melbourne Herald, February 28, 1978) by Defence Minister, James Killen that the planned coastal surveillance of the Exclusive Economic Zone (EEZ) would not be a permanent role of the front line squadrons of the RAAF. The P-3 Orion was costing a very high $2,400 per hour to operate on the watch of 12,500 miles of coastline to the 12 mile off shore limit. To patrol to the proposed extension of the new 200 mile EEZ limit was to massively escalate operating costs.

Sometime in 1976, Short Bros Ltd of Northern Ireland proposed the SD3-MR Seeker, a maritime patrol variant of their SD3-30 commuter aircraft. Sensing that the Australian Government would be close to requesting new equipment for coastal surveillance and not wishing to leave the market to the GAF Searchmaster, Short Bros made a formal co-operative approach with the SD3-MR Seeker to CAC on February 10, 1978 one month before the Searchmaster 'L' commenced flying. In response Chief Engineer John Kentwell, requested an evaluation by Jim Caterson and Wal Watkins.

The Seeker had a crew of four, a 360° vision search radar, an additional fuselage flexible fuel tank for 450 gallons, observation bubble windows and a capacious fuselage with a rear loading ramp for aerial dropping of life rafts etc. CAC was offered the role of outfitting the aircraft to surveillance standard. The company's first response was an evaluation of the Seeker in relation to the Fokker F27M Maritime, the GAF Searchmaster 'L' and five other possible types. The final detailed examination was held between the Seeker, the Searchmaster 'L', the F27M and with the Cessna Citation III as a late unlikely contender from CAC's Rex Aviation subsidiary business. The best economic operating altitude for the Citation was 30,000 ft which put it out of practical consideration. Jim Caterson and Wal Watkins working without an official Air Staff Requirement, nor aware of the intensity or scope of the expected patrols took into consideration generally available data to generate a number of possible flight profiles.

The most effective mission profile was to fly a 50 nm track from shore, the other a 150 nm flight out to near the EEZ limit twice daily. This operation flown at 2,000 feet altitude by three most appropriate aircraft would have resulted in:

Aircraft	Total Annual Operating Cost (A$ Millions)	Average Cost per sq mile scanned
36 Searchmasters	$20.47M	S8.53
20 Seekers	$16.73M	$6.97
20 F27M Maritime	$28.26M	$11.78

This did not allow for the occasions when an aircraft was required to remain on station or for any eastern, southern or Tasmanian coastal flight areas. Fewer aircraft were required to fly daily single pass radar surveillance flights. The Seeker was considered to be a valid contender for Australian coastal patrol operations within the EEZ and was more cost effective than either the GAF Searchmaster 'L' or F27M. Compared with the Searchmaster 'L', the Seeker had greater range, endurance and equipment potential. Its larger cabin size and volume would provide a greater equipment variation and

The civilian airliner version of the Short Brothers SD330.
Roger McDonald Collection

better crew comfort, which would have been further improved by the higher wing loading, suggesting more comfortable ride qualities.

The SD3-MR could match the F27M in range and endurance but had less potential for future equipment growth. It lacked pressurisation whilst its procurement and direct operating costs were considerably less. In addition its crew requirement was least, measured against the distance surveyed. Including costs for government furnished equipment, the indicated selling price for the Seeker was between $2.5M to $2.7M. The comparative aircraft unit cost including spares holding and all equipment for coastal surveillance was:

GAF Searchmaster 'L'	$1.25M
Shorts SD3 MR Seeker	$3.2M
Fokker F27M Maritime	$6.0M

On productivity, number of aircraft and search area costs, the Short Bros Seeker was the most economical choice. CAC was willing to advance the proposal further but the Maritime Border Command made use of the RAN's Grumman S-2G Tracker aircraft (prior to their retirement) and the RAAF's P-3 Orion, both severely handicapped by lack of Service funds for flying time and also affecting the amount of fuel available for normal Service training activities. Border Command then moved into an evolving two tier structure of mainly pressurised, chartered, civilian operated aircraft.

Bibliography:CAC/Short Bros Ltd SD3 MR Seeker
Aircraft- May 1978
Watkins, W. (March 6, 1978). 'Short Seeker' for Australian Coastal Surveillance, Preliminary Assessment. Commonwealth Aircraft Corporation.

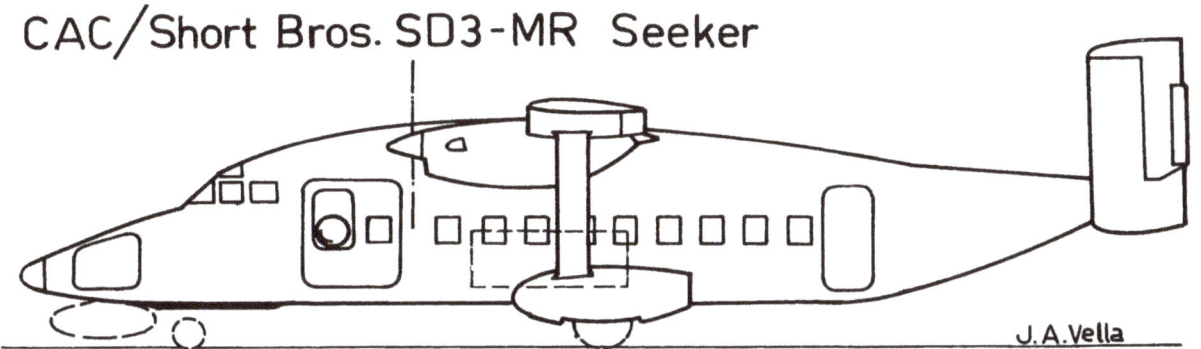

WINJEEL TRAINER – NEW PISTON ENGINE
September 1978

A preliminary unsolicited Company report generated in September 1978 outlined some options for replacing the P & W R985 Wasp Junior 450 hp radial engine in the CA-25 Winjeel Basic Trainer by a general aviation piston engine of a similar rating. For twelve months CAC had anticipated a RAAF request to build a new batch of fifty airframes or implement a re-engineing program with the added benefits of reduced noise and a smaller multi-bladed propeller.

Aircraft Comparison

The primary engine under consideration was the 435 hp Teledyne-Continental GTSIO-520K geared, turbo supercharged, flat six with a 96 inch diameter propeller. With cleaner, flatter cowl lines, the forward flight vision space would have been improved from the 9° of the radial engine to about 15°. Other selections were the 425 hp Lycoming TIGO-541K and two US production auto engines fitted to sport aircraft-the Geschwender 400 (Ford V8) of 400 hp and the 475 hp Stage 2 Development Corp V8450A. Both were fully capable of aerobatic manoeuvres.

	Aircraft Comparison		
Unit	P & W R985 Wasp Junior 450 hp	Teledyne Continental GTSIO-520K 435 hp	Change %
Weight empty (lb)	3400	3300	
Weight TO (lb)	4360	4260	
Max speed at SL (kts)	160	168	5
Max speed at 15,000 ft (kts)	158	192	21.5
Climb rate at 15,000 ft (ft/min)	500	1400	180
Time to 15,000 ft (mins)	17	10	-41

Bibliography: Winjeel Trainer New Piston Engine
Watkins, W. (September 5, 1978). Engineering Report AA390. Winjeel, New Engine Installation. Commonwealth Aircraft Corporation.

WINJEEL TRAINER – TURBOPROP ENGINE
APRIL 1979

In 1979 the RAAF made an informal request of CAC to ascertain the costs of a production run of new Winjeel airframes fitted with a turboprop engine and making use of existing Winjeel tooling.

With the P & W R985 Wasp Junior radial engine of the in-service Winjeel aircraft no longer in production, there was concern in the Air Force Engineering Branch on the future availability of spare parts support. Report AA407 of April 30, 1979 outlined the scope of installing a P & W (Canada) PT6A-25 turboprop engine de-rated to 410 hp to a production run of 100 airframes.

Compared with the 685 lb weight of the Wasp Junior, the PT6 weighed a mere 335 lb. There had to be a forward re-positioning of radio and electrical items to the front of the aircraft to compensate for this lower weight. A 90 inch diameter three bladed propeller would have been located 18 to 20 inches ahead of its original position. The alternate Allison 250-E17 turboprop was not favoured as its extreme lightness would have required a substantial lengthening to the front of the aircraft. The notional production run of 100 new Winjeel airframes would have entailed 1.8 million hours of work and cost about $40.5M following a development phase of $954,000.

	Aircraft Comparison		
Unit	P & W R985 Wasp Junior 450 hp	P & W PT6A-25 Torque limited to 410 shp	Change %
Weight empty (lb)	3400	2920	
Weight TO (lb)	4360	3970	
Max speed at SL (kts)	160	166	3.4
Max speed at 15,000 ft (kts)	158	195	23.4
Climb rate at SL (ft/min)	1235	1420	15
Climb rate at 15,000 ft (ft/min)	530	1595	191
Time to 15,000 ft (mins)	16.4	10.1	-38.4

Bibliography: Winjeel Trainer Turboprop Engine
Watkins, W. (April 30, 1979) . Engineering Report AA407. Winjeel, PT6A Installation. Commonwealth Aircraft Corporation.

AAC/CA-34 WAMIRA BASIC PILOT TRAINER AIRCRAFT
July 1979

The new Basic Pilot trainer aircraft was to be built to replace the RAAF's fleet of CT-4A Airtrainers. Air Force Staff Target AFST 5044 was raised in October 1978. It set out to establish a design criteria to build a more structurally sound and reliable trainer (the only such in the world) to expensive Military Specifications criteria, believing this approach would also attract overseas interest and sales.

Design Expectations

The RAAF requested 65 (later increased to 69) aircraft to be delivered from mid-1986 when the 'Life of Type' of the existing CT-4A Airtrainers was expected to be reached, (an unproven and untested expectation) which subsequent fatigue testing proved pessimistic. The Air Force demanded an exacting design where some of its expectations included:

- A trainer aircraft that would allow ab-initio training of students with no-prior flying experience and used for 50% or for the first 100 hours of pilot training time (whereas flying time on the CT4 was limited to the first 60 hours).
- Design & certification to MILSPECS for high performance, long service life and rapid line maintenance
- A project to equip the Australian aerospace industry with advanced design capability.
- Offer prospects to overseas orders to defray design and development costs.

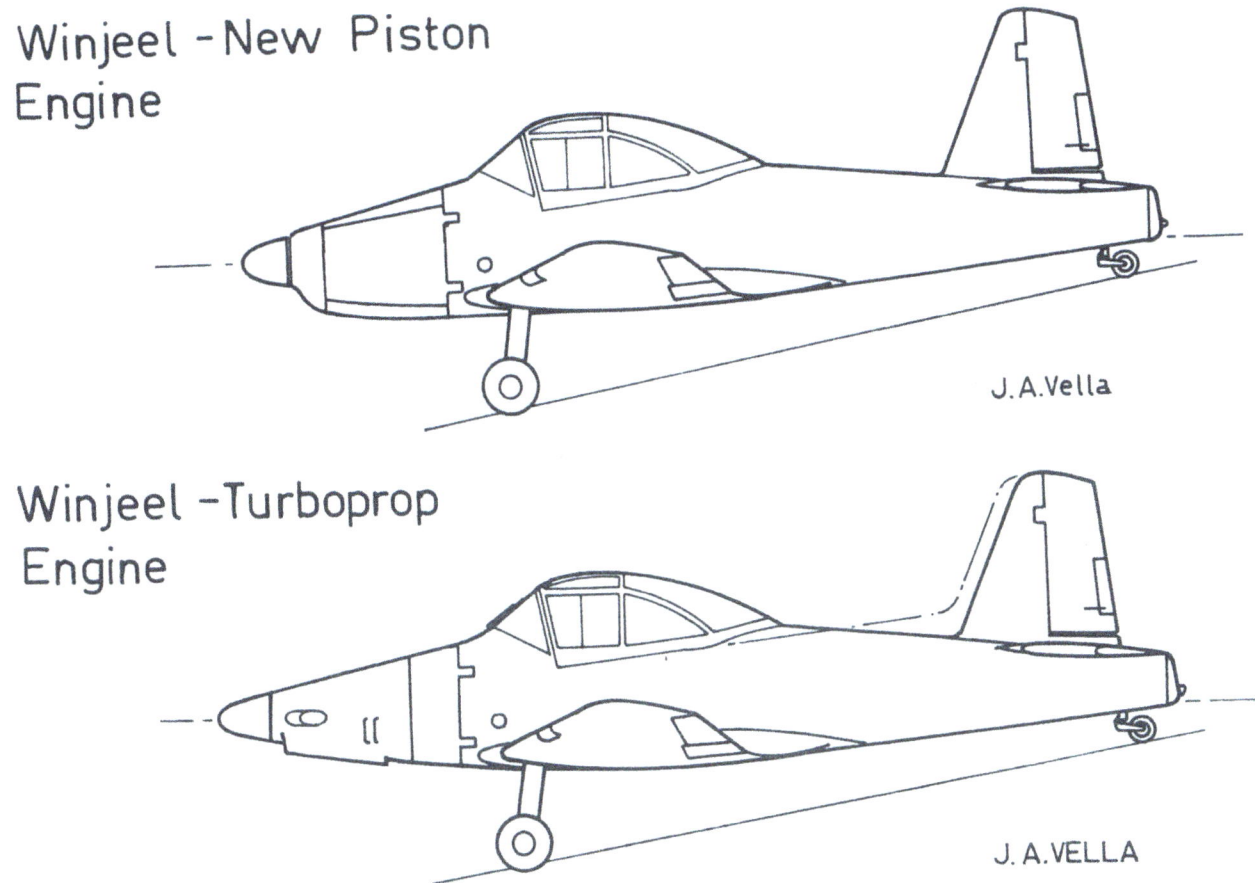

- To carry out comprehensive aerobatic sequences at or above 10,000 feet in a tropical environment including sustaining 2.5g turns in these conditions.
- Two back-to-back sorties with a total endurance of 3 hours with 50 minutes reserve.
- A maximum endurance of 5 hours on internal fuel.
- A minimum structure life of 20 years and 8,000 flying hours.
- 2,000 feet / min initial rate of climb.
- A structural design based on flight load limits of +7.0g & -3.5g at max. training mission weight of 4,410 lb but up to 5,730 lbs for alternate roles.
- Nose wheel steering through the rudder pedals.
- Soft field operation and 13 ft / sec vertical landing velocity.
- A side-by-side cockpit arrangement with provision for two other passengers in removable seats.
- Target of 2 maintenance man-hours/flight hour; high reliability system LRUs.
- A non-pressurised cabin with dilute/demand oxygen capacity up to 25,000 feet.
- An Environmental Control System that would produce comfortable cockpit conditions of between 20-27° C within 5 minutes of start-up following a pre-flight soak of up to 4 hours with the canopy open in a temperature of 45°C.
- Constructing two prototype aircraft, one fatigue airframe and one equivalent static test airframe. The second prototype to be the RAAF production evaluation aircraft and both prototypes to eventually join the service fleet.
- An aircraft with an expandable role capability such as FAC (not specified as part of the AAC spec).

Feasibility Study & Phase 1 Project Definition

In July 1979 the Australian Aircraft Industry Study Group (AISG) commenced a feasibility study funded to $340,000 and reported in July 1980 that without any existing or projected (overseas) trainer studies able to fully meet the RAAF requirements, a local design could be embarked on with a low associated technical risk. Jim Caterson, Senior Engineer Flight Technology and Wal Watkins, Support Engineer (Engine Performance) were CAC personnel seconded to the Industry Study. In AISG's estimation, local design, development and production would cost $103.3M (at June 1980 prices), some $30M or 30% more than the purchase of an overseas design. A prototype aircraft could be flight tested in late 1983, first production aircraft completed in early 1986 with the prospects of about 150 overseas sales. The AISG suggested the formation of a consortium of its own members to implement the project. In October/November 1979 John Kentwell, Gordon Bennett (GAF) and Peter Smith (HDH Commercial Manager) toured to test interest in the design and were surprised in the interest shown by Canada, Sweden, the UK and USA.

James Killen, Defence Minister in the Liberal Country Party Government approved the project on December 1, 1981 for design, development and production at a total outlay of $155M (August 1981 prices) based on the RAAF's update of the AISG estimates; a decision favoured by its promoter, the Chief of Air Force Technical Staff (CAFTS), AVM Joseph Anthony Dietz, a strong supporter of the project.

AVM Dietz, against the wishes of many pilots stuck to the two-tier training system ie 40 hours basic followed by 100 hours advanced training. Side by side seating seemed logical for first time fliers as had been in the UK, Australia, Sweden and USA designs. Tandem seating was favoured elsewhere in the world. With RAAF instructors, it was split 50% either way. (In the RAF, tandem seating was seen to reduce stress on fairly inexperienced trainees if they had become used to not sitting next to instructors when their syllabus moved to the high performance tandem HS Hawk). With demand for higher speed at lower levels on the increase, a tandem seating configuration provided slightly less airframe drag. An extra trainee passenger seat; a seat for tech support as the RAAF planned to operate the aircraft away from main bases at times or space for the carriage of tools were requested. Larger, lower pressure tyres for grass field operation as at RAAF Point Cook were mandated. Wet assembly was planned. This was an anti-corrosion measure of applying protective coatings

of a gel or sealant between adjacent metal surfaces and around fasteners to eliminate electrolytic corrosion.

During the Phase 1 Project Definition, completed in April 1982, the ASIG working as a de-facto consortium under a $4.33M GAF led contract; produced initial design, a development cost plan and a detailed development specification. The RAAF made use of some 14 MILSPEC documents spread across flight dynamics, human engineering, system safety, flight loads, maintenance and more. Even at this early stage, industry had its misgivings about its own capability and interface problems with the RAAF. The low level 24% of R & D in the aerospace industry became evident: GAF's share was 18.6% but only 5.4% went to the private sector.

In 1981 the AISG sought and invited a review in Australia by J. Stamper, technical director of British Aerospace and president of the Royal Aeronautical Society. He found adequate technical competency but highlighted *"the RAAF emphasis on control which could lead to a heavily biased administrative approach which might be a recipe for a well-documented history of failure"*.

Australian Aircraft Consortium

It was realised by all parties that the aircraft design expertise of the total industry would need to be pooled and that CAC had a significant proportion of that expertise. In the climate of the day ie. in accord with the Government policy of 'rationalisation by specialisation' GAF appeared certain to be appointed the prime contractor. The private HDH and CAC and indeed some senior personnel in GAF and the RAAF did not consider GAF had the necessary business acumen (in view of the problems with the GAF Nomad utility aircraft) to manage the project. Nor were CAC and HDH keen to relinquish to the public service controlled GAF, their senior design engineers, design draftsmen and technical staff in whom they had a large resource investment. Maximum use was to be made of apprentice labour to provide and extend industry experience. This was to create its own learning problems.

The Australian Aircraft Consortium Pty Ltd (AAC) was constituted in January, registered in March 1982 in the ACT and located in Todd Rd, Port Melbourne. The Advanced Jet Trainer, (RAAF AFST 5045) follow-on, to the expected 1990s replacement for the Macchi MB 326H was also seen as possible future work. The AAC was a three-way split independent company managed by a board consisting of the shareholder's six directors ie D. Dalziel; J.Kentwell(CAC); M.Lynch; M.Morrison(GAF): B.Price; S.Schaetzel (HDH) and two independents, of whom Jack Davenport, businessman and former RAAF WW2 pilot was chairman. GAF, CAC and HDH were also the AAC's main sub-contractors and the principal source of its seconded employees. Fourteen former CAC drafting staff and engineers became AAC employees as part of the core team including Jim Caterson, D. A. Betts, D. Collier, J. Moorhouse, D. Kamil, M. J. Howlett, Wal Watkins, Jim Adams, B. Maddoch and R. Maucer; whilst at the CAC premises, another 18 design staff and engineers were directly concerned with detail design.

On June 16, 1982, Ian Viner, Minister for Defence Support signed a $35.9M contract with the AAC's Malcolm Morrison, Manager GAF and Stan Schaetzel, Technical Director, HDH for the aircraft design and development (Phase 2) of the A10 *Wamira* – an indigenous language alternative name for throwing stick. A name (it was stated) that would project young Australian pilots into their flying career. *Wamira* also followed the tradition of assigning trainer aircraft indigenous names starting with the letter 'W' eg, *Warrigal*, *Wirraway* and *Winjeel*.

Phase 2 Design & Development

The AAC had no production or test facilities, sub-contracting such activities to its shareholders and to other specialist organisations such as the ARL (approx 1,000 hours) using the newly established method of rotary balance and conventional dynamic model testing and through a government to government (no outlay) agreement, using NASA's Langley, Virginia USA, Vertical Spin Facility (approx 200 hours and 1,000 free-flight model tests) contracted through Bihrle Applied Research (Virginia), for specialist client model manufacture and simulated aircraft testing.

Phase 2 required the core team of senior designers at the AAC premises to develop the layout of the aircraft and its main components following which Detail Design Documents (DDD) would be issued to the main sub-contractors to detail design and then fabricate after vetting by the AAC. About 50 staff comprised the AAC technical team. The general breakdown of design and construction packages were for: Power unit, nose fuselage structure, empennage and most aircraft systems to come from CAC; wing and landing gear from HDH; wheels and brakes from Dunlop and GAF responsible for the fuselage, final assembly and flight test. There was a prohibition to the use of castings, a source of possible corrosion.

Because of the concern for its own funds and the industry's capability to meet the demanding requirements to cost and time, the RAAF insisted on the application of strong management control through the AAC for strict design and configuration control processes and project performance requirements. In spite of these rigid arrangements and to some degree because of them, Phase 2 slipped and costs (on a cost plus reimbursement basis) leapt from the initial $35.9M to $46M (at August 1981 prices) to build the two prototypes. The aircraft mock-up was to be completed by December 1973; structural tests to start in April 1984; prototype roll-out in December 1984 with first flight in February 1985. The first production delivery in October 1987; RAAF type approval in July 1988 and the entire order delivered by August 1990, a slippage of about 12 months.

Leadership of the AAC A10 was: Dr J. North, Project Manager & Assistant General Manager; Alan J. Smith, General Manager & Chief Designer, 1990/82, 1984/85 (previously project design, guided weapons, GAF); Robert Dengate, Chief Designer, 1982/84 (previously Chief designer, HDH); Jim Caterson, Deputy Chief Designer,1982/85 (previously Senior Engineer Flight Technology, CAC) and Peter Debnam, General Manager, 1985.

Phase 2 Difficulties

The project was displayed at the 1983 Paris Air Show by which time the unit cost was being given as $1M ± 10%. The Auditor General's Department (auditor J. V. Monagham) examined the project in December 1984. It found that short on aircraft design/construction experience, there was a substantial initial underestimation of project costs by the AISG. Audit of GAF's financial statements had disclosed significant errors in the recording of transactions and departures from a number of basic accounting procedures and controls. The Joint Parliamentary Public Accounts Committee examined the project during April and May 1985 and considered it to be the least successful of 16 Defence projects investigated. Design and development work had slipped some thirteen months, the first flight had now been put back to March 1986 and the estimated cost of completing Phase 2 had doubled to $94.8M whilst total project cost had leaped to $313.2M (December 1984 prices), three times the original estimate. To March 1985, 80% of the aircraft's design was complete but only two out of the 35 structural design packages and none of 15 system packages had been accepted by the AAC from its sub-contractors. The slippage started from an eight month delay in the commencement of design work and the issuing of the Detailed Design Documents. Priority was given to

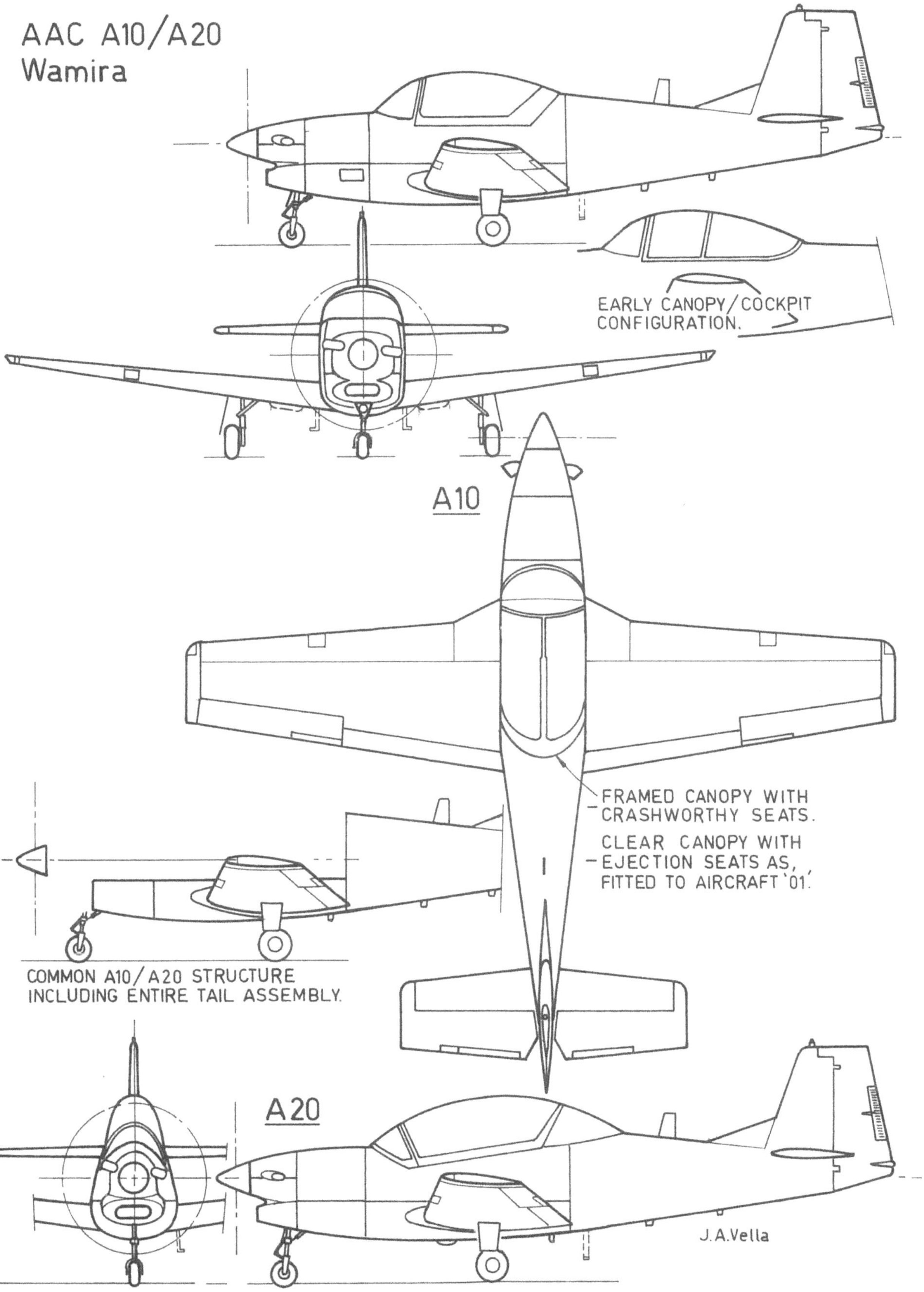

AAC A10/A20 Wamira

EARLY CANOPY/COCKPIT CONFIGURATION.

A10

FRAMED CANOPY WITH CRASHWORTHY SEATS.

CLEAR CANOPY WITH EJECTION SEATS AS FITTED TO AIRCRAFT '01'.

COMMON A10/A20 STRUCTURE INCLUDING ENTIRE TAIL ASSEMBLY.

A20

J.A.Vella

AAC Wamira Rotary Balance test model. **DSTO/ARL**

AAC Wamira Dynamic Spin test model. **DSTO/ARL**

01 partial fuselage structure at GAF. **GAF Heritage Group**.

01 fuselage structure work underway at GAF. Structural-test fuselage taking shape at the right rear. **GAF Heritage Group**

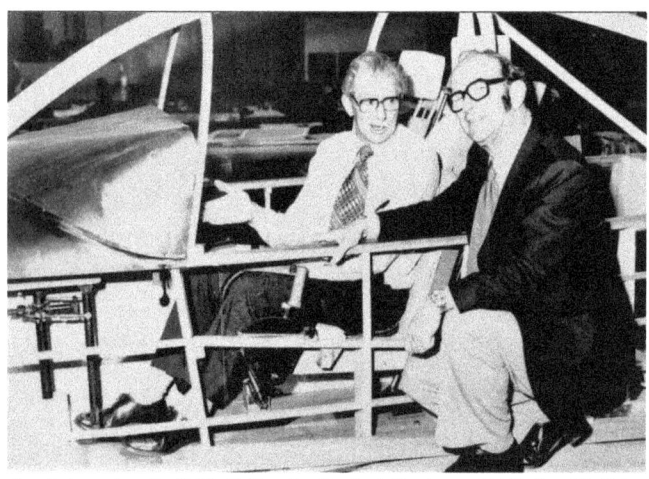
Jim Adams(seated) CAC Wamira Project Engineer & Walter Watkins project Support Engineer responsible for the aircraft mock-up.**HDHV**

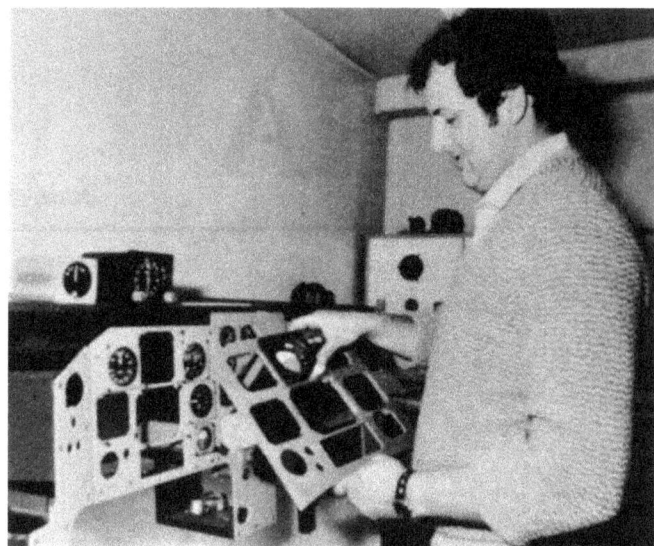
Wamira prototype cockpit instrument panel work at CAC. **GAF Heritage Group**

Wamira prototype delivered by the RAAF to the Moorabbin Air Museum on August 9,2019

A second low loader transport delivered the wings, canopies & various cockpit mock-ups etc *Ewan McArthur*

structural rather than systems design which the AAC considered a convenient way to operate in the circumstances.

Two of the contractual major technical milestones had slipped substantially due to a difference of opinion between the AAC and the RAAF. The Cockpit Mock-Up conference set for June 1983 was not finalised until August 1984, a delay of 14 months, whilst the Installation and Access conference meant for July 1983 was not settled till April 1985, twenty-one months late. The full scale mock-up completed August 1983 was 8 months late. The estimated five month slippage in detail design work was the time taken to arrive at final design solutions acceptable to the RAAF (at a very early stage in the project) including both cockpit and Line Replacement Unit (LRU) access and maintainability issues. Although not part of the delay, it was the AAC's conclusion that the Air Force's stringent air conditioning requirement could not reasonably be met. A more cost effective solution would have been using aircraft shelters to cope with full heat soak conditions. But a fixed structure could not be funded from the finance vote used to acquire aircraft.

AVM Tony Deitz died suddenly on January 15, 1985. AVM Ian Sutherland took over from February 22,1985 to July 5, 1989. His successor AVM Brain Graff was the last in the role (November 5, 1989) following an amalgamation of both the CAFTS and CAFM positions into Materiel, Engineering & Supply functions in a new Materiel Division in HQ Logistics Command.

Defence, finally realising the slow progress, carried out a restructuring, approached several commercial concerns, including major American aerospace companies to conduct audits of costing and management controls. When all the firms refused to become involved, Defence set up an Inter-Departmental Committee (IDC) to review the project and determine its future. Reporting several months late in June 1985 it then forecast a final 69 aircraft cost in excess of $350M with little scope for cost reduction under the existing unfavourable managerial arrangement. It suggested a technical review to reduce costs and the possibility of adopting the local construction of an overseas design. The IDC also mentioned three items ie the changes to passenger accommodation; the deferral of crashworthy pilot seats and the relocation of fuel tanks from the wings to the fuselage could have had impacts on the design schedule. This was strongly rejected by Deputy Chief Designer Jim Caterson in correspondence with the author.

The third seat on the port side facing aft was now for a ground engineer on cross-country flights, not for the second trainee. The original need for the extra two seats was reduced to one with an agreed airworthiness installation based on the civil FAR 23 requirements, not to the full military spec of crash worthy seats. The air-conditioning unit was to be located next to the seat. Doubts then arose about passenger emergency, ground or airborne egress (by parachute in the latter case) and the passenger seat position was not included in the contract. The issue remained clouded by the RAAF's indecision about ejection seats for production aircraft.

The original specification requested energy-absorbing crashworthy seats to limit vertical forces on the crew to 11g. A cavity depth of about 13 inches within which the energy absorption seat system would stroke through a hinged floor panel, magnified the problems associated with the design of the fuselage and all systems located in the area. ARL established the design criteria for the seats. The AAC raised its concerns in 1983 on the time taken, incurring a six month delay, the large associated expense and the cost-effectiveness of these seats. The RAAF backed down but the damage had been done.

Ejection seats were proposed by the AAC (Jim Caterson) in 1980 and supported by the RAAF General Duties Branch but rejected by the RAAF Maintenance Branch on the grounds of proven turbo prop engine reliability and the added need to provide armament maintenance trades increasing through-life operational expense at training units. The AAC engineered the installation as much as possible in compliance with the MILSPEC to facilitate the inevitable future approval requirement for ejection seats as found in the overseas Embraer Tucano and Pilatus PC-9 trainers. However, it was agreed that the prototypes would be fitted with ejection seats to provide maximum pilot safety whilst subjecting an unknown aircraft to the extremes of the design envelope as quickly as possible. This led, at the end of 1984 to a change from the framed, emergency opening / manual bale out, ground egress canopy design to a one piece unit required for ejection seats that in turn meant doing away with the turn-over truss and relying on the windscreen bow, propeller and the top of the ejection seat seats to provide for turnover protection. Master reference models, tools and parts built by CAC had to be scrapped.

Fuel storage was moved from the integral tank in each wing with a collector tank to that of a single crashworthy bladder tank located between the wing front and rear carry-through structure spar below the rear cabin floor space. The complexity and maintenance cost of the original tank design was considered to be an unwarranted development risk. The re-location was also required to improve the aircraft's aerobatic performance.

CAC's Involvement

At the end of the Design Definition Phase the practical and sensible recommendations for the division of work between the three main companies would have had CAC building the fuselage and its main systems, HDH the similar work on the wings, with GAF carrying out ancillary structures and systems, final assembly and test. The Department of Productivity overturned this as it went against its rationalisation policy and CAC could not be seen to be doing significant and identifiable airframe sub-assemblies. It was shunted aside. The task of providing an equitable workload in a sensible manner then became very difficult. It was not achieved because CAC was left with a heterogeneous collection of mechanical and fluid systems which had to be designed into structures being engineered and revised by others. The interface problems with the greatest amount of change occurring in the systems were enormous. This badly instituted breakdown of work was a significant factor in the cost over-runs.

The detail design and manufacturing allotted to CAC to contract CA-34 for the first aircraft included the complete engine installation, fuselage nose structure, intake and cowlings, canopy and windscreen master reference tooling, horizontal tail, rudder and elevators, flight instruments, fuel system detail design subcontractor, flying controls and oxygen system assemblies, environmental control system, electrics (for the landing gear,flaps & trim tabs), avionics, pitot static system, windscreen / canopy frame, ejection seats. CAC was also to design, build and test a windscreen impact strike gun and the airframe static structural test rig. Its work was overseen by John Kentwell, Manager Engineering and Walter Watkins,Design Engineer.

AAC A20 for the RAF

As the AAC sought overseas sales it became obvious that both the side-by-side seating and MILSPEC design had little appeal. AM David Evans, Chief of Air Staff from 1982 developed late doubts about both issues and that the initial assumptions had been incorrect.

The AAC linked with independent Westland Ltd (UK) in mid-July 1984, with Westland holding a 48% share to manage and promote the A10 and also build the A20 derivative parts of the Wamira in the

The full scale mockup developing slowly sitting on trestles in the GAF Experimental Workshop at week 28. **GAF Heritage Group**

A sad looking cargo arriving at the Moorabbin Air Museum. August 9, 2019. **Ewan McArthur**

More uncertainty, further late design interference. Another change in the AAC Wamira A10 canopy configuration frustrating the Company Clowns. **Roger Ward**

UK to bid for the Royal Air Force's eventual order of 130 aircraft to request AST 412 for a new basic trainer to replace the Hunting Jet Provost. Sir Basil Blackwell, Westland's chairman was upbeat about it and a joint Board was formed. In turn Westland offered the AAC joint development in an unidentified 30 seat helicopter concept.

The A20's tandem cockpit seat arrangement was laid out to be nearly identical to that of the RAF's operational jet trainer, the HS Hawk. The tandem cockpit fitted into the space for the two extra seats in the A10 within the same overall length with changes limited to aft of the firewall. Fuel was reduced for a shorter 2 hours flight training regime. The tandem fuselage gave an extra 11kts speed at SL. With an airframe commonality of about 80%, the AAC was to build those parts common to both the A10 and A20. The AAC estimated it would cost A$10M to develop the design of the A20.

The Clowns' work on an enlarged "Whamira"rudder was to be put on hold (for costs savings) until flight testing had taken place. Note the AAC staff member on the right. **Roger Ward**

The AAC A20 submission with an Engineering Mock-Up(EMU) was one of the four finalists that included the Pilatus PC-9, Hunting/NDN-1T Firecracker, the Shorts/Embraer EMB-312 Tucano. Its short listing was leaked by the Financial Times (UK) on March 13, 1984. The A20 was looked upon as the best design to meet the RAF's need. It was also the newest, the most expensive, least developed and least certain contender. It was offered in two variants: the A20 with PT6A-25C engine rated at 750 shp and 3 bladed propeller and the A20/2 with PT6-25C/2 engine rated at 850 shp with a four bladed propeller as well as the last ditch 1,000 shp Garrett AiResearch TPE331-101H engine. Westland Ltd displayed the A20 Engineering Mock-UP (EMU) at the 1984 SBAC Farnborough Air Display & Exhibition. It was then stored until acquired by the Moorabbin Air Museum in 2018. The NDN-1T Firecracker, the only UK entrant, had the support of the British Parliament whereas it complained that " *the A20 cannot be a serious contender*"....."*Why should we fund development of an Australian aircraft when we rejected a proposal by BAe to fund its own project...*" The Tucano was announced the winner in December 1984 and would be built by Shorts of Belfast. It was the cheapest, most extensively modified, over-budget, very late, difficult to line-maintain aircraft, but was 30 years in service.

In an opening for potential A10 sales and in a bid to defray development costs, a Memorandum of Understanding was signed in early 1985 with the China National Aerotechnological Export & Import Corporation (CNAEIC) with a follow-up delegation visiting Melbourne. Wamira parts made in China would reduce costs considerably and lead to the possible sale of the aircraft to the Air Force of the People's Liberation Army. This in turn led to an expressed interest in the possible follow-on AAC new jet trainer design and co-production.

Participation Cost Saving Ideas

The project was running 15 months late. In advance of the Defence Inter-Departmental Committee's recommendation of June 1985 for a costs technical review, a sizeable team at CAC comprised of A. Cassidy, Chief Design Engineer; I. Grundy, Senior Production Engineer; D. Castledine, Wamira Project Manager; Peter Howell, Senior Engineer Mechanical; R. Macartney, Senior Engineer Structures; John Manderson, Senior Engineer Electrical; T. Pashai, Weights Engineer; D. Samarsky, Mechanical Engineer; C. Allott, Sales & Contracts and S. Bacon from Purchasing, worked on an extensive costs reduction analysis of CAC's areas of responsibility in the aircraft's structure for the following program Phases 3 & 4.

It reported quickly on July 5, 1985 with a suggestion to simplify the nose-wheel steering; a cable system to replace the push-rod flying controls; replacement of the crashworthy seats by fixed or ejection seats (the latter requested by the Royal Air Force spec); increasing the time of the RAAF's ECS 5 minute pull-down from hot, solar soaking to the generally acceptable 30 minutes wait. Fit an alternative hinged canopy of reduced size and limited bird strike rating or allow a simplification of the entire canopy rails and canopy / fuselage interface; use a single curvature, cast acrylic, less costly windscreen transparency. Delete the double curvatures in the front fuselage areas; redesign for one hinged engine cowl each side; introduce a one piece carry-through horizontal tail with cost and weight fatigue advantages. Change the crashworthy fuel tank to a normal bag tank. Hold back on plans for an enlarged (better spin) rudder until the flight testing phase. All this and re-assessment of other structural fabrication detail, the re-thinking on the wet assembly and protective treatment requirements would, if removed from RAAF management strictures, was estimated to save $935,692 in CAC's design package.

L-R: Robert Dengate, Chief Designer 1982/84; Dr Jim North, Project Manager & Assistant GM; Alan Smith GM & Chief Designer 1990/82. **GAF Heritage Group**

Foreign Competition

Following the IDC report of June 1985 the Government directed Defence in July to quickly conduct an alternative trainer competition. Meanwhile, negotiations that had been underway in the background saw HDH acquire total ownership of CAC on July 1, 1985 and therefore a two thirds share of the AAC. The Government also followed with the transfer to HDH of its GAF one third share in the Consortium giving HDH total control of the AAC.

Stan Schaetzel, Technical Director of HDH became Managing Director of the AAC as the interim chief executive in charge of preparing a revised A10B bid and to ensure that the prototype would roll out on December 1, 1985. Industry had difficulty throughout the project to find a suitable permanent chief executive of the AAC. Its Board on many occasions acted as an executive committee rather than a board of review.

On 7 July, Defence Minister Kim Beazely announced HDH would be given the opportunity to rescue a revised A10B Wamira proposal against possible collaborative production under licence of turboprop trainer aircraft designs from the Short Bros / Embraer Super Tucano and Pilatus Aircraft Ltd. A DoD team visited Shorts and Piliatus during August 1985. Meanwhile financial approval for Phase 2 was increased to $64.4M but industry activity levels were reduced to ensure funds would last until December 1985 (the start of the factory summer holiday break). Spending rates were running at half those of earlier in the year. Before work was cut back, the AAC had estimated that the design to the current specification was about 90% complete with about nine months of outstanding construction work on the first prototype before first flight. CAC's design component was never completed.

What Had Been Achieved

The fatigue test specimen wing was delivered by HDH to the University of NSW for static testing on May 31, 1985. The fully fitted prototype wing was sent to the GAF complex in early August 1985 for fitting to airframe 01 where the centre and rear fuselage sections had reached the skinning stage. Fracture mechanics theory, damage tolerance and durability design techniques were introduced with assistance from McDonnell Douglas to create good design structure detail, using quality materials, corrosion prevention measures and applying stress levels so that initial flaws in the manufacturing process and material defects would not grow to critical size and involve excessive repair costs. The wing to fuselage joint had reached 16,000 hours of fatigue testing at the ARL. Structural testing had achieved 32,000 hours meeting the required safe life of 8,000 hours. GAF had evolved a complex flight test instrumentation system far in advance of anything previously used in Australia comprising the airborne component, a ground display and processing facility and an automatic test and calibration system capable of acquiring data from 450 parameters.

Promoting the future A20 in FLIGHT International in September 1984. **J.A. Vella Collection**

CAC's impact strike gun was used to test the wing leading edges. They collapsed on impact test, were re-designed and re-built.

Tenders which closed on September 16, 1985 were received from HDH with the revised A10B Wamira and Pilatus Aircraft with an improved PC-7 Mk 2 or the PC- 9. The Short Bros / Embraer joint Super Tucano bid did not submit. The PC-7 was the cheapest. HDH had continued A10B development with a simplified design in which the RAAF had a much reduced day-to-day involvement. In Phase 3 (Production Tooling and acquiring long-lead items) and Phase 4 (Production Bidding) HDH had carried out a review with consultants from Aermacchi (Italy) and examined GAF's operations in order to curb costs. The A10B was offered at a firm fixed price of $184M on a baseline configuration, with improvement options comparable to that of the Pilatus PC-7 Mk 2. The change to cost effectiveness was now considered by Defence to be more important than *pure performance*.

The first and only prototype AAC Wamira A10 in partial assembly state at the Government Aircraft Factory. **Australian Aircraft Consortium**

Finished in an orange & white paint scheme what may have become Wamira A23-001 just prior to its political cancellation in December 1985. **Australian Aircraft Consortium**

Specifications	A10 Wamira (A20 noted where different)			
Powerplant	A10: One 750 shp Pratt & Whitney (Canada) PT6A-25D turboprop engine flat rated at 620 shp for TO, driving a three bladed 7 ft 6 inch diameter propeller A20: as above A20/2: One 850 shp Pratt & Whitney (Canada) PT6A-25C/2 driving a four bladed propeller			
Performance	(At max training weight)	A10	A20	
	Max speed at SL	218 kts	239 kts	
	Cruising speed at SL	213 kts	NA	
	Cruising speed at 15,000 ft	215 kts	167 kts	
	Max speed at 15,000 ft	226 kts	NA	
	Vne	320 kts	NA	
	Limit speed 280 kts to 16,000 ft, then Mach 0.58 above 16,000 ft		NA	
	Service ceiling	31,000 ft	32,600 ft	
	Time to 10,000 ft	6 mins	NA	
	Rate of climb at SL	2,760 ft / min	3,050 ft / min	
	Stall speed flaps lowered	59 kts	NA	
	Approach speed	71 kts	57 kts	
	TO distance over 50 ft	1,180 ft	1,020 ft	
	Landing distance over 50 ft	1,640 ft	1,180 ft	
	Endurance with 50 mins reserve	3 hrs	NA	
	TO control capability in 30 kt crosswind		NA	
	Landing capability in 20 kt crosswind		NA	
Weights		A10	A20	
	Empty equipped	3,546 lbs	Empty 3,188 lbs	
	Max fuel load	1,043 lbs	983 lbs	
	Fuel capacity	120 gall	NA	
	Max TO training	4,850 lbs	4,630 lbs	
	Max alternate roles	6,173 lbs	NA	
Dimensions	Wing span	36 ft 1 in	Chord at C/L	9 ft 11.25 ins
	Chord at tip	3 ft 11.5 ins	Aspect ratio	6.05
	Wing gross area	215.3 sq ft		
	Airfoil section NACA 23018 (Root)		Airfoil section NACA 23012 (Tip)	
	Length (A10)	33 ft 9.5 ins	Length (A20)	33 ft 1.5 ins
	Tailplane span	14 ft 9 ins	Tailplane chord at C/L	4 ft 7.5 ins
	Tailplane chord at tip	3 ft 2.8 ins	Tailplane area	58.1 sq ft
	Height	12 ft 1.75 ins	Fin tip chord	3 ft 2 ins
	Chord at base of fin	6 ft 2.75 ins	Vertical tail area	6.9 sq ft
	Wheel base	10 ft 2 ins	Track	13 ft 1.5 ins
	Undercarriage sink rate	13 ft/sec	Max compression stroke	11 ins
Armament	A10 Underwing stations inboard 2 x 550 lb Underwing stations outboard 2 x 330 lb Total underwing load 1,760 lbs One centre line wet/dry station		A20 Underwing stations 4 off NA Total underwing load 1,322 lbs NA	

However the tender evaluation team adjusted and raised the A10B bid, *'by various contingencies'*, to $270M under strong protest from HDH. On December 16, 1985 it selected the Pilatus PC-9 (certified to civilian FAR 23 rules) for local manufacture, starting mid-1986 and costing a fixed $240M. Wamira design work ceased leaving an incomplete, largely cosmetic airframe. With $68M already expended on design and development, the total Wamira cost was now estimated would end up at $337M. Two days after the selection of the PC-9 the last A10B drawing was signed off and all work at HDH ceased in March 1986. Some 70 Australian firms were to supply items.

The RAAF chose to accept the excessively more powerful PC-9 (950 shp) in comparison with the Wamira's 650 shp; the tandem seating, the lack of initial grass field ability and ab-initio capability, stall and approach speeds in excess of its request and performance figures for a SL temperature of 20°C as against the original requirement for 35°C. It hoped it would save $20M each year by going back to the CT4A Airtrainer ($300/hr) as a grading aircraft for the first 20 to 25 hours of initial flying and using the PC-9 ($900/hr) for 120 hours of training, cutting back the expensive ($1,500/hr) MB326H jet phase to about 60 hours. In accepting the bids the RAAF had altered the baseline of its requirements and moved from an over-specified costly local design to reduce costs and then to somehow acquire a new alternative trainer.

The PC-9 did not comply with the major requirements of AFST 5044.

Failure Analysis

The extensively documented reasons set out in the Australian Parliament Joint Committee of Public Accounts and the Auditor General's Report on the failure of the Wamira, points the blame to the Air Force. A summary follows:

- There were inadequacies and omissions in the initial definition and evaluation of the project before moving to Phase 2 such as underestimated cost, time scale and technical risks and were not subjected to sufficient rigorous evaluation before approval.
- Clarification of the specification before start of Phase 2 on occasions took a long time to resolve. Large number of specification changes hampered development of a baseline control configuration and for the AAC to control the design.
- The estimates of overseas sales prospects were based on simple, very optimistic world-wide need projections.
- 'Life of type' estimates for the existing CT4A Airtrainer fleet estimates were inadequate. The original 2,500 to 3,000 hours of fatigue life were found a few years later by ARL to be at 5,000 hours or well above.
- For the RAAF wanting to design and certify an aircraft to MILSPEC standards in the hope of increasing its marketability (including to the USAF) when the local industry lacked MILSPEC design experience. Its use in an inflexible and authoritarian way created major design problems. The parallel objectives of marketability and the development of design expertise came into conflict in the varying interpretations given to the some 200 contractual specifications.
- Whereas the AAC was expecting *'reasoned practical compromise'* in meeting design objectives, the RAAF insisted on strict compliance otherwise the purpose of the project would be defeated.
- AAC criticised the multiplicity of official contact points and insistence on an extreme number of various reports (33 copies) required, which forced the AAC to *'accommodate many interpretations of particular requirements'*.
- There were two ends to every complaint: one at the AAC in Melbourne, the other at Canberra
- A lack of delegation authority to the RAAF representatives at the AAC site sometimes led to many working level decisions changed in Canberra months later.
- The issuing of a very rigid Specification AC180 which defined many design solutions giving the AAC designers virtually no room to move.
- The RAAF dominated the mock-up assessments, wanting absolute correct design details before moving on, whereas the AAC had expected the record of a change or alteration and its later incorporation in the detail design work.
- Some RAAF assessors had difficulty interpreting drawings and lacked design and general post graduate R & D experience as compared with their USAF counterparts.
- The importance at getting the design right from the very start was unwarranted as any aircraft design would go through various modifications before production approval.
- Poor Air Force management with the division of responsibility split between the Chief of Air Force Materiel (CAFM) who strongly backed the project and the Chief of Air Force Technical Services(CAFTS), the latter driving the project on narrow technical iterations without constraint on cost and schedule considerations leading it towards cancellation. There should have been a single RAAF interface with the AAC.
- The RAAF had highly competent aircraft engineering maintenaance. It had very little aircraft design experience.

Contributing Project Failures

- Management problems between the AAC, its sub-contractors and within the sub-contractors themselves made it difficult to co-ordinate the design process. CAC was not exempt in this.
- The AAC lacked a managing director.
- The industry should not have accepted the Phase 2 contract, which in many paragraphs, had open-ended provisions *'to the satisfaction of the design approving authority'* ie the Chief of Air Force Technical Services.
- The cost-plus system worked against efficient control within the sub-contractors.
- The local aerospace industry lacked a commercial or competitive approach and the project showed up the deficiencies of cost-plus re-imbursement contracts.
- There should have been one prime contractor in charge and each sub-contractor should have been allowed to supply fully stuffed discrete assemblies to avoid the many interface problems.
- Most significantly, both the Auditor General and the RAAF agreed the project should have been managed by one contractor.
- The Air Force was not technically or procedurally ready for the project in 1980 due to its pre-occupation with the introduction of the F/A-18 Hornet fighter.
- The Air Force due to its lack of experience launched heavy USAF project control procedures without regard to their appropriateness or cost-effectiveness in the Australian context, a manner described as *'USAF style pubescent kids in uniform acting as 'clipboard managers'* that cost everyone an enormous waste of time and money.
- The RAAF's definition and evaluation of its requirements was inadequate with the result the project was compromised at the outset by ill-considered and conflicting objectives, bad timing and poor estimates.
- RAAF project management was not up to date with the known risks of local design and development in which industry had no recent experience (nor with MILSPECS).

- RAAF was not concerned as much in project delay as in the escalation of costs in a reduced RAAF budget, which threatened higher priority projects as the F/A-18 Hornet; the development costs of the new E-7A Wedgetail AEW & C and conversion of B707 transports into aerial tankers. It had spent $68M up to cancellation.
- RAAF team members were promoted or transferred resulting in different views brought in by different officers There were three changes of CAFM during Wamira (1981-86): AVM Henry Hughes (Jan 1979-Nov 81); AVM Roy Frost (Mar 1982-July 82); AVM Alan Heggen (July 1982-July 87)
- CAS AM David Evans wanted the aircraft to succeed for the sake and future of the local industry; but believed the AAC was distracted by their plans to submit a tandem seat design for the RAF, whilst in retrospect he thought the decision to embark on the MILSPECS concept was unwise.

In a letter to *Aircraft* (November 1985), AVM Alan Heggen(CAFM) denied RAAF was the major cause of the trouble. *"Whilst it was not untrue, the criticism ignored the implications and processes involved in approving design features, a normal and technically prudent process which normally took less than six months. Normally there would have been one team responsible for such a design, not four with one of them trying to make the other three match each other and over-ruling their considered decisions, even if that was the customer."*

Questioned by the Senate Estimates Committee (Defence Industry Newsletter) AVM Heggen said in part *"the reasons were that the contractor was not able to provide data in the detail that the costs and schedule control system required. Another was that the very nature of a design and development project meant that there was no finite and recognisable end to the design and development task and it was difficult to measure the total extent of the task. While it was possible to determine how much work had to be done and what stage was reached, it was not possible to measure precisely what remained to be done...because...new work and new tasks emerged from time to time."*

ADSTE-The Association of Drafting, Supervisory & Technical Employees in its 1985 review noted the 'interface' inability to exchange electronically between the contractor's disparate sites designs generated by CAD/CAM; the lengthy delays in making design choices;the RAAF interference in design eroded industry's capacity to be efficient and led to second-guess and anticipate their demands. The time taken, initially six months, averaging 200 days to approve drawings. The AAC developed *'a them and us'* siege mentality in its relationship with the contractors and was unable to fulfil its role of design co-ordinator due to conflicting pressures. It tended to introduce changes near the end of a detail design stage. CAC, in one instance produced 15 versions of the same design item. The AAC checked all drawings repeating what had already been done by the contractors. Production drawings meant from the outset for a prototype airframe was a problem. It generated a huge volume of paperwork when changes were made. The differences in salaries and conditions between the three companies employees created friction.

Stan Schaetzel summed up the project loss: *"The failure to get it elected for local use in favour of an overseas design which does not fully not fully meet AFST 5044, is not only a reflection on the capabilities of the manufacturing industry but of the whole Australian engineering profession. It needs to be examined and understood."*

The A10 Wamira was the first locally designed and built airframe at the request of the RAAF since the CA-25 Winjeel of 1952; a gap of some 29 years. The office of the CAFTS (as reported to Parliament) wanted the project to succeed with his configuration and was in a prolonged managerial conflict with the office of the CAFM with resultant major internal delays, changes and inflexible decisions to the detriment of the project.

HDH continued to hope for overseas sales with commercial rights for the modified A10B variant but without its MILSPEC. The opening with China did not succeed. There was no confidence in a design that the RAAF had not accepted.

On October 24, 1990 the AAC resolved to end, winding-up on June 26, 1991. The incomplete airframe was noted at RAAF Base Wagga, NSW in October 1986, then moved to the RMIT University school at Point Cook. It was donated and delivered to the Moorabbin Air Museum on August 9, 2019. Endeavour Aerospace Pty Ltd was reputed to have purchased the design rights from the Government in 2000 intending to resume the project in some manner. It was de-registered on March 15, 2016.

By comparison, the USAF chose the Fairchild Republic T-46, side by side Next Generation Trainer (NGT) on July 2, 1982. It flew on October 26, 1985 six months late, was cancelled in 1986 due to doubled cost overruns, poor engine performance, bad program management. It led to the demise of Fairchild Republic Corporation on December 31, 1987. The Wamira A10 was looked at favourably and was to be offered for the NGT request. The USAF and US Navy selected the Beechcraft T-6A Texan II, a highly modified version of the PC-9 in 1989 to replace the T-37, T-46 and T34. It flew in 1998, suffered massive cost escalation, a unit price of US$S4.3M and entered service in 2001.

Bibliography: AAC/CA-34 Wamira Basic Pilot Trainer Aircraft

Aircraft - (March 1981, November 1983, March 1985, July 1985, September 1985, January 1986).

Aircraft Industry Study Group. File Phase 3 costs.(March 5, 1981). 435-3-1.

Australia. Parliament. Joint Committee of Public Accounts (1986). Report 243 - Review of Defence Project Management. Vols 1 & 2.

Australian Aircraft Consortium (1984). A10 Basic Trainer & A20 Tandem Trainer brochures.

Australian Aircraft Consortium. (1985). [Program Newsheets]

Australian Aircraft Consortium Wamira. *Air International*. Vols. 26, 27, 28, 29.

Cassidy, A. (Chief Design Engineer). (June 24,1985). AA CA34-24. Review of RAAF & RAF Specs. for a Basic Pilot Training Aircraft. Commonwealth Aircraft Corporation.

Cassidy, A. (Chief Design Engineer). (July 5,1985). AA-CA34-26. Potential Cost Reductions for Wamira Phase 3 & 4 Program. Commonwealth Aircraft Corporation.

Caterson, J. (AAC Deputy Chief Designer); Kentwell, J. (CAC Chief Engineer); Dengate, R; Collier, D. & Watkins, W. (1985-1986) [Correspondence & topic texts verification]

Commonwealth Aircraft Corporation. *Pursuit, Air Tales*.(Various)

Commonwealth Aircraft Corporation. (Undated). A10 Production Parts Breakdown Chart.

Commonwealth Aircraft Corporation. AA CA34-24. Review of RAAF & RAF Specs for a Basic Pilot Training Aircraft.

Commonwealth Aircraft Corporation. AA CA34-26. Potential Cost Reductions for Phase 3 & 4.

Defence Update. (June 1985, Sept 1985). *Australian Aviation*- (June 1985, September 1985).

The Clowns escape. The AAC Wamira A10B bombs out and the CA-37 Pilatus PC-9A wins the renewed Basic Trainer selection process.
Roger Ward

Dept of Defence (November 20,1989). Re-organisation of Materiel Division AE88-21468.

Evans, David, CAS AM (2011). *Down to Earth. A Home-Built Training Aircraft for the RAAF.* Air Development Centre, Canberra.

Institution of Engineers Australia.(March 1987). Aerospace Industry Working Party Report.

Man & Aerial Machines . 1990. John Hopton. Prahran, Victoria

Martin,Colin; Drobik, Jan; Malone, Peter. DSTO/ARL. *Hawker and The Spin.* 2001 RAAF History Conference.

Muir, Tom (June 1985). '*Why the Wamira Missed.*' ADSTE (Melb)

Sarrailhe, S.R. Australia. DSTO/ARL. (April 1981) AR-002-987. Proposed Crashworthiness Requirements for the Australian Basic Trainer Aircraft.

Schaetzel, Stan (March 1986). '*Why Can't Australia Make its Own Defence Hardware*'. *Institute of Engineers Australia Journal.*

Smith, T. (Manager Sales & Contracts, Aircraft Division).(August 24,1983). AA-C34-15 Trainer Project Phase 3 Estimate. Commonwealth Aircraft Corporation.

Smith, T. (Manager Sales & Contracts, Aircraft Division).(September 1, 1983). AER/AD7345. Trainer Project Phase 3 Re-estimate. Commonwealth Aircraft Corporation.

Trove. National Library of Australia. *Endeavour Aerospace.*

Trove. RAAF News (1989,1990,1993). *New Materiel Division; Engineering Branch Farewelled; Senior Engineer Retires.*

Vella J. A. (1985). 'The Wamira A10 Project'. *Aviation Heritage*, AHSA. Vol. 24/3.

'Why the Wamira Never Got Airborne'. *Chartered Engineer.* (Victoria). (March 21,1986).

WINJEEL AFST 5044, BASIC TRAINER PROPOSAL[1]
April 1980

AFST 5044 Basic Trainer requirement issued in October 1978 was to become the troubled and controversial A10 Wamira design of the Australian Aircraft Consortium.

In the early part of 1980 the RAAF was showing concern at the indicative high cost and resources which were required to develop and produce the Indigenous New Design (A10 Wamira) under non-commercial, collaborative, work-sharing and untried management procedures with inexperienced contractual labour. If the new trainer was not available by 1986, budget cuts and re-planning consequences were feared. If things were to go wrong, a fall back option should have been in place.

Unofficially, Wal Watkins created the possibility of this fall-back option in a study making use of extensively modified new build Winjeel airframes. This proposal would have required only 20-25% of the pre-production development effort of a completely new design. Significantly it would have provided the preferred side-by-side cockpit seating arrangement and met the RAAF's critical 2.5g steady turn manoeuvre requirement at 10,000 ft.

The major modifications required to match the AFST 5044 requirements were:
- A turboprop engine installation
- Tricycle undercarriage
- An increase in fuel capacity
- The addition of air-conditioning
- New avionics and instrumentation
- Structural and life extension modifications to known deficient areas
- Possible extension of fin and dorsal areas

All of these major modifications would have satisfied as separate packages the work sharing arrangements for industry during the Design and Development Phase. There was also the scope for involvement in GRP composites for complex curvature non-structural panel areas. The preferred engine with inverted flight capability was the P & W (Canada) PT6A-25 from a selection which considered the Rolls Royce RB318 and the Garrett AiResearch TPE-331) matched with a 90 inch diameter three or four bladed propeller. Major electrical equipment re-location was necessary to compensate for the much lighter engine weight together with the possibility of a slight (about 3 in) rearward shift of the original wing placement. The difficult ECS demand would have been met with the straight adoption of the system installed in the Beechcraft T-34C Mentor, utilizing a general aviation unit (or ultimately building a specifically tailored system).

Project Definition, Development and Production

Some 8,860 hours and $445,000 (1980 prices) in a time frame of 20 months was required for Project Definition. The Design and Development Phase would have been partly implemented using two or three spare Winjeel airframes and used engines loaned by the manufacturers to make a gradual introduction of the major modifications required to match the AFST 5044 requirements with first flight of a prototype test airframe 12 months from the start of design.

Winjeel - AFST 5044 Basic Trainer Proposal [1]

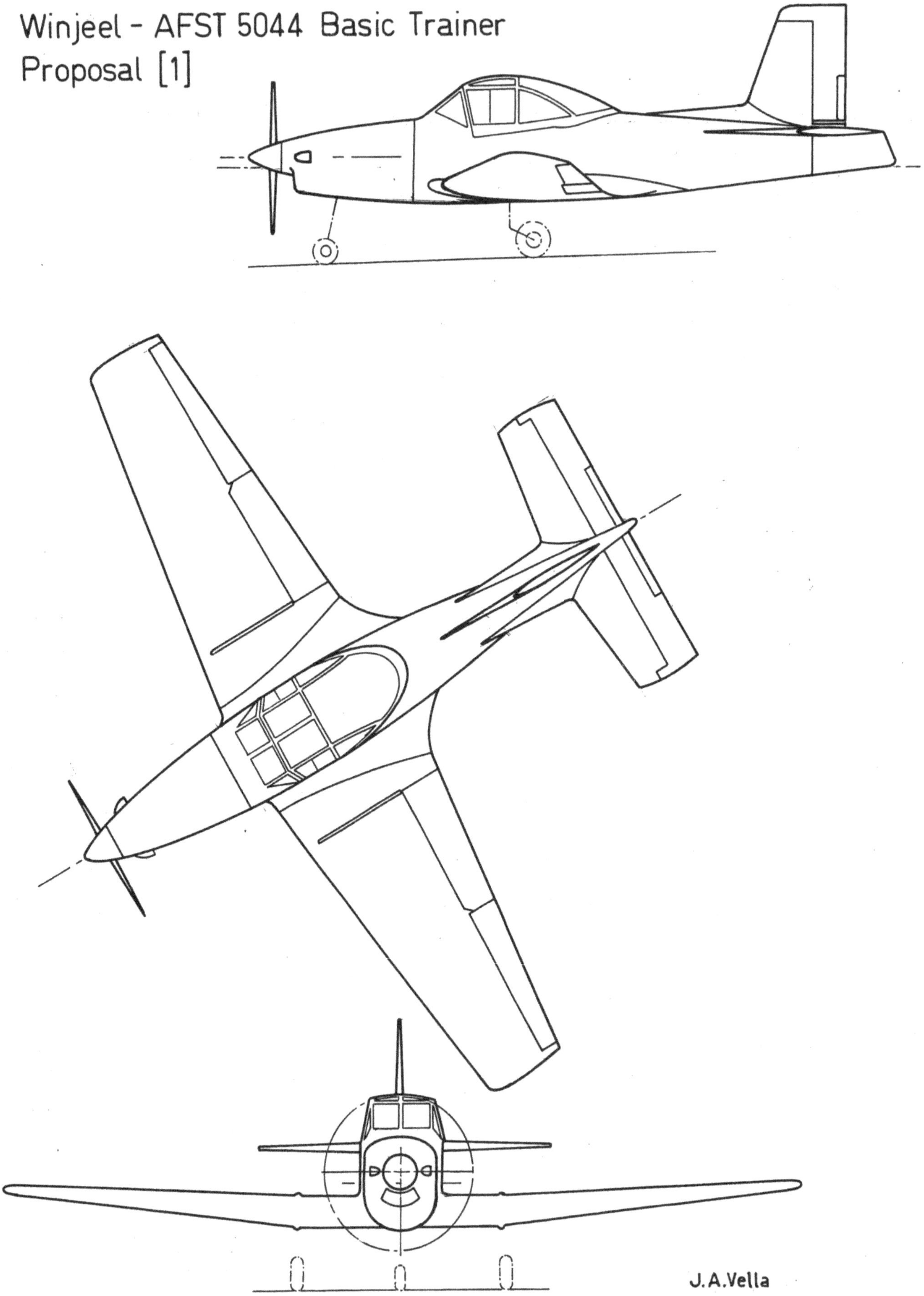

J.A.Vella

Table 1: Winjeel AFST 5044 Basic Trainer Proposal [1]. Pre-Production Costs [1980 Values]

	Indigenous New Design		Winjeel Modification	
	A$ Million	Man hours (x 1,000)	A$ Million	Man hours (x 1,000)
Project definition	2.22	68.3	0.45	8.8
Design & development	22.37	723.4	4.4	149.8
Production investment	7.97	299.2	2	59.7
Total pre-production	32.56	1090.9	6.85	218.4
Production (65 aircraft)	42.49	1217	43.57	1362.5
Total program	**A$75.05M**	**2307.9**	**A$57.27M**	**1580.9**

Whilst the Aircraft Industry study Group put its 1980 estimate for the Design and Development costs for the Indigenous New Design at $22.4M (which was to move higher as time went on) for two prototypes, that for the Winjeel based design was for $4.4M, a notional saving of $18M. The use of existing and modified production tooling was to cost $2M, whilst $7.97M was the envisaged cost for Indigenous New Design tooling. However the estimated production costs for the two concepts based on Indigenous New Design cost estimation procedures were nearly identical ie $42.9M for the Indigenous New Design and S43.57M for the Winjeel derivative based on the production of 65 airframes. Table 1 shows an estimated saving of $17.78M and 727,000 man hours in the overall program in favour of the modified Winjeel concept.

Comparative unit costs based on the RAAF initial request for 65 aircraft would have been:

$1,154,000 for the Indigenous New Design
$776,000 for the Winjeel Modification

Delivery of the first modified production Winjeel in this scheme was expected for the beginning of 1984, the last at around July 1986. The idea was a viable low risk proposition which was not circulated or publicized as there was an embargo placed on individual trainer design initiatives from the shareholder member companies forming part of the Australian Aircraft Consortium building the A10 Wamira.

Bibliography: Winjeel AFST 5044 Basic Trainer Proposal [1]
Watkins, W. (April 4, 1980). Engineering Report AA458. A Basic Trainer Proposal, Winjeel Modification. Commonwealth Aircraft Corporation.

WINJEEL AFST 5044 BASIC TRAINER PROPOSAL [2] 1980

This concept was a further development down the path taken in study AA458, the use of a modified Winjeel airframe to fulfill the need for an alternate new Basic Trainer for the RAAF.

In this instance the aim was to lower structure weight, reduce the wing area and increase the wing loading, thereby raising the speed to simulate the handling characteristics of some swept wing jets. By reducing the thickness/chord ratio and aspect ratios over the wing root sections, the extended inner wing leading edges would highlight the relationship between speed decay and rate of sink at nose-up attitudes over a wider range than was achievable with higher aspect ratio wings, developing in pilot students an angle of attack awareness early in their training career.

The span was to be reduced to 33 feet in a parallel planform wing of 5.5 feet chord with an area of 180 sq ft. This changed the wing loading and aspect ratios to around 23.25 lb/sq ft and 6.0 respectively from the original area of 250 sq ft; a wing loading of 17.2 lb/sq ft and an aspect ratio of 6.5.

The horizontal tail unit was also reduced in area and re-designed in an approximate configuration to that of the MB326H item. Whilst the ideas in this step were of a preliminary nature they highlighted the soundness and the development potential of the Winjeel.

This was to be the last time a modification was proposed for the Winjeel airframe. The number of known modification and configuration changes planned for the Winjeel described in this history starting with the CA-22 prototype, number nineteen(19). The only new lease of life the aircraft was to experience was in the hands of private owners following its retirement from the RAAF.

Bibliography: Winjeel AFST 5044 Basic Trainer Proposal [2]
Watkins, W. (1986). [Private notes & interviews].

CA-35 LADS Installation
1980-1987

LADS (Laser Airborne Depth Sounder) was an aerial hydrographic survey technique developed in Australia by an Australian group of companies headed by Thorn-EMI Electronics funded by the Royal Australian Navy. It was a concept derived from WRELADS I (Weapons Research Establishment Laser Airborne Depth Sounder I), an extensive R & D program led by the highly honoured Dr Mike Penny principal scientist from the Surveillance Research Laboratory of the Defence Science & Technology Organisation. An airborne laser land profiler WREMAPS II, started in 1969, designed and built in 1971 by the WRE, was flight tested in VH-FWG, a Beechcraft Queen Air of Union Air backed up with a Wild RC10 aerial camera. The laser platform was then modified to profile the sea bed and flight tested as the new WRELADS (backed up with an RC10 camera) in June 1975 on Beechcraft Queen Air aircraft VH-RUU also of Union Air, Toowoomba, Queensland.

From October 1976 testing took place off the South Australia and Queensland coasts. This progressed to the WRELADS II system platform designed and installed by AEL Engineering in the RAAF's ARDU C-47B (A65-86) aircraft in 1978-79 for initial test and evaluation by the RAN's Hydrographic Unit across a variety of Australian coastal conditions and sea states.

The impetus for the development of the WRELADS equipment was the large volume of hydrographic survey work required to be carried out by the Royal Australian Navy and the protracted timescale inherent in carrying out this task with shipborne systems in an area of national responsibility of approximately 1/8th of the earth's surface.

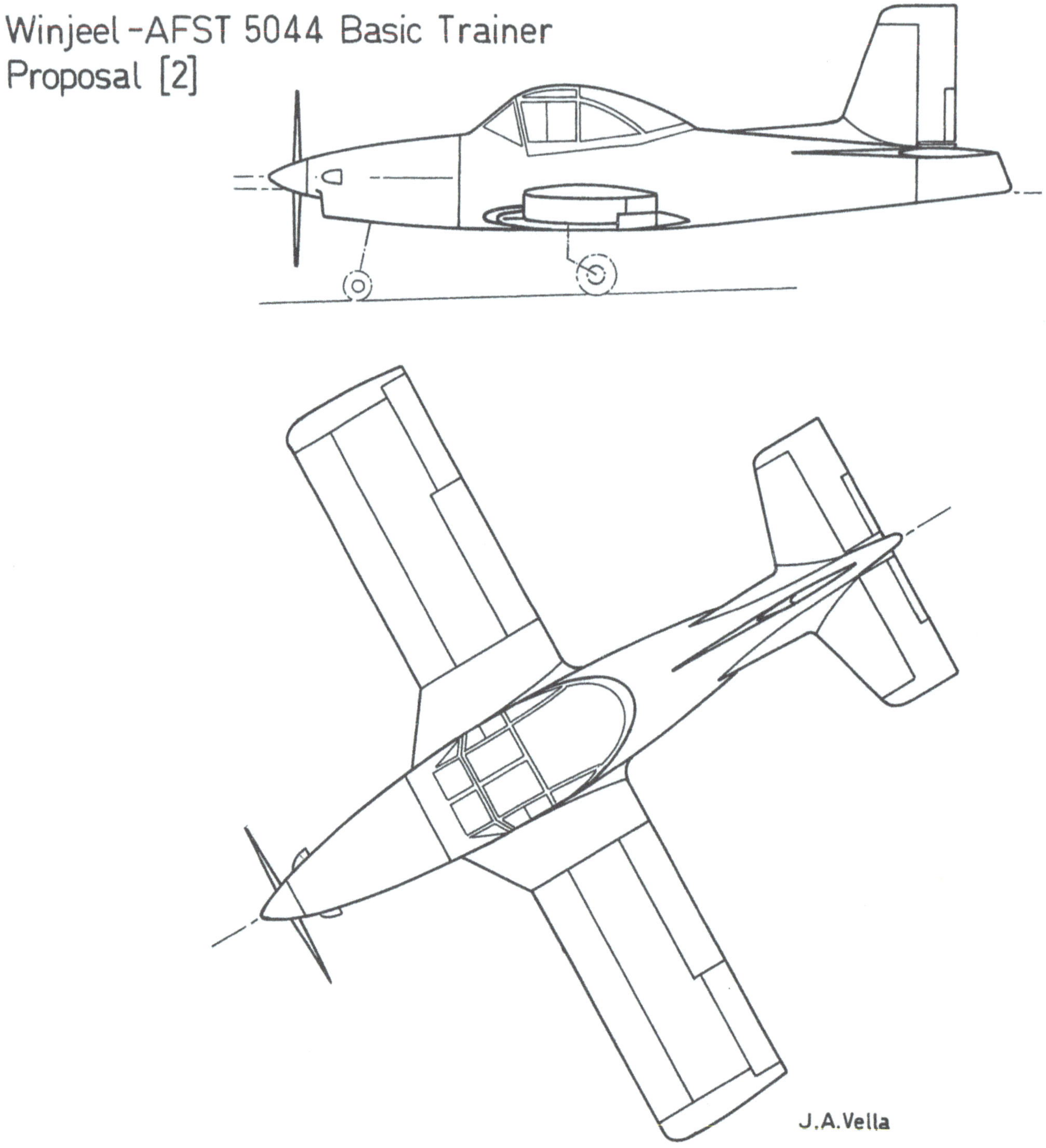

Winjeel-AFST 5044 Basic Trainer Proposal [2]

J.A. Vella

Naval Staff Requirement NSR 1102 was raised for an airborne system capable of incorporating the WRELADS II platform. CAC under sub-contract to EMI, participated in an initial $10,000 study phase that had its beginnings in the middle of 1980 to evaluate the aircraft requirements for an operational system. The follow-on Project Definition Study, a twelve month phase, also under the leadership of Thorn-EMI Electronics was allocated to various sub-contractors in their areas of specialization. This began in February 1982 and ended in May 1983 with Fairey Aviation (Aust) responsible for the mechanical design; Quentron for the laser equipment and CAC for aircraft structure modifications and the re-design of the on-board equipment. Software design developers, Computer Sciences Australia, was later added to the group.

Under project CA-35, CAC was to be responsible for the design of the mounting of the avionics racks, aircraft rewiring, ECS revision to cater for increased heat loads, the system console structure and the fitting of the laser scanning window or aperture in the lower fuselage. From 1973 CAC had built up extensive experience in this type of work when it was tasked with the CA-33 contract modifying the RAAF P-3C Orion fleet for the Marconi AQS-901 acoustic signal processing system and its associated equipment changes.

New Aerial Platform

As a result of the C-47 trials it became obvious that a number of improvements were needed for an operational system such as:

- A pressurized aircraft to allow economical cruising to and from station and for ferrying
- Use of an autopilot coupled to the WRELADS navigation computer for flight control and improved attitude stability of the aircraft given coastal turbulence conditions
- Reduction of on-board personnel numbers to operate WRELADS
- Greater onboard AC power
- Increased aircraft equipment and passenger ferry space

System Description

LADS was designed to operate in the waters of the shallow continental shelf in day and night conditions measuring sea depths in the range of six to 150 feet (the maximum depth depended on water turbidity) with an accuracy, following computer processing of better than 18 inches. It used two laser beams directed vertically downwards as the aircraft flew overhead. One beam was of infra-red wavelength and was reflected from the surface of the water providing a constant reference for depth measurement. The green beam was of a wavelength that could penetrate to considerable depth in the water and reflect off the sea floor. The variation in return time for the green beam, corrected against the infra-red reference beam was a direct measure of the water's depth and allowed the sea bottom to be profiled. The operational technique was to fly in pre-planned tracks over the area to be surveyed at an altitude of 1,500 feet and a speed of 135 kts. Under these flying conditions, LADS took depth soundings spaced 30 feet apart produced by the green beam as it was deflected by scanning mirrors over a traverse arc of +/- 15 degrees in a controlled sequence with an area coverage of 194,000 sq ft / second of mission time. At this stage the leading US physicist in the field of laser hydrography, Dr Gary Gunther had already described the Australian LADS as the most sophisticated and successful experimental system of its kind in the world.

Aircraft Selection

NSR 1102 had stipulated the need for a twin engine, pressurized, air conditioned aircraft with a speed of 136 kts (TAS), a time on station of four hours and a ferry range of not less than 1,200 nm. The Requirement sought the use of a commercial aircraft in which it would be possible to remove the WRELADS equipment and reinstate the aircraft back to its original configuration. The aircraft which met these criteria at that time were the Fokker F27 Friendship, the Fokker F27M Maritime and the Hawker Siddeley HS748. The F27 was especially well suited with ample internal volume, electrical and air conditioning capacity and a high placed wing which gave an unobstructed lower fuselage for locating a laser viewing hatch. It was also in widespread local airline use which enhanced its prospects of selection due to in-service back-up support; whereas the HS748 was hampered by the structure of its low set wing. Had the pressurisation requirement been waived, the probable airframe contenders were stated as being the CASA C212 Aviocar, the Shorts 330 and a version of the DHC-5D Buffalo.

L.A.D.S. test aircraft A65-86. RAAF Edinburgh, ARDU, S. Aust. April 5,1981. Aircraft has a temporary dorsal intake/vent mid-fuselage offset to stbd behind the blade antenna **David Anderson 715058101S**

Needing to familiarize themselves with the structural modifications already carried out to create the F27M Maritime, CAC's John Manderson, Ken Bateman and Murray Scott visited the Fokker Netherlands Company. Rather than retain the original 32 inch by 32 inch aperture in the bottom of the fuselage (as requested by the Defence Research Centre, Salisbury) that would have remained open during survey operations, it was decided to opt for an F27M modification of an 8.8 sq ft opening covered by an optical standards window protected by electrically operated externally-run hatch covers. In the event of a forced ditching at sea improved crew survival prospects were anticipated if further F27M features such as an upper fuselage escape hatch above the starboard observer station and the underwing pylon mounted tanks were adopted.

The pylon tanks of 209 Imp gall capacity, besides giving an increase in range and relief in wing root bending stress would act as stabilizers on a ditched aircraft in a manner similar to a flying boat reducing the roll angle and possibly preventing the wing tip from contacting the water. A windshield de-salting system for low overwater flying was also suggested. The overseas visit also took in Smiths Instruments (UK) for data instrumentation and Sperry (USA) for the interfacing of the preferred autopilot and the automatic navigation/track-keeping equipment. This equipment was to comprise of the Rook-Cubic Western Data Argo DM54 navigation/processing rack which was to provide automatic track-keeping and height control with a consistent positional accuracy to 45 feet in conjunction with ground reference beacons; the Depth Sounder Rack which included the laser and power supplies, video camera, data recorders and processors. The System Console was designed for one person operation with provision for a second assistant or training position.

The project ran into early problems as it became obvious to CAC that the Defence work definition specification lacked the necessary

The nose art (on both sides) of A65-86 of WRELADS/ARDU/DRC/RAN Hydrographic Service bodies involved in the L.A.D.S project. July 2, 1981 ,RAAF Edinburgh ,S.Aust. **David Anderson 719098105S**

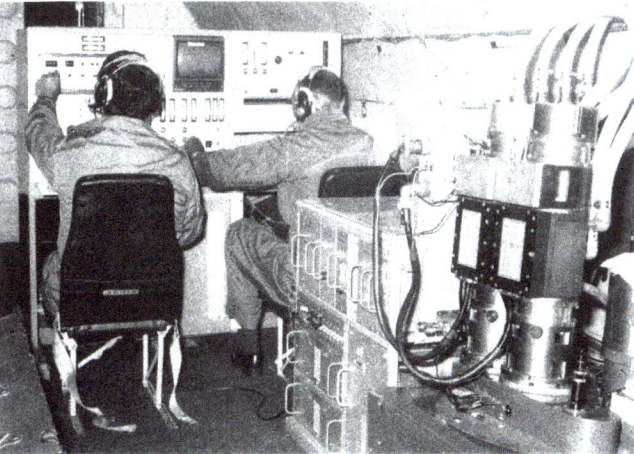

The experimental L.A.D.S. installed in the RAAF's Aeronautical Research & Development Unit C-47B, A65-86. **Department of Defence**.

VH-EWP in the 'NAVY Hydrography' eye-catching colour scheme of white, light grey, black, red, blue and the kangaroo aircraft roundels. Date, unknown; location (most probably Essendon, VIC) photographer unknown. **Roger McDonald Collection**

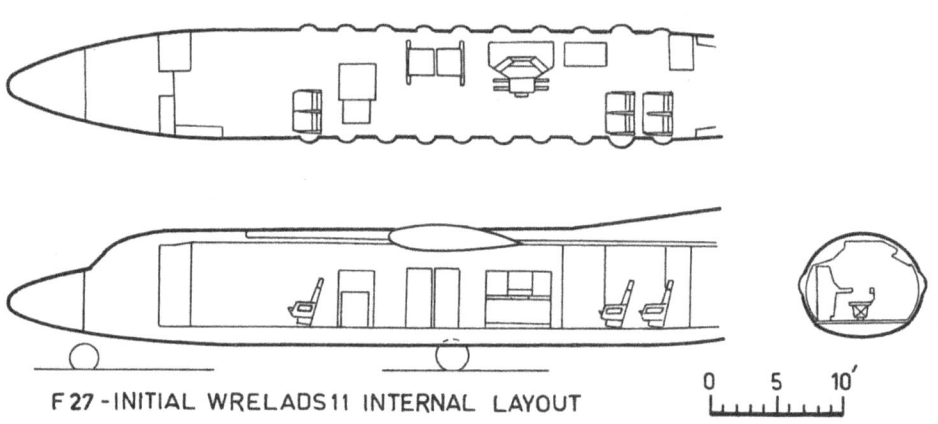

F 27 - INITIAL WRELADS 11 INTERNAL LAYOUT

CA-35 Laser Airborne Depth Sounder Installation

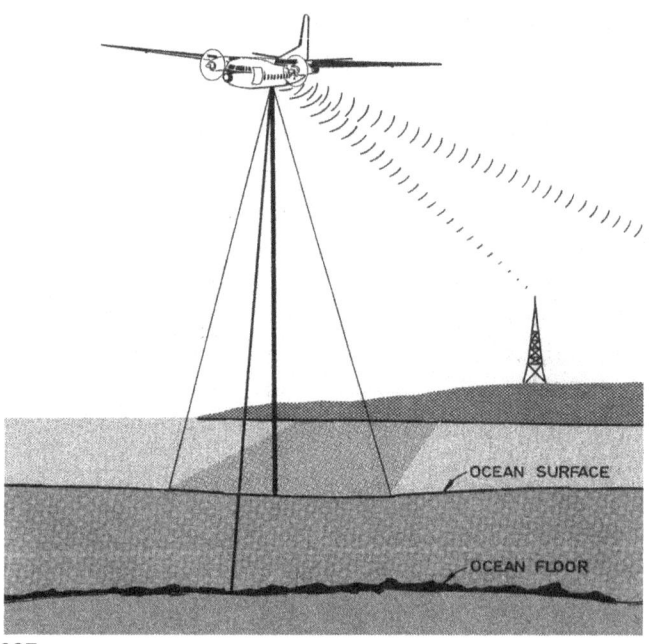

L.A.D.S. Aircraft. Fokker Friendship F27 VH-EWP with the laser rangefinder window in-line with the leading edge of the wing, cover open. October 27, 2007. **Roger McDonald**.

depth and detail. Its parameters were little removed from the demonstration system WRELADS II installed in the Air Force C-47, whereas CAC's aircraft assessment revealed the need for a vastly more efficient package with a greatly increased level of automation and consistent operation reliability. The necessity to re-write the specification to cater for a pressurised airframe and a more refined depth sounder system, stalled design work for about six months, creating cost and time-scale overruns with the inevitable budget blow-out for the Navy.

The program eventually came under the total control of the Defence Research Centre, Salisbury (DRCS), South Australia, a part of the DSTO, with the Navy, preparing to issue tenders in 1987 for a ten year program of aerial operation. Some $3M was earmarked for expenditure during 1987/88 from an eventual total program cost of $40M (1987 prices) with a planned in-service date of 1991.

By October 1986, CAC's commitment to the project had been reduced to the structural alterations of the lower fuselage for the laser viewing window with input from Fokker design.

On May 24, 1989 Defence announced that F27-500, VH-EWP of East-West Airlines, would be purchased and be extensively modified over 30 months in an $11M project to design and fit an operational system led by BHP Engineering, BAE Systems, Vision Systems and Honeywell at Adelaide Airport. East-West Airlines was to crew and operate VH-EWP within the contract. With WRELADS II installed, VH-EWP was completed on January 28, 1992 culminating 20 years and $50M of R & D. It was accepted for service by the Navy on October 8, 1993. Some $300M to $500M was estimated would be saved across 10 years using the new aerial surveying method as against the Navy's standard, slower multi-ship method.

Vision Systems and its subsidiary LADS Corp acquired DHC Dash 8-202 aircraft (VH-LCL) in January 1998 in which to install a smaller, more accurate LADS Mk 2 platform for general commercial use (separate from the NAVY's VH-EWP) both in Australia and on extended international deployments. Forty square nautical miles could be surveyed in a 7 hour sortie. Tenix Defence (LADS Corporation) acquired both companies in March 2000. National Air Support owned by Cobham UK was on contract to manage and support all operations of VH-LCL from 1998. In 2009 ,VH-LCL painted in Navy markings replaced VH-EWP.

CAC's airborne systems package design input into the concept was part of its success in its various iterations in different airframes from 1982 and for the following 35 years.

Bibliography: CA-35 LADS Installation Sub-Contract
Adf Serials. Army Beechcraft A65 & B70 Queen Air aircraft.
Aircraft & Aerospace. *Tenix LADS Corporation*. March 2003.
Clegg, J.E; Penny M.F. (January 1978). *Depth- Sounding from the air by laser beam*. Defence Department.
Commonwealth Aircraft Corporation. (1980). Minutes of CAC Board Meeting.
Commonwealth Aircraft Corporation (October 31,1980). Engineering Report AA475. WRELADS Engineering Study. Assessment of Aircraft Requirements.
Commonwealth Aircraft Corporation. (February 1981). Engineering Report AA512. LADS Aircraft Specification Draft.
Commonwealth Aircraft Corporation. (September 1,1981). Engineering Report AA521. Assessment of F27 Modification for LADS.
Hawkins, Max. 'Good prospects for exports of Australian LADS system'. Australian Aviation. (April 1992).
LADS, New Platform.(2015). *Australian Warship*, Issue no. 90.
LADS brochure.Thorn-EMI Electronics. (March 1982).
Laser Airborne Depth Sounder'. *Pacific Defence Reporter*. (June 1981).

AP1035 - REMOTELY PILOTED CROP SPRAYING HELICOPTER
June 1980

Early in 1980 CAC was invited by project management consultants Electronic Systems and Management Services Ltd, (ESAMS) Sydney, NSW (known as EASAMS in Europe), an independent (1976) company within GEC, to participate in a funded study to evaluate the viability of a design of a remotely controlled and independently operated helicopter it had under consideration from an unidentified client.

(ESAMS had been part of the 1971, EX300 Barra Sonobuoy project team). This unmanned helicopter was aimed at the night time, hazardous crop spraying operation for night feeding crop insects. A helicopter by virtue of its relatively slow speed and swirling air movement generated by the blade action would enhance the directing of released chemical spray at the vulnerable underside of the foliage of the affected plant crop.

Aircraft Description
The helicopter was remotely piloted, controlled solely by the action and interaction of the rotors as commanded by an auto-pilot and the remote pilot inputs from a control console. The flight action was of a constant forward speed/height flight with a conversion manoeuvre to a reverse constant/height travel on a path parallel to the previous flight path, all actions being automatic and correlated in space through constant interrogation from transponder aerials set up on the land boundaries of the operation. It was originally proposed with a 420shp Turbomeca Artouste turboshaft engine.

Jim Caterson and John Manderson's mechanical, aerodynamic and structural evaluation study was to consider replacing the French turboshaft by the Allison 250-C20 of a similar rating, located lengthwise along the longitudinal axis of the tubular frame with a common drive to the port and starboard rotors and to also reduce the structure weight. The two-bladed hinge-less rotors counter-rotated, the plane of each rotor disc was inclined at 85° to produce a dihedral effect. The open frame welded steel tube structure was to be in modular form for ease of repair and transportation with a concentration of the flight control equipment, spray tank, fuel and

Specifications	AP1035 Remotely-Piloted Crop Spraying Helicopter	
Powerplant	One GM Allison 250-B17C (C20) turboshaft engine of 417 shp at take-off	
Performance	Operating speed	60kt
	Vertical rate of climb at 10° C & 2,500 lb	960 ft/min
	Rate of climb at 10° C & 2,500 lb	1,680 ft/min
Weights	Engine dry weight	160 lb
	Empty	1,380 lb
	Max TO	2,500 lb
Dimensions	Rotor 12 ft dia, mounted at 15 ft centres	
	Basic airframe length	27 ft 6 ins
	Width	17 ft 6 ins
	Height	15 ft 8 ins
	Overall length to end of spray boom	90 ft

AP 1035

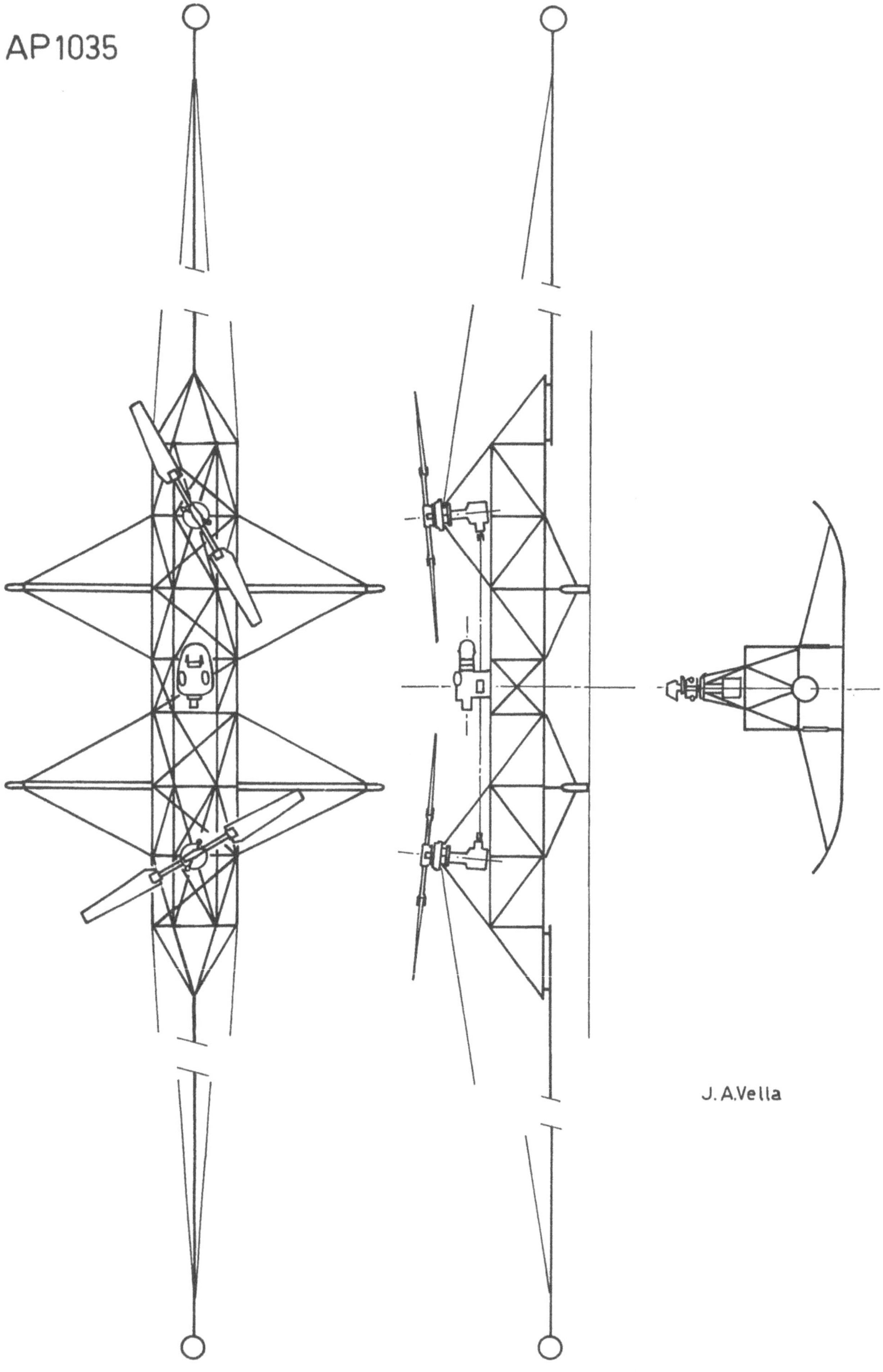

J. A. Vella

oil tanks on the vehicle centre line. Aerodynamic spheres at the ends of the 90 foot span, cantilevered wire braced spray rig booms, provided aerial damping and housed the command/control aerials. The entire assembly which sat on two spring dampened skids was much lighter and offered a greater disposable payload than the original Turbomeca Artouste powered design.

The study was confident that with further development to improve the out-of-ground-effect climb and further analysis of the stability and control characteristics, the design would achieve its original intent.

Bibliography: AP1035 Remotely Piloted Crop Spraying Helicopter

Commonwealth Aircraft Corporation. (June 4, 1980). Engineering Report AA463. ESAMS-Remotely Piloted Helicopter Project. Aerodynamic Design Evaluation.

AP1051 - PROJECT KAHU, RNZAF A-4 SKYHAWK MODERNISATION
1983 - 1985

During 1982 the Royal New Zealand Air Force released a Request for Proposals for the modernisation of its fleet of 22 McDonnell – Douglas A-4 Skyhawk fighter bombers. This significant and extensive Project Kahu (Maori indigenous language for 'Hawk') avionics upgrade program was estimated to cost some NZ$148M and was intended to bring these aircraft to about a 90% attack capability of the General Dynamics F-16 Fighting Falcon but for a sixth of that aircraft cost.

Responses were received from a number of vendors, including Israeli Aircraft Industries (IAI) but no decision was made because of funding and defence review considerations. In April 1984 after initial approaches from IAI for a combined IAI/CAC bid, CAC's senior management visited New Zealand for broader discussions. CAC'S Gerry Roberts, Neil Spence, John Manderson and Peter Howell were on the engineering team assigned to the project definition phase.

The following month CAC elected to bid as a prime contractor with IAI as the major sub-contractor. This was closely followed by a CAC evaluation team visit to Israel. Original perceptions of the total A-4 enhancement deal included the significant hardware tasks associated with the conversion of the A-4G variant acquired from the Royal Australian Navy to RNZAF A-4K configuration; a structural refurbishment program and a new navigation/attack package comprising of integrated weapons delivery, stores management, radar altimeter, INS, communications and sensors.

However the only section of the modernisation to be released to overseas industry was the avionics component, the other elements were retained for indigenous NZ resources. CAC's knowledge of the avionics systems under consideration was limited and as such the bulk of the design component of the submission came from Israel.

The link with IAI was attractive in that it offered the least technical risk as the principal systems which were offered were already operational in the Israeli Air Force's extensive A-4 Skyhawk light bomber fleet. IAI being also the supplier of a large proportion of the required avionics equipment drastically reduced the number of sub-contractors and streamlined the contractual arrangements. A number of other possible teaming arrangements had been considered and discussions were held with Ferranti, Boeing, and Marconi GEC. None of these companies had a basic suite developed and proven for A-4 integration. In most instances multiple contractor development programs with consequent risks appeared inevitable. CAC's prime contractor functions with IAI were for prototype development, project management, supply of IAI avionics and the manufacture of the necessary conversion kits.

This desire to pursue the prime role in Project Kahu was based on the hope of expanding on the experience of the P-3C Orion and Macchi MB326H system integration work already undertaken for the RAAF. Additionally, extending defence support into New Zealand in view of the then ANZUS alliance restrictions brought on by New Zealand's ban on visits of nuclear armed or powered ships, was an opportunity worth developing.

The bid submitted on July 30, 1984 and supported by an informal presentation to RNZAF Air Staff was rejected by the NZ Ministry of Defence Support Branch in October 1984. It was considered to be conservative in a technical sense in that it lacked an attempt to meet the RNZAF requirement for radar with air and sea search capabilities. It did not include a digital data transfer bus which would have simplified the integration of the various systems and components and to closely match the cockpit configuration required by the RNZAF. This lack of data bus precluded future weapons flexibility. Although the IAI weapons delivery and navigation systems were impressive, there was concern for the high cost of what was basically a fully (IAI) developed system and the amount of space it occupied such as the retention of the dorsal equipment hump.

Through the proven significant combat experience with their A-4 Skyhawk fleet in the Arab / Israeli conflicts, the Israeli's belief of what was needed for the RNZAF did not coincide or meet with what the customer requested – a strange bid strategy that puzzled the CAC team. The IAI involvement had become a matter of concern in New Zealand over long term or stretched logistic support. Additionally, CAC was in direct competition with Air New Zealand for the system

RNZAF McDonnell Douglas A4K ,NZ6215. Avalon, Airfield, Victoria. March 23, 1995. **J. A. Vella**

RNZAF Mc Donnell Douglas A4K, NZ6215,NZ6126. Avalon Airfield, Victoria. March 23, 1995. **J. A. Vella**

installation/integration work package, a factor that could have had some influence. This was in spite of concern for the capacity of the NZ aviation industry to handle the whole KAHU project. However CAC's good reputation, particularly on the engineering side was reinforced during Project KAHU presentations. It was highly regarded as a regional defence aircraft industry.

In January 1986 Smiths Industries SLI Ltd Avionics Corp began the co-ordination of the revamping of the avionics and attack systems. This work, together with the structural upgrading of the entire fleet was completed in December 1990.

Bibliography: AP1051-Project KAHU RNZAF A-4 Skyhawk Modernisation

Air International. (February 1987, November 1990).Key Publishing, Lincs, UK.

Commonwealth Aircraft Corporation. (March 1985).[In-House Memorandum Notes].

Commonwealth Aircraft Corporation. (July 25, 1984). Drg. AP 1051 Royal New Zealand Air Force Skyhawk Modernisation Proposal.

Roberts, G.A. (March 20, 1985). Royal New Zealand Air Force Skyhawk Modernisation. CAC Involvement to March 1985. Commonwealth Aircraft Corporation.

CHAPTER 11. POST MERGER PROJECTS
CA-37 PILATUS PC-9/A BASIC & ADVANCED TRAINER AIRCRAFT
July 1986

Although the construction and assembly program of the Swiss Pilatus Aircraft PC-9/A followed CAC's merger with HDHV, it fell inside what would have been CAC's 50th anniversary on October 17,1986.

In replacing the cancelled local AAC A10B Wamira Basic Pilot Trainer Aircraft, the Federal Government entered into a $230M contract on July 10, 1986 for the building and assembly of 67 flying examples of the PC-9/A and one static test specimen. Sixty nine aircraft were originally sought ($240M) but this was reduced to 67 airframes to compensate for escalation in costs. All but the first two (Pilatus c/n 501, 502) of the 67 aircraft were to be built, fitted out and assembled locally by HDH at their Bankstown, NSW plant.

The fixed price contract was unique in that it was the first occasion in which the production licence was held not by the Government but by the builder (HDH) providing the incentive for seeking further sales. Pilatus reserved constructor numbers 501 to 599 for HDH planned and possible production orders. The company was also to provide a total product support package covering the first three years of RAAF operation from flight line maintenance to major repairs and training.

While HDH Bankstown was the prime contractor, the main manufacturing tasks were to take place in Melbourne. HDH Victoria (HDHV, formerly CAC) would be responsible for the one piece wing, flaps and ailerons; (Dunlop and Transavia) with the main undercarriage. Composite material bay doors were offered for sub-contract. The wings for aircraft c/ns 503 to 508 were delivered as complete assemblies ex-Pilatus; 509 and 510 would arrive as sub-assemblies and c/n 511 would be almost entirely of local content, whilst the wing control systems and landing gear components for all aircraft through to No 19 would also be ex-Pilatus, Stans,Switzerland.

HDHV would take about 30% of the airframe work whilst ASTA's share (the former GAF) would be about 40%. The portion of the work allocated to HDHV was assigned the contract number CA-37.

ASTA's lead-in assembly program was similar to that of HDHV: complete fuselage assemblies, along with kits of system components, horizontal tail and elevator assemblies up to aircraft No 8 would be supplied by Pilatus. Thereafter smaller sub-assemblies were received up to airframe No 19 with ASTA's local input commencing with airframe No 20. Their involvement included the engine mounting, cockpit instrumentation metalwork and the canopy frame. The moulding of the canopy and the supply of the nosewheel would both be subject to sub-contact from aircraft No 20 onwards. The final task of assembling the aircraft belonged to HDH Bankstown, NSW through eight stages where the fuselage was fitted out with the controls, hydraulics, air conditioning, electrical/radio/avionics and engine looms, cockpit instruments, panels, ejection seats, engine module, flying surfaces and undercarriage followed by painting, inspection and test flight. The static test airframe destined for ARL came from the 10th locally built wing and the 18th locally built fuselage.

The PC-9/A had been optimised for sealed runways unlike the grass field capability which the RAAF had requested. Prior to the finalization of the contract Pilatus had demonstrated a working arrangement for the necessary low pressure tyres to be accommodated within the wing without a major redesign change, but with a recourse to bulged fairing doors. This was expected to require about 11,000 manhours of design and development in Australia to correct its shortcomings. This 'grass amenable' undercarriage provided a sink rate of 10 ft/sec, whereas that specified for the A10 Wamira Trainer local design had called for a sink rate of 13 ft/sec. Aircraft Nos 1-3 were scheduled for delivery in 1987; 4-10 in 1988; 11-24 in 1989; 25-43 in 1990 and 44-67 in 1991.

Production was to build up to two aircraft each month from airframe No 30 with the intention of RAAF acceptance in 1987 and of phasing the PC-9/A into the RAAF instructional syllabus during 1989. This was delayed slightly by problems of equipment quality. The CA-37 PC-9/A contract price was reduced from an original $34,88M to $30,30M by a lowered labor rate of $42.60/ hour.

Besides the change-over to low pressure tyres, other modifications and additions to the Australian PC-9/A were: engine secondary display panel revisions; anti-collision beacons fitted to the upper and lower aircraft fuselage; an oxygen pressure reduction valve; a fatigue data recorder; engine cowl inlet and ducting revisions. Permanently fastened metal-to-metal surfaces were wet assembled using corrosion suppressant barium chromate compound. The aircraft was inferior to the Wamira particularly in the area of damage tolerant design.

A23-007 of the Aircraft Research & Development Unit. RAAF Point Cook. Victoria. February 12 ,1995. **J. A. Vella**

CA-37 Pilatus PC-9A. A23-052. RAAF Roulettes Display Team. Avalon Airfield, Victoria..March 1999. **J. A. Vella**

The Clowns' last comment on Basic Trainer Aircraft configuration. **Roger Ward**

RAAF B707-338C, A20-629 of 33 Sqdn prior to the start of tanker conversion in the new HDHV hangar erected for the project. **Robert Anderson. RJA041218N.**

The Flight Refuelling Ltd Mk 32B pod. **Air Power Aust. Carlo Kopp**

The aircraft was not used in the basic flight training role. The RAAF went back from the start of 1993 to using a new fleet of AESL CT-4B Airtrainers with the side-by-side seating arrangement identical to that of the acrimoniously cancelled Wamira A10B. The RAAF allocated it the Series 3 aircraft ident A23 previously reserved for the cancelled Wamira Basic Trainer.

The PC-9/A was operated by 2 FTS at RAAF Pearce; Central Flying School/Roulettes display team at RAAF East Sale; No 4 Forward Air Control Development Unit at RAAF Williamtown, 76 and 77 Squadrons and ARDU at RAAF Base Edinburgh. Aircraft A23-020; 022; 031 and 032 were operated by the FAC Flight.

After approximately 30 years in service, withdrawal of the PC-9/A commenced in 2019 with the arrival of its replacement, the Pilatus PC-21 which together with a range of advanced ground simulators and training aids became both a basic and advanced trainer taking over from the PC-9/A and finally replacing the AESL piston engine, Avgas based, CT-4B Airtrainer step. The 49 new aircraft were built, finished and flown out from Stans direct to the RAAF.

Bibliography: CA-37 Pilatus PC-9/A Basic & Advanced Trainer

Australian Aviation. (May 1987, June 1987).

Bullen, R.D. (1987). PC-9 Program Manager HDH Ltd. [Interview].

Rees, D.D. (1987). Corporate Manager Market Development & Publicity HDHV. [Interview].

Kennedy J. (1987). PC-9 Project Manager HDHV. [Interview].

Whitney, J. (1987). PC-9 Project Manager HDH Ltd. [Correspondence].

CA-38 AERIAL REFUELLING TANKER CONVERSIONS 1989-1992

First suggested in 1982/83 and approved in the 1987 Defence White Paper under Project Air 5080, the RAAF issued a Request For Tender in June 1986 for the conversion of four of its six Boeing B707-338C (ex-Qantas) aircraft to the Aerial Air Refuelling (AAR) training role. On June 23, 1988 the Bedck Division of Israeli Aircraft Industries (IAI) was nominated project leader. It was originally listed as a $15M project. However in *'Taking the Lead-The RAAF 1972-1996'* it is listed as being allocated $45M and ended up costing $60M. HDHV was the main sub-contractor to install two underwing hose and drogue Flight Refuelling Ltd Mk 32B pods to each aircraft. This was to support the RAAF's airborne air refuelling probe-equipped, McDonnell-Douglas F/A-18 Hornet fighter fleet and to build up aerial refuelling experience for a future larger replacement aircraft.

Conversion work was centred at Melbourne's Tullamarine Airport in a newly erected HDHV hangar. Upgrade kits were provided by IAI (who had previously carried out similar work for the Israeli Air Defence Force) to install hydraulic powered fuel pumps submerged in the centre section fuel tank, which delivered fuel through new piping to the two pods. The addition of two new hydraulic fluid pumps to the accessory drive of engines 1 and 4 was done to back up the drives on engines 2 and 3. The self contained pods provided their fuel delivery working pressure and drove the vane pump/motor via their variable pitch, computer controlled, ram air turbine. The pods with an average flow rate of 2,800 lb/min, weighed 1,190 lb each for which the outer wings were strengthened. Fuel could only be delivered from the B707's own wing tanks supply. Design problems on the main fuel pump forced a five-month delay. Piping for a possible future centre-line refuelling boom was not installed, however during static ground fuel flow tests, equipment failure at that sealed take-off junction

B707-338C, A20-629 and the HDHV technical team at Tullamarine Airport, Victoria. **Ron Jenkins**

Boeing B707-338C A20-623 of 33 Sqdn, Tullamarine, Victoria. March 26, 2006. **George Canciani**

Boeing B707-338C A20-629 of 33 Sqdn, RAAF Richmond. NSW October 22, 2006. **George Canciani**

Remote TV camera in the new rear ventral turret operated by the flight engineer during air refuelling. **Ron Jenkins**

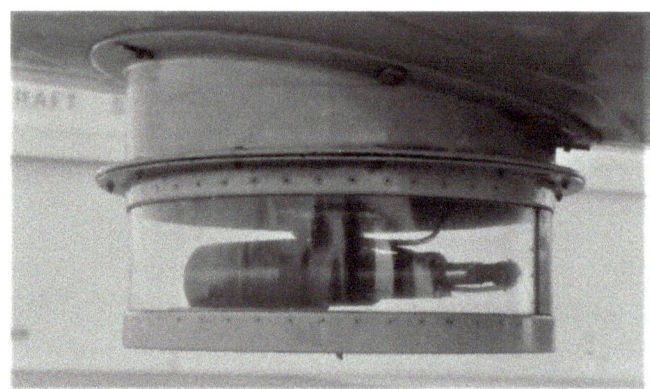

Side profile of the remote TV camera on B707-338C, A20-624. **Robert Anderson. FGH040818P.**

flooded the hold. Floodlights were fitted to illuminate the aircraft tail surfaces as well as infrared flood lights to illuminate the receiver aircraft during night operations. Refuelling operations were viewed through a remote TV camera fitted in a turntable assembly inside a new ventral, rear fuselage turret located just ahead of the rear cabin doors. The AAR process was operated by the flight engineer from new refuelling monitoring panels. The navigator's station was transformed into a mission co-ordinator station with a mission avionics CRT display.

New INS, TACAN, IFF and upgraded comms etc were required to allow receiver aircraft to locate and rendezvous with the tanker. Project management was divided between some six RAAF engineers and flight test personnel, Logistics Command, Airworthiness, 486 Maintenance Squadron, 33 Squadron aircrew and the prime contractor IAI. The HDHV component managed by Anthony Carolan was responsible for the design, manufacturing, assembly and aircraft installation. The project had a successful outcome for HDHV/CAC.

A20-629 (VH-EAI) was the first aircraft completed in February 1990 followed by A20-627 (VH-EAG) in April 1991; A20-624 (VH-EAD) and A20-623 (VH-EAC) for service with 33 Squadron.

As part of the Air Lift Group 84 Wing they operated over Iraq and Afghanistan from February 1998 in Allied Coalition and United Nations AAR operations.

Bibliography: CA-38 Aerial Refuelling Tanker Conversions

Kopp Carlo. *The RAAF Tanker Program.* Australian Aviation, May 1990.

Lax, Mark. (2020) *Taking the Lead, The RAAF 1972-1996.* Big Sky Publishing, NSW.

Richardson, David GRP CPT . [Correspondence] (2019).

CA-39 McDONNELL-DOUGLAS MDX/MD900 EXPLORER HELICOPTER
1989-1999

In March 1989 HDH committed $60M for a 20% share in the design and build of prototypes of the McDonnell Douglas Helicopter Company (formerly Hughes Helicopters) MDX/MD900 Explorer NOTAR (no tail rotor), anti-torque system helicopter. This project was part of the offset credit for the acquisition of the RAAF's F/A-18 Hornet fighter aircraft. Work at Bankstown included the design of the cabin fuselage and the building of composite parts.

Fisherman's Bend designed, manufactured, subcontracted all of the fabrication tooling and various assembly jigs and sheet metal details together with the final assembly with engines, all inspected by resident McDD and FAA reps. Flight testing was to be in the USA. A big gamble, the project suffered a large financial loss with on-going delamination problems due to faulty workmanship in the composites production process. Several aircraft were scrapped. Reports vary

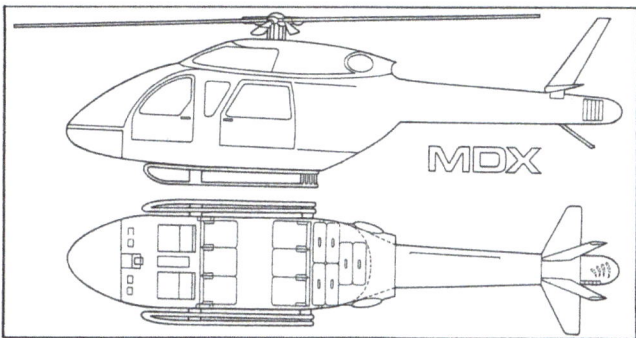

The McDonnell Douglas MDX NOTAR helicopter. **AIRCRAFT/Herald & Weekly Times**

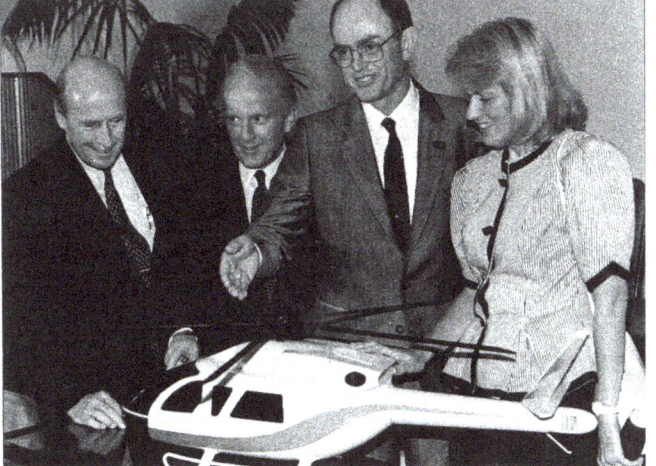

At the MDX signing ceremony Canberra, March 1989. L-R Pete Conrad, VP McDonnell Douglas Corp; Senator John Button, Minister for Industry, Technology & Commerce; Bruce Hattersley, Managing Director, HDH Ltd, and Ros Kelley, Minister for Defence Science. **AIRCRAFT/Herald & Weekly Times**

between 20 or 50 or 200 static test and production body assemblies being delivered before HDH under BTR Nylex ownership, decided to cut its losses and transferred the program to Tusas Aerospace Industries (TAI) in Ankara, Turkey which had extensive composites construction facilities. HDH/CAC personnel took part in the handover and follow-on training at TAI.

Boeing Aerospace (USA), in its takeover of McDD, inherited their light helicopter division then moved to divest itself of the MD900 and rest of its other helicopter range as a non-core activity in February 1999 but retained the highly successful AH-64 Apache attack helicopter. The Explorer was taken up by McDonnell Douglas Helicopters Inc (MDHI) located at Mesa, Arizona, a subsidiary of the Dutch based RDM Industrial Group. MDHI tried hard to reduce the MD900 high unit price. It proved incapable of delivering vital parts to operators in time via its large dispersed delivery supply chain. It ran into US certification problems with an overweight configured MD900 aircraft for one customer. It accumulated big debts but was rescued by the New York financial firm of Patriarch Partners in August 2005. The design had significant competition in the Eurocopter EC-135. About 139 examples were built or found customers.

Bibliography: CA-39 McDonnell Douglas Explorer Helicopter
Aircraft, HDH MDX Deal, March 1989.

Interavia, Notar, April 1988.

MDX-The New Helicopter Concepts. *Air Pictorial*, April 1989.

Rotor & Wing, MD Reborn, August 1999, March 2001.

Sullivan, Michael (1991-2000). HDHV Senior Production Planner. [Correspondence].

CA-40 LOCKHEED P-3C ORION ESM UPGRADE 1990-1995

HDHV with prime contractor Israeli Aircraft Industries in Project Air 5140 installed an additional Elta ALR-2001 Electronic Support Measures (ESM) sensor station. This gave the P-3C fleet a huge leap in its electronic intelligence gathering (ELINT) capability.

CA-41 GENERAL DYNAMICS F-111C AVIONICS UPDATE PROGRAM 1993-1997

Rockwell International teamed with subcontractor HDHV in August 1990 in a successful bid for Project AIR 5225, an extensive digital Avionics Update Program (AUP) on 21 aircraft of the RAAF's RF/F-111C bomber fleet. This was to improve the reliability, decrease the maintenance load and extend its life by 20 years to 2010. The A$474M project cost was split evenly between US and Australian industry.

Following Boeing's acquisition of Rockwell in 1996, Boeing Australia became the prime AUP contractor. The last modified F-111C aircraft (A8-148) was delivered in November 1999. The HDH/CAC known work included the manufacture of wiring looms and rewiring the weapons pylons for the digital upgrade. The project improved the aircraft's MTBF of its avionics from that of 3.5 hours to 179 hours.

CA-42 DETAILS UNKNOWN
CA-43 DETAILS UNKNOWN

CA-44 Sikorsky S-70B-2 & S-70A-9 HELICOPTERS

HDH took part in the assembly at Bankstown of the first batch of eight Sikorsky S70A-2 Seahawk helicopters for the RAN. By mutual agreement it withdrew for that part of the contract because the slow supply of parts, the complexity of the electronics and the lack of data from Sikorsky had become a problem. The eight aircraft were built in Florida instead and the project was passed to Aerospace Technologies of Australia (ASTA) in 1989 to complete the assembly of the second batch. This allowed HDH to devote its manpower to meeting its commitment to the assembly program of the Army's 37 Blackhawk helicopters.

CHAPTER 12. AERO ENGINE WORK

CAC ENGINE WORK – SUMMARY

Some 2,256* engines were built by CAC since 1936. This number, available at the time of compiling this work, included the engines which were purchased as lead-in examples. The equivalent number of engines built as production spares is not known. Table 1 lists only the engines in which CAC had a major production involvement, thus excluding the GE F404 and T700 turboshaft.

Repairs and total overhauls are known to have exceeded 4,000 engines. This figure omits a large amount of the then (1987) ongoing ATAR, Viper, F404 ,T700 jet engine and turboshaft support.

The Department of Aircraft Production Aircraft Advisory Committee Meeting notes of WW2 form the basis of the dates and entries for the entire engine requirements of that period. Some of the entries do not relate directly to CAC manufacturing, nevertheless they are included to provide a link to the airframe requirements and production planning of that period. Herb Knight, Engine Department Manager and CAC's second General Manager, was in his retirement, the author's source for much general oral information, hand written correspondence and insight regarding his time as manager of the aero engine division.

*Another CAC document has this figure at 2,500.

CAC / PRATT & WHITNEY R-1340 S1H1G WASP Radial Engine

The conditions of the original manufacturing licence of Pratt & Whitney engines with its parent company the United Aircraft Corporation of November 25, 1936 requested a fee of US$50,000 (£12,720) for the manufacturing data and specifications,US$500 for every engine built during the first 12 months and US$5,000 every six months thereafter.

The contract dated April 6, 1937 was valid for five years but was later extended a further five years to April 1947. United Aircraft Corporation agreed to forgo any royalty payments beyond April, 1944. The terms and conditions of the original agreement were to run for a period of ten years. At his second visit to United Aircraft, Wackett was successful in having the payment of royalties curtailed after the initial five year term. To the end of the royalty period, United Aircraft had received US$499,550 for engines and spares and US$155,712 based on a 7.5% royalty for the cost of locally manufactured parts.

On March 3, 1942, CAC reported to the Aircraft Production Commission that it had achieved an output of six completed engines each week and the equivalent of another two engines each week in replacement spare parts. The last of the 680 Wasp engines was completed on October 30, 1943. Herbert Knight was keen to remark that Wassilief, a engineering firm in South Melbourne, produced the silver-lead bearings for both the R-1340 and R-1830 master rods. The former were plain sleeves; the latter of the split variety. Both were of very high quality precision design with the final indium plating carried out by CAC.

On February 7, 1942 the DAP advised Wackett that R.W. Cameron & Co were shipping out two consignments of 400 ungeared R-1340 engines in February and April for use by the Armoured Fighting Vehicles Division of the Ministry of Munitions at Port Melbourne in the Australian Cruiser Tank Mk 1 *Sentinel* (Aust AC1). CAC had already supplied three engines to that Division for evaluation on December 18, 1941 and Wackett offered his assistance with the project having already had CAC run a series of tests on the *Scorpion* (direct drive Wasp) armoured fighting vehicle engine of behalf of the Division.

However the prime technical responsibility and project management within the Armoured Fighting Vehicles Division to convert the Wasp engines to cope with the difficult gear box torque was deemed by Wackett to be fundamentally wrong. There was no organisation in place to tackle the tank's power plant problem. He changed his mind, wanted nothing further to do with the concept and withdrew from it on June 15, 1942.

The tank project was subsequently abandoned in July 1943 with the war emphasis turning to building railway locomotives and supporting incoming American tanks. By 1946, three hundred and fifty of these American built engines were converted with CAC built reduction gear drives for use on the Wirraway production lines. The

Bench work in the Engine Factory.
L.J.Wackett /MS4858/NLA

Pratt & Whitney (CAC) R-1340 Wasp radial engine. The first engine and the second most numerous type built by CAC. **HDHV**

Table 1: Piston Engines Produced By CAC					
Licensor	Engine Model	HP	Number Produced	Factory	Application
P & W	R1340	600	680	Fisherman's Bend	CAC Wirraway, Ceres
P & W	R1830	1200	870	Lidcombe	GAF Beaufort
CAC/P & W	R795	450	2	Fisherman's Bend	CAC prototypes for Winjeel CA-22
Rolls Royce	Merlin 102	1760	108	Lidcombe	GAF Lincoln
Piston Engines Sub-Total			1660		

Table 2: Jet Engines Produced By CAC

Licensor	Engine Model	Thrust (lbs)	Number Produced	Factory	Application
Rolls Royce	Nene 2-VH	5000	114	Fisherman's Bend	HDH Vampire
Rolls Royce	Avon Mk 1	6500	44	Fisherman's Bend	GAF Canberra
Rolls Royce	Avon Mk 109	7350	47	Fisherman's Bend	GAF Canberra
Rolls Royce	Avon Mk 20	7500	52	Fisherman's Bend	CAC Sabre
Rolls Royce	Avon Mk 26	7500	75	Fisherman's Bend	CAC Sabre
SNECMA	ATAR 09C	13230	140	Fisherman's Bend	GAF Mirage IIIO
Bristol Siddeley	Viper ASV 11	2500	119	Fisherman's Bend	CAC MB326H
Jet Engines Sub Total			591		
Total All Engines			2251		

R-1340 was also used on the CA-28 Ceres aerial agriculture application aircraft.

The reality of the first aero engine mass production in Australia was the prodigious effort of engineering turnaround in metals availability, sub-contractor establishment and continued reliability where almost none had existed previously, at least not to the exacting degree of quality and quantity required for the sustenance of a wartime endeavour, as it subsequently became.

Most importantly, the industry was able to rescue hundreds of engines damaged by use in harsh operational conditions and put them back in service, achieving a saving of both time and money.

CAC / PRATT & WHITNEY R-1830 S1C3-G TWIN WASP Radial Engine

The office of the Prime Minister's Department informed CAC on November 15, 1939 of the Government's desire to build a factory to produce the P&W Twin Wasp to meet the needs of the DAP Beaufort bomber project and siting it in the Sydney metropolitan area was expected to tap a new resource of manpower. CAC was to choose the location (Lidcombe, NSW), arrange the plant layout and erection and to manage and operate the facility on behalf of the Commonwealth Government.

Planning centred on an output of 40 engines each month working to a two-shift routine, building up to 48 engines each month during 1943. The long term aim was to convert the R-1340 Wasp production line at Fisherman's Bend to the construction of the S1C3-G also at the rate of 48 engines each month. This transfer did not eventuate because the necessary machine tools on request from the United States did not materialize.

When the 14 cylinder 1,200 hp, R-1830 S1C3-G radial engine was selected for local manufacture the more powerful two stage S3C3-G variant had not been available. On its later availability it was considered neither practical nor desirable, having regard to the delay which would have been incurred in embarking on production, to switch over to the manufacture of the higher powered variant.

Arrangements were made for the supply of materials for a total of one thousand S1C3-G engines and spares in anticipation of Beaufort and the later CA-11 Woomera bomber requirements. Limited production was underway by the end of March, 1941 and the first delivery was made in November. The local introduction of the engine was assisted by the arrival from the United States by June 1942 of 155 examples of the engine, thirty of which were in component spares. Early difficulties were encountered in the cutting of bevel reduction gears. CAC was not alone in this, P&W had come across the same problems but the issuing of revised manufacturing data overcame this set-back. In spite of this difficulty 511 Twin Wasps had been delivered to December 31, 1943 five engines less than the scheduled number. Local content level reached the high mark of 95%.

The USAAC was a second customer for R-1830 spare parts. A £2M order, the equivalent to 250 new-build engines or six months work was placed in March 1944. Work on this contract stopped before the order was half finished because of the withdrawal of United States forces from Australia. For a time in 1944, this extra workload created a drop in output of completed new engines to 20 each month.

At the end of the war (August 31, 1945) the tally of completed engines stood at 870, not including the spares production equivalent to 130 completed engines. With the changeover of production at Lidcombe to the build of Rolls Royce Merlin engines, the machine tools and tooling for the production of R-1830 spares were transferred to Fisherman's Bend. This was very useful in the overhaul of the Twin Wasp on civil DC-3 aircraft coming into local service. The breakdown in model numbers is not available but the company overhauled 307 Twin Wasps for the RAAF and 1,071 examples for the USAAC during WW2. It is likely that the latter figure includes the USAAC's larger R-2800 engines.

The production licence fees for this, the second engine from United Aircraft Corporation to be built in Australia for the Commonwealth Government, included an initial lump sum payment of US$95,000 (A£30,000); US$750 for each engine built, and 6% of the value of manufactured spare parts. The terms to January 29, 1946; the end of the five year licence agreement had netted United Aircraft US$519,000 for the building of engines and A£162,295 for manufactured spares.

One very important component of both the R-1340 and R-1830 engines which was still imported, was the sodium cooled exhaust valves. The R-1340 used a hollow stem valve and the R-1830 a hollow stem and head valve. These valves had given excellent service but as the age of engines increased it was possible the rejection rate could increase and valves could be difficult to obtain from the manufacturers – Thompson Products in the United States. The sodium cooled valve was probably the most important factor in the success of American air cooled radial engines. It permitted even the largest engines to be operated successfully with two-valve (inlet and exhaust) heads. This enabled the most favourable shape of the heads and the cooling fins.

Following the successful approach to Thompson Products for a manufacturing licence, both types of valve were forged locally. However it was not necessary to proceed with quantity production as the war finished shortly after the start of local manufacture. James

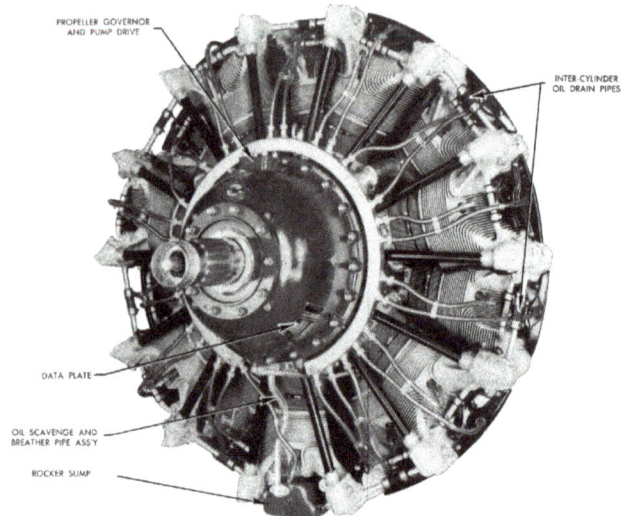

Pratt & Whitney (CAC) R-1830 Twin Wasp radial engine, the first twin-row radial engine produced by CAC. **HDHV**

H. Kirby who had been Lidcombe's manager since February 1941, resigned from the position in July, 1946.

In July 1982 CAC was still in the unique position of supplying R-1340, R-1830 and R-2000 engine cylinder heads to customers in the United States.

PRATT & WHITNEY R-1830 S3C4-G TWIN WASP Radial Engine

CAC was not involved in the manufacturing of this, more powerful, version of the Twin Wasp. It was the engine fitted in the Boomerang series as well as in some production blocks of the DAP Beaufort bomber.

With the design of the Boomerang fighter, the use of this engine became a priority allocation, the Department of Aircraft Production documenting in February 24, 1942 the need for 400 examples of the engine for the following year's aircraft production. This demand was raised shortly after to 1,038 engines to be imported and delivered by August 1943. Total deliveries to June 1942 had been 128 engines. DAP Beaufort production aircraft numbers 1 to 50 and 181 to 450 were earmarked to receive the S3C4-G Wasp.

WRIGHT R-2600 CYCLONE Radial Engine

The 451st and subsequent examples of the DAP Beaufort bomber were planned to have the Wright R-2600 Cyclone radial engine. CAC's developing CA-11 Woomera bomber was also a candidate for this engine as part of a planned future improvement of its performance. To meet the operational need during 1944/45, orders for 600 examples of the 1,600/1,750 hp R2600B and sufficient spares had to be placed by 1943.

On April 21, 1942 the DAP had confirmation that one hundred and forty-five R-2600B engines had been allocated for delivery by the United States. Ten engines were to be received in June and July and twenty-five each month thereafter to December. These, CAC planned to use on a growth version of the Boomerang. (Refer to Proposal P176).

However the United States Joint Aircraft Committee refused to make any further allocations beyond a small number, (about 10 engines), to be used on the DAP Beaufort and CA-4 Wackett bomber for type trials. Further allocations would only have been possible if these re-engined aircraft displayed an improved level of performance.

The only way of closing the gap between the supply of the S1C3-G engines manufactured at Lidcombe and the operational need, was to import quantities of either the P&W S3C4-G or the Wright R2600B, or both. The Manpower Authority was consulted as to the feasibility of establishing a Wright Cyclone production line. Lawrence Wackett took this a step further by advocating to the Aircraft Advisory Committee on August 4, 1942 that the test house facilities and tooling to be established at CAC as part of the support program for the overhaul of R2600 engines of the USAAC, also be used as the basis for the local production of the engine. This would have been further assisted by including the tooling the RAAF had in use at Wagga for the overhaul of the R2600.

The USAAC withdrew from Australia before the project at Fisherman's Bend had got underway. The matter was deferred and no engines were received for incorporation into any prototype trial aircraft and no production was undertaken.

PRATT & WHITNEY / CAC R-2000 Radial Engine

The R-2000 engine came into prominence at CAC through plans to incorporate a more powerful engine into the Boomerang fighter and Woomera bomber airframes. (Refer to aircraft texts). The object was to increase the engine size to overcome heating problems when the R-1830 was operated at full load under tropical conditions.

R-2000 modification drawings were brought from the United States by a Pratt & Whitney engineer during July or August 1942. The basic alteration to an R-1830 S1C3-G fourteen cylinder radial engine (then in production by CAC) was to increase the displacement capacity from 1,830 cubic inches to 2,000 cubic inches and install a geared fan to force cooling air over the cylinders. The DAP meeting of October 19, 1942 revealed that the Air Board had given the authority for CAC's Lidcombe factory to assemble five examples of the R-2000 engine. It was the Board's hope that if the engine was successful it would become the basic Boomerang engine, releasing the S3C-4G unit for the DAP Beaufort.

By January 1943 the first engine, fitted with an 8.47 to 1 blower, was undergoing initial testing at Lidcombe, NSW. Its performance was equivalent to the S3C4-G fitted with a two stage blower. The second R-2000 was built with a 7.15 to 1 blower and on completion the engines were sent to Fisherman's Bend for serious trials. During the early testing phase the cast magnesium cooling fan blades suffered metal failure. A redesign was undertaken in forged aluminium which followed closely on the BMW fan fitted on the front of the engine in the German Focke Wulf Fw 190 fighter.

After 60 hours of testing the emphasis was on the R-2000 with the 7.15 blower, production of which was considered to be more feasible than tooling up for the S3C4-G. Test bench figures were 1,300 hp at 2,700 rpm at take-off and 1,100 hp at 2,250 rpm at 4,000 ft. On August 2, 1943 two articulating connecting rods failed under test but were replaced by strengthened substitutes. The third engine was fitted with 16:9 spur reduction gears to obviate the production of the de-coupled nose and save on a considerable number of ball bearings, but in October this gearing failed and the engine reverted to testing with a bevel gear reduction.

The re-designed fan was a success in its 50 hour ground test. Compared with the United States version of the R-2000 which involved a re-design of cylinder heads to gain extra cooling, CAC's approach was to gain the main increase in horsepower through an increase in cylinder capacity and the use of forced cooling air. Wackett's hopes and aspirations for the R-2000 grew as the engine underwent progressive testing. He hoped the engine design would be one which CAC could claim as its own and one which would find a place in post war civil aviation.

Substituting the R-2000 for the R-1830 in aircraft which were then in service would extend the military usefulness of those machines by some 12 months. The engine was now expected to produce 1,300 hp in continuous operation, 1,350 hp for 5 minutes and would result in a 500 ft / minute better rate of climb and a 15 mph increase in speed. By November 8, 1943 all five authorised build engines had been completed and an output of 1,350 hp, with 52 inches of boost at full power, without a fan was achieved. The next step was to enlarge the inlet valves to produce 1,400 hp for take-off with 56 inches of boost (this was achieved in March 1944).

Towards the end of 1943, the fan was given its flight test on Boomerang A46-157, a standard production aircraft powered by the S3C4-G engine. This was able to give a sustained climb to 25,000 feet with engine cowling gills shut, without exceeding 240°F on the hottest cylinder. The engine was a source of continuous frustration because of repeated interruptions in the type trial due to failures caused by build errors, carelessness in the fitting of the cooling baffles or other defects. These were not related to the engine changes introduced as part of the upgrade, but with components which were in everyday use in thousands of engines but which, in a particular engine that had been selected for test, subsequently appeared to have been below standard. There were two instances of master rod bearing failure because of a defective centre main bearing liner.

In June 1944 one engine was finally dispatched to the CSIR for official type testing. This engine suffered a mishap in September when, through an oversight, a plug in the lubricating system was not removed. The fan seized up and the engine was damaged. This led to disagreement between CAC and CSIR on the method of engine testing which was resolved in time for a second R-2000 to be accepted by CSIR in November. A fan-cooled R-1830 was also delivered for a basis of comparison. By September 30, 1945 with nearly 90% of testing complete, a piston of one of the test engines was destroyed because of excessive ring wear and distortion. The program came to an end without a single R-2000 engine getting airborne.

Two of the five engines were earmarked for test installation on a DAP Beaufort. However, the DAP Division did not react very favourably to this gesture as the aircraft cowlings would have needed to be extended forward to accept the cooling fan. Without the fan, the installation would not have been effective.

The question of infringement of the licence arrangement with United Aircraft brought about a series of written exchanges with CAC. It was CAC's opinion and contention that the fan-cooled R-2000 engine fell outside the scope of the R-1830 Twin Wasp licence agreement.

PRATT & WHITNEY R-2800 DOUBLE WASP Radial Engine

The subject of building a new, bigger aero engine was revived by Wackett on October 27, 1942 in a memo sent to the DAP favouring the 1,950 hp Pratt & Whitney R-2800, 18 cylinder Double Wasp radial engine. His comments were based on a technical report prepared by Herb Knight outlining the extreme simplicity of this engine in comparison with the R-1830 and its similarity to the R-1340 Wasp which CAC was building at Fisherman's Bend. Wackett argued for modifying or discarding the plan to upgrade the Boomerang with the Wright Cyclone R-2600 and move instead into obtaining a licence to build the R-2800 at the rate of 40 engines each month incorporating the engine into the design of a new fighter. On November 9, 1942 he presented the merits to be gained from the one organisation building both the engine and designing the airframe. The Board of Directors meeting on that day approved Wackett's plans with the big engine.

The Lidcombe plant was overhauling one P&W R-2800 per day for the USAAC for a requirement of 30 engines each month. The planned factory expansion was to make it possible to overhaul thirty R-2800 and sixty R-1830 engines each month.

On November 30, 1942 Herb Knight requested a loan of one R-2800 from Lidcombe to enable a study of its construction to be made and to investigate in detail the capability of CAC's machine tools to fabricate all components of the engine (see also CA-15). Lidcombe dispatched an engine on April 15, 1943. The situation was analysed as being highly dependant on the availability of tooling. Utilizing all of the local tool-making facilities and with appropriate priorities organised in the United States, it was expected to take at least 18 months to establish all of the production tooling. There was a further 12 month wait assuming a reasonable quantity of forgings was available from the United States before there would have been full absorption of the company's facilities. The proposal got no further other than a later attempt in April 1944 to seek specifications and manufacturing data to build R2800 spares for USAAC.

Bibliography: R-1340; R-1830; R-2600; R-2000; R-2800 Radial Engines

Commonwealth Aircraft Corporation. Scorpion Engine. (1941-1942). File No 1.

CAC wartime factory progress reports & the fortnightly wartime meetings of the Department of Aircraft Production.

WRIGHT R-3350 CYCLONE Turbo Compound Radial Engine Spares

CAC was given a proposal on November 16, 1948 by the secretary of the DAP that the company build spare parts for the challenging complex Wright Cyclone R-3350 engines fitted on the 18 Lockheed Constellation aircraft operated by Qantas Empire Airways. The cost of the volume of high usage spares had reached US$1.5M a year. There is no evidence that CAC took on this work.

ROLLS ROYCE Nene 2-VH Turbojet

The DAP became aware on August 29, 1946 of Federal Cabinet's approval to make an initial purchase of 50 De Havilland Vampire fighter aircraft and to substitute the 5,000 lb thrust Rolls Royce Nene turbojet engine in place of the original 3,500 lb thrust Rolls Royce

Goblin. The first order for 60 engines was placed on September 2,1946. Hugh Francis, CAC's Aircraft Factory Manager and Chief Aeronautical Engineer who had led a team of twelve of the company's airframe and engine specialists on a jet engine and airframe study tour of the United Kingdom in August 1945, initiated the Nene licence negotiations with Rolls Royce.

The Aircraft Division's engineering representatives on the team had a dual interest as that division was to handle the production of the sheet metal components of the engine. These CAC staff provided an important nucleus of expertise in the industry when a rapid expansion of industrial effort was needed to cope with the entry into the Nene project and the much larger Avon turbojet program which soon followed.

On February 2, 1947 the Australian Government reached an agreement for the licence production of the Nene for a lump sum fee of £50,000; together with £200 for every engine built and £5,000 for each of the first four years of the licence. The CAC team that was sent over to familiarize itself with the Nene layout arrived at Rolls Royce, UK in March 1947 but found their entry to the premises barred until the Australian Government had handed over half of the agreed lump sum.

Meanwhile fitting the Nene in the single seat Vampire for the RAAF necessitated a series of changes to the design of the engine. Because of its weight it was necessary to mount the engine further forward. This was not possible, so in order to achieve the correct aircraft balance Rolls Royce changed the large aluminium alloy structural components to magnesium. The balance was still incorrect, so the detachable nozzle on the jet pipe with its two joining flanges and multitude of bolts was discarded in favour of a fixed nozzle. Due to the closeness of the engine to the pilot a special stressing requirement was applied to the Vampire airframe to cover a 25g crash landing situation. Very early in the project, CAC was advised the magnesium components had not been checked to meet the special 'crash' landing case so that it became necessary to produce local modifications to increase the strength of the four attachments of the compressor casing to the attachment points of the supporting steel tube structure.

The turbine blades and turbine nozzle guide vanes were likely to be high usage items. National Forge (Melbourne) undertook production of the turbine blades and CAC machined all the faces on an eight spindle copy milling machine. The stator nozzle guide vanes were produced as precision castings by the lost wax process and CAC requested that the Government obtain an *Austenal* licence for the process. This was refused as it was officially claimed by DAP that any competent dental mechanic could handle the work. This took no account of the high metallurgical standard needed for the vanes and the turbine blades, both of which were subject to thermal shock and creep. Finally it was accepted that a licence would be necessary and a precision casting unit was established at CAC. Major new sheetmetal fabrication and production techniques on specialised machinery were introduced. Hampered by the government poor decision making process, some components had to be always imported.

Other machines were adapted to work on the two-sided compressor discs. In turn the Aircraft Division installed continuous electric seam welding equipment to handle large volumes of work on combustion and exhaust components. Another 38 engines were ordered on October 26,1950 followed by a further 16, brought on by a heavy Vampire training program in support of the Korean war.

The first Nene, one of eight units assembled from imported components was tested in October 1948. Australian content was

The Rolls Royce Nene centrifugal turbojet, the first jet engine in RAAF service. **HDHV**

around the 90% level by the fifteenth engine. Production at the rate of one engine every two weeks ran from December 1948 to July 27,1954 with a brief production peak of one engine per week to total 114 examples. One hundred and eight modifications were generated locally and some 3,400 tooling items were used.

ROLLS ROYCE MERLIN 102 Liquid Cooled Engine

The Merlin 102 was originally intended for the cancelled twelve aircraft of the GAF Avro Tudor 1 project. One hundred and eight units were built at Lidcombe between 1945 and May 1952 for installation in the GAF Lincoln bomber / maritime patrol aircraft from the order placed in March 1944..

CAC R795 CICADA Radial Engine

CAC manufactured the Pratt & Whitney R-1340 Wasp and the R-1830 Twin Wasp radial engines to a combined total in excess of 1,500 engines together with large quantities of critical spare parts. Some of the extremely arduous operation conditions of WW2 under which aircraft fitted with these engines operated, demonstrated the reliability and durability of these engines as well as the importance of the availability of an efficient spares supply. A high level of local self-sufficiency was achieved and it was possible to increase this aspect significantly by component redesign in several areas had the need arisen.

The RR Merlin in-line liquid cooled engine travelling assembly line at CAC's Lidcombe, NSW plant. **HDHV**

CAC R795 Cicada

In respect of the prototype CA-22 Winjeel Basic Trainer which was requested in 1948, an engine of an estimated 450 hp capacity was considered to be of adequate performance and would offer the required levels of reliability and durability whilst operating under severe operational conditions. Limited finance was authorised by the government for the design and local production of two prototype test engines. For this reason and to minimize the time involved it was decided to make maximum use of existing materials, tooling and readily available P&W R-1830 Twin Wasp production facilities.

The design that was settled on was of a seven cylinder single row radial engine based on the use of the front and rear crankcase section forgings of the R-1830 and the modified crankshaft and connecting rod assemblies of the R-1340. Adjusting the bore and stroke to 5.375 inches and 5.0 inches respectively, a displacement of 795 cubic inches was achieved.

Through the generous use of cooling fins for both cylinder heads and barrels and the provision of pressure type deflectors to force a high velocity flow of cooling air through the finning of the cylinder assemblies, the engine output was judged to match that available from the contemporary 450 hp nine cylinder Pratt & Whitney R-985 Wasp Junior engine. This was further emphasised by the use of a high compression ratio (6.7:1) and higher revolutions (2,600 rpm) to make up for the lower capacity. The engine was 125 lbs heavier than the Wasp Junior so its fuel consumption would have been greater.

Fewer cylinders meant a reduced maintenance and production commitment. Additionally it presented the opportunity of increasing the strength of some of the more highly stressed components. An engine of this size would normally have been of the direct drive type but it was decided that gearing would have the advantage of improving propeller efficiency and reducing propeller noise. In the interest of weight reduction and simplicity of production, a completely new spur gear design was adopted. The propeller shaft, offset in the vertical plane from the crankshaft, turned at a ratio of 0.8:1 to the engine speed.

Provision was made in the design of the nose section of the propeller shaft for the installation of either a constant speed or a Hydromatic type propeller. These were available from the Hawker de Havilland Company, Bankstown, NSW who completed two prototype propellers for the Cicada. Their design was based on units in production in the UK on the English engines on the de Havilland

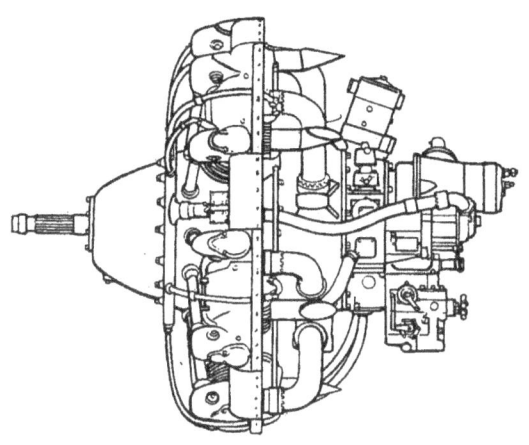

Dove and Percival Prince aircraft but modified to follow the American standards on the Cicada. They were were three bladed lightweight Hydromatic, fully feathering, capable of reverse pitch, but with a reversed right hand rotation, 99 inches in diameter, with a potential for an increase to 108 inches in a larger or multi-engine installation.

Throughout the manufacturing programs of the R-1340 and R-1830 engines it was necessary to satisfy the need for ball and roller bearings through overseas imports. For the Cicada, the deliberate step was taken to replace these as far as possible by plain bearings.

Damaged internal components in one of the test mishaps with the CAC Cicada test engines. **HDHV**

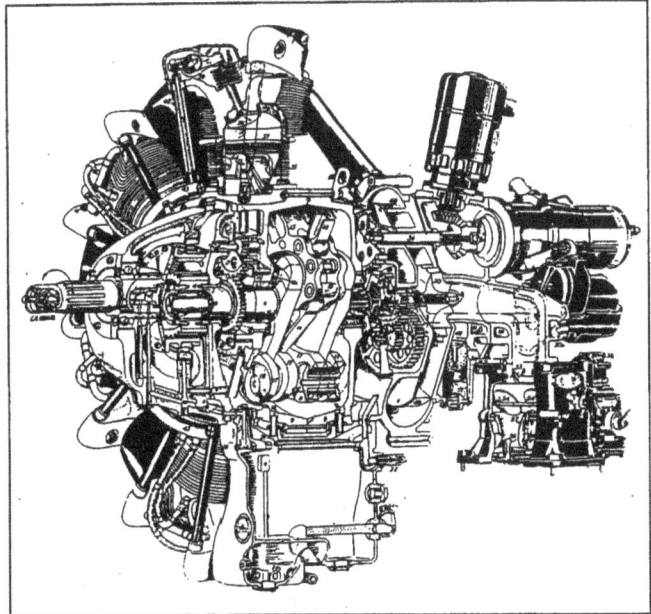

A cut-away drawing of the Cicada. **L.J.Wackett/MS4858/NLA**

Damaged internal parts from one of the structural failures during qualification testing of CAC's Cicada radial engine. **HDHV**

Specifications	CAC R795 seven cyl, air cooled radial engine of 450 hp at 2,600 rpm at SL
Technical Data	10:1 supercharger 0.8:1 reduction gear Injection type carburettor Bore 5.375 ins Stroke 5 ins Swept volume 795 cu ins(13.1 litres)
Weights	Dry 770 lb
Dimensions	Diameter 46.5 ins Length 58 ins

Their adoption meant internal friction in the engine would result in some loss of efficiency but it was preferable to accept that loss rather than the possibility of a breakdown in supply of bearings from overseas. The manufacture of critical plain bearings such as those for master connecting rods had already been successfully achieved in Australia.

CAC's first indicative cost estimate of January 31, 1949 for the research and development phase of the two test engines was put at £60,000 but the Government stated in September 1949 that it would not go above £50,000.

Design was completed in October 1950 and work on construction of the prototype engines began in November. It proceeded in fits and starts due to the more important dictates of the CAC/Rolls Royce Avon engine production plans, however by February 1952 both Cicadas had developed full take-off power without any difficulty. Because of the constraints of a limited budget, advantage was taken of the stock of BTH magnetos which had accumulated in RAAF stores and were offered to CAC. The BTH units were stated to be suitable for operation in either direction of rotation and to fit in with the existing layout in the engine rear section. Installed on Avro Anson aircraft their direction of rotation was opposite to that of the Cicada. Many of them had been used for unknown number of hours and presumably some distortion of the teeth in one of the non-metallic gears had taken place.

This appeared to be the only explanation of the failure of one of the magnetos and consequent loss of timing whilst engine No 2 was on full power test. This magneto failure, occurring during July 1952, was the third BTH unit to fail but on this occasion it resulted in structural damage in the power section of the engine, notably of a number of cylinders and articulating connecting rods. The damage was put at about £1,000 and the rear section of the engine was re-built, necessitating new castings (£4,500). A locally manufactured generator was introduced. Scintilla magnetos, as used on the R-1340 and R-1830 were fitted instead and an injection type carburettor chosen so as to prevent the icing problem experienced with the Wasp engine.

CAC sought a new funding estimate of £65,000 to cover the design revisions and to cope with an extended type test of 300 hours. Previous type test requirements had stipulated 100 hours of testing. The work of repairing the damaged No 2 engine, modification of both engines and rebuilding new rear sections rather than modifying the original entailed a greater expense and the upward creep for more funds continued. CAC requested £75,800.

The new 300 hour type-trial commenced in February 1953. It was to be run over 40 working days. By March each engine had amassed 200 hours of development testing and the Cicada engine installation design for the Winjeel was completed. With each request for more funds Wackett stressed to the Department of Aircraft Production the need for Australian self-sufficiency and the importance of adhering to the development program in-spite of the setbacks. A setback occurred in April through the failure of a crank-pin bolt. The second engine was then prepared and brought up to test status and almost immediately the new connecting rod seized. This brought about an investigation by the Defence Research Committee headed by Professor Martin. The two engines had amassed a combined 750 hours running time.

In May 1953 CAC sought to raise the level of expenditure to £77,500 but at this juncture the Air Force had become committed to installing used Wasp Junior engines in the Winjeel, at least for the first 30 aircraft and to continue with the Cicada as a research and development project.

A85-618, the first CA-22 Winjeel prototype was to receive one of the Cicadas in September. To finance the flight test phase a further funding increase was sought to bring the total to £85,800 but the Department of Defence would not under any circumstance allow expenditure outlays to now exceed £80,000.

The following month the engine suffered its second rear crankshaft bearing seizure 100 hours into its type test and after 1,000 hours of combined engine time. This was corrected by providing a direct oil feed instead of one through the crankshaft. This did not mean all difficulties had come to a happy juncture as on 11 November there was another crankshaft failure. This was the same crankshaft in use when the engine had suffered its magneto failure and unknowingly it had been damaged but gone unnoticed.

Not content with waiting for official funding the company spent £1,748 from its project profit of £4,928 to keep the program alive. This took the total outlay to June 1954 to £79,753 including the CAC component.

It was not until October that matters had been sorted out and testing had resumed once more. The DAP's not-to-exceed £80,000 limit was reached on August 6, 1954. The status at the end of the project on February 7, 1955 when CAC was to account to the Department of Defence Production, was comprised of one complete engine assembled to Engine Build No 9 status, an unserviceable second Cicada and about 1,000 engineering drawings, reports and design schemes. All components were held in store awaiting a resumption of the type test if and when required.

On May 24, 1954 CAC received a surprise expression of interest looking to use the Cicada on the Air Tractor agricultural farming aircraft built by the Central-Lamson Aircraft (f/f 10/12/1953) Company of Washington, USA. The Air Tractor prototype had been flying for six months powered by a Pratt & Whitney Wasp Junior radial engine. CAC was not able to promise production engine deliveries till the end of 1956.

£250,000 was required to set up a Cicada production line. Had this step been achieved the Winjeel would have been as near to a complete Australian designed mass production aircraft as was possible to achieve taking into account the small production run. CAC did not expect the nagging mechanical setbacks that were thrown up, whilst the Government never came to grips with the extent of the development schedule that was needed. Herb Knight was most disappointed with the end result. (Refer also to the P265/XP56 Wallaby Feeder Liner proposal.)

Bibliography : CAC R795 Cicada Radial Engine

Commonwealth Aircraft Corporation. (1949-1953).CAC Production Reports to Department of Aircraft Production.

Commonwealth Aircraft Corporation (1949-1955). Cicada Engine Correspondence Files.

Commonwealth Aircraft Corporation (1949-1954). Cicada Engine Project. File E166.

Flight. (April 9, 1954)

Knight, Herbert. (May 19,1953). Cicada Engine Project Costs.

Knight, Herbert. (January-April 1987). General Manager 1961-1969. [Correspondence]

ROLLS ROYCE AVON Turbojet

The company's second jet engine project was the axial flow Rolls Royce Avon Mk 1. Herb Knight arrived in the UK on June 9, 1950 to set up a CAC team at RR to arrange for tooling and materials. Colin Bellward followed in November. The Avon was a huge engineering challenge.

In an address to the Institute of Production Engineers in September 1955 Wackett explained the complexity of the Avon production RA-7(Mk 20), its many suppliers, machining of 15,000 parts for each engine, the use of 12,500 special tools, 500 machine tools, plant outlay of £4M and an output of 2 engines/week. The RA-3 (Mk 1) was hardly fit for service when first used, with continual problems and modifications underway during production. The same difficulties occurred with the RA-7; an enormous engineering and technical undertaking by CAC and its suppliers. This required a large commitment from National Forge for aluminium alloy and bronze compressor blades 'close' forged to size and shape leaving the tip root attachments and the leading and trailing edges to be machined. There was the turning and boring of the compressor and turbine shafts and the simultaneous machining of 12 grooves in the split compressor casing to accept the stator blade roots.

The installation of the Avon in the Sabre airframe and the subsequent compressor surge that was experienced in the tropics during gun firing trials was overcome by Rolls Royce with the re-matching of the compressor and turbine. This resulted in a reduction of thrust which CAC restored to 7,500 lb by modifying the exhaust jet pipe. The increase in jet pipe efficiency was achieved by changing the fairings on the inner cone support tubes from symmetrical to asymmetrical in shape. Early engine vibrations were traced to the drive shaft between the the engine and the accessory drive gearbox. A strengthened drive shaft solved the problem.

RA- 3 Mk 1- 6,500 lb thrust

Between November 1953 and May 1957 forty-four engines (CAC 1-40) were built. The first engine ran in September, 1953. All were built for the GAF Canberra Mk 20 / Mk 21 bomber/trainer aircraft.

RA-7 Avon 100 Series Mk 109 - 7,350 lb thrust

Between March 1956 and August 1958 forty-seven Mk 109 engines (CAC 401-447) were built for the Canberra Mk 20 bomber.

In-line machining of Avon engine components 'Dept Crankcase Section'. **HDHV**

(160 serial numbers for the Mk 1 and Mk 109 engines were in use by the RAAF including the 91 CAC built engines).

RA-7 / RB 65 Mk 20 - 7,500 lb thrust

Fifty-two engines built between March 1955 and September 1967 for the CA-27 Mk 31 Sabre. Twenty engines (Nos 3064-3083) were imported at the start of the program.

RA-7 / RB 65 Mk 26 - 7,500 lb thrust

Seventy-five engines built between May 1957 and June 1961 for the CA-27 Mk 32 Sabre. A long way into the local Sabre program 20 more Mk 26 engines were requested. Parts which made this engine special to the CA-27 Sabre were built by CAC, shipped to Rolls Royce, UK where they were incorporated into the new engines (Nos 3427-3436, 3441-3450). This engine had greater compressor stall tolerance than the Mk 20. The modifications included increasing the high pressure turbine blades angle of incidence by 8°; increasing the throat areas of the high pressure nozzle guide vanes to 142 sq ins and adding a fuel dipper unit.

Avon engines built to local requirements incorporated 285 modifications. Manufactured spares approximated about a third of the total engines built. CAC Mk 20 / Mk 26 were numbered CAC 101-227. In addition the company maintained Avon engines used in local industrial applications and in the donated AURI and RMAF CA-27 Sabres.

The Avon engine series assembly line. **HDHV**

SNECMA ATAR 9C Turbojet

The SNECMA ATAR 09C3/03Z turbojet (from Atelier Technique Aeronautique Richenback) for which CAC was prime contractor, was the first reheat jet engine to be manufactured in Australia. A rugged 13,230 lb reheat thrust unit was for the GAF/Marcel Dassault Mirage IIIO fighter of the RAAF. More complex than the Avon, its design origin heritage reached back to the German turbojets of WW2.

The nine stage compressor and two stage turbine meant a large increase in the production of blades (compared with the previous RR Avon engine) requiring the installation of further eight-spindle milling machines. The low pressure nozzle guide vanes were precision cast as in the Avon whilst the air cooled high pressure guide vanes were of folded heavy gauge sheet construction.

Once again the Government would not approve the purchase of some required special machining tools and in the case of the Curvic Coupling of the two turbine stages, the problem was overcome by CAC engineers modifying a second-hand machine acquired in the United States and adapting it for ATAR components fabrication. The British Shaw casting process that used solid patterns instead of the wax type used in the Austenal process was used for the precision cast, heat resisting components in the controllable nozzle of the jet pipe.

With a chain of local supply companies, CAC built the engine to an initial 80% local content value but ended up nearer to 90%. Some local content was introduced from the 19th engine with progressively increased input until by the 32nd engine almost all the selected build components were being manufactured locally.

SNECMA ATAR 09C engines for the RAAF Mirage IIIO supersonic multi-role fighter coming together with their reheat units. **HDHV**

SNECMA ATAR 09C engine assembly. **David Anderson. 704072052P**

The ATAR started in Australia with the 09C3 model which was difficult and tedious to overhaul with SNECMA's intention that the replacement of damaged compressor blades could be carried out in the field. This required the moment balancing of all blades and holding a full range of spares for all categories of moment balance at RAAF units. Good in theory, but in practice impossible to organise. From 1964 SNECMA brought the engines up to 09C4 standard.

The importance of local production support was exemplified by the return to CAC early in the service life of the Mirage of a large number of engines with damaged compressor blades. This was before a single engine had reached its normal overhaul strip down. The demand for replacement blades was so great that the spares holding purchased from France to secure the first year of operation was entirely exhausted. The repair program was achieved by the diversion of blades from local production. Further changes in 1966 were introduced to bring all engines up to 09C5 status. The 09C5 had a completely new compressor structure and the whole unit had to be dismantled to replace one damaged blade. The assembly of the compressor was attained by shrink fitting of the discs and bolting using friction locking nuts, the friction grip of each being re-established before assembly. This level of complexity surprised the RAAF with the length of time it took to repair a damaged engine.

SNECMA introduced 09C6, 09C7 and 09C8 level modifications but only the 09C8 scheme was locally adopted, and that only in part. The ATAR inventory totalled 192 engines of which 21 were built by SNECMA, bulk stripped and re-built by CAC. Whilst 140 were constructed from parts progressively introducing local manufacture, 31 complete units were bought in for use on the late order for 16 dual-seater Mirage IIIOD. CAC supplied A$940,000 worth of turbine blades and engine intake casings to France as offset work.

About 450 engine modifications and 60 to 70 fuel system alterations were introduced to the middle of 1987. Some 15 to 20% of the total modifications were locally raised. Production ran from September 1964 to June 1969.

Engines passed back through the CAC engine division on 1,390 occasions for overhaul, repair and bay servicing.

BRISTOL SIDDELEY VIPER 22-11 Turbojet

This 2,500 lb thrust engine was built for the CA-30 Macchi MB326H jet trainer. Colin Bellward led a CAC and HdH team to Bristol Siddelely (UK) from November 1965 to set up the production material process. HdH were the Australian agents and were to build

Bristol Siddeley Viper ASV 22-11 turbo-jet as used on the Macchi MB326H. **HDHV**

CAC's nameplate on Bristol Siddeley Viper engine.
David Anderson. 1372PNG

components to 25% of total engine manhours. Thirty four engines were brought in during the early lead-in phase and 113 units were produced between May 1968 and May 1972. Some 119 main engine modifications had been phased in to the middle of 1987. The majority of Viper overhaul work was carried out by HDH in Perth. The Government paid £52,000 for the manufacturing licence and the first Viper engine assembled in Australia followed by £15,000 for the twenty-first engine assembled locally and £1,100 for each Viper engine built, together with 5% of Bristol Siddeley's net selling price for all spare parts manufactured. National Forge produced turbine and compressor blanks.

Bibliography: Bristol Siddeley Viper 22-11 Turbojet
Licence Agreement Between Bristol Siddeley Engines Ltd & The Commonwealth of Australia, Filton UK

GENERAL ELECTRIC F404 Turbofan

This advanced, reheat turbofan engine delivering 10,600lb thrust dry and 16,000 lb with reheat was to power the RAAF's fleet of 75 McDD F/A-18A & B Hornet fighter aircraft (two in each aircraft). Largely an assembly program with little direct manufacturing. CAC built 27 components comprising 100 parts of engine technology transfer including 73 aircraft-mounted accessory drive gear boxes, fan blades, casings, inlet guide vanes, bearing seals and housings. The first seven engines arrived assembled, 17 were assembled from modules. CAC was to assemble 161 engines plus spare modules and 185 sets of engine components with the last of the $200M contract of 1981 delivered in October 1989.

The $8.7M Government owned Aero-Engine Test Facility, designed by AECON(USA), built by the Dept of Housing & Construction was located in the SE corner of the CAC away from the other test houses. Totally air cooled, it sent test parameters back to GE during test running. It operated from September 26, 1984, leased to CAC who was committed to AIT-Assembly Inspection Test (Manufacture) and engine test; DLM-Depot Level Maintenance (Overhaul); ILM-Intermediate Level Maintenance (Repair) and associated component repair for spares.

The RAAF sent faulty modules to CAC for either repair or overhaul pending damage surveyed and status of life-limited parts. CAC did similar lucrative module work for the US Navy. At its peak this doubled their F404 work. One USN aircraft carrier provided as much F404 work as the whole RAAF. The only F404 engine tested after the AIT phase was the periodical running of the certification/calibration F404-400 engine which the RAAF eventually took away. The F404's efficient design of six separate modules did away with the need to strip down complete jet engines to get to a

General Electric GE F404-GE-400 low bypass, 16,000 lb thrust afterburning turbofan engine for the F/A-18A & B Hornet fighter. **GE**

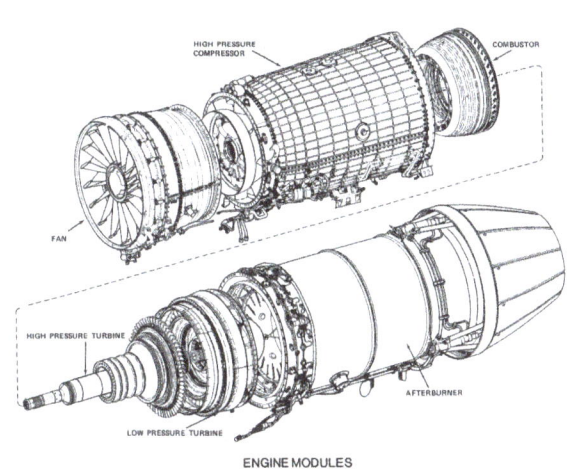

GE F404 turbofan engine six(6) module repair & service breakdown. **CAC**

problem. It allowed the RAAF to assemble the modules themselves with a module changer (ie engine suspended via 3 supporting frames) and test run complete engines on two outdoor test benches to verify post-module change for performance and proof of fault rectification at RAAF Base Williamtown. A $3M addition to the Test House in 1988 allowed it to test the GE T700 helicopter turboshaft and follow identical AIT, DLM and ILM phases to keep the Test House operational as a back-up to the RAAF carrying out all F404 testing themselves.

Late in 1994 the Government informed CAC the overhaul, repair and testing of the RAAF's engine modules was to continue with Aviation Enterprises (TAE), an offshoot of Air New Zealand on the basis of a yearly $2.5M, favourable exchange rate deal. This cross-Tasman Sea hardware exchange was justified by the Defence Minister's statement...'*with the Government's practice of best value for money.*' TAE had been maintaining the Allison T56 turboshaft engines on the RAAF's C-130 fleet, but had no experience with this class of engine. Government owned F404 engine tooling was sent to NZ to carry out the work but not the CAC developed, value adding production technique such as plasma coatings on the combuster liners and fan blades that won it USN work and repair accolades. Their work on USN engines put it many years ahead of the service life of the equivalent RAAF'S engines.

With the big loss of the F404 through-life work in Melbourne, BTR-Nylex Ltd, the (1992) new owners of Hawker Siddeley Group/HDH, decided to move the GE T700 engine testing to HDH Bankstown and demanded the Government's prompt removal of Test House No

GE F404 titanium engine fan casing production. **Tony Todaro**

Final check of F404 engine in cell before a test run. **Tony Todaro**

F404 thrust trolley being prepared for engine installation. **Tony Todaro**

The Government's Aero Engine Test Facility (1984-95) built at CAC to test the GE F404 engines for the F/A-18 Hornet fighter. **CAC**

The Government funded and built advanced engine test facility to test and support the GE F404 engine. An example under test is visible from the test & control room (above and below). **HDHV**

Engine Test House No 4. Fuel farm & start air storage for F404 engine manufacture testing. **Tony Todaro**

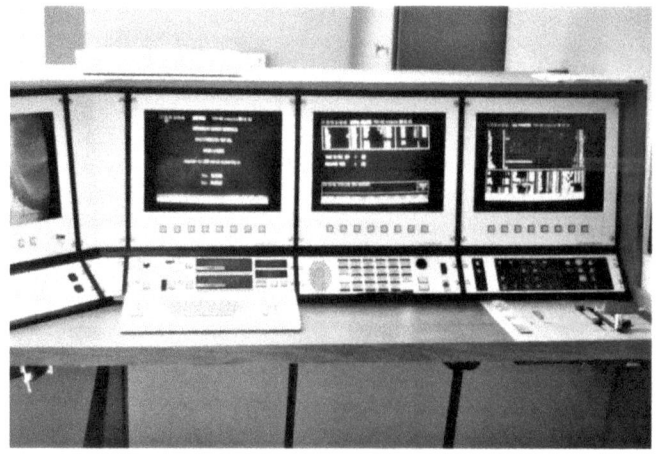

4 from HDHV land, otherwise it would be asked to pay significant rental fees. 62 Turbine Overhaul & Repair Centre personnel were made redundant. Defence Minister Robert Ray announced the closure (followed by the demolition) of the the facility on January 16, 1995 acknowledging it was BTR's economic decision. All this created a dramatic critical shortage of serviceable engines for some five years lasting till 1999, forcing the RAAF to borrow 10 engines from Canada. It also ended CAC's long, on-going, offset F404 work for the US Navy. (which TAE lacking the production expertise did not win)

In 2005 TAE set up engine test facilities in Queensland.

General Electric T700 Turboshaft

This 1950shp turboshaft was used in the Sikorsky Blackhawk/Seahawk helicopters. Engine parts were built for Sikorsky in a A$6M offset deal in 1987/88. For a further A$1.2M, fifty engines were assembled for the same helicopters in service with the RAAF and RAN.

Other Turbine Overhaul Work

The fuel rig test room; the oil rig test room; ATAR gas starter -generator rig; the earlier Bell 206B Kiowa power train; the later Sikorsky Blackhawk/Seahawk helicopter intermediate and tail tail rotor gear boxes using the 500hp electric dynamometer test rig were never given test cell status. They were built into sound proof rooms or cells within the No 1 & 2 Test House complex, a large building with many rooms/rigs/cells and a maze of narrow red brick corridors. The F/A-18 Hornet AMAD (Airframe Mounted Accessory Drive Gearbox) test rig was set up within Test House Cell No 1, as it was no longer used for jet engine testing. Defence was so impressed with this work at Fisherman's Bend, it insisted that gear box work be added to the T700 engine contract to force HDH do the work at Bankstown, NSW.

Sikorsky Blackhawk/Seahawk power train test rig-500hp drive test, electric motor (lower left). Load resistance motor (top upper right). Drive shafts to the intermediate & tail rotor gear boxes are enclosed for safe running. **Tony Todaro**

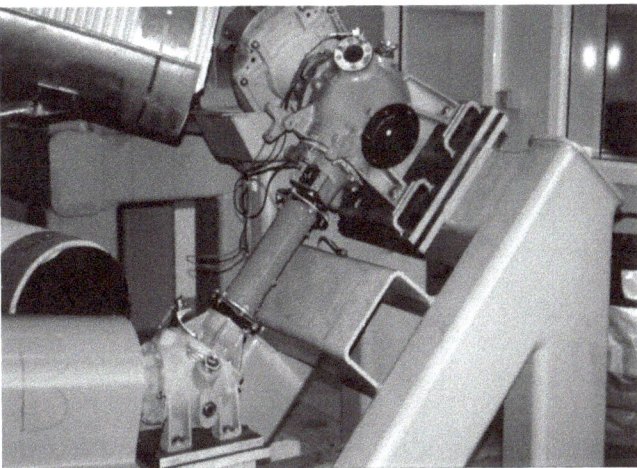

Sikorsky Blackhawk/Seahawk helicopters intermediate gear box (lower left) & exposed drive shaft to the tail rotor gear box (upper). **Tony Todaro**

Tony Todaro setting up to run a Sikorsky Blackhawk/Seahawk helicopter power train test. **Tony Todaro**

Combined CAC & GAF Open Day included displays of the Mirage and MB326H airframe final assembly parts; ATAR & Viper engines production components, major aircraft contractor suppliers, a 39 passenger COMAIR bus & GAF Jindivik in Plants 1, 3, 4 & 5. Flying displays were provided by Winjeel, Sabre, MB326H, Canberra & Mirage aircraft. Cameras were not allowed on site. March 23, 1968. **J.A.Vella Collection**

Above & below: Engine Test Houses Nos 1 & 3. **Tony Todaro**

The detuner exhaust on roll-back tracks at Engine Test House No 3. Designed, built and completed by CAC in 1962 to test the RR Avon engines series and others beyond to 30,000 lb thrust. The cooling water storage tank is in the centre. Detuner No 2 is to the right. **CAC**

Engine Test House No 2. **Tony Todaro**

CAC's cast aluminium emblem over Engine Test House No 3.

Advertisement in **AIRCRAFT** journal, December 1964. **J.A. Vella Collection**

Appendices

Appendix 1:

CAC COMPANY DATA

CHAIRMEN OF THE CAC BOARD

H G Darling	1936-1950
M L Darling	1950-1957
Sir Sydney Rowell	1957-1968
Sir Frederick Scherger	1968-1974
N F Stevens	1974-1985
M B S Price	1985

EMPLOYEE NUMBERS

Date	Number of Personnel
APRIL 1938	490
MARCH 1939	1350
JANUARY 1940	2580
MAY 1941	4600
NOVEMBER 1941	5141
MAY 1942	5908
JANUARY 1944 (Fish. Bend, includes 1,244 females)	7400
JANUARY 1944 (Lidcombe, NSW)	3243
AUGUST 1945 (Fish. Bend, includes 753 females)	5408
AUGUST 1955	4635
AUGUST 1961	2300
DECEMBER 1964	3000
DECEMBER 1966	3484
OCTOBER 1971	2042
AUGUST 1976	1510
JUNE 1984	1872
JUNE 1985	1811
OCTOBER 1986	1306
OCTOBER 1986 (HDH/CAC Group)	3300
1995 (BTR Nylex/HDH)	<800

Appendix 2:

THE GOVERNMENT'S CONTROL OF THE AIRCRAFT INDUSTRY

1939	July 1	Department of Supply & Development
1939	July 1	Aircraft Construction Branch formed
1940	March 3	Aircraft Production Commission formed
1942	January 1	Department of Aircraft Production established
1941	December	Aircraft Production Commission abolished
1942	January 13	Aircraft Advisory Committee formed
1942	(Late)	Beaufort Division formed within the DAP
1945	May	Aircraft Advisory Committee abolished
1946	November	Department of Aircraft Production disbanded
1947	(Late)	Government Aircraft Factories formed (formerly the Beaufort Division)
1948	April	Department of Supply & Development formed
1950	March	Department of Supply established
1951	May	Department of Defence Production
1958	April	Department of Supply re-established

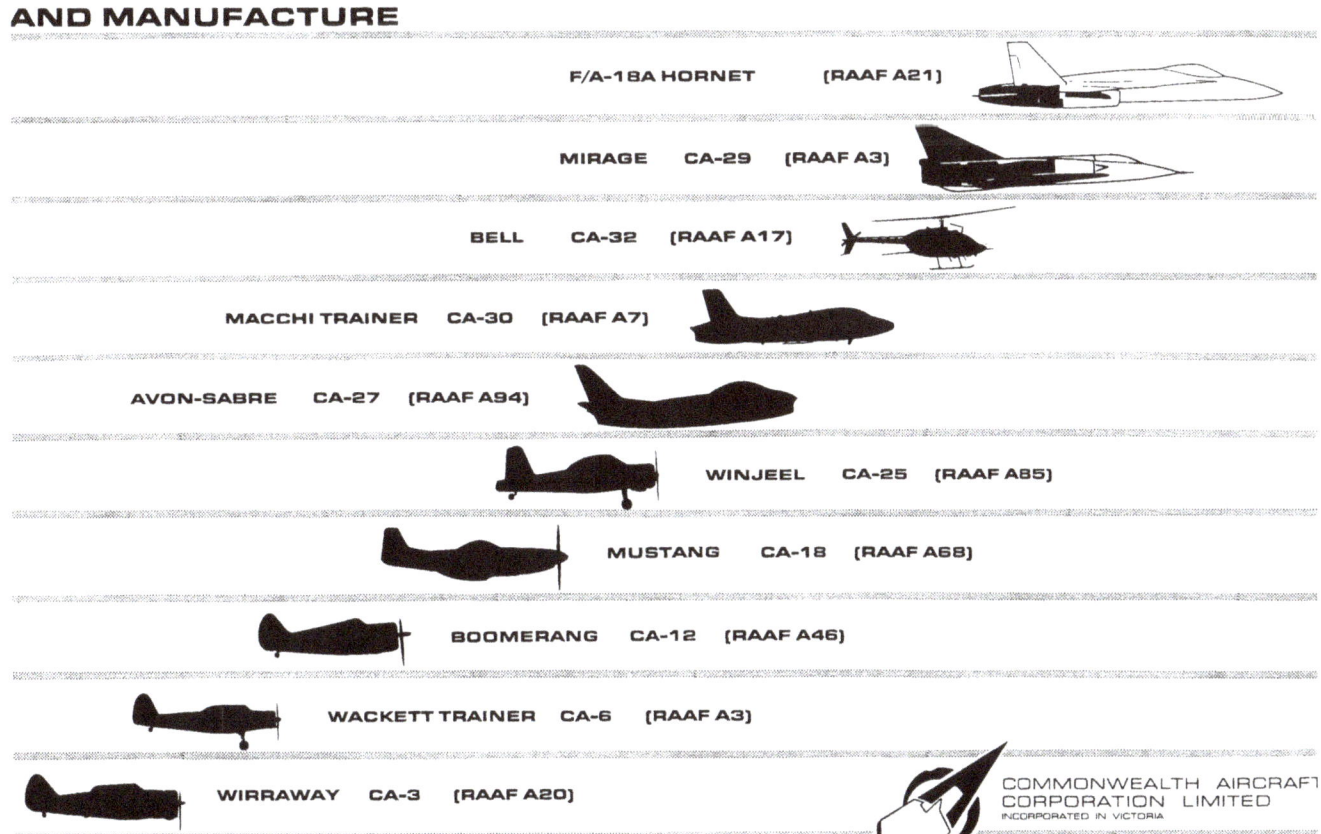

Appendix 3: CAC LOGOS

The series of logo designs depict the Company's movement with the market. The slim three 'feathers' gannet seabird logo was first seen on LJW 7 Gannett (A14-3) built in CAC's name at Tugan Aircraft Ltd, NSW. It was revised sometime to a shorter, compact, five 'feathers' design (above). Production airframes from the Wirraway and onwards past WW2 carried the logo. Applied in left and right side forward pointing versions, it disappeared from some aircraft during in-service repaints. The combination of the names of Frank Gannon(Tugan Aircraft Ltd) and L.Wackett is believed to be the origin of the gannet logo for the new CAC.

In the late 1960s or early 1970s a logo in the shape of a modified triangle form emerged. A stylised delta shape aircraft within that outline made up the letters 'CAC'. The design had a short life span and its application seems to have been limited to letterheads and some publicity related material.

This design by Barry Klemke first appeared in August 1979 and was intended to express the broadened aspirations of CAC protecting Australia, whilst receiving Australia's support in its move into the world scene. The stylised letter 'C' represents the arms of a callipers and the 'A' characterises flight and forward thrust.

The corporate symbol of the new owners of CAC introduced in 1987 established the image of Hawker de Havilland Victoria Ltd.

A typical CAC constructor plate. This one is from CA-16 Wirraway Mk III c/n 1173, built Sept 1945. **J.A.Vella Collection**

Examples of adhesive labels applied to equipment. **J.A.Vella Collection**

Fifty Years Commemorative Plaque. 1936-1986. **J.A.Vella Collection**

CAC was part of the HDH, GAF consortium building the failed A10 Wamira Basic Trainer aircraft. **GAF Heritage Group**

Appendix 4:

SELECTED DESIGN AND PROGRAM MANAGEMENT PERSONNEL

Abbott, R.L. (Bill): CAC GM from January 1,1970. Former Chief Engineer of GMH. GM and director of British Motor Corporation Leyland (Aust); private pilot. Expanded general aviation and commercial work activities. Chairman of Rex Aviation. Retired August 31, 1976; (d. November 6, 1995).

Air, Thomas W. (Bill): Shipwright, naval architect, engineer at the Cockatoo Dockyard Aviation Division. Designed the T.W.A.- 4, a wooden four seater light aircraft powered by a 210hp Menasco engine in 1936. One example was built by Palcar Manufacturing Co Ltd and flew on November 23, 1938. At North American Aviation prior to NA-33 production. CAC's first and for 15 years, CAC Chief Engineer, Airframes. Responsible for translating into shape the aeroplane ideas of L.W. Wackett prior to and during WW2. Left CAC in 1948 for Technico Instruments (Aircraft) as factory manager. Re-joined CAC in November 1949 as Chief Engineer Aircraft Division on a salary of £116 / month. However due to the poor pay resigned in October 1952. At de Havilland (Stevenage, UK) in 1953 on the Black Knight Intermediate Range Ballistic Missile(IRBM)development. In 1960 Chief Engineer of Ballistic Missiles. 1964 Director Engineering HDH, Australia.

Archer, J.A.Lee: RAAF Beaufighter & Mosquito pilot in WW2; ARDU test pilot including testing of CA-15. Civilian test pilot at end of WW2 with RAE, Farnborough. Formed International Helicopter Pty Ltd in 1960 with a Hughes Helicopters (Aust) franchise. Joined CAC in 1967 as Manager Helicopter Division & CAC Manager for SE Asia & International Sales Manager. Retired December 1982.

Board, Greg: Instructor at Boomerang OTU, Mildura. Joined CAC as test pilot March 1,1943. CA-11 f/f on July 7, 1944. Departed CAC February 2,1945.

Boss-Walker, Hubert: Graduated RMC Duntroon & No 1 FTS December 31,1931. 1932-36 with RAF No 57 Sqdn. Joined CAC March 1939. Made Wirraway f/f on March 27, 1939; CA-2 f/f on September 11 or 19,1939; CA 4 f/f on September 14,1941. Left CAC October 10, 1941. In fatal crash due to a structural failure while test flying DH Mosquito A52-12 on June 12, 1944 for de Havilland, Bankstown,NSW.

Carolan, Anthony: ex-HDH, Hawker Siddeley (UK). General Manager HDH Victoria from April 1986.

Carter, James Ogilvie: RAF & RAAF. Joined CAC Sept 26, 1941 as assistant test pilot to Hubert Boss-Walker. Flight tested Wirraways & Boomerangs. In fatal crash on January 15,1943 on his first familiarization test flight on CA-4.

Caterson, Jim: With Victa on Airtourer design. 1962 CAC Draftsman; Flight Test Engineer; ARDU RAAF Base Laverton; 1976 Senior Engineer Flight Technology; 1982-85 AAC (Wamira) Deputy Chief Designer; 1986 HDH Victoria Chief Aircraft Engineer; Systems Engineering Manager.

Dalziel, John David (Jock): GM of BHP Whyalla Shipyards replaced Bill Abbott as GM on Sept 1, 1976. Continued the expansion of commercial work. Director of Rex Aviation. Retired on July 31, 1985 after CAC merged with HDH.

David, Frederick William (Fred): (b. February 17,1900; d. September 28,1992 or June 3,1992). Arrived Melbourne March 23,1939. Chief Designer during WW2. Made a name change. Responsible for CA-12, CA-15 and improvements on the CA-11. Friederich Wilhelm Dawid was born in Austria. Graduated in 1922. Started with Ernst Heinkel Flugzeugwerke AG in 1925; then at Fiesler Flugzeugbau from 1934; had to leave Germany because of his Jewish heritage and was placed (by Prof Ernst Heinkel) as a Structure Engineer on behalf of the Imperial Japanese Navy with Aichi Tokei Denki Kabushiki Kaisa (Aichi Clock & Electric Company) with whom Heinkel's designs had a previous connection from 1925 with a series of reconnaissance aircraft suitable for catapult launching. The work was one of strict security with little indication of what aircraft designs Aichi was embarked upon. As a foreigner, contact with aircraft hardware was restricted to night time visits to the factory floor to inspect airframe structure problems with a torch. In retrospect the aircraft he worked on was the Aichi D3A1 (Val) Type 99 carrier-borne dive bomber. When Japan entered the war on the side of Nazi Germany Friederich came to CAC in April 1939 having been recommended to Wackett by the resident Australian Consul in Japan. He was technically an enemy alien and was required to report to a local police station. Spent time at the RAE (UK) in 1946 and took up the position in 1947 at the ARL as Superintendent of the Aerodynamics Department at the instigation of the DoS to work on the new GAF Jindivik remote piloted aircraft.

Faggetter, Edwin Frederick (Ted):(1909-2001) Project Design Engineer joined CAC in 1938 coming from Short Bros, Supermarine, Airspeed, Saunders & Roe & Westland (UK). Set up Australian Dunlop Aviation Division at Bayswater, Victoria in 1948.

Fleming, Ian Bowman: CAC Flight Test Observer/ Engineer (1939-44). To the UK at end of WW2. At the request of the DoS was moved to DAP/GAF to lead the Pika & Jindivik design team. Controller of Guided Weapons and Aircraft in Department of Supply.

Francis, Hugh: Chief Engineer of the Technical Department of Armstrong Whitworth (UK). CAC Aircraft Factory Superintendent during WW2. Left in 1948.

Frewin, Ken: 1933 pilot with Tasmanian Aerial Services & Holyman Airways. From 1936 tested the imported, locally assembled DC-2 airliners for Holyman Airways Ltd. January 1940: flying instructor at RAAF Pt Cook, Camden & Wagga. Joined CAC in Sept/Oct 1941. CA-12 f/f on May 29,1942. Dismissed July 14, 1942. Resigned August 8, 1942.

Hattersley, Bruce: ex-HDH production manager; acting HDH/CAC GM from August 1, 1985 till March 1986.

Humphries, Douglas G. 1940 joined CAC. Major involvement in the CA-15 design under Fred David. Chief Design Engineer replacing Tommy W. Air. In UK 1947/48 for jet and supersonic aircraft design studies. Design leader on the CA-22, CA-23 & CA-28. Left January 1958 to join T.W. Air at de Havilland (UK) for Blue Streak IRBM & Ariane space launcher design.

Irving, Louis: Performance Engineer DCA; 1953 CAC Flight Test Engineer; 1970 Engineering Manager.

Kentwell, John: (Sydney) 1947 with Bristol Aeroplane Co. working on the Brabazon & Brittannia airliners. At CAC April 1951 as Senior Structures Engineer. 1953 CAC resident rep at NAA. 1959-70 Chief Design Engineer; 1977-86 CAC/HDHV Chief Engineer & Manager Engineering. Retired July 1986.

Jones, E.J. (Ernie): Joined CAC in 1937 as Drawing Office Structures Group Leader; Administrative Chief Draftsman; Aircraft Factory Manager & responsible for the establishment of overseas offices with all major aircraft programs from Avon Sabre to MB326H. Retired April 1971.

Knight, Herbert: graduated from University of Qld in 1926, spent three years with Westland Aircraft (UK) as a stress analyst; with Imperial Airways during their operation of the Handley Page HP42; as a civilian technical officer in the Directorate of Technical Services at RAAF HQ (Melb) and a technical assistant (time keeper) to the race committee in the Melbourne finish of the 1934 London to Melbourne Centenary Air Race; with the Civil Aeronautics Board; joined CAC in 1937 and worked on the conversion of the NA33 to the Wirraway. From 1941 was Engine factory manager and superintendent to December 1960. From January 1, 1961, CAC's second General Manager. Retired on December 31, 1969.

Rees, David Roy: In charge of Canberra Mk2 & Mk6 Line Servicing, RAF, UK. Held various Flight Dynamics design leadership roles on P1127, Harrier & P1154 VTOL projects with Hawker Siddeley (UK). At CAC Senior design Engineer(Flight Technology) 1967-73. Project Control Manager 1973-75; Manager Planning, Production Control; Marketing Manager of Defence Operations; Public Affairs officer; Manager Market Development to 1985. President R.Ae.S. of Aust. 1985-87

Reid, Charles J.: 1940 CAC Draftsman; Chief Aerodynamicist; Senior Design Engineer Flight Technology. Retired 1981.

Ring, Ian Hayward: From Adelaide. 1936-1940 in design offices of Vickers & A.V.Roe (UK). 1940 CAC Assistant Design Engineer. At RAE to 1947; at CAC 1953 to 1970 Chief Engineer; Manager Engineering Division; Commercial Manager. Salary of £3,417 at August 12,1960. 1972 Program Controller; General Manager Defence Division. Retired 1980. (d. August 5,2004)

Schofield, James: RAAF graduate. Flew with RAF 451 & 127 Sqdns. Completed RAAF No 4 Test Pilots Course on January 29, 1945. Joined CAC. CA-17 f/f on April 30, 1945. CA-15 f/f on March 4, 1946. Left CAC for DCA 1947.

Schulz, Reg V.: Joined CAC October 2, 1937 as Design Draftsman; Mechanical Engineer; CA-1 to CA16 & CA-4 Project Engineer. Production Engineer Aircraft Division 1945-59.

Stern, Lionel: Chief Draftsman. Departed CAC at end of WW2 for Repco Engineering.

Wackett (Sir), Lawrence J: (b. January 2,1896; d.March 18,1982) Born in Qld. Duntroon graduate; pilot in the Aust Flying Corp. Designer of six aircraft of his name. First General Manager of CAC. Production engineer, practical innovator, ideas person, inventor, held patents for some fabrication tooling for metal roof tiles; brilliant at mathematics, volatile virtuoso personality; limited working knowledge of aerodynamics or structures. Thomas W. Air helped translate Wackett's aeronautical ideas into shape. Salary of £7,200 at August 12, 1960. Created Knight Bachelor in April 1954; retired Dec 1960.

Watkins Walter (Wal): CAC 1940 Design Draftsman; 1945 winner of 'Aircraft' magazine post- WW2 light aircraft design. 'Rover' was a high wing, V-tail, three seater powered by 115hp Lycoming driving two wing-mounted counter-rotating pusher propellers. 1946-51 with De Havilland (UK) on DH Comet airliner & DH 108 tailless swept wing designs; CAC Leader Drawing Office Preliminary Design Group 1952-58; Project Support Engineer 1958-83.

Appendix 5:

AN EXPLANATION OF CONSTRUCTOR NUMBER REVISIONS

The identification of the constructor numbers allocated to the CA-11, CA-14/14A and CA-15 has long been the subject of doubt when other number allocations and actual constructor plate data is taken into consideration. This summary attempts to revise the numbers given in CAC published lists and other publicity material.

The most prominent of these company items is the compilation from Section 1, Page 82 of the Drawing Office Manual of September 1970 of the Aircraft Contract Numbers, Description and Serial Numbers.

1. A total of 250 Boomerang aircraft was built and the CA-14/14A was included in that total. Constructor plates on Boomerang aircraft awaiting disposal at Oakey, Qld in 1948 were checked by Jack Prior (AHSA). His records and constructor plates which were removed revealed that:

(Batch no. T9) A46-249 had a c/n 1073, i.e. up one number (should have been 1072);

(Batch no. S5) A46-235 had a c/n 1059, i.e. up one number (should have been 1058); whilst

(Batch no. R5) A46-225 had a c/n 1048 which was correct for its position on the line.

In this re-arrangement of numbers, Richard Hourigan (AHSA) has concluded that somewhere between c/n 1049 and c/n 1057, a constructor number, selected at random, was allocated to either the CA-14 or CA-15. A letter from the Department of Supply (August 8, 1963) states that CAC suggested this, then advising that the CA-14 was c/n 1074. The CA-14 was flying (accepted by the RAAF on April 17,1943) before any of the CA-19 aircraft (first CA-19 accepted by the RAAF on May 25,1944) had flown.

The CA-19 was built in batches of ten aircraft. The 'R' batch ended with A46-230, c/n 1053. By deduction, if A46-235, c/n 1059, was batch number 'S5', then the 'S' batch commenced with aircraft A46-230, c/n 1055. This left c/n 1054 unallocated but most probably the number for the CA-15. The often quoted c/n 1073 for the CA-14 could not possibly be so if a plate (as described earlier) with that number on it was located and removed from Boomerang A46-249 wreck at Oakey, Qld.

2. Additionally, CAC published material gives the CA-17/CA-18 Mustangs as commencing with c/n 1226, when actual plate numbers and DCA civil register data of CAC Mustangs which did appear on the civil register, places all the Mustangs one hundred (100) numbers higher, eg. '1524' was A68-199 and became VH-BOZ and '1444' was A68-119 which became VH-IVI.

3. Having arrived at the above, a gap of 115 numbers appears between c/n 1210 and c/n 1325 which would apply to the CA-11 Woomera. This however creates an anomaly as only 105 examples of the Woomera are known to have been on ordered. The constructor number of the only CA-11 to fly has been quoted as 1225.

Contract CA-16 for Wirraways was to run to 150 aircraft, A20-623 to 773, ie c/n 1075 to 1224, which is where the CA-11, with a c/n 1225, seems to fit in. In fact production stopped at A20-757, c/n 1209, after 135 aircraft were built. Yet, the CA-11 may also have been c/n 1325, ie the number before c/n 1326, the start of the CA-17 Mustang line.

Appendix 6

DESIGN FAMILIES
BY THE PROPOSED USE OF COMMON ORIGIN COMPONENTS AND SYSTEMS

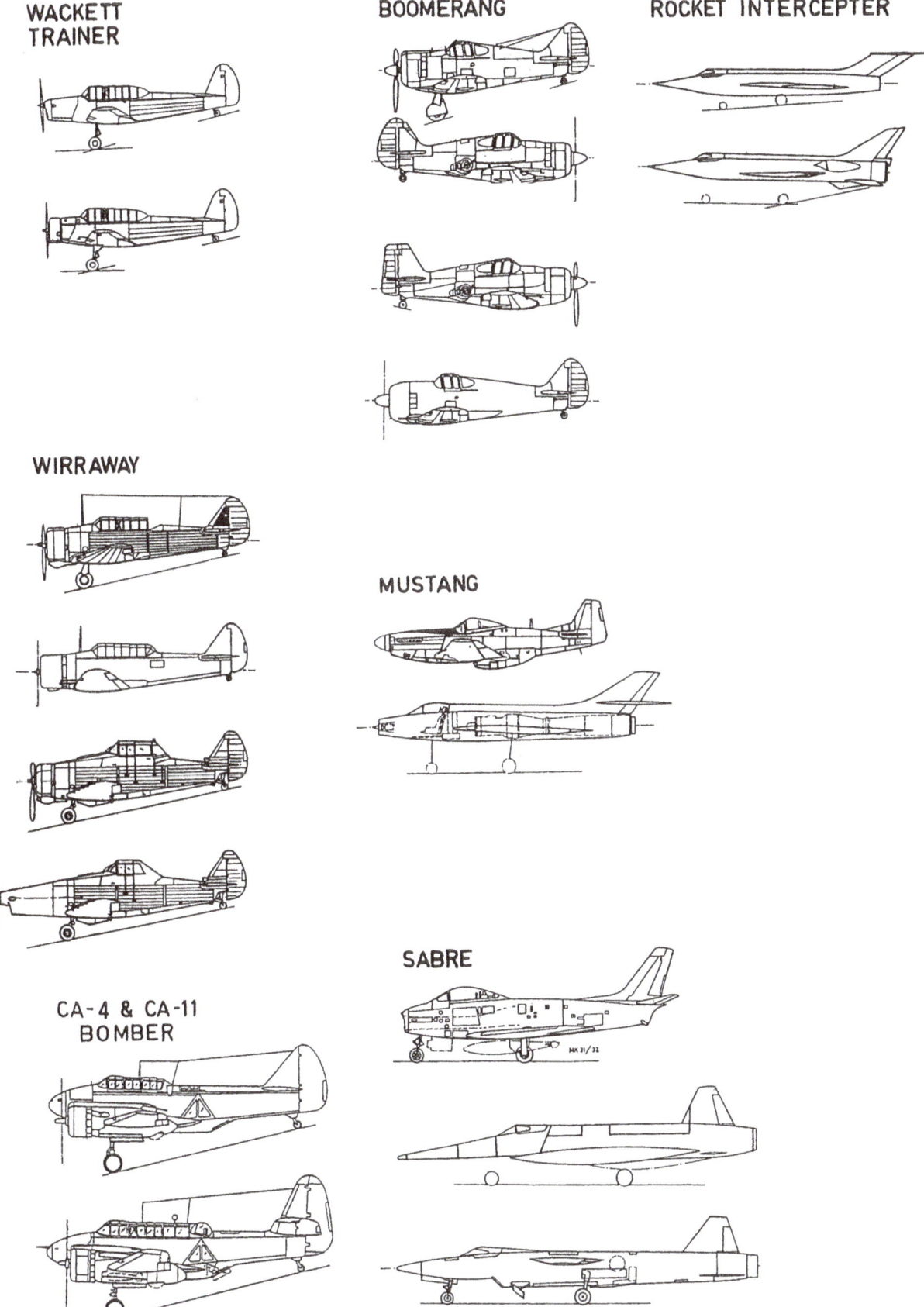

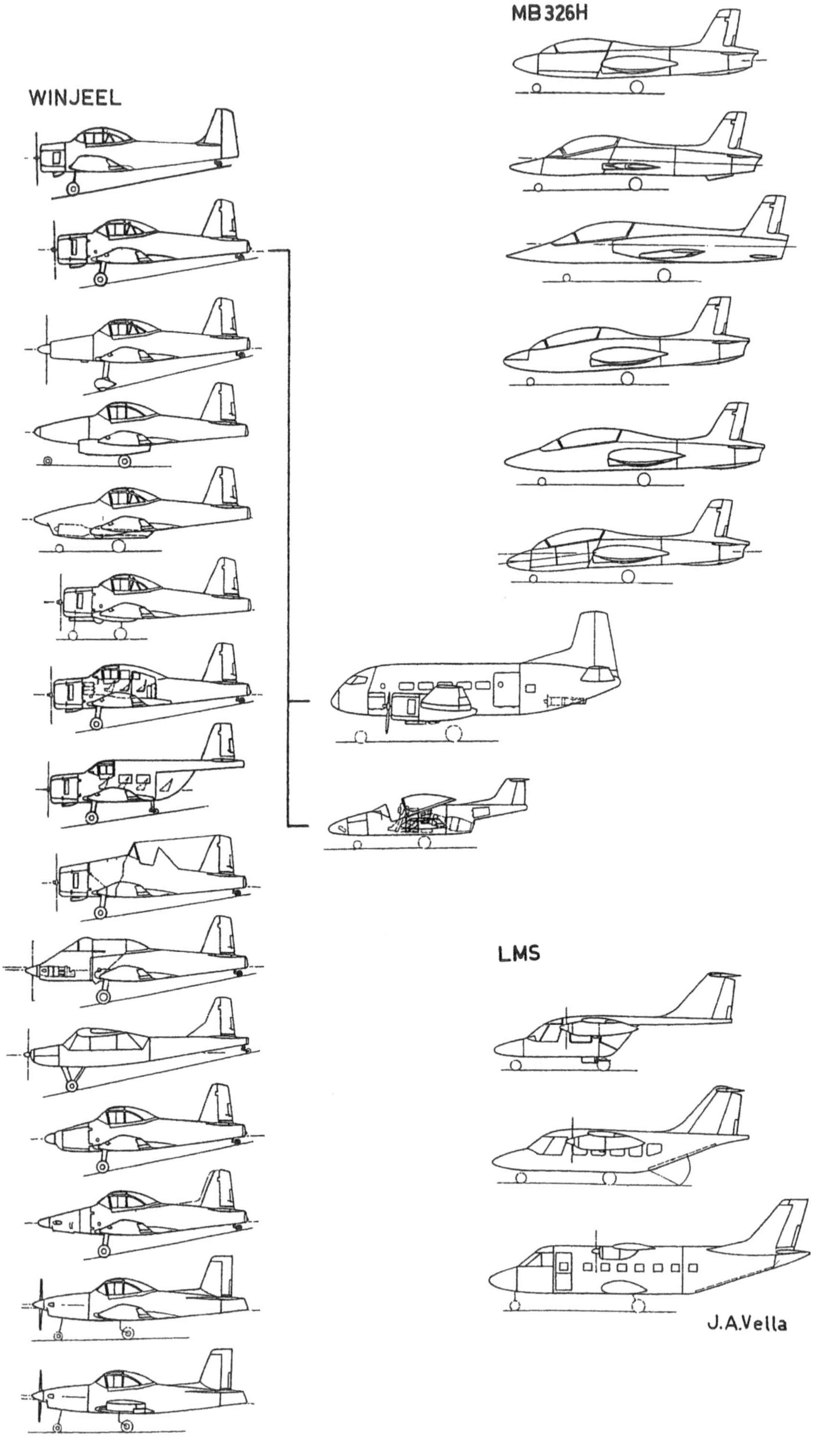

WINJEEL

MB 326H

LMS

J.A.Vella

Appendix 7

ORGANISATION CHARTS

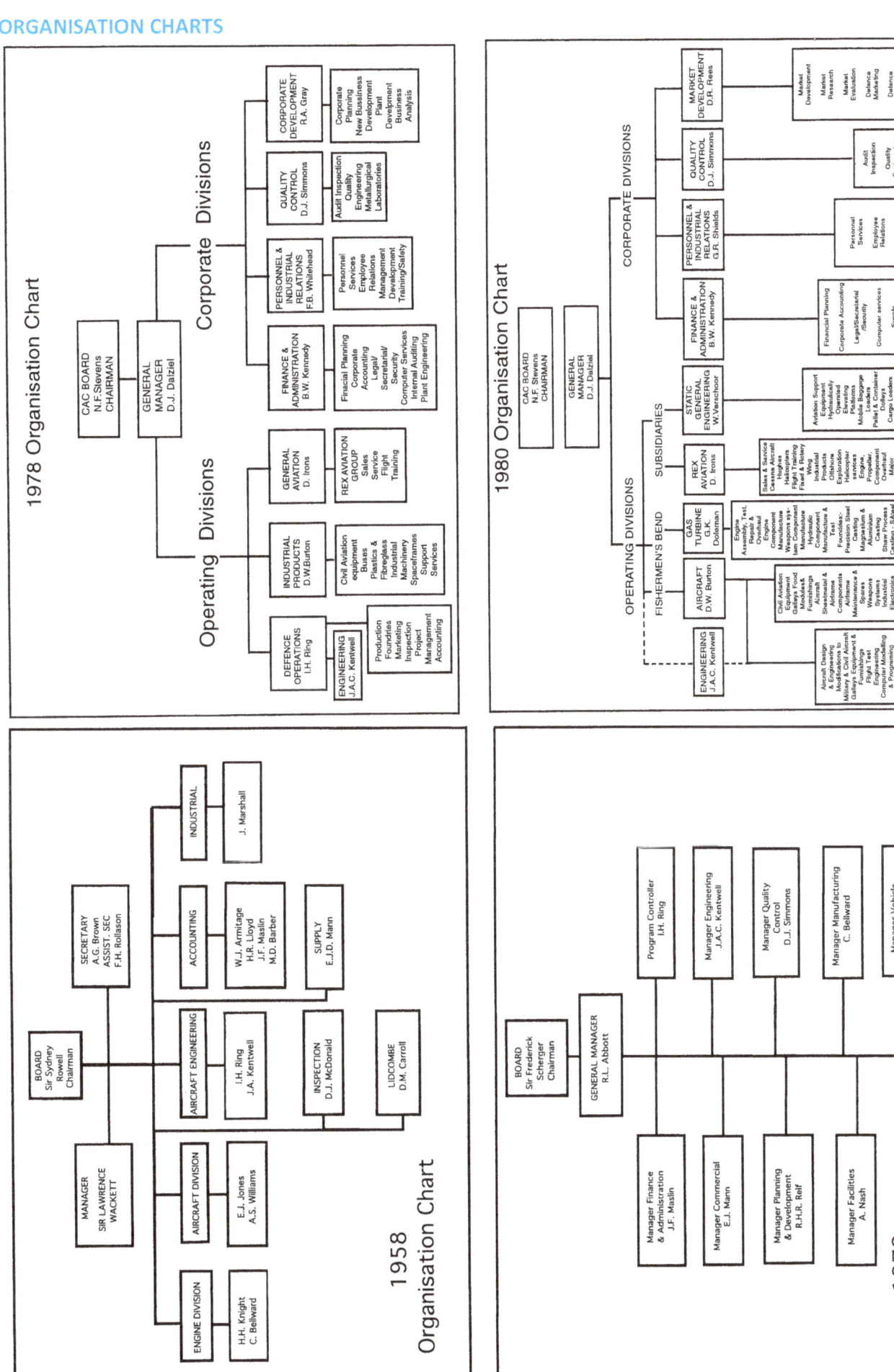

Appendix 8

FACTORY LAYOUT c.1986

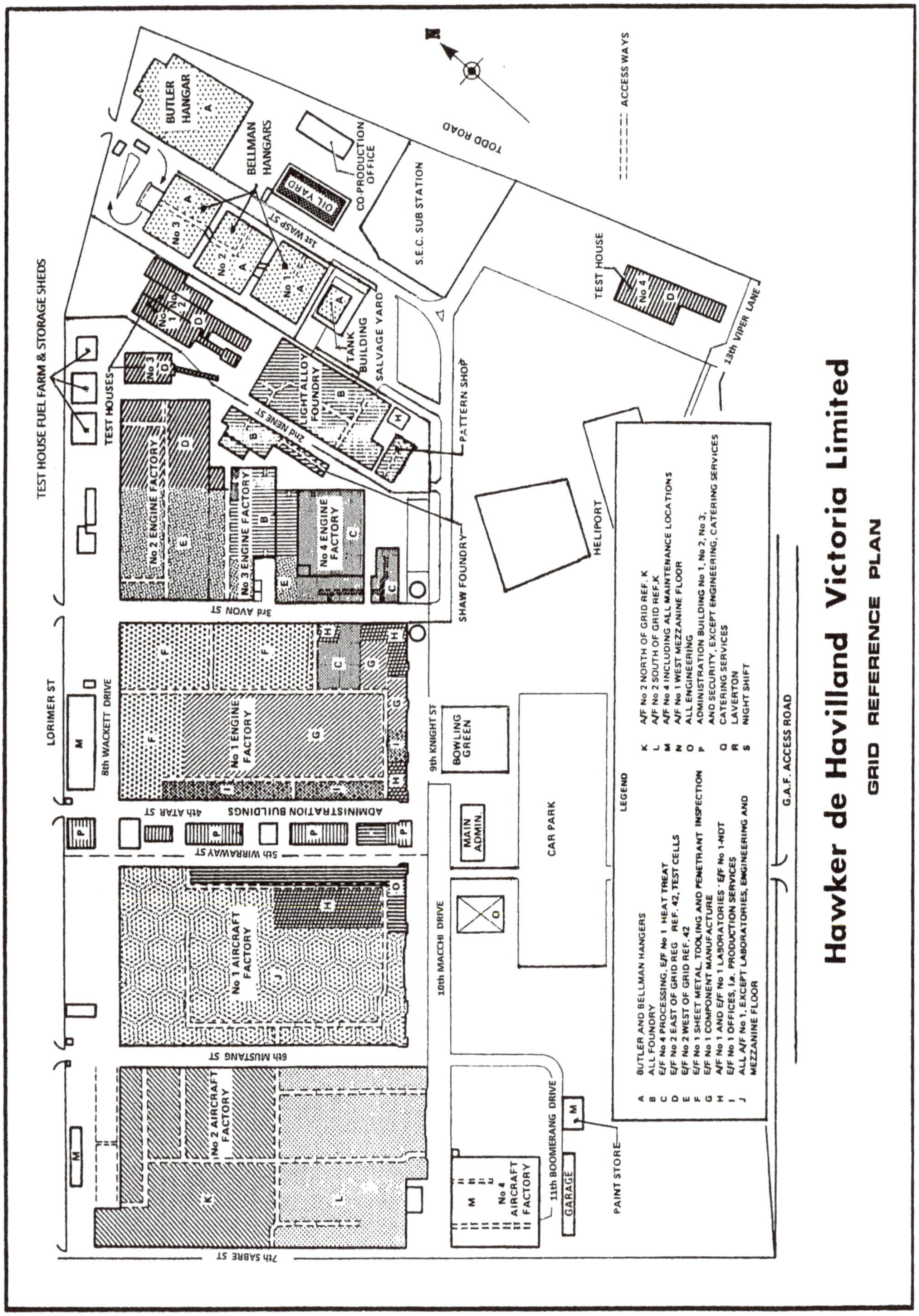

Appendix 9

CONTRACT NUMBER LIST (AS ISSUED BY CAC)

DRAWING OFFICE MANUAL

SECTION 1   PAGE B2   September 1970

DRAWING OFFICE PROCEDURES

Aircraft Contract Numbers, Description and Serial Numbers

C.A.C. CONTRACT NUMBER	AIRCRAFT DESCRIPTION	NUMBER MANUF.	R.A.A.F. TYPE	C.A.C. SERIAL No.
	GANNET PRIOR TO INTRODUCTION OF			
	WIDGEON AMPHIBIAN NUMBERING SYSTEM.			
CA-1	WIRRAWAY - SINGLE ROW WASP S1-H1-G ENGINE	40	A20	1-40
CA-2	WACKETT TRAINER - PROTOTYPE - GYPSY 4 ENGINE	2	A3	101, 102
CA-2A	WACKETT TRAINER - PROTOTYPE - GYPSY 6 ENGINE	-	-	-
CA-2B	WACKETT TRAINER - PROTOTYPE - WARNER SCARAB ENGINE	-	-	-
CA-3	WIRRAWAY	60	A20	41-100
CA-4	WOOMERA BOMBER - PROTOTYPE - TWIN ROW WASP ENGINES	1	A25	435
CA-5	WIRRAWAY	32	A20	103-134
CA-6	WACKETT TRAINER - WARNER SCARAB ENGINE	200	A3	235-434
CA-7	WIRRAWAY	100	A20	135-234
CA-8	WIRRAWAY	200	A20	436-635
CA-9	WIRRAWAY	187	A20	636-823
CA-10	WIRRAWAY DIVE BOMBER CANCELLED			
CA-10A	WIRRAWAY DIVE BOMBER CANCELLED			
CA-11	WOOMERA TORPEDO AND DIVE BOMBER - TWIN ROW WASP S3-C3-G ENGINE	1	A23	1225
CA-12	BOOMERANG INTERCEPTOR - TWIN ROW WASP - S3-C4-G ENGINE	105	A46	824-928
CA-13	BOOMERANG	95	A46	929-1023
CA-14	BOOMERANG (WITH TURBO SUPERCHARGER) PROTOTYPE	1	A46	~~1074~~
CA-14A	BOOMERANG (MODIFIED TAIL, AND TURBO SUPERCHARGER) PROTOTYPE CANCELLED			
CA-15	FIGHTER PROTOTYPE - ROLLS ROYCE GRIFFON ENGINE	1	A62	~~1073~~
CA-16	WIRRAWAY - DIVE BOMBER	150	A20	1075-1224
CA-17	MUSTANG FIGHTER - MK.20 PACKARD MERLIN ENGINE	80	A68	1226-1305
CA-18	MUSTANG FIGHTER - MK.21 PACKARD MERLIN ENGINE	120	A68	1306-1425
CA-19	BOOMERANG	49	A46	1024-1072
CA-20	WIRRAWAY DIVE BOMBER CANCELLED			
CA-21	MUSTANG TRAINER - TWO SEATER CANCELLED			
CA-22	WINJEEL TRAINER PROTOTYPE - WASP JUNIOR ENGINE	2	A85	1426, 1427
CA-23	FIGHTER - TWIN JET, ALL WEATHER CANCELLED			
CA-24	HAWKER FIGHTER - P1071 CANCELLED			
CA-25	WINJEEL TRAINER - WASP JUNIOR ENGINE	~~60~~	A85	1-60
CA-26	SABRE FIGHTER - PROTOTYPE - R.A.7 AVON ENGINE	1	A94	1428
CA-27	SABRE FIGHTER - R.A.7 AVON ENGINE	90	A94	1-90
		21	A94	91-111
CA-28	CERES AGRICULTURAL AIRCRAFT - SINGLE ROW WASP		CIVIL	-
CA-29	MIRAGE FIGHTER - ATAR ENGINE (WING & FIN ONLY)	111	A3	-
CA-30	MACCHI MB326 TRAINER - VIPER ENGINE	97	A7	
CA-31	SUPERSONIC TRAINER - CANCELLED	-	-	-

Appendix 10

PRODUCTION AIRCRAFT LIST (AS ISSUED BY CAC)

COMMONWEALTH AIRCRAFT CORPORATION PTY. LTD.

The Company's first aircraft were the NA16 and 33 which were used as received from North American Aviation, Inc. and evaluated by the RAAF. They had RAAF Nos. A20-1 and 2 respectively. Various modifications including fitment of two forward firing machine guns, bomb gear, camera and radio were suggested and incorporated. The name "Wirraway" was given to this series of aircraft the first of which flew on March 8th 1939. Further types of aircraft were manufactured as listed below:

AIRCRAFT TYPE	CAC CONTRACT NO.	SERIAL NO.	RAAF NO.
Wirraway GP MK.1	CA1	1-40	A20-3-42(MK1)
" "	CA3	41-100	"43-102(MK11)
" "	CA5	103-134	"103-134 "
" "	CA7	135-234	"135-234 "
" " /Trainer	CA8	436-635	"235-434 "
" Dive Bomber	CA9	636-823	"435-622 "
" GP	CA10&10A Cancelled	-	-
" Dive Bomber	CA16	1075-1224	A20-623-772 (MK111)
" " "	CA20 Cancelled	-	-
Wackett Trainer Prototype (Gipsy4)	CA2	101,102	A3-1001/1002
" " " (Gipsy6)	CA2A	-	"
" " " (Warner Scarab)	CA2B	-	"
" " " "	CA6	235-434	"
Woomera Bomber	CA4	435	A23-1001
" "	CA11	1225	A23-1
" "	CA11A	Not Completed	-
Boomerang Fighter Intercepter	CA12	824-928	A46-1-105
" " "	CA13	929-1023	" 106-200
" " " (With supercharger)	CA14 (	1073	) " 1001
" " " (With supercharger, square fin & rudder)	CA14A (		)
" "	CA19	1024-1072	" 201-249
Fighter RR Griffon	CA15	1074	A62-1001
Mustang Fighter Packard Merlin	CA17	1226-1305	A68-1(MK20)
" " " "	CA18	1306-1425	A68 (MK21)
" " " " (Survey)	"		" (MK22)
" " RR Merlin 66 or 70	"		" (MK23)
	CA21(Two seater-Cancelled)		-
Winjeel Trainer 1st prototype	CA22	1426	A85
" " 2nd "	"	1427	A85-364
" " Production	CA25	1-60	" 618-678
Fighter(twin jet, all-weather)	CA23 Cancelled	-	-
" (Hawker P1071)	CA24 Cancelled	-	-
Sabre Fighter Prototype	CA26	1428	A94-101(MK30)
" " Production	CA27)		" 901-942
	")	1-90	(MK31)
" " "	")		" 943-990)
" " "	"	91-111	" 351-371) MK32
Ceres Agricultural Aircraft. Civil	CA28	-	-
Mirage 111 Fighter Sub-contract	CA29	-	A3
Macchi Jet Trainer MB326H	CA30	-	A7

CAC AIRCRAFT CONSTRUCTOR NUMBERS

CAC CONSTRUCTOR NUMBER	CAC CONTRACT NUMBER	AIRCRAFT	CAC AIRCRAFT NUMBER	BATCH OR PHASE NUMBER	RAAF IDENTITY	NUMBER MANUF.
1 – 40	CA-1	Wirraway I	–	–	A20-3 to 42	40
41 – 100	CA-3	Wirraway II	–	–	A20-43 to 102	60
101	CA-2	Wackett Trainer	–	–	A3-1001	1
102	CA-2	Prototypes (Previously A3-1 and A3-2)	–	–	A3-1002	1
103-134	CA-5	Wirraway II	–	–	A20-103 to 134	32
135-234	CA-7	Wirraway II	–	–	A20-135 to 234	100
235-239	CA-6	Wackett Trainer (200 aircraft)	CA-6-1 to 5	A1 to A5	A3-1 to 5	5
240-244	CA-6	"	CA-6-6 to 10	B1 to B5	A3-6 to 10	5
245-254	CA-6	"	CA-6-11 to 20	C1 to C10	A3-11 to 20	10
255-274	CA-6	"	CA-6-21 to 40	D1 to D20	A3-21 to 40	20
275-294	CA-6	"	CA-6-41 to 60	E1 to E20	A3-41 to 60	20
295-314	CA-6	"	CA-6-61 to 80	F1 to F20	A3-61 to 80	20
315-334	CA-6	"	CA-6-81 to 100	G1 to G20	A3-81 to 100	20
335-354	CA-6	"	CA-6-101 to 120	H1 to H20	A3-101 to 120	20
355-374	CA-6	"	CA-6-121 to 140	J1 to J20	A3-121 to 140	20
375-394	CA-6	"	CA-6-141 to 160	K1 to K20	A3-141 to 160	20
395-414	CA-6	"	CA-6-161 to 180	L1 to L20	A3-161 to 180	20
415-434	CA-6	"	CA-6-181 to 200	M1 to M20	A3-181 to 200	20

CAC CONSTRUCTOR NUMBER	CAC CONTRACT NUMBER	AIRCRAFT	CAC AIRCRAFT NUMBER	BATCH OR PHASE NUMBER	RAAF IDENTITY	NUMBER MANUF.
435	CA-4	Wackett Bomber	–	–	A23-1001	1
436-635	CA-8	Wirraway II	–	–	A20-235 to 434	200
636-823	CA-9	Wirraway II	–	–	A20-435 to 622	188
824-838	CA-12	Boomerang I	1 to 15	–	A46-1 to 15	15
839-848	CA-12	(105 aircraft)	16 to 25	C1 to C10	A46-16 to 25	10
849-868	CA-12	"	26 to 45	12-D1 to 12-D20	A46-26 to 45	20
869-888	CA-12	"	46 to 65	E1 to E20	A46-46 to 65	20
889-908	CA-12	"	66 to 85	F1 to F20	A46-66 to 85	20
909-928	CA-12	"	86 to 105	G1 to G20	A46-86 to 105	20
929-948	CA-13	Boomerang II	106 to 125	H1 to H20	A46-106 to 125	20
949-968	CA-13	(95 aircraft)	126 to 145	J1 to J20	A46-126 to 145	20
969-988	CA-13	"	146 to 165	K1 to K20	A46-146 to 165	20
989-1008	CA-13	"	166 to 185	L1 to L20	A46-166 to 185	20
1009-1023	CA-13	"	186 to 200	M1 to M20	A46-186 to 200	20
1024-1033	CA-19	Boomerang II	201 to 210	N1 to N10	A46-201 to 210	10
1034-1043	CA-19	(30 aircraft)	211 to 220	P1 to P10	A46-211 to 220	10
1044-1053	CA-19	"	221 to 230	R1 to R10	A46-221 to 230	10
1054	CA-15	Fighter (Prototype)	–	–	A62-1001	1
1055-1064	CA-19	**Boomerang II**	231 to 240	S1 to S10	A46-231 to 240	10
1065-1073	CA-19	(19 aircraft)	241 to 249	T1 to T9	A46-241 to 249	9

CAC CONSTRUCTOR NUMBER	CAC CONTRACT NUMBER	AIRCRAFT	CAC AIRCRAFT NUMBER	BATCH OR PHASE NUMBER	RAAF INDENTITY	NUMBER MANUF.
1074	CA-14/14A	Boomerang Turbo supercharger Prototype	–	–	A46-1001	1
1075-1209	CA-16	Wirraway III (was to be 150 aircraft and stop at c/n 1224)	–	–	A20-623 to 757	135
1210-1325	CA-11/11A	Woomera Intended Production (105 a/c)		–	A23-1 to 105?	115?
1326-1405	CA-17	Mustang Mk 20	–	–	A68-1 to 80	80
1406-1419	CA-18	Mustang Mk 22(PR)	–	–	A68-81 to 94	14
1420-1445	CA-18	Mustang Mk 21	–	–	A68-95 to 120	26
1446-1511	CA-18	Mustang Mk 23	–	–	A68-121 to 186	66
1512-1525	CA-18	Mustang Mk 22(PR)	–	–	A68-187 to 200	14
	CA-21	Mustang order for 250 a/c cancelled				
1526	CA-22	Winjeel Prototype	–	–	A85-618	1
1527	CA-22-T2	Winjeel Prototype	–	–	A85-364	1
1528	CA-26	Sabre Mk 30 Prototype	–	–	A94-101	1
25-1 to 62	CA-25	Winjeel Production	–	–	A85-401 to 462	62
27-1 to 22	CA-27	Sabre Mk 30	–	–	A94-901 to 922	22
27-23 to 42	CA-27	Sabre Mk 31	–	–	A94-923 to 942	20

CAC CONSTRUCTOR NUMBER	CAC CONTRACT NUMBER	AIRCRAFT	BATCH OR PHASE NUMBER	RAAF IDENTITY	NUMBER MANUF.
27-43 to 70	CA-27	Sabre Mk 32	–	A94-943 to 970	28
27-71 to 90	CA-27	Sabre Mk 32	–	A94-971 to 990	20
27-91 to 111	CA-27	Sabre Mk 32	–	A94-351 to 371	21
28-1	CA-28	Ceres Type 'A'	–	–	1
28-2 to 6 and 18	CA-28	Ceres Type 'B'	–	–	6
28-7 to 17 and 19 to 21	CA-28	Ceres Type 'C'	–	–	14
6351	CA-30	Macchi MB326H (97 aircraft)	–	A7-001	
6370	CA-30	"	–	A7-002	
6371	CA-30	"	–	A7-003	
6374	CA-30	"	–	A7-004	
6377	CA-30	"	–	A7-005	
6380	CA-30	"	–	A7-006	
6373	CA-30	"	–	A7-007	
6376	CA-30	"	–	A7-008	
6379	CA-30	"	–	A7-009	
6382	CA-30	"	–	A7-010	
6383	CA-30	"	–	A7-011	
6385	CA-30	"	–	A7-012	
6381	CA-30	"	–	A7-013	

Aer Macchi c/n's (bracket covers 6351–6381)

CAC CONSTRUCTOR NUMBER	CAC CONTRACT NUMBER	AIRCRAFT	CAC AIRCRAFT NUMBER	BATCH OR PHASE NUMBER	RAAF IDENTITY	NUMBER MANUF.
30-14	CA-30	Macchi MB326H	Aer Macchi c/n's	—	A7-014	
6387	CA-30	"		—	A7-015	
6388	CA-30	"		—	A7-016	
6389	CA-30	"		—	A7-017	
6391	CA-30	"		—	A7-018	
6392	CA-30	"		—	A7-019	
6394	CA-30	"		—	A7-020	
6395	CA-30	"		—	A7-021	
30-22 to 72	CA-30	"	—	—	A7-022 to 072	
30-73 to 78	CA-30	"	—	—	N14-073 to 078	
30-79 to 83	CA-30	"	—	—	A7-079 to 083	
30-84 to 87	CA-30	"	—	—	N14-084 to 087	
30-88 to 97	CA-30	"	—	—	A7-088 to 097	97 total
44501-44512	CA-32	Bell 206B-1 (Bell c/ns - fully imported aircraft)			A17-001 to 012	12
44513-44549	CA-32	Bell 206B-1 (Bell c/ns - part imported, part locally built aircraft.)			A17-013 to 049	37
44550(44706)	CA-32	Bell 206B-1	(Bell c/ns in '700' group were for civil airframes. Aircraft were converted to military role and given '500' group c/ns.)		A17-050	
44551(44707)	CA-32	"			A17-051	
44552(44703)	CA-32	"			A17-052	
44553(44704)	CA-32	"			A17-053	
44554(44705)	CA-32	"			A17-054	

CAC CONSTRUCTOR NUMBER	CAC CONTRACT NUMBER	AIRCRAFT	CAC AIRCRAFT NUMBER	BATCH OR PHASE NUMBER	RAAF IDENTITY	NUMBER MANUF.
44555 (44701)	CA-32	Bell 206B-1	—	—	A17-055	
44556 (44702)	CA-32	"	—	—	A17-056	7
						(56 total)
501-567	CA-37	Pilatus PC9	—	—	A23-001 to 067	67
		(c/n's to 599 Reserved for HDH)				

In association with Rigfield Constructions & Mero Raumstruktur GMBH(West Germany) CAC was responsible for the tube frame spire above the Victorian Arts Centre (Melbourne)

*Depicting in **AIRCRAFT** journal the line-up of engines built by the company up to the BS Viper but not the GE F404. **J.A. Vella Collection***

Appendix 12:

CAC PROJECT AND DRAWING NUMBER SYSTEMS

A variety of project, proposal and drawing number systems were employed at CAC. A number of these systems ran in parallel and were used to differentiate engineering groupings.

A and AA Numbers:

The original aircraft company engineering reports were prefixed by the letter 'A' followed by a numeral. In the early 1950s a sequence of 'AA' prefixes was introduced and the earlier 'A' reports were re-numbered with the new prefix whilst at the same time superseding or omitting obsolete reports.

ADO Numbers:

Were generally intended to document drawing office hardware and furniture items and included the recording of aircraft test gear items, aircraft mock-up designs, loft drawings and standard dimensional layout drawings. No dates were recorded and the system appears to have lapsed in 1969.

AP Numbers:

A new series of proposal numbers was started on June 1, 1968. This replaced the 'P' number system and was divided into separate categories of:

AP 1001 onwards -New Aircraft Proposals

MP 1000 onwards-New Miscellaneous Proposals

VP 1001 onwards -New Vehicle Proposals

AX Numbers :

'AX' prefixed numbers were given to Aircraft Experimental work which was of an exploratory and research nature ie fabrication techniques, aircraft constructional hardware etc. This series, started in 1943 was terminated as obsolete in June 1968.

CA Numbers:

Commonwealth Aircraft contract numbers as project designations were applied in a similar fashion to the NA numbers given by North American Aviation to their designs. In the case of CAC, the numbers related to firmed up designs or manufacturing contracts.

EX Numbers:

This was the Miscellaneous Contract Drawing List. It was started in the late 1940s to include house production components and went on to include such diverse headings as bus interiors, planetarium structures, repair and modification schemes for in service military aircraft, fatigue life monitoring installations, missile handling systems, etc. The system was current to the end of CAC.

FL Numbers:

Encompassed factory and office plan layouts

ME Numbers:

Method of Engineering Data Sheets

MP Numbers:

Miscellaneous Proposal drawings

PA Numbers:

Production Aids drawings

PE Numbers:

Plant Engineering Equipment drawings

SP Numbers :

MERO AG Spaceframe structural proposal drawings

TE Numbers:

Test Equipment items came under this heading and included such things as fatigue test rigs and all manner of test gear. This system was continued by HDH (V) under the control of the Engineering Test Section.

P Numbers:

This was a system which encompassed some full aircraft outlines but was primarily concerned with aircraft structural detail, components and modifications, missile handling equipment and a large amount of structural and body detail design for passenger buses. This scheme was terminated on June 1, 1968 at proposal P550 and replaced by a new AP (New Aircraft Proposals); MP (Miscellaneous Proposals) and VP (New Vehicle Proposals) series.

XP Numbers:

This series was exclusively reserved for aircraft proposals. Numbers were sequentially applied from 1952 onwards to concepts from the Preliminary Design Group and were retrospectively applied to designs prior to that date. This numbering system stopped at the XP77 Ceres in 1956 and was finally done away with in June 1968 to be replaced by the new AP (New Aircraft Proposals) listing.

Appendix 13:

DESIGN ORIGIN BACKGROUND

The process of preliminary design was initiated by the Chief Engineer Thomas W. Air, with Lawrence Wackett's agreement. It involved the Engineering Department in varying degrees and at various levels from 1948 onwards. The formation of a Preliminary Design Group in the Drawing Office was initiated by the Chief Designer Douglas Humphries and the Senior Design Engineer Ian Ring as a means of making the effort more cost effective. Working together with Charles Reid, Wal Watkins was appointed the Group Leader of the Preliminary Design Group in late 1952 at the request of the Administrative Chief Draftsman, Ern Jones.

The effort put into innovative design work was a continuation of Wackett's creative philosophy. He gave it his full support without trying to control the work believing it was necessary to be involved in design work to keep engineering skills at peak level as it could also determine the future of the company.

Ian Ring assumed the position of Chief Engineer in 1953 and maintained a continuous effort to increase the design process and its promotion to the Government and the RAAF. The overall design achievement of what was undoubtedly Australia's leading aircraft design group peaked in the years 1941 to 1944 and 1947 to 1954; coming through the CA-23; CA-25 Winjeel; CA-27 Sabre re-design work; a new jet trainer; the series of rocket based interceptors; a feeder liner and Mach 2 Air Superiority Fighters. It peaked again between 1964 and 1969 on the CA-31 and the AA-107 when an intense political and publicity campaign was conducted to promote these big projects.

Slowly the airframe structural design philosophy had moved away from one based on distributed loading such as was applied to the CA-23, XP63 through to XP68 to one employing boom / spar principles. The experience of the draftsmen and engineers in the company's employment was probably underestimated by the management, the shareholders and the RAAF. The Preliminary Design Group was disbanded in 1958. From 1960 and after Wackett's retirement, it had become an ad hoc setup with drafting staff and engineering support seconded to a design task as required.

The company's aircraft designs were nearly always isolated, step by step developments of an earlier proven outline, concept or airframe, only taking small risk steps in order to maintain minimum development costs. The concepts and ideas were aware of other countries' aeronautical engineering efforts during the same time frames with the general thrust or themes predominating in the areas of trainers, agricultural and STOL designs; chosen because their size was within the engineering capacity of the company. Their proposals and designs ran for periods ranging from five days to four years.

That CAC was not able to roll out an unbroken stream of home grown designs and commit them to production was not the fault of the design team. The company was originally set up as a national gesture for the building of military aircraft to support the Air Force in the defence of Australia. Part of the original agreement which the company had with the Government was that at any given time it had to abandon its commercial work if the Defence Department required the full facilities of CAC. By this agreement, CAC had virtually written away its right to engage in long term private programs of a large scale inhibiting the ambitions of most within the organisation. The intention in 1936 was to also eventually build civil aircraft.

Engineering plant owned by the Government was mixed in with CAC owned plant and CAC could not use this Government equipment (it could at the beginning) unless a high usage fee was paid. This was intended to prevent CAC from embarking on too much of its own work and for the upkeep of the unused and mostly worn plant (part of the Defence Mobilization Reserve) the Government paid out a Reserve Capacity Funding so that staff could be employed to keep the idle plant in running order.

The Reserve Capacity Funding (RCF) applied to CAC, HDH and GAF was based on the concept that certain resources in the industry were essential to the maintenance of Defence Industrial Capability. At CAC

$$RCF = \left[1 - \frac{WD}{WR}\right] \times [Cf - RC \times WC]$$

the formula for estimating Reserve Capacity Funding was expressed as:

WD= Defence Workload in direct manhours/year

WR=Defence Max Capacity Workload for Mobilisation

Cf=Fixed Essential Resource Costs ($)

WC=Commercial Offset Workload in direct manhours/year

RC=Cost Rate/manhour ($/mhour)

If CAC's defence workload utilised all of the Max Defence Capacity(WD), Commercial Offset Capacity(WC) would be zero, since there would be no capacity for commercial work. The cost-plus charging basis limited it to a ridiculously small profit margin.

Unless the Government of the day or the Air Force could be interested in a proposal, there was no other market available or possible, unless overseas collaboration was tested. Very serious efforts were made (without Government support) to interest S.E. Asian countries in collaborating in the design and manufacture of small military support aircraft but it became apparent that these nations were looking for aid, not participation. Whilst at times certain senior RAAF officers gave full support and encouragement to CAC, RAAF policy was generally antagonistic to any local industry as it was seen to intrude into their closed world of equipment selection and the word *'design'* created fear. The management of the Engineering Department made original design work a strong feature of company policy as part of the essential well-being of the organisation. This was reflected in fields other than aircraft design, eg: six different model passenger buses; cancer treatment equipment; the very successful engineering group of Ikara and Branik launcher systems; Barra sonobuoy development; various extensive P-3C Orion system updates; the conversion of RAAF B707 transports to aerial tankers and RAAF C-130H Hercules transports ESM upgrades.

ADDENDA

1. AARG / MAM / ANAM

The various titles used by this museum have included the Australian Aircraft Restoration Group (AARG); Moorabbin Air Museum (MAM); Australian National Aviation Museum (ANAM) and back again to MAM. The museum's collection is based at Moorabbin Airport to the SE of Melbourne and it has operated since 1962. CAC directors Sir Frederick Scherger and Sir Robert Law-Smith visited the museum collection in 1969 and showing a lot of interest donated $500 towards their building fund. ($1,630 in 2021 values)

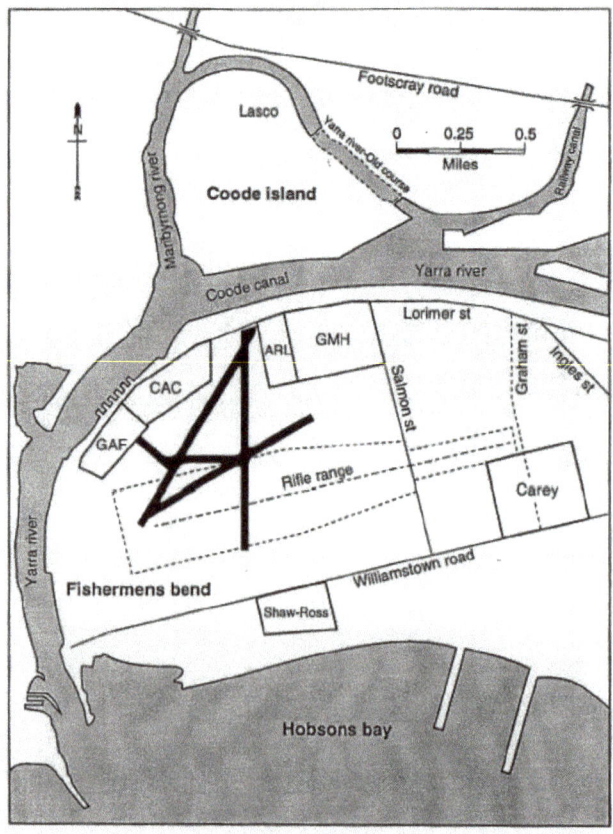

Close proximity locations of CAC/GAF/ARL/GMH & the earlier landing grounds of Graham Carey 1919-21; Shaw-Ross 1920-29 & Larkin Aircraft Supply Company (LASCO) 1921-34. **ARL/DSTO**

PHOTOGRAPHIC ADDENDUM

(L-R). Aircraft Factory 1; the original Administration Building & Engine Factory 1. **L.J. Wackett /MS4858 /NLA**

Wackett Widgeon I, G-AEKB in revised amphibian layout with Aircraft Disposal Company (ADC) Nimbus 6 cyl in-line, 300hp, water-cooled engine (1927). 'No one had any use for it.' The 'EKB' in the registration stood for <u>E</u>ric <u>K</u>endall <u>B</u>owden-Defence Minister who supported LJW & his design. LJW ignored the allocated registration G-AUFO. Cost estimate ...$5,000. Final cost ... $14,360. **Neil Follett Collection**

Wackett Warbler airframe structure (1923-24). Light Plane Competition, NSW Aero Club. **David Anderson. A695 907072093P**

Wackett Widgeon II,1928 with the Armstrong Siddeley Jaguar engine near Perth on the Swan River, West Australia. ' was not designed for any specific purpose and it did not appear to meet any useful military requirement'....Auditor-General. Cost estimate...$8,000. Final cost. ....$18,478. **State Library West Australia**

The Warbler with pusher engine at the Australian Aerial Derby(1924) built whilst LJW was being mentored by Frank S. Barnwell of Bristol Aeroplane Co. **David Anderson. A695 710072014P**

The Wackett designed Wizard 2 cylinder, 25 hp engine for the Warbler. **David Anderson. A695 707072092P**

Wackett Warrigal I trainer with Armstrong Siddeley Lynx engine. Was unsuccessful. Cost was $7,450 above estimate. Received adverse report from No 1 FTS. The Westland Wapiti was used in the training & instructional role instead. **David Anderson. A695 707072090P**

Wackett Warrigal I trainer (1929). **David Anderson. FH 18111807P**

Wackett Warrigal II, Army Co-operation Aircraft (1930). **David Anderson. A688 711072018P**

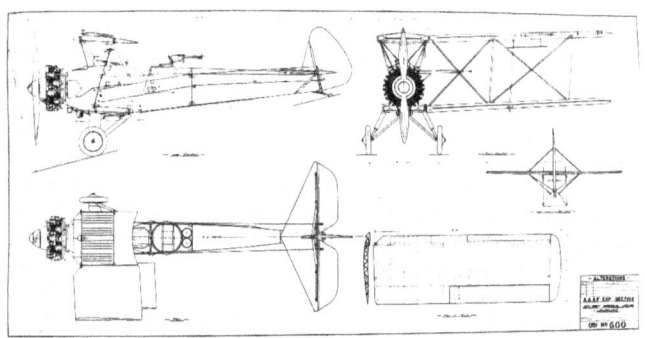

RAAF Experimental Section drawing of Warrigal II with Armstrong Siddeley Jaguar engine. **L.J. Wackett / MS4858 /NLA**

Wackett Warrigal II with Armstrong Siddeley Jaguar engine. **David Anderson. A688 7110072019**

The L J Wackett hydroplane designs at Cockatoo Dockyard, 'Century Tire' & 'Cettien' (below) won the Aust Motor Boat Championship Unlimited, Griffith Cup in 1924/25 & 1934 respectively. **L.J.Wackett / MS4858 /NLA**

L J Wackett built an unidentified hydroplane of his own but deliberately destroyed it after nearly losing his life in it. He is possibly driving 'Wild Fire II' and handling launch of 'Wild Fire'(bottom R) at Cockatoo Island Dockyard on Sydney harbour. **L. J. Wackett./ MS4858**

The sole LJW6 Codock, VH-URP designed & built to an order for Charles Kingsford Smith after its f/f on March 6,1934, Mascot, NSW. (L-R) L.J. Wackett; M.P. Allsop (Vacuum Oil Co.); Sir Charles Kingsford Smith; Beau Sheil (Vacuum Oil N.Z rep) & Sqdn Ldr F.W.'Tiny' White. **L.J. Wackett /MS4858 /NLA**

The sole LJW6 Codock six passenger aircraft of three ordered for a new domestic airline, Dominion Airways, in New Zealand. Troubles with the Napier Javelin engines & the loss of his anticipated Australia-Singapore Empire mail contract to Qantas Ltd, ended this particular Sir Charles Kingsford Smith's business plan. **J.A.Vella Collection**

L. J. Wackett & 'Smithy' inspect the extra tanks built into his Lockheed Altair, 'Lady Southern Cross',VH-USB (1934) for the first west-east crossing of the Pacific. **L.J. Wackett /MS4858 /NLA**

LJW7 Tugan Gannet, A14-1 in RAAF markings. **Neil Follett Collection**

LJW7 Tugan Gannet, VH-UYE (& VH-UVY) with auxiliary fins installed, Mascot Aerodrome, 1936. **Neil Follett Collection**

A14-3 in RAAF markings & possibly first application of the CAC (slim version) logo on the fin, RAAF Laverton. **The Collection P7424-0013**

Members of the Aircraft Advisory Committee-WW2.

The work of political cartoonist Samuel G. Wells, 1941. **1**. Senator Don Cameron-Minister of Aircraft Production; **2**. V.F. Letcher-Asst Sec.(Admin) DAP; **3.** D. McVey-Sec. DAP; **4.** N.Roberts-Trade Unions; **5.** Grp Capt A.W. Murphy-RAAF; **6.** L.J.W-Chief Technical Adviser; **7.** F.J. Shea-Director Aircraft Maintenance Div.; **8.** John Storey-Director Beaufighter Div.; **9.** Laurie Coombes-C.S.I.R.; **10.** W.T. Harris-Asst Sec (Finance) DAP; **11.** H.G.Darling-Chairman CAC Ltd; **12.** E.V. Nixon-Treasury (away sick). **Melbourne Herald & L.J.Wackett /MS4858 /NLA**

The home guard marching down Lorimer Street in front of CAC with the Yarra River to the left. **David Anderson. 03 032015P**

Wartime factory employees boarding the Fisherman's Bend buses at the end of their work shift. **David Anderson. A124 07032031P**

Wartime day shift workers leaving CAC & DAP along Lorimer Street, Port Melbourne. **David Anderson. A124 07032049P**

CAC factory extension work, January 1942. **David Anderson. 701022069P.**

The rudimentary Melbourne & Metropolitan Tramways Board buses. Canvas covered, wooden framed 'dogboxes', sheeted with pressed wood fibre board, lining up in front of CAC to travel to Queens Bridge Street, Melbourne. **David Anderson. A124 07032007P**

Wartime ambulance presented by CAC employees & staff. **David Anderson. 03032007P**

Company employees rushing to board their transport home. **David Anderson. A124 07032009P**

Ambulance presentation outside the partly camouflaged factory entrance & sandbagged trenches.. **David Anderson. 03032012P**

Wirraway production airframes lined up. Visible are CA-16 A20-669 to 671. **David Anderson. 722062004P**

A20-155. Two CA-7 Wirraways at rural Mittagong, NSW during WW2. **Berrima District Historical Society**

A20-395. CA-8 in trainer markings from the School of Army Co-Operation, Canberra, ACT. 1941. **J.A. Vella Collection**

Early production CA-1 Wirraway line-up. **David Anderson. 707072010P**

A20-649. CA-16. Wirraway Restoration discussion.(L-R) Kevin Duffy (Sqdn Ldr, Engineering); Frank Joliffe; & Ian Royle (CAC/MAM). RAAF Point Cook. January 27, 1974. **J.A. Vella**

A20-2, the NA-16-2K on display for the Victory Bonds Loan Parade, Swanston Street, Melbourne. April 28, 1944. **J.A. Vella Collection**

Wirraway formation from 2 SFTS, Wagga, NSW. 1940. **J.A. Vella Collection**

Rolling out the MAM's A20-649 out of Hangar 185 for its first test engine run. RAAF Point Cook. August 23, 1974. **J.A. Vella**

A20-649. (VH-WIR ntu) Flying restoration. RAAF Point Cook. December 8, 1974. Exported 1993. **J.A.Vella**

A20-653. (VH-BFF) RAAF Point Cook. November 13, 1977. **J.A.Vella**

A20-687. CA-16. In the colours of A20-561, QE-B (6 Sqdn) of RAAF Museum Point Cook.(Non-flying). November 13,1977. RAAF . **J.A.Vella**

A20-10 of the Moorabbin Air Museum. The oldest surviving Wirraway GP aircraft on a RAAF transport returning after static exhibition at RAAF 50th Anniversary Air Display at RAAF Laverton, VIC .May 2 ,1971. **J.A.Vella**

A20-561 at home at CAC's 40th Anniversary Open Day. April 1977. **J.A.Vella**

CA-2,A3-1/A3-1001 prototype without the outer wing slots at Fisherman's Bend. **David Anderson. 722062020P**

A20-653. CA-16. In the colours of BF-F (9 Sqdn) of RAAF Heritage & History Branch. First civil registered restored Wirraway. Work began 1971 with f/f December 4, 1975. February 28, 1976. Essendon, Victoria. **J.A.Vella**

CA-2, A3-1/A3-1001 prototype with metal prop, Gipsy Major engine & unique cockpit canopy sections. **David Anderson. 722062018P**

Load testing of the CA-6 Wackett Trainer wing. **David Anderson. 584 722062019P**

A3-22. CA-6 Wackett Trainer in the RAAF standard earth brown, foliage green and trainer yellow belonging to the Moorabbin Air Museum. November 13, 1977. **J.A.Vella**

Mating a CA-6 Wackett Trainer fuselage frame to its wing assembly. **David Anderson. 583 722062016P**

A3-100. CA-6 in the later all over Trainer Yellow scheme. **Neil Follett Collection**

CA-6. A3-52 ex-7 SFTS, Deniliquin, NSW crashed at Evans Head, NSW. Crew from 7 CRD, Tocumwal, NSW reducing it to components. October 19, 1944. **Neil Follett Collection**

VH-DGR (ex-A3-120). CA-6 Wackett Trainer. Mudgee, NSW. September 1968. **Geoff Goddall**

VH-BEC (ex A3-139). CA-6 Wackett Trainer. Moorabbin, Victoria. 1961. **Neil Follett Collection**

VH-AIV (ex A3-23). CA-6 Wackett Trainer. Bankstown Airport, NSW. 1954. **Lorrie Molent/ARL**

VH-CXS & VH-ENM. Yeoman YA-1 Cropmasters. Wee Waa, NSW. June 2, 1975. **Geoff Goodall**

VH-AJH (ex A3-49). Kingsford Smith KS-3, the last example of four conversion/builds with the hopper installed in the previous rear cockpit position. Jandakot, West Aust. January 8, 1974. **Geoff Goodall**

A46-2. The second CA-12 Boomerang. **Andrew Carlile**

Yeoman YA-1 Cropmaster VH-CXS. One of 20 built of a design based on some CA-6 structural parts. Albury, NSW. September 1965. **Geoff Goodall**

A46-47. CA-12. 2 OTU, Mildura, Victoria. 1942. **J.A.Vella Collection**

VH-CSX. Yeoman YA-1 Cropmaster. Wee Waa, NSW. April 5,1978. **Geoff Goodall**

A46-205. CA-19 Boomerang (Batch N5-fifth production CA-19). Fishermans Bend, Victoria.. **Neil Follett Collection**

A46-30. CA-12. 'B' (85 Sqdn Interceptor) did not display their 'SH' Sqdn code in service. RAAF Museum Point Cook. (Non-flying). February 29, 2004. **J.A.Vella**

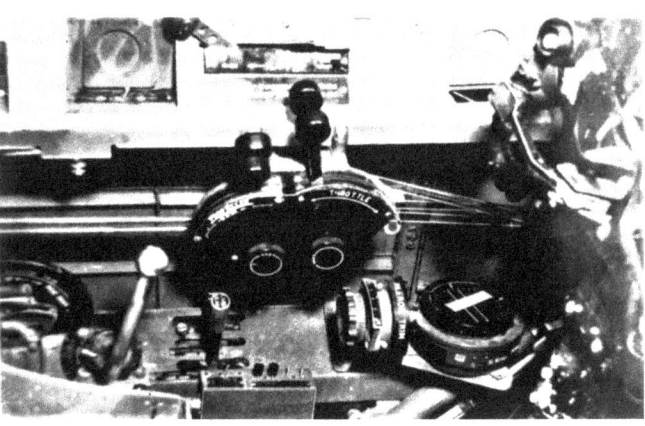

CA-11 Woomera. Front cockpit port side.

A46-63. CA-12 (VH-XBL), LB-L, (5 Sqdn). RAAF Point Cook. February 28, 2010. **J.A.Vella**

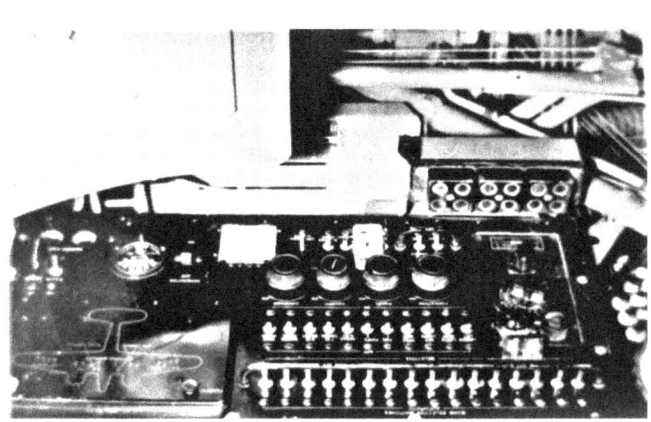

CA-11 Woomera. Front cockpit stbd side.

A46-122. CA-13 Boomerang. MH-R (3 Sqdn) of RAAF Heritage & History Branch. March 13, 2016. Tyabb,Victoria. **J.A. Vella**

CA-11 Woomera. Rear cockpit port side.

CA-19 (VH-BOM). MH-Y (83 Sqdn), 'Millingimbi Ghost' with incorrect roundel & tail markings. Eventually retired to the RAAF Amberley Heritage Centre. February 16,1999. Avalon, Victoria. **J.A.Vella**

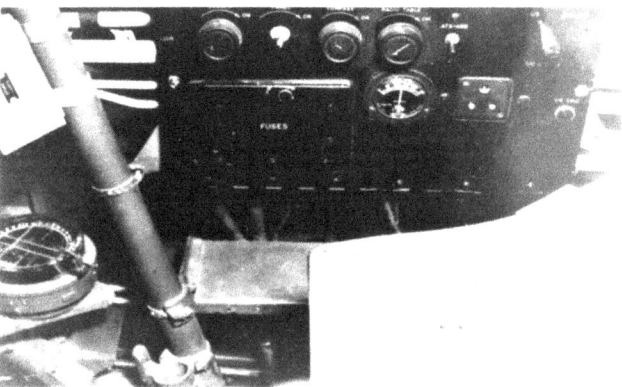

CA-11 Woomera. Rear cockpit stbd side. **All views R.Schulz**

CA-4. A23-1001 with two torpedoes, their steadying arms omitted. **David Anderson. 337 17012070P**

Above & below. A68-118 (VH-AGJ). CA-18 Mk 21. Tyabb, Victoria. March 14,2004 & RAAF Point Cook, February 28, 2010. **J.A.Vella**

Timber wall frames construction as part of the post war stop gap pre-fab housing project. **L.J.Wackett/MS48458/NLA**

A68-104 (VH-BOB). CA-18 Mk 21. RAAF Point Cook. February 24,2008. **J.A.Vella**

A68-105 (VH-JUC). CA-18 Mk 21. Finished as KH677, CV-P, 3 Sqdn, RAAF, Italy, 1945. RAAF Point Cook. December 17,2003. **J.A.Vella**

A68-107 (VH-AUB). CA-18 Mk 21. Tyabb, Victoria. March 14,2004 **J.A.Vella**

A68–170 (VH-SVU). CA-18 Mk 23. Finished as A68-750, AM-G, 77 Sqdn, Occupation of Japan 1947. Was previously known as 'Duffy's Delight'..its then Pt. Cook resident RAAF engineer. RAAF Point Cook. February 24, 2008. **J.A.Vella**

CA-15, A62-1001 prototype, Fisherman's Bend, May 4,1946, the day of its first flight. **David Anderson. A520 720022007P**

CA-22 Winjeel forward fuselage mock-up. **David Anderson. 727051583P**

The company airfield fire truck (ladder retracted) & a cheerful crew, May 4,1946. On standby for the first flight of the CA-15. **David Anderson. A520 720022013P**

CA-22/CA-25 wooden model in the ARL wind tunnel. **David Anderson. 729051526P**

CA-15. A62-1001. Crash following hydraulic failure. RAAF Pt Cook, December 10,1946. **David Anderson. A560 20714012070P**

CA-22, A85-364. First prototype in its initial tailplane arrangement. **David Anderson. 727051556P.**

Propeller overhaul shop. Black spinner (centre) is off the CA-15. **David Anderson. 722062001P**

CA-22, A85-618. Winjeel second prototype with the original tail assembly but with a small dorsal fin, 1951, over Port Philip Bay with Williamstown in the background. **David Anderson. A752 727032036P**

CA-22 Basic Trainer instrument panel. **David Anderson. 727051579P.**

CA-25 Winjeel fuselage & cockpit production parts awaiting assembly. **David Anderson. 729051504P.**

A85-618. Fin/rudder in the original position. Spin recovery parachute housing on mid dorsal fuselage. **David Anderson. 727051569P**

CA-25 Winjeel, A85-423 & 425. Early placement with the BFTS, Uranquinty, NSW with the old UK style roundels & orange / yellow trainer fuselage band. **David Anderson. A800 706072002P**

A85-618. Fin moved forward & spin recovery parachute housing relocated to the extreme rear fuselage end.
David Anderson. 727051576P

CA-25 Winjeel, A85-401, first production example, tufted for airflow testing. **David Anderson. 729051551P**

CA-25 Winjeel. A protracted manufacturing & assembly program. **David Anderson. 727051599P**

CA-25, A85-445 with whip aerial and blade antenna in FAC training configuration. 1969. Avalon Airfield. **David Anderson. 730051521P**

A85-410, 411, 415 & 426 of 4 Flight Forward Air Control training unit near RAAF Williamtown, NSW. **David Anderson. 727051578P**

CA-27 Sabre early production work as indicated by the original old UK style RAAF roundel & the employee's beret. **David Anderson. 722062013P**

1962: CAC's 25th Anniversary was during the busy period of the CA-27 Sabre production of 111 aircraft, their Avon engines and those for the GAF Canberra bomber. **J.A. Vella Collection**

CA-27 Sabre general assembly area. **David Anderson. 722062011P**

A94-928, 910 with the early (centre) & final cannon blast exit designs. Sept 1958. ARDU RAAF Laverton. **David Anderson. A816 717032096P**

A85-426. FAC Winjeel in 76 Sqdn markings visiting RAAF Point Cook. **J.A. Vella**

Left & Above: Prototype CA-26 Sabre, A94-101. Preparing and transporting it along the Geelong Road to its first flight on August 3, 1953 at Avalon Airfield, Lara, Victoria. **CAC**

A94-357 Sabre Mk 32. RAAF exercise at Darwin with inert Sidewinder AAM. **RAAF**

A95-965 Sabre Mk 32 of 77 Sqdn in the green nose, green / white checks with black outline on the fin. **RAAF**

A94-355 Sabre Mk 32 of 'Black Diamonds' 75 Sqdn, RAAF Williamtown display team, 1964. **J.A. Vella**

Line-up of 3 Sqdn Sabres at RAAF Butterworth, Malaysia following a complex movement operation from Williamtown. Oct 1958. **RAAF**

FM1362 ex A94-362 Sabre Mk 32 of 11 Sqdn Royal Malayasian Air Force with well used cannon blast panels. **J.A. Vella Collection**

(Above) A94-901 Sabre Mk 30 of 'Black Panthers' & A94-947 Mk 32 (below) of 'Red Diamonds' display teams from 76 Sqdn. **J.A. Vella**

(Above) A94-906 Sabre Mk 30 in the yellow & black tiger emblem colours of 2 (F) OCU RAAF Williamtown, 1962.

(Right) A94-915 Sabre Mk 30 of the 'Marksman' display team also of 2 (F) OCU in the yellow & black markings, RAAF Williamtown, October 1, 1968. **J.A. Vella**

Advertisement in **AIRCRAFT** journal. November 1953.
J.A. Vella Collection

Advertisement in **AIRCRAFT** journal. November 1955. **J.A.Vella Collection**

A7-007. Early CA-30 MB326H on the factory assembly line. Fisherman's Bend. **David Anderson. 722081605P**

CA-28. Ceres. VH-CEK flown by Roy Goon at Aerial Agriculture convention, Wagga, NSW. November 1960. **Geoff Goodall/Kurt Finger**

CA9-763, the curiously titled Wirraway A20-570 (radio callsign VH-AAZ). CAC's company aircraft used to familiarize prospective CA-28 Ceres owner/pilots. **Richard Hourigan**

VH-SSY. CA-28 Ceres with three other sad looking temporarily retired Ceres of Airfarm Associates still in their striking deep scarlet/yellow colour scheme. Tamworth, NSW. September 24, 1972. **J.A.Vella**

At the combined investiture March 4, 1954 (Melbourne) by Queen Elizabeth of Sir Lawrence Wackett, Sir George Jones & Sir Richard Williams. **L.J.Wackett / MS4858 /NLA**

RAAF C-130H awaiting RWR & ESM equipment installation in the HDHV/Tenix Defence Systems hangar sometimes known as the Skunk Works or Blunderdome by the technical staff. **Roger Ward**

David Anderson receiving the inaugural H. Knight (General Manager) award for exceptional study achievement.

The end of that part of Project Echidna of fitting RWR & ESM equipment on the RAAF's twelve C-130H Hercules at Tullamarine Airport, Victoria. **Roger Ward**

More commercial work. CAC designed SASSI Clay Crushing machine. Built by 4th year apprentices Bob Simmons (L) & David Anderson. **David Anderson**

Tactical Air Defence Radar System AN/TPS-77 mobile radar equipment cabin. Four sets were built at Fisherman's Bend and tested by HDHV/Tenix/BAE Systems

Lockheed Martin AN/TPS-77 RAAF Long Range Radar

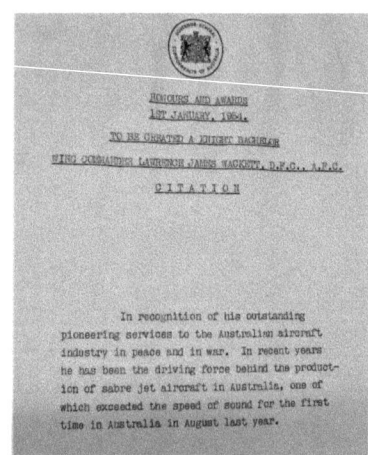

The January 1, 1954 Knighthood Citation for Wackett's achievement with the CA-27 Sabre project. **L.J.Wackett/MS4858/NLA**

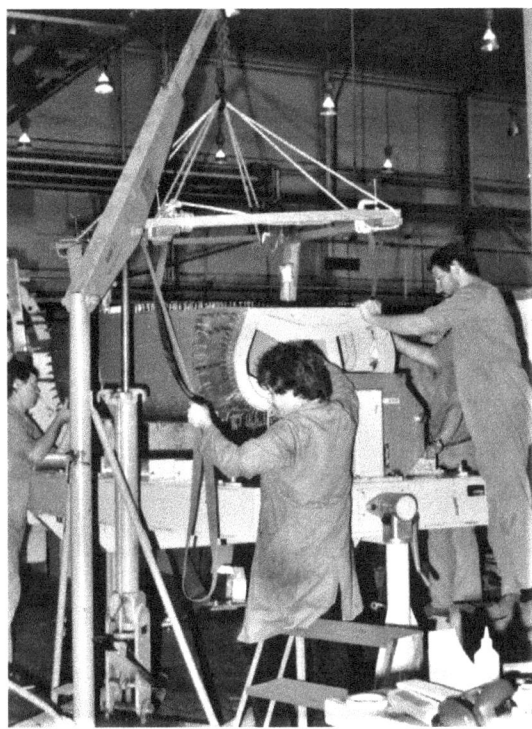

Left & Above: AAC Wamira. Testing the instrument panel blank & placing the engine lower trunk at GAF. Wamira project was intended to familiarize as many apprentices as practical in aircraft construction techniques. **GAF Heritage Group**

'Wamira Dreaming'. What may have been! Depiction of A23-068 of 1 BFTS, over RAAF Point Cook, Victoria, the penultimate A10 of the cancelled RAAF's initial 69 aircraft order. **GAF Heritage Group**

Left: The anger and frustration following the cancellation of the project was displayed by GAF /AAC project staff by the knife and fake blood in stabbing the fuselage of the developing full scale mock-up at week 51. **GAF Heritage Group**

Wamira (Continued). CAC, prevented from building airframe parts had the difficult role of fitting systems into sub-assemblies built by GAF & HDH. **GAF Heritage Group**

What might have been? Tandem seat Wamira A20 of the Royal Air Force over the chalk cliffs of England. **GAF Heritage Group**

The huge hydrodynamic test tank used for developing and testing of the Barra sonar submarine detection buoys (floating in the centre of the tank. **HDHV**

The CAC designed Ikara launcher in the Butler hangar. The MH & LS ship training rig was behind the screened off non-access area. CAC Open Day April 1977. **J.A.Vella**

GAF Turana Target Drone (Navy) test round leaving the CAC Ikara launcher on HMAS Swan (DE) in 1978. Turana propulsion had a different rocket boost engine to the GAF Ikara together with a 180 lb thrust Microturbo 022-01 turbojet. The short lived Womba anti-ship missile idea based on a developed Turana was another common airframe candidate for the CAC launcher.
HARS Aviation Museum/Fleet Air Arm Association/ Phil Thompson

An IKARA test vehicle less its dorsal fin & push-on wings with a torpedo in test markings for parachute drop tests under the wing of RAF Canberra B(I)8 WT333 attached to 2 Trials Unit, RAAF Edinburgh, S. Aust operating out of Avalon Airfield, Victoria assigned to GAF from November 28, 1966, on either or both RAN & RN trials. WT333 was back in the UK on July 17, 1969. **ADF Serials/GAF/ Robert Nash/JAV**

Car & motorbike weekend races were a feature on the Fisherman's Bend airstrip. The October 1955 event is one example. **CAC**

Post merger. Chaos, confusion & congestion following the transfer of stored material from Aircraft Factory 2 into Aircraft Factory 1. **Roger Ward**

Above & Below: Front (aircraft) & rear (tombstone) images on a staff sponsored T-shirt to mark the closure and names of personnel who lost their jobs at the BTR Nylex/HDHV's demise of the highly respected Engine Repair & Overhaul Workshop in 1995. **Tony Todaro**

Precision casting. Disposal auction by HDHV on May 30, 1988 ended 50 years of this self-reliant, highly developed, varied and extensively used activity. **Tony Todaro**

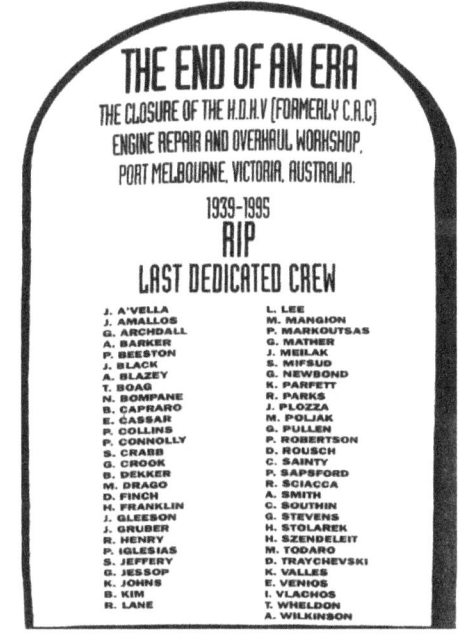

(Above & below) Aircraft Factory 1, cleared, forlorn. The end of history. **Tony Todaro**

(Above & below) Aircraft Factory 2 emptied, ready for the wreckers. **Tony Todaro**

Manufacture of General Electric F404 engine air seals. **Tony Todaro**

CAC's building assets being progressively torn down. **Tony Todaro**

The only remnant of CAC in 2020 is the re-purposed former 'White House' new administration building block in an entirely new industrial estate on the former CAC site. **Tony Todaro**

Demolition underway of the original CAC administrative building block. **CAC**

Offset and commercial work after the CAC/HDH merger:

Clockwise from top right: 1 & 2. Completed HS Nimrod MR2(RAF UK) underwing weapons pylons. 3. Pylon assembly jig. 4. C27J Alenia AerMacchi Spartan transport main rear loading ramp being moved to the next production stage. 5. A near completed short ramp section. 6. The C27J Sparton. Ten (10) examples acquired by the RAAF as the DHC-4 Caribou replacement. 7. HS Hawk trainer air brake in construction jig. 8. A completed horizontal stabilizer assembly. 9. Stabilizer frame in the assembly jig. **Michael Sullivan**

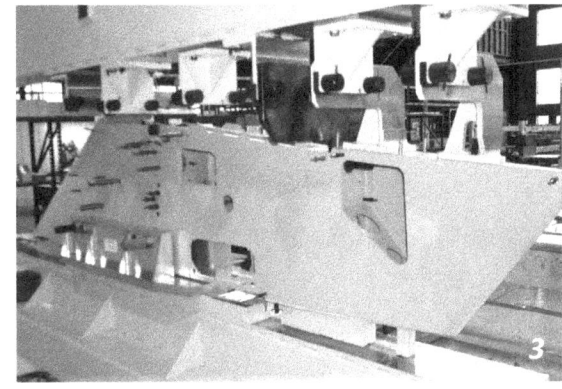

Non-conforming parts review: Panel reps from Dept of Quality Assurance(DQA); Northrop; McDonnell Douglas; HDH Quality; HDH Engineer & Roger Ward waving Material Review Reports (MRR)(top upper left).Roger, a Quality Inspector did not really dress like that. One US rep is bending a six inch rule to emphasise a point. **Roger Ward**

More chaos - post merger. An exchange of dollars to find storage space in Aircraft Factory 1 for material from Aircraft Factory 2 in failed attempt to lease out Aircraft Factory 2. **Roger Ward**

Faulty F/A-18 engine nozzles going cheap. **Roger Ward**

'Welcome Home'- post merger action of moving the entire AF1 Planning Department from the AF1 mezzanine into the Engine Shop & moving them back again two weeks later. **Roger Ward**

'Situation Back to Normal'- HDH takeover, no change, expected. The CAC poor clown on skateboard & banjo strumming mate welcome HDH clown arriving in a flash vehicle. **Roger Ward**

Regretting the merit of the decision. **Roger Ward**

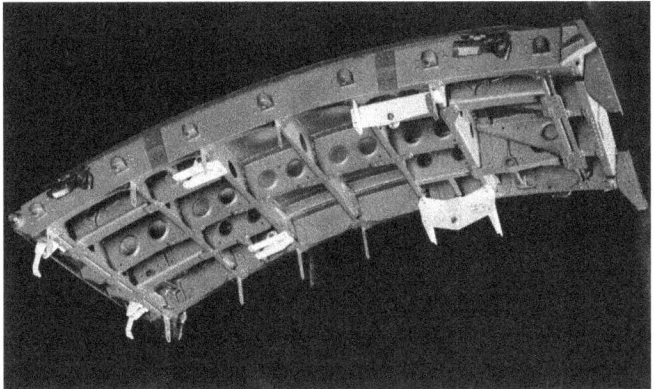
ATAR engine high pressure nozzle guide vane assembly being prepared for vacuum heat treatment. **HDHV**

CAC commercial work. Cabin exit doors for the Lockheed wide-body L-1011 Tristar airliner. **HDHV**

HDHV. A cabin of the ill-fated MDX helicopter project. **Ross Garlick**

Advertisement in the RAAF Laverton Air Display program of 27 March 1977. **Tony Todaro**

A reflection by former employees on the failed HDHV restructuring of the CAC 'culture' by stripping all the Leading Hands & Foreman of their duties, responsibilities & pay & replacing them with one third their number by Supervisors. It crushed productivity & morale. **Anonymous/CAC ex Employees Website**

Left. The Clowns brain storming to improve business productivity in 1987 post-merger with HDH after a structural reorganisation to change the factory floor 'culture' at CAC failed. **Roger Ward**

Index

A

Aerial Air Re-fuelling	302
Aeronautical Research Laboratory	35
AF/ARN-801 'Wombat'	xix
Air Force of the People's Liberation Army.	287
Air Staff Requirement	
Air Force Staff Target AFST 5044	xxxvii, 281, 290, 292, 294
Air Staff Requirement (AIR) 65	233
Air Staff Requirement AIR/64 Issue 2	215
Air Staff Requirement AIR/67	224
Air Staff Requirement ASR 120/78	253
Air Staff Requirement No 55 Issue 2	236
Air Staff Target AST 120/84	274
British Air Ministry Spec G24/35	x
Project Air 5225	304
Project Air 5276	261
Project Air 5375	xxxi
Project Air 5416	xxx
RAAF ASR 120/72	258
RAAF Development Spec No 241	35
RAAF Requirement (OR AIR 7)	96
RAAF Spec. Eng AC163	237
RAAF Spec.Eng. AC159	237
RAAF Specification 2/42	52
RAAF Specification 2/43	71, 72
RAAF Specification 3/38	15, 29
RAAF Specification AC94	142
Royal Air Force ASR No 397	252
Royal Air Force AST 362	215, 216
Royal Air Force AST 412	287
Specification AC180	290
Specification AC77	123
Specification AC79A	96
Specification AC85	105
Technical Requirement AC77	91, 123
Aircraft	
AA-106	216
AerMacchi MB326G	255
AerMacchi MB339	201, 253, 255
Aerospatiale AS350B Ecureuil (Squirrel)	243
AESL Airtourer	224
AESL Airtrainer CT-4A	225, 281, 302
AESL CT-4B	226, 302
Alenia C27J Spartan	xxx
Avro Anson	xiv, 17, 311
Avro Athena T1	87
Avro Cadet	19
Avro X	ix
BAC Jet Provost	208
BAC P59/P62 trainers	216
BAC Strikemaster Mk 88	211
BAC/SEPECAT Jaguar	216, 219
Beagle Pup	224, 225
Bede Aircraft BD-5	262
Beechcraft T-6A Texan II	291
Bell 206B/OH-58	236
Bell 47G Sioux	236
Bell AH-1G HueyCobra	223
Bell UH-1B Iroquois	245
Bell X-1	121, 127
Blackburn Botha	x
Blanik glider	257
BN-2T turbine Islander	228
Boeing 747	xxvi, xxix
Bristol Beaufort	x, xiii, 35, 52
Canadair CL-13 Sabre	114
Canadair CL-41 Tutor	208
Cessna C172	251
Cessna C175	248
Cessna Citation III	280
Cessna O-2	263
DAP Beaufighter	53
DAP Beaufort	xiv, xvi, xxii, 9, 27, 35, 37, 44, 52-54, 56, 58, 70, 85, 86, 307, 308, 318
Dassault Mirage III	181
Dassault/Dornier Alpha Jet	253
DCA3	85
DCA5	85
de Havilland Canada DHP-72	270
DH82 Tiger Moth	4, 17, 19, 24
DHC-4 Caribou	xxxvii, 270
DHC-5 Buffalo	270, 274, 296
DHC-6 twin Otter	230, 235, 272
DHC-7	232, 271
Dornier Do28	251
Douglas C-47	52
Douglas DC-2	23
EE Lightning	104, 181
Embraer EMB-312 Tucano	287
F4U Corsair	12
Fairchild Republic T-46	278, 291
Fairey Battle	17, 44
Fokker F27 Friendship	xvii, xix, xxii, 192, 296
Fokker F27M Maritime	280
Follant Gnat Trainer	252
Fuji FA200	224
Fuji T1F-3	208
GAF Nomad	xxiv, xxvi, xxxi, xxxvii, 223, 227, 231, 235, 236, 252, 263, 264, 270, 271, 279, 283
GAF Nomad Searchmaster 'L'	279
Grumman S-2E/G Tracker	245
Grumman S-2G Tracker	280
Hawker P1052	105
Hawker Seahawk	105
Hawker Siddeley 1182	252
Hawker Siddeley HS748	xxvii, 296
Hawker Siddeley Nimrod	xxx, 244, 245, 258
Helio Super Courier	232
Hughes 369/500/OH-6A Cayuse	214
Hughes 500C	268
Hunting Percival Jet Provost T2	208
Kawanishi H6K4 'Mavis'	11
KS 3 Cropmaster	25
Libelle glider	257
LJW6 Codock	ix, 338
LJW7 Tugan Gannet	x, xi, 338
Lockheed F-104A Starfighter	153, 180
Lockheed F-104G Starfighter	181
Lockheed L-400	275
Lockheed P2V-4 & 5 Neptune	xix
Lockheed P-3B Orion	xxiv
Lockheed P-3C Orion Update II	258
Lockheed P-3C Orion Update III/2	259
Lockheed SP-2H Neptune	xix, 258, 260
Lockheed Tristar	xxvi
Mc Donnell-Douglas A-4 Skyhawk	300
McDonnell-Douglas F/A-18 Hornet	302
MDX/Explorer NOTAR	303
Miles Magister	15, 19
Mitsubishi A6M3 Zero	12

NDN-1T Firecracker	287
Nord 262	226
North Amerian A-3J/RA5C Vigilante	xix
North American NA-16	xi, 1-3, 6, 13, 14, 16
North American NA-33	3, 5, 14
North American NA-50	55
North American OV-10 Bronco	263
North American TF-86 Sabre	114
North American TP-51 Mustang	87
Northrop N156F	180, 182
Northrop T-38 Talon	195, 216, 223
Pilatus Aircraft Works	236
Pilatus PC-8D Porter	251
Potez 94	208
Project 'N' Nomad	223
Republic F-105	181
SAAB 105	208
SAAB Fairchild 340	229
SAAB J-35 Draken	181
Saab JA37 Viggen	xxvi
Salto glider	257
Shorts SD3-MR Seeker	xxxvii, 279
SIAI Marchetti S211	279
Sikorsky Blackhawk	304
Sikorsky MH53E Sea Dragon	xxix
Sikorsky S61N	xxvi
Sikorsky S70A-2 Seahawk	304
Southern Cross	ix
Sud Aviation/Westland SA341 Gazelle	236
Supermarine Spitfire Mk VIII	86, 90
Supermarine Type 541	107
Vasama glider	257
Victa Aircruiser	224
Wackett Warbler	viii, 336
Wackett Warrigal I	ix, 337
Wackett Warrigal II	ix, 337
Wackett Widgeon I	viii, 336
Wackett Widgeon II	336
Westland Lysander	xi, xxxiii, 155
Westland Scout	236
Westland Sud-Aviation SA341 Gazelle	215
Wirraway	iv, xiii-xv, xxxvi, 1, 3-4, 6, 8-14, 16-20, 28-31, 35, 37-39, 44, 51, 55-57, 63, 65, 85, 127, 170, 172, 174, 179, 305, 306, 321
Yakelov 40	xxv
Yeoman YA-1 Cropmaster	25
Aircraft Development Mission	103
Aircraft Production Commission	xiii, 14, 18, 19, 29, 35, 305, 318
Aircraft Research and Development Unit	83, 93, 111, 257, 258
American S.W. Pacific Command	53
AN/AQA-7 DIFAR	258
AN/AQS-901	244, 259-260
Anglo/Australian program	216
ARDU	v, 94, 111, 114, 118, 188, 211, 226, 241, 258-259, 263, 296, 302, 320
ARL	v, xxviii, 35, 52, 93, 94, 96, 259, 283, 286, 290, 301
Army Aviation Corp	214, 241
11 Supply Battalion	241
161 Recce Squadron	241
162 Recce Squadron	241
171 Operations Support Squadron	241
School of Army Aviation	241
Army Light Helicopter	236
Auditor General's Department	283
Australian Aircraft Consortium Pty Ltd	283
Australian Aircraft Industry Study Group	282
Australian Cruiser Tank	10, 305
Australian Flying Corps	viii

B

BAE/Ansett Flying College	226
Barra Sonobuoy	xxiv, xxv, xxxvii, 244, 246, 258, 298, 335
Beaufort Division	xiv-xvi, 318
Bellman hangar	xv, xvi, xviii, 245
Blue Jay	xxxvi, 163-165, 193
Bonded panel fabrication	238
Branik	xxii, xxv, xxxvii, 228, 335
Brazilian Navy	xxii, xxv, 228
British Minister for Defence	215
Butler hangar	xiii, 245

C

CA-30 Mk 2A / 2C / 2E variants	253
CA-30 Mk 2B / 2D / 2F variants	253
CA-4 crash	47
CAC's South East Asia Manager	263
Calloy	xxvi
Chief of Air Force Materiel	256, 290, 291
Chief of Air Force Technical Services	290
Chief of Air Force Technical Staff	282
Citizen Air Force	
21 City of Melbourne (Fighter) Squadron	91
22 City of Sydney (Fighter) Squadron	91
23 City of Brisbane (Fighter) Squadron	91
24 City of Adelaide (Fighter) Squadron	91
Coastal Surveillance Aircraft	263
Cockpit Mock-Up conference	286
Companies	
A V Jennings	xvii
AAC- Westland Ltd (UK)	286
AerMacchi	209, 219, 255, 256
Aero Engine Services Ltd	225, 230
Aichi Tokei denki Kabushiki Kaisha	35
Air Parts (NZ) Ltd	225
Airfarm Associates	170, 172, 174-176, 179
Airland Improvements	179
Aluminium Company of America	xiv, 3
Amalgamated Wireless Australia(AWA)	230
Ansett Airways	24
Ansett-ANA	229
ASTA	v, 261, 301, 304
Austimpro	53
Australian Chemical Industries	52
Australian Metal Productions	52
Australian National Industries	xxix
AVCOM Industries	248
Babb Co. Inc	123
Bachan Aerospace	xxviii
BAE Systems	298
Bell Australia (BA)	237
Bell Helicopter Company (BHC)	236
BHP Engineering	298
BHP's Shipyard Division	xxvii
Bihrle Applied Research	283
Boeing	xxix, xxxii, 155, 229, 300, 304
Bristol Aeroplane Co (Aust)	124
British Motor Corporation	xx, xxi, 320
Broken Hill Associated Smelters	v, xi
Broken Hill Pty Ltd	261
Brookes Robinson	52
Canadair	108, 111, 114, 208

Chrysler Motor Car Annexe	xxii
Clyde Engineering	8, 11, 23
Cobham UK	298
Commercial Aviation Pty Ltd	xxvii
Commonwealth Aircraft Corporation	iii, v, x, xi, xxx, xxxi, xxxiii, 1, 14, 29, 31, 33, 54, 66, 70, 71, 83, 86, 91, 94, 96, 105, 108, 119, 123, 127, 131, 134, 137, 142, 145, 153, 161, 162, 164, 165, 167, 179, 180, 188, 193, 199, 206, 208, 215, 223, 224, 226, 228, 229, 233, 235, 236, 243, 246, 248, 252, 253, 256, 261-262, 268, 270, 271, 274, 275, 279, 281, 291, 294, 298, 301, 308, 312
Commonwealth Steel	xxix
Commuter Aircraft Corporation	232
Computer Devices of Canada	261
Coondair Pty Ltd	179
de Havilland	v, xii, xxi, xxii, xxiv, xxxi, xxxii, 9, 11, 13, 15, 18, 51, 53, 61, 65, 71, 83, 89-91, 95, 103, 106, 124, 137, 139, 142, 162-165, 209, 232, 238, 248, 271, 308, 310, 319-321
Doggett Aviation	179
Dunlop	xvi, 52, 124, 209, 283, 301, 320
Electronic Systems & Management Services Ltd	298
EMIE Lorell	xxvii
Endeavour Aerospace Pty Ltd	291
English Electric	xviii, 104, 181, 215
Ernest Heinkel	35
ESAMS Ltd. Aust	244
Fairchild Republic Corporation	291
Fairey Aviation (Aust)	295
Flight Refuelling Ltd	302
GAC (Aust) Pty Ltd	229
GAF	iii, v, xvi, xviii-xxi, xxiii, xxv, xxvi, xxviii, xxxvii, 93, 108, 111, 118, 124, 133, 134, 172, 174, 182-184, 187, 208, 209, 216, 227, 229, 231, 235-236, 238, 243, 248, 252, 263-264, 271, 272, 274, 280, 283, 285, 287-288, 301, 306, 309, 312, 313, 320, 335
General Aeronautique Marcel Dassault (GAMD)	181
General Aircraft Corporation	228, 230
General Motors	v, vii, xi, 52, 108, 241
GMH	v, viii, xi, xv, xvii, 11, 18, 23, 85
Grumman Aerospace Corporation	265
Harland Engineering	55
Hawker de Havilland	v, xvi, xxi, xxiv, xxix, xxxi, xxxii, 209, 238, 310, 319
HDH	iii, v, xxi, xxiii, xxiv, xxvii, xxviii, xxx, 188, 209, 211, 238, 252, 261, 274, 283, 290, 301, 302, 318, 320, 335
Helio Aircraft Corporation	229
HSA Kingston, UK	252
Hughes Helicopters	xx, 214, 268, 303, 320
Imperial Chemical Industries	v, vii
International Helicopters Pty Ltd	214
Israeli Aircraft Industries	300, 302
Jayrow Helicopters	215
Jetair Australia Ltd	230
LADS Corp	298
Limberlost Lumber Mills	xvii
Lund Aviation Inc	13, 124
Marconi (UK)	244
Marshall's Spreading Service	179
Mero Raurnstruktur GMBH	xxvii
Morane Saulnier	248
Myttons	11, 52
National Air Support	298
New England Aerial Topdressing	179
New Zealand National Airways Corporation	230
North American Aviation	vi, xi, 1-3, 6, 14, 17, 71, 72, 86-87, 108, 111, 114, 119, 123, 127, 144, 162, 320, 334
NZ Aerospace Industries (NZAI)	225
Pacific Airmotive Corporation	229, 230
Philips Industries	244
Pilatus Aircraft Works	236
Plessey Electronics (Aust)	244
Plessey Pacific	246
Proctor's Rural Services	174, 175, 179
Qantas Airways	xxv, 229, 235
Quentron	295
R W Cameron & Co	16
RAGNAR Pty Ltd	19
Ready Mix-Concrete Pty Ltd	53
Reims Aviation	251
Repco Brabham	xxv
Rex Aviation	xxi, xxiii, xxvii, 215, 248, 252, 270, 280, 320
Richards Industries	8, 11, 52, 65
Rockwell	xxxii, 304
Rolls Royce	vi, xvii, xxvii, xxix, 76, 81, 82, 89, 90, 96, 98, 102, 105-108, 110, 114, 117, 121, 133, 142, 143, 145, 153, 155, 160, 165, 167, 181-182, 188, 197, 199, 202, 216, 221, 247, 251-253, 256, 262, 306, 309, 311-312
Rook-Cubic Western Data	296
Rossair Ltd	248
RR Light Aircraft Engine Division (UK)	262
Ruskins Motor Bodies	52
Shell Australia	52
Short Bros Ltd	280
Smiths Instruments (UK)	296
Southern Panel	52
Static General Engineering	xxvii, xxviii
Super Spread Aviation	170, 179
Super Spread Pty Ltd	170
Tennix Defence (LADS Corporation)	298
Thorn-EMI Electronics	259, 295, 298
Toorongo Logging Co	xvii
Tugan Aircraft Co	viii, x, xii, xiii, 1, 2, 6, 16, 37
Union Air	294
United Aircraft Corp	305, 306
Vershoor	xxvii
Vickers Barrow	228
Vision Systems	298
Warner Aircraft Corp	17
Westland Helicopters	xxix
Whittle's Power Jets	xvi
Consultants W.D. Scott	xxvii
Coombs Modular Steel House	xxvi

D

DAP's Beaufort division	xvi
DDG Class	190-191, 228
de Havilland Firestreak	118, 162-164, 193
Defence Inter-Departmental Committee	287
Defence Operations Division	xxvii
Defence Research Centre, Salisbury	v, 245, 296
Deliverette	xv
DEPAIR	v, 9, 72
Department of Air	v, xiv, 6, 14, 23, 70, 81, 83, 94, 105, 208, 214, 236, 243, 255, 305, 307, 308, 312, 318
Department of Civil Aviation	v, xxv, xxviii, 25, 87, 193, 230
Department of Defence	v, x, 111, 118, 172, 181, 189, 192, 211, 255, 263, 279, 296, 311, 318
Department of Foreign Affairs	114, 263
Department of Manufacturing Industry	xxiv, 215, 241
Department of Productivity	236, 286
Department of Supply	v, xxii, 4, 19, 94, 105, 110, 111, 181, 183, 188, 192, 208, 211, 216, 233, 243, 252, 256, 318, 320, 321
Department of Trade	229

Department of Transport	271
Design Definition Phase	286
Detail Design Documents	283
Durability & Damage Tolerance Assessment	211

E

East-West Airlines	298
Empire Air Training Scheme	v, 4, 10, 17, 23
Engineering Mock-Up(EMU)	287
Engines	
Avco Lycoming IO-540	251
Avco Lycoming IO-720-AIA	207
Avco Lycoming O-360	252
Avco Lycoming TIGO-541K	281
Bristol Centaurus CE-12SM	76
Bristol Siddeley BS358	199
BS Viper 22-11	209, 255, 275, 276, 313
BS Viper 500	243, 253, 255
BS Viper 600	197, 246
BS Viper 632-43	253, 255, 256
CAC R795 Cicada	123, 139, 309, 312
DH Gipsy Major Series II	15, 16
DH Gipsy Six	xii, 16
Garrett Airesearch TFE-311	278
Garrett AiResearch TPE-331	227, 292
Garrett AiResearch TPE331-101H	287
GE CF6-80/CFM56	xxvi
GE F404	xxviii, xxx, 305, 314-315
GE J47	110
GE J85-15	199
GE J85-J1A	195
Geschwender 400 (Ford V8)	281
GM Allison 250	215, 227, 228, 235, 268, 281
GM Allison 250-C20	236
GM Allison T56	xxvi
Napier Scorpion	162
P & W (Canada) JT15D-5	276
P & W (Canada) PT6	193
P & W (Canada) PT6-25C/2	287
P & W (Canada) PT6-30	229
P & W (Canada) PT6A-20	223, 281
P & W (Canada) PT6A-25	281
P & W (Canada) PT6A-40	230, 233
P & W / CAC R2000	xxviii, 48, 51, 52, 65, 70, 308
P & W R1340 Wasp	xiii, xiv, xxviii, 2, 4, 10, 13, 30, 33, 70, 71, 85, 172, 177, 223, 305-309, 311
P & W R1830 S1C3-G Twin Wasp	48, 52, 61, 307
P & W R2800	308
P & W R2800-10W	72, 74
P & W R2800-21 Double Wasp	71
P & W R2800-22W	72
P & W R2800-43	71
P & W R2800-57W	74, 75, 77, 83
P & W R985 Wasp Junior	123, 281
Packard Merlin V1650-7	89, 90
Ralph Sarich Orbital Engine	261
Reaction Motors XLR-11-RM-5	127
Revmaster R2100D(VW)	262
RR Avon 100 Series	312
RR Avon 200 Series RA24R	146
RR Avon RA.14	133
RR Avon RA.19R	155
RR Avon RA.3	102, 110
RR Avon RA.3 Mk 1	312
RR Avon RA.7 / RB65	312
RR Avon RA-7	103, 119, 121, 131
RR Derwent 8 RD7	xxxvi, 142, 189
RR Griffon 121	81
RR Griffon 125	76
RR Griffon 61	82, 83
RR Griffon 85	81
RR Merlin 102	309
RR Merlin 66/70	90
RR Nene 2-VH	xvii, 106, 306, 308
RR RA.3 Mk1	312
RR RB108	165
RR RB93	143, 145
RR/Turbomeca RB172/T260 Adour	197
Sarich Orbital Engine	xxxvii, 262
SNECMA ATAR 09C	v, xx, xxvii-xxx, 181-183, 186, 188, 239, 305, 306, 313, 316
Stage 2 Development Corp V8450A	281
Teledyne Continental GTSIO-520K	281
Teledyne Continental Tiara	235
Teledyne Continental TSIO-520	265, 268, 273
Turbomeca Aspin II	134
Turbomeca Larzac	256
Turbomeca Marbore II	137
Warner Super Scarab	17, 20, 28
Wright Cyclone R3350	308
Wright R2600B	52, 307
Eureka Stockade Aviation Museum	223
Exclusive Economic Zone	v, 263, 279

F

F40-Niteroi	228
F41 - Defensora	228
F44 - Independencia	228
F45 - Uniao	228
FAR 23 rules	224
Federal Labor Government	188, 238
Fighter Factory	181
Finlay National Award	xix
Fitzgerald Committee	xxii
Flight Refuelling Ltd	302
Forest Products Division	11, 18
Forward Air Control Aircraft	xxxvii, 233, 235, 263
Frank Matich racing wheel castings	xxv

G

GAC Transport Division	229
Gliding Federation of Australia	v, 251, 257, 258

H

Harpoon anti-ship missile	xxvi
Helicopter Division.	214
House of Representatives	xxi, 118, 199, 206, 211, 214, 223

I

Ikara	xxi, xxii, xxv, xxxvii, 189-191, 228, 245
Indigenous New Design	292
Indonesian Air Force (AURI)	118
Industries Assistance Commission	xxiv, xxxiii, 241, 243, 263, 268
Industry Work Package	256
Inter-Departmental Committee	286, 287

Israeli Air Defence Force	302

J

Jindivik	xvi, xxii, 118, 182, 320
Joint Parliamentary Public Accounts Committee	283

K

Kernot Memorial Medal	xix
Knight Bachelor	xix, 321
Konfrontasi	118

L

Laser Airborne Depth Sounder	294, 298
Lend-Lease	62, 70, 74, 90
Leopard 1 Battle Tank	xxvi
Line Replacement Unit	286
LOTEX	vi, xxiv, 184, 211, 213
Lower Yarra Bridge	xviii

M

Malkara	xxii, 182
Memorandum of Understanding	287
Metal adhesive bonded blades	238
MILSPEC	286, 290
Minister for Air	xiii, xxi, xxiv, 6, 14, 17, 105, 110, 118, 142, 183, 199, 252
Minister for Aircraft Production	xiii, xxiv, 6, 14
Minister for Defence	xi, xxxiii, 1, 4, 14, 16, 96, 181, 199, 215, 219, 225, 230, 236
Minister for Science & Consumer Affairs	xxiv
Minister for Science and Technology, Singapore	264, 278
Minister for Supply	xiii, xxii, 182, 208, 219, 230
Moorabbin Air Museum	263, 285, 287, 291
MoS	vi, 104
Myer	xvii

N

NASA Langley, Vertical Spin Facility.	283
Navy Staff Requirement NSR 1102	295
Navy Staff Requirement NSR 4/67	236
Netherlands East Indies Army Air Force	25
Next Generation Trainer	278, 291
Nulka Active Ship Missile Decoy Rocket System	xxvi
Nymphea	xxvii

O

Ocean Digger	xxvii
Omega	xxiv, 261
Oswald Watt Medal	xix

P

Pappas, Evans, Carter and Koop	xxix
passenger bus bodies.	xvii

People	
Abbott (Bill) R L	xx, xxi, xxiii, xxvii, 230, 248, 251, 264, 320
Adams Jim	285
Air (Bill) Thomas W	xiii, xvi, 2, 16, 95, 320
Allott C	287
Anderson (D.G.) Sir Donald	240
Anderson Senator Ken	xxii, 219, 223, 228
Archer Flt Lt J Lee	83
Archer Lee	iii, 12, 118, 215, 243, 264, 268, 278, 320
Atcherley AVM R L	106
Bacon S	287
Baker Dennis	iii, 245, 259, 260
Baldwin Stanley	x
Barnard Lance	xxiii, 241
Barnwell Frank S	viii, 336
Barrett Geoff	170
Bateman Ken	296
Beazely Kim	288
Beck Ted	3
Becker Harry	36, 72, 93
Bellward Colin	xvi
Bennett Gordon	282
Betts D A	283
Billington Cecil	215
Blackwell Sir Basil	287
Board Greg	320
Bollinger Dr Lynn	228, 233
Bolton Allan	xvi
Boss-Walker Hubert	xvi, 4-6, 16, 37, 38, 43, 56, 320
Bostock AVM W D	71
Bowden E K	viii
Brain Lester	xxii
Brett Lt General G	57
Brooke-Popham ACM Sir Robert	43
Brookes Sqdn Ldr W	11
Brooks Richard	xvi
Brown Arch A G	xi, 6, 36, 44, 170, 172
Brown George	xvi
Brown J T	26, 29
Bruce High Commissioner Stanley	x
Burgess J D	245
Burnett(RAF) ACM Sir Charles	19
Burton D W	xxvii
Button Senator John	xxx, 44, 304
Cameron Clyde	xxiv
Cameron Don	xiv, xxiv
Campbell Jim	237
Carey Graham	xii
Carolan Anthony	iii, xxx, 320
Carpender(USN) Vice Admiral Arthur	xv
Carter James	xvi, 6, 58, 320
Casey Richard G	5
Cassar Alf	245
Cassidy A	287, 291
Castledine D	287
Caterson Jim	iii, 209, 241, 275, 280, 282, 320
Chenery E R	10
Chifley PM Ben	105
Chittock Alfred	245
Clapp Harold W	xiii
Cobham B	iii
Collier D	iii, 291
Coombes Laurie	35, 338
Corbett Arthur	85
Coulston Sgt J	12
Creasey Ray	215, 216
Cuming Sqdn Ldr Derek R 'Jell'	53, 83, 181
Curtin PM John	xiv, xxii

Dalziel (Jock) D J	iii, xxiv, xxvii, xxx, 268, 279, 320
Darling Harold	5
Davenport-Brown(RAF) Flt Lt W	44
David (Fred) Friedrich	xvi, 35, 320
Debnam Peter	283
Dengate Robert	283
Dietz AVM Tony	282
Doleman Gordon	xxvii
Douglas Snr Donald	229
Eaton Air Cdre Brian	208
Ellem John	261
Ellington (RAF) AM Sir Edward	2
Eltringham Don	263
Enderby Ken	241
Faggetter Edwin (Ted)	xvi, 320
Fairbairn David	xxi, 183, 219, 225
Fairhall Allen	199
Fedden Sir Roy	xix, 192
Fehr J. Kornel	229
Fleming Ian	xvi, 41, 43, 55, 72, 91, 188, 215, 252, 320
Foden Peter	245
Foster George	xvi
Francis Hugh	xvi, 55, 81, 320
Fraser Malcolm	xxi, 211, 219, 223, 236
Frewin Ken	320
Frost AVM Roy	291
Gannon Frank	ix
Goon Roy	172, 174, 175
Gornall William	215
Graff AVM Brian	286
Grey C G	x, 4, 6, 297
Grundy I	287
Hardman(RAF) AM Sir Donald	104
Harper Flt Lt James	43
Harper Sqdn Ldr James	47
Harrison H C	viii, xii, 1, 58
Hartnett Laurence J	vii, viii, xi, xii, xxxiii, 18, 265
Hattersley Bruce	xxx, 320
Heffernan Flt Lt Patrick	2
Heggen AVM Alan	291
Henty Senator Norman	208
Hives Ernest W	82, 108
Howell Peter	245, 287, 300
Howlett M J	283
Howson Peter	199
Hudson Ray	237
Hughes AVM Henry	291
Hulme Alan S	182
Humphries Douglas	xvi, 35, 55, 70, 72, 76, 103, 119, 121, 127, 131, 137, 142, 165, 320
Hunter Ken	261
Hutchinson Les	245
Irons David	248
Irving Louis	172, 201, 261, 263, 320
Jablonsky Bruno	74
Jones Air Cmdr George	52
Jones CAS, AVM George	iii, xviii, 29, 52, 70, 91, 96, 104-106, 108, 110, 123, 142, 188, 320
Jones Ern	iii, 16, 20, 55, 87, 106, 110, 123, 124, 334
Katter Robert C	xxv, 241
Keating Paul	211, 219
Keevers Brian	195, 215, 216
Kenney Lt General George	62
Kentwell John	xxvii, xxxi, 111, 119, 162, 163, 180, 189, 192, 195, 215, 216, 228, 235, 246, 252, 280, 282, 286, 291, 320
Killen James	279, 282
Kindelberger J H	1, 86, 87
Kingsford Smith Charles	ix, 25, 338
Kingsford-Smth Rollo	xxix
Kirby J N	3, 11, 52, 307
Knight Herbert	iii, xi, xiii, xvii, xx, xxi, xxxiii, 14, 30, 55, 98, 106, 119, 181, 214, 305, 308, 311, 312, 321, 351
Laby Professor Thomas	36
Lemberg E	245
Letcher Victor	107, 110, 119, 338
Lewis, Essington	vii, xi, 86
Lipscombe Paul	237
Lodge Maurice	3, 57, 87, 106
Lumby Charles	47
Lunney Keith	245
Lyons PM Joe	x-xi
MacArthur General Douglas	xv, 62, 85, 87
Macartney R	287
Maddoch B	283
Manderson John	287, 296, 300
Marshall Sid	245
Marshall Wg Cmdr Geoff	93
Mason Roy	215
Maucer R	283
McCoubrie Leon	iii, 245
McGrath Sir Charles	xxiii, xxxiii
McLachlan AM I D	182
McVey Daniel	85, 86
Melbourne Jim	xvi
Meng Dr L C	265
Menzies Robert Gordon	5, 108, 142
Miles John	83, 87, 93, 105, 111, 124
Millicer Henry	94, 224
Moharich Joe	240
Mole Ian	245
Monagham J V	283
Monash John	viii
Morrison Bill	263
Morrison Malcolm	283
Murphy A W	viii, 1
Nixon S V	5
North Dr J	283
Page Frederick W	215
Paltridge Senator Shane	208
Park Sir Keith	105
Parkhill, Archdale	vii, viii, xi, xxxiii, 1-3, 14
Pashai T	287
Patching Alan	iii, 94, 251
Patterson Bill	278
Pazmany Ladislao	262
Pfitzner Leigh	245
Price Ralph	xvi, 16, 35, 55
Rees David	iii, xxvi, xxx, xxxiii, 201, 206, 215, 216, 226, 228, 233, 235, 246, 248, 252, 253, 256, 261, 302, 321
Reid Charles	iii, xxvi, 103, 110, 121, 127, 133, 142, 145, 153, 160, 180, 195, 208, 215, 216, 223, 235, 236, 243, 245, 246, 248, 252, 256, 275, 321
Rich Bob	237
Richardson Geoffrey (Geoff)	170
Ring Ian	iii, xvi, xx, xxi, xxvii, xxxiii, 9, 13, 18, 27, 37, 55, 58, 64, 72, 93, 98, 103, 105, 110, 124, 134, 143, 162, 165, 170, 181, 188, 203, 206, 237, 240, 243, 277, 279, 308, 321, 334
Roberts Gerry	300
Robertson Sqdn Ldr Ken	93
Rowell Sir Sydney	xx, 318
Rowland Wg Cdr James	182
Saget Jean-Marie	182
Salmond (RAF) AM Sir John	ix
Samarsky D	287

Sarich Ralph	261
Scascighini Les	53
Schaetzel Stan	283, 288
Scherger ACM Sir Frederick	xviii, xx, xxii, xxxiii, 2, 14, 104, 105, 110, 181, 318
Schofield James	xvi, 82, 91, 321
Schulz Reg	iii, xv, 3, 35-38, 43, 47, 48, 50, 51, 53, 54, 64, 88, 106, 116, 124, 321
Scott Flt Lt Bill	93, 111, 172
Scott Murray	296
Scott-Hall Stewart	104
Shelton Tom	216
Shepherd M L	vii
Slessor (RAF) CAS Sir John	104
Smith Neville	iii, 237
Smth Alan J	283
Solvey Joe	55
Spence Neil	300
Spiteri J	252
Stamper J	283
Stanwycks John	237
Stern Lionel	35
Sullivan Michael	iii
Susans Grp Cpt Ron T	182
Sutherland AVM Ian	286
Townley Athol	181
Trimble Tom	216
Turl Leo	ix
Wackett Lawrence	vii-x, xii-xix, xxii, xxv, xxxiii, xxxiv, xxxvi, 1-5, 8, 9, 14, 16-20, 22-26, 28-31, 35-37, 39, 43, 44, 47, 50, 53, 54, 56, 58, 62, 64, 71-72, 85-87, 91, 95, 104, 106-108, 110, 111, 114, 119, 123-124, 137, 164, 170, 172, 175, 181, 182, 224, 305, 307, 308, 311, 312, 319-321, 336-338, 342, 351
Waldrup Herb	240
Ward Dr R G	261
Watkins Walter	iii, xxvi, 99, 103, 129, 137, 145, 170, 181, 195, 206, 208, 215, 216, 219, 222, 230, 235, 248, 251, 252, 256, 261, 263-264, 266, 268, 270-271, 276, 278-281, 283, 285, 286, 291, 294, 321, 334
Westrup Ron	265
Wheeler Frank T	xiii
White Thomas W	105
Whitlam PM Gough	xxiv, 238
Williams Arthur	55, 228
Williams AVM Richard	vii, viii, xi, xxxiii, 17, 351
Wimperis H E	35
Zelt Earl	240
Philco Sidewinder	xix

Places

Andir	26
Avalon Airfield	xviii, xix, xxii, xxv, 111, 113, 118, 172, 183, 184, 209-210, 213, 236, 261, 300, 302, 348, 354
Bankstown	xxiii, 8, 11, 25, 88, 124, 209, 211, 215, 226, 252, 301, 304, 310, 320
Benalla	20, 25, 257
Bouganville Island	12
Brisbane Airport	237
Cape Willoughby	260
Cloncurry, Qld	241
Cockatoo Dockyard	ix, xiii, 320
Deniliquin, NSW	10
Emu Field, Maralinga	91
Essendon Airport	i, xxiii, 258, 259, 274
Fisherman's Bend	iii, xii, xiv, xvi-xviii, xxii-xxiv, xxvii, xxxi, xxxii, 2, 3, 10, 17, 23, 38, 43, 47, 64, 65, 76, 80, 85, 88, 93, 98, 111, 118, 124, 170, 172, 174, 176, 209, 211, 212, 215, 259, 303, 305-308, 339, 341, 346, 351, 354
Gona, PNG	12
Highett	xiv, xvi
Indonesia	v, 118, 209, 264
Iswahyudi Air Base, East Java	118
Kalidjate	26
Kalkadoon Park, Mt Isa, Qld	241
Kentwell John	iii
Kilmore	52
Labuan	12
Laverton	xviii, 2, 4, 11, 15-17, 19, 23, 43, 44, 48, 53, 65, 87, 114, 115, 118, 184, 211, 212, 214, 257-258, 320, 338, 348
Lidcombe	xiv, xvi, xviii, xix, xxiii, xxxiv, 43, 54, 71, 76, 90, 124, 170, 305-309
Malaysia	xxvii, 115, 216, 264
Mallala	13
Martlesham Heath Experimental Station	viii
Mascot Aerodrome	viii, ix, xi, 23, 25
Mt Gambier	24
Nayook	xvii
North Island, NZ	228
Orfordness Experimental Station	viii, 39
Phuc Tuy province	237
Preston Division, Warton	215
Randwick	36
Singapore	xxvii, 11, 43, 114, 181, 211, 216, 264, 265, 268, 271, 278, 279
South Vietnam	223, 236, 237, 263
Spencer Gulf	260
St Vincent Gulf, S.Aust	245
Tamworth Airport	226
Tanjung Priok	26
Thailand	55, 118, 209, 264
Tjilitan (Djakarta, West Java ML)	26
Tocumwal	xviii, 25, 91
Tullamarine Airport	258, 302
Ubon, Thailand	118
Uranquinty	10, 12, 94, 127
Varese, Italy	209
Victor Harbour	260
Vunakanau, Rabaul	11
Waikerie	257
Warringah	xi, xxxiii, 2, 14
Wichita, Kansas	248
Woodside	260
Yorke Peninsula	260
Youngstown, Ohio	233

Projects

A Commercial Aircraft Replacement for the Winjeel Trainer	224
AAC / CA-34 Wamira Basic Pilot Trainer Aircraft	281
An Aerial Top-Dressing Aircraft	206
AP1001 BAC / CAC AA-107 Close Support / Trainer Aircraft	215
AP1002 CAC / Hawker Siddeley HS1182(Hawk) Jet Trainer	252
AP1035-Remotely Piloted Crop Spraying Helicopter	298
AP1051-Project KAHU, RNZAF A-4 Skyhawk Modernisation	300
Blue Jay Missiles on DH Sea Venom Fighter	165
Britten-Norman Islander with Turboprop Engines	226
C-130 'Tubby' Hercules	274
CA-1,3,5,7,8,9,10 & 16 NA-16 Wirraway G.P. Aircraft / Trainer	1
CA-12,13,14,14A & 19 Boomerang	54
CA-24 Hawker P1081 Day Fighter Aircraft	105
CA-25 Winjeel	123
CA-26/CA-27 North American F-86 Sabre Fighter	108

CA-28 Ceres Turbo Prop Conversion	223
CA-29 GAMD Mirage IIIO Fighter Sub-Contract	180
CA-30 Aer Macchi MB326H Trainer Aircraft	208
CA-30 Mk 2 MB326H Jet Trainer	253
CA-31 Supersonic Trainer/Close Support Aircraft	195
CA-32 Bell 206B-1 L.O.H. (Kalkadoon)	236
CA-33 P-3 Orion Systems Upgrade	258
CA-36 Apprentice Training Project (Pazmany PL-4A)	262
CA-37 Pilatus PC-9A Basic & Advanced Trainer Aircraft	302
CA-38 Aerial Refuelling Tanker Conversions	302
CA-39 McDonnell-Douglas Explorer Helicopter	303
CA-4 Wackett Bomber & CA-11 Woomera Bomber	35
CA-40 Lockheed P-3C Orion ESM Upgrade	304
CA-41 General Dynamics F-111C AUP	304
CA-42 Unknown	304
CA-43 Unknown	304
CA-44 Sikorsky S-70B-2 & S-70A-9 Helicopters	304
CAC / Short Bros Ltd SD3-MR Seeker	279
CAP 201 Macchi MB326H Replacement Trainer Aircraft	246
CA-X Universal Lightweight Trainer	275
Cessna Compacts, Aerobat A157,Twins & Glider Tug	248
Conceptual STOL Feeder Liner	192
EX200 / EX220 Ikara Missile Handling & Launch System	188
EX260 Branik Missile Handling & Launch System	228
EX300 Barra Sonobuoy	243, 246
Fighter Requirements Criteria 1953-1960	146
GAC-100 Commuter Aircraft	228
GAF Nomad Technical Assessment	235
Light Helicopter Crane / Jeep	268
Light Military/Civil Transport (LMS Derivative)	268
Light Surveillance Aircraft (Cessna 402A Mod)	270
Light Utility Transport Aircraft	271
Light Weight Jet Trainer	278
Macchi MB326H (Modification)	243
P143 Ab-Initio Trainer Aircraft	15
P144 / P148 Twin Engine Bomber Reconnaissance Aircraft	30
P147 Single Engine Two Place Multi-Gun Fighter Aircraft	30
P149 Twin Engine Fighter Aircraft	31
P150 Twin Engine General Purpose Aircraft	33
P175 Anti-Tank Aircraft	66
P177 Four Engine Transport Aircraft	83
P178 / CA-15 Fighter Aircraft	71
P182/ P184 /P185 /P186 Fighter Aircraft Grumman F9F Panther Derivatives	94
P189 / P193 / CA-22 Winjeel Trainer Aircraft Prototypes	91
P196 Twin Seat All-Weather Fighter Aircraft	96
P223 CA-23 All-Weather Fighter Aircraft	96
P247 / XP48 & P248 / XP49 Winjeel, R.R. Dart Turboprop Trainer Aircraft	133
P256 / XP54 Winjeel, Twin Aspin II Turbojet Trainer	134
P260 / XP55 Jet Trainer	134
P265 / XP56 Wallaby Feederliner	137
P267 / XP58 Winjeel, Twin Marbore II Turbojet Trainer	134
P269 / XP59 Jet Trainer	134
P271 / XP63 Jet Trainer, R.R.Derwent Turbojet	142
P277 / XP61 Winjeel Ambulance	142
P302 / XP69 Improved Avon Sabre	161
P312 / P313 Sabre, In-Flight Re-Fuelling	162
P314 / XP70 Winjeel-Tricycle Undercarriage	161
P321 / XP71 Sabre, Rocket Boost [1]	162
P322 / XP72 Sabre, NASARR Installation	163
P402 Sabre, Rocket Boost [2]	179
Project KAHU	xxxvii, 300
Rocket Interceptor[1]	121
Sarich Orbital Engine for Aircraft Application	261
The Hughes Franchise-A Conflict of Helicopter Interests	214
The Light Military Support Aircraft	263
Turbofan Boost Engine on Short Haul Twin Turboprop Aircraft	226
Winjeel FAC 101D Forward Air Control Aircraft	233
Winjeel for Glider Towing	257
Winjeel Trainer- Turboprop Engine	281
Winjeel, Turboprop Agricultural Aircraft	193
Winjeel-AFST 5044 Basic Trainer Proposal [1]	292
Winjeel-AFST 5044 Basic Trainer Proposal [2]	294
XP46 Single Seat Day Fighter Aircraft	119
XP47 Rocket Interceptor[2]	127
XP62 Four Engine Light Interceptor	143
XP64 / 65 / 66 Warrior- Air Superiority Fighter	146
XP67 / XP68 Fighter Aircraft	153
XP73 Jet Trainer & XP74 Executive Transport Aircraft	165
XP75 Winjeel Utility Aeroplane [1]	167
XP75 Winjeel Utility Aeroplane [2]	167
XP76 Winjeel Agricultural Aircraft	167
XP77 / CA-28 Ceres Agricultural Aircraft	167

R

RAAF Archerfield	10
RAAF Base Butterworth	118
RAAF Base East Sale	127, 302
RAAF Base Edinburgh	258-260, 302
RAAF Base Laverton	2, 4, 41, 83, 91, 114, 241, 257, 320
RAAF Base Pearce	302
RAAF Base Point Cook	127, 226
RAAF Base Richmond	245
RAAF Base Townsville	258
RAAF Base Williamtown	118
RAAF Darwin	10
RAAF Support Command	184, 257
RAE Farnborough	xvi, 16
Rationalization	xxi-xxv, xxviii, xxxi, 241, 263
Raytheon AIM-9B Sidewinder	118
Reserve Capacity Funding	xxiii, xxv, xxxi, 335
Rhodesian Air Force	225
RNZAF	vi, xxxvii, 12, 91, 209, 253, 260, 300
Roulettes display team	214, 302
Royal Aircraft Establishment	vi, xvi, 98, 105, 216
Royal Australian Navy	
Fleet Air Arm	i, 12, 14, 107, 164, 209, 214, 236, 241, 242
Fleet Air Arm HC-723 Sqdn	241, 242
Fleet Air Arm VC-724 Sqdn	209, 214
HMAS Albatross, Nowra	209
RAN River Class	228
RAN Wirraways	13
Royal Malaysian Air Force	114, 118
Royal Thai Air Force	226
Royal Victorian Aero Club	19, 248

S

SAAB-Svenska	xxvi
SBAC Farnborough Air Display & Exhibition, 1984.	287
Singapore Minister for Science and Technology	264
Snake Eye bomb	xxiv
Spaceframes	xxvii

SSQ-801 Barra Sonobuoy	244
Swiss flying club	225

T

Tactical Transport Aircraft Study	274
Technical Director, HDH	283
Telecommunication Research Establishment	vi, 104
Telstars display team	214
Tennix Defence (LADS Corporation)	298
Test Pilots	
Board Greg	xvi, 53, 62, 65, 87
Boss-Walker Hubert	xvi, 4, 16, 37, 38, 43, 56, 320
Carter James	xvi, 6, 47, 58
Frewin Ken	xvi, 41, 43, 47, 56, 57
Schofield James	xvi, 80, 82, 87-88, 91, 321
Trease Bob	240, 241
The Learning Curve effect	xx
Trainer Evaluation Aircraft	256

U

UK Ministry of Defence	252
Ultra-Light Aircraft Association of Australia	262
Units	
1 AD	20, 52, 83
1 AFTS	13
1 APU	53, 83, 93
1 BFTS	13, 127
1 CRD	53
1 FTS	226, 320
1 WAGS	23, 25
10 CU	12
10 Squadron	258-260
11 EFTS	20, 25, 28
11 Squadron	260
12 Squadron	11
2 (F) OTU	118
2 AD	9
2 CRD	25
2 FTS	302
2 OCU	118
2 SFTS	9
2 WAGS	23
25 Squadron	211
292 Training Squadron	261
3 EFTS	20, 24, 28
3 Squadron	viii, 118
3 Tactical Reconnaissance Squadron	91
3 WAGS	23
30 Squadron	12
33 Squadron	303
4 CU	12
4 Forward Air Control Development Unit	302
4 Squadron	9, 65
4 Tactical Reconnaissance Squadron	91
486 Maintenance Squadron	303
492 Maintenance Squadron	261
5 OCU	115, 118
5 Squadron	9, 11, 64
54 Squadron	12
60 Squadron	12
7 AD	24
75 Squadron	91, 118
76 Squadron	91, 118, 188
77 Squadron	91, 118
78 Fighter Wing	91, 118
78 Squadron	91
8 EFTS	23
8 OTU	23, 65
81 Fighter Wing	91
82 Squadron	12, 91
83 Squadron	65
84 Squadron	65
85 Squadron	65
86 Squadron	91
86 Wing	i
92 Wing	261
Basic Flying Training School	127, 226
CAF	v, 25, 91
Central Flying School	v, 23, 56, 91, 127, 211, 302
CFS	v, 20, 25, 127, 210, 211
CMU, Narrandera	25
CMU, Tamworth	25
NAV-W	24
RSU	vi, 52
SFTS	9, 17, 19
University of NSW	288
UYS-503	261

V

Variable Wing Sweep	vi, 219
Victa's Aircraft Division	224
Vosper Thornycroft Ltd.(UK)	228

W

Weapons Research Establishment	vi, 118, 188, 294
World Gliding Championships	257
WRELADS I	295, 298
WRELADS II	294
WREMAPS II	294

Y

Yarra River	xii-xiv, xvi, xviii, xxviii, 189, 242, 339

www.ingramcontent.com/pod-product-compliance
Lightning Source LLC
Chambersburg PA
CBHW041709290426
44109CB00028B/2830